Ethical Theory and Business

THIRD EDITION

Edited by

Tom L. Beauchamp
Kennedy Institute of Ethics
Georgetown University

Norman E. Bowie
Center for the Study of Values
University of Delaware

Prentice Hall, *Englewood Cliffs, New Jersey 07632*

LIBRARY OF CONGRESS
Library of Congress Cataloging-in-Publication Data

Ethical theory and business : edited by Tom L. Beauchamp, Norman E.
Bowie.
    p.   cm.
  Includes bibliographies.
  ISBN 0-13-290503-5
  1. Business ethics. 2. Business ethics--Case studies.
3. Industry--Social aspects--United States. 4. Industry--Social
aspects--United States--Case studies. 5. Corporation law--United
States--Cases. 6. Consumer protection--Law and legislation--United
States--Cases.   I. Beauchamp, Tom L. II. Bowie, Norman E., 1942-

HF5387.E82 1988
174'.4--dc19   87-25457
                                                     CIP

Cover design: *George Cornell*
Manufacturing buyer: *Margaret Rizzi*

 © 1988, 1983, 1979 by Prentice-Hall, Inc.
A Division of Simon & Schuster
Englewood Cliffs, New Jersey 07632

All rights reserved. No part of this book may be
reproduced, in any form or by any means,
without permission in writing from the publisher.

Printed in the United States of America
10 9 8 7 6 5 4 3 2

ISBN 0-13-290503-5   01

Prentice-Hall International (UK) Limited, *London*
Prentice-Hall of Australia Pty. Limited, *Sydney*
Prentice-Hall Canada Inc., *Toronto*
Prentice-Hall Hispanoamericana, S.A., *Mexico*
Prentice-Hall of India Private Limited, *New Delhi*
Prentice-Hall of Japan, Inc., *Tokyo*
Simon & Schuster Asia Pte. Ltd., *Singapore*
Editora Prentice-Hall do Brasil, Ltda., *Rio de Janeiro*

Contents

CHAPTER FOUR
Protecting Consumers, Workers, and the Environment   194

CHAPTER FIVE

Rights and Obligations of Employers and Employees 257

CHAPTER SIX

Discrimination and Employment Practices 330

CHAPTER SEVEN
Advertising and Disclosing Information 398

Preface

When the first edition of *Ethical Theory and Business* went to press in late 1977, business ethics had received very little attention by philosophers and was hidden under other labels in business schools. Much has changed since 1977. The American Assembly of Collegiate Schools of Business has insisted that ethics be a part of the business student's education, and an increasingly sophisticated literature has emerged in business ethics.

The second edition published in 1983 was no mere cosmetic change. It was radically reshaped. In preparing that edition, we vowed we would not labor so intensely on the third edition. We made a vow we could not keep. The same forces of change that convinced us to restructure the first edition still exist. Consequently, the third edition is as different from the second as the second from the first. The chapter on ethical theory has been expanded and includes a discussion of the case method. We have added an entirely new chapter on topics in accounting, investment, and finance. There is also new material on the topics of obligations of business to consumers, compara-

ble worth, and stakeholder theory. In all, thirty-five articles are new.

However, many familiar landmarks remain. We have retained all the chapter topics from the second edition with the exception of "Conflicts of Interest and Roles." Employee rights, whistleblowing, advertising ethics, affirmative action, and the obligations of business to protect the environment remain staple topics. We have also retained the chapters on economic justice, regulation, and corporate responsibility. Twenty-three articles are carried over into this edition.

We have received many helpful suggestions for improving this anthology. It is impossible to recognize them all, but special thanks should be given to John Abbarno and Tom Dunfee, as well as to careful reviews given by Robert Ashmore, J. David Newell, Michael A. Payne, and Michael S. Pritchard. Both Sandy Manno and Manuel Fernandez shepherded draft after draft of this new edition through our offices—always with patience and good humor.

CHAPTER ONE

Ethical Theory and Its Application to Business

Tom L. Beauchamp

The problems and issues discussed in this book have emerged from professional practice in many areas of business, as well as psychology, law, economics, engineering, and international relations. The unifying theme in the volume, however, is that of moral reflection, and ethical theory is the field that traditionally has promoted such reflection. The goal of this first chapter is to provide a foundation in ethical theory sufficient for reading and criticizing essays in the ensuing chapters. An analytic framework is presented of the topics and forms of reasoning found in moral philosophy, as they are applied to problems in business. The first part of this chapter is entitled "Fundamental Concepts and Problems" because it introduces basic and recurring distinctions, definitions, and issues. The second part examines the most influential and relevant types of normative ethical theory. The third part is devoted to the topic of the use of "the case method" as a source of moral reflection.

PART ONE: FUNDAMENTAL CONCEPTS AND PROBLEMS

Morality and Ethical Theory

The term *morality* has a broad meaning that extends beyond the moral philosophy and professional codes of conduct adopted by corporations and professional associations. Morality is concerned more generally with practices defining right and wrong. These practices, together with other kinds of customs, rules, and practices, are transmitted within cultures and institutions from generation to generation. Morality, then, denotes a social institution, composed of a set of standards pervasively acknowledged by the members of the culture in which it is entrenched. In this respect, it has an objective status as a body of guidelines for action. Like political constitutions and natural languages, morality exists prior to the acceptance (or rejection) of its standards by particular individuals. That is,

1

individuals do not create their morality by making their own rules, and morality cannot be purely a personal policy or code.

Sometimes morality is cynically or frivolously dismissed, as if it were no more significant than superstition, but this claim too is untenable: Morality is essential to social stability and the preservation of human decency, and the fact that it is sometimes ignored serves only to emphasize its significance. Businesspersons too often do not appreciate how pervasively moral practices and rules already govern their conduct. In the context of a complex sale of property, I was once introduced to a large commercial property owner as a professor of business ethics. His response was typical of my experiences on the occasions when I have been so introduced: "There is no ethics in business," he said. "They want more for their property and I want to give them less. What's ethical about that?" But 15 minutes later he was engaged in establishing a sale price that would be considered "fair," not only by the market value of real estate in the area, but also fair to the family selling the property. When some questions arose about the value of a parking lot belonging to the property, this businessman noted that its value had already been factored in. He then appealed to his and his partner's impeccable reputations for honesty and integrity in making such assessments. He noted, probably correctly, how easy it would be for him to take advantage of a seller, because of his own superior experience and knowledge of the market.

At this point he turned to me and began to discourse on the importance of *trust* in a context in which the family selling the property could not possibly understand the many complexities of rental arrangements and other dimensions of ownership in the property. "I don't believe in ethical *rules* for business," he said, "but I do believe in ethical *virtues* for businessmen." This was the man who only an hour before had said, "There is no ethics in business." In the end, the transaction probably could not have been completed without the presence of the very trust he mentioned, together with established practices of fair play for arriving at a fair price on the property. A long history of honest dealings between the family, the buyers, and the family's accountant also made a difference in this context, because the value of the property was extraordinarily difficult to assess, even by expert appraisers. Without these moral relationships the entire transaction would likely have failed, and the property would have been sold at auction. This is an example of how morality is often at work in subtle, almost unnoticed ways in business relationships and transactions.

The word *morality*, however, does not capture various aspects of the analysis we will encounter in this volume. In contrast to *morality*, the terms *ethical theory* and *moral philosophy* suggest reflection on the nature and place of morality. These words refer to attempts to introduce clarity, substance, and precision of argument into the domain of morality. Many people go through life with an understanding of morality largely dictated by their culture. Other persons, however, are not satisfied simply to conform to the morality of society. They want difficult questions answered: Is what our society forbids really wrong? Is what our society values really good? What is the purpose of morality? Does religion have anything to do with morality? Do the moral rules of society fit together in a unified whole? If there are conflicts and inconsistencies in our practices and beliefs, how should they be resolved? What should we do when we face a moral problem for which society has, as yet, provided no instruction?

Moral philosophers seek to answer such questions and to put moral beliefs and social practices of morality into a more unified and defensible package of guidelines and concepts. Sometimes this task involves challenging traditional moral beliefs, assessing the quality of moral arguments, and suggesting modifications in existing beliefs. Morality, we might say, consists of what persons ought to do in order to conform to society's norms of behavior, whereas ethics consists of the philosophical reasons for—or against—the morality stipulated by society. Usually the latter effort centers on *justification* (see pp. 8–9). Philosophers seek to justify a system of standards or some moral point of view on the basis of carefully analyzed and defended theories and principles such as respect for autonomy, distributive justice, equal treatment, human rights, beneficence, and utility—some of the principles commonly employed in contemporary moral philosophy.

Most moral principles are already embedded in public morality and policies, but generally only in a vague and underanalyzed form. Justice is a good example. A recurrent topic in the pages of the *Wall Street Journal, Forbes, Business Week,* and other leading popular journals of business is the justice or fairness of the present system of corporate and individual taxation. However, an extended or detailed analysis of justice is virtually never provided in these periodicals. Such matters are usually left at an intuitive or party-line level, where it is easy to presuppose the correctness of a moral point of view, but difficult to argue for it.

In this Introduction, the terms *ethical* and *moral* will be taken as identical in meaning, and *ethics* will be used as a general term referring to both moral beliefs and ethical theory. *Moral philosophy, ethical theory,* and *philosophical ethics,* by contrast, will be reserved for philosophical theories, including philosophical reflection on social morality. Although popular discussions of moral problems use moral language, they seldom invoke ethical theory and its techniques.

Morality and Prudence

Most students do not encounter moral philosophy until they are in college or graduate school. Morality, however, is learned by virtually every young child as part of the acculturation process. The first step in this process is learning how to distinguish moral rules from rules of prudence (self-interest). This task can be difficult, because the two kinds of rules are often learned together, without being distinguished by their teachers. For example, we are constantly reminded in our early years that we must observe such rules as "Don't touch the hot stove," "Don't cross the street without looking both ways," "Brush your teeth after meals," and "Eat your vegetables." Most of these oughts and ought nots are instructions in our self-interest; that is, they are instructions in prudence. However, we are later given oughts or ought nots of a moral kind. We are told either by our parents, teachers, or peers that there are certain things we ought or ought not to do because these actions affect the interests of other people: "Don't pull your sister's hair." "Don't take money from your mother's pocketbook." "Share your toys." "Write a thank-you note to Grandma." As we grow up, we learn what society expects of us in terms of taking the interests of other people into account. We thus learn what society expects in the way of moral behavior.

Unfortunately it is often difficult to distinguish between morality and prudence in business judgments. Morality and prudence can even be bound together in a single statement. A simple example of both moral and prudential reasoning at work in business is found in an executive decision at Procter and Gamble to take off the market its Rely brand tampons, which had been causally linked to toxic shock syndrome.[1] Procter and Gamble had invested twenty years of research and approximately $75 million in the product's preparation. But the company became convinced, after its own investigation, that there was a possible causal connection to the toxic shock condition. At first, when scientific research seemed to offer some evidence that the material in the tampons did not encourage bacterial growth, Edward G. Harness, chairman of the board and chief executive officer, said he was "determined to fight for a brand, to keep an important brand from being hurt by insufficient data in the hands of a bureaucracy."[2] However, by September 18, 1980, Procter and

Gamble stopped production of the Rely tampon, in part because of negative publicity and a report from the Center for Disease Control that linked Rely statistically to toxic shock syndrome—a report Procter and Gamble's physicians, microbiologists, and epidemiologists were unable to refute. "That was the turning point," Mr. Harness said. The company subsequently pledged its research expertise to the Center for Disease Control to investigate toxic shock syndrome and agreed to finance and direct a large educational program about the disease, as well as issue a warning to women not to use Rely. Referring to the Rely case, Mr. Harness later made the following public announcement:

> Company management must consistently demonstrate a superior talent for keeping profit and growth objectives as first priorities. However, it also must have enough breadth to recognize that enlightened self-interest requires the company to fill any reasonable expectation placed upon it by the community and the various concerned publics. Keeping priorities straight and maintaining the sense of civic responsibility will achieve important secondary objectives of the firm. Profitability and growth go hand in hand with fair treatment of employees, of direct customers, of consumers, and of the community.[3]

Here prudence and morality flow together, perhaps as justifications for different audiences at whom the statement is directed.

People sometimes say that morality is nothing but prudence, because executives like Mr. Harness only appeal to moral notions for the reason that the appeal is good for business. That is, morality serves only a prudential purpose on the route to profits. The implication is either that ethical issues do not matter much to people in business or that business presents no distinctive ethical problems. Such views seem odd, as we noted earlier, because the existence of business relationships depends in significant respects on moral relationships of trust, honesty, and fairness, not as prudence but as a set of moral relationships. Imagine trying to practice business in a context in which lying, stealing, and other immoral actions were routine. Business could not be practiced in such an arrangement, because business requires a society in which contracts are generally honored and property is respected. No organization can expect to survive in business if it cannot gain the faith and trust of the parties with which it deals. Moreover, bribery, kickbacks, fraud, and certain monopolistic activities in the restraint of trade have all been judged inappropriate, precisely because they involve immoral practices that will undermine business association. For these reasons there are standards of good business practice, some of which are written into the aforementioned business codes of ethics.

A simple example is found in two scandals that undermined confidence in United States auction houses in the mid–1980s. In 1986 it was discovered that in May 1981 David Bathurst, then President of Christie's in New York, had lied about the sale of two paintings by Gauguin and Van Gogh, saying they had been sold when in fact Christie's could not get a good price and so clandestinely took them back in house. Bathurst was "protecting the market," as it is sometimes put. Then, in 1985, Sotheby's had to recall some Hebrew manuscripts and a rare book it had auctioned because clear title to the property had never been obtained. These two scandals prompted widespread questioning about the manipulation of the market at auction houses, about how prices are set, how sales are reported, how insider information is used, how insurance values are set, how works are "bought in" by the house if the price is not high enough, and so on. Suddenly general confidence in auction houses was shaken. Not just works of art, but everything from rare books to real estate came under suspicion. Businesspersons looked to alternatives. Although Sotheby's and Christie's are businesses that together bring in over a billion dollars per year, their business requires a certain level of trust and honesty or they will fall to their competitors, and perhaps even endanger the existence of major auction houses. Everyone knows that dealers and buyers can be fooled and manipulated at auctions, but there must be at least a threshold level of honesty and fair dealing or there will no longer be an institution of auctioneering.[4] Whether the reason for having these rules is prudence or independent respect for morality is, however, an open question.

Obviously, the morality of many accepted business practices can be questioned—perhaps because they are based on prudence rather than morality, but also because some actions that were long accepted or at least condoned in the business community eventually have become rightly condemned as immoral—for example, the discharge of waste into the air and water, plant relocation purely for economic gain, large political contributions to those who support the "right" business interests, and employment practices that discriminate against minorities. Because business activity takes place within a larger social framework, businesspersons are sometimes forced to reflect on these moral judgments of their activities, even when they cringe at the thought—not necessarily because it is prudent to do so, but because it is right to do so. However, it is generally believed, for good reason, that the practice of morality is in the interest of business, and this is one justifiable motive for acting in accordance with morality.

Morality and Law

Most of the chapters in this book contain selections from case law (judge-made law expressed in court decisions). Often selections in the chapters will mention statutory law (federal and state statutes and their accompanying administrative regulations). Law in these forms has brought important issues before the public. Case law, in particular, has established influential precedents that provide material for reflection on both legal and moral obligations. Yet it is vital to distinguish *moral* evaluation form *legal* evaluation. Issues of legal liability, costs to the system, practicability within the litigation process, and questions of compensation may demand that legal re-

quirements be different from moral requirements.

Despite an important intersection between morals and law, the law is not the repository of our moral standards and values, even when the law is directly concerned with moral problems. A law-abiding person is not necessarily morally sensitive or virtuous, and from the fact that something is legally acceptable, it does not follow that it is morally acceptable. Numerous failures to fulfill agreements in business do not involve legal violations of contract, but may nonetheless involve moral violations of promise keeping, and may therefore be gravely wrong from the moral point of view, even though legally innocent. Questions are raised in later chapters about the morality of many business actions, such as plant relocation and mergers that cause unemployment, even though such actions are not illegal.

To get at the differences between moral and legal appraisals, consider a case in which the Mobil Corporation and the Washington Post Company became entangled in a bitter dispute. The *Washington Post* published an article alleging that William P. Tavoulareas, President of Mobil Oil, had abused his position and had misappropriated Mobil's corporate assets to set up his son in the shipping business. Tavoulareas, in turn, sued the *Post* for libel. In a tortuous journey through the courts, some judges ultimately reached a verdict in Tavoulareas' favor, whereas other judges ruled against him. Suppose Tavoulareas is legally innocent of any wrongdoing; that is, suppose he did not legally misuse his position or Mobil's assets. It does not automatically follow that he is morally innocent of wrongdoing in using his position to assist his son or to use corporate assets unfairly. Now, to change the supposition for purposes of contrast, suppose the *Post* is legally innocent of the charge of libel. The newspaper may nonetheless be guilty of moral violations of false description, incompetent journalism, invasion of privacy, and so on. Legal innocence does not preclude gross violations of professional ethics. In discussions of guilt, obligation, responsibility, and the like in the abstract, it is essential to establish whether a legal or a moral perspective is under consideration. Guilt or innocence in the one domain does not entail guilt or innocence in the other.

Issues of law and morality are commonly treated in public debate as though the only matter of abiding concern worthy of public scrutiny is whether a person has conformed to or violated the law. However, the more pressing and important matter often concerns morality. Anthony Lewis of the *New York Times* published a column on the *Post*/Tavoulareas case in which he wrote as follows: ''As it happens, I personally thought the Tavoulareas story was an overblown and unconvincing tale not worth the play or space. But . . . the press could not operate with any semblance of freedom if judges made a practice of second-guessing editorial decisions.''[5] Lewis offered a moral condemnation covered by a legal absolution, and then concluded as though the legal issues alone were the important ones in the case.

This comment is typical of much thought about problems in business where both legal and moral concerns are present. No matter how morally defective a particular conduct may be, the presumption goes, it must not be subject to legal control or sanctions. A potential problem with this approach is what often forms its bottom line: The conduct is judged acceptable in general because (1) there is no legal violation and (2) there ought not to be any new legal standard enacted that would hold the person liable. Ignored is that the acceptability of the conduct may be inappropriate and condemnable by the standards of morality.

A related form of confusion involves the belief that if a person is found guilty under the law, the person is therefore morally guilty. Such judgments are not necessarily correct and always depend on the moral acceptability of the law on which the judgment is reached. For example, before the Foreign Corrupt Practices Act was signed into law (on December 20, 1977) by President Jimmy Carter, slush funds, bribes, and the like had not been illegal

for American corporations dealing with foreign governments. After the new and stringently restrictive legislation was enacted (perhaps as an overreaction to the Watergate scandals that motivated its passage), an intense and still ongoing debate surrounded the act's implications because it served to frustrate many business practices that are deemed not only acceptable in various foreign cultures but necessary to the conduct of business. Many today believe there is nothing *unethical* or corrupt in these now *illegal* acts. The real problem, they contend, is a shortsightedness in the legislation.

Furthermore, the law has often been accused, with some justification, of resulting in moral unfairness through court judgments rendered against corporations. Here are some examples:[6] (1) Monsanto Chemical was successfully sued for $200 million, although the presiding judge asserted that there was no credible evidence linking Monsanto's Agent Orange to the severe harms that had been described in the case. (2) Chevron Oil was successfully sued for mislabeling its cans of paraquat, although the offending label conformed exactly to federal regulations, which permitted no other form of label to be used. (3) Although whooping cough vaccine indisputably reduces the risk of this disease for children who receive the vaccine, almost no manufacturer will produce it because of fear of costly suits brought under product liability laws. In each of these cases it is easy to understand why critics have considered various regulations, legislation, and case law morally disgraceful.

Law and morality should therefore be kept distinct. The two often brush in close contact—as in the legal cases reprinted at the ends of most of the following chapters—because they share concerns over matters of basic social importance. Principles, duties, and criteria of evidence are often shared by morality and law, and laws may be shaped by moral principles and established to protect moral interests. Law, in certain respects, is our agency for translating morality into explicit social guidelines and practices. But these generalizations about the intersection of law and morality could also be applied to religion, economics, politics, and many overlapping disciplines and areas of conduct, all of which should be kept as separate as possible from morality.

Business ethics in the United States is currently involved in an entangled, complex, and mutually stimulating relationship with law. The law often appeals to moral duties and rights, places sanctions on violators, and in general strengthens the social importance of moral beliefs. Nevertheless, the law rightly backs away from attempting to legislate against everything that is morally wrong. In recent years the judges have been searching in their opinions for extra-legal mechanisms such as peer review, committees, codes of ethics, and self-regulatory procedural mechanisms that will limit the involvement of the law and escape involvement by legislatures, regulatory agencies, and the courts. (See Chapter Three.) As the courts and legislatures become even more pressed for time, it seems inevitable that procedures to protect ethical interests that are outside the reach of the law will assume greater significance.

Approaches to the Study of Morality

Morality and ethical theory can be studied and developed by a variety of methods, but four general approaches have dominated the literature. Two of these approaches describe and analyze morality presumably without taking moral positions; two other approaches do involve taking moral positions and involve appeal to ethical theory. These four approaches can be outlined as follows:

> Descriptive approaches
> > Scientific studies
> > Conceptual studies
> Prescriptive approaches
> > General normative ethics
> > Applied normative ethics

These categories do not express rigid and always clearly distinguishable approaches. In-

deed, they often overlap in a single work. Nonetheless, when understood as broad, polar, contrasting positions, they can serve as models of inquiry, and thus as valuable distinctions.

First among the two descriptive fields of inquiry is the *scientific study* of ethics. The factual description and explanation of moral behavior and beliefs as performed by anthropologists, sociologists, and historians is typical of this approach. Here moral attitudes, codes, and beliefs are described. These include sexual practices, codes of honor, and rules governing permissible killing in a society. Examples can be found in certain *Harvard Business Review* articles and *Forbes* magazine polls that report what business executives believe is morally acceptable and morally unacceptable.

The second descriptive field involves the *conceptual study* of ethics. Here the meanings of central terms in ethics such as *right, obligation, justice, good, virtue,* and *responsibility* are analyzed, and forms of moral reasoning are studied. Crucial terms in business ethics such as *trade secret* and *affirmative action* can be given the same kind of careful conceptual attention. The proper analysis of the term *morality* (as in the first few pages of this Introduction) and the distinction between the moral and the nonmoral are typical examples of such conceptual problems in general ethics. (Descriptive ethics and conceptual studies may not be the only forms of nonnormative inquiry. For example, there may be biological bases of moral behavior that deserve investigation.)

One conceptual matter of interest is that persons in business often seem to mean something rather different by the term *ethics* than do philosophers. *Ethics* is sometimes implicitly understood in the business community as a code word for a set of rules of correct conduct, in the sense of things one must do in order to stay in good standing in the community or to avoid trouble with the law or with one's associates. Ethics may be implicitly conceived as something that is not a generally required or a publicly generalizable matter, because its rules are "in-house" or "in the profession." For example, an extensive set of rules of confidentiality of information and privacy rights has been developed at the Northwestern National Bank in Minneapolis, governing both customer and employee information stored in its computers. The bank is proud of its comprehensive and exacting rules, but these rules are thought of as a private list of principles for that bank and not something company officials would think of as required of all banks or would wish to pass on to similar businesses. Clearly, not all codes or sets of ethical principles in business can be so interpreted, because companies are often eager to make their principles and practices public and to see them generalized. The important concept is that the idea of a private code or one not meant to apply broadly to persons in a similar setting is generally foreign to what philosophers mean when they use the terms *morality* and *ethics*.[7]

General normative ethics is a prescriptive study that attempts to formulate and defend basic moral norms governing moral life. Normative moral philosophy thus aims at determining what *ought* to be done, which may need to be distinguished from what *is* in fact practiced. Ideally, an ethical theory will provide reasons for adopting a whole system of moral principles or virtues. The most prominent and general of these theories are utilitarianism and deontology. Utilitarians argue that there is one and only one fundamental principle determining right action, which can be roughly stated as follows: "An action is morally right if and only if it produces at least as great a balance of value over disvalue as any available alternative action." Deontologists, by contrast, have argued that one or more fundamental principles of ethics differ from the principle of utility. These are usually principles of duty, such as "Never treat another person merely as a means to your own goals." We shall examine both forms of these theories, together with other dimensions of ethical theory, in Part Two of this Introduction.

The principles of general normative ethics are commonly used to treat such specific moral problems as abortion, widespread hunger, corporate responsibility, and racial and sexual discrimination. This use of ethical theory is referred to as *applied ethics*. Philosophical treatment of medical ethics, engineering ethics, journalistic ethics, jurisprudence, and business ethics involves distinct areas of the application of general ethical principles to moral problems that arise in these professions. Substantially the same general ethical principles apply to the problems across these professional fields and in areas beyond professional ethics as well. One might appeal to principles of justice, for example, in order to illuminate and resolve issues of taxation, health care distribution, environmental responsibility, criminal punishment, and reverse discrimination (see Chapters Four, Six, and Nine). Similarly, principles of veracity (truthfulness) apply to debates about secrecy and deception in international politics, misleading advertisements in business ethics, balanced reporting in journalistic ethics, and the disclosure of the nature and extent of an illness to a patient in medical ethics. Increased clarity about the general conditions under which truth must be told and when it may be withheld presumably would enhance understanding of what is required in each of these areas. (See portions of Chapters Seven and Eight.)

Applied ethics and the exercise of sound judgment in business practice are central to most essays and cases in this volume. An interdisciplinary approach to ethics has been frequently employed in recent years in contexts of public policy and business ethics, where practitioners bring experience and technical information to the discussion, while moral philosophers contribute familiarity with traditions of ethical reflection, insights into various distinctions and categories that can illuminate moral issues, and skill in probing the presuppositions and implications of positions.

Justification in Ethics

The chapters in this book contain selections by authors who take moral (and sometimes legal) positions on issues. To take such a defensible position should not merely be to express a personal opinion on a moral matter. People often act as if they had the weight of morality behind their pronouncements when we wonder whether the proclaimed moral position has any real basis in morality. Almost everyone interested in moral problems at some point asks questions about whether views about what is morally good and right can be justified. If so, what counts as an adequate justification? An easy answer to this question is to say that moral judgments are justified by giving reasons for them. However, not all reasons are good reasons, and not all good reasons are sufficient for justification. For example, a good reason for regulating various business practices—such as those of industries involved in the use of radioactive products—is that they present a clear and present danger to other persons. Many have believed that this reason is also sufficient to justify a broad set of regulatory practices, such as government protection against environmental contamination.

By contrast, some propose as a good reason for government regulation the idea that persons in business cannot be trusted to police themselves; many people do not consider this a good reason because it involves a deprivation of liberty. If someone holds that past failures of self-regulatory mechanisms constitute a good and sufficient reason to justify federal regulation, we expect that person to give us some further account as to why this reason is both good and sufficient. We expect references, for example, to the dire consequences for the public interest if government fails to intervene. We expect the invocation of certain principles about the importance of protecting against inadvertent tragedies such as the near disaster at the Three Mile Island nuclear generating station. We thus expect the person to offer a set of reasons that amounts to an argued defense of his or her perspective on the issues.

Every belief we hold is subject to challenge of this sort and therefore to justification by reasoned argument. No matter what we believe about the justifiability of certain business practices, our views are subject to criticism and require defense. But just as there are

good and bad reasons, so there are good and bad arguments. We must know whether the premises are acceptable in order to know whether an argument proves or justifies anything.

The Concept of Conscience

"I cannot in good conscience continue my . . . association with Mellon Bank Corporation." So said J. David Barnes, a member of the bank's advisory board of directors, upon tendering his resignation.[8] Mellon Bank had offered to lend $150 million to T. Boone Pickens of Mesa Petroleum in his attempt to get control of Phillips Petroleum, or, as some prefer to say, in his attempt at greenmail. (See Chapter Eight.) In effect, Barnes resigned because he could not in good moral conscience condone the bank's money going to a person he regarded as a morally unscrupulous operator.

The slogan "Let your conscience be your guide" has long been for many the bottom line in moral justification, and this slogan remains influential in popular ethical writings and articles on business ethics. In a society in which considerable latitude of autonomous choice is allowed in circumstances of open social disagreement, it is easy to see why autonomous agents would appeal to their own heartfelt reasons as a justification for various forms of resistance to social pressures and arrangements. There is a distinguished literature on conscientious objection that points to the importance of preserving autonomous disagreement in such contexts, and appeals to conscience may be based on carefully structured justifications. We shall encounter several instances of conscientious objection in the section on whistle blowing (see Chapter Five).

An intriguing case of conscience occurred in 1965 when a physical plant superintendent at Eastern Illinois University repeatedly protested what he believed to be faulty construction plans for a new campus building expansion program. Against the advice of a close friend, he did not simply report his evaluation; he objected vigorously and repeatedly. His complaints, however, fell on unsympathetic ears in the university administration, and soon his pay was cut $100 a month, his responsibilities were diminished, and a psychiatric examination was recommended for him by the president of the University. Subsequently his contract was not renewed, and he resigned. After some public furor, the governor of Illinois appointed a committee of engineering experts to investigate the alleged construction irregularities. The plant superintendent, Gerald Cravey, offered the following reasons for his dogged insistence on revisions in the construction plans: "I sometimes think that my friend's advice would have been the best course. But I still had to live with myself. Today I can look myself in the mirror when I shave. I couldn't if I had kept quiet about what I saw."[9]

Despite our admiration for such a person of conscience, philosophers have generally judged appeals to conscience alone—that is, independent of a justification that is general and not merely unique to the person—as insufficient and untrustworthy as rational and impartial bases for ethical judgments. Consciences vary radically from person to person and time to time, and are often altered by circumstance, religious belief, childhood, and training. For example, Stanley Kresge, the son of the founder of S.S. Kresge Company—now known as K-Mart Corporation—is a teetotaler for religious reasons. When the company started selling beer and wine, Mr. Kresge sold all his stock. His conscience, he said, would not let him make a profit on alcohol. But the company dismissed his objection as a matter of "his own business" and asserted that it sees nothing whatever wrong with earning profits on alcohol.[10] Similarly, views about the right to publish pornography and rights of the press are matters of brisk debate and deep conviction, but these conscientious beliefs alone hardly resolve the issues.

Consciences are also subject to impulse and whim, and are rather more acute, for instance, when a police officer is sighted that when there are no enforcers nearby. Appeals to the rightness of an action on the grounds of individual conscience can even be rational-izations for immoral acts. Political assassins and terrorists, for example, commonly appeal to conscience as a source of justification for their actions.

Within the culture of business, references to conscience can also be used in a broad sense to refer to a person's overall moral character or moral defects as well as to a morally conscientious person or corporation. Here is a typical statement of this sort:

> [In] socially responsible investing . . . securities are selected not only on their financial merits but also on judgments of *conscience.*
>
> At least five state governments and 14 cities have passed laws requiring their pension manager to get rid of shares in companies that do business in South Africa. . . .
>
> [The] Calvert Social Investment Managed Growth [is] a mutual fund whose scruples extend beyond South Africa to include companies that pollute the environment, produce nuclear energy, have a history of poor labor relations, or manufacture weapons.[11]

Here conscience refers to the exercise of moral judgments about investing based on moral judgments of corporate responsibility and performance.

Consider also the following comment by CBS chairman Thomas Wyman, intended as a criticism of cable TV owner Ted Turner, who at the time was engaged in a hostile financial bid for ownership of CBS: "He [Turner] is not qualified because he doesn't have the conscience. When what you are broadcasting goes out to 70 million people, you better be thinking about something broader than the things I think occupy his thinking, and that includes money."[12] This is a typical form of moral criticism in business. The comment, in effect, asserts that Turner does not have a sufficiently developed sense of moral responsibility for the job. Even if he has a conscience that informs him of his responsibilities, it is not well tutored enough and fails to reflect a morally sound perspective.

Comments such as Wyman's are often derived from practical experience and are left at an intuitive level without adequate supporting moral argument or analysis. It is open to

Turner to respond that his conscience is more advanced than Wyman's, in which case we come to a moral standstill unless further grounds are adduced for what is to count as a morally responsible exercise of executive authority in broadcasting. The reliability of conscience is thus not self-certifying, and a justification for one's convictions is needed from some source external to conscience itself. But can there be such a source? Are the ideas of both conscience and justification in the end reducible to mere individual rules and nothing more? This problem takes us straight to the issue of relativism and objectivity in morals.

Relativism and Objectivity of Belief

One of the most important problems with personal belief and justification is generally referred to as relativism. Cultural and individual variations in moral judgment have prompted several questions: Are there correct or objective justifications in morals? Could there be a neutral standpoint from which to view moral disagreements? Some have contended that moral views simply express how one feels or how a culture accommodates the desires of its peoples. Such doubts about an objective basis in morality spawn issues of relativism and disagreement in morals, as we shall see in this and succeeding sections. Each of these problems raises questions about whether an objective morality is possible and whether reason has any substantial role to play in ethics.

Cultural and Individual Relativism. Moral relativists contend that all moral beliefs and principles are relative to individual cultures or individual persons. This position is defended by appeal to data indicating that moral rightness and wrongness vary from place to place and that there are no absolute or universal moral standards that have applied to all persons at all times. Proponents of relativism add that the concept of rightness depends on individual or cultural beliefs and that rightness and wrongness are therefore meaningless notions if isolated from the specific contexts in

which they have arisen. Practices of business payoffs, employee treatment and loyalty, and corporate taxation are but three among thousands of possible examples. Practices of bribery, the form taken by codes of ethics, and the way employees are treated are thus all relative to cultures, institutions, and individuals.

An issue in business ethics that has commanded widespread attention in recent years is the way in which women are used in the Japanese labor force, by contrast to employment practices in North America. In both nations the percentage of women in the workforce is dramatically higher than in previous generations, and there are national laws against sex discrimination. But in Japan the traditional subservient role of women has been perpetuated longer than in many parts of the world. Women are paid little over half the salary of men for comparable work, and Japan has no effective laws or moral rules of equal pay for equal work. Women are widely used for cheap labor by exporters, for example, in order to hold down costs and remain competitive with third-world suppliers. Women in Japanese offices have two main tasks: serving tea and serving male orders. Jobs are categorized by sex. Many practices in employment, promotion, and child-rearing that would be labeled discriminatory in the United States are deeply embedded parts of Japanese training and culture; these practices are accepted pervasively by men and (to a lesser but still major extent) by women. In virtually every industry women must work far harder to advance in a career than do men. Eighty percent of Japan's top 1,118 companies who interview university graduates screen out women and interview only men. These same companies recruit fewer well-educated women in roles designed to support male employees, and women are granted fewer rights against being fired and fewer protections against inferior working conditions.[13]

Most who have studied Japanese practices would agree that Japan is changing and that equality is making some headway. Nonetheless, this description of the rules and practices governing Japanese women workers can be used to illustrate the problem of relativism at two levels. First, there do seem to be cultural differences in the way women are treated in various cultures. These cultural differences are also connected to general moral views about rights, discrimination, equal treatment, and so on. A culture like Saudia Arabia exhibits very different views about the role of women from those exhibited in Japan, which differ in other ways from those in North America. Second, there are also differences within Japanese culture: The outlook of more career-minded and less passive women differs strikingly from the outlook of executive males and passive women.

These problems of apparent moral diversity offer a serious challenge to moral philosophy. Although the thesis that relativism is a correct and highly significant doctrine has at times been a fashionable view in the social sciences, moral philosophers have tended to reject relativism. Among the best known arguments advanced against it is that there is a universal structure of human nature or at least a universal set of human needs that leads to the adoption of similar, or even identical, basic moral principles in all cultures. A related argument is that despite differing practices and beliefs, people do not clearly disagree about ultimate moral standards. For example, if personal payments for special services are common in one culture and punishable as bribery in another, then it is undeniable that these customs are different, but it does not follow that the moral principles underlying the customs are relative. The two cultures may agree about basic principles of morality, yet disagree about how to apply these principles in particular situations. For example, one culture may believe that practices of grease payments produce a social good by eliminating government interference and lowering the salaries paid to functionaries, while another culture believes a social good is introduced by eliminating all special favors. Both justifications look to the overall social good, but they apply this principle in disparate, apparently competing ways.

This possibility indicates that a basic or fundamental conflict between cultural values could only occur if apparent cultural disagreements about proper principles or rules occurred at the deepest levels of moral rules. Otherwise, the apparent disagreements can be understood in terms of, and perhaps be arbitrated by, appeal to deeper rules. If a moral conflict were truly fundamental, than the conflict could not be removed even if there were perfect agreement about the facts of a case, about the concepts involved, and about background beliefs.

To take still another step, suppose that certain persons do not agree on the same basic or fundamental norm or set of norms. It does not follow from this disagreement that there is no ultimate norm or set of norms in which everyone *ought* to believe. Consider an analogy to religious disagreement: From the fact that people have incompatible religious or atheistic beliefs, it does not follow that there is no single correct set of religious or atheistic propositions. Given anthropological data, one might be skeptical that there could be a compelling argument in favor of one system of religion or morality. But nothing more than skepticism seems justified by the facts adduced by anthropology, and nothing more than this skepticism would be justified even if fundamental conflicts of belief were discovered. Skepticism of course presents serious philosophical issues, but alone it does not support relativism, because ethical theory is free to try to determine which is the best set of moral beliefs—as we shall see in Part Two of this chapter.

Cultural Objectivity and Moral Stultification. One way to evaluate various (but perhaps not all) problems of relativism is to focus (1) on the objectivity of morals within cultures and (2) on the stultifying consequences of a serious belief in moral relativism. Let us consider (1) and (2) in order.

(1) We noted previously that morality is concerned with practices of right and wrong transmitted within cultures from one generation to another. The terms of social life are set by these practices, whose rules are pervasively acknowledged and shared in that cul-

ture. Within the culture, then, there is a significant measure of moral objectivity, because morality by its very nature does not exist through a person's subjective opinion. Individuals cannot create it by stipulation or correctly call a personal policy a morality. Such moral individualism would be as dubious as anarchism in politics and law, and none of us readily accepts a declaration by another person that his or her political and legal beliefs are validly determined by himself or herself alone.

It is, of course, true that some moral codes and practices must be formulated within social institutions and will be modified over time. But this fact does not mean that moral rules can be created without regard for the prevailing morality or invented like the latest technology. A corporation cannot develop its professional ethics from whole cloth. For example, a hospital corporation like Humana cannot draw up a code that brushes aside the need for confidentiality of patient information, or that permits surgeons to proceed without adequate consents from patients; and a brokerage house cannot simply define a conflict of interest in any way it wants as part of its moral code. If its definition and rules of conflict of interest deviate significantly from the standard or accepted definition, they can be rejected as subjective and mistaken.

Room for invention or alteration in morality is thus restricted by the broader understanding of morality in the culture. Rules cannot be *moral* standards or beliefs simply because they are so labeled. If relativism means they can be so invented or labeled, then relativism is mistaken. This defense of objectivity is not transcultural, and so must admit that *cultural* relativism may be true. But it supplies a strong reason for doubt about *individual* relativism. The second evaluation of relativism may help with cultural forms.

(2) The consequences of accepting relativism should be considered insofar as these consequences might have the effect of preventing serious reflection on and resolution of moral problems. Consider this analogy: If a husband and a wife have a serious disagree-

ment over whether to have another child because they have different views of family life and of their relationship, the problem will not vanish simply by declaring that their views about further children are relative to their different views about family life and relationships. The problem needs resolution, and among reasonable persons resolution will come only through hard thinking and perhaps considerable negotiation and compromise.

Similarly with moral problems, even if extraordinarily different viewpoints do prevail, a resolution is still needed. From this perspective, moral reflection that transcends human differences is needed *even if relativism is entirely true*. When two parties argue about some serious, divisive, and contested moral issue—killing animals or withholding information from contracting parties, for example—we tend to think that some genuinely fair and justified compromise may be reached, or perhaps we remain uncertain while anticipating the emergence of the best argument. We seldom infer from the mere fact of a conflict between beliefs that there is no way to establish one view as correct or as better argued than the other. The more absurd the position advanced by one party, the more convinced we become that some views being defended are mistaken or require supplementation. We are seldom tempted to conclude that there could not be any correct ethical perspective or any reasonable negotiation that might resolve disputes among reasonable persons. One use of ethical theory is to provide a structured approach to moral reasoning that enables us to work on such problems.

We shall turn to ethical theories in Part Two of this Introduction, but moral disagreements and their resolution need further discussion now.

Moral Disagreements

In any pluralistic culture there are many potential dilemmas involving conflicts of value. In this volume we will examine a few instances, such as not disclosing pertinent information in business deals, whistle blowing in industry, advertising on children's television, preferential hiring policies, and the like. Nevertheless, there are ways to resolve or at least reduce the level of some disagreements. Let us examine several methods that have been employed in the past to deal constructively with moral disagreements, each of which deserves recognition as a method of easing disagreement and conflict.

Obtaining Objective Information. Moral disagreements can sometimes be at least partially resolved by obtaining factual information on which points of moral controversy turn, particularly when the criteria establishing legitimate information are rigorous and demand objectivity. It has often been uncritically assumed that moral disputes are (by definition) produced solely by differences over moral judgments or principles, and not by a lack of information. This assumption is overly simplistic. Moral disputes often have nonmoral elements as central ingredients. For example, debates over the allocation of tax dollars to prevent accidents or disease in the workplace often became bogged down in factual issues of whether particular measures such as masks or lower levels of toxic chemicals actually function to prevent death and disease. (See Chapter Four, under "Worker Safety.")

In a publicized controversy over the morality of "exaggerated claims" in advertising, the Federal Trade Commission (FTC) alleged that the Standard Oil Company of California (SO-CAL) was guilty of intentionally misleading the public with its commercials for Chevron gasoline containing the additive F-310. Among the most damaging of the FTC's charges was the claim that SOCAL was falsely representing its F-310 additive as a unique product, therefore deceiving and misleading the public. Preliminary conferences and investigations, however, substantiated the validity of SOCAL's claims regarding its product's uniqueness, and the FTC thereupon withdrew its now demonstrably unfounded charges. While the dispute regarding other aspects of the F-310 advertising campaign was to continue, the appeal to the factual record had narrowed and

focused the ground of disagreement and therefore advanced the moral and legal controversy toward a resolution.

Controversies like those over the use of saccharin in diet sodas, toxic substances in the workplace, fluoridation of public waters, and the manufacture, dissemination, and advertisement of vaccines for medical use are laced with issues of both values and facts. The arguments used by disagreeing parties may turn on a dispute about liberty or justice, and therefore may be primarily moral; but they may also rest on factual disagreements over, for example, the efficacy of a product. New information thus may have only a limited bearing on the resolution of some of these controversies, while in others it may have a direct and almost overpowering influence.

Definitional Clarity. Controversies have been settled by reaching conceptual or definitional agreement over the language used by disputing parties. In some cases stipulation of a definition or a clear explanation of what is meant by a term may prove sufficient, but in other cases agreement cannot be so conveniently achieved. Controversies discussed in Chapter Six over the morality of affirmative action, reverse discrimination, and comparable worth, for example, are often needlessly complicated because different senses of these expressions are employed, and yet disputing parties may have much invested in their particular preferred definitions. If there is no common point of contention in such cases, then parties will be addressing entirely separate issues through their conceptual assumptions and thus will not even have a bona fide moral disagreement.

While conceptual agreement provides no guarantee that a dispute will be settled, it should at least facilitate direct discussion of the outstanding issues. For this reason, many essays in this volume dwell at some length on problems of conceptual clarity. (This is the area of ethics described earlier as "conceptual studies.")

Adopting a Code. Resolution of moral problems can also be facilitated if disputing parties can come to an agreement on a common set of moral principles or adopt a common code to govern their behavior. If this agreement requires a shift between two starkly different moral points of view, agreement will of course rarely if ever be achieved. Differences that divide persons at the level of their most cherished principles are deep divisions, and conversions are infrequent. Various forms of discussion and negotiation can, however, lead to the adoption of a new or changed moral framework that can serve as a common basis for discussion.

A typical example is the following: General Dynamics, the third largest defense contractor in the United States, was heavily criticized in May 1985 for "padding" bills through overhead charges, and for giving a series of gifts to Admiral Hyman G. Rickover. General Dynamics protested its innocence, as did other defense contractors who were criticized in subsequent weeks. They appealed to a lack of explicit rules to determine proper conduct. Secretary of the Navy John Lehman then insisted that the company adopt a "rigorous code of ethics" that was acceptable to the Navy. The purpose of this code was to fix the terms of billing and gift giving so that permissible and impermissible actions were thoroughly understood by all parties, and so that specific reasons could be advanced when *apparently* immoral behavior occurred. Because the terms of the Navy's agreement with defense contractors had been too loose, the door had been open to abuse and misunderstanding. The code would also be used, Secretary Lehman said, to fix the meaning of "keeping the public trust," not only for General Dynamics but for all defense contractors.

The *Washington Post* rightly pointed out (in an editorial) that the code should also be used to address many "serious questions about what the Defense Department's relationship should be with its contractors." For example, how should big weapons contracts be competitively negotiated? And what kinds of control should the government exert? The *Post* reasoned that if such "larger issues" were governed by explicit, well-framed rules in the code, we would then have a better grasp on

what it means for both the Navy and its private contractors to "serve the public."[14] As we shall see repeatedly in this volume, problems of moral controversy are often handled in professional communities and in government by drafting and agreeing to codes of professional ethics. Questions about the adequacy and comprehensiveness of such codes are addressed in several chapters.

Example-Counterexample. Resolution of moral controversies can be aided by a method of example and opposed counterexample. Here cases or examples favorable to one point of view are brought forward and counterexamples to these cases are thrown up by a second party against the examples and claims of the first. For instance, in a famous case against AT&T, a dispute over discriminatory hiring and promotion between the company and the Equal Employment Opportunities Commission (EEOC) was handled by the citation of statistics and examples that allegedly documented the claims made by each side. AT&T showed, for example, that 55 percent of the people on its payroll were women and that 33 percent of management positions were held by women. To sharpen its allegation of discriminatory practices in the face of this evidence, the EEOC countered by citing a government study that demonstrated that 99 percent of all operators were female, while only 1 percent of craft workers were female. Such use of example and counterexample serves as a format for weighing the strength of conflicting considerations.

Analysis of Arguments and Positions. Finally one of the most important methods of philosophical inquiry is that of exposing the inadequacies in and unexpected consequences of arguments and positions (in the sense of *argument* previously introduced). There are many ways of attacking or exposing an argument or position. If a moral argument leads to conclusions that a proponent is not prepared to defend and did not previously anticipate, then part of the argument will have to be changed, and the distance between those who disagree will perhaps be reduced by this process. Inconsistencies not only in reasoning but also in organizational schemes or pronouncements can be invoked. This style of argument can be supplemented by one or more of the previously mentioned four ways of reducing moral disagreement. Works published in philosophical journals and editorials in newspapers often take precisely these forms of argument, using counterexamples and proposing alternative frameworks. However, in an actual context of controversy sharp attacks or critiques are unlikely to eventuate in an agreement unless a climate of reason prevails. A fundamental axiom of successful negotiation is "reason and be open to reason." It holds for moral controversy as well as any other kind of controversy.

Many moral disagreements may not be resolvable by any of the five methods we have discussed. No contention is made here that moral disagreements can always be resolved, or even that every reasonable person must accept the same method for approaching such problems. We may never have a single ethical theory or a single method adequate to resolve all disagreements, and the pluralism of belief in our culture often presents a considerable barrier to closure. There is always a possibility of continual disagreement, and the resolution of crosscultural conflicts such as those faced by multinational corporations may prove especially elusive. However, if something is to be done about these problems of justification in contexts of disagreement, a resolution seems most likely to occur if methods like those outlined in this section are used.

The Problem of Egoism

Many attitudes in business have been analyzed as fundamentally *egoistic*. The claim is that each executive and corporation acts from prudence, as we earlier defined it—that is, each business is out to promote its own interests. Some say the corporation has no other real interest, because it should strive to be as successful in competition as possible.

The philosophical theory called egoism has familiar origins. Each of us has been confronted with occasions on which a choice must be made between spending money on ourselves or on some worthy charitable enterprise. For example, when one elects to purchase new clothes for oneself rather than contribute to a university scholarship fund for poor students, self-interest is given priority over the interests of those students. Egoism generalizes beyond these occasions of choice to all human choices. The egoist contends that all choices either do involve or should involve self-promotion as their sole objective. Thus, a person's or a corporation's only goal and perhaps only duty is self-promotion. No sacrifices and no other obligations are owed to others.

We can begin to examine egoism by distinguishing its two main varieties—psychological egoism and ethical egoism.

Psychological Egoism. Psychological egoism is the view that everyone is always motivated to act in his or her own perceived self-interest. This theory concerns human motivation and offers an explanation of human conduct, in contrast to a justification of human conduct. It says that people always do what pleases them or what is in their own interest. Popular ways of expressing this viewpoint include: "People are at heart selfish, even if they appear to be unselfish"; "People always look out for Number One first"; "In the long run, everybody always does what he or she wants to do or whatever is least painful"; and "No matter what a person says, everybody always acts for the sake of personal satisfaction."

Psychological egoism presents a serious challenge to moral philosophy. If it is correct, there could be no purely altruistic or moral motivation (as the term *morality* is commonly used). Normative ethics presupposes that one *ought* to behave in accordance with certain moral principles, whether or not such behavior promotes one's own interests. If people are so constituted that they must always act in their own interest, then it would be absurd ever to ask them to act contrary to this self-interest. Thus, if psychological egoism is true, the whole enterprise of normative ethics seems futile.

Those who accept psychological egoism do so because they are convinced by their observation of themselves and others that people are entirely self-centered in their motivation. Conversely, those who reject the theory are likely to do so because they see many examples of altruistic behavior in the lives of friends, saints, heroes, and public servants, and because contemporary anthropology, psychology, and biology offer many compelling studies of sacrificial behavior. Even if it is conceded that people are basically selfish, critics of egoism say it seems undeniable that there are at least *some* outstanding examples of preeminently unselfish actions—for example, generous corporations who cut profits in order to provide public services (see Chapter Two, pp. 59–62), and employees who blow the whistle on unsafe or otherwise improper business practices, when they stand to lose their jobs and suffer social ostracism because of their actions. (See pp. 262–63 in Chapter Five.)

The defender of psychological egoism is not impressed by the exemplary lives of saints and heroes or by social practices of sacrifice. The psychological egoist will point out that the position does not hold that people always behave in an outwardly selfish manner. No matter now self-sacrificing a person's behavior may be at times, egoists maintain, the desire behind the action is always selfish, one is ultimately out for oneself—whether in the long or the short run, and whether one knows it or not. In their view, an egoistic action is perfectly compatible with behavior that we categorize as altruistic. For example, many corporations have adopted "enlightened self-interest" policies through which they are responsive to community needs and promote worker satisfaction because they believe their actions will promote their image and ultimately their earnings. The clever person or corporation can appear to be the most unselfish agent around, but whether the actions are really egoistic depends on the motivation be-

hind the appearance. Apparently altruistic agents may simply believe that an unselfish appearance best promotes their own long-range interests. From the egoist's point of view, the fact that some sacrifices (pseudo-sacrifices?) may be necessary in the short run does not count against egoism.

A typical example in business is the following: In mid–1985 Illinois Bell argued before the Illinois Commerce Commission that its competitors should be allowed full access to markets, and thus that there should be no regulation to protect Illinois Bell from its competitors. Illinois Bell had long been protected by such regulation and under it had grown to be a successful, $2.7 billion company. Why, then, was it now arguing that a complete free market would be the fairest business arrangement? *Forbes* magazine asked, "Is this 'altruism' or is it 'enlightened self interest'?" *Forbes* editors answered that, despite the appearance of altruism, what Illinois Bell wanted was "to get the state regulators off their backs" in order to be able to compete more successfully with fewer constraints and to avoid losing business to large companies that could set up their own telephone systems. Self-interest, not fairness was, according to *Forbes,* the proper explanation of Illinois Bell's behavior.[15]

The psychological egoist maintains that all persons who expend effort to help others, to promote fairness in competition, to promote the general welfare, or even to risk their lives for the welfare of others are really acting to promote themselves. In loving others, for example, we strengthen their love for us. By sacrificing for our children, we take satisfaction in their achievements. By following society's moral codes, we avoid both the police and social ostracism. The psychological egoist concedes that people often do act contrary to their self-interest and that some people seem to act contrary to their self-interest most of the time. People simply make mistakes in assessing what is in their self-interest, and a few people stupidly overlook their best interest. Thus, the psychological egoist is not saying that people act in terms of their real self-interest. The egoist is only committed to the view that everyone always is motivated to act in accordance with perceived self-interest.

Is psychological egoism a correct theory? To answer this question, as a matter of psychological fact, is a task too complicated for us to consider here. However, because there do seem to be cases of genuinely altruistic acts that are clearly not in the interest of the individual performing them—for example, giving up one's life to save another—we should make some attempt to assess the adequacy of the egoist's arguments. It is tempting for the psychological egoist to make the theory necessarily true because of the difficulties in proving it to be empirically true. When confronted with what looks like genuinely altruistic acts, egoists may appeal to unconscious motives of self-interest or claim that every act is based on some desire of the person performing the act and that acting on that desire is what is meant by *self-interest*.

The latter explanation may be only a conceptual or verbal trick: The egoist may only have changed the definition of *self-interest*. At first, self-interest meant acting to advantage oneself. Now self-interest has been redefined to mean acting on any interest one has. But the central question remains unresolved: Are there two different kinds of human motives? Do we sometimes have an interest in acting for ourselves and sometimes on behalf of others, or do we simply act for ourselves? We often do act in terms of our own self-interest, and often our interests and the interests of others coincide, but philosophy and psychology have yet to establish that we never act contrary to our perceived self-interest. For this reason psychological egoism remains a speculative hypothesis.

Ethical Egoism. The second type of egoistic theory may be roughly defined as the theory that the only valid standard of conduct is the obligation to promote one's own well-being above everyone else's. Whereas psychological egoism is a psychological theory about human motivation, ethical egoism purports to be a general theory about what we ought to do.

According to psychological egoism, we always *do* act on the basis of perceived self-interest. According to ethical egoism, we always *ought* to act on the basis of perceived self-interest.

The legendary advice that we should always try to maximize our personal good is generally conveyed through maxims such as, "You're a sucker if you don't always look out for yourself first and others second." This maxim is unacceptable by the norms of common morality, which requires that we return a lost wallet to a known owner and that we correct a bank loan officer's errors in our favor. Yet, why should we look out for the interests of others on such occasions? This question has troubled many reflective persons, some of whom have concluded that acting against one's own interest is actually contrary to reason. These thinkers regard conventional morality as tinged with irrational sentiment and indefensible constraints on the individual. They are the supporters of ethical egoism. Their view is not that we ought never to take the interests of others into account, but rather that we should consider the interests of others only when it suits our own interests.

The important question is what society would be like if ethical egoism were the conventional, prevailing theory of proper conduct. Some philosophers and political theorists have argued that anarchism and chaos would result from ethical egoism unless certain preventive measures were adopted. A classic statement of this position was made by the philosopher Thomas Hobbes: Imagine a world with limited resources, where persons are approximately equal in their ability to harm one another, and everyone acts exclusively in his or her own interest. Hobbes argued that in such a world everyone would be at everyone else's throat; such a state of nature would be plagued by anxiety, violence, and constant danger. As Hobbes put it, life would be "solitary, poor, nasty, brutish, and short." However, Hobbes also assumed that human beings were sufficiently rational to recognize their own interests. To avoid the war of all against all he urged that his readers form a powerful state to protect themselves.

Egoists accept Hobbes's view in the following form: Any clever person will realize that he or she has no moral obligations to others besides those he or she voluntarily assumes. One should accept moral rules and assume specific obligations only when doing so promotes one's self-interest. Even if one agrees to live under a set of laws of the state that are binding on everyone, one should obey rules and laws only in order to protect oneself and to bring about a situation of communal living that is personally advantageous. One should also back down on an obligation whenever it becomes clear that it is to one's long-range disadvantage to fulfill the obligation. Thus, when confronted by a social revolution, the questionable trustworthiness of a colleague, or an incompetent administration at one's place of employment, one is under no obligation to obey the law, fulfill one's contracts, or tell the truth. These obligations exist only because one assumes them, and one ought to assume them only as long as doing so promotes one's own interest.

What can be said by way of criticism of this form of ethical egoism? One important criticism is that the theory gives incompatible directives in circumstances of moral conflict: If everyone acted egoistically, it seems reasonably certain that protracted conflicts would occur, just as many international conflicts now arise among nations primarily pursuing their own interests. According to ethical egoism, both parties in a circumstance of conflict ought to pursue their own best interests exclusively, and it is morally right for both to do so. For example, it is in the interest of a consumer activist to stop production and distribution of an automobile of allegedly hazardous design, and it is no less in the interest of the automobile manufacturer to prevent the consumer activist from stopping production and distribution of the model. Egoism urges both parties to pursue their interests exclusively and holds both pursuits to be morally right.

The oddity of this situation can be high-lighted by imagining that the consumer activist is an egoist. In order to be a consistent egoist, the activist must hold to a theory that the automobile manufacturer ought to pursue its interest, which would involve thwarting the activist's consumer objectives (all ought to pursue their interests and thwart others if necessary). In thus striving for theoretical consistency, the egoist supports a theory that works against his or her own interest, and so seems to fall into inconsistency. The egoist says that everyone ought to seek his or her own maximal satisfaction, even though the pursuit by everyone of their interests would negatively affect the egoist's own pursuit of maximal satisfaction.

The most plausible egoistic reply to this objection is that it springs from a misunderstanding of the rules and policies that an ethical egoist would actually promote. If everyone were to act on more or less fixed rules such as those found in conventional moral and legal systems, this arrangement would produce the most desirable state of affairs from an egoistic point of view. The reason is that such rules arbitrate conflicts and make social life more agreeable. These rules would include, for example, familiar moral and legal principles of justice that are intended to make everyone's situation more secure and stable.

Only an unduly narrow conception of genuine self-interest, the egoist might argue, leads critics to think that the egoist would not willingly observe such rules of justice when it is in one's self-interest to do so, as it usually is. If society can be structured to resolve personal conflicts through courts and other peaceful means, the egoist will see it as in his or her interest to accept those binding social arrangements—just as the egoist will see it as prudent to treat other individuals well in personal contacts with them. Notice that the egoist is not saying that his or her best interests are served by promoting the good of others, but rather that personal interests are served by observing impartial rules irrespective of the outcome for others. The egoist does not care about the welfare of others except insofar as it affects her or his own welfare, and it is this alone that motivates acceptance of the conventional rules of morality.

Egoistic Business Practices and Utilitarian Results. A different view from that of Hobbes, and one that has been extremely influential in the personal philosophy of the business community, is found in Adam Smith's economic and moral writings. Smith believed that the public good evolves out of a suitably restrained clash of competing individual interests. As each person pursues his or her own self-interest, the interactive process is guided by an "invisible hand," so that the public interest is achieved. It is ironic that, according to Smith, individual egoism in commercial transactions leads not to the war of all against all, but rather to utilitarianism, that is, the largest number of benefits for the largest number of persons. The free market is, Smith thought, a better method of achieving the public good than the highly visible and authoritarian hand of Hobbes's all-powerful sovereign state.

To protect individual freedom, Smith thought government should be limited. At the same time, he recognized that concern with freedom and self-interest could get out of control, and hence he proposed that a minimal state and regulatory activity is required to provide and enforce the rules of the competitive game. Smith's picture of a restrained egoistic world has captivated many in the business community. They do not picture themselves as selfish and indifferent to the interests of others, and they recognize that a certain element of cooperation is essential if their own interests are to flourish. At the same time, they recognize that when their interests do conflict with the interests of others within the established rules of the competitive game, they should pursue their own interests. Within the rules of business practice, they see business ethics as the ethics of a suitably restrained egoist. It is egoistic because it is an ethic based on the active pursuit of one's own interest. It is restrained because self-interest must be kept within the bounds of the prevailing rules of business practice.

Consider pricing and production by the thirteen nations that are members of OPEC (Organization of Petroleum Exporting Countries). These nations all believe that the group's best interest is generally served by an industrious pursuit of self-interest by each member nation. However, OPEC's raison d'être and strength as a group are its ability to set and hold oil prices at a sufficiently high level so that each member gets the maximum benefit from the protection of that price level. A problem has arisen in times of falling petroleum spot market prices, because each member nation has an incentive to "cheat" on OPEC rules by defecting from the official price level. Explicitly acknowledging that OPEC member nations cannot trust each other in this circumstance, OPEC hired a Dutch accounting firm (KMG Klynveld Kraaugenhoff & Co.) to monitor each member state's actual pricing and production figures. Thus, although OPEC aims to maximize the self-interest of all member nations and promote that good, it also restrains individual action that threatens the vital interests of other member nations.[16]

Many in the business community have actively supported the view that a suitably restrained egoism leads to utilitarian outcomes (even if not to the full utilitarian moral philosophy). This in fact is one of the defenses of a free market economy: Competition advances the good of corporations, and competition among individual firms advances the good of society as a whole. Hence, a popular view of business ethics might be captured by the phrase, "ethical egoism leads to utilitarian outcomes." As Adam Smith put it, corporations and individuals who pursue their individual interests also thereby promote the public good, so long as they abide by the rules that protect the public.

A controversial figure who defends his actions through this line of argument is America's highest-paid corporate executive (see p. 551 in Chapter Nine), the previously mentioned T. Boone Pickens, Chairman of Mesa Petroleum Company. Pickens is a corporate "raider" (see pp. 476–78 in Chapter Eight): He works to spot undervalued corporations, and then threatens to take them over. Using speculative stock purchases and hostile tender offers, raiders strike fear in the hearts of corporate managers, who sometimes modify their growth plans to defend the corporation from the takeover attempt. Pickens believes that he is simply drawing attention to undervalued companies whose true value comes to light through his activities; this benefits the stockholders (who he proclaims are the only real owners of public corporations), whose stock suddenly increases in monetary value. Pickens's immediate ambition is self-interest—profit for himself and his company—but he claims that the public in general is a large benefactor of his efforts to improve his own financial position.

Many corporate managers vigorously disagree with Pickens, and many also disagree with the confident optimism underlying Adam Smith's more general perspective. They also reject all forms of egoism. We can begin to understand why by turning to the study of ethical theory, and to utilitarian ethical theories in particular.

PART TWO: NORMATIVE ETHICAL THEORY

Early in Part One we observed that *morality*—as contrasted with ethical theory—denotes a social institution, composed of a set of standards pervasively acknowledged by the members of the culture in which it is entrenched, and thus that individuals do not create their morality by making their own rules. If there is to be a meaningful ethics in the culture of business, those who share this morality while engaging in business practice must be able to implement standards that are more than hopeless abstractions. We need both an acceptable *theory* of business responsibility—as expressed in business and philosophical journals, conferences on business ethics, and the like—and a way to make the theory institutionalized in *practice*.

Perhaps the central question at stake in Part Two is, "What constitutes an acceptable standard for practice and by what authority is the standard acceptable?" One time-honored answer is that the acceptability of a moral standard is to be determined by prevailing conventions in business or authoritative profession-generated documents such as codes. Many businesspersons find this viewpoint congenial and thus often do not see the need for revisions of prevailing practices, which they find comfortable and adequate. However, some businesspersons and many critics of business who are concerned about relating ethical theory to practice may take the competing view that traditional or operative standards are often incomplete, poorly understood, and inconsistent—as well as suffering from the lack of a uniform theory that would make the body of rules consistent and coherent. Those who take this viewpoint are inclined to revise or possibly ignore business practices, and they often look to some system of ethical theory to provide a basis for revisions.

Any account of professional standards ideally should begin with their historical and institutional roots, not merely—as philosophers often attempt in their work—with the conceptual and normative foundations of a philosophical ethical theory. Only if we do not allow ourselves to get too distant from the historical and cultural contexts in which conceptions of business ethics arose can we hope to spot defects in the practices and gain a meaningful appreciation of moral issues in business. However, in our current discussion of professional ethics we must telescope history dramatically in order to present the main outlines of the gradual development of professional standards in business.

To make matters still more complicated, moral standards operative in the professions often have grown up in constant interaction with a body of law; some legal doctrine may even have been fashioned to handle specific areas of business conduct. Both the law and the moral standards operative in professional settings may have taken a considerable period of time to reach the shape that we now recognize. Furthermore, this developmental history generally has occurred under the impact of broad cultural influences such as the civil rights and consumer protection movements, and an adequate understanding of the professional standards can only be reached by framing them in the context of these larger cultural phenomena. With these cautions in mind, we can examine two important tests of reasonableness in business conduct.

Professional Standards: The Role of Tradition and Practice

The two apparently competing standards— both of which have a rich history of discussion and use in legal contexts—will be referred to here as the professional practice standard and the reasonable person standard.

The Professional Practice Standard. The first standard holds that duties and other standards of moral conduct are determined by the customary practices of a professional community. Proponents of this standard argue that a businessperson is charged professionally with various responsibilities (for example, avoiding harm, honoring warranties, removing conflicts of information, and obeying legal requirements) and must use proper professional criteria for determining appropriate actions. Custom in the profession establishes the standards of obligatory conduct, such as "due care." Any person without expert knowledge is unqualified to establish what should be done, and for this reason the professional community is the appropriate source. This rule is applied in cases where wrong conduct is suspected in order to determine the duty of due care in the person's performance. For example, the standard is familiar to the courts in their handling of negligence cases, where it must be possible to assess responsibility and liability for harm, usually because a client, patient, or customer seeks to punish the responsible party, be compensated, or both.

We need not dwell here on the important topic of legal liability or compensation, but the legal model of responsibility for harmful action does suggest a useful general framework that can be adapted to express the idea of moral responsibility in business. In this model, care is a central concept for assessing moral responsibility for harmful outcomes: Anyone who is not sufficiently careful automatically invites moral blame as well as legal penalty. To be morally blameworthy a harm must be caused by carelessness resulting from failure to discharge a socially, legally, or morally imposed duty to take care or to behave reasonably toward others. Therefore negligence or unintentional, careless action can be analyzed in terms of the following essential elements of a professional model:

1. An established professional duty to the affected party must exist.
2. Someone must breach that duty.
3. The affected party must experience a harm.
4. This harm must be caused by the breach of duty.

Professional malpractice is thus an instance of negligence in which professional standards of care have not been followed—for example, when an accountant fails to follow generally accepted accounting practices in auditing a firm. Of course, the model of a person as negligent is hardly a foolproof method of assessing responsibility for causing harm in business. For example, harm might be caused by a decision that was reached through the efforts of many parties, including executives, members of the board, venture capitalists, and consultants. Here a diffusion of responsibility occurs, and it is often difficult or even impossible to determine who, if anyone, made the decision or performed the action that caused the harm—an issue that receives further attention in Chapter Two. Another limitation is that avoiding harm to others sometimes involves acts of exceptional courage of a kind that has not generally been required in the professions or elsewhere.

One area of massive uncertainty in contemporary business involves a failure by professionals, such as accountants, to probe deeply enough in an investigative report, so that persons are harmed by not having information that the professional had the responsibility to uncover. For example, since a scandal at McKesson & Robbins in 1940, the Securities and Exchange Commission has held that an accountant performing a corporate audit has a duty to uncover gross management overstatements. Although accountants have long resisted the idea that they are negligent because they have not uncovered management fraud, some recent legal cases have suggested that the courts expect accountants to uncover fraud, no matter how subtle. (See pp. 475–76.) By this demanding standard, auditors who fail to catch red flags that professional standards determine to be suspicious would be responsible for harms that result from their negligence.

Despite its popularity in business as an expression of standards of professional responsibility, the professional practice standard has shortcomings worthy of discussion. First, this particular professional standard of duty (and negligence) would surely be too high for some areas of practice. Even when the utmost care is exercised in some circumstances, it is possible that some critical factor has been omitted or distorted because of lack of access to sources or documents. Second, it can be questioned whether a customary standard of disclosure actually exists within the relevant fields of business, and how much consensus is required for the establishment of such a standard—that is, for a norm to count as a standard prevalent in practice. A third objection is that truly negligent care might be perpetuated if relevant professionals generally offer the same inferior set of precautions, warranties, technology, auditing strategies, and so on—whether through ignorance, as a genuine conviction, or for reasons of professional solidarity. If the elements of negligent behavior are to serve as a workable model for business settings, the established duty cannot be set at such a low level that virtually any conduct is acceptable.

Another more fundamental objection centers on a basic assumption of the professional practice standard: that the relevant professionals actually have sufficient expertise to know what the proper precautions, information, warranties, auditing strategies, and the like should be. This assumption is empirical, yet there are no reliable data on these issues, and current research on the effects of professional standards is both sketchy and inconclusive. One might also doubt that professional standards should be set by the professionals even when they do possess the relevant expertise. A good bet is that customers, employees, and consumers will desire more detailed disclosures or more extensive precautions as standards of due care than would a circle of professionals practicing the business. Ultimately, decisions about due care are not merely professional judgments, and thus critics maintain that they should not be reserved to the professional alone, or even primarily.

Another problem with the due care principle has arisen over how to assess the obligations of manufacturers when their products prove to be defective even though no negligence was involved on their part. An implication of the due care principle is that a manufacturer is not liable when a product defect results in harm to others if the manufacturer could not have foreseen or prevented the harm. There are problems both about how much care is sufficient and over whether it is fair to hold corporations liable if defects could not have been corrected under any reasonable standard. As we see in Chapter Four, this problem of "strict liability" is a complicated problem intrinsic to professional responsibility.

The Reasonable Person Standard. These objections to the professional practice standard suggest the need to adopt a different standard that is designed to protect employees, clients, customers, and the public more adequately. Such a standard is often expressed in terms of what the reasonable person would do. Under this standard, customers or public representatives, say, are to judge whether professional determinations are adequate in terms of standards of reasonableness, and a professional's conduct may therefore be found negligent or otherwise deficient even if his or her behavior conforms perfectly to recognized and routine professional practice. For example, it might be argued that warnings by various drug manufacturers of the side effects of drugs are incomplete or nonexistent and that the problem of making adequate warnings and disclosures requires the judgment of the reasonable person and exceeds the skill and knowledge found across the industry.

The well-known legal model of the "reasonable person," known in English common law since 1783 as the "reasonable man" standard, has been interpreted so that it must be applied by a factfinder (a jury or sometimes a judge) who must evaluate conduct objectively. The standard is objective in that it is designed to incorporate the common body of assumptions that the members of a society make about their fellow citizens in order to cooperate efficiently. For example, the reasonable-person standard provides a basis on which parties to contracts can avoid hidden misunderstandings. The reasonable person is simply a constructed composite of reasonable persons in society and is never to be understood as a specific person or as the average person.

In theory, then, the law does not look to average persons or statistical norms when deciding whether a person or an act is reasonable—although no doubt this often happens in actual practice. The law asks a jury or some other body to reflect on social standards of reasonableness, and to frame the judgment to be reached entirely in those terms. This standard is commonly invoked in the courtroom to investigate how much information a reasonable person needs to know about such matters as risks, alternatives, and consequences in order to make prudent choices that are adequately informed. The legal litmus test under this standard for determining the extent of an adequate disclosure of information, for example, is the *materiality*—that is, significance—of information to the de-

cision-making process of the person to whom the disclosure was made.

Although here we are reflecting morally rather than legally, it is possible to take a similar approach in applying the reasonable-person standard to problems of business ethics. Here the reasonable person is to be understood from the point of view of a customer, employee, consumer, business competitor, or client's needs, rather than from the point of view of the routine practices or policies found in business. The reasonable person should behave as reasonable consumers and customers would expect of the moral person.

Thus far, then, neither standard seems adequate as a grounding for professional ethics.

The Role of Philosophical Ethics. To the extent business ethics leaves room for improvement, revision, expansion, and even novelty, philosophical ethics seems to have an important role to play. The dark side of this opportunity is that traditionally philosophical ethics has been largely divorced from the development of rules, forms of practice, and the general literature of business. In recent years, however, philosophical ethics has been increasingly invoked to help shape both old and new problems of corporate responsibility, and we have begun to appreciate that although the sources of ethics in business and the sources of ethics in philosophy have historically been starkly different—like two animals from entirely separate domains of the animal kingdom—both philosophical ethics and professional ethics often develop from already existent movements, events, and issues in social ethics and politics.

So does the law, and it serves justice to remember the profound impact of the law and the pioneering character of the landmark cases found in most of the chapters in this volume. The law's effect on thinking about many moral problems has often outstripped the thinking in either business or philosophy and has stimulated both disciplines to new proposed solutions. The influential role of the courts in moral problems can perhaps be explained by the fact that the courts already had in place a structure that was better equipped to address the issues than did either business or philosophy. Civil liberties, self-determination, fraud, bodily integrity, battery, trespass, the fiduciary relationship, contract, and the like are in some respects still more fully developed and applicable to social problems than are parallel philosophical principles.

In business there is rarely to be found such a ready set of internal principles as those in law, and there is no real resource for reflection on moral problems of the sort found in philosophy. Developments in business ethics that move beyond professional practice standards therefore tend to come from either law or philosophy. It should not be supposed that business morality always requires supplementation by law and philosophy, but there are many occasions on which this supplementation presents efficiency, clarity, and comprehensiveness in the treatment of moral problems by bringing an applicable external source or framework. Sometimes business is even jolted from an exclusive preoccupation with a certain settled viewpoint—possibly its professional standards—to see more viable alternatives.

In the remainder of Part Two, we turn our attention more to ethical theory than to either legal theory or professional practice in business. Our objective is to achieve a deeper appreciation and analysis of the uncertainties surrounding contemporary business ethics and the ways in which ethical theory may play a role in their clarification and resolution. My assumption will be that ethical theory cannot simply be rushed in to establish justifications and overturn well established parts of the moral viewpoint found in business, but that ethical theory also can provide philosophical arguments that reduce pervasive vagueness and that present reasoned patterns of justification and programs of reform. Philosophical theory presents a reconstruction of concepts and claims that refine, sharpen, and challenge what we have thought historically and what in the literature should have been meant when

vague appeals were made. A philosophical theory thus should be influenced by history in business and by a knowledge of practice, but not imprisoned by these traditions.

Utilitarian Theories

In contemporary philosophy, ethical theories are commonly divided into two broad, fundamental types, teleological and deontological. Presumably the two approaches provide radically different perspectives on the moral life and entail different conclusions about what ought to be done. However, they have never been demonstrated to be inconsistent, and their exact similarities and differences deserve close study.

Teleological theories hold that the moral worth of actions or practices is determined solely by the consequences of the actions or practices. The most widely studied teleological theory is utilitarianism, which holds that an action or practice is right (when compared to any alternative action or practice) if it leads to the greatest possible balance of good consequences or to the least possible balance of bad consequences in the world as a whole. In taking this perspective, utilitarians invite consideration of the overall purpose or function of morality as a social institution. The purpose of the institution of morality, they maintain, is to promote human welfare by minimizing harms and maximizing benefits. A good example of this approach to the moral life is found in Chapter Three of this volume, where certain authors see the purpose of government regulation and the use of cost/benefit analysis in utilitarian terms.

Mill's Utilitarianism. The first developed utilitarian philosophical writings were those of David Hume (1711–1776), Jeremy Bentham (1748–1832), and John Stuart Mill (1806–1873), and the major theoretical exposition of utilitarianism is still Mill's *Utilitarianism* (1863). In this work Mill discusses two foundations or sources of utilitarian thinking: a *normative* foundation in the principle of utility and a *psy-*

chological foundation in human nature. He proposes the principle of utility, or the "greatest happiness principle" as the foundation of normative ethical theory: Actions are right, he says, in proportion to their tendency to promote happiness or absence of pain, and wrong insofar as they tend to produce pain or displeasure. Pleasure and freedom from pain, Mill argues, are alone desirable as ends; all desirable things (which are numerous) are therefore desirable either for the pleasure inherent in them, or as means to the promotion of pleasure and the prevention of pain.

Mill's second foundation of utilitarianism derives from his belief that most, and perhaps all, persons have a basic desire for unity and harmony with their fellow human beings. Just as we feel horror at crimes, he says, so we have a basic moral sensitiveness to the needs of others. His view seems to be that the purpose of morality is at once to tap natural human sympathies so as to benefit others, while at the same time controlling unsympathetic attitudes that cause harm to others. The principle of utility is conceived as the best means to these basic human goals.

Essential Features of Utilitarianism. Several essential features of utilitarianism may be extracted from the reasoning of Mill and other utilitarians. First, utilitarianism is committed to the maximization of the good and the minimization of harm and evil. It asserts that we ought always to produce the greatest possible balance of positive value for all persons affected, or the minimum balance of disvalue. The obvious means to maximization is efficiency, a goal that persons in business generally find congenial, because efficiency is highly prized throughout the economic sector. Efficiency is a means to higher profits and to lower prices, and the struggle to be maximally profitable seeks to obtain maximum production from limited economic resources. The utilitarian commitment to the principle of optimal productivity through efficiency is an essential part of the traditional business conception of society and standard part of business practice. In this respect the enterprise of

business harbors a fundamentally utilitarian conception of the good society.

The need both to minimize harm and to balance risks against benefits has been a perennial concern of the business community. Corporations like Allied Corporation and Lockheed California Company—two corporations beset by corporate scandals in the 1970s—have held regular management ethics seminars on the topic of assessing the "lesser of evils" in a business circumstance where necessarily there will be some evil outcome. Even more frequent is the need to bring about the best possible outcome in a tradeoff situation—a circumstance most businesses face almost daily when weighing harms and benefits as part of the decision making process. Practitioners of any profession must face these choices. Physicians, for example, who pledge to do no harm are not pledging never to cause harm, but rather to strive for a balance of benefits over harms.

Thus, the primary obligation is to weigh benefits against harms, benefits against alternative benefits, and harms against alternative harms. For example, those in the petroleum industry know that oil and gas operations exist tenuously with wetlands areas, waterfowl, and fish. But it is not an either/or situation: Corporate and public policies often balance possible environmental harms against industrial productivity and its benefits. Similarly, those in the nuclear power industry know that U.S. power plants are built with heavy containment structures to withstand most internal failures; but we also know that there could be a major disaster such as that at Chernobyl, Russia, in 1986. In building such structures we balance public benefit, predicted cost savings, the probability of failure, and the magnitude of harm in the event of failure. The utilitarian believes that such examples from public policy exhibit a general truth about the moral life.

However, there is more to most accounts of utilitarianism than efficiency, reducing evil, and maximizing positive outcomes in the tradeoff situation, and hence a second essential feature must be considered. This feature is the utilitarians' theory of intrinsic value. Efficiency itself is simply an instrumental good; that is, it is valuable strictly as a means to something else. In the corporation, efficiency is valuable as a means to growth and to maximizing profit. Within the free enterprise system of competing firms, efficiency is valuable as a means toward maximizing the production of goods and services. Within utilitarian moral theory, efficiency is the means for maximizing the good. But what is "good" according to the utilitarian?

We can begin to form an answer to this question by considering, as an illustration, the working of the stock market. Daily results on Wall Street are not intrinsically good; they are extrinsically good as a means to other ends, such as financial security and happiness. Utilitarians believe that what we really ought to seek in life are certain experiences and conditions that are good in themselves without reference to their further consequences, and that all values are ultimately to be gauged in terms of these intrinsic goods. Health, friendship, and freedom from pain would be included among such values. An intrinsic value, then, is a value in life that we wish to possess and enjoy just for its own sake and not as a means to something else.

However, utilitarians are in disagreement as to what constitutes the complete range of things or states that are good. Bentham and Mill are hedonists; they believe that only pleasure or happiness (which are synonymous terms in this context) can be intrinsically good. Everything besides pleasure is merely instrumentally good to the end of pleasure. *Hedonistic* utilitarians, then, believe that any act or practice that maximizes pleasure (when compared with any alternative act or practice) is right. They insist that "pleasure" covers a broad range of experiences and states of affairs, including most satisfactions we find in life. Nonetheless, later utilitarian philosophers have argued that other values besides pleasure possess intrinsic worth—for example, friendship, knowledge, courage, health, and beauty. Utilitarians who believe in multiple intrinsic values are referred to as *pluralistic* utilitarians.

In recent philosophy, economics, and psychology, neither the approach of the hedonists nor that of the pluralists has prevailed. Both approaches have seemed relatively useless for purposes of objectively aggregating widely different interests in order to determine maximal value and therefore right action. Another approach is to appeal to individual preferences. The concept of utility is understood from this perspective not in terms of states of affairs such as happiness, but rather in terms of the satisfaction of individual preferences, as determined by a person's behavior. In the language of business, utility is measured by what a person purchases or otherwise pursues. Accordingly, to maximize a person's utility is to provide that which he or she has chosen or would choose from among the available alternatives. To maximize the utility of all persons affected by an action or policy is to maximize the utility of the aggregate group.

While this preference-based utilitarian approach to value has been viewed by many as superior to its predecessors, it has not proved to be trouble-free as a moral theory. A major theoretical problem arises when individuals have morally unacceptable preferences. For example, a person's strong sexual preference may be to rape young children, or an employment officer may prefer to discriminate against women, yet such preferences are morally intolerable. We reject such preferences as harmful and without any positive value. Utilitarianism based purely on subjective preferences is satisfactory, then, only if a range of acceptable preferences can be formulated. This latter task has proved difficult in theory, and it may even be inconsistent with a pure preference approach.

Nonetheless, some plausible replies to this objection are open to utilitarians. First, because most people are not perverse and do have morally acceptable values (albeit sometimes odd ones), utilitarians believe they are justified in proceeding under the assumption that the preference approach is not fatally marred by a speculative problem. As Mill noted, any moral theory may lead to unsatisfactory outcomes if one assumes universal idiocy. Second, because perverse desires have at times worked against the larger objectives of utilitarianism (maximal public welfare) by creating unhappiness, the utilitarian could argue that such desires (preferences) should never be permitted to count in the calculus of preferences. We discount preferences to rape children and to discriminate against women not only because they obstruct the preferences of children and women, but because, more generally, such preferences eventuate in unhappiness and conflict in society. Preferences that serve merely to frustrate the preferences of others are thus ruled out by the goal of utilitarianism (though experience may be needed to know this). As Mill argued, the cultivation of certain kinds of desires and the exclusion of antithetical desires is built into the ideal of utilitarianism.

Still, even if most people are not perverse and if the ideals of utilitarianism are well entrenched in society, some rational agents may have preferences that are immoral or unjust. A major problem for utilitarian theory is that it may need a supplementary criterion of value other than mere preference. Many critics have suggested that at least one or more principles of justice must supplement the principle of utility.

A third essential feature of utilitarianism is its commitment to the measurement and comparison of goods. On the hedonistic view, we must be able to measure pleasurable and painful states and be able to compare one person's pleasures with another's in order to decide which is greater. Bentham, for example, worked out a measurement device that he called the hedonic calculus. He thought he could add the quantitative units of individual happiness, subtract the units of individual unhappiness, and thereby arrive at a measure of total happiness. By the use of this hedonic calculus we allegedly can measure and compare individual happiness and can ultimately determine the act or practice that will provide the greatest happiness to the greatest number. Historically, many economists have maintained that the maximum of goods and serv-

ices can be squeezed from scarce resources through a free-market, competitive economy. These economists also believed that in maximizing the production of valued goods and services, happiness would be maximized as well. Utilitarian analysis provided the bridge for that conclusion.

Consider a thousand people who are planning a vacation for a week in July. There are 250 ocean front sites, 250 sites in the mountains, 250 sites on a lake, and 250 sites near the ocean but not on it. The thousand people express their preferences for the sites. If there are too many requests for the lake, the price of the lake sites will rise. Those who least prefer the lake (at the established price, anyway) will choose some other vacation site. By replacing Bentham's hedonic calculus with the measuring stick of *price* and *preference*, economists have argued that an economy constructed along the lines of the postulates of free competition maximizes utility. Economic theory was thus utilitarian at its core, and business theory borrowed and built upon that utilitarian base.

A Narrow Utilitarian Theory Based on Economic Efficiency. An extremely narrow utilitarian view that is now increasingly accepted by some influential figures in American legal and economic circles is that every facet of society, from institutions such as motherhood and universities to those of gasoline refining and criminal punishment, can and should be analyzed in terms of economic efficiency—that is, highest benefit at the least cost. Often referred to simply as ''law and economics,'' this influential branch of legal scholarship holds that we can query whether virtually any social institution is economically efficient and then seek to restructure it along lines of greater efficiency. Any law or practice that does not serve this goal should be restructured so that it does.

A famous and controversial example comes from an examination of adoption practices and laws by a former University of Chicago law professor and now federal judge, Richard Posner.[17] He argued that current state laws in the United States tend to create and then to perpetuate the well-known shortage of babies available for adoption. The natural consequence is an illegal black market. Economic efficiency and social utility would be increased, he argued, if qualified potential parents could purchase infants on the open market, paying fees to women who could carry babies to term instead of having abortions, and then would place the child through an adoption agency for a private sale. Consumer satisfaction would increase, the cost of babies would be far less than it now is on the black market, and babies would be far better off because purchasers tend to care more for what they purchase than what they get free.

The larger social vision, in effect, is that society should be structured in terms of utilitarian economics; the entire category of social significance is viewed in economic terms, and all values can be reduced to economic value. For example, the right of privacy has been attacked on grounds that withholding many personal facts tends to undermine efficiency in hiring, taxing, and even marriage. Both nonutilitarian critics and utilitarians who take a broader view of social and personal value have condemned this theory as too narrow. In particular, they have criticized the theory as attempting to replace the social value of human welfare with the value of free-market competition, thus overemphasizing the relevance of economics for social affairs. The argument, essentially, is that the good of efficiency must be tempered in many cases by fairness (justice). An additional criticism is that the theory wrongly assumes that the main purpose of human action is to maximize economic wealth.

While this criticism may have merit, it is important to reflect on the potential impact this utilitarian economic theory could have in business, law, and government. To take one small example, this theory has already had a major impact on anti-trust law in the United States; courts have become tolerant of competitive, aggressive, but highly efficient business practices that in the past would have been judged illegal. The theory has also had significant impact on corporate law, when, for example, takeovers are now widely regarded as improving the economy by shifting assets to better management. Looking at competitive practices less in terms of the businesses that are harmed and more in terms of fostering competition and thereby increasing overall efficiency could potentially have a revolutionary effect on institutions that had not formerly been evaluated from this perspective. Some now believe that for-profit hospitals, for example, have already set us on this path for health-care institutions. It is not difficult to see how such a view could be pushed in many other basic institutions, such as public schools, public utilities, and foreign trade.

This general approach is an instructive example of a narrow but now influential conception of utilitarianism at work in business and law. It is also not difficult to see why other utilitarians and critics of utilitarianism would find it too confining, and even immoral.

Act and Rule Utilitarianism

Utilitarian moral philosophers are conventionally divided into two types, act utilitarians and rule utilitarians. An act utilitarian argues that in all situations one ought to perform that act which leads to the greatest good for the greatest number. Utilitarianism aims at maximizing value, and the most direct means to this goal would seem to be that of maximizing value on every single occasion. The act utilitarian thus regards rules such as ''You ought to tell the truth in making contracts'' as useful guidelines, but also as expendable. An act utilitarian would not hesitate to break any moral rule if breaking it would lead to the greatest good for the greatest number in a particular case. Rule utilitarians, as we shall see, reserve a more significant place for rules, which they do not regard as expendable merely on grounds that utility will be maximized in the circumstances.

Consider the following case, in which American business practices and standards run up against the quite different practices of the Italian business community. The case turns on the tax problems encountered by the Italian subsidiary of a major American bank. It seems that in Italy the practices of corporate taxation typically involve elaborate negotiations between hired company representatives and the Italian tax service, and that the tax statement initially submitted by a corporation is always regarded as a dramatically understated bid intended only as a starting point for the negotiating process. In the case in question, the American manager of the Italian banking subsidiary decided, against the advice of locally experienced lawyers and tax consultants, to ignore the native Italian practices and file a conventional American-style tax statement (that is, one in which the subsidiary's profits for the year were not dramatically understated). Among his reasons for this decision was the belief that to conform to the local customs would be to violate the important moral rule of truth telling.[18]

An act utilitarian might well take exception to this conclusion. Admittedly, to file an Italian-style tax statement would be to violate a moral rule of truth telling; but the act utilitarian would argue that such a rule is only a rule of thumb and can justifiably be violated in order to produce the greatest good. In the present case, the argument would go, the greatest good would evidently be done by following the local consultants' advice and conforming to the Italian practices. Only by following those practices will the appropriate amount of tax be paid. This conclusion is strengthened by the ultimate outcome of the present case: The Italian authorities forced the bank to enter into the customary negotiations, a process in which the original, truthful tax statement was treated as an understated opening bid, and a dramatically excessive tax payment was consequently exacted.

In contrast to the position of act utilitarians, rule utilitarians hold that rules have a central position in morality that cannot be compromised by the demands of particular situations. Such compromise would threaten the general effectiveness of the rules, the observance of which would maximize social utility. An example of rule utilitarian reasoning is found in

a case involving John Zaccaro, the husband of 1984 vice-presidential candidate Geraldine A. Ferraro. In late 1982 Zaccaro was appointed the guardian of an elderly woman's estate. For his own business purposes, Zaccaro borrowed $175,000 from the estate to be repaid at 12 percent interest. Zaccaro was also to have been paid a fee for overseeing the investments. The propriety of Zacarro's actions wound up in court, where it was determined that he had not acted dishonestly or with malicious intent and may well have made more dividends for the elderly woman than she would have reaped through more conservative investing. In effect, the court found that Zaccaro may have maximized the utility of everyone who was directly affected in the circumstances. Nonetheless, Zaccaro had placed himself in a position of conflict of interest, and the court found that "the rule is inflexible that a trustee shall not place himself in a position where his interest is or may be in conflict with his duty." For his part, Zaccaro maintained that he acted in good faith and benefited the woman as best he could, but said, "I understand and accept the decision of the court that general principles of law must nevertheless be applied rigidly to guide the actions of other conservators."[19] In effect, both the judge and Zaccaro were agreeing that rule utilitarianism takes precedence over act utilitarianism; even if Zaccaro had maximized everyone's utility in the circumstance his act violated a basic, inflexible rule that had to take precedence.

For the rule utilitarian, then, actions are justified by appeal to abstract rules such as "Don't deceive," "Don't bribe," and "Don't break promises." These rules, in turn, are justified by an appeal to the principle of utility. The rule utilitarian believes this position can escape the objections to act utilitarianism, precisely because rules are not subject to change by the demands of individual circumstances. Utilitarian rules are in theory firm and protective of all classes of individuals—just as human rights (as we will see later) are rigidly protective of all individuals regardless of social convenience and momentary need.

Act utilitarians, however, have a reply to the criticisms advanced by rule utilitarians. They argue that there is a third possibility that lies between never obeying a rule and always obeying it—that it should only sometimes be obeyed. An example of this act utilitarian form of reasoning is found in the defense offered by A. Carl Kotchian, former president of Lockheed Corporation, of $12 million in "grease payments" made to high Japanese officials in order to facilitate sales of his TriStar plane. Kotchian recognized that "extortion," as he called it, was involved and that American rules of business ethics forbid such payments. Kotchian advanced two arguments in defense of his payments: (1) "Such disbursements did not [at the time] violate American laws," and (2) "the TriStar payments . . . would provide Lockheed workers with jobs and thus redounded to the benefit of their dependents, their communities, and stockholders of the corporation." Kotchian went on to argue that the financial consequences of "commercial success" and the public interest in both Japan and the United States were sufficient to override "a purely ethical and moral standpoint."[20] This is precisely the form of reasoning that rule utilitarians have generally rejected but act utilitarians have defended as at least meriting serious consideration.

In the end the act-utilitarian view seems to invoke a prediction that we will be better off in the moral life if we sometimes obey and sometimes disobey rules, because this kind of conduct will not fundamentally erode either moral rules or our general respect for morality. The rule utilitarian would, of course, challenge the part of this argument that claims that less rather than more damage will be done to the institution of morality by adopting an act-utilitarian position. Much current debate within utilitarianism focuses on this issue.

It is also appropriate to ask whether rule utilitarians can escape the very criticisms they level at act utilitarians. There are often conflicts between moral rules: for example, rules of confidentiality conflict with rules protecting individual welfare. We shall see in Chapter Five that many people believe an employer's rights can easily conflict with the rights of employees, as cases of whistle blowing illustrate. If the moral life were so ordered that we always knew which rules and rights should receive priority, there would be no serious problem for moral theory. Yet such a ranking of rules seems clearly impossible. Mill briefly considered this problem. He held that the principle of utility should itself decide in any given circumstance which rule is to take priority. However, if this solution is accepted by rule utilitarians, then their theory must on some occasions rely on the principle of utility to decide in particular situations which action is preferable to which alternative action in the absence of a governing rule.

The rule utilitarian has a reply to this criticism, namely that a sense of relative weight and importance would, insofar as is possible, be built directly into moral rules. For example, the rule utilitarian might argue that rules prohibiting false and misleading advertising of products are of such vital social significance (that is, have such paramount social utility) that they can never be overridden by an appeal to rules that allow manufacturers the freedom to advertise and market their products. Of course, rule utilitarians must concede, in the end, that weights cannot be so definitively formulated and built into principles that irresolvable conflicts among rules will never arise. What they need not concede is that this problem is unique to rule utilitarianism. Every moral theory that accepts a plural number of rules has certain practical limitations in cases of conflicts between the rules. It will nonetheless be possible to distinguish theories that require strict observance of rules from those, such as act utilitarianism, that do not.

Criticisms of Utilitarianism

The Problem of Quantifying Goodness. Several major criticisms of utilitarian theories in general have been put forward, one of which centers on the question: Can units of happiness or some other utilitarian value be measured and compared so as to determine the best among alternatives? How is Congress to compare, for example, the value of a financial support program for the automobile industry with the value of regular inspections of plants in order to prevent occupational disease? This criticism might be called the comparison problem or the apples-and-oranges problem. This difficulty in comparing different experiences clearly extends in practical ways to business firms. For example, one device suggested for measuring corporate responsibility is the corporate social audit. In addition to providing a financial picture of the company, the social audit is supposed to provide a picture of the company's sense of social responsibility. However, problems have arisen over how to measure and compare a corporation's ethical assets and liabilities that have left the corporate social audit in a relatively primitive state. (We will examine the corporate social audit in Chapter Two.)

Bentham's theory that pleasure alone is good and that it can be quantified has been a special object of attack. Even Mill charged that, on Bentham's account, it would be better to be a satisfied pig than a dissatisfied Socrates. Human experience, Mill argues, is such that some pleasures are qualitatively better than others. For example, Socratic pleasures of the mind are qualitatively better than purely bodily pleasures. Mill thus had to explain how "qualitative betterness" can be weighed and compared, but he came up with no satisfactory explanation. Moreover, it appears to many modern philosophers that Mill's strategy does not even preserve hedonism. What special quality could a somewhat less pleasurable experience have that makes it better? It cannot be the pleasure alone, but must not hedonism then be given up (since it is theoretically committed to the view that pleasure is the sole good)?

Utilitarians who were not hedonists encountered other serious problems with quantification. Economists, for example, either simply appropriated the word "utility" to denote that experience of satisfaction of preference in which economists were interested, or they abandoned the word "utility" and talked about "preference ordering" instead. Many still doubt that construing utility in these ways will resolve the measurability problem. Suppose Jim prefers to spend his 97 cents on milk, and Sally prefers to spend her 97 cents on bread. Suppose neither Sally nor Jim has any money and they have only $1.30 to distribute between them. What can utilitarianism advise when utility is limited to preference orderings? It seems that no advice is possible unless some inferences are made that enable us to go from known preferences to other considerations of welfare and happiness.

The utilitarian reply to these criticisms is that the alleged problem is either a pseudo-problem or else one that affects all ethical theories: We make crude, rough and ready comparisons of values every day, including pleasures and dislikes. For example, we decide to go as a group to a bar rather than have an office party, because we think the bar function will satisfy more members of the group. Utilitarians readily acknowledge that accurate measurements of others' goods or preferences can seldom be provided because of limited knowledge and time. In everyday affairs such as purchasing supplies, administering business, or making legislative decisions, severely limited knowledge regarding the consequences of our actions is often all that is available. What is important, from the utilitarian moral perspective, is that one conscientiously attempts to determine the most desirable action and then with equal seriousness attempts to perform that action.

The Problem of Unjust Consequences. Utilitarianism has also been criticized on grounds that it can lead to injustice. The chief complaint is that the action that produces the greatest balance of value for the greatest number of people may bring about unjustified harm or disvalue to a minority. Consider an extreme example. Suppose a slave society produced the greatest happiness for the greatest number. Would a utilitarian have to say that the practice of slavery in that particular society is morally obligatory?

One standard response of a utilitarian is to deny that the world of human relations would ever be such that slavery would in fact lead to the greatest happiness for the greatest number. Such a response may not be adequate, however. Many political philosophers and legal theorists have argued that documents such as the Bill of Rights in the United States Constitution contain rules that prohibit or constrain utilitarian calculations rather than serve as examples of utilitarian policy decision. The Bill of Rights, they say, was inserted into the Constitution because those rights protect individuals against slavery and other practices even if they are not rights that lead to the greatest good for the greatest number. Their justification thus seems nonutilitarian, because their purpose is to protect citizens from being sacrificed in the name of the public good.

In the last opinion he ever wrote for the Supreme Court (in July 1986), Chief Justice Warren Burger affirmed an earlier opinion in the following words: "The fact that a given law or procedure is efficient, convenient and useful in facilitating functions of government, standing alone, will not save it if it is contrary to the Constitution. Convenience and efficiency are not the primary objectives—or the hallmarks—of democratic government."[21] Burger's criticism captures the essence of what many have argued against utilitarianism: that it fails to account for basic principles that cannot be modified in the name of efficiency, productivity, and convenience.

In evaluating possible utilitarian replies to these criticisms, it is important to remember that utilitarians insist that all entailed costs and benefits of an action or practice must be weighed in any process of evaluation. In the case of employee and consumer rights, for example, the costs will often include protests from labor and consumer groups, impairment to social ideals, further alienation of employees from executives, the loss of customers to competitors, and so on. Second, rule-utilitarian analyses emphatically deny that single cost/benefit determinations are always acceptable. Such utilitarian analyses propose

that general rules of justice (justified by broad considerations of utility) ought to constrain particular actions or uses of cost/benefit calculations in all cases. They would also believe that the above criticisms of utilitarianism are short-sighted, because they focus on injustices that might be caused through a superficial or short-term application of the principle of utility. In a long-range view, utilitarians argue, promoting utility never eventuates in overall unjust outcomes. Whether utilitarianism is compatible with justice will be discussed again in Chapter Nine.

Deontological Theories

An underlying assumption of the previous criticisms of utilitarianism is that an adequate ethical theory cannot be entirely teleological or consequential. Deontological theories (derived from the Greek for "duty") maintain that the concept of duty is in some respect independent of the concept of good and that some actions are right or wrong for reasons other than their consequences. Factors other than good outcomes, then, justify at least some moral judgments and actions. The fairness of distribution, keeping a personal promise, repaying a debt, and abiding by a contract would be right, according to these theories, whether or not utility was maximized.

Deontologists argue that a variety of relationships between persons have significance for reasons other than the consequences of these relationships. Here are some examples:

1. Businesspersons tend to treat each customer according to the history of their relationship. If the person is a regular customer and the merchandise being sold is in scarce supply, the customer will be given preferential treatment, because a relationship of commitment and trust has already been established.
2. The consequences of a banker's computer-rigged theft that throws his bank into insolvency are far greater than those of a railway station clerk's persistent cheating of customers out of nickels and dimes. Yet the motives of the two persons seem equally wicked and corrupt.
3. Being a parent or a fiduciary agent places a per-

son in a special relation of obligation. In the event of a burning apartment house, a father presumably ought to save his child first, even if the world would be better off if he saved someone else in the building who was more valuable to society.

4. A fiduciary too is obligated to act for a client or customer's best interest and not with a view to society's utilitarian interests.

For the deontologists, in short, there are many special, nonconsequential relations such as friendships, parent-child relations, and business affiliations that intrinsically establish and enrich the moral life. Deontological convictions such as these play as important a part in some aspects of business ethics as utilitarian ones. This is not to suggest that utilitarians denigrate or downgrade such relationships. They do not. The point is that deontologists do not believe that such relationships can be justified on consequentialist grounds.

An important difference between utilitarians and deontologists arises from the characteristic means/end reasoning used by utilitarians. Utilitarians focus on goals and on the most efficient means to goals that maximize value—a conception of the moral life that both scientists and businesspersons generally find congenial because the conception is so congruent with business and scientific reasoning. Deontologists, however, think it is mistaken to conceptualize the moral life—even the moral life in the business community—in such terms.

Consider the following example.[22] In his imposing novel of big business in Hong Kong, *Noble House,* James Clavell tells the story of a decision made in 1894 by the most powerful business leader in the colony. The city was at the time threatened by bubonic plague, and tens of thousands were dying. The elimination of the rat population was thought essential to the elimination of the plague bacillus; yet in the poverty-ridden hillside village of Tai-ping Shan the superstitions of the inhabitants led them to do nothing to assist in the effort to drive out the rats. In the face of this monumental ignorance, and with deaths mounting daily by the continued spread of the

plague, the business leader acted as follows: "I had Tai-ping Shan put to the torch by night, the whole monstrous stenching mountainside. That some inhabitants were consumed is on my conscience, but without the cleansing fire the Colony was doomed and hundreds of thousands more doomed." Whereas such consequential reasoning seems characteristic of (act) utilitarianism, deontologists urge that the rights and claims of villagers in Tai-ping Shan should never even be conceived in terms of social utility. Despite their staggering and ineliminable ignorance, their rights and person transcend utilitarian calculations.

As a second example of differences in utilitarian and deontological thinking, consider a survey conducted by researchers K. Ann Coleman Stolurow and Dale W. Moeller.[23] Stolurow and Moeller were interested in the frequency with which x-rays are routinely used as part of dental checkups. They conducted a telephone survey of dental offices in the Boston area and found that in 95 percent of the offices surveyed x-ray procedures are customarily ordered in connection with the initial investigation of new patients, and that in nearly half of those offices the procedures employed involve full mouth x-rays. To obtain accurate information, these researchers presented themselves over the telephone as new residents in the Boston area inquiring about available dental services, and they asked a series of specific questions that followed a prepared written survey instrument, wholly undisclosed to the dentists or their offices. This misrepresentation apparently contributed significantly to the accuracy of the results, because the data obtained showed a frequency of dental x-ray use far greater than that reported by an earlier study in which the researchers did not conceal their purposes. However, their use of deception raises ethical issues of whether the researchers violated the moral rights of the participants or unjustifiably invaded privacy.

Many (act) utilitarians would likely consider this study justifiable: There are public benefits of obtaining accurate information about dental x-rays. The information, for instance, might form the basis on which the American Dental Association would refocus its ongoing efforts to reduce unnecessary x-ray exposure from lessening dosage levels to cutting down on the frequency of exposure. One also might draw an analogy with consumer surveys, noting that the survey sought to evaluate a contractual service between providers and customers. The utilitarian could then argue that the terms of the contract give potential customers grounds to know accurate information about the service, and that this customer interest overrides conflicting rights of dental office owners and employees. A deontologist, by contrast, is likely to find indefensible the deception and invasion of privacy essential to the very conduct of the study.

Perhaps the most common problem of this sort that arises in business is breach of contract and fiduciary duty, sometimes accompanied by deceit and misrepresentation. This often occurs in business when there exists an unclear legal situation, some form of underdeveloped moral commitment between parties, or a situation in which one party sees an opportunity that involves evading or hedging on the moral commitment. For example, in early 1985 the Unocal Corporation sharply criticized its principal bank, Security Pacific Corporation, for knowingly making loans of $185 million to a group that intended to use the money to buy shares in Unocal for purposes of a hostile takeover acquisition. Fred Hartley, Chairman and President of Unocal, argued that the banks and investment bankers were "playing both sides of the game." Not only, he said, had Security Pacific promised not to finance such takeover attempts three months before doing so, but had acted under conditions "in which the bank [has] continually received [for the last 40 years] confidential financial, geological, and engineering information from the company."[24]

Let us assume that the facts of this case are as Unocal presents them. (In fact, the parties spearheading the takeover later sued Unocal for intimidating and coercing Security Pacific and other banks into dropping their promised financing; but we need not consider here this added moral and legal complication.) Let us further assume that the consequences of the hostile takeover for the banks, shareholders, and the takeover party were highly beneficial from a utilitarian point of view. A deontologist is likely to argue that despite the maximization of utilitarian value for the majority of persons affected, the relationship between Unocal and Security Pacific should be the primary focus of any moral assessment of the situation. A forty-year history in which the bank has stockpiled confidential information cannot, from a deontological perspective, simply be case aside for the value of utilitarian benefit. Security Pacific, then, would indeed be guilty of a breach of fiduciary duty and violation of confidentiality, at the very least. (A rule utilitarian might, of course, agree with the deontologist in this assessment.)

The Assessment of Motives

Deontologists commonly insist on the importance of the motives and the character of human actors, quite apart from the consequences planned or produced by the agent. A utilitarian will agree that motives are critical to our assessment of persons, but will insist that right motives are determined exclusively by the intention to produce the best possible consequences. Deontologists tend to regard this form of assessment as too restricted in scope. Whatever one's view may be of this dispute between deontologists and utilitarians, there are two significant moral problems about the motives that underlie human actions: (1) whether one's motive is intentional so that one can be held accountable for an outcome and (2) whether certain kinds of motives are morally superior. Let us take up each problem in turn.

The first problem deals with whether a person intended a certain event that occurred, and therefore whether for that reason the person is responsible for the outcome. We often intend one thing to occur but another unintended consequence occurs—as when one intends to throw an electric power switch but mistakenly grasps a lever that shuts off the water. Often we are not responsible for doing what we did not intend to do, but not always. We can be held responsible if we should have known to do (or not do) what we did (or failed to do). We can sometimes rightly be held negligent even in the absence of any intention on our part to perform (or not perform) an action.

Such judgments can have enormous importance in business ethics. This was dramatically illustrated in a February 1983 event, when Stefan Golab collapsed and died while working at Film Recovery Systems Corporation in Illinois. Golab's job was cleaning the barrels of cyanide in which x-rays were dipped in order to recover silver from film. A coroner ruled that cyanide fumes killed him. An investigation by state authorities showed that managers at Film Recovery Systems had failed to caution workers about the dangers of the cyanide, although the cyanide suppliers had warned the managers of the dangers. The state charged that the owners and managers had "knowingly created a strong probability of death." A murder charge and conviction was upheld against both the owners and the managers—the first time in U.S. history that a murder charge was sustained against an employer.[25] However, this case appears to be morally more complicated than the legal judgment indicates. The owners knew little of the day-to-day operations in the plant, and the managers themselves worked near the vats of cyanide, apparently believing that they were using chemicals that were not dangerous. Many cases of moral assessment in business ethics similarly turn on what we believe about the knowledge and intentions of other actors, especially when we view them as negligent or irresponsible.

To understand the deontologist's point of view on question (2) about motives, consider the example of three different people making personal sacrifices for a sick relative. Fred makes the sacrifices only because he fears social criticism that would result if he didn't. He hates making the sacrifices and secretly resents having to be involved. Bill, however, is naturally a kind-hearted person. He does not

view the sacrifice as a genuine sacrifice at all. He is motivated by the satisfaction that comes from helping others. Sam, by contrast, derives no personal satisfaction from taking care of his sick relative. He would rather be doing other things, and he takes care of his sick relative purely from a sense of duty.

Let us assume that in the cases of these three differently motivated persons, the consequences of their actions are equally good, because the sick aunt is adequately cared for, a result each actor intends. Suppose we ask, however, which person is behaving in a morally praiseworthy manner. On a utilitarian theory such a question might be hard to answer, especially if act utilitarianism were in question, because the good consequences are identical and are intended by each of the actors. Many deontologists believe, however, that in moral evaluation motives count substantially. But which motive is morally superior? Nearly everyone would agree that Fred's motive is not a moral motive at all. It is a motive of prudence and springs from fear. This is not to say that Fred's action does not have good consequences that are intended by Fred. However, Fred does not deserve any moral credit for his act because it is not a morally motivated act. To recognize the prudential basis of the action does not, of course, detract from its good consequences. Indeed, given the purpose or function of the business enterprise, the motive of self-interest may be the most appropriate motive to ensure good consequences. The point a deontologist might make is that a business derives no special moral credit for acting in its own interest, even if society is benefited by and pleased by the action.

If Fred's motive is not moral, what about Bill's and Sam's? Here deontologists disagree about an appropriate answer. Some identify morally correct motivation with altruistic motivation. Bill's behavior is morally right because his action is motivated by a concern for others. This altruistic attitude is absent in Sam's case, and hence Sam's action seems to some morally inferior. However, the eighteenth-century philosopher Immanuel Kant

(1734–1804)—the most influential of all deontological writers—argues on behalf of the moral superiority of Sam's motive. Kant thinks that Bill deserves no more moral credit than Fred. Bill is inclined by his nature to do the right thing. He is lucky or has been well trained by his family, but this merits no moral praise. Kant believes that an act is morally praiseworthy only if done neither for self-interested reasons nor as the result of a natural disposition, but rather from *duty*. Let us now look further at his views in the context of his general ethical theory.

Kantian Ethics

Kant emphasizes performing one's duty for the sake of duty and not for any other reason—one indication that he espouses a pure form of deontology. He insists that all persons act not only in accordance with duty but for the sake of duty. That is, the person's motive for acting must be a recognition of the act as resting on duty. It is not good enough, in Kant's view, that one merely performs the morally correct action, because one could perform one's duty for self-interested reasons having nothing to do with morality. For example, if an employer discloses a health hazard to an employee only because he or she fears a lawsuit, and not because of a belief in the importance of truth telling, then such an employer acts rightly but deserves no moral credit for the action.

Kant tries to establish the ultimate basis for the validity of moral rules of duty in pure reason, not in intuition, conscience, or utility. Morality, he contends, provides a rational framework of principles and rules that constrain and guide everyone, independent of their own personal goals and preferences. He believes that all considerations of utility and self-interest are secondary, because the moral worth of an agent's action depends exclusively on the moral acceptability of the rule according to which the person is acting—or, as Kant prefers to say, moral acceptability depends on the rule that determines the agent's

will. An action has moral worth only when performed by an agent who possesses what Kant calls a good will; and a person has a good will only if moral duty based on a valid rule is the sole motive for the action.

Kant develops this notion into a fundamental moral law that he characterizes as a categorical demand that persons be treated as ends in themselves and never solely as means to the ends of others. In other words, persons must be treated as having their own autonomously established goals and must never be treated purely as the means to another's personal goals. In another (separately developed) formulation, the principle is stated as follows: "I ought never to act except in such a way that I can also will that my maxim should become a universal law." Kant calls this principle the "categorical imperative." It is categorical because it admits of no exceptions and is absolutely binding. It is imperative because it gives instruction about how one must act. He gives several examples—all controversial—of moral maxims that are made imperative by this fundamental principle: "Help others in distress," "Do not commit suicide," and "Work to develop your abilities."

As the above formulation suggests, Kant emphasizes the notion of "rule as universal law." Rules that determine duty are made correct by their universality, that is, the fact that they apply consistently to everyone. This criterion of universality offers some worthwhile lessons for ethics in business. Some of the clearest cases of immoral behavior involve a person trying to make a unique exception of himself or herself purely for personal reasons. Obviously such conduct could not be made universal, or else the very rules presupposed by the idea of "being an exception" would be destroyed. For example, if a corporation kites checks in order to reap a profit in the way E. F. Hutton did in a scandal of the early 1980s, it makes itself an exception to the system of monetary transfer, thereby cheating the system, which is established by certain rules. This conduct, if carried out consistently by other corporations, would violate the very rules presupposed by the system, thereby rendering the system inconsistent, that is, having inconsistent rules of operation.

An example of this Kantian form of reasoning was found in 1969 when some self-announced "entrepreneurs" took pictures from the air of a new E.I. DuPont de Nemours methanol plant in Beaumont, Texas. (Methanol is a chemical used in making antifreeze and was then secret and unpatented.) DuPont sued, alleging wrongful obtaining of trade secrets. Those who took the pictures claimed that there had been no wrongdoing. The pictures had been taken in public airspace, they reasoned, and so were in the public domain. The court upheld DuPont's position. Its argument was that society cannot "accept the law of the jungle as the standard of morality expected in our commercial relations." The court contended that moral standards apply universally in these transactions, and then issued the following universal rule: "To obtain knowledge of a process without spending the time and money to discover it independently is *improper* unless the holder voluntarily discloses it or fails to take reasonable precautions to ensure its secrecy."[26] The court's point seems to be that if the behavior of stealing trade secrets were universalized, then the very rules underlying the idea of trade secrets would be inconsistent with the rules used to steal them. The rules of theft therefore cannot be consistently universalized or else we would have "the law of the jungle."

Kant's view, then, is that such practices as invasion of privacy, theft, line cutting, cheating, kickbacks, and bribes are "contradictory"; that is, they are not consistent with what they presuppose. Consider cases of promising, information disclosure, and lying—as found in Chapter Seven. If one were consistently to recommend the rule "lie when it works to your advantage," our conventional practices of truth-telling would be inconsistent with such a rule of behavior. The universalization of rules that allow lying would entitle everyone to lie to you, just as you can lie to them. In this event, one could never tell if a person were telling the truth or lying. Such a rule would thus be inconsistent with the practice of truthtelling that it presupposes. Simi-

larly, cheating is inconsistent with the practice of examinations that it presupposes. How could one cheat if there were no examinations that assumed honesty? Kickbacks and bribes are inconsistent with various business practices or expectations regarding the conduct of public officials. All such practices are inconsistent with a rule or practice that they presuppose. Kant's point is implicitly recognized by the business community when corporate officials despair of the immoral practices of other corporations and denounce executives engaging in underhanded practices as undermining the business enterprise itself.

Respect for Persons

Our examination of Kant's philosophy is not yet complete. Some have thought that Kant holds categorically that we can never treat another as a means to our ends. This bald interpretation, however, misrepresents his views. Kant does not prohibit this use of persons categorically and without qualification. He argues only that we must not treat another exclusively as a means to our own ends. When employees are ordered to perform odious tasks, they are treated as a means to an employer's or supervisor's ends, but they are not exclusively used for others' purposes, because they do not necessarily become mere servants or objects. His imperative demands only that such persons be treated with the respect and moral dignity to which every person is entitled at all times, including those times when they are used primarily as means to the ends of others. To treat persons merely as means, strictly speaking, is to disregard their personhood by exploiting or otherwise using them without regard to their own interests, needs, and conscientious concerns.

Kant's claim that people must always treat each other as ends in themselves and never as means has been developed as a principle of respect for persons. To treat persons according to Kant's rule is to treat their decisions and values with respect. To fail to respect persons is to treat them as mere means in accordance with our own ends, and thus as if they were not independent agents. To exhibit a lack of respect for persons is either to reject a person's considered judgments or to deny the person the liberty to act on those judgments. For example, an intentional suppression of information to someone, on the basis of which they might have decided not to purchase a house or automobile, might involve such disrespect because of the control exerted by the suppression of information.

"Respect for persons" has sometimes been expressed in corporate contexts as "respect for the individual." Japanese companies have often been praised for placing a higher premium on the individual needs and service records of their employees than do most American corporations (although they are also criticized as paternalistic and discriminatory against women, as we discussed earlier). Hewlett-Packard, however, is one American firm that has been compared favorably to the Japanese system and praised for its employee relationships. Because Hewlett-Packard does not fire employees (instead using partial-hour layoffs and similar strategies) and attempts to make the corporate setting as pleasant as possible for all workers, its employees tend to be tenaciously loyal and highly productive. Whatever its reasons for the policy, Hewlett-Packard has earned a reputation as a corporation that respects the individual.

Respect for the human being is often said by deontologists in the Kantian tradition to be demanded—and not just optional at a corporation's discretion—because human beings possess a moral dignity, and therefore it is always inappropriate to treat them as if they had merely the conditional value possessed by animals and natural objects. Respect for persons, thus construed, may easily seem to come into conflict with the constraints of economic interactions. Many people would, for instance, see this Kantian principle at issue in a case involving the Plasma International Company.[27] The case developed in the wake of a disaster in Nicaragua that produced a sudden need for fresh blood to be used in transfusions. Plasma International had obtained the blood in underdeveloped West

African countries (often paying as little as 15 cents per pint), and the transaction ultimately yielded the firm nearly a quarter of a million dollars in profits. Because they gave vulnerable West Africans just pennies for a substance whose importance to the situation in Nicaragua was then exploited for tremendous economic gain, Plasma International was accused of treating human beings as though they possessed the merely conditional value of lower animals or natural objects. The company seemed to deny people the respect appropriate to their special dignity. Here human dignity and respect for persons are invoked as potential constraints on free market activities.

Prima Facie Duties and Common Sense Morality

An important theory developed by deontologist W. D. Ross is based on his account of *prima facie duties.* He argues that there are several basic rules of moral duty, and that they do not derive from either the principle of utility or Kant's categorical imperative. For example, our promises create duties of fidelity, wrongful actions create duties of reparation, and the generous gifts of our friends create duties of gratitude. Ross defends several additional duties, such as duties of self-improvement, nonmaleficence, beneficence, and justice.

Unlike Kant's system and the utilitarian system, Ross's list of duties is not based on any overarching principle. He defends it simply as a reflection of our ordinary moral beliefs and judgments. He argues that we must find the greatest duty in any given circumstance by finding the greatest balance of right over wrong in that particular context. In order to determine this balance, Ross introduces the distinction between prima facie duties and actual duties. Prima facie indicates a duty that always must be acted upon unless it conflicts on a particular occasion with an equal or stronger duty. Such a duty is always right and binding, all other things being equal. A prima facie duty becomes a duty to be acted on in particular circumstances if it is *not* overridden or outweighed by some competing moral demand. One's actual duty is thus determined by an examination of the respective weights of the competing prima facie duties. Obviously prima facie duties are not absolute, but at the same time they are far more binding than mere rules of thumb.

For example, Ross considers promise keeping a prima facie duty. Does this mean that one must always, under all circumstances, keep one's promise—as if promise keeping were a true categorical imperative? No, there certainly are situations in which breaking a promise is justified. Minor defaults on a promise are justified whenever disastrous harms would be inflicted on another if one were to keep the promise. To call promise breaking prima facie wrong means that promise breaking is wrong, unless some more weighty moral consideration in the circumstances is overriding. Should the duty to keep promises come into conflict with the duty to protect innocent persons—as when one breaks a promise in order to protect someone from harm that would occur if the promise were kept—then the actual duty may be to protect innocent persons (thus overriding the prima facie duty of promise keeping).

The idea that moral principles are absolute values has had a long, but troubled history. Both utilitarians and Kantians have defended their basic rule (the principle of utility and the categorical imperative) as absolute, but the claim that any rule or principle is absolute has been widely challenged. For Ross's reasons, among others, moral philosophers have with increasing frequency come to regard all duties and rights not as inflexible standards, but rather as strong prima facie moral demands that may be validly overridden in circumstances of competition with other moral claims. The idea of an exception-free hierarchy of rules and principles has virtually vanished, as has the claim to be able to arrange moral principles in a hierarchical order that avoids conflict. This position also seems to entail that in cases of conflict there may not be

a single right action, because two or more morally acceptable actions may be unavoidably in conflict and may prove to be of equal weight in the circumstances.

An example is found in John Stuart Mill's celebrated thesis that a principle of maximally free speech serves the public interest better than any system of control, on grounds that truth most consistently emerges from a free marketplace of ideas. Mill was no free-speech absolutist (even if he was an absolutist about the principle of utility). He argued that no one should be free to wantonly violate someone else's rights, unjustly damage another's reputation, disclose secrets vital to the public interest, and so on. Some of the most committed utilitarians (including Mill) and libertarians have advocated placing some restraints—moral and legal—on freedoms of speech.

There has been an increasing tendency in recent moral theory to believe that the many different kinds of moral principles—for example, utility, justice, and respect for persons—are equally weighted in abstraction from particular circumstances. Thus, justice has the same claim to status as a moral principle as does freedom. This point has proven particularly controversial, however, because many philosophers believe that some principle—be it respect for autonomy, or utility, or justice—is more basic or has greater weight than other principles. This problem of how to properly value or weight different moral principles remains unresolved in contemporary moral theory.

Criticisms of Deontological Theories

An important criticism of deontological theories often expressed by utilitarians should now be considered, together with a response that deontologists might offer. The criticism is that deontologists covertly appeal to utilitarian consequences in order to demonstrate the rightness of actions. John Stuart Mill argues that even Kant's theory does not avoid appeal to the consequences of an action in determining whether it is right or wrong. On Mill's interpretation of Kant, the categorical imperative demands that an action should be morally prohibited if "the consequences of (its) universal adoption would be such as no one would choose to incur." Kant fails "almost grotesquely," as Mill puts it, to show that any form of certification of a moral rule appears purely by universalizing rules of conduct or by appealing to the idea of consistency. Mill argues that Kant's theory relies on a subtle but essential appeal to the utilitarian principle that if the consequences of the universal performance of a certain type of action can be shown to be undesirable overall, then that sort of action is wrong.

One possible defense of Kant against this criticism is the following. It is inaccurate from the outset to say that Kant disregards consequences, or even that he believes an action is morally right (or wrong) without regard to its consequences. Kant holds only that the features of an action that make it right are not dependent upon any particular outcome. If the consequences of an action cannot be separated from the nature of the action itself, they too must be considered when an agent universalizes the action in order to determine whether it is permissible. According to this line of defense, Kant's theory is not dependent on any appeal to consequences for its justification.

On the other hand, almost no moral philosopher finds Kant's system fully satisfactory. Even his contemporary defenders tend to have no stronger argument than that Kant provides the elements that are essential for a sound moral position. For example, by using Kantian elements as a basis, some philosophers have attempted to construct a more encompassing deontological theory. They use the Kantian notion of respect for persons as a ground for providing moral theories of justice and rights. There is still considerable controversy, however, as to whether deontological theories are adequate to this task and whether they have been more successful than utilitarian theories. Let us turn, then, specifically to theories of (1) justice and (2) rights, which we will consider here as being defensible on either utilitarian or deontological grounds.

Theories of Justice

Human society is a cooperative enterprise structured by various moral, legal, and cultural rules and principles. These rules and principles form the terms of cooperation in society, the implicit and explicit arrangements and agreements under which individuals are obligated to cooperate or abstain from interfering with others. Sociology, history, cultural anthropology, and social philosophy are all concerned with how rules and principles defining cooperation evolve, are adapted to new situations, and acquire social legitimacy. Philosophers, however, have typically been less interested in questions of history and social science than in questions concerning the justice of the terms of cooperation. For example, philosophers pose questions such as, What gives one person or group of people a right to expect cooperation from another person or group of people in some societal interchange (especially an economic one) if the former benefit and the latter do not? Is it just for some citizens to have more property than others? Is it right for one person to gain an economic advantage over another, if both abide strictly by existing societal rules?

A study performed for the U.S. Federal Reserve in mid–1986 by the Survey Research Center of the University of Michigan showed that in the United States wealth has become far more concentrated in the two decades between 1963 and 1983. The top one-half of one percent (0.5%) of U.S. citizens owned 35 percent of the wealth—up from 25 percent in 1963. Although the share of wealth owned by the top one-half percent was rising rapidly during this period, the share of every other group below the top one-half percent was declining. These two decades reversed a long-standing trend before this period toward less concentration at the top. These figures raise profound questions, in the minds of some philosophers, about the justice of tax shelters, executive compensation, corporate taxation, and the like.

Economists have sometimes complained about the way philosophers approach fairness and justice, on grounds that these concepts have no real role or place in "fair" or "free market arrangements. A "fair price" or "fair trade" is not a matter of moral fairness at all, they say: Prices may be low or high, affordable or not affordable, but not fair or unfair. It is simply unfortunate, not unfair, if one cannot afford to pay for them. The reason is the market-established nature of prices. To speak of "unfair" prices or trade is to express an opinion, but there is nothing objective in such a judgment. Their reasoning is that from a market perspective any price is fair, and no price is unfair.

In one respect this reasoning seems unassailable: In a free market context, fairness in pricing is market controlled. But there still may be insistent questions of fairness that are legitimate in the free market situation: For example, is the market itself a fair arrangement? What makes it fair, if so? If coercion is used in the market to set prices, is this maneuver unfair? If goods such as health care and education are distributed nationally or internationally with vast inequality, can high prices on essential items such as health care goods and university tuitions be fair? These are the kinds of questions of fairness that are raised under the topic of justice.

Some philosophers have held that principles of justice have a moral priority (or weight, as discussed previously) over all other moral principles, or at least that all the major issues of moral, social, and legal philosophy should be framed within a theory of distributive justice. But what is justice, and wherein does its uniqueness lie? Justice has been explicated in terms of the concepts of fairness, entitlement, and "what is deserved." A person has been treated justly when he or she has been given what is due or owed, what he or she deserves or can claim as a matter of entitlement. The more restricted expression *distributive justice* refers to the proper distribution of social benefits and burdens through a cooperative enterprise structured by moral, legal, and cultural rules and principles. The distribution in question is often of social goods—for example, economic benefits and fundamental political rights. But social burdens or risks must also be distributed in many cases. Paying taxes and being drafted into the armed services to fight a war are distributed burdens, while Medicare checks and grants to do research are distributed benefits.

As we shall see in Chapter Nine, recent literature on distributive justice has tended to focus on considerations of fair economic distribution, especially unjust distributions in the form of inequalities of income between different classes of persons and unfair tax burdens on certain classes of persons or types of business. But there are many problems of distributive justice besides strictly economic ones, including the issues raised in prominent contemporary debates over preferential hiring, comparable worth, and reverse discrimination—topics discussed in Chapter Six.

We often express what a person is owed—and therefore what is just—through specific rules and laws, such as those governing gambling, food stamp allocation, medicare coverage, plagiarism, allocation of exotic lifesaving medical resources, admission procedures for universities, and the like. These rules may be evaluated, criticized, and revised by reference to more abstract moral principles such as equality of persons, nondiscriminatory treatment, property ownership, protection from harm, compensatory justice, retributive justice, and so on. The word *justice* is used broadly to range over both these very general principles and more specific rules that these principles help us develop for specific kinds of situations. Without both kinds of guidelines—the general and the specific—it would often be difficult to express what counts as a violation of fairness or justice, especially in the context of professional ethics.

Sometimes in business ethics we confront a noticeably abstract issue, such as the general justifiability of preferential programs in hiring, and sometimes we are confronted with quite concrete and specific charges of unfairness. Consider the following example of a concrete charge: *Money* magazine ran an exposé on

Merrill, Lynch, Pierce, Fenner, and Smith, titled "The Stumbling Herd", that depicted Merrill Lynch as engaged in systematic unfairness in dealing with clients.[28] To illustrate the accusation of systematic unfairness, *Money* charged that Merrill Lynch does not take an attitude of fiduciary responsibility toward its clients, as a brokerage house should: "Commissions and other incentives encourage Merrill Lynch brokers to push what the company needs to sell—not necessarily what the client needs to buy. And the firm's phenomenal growth has come at the cost of deteriorating customer service and increased back-office botches." *Money* suggested that Merrill Lynch was not morally principled and needed rules to provide the service required of a responsible brokerage house.

These charges met a predictably hostile reaction from Merrill Lynch, which labeled the story unfair for other reasons (in effect charging a breach of journalistic ethics).[29] This encounter over problems of fairness is typical in business. Contained within the example are questions of fairness to clients, fairness to the facts, fairness in advertising, fairness to the general public, fairness to special publics, fairness to employers, and so on. These comments reveal what a sweeping, morally generic notion justice is.

Rival Theories and Competing Principles. Some philosophers have believed that our diverse judgments and beliefs on such heterogeneous matters can be brought into systematic unity through a general theory of justice; justice has been analyzed differently, however, in rival and often incompatible theories. (On general theories of justice, see pp. 552–59 in Chapter Nine.) All theories of justice tend to share one principle: Like cases should be treated alike—that is, equals are to be treated equally and unequals unequally. This principle is referred to as the formal principle of justice, or sometimes the formal principle of equality. It asserts that no matter which particulars are under consideration, if persons are equal in those respects, they should be treated alike. Unfortunately, the formal principle of justice does not tell us how to determine equality or proportion in any given case, and it therefore lacks substance as a specific guide to conduct. In any group of persons there will be many ways in which the members of the group are both similar and different, and we therefore must add to the formal principle an account of equality that specifies the relevant respects in terms of which persons are to be treated equally.

Here is a simple example. A longstanding principle on leading stock exchanges is the so-called "one share, one vote principle" or "equal voting rights principle," which states that any company traded on the stock exchange must allow persons holding common stock to cast one vote for each share held. This rule is required as part of the system of corporate governance for companies traded, and is generally considered a matter of justice by attentive stock exchange officials. In May 1985, Gordon Macklin, president of the National Association of Securities Dealers, argued that the over-the-counter market (OTC) should not follow the one share, one vote principle and instead should allow companies to have two classes of common stock with unequal voting rights—as had already been done by several corporations, including Hershey Foods Corporation and Dow Jones & Company, publisher of the *Wall Street Journal*. In July 1986 the New York Stock Exchange ended a 60-year-old "one-share, one-vote" rule and followed the OTC. Nothing in the formal principle of justice rules out unequal voting rights or declares them unjust; even classes of stock that would have no voting rights could be created under this rule. The formal principle merely says that whatever class of stock you own you must be treated equally under that classification. If you hold a class of stock with no voting rights, you must be treated like all other persons in that class: You must not vote!

Thus the formal principle leaves room for differences in the interpretation of how justice applies to particular situations. Systematic theories of justice attempt to be more specific than the formal principle by elaborating in detail how people are to be compared and what it means to give people their due. Philosophers attempt to achieve the needed precision and specificity by developing material principles of justice—so called because they put material content into a theory of justice. Each material principle of justice identifies a relevant property on the basis of which burdens and benefits should be distributed. The following is a sample list of major candidates for the position of justified principles of distributive justice (through longer and shorter lists have been proposed):

1. To each person an equal share,
2. To each person according to individual need,
3. To each person according to that person's rights,
4. To each person according to individual effort,
5. To each person according to societal contribution,
6. To each person according to merit.

A theory might accept more than one of these principles; indeed, some theories of justice accept all six as valid. Most societies use several, in the belief that different rules are appropriate to different situations.

A particular case from business practice may help to make clearer the variety of and potential conflict among material principles of justice. The case involves one Mark Dalton, a histology technician in the employ of a large chemical company.[30] Dalton was an excellent worker, but during a week-long sick leave a company nurse discovered that he had a chronic kidney disease. Furthermore, it was discovered that the permissible chemical vapor exposure levels of Dalton's job might exacerbate his kidney condition. The company management found another job at the same rate of pay for which Dalton was qualified, but it turned out that two other employees eligible for promotion were also interested in the position. Both employees had more seniority and better training than Dalton, and one

was a woman. In this situation, each of the three employees can appeal to a different material principle of justice to substantiate his or her claim to the available position. Dalton can cite the material principle of need, arguing that his medical condition requires that he be offered the new position. With their superior experience and training, each of the other two employees can invoke material principles of merit, societal contribution, and perhaps individual effort on behalf of their claims to the position. Additionally, considerations of equal opportunity might give the woman valid grounds for claiming that justice should take account of her special individual rights, introducing yet another material principle.

While this case is meant to illustrate the possible complexity of appeals to justice, most general theories of justice attempt to systematize and simplify our diverse moral beliefs by selecting and emphasizing one or more of the material principles. As we shall see in detail in Chapter Nine, *egalitarian* theories of justice emphasize equal access to or division of primary goods; *Marxist* theories emphasize need and the contribution made by labor; *libertarian* theories emphasize rights to social and economic liberty; and *utilitarian* theories emphasize a mixed use of such criteria so that public and private utility are maximized.

Just Procedures and Just Results. In the literature on justice there also exists an important distinction between just procedures and just results. The term *distribution* may refer to the procedure of distributing, or it may refer to the result of some system of distribution. Ideally it is preferable to have just procedures and just results, but it is not always possible to have both. For example, one might achieve a just result in distributing wealth, but one might use an unjust procedure, such as undeserved taxation of certain groups, in order to achieve it. By contrast, just procedures sometimes eventuate in unjust results, as when a just procedure such as a fair trial reaches unjust results when the innocent are found guilty. In discussions of justice the system itself is often in question, even though those who are criticizing the system may be pointing to unjust results of the system. It is important to be clear on whether the procedures, the results, or both are under consideration.

Many problems of justice that we must handle as a cooperative society involve designing a system or set of procedures that provides as much justice as possible. Once we agree on appropriate procedures, then as long as a person is treated according to those procedures, the outcome must be declared just—even if it turns out to produce inequalities that seem by other standards unjust. Naturally, if procedural justice is the best we can do—as, for example, in the criminal justice system—we should accept the results of our procedural system with a certain amount of humility, and where possible we should perhaps make allowances for inevitable inequalities—and possibly for inequities and misfortunes.

Because unfortunate (but not necessarily unfair) outcomes are inevitable in purely procedural systems, shifting the issue from results to procedures—as is often done by taking votes in a majoritarian system—will not avoid all ethical controversy. Moreover, the various traditional theories of ethics will provide competing theories of criteria of just procedures as well as of just outcomes. Within the American system, of course, representative democracy acts as something of a final procedure, but agreement on this procedure will clearly not suffice to quiet all controversy about just treatment, especially when majority votes eventuate in outcomes that are unfair to minorities.

In Chapter Nine we will study rival theories of justice and the controversies they generate over just procedures and just results. It would be unfortunate if the discussion here (or there) led the reader to the conclusion that theories of justice are in perpetual warfare and in the end yield no insights into real life circumstances of injustice. One perspective from which to judge competing conceptions of justice is by using the method John Rawls calls *reflective equilibrium.*[31] Rawls agrees with many moral philosophers that there are para-

digm cases of unjust behavior, such as punishing the innocent, and of just behavior, such as an impartial and thorough court of appeals. He assumes, then, that no moral principle can be adequate if it would permit such cases of immoral behavior as punishing the innocent or if it would not praise a court that found an innocent person not guilty. If all moral issues had such paradigm-case resolutions, there would be no need for moral principles.

However, many moral issues have no clear parallel solution; for example, problems of deceptive advertising and environmental responsibility present numerous dilemmas (see Chapters Four and Seven). The purpose of moral principles such as principles of justice is more to assist persons in reasoning through the difficult decisions generated by these dilemmas. As we actively engage in making moral judgments, there is an interplay between the principles we use and the cases to which we apply our principles. We start with paradigm cases about certain acts that are either obviously morally right or morally wrong. We then search for principles that are consistent with these paradigm cases, are consistent with each other, and assist us in resolving difficult moral problems. These principles are then tested to see if they yield counterintuitive results. If so, they are readjusted or are given up and new principles are developed. Moral inquiry and moral practice in virtually every prominent theory of justice reflect this mutual testing of cases against principles and principles against cases. These theories thus may be viewed as general attempts to put all our moral judgments into as consistent a framework as possible.

The use of such reasoning in business ethics is similar. The competitive free enterprise system is viewed by businesspersons as a justified procedure for organizing economic institutions—although the competitive free enterprise system is also a good example of procedural justice that can lead to unfortunate outcomes, especially for the disabled or those who suffer unavoidable and uninsurable economic tragedies. When criticized, some economists and business leaders admit that free enterprise distribution can and sometimes does lead to unfortunate results, but they argue that no other scheme is procedurally more satisfactory.

Theories of Rights

Thus far in our discussion of normative theories (in Part Two of this chapter) we have generally spoken of *obligations* or *duties*. Principles and rules in deontological and utilitarian theories have been understood as principles and rules of obligation. Yet much of the modern ethical discussion that we shall encounter throughout this volume turns on ideas about rights, and many public policy issues concern rights or attempts to secure rights.

Our political tradition itself has developed from a conception of *natural rights*. However, until the seventeenth and eighteenth centuries, problems of political philosophy were rarely discussed in terms of rights, perhaps because duties to lord, king, state, church, and God had been the dominant focus of political and ethical theory. New political views were introduced at this point in history, including the notion of universal natural rights. These rights were thought to consist primarily of rights not to be interfered with, or liberty rights, and were especially treasured as rights against state intrusion or control. Proclamations of such rights as those to life, liberty, property, a speedy trial, and the pursuit of happiness subsequently formed the core of major political and legal documents.

Thus, historically, the notion of *natural* (or *human*) rights emerged from a need to check the sovereign power of states. Rights quickly came to be understood as powerful assertions of claims that demand respect and status. To say that a person or persons possess a right to *X* is to say more than that the sovereign power tolerates their having something or exercising some power; it says that it would be wrong for them not to have *X*, because they have a justified claim to *X*. Rights, then, are justified claims that individuals and groups can make upon others or upon society.[32]

The doctrine of individual rights, as applied within business institutions, has not traditionally been a major focus of business ethics, but this situation may now be changing. Employees were and still are fired for what superiors consider disloyal conduct, and employees traditionally have had no internal right to "blow the whistle" on corporate misconduct. Many alleged abuses of management privileges and authority have also been cataloged, and at present protections against unjust business practices are being demanded, sometimes within companies and sometimes in court. The development of theories of employee rights, consumer rights, and stockholder rights; the clashes among rights claims; and the alleged clash between utilitarianism and nonutilitarian rights theories provide the framework for major contemporary debates within business ethics. (See especially Chapter Four.)

Types of Rights. The bases or origins of rights have also been disputed. One thing seems clear: Rights have diverse origins. If I swear to you that I will tell the whole truth and nothing but the truth, you acquire a right to be told the truth because of my promise. Still other rights are transmitted because of family ties or traditions. These rights all rest on contingent relations of circumstance. Without the special circumstance there would be no rights of that sort. These rights are therefore called *special* rights. But there are also *general* rights, which everyone holds. Many philosophers have maintained that these rights are *fundamental*, and that we have them, irrespective of merit, just because we are human. This humanity is said to confer rights to impartial treatment in matters of justice, freedom, equality of opportunity, and so on. Thus, when members of minority groups complain about discriminatory hiring practices that destroy their human dignity and self-respect (see Chapter Six), one interpretation of these complaints is that those who register them believe that their general moral rights are being violated.

The language of moral rights is greeted by some with skepticism, and even ridicule because of the apparently absurd proliferation of and the conflict among diverse rights claims (especially in recent political debates). For example, it has been claimed by some parties that a pregnant woman has a right to have an abortion, while others claim that fetuses have a right to life that precludes the right to have an abortion. As we shall see throughout this volume, rights language has been extended in recent years to include such controversial rights as the right to financial privacy, rights of workers to information, rights to a pollution-free environment, rights to a job, and the rights of special interest groups.

One such extension of rights can be found as the result of a crucial court decision. In *Cleveland Board of Education* v. *Loudermill,* the U.S. Supreme Court ruled that state and municipal employees have the legal right to both a formal notice and a hearing before being fired. Some now speak confidently of such a moral right for employees of private corporations—and even of a property right to a job (see pp. 260–62). Such claims often involve a moral extension of legal declarations as well as an extension from the public to the private sphere. Another extension, largely confined to the domain of morality, is found in recent discussions of the decisions made by female employees of chemical companies to undergo voluntary sterilization in order to retain their jobs. This practice raises a number of moral issues about rights. Spokespersons for various chemical companies—DuPont, for example—have argued that unborn fetuses have moral and legal rights that the companies, as employers of fertile women, are obliged to protect—the implication being that these obligations justify company decisions to remove nonsterilized women from high paying but potentially dangerous positions.[33] Opponents of such policies argue that the fertile female employees themselves have counter-

vailing moral and economic rights that need to be taken into account.

The intractability of such appeals to rights highlights the importance of analyzing the moral and legal foundations of rights claims, and it will therefore prove useful to examine some other distinctions regarding the nature and types of rights that have emerged in ethical theory.

Prima Facie and Absolute Rights. Prima facie duties were discussed in the earlier section on deontological theories. Such duties are strong moral demands but ones that may be overridden in particular circumstances by more stringent competing moral demands. Such competition also occurs in the case of rights as well, as we noticed in discussing the rights of unborn fetuses and fertile female employees in hazardous chemical workplaces. Many writers in ethics now agree that a person can only validly exercise a right to something if sufficient justification exists—that is, when a right has an overriding status. Rights such as a right to equal economic opportunity, a fetus's right to physical well-being, and a right to be saved from starvation thus may have to compete with other rights. Hence many situations in which rights are in conflict inevitably produce protracted controversy and remind us of the need to balance with great discretion the competing rights claims.

A typical example is found in the 1978 Financial Right to Privacy Act, passed by the U.S. Congress. This act extended a broad right to privacy to bank customers—in particular, a right to prevent prying federal eyes from inspecting private records. However, in 1985 Congress began to consider a new act that would either nullify or heavily qualify the 1978 act. The reason for the change was to strengthen federal authorities in their battle against money-laundering—that is, hiding illegal sources of money. Various major United States banks, especially in Boston and New York, had been found guilty of not reporting—as is legally required—cash transactions over $10,000, and a subsequent investigation found money laundering to be a major national problem. The difficulty that faced Congress was how to balance bank customer's rights to privacy against rights of federal authorities to investigate crime and enforce the law. This balancing proved extremely difficult, especially on two touchy matters: (1) whether customers have a right to know that they are under investigation and, if so, by what agency, and (2) whether court orders must be obtained before bank records can be turned over to federal officials. The banking community generally favored a strongly protected right to privacy, whereas federal enforcement officials preferred a weakly worded right so that their right to enforce the law could more easily override the right to privacy. Congress' job was to balance the competing claims, interests, and conflicting rights.

On some occasions human rights have conflicted with the free-market rights cherished by much of the business community and by libertarian theories of justice. For example, American banks such as First National Bank of Chicago, Bank of America, Manufacturers Hanover, and Citicorp have in recent years eagerly resumed credit to East German banks. They had abandoned credit offerings in 1981 because of political developments in Poland that then cast a dark shadow of uncertainty across Eastern Europe. East Germany had been desperately in need of the money, particularly at the favorable terms extended by American banks such as First Chicago. Formerly, East Germany had been able to obtain Western loans only through West Germany, which extracted concession agreements from East Germans in return for the loans; these agreements increased visits, and immigration to West Germany from East Germany was permitted. These were widely labelled as "human rights concessions" on the part of East Germany. When American banks signed agreements with East Germany, they likely knew that this delicate balance would be disturbed, but they judged that their right to pursue business interests should prevail—or, as some critics accused, they simply failed to

consider that the human rights of East Germans could rival their free-market rights.

Negative and Positive Rights. Philosophers have often drawn a distinction between positive and negative rights. A right to well-being—generally the right to receive goods and services—is a positive right, and a right to liberty—generally a right to not be interfered with—is a negative right. The right to liberty is a negative right because no one has to do anything to honor it. Presumably all that must be done to honor negative rights is to leave people alone. The same is not true with respect to positive rights. To honor those, someone has to provide something. For example, if a person has a human right to well-being and is starving, then someone has a duty to provide that person with food.

This distinction between positive and negative rights has often led those who would include a right to well-being on the list of human rights to argue that the duty to provide for positive rights falls on the state. This distinction has intuitive appeal to many businesspersons, because they wish to limit the power of the state to regulate business, that is, to interfere with free trade. Their view is that business should be free to provide goods and services that turn a profit, and the state should let business do this without interference. But, as for the positive rights of citizens, this task falls upon the state—not upon business—if there are positive rights at all.

The existence of apparently intractable conflicts among rights is one of the more troublesome aspects of contemporary rights theory. This conflict is not simply between negative and positive rights. Conflicts among negative rights also occur. An illustration is provided by a strike at the Adolph Coors brewery in Golden, Colorado.[34] In April 1977, 1,400 workers at the brewery left their jobs in what was to become a prolonged and bitter walkout. At first, the industrial action appeared to turn on technical questions involving seniority, the nature of the work week, and so on, but more general issues of employee rights and employer obligations gradually came to the fore as the dispute wore on. Citing such practices as the use of lie detector tests in screening job applicants and the tendency of company interviewers to ask non-job related questions, union spokesmen claimed that Coors' management was not fulfilling its moral obligation to respect employee rights to privacy. Such negative rights, an argument on behalf of the striking workers might go, carve out a sphere or zone of protected activity with which the employer is morally obliged not to interfere. On the other hand, Coors argued that it has the right to pursue its business in ways it believes are most conducive to profit.

Conclusion

In Part Two of this introductory chapter several central concepts and issues in ethical theory have been examined. The objective has been to explore major options and distinctions so as to promote critical reflection on the cases and articles in subsequent chapters. Many authors whose writings are found in these chapters would not subscribe without qualification to theories such as utilitarianism or deontology as they have been described in this chapter. Nonetheless, the broad characterizations found here should prove useful for understanding the general orientation of these authors.

Philosophy can help us find a reasoned and systematic approach to moral problems, but it does not supply mechanical solutions or definitive procedures for decisionmaking. This lack of finality is no cause for skepticism. Moral philosophy can yield well-constructed arguments and criticisms that help us explore and advance the issues, but practical wisdom and sound judgement are philosophy's indispensable allies in decisionmaking contexts. Though moral dilemmas require a balancing of competing claims in untidy circumstances, we can at least be reassured that in the contribution it has to make philosophy is neither inferior nor superior to other forms of reason-ing, such as those found in law, economics, and the behavioral sciences.

PART THREE: THE ANALYSIS OF CASES

In every subsequent chapter of this volume, the reader will find either legal cases or cases of business activities intended for discussion. These are not materials that derive from or even mention ethical theory, yet they merit moral analysis. The "case method," as it is often called, has long been used in law and business for such purposes. However, only recently has philosophical ethics drawn attention to the importance of case studies and the case method, and "the method" at work is still controversial and unsettled.

Daniel Callahan and Sissela Bok have suggested that "case studies are employed most effectively when they can readily be used to draw out broader ethical principles and moral rules . . . [so as] to draw the attention of students to the common elements in a variety of cases, and to the implicit problems of ethical theory to which they may point."[35] Yet it is not obvious how to apply theory, draw out principles, or find common elements. The history of reflection on case analysis in law and business has much to teach us about discovering, modifying, and applying ethical principles. Their histories, as they have developed in American universities, also have much to teach about how *not* to use "the case method."

The Case Method in Law

The most extensive body of thought on strategies for analyzing cases is found in the law, where case law establishes precedents of evidence and justification. The earliest developments in the history of the legal use of the case method occurred around 1870, when Christopher Columbus Langdell revolutionized academic standards and teaching techniques by introducing the case method at the Harvard Law School.[36] Langdell's casebooks were composed of cases selected and arranged to reveal to the student the pervasive meaning of legal terms, as well as the rules and principles of law. He envisioned a dialectical or Socratic manner of argument that teachers would employ in order to show students how concepts, rules, and principles are found in the legal reasoning of the judge(s) who wrote the opinions. A teacher or legal scholar was supposed to extract fundamental principles, much in the way a skillful biographer might extract the principles of a person's reasoning by studying his or her considered judgments.

However, Langdell's "principles" did not prove to be uniform across courts, context, or time, and incompatible and even rival theories or approaches by judges tended to be controlling in many precedent cases. Nevertheless, when Langdell's vision faded, there were important reasons why the case method, with appropriate modifications, ultimately prevailed in American law schools. Analysis of cases offers teachers and students a powerful tool for generalizing from cases. Spanning the tangled web of details in particular cases are principles of legal reasoning, because judges must have some general basis from which to write the opinions that constitute the cases. Legal theory and its fundamental doctrines can thus be both found in and applied to cases that have come before courts. Moreover, and very importantly, training in the case method sharpens skills of legal reasoning—both legal analysis and legal synthesis. One can tear a case apart and then construct a better way of treating similar cases. In the thrust-and-parry classroom setting, teacher and student alike need to think through a case and its rights and wrongs. The method thus prepares the student for the practice of the law—the application to new cases—and not merely for theoretical wisdom about law.

The case method in law has come to be understood, then, as a way of learning how to assemble facts and to judge the weight of evidence to enable the transfer of that weight to new cases. This is done by generalizing and mastering the principles that control the trans-fer, usually principles at work in the reasoning of judges.

The Case Method in Business

When the Harvard Business School was opened in 1908, its first Dean, Edwin F. Gay, used the Law School curriculum as a prototype for courses on commercial law, and eventually as a model throughout the business school. By 1919 the method had taken hold, and eventually came to dominate business schools that emphasize deliberation and decisionmaking—making analyses, weighing competing considerations, and reaching a decision in complex and difficult circumstances.[37] Judgment is taught in this method rather than doctrine, principle, or fact. Cases that involve puzzles and dilemmas having no definitive solution by reference to principles or precedents are preferred for instructional purposes over those that fail to present a difficult dilemma. Cases are developed to recreate a managerial situation in which moral dilemmas are confronted. Cases are not primarily used to illustrate principles or rules, because the latter abstractions are invariably inadequate for final resolutions in real-world business situations. The objective is to develop a capacity to grasp problems and to find novel solutions that work in the context: Knowing how to think and act is thus more prized than knowing that something is the case.

This use of the case method in business schools springs from an ideal of education that puts the student in an environment in which decisions must be taken after an initial immersion into the facts of a complex situation. Theories and generalizations are downplayed, and the skills of thinking and acting in complex and uncertain environments are upgraded in importance. The essence of the case method is to present a situation replete with the facts, opinions, and prejudices an executive might encounter (often an actual case), and to lead the student to make decisions in such an environment.

No assumption is made in this method that

there is a right answer to any problem that is presented, but only that there are more or less successful ways of handling problems. Understanding argument and analysis (roughly as outlined in Part One of this Introduction) are thus more important than understanding substantive theories (of roughly the sort outlined in Part Two). These forms of understanding need not be seen as antagonistic or even competitive, but the case method in business schools has always placed the premium on the problem-based form of analysis rather than on analysis by use of theory. It also has never emphasized the authority-based method relied on in law schools, where judges and the body of law are overriding authorities. Not unlike the Protestant rejection of authority in the Roman Catholic Church, there is no overriding authority in the case method in business.

Using Ethical Theory for Case Analysis

There are, of course, dangers in transferring the case methods in either law or business to philosophical ethics and business ethics. Not much is drearier than a tedious and unrewarding exposure to the moral opinions of those who are ignorant of theoretical materials that transmit the kind of sustained philosophical reflection outlined in Parts One and Two. This indicates that cases involving ethics in business should be informed by theory although theory should not remain isolated from modification by case study. But why?

First, it seems mistaken to say that ethical theory is not extracted from the examination of cases but only applied to cases. Cases not only provide data for theory, but they are theory's testing ground as well. Revealing cases lead us to modify and refine our theoretical commitments, especially by pointing to inadequacies in or limitations of theories. In thinking through the possible role of case analysis in ethics, we might consider again John Rawls's account of reflective equilibrium (as described previously on p. 45, and now modestly redescribed for present purposes). In developing an ethical theory, he argues, it is ap-

propriate to start with the broadest possible set of our considered judgments about a subject such as justice, and to erect a provisional set of principles that reflects them. These principles can then be pruned and adjusted by bringing cases under them.

If, for example, some problems in business ethics are under examination, widely accepted principles of right action (moral beliefs) might be taken, as Rawls puts it, "provisionally as fixed points," but also as "liable to revision." Paradigm cases of what clearly are right courses of action could first be examined, and a search could then be undertaken for principles consistent with our judgments about these paradigm cases. These principles could be tested by reference to other paradigm cases and other considered judgments found in similar cases. Through this process moral theories and principles could be made to cohere with all our considered judgments about particular cases. That is, general ethical principles and particular judgments could be brought into equilibrium. Principles and theory are justified by the process. Presumably the more complex and far-reaching the cases that force revisions, the richer the resultant theory will be. Traditional ethical theory, from this perspective, has as much to learn from applied contexts as the other way around. Arthur Caplan has put the point well:

> There are many ways currently in vogue for constructing theories in ethics. . . . [Rawls's and Nozick's] are not the only starting points for moral theorizing. One might want to start with a rich base of moral phenomena and, inductively, construct a moral theory that captures the richness and complexity of moral life. . . . Far from being atheoretical, . . . enterprises in applied ethics compel attention to deep philosophical questions about optimal research strategies in ethical theorizing. . . . Theoreticians are always in danger of oversimplifying, over-idealizing, or underestimating the complexity of human behavior.[38]

Our greatest philosophical writings have been plagued by the latter problems, and by a still deadlier difficulty: No theory adequate to serve as the foundation for application to concrete moral problems has ever been devised. Accordingly, presumptions of a unilateral direction to the flow of ethical knowledge and of a special professional expertise for ethics entail a posture of insularity and arrogance that practitioners of ethical theory adopt at great peril.

From this perspective, moral thinking is like other forms of theorizing in that hypotheses must be tested, buried, or modified through experimental thinking. Principles can be justified, modified, or refuted—and new insights gained—by examination of cases that function as experimental data. Similarly, our developed principles allow us to interpret the cases and arrive at moral judgments in a reflective manner. One promise of the case method is the opportunity it creates to increase the development and applicability of ethical theories by more careful attention to complicated, quite real cases that provide opportunities for testing the scope, consistency, and adequacy of those theories.

A complaint heard frequently among university administrators and teachers in recent years is that their students learn technical skills but never develop skills of moral reasoning that can be applied to real life situations. Derek Bok, President of Harvard, has complained (in his book *Beyond the Ivory Tower*) that students learn too much about how to increase profits and too little about an "applied ethics" that could teach them how to confront moral dilemmas. Steven Muller, President of Johns Hopkins, has complained that the modern university teaches marvelous lessons learned from the scientific method, but has failed to teach that this method is neutral to moral values. While this method works marvelously, it does not work for everything, he notes. The call from these and hundreds of similar sources is for an environment in the university in which informed decisionmaking skills involving moral judgment are taught together with the technical skills and theoretical wisdom that seem to dominate in importance

at the present time. The case method has often been cited as a promising entrée—although not a sufficient condition—for teaching moral reflection to augment scientific and theoretical education.

We can with profit, at this point, recall our earlier discussions of relativism and moral disagreement (see pp. 11–13). Often when attending to difficult cases many points of view will bounce about the classroom, and it may seem that the controversies are intractable and not subject to a persuasive form of analysis that transcends mere personal opinion. Far from an environment of learning, students may feel more like a bulletin board to which hundreds of opinions are tacked. It would be a mistake, however, to jump too quickly to the conclusion that such discussion eventuates in opinion only. Many apparent dilemmas do turn out, under discussion, to be partially resolvable and often a consensus position emerges, even if no one ever entirely agrees on the best reasons for defending the position.

It is also important to study cases with an eye to ways in which dilemmas and disagreements can be avoided or minimized. A study of cases in order to detect steps that management might take to avoid problems can be profitable, as can reflection on procedures that might have deflected or defused a problem. This suggests a need to examine cases in terms of alternative strategies and actions. There will invariably be many alternatives that could be proposed, but just as invariably they will not all be equally good. Even if intractable disagreement does set in, learning how to spot problems and resolve or deflect them may turn out to be as important as the substantive issues themselves.

One temptation is to be avoided, however. Those who study the facts of cases invariably want more facts. They see a solution as dependent on knowing more than is known about what transpired. If additional data can be discovered, they think, the problems can be handled and the dilemmas disentangled. A related temptation is to doctor the known facts, thus presenting a hypothetical or new case, rather than an actual case. Both the temptation to put off decisions by searching for more facts and the use of hypothetical facts can have a place in case study, but generally these maneuvers should be avoided. Cases are often interesting because only limited information is known or can be known. One is called on to treat the problem under these real-life conditions of scarcity of information. Professional business works under such conditions day in and day out. There is every reason to want to understand that context as it is, and not merely as it might be in some possible world.

NOTES

1. Our discussion of this case is indebted to Richard Wokutch's write-up found in the cases at the end of Chapter Two in this volume and also to Elizabeth Gatewood and Archie B. Carroll, "Anatomy of a Corporate Social Response: The Procter & Gamble Rely Case," *Business Horizons* (September 1981).
2. Dean Rotbard and John A. Prestbo, "Killing a Product," *Wall Street Journal,* November 3, 1980, p. 21.
3. Edward G. Harness, "Views on Corporate Responsibility," *Corporate Ethics Digest* 1 (September–October 1980).
4. See "For a Few Dollars More," *Newsweek,* July 29, 1985, pp. 59–60; "Christie's Scandal Underlines Mutual Dependence of Dealers, Auction Houses," *International Herald Tribune,* August 10–11, 1985, p. 7.
5. Anthony Lewis, "Getting Even," *New York Times,* April 11, 1985, p. 23.
6. Taken from Peter Huber, "The Press Gets Off Easy in Tort Law," *Wall Street Journal,* July 24, 1985, editorial page.
7. We are indebted to John Cronquist for some of the observations in this paragraph.
8. "Odds & Ends," *Wall Street Journal,* December 13, 1984, sec. 2. p. 1.
9. This case is reprinted in Robert J. Baum, ed., *Ethical Problems in Engineering,* 2nd ed., vol. 2, *Cases* (Troy, N.Y.: Rensselear Polytechnic Institute, 1980), 58–62; quotation on p. 58.

10. See "Principle Sale," *Wall Street Journal,* May 22, 1985, p. 35.
11. Richard A. Lynch, "Domenic Colasacco Makes Ethical Qualms Pay Dividends," *Money,* May 1985, p. 228.
12. Moneyline, *USA Today,* March 14, 1985, Money section, p. 1.
13. See "Japan's Secret Economic Weapon: Exploited Women," *Business Week,* March 4, 1985, pp. 54–55; "Changing Roles: More Women in Japan Get Jobs, Shaking Up Traditional Marriages," *Wall Street Journal,* May 14, 1985, pp. 1, 24; "Japanese Law Aims at Sex Discrimination," *Washington Post,* July 3, 1985, sec. A, pp. 9, 20.
14. "The Navy and General Dynamics" (editorial), *Washington Post,* May 24, 1985, sec. A, p. 26.
15. "Bowing to the Inevitable," *Forbes,* August 12, 1985, p. 66.
16. See "Dutch Accountants Take on a Formidable Task: Ferreting Out 'Cheaters' in the Ranks of OPEC," *Wall Street Journal,* February 26, 1985, "International" section.
17. See Richard Posner, *Economic Analysis of Law,* 3rd ed.
18. Tom L. Beauchamp, ed., *Case Studies in Business, Society, and Ethics* (Englewood Cliffs, N.J.: Prentice-Hall, 1983), 247–49.
19. As quoted in Charles R. Babcock, "Zaccaro Ousted as Guardian of Elderly Woman's Estate," *Washington Post,* August 31, 1984, sec. A, pp. 1, 8.
20. A. Carl Kotchian, in his article, *Saturday Review,* July 9, 1977.
21. See Al Kamen, "Budget Law Rejected by High Court," *Washington Post,* July 8, 1986, p. 1.
22. James Clavell, *Noble House* (New York: Delacorte Press, 1981), 857.
23. K. Ann Coleman Stolurow and Dale W. Moeller, "Dental X-Ray Use in Boston," *American Journal of Public Health* 69 (July 1979): 709–710.
24. See Jennifer Hull, "Unocal Sues Bank," *Wall Street Journal,* March 13, 1985, p. 22, and Charles McCoy, "Mesa Petroleum Alleges Unocal Coerced Banks," *Wall Street Journal,* March 22, 1985, p. 6.
25. "Murder in the Front Office," *Newsweek,* July 8, 1985, p. 58.
26. Quoted from George A. Steiner and John F. Steiner, *Casebook for Business, Government, and Society,* 2nd ed. (New York: Random House, 1980), 151.

27. T. W. Zimmerer and P. L. Preston, "Plasma International," in Beauchamp, *Case Studies,* 157–58, and in R. D. Hay, et al., eds., *Business and Society* (Cincinnati: South-Western, 1976).
28. Marlys Harris, "The Stumbling Herd," *Money,* November 1984, p. 258.
29. Letters to the Editor, *Money,* December, 1984, p. 224.
30. This case report by Robert E. Stevenson is found in *Hastings Center Report* 10 (December 1980): 25.
31. John Rawls, *A Theory of Justice* (Cambridge, Mass.: Harvard University Press, 1971), 20–21, and Norman Daniels, "Wide Reflective Equilibrium and Theory Acceptance in Ethics," *Journal of Philosophy* 76 (1979): 256–282.
32. See Alan Gewirth, *Reason and Morality* (Chicago: The University of Chicago Press, 1978). For an abbreviated discussion, see "The Basis and Content of Human Rights" in *Human Rights Nomos XXIII,* ed. J. Roland Pennock and John W. Chapman (New York: New York University Press, 1981), 119–147.
33. See, for example, Philip Shabecoff, "Industry and Women Clash Over Hazards in the Workplace," *New York Times,* January 3, 1981, and the DuPont case in Beauchamp, *Case Studies.*
34. This case is taken from Vincent Barry, *Moral Issues in Business* (Belmont, Calif.: Wadsworth, 1979), 149.
35. Daniel Callahan and Sissela Bok, *The Teachings of Ethics in Higher Education* (Hastings-on-Hudson, N.Y.: The Hastings Center, 1980), 69. See also Thomas Donaldson, "The Case Method," in his *Case Studies in Business Ethics* (Englewood Cliffs, N.J.: Prentice-Hall, 1984), 1–12.
36. Langdell's first casebook on *Contracts* is treated in Lawrence M. Friedman, *A History of American Law* (New York: Simon and Schuster, 1973), 531–32. The general account of the case method in this section is indebted to this source, and also to G. Edward White, *Tort Law in America: An Intellectual History* (New York: Oxford University Press, 1980).
37. See M. P. McNair, ed., *The Case Method at the Harvard Business School* (New York: McGraw-Hill, 1954).
38. Arthur L. Caplan, "Ethical Engineers Need Not Apply: The State of Applied Ethics Today," *Science, Technology, and Human Values* 6 (Fall 1980): 24–32.

Suggested Supplementary Readings

Business Ethics and Ethical Theory

DeGeorge, Richard T. *Business Ethics.* New York: Macmillan, 1982.
Donaldson, Thomas. *Corporations and Morality.* Englewood Cliffs, N.J.: Prentice-Hall, 1982.
Regan, Tom, ed. *Just Business.* New York: Random House, 1984.
Velasquez, Manuel. *Business Ethics: Concepts and Cases.* Englewood Cliffs, N.J.: Prentice-Hall, 1982.

Ethical Theory and Morality

Beauchamp, Tom L. *Philosophical Ethics.* New York: McGraw-Hill, 1982.
Frankena, William K. *Ethics.* 2nd ed. Englewood Cliffs, N.J.: Prentice-Hall, 1973.
MacIntyre, Alasdair. *A Short History of Ethics.* New York: Macmillan, 1966.
Mackie, John. *Ethics: Inventing Right and Wrong.* Harmondsworth, Eng.: Penguin Books, 1977.
Nielsen, Kai. "Problems of Ethics." In Vol. 3 of *Encyclopedia of Philosophy,* edited by Paul Edwards, 117–134. New York: Macmillan and Free Press, 1967.
Rachels, James. *The Elements of Moral Philosophy.* New York: Random House, 1986.
Taylor, Paul W., ed. *Problems of Moral Philosophy.* 3d ed. Chapter 1. Belmont, Calif.: Wadsworth, 1978.

Justification

Griffiths, A. Phillips. "Ultimate Moral Principles: Their Justification." In Vol. 8 of *Encyclopedia of Philosophy,* edited by Paul Edwards, 117–182. New York: Macmillan and Free Press, 1967.
Held, Virginia. "Justification: Legal and Political." *Ethics* 86 (October 1975): 1–16.

Relativism, Disagreement, and Objectivity

Brandt, Richard B. "Ethical Relativism." In Vol. 3 of *Encyclopedia of Philosophy,* edited by Paul

Edwards, 75–78. New York: Macmillan and Free Press, 1967.

Krausz, Michael, and Jack W. Meiland, eds. *Relativism*. Notre Dame, Ind.: University of Notre Dame Press, 1982.

Ladd, John, ed. *Ethical Relativism*. Belmont, Calif.: Wadsworth, 1973.

Egoism

Brandt, Richard B. *Ethical Theory*, Chapter 14. Englewood Cliffs, N.J.: Prentice Hall, 1959.

Kalin, Jesse. "On Ethical Egoism." In *Studies in Moral Philosophy*, American Philosophical Quarterly Monograph Series no. 1, 1968, pp. 26–41.

MacIntyre, Alasdair. "Egoism and Altruism," in Vol. 2 of *Encyclopedia of Philosophy*, edited by Paul Edwards, 462–466. New York: Macmillan and Free Press, 1967.

Milo, Ronald D., ed. *Egoism and Altruism*. Belmont, Calif.: Wadsworth, 1973.

Utilitarianism

Frey, R. G., ed. *Utility and Rights*. Minneapolis, Minn.: University of Minnesota Press, 1984.

Gorovitz, Samuel, ed. *Mill: Utilitarianism, with Critical Essays*. New York: Bobbs-Merrill, 1971.

Mill, John Stuart. *On Liberty,* London: J. W. Parker, 1859. (Widely reprinted.)

Miller, Harlan B., and William H. Williams, eds. *The Limits of Utilitarianism*. Minneapolis, Minn.: University of Minnesota Press, 1982.

Sen, Amartya, and Bernard Williams, eds. *Utilitarianism and Beyond*. Cambridge: Cambridge University Press, 1982.

Deontology

Donagan, Alan. *The Theory of Morality*. Chicago: University of Chicago Press, 1977.

Kant, Immanuel. *Foundations of the Metaphysics of Morals,* translated by Lewis White Beck. Indianapolis: Bobbs-Merrill, 1959.

Nell, Onora. *Acting on Principle, An Essay on Kantian Ethics*. New York and London: Columbia University Press, 1975.

Rawls, John. *A Theory of Justice*. Cambridge, Mass.: Harvard University Press, 1971.

Ross, William D. *The Right and the Good*. Oxford: Oxford University Press, 1930.

Justice

The entries below are introductions to the subject of Justice. See Chapter Nine for more advanced reading on topics of justice.

Benn, Stanley I. "Justice." In Vol. 4 of *Encyclopedia of Philosophy,* edited by Paul Edwards. New York: Macmillan and Free Press, 1967.

Feinberg, Joel. *Social Philosophy,* Chapter 7. Englewood Cliffs, N.J.: Prentice-Hall, 1973.

Moral and Legal Rights

Dworkin, Ronald. *Taking Rights Seriously*. Cambridge, Mass.: Harvard University Press, 1977.

Feinberg, Joel. *Social Philosophy,* Chapters 4–6. Englewood Cliffs, N.J.: Prentice-Hall, 1973.

Gewirth, Alan. *Human Rights*. Chicago: University of Chicago Press, 1982.

Lyons, David, ed. *Rights*. Belmont, Calif.: Wadsworth, 1979.

Shue, Henry. *Basic Rights: Subsistence, Affluence, and U.S. Foreign Policy*. Princeton: Princeton University Press, 1980.

Waldron, Jeremy. *Theories of Rights*. Oxford: Oxford University Press, 1984.

Wellman, Carl. *A Theory of Rights*. Totowa, N.J.: Rowman and Allanheld, 1985.

Werhane, Patricia H., A.R. Gini, and David T. Ozar, eds. *Philosophical Issues in Human Rights*. New York: Random House, 1986.

White, Alan R. *Rights*. Oxford: Oxford University Press, 1984.

Case Studies in Ethics and Business

Beauchamp, Tom L. *Case Studies in Business, Society, and Ethics*. Englewood Cliffs, N.J.: Prentice-Hall, 1983.

Donaldson, Thomas. *Case Studies in Business Ethics*. Englewood Cliffs, N.J.: Prentice-Hall, 1984.

Goodpaster, Kenneth E. *Ethics in Management*. HBS Case Studies. Boston: Harvard Business School, 1984.

CHAPTER TWO

Corporate Responsibility

INTRODUCTION

Most discussions of business ethics begin with horror stories of business wrongdoing: Company T has polluted the environment, Company U has engaged in fraudulent Eurobond trading, Company V has been found guilty of overcharging the public for gasoline, Company W has been kiting checks, and Company X is charged with sex discrimination. The *Wall Street Journal* will often carry over 100 stories a month of this sort, from which we might infer that there is a basic pattern of questionable practices in business.

However, as business persons constantly point out, many companies also behave in ways that are morally commendable. In their best seller *In Search of Excellence*, Thomas Peters and Robert H. Waterman argue that, among other things, many of the most successful companies remain close to their customers and consider their employees their most important product. For example, Frito-Lay provides a level of customer service that in the short run cannot be justified on economic grounds: "It (Frito-Lay) will spend several hundred dollars sending a truck to restock a store with a couple of $30 cartons of potato chips. . . . The institution is filled with tales of salesmen braving extraordinary weather to deliver a box of potato chips or to

help a store clean up after a hurricane or an accident."[1] Hewlett Packard does not fire employees in recessionary or hard times; everyone shares the pain by taking a pay cut, occasionally with "free" days off to cushion the blow. The Dana Corporation did away with time clocks. At Delta Airlines a committee of flight attendants chooses the uniforms. At IBM, the company philosophy is respect for the individual.[2] This list of commendable policies adopted by corporations could be almost endlessly expanded. The horror stories together with the honor-roll stories suggest a very mixed picture of businesses living up to their responsibilities.

In the first section of this chapter the articles explore questions of the nature of corporate responsibility and the extent to which corporations can be held responsible. The second section focuses on the debate over the duties, if any, that corporations have to various persons and groups.

HOLDING THE CORPORATION RESPONSIBLE

The first three articles in this chapter consider whether it is possible to hold a corporation responsible as a moral agent and, if so, under what conditions and in what ways.

Consider, as an example of this problem, the Union Carbide disaster in Bhopal, India, where 2,000 people died from a deadly cloud of gas.[3] In what respect can Union Carbide be held responsible for those 2,000 deaths? It might be argued that Union Carbide can be held causally responsible in that the company either acted or failed to act in a manner that caused the deaths. Issues about whether a corporation is an agent are important because many believe that only agents can be praised or blamed. If Union Carbide was not a genuine agent, Union Carbide could not have caused the 2,000 deaths in Bhopal, India, and hence could not be morally blamed for them. (Of course, a Union Carbide employee may have been an agent that caused the deaths and hence this agent could be morally blamed for them.)

But what does it mean to say that Union Carbide acted (or failed to act)? An *action* is not just a *happening* or an event that causes something. If a hurricane hits the coast, destroys thousands of buildings, and produces tidal flooding in which 100 people drown, a series of disastrous events caused by the hurricane has occurred, but the hurricane has not acted. By contrast, if an arsonist sets fire to a hotel and 100 people burn to death, there is something more than a series of disastrous causal occurrences. The arsonist has acted and caused the fire.

What distinguishes the arsonist from the hurricane? Many philosophers would argue that the arsonist intentionally brought about the event and acted with knowledge as well as intent. Agency or action seems to require such conditions. But is a corporation an agent with intentions and knowledge? Some would argue that the corporation more closely resembles a hurricane than an arsonist, and thus is no more an agent than the hurricane. However, a corporation, unlike a hurricane, is composed of agents. Some therefore propose that the term "Company X" is just a shorthand way of talking about some individual person or set of persons within the company.

As one English jurist said, "A company has no body to kick and no soul to damn, and by God, it ought to have both." Corporate executives on this view, are agents but corporations are not. In their respective articles in this chapter, both Richard De George and Manuel Velasquez accept the view that corporations are not agents in the relevant sense.

Others disagree with any answer that reduces the referent of "Company X" to the individuals that compose Company X. They believe that although one can speak meaningfully of holding the president of a company responsible for some act that he or she did, company decisions often are not the result of the actions of any one individual or set of identifiable individuals, but rather emerge from the interactions among company officials, including group decision making. For example, a policy statement prepared by the Vice President for Corporate Planning might be prepared and distributed to the board of officers in advance of a board meeting. Each board member will have an idea of what the policy should be, and the final policy statement issued by the board on behalf of the company will not be identical with any of the various statements originally presented at the meeting.

What, then, makes the board's vote or policy an *action* of the corporation? One contemporary philosopher, discussed by Velasquez, has used the notion of a corporate internal decision structure to show how a corporation might be considered an agent.[4] A corporate internal decision structure consists of a statement of corporate policy that spells out the purpose of the corporation and an organizational flow chart that tells how the corporate purpose is to be enacted. A board that carries out corporate policy as prescribed by the flow chart is exhibiting corporate agency, that is, the corporation is acting in accordance with its plans and objectives. Kenneth Goodpaster and John Matthews agree, in their contribution to this chapter, that corporations qua corporations sufficiently resemble human agents and thus can be morally responsible. In holding corporations responsible, Goodpaster and

Matthews emphasize decision-making responsibility. Corporations are capable of rational action and the decisions of the corporation can be rationally evaluated. Corporate decisions can even be described as impulsive or nonimpulsive, long-term or short-term, consistent or inconsistent with corporate policy, and likely or unlikely to enhance shareholder profit.

If corporate decisions can be criticized for being impulsive, they can also be criticized for treating people irresponsibly. A corporate decision is morally responsible only if the corporate internal decision structure insures that all relevant persons affected by the corporate decision are treated with respect. Hence, if the corporate internal decision structure does not have a means for an employee to address a grievance against a supervisor, then in that respect the corporation's decision making is not morally responsible.

Of course, one need not, as Velasquez points out, hold the corporation morally responsible in order to condemn cases of corporate wrongdoing. What one needs to do is search out the individuals within the corporation who are directly responsible for the act and then hold those persons responsible. Indeed, Velasquez argues that unfortunate consequences result if the focus for holding a corporation morally responsible is on the corporation per se rather than on an individual or set of individuals within it.

An alternative position to that of both Goodpaster/Matthews and Velasquez is that neither a corporation nor corporate employees should be held morally responsible.[5] It can be argued that a corporation is created with an end toward profit and that, as an artificial creation, the corporation is not an autonomous agent and hence is not an object we can morally evaluate. Moreover, each employee has a specific role (function) which he or she is to carry out in accordance with organizational goals. With respect to these organizational goals, persons do not act autonomously, as individuals, because they are required to act as they do. Hence, the actions of corporate employees cannot be morally

evaluated. Neither the corporation itself nor corporate employees can be held morally responsible.

This argument is questionable. It seems unsatisfactory to hold that both corporations and corporate employees should be given moral immunity, and that any corporate action would be morally legitimate if it contributed to the corporate goal of profit making. If individual lying or stealing on behalf of individual interests are wrong, are not lying or stealing on behalf of interests in corporate profit equally wrong? And must not someone be held responsible?

GOOD BUSINESS PRACTICES AND THE PURPOSE OF BUSINESS

It is one thing to show that a corporation can be held morally responsible. It is another to show *what* its moral responsibilities are. In addressing this matter we need to consider whether the sole purpose of a corporation is to obtain profit. There is currently a considerable debate as to whether the only goal—or even the primary goal—of a corporation is profit making, especially if that position excludes the legitimacy of moral goals that might compete with or even undermine profit-making activities.

As a businessperson considers some of the objectives and criticisms of traditional business goals, functions, and practices, sooner or later he or she will undoubtedly ask, "What constitutes a good business practice?" What does it mean to be a good thing, whether the thing in question is a toy, a business, a parade, or whatever? Over two thousand years ago, Greek moral philosophers posed this question about many items. Suppose, for example, we want to know what a good racehorse is. On the first level, a good racehorse is a horse that wins races. By studying the horses to learn what characteristics contribute to the winning of races—speed, agility, discipline, and so on—we learn the characteristics of a good racehorse. And so it is with tools, works of art, and methods of accounting.

Using this functional analysis, Plato (427–347 B.C.) and Aristotle (383–322 B.C.) attempted to give an account of the good state. Plato considered the various groups of classes within the state and inquired into the appropriate function of each class. So long as each class within the state is performing its proper function, he argued, then the state is good. However, if members of one class aspire to perform the activities of another class, the state will become disordered and no longer a good state. Plato focused on three classes: the business and labor community (as we shall call it here), the armed forces or soldiers, and the rulers or top agents of national policy. The rulers he took to be analogous to reason in the human person, the soldiers analogous to will, and the labor and business community analogous to appetite.

Businesspersons and workers might be annoyed at being compared with the "lower" aspect of the human person. However, one influential view held by some businesspersons is similar. These businesspersons would agree with Plato that the appropriate function of the business community is to provide for the material needs of the citizens of the state in an efficient manner. Many would also agree with Plato that the making of policies that promote the general good of the state is the proper function of government, and that when members of the business community try to bring about the public good without legitimate authorization, such action will only lead to a confusion of functions and to general disorder.

On such matters, Plato and the contemporary economist Milton Friedman are in agreement. In Friedman's view, the statement "The business of business is business" is not an empty definition but a program for the good or well-ordered state. Friedman defends a "classical" or "narrow" view of corporate social responsibility, which limits corporate responsibility to making profits for its shareholders. Defenders of this narrow view indicate that business has only one appropriate function, which is making profit. This is the sole characteristic of a good business, and it also delineates the sole moral responsibility of the business. In making a profit a corporation thereby provides "service to the community," and it is not under any obligation to provide any other service.

According to this viewpoint, each group within a free and good society should simply work at performing its particular function well. Various groups, each with distinctive and discrete functions, serve society accordingly. There are multiple centers of power and control, and power is kept from becoming concentrated in too few hands. One assumption is that a major danger to democracy and to individual freedom is the centralization of power, especially government power.

Many concerned persons fear that calls for increased social responsibility on the part of businesspersons will in the end only increase government control. It is generally recognized that the function of government is to look after the public interest. If business were to expand its function from making profits to looking after the public interest, it would be acting in ways appropriate to government, and hence would risk putting itself under government control. Other businesspeople fear that calls for increased corporate responsibility will put too much power in the hands of corporate officials, who, unlike government officials, are not elected representatives charged with determining the public good.

CORPORATE SOCIAL RESPONSIBILITY: ITS NATURE AND SCOPE

The classical view that a corporation's primary and perhaps sole responsibility is to maximize the profit of stockholders is embodied in a legal opinion included in this chapter, *Dodge* v. *Ford Motor Company*. The Court ruled that the benefits of higher salaries for Ford workers and the benefits of lower Ford auto prices to consumers must not take priority over the interests of the stockholders. According to *Dodge,* the interests of the stockholder are supreme.

It was not until 1953 in the case of *A.P.*

Smith Manufacturing Company v. *Barlow et al.*, that corporate officials had something approaching legal permission to undertake acts designed to promote the public good. This case, and the subsequent appeal decision, partially reprinted in this chapter, mark a watershed in the history of the development of corporate responsibility. Judges Stein and Jacobs recognize that the corporate good and the good of society are bound together: To twist a saying, "What is good for America is good for General Motors." From this perspective, legal recognition of the interrelation of public good and corporate good permits a broader view of corporate social responsibility.

One of the requirements for good law is that the law provide stability and hence predictability for citizens to achieve their goals and purposes. The body of law represents a contract that a state has with its citizens and institutions. Any incorporated business has a charter—a form of contract—in which society permits the corporation to do business. It is presumed in the arrangement that business practices will lead to the public good. Original charters were based on the assumption that the pursuit of profit yields utilitarian results. In other words, the narrow view of corporate responsibility represented by Friedman was assumed to serve the overall interest of the public at large. If that assumption were successfully challenged, one might have grounds for justifying a broader conception of social responsibility. Much of the current interest in business ethics reflects the views of those who are now challenging this traditional view.

Any fundamental change in our society's understanding of the function of business or of the basis on which society charters corporations raises issues of its own. Those like Friedman who take the narrow view of corporate responsibility could raise the following moral objection in the face of a social demand that the contract with business be changed. The making of a contract is a type of promise making, and just as one party cannot simply break a promise whenever the keeping of the promise would be inconvenient, so society cannot change the rules under which business operates whenever it would be convenient or useful for society to do so. Would society, then, be treating business unjustly if it demanded changes in the very rules established from the start as the rules of the practice?

These questions about corporate responsibility have often arisen when a corporation has an all too single-minded focus on making a profit, to the exclusion of other potentially important social considerations. This is not to deny that a corporation has a right to make a profit, but it does not have a right to use any means it might choose to the end of profit. Chemical companies must restrain their release of toxic wastes, real estate brochures must fairly present information to potentially unwary purchasers, corporate annual reports must not hide qualifications by accounting firms, and so on.

The essay in this chapter by John Simon, Charles Powers, and Jon Gunneman maintains that all individuals and social institutions ought to adhere to certain moral standards which these authors refer to as "the moral minimum." If there is a genuine moral minimum, to which all institutions, including business, must adhere, then the pursuit of profit in violation of the moral minimum is morally irresponsible. In explaining the concept of the moral minimum, they draw on a distinction between negative injunctions and affirmative duties, a distinction that rests on a further distinction between not causing harm and doing everything one can to promote the good. They argue that although society cannot legitimately impose affirmative duties to promote the social welfare on corporations, society certainly can legitimately impose negative injunctions on corporations; that is, society can legitimately insist that corporate activities not cause harm and that corporations therefore must take active steps to prevent potentially harmful activities. These authors recognize, however, that many of our actions only indirectly cause harm and hence that some criteria are needed for determining what harms fall under a person's or a corporation's responsibility.

Others argue that the classical theory, which gives priority to the stockholder, is unfair. In the essay by William Evan and Edward Freeman, the notion of a corporate stakeholder is developed. Corporate stakeholders are persons or groups having an essential interest in the activities of the corporation. Suppliers, customers, employees, stockholders, management, and the local community are all stakeholders. Why should the interests of one stakeholder have priority over the others, especially since the employees and managers usually have a far greater stake in the corporation than the stockholders? Stockholders are often absentee owners who can afford to lose. Many employees, managers, and even local communities have much more than investment capital at stake. Their very livelihoods are at stake. Evan and Freeman argue that a moral theory of the purpose of the corporation must require that the interests of all the stakeholders be considered.

Finally, some believe that corporations have moral responsibilities beyond adhering to the moral minimum and respecting the interests of all the various stakeholders. These persons believe that corporations have an affirmative obligation to contribute to the general good of society. Here is a fairly typical example taken from the 1984 Annual Report (submitted in 1985) of Pacific Gas and Electric Company: In its report, Pacific Gas and Electric presents an extensive section on its "Community Activities." It summarizes some of its major activities as follows: "Helping senior citizens, providing free weatherization for the needy, tutoring educationally deprived youngsters, supporting charitable fund drives—off the job as well as on, Pacific G&E as a company and employees as individuals do their share to enhance the quality of life in the communities we serve." Pacific G&E also cites its reason for these community activities: "Along with the franchise we have been granted to provide such service (gas and power lines) goes a responsibility we feel deeply: the need to do our share in enhancing the quality of life in the communities we serve" (p. 18). Presumably Pacific G&E believes it has a moral obligation to engage in the above activities even at a calculated cost to profits.

Whether corporations actually have an affirmative obligation to benefit society is a matter of ongoing controversy. Some, like Friedman, believe that the corporation has no moral obligation whatever to be generous; the scope of its "social" responsibility is strictly limited to those to whom a share of the profits is owed. They may also believe that it is actually immoral to be generous to those who do not strictly deserve the profits, because one is expropriating and giving away a share of the profits to persons who have no valid claim on those profits, that is, no right or entitlement to them.

By contrast to Friedman's views, those who think that the corporation has duties of generosity, beneficence, and charity think the corporation does have an obligation to give charitably to the wider community, which sustains it by purchasing its products, providing a municipality for commerce, and so on. In this view, the very reciprocity between those who buy and sell products sets up a relationship of mutual obligation. They argue that such obligations rest on three grounds: competence, gratitude, and the responsibilities of citizenship. Because many corporations have both great power and considerable expertise in motivating people to meet goals productively, these corporations ought to use that power and expertise to benefit society. The social power and expertise of the corporation should be used to benefit the public because of the principle that one owes debts of gratitude to those who provide benefits, and corporations have benefitted handsomely from society. A related argument comes from the responsibilities of citizenship: If the individual members of society have an obligation to improve society, why not corporations too?

Except for adherents of the classical view,

all positions on the moral responsibilities of corporations require that a balancing of harms and benefits take place in the assessment of corporate responsibility: Some pollution is necessary if persons are to be employed. Some hazards in the workplace are unavoidable as well. Protection of trade secrets requires limitations on freedom. The reality of the business world and the context of federal regulations is that such tradeoffs must be made. Students interested in how professional philosophers with business experience try to deal with those tradeoffs can consult the essay by John Kavanagh, which discusses the several problems of responsibility that a corporation faces when it wants to close down or relocate a plant. If profit were the sole concern, many plants would be closed or relocated. But plant closings cause real harm to the communities in which they are located, and in a one-company town, the harm can be catastrophic. The principle, "maximize profit no matter what the impact," thus appears to violate morality. Yet the opposing principle, "never close a plant on economic grounds," is unrealistic and, if followed, would frustrate the legitimate purpose of the pursuit of profit. Kavanagh tries to find acceptable moral principles that would enable businesspersons to

balance the company's duty to pursue profit against the company's obligation to the community in which the plant exists.

Kavanagh, like the other authors in this chapter, invites us to reflect on the meaning of the widely used expression "a corporation with a conscience." As the readings in this chapter clearly reveal, this expression is subject to several rival and probably incompatible interpretations.

NOTES

1. Thomas J. Peters and Robert H. Waterman, Jr., *In Search of Excellence* (New York: Warner Books, 1982), 164.
2. *Ibid.*, pp. 238, 244, 250, 255.
3. See Cathy Trost "Bhopal Disaster Spurs Debate Over Usefulness of Criminal Sanctions in Industrial Accidents," *Wall Street Journal*, January 7, 1985, p. 18.
4. Peter French, "The Corporation as a Moral Person," *American Philosophical Quarterly* 3 (1979): 207–215; See Manuel Velasquez, "Why Corporations Are Not Morally Responsible for Anything They Do" in this chapter, pp. 69–76.
5. See John Ladd, "Morality and the Ideal of Rationality in Formal Organizations," *Monist* 54 (1970): 488–516.

Can Corporations Have Moral Responsibility?

Richard T. De George

The notion of collective moral responsibility has received relatively little treatment in the Anglo-American philosophical literature.[1] This is surprising, given the increasingly

widespread practice of ascribing moral responsibility to groups, peoples, and other collections of individuals. After World War II it was common for people to speak of the

From Richard T. De George, "Can Corporations Have Moral Responsibility?" in "Collective Responsibility in the Professions," ed. Michael A. Payne, *University of Dayton Review*, 5 (Winter 1981–82): 3–15. Reprinted by permission.

moral responsibility of the German people for Nazi atrocities; during the Vietnam War many people accused America of immorality in carrying on an immoral war and using immoral tactics such as defoliation and napalm bombings; the whites in the United States have been said to be morally responsible for the plight of the blacks and responsible for making due reparation; and so on. There are many issues involved in the ascription of collective moral responsibility. In this paper I shall focus on collective responsibility as it pertains to corporations.

Corporations make for a special case of discussion of collective responsibility because they are a special kind of entity. Chief Justice Marshall, in *Dartmouth College* v. *Woodward* in 1819 gave the corporation its classical formulation: "A corporation is an artificial being, invisible, intangible, and existing only in contemplation of law. Being the mere creature of law, it possesses only those properties which the character of creation confers upon it, either expressly, or as incidental to its very existence. These are such as are supposed best calculated to effect the object for which it was created."[2] Corporations are not natural persons, they do not have the properties of natural persons, and they have neither all the liberties nor all the liabilities of natural persons. These are the minimum legal facts which every theory concerning a corporation must acknowledge and take into account.

Now there are two views of the moral responsibility of the corporation with which I shall begin my analysis. Each is deficient in some respects. But each raises issues which it is important to be clear about. The first I shall call the Organizational View; the second the Moralistic View.

The Organizational View starts from the legal definition of the corporation and draws out some of its implications. The literature on organizations is immense, and the Organizational View of corporations has been developed by sociologists and organizational theorists.[3] The view of the corporation developed by them has not been universally accepted, though it has been accepted by a large number of businessmen and workers, as well as by theoreticians.

According to the Organizational View, a corporation is a legal entity established for certain limited purposes—profit, production, the provision of services, and similar restricted ends. It is organized to fulfill these specific tasks. As Chief Justice Marshall noted, it has only those properties which its charter confers upon it. It is not a natural person, and is a person at all only for legal purposes. Since a corporation is not a natural person it needs human agents if it is to function. The human agents, however, when they act as parts of the corporation do not act for themselves, as natural individuals in their private capacity. They act as impersonal agents of the corporation in order to fulfill the corporation's ends. Each person working within the corporation has a function which he is to carry out in accordance with the stated ends of the organization. Each person is replaceable by other people. The corporation has "the blessings of potentially perpetual life and limited liability,"[4] which its individual employees in their personal lives do not have. In acting for the corporation an individual person does not act for himself but for the corporation. As long as his actions are part of the proper task assigned him and in accordance with the proper ends of the corporation, the actions are corporate actions, and the liability incurred are the corporation's liabilities. To the extent that an individual cheats the corporation, manipulates it, or in other ways acts contrary to its ends and his function, he incurs personal liability. But these are actions he performs as a person in his own right and not as an agent of the corporation.

Now on this view a corporation is a legal person only. It is not a moral person. To speak of it in moral terms, therefore, is to make a category mistake.[5] It is to take a corporation for a kind of entity which it is not. Since, moreover, its employees, when acting in their official capacity as impersonal agents of the corporation, are not acting in their own right, it is also a mistake to try to impute moral responsibility to them for their actions. This confuses their status as natural and hence moral persons, with their impersonal, legal functions. Individuals in a corporation should not let their personal moral notions supercede the ends of the corporation. If a corporation is established to produce goods and profits, and some members of the corporation feel that more good could be done by giving the profits to charity than distributing dividends to shareholders, as agents of the corporation they are not empowered to follow their own moral bent. To do so would be to make them legally liable as individuals for improper use of corporate assets. The Organizational View maintains, therefore, that moral responsibility cannot properly be assigned either to a corporation for its actions, nor to the agents of a corporation when they act as corporate agents. As legal entities corporations can be legally restrained and can have legal responsibility. But they cannot logically be held morally responsible or have moral responsibility. For they are not moral agents or entities.

Now some organizational theorists conclude from this description that morality is not part of a corporation's concern. Laws must be complied with. But moral concerns have no place in its structure. This is true both in the external dealings of the corporation, when it acts to achieve its ends, and also in the internal structuring of the organization. If people are hired by managers to work for the organization, moral notions which the manager may have about wages and rights should not color his official actions. Workers are free to accept a job with the corporation or not. No one should be forced to work for a corporation. But if someone does agree to work for a corporation, then he agrees to the conditions the corporation attaches to his position. Both the freedom of the worker to enter a contract and the freedom of the corporation to hire individuals is guaranteed by law. As long as all parties abide by the law, personal moral judgments are irrelevant.

This view is accepted, I have indicated, by many workers as well as by many managers and owners of corporations. And holding this view they are understandably annoyed by those outside the corporation who wish to evaluate it from a moral point of view, who wish to impose their moral views on its activities. If producing napalm bombs is legal, and if in fact the government is the prime purchaser, then those who from some moral point of view claim that producing napalm bombs is immoral, that Dow Chemical is immoral to produce them, and that any employees of that company who continue to work for it are immoral because they are taking part in an immoral activity, are simply mistaken. Those who make such charges may be moral people. But they are confused. They fail to understand that a corporation is a legal, not a moral person, and that the persons who work for a corporation work not as persons exercising their own moral views but as impersonal agents restrained by the ends and structures of the corporation.

For those who hold this Organizational View it is proper to discuss the legal responsibility of corporations and of persons within a corporation, but it is improper to speak of either's moral responsibility, individual or collective.

For those who hold what I have called the Moralistic View, these conclusions are simply morally outrageous. If it is a category mistake to apply moral language to corporations, then corporations in effect have moral immunity. Thus, while murder by an individual can be morally condemned, Murders, Inc., cannot be faulted from a moral point of view for pursuing its goal, nor can its agents for doing what is necessary to achieve the corporation's ends. To pick a case in which the end is not illegal, Hitler's SS, if incorporated, could not be morally faulted for exterminating Jews. Nor can Advertisers, Inc., be morally faulted for its ads, providing they are within the letter of the law, nor Shoddy, Inc., if it produces dangerous tools not prohibited by law. All of them may be legally restrained; but they are morally immune. This is so preposterous, the advocates of the Moralistic View claim, that the Organizational View is obviously fundamentally and dangerously mistaken. Individuals do not cease to be moral persons simply because they are employed by corporations; nor are corporations or other organizations or legal entities, such as nations, immune from moral evaluation and criticism. To hold such a view is to fail to understand the nature of morality, and to fail to understand that all human activities are subject to moral evaluation. Incorporation does not render one morally immune.

Now in favor of the Moralistic View is the fact that people do morally evaluate corporations and other similar organizations and collective entities. If it is immoral to do x, then it is immoral whether it is done by an individual or by a corporation. To hold otherwise might be a legal nicety, but it fails to take account of a widespread moral practice. A widespread moral practice may be an erroneous practice. But in this case the practice is held to be erroneous only because of a theory of organizations. And the defense of that theory, the reason why we should adopt that one rather than some other one, is by no means compelling. Given a choice between holding the Organizational View with the implication that all moral judgments of corporations are mistaken, and holding an alternative view which better accounts for the fact that people do morally judge the actions of corporations, it seems to me the latter is to get preference. We should admit that the Organizational View is at least in part deficient and see whether it can be remedied, though to say it is deficient is not to say that it is completely mistaken. Moreover, if the Moralistic View claims that corporations are moral agents in the same way and in the same sense that natural persons are, it also is mistaken. In claiming that a corporation which makes napalm bombs is acting immorally, or that a corporation which exploits its workers is acting immorally we seem to be saying something quite appropriate, and the claim that we are mak-

ing a category mistake seems arbitrary. But if we speak of the moral feelings of the corporation, or of its pangs of conscience, or of its moral shame, we would obviously be speaking metaphorically at best. Though individuals within a company may express shame or pangs of conscience, corporations cannot; nor is it clear that the individuals within the corporation, if they do express shame for the company's actions, do so as agents of the corporation. . . . Corporations are simply not moral agents with feelings, emotions, conscience, and so on. . . .

But all this does not answer the question of whether corporations can be morally responsible for actions, and if so in what sense. . . . A corporation has a public face and its public face is corporate. Its responsibility when looked at in this way is also corporate. In dealing with other firms, in dealing with customers, in dealing with government, it always deals in its corporate mode. The corporation acts, commits itself, delivers and produces goods, abides by or breaks the law, and so on. When, from a moral point of view, we judge the actions of the corporation, we hold the corporation responsible and accountable. We are not, in most cases, either knowledgeable or particularly concerned with the individuals within the corporation. . . .

From within, how is moral responsibility assigned, imputed, and assumed? The first reply is that it may not be. A corporation can be forced by the power of the state to obey its laws. Those within the corporation know this and react accordingly. But from within, those who work for a corporation know that they are not legally bound to be moral, providing the corporation's immoral behavior is not illegal. This is the position of the Organizational View, which rejects the moral ascription from outside and so consistently does not bother with it from inside.

But this situation is no different from individual moral responsibility. For if others ascribe moral responsibility to a natural person, the individual himself need not acknowledge or assume such responsibility. He may differ with them about the appropriateness of the ascription, or he may simply be amoral. Those who agree with the imputation can impose moral sanctions. But these may not be able to force compliance, much less internal assumption of the imputed moral responsibility. In the case of corporations, the fact that those within it may not acknowledge or assume the moral responsibility imputed to it by others proves little. However, if members of the moral community admit that *x*, e.g., theft, is immoral, and if they wish to be consistent, they should admit that it is immoral for corporate as well as for natural persons.

But who within the corporation is responsible for assuming the moral responsibility of a corporation correctly ascribed to it from outside? To answer this question we should look more closely at how moral responsibility can be ascribed from without and assumed from within. A corporation is a single entity for purposes of external action. That is its external face. But from within it is a collection of individuals, each of whom fills certain positions within an organizational structure, and each of whom has certain functions related to the corporation's internal activity. Those outside can sometimes appropriately pierce the external shield of a corporation to ascribe responsibility to those within it, though most frequently they do not. Those within the corporation can assume the responsibility of the corporation jointly or can themselves divide it up. . . .

Now consider five different ways of internally assigning responsibility for corporate actions. We can consider them five models. . . . On the first model, each individual is assigned and/or assumes the full responsibility assigned to the corporation from without. . . . Thus, if a corporation decides to move out of a town paying no attention to what such an action will do to its workers and to the town, the corporation's action might be judged to be immoral. Internally that decision may be one for which each member of the board of directors, for instance, is held fully responsible, though each cast only one vote out of many. Even if a

member voted against the action, if it was taken by the board and implemented, and if he did not dissociate himself by resigning, then he bears full responsibility for the action. If the action is immoral, each bears full moral responsibility for it. The responsibility here is collectively held fully by each individual.

The second model is similar to the first, but it assigns only partial responsibility either to all the members of the corporation or, as a variant, only to those involved in any decision or action taken by a corporation. Thus if a board decides on the issue above, and each person casts only one vote, and if ten votes were required for a motion to pass, each person who voted for it would bear a proportional amount of responsibility, the proportion being divided by the number of affirmative votes. This view wishes to take into account that no one individual acting alone took the decision and that no one individual acting alone could have passed the motion. It was truly a joint action, and must be treated as such. To call it a joint action is to acknowledge joint and partial responsibility, which in this case means dividing it among all those who took part. Those who voted against the measure but did not resign when it was passed may or may not be assigned responsibility on this model. . . .

The above two models break down all corporate responsibility into individual responsibility. In the third model, the corporation is held fully responsible for its actions as well as all the individuals involved in it, with individual responsibility assigned as in model one above. Thus, for instance, a worker in a corporation who had no part in making a decision which leads to the immoral action on the part of a corporation judges the corporation to have acted immorally as well as imputing responsibility to those who made the decision. Does he have, he may ask, the moral obligation to leave a corporation which acts in this manner? Should he assume some responsibility for the corporation's action simply because he works for it and thus helps enable it to act immorally? This way of looking at the moral responsibility of those within a corporation is different from considering the immorality of a corporation's actions to be reducible to those making the decision.

The fourth model is full corporate responsibility with individual responsibility assigned as in model two.

The fifth model assigns responsibility for corporate actions only to the corporation as such, not to any of the members in it individually. This model concedes that corporate actions are not simply the sum of individual actions but that they are actions attributable to the corporation, a separate entity which exists over and above its individual members. The individual members are mortal and replaceable. The corporation is not a fiction, but an organization and a continuing legal person, with a history, traditions, typical ways of acting, rules that govern its behavior, standards which may not be the making of any of the individuals presently employed by the company or by any of its present owners, and so on. If moral responsibility had to be accepted, this would be the model the Organizational View suggests. It is held only collectively and not distributively. . . .

There are a group of other problems which remain. Which of these models is correct, it may be asked? How are we to decide among the models of collective responsibility as applied to corporations? Who *really* has moral responsibility for corporate actions?

Once again we can turn to law for a clue. In some recent cases the courts have come to feel that fines against corporations, even if the fines are large, are not as effective a way of policing corporate activities as the courts would like. For the fines can in some instances be passed off onto consumers. If this is not possible, then frequently the shareholders, who may have had no knowledge of the activity in question, suffer the consequences. Judges, courts, and legislatures have therefore found it advisable in some instances to hold members of the board legally liable for the actions of the cor-

poration. The theory is that if those who make the decisions are held liable for them personally, if they will go to jail for illegal actions, they will be more careful not to engage in illegal practices than if the penalty for such action is simply a fine paid by the corporation from its assets. What the company gains from its illegal actions might even be worth the price of the fine. It is less likely to be viewed by a board member as being worth a personal term in prison. . . .

Now the point to which I wish to draw attention is that in answer to the question of who really has legal responsibility, we must go to the laws and to specific interpretations, and we learn that legal responsibility can be and is assigned in a variety of ways. It can be assigned to the corporation as well as to members within it or only to members within it. The assigning of responsibility in each of these ways carries with it appropriate penalties for violation of the responsibility, penalties which fall either on the corporation or both on the corporation and on individuals within it, or only on individuals within it. In answer to the question, but which one of these is proper, the response is that all of them are, if they fulfill the function they are intended to fulfill. Laws have certain purposes, and if they are to control in certain ways the actions of corporations and of people within corporations, then they are effective insofar as they fulfill their aims. There is no one correct way of legally assigning responsibility with respect to corporate activity. . . .

Now I suggest that the situation is similar with respect to the moral responsibility of corporations. That a part-time janitor working for a corporation should be held fully morally responsible for the immoral actions done by that corporation may sound extreme. In most cases it undoubtedly would be an extreme view. But in others, if the actions of a corporation are truly morally heinous, and if working for the company in any way is to condone its actions, then the janitor might be held morally responsible for the company's actions. But obviously we would like to know what it means to hold someone morally responsible, and what it means to hold a company morally responsible, and what it means to hold both the company and its employees responsible, and so on; and we would want to know what difference it makes if we hold the company but not the employees responsible, and vice versa, and so on through the list of possibilities. Those within the corporation can raise parallel questions. If the janitor is morally responsible we might expect him, on realizing this, to quit. If the manager is morally responsible we might expect him, on realizing this, to change the corporation's policies, assuming it is possible for him to do so. Ascribing responsibility and assuming it might imply responsibility to act in differing ways, depending on one's position. . . .

The thrust of my paper on this point by now, however, should be clear. There is no one sense of moral responsibility which we must discover and in discovering it find whether there is collective moral responsibility and where and how it applies. Morality is a social institution. This does not mean that it is arbitrary, nor necessarily that it is conventional in some narrow meaning of that term. But moral responsibility, just as other moral terms, can be clarified. The clarification should start with some basis in common moral experience. But the concept may well have to be reformulated, more accurately stated for certain purposes, its implications spelled out and evaluated. This is, in fact, the approach that I think should be taken with the notion of collective moral responsibility. . . .

Society, in my view, should not accept the thesis of the Organizational View that the agents of the corporation and the corporation cannot be morally evaluated. They can and should be, since they affect the lives of the members of society and the society as a whole.

Where corporations are so structured that it is difficult for anyone to know whether he is responsible for any particular action or where it is difficult to pinpoint responsibil-

ity, I believe that it should be reorganized so that individuals can know what they are responsible for and so that others can hold them responsible for it. Within the organization I would expect that the moral level of corporate activity would probably rise, if this were the case. If the individual moral responsibility of those within the corporation were clear and if their moral decisions were respected, then the overall result would be that there would be moral pressure brought to bear within a corporation so that each of these involved in decisions concerning the corporation would consider the actions of the corporation and their own participation in those actions from a moral point of view. . . .

NOTES

1. See D. E. Cooper, "Collective Responsibility," *Philosophy*, XLIII (1968), pp. 258–268; Joel Feinberg, "Collective Responsibility," *The Journal of Philosophy*, LXV (1968), pp. 674–688; Virginia Held, "Can a Random Collection of Individuals Be Morally Responsible", *The Journal of Philosophy*, LXVII (1970), pp. 471–481; H. E. Lewis, "Collective Responsibility," *Philosophy*, XXIII (1948), pp. 3–18; and W. H. Walsh, "Pride, Shame and Responsibility," *The Philosophical Quarterly*, XX (1970), pp. 1–13. See also Peter French (ed.), *Individual and Collective Responsibility: The Massacre at My Lai* (Cambridge, Mass.: Schenkman Publishing Co., 1972) which contains some of the above mentioned essays in reworked form, as well as some other essays.
2. Chief Justice Marshall, Dartmouth College v. Woodward, 4 Wheat. 518.636 (1819).
3. See, among others, Herbert A. Simon, *Administrative Behavior*, 2nd ed., (New York: Free Press, 1965); Peter M. Blau and W. Richard Scott, *Formal Organizations*, (San Francisco: Chandler Publishing Co., 1962); and David Silverman, *The Theory of Organizations*. (New York: Basic Books, 1971).
4. Mr. Justice Rehnquist, dissenting, First National Bank of Boston vs. Francis X. Belloti, No. Us 76–1172 (1978).
5. See John Ladd, "Morality and the Ideal of Rationality in Formal Organizations," *The Monist*, LIV (1970), p. 500.

Why Corporations Are Not Morally Responsible for Anything They Do

Manuel G. Velasquez

Does it really make any sense to say that corporations are "morally responsible" for their wrongful actions? Granted, we often and easily assume that saying this makes perfectly good sense. But a moment's reflection might make us pause before so easily attributing moral responsibility to corporate groups. It is relatively clear what we mean when we say that a human individual is morally responsible for some wrongful act. Simplifying somewhat, we mean, at least, that the individual personally performed or helped to perform the act, that she did so intentionally, and that she is justifiably liable to blame and perhaps punishment. It is not equally clear what we mean when we say that a group of individuals is morally responsible for a wrong—that the Ford Motor Company, for example, is "morally responsible" for causing the deaths of many of those killed in Pinto accidents. Clearly we do not mean that everyone in Ford caused or helped to cause these deaths. Nor do we mean that everyone in Ford should be blamed or punished. Perhaps we mean that the responsibility attaches not to each individual in the group but to "the group as a whole." But what is "the group as a whole" if not every individual in the group?

These are puzzling questions. They are questions that I want to address because of their pivotal importance to the way in which we approach ethical issues in business. On the one hand, some authors assume that only human individuals can properly be held morally responsible and, consequently,

think that the proper subject of a business ethic is the individual business person.[1] Other authors assume that moral responsibility should also be attributed to corporate groups, as entities distinct from their members, and, consequently, hold that the corporation must be the (or at least *a*) primary subject of a business ethic.[2] I want to show that this second approach is largely mistaken: I will argue that it makes sense to say that a corporation is morally responsible for a wrongful act only as an elliptical (and somewhat dangerous) way of saying that certain human individuals are morally responsible for that act.

I

To fix our sights let me begin by identifying the kind of responsibility that is at issue here, and let me do this by distinguishing different kinds of responsibility. First, the term *responsible* is sometimes used to mean "trustworthy" or "dependable," as when we say, for example, "Gonzales is a responsible administrator.". . . Second, the term *responsibility* is sometimes used to mean "obligation" or "duty" as in "The responsibility of business is to serve the public," or "Business has the responsibility of serving the public." In this second sense, the term is usually used to look toward the future, toward what still has to be done. Third, *responsibility* is sometimes used to indicate that an action or its consequences are attributable to a certain agent,

From Manuel G. Velasquez, "Why Corporations Are Not Morally Responsible for Anything They Do," *Business & Professional Ethics Journal,* 2 (Spring 1983): 1–4, 6–17. Copyright Manuel G. Velasquez. Reprinted by permission.

as in "Jones is responsible for yesterday's highway accident.". . .

Now it is this third type of responsibility that concerns me and it is the type to which I will be referring when I use the term *moral responsibility*. This type of responsibility is rendered explicit in the classical (i.e., the nineteenth-century common law) notion of criminal responsibility, which is often taken to be a legal rendition of our common understanding of moral responsibility, but one that is subject to the practicalities of legal enforcement. In its classical form, criminal responsibility requires both an *actus reus* and *mens rea*. That is, the accused will be found criminally responsible for a wrongful act only if (1) he personally brought about the wrongful act (i.e., the act was the conventional or causal result of his own bodily movements) or he personally helped to bring it about or he failed to prevent the act when he could have and should have, and (2) he did so intentionally (i.e., he was in voluntary control of the bodily movements that resulted in the act and he knowingly carried out those bodily movements in order to bring about that act or knowingly refrained from carrying out the bodily movements that could have prevented the act). . . .

The philosophical roots of this notion of responsibility stretch back to scholastic doctrines on "imputability." These doctrines are nicely summarized in Kant's *Metaphysics of Morals,* where he writes:

> An action is called a "deed" insofar as it stands under laws of obligation and, consequently, insofar as the subject is considered in this under the aspect of the freedom of his will. Through such an act, the agent is regarded as the originator of the effect, and this effect together with the action itself can be imputed to him if he is previously acquainted with the law by virtue of which an obligation rests on him. . . . Imputation in its moral meaning is the judgement by which someone is regarded as the originator (*causa libera*) of an action, which is then called a "deed" (*factum*) and stands under laws.[3]

As Kant's summary indicates, to say that an action or an effect is to be morally imputed to an agent is to say that the action or the effect "originated" with that agent and that the agent knew the action was morally right or wrong. . . .

In any case, the core concept of moral responsibility that I am trying to identify is the concept that is present in both the philosophical and the legal notions: moral responsibility is the kind of responsibility that is attributed to an agent only for those actions that *originate* in the agent, insofar as the action derived from the agent's intentions (the *mens rea* requirement) and from the same agent's bodily movements (the *actus reus* requirement). . . . An agent originates an action in this sense when (1) he forms a plan of action or intention in his mind and (2) he executes this intention through bodily movements over which he has direct control. . . .

As a glance in the pages of a dictionary will show, the meaning of this kind of responsibility is conceptually tied to another set of notions: liability to blame and punishment. To say that a person is morally responsible for an act is to say that the person is justly liable to blame and punishment. But neither blame nor punishment are appropriate (i.e., morally justified) when a person is not morally responsible for an act in the sense that I am trying to identify. . . .

II

Now let me return to the main question: Does it make any sense to say that corporations are morally responsible for the wrongs they commit in the sense of responsibility that I have just identified? Peter French has laid out the most extended and strongest arguments for the view that moral responsibility can legitimately be attributed to a corporation as an entity logically distinct from its members.[4] The defects of such a view will become obvious if we examine his argument. French argues that corporate organizations can be held morally responsible for their acts because (1) they perform actions that can be attributed only to the corporate organization and not to any of its members and (2) they perform these actions with intentions that can be attributed only to the corporate organization and not to any of its members. Corporate organizations, then, seem to act and they seem to do so intentionally.

French's arguments are significant because they try to show precisely what must be shown if one is to demonstrate that corporations are morally responsible for their acts—namely, that corporations embody the two requirements that are at the heart of the philosophical and legal notions of responsibility: an *actus reus* and *mens rea*. Nonetheless, French is wrong. He is wrong because corporate acts do not originate in the corporation but in the corporation's members.

Consider, first, the requirement of an *actus reus*. Obviously the acts attributed to corporations are not acts that are performed by the corporation as an entity distinct from its members, since corporations do not act except through their members. A corporation may be considered either as a fictitious legal entity to which actions are conventionally attributed or as a real organization comprised of several members whose own actions causally bring about or constitute the corporate act. . . . Considered as a fictitious legal entity the corporation obviously does not perform any bodily acts itself and it is only by way of a convenient fiction that acts performed by others are conventionally attributed to the corporation.[5] On the other hand, considered as a real organization, the corporation is related to its members as an organized group is related to the individuals who comprise the group. It may thus appear that when a corporate member acts the corporation may be said to have performed the act of the member, much as when a person's bodily limb moves the person is said to have moved his limb. But this similarity is deceptive because a group, unlike a body, is made up of autonomous individuals. The individuals who make up the organization are autonomous in the sense that each individual can choose not to carry out the direct bodily movements necessary to bring about the corporate act. And this autonomy is due to the fact that the body of each member is under the direct control not of the corporation but of the individual member. But moral responsibility for an act, as we have seen, can be attributed only to that agent who originated the act in his own body, that is, in the movements of a body over which he has direct control. In corporate agency, action does not originate in a body belonging to the corporation to whom the act is attributed, but in bodies belonging to those human beings whose direct movements constituted or brought about the act that is then attributed to the corporation. . . .

It is true, as French points out, that some corporate acts cannot be "attributed" to its members in the sense that such acts cannot be *predicated* of its members. When one corporation merges with another, for example, we cannot say of any individual member that he has himself "merged." But this does not imply that the individual member is not morally responsible for such corporate acts. . . . There are a variety of corporate acts that can be predicated only of the corporation (such as mergers, entering into certain contractual arrangements, bringing legal suits, etc.) and that cannot be predicated of the corporation's members. Nevertheless, the corporation's members can be morally responsible for such acts, since they are the ones who bring about all corporate acts. . . .

French is also wrong in claiming that the intentions we attribute to corporations are the kind on which moral responsibility rests. He is wrong, that is, with respect to the *mens rea* requirement. According to French, corporate "intentions" may be inferred from the corporation's official policies, decision-making procedures, and lines of authority, to which corporate members must adhere and which are typically designed to ensure that the concatenated decisions and actions of these corporate members will achieve certain objectives. French calls this system of policies, procedures, and lines of authority a "CID" (for Corporate Internal Decision) structure that "accomplishes a subordination and synthesis of the intentions and acts of various biological persons into a corporate decision." Although no particular member of the corporation may intend to achieve the objectives mandated or generated by the CID structure, nonetheless the corporation may be said to "intend" to achieve those objectives. And these intentions, according to French, are sufficient to render corporate acts "intentional."

... But an act is intentional only if it is the carrying out of an intention formed in the mind of the agent whose bodily movements bring about the act. The intentions French attributes to corporations ... do not mark out corporate acts as intentional because the intentions are attributed to one entity (the corporation) whereas the acts are carried out by another entity (the corporate members).

The underlying reason for corporate policies and procedures being unable to generate intentional action is that the concept of intentional action, as I have suggested, is rooted in the concept of an agent with a certain mental and bodily unity that corporations do not have. Intentional agents are mental insofar as they have minds by which they form plans or intentions; they are bodily insofar as they have bodies whose movements they directly control; and they are a unity insofar as the agent who forms intentions also directly controls the bodily movements by which those intentions are executed. It is in virtue of this fact—this unity—that I am said to originate actions (when the actions are the carrying out of intentions I originally formed) and it is also in virtue of this unity that my actions can be intentional: intentional action in the world requires a unity of mind and physical instrumentality. Corporate agents, as we know them, do not have this kind of unity and con-

sequently their "intentions" do not connect with their actions in the proper way. . . .

Who, then, is morally responsible for the acts of a corporation? There is no single answer to this question. To the extent that certain members of a corporation each intentionally decide to bring about a corporate act together, those members are each morally responsible for that corporate act. To the extent that a corporate act is the result of policies and procedures that were intentionally designed by certain persons to produce precisely that type of act, those persons are morally responsible for that act. And to the extent that a corporate act is the unintentional result of the concatenated actions of several corporate members, none of whom knew about or intended that outcome, the corporate act may be an act for which no one is morally responsible: it is an unintentional happening.

III

Let me leave French's views now and turn to a second set of arguments that show that corporations as distinct from their members cannot be morally responsible for what they do.

Obviously, we often say that this or that corporation is morally responsible for a wrongful act and that it should be blamed or punished for the act. Two questions regarding this statement must be addressed here: (1) What is the entity to which we can be referring when we say "the corporation" and (2) What can we mean by saying that that entity (and not another) is morally responsible and should be blamed and punished?

There are, I believe, three main answers to the first question. [As indicated earlier,] we sometimes use the term *corporation* to refer to a legal but fictitious entity recognized by the law. In this sense the term refers to an entity distinct from the group of human beings that constitutes its members. We sometimes use the term to refer to an organization of human beings, and then it may refer to one of two things. First, it may refer to the set of relationships that obtain among a certain group of human beings. In this sense, "the corporation" refers to the structured set of relationships that allows us to identify a group of human beings and their activities as a corporate organization. Second, when referring to the corporation as an organization we may simply be referring to the group of human beings that constitute the members of the corporation. In this sense, "the corporation" refers to the human beings who make up the corporate organization.

There are, then, three main entities we may be referring to when we use the term *corporation:* (a) the fictitious legal entity, (b) the organization as a structured set of relationships, and (c) the organization as a set of human beings. We may safely set aside the first sense. . . . People who hold corporations morally responsible for their acts have in mind real agents that exert physical causality upon the world independently of the law. That is, they are referring to the corporations as an organization either in sense (b) or in sense (c).

Let us turn, then, to the second question: What can one mean by saying that the corporation in sense (b) or in sense (c), and not some other entity, is morally responsible for a wrong and should be blamed or punished? Consider sense (b) first. In attributing moral responsibility for a wrongful act to a corporation in sense (b), one is attributing moral responsibility to a structured set of relationships, and one is implying that this structured set of relationships, and not some other entity, should be blamed and punished for the act. But there are two reasons for thinking that this cannot be what people have in mind when claiming that corporations are morally responsible for a wrongful act. First and most obvious is the fact that it makes little sense to speak of "punishing" relationships. In what sense can relationships feel the shame that is the appropriate response to being blamed and in what sense can relationships experience the suf-

fering or loss that accompanies punishment? When people claim that corporations are morally responsible for some wrongdoing and should be blamed or punished for that act, they are not talking about "punishing" relationships. Second, in saying that a set of organizational structures, and not some other entity, is morally responsible for an act, we imply that only those organizational structures, and not the organization's members, should receive the punishment consequent on that attribution of moral responsibility.. . . . All that a corporation's members should have to suffer is the blame and punishment consequent on their own moral responsibility; to make them suffer the punishment that should have been levied on the corporate structure would be to punish them twice. But in fact it is not possible to impose blame or punishment upon an organizational structure without having that blame or punishment fall on the shoulders of the corporation's members. It is the members who will feel all the effects and bear all the injuries if the corporation's structures are "fined," if its "public image" is "tarnished," or if these structures are altered or perhaps even dissolved. These members are therefore being unjustly forced to bear the punishment for another entity's moral responsibility (in addition to any punishment they may have to bear for their own moral responsibility for the act). And such unfair shifting of punishment *away* from the morally responsible party is certainly not what one has in mind when one says that corporations are morally responsible for their acts and should therefore be blamed and punished for them.

That leaves us, then, with sense (c): in saying that corporations are morally responsible for wrongful acts, we would have to mean that the group of human beings who constitute the corporation's members are morally responsible for that act and should bear the blame and punishment for the act. But here, again, it is possible to have a number of different things in mind. . . .

It is clear enough, I believe, that when

people say that a corporation is morally responsible for a wrongful act and thereby imply that it should be blamed and punished for that act, they cannot properly mean that blame and punishment should be distributed to *every* member of the corporation. For some members of the corporation may have been innocently ignorant of that wrongful act, may have done nothing whatsoever to contribute to the act, and may have been in no position to prevent the act. It would obviously be wrong to impose punishment and blame on such persons for acts of which they were ignorant and with which they had no causal connection. To punish and blame such people (who might include janitors, secretaries, stockholders, etc.) would clearly violate the moral principles on which, as I argued, liability to blame and punishment rests. I take it that when people say that a corporation is morally responsible for a wrongful act and should therefore be blamed and punished, they are not advocating punishment of the innocent. . . .

Saying that a corporation is morally responsible for some wrongful act is acceptable only if it is an elliptical way of claiming that there are some people in the corporation who are morally responsible for that act and who should therefore be blamed and punished. Who would these people be? Since it violates our moral principles to impose blame and punishment on those in whom a wrongful act did not originate, we must be elliptically referring to those people in the corporation who intentionally brought the act about through their direct bodily movements or who knowingly contributed to the act (or, in case of omissions, who knowingly failed to carry out the direct bodily movements they could and should have carried out to prevent it). We are often forced to adopt this elliptical way of speaking because, as outsiders, we are usually ignorant of the inner workings of a corporation. Suspecting that some members of a corporation knew that an act they were intentionally carrying out (or helping to carry out, or failing to prevent) was wrong, but not knowing who those members were, we refer to them under the rubric of "the corporation" and say that the corporation is morally responsible for the act. . . . To say that a corporation is morally responsible for some wrongful act, then, is but an elliptical way of saying (if what one is saying makes sense) that some people within the corporation are morally responsible for the act; it is not a way of attributing moral responsibility to some entity or structure called "the corporation" or to the entire corporate membership (except in the special case in which every individual intentionally contributed to the wrongful act). It is thus incorrect to attribute moral responsibility to the corporation as such.

Someone may object that when a company like Ford manufactures a product that injures a number of people, there is a sense in which everyone in the company contributed to the product and thereby contributed to the injuries. Moreover, when law courts compensate victims of such products, all the members of the company end up paying for the compensation (in the form of lowered salaries, decreased earnings, etc.) and all are thus in effect punished for the injurious act. This shows, someone may want to object, that we hold each member in a corporation morally responsible for wrongful corporate acts, whether that member intentionally helped to carry them out or not, and we are quite willing to punish each one merely for being a member of the corporation.

Such an objection, however, would be based on a confusion of different types of responsibility. Nothing that I have said here precludes us from claiming that entire corporate groups may be held "responsible" for a wrongful act in any of the *other* senses of responsibility that I identified at the beginning of this essay. But it is important not to confuse attributions of responsibility in these other senses with attributions of moral responsibility. For example, corporations "as a whole" may legitimately be held *causally* responsible for an act or an effect. It thus makes perfectly good sense to attribute to *every* member of a corporation the *causal* responsibility for producing the products the corporation manufactures. But attributing causal responsibility to a corporate group is clearly not the same as attributing moral responsibility.

Although the issue is more complicated, it also makes perfectly good sense to attribute "compensatory" responsibility for an injury to *every* member of a corporation, even though not every member of the corporation may be morally responsible for the injury. When a party has been injured, of course, we generally rule that the injured party should be compensated by the person who is morally responsible for the injury. But we often abandon this rule when considerations of efficiency, fairness, ability to pay, causal connections, or risk distribution lead us to separate compensatory responsibility from moral responsibility. The law of torts holds, for example, that when an employee injures a third party in the course of the employee's work, the injured party is to be compensated by the employer because the injured party thereby has a greater chance of recovery (since the employer has a "deeper pocket" than the employee) and because the employer can more easily spread the risk for such injuries by purchasing insurance. Here considerations of social efficiency and risk distribution lead us to pin compensatory responsibility for an injury upon an employer, who may not be morally responsible for the injury, and through the employer upon the insurer, who must ultimately compensate the injured party. . . .

It is clearly important to keep the various senses of responsibility distinct. It is also important not to run together the meaning the term *moral responsibility* may have when it is applied to human individuals with the meaning it may have when it is applied to corporate organizations. For as used of human beings, the term is embedded in a system of psychological, physiological, and moral notions that distinguish human beings and their modes of acting from corporate groups and the modes of action proper

to them. The differences between a human being and a group of human beings are so obvious and enormous that it is quite astonishing to find people wanting to assimilate one to the other. . . .

IV

I will end by giving two reasons for thinking it is dangerous to accept the erroneous view that the corporation is a moral agent, that is, an agent that is morally responsible for its actions. First, if we accept the view that moral responsibility for wrongful corporate acts rests with the corporation, we will tend to be satisfied with blaming or punishing only the corporate entity. Instead of pointing our blame and aiming our punishment at the people who carried out the actions that produced these wrongs, we will do nothing but futilely wave our hands before the corporate veil. If we are to deter corporate wrongdoing and be assured that corporate members will comply with our moral and legal norms, our blame and punishment must travel behind the corporate veil to lodge with those who knowingly and intentionally bring about the corporation's acts. Since corporate acts originate in them, they must be blamed and punished for those acts.

Second, and perhaps more important, viewing the corporation as an entity that can "act" and "intend" like a large-scale personality will result in our being tempted to look upon the corporation as a larger-than-human person whose ends and well-being are more important than those of its members. We will be tempted, that is, to look upon the corporation as organic theories of the state looked upon the state: since the corporation is a whole person (with its own group mind) and the member merely a part, the interests of the corporation's members may legitimately be sacrificed to the corporation's interests and the good of the individual may be subordinated to the corporation's good. . . . As loyalty to the corporation becomes the basic virtue and service to the corporation the basic moral act, the individual will end by being swallowed up by the corporation.

NOTES

1. See Manuel Velasquez, *Business Ethics: Concepts and Cases* (Englewood Cliffs, NJ: Prentice-Hall, 1982), p. 17; Michael Keeley, "Organizations as Non-Persons," *Journal of Value Inquiry* 15 (1981): 149–55.
2. See Thomas Donaldson, *Corporations and Morality* (Englewood Cliffs, NJ: Prentice-Hall, 1982), pp. 32–34. . . . See also David T. Ozar, "The Moral Responsibility of Corporations," in *Ethical Issues in Business: A Philosophical Approach,* ed. Thomas Donaldson and Patricia Werhane (Englewood Cliffs, NJ: Prentice-Hall, 1979), pp. 294–99; Kenneth E. Goodpaster and John B. Matthews, Jr., "Can a Corporation Have a Conscience?" *Harvard Business Review* 60 (1982):132–41.
3. Immanuel Kant, *The Metaphysical Elements of Justice,* trans. John Ladd (New York: Bobbs-Merrill Company, 1968), pp. 24, 29.
4. Peter French, "The Corporation as a Moral Person," *American Philosophical Quarterly* 16 (July 1979): 297–317. Similar arguments appear in Ozar, op. cit.; Goodpaster and Matthews, op. cit.; Thomas Donaldson, "Moral Agency and Corporations," *Philosophy in Context* 10 (1980): 51–70; and D. E. Cooper, "Collective Responsibility," *Philosophy* 43 (1968): 258–68.
5. See Larry May, "Vicarious Agency," a paper delivered at the University of Illinois at Chicago Circle, May 15, 1981, for the Conference on Business and Professional Ethics.

Can a Corporation Have a Conscience?

Kenneth E. Goodpaster and John B. Matthews, Jr.

If people are going to adopt the terminology of "responsibility" (with its allied concepts of corporate conscience) to suggest new, improved ways of dealing with corporations, then they ought to go back and examine in detail what "being responsible" entails—in the ordinary case of the responsible human being. Only after we have considered what being responsible calls for in general does it make sense to develop the notion of a corporation being responsible.*

Christopher Stone

*From *Where the Law Ends* © 1975 by Christopher D. Stone. Reprinted with permission of Harper & Row, Publishers, Inc.

During the severe racial tensions of the 1960s, Southern Steel Company (actual case, disguised name) faced considerable pressure from government and the press to explain and modify its policies regarding discrimination both within its plants and in the major city where it was located. SSC was the largest employer in the area (it had nearly 15,000 workers, one-third of whom were black) and had made great strides toward removing barriers to equal job opportunity in its several plants. In addition, its top executives (especially its chief executive officer, James Weston) had distinguished themselves as private citizens for years in community programs for black housing, education, and small busi-

From Kenneth E. Goodpaster and John B. Matthews, Jr., "Can a Corporation Have a Conscience?" *Harvard Business Review* (January/February 1982). Reprinted by permission of the *Harvard Business Review.* Copyright © 1982 by the President and Fellows of Harvard College; all rights reserved.

ness as well as in attempts at desegregating all-white police and local government organizations.

SSC drew the line, however, at using its substantial economic influence in the local area to advance the cause of the civil rights movement by pressuring banks, suppliers, and the local government:

> As individuals we can exercise what influence we may have as citizens, but for a corporation to attempt to exert any kind of economic compulsion to achieve a particular end in a social area seems to me to be quite beyond what a corporation should do and quite beyond what a corporation can do. I believe that while government may seek to compel social reforms, any attempt by a private organization like SSC to impose its views, its beliefs, and its will upon the community would be repugnant to our American constitutional concepts and that appropriate steps to correct this abuse of corporate power would be universally demanded by public opinion.

Weston could have been speaking in the early 1980s on any issue that corporations around the United States now face. Instead of social justice, his theme might be environmental protection, product safety, marketing practice, or international bribery. His statement for SSC raises the important issue of corporate responsibility. Can a corporation have a conscience?

Weston apparently felt comfortable saying it need not. The responsibilities of ordinary persons and of "artificial persons" like corporations are, in his view, separate. Persons' responsibilities go beyond those of corporations. Persons, he seems to have believed, ought to care not only about themselves but also about the dignity and well-being of those around them—ought not only to care but also to act. Organizations, he evidently thought, are creatures of, and to a degree prisoners of, the systems of economic incentive and political sanction that give them reality and therefore should not be expected to display the same moral attributes that we expect of persons.

Others inside business as well as outside share Weston's perception. One influential philosopher—John Ladd—carries Weston's view a step further:

> It is improper to expect organizational conduct to conform to the ordinary principles of morality. We cannot and must not expect formal organizations, or their representatives acting in their official capacities, to be honest, courageous, considerate, sympathetic, or to have any kind of moral integrity. Such concepts are not in the vocabulary, so to speak, of the organizational language game.[1]

In our opinion, this line of thought represents a tremendous barrier to the development of business ethics both as a field of inquiry and as a practical force in managerial decision making. This is a matter about which executives must be philosophical and philosophers must be practical. A corporation can and should have a conscience. The language of ethics does have a place in the vocabulary of an organization. There need not be and there should not be a disjunction of the sort attributed to SSC's James Weston. Organizational agents such as corporations should be no more and no less morally responsible (rational, self-interested, altruistic) than ordinary persons.

We take this position because we think an analogy holds between the individual and the corporation. If we analyze the concept of moral responsibility as it applies to persons, we find that projecting it to corporations as agents in society is possible.

DEFINING THE RESPONSIBILITY OF PERSONS

When we speak of the responsibility of individuals, philosophers say that we mean three things: someone is to blame, something has to be done, or some kind of trustworthiness can be expected. (See the *Exhibit* on page 78.)

Three Uses of the Term *Responsible*

The causal sense	"He is responsible for this." Emphasis on holding to account for past actions, causality.
The rule-following sense	"As a lawyer, he is responsible for defending that client." Emphasis on following social and legal norms.
The decision-making sense	"He is a responsible person." Emphasis on an individual's independent judgment.

Holding Accountable

We apply the first meaning, what we shall call the *causal* sense, primarily to legal and moral contexts where what is at issue is praise or blame for a past action. We say of a person that he or she was responsible for what happened, is to blame for it, should be held accountable. In this sense of the word, *responsibility* has to do with tracing the causes of actions and events, of finding out who is answerable in a given situation. Our aim is to determine someone's intention, free will, degree of participation, and appropriate reward or punishment.

Rule Following

We apply the second meaning of *responsibility* to rule following, to contexts where individuals are subject to externally imposed norms often associated with some social role that people play. We speak of the responsibilities of parents to children, of doctors to patients, of lawyers to clients, of citizens to the law. What is socially expected and what the party involved is to answer for are at issue here.

Decision Making

We use the third meaning of *responsibility* for decision making. With this meaning of the term, we say that individuals are responsible

if they are trustworthy and reliable, if they allow appropriate factors to affect their judgment; we refer primarily to a person's independent thought processes and decision making, processes that justify an attitude of trust from those who interact with him or her as a responsible individual.

The distinguishing characteristic of moral responsibility, it seems to us, lies in this third sense of the term. Here the focus is on the intellectual and emotional processes in the individual's moral reasoning. Philosophers call this "taking a moral point of view" and contrast it with such other processes as being financially prudent and attending to legal obligations.

To be sure, characterizing a person as "morally responsible" may seem rather vague. But vagueness is a contextual notion. Everything depends on how we fill in the blank in "vague for _____ purposes."

In some contexts the term "six o'clockish" is vague, while in others it is useful and informative. As a response to a space-shuttle pilot who wants to know when to fire the reentry rockets, it will not do, but it might do in response to a spouse who wants to know when one will arrive home at the end of the workday.

We maintain that the processes underlying moral responsibility can be defined and are not themselves vague, even though gaining consensus on specific moral norms and decisions is not always easy.

What, then, characterizes the processes underlying the judgment of a person we call morally responsible? Philosopher William K. Frankena offers the following answer:

"A morality is a normative system in which judgments are made, more or less consciously, [out of a] consideration of the effects of actions ... on the lives of persons ... including the lives of others besides the person acting. ... David Hume took a similar position when he argued that what speaks in a moral judgment is a kind of sympathy. ... A little later, ... Kant put the matter somewhat better by characterizing morality as the business of respecting persons as ends and not as means or as things. . . . "[2]

Frankena is pointing to two traits, both rooted in a long and diverse philosophical tradition:

1. **Rationality.** Taking a moral point of view includes the features we usually attribute to rational decision making, that is, lack of impulsiveness, care in mapping out alternatives and consequences, clarity about goals and purposes, attention to details of implementation.
2. **Respect.** The moral point of view also includes a special awareness of and concern for the effects of one's decisions and policies on others, special in the sense that it goes beyond the kind of awareness and concern that would ordinarily be part of rationality, that is, beyond seeing others merely as instrumental to accomplishing one's own purposes. This is respect for the lives of others and involves taking their needs and interests seriously, not simply as resources in one's own decision making but as limiting conditions which change the very definition of one's habitat from a self-centered to a shared environment. It is what philosopher Immanuel Kant meant by the "categorical imperative" to treat others as valuable in and for themselves.

It is this feature that permits us to trust the morally responsible person. We know that such a person takes our point of view into account not merely as a useful precaution (as in "honesty is the best policy") but as important in its own right.

These components of moral responsibility are not too vague to be useful. Rationality and respect affect the manner in which a person approaches practical decision making: they affect the way in which the individual processes information and makes choices. A rational but not respectful Bill Jones will not lie to his friends *unless* he is reasonably sure he will not be found out. A rational but not respectful Mary Smith will defend an unjustly treated party *unless* she thinks it may be too costly to herself. A rational *and* respectful decision maker, however, notices—and cares—whether the con-

sequences of his or her conduct lead to injuries or indignities to others.

Two individuals who take "the moral point of view" will not of course always agree on ethical matters, but they do at least have a basis for dialogue.

PROJECTING RESPONSIBILITY TO CORPORATIONS

Now that we have removed some of the vagueness from the notion of moral responsibility as it applies to persons, we can search for a frame of reference in which, by analogy with Bill Jones and Mary Smith, we can meaningfully and appropriately say that corporations are morally responsible. This is the issue reflected in the SSC case.

To deal with it, we must ask two questions: Is it meaningful to apply moral concepts to actors who are not persons but who are instead made up of persons? And even if meaningful, is it advisable to do so?

If a group can act like a person in some ways, then we can expect it to behave like a person in other ways. For one thing, we know that people organized into a group can act as a unit. As business people well know, legally a corporation is considered a unit. To approach unity, a group usually has some sort of internal decision structure, a system of rules that spell out authority relationships and specify the conditions under which certain individuals' actions become official actions of the group.[3]

If we can say that persons act responsibly only if they gather information about the impact of their actions on others and use it in making decisions, we can reasonably do the same for organizations. Our proposed frame of reference for thinking about and implementing corporate responsibility aims at spelling out the processes associated with the moral responsibility of individuals and projecting them to the level of organizations. This is similar to, though an inversion of, Plato's famous method in the *Republic,* in which justice in the community is used as a model for justice in the individual.

Hence, corporations that monitor their employment practices and the effects of their production processes and products on the environment and human health show the same kind of rationality and respect that morally responsible individuals do. Thus, attributing actions, strategies, decisions, and moral responsibilities to corporations as entities distinguishable from those who hold offices in them poses no problem.

And when we look about us, we can readily see differences in moral responsibility among corporations in much the same way that we see differences among persons. Some corporations have built features into their management incentive systems, board structures, internal control systems, and research agendas that in a person we would call self-control, integrity, and conscientiousness. Some have institutionalized awareness and concern for consumers, employees, and the rest of the public in ways that others clearly have not.

As a matter of course, some corporations attend to the human impact of their operations and policies and reject operations and policies that are questionable. Whether the issue be the health effects of sugared cereal or cigarettes, the safety of tires or tampons, civil liberties in the corporation or the community, an organization reveals its character as surely as a person does.

Indeed, the parallel may be even more dramatic. For just as the moral responsibility displayed by an individual develops over time from infancy to adulthood,[4] so too we may expect to find stages of development in organizational character that show significant patterns.

EVALUATING THE IDEA OF MORAL PROJECTION

Concepts like moral responsibility not only make sense when applied to organizations but also provide touchstones for designing more effective models than we now have for guiding corporate policy.

Now we can understand what it means to invite SSC as a corporation to be morally responsible both in-house and in its community, but *should* we issue the invitation? Here we turn to the question of advisability. Should we require the organizational agents in our society to have the same moral attributes we require of ourselves?

Our proposal to spell out the processes associated with moral responsibility for individuals and then to project them to their organizational counterparts takes on added meaning when we examine alternative frames of reference for corporate responsibility.

Two frames of reference that compete for the allegiance of people who ponder the question of corporate responsibility are emphatically opposed to this principle of moral projection—what we might refer to as the "invisible hand" view and the "hand of government" view.

The Invisible Hand

The most eloquent spokesman of the first view is Milton Friedman (echoing many philosophers and economists since Adam Smith). According to this pattern of thought, the true and only social responsibilities of business organizations are to make profits and obey the laws. The workings of the free and competitive marketplace will "moralize" corporate behavior quite independently of any attempts to expand or transform decision making via moral projection.

A deliberate amorality in the executive suite is encouraged in the name of systemic morality: the common good is best served when each of us and our economic institutions pursue not the common good or moral purpose, advocates say, but competitive advantage. Morality, responsibility, and conscience reside in the invisible hand of the free market system, not in the hands of the organizations within the system, much less the managers within the organizations.

To be sure, people of this opinion admit, there is a sense in which social or ethical issues can and should enter the corporate mind, but the filtering of such issues is thorough: they go through the screens of custom, public opinion, public relations, and the law. And, in any case, self-interest maintains primacy as an objective and a guiding star.

The reaction from this frame of reference to the suggestion that moral judgment be integrated with corporate strategy is clearly negative. Such an integration is seen as inefficient and arrogant, and in the end both an illegitimate use of corporate power and an abuse of the manager's fiduciary role. With respect to our SSC case, advocates of the invisible hand model would vigorously resist efforts, beyond legal requirements, to make SSC right the wrongs of racial injustice. SSC's responsibility would be to make steel of high quality at least cost, to deliver it on time, and to satisfy its customers and stockholders. Justice would not be part of SSC's corporate mandate.

The Hand of Government

Advocates of the second dissenting frame of reference abound, but John Kenneth Galbraith's work has counterpointed Milton Friedman's with insight and style. Under this view of corporate responsibility, corporations are to pursue objectives that are rational and purely economic. The regulatory hands of the law and the political process rather than the invisible hand of the marketplace turns these objectives to the common good.

Again, in this view, it is a system that provides the moral direction for corporate decision making—a system, though, that is guided by political managers, the custodians of the public purpose. In the case of SSC, proponents of this view would look to the state for moral direction and responsible management, both within SSC and in the community. The corporation would have no moral responsibility beyond political and legal obedience.

What is striking is not so much the radical difference between the economic and social philosophies that underlie these two views of the source of corporate responsibility but the conceptual similarities. Both views locate morality, ethics, responsibility, and conscience in the systems of rules and incentives in which the modern corporation finds itself embedded. Both views reject the exercise of independent moral judgment by corporations as actors in society.

Neither view trusts corporate leaders with stewardship over what are often called noneconomic values. Both require corporate responsibility to march to the beat of drums outside. In the jargon of moral philosophy, both views press for a rule-centered or a system-centered ethics instead of an agent-centered ethics. In terms of the *Exhibit,* these frames of reference countenance corporate rule-following responsibility for corporations but not corporate decision-making responsibility.

The Hand of Management

To be sure, the two views under discussion differ in that one looks to an invisible moral force in the market while the other looks to a visible moral force in government. But both would advise against a principle of moral projection that permits or encourages corporations to exercise independent, noneconomic judgment over matters that face them in their short- and long-term plans and operations.

Accordingly, both would reject a third view of corporate responsibility that seeks to affect the thought processes of the organization itself—a sort of "hand of management" view—since neither seems willing or able to see the engines of profit regulate themselves to the degree that would be implied by taking the principle of moral projection seriously. Cries of inefficiency and moral imperialism from the right would be matched by cries of insensitivity and illegitimacy from the left, all in the name of preserving us from corporations and managers run morally amok.

Better, critics would say, that moral philosophy be left to philosophers, philanthropists, and politicians than to business leaders. Better that corporate morality be kept to glossy annual reports, where it is safely insulated from policy and performance.

The two conventional frames of reference locate moral restraint in forces external to the person and the corporation. They deny moral reasoning and intent to the corporation in the name of either market competition or society's system of explicit legal constraints and presume that these have a better moral effect than that of rationality and respect.

Although the principle of moral projection, which underwrites the idea of a corporate conscience and patterns it on the thought and feeling processes of the person, is in our view compelling, we must acknowledge that it is neither part of the received wisdom, nor is its advisability beyond question or objection. Indeed, attributing the role of conscience to the corporation seems to carry with it new and disturbing implications for our usual ways of thinking about ethics and business.

Perhaps the best way to clarify and defend this frame of reference is to address the objections to the principle found in the ruled insert on pages [83–86]. There we see a summary of the criticisms and counterarguments we have heard during hours of discussion with business executives and business school students. We believe that the replies to the objections about a corporation having a conscience are convincing.

LEAVING THE DOUBLE STANDARD BEHIND

We have come some distance from our opening reflection on Southern Steel Company and its role in its community. Our proposal—clarified, we hope, through these objections and replies—suggests that it is not

sufficient to draw a sharp line between individuals' private ideas and efforts and a corporation's institutional efforts, but that the latter can and should be built upon the former.

Does this frame of reference give us an unequivocal prescription for the behavior of SSC in its circumstances? No, it does not. Persuasive arguments might be made now and might have been made then that SSC should not have used its considerable economic clout to threaten the community into desegregation. A careful analysis of the realities of the environment might have disclosed that such a course would have been counterproductive, leading to more injustice than it would have alleviated.

The point is that some of the arguments and some of the analyses are or would have been moral arguments, and thereby the ultimate decision that of an ethically responsible organization. The significance of this point can hardly be overstated, for it represents the adoption of a new perspective on corporate policy and a new way of thinking about business ethics. We agree with one authority, who writes that "the business firm, as an organic entity intricately affected by and affecting its environment, is as appropriately adaptive . . . to demands for responsible behavior as for economic service."[5]

The frame of reference here developed does not offer a decision procedure for corporate managers. That has not been our purpose. It does, however, shed light on the conceptual foundations of business ethics by training attention on the corporation as a moral agent in society. Legal systems of rules and incentives are insufficient, even though they may be necessary, as frameworks for corporate responsibility. Taking conceptual cues from the features of moral responsibility normally expected of the person in our opinion deserves practicing managers' serious consideration.

The lack of congruence that James Weston saw between individual and corporate moral responsibility can be, and we think should be, overcome. In the process, what a number of writers have characterized as a double standard—a discrepancy between our personal lives and our lives in organizational settings—might be dampened. The principle of moral projection not only helps us to conceptualize the kinds of demands that we might make of corporations and other organizations but also offers the prospect of harmonizing those demands with the demands that we make of ourselves.

IS A CORPORATION A MORALLY RESPONSIBLE 'PERSON'?

Objection One to the Analogy:

Corporations are not persons. They are artificial legal constructions, machines for mobilizing economic investments toward the efficient production of goods and services. We cannot hold a corporation responsible. We can only hold individuals responsible.

Reply:

Our frame of reference does not imply that corporations are persons in a literal sense. It simply means that in certain respects concepts and functions normally attributed to persons can also be attributed to organizations made up of persons. Goals, economic values, strategies, and other such personal attributes are often usefully projected to the corporate level by managers and researchers. Why should we not project the functions of conscience in the same way? As for holding corporations responsible, recent criminal prosecutions such as the case of Ford Motor Company and its Pinto gas tanks suggest that society finds the idea both intelligible and useful.

Objection 2:

A corporation cannot be held responsible at the sacrifice of profit. Profitability and financial health have always been and should continue to be the "categorical imperatives" of a business operation.

Reply:

We must of course acknowledge the imperatives of survival, stability, and growth when we discuss corporations, as indeed we must acknowledge them when we discuss the life of an individual. Self-sacrifice has been identified with moral responsibility in only the most extreme cases. The pursuit of profit and self-interest need not be pitted against the demands of moral responsibility. Moral demands are best viewed as containments—not replacements—for self-interest.

This is not to say that profit maximization never conflicts with morality. But profit maximization conflicts with other managerial values as well. The point is to coordinate imperatives, not deny their validity.

Objection 3:

Corporate executives are not elected representatives of the people, nor are they anointed or appointed as social guardians. They therefore lack the social mandate that a democratic society rightly demands of those who would pursue ethically or socially motivated policies. By keeping corporate policies confined to economic motivations, we keep the power of corporate executives in its proper place.

Reply:

The objection betrays an oversimplified view of the relationship between the public and the private sector. Neither private individuals nor private corporations that guide their conduct by ethical or social values beyond the demands of law should be constrained merely because they are not elected to do so. The demands of moral responsibility are independent of the demands of political legitimacy and are in fact presupposed by them.

To be sure, the state and the political

process will and must remain the primary mechanisms for protecting the public interest, but one might be forgiven the hope that the political process will not substitute for the moral judgment of the citizenry or other components of society such as corporations.

Objection 4:

Our system of law carefully defines the role of agent or fiduciary and makes corporate managers accountable to shareholders and investors for the use of their assets. Management cannot, in the name of corporate moral responsibility, arrogate to itself the right to manage those assets by partially non-economic criteria.

Reply:

First, it is not so clear that investors insist on purely economic criteria in the management of their assets, especially if some of the shareholders' resolutions and board reforms of the last decade are any indication. For instance, companies doing business in South Africa have had stockholders question their activities, other companies have instituted audit committees for their boards before such auditing was mandated, and mutual funds for which "socially responsible behavior" is a major investment criterion now exists.

Second, the categories of "shareholder" and "investor" connote wider time spans than do immediate or short-term returns. As a practical matter, considerations of stability and long-term return on investment enlarge the class of principals to which managers bear a fiduciary relationship.

Third, the trust that managers hold does not and never has extended to "any means available" to advance the interests of the principals. Both legal and moral constraints must be understood to qualify that trust—even, perhaps, in the name of a larger trust and a more basic fiduciary relationship to the members of society at large.

Objection 5:

The power, size, and scale of the modern corporation—domestic as well as international—are awesome. To unleash, even partially, such power from the discipline of the marketplace and the narrow or possibly nonexistent moral purpose implicit in that discipline would be socially dangerous. Had SSC acted in the community to further racial justice, its purposes might have been admirable, but those purposes could have led to a kind of moral imperialism or worse. Suppose SSC had thrown its power behind the Ku Klux Klan.

Reply:

This is a very real and important objection. What seems not to be appreciated is the fact that power affects when it is used as well as when it is not used. A decision by SSC not to exercise its economic influence according to "non-economic" criteria is inevitably a moral decision and just as inevitably affects the community. The issue in the end is not whether corporations (and other organizations) should be "unleashed" to exert moral force in our society but rather how critically and self-consciously they should choose to do so.

The degree of influence enjoyed by an agent, whether a person or an organization, is not so much a factor recommending moral disengagement as a factor demanding a high level of moral awareness. Imperialism is more to be feared when moral reasoning is absent than when it is present. Nor do we suggest that the "discipline of the marketplace" be diluted; rather, we call for it to be supplemented with the discipline of moral reflection.

Objection 6:

The idea of moral projection is a useful device for structuring corporate responsibility only if our understanding of moral responsibility at the level of the person is in some sense richer than our understanding of moral responsibility on the level of the organization as a whole. If we are not clear about individual responsibility, the projection is fruitless.

Reply:

The objection is well taken. The challenge offered by the idea of moral projection lies in our capacity to articulate criteria or frameworks of reasoning for the morally responsible person. And though such a challenge is formidable, it is not clear that it cannot be met, at least with sufficient consensus to be useful.

For centuries, the study and criticism of frameworks have gone on, carried forward by many disciplines, including psychology, the social sciences, and philosophy. And though it would be a mistake to suggest that any single framework (much less a decision mechanism) has emerged as the right one, it is true that recurrent patterns are discernible and well enough defined to structure moral discussion.

In the body of the article, we spoke of rationality and respect as components of individual responsibility. Further analysis of these components would translate them into social costs and benefits, justice in the distribution of goods and services, basic rights and duties, and fidelity to contracts. The view that pluralism in our society has undercut all possibility of moral agreement is anything but self-evident. Sincere moral disagreement is, of course, inevitable and not clearly lamentable. But a process and a vocabulary for articulating such values as we share is no small step forward when compared with the alternatives. Perhaps in our exploration of the moral projection we might make some surprising and even reassuring discoveries about ourselves.

Objection 7:

Why is it necessary to project moral responsibility to the level of the organization? Isn't the task of defining corporate responsibility and business ethics sufficiently discharged if

we clarify the responsibilities of men and women in business as individuals? Doesn't ethics finally rest on the honesty and integrity of the individual in the business world?

Reply:

Yes and no. Yes, in the sense that the control of large organizations does finally rest in the hands of managers, of men and women. No, in the sense that what is being controlled is a cooperative system for a cooperative purpose. The projection of responsibility to the organization is simply an acknowledgement of the fact that the whole is more than the sum of its parts. Many intelligent people do not an intelligent organization make. Intelligence needs to be structured, organized, divided, and recombined in complex processes for complex purposes.

Studies of management have long shown that the attributes, successes, and failures of organizations are phenomena that emerge from the coordination of persons' attributes and that explanations of such phenomena require categories of analysis and description beyond the level of the individual. Moral responsibility is an attribute that can manifest itself in organizations as surely as competence or efficiency.

Objection 8:

Is the frame of reference here proposed intended to replace or undercut the relevance of the "invisible hand" and the "government hand" views, which depend on external controls?

Reply:

No. Just as regulation and economic competition are not substitutes for corporate responsibility, so corporate responsibility is not a substitute for law and the market. The imperatives of ethics cannot be relied on—nor have they ever been relied on—without a context of external sanctions. And this is true as much for individuals as for organizations.

This frame of reference takes us beneath, but not beyond, the realm of external systems of rules and incentives and into the thought processes that interpret and respond to the corporation's environment. Morality is more than merely part of that environment. It aims at the projection of conscience, not the enthronement of it in either the state or the competitive process.

The rise of the modern large corporation and the concomitant rise of the professional manager demand a conceptual framework in which these phenomena can be accommodated to moral thought. The principle of moral projection furthers such accommodation by recognizing a new level of agency in society and thus a new level of responsibility.

Objection 9:

Corporations have always taken the interests of those outside the corporation into account in the sense that customer relations and public relations generally are an integral part of rational economic decision making. Market signals and social signals that filter through the market mechanism inevitably represent the interests of parties affected by the behavior of the company. What, then, is the point of adding respect to rationality?

Reply:

Representing the affected parties solely as economic variables in the environment of the company is treating them as means or resources and not as ends in themselves. It implies that the only voice which affected parties should have in organizational decision making is that of potential buyers, sellers, regulators, or boycotters. Besides, many affected parties may not occupy such roles, and those who do may not be able to signal the organization with messages that effectively represent their stakes in its actions.

To be sure, classical economic theory would have us believe that perfect competition in free markets (with modest adjustments from the state) will result in all relevant signals being "heard," but the abstractions from reality implicit in such theory make it insufficient as a frame of reference for moral responsibility. In a world in which strict self-interest was congruent with the common good, moral responsibility might be unnecessary. We do not, alas, live in such a world.

The element of respect in our analysis of responsibility plays an essential role in ensuring the recognition of unrepresented or under-represented voices in the decision making of organizations as agents. Showing respect for persons as ends and not mere means to organizational purposes is central to the concept of corporate moral responsibility.

NOTES

1. See John Ladd, "Morality and the Ideal of Rationality in Formal Organizations," *The Monist,* October 1970, p. 499.
2. See William K. Frankena, *Thinking About Morality* (Ann Arbor, University of Michigan Press, 1980), p. 26.
3. See Peter French, "The Corporation as a Moral Person," *American Philosophical Quarterly,* July 1979, p. 207.
4. A process that psychological researchers from Jean Piaget to Lawrence Kohlberg have examined carefully; see Jean Piaget, *The Moral Judgment of the Child* (New York, Free Press, 1965) and Lawrence Kohlberg, *The Philosophy of Moral Development* (New York, Harper & Row, 1981).
5. See Kenneth R. Andrews, *The Concept of Corporate Strategy,* revised edition (Homewood, Ill., Dow Jones-Irwin, 1980), p. 99.

The Social Responsibility of Business Is to Increase Its Profits

Milton Friedman

When I hear businessmen speak eloquently about the "social responsibilities of business in a free-enterprise system," I am reminded of the wonderful line about the Frenchman who discovered at the age of 70 that he had been speaking prose all his life. The businessmen believe that they are defending free enterprise when they declaim that business is not concerned "merely" with profit but also with promoting desirable "social" ends; that business has a "social conscience" and takes seriously its responsibilities for providing employment, eliminating discrimination, avoiding pollution and whatever else may be the catchwords of the contemporary crop of reformers. In fact they are—or would be if they or anyone else took them seriously—preaching pure and unadulterated socialism. Businessmen who talk this way are unwitting puppets of the intellectual forces that have been undermining the basis of a free society these past decades.

The discussions of the "social responsibilities of business" are notable for their analytical looseness and lack of rigor. What does it mean to say that "business" has responsibilities? Only people can have responsibilities. A corporation is an artificial person and in this sense may have artificial responsibilities, but "business" as a whole cannot be said to have responsibilities, even in this vague sense. The first step toward clarity in examining the doctrine of the social responsibility of business is to ask precisely what it implies for whom.

Presumably, the individuals who are to be responsible are businessmen, which means individual proprietors or corporate executives. Most of the discussion of social responsibility is directed at corporations, so in what follows I shall mostly neglect the individual proprietors and speak of corporate executives.

In a free-enterprise, private-property system, a corporate executive is an employee of the owners of the business. He has direct responsibility to his employers. That responsibility is to conduct the business in accordance with their desires, which generally will be to make as much money as possible while conforming to the basic rules of the society, both those embodied in law and those embodied in ethical custom. Of course, in some cases his employers may have a different objective. A group of persons might establish a corporation for an eleemosynary purpose—for example, a hospital or a school. The manager of such a corporation will not have money profit as his objectives but the rendering of certain services.

In either case, the key point is that, in his capacity as a corporate executive, the manager is the agent of the individuals who own the corporation or establish the eleemosynary institution, and his primary responsibility is to them.

Needless to say, this does not mean that it is easy to judge how well he is performing his task. But at least the criterion of performance is straightforward, and the persons among whom a voluntary contractual arrangement exists are clearly defined.

From Milton Friedman, "The Social Responsibility of Business Is to Increase Its Profits," *New York Times Magazine,* September 13, 1970. Copyright © 1970 by The New York Times Company. Reprinted by permission.

Of course, the corporate executive is also a person in his own right. As a person, he may have many other responsibilities that he recognizes or assumes voluntarily—to his family, his conscience, his feelings of charity, his church, his clubs, his city, his country. He may feel impelled by these responsibilities to devote part of his income to causes he regards as worthy, to refuse to work for particular corporations, even to leave his job, for example, to join his country's armed forces. If we wish, we may refer to some of these responsibilities as "social responsibilities." But in these respects he is acting as a principal, not an agent; he is spending his own money or time or energy, not the money of his employers or the time or energy he has contracted to devote to their purposes. If these are "social responsibilities," they are the social responsibilities of individuals, not of business.

What does it mean to say that the corporate executive has a "social responsibility" in his capacity as businessman? If this statement is not pure rhetoric, it must mean that he is to act in some way that is not in the interest of his employers. For example, that he is to refrain from increasing the price of the product in order to contribute to the social objective of preventing inflation, even though a price increase would be in the best interests of the corporation. Or that he is to make expenditures on reducing pollution beyond the amount that is in the best interests of the corporation or that is required by law in order to contribute to the social objective of improving the environment. Or that, at the expense of corporate profits, he is to hire "hardcore" unemployed instead of better qualified available workmen to contribute to the social objective of reducing poverty.

In each of these cases, the corporate executive would be spending someone else's money for a general social interest. Insofar as his actions in accord with his "social responsibility" reduce returns to stockholders, he is spending their money. Insofar as his actions raise the price to customers, he is spending the customers' money. Insofar as his actions lower the wages of some employees, he is spending their money.

The stockholders or the customers or the employees could separately spend their own money on the particular action if they wished to do so. The executive is exercising a distinct "social responsibility," rather than serving as an agent of the stockholders or the customers or the employees, only if he spends the money in a different way than they would have spent it.

But if he does this, he is in effect imposing taxes, on the one hand, and deciding how the tax proceeds shall be spent, on the other.

This process raises political questions on two levels: principle and consequences. On the level of political principle, the imposition of taxes and the expenditure of tax proceeds are governmental functions. We have established elaborate constitutional, parliamentary and judicial provisions to control these functions, to assure that taxes are imposed so far as possible in accordance with the preferences and desires of the public—after all, "taxation without representation" was one of the battle cries of the American Revolution. We have a system of checks and balances to separate the legislative function of imposing taxes and enacting expenditures from the executive function of collecting taxes and administering expenditure programs and from the judicial function of mediating disputes and interpreting the law.

Here the businessman—self-selected or appointed directly or indirectly by stockholders—is to be simultaneously legislator, executive and jurist. He is to decide whom to tax by how much and for what purpose, and he is to spend the proceeds—all this guided only by general exhortations from on high to restrain inflation, improve the environment, fight poverty and so on and on.

The whole justification for permitting the corporate executive to be selected by the stockholders is that the executive is an agent serving the interests of his principal. This justification disappears when the corporate executive imposes taxes and spends the proceeds for "social" purposes. He becomes in effect a public employee, a civil servant, even though he remains in name an employee of a private enterprise. On grounds of political principle, it is intolerable that such civil servants—insofar as their actions in the name of social responsibility are real and not just window-dressing—should be selected as they are now. If they are to be civil servants, then they must be elected through a political process. If they are to impose taxes and make expenditures to foster "social" objectives, then political machinery must be set up to make the assessment of taxes and to determine through a political process the objectives to be served.

This is the basic reason why the doctrine of "social responsibility" involves the acceptance of the socialist view that political mechanisms, not market mechanisms, are the appropriate way to determine the allocation of scarce resources to alternative uses.

On the grounds of consequences, can the corporate executive in fact discharge his alleged "social responsibilities"? On the other hand, suppose he could get away with spending the stockholders' or customers' or employees' money. How is he to know how to spend it? He is told that he must contribute to fighting inflation. How is he to know what action of his will contribute to that end? He is presumably an expert in running his company—in producing a product or selling it or financing it. But nothing about his selection makes him an expert on inflation. Will his holding down the price of his product reduce inflationary pressure? Or, by leaving more spending power in the hands of his customers, simply divert it elsewhere? Or, by forcing him to produce less because of the lower price, will it simply contribute to shortages? Even if he could answer these questions, how much cost is he justified in imposing on his stockholders, customers and employees for this social purpose? What is his appropriate share and what is the appropriate share of others?

And, whether he wants to or not, can he get away with spending his stockholders', customers' or employees' money? Will not the stockholders fire him? (Either the present ones or those who take over when his actions in the name of social responsibility have reduced the corporation's profits and the price of its stock.) His customers and his employees can desert him for other producers and employers less scrupulous in exercising their social responsibilities.

This facet of "social responsibility" doctrine is brought into sharp relief when the doctrine is used to justify wage restraint by trade unions. The conflict of interest is naked and clear when union officials are asked to subordinate the interest of their members to some more general purpose. If the union officials try to enforce wage restraint, the consequence is likely to be wildcat strikes, rank-and-file revolts and the emergence of strong competitors for their jobs. We thus have the ironic phenomenon that union leaders—at least in the U.S.—have objected to Government interference with the market far more consistently and courageously than have business leaders.

The difficulty of exercising "social responsibility" illustrates, of course, the great virtue of private competitive enterprise—it forces people to be responsible for their own actions and makes it difficult for them to "exploit" other people for either selfish or unselfish purposes. They can do good—but only at their own expense.

Many a reader who has followed the argument this far may be tempted to remonstrate that it is all well and good to speak of Government's having the responsibility to impose taxes and determine expenditures for such "social" purposes as controlling pollution or training the hard-core unemployed, but that the problems are too urgent to wait on the slow course of political processes, that the exercise of social responsibility by businessmen is a quicker and surer way to solve pressing current problems.

Aside from the question of fact—I share Adam Smith's skepticism about the benefits that can be expected from "those who affected to trade for the public good"—this argument must be rejected on grounds of principle. What it amounts to is an assertion that those who favor the taxes and expenditures in question have failed to persuade a majority of their fellow citizens to be of like mind and that they are seeking to attain by undemocratic procedures what they cannot attain by democratic procedures. In a free society, it is hard for "evil" people to do "evil," especially since one man's good is another's evil.

I have, for simplicity, concentrated on the special case of the corporate executive, except only for the brief digression on trade unions. But precisely the same argument applies to the newer phenomenon of calling upon stockholders to require corporations to exercise social responsibility (the recent G.M. crusade for example). In most of these cases, what is in effect involved is some stockholders trying to get other stockholders (or customers or employees) to contribute against their will to "social" causes favored by the activists. Insofar as they succeed, they are again imposing taxes and spending the proceeds.

The situation of the individual proprietor is somewhat different. If he acts to reduce the returns of his enterprise in order to exercise his "social responsibility," he is spending his own money, not someone else's. If he wishes to spend his money on such purposes, that is his right, and I cannot see that there is any objection to his doing so. In the process, he, too, may impose costs on employees and customers. However, because he is far less likely than a large corporation or union to have monopolistic power, any such side effects will tend to be minor.

Of course, in practice the doctrine of social responsibility is frequently a cloak for actions that are justified on other grounds rather than a reason for those actions.

To illustrate, it may well be in the long-run interest of a corporation that is a major employer in a small community to devote resources to providing amenities to that community or to improving its government. That may make it easier to attract desirable employees, it may reduce the wage bill or lessen losses from pilferage and sabotage or have other worthwhile effects. Or it may be that, given the laws about the deductibility of corporate charitable contributions, the stockholders can contribute more to charities they favor by having the corporation make the gift than by doing it themselves, since they can in that way contribute an amount that would otherwise have been paid as corporate taxes.

In each of these—and many similar—cases, there is a strong temptation to rationalize these actions as an exercise of "social responsibility." In the present climate of opinion, with its widespread aversion to "capitalism," "profits," the "soulless corporation" and so on, this is one way for a corporation to generate goodwill as a by-product of expenditures that are entirely justified in its own self-interest.

It would be inconsistent of me to call on corporate executives to refrain from this hypocritical window-dressing because it harms the foundations of a free society. That would be to call on them to exercise a "social responsibility"! If our institutions, and the attitudes of the public make it in their self-interest to cloak their actions in this way, I cannot summon much indignation to denounce them. At the same time, I can express admiration for those individual proprietors or owners of closely held corporations or stockholders of more broadly held corporations who disdain such tactics as approaching fraud.

Whether blameworthy or not, the use of the cloak of social responsibility, and the nonsense spoken in its name by influential and prestigious businessmen, does clearly harm the foundations of a free society. I have been impressed time and again by the schizophrenic character of many businessmen. They are capable of being extremely far-sighted and clear-headed in matters that are internal to their businesses. They are incredibly short-sighted and muddle-headed in matters that are outside their businesses but affect the possible survival of business in general. This short-sightedness is strikingly exemplified in the calls from many business-men for wage and price guidelines or con-trols or income policies. There is nothing that could do more in a brief period to de-stroy a market system and replace it by a cen-trally controlled system than effective gov-ernmental control of prices and wages.

The short-sightedness is also exemplified in speeches by businessmen on social re-sponsibility. This may gain them kudos in the short run. But it helps to strengthen the already too prevalent view that the pursuit of profits is wicked and immoral and must be curbed and controlled by external forces. Once this view is adopted, the external forces that curb the market will not be the social consciences, however highly devel-oped, of the pontificating executives; it will be the iron fist of Government bureaucrats. Here, as with price and wage controls, busi-nessmen seem to me to reveal a suicidal im-pulse.

The political principle that underlies the market mechanism is unanimity. In an ideal free market resting on private property, no individual can coerce any other, all coopera-tion is voluntary, all parties to such coopera-tion benefit or they need not participate. There are no values, no "social" responsibili-ties in any sense other than the shared values and responsibilities of individuals. Society is a collection of individuals and of the various groups they voluntarily form.

The political principle that underlies the political mechanism is conformity. The indi-vidual must serve a more general social in-terest—whether that be determined by a church or a dictator or a majority. The indi-vidual may have a vote and say in what is to be done, but if he is overruled, he must conform. It is appropriate for some to re-quire others to contribute to a general social purpose whether they wish to or not.

Unfortunately, unanimity is not always feasible. There are some respects in which conformity appears unavoidable, so I do not see how one can avoid the use of the politi-cal mechanism altogether.

But the doctrine of "social responsibility" taken seriously would extend the scope of the political mechanism to every human ac-tivity. It does not differ in philosophy from the most explicitly collectivist doctrine. It differs only by professing to believe that collectivist ends can be attained without col-lectivist means. That is why, in my book "Capitalism and Freedom," I have called it a "fundamentally subversive doctrine" in a free society, and have said that in such a soci-ety, "there is one and only one social respon-sibility of business—to use its resources and engage in activities designed to increase its profits so long as it stays within the rules of the game, which is to say, engages in open and free competition without deception or fraud."

The Responsibilities of Corporations and Their Owners

John G. Simon, Charles W. Powers, and Jon P. Gunnemann

...Our analysis of the controversies surrounding the notion of corporate responsibility—and the suggestion that the university as an investor should be concerned with corporate responsibility—proceeds in large part from our approach to certain issues in the area of social responsibility and public morals. In particular, we (1) make a distinction between negative injunctions and affirmative duties; (2) assert that all men have the "moral minimum" obligation not to impose social injury; (3) delineate those conditions under which one is held responsible for social injury, even where it is not clear that the injury was self-caused; and (4) take a position in the argument between those who strive for moral purity and those who strive for moral effectiveness.

NEGATIVE INJUNCTIONS AND AFFIRMATIVE DUTIES

A distinction which informs much of our discussion differentiates between injunctions against activities that injure others and duties which require the affirmative pursuit of some good. The failure to make this distinction in debate on public ethics often results in false dichotomies, a point illustrated by an article which appeared just over a decade ago in the *Harvard Business Review*. In that article, which provoked considerable debate in the business community, Theodore Levitt argued against corporate social responsibility both because it was dangerous for society and because it detracted from the primary goal of business, the making of profit. We deal with the merits of these arguments later; what is important for our immediate purpose, however, is Levitt's designation of those activities and concerns which constitute social responsibility. He notes that the corporation has become "more concerned about the needs of its employees, about schools, hospitals, welfare agencies and even aesthetics," and that it is "fashionable ... for the corporation to show that it is a great innovator; more specifically, a great public benefactor; and, very particularly, that it exists 'to serve the public.'"[1] Having so delimited the notion of corporate responsibility, Levitt presents the reader with a choice between, on the one hand, getting involved in the management of society, "creating munificence for one and all," and, on the other hand, fulfilling the profit-making function. But such a choice excludes another meaning of corporate responsibility: the making of profits in such a way as to minimize social injury. Levitt at no point considers the possibility that business activity may at times injure others and that it may be necessary to regulate the social consequences of one's business activities accordingly....

Our public discourse abounds with similar failures to distinguish between positive and perhaps lofty ideals and minimal re-

From John G. Simon, Charles W. Powers, and Jon P. Gunnemann, "The Responsibilities of Corporations and Their Owners," in *The Ethical Investor: Universities and Corporate Responsibility.* Copyright © 1972 by Yale University Press, New Haven, Conn. Reprinted by permission of the publisher.

quirements of social organization. During the election campaigns of the 1950's and the civil rights movement of the early 1960's, the slogan, "You can't legislate morality," was a popular cry on many fronts. Obviously, we have not succeeded in devising laws that create within our citizens a predisposition to love and kindness; but we can devise laws which will minimize the injury that one citizen must suffer at the hands of another. Although the virtue of love may be the possession of a few, justice—in the minimal sense of not injuring others—can be required of all.

The distinction between negative injunctions and affirmative duties is old, having roots in common law and equity jurisprudence.[2] Here it is based on the premise that it is easier to specify and enjoin a civil wrong than to state what should be done. In the Ten Commandments, affirmative duties are spelled out only for one's relations with God and parents; for the more public relationships, we are given only the negative injunction: "Thou shalt not. . . . " Similarly, the Bill of Rights contains only negative injunctions.

AVOIDANCE AND CORRECTION OF SOCIAL INJURY AS A "MORAL MINIMUM"

We do not mean to distinguish between negative injunctions and affirmative duties solely in the interests of analytical precision. The negative injunction to avoid and correct social injury threads its way through all morality. We call it a "moral minimum," implying that however one may choose to limit the concept of social responsibility, one cannot exclude this negative injunction. Although reasons may exist why certain persons or institutions cannot or should not be required to pursue moral or social good in all situations, there are many fewer reasons why one should be excused from the injunction against injuring others. Any citizen, individual or institutional, may have competing obligations which could, under some circumstances, override this negative injunction. But these special circumstances do not wipe away the prima facie obligation to avoid harming others.

In emphasizing the central role of the negative injunction, we do not suggest that affirmative duties are never important. A society where citizens go well beyond the requirement to avoid damage to others will surely be a better community. But we do recognize that individuals exhibit varying degrees of commitment to promote affirmatively the public welfare, whereas we expect everyone equally to refrain from injuring others.

The view that all citizens are equally obligated to avoid or correct any social injury which is self-caused finds support in our legal as well as our moral tradition. H. L. A. Hart and A. M. Honoré have written:

> In the moral judgments of ordinary life, we have occasion to blame people because they have caused harm to others, and also, if less frequently, to insist that morally they are bound to compensate those to whom they have caused harm. These are the moral analogues of more precise legal conceptions: for, in all legal systems liability to be punished or to make compensation frequently depends on whether actions (or omissions) have caused harm. Moral blame is not of course confined to such cases of causing harm.[3]

We know of no societies, from the literature of anthropology or comparative ethics, whose moral codes do not contain some injunction against harming others. The specific notion of *harm* or *social injury* may vary, as well as the mode of correction and restitution, but the injunctions are present. . . .

We asserted earlier that it is easier to enjoin and correct a wrong than it is to prescribe affirmatively what is good for society and what ought to be done. Notions of the public good and the values that men actively seek to implement are subjects of intense disagreement. In this realm, pluralism is almost inevitable, and some would argue that it is healthy. Yet there can also be disagreement about what constitutes social injury or harm. What some people think are affirmative duties may be seen by others as correction of social injury. For example, the notion that business corporations should make special effort to train and employ members of minority groups could be understood by some to fulfill an affirmative duty on the part of corporations to meet society's problems; but it could be interpreted by others as the correction of a social injury caused by years of institutional racism. As a more extreme example, a Marxist would in all probability contend that *all* corporate activity is socially injurious and that therefore all social pursuits by corporations are corrective responses rather than affirmative actions.

Although the notion of *social injury* is imprecise and although many hard cases will be encountered in applying it, we think that it is a helpful designation and that cases can be decided on the basis of it. In the law, many notions (such as *negligence* in the law of torts or *consideration* in the law of contracts) are equally vague but have received content from repeated decision making over time. We would hope that under our proposed Guidelines similar "case law" would develop. Moreover, our Guidelines attempt to give some contents to the notion of *social injury* by referring to external norms: *social injury* is defined as "particularly including activities which violate, or frustrate the enforcement of, rules of domestic or international law intended to protect individuals against deprivation of health, safety or basic freedoms."

In sum, we would affirm the prima facie obligation of all citizens, both individual and institutional, to avoid and correct self-caused social injury. Much more in the way of affirmative acts may be expected of certain kinds of citizens, but none is exempt from this "moral minimum."

In some cases it may not be true—or at least it may not be clear—that one has caused or helped to cause social injury, and yet one may bear responsibility for correct-ing or averting the injury. We consider next the circumstances under which this responsibility may arise.

NEED, PROXIMITY, CAPABILITY, AND LAST RESORT (THE KEW GARDENS PRINCIPLE)

Several years ago the public was shocked by the news accounts of the stabbing and agonizingly slow death of Kitty Genovese in the Kew Gardens section of New York City while thirty-eight people watched or heard and did nothing.[4] What so deeply disturbed the public's moral sensibility was that in the face of a critical human need, people who were close to that need and had the power to do something about it failed to act.

The public's reaction suggests that, no matter how narrowly one may conceive of social responsibility, there are some situations in which a combination of circumstances thrusts upon us an obligation to respond. Life is fraught with emergency situations in which a failure to respond is a special form of violation of the negative injunction against causing social injury: a sin of omission becomes a sin of commission.

Legal responsibility for aiding someone in cases of grave distress or injury, even when caused by another, is recognized by many European civil codes and by the criminal laws of one of our states:

(A) A person who knows that another is exposed to grave physical harm shall, to the extent that the same can be rendered without danger or peril to himself or without interference with important duties owed to others, give reasonable assistance to the exposed person unless that assistance or care is being provided by others. . . .

(C) A person who wilfully violates subsection (A) of this section shall be fined not more than $100.00.[5]

This Vermont statute recognizes that it is not reasonable in all cases to require a person to give assistance to someone who is endang-

ered. If such aid imperils himself, or interferes with duties owed to others, or if there
are others providing the aid, the person is
excepted from the obligation. These conditions of responsibility give some shape to
difficult cases and are in striking parallel
with the conditions which existed at Kew
Gardens. The salient features of the Kitty
Genovese case are (1) critical need; (2) the
proximity of the thirty-eight spectators; (3)
the capability of the spectators to act help-
fully (at least to telephone the police); and
(4) the absence of other (including official)
help; i.e., the thirty-eight were the last resort.
There would, we believe, be widespread
agreement that a moral obligation to aid
another arises when these four features are
present. What we have called the "moral
minimum" (the duty to avoid and correct
self-caused social injury) is an obvious and
easy example of fulfillment of these criteria—so obvious that there is little need to
go through step-by-step analysis of these factors. Where the injury is not clearly self-
caused, the application of these criteria aids
in deciding responsibility. We have called
this combination of features governing difficult cases the "Kew Gardens Principle."
There follows a more detailed examination
of each of the features:

Need. In cases where the other three criteria are constant, increased need increases
responsibility. Just as there is no precise definition of social injury (one kind of need),
there is no precise definition of need or way
of measuring its extent.

Proximity. The thirty-eight witnesses of
the Genovese slaying were geographically
close to the deed. But proximity to a situation of need is not necessarily spatial. Proximity is largely a function of notice: we hold
a person blameworthy if he knows of imper-
ilment and does not do what he reasonably
can do to remedy the situation. Thus, the
thirty-eight at Kew Gardens were delinquent
not because they were near but because
nearness enabled them to know that some-

one was in need. A deaf person who could
not hear the cries for help would not be considered blameworthy even if he were closer
than those who could hear. So also, a man in
Afghanistan is uniquely responsible for the
serious illness of a man in Peoria, Illinois, if
he has knowledge of the man's illness, if he
can telephone a doctor about it, and if he
alone has that notice. When we become
aware of a wrongdoing or a social injury, we
take on obligations that we did not have
while ignorant.

Notice does not exhaust the meaning of
proximity, however. It is reasonable to maintain that the sick man's neighbors in Peoria
were to some extent blameworthy if they
made no effort to inquire into the man's welfare. Ignorance cannot always be helped, but
we do expect certain persons and perhaps
institutions to look harder for information
about critical need.[6] In this sense, proximity
has to do with the network of social expectations that flow from notions of civic duty, duties to one's family, and so on. Thus, we expect a man to be more alert to the plight of
his next-door neighbor than to the needs of
a child in East Pakistan, just as we expect a
man to be more alert to the situation of his
own children than to the problems of the
family down the block. The failure of the
man to act in conformance with this expectation does not give him actual notice of need,
but it creates what the law would call *constructive notice.* Both factors—actual notice
and constructive notice growing out of social expectation—enter into the determination of responsibility and blame.

Capability. Even if there is a need to
which a person has proximity, that person is
not usually held responsible unless there is
something he can reasonably be expected to
do to meet the need. To follow Immanuel
Kant, *ought* assumes *can.* What one is reasonably capable of doing, of course, admits to
some variety of interpretation. In the Kew
Gardens incident, it might not have been
reasonable to expect someone to place his
body between the girl and the knife. It was

surely reasonable to expect someone to call the police. So also it would not seem to be within the canons of reasonability for a university to sacrifice education for charity.... But if the university is able, by non-self-sacrificial means, to mitigate injury caused by a company of which it is an owner, it would not seem unreasonable to ask it to do so.

Last Resort. In the emergency situations we have been describing, one becomes more responsible the less likely it is that someone else will be able to aid. Physical proximity is a factor here, as is time. If the knife is drawn, one cannot wait for the policeman. It is important to note here that determination of last resort becomes more difficult the more complex the social situation or organization. The man on the road to Jericho, in spite of the presence of a few other travelers, probably had a fairly good notion that he was the only person who could help the man attacked by thieves. But on a street in New York City, there is always the hope that someone else will step forward to give aid. Surely this rationalization entered into the silence of each of the thirty-eight: there were, after all, thirty-seven others. Similarly, within large corporations it is difficult to know not only whether one alone has notice of a wrongdoing, but also whether there is anyone else who is able to respond. Because of this diffusion of responsibility in complex organizations and societies, the notion of last resort is less useful than the other Kew Gardens criteria in determining whether one ought to act in aid of someone in need or to avert or correct social injury. Failure to act because one hopes someone else will act—or because one is trying to find out who is the last resort—may frequently lead to a situation in which no one acts at all. This fact, we think, places more weight on the first three features of the Kew Gardens Principle in determining responsibility, and it creates a presumption in favor of taking action when those three conditions are present.

NOTES

1. Theodore Levitt, "The Dangers of Social Responsibility," *Harvard Business Review* (Sept.–Oct. 1958): 41–50.
2. We are grateful to President Edward Bloustein of Rutgers University for suggesting this terminology and for inviting our attention to its historical antecedents. Further analysis of the distinction between *negative injunctions* and *affirmative duties* is given in the following sections of this chapter.
3. H. L. A. Hart and A. M. Honoré, *Causation in the Law* (Oxford, 1959), p. 59.
4. See A.M. Rosenthal, *Thirty-Eight Witnesses* (New York, 1964).
5. "Duty to Aid the Endangered Act," *Vt. Stat. Ann.*, Ch. 12, §519 (Supp. 1968). See G. Hughes, "Criminal Omissions," 67 *Yale L. J.* 590 (1958).
6. See, for example, Albert Speer's reflection on his role during the Hitler regime: "For being in a position to know and nevertheless shunning knowledge creates direct responsibility for the consequences—from the very beginning." *Inside the Third Reich* (New York, 1970), p. 19.

A Stakeholder Theory of the Modern Corporation: Kantian Capitalism

William M. Evan and R. Edward Freeman

I. INTRODUCTION

Corporations have ceased to be merely legal devices through which the private business transactions of individuals may be carried on. Though still much used for this purpose, the corporate form has acquired a larger significance. The corporation has, in fact, become both a method of property tenure and a means of organizing economic life. Grown to tremendous proportions, there may be said to have evolved a "corporate system"—which has attracted to itself a combination of attributes and powers, and has attained a degree of prominence entitling it to be dealt with as a major social institution.[1]

Despite these prophetic words of Berle and Means (1932), scholars and managers alike continue to hold sacred the view that managers bear a special relationship to the stockholders in the firm. Since stockholders own shares in the firm, they have certain rights and privileges, which must be granted to them by management, as well as others. Since the greatest good of all results from the self-interested pursuit of business, managers must be free to respond quickly to market forces. Sanctions, in the form of "the law of corporations," and other protective mechanisms in the form of social custom, accepted management practice, myth, and ritual, serve to reinforce the assumption of the primacy of the stockholder.

The purpose of this paper is to pose several challenges to this assumption, from within the framework of managerial capital-

ism, and to suggest the bare bones of an alternative theory, *a stakeholder theory of the modern corporation*. We do not seek the demise of the modern corporation, either intellectually or in fact. Rather, we seek its transformation. In the words of Neurath, we shall attempt to "rebuild the ship, plank by plank, while it remains afloat."[2]

Our thesis is that we can revitalize the concept of managerial capitalism by replacing the notion that managers have a duty to stockholders with the concept that managers bear a fiduciary relationship to stakeholders. Stakeholders are those groups who have a stake in or claim on the firm. Specifically we include suppliers, customers, employees, stockholders, and the local community, as well as management in its role as agent for these groups. We argue that the legal, economic, political, and moral challenges to the currently received theory of the firm, as a nexus of contracts among the owners of the factors of production and customers, require us to revise this concept along essentially Kantian lines. That is, each of these stakeholder groups has a right not to be treated as a means to some end, and therefore must participate in determining the future direction of the firm in which they have a stake.[3] . . .

The crux of our argument is that we must reconceptualize the firm around the following question: For whose benefit and at whose expense should the firm be managed? We shall set forth such a reconceptualization in the form of a *stakeholder theory of the firm*. Fi-

---

Used by permission of the authors.

nally, we shall critically examine the stakeholder view and its implications for the future of the capitalist system.

II. THE ATTACK ON MANAGERIAL CAPITALISM

The Legal Argument

The law of corporations gives a relatively clear-cut answer to the question: In whose interest and for whose benefit should the modern corporation be governed? It says that the corporation should be run in the interests of the stockholders in the firm. Directors and other officers of the firm have a fiduciary obligation to stockholders in the sense that the "affairs of the corporation" must be conducted in the interests of the stockholders. And stockholders can theoretically bring suit against those directors and managers for doing otherwise. It says further that the corporation exists "in contemplation of the law," has personality as a "legal person," limited liability for its actions, and immortality, as its existence transcends that of its members.[4]

The basic idea of managerial capitalism is that in return for controlling the firm, management vigorously pursues the interests of stockholders. Since the corporation is a legal person, existing in contemplation of the law, managers of the corporation are constrained by law. Until recently there was no constraint at all. In this century, ... the law has evolved to effectively constrain the pursuit of stockholder interests at the expense of other claimants on the firm. It has, in effect, guaranteed that the claims of customers, suppliers, local communities, and employees are in general subordinated to the claims of stockholders. ...

Central to the managerial view of the firm is that management can pursue market transactions with suppliers and customers in an unconstrained manner.[5] The existence of marketplace forces will insure that fair prices for goods will be taken. This supplier-firm-customer chain has been constrained by a number of legislative and judicial acts. The doctrine of "privity of contract," as articulated in *Winterbottom* v. *Wright* in 1842, has been eroded by the developments in products liability law. Indeed, *Greenman* v. *Yuba Power* gives the manufacturer strict liability for damage caused by its products, even though the seller has exercised all possible care in the preparation and sale of the product and the consumer has not bought the product from nor entered into any contractual arrangement with the seller. Caveat emptor has been replaced, in large part, with caveat venditor.[6] The Consumer Product Safety Commission has the power to enact product recalls, and in 1980 one U.S. automobile company recalled more cars than it built.... Some industries are required to provide information to customers about a product's ingredients, whether or not the customers want and are willing to pay for this information.[7]

The supplier-firm-customer chain is far from that visualized by managerial capitalism. Firms, in their roles as customers and suppliers of other firms, have benefitted from these constraints, and they have been harmed to the degree to which the constraints have meant loss of profit. However, we can say that management is not allowed to pursue the interests of stockholders at the expense of customers and suppliers.

The same argument is applicable to management's dealings with employees. The National Labor Relations Act gave employees the right to unionize and to bargain in good faith. It set up the National Labor Relations Board to enforce these rights with management. The Equal Pay Act of 1963 and Title VII of the Civil Rights Act of 1964 constrain management from discrimination in hiring practices; these have been followed with the Age Discrimination in Employment Act of 1967.[8] The emergence of a body of administrative case law arising from labor-management disputes and the historic settling of discrimination claims with large employers such as AT&T have caused the emergence of a body of practice in the corporation that is consistent with the legal guarantee of the rights of the employees. . . . The law has protected the due process rights of those employees who enter into collective bargaining agreements with management. As of the present, however, only 30 percent of the labor force are participating in such agreements; this has prompted one labor law scholar to propose a statutory law prohibiting dismissals of the 70 percent of the work force not protected.[9] . . .

The law has also protected the interests of local communities. The Clean Air Act and Clean Water Act have constrained management from "spoiling the commons." In an historic case, *Marsh* v. *Alabama,* the Supreme Court ruled that a company-owned town was subject to the provisions of the U.S. Constitution, thereby guaranteeing the rights of local citizens and negating the "property rights" of the firm. Some states and municipalities have gone further and passed laws preventing firms from moving plants or constraining when and how plants can be closed, and there is much current legal activity in this area to constrain management's pursuit of stockholders' interests at the expense of the local communities in which the firm operates. . . .

We have argued that the result of such changes in the legal system can be viewed as giving some rights to those groups that have a claim on the firm, for example, customers, suppliers, employees, local communities, stockholders, and management. It raises the question, at the core of a theory of the firm: In whose interest and for whose benefit should the firm be managed? The answer proposed by managerial capitalism is clearly "the stockholders," and we have argued that the law has been progressively circumscribing this answer.

The Economic Argument

In its pure ideological form managerial capitalism seeks to maximize the interests of stockholders. In its perennial criticism of government regulation, management espouses the "invisible hand" doctrine. It contends that it creates the greatest good for the greatest number, and therefore government need not intervene. However, we know that externalities, moral hazards, and monopoly power exist in fact, whether or not they exist in theory. Further, some of the legal apparatus mentioned above has evolved to deal with just these issues.

The problem of the "tragedy of the commons" or the free-rider problem pervades the concept of public goods such as water and air. No one has an incentive to incur the cost of clean-up or the cost of nonpollution, since the marginal gain of one firm's action is small. Every firm reasons this way, and the result is pollution of water and air. Since the industrial revolution, firms have sought to internalize the benefits and externalize the costs of their actions. The cost must be borne by all, through taxation and regulation; hence we have the emergence of the environmental regulations of the 1970s.

Similarly, moral hazards arise when the purchaser of a good or service can pass along the cost of that good. There is no incentive to economize, on the part of either the producer or the consumer, and there is excessive use of the resources involved. The institutionalized practice of third-party payment in health care is a prime example.

Finally, we see the avoidance of competitive behavior on the part of firms, each seeking to monopolize a small portion of the market and not compete with one another. In a number of industries, oligopolies have emerged, and while there is questionable evidence that oligopolies are not the most efficient corporate form in some industries, suffice it to say that the potential for abuse of market power has again led to regulation of managerial activity. In the classic case, AT&T, arguably one of the great technological and managerial achievements of the century, was broken up into eight separate companies to prevent its abuse of monopoly power.

Externalities, moral hazards, and monopoly power have led to more external control on managerial capitalism. There are de facto constraints, due to these economic facts of life, on the ability of management to act in the interests of stockholders....

III. A STAKEHOLDER THEORY OF THE FIRM

Foundations of a Theory

... Arguments that question the legitimacy of the modern corporation based on excessive corporate power usually hold that the corporation has no right to rule for its constituents. Each person has the right to be treated, not as a means to some corporate end, but as an end in itself. If the modern corporation insists on treating others as means to an end, then at minimum they must agree to and hence participate (or choose not to participate) in the decisions to be used as such. If our theory does not require an understanding of the rights of those parties affected by the corporation, then it will run afoul of our judgments about rights. Thus, property rights are not absolute, especially when they conflict with important rights of others. The right to property does not yield the right to treat others as means to an end. Property rights are not a license to ignore Kant's principle of respect for persons. Any theory of the modern corporation that is consistent with our considered moral judgments must recognize that property rights are not absolute.

Arguments that question the legitimacy of the modern corporation based on externalities or harm usually hold that the corporation is accountable for the consequences of its actions. Persons are responsible for the consequences of their actions through the corporation, even if those actions are mediated. Any theory that seeks to justify the corporate form must be based partially on the idea that the corporation and its managers as moral agents can be the cause of and be held accountable for the consequences of their actions.

In line with these two themes of rights and effects, ... we suggest two principles that will serve as working rules, not absolutes, to guide us in addressing some of the foundational issues. We will not settle the thorny issues that these principles raise, but merely argue that any theory, including the stakeholder theory, must be consistent with these principles.

Principle of Corporate Rights (PCR): The corporation and its managers may not violate the legitimate rights of others to determine their own future.

Principle of Corporate Effects (PCE): The corporation and its managers are responsible for the effects of their actions on others.

. . . .

The Stakeholder Concept

Corporations have stakeholders, that is, groups and individuals who benefit from or are harmed by, and whose rights are violated or respected by, corporate actions. The notion of stakeholder is built around the Principle of Corporate Rights (PCR) and the Principle of Corporate Effect (PCE).... The concept of stakeholders is a generalization of the notion of stockholders, who themselves have some special claim on the firm. Just as stockholders have a right to certain actions by management, so do other stakeholders have a right to their claim. The exact nature of these claims is a difficult question that we shall address, but the logic is identical to that of the stockholder theory. Stakes require action of a certain sort, and conflicting stakes require methods of resolution....

Freeman and Reed (1983)[10] distinguish two senses of *stakeholder*. The "narrow definition" includes those groups who are vital to the survival and success of the corporation. The "wide definition" includes any group or individual who can affect or is affected by the corporation. While the wide definition is more in keeping with (PCE) and (PCR), it

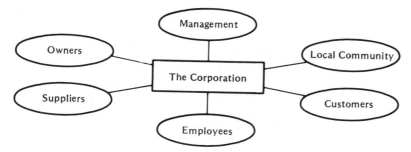

FIGURE 1. A Stakeholder Model of the Corporation.

raises too many difficult issues. We shall begin with a more modest aim: to articulate a stakeholder theory using the narrow definition.

Stakeholders in the Modern Corporation

Figure 1 depicts the stakeholders in a typical large corporation. The stakes of each are reciprocal, since each can affect the other in terms of harms and benefits as well as rights and duties. The stakes of each are not univocal and would vary by particular corporation. We merely set forth some general notions that seem to be common to many large firms.

Owners have some financial stake in the form of stocks, bonds, and so on, and expect some kind of financial return. Either they have given money directly to the firm, or they have some historical claim made through a series of morally justified exchanges. The firm affects their livelihood or, if a substantial portion of their retirement income is in stocks or bonds, their ability to care for themselves when they can no longer work. Of course, the stakes of owners will differ by type of owner, preferences for money, moral preferences, and so on, as well as by type of firm. The owners of AT&T are quite different from the owners of Ford Motor Company, with stock of the former company being widely dispersed among 3 million stockholders and that of the latter being held by a small family group, as well as a large group of public stockholders.

Employees have their jobs and usually their livelihood at stake; they often have specialized skills for which there is usually no perfectly elastic market. In return for their labor, they expect some security, wages, and benefits, and meaningful work. Where they are used as means to an end, they must participate in decisions affecting such use. In return for their loyalty, the corporation is expected to provide for them and carry them through difficult times. Employees are expected to follow the instructions of management most of the time, to speak favorably about the company, and to be responsible citizens in the local communities in which the company operates. The evidence that such policies and values as described here lead to productive company-employee relationships is compelling. It is equally compelling to realize that the opportunities for "bad faith" on the part of both management and employees are enormous. "Mock participation" in quality circles, singing the company song, and wearing the company uniform solely to please management, as well as management by authoritarian supervisors, all lead to distrust and unproductive work.

Suppliers, interpreted in a stakeholder sense, are vital to the success of the firm, for raw materials will determine the final product quality and price. In turn the firm is a customer of the supplier and is therefore vital to the success and survival of the supplier. When the firm treats the supplier as a valued member of the stakeholder network, rather than simply as a source of materials, the supplier will respond when the firm is in need. Chrysler traditionally had very close ties to its suppliers, even to the extent that led some to suspect the transfer of illegal payments. And when Chrysler was on the brink of disaster, the suppliers responded with price cuts, accepting late payments, financing, and so on. Supplier and company can rise and fall together. Of course, again, the particular supplier relationships will depend on a number of variables such as the number of suppliers and whether the supplies are finished goods or raw materials.

Customers exchange resources for the products of the firm and in return receive the benefits of the products. Customers provide the lifeblood of the firm in the form of revenue. Given the level of reinvestment of earnings in large corporations, customers indirectly pay for the development of new products and services. Peters and Waterman (1982)[11] have argued that being close to the customer leads to success with other stakeholders and that a distinguishing characteristic of some companies that have performed well is their emphasis on the customer. By paying attention to customers' needs, management automatically addresses the needs of suppliers and owners. Moreover, it seems that the ethic of customer service carries over to the community. Almost without fail the "excellent companies" in Peters and Waterman's study have good reputations in the community. We would argue that Peters and Waterman have found multiple applications of Kant's dictum, "Treat persons as ends unto themselves," and it should come as no surprise that persons respond to such respectful treatment, be they customers, suppliers, owners, employees, or members of the local community. The real surprise is the novelty of the application of Kant's rule in a theory of good management practice.

The local community grants the firm the right to build facilities and benefits from the tax base and economic and social contributions of the firm. In return for the provision of local services, the firm is expected to be a good citizen, as is any person, either "natu-

ral or artificial." The firm cannot expose the community to unreasonable hazards in the form of pollution, toxic waste, and so on. If for some reason the firm must leave a community, it is expected to work with local leaders to make the transition as smooth as possible. Of course, the firm does not have perfect knowledge, but when it discovers some danger or runs afoul of new competition, it is expected to inform the local community and to work with the community to overcome any problem. When the firm mismanages its relationship with the local community, it is in the same position as a citizen who commits a crime. It has violated the implicit social contract with the community and should expect to be distrusted and ostracized. It should not be surprised when punitive measures are invoked.

We have not included "competitors" as stakeholders in the narrow sense, since strictly speaking they are not necessary for the survival and success of the firm; the stakeholder theory works equally well in monopoly contexts. However, competitors and government would be the first to be included in an extension of this basic theory. It is simply not true that the interests of competitors in an industry are always in conflict. There is no reason why trade associations and other multi-organizational groups cannot band together to solve common problems that have little to do with how to restrain trade. Implementation of stakeholder management principles, in the long run, mitigates the need for industrial policy and an increasing role for government intervention and regulation.

The Role of Management

Management plays a special role, for it too has a stake in the fiction that is the modern corporation. On the one hand, management's stake is like that of employees, with some kind of explicit or implicit employment contract. But, on the other hand, management has a duty of safeguarding the welfare of the abstract entity that is the corporation, which can override a stake as employee. In short, management, especially top management, must look after the health of the corporation, and this involves balancing the multiple claims of conflicting stakeholders. Owners want more financial returns, while customers want more money spent on research and development. Employees want higher wages and better benefits, while the local community wants better parks and day-care facilities.

The task of management in today's corporation is akin to that of King Solomon. The stakeholder theory does not give primacy to one stakeholder group over another, though there will surely be times when one group will benefit at the expense of others. In general, however, management must keep the relationships among stakeholders in balance. When these relationships become unbalanced, the survival of the firm is in jeopardy.

When wages are too high and product quality is too low, customers leave, suppliers suffer, and owners sell their stocks and bonds, depressing the stock price and making it difficult to raise new capital at favorable rates. Note, however, that the reason for paying returns to owners is not that they "own" the firm, but that their support is necessary for the survival of the firm, and that they have a legitimate claim on the firm. Similar reasoning applies in turn to each stakeholder group.

A stakeholder theory of the firm must redefine the purpose of the firm. The stockholder theory claims that the purpose of the firm is to maximize the welfare of the stockholders, perhaps subject to some moral or social constraints, either because such maximization leads to the greatest good or because of property rights. The purpose of the firm is quite different in our view. If a stakeholder theory is to be consistent with the principles of corporate effects and rights, then its purpose must take into account Kant's dictum of respect for persons. The very purpose of the firm is, in our view, to serve as a vehicle for coordinating stakeholder interests. It is through the firm that each stakeholder group makes itself better

off through voluntary exchanges. The corporation serves at the pleasure of its stakeholders, and none may be used as a means to the ends of another without full rights of participation in that decision. We can crystallize the particular applications of PCR and PCE to the stakeholder theory in two further principles. These stakeholder management principles will serve as a foundation for articulating the theory. They are guiding ideals for the immortal corporation as it endures through generations of particular mortal stakeholders.

Stakeholder Management Principles

P1: The corporation should be managed for the benefit of its stakeholders: its customers, suppliers, owners, employees, and local communities. The rights of these groups must be ensured, and, further, the groups must participate, in some sense, in decisions that substantially affect their welfare.

P2: Management bears a fiduciary relationship to stakeholders and to the corporation as an abstract entity. It must act in the interests of the stakeholders as their agent, and it must act in the interests of the corporation to ensure the survival of the firm, safeguarding the long-term stakes of each group.

P1, which we might call The Principle of Corporate Legitimacy, redefines the purpose of the firm to be in line with the principles of corporate effects and rights. It implies the legitimacy of stakeholder claims on the firm. Any social contract that justifies the existence of the corporate form includes the notion that stakeholders are a party to that contract. Further, stakeholders have some inalienable rights to participate in decisions that substantially affect their welfare or involve their being used as a means to another's ends. We bring to bear our arguments for the incoherence of the stockholder view as justification for P1. If in fact there is no good reason for the stockholder theory, and if in fact there are harms, benefits, and rights of stakeholders involved in running the modern corporation, then we know of no other starting point for a theory of the corporation than P1.

P2, which we might call The Stakeholder Fiduciary Principle, explicitly defines the duty of management to recognize these claims. It will not always be possible to meet all claims of all stakeholders all the time, since some of these claims will conflict. Here P2 recognizes the duty of management to act in the long-term best interests of the corporation, conceived as a forum of stakeholder interaction, when the interests of the group outweigh the interests of the individual parties to the collective contract. The duty described in P2 is a fiduciary duty, yet it does not suffer from the difficulties surrounding the fiduciary duty to stockholders, for the conflicts involved there are precisely those that P2 makes it mandatory for management to resolve. Of course, P2 gives no instructions for a magical resolution of the conflicts that arise from prima facie obligations to multiple parties. An analysis of such rules for decision making is a subject to be addressed on another occasion, but P2 does give these conflicts a legitimacy that they do not enjoy in the stockholder theory. It gives management a clear and distinct directive to pay attention to stakeholder claims.

P1 and P2 recognize the eventual need for changes in the law of corporations and other governance mechanisms if the stakeholder theory is to be put into practice. P1 and P2, if implemented as a major innovation in the structure of the corporation, will make manifest the eventual legal institutionalization of sanctions. . . .

Structural Mechanisms

We propose several structural mechanisms to make a stakeholder management conception practicable. We shall offer a sketch of these here and say little by way of argument for them.

1. *The Stakeholder Board of Directors.* We propose that every corporation of a certain size yet to be determined, but surely all those that are publicly traded or are of the size of those publicly traded, form a Board of Directors comprised of representatives of five stakeholder groups, including employees, customers, suppliers, stockholders, and members of the local community, as well as a representative of the corporation, whom we might call a "metaphysical director" since he or she would be responsible for the metaphysical entity that is "the corporation." Whether or not each representative has an equal voting right is a matter that can be decided by experimentation; issues of governance lend themselves naturally to both laboratory and organizational experiments.

These directors will be vested with the duty of care to manage the affairs of the corporation in concert with the interests of its stakeholders. Such a Board would ensure that the rights of each group would have a forum, and by involving a director for the corporation, would ensure that the corporation itself would not be unduly harmed for the benefit of a particular group. In addition, by vesting each director with the duty of care for all stakeholders, we ensure that positive resolutions of conflicts would occur. While options such as "stakeholder derivative suits" would naturally evolve under the law of corporations as revised, we are not sanguine about their effectiveness and prefer the workings of the political process, as inefficient as it may be. Therefore, representatives of each stakeholder group would be elected from a "stakeholder assembly" who would initially meet to adopt working rules, charters, and so on, and whose sole purpose would be to elect and recall representatives to corporate boards. The task of the metaphysical director, to be elected unanimously by the stakeholder representatives, is especially important. The fact that the director has no direct constituency would appear to enhance management control. However, nothing could be further from the truth. To represent the abstract entity that is the corporation would be a most demanding job. Our metaphysical director would be responsible for convincing both stakeholders and management that a certain course of action was in the interests of the long-term health of the corporation, especially when that action implies the sacrifice of the interests of all. The metaphysical director would be a key link between the stakeholder representatives and management, and would spearhead the drive to protect the norms of the interests of all stakeholders.

2. *The Stakeholder Bill of Rights.* Each stakeholder group would have the right to elect representatives and to recall representatives to boards. Whether this is done on a corporation-by-corporation, an industry-by-industry, or a country-by-country basis is a matter for further discussion. Each stakeholder group would have the right to free speech, the right to grievance procedures inside the corporation and if necessary in the courts, the right to civil disobedience, and other basic political rights.

3. *The Management Bill of Rights.* Management would have the right to act on its fiduciary duty, as interpreted and constrained by the Board and the courts, the right to safeguard innovation and research and development, the right to free speech, grievance procedures, civil disobedience, and so on.

Both Bills of Rights merely recognize the fact that organizational life is pervasive in our society. If we are not to become what Orwell envisioned, then our organizations must guarantee those basic political freedoms, even at the cost of economic efficiency. If organizational members are to find meaningful work by participating actively in the modern corporation, then we must ensure that the principles of Jeffersonian democracy are safeguarded.

4. *Corporate Law.* The law of corporations needs to be redefined to recognize the legitimate purpose of the corporation as stated in P1. This has in fact developed in some areas of the law, such as products liability, where the claims of customers to safe products has emerged, and labor law, where the claims of employees have been safeguarded. Indeed, in such pioneering cases as *Marsh* v. *Alabama* the courts have come close to a stakeholder perspective. We envision that a body of case law will emerge to give meaning to "the proper claims of stakeholders," and in effect that the "wisdom of Solomon" necessary to make the stakeholder theory work will

emerge naturally through the joint action of the courts, stakeholders, and management.

While much of the above may seem utopian, there are some very practical transitional steps that could occur. Each large corporation could form a stakeholder advisory board, which would prepare a charter detailing how the organization is to treat the claims of each stakeholder. Initially this stakeholder advisory board would serve as an advisor to the current board of directors, and eventually it would replace that board. Simultaneously, a group of legal scholars and practitioners, such as the American Law Institute, could initiate discussion of the legal proposals and methods to change corporate charters, while business groups such as the Business Roundtable could examine the practical consequences of our proposals. Given the emergence of some consensus, we believe that a workable transition can be found. . . .

NOTES

1. Cf. A. Berle and G. Means, *The Modern Corporation and Private Property* (New York: Commerce Clearing House, 1932), 1. For a reassessment of Berle and Means' argument after 50 years, see *Journal of Law and Economics* 26 (June 1983), especially G. Stigler and C. Friedland, "The Literature of Economics: The Case of Berle and Means," 237–68; D. North, "Comment on Stigler and Friedland," 269–72; and G. Means, "Corporate Power in the Marketplace," 467–85.

2. The metaphor of rebuilding the ship while afloat is attributed to Neurath by W. Quine, *Word and Object* (Cambridge: Harvard University Press, 1960), and W. Quine and J. Ullian, *The Web of Belief* (New York: Random House, 1978). The point is that to keep the ship afloat during repairs we must replace a plank with one that will do a better job. Our argument is that Kantian capitalism can so replace the current version of managerial capitalism.

3. Kant's notion of respect for persons (i.e., that each person has a right not to be treated as a means to an end) can be be found in I. Kant, *Critique of Practical Reason* (1838 edition). See J. Rawls, *A Theory of Justice* (Cambridge: Har-

vard University Press, 1971) for an eloquent modern interpretation.

4. For an introduction to the law of corporations see A. Conard, *Corporations in Perspective* (Mineola, NY: The Foundation Press, 1976), especially section 19; and R. Hamilton, *Corporations* (St. Paul: West Publishing, 1981), Chapter eight.

5. For a modern statement of managerial capitalism, see the literature in managerial economics, for example R. Coase, "The Nature of the Firm," *Economica* 4 (1937): 386–405; M. Jensen and W. Meckling, "Theory of the Firm: Managerial Behavior, Agency Costs and Ownership Structure," *Journal of Financial Economics* 3 (1976): 305–60; and O. Williamson, *The Economics of Discretionary Behavior* (London: Kershaw Publishing, 1965).

6. See R. Charan and E. Freeman, "Planning for the Business Environment of the 1980s," *The Journal of Business Strategy* 1 (1980): 9–19,

especially p. 15 for a brief account of the major developments in products liability law.

7. See S. Breyer, *Regulation and its Reform* (Cambridge: Harvard University Press, 1983), 133 for an analysis of food additives.

8. See I. Millstein and S. Katsh, *The Limits of Corporate Power* (New York: Macmillan, 1981), Chapter four.

9. Cf. C. Summers, "Protecting All Employees Against UnJust Dismissal," *Harvard Business Review* 58 (1980): 136 for a careful statement of the argument.

10. See E. Freeman and D. Reed, "Stockholders and Stakeholders: A New Perspective on Corporate Governance," in C. Huizinga, ed., *Corporate Governance: A Definitive Exploration of the Issues* (Los Angeles: UCLA Extension Press, 1983).

11. See T. Peters and R. Waterman, *In Search of Excellence* (New York: Harper and Row, 1982).

Ethical Issues in Plant Relocation

John P. Kavanagh

The location of a major new manufacturing plant in a community is often the occasion of great rejoicing. City fathers welcome the enterprise as a vital addition to the town's economy. Visions of augmented tax base to support municipal services, jobs for the unemployed and for entrants into the work force, opportunities for local entrepreneurs to expand markets for goods and services, additional sources of support for civic and charitable endeavors, new challenges for educators to provide education and training—all these contribute to the euphoria of a new plant in the community.

Contrast this picture with that of a community experiencing the shutdown or relocation of a major plant, particularly one

which has operated in the community for many years. Many people are hurt. For some it means actual hardship; others find their future expectations diminished to the point of despair. The community as a whole feels a shock to its economic vitality and perhaps to its fiscal stability as well.[1]

Yet economists assure us that changes in business locations are merely "adjustments to economic forces and are to be expected in any large and dynamic economy."[2] Even the severest critics of plant relocations who advocate laws to regulate such movements agree that prudent use of scarce resources "often calls for the removal of resources from some activities to more productive functions elsewhere"; they only want "to as-

Used by permission of the author, who gratefully acknowledges support from the Rockefeller Foundation and the Center for the Study of Values, University of Delaware.

sure that the transfer of capital from one use in one location to another elsewhere will not ride roughshod over the needs of the people and the communities involved."[3]

The thesis which I would like to establish is simple, but it has relatively far-reaching implications. In its basic form it may be stated:

In deciding whether or not to relocate a manufacturing operation, a company has moral obligations to its employees and to the community in which the operation is located which require that the company

1. take into account the impact of the proposed move on employees and the community;
2. avoid the move if reasonably possible;
3. notify the affected parties as soon as possible if the decision is to make the move; and
4. take positive measures to ameliorate the effects of the move.[4]

In making a decision whether or not to move, companies often do not take into account the impact on employees and the community. The management weighs economic reasons very carefully. It considers the effect on production, sales, public relations and, ultimately, profit. On the basis of reasonable assumptions, it projects the outcomes expected to result from each of the options under consideration. Too often, however, there is no place in the economic calculus for any recognition of the effect the move will have on the work force or the community. Our thesis asserts that the company is not morally free to ignore this impact, since employees and members of the community are not mere things but people, whom the company has an obligation not to harm.[5] This moral fact not only deserves consideration along with economic facts but should be the overriding consideration unless there are countervailing moral reasons.

If the company takes this obligation seriously, it ought to start with a strong presumption that the move should be avoided if at all reasonably possible. It should consider every reasonable alternative: rehabilitation of the existing facility, construction of a new plant within the same community, renegotiation of the labor contract, financial assistance from civic or governmental sources, negotiation of special tax incentives, even acceptance of less than maximum profit return. Only after ruling out other available options should the company decide in favor of the move.[6]

After giving serious consideration to other alternatives, the company may still decide it has no reasonable choice but to move. In that case, two obligations remain: the company should notify the affected parties as soon as possible, and it should do whatever is necessary to ameliorate the effects of the move.

Timely notification is important. If given before the final decision is taken, it might provide the opportunity for labor organizations, civic groups, or government agencies to offer options which would enable the company to continue operations. In any event, notification is essential to permit planning for an orderly transition and preparation of programs to accommodate the change.

Ameliorating the effects of the move is not likely to be easy. Companies often offer employees the opportunity to transfer to the new location; for some this might be acceptable, but for others it would be a real hardship. Alternatively, the company might provide effective out-placement efforts as well as income maintenance for displaced workers, at least during a transition period.

To offset adverse effects on the community, the company should make a serious attempt to find a new employer to replace the lost job opportunities. A large corporation might be able to find a replacement within its own organization. Another approach would be to seek another employer among customers, vendors, competitors, or other companies who could utilize the facilities and work force being abandoned. The departing company might donate its plant, if still usable, to the community or local development organization. In some cases the better offer might be to demolish existing facilities and make the improved site available, along with financial help to the local agency concerned with promoting the location of new industries.[7]

These steps may help to make the community whole again, but some situations may require additional effort. In close consultation and cooperation with municipal officials, the company may have to work out a plan to relieve the community of financial burdens of infrastructure improvements, for instance, which were made to serve the company's special needs.

ARGUMENT IN SUPPORT OF THESIS

It should be a little clearer now what the proposed thesis means. Before proceeding to argue directly in favor of this position, however, I would like first to establish the following "Externalities Lemma":

> By locating and operating a manufacturing plant (or similar job-creating operation) in a community, a company produces certain externalities, affecting both workers and the community, which are pertinent to the relocation issue.

The term "externalities" is common enough in the literature of economics. It refers to unintended side effects—good or bad—which an operation produces along with its intended product. In recent years environmentalists have emphasized externalities which affect the quality of the air or water in the vicinity of manufacturing plants. A firm really interested in producing paper, for example, also produces physical and chemical waste products which may affect the surrounding environment adversely if not properly controlled. The company has no interest in producing these products nor any direct intention of doing so, but in doing what it does intend—making paper—it also perforce produces these unwanted products.[8]

Environmentalists have successfully urged that companies should "internalize" these externalities by recognizing them as real even though unintended products and making them part of the economic system. In some cases the companies have been able to eliminate or minimize the externalities by modifying processes. In other instances, they have been able to convert them into useful products, for example, by recycling spent pulp liquor to provide purified chemicals usable a second time in the process or by converting them to products which could be sold for some other purpose. When conversions of this kind have proved to be impractical, companies have internalized the externalities by finding ways to treat or dispose of the effluent safely and including costs incurred as production expenses reflected in price and profit computations.

The "Externalities Lemma" asserts that the operation of a plant results in certain externalities pertinent to the issue of plant relocation. Although the company's intention is simply to manufacture and distribute its product, the act of doing so produces unintended results which seriously affect its workers and the community in which the company operates.

When a person agrees to work for a company, her pay is a return for effort expended to produce the product. These wages, however, do not take into account the myriad relationships which the employee builds up as a result of accepting the job. In addition to providing labor for the company, the worker adopts a life style which contributes to the work. Many people move their place of residence, enroll children in school, join local churches, become members of clubs, take interest in civic affairs—in short, make a total commitment of their lives to the community and the company. They build up a whole network of relationships based on their association with the company.

These life style commitments are advantageous to the worker, to be sure. They enable him to live a fully rounded life. But the advantage is not one-sided. The company benefits from having an employee involved in these relationships. The situation enhances the worker's ability to do his job, encourages loyalty to the company, and facilitates the employee's continuing progress in learning to do his job effectively.

The stable relationships developed benefit the community as well, but the company's presence also affects the community in other ways. City engineers adjust traffic patterns to accommodate traffic generated by workers going to or leaving the plant as well as incoming and outgoing freight movements. The municipality may have to plan, build, and maintain water and sewerage facilities on a much larger scale to serve the company's needs. Police and fire departments may require more personnel and equipment because of the plant's presence.

Assuming an equitable tax structure, the company will pay its fair share for services provided. Other taxpayers are usually willing to contribute as well because of the indirect benefits they receive. The whole system can work smoothly because of the symbiotic relationship between the plant, its workers, and the community. Merchants, purveyors of services, schools, and private support agencies of all kinds prosper so long as the relationship continues.

When a major plant discontinues operations, however, it becomes evident that an unintended situation has been created. Not only are employees out of work, deprived of their livelihood or dependent on others for it, but the community itself suffers. Businesses dependent on the company or its employees feel the impact. The municipality and its taxpayers are left with more employees and infrastructure than they need, with continuing cost burdens far out of proportion with revenue. Schools, churches, and private associations all find themselves overbuilt as people leave or are unable to contribute to their support.

Results of the kind described are especially obvious in a small community with a single major employer. In such circumstances it is easy to isolate the phenomenon.

The same effects occur, however, in larger communities with more complex economies, only they tend to be less easily observed. In the larger setting the impact on the total community may be somewhat less, but it is no less real on those affected. What remains in any case is the whole web of relationships built up which would not exist if the company had not started the operation and particularly if it had not continued over a relatively long period. The company did not intend to create this web, but it is there nevertheless because of the plant—and the operation could not have survived without it.

In light of what we can observe, the "Externalities Lemma" seems to be inescapably true. If that is indeed the case, it is not difficult to establish our thesis. One of the dicta accepted in the law of property, clearly grounded in basic ethical principles of fairness and justice, is the maxim *sic utere tuo ut alienum non laedas*—use that which is yours in such a way that you do not injure another. A company which has established a plant in a community, particularly when it had continued the operation over a long period, would clearly be injuring others if it closed or moved that operation without taking into account—in a significant way—the impact of that move on its workers and the community. By its presence the plan has created the externalities described. It is the company's moral obligation to internalize them—to replace its divot, so to speak. It can move toward meeting this obligation by undertaking the kind of actions discussed above.

One might object that the injury or harm done the workers is not really the kind of harm which the *sic utere* principle proscribes. Certainly the harm is not intentional; the company intends merely to use its capital to the best advantage in making a profit. Even unintentional harm, however, may be morally wrong; in any event, it is reasonable to ask for moral justification of the harmful actions.

The employer might invoke the Common Law concept that the employment relationship is strictly "at-will"—that an employer is free to discharge an employee whenever she chooses, for any reason or no reason at all. Even the Common Law, however, has come to recognize that rigid application of this doctrine cannot withstand the moral criticism arising out of contemporary social and economic circumstances. At the very least, our sense of equity demands that the employer justify the discharge by showing that race, gender or age discrimination, or retaliation for lawful exercise of rights, did not motivate the harmful action.

Almost any moral system recognizes that every moral agent has an obligation to treat human beings as persons rather than as things. Hiring a person creates a special kind of relationship. For the employer it is not like buying a piece of material or a machine: these are things, which the buyer is free to use as a means of achieving an end, with no moral responsibility owed to the purchased objects. But the employer is not free, morally speaking, to use an employee as a thing, as simply a means to an end. Since the employee is a person, the employer has an obligation to respect her integrity as a person: her feelings, values, goals, emotional relationships, cultural attachments, self-regard. As an autonomous living entity the employee is the center of a complex web of relationships and it is this whole composite with which the employer becomes involved. Obviously, the employer is not responsible for everything which happens to or within this web; but he is responsible for whatever his actions change or otherwise affect. The relationships mentioned in discussing the "Externalities Lemma" are ones which the employer's actions affect adversely in (un-mitigated) plant closure decisions. Even though the company no longer needs its workers as a means to its end of profitable production, it may not with moral impunity treat them like excess material or machines, but has an obligation to protect them from the adverse consequences brought about by the company's use of them.

A company which closes or relocates a plant without ameliorating actions is acting unfairly toward its employees and the community. The general idea of fairness is that anyone who chooses to get involved with others in a cooperative activity has to do his share and is entitled to expect others involved to do likewise.[9]

In the kind of situation we are concerned with there is a reasonably just cooperative arrangement under which a person agrees to work for a company; the primary *quid pro quo* is the employer's fair day's pay for the employee's fair day's work. But each party to the agreement has additional legitimate expectations about the other. The employer expects the worker to make a commitment to the job; one of the largest corporations has this to say:

> . . . The challenges of the workplace impose strong mutual responsibilities upon General Motors and its employees. . . .
>
> An employee's most basic responsibility is to work consistently to the best of his or her ability—not just to follow instructions, but to ask questions, think independently, and make constructive suggestions for improvement.
>
> A first-rate job requires employees to maintain their good health and mental alertness, to be prompt and present on the job, to cooperate with fellow workers, and to be loyal to the Corporation—its people and products. Because GM people *are* General Motors—in the eyes of their friends and neighbors—employees also are encouraged to take interest in the basic goals, problems, and public positions of the Corporation.
>
> . . . General Motors encourages employees as individual citizens to involve themselves in community service and politics. . . . [10]

The employee, in turn, expects the company to do somewhat more than simply pay agreed-on wages. For example, no one would question that being provided a safe and at least tolerably pleasant workplace is within the worker's legitimate expectations. Beyond that, if it is fair for the company to expect that employees will take all the actions and have all the attitudes which a company like General Motors encourages and considers requisite to "a first-rate job" it also seems reasonable for workers to expect that the employer will not suddenly shut up shop and leave them high and dry with unpaid mortgages (on houses bought so they could be "prompt and present on the job" and involved in "community service and politics"), children in school, and commitments to various people or organizations; all this is part of a lifestyle to which they committed themselves when they entered into their agreement to work for the company—the kind of agreement which the GM statement calls a "partnership which can help assure the Corporation's success in the years to come, as well as contribute to an improved quality of life for the men and women of General Motors."[11]

There is nothing extraordinary in all this. In most social relationships the parties involved in an agreement have legitimate expectations which are often not expressed in the agreement itself. Fairness requires that a company either avoid a move which would cause grave hardship to workers or at least take action which would render the action harmless, since this is a legitimate expectation of the implicit "partnership" agreement between employer and employee.

NOTES

1. These initial observations, as well as several others throughout the paper, are based on the author's direct involvement in plant relocation situations in the course of more than twenty-five years of work as a senior official in Michigan state government agencies concerned with economic development programs. There is also a wealth of empirical literature on the subject referenced in the publications cited below by McKenzie; Bluestone and Harrison; and Stern *et al.*

2. Richard B. McKenzie, *Restrictions on Business Mobility* (Washington: American Enterprise Institute for Public Policy Research, 1979), p. 1.

3. Barry Bluestone and Bennett Harrison, *Capital and Communities* (Washington: The Progressive Alliance, 1980), p. ii.

4. For brevity's sake I will generally speak of "relocation," although I mean also to include discontinuation of operations in the community without removal to another location.

5. The question of whether a company, a corporation or any collective can be the subject of moral acts is much controverted, but it is not the point at issue here. For those who reject the collective responsibility position, substitute the phrase "those persons morally responsible for the actions of the company" for the "company." In support of collective responsibility, see Peter A. French, "The Corporation as a Moral Person," *American Philosophical Quarterly,* 16 (1979), p. 207.

6. See John M. Clark, *Economic Institutions and Human Welfare* (New York: Alfred A. Knopf, 1957), pp. 195–197, for an interesting discussion from an economist's view point of social obligations of a company in a relocation situation.

7. One plan which has received considerable attention calls for the company to transfer ownership to former workers or the community or a joint community-employee corporation. This has worked well in particularly favorable circumstances but has failed in other cases. See Robert N. Stern, K. Haydn Wood, and Tove Helland Hammer, *Employee Ownership in Plant Shutdowns* (Kalamazoo, Michigan: The W. E. Upjohn Institute for Employment Research, 1979). A current (November, 1981) instance is a planned purchase of the New Departure-Hyatt Bearing Division of General Motors Corp. at Clark, N.J. by former employees after GM announced its intention to close the plant.

8. Externalities can be beneficial. A paper operation may require management of forest resources to assure an adequate supply of timber. This may open previously inaccessible land for recreational use. Although the company may only intend to improve its timber holdings, it may also enhance the wildlife capabilities of the forest. The paper plant itself may become a tourist attraction, providing an unintended benefit to the community.

9. See John Rawls, *A Theory of Justice* (Cambridge, Mass.: Harvard University Press, 1971), p. 343.

10. *1980 General Motors Public Interest Report,* p. 83.

11. Citing of General Motors' statement should

not be interpreted as critical of that company; the Corporation has a policy of replacing obsolete plants with new facilities in the same area "whenever it is economically feasible" and also, under its union contracts and salaried worker policies, pays substantial compensation to laid-off employees. GM has currently committed $10 billion to the rehabilitation and replacement of production facilities in Michigan alone.

Dodge v. Ford Motor Co.

... When plaintiffs made their complaint and demand for further dividends, the Ford Motor Company had concluded its most prosperous year of business. The demand for its cars at the price of the preceding year continued. It could make and could market in the year beginning August 1, 1916, more than 500,000 cars. Sales of parts and repairs would necessarily increase. The cost of materials was likely to advance, and perhaps the price of labor; but it reasonably might have expected a profit for the year of upwards of $60,000,000.... Considering only these facts, a refusal to declare and pay further dividends appears to be not an exercise of discretion on the part of the directors, but an arbitrary refusal to do what the circumstances required to be done. These facts and others call upon the directors to justify their action, or failure or refusal to act. In justification, the defendants have offered testimony tending to prove and which does prove, the following facts: It had been the policy of the corporation for a considerable time to annually reduce the selling price of cars, while keeping up, or improving, their quality. As early as in June, 1915, a general plan for the expansion of the productive capacity of the concern by a practical duplication of its plant had been talked over by the executive officers and directors and agreed upon; not all of the details having been settled, and no formal action of directors having been taken. The erection of a smelter was considered, and engineering and other data in connection therewith secured. In consequence, it was determined not to reduce the selling price of cars for the year beginning August 1, 1915, but to maintain the price to accumulate a large surplus to pay for the proposed expansion of plant and equipment, and perhaps to build a plant for smelting ore. It is hoped, by Mr. Ford, that eventually 1,000,000 cars will be annually produced. The contemplated changes will permit the increased output.

The plan, as affecting the profits of the business for the year beginning August 1, 1916, and thereafter, calls for a reduction in the selling price of the cars. ... In short, the plan does not call for and is not intended to produce immediately a more profitable business, but a less profitable one; not only less profitable than formerly, but less profitable than it is admitted it might be made. The apparent immediate effect will be to diminish the value of shares and the returns to shareholders.

It is the contention of plaintiffs that the apparent effect of the plan is intended to be the continued and continuing effect of it, and that it is deliberately proposed, not of record and not by official corporate declaration, but nevertheless proposed, to continue the corporation henceforth as a semi-eleemosynary institution and not as a business

---

204 Mich. 459, 170 N.W. 668, 3 A.L.R. 413. Majority opinion by Justice J. Ostrander, Supreme Court of Michigan.

institution. In support of this contention, they point to the attitude and to the expressions of Mr. Henry Ford. . . .

"My ambition," said Mr. Ford, "is to employ still more men, to spread the benefits of this industrial system to the greatest possible number, to help them build up their lives and their homes. To do this we are putting the greatest share of our profits back in the business."

"With regard to dividends, the company paid sixty per cent, on its capitalization of two million dollars, or $1,200,000, leaving $58,000,000 to reinvest for the growth of the company. This is Mr. Ford's policy at present, and it is understood that the other stockholders cheerfully accede to this plan."

He had made up his mind in the summer of 1916 that no dividends other than the regular dividends should be paid, "for the present."

"Q. For how long? Had you fixed in your mind any time in the future, when you were going to pay—A. No.
"Q. That was indefinite in the future? A. That was indefinite; yes, sir."

The record, and especially the testimony of Mr. Ford, convinces that he has to some extent the attitude towards shareholders of one who has dispensed and distributed to them large gains and that they should be content to take what he chooses to give. His testimony creates the impression, also, that he thinks the Ford Motor Company has made too much money, has had too large profits, and that, although large profits might be still earned, a sharing of them with the public, by reducing the price of the output of the company, ought to be undertaken. We have no doubt that certain sentiments, philanthropic and altruistic, creditable to Mr. Ford, had large influence in determining the policy to be pursued by the Ford Motor Company—the policy which as been herein referred to.

It is said by his counsel that—

"Although a manufacturing corporation cannot engage in humanitarian works as its principal business, the fact that it is organized for profit does not prevent the existence of implied powers to carry on with humanitarian motives such charitable works as are incidental to the main business of the corporation." . . .

In discussing this proposition counsel have referred to decisions [citations omitted]. These cases, after all, like all others in which the subject is treated, turn finally upon the point, the question, whether it appears that the directors were not acting for the best interests of the corporation. We do not draw in question, nor do counsel for the plaintiffs do so, the validity of the general proposition stated by counsel nor the soundness of the opinions delivered in the cases cited. The case presented here is not like any of them. The difference between an incidental humanitarian expenditure of corporate funds for the benefit of the employees, like the building of a hospital for their use and the employment of agencies for the betterment of their condition, and a general purpose and plan to benefit mankind at the expense of others, is obvious. There should be no confusion (of which there is evidence) of the duties which Mr. Ford conceives that he and the stockholders owe to the general public and the duties which in law he and his codirectors owe to protesting, minority stockholders. A business corporation is organized and carried on primarily for the profit of the stockholders. The powers of the directors are to be employed for that end. The discretion of directors is to be exercised in the choice of means to attain that end, and does not extend to a change in the end itself, to the reduction of profits, or to the nondistribution of profits among stockholders in order to devote them to other purposes. . . . As we have pointed out, and the proposition does not require argument to sustain it, it is not within the lawful powers of a board of directors to shape and conduct the affairs of a corporation for the merely incidental benefit of shareholders and for the primary purpose of benefiting others, and no one will contend that, if the avowed purpose of the defendant directors was to sacrifice the interests of shareholders, it would not be the duty of the courts to interfere.... It is obvious that an annual dividend of 60 per cent, upon $2,000,000, or $1,200,000, is the equivalent of a very small dividend upon $100,000,000, or more.

The decree of the court below fixing and determining the specific amount to be distributed to stockholders is affirmed....

A. P. Smith Manufacturing Co. v. Barlow

The Chancery Division, in a well-reasoned opinion by Judge Stein, determined that a donation by the plaintiff The A. P. Smith Manufacturing Company to Princeton University was *intra vires*. Because of the public importance of the issues presented, the appeal duly taken to the Appellate Division has been certified directly to this court under Rule 1:5–1(a).

The company was incorporated in 1896 and is engaged in the manufacture and sale of valves, fire hydrants and special equipment, mainly for water and gas industries. Its plant is located in East Orange and Bloomfield and it has approximately 300 employees. Over the years the company has contributed regularly to the local community chest and on occasions to Upsala College in East Orange and Newark University, now part of Rutgers, the State University. On July 24, 1951 the board of directors adopted a resolution which set forth that it was in the corporation's best interests to join with others in the 1951 Annual Giving to Princeton University, and appropriated the sum of $1,500 to be transferred by the corporation's treasurer to the university as a contribution towards its maintenance. When this action was questioned by stockholders the corporation instituted a declaratory judgment action in the Chancery Division and trial was had in due course.

Mr. Hubert F. O'Brien, the president of the company, testified that he considered the contribution to be a sound investment, that the public expects corporations to aid philanthropic and benevolent institutions, that they obtain good will in the community by so doing, and that their charitable donations create favorable environment for their business operations. In addition, he expressed the thought that in contributing to liberal arts institutions, corporations were furthering their self-interest in assuring the free flow of properly trained personnel for administrative and other corporate employment. Mr. Frank W. Abrams, chairman of the board of the Standard Oil Company of New Jersey, testified that corporations are expected to acknowledge their public responsibilities in support of the essential elements of our free enterprise system. He indicated that it was not "good business" to disappoint "this reasonable and justified public expectation," nor was it good business for corporations "to take substantial benefits from their membership in the economic community while avoiding the normally accepted obligations of citizenship in the social community." Mr. Irving S. Olds, former chair-

---

98 A 2d 581 (1953). Opinion by Judge J. Jacobs, Supreme Court of New Jersey.

man of the board of the United States Steel Corporation, pointed out that corporations have a self-interest in the maintenance of liberal education as the bulwark of good government. He stated that "Capitalism and free enterprise owe their survival in no small degree to the existence of our private, independent universities" and that if American business does not aid in their maintenance it is not "properly protecting the long-range interest of its stockholders, its employees and its customers." Similarly, Dr. Harold W. Dodds, President of Princeton University, suggested that if private institutions of higher learning were replaced by governmental institutions our society would be vastly different and private enterprise in other fields would fade out rather promptly. Further on he stated that "democratic society will not long endure if it does not nourish within itself strong centers of non-governmental fountains of knowledge, opinions of all sorts not governmentally or politically originated. If the time comes when all these centers are absorbed into government, then freedom as we know it, I submit, is at an end." . . .

When the wealth of the nation was primarily in the hands of individuals they discharged their responsibilities as citizens by donating freely for charitable purposes. With the transfer of most of the wealth to corporate hands and the imposition of heavy burdens of individual taxation, they have been unable to keep pace with increased philanthropic needs. They have therefore, with justification, turned to corporations to assume the modern obligations of good citizenship in the same manner as humans do. Congress and state legislatures have enacted laws which encourage corporate contributions, and much has recently been written to indicate the crying need and adequate legal basis therefor[e]. . . .

During the first world war corporations loaned their personnel and contributed substantial corporate funds in order to insure survival; during the depression of the '30s they made contributions to alleviate the desperate hardships of the millions of unemployed; and during the second world war they again contributed to insure survival. They now recognize that we are faced with other, though nonetheless vicious, threats from abroad which must be withstood without impairing the vigor of our democratic institutions at home and that otherwise victory will be pyrrhic indeed. More and more they have come to recognize that their salvation rests upon sound economic and social environment which in turn rests in no insignificant part upon free and vigorous non-governmental institutions of learning. It seems to us that just as the conditions prevailing when corporations were originally created required that they serve public as well as private interests, modern conditions require that corporations acknowledge and discharge social as well as private responsibilities as members of the communities within which they operate. Within this broad concept there is no difficulty in sustaining, as incidental to their proper objects and in aid of the public welfare, the power of corporations to contribute corporate funds within reasonable limits in support of academic institutions. But even if we confine ourselves to the terms of the common-law rule in its application to current conditions, such expenditures may likewise readily be justified as being for the benefit of the corporation; indeed, if need be the matter may be viewed strictly in terms of actual survival of the corporation in a free enterprise system. The genius of our common law has been its capacity for growth and its adaptability to the needs of the times. Generally courts have accomplished the desired result indirectly through the molding of old forms. Occasionally they have done it directly through frank rejection of the old and recognition of the new. But whichever path the common law has taken it has not been found wanting as the proper tool for the advancement of the general good. . . .

In the light of all of the foregoing we have no hesitancy in sustaining the validity of the donation by the plaintiff. There is no suggestion that it was made indiscriminately or to a pet charity of the corporate directors in furtherance of personal rather than corporate ends. On the contrary, it was made to a preeminent institution of higher learning, was modest in amount and well within the limitations imposed by the statutory enactments, and was voluntarily made in the reasonable belief that it would aid the public welfare and advance the interests of the plaintiff as a private corporation and as part of the community in which it operates. We find that it was a lawful exercise of the corporation's implied and incidental powers under common-law principles and that it came within the express authority of the pertinent state legislation. As has been indicated, there is now widespread belief throughout the nation that free and vigorous non-governmental institutions of learning are vital to our democracy and the sys-

tem of free enterprise and that withdrawal of corporate authority to make such contributions within reasonable limits would seriously threaten their continuance. Corporations have come to recognize this and with their enlightenment have sought in varying measures, as has the plaintiff by its contribution, to insure and strengthen the society which gives them existence and the means of aiding themselves and their fellow citizens. Clearly then, the appellants, as individual stockholders whose private interests rest entirely upon the well-being of the plaintiff corporation, ought not be permitted to close their eyes to present-day realities and thwart the long-visioned corporate action in recognizing and voluntarily discharging its high obligations as a constituent of our modern social structure.

The judgment entered in the Chancery Division is in all respects Affirmed.

CASE 1. Shutdown at Eastland

When Speedy Motors Company closed its assembly plant in Eastland, Michigan, lobbyists for organized labor cited the case as one more reason why the Federal government should pass a law regulating plant closings. With less than a month's notice, the company laid off nearly 2,000 workers and permanently shut down the facility, which had been in operation more than 20 years. The local union president called the action "a callous and heartless treatment of the workers and of the community."

Company executives defended the decision as inevitable in view of the harsh competitive realities of the automotive industry. "Purchases of the Speedy model produced at Eastland have fallen to almost nothing and there is nothing we can do about changes in

consumer preferences," a company spokesman said.

Labor lobbyists insist that instances such as this show the need for a Federal law which would require companies to give as much as two years' notice before closing a major factory, unless they can demonstrate that an emergency exists. The proposed legislation would also require the employer to provide special benefits to workers and the community affected by the shutdown.

"Closing plants needlessly and without warning is an antisocial, criminal act," a union leader said. "Giant corporations don't give a thought to the hardships they are imposing on long-time employees and communities that depend on their jobs. The only thing they consider is their profit."

Adapted from a case by John P. Kavanagh, Emeritus Assistant Professor of Philosophy, Center for the Study of Values, University of Delaware. Reprinted by permission.

Opponents of the legislation maintain that the proposed law would strike at the heart of the free enterprise system. "Companies must be free to do business wherever they choose without being penalized," a corporate spokesman argued. "Plant closing legislation would constitute unjustified interference in private decision making. Laws which restrict the ability of management to operate a business in the most efficient manner are counterproductive and in direct conflict with the theory of free enterprise."

Questions

1. Does the closing of a plant when it ceases to be profitable violate the "moral minimum"?
2. Should one of the rules of the game in a new social contract between society and business stipulate procedures for a morally justified plant closing?
3. Who should take primary responsibility for those laid off or terminated due to a plant closing?

CASE 2. The Sloane Products Case

Sloane Products is a regional manufacturer of metal dispensers for paper products used in restaurants, hotels, and passenger terminals. The products bear the Sloane brand and are advertised in trade journals. Sloane sells its products through wholesalers. There is no information on the amount of output eventually sold in minority-operated establishments. Sloane assumes the amount is relatively small. The manufacturing plant, however, is in an older metropolitan area with a large black population, though the plant itself is far from the center of the black neighborhoods and the firm has only a few black employees.

In response to pleas from the metropolitan chapter of the National Alliance of Business, Sloane's board adopted the following policy on minority purchasing:

Sloane managers are expected to make extra efforts to find minority suppliers and even to help minority enterprises adjust to Sloane's purchasing requirements. The board's instructions also made it clear that the effort was not expected to impose any serious disruption on Sloane's operations.

Right after the procurement directive was issued, Frank Gambetta, head of purchasing,

had found a local firm, Diamond Carton Company, a black owned and managed producer of corrugated boxes for shipping merchandise. For quotation purposes, Gambetta's office had given Diamond information on quantity, quality, sizes, and delivery requirements.

Diamond had admitted being new to the business but assured the people at Sloane that Diamond could meet the product and delivery specifications.

Diamond had sent quotations to Gambetta's office. After some negotiation, Diamond was awarded a contract by Sloane, who then reduced quantities purchased from other sources.

However, Diamond did not provide samples for pre-production approval at the time specified in the original agreement. When samples eventually appeared, they proved to be below standard. Gambetta and production chief Sam Fritzel then spent time helping the managers at Diamond work out the defects, and eventually Diamond did produce samples that could be approved.

First production deliveries were satisfactory, but since then every delivery has been either late or substandard. This has been going on for four months.

Adapted from a case by Lawrence G. Lavengood, Professor of Business History, Graduate School of Management, Northwestern University. Reprinted by permission.

Fritzel is ready to end the agreement on the grounds that the relationship with Diamond is disrupting Sloane's operations.

Questions

1. Has Sloane done enough for Diamond to justify ending the agreement at the present time?

2. Is the fact that the relationship with Diamond is disrupting Sloane's operation good enough reason by itself for ending the agreement?

3. If Sloane does end the agreement with Diamond, does it have any obligation to find another minority supplier?

4. Given Sloane's geographical location, does it have any special moral obligation to the black community at all?

CASE 3. Procter and Gamble and Toxic Shock Syndrome

In September 1980, Procter and Gamble reached a consent agreement with the Food and Drug Administration (FDA) to "demarket" its new super absorbent Rely tampon which had been twenty years in development. This agreement was reached one week after Procter and Gamble representatives were confronted by the FDA with results of a Center for Disease Control (CDC) study which found a strong correlation between the use of Rely tampons and Toxic Shock Syndrome (TSS). By then, TSS, a disease characterized by vomiting, high fever, diarrhea, and a rapid drop in blood pressure resulting in shock, had been blamed as the cause of death for 25 women in 1975. Subsequent deaths brought this number to about 100 by 1984.

Procter and Gamble was initially made aware of evidence linking tampon usage with TSS in June 1980 when it, along with other tampon manufacturers, received the results of a preliminary CDC study. Shortly thereafter, Procter and Gamble conducted its own studies of Rely, and found no significant link between TSS and this particular brand of tampons. Given a week to respond to the September CDC study, Procter and Gamble quickly assembled a previously selected independent panel of health and scientific experts to review the CDC findings. This panel reported that they did not find convincing evidence linking Rely in particular to TSS (as opposed to tampons in general). On the other hand, they reported that they could not refute the claims of the CDC study either.

As a result of this panel's findings, Procter and Gamble immediately discontinued sales of Rely. When its representatives next met with the representatives of the FDA, Procter and Gamble signed the consent agreement calling for the "withdrawal" of Rely from the market. Under this agreement Procter and Gamble attempted to buy back all of the product which was still in the hands of consumers or retailers through a concentrated campaign consisting of 340,000 letters and telegrams sent to retailers, and radio, television, and print advertisements directed at consumers.

According to the consent agreement, Procter and Gamble did not have to declare the product unsafe or defective and in fact they stated they had no evidence that it was. The motivation for reaching this agreement was at least partly the fear of being forced by the FDA into a "product recall" in which they would have to admit the product was unsafe—an admission that would certainly be used in product liability litigation. Procter and Gamble is also particularly sensitive

---

This case was prepared by Richard Wokutch, Associate Professor of Management, Virginia Polytechnic Institute and State University. Reprinted by permission.

to adverse publicity and this product withdrawal was viewed as a way to cut its losses on this dimension.

Toxic shock syndrome remains a mystery. New occurrences of the disease continue even after the withdrawal of Rely. Scientists believe it is caused by a virulent strain of bacteria, and evidence persists that contraction of the disease is linked to certain forms of tampon usage, but the precise connection is unclear. Both men and nonmenstruating women have contracted the disease.

For Procter and Gamble the withdrawal of Rely from the market was estimated to have cost $75 million after taxes (compared with total corporate profits of $640 million in the preceding year). Procter and Gamble was also left with no product in the $1 billion per year menstrual-products market, although they were considering new entries. The company's reputation, which suffered during the controversy, seems to have largely been redeemed. A public opinion survey conducted after the withdrawal found that the public gave Procter and Gamble high marks for its quick action.

A number of legal claims against Procter and Gamble are slowly making their way through the courts. Although accurate figures are hard to come by, several sources estimate that approximately 400 lawsuits were filed against Procter and Gamble for an esti-

mated $4 billion. Other tampon manufacturers have also been sued.

The results of the lawsuits settled to date are even more difficult to assess since many were settled out of court. Most settlements, however, appear to have been for far less than the plaintiffs requested. Still, in the aggregate the financial burden to Procter and Gamble has been substantial.

In 1984 Procter and Gamble reentered the menstrual market with "Always," a line of absorbent sanitary napkins.

Questions

1. When confronted with the September CDC study, what were Procter and Gamble's response options?
2. Was the selected response strategy the most "socially responsible"? Was it the most profitable?
3. If Procter and Gamble had not been faced with the prospect of a government-mandated "product recall" do you think they would have responded any differently? What do you think they should have done in such a circumstance?
4. Discuss the factors you would consider in marketing a product where there is uncertainty about the risks involved.

CASE 4. The Crash on Mount Erebus

On November 28, 1979, a DC-10 operated by Air New Zealand and with 237 sightseers and 20 crew members aboard crashed into Mt. Erebus in Antartica. There were no survivors. Subsequent investigation revealed that the DC-10 had been flying under visual flight rules with visibility of 23 miles. The aircraft was at 2,000 feet when it crashed into the side of 12,000-foot-high Mt. Erebus.

A Royal Commission was created to inves-

tigate the cause of the disaster. Air New Zealand argued that the crash had been caused by pilot error. Captain Collins had been 27 miles off course and had been flying too low.

The Royal Commission uncovered evidence that disputed the pilot error theory. A DC-10 is navigated by a computer system such that once a series of coordinates has been fed into the aircraft's computer, the plane can fly by itself between points in ac-

The details of this case were taken from Peter A. French, "The Principle of Responsive Adjustment in Corporate Moral Responsibility: The Crash on Mount Erebus," *Journal of Business Ethics* 3 (May 1984): 101–111.

cordance with the computer's instructions. At a briefing 19 days before the flight, Captain Collins was told that the coordinates for the route of flight would be the standard ones for tourist flights of this kind. In fact a different set of coordinates was entered into the computer. Collins followed the computer track.

But why would Captain Collins, operating with a visibility of 23 miles, fly his plane into the mountain? The explanation is that the pilot probably experienced whiteout—an atmospheric effect that produces a loss of depth perception, flattening out even mountainous terrain.

Why had the coordinates been changed between the time of Captain Collins' briefing and the time of the actual flight? The change had been ordered by the operations

manager for DC-10 aircraft in New Zealand. Although the change was made for good reasons, Captain Collins was never informed of the change.

Questions

1. Can the responsibility for the Mt. Erebus crash be traced to a specific person or to several persons within Air New Zealand?
2. Does it make sense to claim that the responsibility for the crash rests with Air New Zealand but that it does not rest with any specific individual Air New Zealand employees?
3. What procedures should Air New Zealand adopt to fulfill its obligations for public safety?

Suggested Supplementary Readings

Andrews, Kenneth R. "Can the Best Corporations Be Made Moral?" *Harvard Business Review* 51 (May–June 1973): 57–64.

Anshen, Melvin. "Changing The Social Contract: A Role For Business." *The Columbia Journal of World Business* 5 (November–December 1970): 6–14.

Blumberg, Phillip I. "Selected Materials on Corporate Social Responsibility." *Business Lawyer* (July 1972): 1275–99.

Bowie, Norman E. *Business Ethics.* Englewood Cliffs, N.J.: Prentice-Hall, 1982.

Brozen, Yale, Elmer Johnson, and Charles Powers. *Can the Market Sustain An Ethic?* Chicago: University of Chicago Press, 1978.

Buchholz, Rogene A. *Essentials of Public Policy For Management.* Englewood Cliffs, N.J.: Prentice-Hall, 1985.

Camenish, Paul F. "Business Ethics." *Business and Professional Ethics Journal* 1 (Fall 1981): 59–69.

Cavanagh, G. F. *American Business Values in Transition.* Englewood Cliffs, N.J.: Prentice-Hall, 1976.

Chamberlain, Neil W. *The Limits of Corporate Responsibility.* New York: Basic Books, 1973.

Committee for Economic Development (CED). *Social Responsibilities of Business Corporations.* New York: CED, 1971.

Dahl, Robert. "A Prelude to Corporate Reform." *Business and Society Review* 1 (Spring 1972): 17–23.

Davis, Keith. "Five Propositions for Social Responsibility." *Business Horizons* (June 1975): 19–24.

Davis, Keith, and Robert L. Blomstrom. *Business and Society: Environment and Responsibility.* 3d ed. New York: McGraw-Hill, 1975.

DeGeorge, Richard T. "Moral Responsibility and Corporations," Chapter 5 in *Business Ethics.* 2d ed. New York: Macmillan, 1986.

Donaldson, Thomas. *Corporations and Morality.* Englewood Cliffs, N.J.: Prentice-Hall, 1982.

Freeman, R. Edward. *Strategic Management: A Stakeholder Approach.* Boston: Pitman, 1984.

French, Peter A. *Collective and Corporate Responsibility.* New York: Columbia University Press, 1984.

———."The Hester Prynne Sanction." *Business and Professional Ethics Journal* 4 (Winter 1985): 19–32.

Gillespie, Norman C. "The Business of Ethics." *The Michigan Business Review* 27 (November 1975): 1–4.

Giunta, Joanne. *Introduction to Corporate Social Responsibility Management.* Philadelphia: Human Resources Network, 1977.

Hastings Law Journal Symposium on Corporate Social Responsibility, *Hastings Law Journal* 30 (5 May 1979).

Hodges, Luther H., and Milton Friedman. "Does Business Have a Social Responsibility?" *Magazine of Bank Administration* 47 (April 1971).

Hoffman, W. Michael. "Business Values and Social Justice: Compatibility or Contradiction?" *Proceedings of the First National Conference on Business Ethics*. Waltham, Mass.: Center for Business Ethics at Bentley College, 1977.

Jacoby, Neil H. *Corporate Power and Social Responsibility*. New York: Macmillan, 1973.

Johnson, Bruce M., ed. *The Attack on Corporate America*. New York: McGraw-Hill, 1978.

Kapp, K. William. *The Social Costs of Private Enterprise*. New York: Schocken Books, 1971.

Ladd, John. "Morality and the Ideal of Rationality in Formal Organizations." *Monist* 54 (October 1970): 488–516.

Mintzberg, Henry. "The Case for Corporate Social Responsibility." *Journal of Business Strategy* 4 (1983): 3–15.

O'Toole, James. *Vanguard Management*. Garden City, N.Y.: Doubleday, 1985.

Peters, Thomas J., and Robert H. Waterman, Jr. *In Search of Excellence*. New York: Warner Books, 1982.

Pichler, Joseph A. "The Liberty Principle: A Basis for Management Ethics." *Business & Professional Ethics Journal* 2, (Winter 1983): 19–29.

Purcell, Theodore V., S. J. "A Practical Guide to Ethics in Business." *Business and Society Review* 13 (Spring 1975): 43–50.

Reprints from Harvard Business Review. Ethics for Executives Series. Cambridge, Mass.: Harvard University Press, contents copyrighted 1955–61, 1966–68.

Sethi, Prakash S. *Up Against the Corporate Wall: Modern Corporations and Social Issues of the Eighties*. 4th ed. Englewood Cliffs, N.J.: Prentice-Hall, 1982.

Tuleja, Tad. *Beyond The Bottom Line: How Business Leaders Are Turning Principles into Profits*. New York: Facts on File Publications, 1985.

Velasquez, Manuel G. *Business Ethics: Concepts and Cases*. Englewood Cliffs, N.J.: Prentice-Hall, 1982.

Walton, Clarence C. *Corporate Social Responsibilities*. Belmont, Calif.: Wadsworth, 1967.

Williams, Oliver, and John Houck, eds. *The Judeo-Christian Vision and the Modern Corporation*. Notre Dame: University of Notre Dame Press, 1982.

CHAPTER THREE

The Regulation of Business

INTRODUCTION

Chapter Two addressed the general problem of corporate responsibility, but the important subject of mechanisms for achieving corporate responsibility will be discussed in this chapter. Here we will focus on how corporate performance is to be monitored, by whom business may legitimately be regulated, and how and by whom the norms of corporate responsibility should be enforced. For example, many tend to think of enforcement in terms of legal liability—a linkage that is hardly surprising in a world in which lawsuits against corporate board members and officers are society's most common vehicle for enforcing accountability and providing redress. But there are other options that are distinctly moral rather than legal in nature, and in many situations one of these other options (or some combination of them) might be superior to the legal approach.

In many respects corporations are analogous to individuals facing a problem in practicing their morality that is commonly referred to as *weakness of will:* They sometimes yield to the temptation to do what they know is morally wrong. There are two fundamental strategies for overcoming weakness of will. One relies on voluntary, internal mechanisms of *self-control* and the other on coercive or manipulative *external constraints* on behavior. These same two strategies have been adopted to overcome weakness of will in business. The two most common internal mechanisms for self-control include business codes of ethics and the corporate social audit. The most pervasive external constraint is government regulation. The strengths and weaknesses of mechanisms for self-regulation and of government regulation are both assessed in this chapter.

SELF-REGULATION

The importance of self-regulation for business is similar to the importance of autonomy for persons, which is grounded in the Western tradition of the importance of individual rights, freedom, and choice, in preference to state control. The principle of respect for autonomy dictates that persons should be free to choose and act without controlling constraints imposed by others. Many believe that this principle holds for corporations no less than for individual persons. Of course, there is an implicit reciprocity of obligations: In return for their autonomy, businesspersons must act responsibly. This leads to the two main reasons supporting self-regulation: First, businesspersons know their business and their roles and commitments better than any outsiders could. Hence, duties seem best established by a knowledgeable community of practitioners. Second, businesspersons are best situated to bring pressures to bear on their members when they fail to perform their duties or when they abuse the public trust. A professional organization of businesspersons with the proper resources can run educational programs about ethics, produce codes of conduct, monitor members' practices, and discipline and punish misconduct.

If this case for self-regulation is sound, then it is reasonable to consider the methods and means by which it can be made to function in practice. Most businesspersons agree that society can expect a high level of ethical conduct on the part of persons engaged in business only if the practices and reward-and-punishment structures of business reinforce that behavior—inculcating appropriate senses of pride, shame, and responsibility. There are many strategies for institutionalizing ethics, some of which require changes in the way corporations are managed. For example, with the Challenger shuttle disaster in 1986, the failure of individuals and general flaws in management combined to cause or contribute to a disaster. Apparently a vice-president of Morton Thiokol yielded to pressure from NASA officials and overruled the judgment of Thiokol engineers that certain parts (the O-rings) might not perform in subfreezing temperatures. In addition, testimony before a presidentially appointed investigatory commission indicated that top officials at NASA were unaware that various safety issues had been brought to the attention of NASA subordinates. The astronauts were apparently the victims of both individual lapses in judgment and flawed lines of communication.

On some occasions all that is needed to ensure moral behavior is a suitable procedure. Substantive requirements are not needed. For example, a number of advertising companies have a routine procedure of making surprise visits to TV stations and checking their records as to whether they in fact broadcast commercials that they contracted to broadcast. Gary Pranzo, director of local broadcasting at Young & Rubicam, considers it "our fiduciary responsibility to our employees to do surprise audits."[1] These checks, then, serve a double moral purpose: They keep broadcasters honest, and they fulfill an advertising agency's fiduciary responsibility to its clients. It is worth noting, in passing, that this same monitoring practice used to be performed by the Federal Communications Commission which stopped investigating stations' commercial logs as part of its massive effort at deregulation.

Other strategies for institutionalizing ethics require changes in the way information is processed. In ascertaining the cause of the crash of Air New Zealand TE-901 into Mt. Erebus (see Chapter Two, pp. 119–120), the Royal Commission that investigated the crash identified the essential cause of the crash as the failure of the airline to inform Captain Collins of the change of the coordinates in the aircraft's internal computer system.[2] Further investigation indicated that this communications failure was not simply the oversight of one individual. Rather, the communications gap resulted from general flaws in management procedure. To avoid another disaster, the management needed to improve the means of communication so that pilots were given complete information as to the coordinates placed into the aircraft's computer. The lesson to be learned from all these cases is that successful self-regulation in business requires persons who are responsible for ethical issues and sound management procedures for effecting ethical results. These procedures include adequate lines of communication, designations of responsibility, and clear opportunities for the ethical ramifications of corporate decisions to be discussed.

Codes of Ethics

Among the most common means to this end of self-regulation is the code of ethics directed at the amelioration of specific professional problems—as, for example, those used by physicians, nurses, bankers, advertising agents, chemical engineers, and lawyers. There are several advantages to such codes: (1) They provide more stable, permanent guides to right and wrong conduct than do human personalities; (2) they provide guidance in ethically ambiguous situations such as conflict-of-interest dangers (see Chapter Eight, pp. 472–475); and (3) they act as a partial check on otherwise unchecked powers of employers.

To illustrate the practical efficacy of these advantages, let us examine two codes to see how they handle conflicts of interest. With respect to insider information, IBM gives the following directives to its employees:[3]

> If IBM is about to announce a new product or make a purchasing decision and the news could affect the stock of a competitor or supplier, you must not trade in the stock of those companies.

> If IBM is about to make an announcement that could affect the price of its stock, you must not trade in IBM stock.

> If IBM is about to build a new facility, you must not invest in land or business near the new site.

And with respect to tips, gifts, and entertainment, IBM says,

> No IBM employee, or any member of his or her immediate family, can accept gratuities or gifts of money from a supplier, customer, or anyone in a business relationship. Nor can they accept a gift or consideration that could be perceived as having been offered because of the business relationship. 'Perceived' simply means this: If you read about it in the local newspaper, would you wonder whether the gift just might have had something to do with a business relationship?

> No IBM employee can give money or a gift of significant value to a customer, supplier, or anyone if it could reasonably be viewed as being done to gain a business advantage.

The *Wilmington News Journal* treats favors and favoritism in its code of ethics in a similar fashion:[4]

> No employee shall accept gifts of money or items of value. Such things as pens and pocket diaries that appear to be worth no more than a few dollars may be accepted. . . .

> Free admissions to any event that is not free to the public are prohibited. If the public pays, the News Journal papers pay. . . .

Sometimes, however, the competitive nature of business makes it impossible for an individual corporation to do the morally appropriate act and survive. Suppose, for example, that textile company A is polluting a river and that expensive technology is now available to enable company A to reduce pollution. On the basis of the harm analysis provided by Simon, Powers, and Gunnemann (see Chapter Two), it seems that company A ought to install the pollution control device. However, suppose that company A can show that all other textile companies are similarly polluting rivers. If company A installs the pollution control devices and the other textile companies do not, company A's products will rise in price and hence will run the risk of becoming noncompetitive. Eventually company A may be forced out of business. The competitive situation thus makes it unfair and, from an *economic* perspective, impossible for company A to do the morally appropriate thing. Only a rule that requires *all* textile companies to install pollution control devices will be fair and effective. It is often maintained that in situations paralleling this textile pollution case, government regulation is the only viable answer.

Another advantage of codes of ethics is that they enable a company to do the morally responsible act that it wants to do but, because of competitive pressures, would otherwise be unable to do. In so doing, as Kenneth Arrow points out in his article, an industrywide code could serve as a viable alternative to government regulation.

Arrow argues that the textile pollution case can potentially be adequately handled by an industrywide code of ethics and that at least some evidence exists that industrywide codes can work. Not all moral problems of personal conflict in society need to be resolved in courts by law or by regulatory agencies. Some are suitably handled by society's general moral codes or even by formal committee decisions. Indeed, if moral codes and practices were not widely efficacious, the courts and the regulatory systems would be overwhelmed.

Nonetheless, there remain substantial problems about how efficacious codes are even when they are taken seriously and are enforced. For example, in 1984 the National Association of Securities Dealers—a national self-regulatory organization for 5,500 member firms—censured and disciplined for the fifth time the Springfield, Virginia, firm of Voss & Co. for violating the NASD's rules of fair practice. The findings indicated egregious abdications of responsibilities to customers and the pocketing of substantial monies. Fines of $4,000 and the suspension of the firm's president for five days were administered as penalties. The NASD noted that "the firm and Voss have demonstrated a chronic inability and unwillingness to comply with applicable requirements."[5] On the one hand, the NASD is to be commended for unusual vigilance. On the other hand, in the light of four previous violations and the substantial amount of money at stake, the punishment administered seems an unlikely deterrent.

Corporate Social Audit

In order to determine whether self-regulation is effective, we need some way of measuring results—something like standard audit and accounting procedures for annual financial reports to stockholders. It has been suggested that the notion of an audit should be extended beyond the state of a corporations' financial health to the state of its moral health. The figures in Figure 1 from the First National Bank of Minneapolis Social-Environmental Audit provide an example of a corporate social audit. When first discussed, the notion of a corporate social audit was enthusiastically received by the business community. The Committee for Economic Development commissioned a study of the corporate social audit, a portion of which is included in this chapter. This study explained the function of a corporate social audit and gave the concept some respectability in the business community. However, a variety of conceptual problems, costs, and difficulties in implementation have muted the initial enthusiasm for the corporate social audit, and some observers predict its imminent demise.

The chief problem with the implementation of corporate social audits comes in knowing what to measure and how to make adequate measurements. The notion of the corporate social audit has utilitarian roots, and problems of measurability that plague utilitarianism similarly constitute a stumbling block to the successful implementation of the corporate social audit. Further discussion of the measurability problems common to both self-regulation and government regulation is found in the concluding section of this chapter on regulating through cost-benefit analysis.

For corporate codes of conduct and corporate social audits to be adequate, codes of conduct must be enforced and the message transmitted that ethics is taken seriously. Phillip T. Drotning of Standard Oil of Indiana has put the point this way:

Several generations of corporate history have demonstrated that any significant corporate activity must be locked into the mainstream of corporate operations or it doesn't get done. Social policies will remain placebos for the tortured executive conscience until they are implemented with the same iron fisted management tools that are routinely employed in other areas of activity to measure performance, secure accountability, and distribute penalties and rewards.[6]

1974 Internal Social-Environmental Audit

FIRST NATIONAL BANK OF MINNEAPOLIS

		1974 Performance Level	Net Percentage Performance Differential '73-'74 (2)	1974 Objectives (3)	1974 Social Performance Index (4)	1975 Objectives (5)
Housing 1 (1)	1. Number of residential mortgage loans originated in 1974 to families living in		35%			
	a.) Minneapolis	a.) 360		+	↑	a.) 360
	b.) Suburbs & St. Paul	b.) 967	30	+		b.) 967
	2. Dollar amount of residential mortgage loans originated in 1974 to families in		25	+	↑	a.) $ 8,861,000
	a.) Minneapolis	a.) $ 8,861,000	20	+	↑	
	b.) Suburbs & St. Paul	b.) $29,324,000		+		b.) $29,324,000
	3. Number of outstanding home improvement loans made to families living in		15			a.) 655
	a.) Minneapolis	a.) 357				
	b.) Suburbs & St. Paul	b.) 744	10			b.) 676
	4. Ratio originated residential mortgage loans to bank's total resources	1:50	5			1:50
	5. Foundation contribution	$10,000	0	$10,920	.92	$10,000
Education 2	1. Number of classes taken by employees paid by bank	363	5%	+	↓	
	a.) internal	164	4	+	↑	
	b.) external	199		+	↓	
	2. Number of employees in bank college gift matching program	48	3	+	↑	55
	3. Employee community involvement man-hours per month	1,129	2	+	↑	1,241
	4. Foundation contribution to educational institutions	$51,750	1 / 0	$50,006	1.03	$55,000
Public Safety 3	1. Accidents on bank premises involving employees — 1974 (Does not include sports)	26	80% / 60 / 40			26
	2. Accidents involving non-employees	14	20 / 0			14
Income 4	1. Clerical employees — monthly income related to area-wide averages	1:1.01				1:1
	2. Clerical employees — composite productivity relation to base 1973	1:1.06				1:1.10
Job Opportunities 5	1. Percent officers, managers and professionals (EEO defined)	a.) 19.8	80% / 60	+	↑	a.) 23.8
	a.) women b.) racial minority	b.) 3.5	40	+	↑	b.) 4.2
	2. Percent of job categories posted	77	20 / 0	75	1.03	77
Health 6	1. Estimated commitment to treatment of alcoholism	a.) $5,460	50%	+ 50%	.61	
	a.) money b.) man-hours	b.) 222		+ 100%	1.39	
	2. Number of days missed due to health problems per capita	a.) 3.43	40	a.) 5.0	a.) 1.7	a.) 3.43
	a.) women b.) men	b.) 1.65	30	b.) 2.3	b.) 4.3	b.) 1.65
	3. Prepaid health services (HMO) as employee health option		20			
	a.) services offered	a.) 0				a.) 0
	b.) dollar	b.) $1,000	10	+	↓	b.) $1,500
	c.) man-hours	c.) 141	0	+	↑	c.) 150
Transportation 7	1. Percent employees taking bus to work	61	50% / 40	50	1.22	65
	2. Percent employees who come to work in car pools	17	30 / 20	30	.56	20
	3. Percent employees who drive to work alone	19	10 / 0	15	.79	15
Participation 8	1. Man-hours per month spent by employees in community activity	4,632	50%	+		5,095
	a.) on bank time	585	40	380	1.54	643
	b.) non-bank time	4,047	30	+	↑	4,451
	2. Percent employees donating to United Way	83	20	+	↑	85
	3. Percent employees voting Nov. '74	75	10 / 0			

FIGURE 1. 1974 Internal Social-Environment Audit for the First National Bank of Minneapolis

1974 Internal Social-Environmental Audit

FIRST NATIONAL BANK OF MINNEAPOLIS

	1974 Performance Level	Net Percentage Performance Differential '73-'74 (2)	1974 Objectives (3)	1974 Social Performance Index (4)	1975 Objectives (5)
Environment 9 (1)					
1. Percent office paper which is recycled	18		+	▲	18.5
2. Energy consumed by bank					
a.) steam	44,727,500		44,355,075	.99	44,727,500
b.) electric (in kilowatt hours 1-1-74 to 12-31-74)	13,095,560		−15%	.91	13,095,560
3. Loan commitments to firms dealing in anti-pollution equipment	$8,382,000				
4. Community involvement commitment in man-hours per month	153				168
5. Foundation contribution	$5,000		$6,037	.83	$5,000
Culture 10					
1. Level of commercial line commitments to cultural institutions	$4,000,000				$4,000,000
2. Community involvement — man-hours/month	333				370
3. Foundation contribution	$115,200		$113,514	.99	$135,200
Human Relations					
1. Number minority business loan applicants	56			▲	
2. Percent approved installment loan applications					
a.) women	82				83
b.) men	83				83
3. Level of minority business purchases	$46,530		$45,440	1.01	$49,000
4. Community involvement — man-hours/month	803		+	▲	883
5. Foundation contribution	$20,500		$18,250	1.12	$23,500
Community Investment (6)					
1. Commitment to lend money to businesses					
a.) Minneapolis	$284,936,000				$284,936,000
b.) Suburbs and St. Paul	$296,127,000				$296,127,000
2. Commitments to lend money to civic institutions at other than market terms					
a.) number	8				
b.) amount	$8,700,000				$8,700,000
3. Dollar volume of commercial mortgage loans originated in					
a.) Minneapolis	$1,143,000				
b.) Suburbs and St. Paul	$3,902,000				
4. Dollar volume commercial construction and land development loans					
a.) Minneapolis	$ 4,685,000		+	▼	
b.) Suburbs and St. Paul	$26,905,000		+	▼	
5. Estimated dollar value of personal loans outstanding/total personal savings deposits	$239,602,000/ $233,568,000		+	▲	
6. Total Foundation Contribution	$421,000		$420,000	1.0	$445,000
Consumer Protection and Services					
1. New consumer services offered	8				8
2. Diversity of perspective — percent of Board members without a primary background as a business executive	8		+	▼	
3. Student loans originated in 1974					
a.) number b.) dollar volume	a.) 1,192 b.) $1,877,000				a.) 1,192 b.) $1,877,000

(1) Numbered categories listed in order of community priority as determined from 1972 First Minneapolis community Social-Environmental Audit.

(2) Net Percentage Performance Differential computed by (a) determining the percentage difference in 1974 against 1973 for each indicator, (b) adding the percentage increases or decreases, and (c) dividing the result by the number of indicators used in the category

to determine the net change. Only indicators appearing in both the 1973 and 1974 audit are considered.

(3) Many 1974 objectives were specified only as increase (+) or decrease (−) because the 1974 corporate planning process was not time coordinated with the audit process.

(4) Where a numerical 1974 objective was specified for an indicator, the 1974 achievement was measured against that objective. 1.00 or

more indicates the objective was met or exceeded. Less than 1.00 indicates the extent to which the objective was not met. If the 1974 objective indicated an increase (+), the 1974 performance is reflected by an ▲ if the objective was met or by an ▼ if it was not.

(5) Objectives are set as a part of the 1975 corporate management plan.

(6) Entitled Community Commitment in 1973.

FIGURE 1, *continued*

Source: First National Bank of Minneapolis. *1974 Annual Report.* Used by permission.

Many suggestions for institutionalizing ethics have been mentioned, and some have been implemented. For example, Theodore Purcell has advocated electing an "angel's advocate" to the board of directors[7]—that is, an expert in matters of business ethics whose responsibility is to certify that the ethical perspective be applied to major corporate decisions. Purcell's idea has been adopted by some companies. One representative of this sort is Leon Sullivan, pastor of the Zion Baptist Church of Philadelphia, and author of the Sullivan principles that serve as guides for companies investing in South Africa. Sullivan was the first black director of the General Motors Corporation and, to use his terminology, served in that role as a public interest director. One danger in appointing a public interest director is that he or she will be identified as "the ethics person." Ethics might then become the sole responsibility of the public interest director, and self-regulation would not have any bona fide institutional position or commitment.

Another route to the adoption of a code of ethics is through an external authority's proposal or requirement. For example, the Office of the Comptroller of the Currency, which regulates the United States's 4,700 nationally chartered banks, urged those banks in 1985 to consider incorporating new national laws on bribery into their codes of ethics and adding provisions about gratuities and arranging quid pro quos. At almost the same time, the Securities and Exchange Commission strongly urged government-securities dealers to establish a national organization that is self-regulative in order to avert problems in the unregulated securities market. SEC officials hinted that if this were not done, federal controls likely would have to be exerted. Another case moves beyond suggestion, to requirement: In the wake of a scandal over bill-padding and influence-peddling at General Dynamics Corp., Navy Secretary John F. Lehman in 1985 suspended the corporation from obtaining new contracts until it established a "rigorous code of ethics" for its corporate officers. Over a billion dollars of pending contracts were immediately affected.[8] This kind of case shows that there can be a significant overlap between internal codes and external government regulation, a subject to which we now turn.

GOVERNMENT REGULATION

History

As social and economic systems in European and North American nations have grown more complex, there has been a correlative increase in the scope of government regulation of business (and of all economic activity). Sometimes the government intervenes for the purpose of shoring up the economic system itself, while at other times intervention is undertaken to support certain socially approved goals. Whatever the exact purpose, government regulation of business is now an enormous undertaking. Because this phenomenon has emerged so rapidly and amid such constant controversy, an historical survey of the setting and reasons for modern regulation of business in the United States will be helpful.

In the nineteenth and early twentieth centuries, an individualist philosophy prevailed in both government and business, according to which the success of business is due largely to individual effort, which the government restricts only at society's economic peril. The proper role of government relative to industry is thus that of encouraging the growth of unregulated business. Action in light of this philosophy led to a situation in which the corporation was privileged: Tariffs intended to prevent foreign competition were erected, corporate taxes were kept at low levels, and the corporation enjoyed an advantaged status under law. Giant corporations quickly began to control the economy of the country. Before the turn of the twentieth century, the 200 largest corporations produced more of the GNP than the next 100,000 largest corporations combined. These monopolies stifled competition and inflated prices. While their corporate profits rapidly increased, wages were decreasing and the cost of living was soaring. At the same time, these corporations engaged in a number of ethically unacceptable practices, such as lowering product quality without warning, watering down the value of stock and so on.

In 1887, the Interstate Commerce Act was passed to protect farmers and small business persons from monopolistic practices, especially by the railroads. A federal regulatory agency, the Interstate Commerce Commission, was created to monitor the railroads, though it was given no real power to do so, and the act thus had little immediate effect. Only three years later, in 1890, the Sherman Antitrust Act was passed to protect small businesses from a wide variety of monopolistic practices. However, for many years thereafter, the courts continued to favor monopolistic interests, and not until Theodore Roosevelt's administration was a stricter interpretation placed on the Sherman Act. Finally, in 1914, both the Clayton Act and the Federal Trade Commission Act were enacted to control anticompetitive practices. The basic idea was to free the free enterprise system from monopoly and deceptive maneuvers.

Shortly thereafter, a World War I boom restored confidence in business, and not until the Depression was there renewed pressure for further regulation. However, from 1930 until the present, a broad range of federal legislation has been enacted to control those business activities believed to involve unfairnesses or inefficiencies analogous to those that earlier had resulted from unregulated industry. Thus, unfair advertising, deceptive trade, sluggish competition, powerful anticompetitive mergers, questionable investment practices, waste discharges, discrimination in hiring, and so on, all gradually came under federal regulation. Many state and local government controls were also enacted. Consequently, federal regulation has come to affect virtually every business in the country. There are now approximately 65 major federal agencies whose regulatory activities have a direct impact on business. As both regulation and deregulation have increased, so have the critical responses.

Presumably, everyone would like to see the federal regulatory process achieve vital social ends without obstructing the productive capacity of the marketplace. We sometimes use shorthand to express this view by saying that we want business regulated "in the public interest." Yet what is the public interest, and do regulatory agencies now function so that this interest is best served? Virtually no one is satisfied with the current state of regulatory practices in the United States or with much of the deregulation that has occurred. Critics across a wide spectrum of political opinion accuse federal agencies of either too much, too little, or inefficient regulation.

Advantages of Government Regulation

Competition is one of the rules of business practice, and the first instances of government regulation grew out of the unanimously recognized authority of government to interpret and enforce the rules of competition. In its initial phase, government regulation was designed to protect both business and the public from anticompetitive practices. This protection included the regulation of natural monopolies (for example, the utilities or telephone companies). In industries like these it was thought to make no sense to have competing companies. This anticompetitive regulatory task was later expanded to protect the public from unfair competitive practices as well. Government regulation expanded to focus on fraud, deception, and dishonesty. In this latter sphere, the public is perhaps most familiar with the government regulation of deceptive advertising by the Federal Trade Commission.

This type of government regulation—when conducted fairly and efficiently—both ought to be and in fact is supported by the business community. Such government regulation ought to be supported by the business community because it is regulation designed to support the rules of business activity itself. Practices that undermine competition, either through monopoly or deceit, cut away at a central tenet of business practice. From a market perspective, failure to support attempts to control and thwart anticompetitive practices would be self-defeating. The presence of regulatory activities increases investor, consumer, and competitor confidence in the integrity of the markets—and thus seems to work to everyone's advantage.

Theory, in this regard, is supported by practice. Complaints regarding deceptive advertising often are brought to the attention of government regulators by the competitors of the alleged offender. It was competing oil companies who successfully challenged Chevron's STP advertising claims. Similarly, it was competing drug companies who complained to the Federal Trade Commission about the claims of Sterling Drug on behalf of Bayer aspirin. Sterling used a report in the *New England Journal of Medicine*, which received partial financial support from the FTC itself, as "objective" proof for the superiority of Bayer aspirin. The competing companies alleged that the ads were misleading and deceptive. That dispute went all the way to the Supreme Court, which turned down the complaints of the competing drug companies (*F.T.C. v. Sterling Drug*). The Bayer aspirin dispute provides a perfect illustration of business reliance on government regulation and of its use of the judiciary to settle a dispute on a rule of business practice. Such government regulation is clearly in the interest of business.

In recent years a number of major corporations have expressed their fear that federal *deregulation* has produced unfairness in their industries; they want regulation back where controls have been lifted. For example, a number of grain and chemical shippers as well as public utilities want to reinstitute ICC controls of coal shipment rates on the same grounds we saw in the nineteenth century: Monopoly railroads are left free to "gouge" all shippers who must use a single railroad. Similarly, many insurance companies have asked that federal controls be applied to banks that are now competing in the insurance industry on grounds that banks are given an unfair advantage. One of the most interesting industries to watch is the airline industry, where major carriers have begun to collaborate in an effort to avoid crowded scheduling, thus assuming the old role of the now defunct Civil Aeronautics Board. Smaller airlines,

which grew up under and generally favor deregulation, have begun to argue that there must be selective government regulation in order to maintain fair competition.

Sometimes unnoticed in the discussion of regulation is the massive *cooperative* interaction between government and industry that requires federal rule making. This cooperation is scarcely unique to the United States: In virtually every nation in the world governments are intimately engaged in planning, financing, contracting, and otherwise subsidizing major sectors of the economy, often in collaboration with private industry. The rationale is to produce social efficiency, enhance international cooperation and competition, lower unemployment, reduce monopoly, stimulate ailing industries, and avoid wasteful duplicative activities such as research. Sometimes notorious business success stories are actually the result of cooperative planning between a government and private industry. The famous devastation of the U.S. steel industry by the Japanese, for example, came about through a plan of the Japanese government. During World War II the United States created a vast network of new and often efficient businesses because of national need—including steel and aluminum industries and pipeline companies—not to mention public utilities, which are actually privately owned by heavily regulated companies.

Government regulation can also serve another interest of business. In the absence of an effective code of ethics, industrywide government regulation would enable the individual firm to undertake the action that is desirable from society's point of view without incurring a competitive disadvantage. For example, by setting universal air quality control standards, all firms polluting the air would be required to install scrubbers. In this way, government regulation enables some companies to do the good they believe should be done, but could not otherwise do because the competitive penalties would be too high. In such situations government regulation assists well-intentioned businesses to be the good citizens they want to be.

Yet another advantage of government regulation is that it controls indifferent or malefi-cent corporations and industries and forces them to adhere to the minimum requirements of responsibility. Much of the growth of gov-ernment regulation can be attributed to the fact that society has broadened its notion of corporate social responsibility and therefore the need for governmental control. The public has demanded government regulation as a check on corporate misbehavior or inaction while simultaneously expanding the list of business activities that it finds ethically inap-propriate or in need of investigation. Some-times it is clear that self-regulatory action within an industry is out of the question as the method of regulation. For example, in recent years there have been a number of legislative battles over the regulation of video display ter-minals for computers, reservation systems, and the like. As this book goes to press, West Germany has an elaborate set of regulations concerning the manufacture and use of these devices, and legislation supported by various labor unions and women's groups has been introduced in 20 states in the United States to limit exposure to video displays in order to re-duce eyestrain, fatigue, backaches, and head-aches thought to be caused by daily use of these terminals in the automated office. None of these bills has passed (one passed the legis-lature in Oregon, but was vetoed by the gov-ernor) because the manufacturers of the equipment have been uniformly opposed to any form of regulation other than by local em-ployers. For example, major manufacturers such as AT&T, Hewlett-Packard, IBM, and Tek-tronix all formed the Coalition for Office Tech-nology to combat the regulatory efforts.[9]

In summary, the expansion of government regulation is the result of at least three factors. First, it results from the universally recognized authority of government to interpret and en-force the rules of business activity. Second, it results from requests from socially enlight-ened corporations that need government-imposed standards to enable them to take socially desirable actions without incurring se-rious competitive disadvantages. Third, it re-sults from the demands of the general public that it be protected against a growing list of

what are viewed as undesirable corporate practices.

Disadvantages of Government Regulation

Despite the advantages for business of some forms of government regulation, government regulation is often viewed on a scale from dis-trust to horror. There are several popular rea-sons why government regulation is opposed. These include:

1. a recognition that government regulation would diminish the power and the prestige of corporate officials;
2. a fear that government officials would interfere with incentives and efficiency and hence re-duce profit;
3. a judgment that government officials do not un-derstand business and hence that its regulations would be unreasonable and unworkable;
4. a judgment that government officials are in no position to comment on the ethics of others;
5. a judgment that the federal government is al-ready too powerful in a pluralistic society so that it is inappropriate to increase the power of government in this way;
6. a judgment that government regulation violates the legitimate freedom and moral rights of em-ployers and stockholders; and
7. a judgment that inviting government to resolve problems of conflict is confrontational and so-cially divisive.

One of the strongest and most influential opponents of government regulation has been Gary Becker, University Professor of Eco-nomics and Chairman of the Economics De-partment at the University of Chicago. He has presented a utilitarian case against regulation, largely by focusing on the role of special-interest groups in a regulatory environment:

Special-interest groups use political clout to ob-tain subsidies, favorable regulations, and other government help that enable them to resist making adjustments to adverse economic con-ditions. . . . Experience in the U.S. and other countries suggests that workers, management, and other interest groups will manipulate any industrial policy to promote their own interests rather than those of the whole country.[10]

Becker chalks up the failure of the U.S. steel industry less to Japanese ingenuity than to excessive demands in the United States by that industry for quotas and tariffs on imported steel, loan guarantees for steel companies, and government-directed programs to reinvest profits. These programs, he argues, raised prices and made U.S. steel noncompetitive. The major economic disasters in Israel, Russia, and Britain stem, in his judgment, from precisely such well-intentioned but ill-fated policies, which in the end do not even serve the special interests that lobby for them.

Although the above seven items and the statement by Becker present an accurate list of widespread objections to government regulation, some objections are either too sweeping—for example, point 4—or self-serving—for example, point 1. Philosophically, what is needed is some general theoretical framework to serve as the basis of criticism and to answer the question, Which regulations are reasonable and which ones are unreasonable? In 1964, Lon Fuller published his important book *The Morality of Law,* which provides eight criteria for evaluating good law and argues that extreme departures from those eight conditions threaten to undermine the legal system itself. In his article later in this chapter, Norman Bowie adapts Fuller's criteria for the special context of government regulation. Many government regulations fall short under the criteria he proposes.

There are also general limitations inherent in the nature of law that limit its effectiveness as a means of regulation. If the only means of ensuring moral conduct were the law, serious social repercussions would result. At best society would be burdened with an expensive enforcement apparatus; at the extreme, society would become either totalitarian or collapse in anarchy. The Internal Revenue Service, for example, admits that it would be powerless to prevent widespread cheating on income taxes, and if such cheating occurred the government could no longer use the income tax. In the article that concludes the Government Regulation section, Christopher Stone discusses some of the features of law that limit its effectiveness as a regulatory device.

Most businesspersons have already moved beyond the point of believing that the law is the definitive or sole word in setting standards of corporate ethics. The view "If it's legal, it's O.K." is not the prevailing notion in most corporations. Nonetheless, the first response of the public whenever it is unhappy is to argue for the passage of new laws. If Stone's analysis is correct, a constant attempt to regulate corporate conduct through law is doomed to failure. First, there is the time-lag problem. Laws are passed only after the damage has been done, and often the damage is severe. What is needed is some way of preventing the damage in the first place, and we cannot reasonably look to the law for that degree or form of protection.

Stone also points out that government regulation works poorly when there is no consensus as to what is right or wrong. In a democracy, the temptation is to identify the problem—for example, the degradation of the environment—and then to create a regulatory body with a broad mandate to "fix" the problem. However, the divisions that prevent Congress from drawing up specific regulations soon plague the regulatory agency itself.

Not all criticisms of government regulation are justified, however. A popular criticism of government regulation is that it is paternalistic because it forces us to do things for our own good on the grounds that it knows what is in our best interest better than we do. Some argue that laws requiring the use of seatbelts or requiring motorcyclists to wear helmets are passed on paternalistic grounds. Studies have shown over and over that the vast majority of drivers do not voluntarily wear seatbelts. Other research shows that many workers oppose various safety regulations—the wearing of helmets or safety goggles for example. In his article, Steve Kelman agrees that paternalistic government regulation is either wrong or subject to criticism. However, he argues that the paternalistic charge is misplaced. His strategy is to show that in some cases the government really may know more than we do, such as when we do not have the information to make individual decisions about the safety of a product. Moreover, as Kelman points out, even if we could get the information, obtaining it is often too costly. Sometimes the psychological cost of facing certain problems such as the prospect of illness and death are so high that we would rather have others think about them instead. What appears to be wrongful paternalism may turn out to be advantageous protection.

Government regulation, then, is neither a complete blessing nor a complete curse. Properly formulated, regulations applied in the appropriate situations can help assure proper corporate behavior. However, the complete job of business ethics cannot be done by regulatory action any more than by case law in the courts.

MORAL REASONING AND COST-BENEFIT ANALYSIS

In recent years, especially in the regulative agencies of government, a particular method has been widely touted as a means of applying legal standards to the regulation of industry. This method is generally referred to as cost-benefit analysis, one segment of which is risk-benefit analysis. This method has also been employed by individual firms. For example, some corporate social audits are based on cost-benefit principles. The purpose is to provide a systematic method to facilitate tasks of decision making—whether decisions apply to the regulation of business or to the corporate management of a business. Since both management and the government have definite goals (for example, the firm strives to maximize profits), they are naturally interested in the most efficient means to those ends. The cost-benefit approach is intended to show how one can bring about the desired result with the least possible expenditure.

The simple idea behind cost-benefit procedures is that one can *measure* costs and benefits by some acceptable device, at the same time identifying uncertainties and possible

tradeoffs, in order to present policy makers or businesspersons with specific, relevant information on the basis of which a decision can be reached. Although such analysis usually proceeds by measuring different quantitative units (for example, the number of worker accidents, statistical deaths, dollars expended, and number of workers fired) cost-benefit analysis (in the ideal) attempts in the end to convert and express these seemingly incommensurable units of measurement into a common one, usually a monetary unit. This ultimate reduction gives the method its power, in the minds of many, because judgments about tradeoffs can be made on the basis of perfectly comparable quantities. For example, it has been argued that among its other uses it can be employed to make financially explicit such tradeoffs (reached in government policy decisions) as those between environmental quality and factory productivity and between the quality of gasoline and the quality of the health of those who produce it.

Vincent Vaccaro, a government employee, has participated in cost-benefit studies. His article, "Cost-Benefit Analysis and Public Policy Formation" is essentially a defense of the practice. However, his defense is tempered by the recognition that cost-benefit analyses are often improperly done and by the recognition that certain issues of distributive justice must be settled before the cost-benefit process begins. Vaccaro thus argues that cost-benefit analysis ought to be constrained by various social goals including moral ones. The critics of cost-benefit analysis remain unconvinced, however.

Cost-benefit analysis has been widely criticized as a technique, especially when suggested for public policy purposes. First, the method has proved difficult to implement. Economists have been concerned largely with spelling out how such analyses can be carried out in *theory* rather than with providing practical and already quantified examples. The fact that many important variables are difficult to ascertain and reliably quantify—so difficult that we may never be very confident about the ending net sum—is a major reason why cost-benefit analysis has not been more widely used and has seemed to many a non-viable technique. This conclusion has been particularly drawn in the case of evaluating projects that would improve the quality of life, as opposed to considerations merely about the purchase of capital goods.

Here one might consider the value and difficulty of using cost-benefit analysis to decide in some particular setting whether self-regulation or government regulation is the most cost-efficient way to regulate. Huge costs are, after all, involved in keeping records, processing information, monitoring and inspecting, disciplining, and so on. Efficient and effective self-regulatory activity will save the public vast sums of money, and has the further advantage of decreasing hostility toward state controllers. But if such activity is inefficient and ineffective, the public may suffer more and pay an even higher price. This is just the sort of decision that cost-benefit analysis is supposed to be able to help us make. But it is no easy (or inexpensive) matter to quantify the costs of the two forms of regulation, while figuring out how to factor in the values of freedom from external control and protection of the integrity and reputation of markets.

A controversial use of cost-benefit analysis occurs when a value is placed on human lives. For example, the Ford Motor Company was widely criticized for putting a cost on human lives when it decided not to spend more money to make a safer gas tank for the Ford Pinto. A cost-benefit analysis showed that the cost of improving the Pinto exceeded the value of the lives saved. Yet, many now agree that if policy decisions are to be made, some value must be placed on human life. To decide as objectively as possible how much money to put into highway safety or into medical research, one needs appropriate data and a means of placing a value on human life. It seems implausible to suppose that those who think that human life is of infinite value want to tax themselves infinitely, or even more than they are taxed now.

However, the standard techniques for measuring human life all have difficulties of another sort. Consider a popular method that discounts to the present the person's expected future earnings. On this method, the life of an older, low-income person is worth less in dollars than that of a young high-income person. This implication prepares the way for a second important objection to cost-benefit analysis, namely that we may not want it for *moral* reasons, and especially for reasons of (distributive) justice. It may be that some cost-benefit analyses will tell us that a particular device would be highly beneficial as compared to its costs, and yet provision of this benefit might function in an economy to deny more basic services to those who desperately need them. Perhaps instead, as a matter of justice, such needy persons ought to be subsidized, either in terms of services or financial awards, no matter what cost-benefit analyses reveal. When this problem is coupled with the generally acknowledged fact that the language of "costs" and "benefits" itself harbors implicit value judgments about positive and negative consequences, it appears that some fundamental moral thinking must be done, not only about whether to accept a *particular* cost-benefit model as decisive, but also about the acceptability of the *notions* of "costs" and "benefits."

Finally, we may have good reason for preferring political solutions to some questions rather than cost-benefit analyses. In the "Cotton Dust Standard Case" included at the end of this chapter, the Supreme Court ruled that OSHA had properly interpreted Congress's directive that the cotton dust standard be set at a level that was as high as the technology permitted rather than at a lower level justified by cost-benefit analysis. Congress can require regulations that are inefficient from a cost-benefit perspective. In the article that concludes this chapter, Mark Sagoff argues against a total reliance on cost-benefit analysis for matters of health and safety even if such reliance would be most efficient.

The federal government in the United States continues to push for both greater efficiency and decreased regulation in many areas. As it does, the role of cost-benefit analysis may substantially increase—a joy to its supporters and a source of irritation to its critics.

NOTES

1. As quoted in Ronald Alsop, "Efficacy of Global Ad Projects Is Questioned in Firm's Survey," *Wall Street Journal,* September 13, 1984, p. 31.
2. Peter A. French, "The Principle of Responsive Adjustment in Corporate Moral Responsibility: The Crash on Mount Erebus," *Journal of Business Ethics* 3 (May 1984): 101–111.
3. IBM Business Conduct Guidelines (internal document), 11–12.
4. *The News Journal's Code of Professionalism and Ethics Sunday News Journal,* August 29, 1982, p. H3.
5. See Bruce Ingersoll, "SEC Says NASD Was Too Lenient In Censure of Broker," *Wall Street Journal,* September 21, 1984, p. 36.
6. Phillip T. Drotning, "Organizing the Company for Social Action," in *The Unstable Ground: Corporate Social Policy,* ed. S. Prakash Sethi (Los Angeles: Melville, 1974), p. 259.
7. Theodore Purcell, "Electing an Angel's Advocate to the Board," *Management Review,* 65 (May 1976): 9–10.
8. See Michael Weisskopf, "Arms Firm Punished by Navy," *Washington Post,* May 22, 1985, pp. A1, A6; James L. Rowe, "Guidelines Urged on Bank Closures," *Washington Post,* April 1, 1985, p. A9; Bruce Ingersoll, "Self-Regulation Urged for Dealers of U.S. Securities," *Wall Street Journal,* March 28, 1985, p. 20; and Nathaniel C. Nash, "Debt Units Facing New Rules," *New York Times,* April 10, 1985, p. 29.
9. Henry Weinstein, "The VDT: Typhoid Mary or a Vision of the Future?" *International Herald Tribune,* August 21, 1985, p. 6.
10. Gary Becker, "The Best Industrial Policy is None At All," *Business Week,* August 5, 1985, p. 14.

Business Codes and Economic Efficiency

Kenneth J. Arrow

This paper makes some observations on the widespread notion that the individual has some responsibility to others in the conduct of his economic affairs. It is held that there are a number of circumstances under which the economic agent should forgo profit or other benefits to himself in order to achieve some social goal, especially to avoid a disservice to other individuals. For the purpose of keeping the discussion within bounds, I shall confine my attention to the obligations that might be imposed on business firms.

. . . Is it reasonable to expect that ethical codes will arise or be created? . . . This may seem to be a strange possibility for an economist to raise. But when there is a wide difference in knowledge between the two sides of the market, recognized ethical codes can be, as has already been suggested, a great contribution to economic efficiency. Actually we do have examples of this in our everyday lives, but in very limited areas. The case of medical ethics is the most striking. By its very nature there is a very large difference in

From Kenneth J. Arrow, "Social Responsibility and Economic Efficiency," *Public Policy* 21 (Summer 1973). Copyright © 1973 by the President and Fellows of Harvard College.

knowledge between the buyer and the seller. One is, in fact, buying precisely the service of someone with much more knowledge than you have. To make this relationship a viable one, ethical codes have grown up over the centuries, both to avoid the possibility of exploitation by the physician and to assure the buyer of medical services that he is not being exploited. I am not suggesting that these are universally obeyed, but there is a strong presumption that the doctor is going to perform to a large extent with your welfare in mind. Unnecessary medical expenses or other abuses are perceived as violations of ethics. There is a powerful ethical background against which we make this judgment. Behavior that we would regard as highly reprehensible in a physician is judged less harshly when found among businessmen. The medical profession is typical of professions in general. All professions involve a situation in which knowledge is unequal on two sides of the market by the very definition of the profession, and therefore there have grown up ethical principles that afford some protection to the client. Notice there is a mutual benefit in this. The fact is that if you had sufficient distrust of a doctor's services, you wouldn't buy them. Therefore the physician wants an ethical code to act as assurance to the buyer, and he certainly wants his competitors to obey this same code, partly because any violation may put him at a disadvantage but more especially because the violation will reflect on him, since the buyer of the medical services may not be able to distinguish one doctor from another. A close look reveals that a great deal of economic life depends for its viability on a certain limited degree of ethical commitment. Purely selfish behavior of individuals is really incompatible with any kind of settled economic life. There is almost invariably some element of trust and confidence. Much business is done on the basis of verbal assurance. It would be too elaborate to try to get written commitments on every possible point. Every contract depends for its observance on a mass of unspecified conditions which suggest that the performance will be carried out in good faith without insistence on sticking literally to its wording. To put the matter in its simplest form, in almost every economic transaction, in any exchange of goods for money, somebody gives up his valuable asset before he gets the other's; either the goods are given before the money or the money is given before the goods. Moreover there is a general confidence that there won't be any violation of the implicit agreement. Another example in daily life of this kind of ethics is the observance of queue discipline. People line up; there are people who try to break in ahead of you, but there is an ethic which holds that this is bad. It is clearly an ethic which is in everybody's interest to preserve; one waits at the end of the line this time, and one is protected against somebody's coming in ahead of him.

In the context of product safety, efficiency would be greatly enhanced by accepted ethical rules. Sometimes it may be enough to have an ethical compulsion to reveal all the information available and let the buyer choose. This is not necessarily always the best. It can be argued that under some circumstances setting minimum safety standards and simply not putting out products that do not meet them would be desirable and should be felt by the businessman to be an obligation.

Now I've said that ethical codes are desirable. It doesn't follow from that that they will come about. An ethical code is useful only if it is widely accepted. Its implications for specific behavior must be moderately clear, and above all it must be clearly perceived that the acceptance of these ethical obligations by everybody does involve mutual gain. Ethical codes that lack the latter property are unlikely to be viable. How do such codes develop? They may develop as a consensus out of lengthy public discussion of obligations, discussion which will take place in legislatures, lecture halls, business journals, and other public forums. The codes are communicated by the very process of coming to an agreement. A more formal alternative would be to have some highly prestigious group discuss ethical codes for safety standards. In either case to become and to remain a part of the economic environment, the codes have to be accepted by the significant operating institutions and transmitted from one generation of executives to the next through standard operating procedures, through education in business schools, and through indoctrination of one kind or another. If we seriously expect such codes to develop and to be maintained, we might ask how the agreements develop and above all, how the codes remain stable. After all, an ethical code, however much it may be in the interest of all, is, as we remarked earlier, not in the interest of any one firm. The code may be of value to the running of the system as a whole, it may be of value to all firms if all firms maintain it, and yet it will be to the advantage of any one firm to cheat—in fact the more so, the more other firms are sticking to it. But there are some reasons for thinking that ethical codes can develop and be stable. These codes will not develop completely without institutional support. That is to say, there will be need for focal organizations, such as government agencies, trade associations, and consumer defense groups, or all combined to make the codes explicit, to iterate their doctrine and to make their presence felt. Given that help, I think the emergence of ethical codes on matters such as safety, at least, is possible. One positive factor here is something that is a negative factor in other contexts, namely that our economic organization is to such a large extent composed of large firms. The corporation is no longer a single individual; it is a social organization with internal social ties and internal pressures for acceptability and esteem. The individual members of the corporation are not only parts of the corporation but also members of a larger society whose esteem is desired. Power in a large corporation is necessarily diffused; not many individuals in such organizations feel so thoroughly identified with the corporation that other kinds of social pressures become irrelevant. Furthermore, in a large, complex firm where many people have to participate in any deci-

sion, there are likely to be some who are motivated to call attention to violations of the code. This kind of check has been conspicuous in government in recent years. The Pentagon Papers are an outstanding illustration of the fact that within the organization there are those who recognize moral guilt and take occasion to blow the whistle. I expect the same sort of behavior to occur in any large organization when there are well-defined ethical rules whose violation can be observed.

One can still ask if the codes are likely to be stable. Since it may well be possible and profitable for a minority to cheat, will it not be true that the whole system may break down? In fact, however, some of the pressures work in the other direction. It is clearly in the interest of those who are obeying the codes to enforce them, to call attention to violations, to use the ethical and social pressures of the society at large against their less scrupulous rivals. At the same time the value of maintaining the system may well be apparent to all, and no doubt ways will be found to use the assurance of quality generated by the system as a positive asset in attracting consumers and workers.

One must not expect miraculous transformations in human behavior. Ethical codes, if they are to be viable, should be limited in their scope. They are not a universal substitute for the weapons mentioned earlier, the institutions, taxes, regulations, and legal remedies. Further, we should expect the codes to apply in situations where the firm has superior knowledge of the situation. I would not want the firm to act in accordance with some ethical principles in regard to matters of which it has little knowledge. For example, with quality standards which consumers can observe, it may not be desirable that the firm decide for itself, at least on ethical grounds, because it is depriving the consumer of the freedom of choice between high-quality, high-cost and low-quality, low-cost products. It is in areas where someone is typically misinformed or imperfectly informed that ethical codes can contribute to economic efficiency.

The Logic, Scope, and Feasibility of the Corporate Social Audit

John J. Corson and George A. Steiner in collaboration with Robert C. Meehan

The corporation, like the government, the hospital, the university, and the church, is being held accountable to its constituencies and to the general public in an unprecedented fashion today.

This demand is an inevitable consequence of the emergence of the compact society in which many more units—business firms, governments, hospitals, colleges, universities, and others—compete with one another in markedly limited living space to serve a people that expect a better quality of life than has previously been available to them. Each unit is being held accountable for contributing to making life safer, more secure, more healthful, more equitable, and more rewarding of honest effort, and to offering greater opportunity for every individual. These two trends (the increasing demand for accountability by the individual unit and the rising expectations as to the acceptable quality of life) underlie the development of the social audit....

Historically, the primary *social* responsibility of the corporation has been to discover and develop goods and services that satisfy the needs of people. The accomplishment of that end—the production of an increasing abundance of steadily improving goods and services—has long been regarded as of such great value to the society as to warrant the earning of profits.[1]

As the basic wants for food, clothing, shelter, and health care of most members of American society have been satisfied, society's expectations have grown to include not only new and better goods and services but other things as well. For example: (1) services of clear social utility that were once provided by government and are now provided by corporations at a *profit;* such services include postsecondary education (e.g., the schools and educational services marketed by Bell and Howell Company) and providing food services for school programs and for aged and invalid persons in their homes; (2) a widening range of amenities, services, and information for employees, consumers, shareholders, and the community, without prospect of profit and at the cost of the corporation.

If the social audit is to catalogue all such activities, verify the costs entailed, and evaluate the benefits produced, it becomes an evaluation of everything a corporation is doing. When the scope is thus defined, it becomes impractical to accomplish a social audit and, indeed, the information it would present would likely be too massive to be useful.

If, on the other hand, the scope of the audit—that is, the activities to be catalogued, verified, and evaluated—is limited, it will not demonstrate to the constituencies the

---

From John J. Corson and George A. Steiner in collaboration with Robert C. Meehan, "The Logic, Scope, and Feasibility of the Corporate Social Audit," in *Measuring Business's Social Performance: The Corporate Social Audit.* Copyright © 1974 by Committee for Economic Development, New York. Reprinted by permission of the publisher.

extent to which the corporation's social performance measures up to what the constituents expect. For example, the social audit will not perform this principal function if it is limited to (1) those activities for which a corporation's executives are particularly concerned about accomplishments and/or costs incurred; (2) those activities about which information is publicized to better the corporation's public image.

Therefore, the scope of the social audit (like the scope of the financial audit) is determined by the informational needs of those it is designed to serve—employees, consumers, concerned shareholders, the general public, and those who influence the shaping of public opinion. In the course of time those needs will undoubtedly change, but in the main they will include the need for information about: (1) statutorily required activities (e.g., the provision of equal employment opportunities for minority group members); (2) voluntary activities (e.g., the making of contributions to health, educational, and cultural agencies and the "adoption" of a local high school); and (3) socially useful activities undertaken for the making of profits (e.g., contracting to provide teaching services in the schools).

The key task for the corporation is to specify what activities are of concern to its constituencies at a particular time.[2] It is a difficult task, and new ways and means must be developed to accomplish it. . . .

Few social audits made today embrace the categories of activities that fall logically within the scope as suggested here. The scope of few if any of these audits is determined by the standard of social expectations that has been proposed. The failure to attain this ideal is to be expected at this early stage in the evolution of this form of appraisal. A methodology for identifying social expectations and appraising corporate social performance is still being developed. To indicate the point that has been reached, we will describe ways of determining what society expects of the corporation and examine existing yardsticks for measuring the corpora-

tion's performance of various social activities.

Society communicates its expectations in several ways. This is done through the crusading of reformers. It is also done by businessmen with social foresight who by taking advanced steps communicate the needs of society by example. Such examples have been set by Henry Ford when he established the $5 per-day wage in the automobile industry, by George Eastman and Marion B. Folsom when in the 1930s Eastman Kodak Company established its wage-dividend and pension policies, and by International Business Machines Corporation and Xerox Corporation more recently in granting leaves at full pay to employees who choose to engage in community activities.

Group pressures are another means by which society communicates its expectations. The National Consumers League in the 1930s and the United Farm Workers in 1972 communicated what they contended were the expectations of the society by mobilizing consumers to force employers to better conditions for their workers. Strikes, boycotts, sit-ins, and demonstrations have been used to convey other expectations to corporate leadership.

In theory, society communicates its expectations to corporate leadership through the voices of the corporation's stockholders. Many recent stockholders' meetings illustrate both the theoretical process as well as its ineffectiveness. A score of issues ranging from the corporation's efforts to curb pollution and employ women to changing its operations in South Africa have been presented by small, articulate minorities in the form of resolutions for stockholder approval which have been regularly voted down. The presentation of such resolutions by a few stockholders, despite their usual rejection, nevertheless forces corporate management to consider whether society expects it to perform the actions proposed.

Society conveys its expectations most clearly when they are finally enacted into law. Prior to 1935, a few employers provided pensions for employees who had spent much of their adult life in their employ. Unemployment and suffering among the aged during the depression of the 1930s attracted public concern and resulted in the enactment of the Social Security Act. By means of this law, society converted a growing public desire and the example of a few employers into an obligation for all employers. Other examples of such actions are apparent in the labeling requirements and product quality standards set by the Food and Drug Administration and the Federal Trade Commission, in the water quality standards established by the state governments, and in the financial reporting practices stipulated by the Securities and Exchange Commission.

Such channels of information provided the corporation executive with indications of society's expectations.[3] However, much of what is transmitted through these channels (other than actual legislation) is distorted by the opposing views of others in the society, is blurred by emotions, or is simply inaccurate. The executive is thus left with the task of weighing these messages and deciding what expectations have gained general acceptance among consumers, employers, stockholders, and citizens so strongly as to suggest, if not require, that the corporation take action. His problem is one of determining what social responsibilities are of such critical and continuing importance to the constituencies his firm serves as to warrant its acceptance of the associated costs and obligations.[4]

The methodology to make this determination has not been perfected but is now being developed. Staff members of the larger corporation usually have an understanding of the demands as well as threats made on the company at the present time and those that will be made in the future. What the corporation more often lacks is the capacity for objectively weighing its obligation to meet such demands. Yet some larger companies, General Electric Company, for instance, have made such assessments.[5] They have demonstrated that decisions can be made by

staff, when guided by clear policy, about the relationship that the corporation strives to maintain to the society.[6] To ensure objectivity the corporation's staff and managers can be aided by market surveys and polls of constituent opinion that provide reliable indications of social expectations. From the results managers then can select those activities they think they should pursue to meet the most urgent needs of society. . . .

Presuming that the scope of a social audit can be determined, what yardsticks are available to measure the costs and accomplishments of activities included in the social audit? Without credible measures of business's social performance the social audit will make little progress. Many business executives hold views similar to that expressed by one respondent to [a] survey, who stated: "Most of the elements involved cannot be quantified in any meaningful way and . . . a balance sheet would result only in an oversimplified representation which might lend itself to puffery." Measures of accomplishment for many activities, as this respondent has accurately pointed out, do not yet exist, and the identification of costs is sometimes difficult. The problems involved in developing measures of accomplishment and in identifying relevant costs are substantial, yet the development of useful measures is progressing.

The financial auditor has numerous acceptable yardsticks for evaluating the financial operations of a business enterprise. They include unit production costs, the ratio of each category of costs to the sales dollar, the current ratio, inventory turnover, the aging of receivables, cash flow analyses, the ratio of net earnings to interest on debt, and others. The social auditor is at an early stage of forging similar yardsticks and faces formidable obstacles in perfecting measures for a number of social activities. . . .

The development of the social audit today is hobbled, as our survey indicates, by confusion as to purpose as well as by difficulties confronted in striving to measure costs and accomplishments. If the social audit is to inform insiders alone, one set of measures focusing on costs and efficiency of performance is needed. If the social audit is designed to meet the demands of outsiders for an assessment of social performance, a different set of measures is required.

If we assume that both needs must be served, the problem of measurement still remains. By definition an audit is a "methodical examination and review," but many businessmen view an audit as necessarily involving quantification, and, as we have stated, the quantification of costs and accomplishments is difficult, the latter more so than the former.

The costs involved in many social activities, although not all, are difficult to isolate. The benefits received by the company itself or those contributed to society are difficult to appraise. For example, what cost/benefit is involved in the maintenance by corporations of deposits in minority-owned and -operated banks? In increasing the proportion of blacks in the corporate work force? If the cost of building a plant in the inner city rather than moving it to the suburbs can be identified, how can the auditor measure the benefits produced for the company? For the community? What is the value to society of contributions to the support of black colleges and universities? Of the service of corporate employees on leave to teach in universities? Of the stimulation of interest in liturgical music?

The quantification that is involved in the financial audit (which conditions thinking as to the nature of a social audit) evolved over many years. Gradually accountants have found ways of quantifying concepts that at an earlier time were dealt with only or primarily as subjective judgments (e.g., cash flow). But even today some important concepts of costs and value are difficult to quantify and are treated in descriptive footnotes to corporate financial statements.

Methods for quantifying accomplishments of social activities are being developed. For those activities that are now required by government, some yardsticks that

quantify what is expected have been established; for example, state and federal governments have established air quality and water quality standards. Yardsticks are evolving for some activities that are generally accepted by corporations as responsibilities they should bear, for example, the proportion of net income the corporation contributes to charitable, educational, religious, and welfare institutions. For many activities that corporations have undertaken, no yardsticks of accomplishment are yet available. To illustrate, there are no yardsticks to measure the performance of a company in helping society to improve its transportation systems or to preserve animal life or to recycle materials. . . . Gradually ways must and, hopefully, will be found to evaluate the worth as well as the cost of many activities that are now unmeasurable. . . .

One-half of the companies responding to our survey stated that they made the results of their audit of social activities available only to the company's executives and directors. Less than half the respondent companies made the results available to the stockholders and to the public. Do these practices constitute the kind of accountability being called for?

When one assesses the demands from constituents and the breadth of the social audits being made by the pioneering companies, the answer must be "No." Yet, an increasing number of corporations are now including statements in their annual and quarterly reports to stockholders describing what they have done in particular fields of social activity.[7] A few corporations use newspaper advertising to tell the general public about social activities they are engaged in,* and some others have prepared special reports describing rather comprehensively their activities and have made them generally available.

---

*For example, the Chase Manhattan Bank advertised in a number of newspapers and journals that "We helped the Black magazine (*Black Enterprise*) that's helping Black businessmen."

Examples of such special reports are those made in 1972, 1973, and 1974 by the General Motors Corporation entitled *Report on Progress in Areas of Public Concern.* These reports explain what General Motors did in these years to meet the problems of automobile pollution and automobile safety. They refine and make more generally known the corporation's policy relative to investments in South Africa, its policy and accomplishments in hiring members of minority groups, its efforts to assist minority group members to conduct their own businesses, and its efforts to seek the views of the consumers of its products and act upon their complaints.[8]

NOTES

1. Criticisms of the "large corporation as a malevolent conscious force" ignore the central fact that "the large bureaucratized industrial enterprise is the principal tool that we have available for providing those resources which are needed to improve the quality of life." Joseph L. Bower, "On the Amoral Organization," in Marris, *The Corporate Society,* p. 178.
2. For a list of fourteen major constituencies likely to exert pressure that the corporation must consider in its strategic planning processes, see Ian H. Wilson, "Reforming the Strategic Planning Process: Integration of Social Responsibility and Business Needs," in Sethi, *The Unstable Ground,* pp. 245–255.
3. For views that have aided us in developing this analysis, see Dow Votaw, "Corporate Social Reform: An Educator's Viewpoint"; and George P. Hinckley and James E. Post, "The Performance Context of Corporate Responsibility," in Sethi, *The Unstable Ground,* pp. 14–23; 293–302.
4. For an ingenious method for making such determinations, see Allan D. Shocker and S. Prakash Sethi, "An Approach to Incorporating Social Preferences in Developing Corporate Action Strategies," in Sethi, *The Unstable Ground,* pp. 67–80.
5. For a discussion and evaluation of some ninety-seven demands made in this company, see Robert M. Estes, "Today's Demands on Business," in *The Changing Business Role in Modern Society,* ed. George A. Steiner (Los Angeles: University of California at Los Angeles, Graduate School of Management, 1974), pp. 160–178.
6. For an excellent example of such policy, see "What Should a Corporation Do?" *Roper Report,* no. 2 (October 1971), pp. 2–3. This contains an excerpt of the philosophy and goals of the Standard Oil Company (N.J.), now the Exxon Corporation.
7. Fry Consultants, *Social Responsibilities II* (Washington, D.C., 1971), p. 2.
8. Other companies that distribute similar reports for public consumption include the Bank of America, CNA Financial Corporation, Dayton Hudson Corporation, Eastern Gas and Fuel Associates, and Ford Motor Company.

The Limits of Business Self-Regulation

Ian Maitland

In a liberal democracy, there are limits to the extent to which socially responsible behavior can be ordered by law. Beyond a certain point, the costs of expanding the apparatus of state control become prohibitive—in terms of abridged liberties, bureaucratic hypertrophy, and sheer inefficiency. This fact probably accounts for the lasting appeal of

From Ian Maitland, "The Limits of Business Self-Regulation," *California Management Review* 27 (1985), © 1985 by the Regents of the University of California. By permission of the Regents.

the concept of self-regulation—the idea that we would be better off if we could rely on the promptings of a corporate "conscience" to regulate corporate behavior instead of the heavy hand of government regulation.

To its advocates, the virtues of self-regulation—or "corporate social responsibility"—seem self-evident. It promises simultaneously to allay business fears of further government encroachment and to restore the public's faith in business. What is more, it asks of business only that it behave in its own enlightened self-interest. While this entails a radical break with the way managers have conceived of their role in the past, it does not make any impossible or self-contradictory demands that an imaginative manager cannot adapt to. In any case, such things as the new awareness of the fragility of the physical environment, the quantum leap in the power of large corporations, and a New American Ideology, all demand no less.

The period from the mid-1950s to the mid-1970s saw a stream of proposals for the moral reconstruction of the corporation. The principal obstacle to self-regulation was diagnosed as managers' single-minded preoccupation with profit maximization. This, in turn, was attributed to intellectual shortcomings—managers' insularity, their failure to keep up with changing values, their inability to see their role in a system-wide perspective, and their attachment to an outmoded ideology which defined the public interest as the unintended outcome of the pursuit of selfish interests. Also implicated were the organizational structure and culture of the modern corporation which supposedly embodied and perpetuated this orientation to profit. The advocates of self-regulation saw their task as being the proselytizing and scolding of managers into a broader definition of their role and the drawing up of blueprints for the socially responsible corporation.

This most recent wave of enthusiasm for self-regulation has largely receded, leaving behind it few enduring achievements. By and large, the exhortations appear to have fallen on deaf ears, or at best to have had only a marginal impact on corporate conduct. The primacy of profit maximization remains unchallenged and we continue to rely—and will do so for the foreseeable future—on legal compulsion administered by the state to regulate the undesirable consequences of economic activity.

If the marriage between the corporation and self-regulation was made in heaven, why has it not been consummated? The failure of self-regulation to live up to its promise is attributable to factors that have, for the most part, been overlooked by its advocates. In their attempts to make over managers' value systems and restructure the modern corporation, they have largely neglected the very real limits on managers' discretion that result from the operation of a market economy. As a consequence of these limits, managers are largely *unable* to consider their firms' impact on society or to subordinate profit-maximization to social objectives, no matter how well-intentioned they are.

A GAME THEORETIC ANALYSIS OF SELF-REGULATION

The crux of this argument is the recognition that an individual firm's interests as a competitor in the marketplace often diverge from its interests as a part of the wider society (or, for that matter, as a part of the business community). In this latter role, the firm is likely to welcome a cleaner environment, but as a competitor in the marketplace it has an interest in minimizing its own pollution abatement costs. It may philosophically favor a free market, but it will probably lobby in favor of protection for itself. This observation is a commonplace one, but its implications are rarely fully explored.

The firm's interests as part of a broader group typically take the form of collective or public goods. Using a rational choice model of behavior, Mancur Olson has demonstrated that it is not in the interest of a group member (let us say, the firm) to contribute to the costs of providing such goods.[1] Public goods (e.g., a cleaner environment or the free market) are goods that are available to all firms irrespective of whether or not they have contributed to their upkeep or refrained from abusing them. Since their availability is not contingent on a firm having contributed, each firm has a rational incentive to free-ride, i.e., to leave the costs of providing them to other firms. However, if each firm succumbs to this temptation, as it must if it acts in its own rational self-interest, then the public good will not be provided at all. Thus, even when they are in agreement, "rational, self-interested individuals will not act to achieve their common or group interests."[2] In a rational world, Olson concludes, "it is certain that a collective good will *not* be provided unless there is coercion or some outside inducement."[3]

The typical objectives of business self-regulation and responsible corporate behavior—such as a cleaner environment—are public goods. Olson's theory therefore provides a basis for explaining why business self-regulation appears so hard to achieve.

Russell Hardin has pointed out that the logic underlying Olson's theory of collective action is identical to that of an n-person prisoner's dilemma (PD).[4] The strategy of not contributing toward the cost of a public good dominates the strategy of paying for it, in the sense that no matter what other firms do, any particular firm will be better off if it does not contribute.

. . . Ford Runge (following A.K. Sen) has argued that what appears to be a prisoner's dilemma proves, on closer inspection, to be an "assurance problem" (AP).[5] According to this theory, the group member (i.e., firm) does not withhold its contribution to a public good based on a rational calculation of the costs and benefits involved (as with the PD) but rather does so because it is unable to obtain the necessary assurance that other firms will contribute their fair share. In other words, the AP substitutes the more lenient assumption that firms prefer equal or fair shares for the PD's assumption that they invariably try to maximize their individual

net gain. Under the AP, we can expect firms to regulate their own behavior in some larger interest so long as they are confident that other firms are doing the same.

But in a market economy, where decision making is highly dispersed, the prediction of other firms' behavior becomes problematic. As a consequence, no individual firm can be sure that it is not placing itself at a competitive disadvantage by unwittingly interpreting its own obligations more strictly than its competitors do theirs. In these circumstances, all firms are likely to undertake less self-regulation than they would in principle be willing (indeed, eager) to accept.

In spite of their differences, both the PD and the AP involve problems of collective action. In the case of the PD, the problem is that it is always in the rational interest of each firm to put its own individual interests ahead of its collective interests. In the case of the AP, the problem is that of coordinating firms' expectations regarding fair shares.

The sub-optimal supply of business self-regulation can be explained largely in terms of the barriers to collective action by firms. There are three levels of self-regulation: the firm level (corporate social responsibility); the industry level (industry self-regulation); and the level of the economy (business-wide self-regulation). It is only at the third level that the necessary collective action is likely to be of a socially benign variety.

THREE LEVELS OF SELF-REGULATION

Corporate Social Responsibility. Contemporary advocates of corporate social responsibility acknowledge the difficulties of implementing it, but they go on to proclaim its inevitability anyway. In their view, it has to work because nothing else will; at best, the law elicits grudging and literal compliance with certain minimal standards when what is needed is corporations' spontaneous and whole-hearted identification with the *goals* of the law.[6] As Christopher Stone says, there are clear advantages to "encouraging people to act in socially responsible ways because they believe it the 'right thing' to do, rather than because (and thus, perhaps, only to the extent that) they are ordered to do so."[7]

Advocates of social responsibility have offered a number of prescriptions for curing firms' fixation on profit maximization. The weakness of these proposals lies in their assumption that social responsibility can be produced by manipulating the corporation. They overlook the extent to which the firm's behavior is a function of market imperatives rather than of managers' values or corporate structure. . . .

This point is . . . illustrated by cases where competitive pressures have prevented firms from acting responsibly even where it would be in their economic interest to do so. Robert Leone has described how aerosol spray manufacturers were reluctant to abandon the use of fluorocarbon propellants (which were suspected of depleting the ozone layer in the stratosphere) even though the alternative technology was cheaper. The problem was that "any individual company that voluntarily abandoned the use of such propellants ran the risk of a sizeable loss of market share as long as competitors still offered aerosol versions of their products [which the public values for their convenience]."[8] In situations of this kind it is not unusual for responsible firms, aware of their own helplessness, to solicit regulation in order to prevent themselves being taken advantage of by competitors who do not share their scruples about despoiling the environment or injuring the industry's reputation. Thus aerosol manufacturers did not oppose the ban on fluorocarbons in spite of the tenuous scientific evidence of their dangers. Similarly, following the Tylenol poisonings, the pharmaceutical industry sought and obtained from the FDA a uniform national rule on tamper-resistant packaging, because no individual firm had wanted to unilaterally incur the expense of such packaging.[9] The list of examples is endless.

In a market economy, firms are usually *unable* to act in their own collective interests be-

cause "responsible" conduct risks placing the firms that practice it at a competitive disadvantage unless other firms follow suit. Where there is no well-defined standard that enjoys general acceptance, it will take some sort of tacit or overt coordination by firms to supply one. Even if that coordination survives the attentions of the Antitrust Division and the FTC, compliance will still be problematic because of the free-rider problem. Arrow has pointed out that a "code [of behavior] may be of value to . . . all firms if all firms maintain it, and yet it will be to the advantage of any one firm to cheat—in fact the more so, the more other firms are sticking to it."[10] We are therefore faced with the paradox that the voluntary compliance of the majority of firms may depend on the coercive imposition of the code of behavior on the minority of free riders. Thus, although it is fashionable to view voluntarism and coercion as opposites—and to prefer the former for being more humane and, ultimately, effective—they are more properly seen as interdependent.[11]

Industry Self-Regulation. If responsible corporate conduct must ultimately be backed by coercion, there remains the question of who is to administer the coercion. Is self-regulation by a trade association or other industry body a practical alternative to government regulation? The classic solution to the public goods dilemma is "mutual coercion, mutually agreed upon."[12] The possibility of "permitting businesses to coerce themselves" has been raised by Thomas Schelling who adds that such an approach "could appeal to firms which are prepared to incur costs but only on condition that their competitors do also."[13]

The record of industry self-regulation in the United States suggests that it does indeed commonly arise in response to the public goods problem. David A. Garvin explains the development of self-regulation in the advertising industry in this way.[14] Michael Porter has noted that self-regulation may be of particular importance to an emerging industry which is trying to secure consumer acceptance of its products. At this stage of its life cycle, an industry's reputation could be irretrievably injured by the actions of a single producer.[15] Thus the intense self-regulation in the microwave industry is understandable in terms of the industry's need to "overcome the inherent suspicion with which many people view 'new' technology like microwave ovens."[16] Nevertheless, industry self-regulation remains the exception in the United States. This is so because it is a two-edged sword: the powers to prevent trade abuses are the same powers that would be needed to restrain trade.

Because of the potential anti-competitive implications of industry self-regulation, its scope has been strictly limited. Anti-trust laws have significantly circumscribed the powers of trade associations. Legal decisions have proscribed industry-wide attempts to eliminate inferior products or impose ethical codes of conduct. Major oil firms were frustrated by the anti-trust statutes when they tried to establish an information system to rate the quality of oil tankers in an attempt to reduce the incidence of oil spills from substandard vessels.[17] Airlines have had to petition the civil Aeronautics Board for antitrust immunity so that they could discuss ways of coordinating their schedules in order to reduce peak-hour overcrowding at major airports.[18]

In short, industry or trade associations appear to hold out little promise of being transformed into vehicles for industry self-regulation. The fear is too entrenched that industry self-regulation, however plausible its initial rationale, will eventually degenerate into industry protectionism.

Business Self-Regulation. If self-regulation at the level of the individual firm is of limited usefulness because of the free-rider problem, and if industry self-regulation is ruled out by anti-trust considerations, we are left with self-regulation on a business-wide basis, presumably administered by a confederation or peak organization. An "encom-

passing" business organization of this sort would be less vulnerable to the anti-trust objections that can be levelled at industry associations. This is so because the diversity of its membership would inhibit such an organization from aligning itself with the sectional interests of particular firms or industries. Because it would embrace, for example, both producers and consumers of steel, it would be unable to support policies specifically favoring the steel industry (such as a cartel or tariffs) without antagonizing other parts of its membership that would be injured by such policies. A business peak organization would thus be constrained to adopt a pro-competitive posture.[19]

How might a peak organization contribute to resolving the assurance problem and the prisoner's dilemma? In the case of the AP, we saw that the principal impediment to cooperation is the difficulty of predicting others' behavior—without which coordination is impossible. By defining a code of responsible corporate conduct—and/or making authoritative rulings in particular cases—a peak organization might substantially remove this difficulty. In particular, if it is equipped to *monitor* compliance with the code, it could provide cooperating firms with the necessary assurance that they were not shouldering an unfair burden.

The point here is not that a peak organization would necessarily be more competent to make ethical judgments or that its code would be ethically superior; it is that the code would be a *common* one that would enable firms to coordinate their behavior. As we have seen, where there is a multiplicity of standards, there is effectively no standard at all, because no firm can be confident that its competitors are playing by the same rules.

A common external code would also help defuse two contentious issues in top management's relations with the firm's stockholders. First, managers would be at least partly relieved of the task of making subjective (and often thankless) judgments about the firm's obligations to various stakeholders—a task for which they are generally not equipped by training, by aptitude, or by inclination. Second, such a code would permit them to heed society's demands that the firm behave responsibly while at the same time protecting them from the charge that their generosity at the stockholders' expense was jeopardizing the firm's competitive position.[20]

So far we have assumed that each firm *wants* to cooperate (i.e., to contribute to the realization of the public good, in this case by acting responsibly) provided other firms do the same. As long as there is some means of coordinating their behavior, then firms can be counted on to cooperate. What happens if we allow for the likelihood that, while most firms may be disposed to comply with the code, some number of opportunistic firms will choose to defect?

A code of conduct—even if only morally binding—can be expected to exert a powerful constraining influence on the behavior of would-be defectors. Such a code would embody "good practice" and so would serve as a standard against which corporate behavior could be judged in individual cases. Consequently, firms which violated the code would be isolated and the spotlight of public indignation would be turned on them. In the cases where moral suasion failed, the code would still offer certain advantages (at least from business's standpoint). First, an adverse ruling by the peak organization would serve to distance the business community as a whole from the actions of a deviant firm and so would counter the impression that business was winking at corporate abuses.[21] Second, the standards defined by the peak organization might become the basis for subsequent legislation or regulatory rulemaking. By setting the agenda in this fashion, the peak organization might forestall more extreme or onerous proposals.

However, the defection of even a handful of firms (if it involved repeated or gross violation of the code) would undermine the social contract on which the consent of the majority was based. Their continued compliance would likely be conditional on the code

being effectively policed. Therefore, it seems inconceivable that business self-regulation could be based on moral suasion alone....

Thus, if we modify the AP to reflect the real-world probability that some number of opportunistic firms will disregard the code, the case for investing the peak organization with some powers of compulsion becomes unanswerable. The case is stronger still if we accept the axiom of the PD that firms will invariably defect when it is in their narrow self-interest to do so. Some form of sovereign to enforce the terms of the social contract then becomes indispensable....

THE CONSEQUENCES OF PEAK ORGANIZATION

Peak (or "encompassing") organizations are not merely larger special interest organizations. By virtue of the breadth and heterogeneity of their membership, they are transformed into a qualitatively different phenomenon. Indeed, peak organizations are likely to exert pressure on the behavior of their members in the direction of the public interest.

In the interests of its own stability, any organization must resist efforts by parts of its membership to obtain private benefits at the expense of other parts. It follows that the more inclusive or encompassing the organization, the larger the fraction of society it represents, and so the higher the probability that it will oppose self-serving behavior (by sections of its membership) that inflicts external costs on the rest of society....

The officers of business peak organizations in Germany, Japan, and Sweden have a quasi-public conception of their role that is far removed from the American interest group model. According to Andrew Shonfield, Germany's two business *Spitzenverbände* "have typically seen themselves as performing an important public role, as guardians of the long-term interests of the nation's industries."[22] The same finding is reported by an American scholar who evidently has difficulty in taking at face value the claims made by leaders of the BDI (Confederation of German Industry): "To avoid giving an impression that it is an interest group with base, selfish and narrow aims, the BDI constantly identifies its own goals with those of the entire nation."[23] Finally, David Bresnick recently studied the role of the national confederation of employers and trade unions of six countries in the formation and implementation of youth employment policies. In Germany, these policies were largely made and administered by the confederations themselves. In Bresnick's words, "The system in Germany has evolved with minimal government regulation and maximum protection of the interests of the young, while promoting the interests of the corporations, trade unions and the society in general. It has reduced the government role to one of occasional intervenor. It has taken the government out of the business of tax collector and achieved a degree of social compliance that is extraordinary."[24]

A similar account is given by Ezra Vogel of the role of the Japanese business peak organization, *Keidanren*.[25] Keidanren concentrates on issues of interest to the business community as a whole and "cannot be partial to any single group or any industrial sector." Vogel reports that Japanese business leaders are surprised at "the extent to which American businessmen thought only of their own company and were unprepared to consider business problems from a broader perspective." In Japan, this "higher level of aggregation of interests within the business community tends to ensure that the highest level politicians also think in comparably broad terms."[26] . . .

While the data on . . . German and Japanese peak organizations are too unsystematic to constitute a strict test concerning the consequences of peak organizations, they do shed a revealing light on the role such an organization might play in the U.S. In particular, in administering a system of self-regulation, a peak organization would be in a position to take into account a broader range of interests than is catered for by our present structures of interest representation. Also, a peak organization might promote more harmonious business-government relations without entailing the cooptation or capture of either one by the other.

PROSPECTS

What are the prospects of [a] system of business self-regulation administered by a peak organization taking root in the U.S.? What incentives would an American peak organization be able to rely on to secure firms' compliance with its standards and rulings? We have seen that, by itself, recognition of the mutuality of gains to be had from a peak organization cannot guarantee such compliance. In order to overcome the free-rider problem, the would-be peak organization must be able to offer firms private benefits or "selective incentives" that are unavailable outside the organization but that are sufficiently attractive to induce firms to comply.[27]

Students of organizations have identified an array of incentives—both positive and negative—that have been used to attract and hold members. These include: selective access to information (e.g., about government actions, technical developments, and commercial practices) under the organization's control; regulation of jurisdictional disputes between members; predatory price-cutting; boycotts; withdrawal of credit; public disparagement; fines; social status; and conviviality. . . . Finally, purposive incentives—"intangible rewards that derive from the sense of satisfaction of having contributed to the attainment of a worthwhile cause"—have provided at least a transient basis for organization. . . .

The difficulties encountered by trade associations that try to influence their members' behavior are compounded in the case of a would-be peak organization. A peak organization has access to fewer selective benefits with which to maintain members' allegiance, and its goals are even further removed from the immediate concerns of most firms. Moreover, these goals tend to be public goods (e.g., maintaining the private enterprise system or avoiding higher taxes). Wilson notes that "no single businessman has an incentive to contribute to the attainment of what all would receive if the organized political efforts are successful." In these circumstances, "the creation and maintenance of an association such as the [U.S.] Chamber, which seeks to represent all business in general and no business in particular, has been a considerable achievement."[28]

The Chamber, of course, seeks only to speak for business's collective interests. It is not difficult to imagine how much more precarious its existence would be if it also tried to set and enforce standards of conduct. It follows that if trade associations have generally been ineffective except when their powers have been underwritten by the government, a peak organization is *a fortiori* likely to be dependent on government support. And, in fact, in Western Europe, it appears that "many of the peak associations . . . reached their hegemonic status with major contributions from the more or less official recognition of key government agencies."[29]

What form would such public support have to take in the U.S.? It might involve waiving anti-trust laws in the case of the peak organization, e.g., by permitting it to punish free-riding behavior by imposing fines or administering boycotts. Government might grant it certain prerogatives—e.g., privileged access to key policy deliberations or agency rule-making, which it might in turn use to obtain leverage over recalcitrant firms. The government might require—as in Japan[30]—that every firm be a registered member of the peak organization. All these actions would serve to strengthen the peak organization vis-à-vis its members.

However, the chances are slight that actions of this kind could be taken in the U.S. In the first place, as Salisbury says, "American political culture is so rooted in individualist assumptions that [interest] groups have

no integral place."[31] In contrast with Europe, associations have not been officially incorporated into the process of policy formation; bureaucrats in the U.S. deal directly with constituent units (individual firms, hospitals, universities, etc.) not with associations.[32] Given the dubious legitimacy of interest organizations in general, it seems improbable that semi-official status or privileged access would be granted to a peak organization.

A second obstacle is the structure of American government. The fragmentation of power in the American system—federalism, separation of powers, legislators nominated and elected from single-member districts—has created multiple points of access for interests that want to influence the policy process. Wilson has persuasively argued that a country's interest group structure is largely a reflection of its political structure. Thus a centralized, executive-led government is likely to generate strong national interest associations and, conversely, "the greater decentralization and dispersion of political authority in the United States helps explain the greater variety of politically active American voluntary associations."[33] In the American context, then, it is virtually inconceivable that a peak organization could secure a monopolistic or privileged role in public policymaking in even a few key areas; but without superior access of this sort it is deprived of one of the few resources available to influence its members' behavior. . . .

CONCLUSION

. . . This article has examined the ways it might be possible for firms to coordinate their behavior (both in their own larger interests and the public interest) while at the same time minimizing the risk that this coordination would be exploited for anti-social purposes. Such a benign outcome could be obtained by permitting collective action to be administered by a business-wide peak organization. At this level of coordination, a competitive market economy could coexist with effective self-regulation. However, the United States—given its distinctive political institutions—is not likely to provide a congenial soil for such an organization to take root.

REFERENCES

1. Mancur Olson, *The Logic of Collective Action,* (Cambridge, MA: Harvard University Press, 1965).
2. Ibid., p. 2.
3. Ibid., p. 44.
4. Russell Hardin, "Collective Action as an Agreeable n-Prisoner's Dilemma," *Behavioral Science,* vol. 16 (1971), pp. 472–79.
5. C. Ford Runge, "Institutions and the Free Rider: The Assurance Problem in Collective Action," *Journal of Politics,* vol. 46 (1984), pp. 154–81.
6. Cf. Henry Mintzberg, "The Case for Corporate Social Responsibility," *Journal of Business Strategy,* vol. 14 (1983), pp. 3–15.
7. Christopher Stone, *Where the Law Ends,* (New York, NY: Harper Torchbooks, 1975), p. 112.
8. Robert A. Leone, "Competition and the Regulatory Boom," in Dorothy Tella, ed., *Government Regulation of Business: Its Growth, Impact, and Future,* (Washington, D.C.: Chamber of Commerce of the United States, 1979), p. 34.
9. Susan Bartlett Foote, "Corporate Responsibility in a Changing Legal Environment," *California Management Review,* vol. 26 (1984), pp. 217–28.
10. Kenneth J. Arrow, "Social Responsibility and Economic Efficiency," *Public Policy,* vol. 21 (1973), p. 315.
11. See Thomas Schelling on "the false dichotomy of voluntarism and coercion," in "Command and Control," in James W. McKie, ed., *Social Responsibility and the Business Predicament,* (Washington, D.C.: Brookings, 1974), p. 103.
12. The phrase is from Garrett Hardin's "The Tragedy of the Commons," *Science,* vol. 162 (1968), p. 1247.
13. Schelling, op. cit., p. 103.
14. David Garvin, "Can Industry Self-Regulation Work?" *California Management Review,* vol. 25 (1983), p. 42.
15. Michael Porter, *Competitive Strategy,* (New York, NY: Free Press, 1980), p. 230.
16. Thomas P. Grumbly, "Self-Regulation: Private Vice and Public Virtue Revisited," in Eugene Bardach and Robert Kagan, eds., *Social Regulation: Strategies for Reform* (San Francisco, CA: Institute for Contemporary Studies, 1982), p. 97.
17. Garvin, op. cit., p. 155, 156.
18. Christopher Conte, "Transport Agency's Dole Vows to Restrict Traffic at 6 Busy Airports if Carriers Don't," *Wall Street Journal,* August 16, 1984, p. 10.
19. Mancur Olson, *The Rise and Decline of Nations,* (New Haven, CT: Yale University Press, 1982), pp. 47–48.
20. These objections lie at the heart of the complaint that the doctrine of corporate social responsibility provides no operational guidelines to assist managers in making responsible choices. The most sophisticated (but, I think, ultimately unsuccessful) attempt to supply an objective, external standard (located in what they call the public policy process) is Lee Preston and James Post, *Private Management and Public Policy,* (Englewood Cliffs, NJ: Prentice-Hall, 1975).
21. See on this point the remarks of Walter A. Haas, Jr., of Levi Strauss quoted in Leonard Silk and David Vogel, *Ethics and Profits* (New York, NY: Simon & Schuster, 1976), pp. 25–27.
22. Andrew Shonfield, *Modern Capitalism,* (New York and London: Oxford University Press, 1965), p. 245.
23. Gerard Baunthal, *The Federation of German Industries in Politics,* (Ithaca, NY: Cornell University Press, 1965), pp. 56–57.
24. David Bresnick, "The Youth Employment Policy Dance: Interest Groups in the Formulation and Implementation of Public Policy," paper presented at the American Political Science Association meetings in Denver, September 2–5, 1982, p. 33.
25. Ezra Vogel, *Japan as Number 1,* (New York, NY: Harper Colophon, 1979), chapter 5.
26. Ibid.
27. This is, of course, the essence of the argument in Olson's *Logic,* op. cit. This section draws heavily on James Q. Wilson, *Political Organizations,* op. cit.; Robert H. Salisbury, "Why No Corporatism in America?," in Philippe Schmitter and Gerhard Lehmbruch, *Trends Toward Corporatist Intermediation,* (Beverly Hills: Sage, 1979); and Philippe Schmitter and Donald Brand, "Organizing Capitalists in the United States: The Advantages and

Disadvantages of Exceptionalism," presented at a workshop at the International Institute of Management, Berlin, November 14–16, 1979.
28. James Q. Wilson, *Political Organizations* (New York, NY: Basic Books, 1973), pp. 153, 161.

29. Salisbury, op. cit., p. 215. See also Wilson, op. cit., p. 82.
30. Vogel, *Japan as Number 1*, op. cit., p. 112.
31. Salisbury, op. cit. p. 222.
32. Schmitter and Brand, op. cit., p. 71.
33. Wilson, op. cit., p. 83; see generally chapter 5.

Regulation and Paternalism

Steven Kelman

Opposition to paternalism plays an important role in the current national debate over the appropriate scope for government regulation, especially consumer protection regulation on behalf of safety and health. It is frequently summoned in condemning calls to ban saccharin or laetrile. It is pronounced likewise against proposals to require people to wear seatbelts or motorcycle helmets. And it appears in criticisms of safety standards for lawnmowers or autos, since such standards, although they neither ban nor mandate use of the product in question, do require that consumers pay for certain safety features if they wish to buy the product. The antipaternalistic contention is simple. If people know the risks of, say, saccharin and choose to run these risks for themselves in order to obtain the benefits they believe they will gain, who are we to interfere with that choice?

I believe that it is correct to oppose paternalism, but incorrect to tar most government consumer protection health and safety regulations with a paternalistic brush. . . .

There are, in other words, good nonpaternalistic arguments for such regulation, although these arguments are often mistaken

for paternalistic ones. In the final section, I will discuss explicitly the question of whether there are ever any occasions when regulation might be justified on avowedly paternalistic grounds. . . .

DECISION-MAKING COSTS AND VOLUNTARY RENUNCIATION OF CHOICE AUTHORITY

In this section, I argue that when there are costs associated with deciding what choice to make, it is rational in some situations for an individual to renounce his authority to make the choice for himself, and to hand over such authority to a third party who will make the choice in the individual's interest. Such third-party choices are not paternalistic, because they are not made against the person's wishes. They introduce a new category, separate both from choices one makes oneself and from choices made paternalistically. Much government safety regulation of consumer products, I believe, falls into this category.

The probability that one would want to

From Steven Kelman, "Regulation and Paternalism," *Public Policy* 29 (Spring 1981). Copyright © 1981 by the President and Fellows of Harvard College.

renounce the authority to choose increases (1) the more that the decision-making costs for the person exceed those for the third party, and (2) the closer the choice the third party makes is to the choice the person would have made. . . .

The costs of decision-making include information-gathering costs, information-processing costs, and possibly psychological costs of choice. Information-gathering costs are the costs of determining the existence of all the relevant features across which the different types of a product can vary and the different values these variables take across the different types of a product. Information-processing costs are the costs of calculating the implication of the different values for a judgment of the benefits of the product, given one's preferences. Psychological costs are the frustration that may be felt from information overload or the trauma that may be experienced from having to make difficult choices.

An immense disservice to intelligent discussion of the safety regulation of consumer products occurs because of the tendency to base such discussions on a small number of dramatic instances—saccharin, seatbelts, laetrile. A statement such as, "People know that it's more risky to drive without seatbelts than with them, and if they choose to take that risk to avoid the discomfort of wearing the belts, that should be up to them," may be made with a straight face. People know the feature they are making a choice about (that is, they know what seatbelts are). They know what values the variable can take (the seatbelts may be worn or not worn). They know the implications of these different values for their judgments about the choice (wearing seatbelts decreases risk but may increase discomfort).

The problem is that such individual dramatic examples are unrepresentative of the universe of choices that consumers would have to make for themselves in a world where they had to make all decisions about the safety features of products they buy themselves. Statements about consumers knowing the risks of failing to use seatbelts

or consuming saccharin and choosing to bear them are plausible. Statements such as the following are far less so: "People know that if the distance between the slats on the infant crib is $2\frac{3}{8}$th inches there is little risk that an infant will strangle himself falling through the slats, while if the distance is $3\frac{1}{4}$th inches the risk is much greater, and if they choose to take this risk to get a crib that is less expensive, that should be up to them." The reader may ask himself if he would feel confident identifying which one of the four following substances that may be present in food is far more risky than the other three: calcium hexametaphosphate, methyl paraben, sodium benzoate, and trichloroethylene. Or he may ask himself how confident he would feel making decisions about what safety features to buy in order to guard against power lawnmower accidents or to protect against a radio exploding or electrocuting him. If he does know, how confident does he feel that he understands the risks associated with various levels of the substance? Is five parts per million of benzene hexachloride a lot or a little? If the bacteria count in frozen egg is one million per gram, should we be alarmed?

What these examples suggest—they could be multiplied manyfold—is that consumers do not ordinarily have anything approaching perfect information for judging the safety of most consumer products themselves, the misleading examples from widely publicized regulatory controversies over issues such as seatbelts and saccharin to the contrary notwithstanding. Compared with their knowledge of product features such as appearance, convenience, or taste, knowledge of safety features is typically very small.

One conclusion sometimes drawn is that lack of knowledge demonstrates lack of concern. If people do not know about safety features, it is sometimes argued, that means they do not care about them. This conclusion does not follow from the premise. When information-gathering costs something, the amount of information gathered depends not only on the perceived benefits of the information but also on how costly it would be to gather. I may "care" about two product features equally, but if information on one is cheap to obtain and information on the other is expensive, I will gather more information on the first feature than on the second. Information on product features such as appearance or convenience is often relatively easy to get. Information on a product's appearance is garnered by simple observation. For a product that does not cost very much and that is frequently repurchased, experience is a cheap way to gain information about the product's convenience or taste. I may buy a certain brand of orange soda or paper tissue and try it. Then I will know whether I like it.

By contrast, gathering information on safety features is often very costly. Frequently, arcane or technical facts must be understood, and the recourse to experience is not available in the same way as with many other product features. Using a risky product does not always lead to an accident. Drinking a brand of orange soda will always lead to information on its taste, but not on its additives. To go through the pain of an injury or illness is a very high cost to pay for gathering information about a product's safety. . . .

The first criterion for a situation in which it would be rational for an individual to hand over decision-making authority to a third party is when the third party can gather the information more cheaply than the individual can. This criterion often applies in the case of safety features. The per consumer cost of gathering safety information is likely to be much less for an expert third party gathering it for a large group of consumers than for an individual. An expert has an easier time finding out about and evaluating different technical safety features. Since only one gathering process need occur, its cost can be divided among the large group for whom it is undertaken, rather than having to be separately borne by each individual consumer assembling similar information for himself.

The second cost associated with the act of choosing is the cost in information-process-

ing. This involves taking information about a product feature and evaluating its significance in light of one's preferences. Memory and other cognitive limitations make it costly or simply impossible to process large amounts of information about a product, even if the information is available. Information-processing costs clearly vary across people and situations, but the more information that must be processed, the higher the processing costs. Furthermore, there is evidence that at some point "information overload" occurs, where the brain has too much information to process. Under the circumstances, one's skill at evaluating information can decrease so much that the choice reflects one's preferences worse than a choice made where less information was available, but could be processed better. . . . Overload may appear not only when we must process a lot of information for a single choice, but also when we must process little information for many choices.

Choice may carry with it psychological costs as well. To be sure, there are many instances, as noted earlier, where people relish the opportunity to choose. In other instances, people might not relish the process, but believe that a choice made by a third party is likely to be so inferior to the choice they make themselves that they are willing to pay possible psychological costs. But this is not always the case. Life would be unbearable if we constantly had to make all decisions for ourselves. Information overload may produce not only evaluations poorer in quality but also feelings of frustration growing out of the realization that our brains are not processing information as well as they usually do. Furthermore, people can find some kinds of decisions very unpleasant to make. These might include choices that are complicated, ones that involve thinking about distasteful things, or ones where all the alternatives are disagreeable. Everyday experience is filled with instances where people try to avoid making unpleasant decisions—if this were not the case, Harry Truman would never have placed the sign "The buck stops here" in his office. Linus, the Peanuts comic strip character, expressed the trauma that can accompany difficult choice when he said, "No problem is so big or so complicated that it can't be run away from." . . .

As with costs of information-gathering, the costs of information-processing and the psychological costs of choice are likely frequently to be lower for an expert third party, as far as safety is concerned, than for the individual. Decisions about safety, because they involve so much technical information, are likely to be those where information overload makes processing costly. They are also likely to be decisions that many people find unpleasant to make. They require that one contemplate the prospect of illness, disfigurement, or even death. They also necessitate thought about tradeoffs between saving money and taking risks—thoughts that most people also find unpleasant, as can be seen by looking at how politicians, agency officials, and even business spokesmen themselves squirm when such topics are raised. In fact, I believe this uneasiness is one of the main reasons why safety decisions are handed over to government. . . .

Objections to the Information Argument for Intervention

Different objections might be made to the argument developed so far. One that is frequently heard runs something like this: if the consumer has difficulty making choices about safety features because he lacks information, then let the government see that the requisite information is provided, rather than mandating safety features or banning products. To do more, the argument goes, would be to throw out the baby of individual choice with the bathwater of imperfect information. . . .

Another objection is sometimes raised: Voluntary renunciation of consumer choice to *some* third party need not justify *government* standards or product bans. Consumers might hire a personal agent to make the choice for them. Or the government might be limited to certify that a product meets whatever safety standards the agency determines to be appropriate. All these methods, it is argued, allow voluntary renunciation of the authority to choose without mandatory government regulation.

I will first consider arguments claiming that the government's role should be limited to information provision—or even that such an information provision role is unjustified. For the government to mandate provision of information or to provide it itself does indeed lower information-gathering costs. To require its dissemination in nontechnical form lowers these costs further. And to make the information conveniently available (as part of labeling) lowers it still further. These steps sometimes do lower decision-making costs enough to make it worthwhile for consumers to retain their authority to choose. An example would be in the area of product quality, where the psychological costs of choice are low and preferences differ widely across consumers. In these cases, government should stick to such tasks. But in other situations, all these steps still would not lower decision-making costs enough to make it rational for a consumer to retain his authority to choose. Under such a regime, consumers still might be confronted frequently with columns of fine print presenting large numbers of product features and risk information about each. The information-processing costs of evaluating this information in the light of one's preferences remain unaffected by the cheaper information-gathering. Any psychological decision-making costs are unaffected as well. . . .

Let us turn now to objections that the third party need not be the government. Consumers might choose to let decisions be made for them by friends they trust or by expert agents they hire to make the decisions in their interests. Mandatory government regulation, the argument continues, is a poor vehicle for making decisions that a consumer chooses to renounce, because it binds not only those who choose *not* to make the choice themselves, but also those who *would* have wanted to do so.

Certainly there are instances where choice by agents that a consumer seeks out might be preferable to decisions by government. Consumers use doctors as agents, for instance, and to some limited extent retail stores act as agents as well. One advantage such choices have is that the agent can be apprised of the client's individual preferences. By contrast, a government agency must make a single choice, despite the existence of diverse preferences among citizens. But in other instances, looking for, paying, and monitoring a privately hired agent would be more expensive than having the government undertake the same tasks. This greater expense might outweigh the advantages of a choice personally tailored to the client's preferences. Furthermore, the private provision of the information-gathering aspect of the agent's job creates the same public goods problems as any private provision of information. And for a person to seek an agent in any individual instance, he must have enough knowledge of the existence of dimensions along which he wishes to judge the product in question to know that he needs an agent in the first place.

Another way for a person to renounce his authority to choose without requiring mandatory government regulation is for the government to certify the safety of products and for the consumer, who wished to renounce his authority, to choose simply to buy the certified product. In certifying a product, the government would decide on appropriate safety features. The only difference would be that it would not be mandatory that all products comply with the features. Only those that did comply, however, would be certified. If a consumer decides to buy a certified product, he in effect has let the government make his decision for him. But those who wish to decide for themselves would have the choice of buying a product without the certified safety feature package.

Choosing to buy certified products might be an appropriate form for voluntary renunciation of the authority to choose. But it might not be a consumer's preferred alternative either. Most important as a reason for preferring mandatory regulation to certification is the fear that despite one's general resolution to buy only certified products, one might be tempted in individual cases to depart from one's resolution and buy noncertified ones. . . .

Even if we end up not giving in to temptation, we might wish to be spared temptation so as to avoid the anxiety costs of realizing that one might, at any time, give in. Thus, a person might well prefer mandatory regulation to certification out of fear that in many specific instances, with one lawnmower in front of him that is certified and another that is not, he might "take a chance" and get the cheaper, noncertified one, although as a general matter of considered reflection he would wish to buy only certified products. People frequently choose to have an alternative withheld from them at later times just to avoid temptation. . . .

It may be accepted that there are people who would rather have government set mandatory safety standards than hire private agents or have the government certify product safety. Yet it still might be protested that others who would prefer to make the decisions themselves (or to hire their own agents or choose with the help of government certification) should not be forced to pay for safety features they do not want.

Under the circumstances, one group or the other will end up being hurt. Either those opposed to mandatory safety standards are harmed by being forced to buy products with mandated features, or those favoring mandatory standards are hurt by having to do without the mandatory standards they seek. Whether the social decision finally made responds to the wishes of the first group or the second has, then, external effects on the group whose wishes are denied. . . . Those seeking mandatory regulation are demanding something that will help themselves and hurt those who would prefer to choose for themselves. The latter group, then, may be seen as passive victims of the acts of those demanding regulation. The *prima facie* duty to do justice suggests sympathy with passive victims against active encroachers. Nevertheless, considerations of the size of the groups seeking and wishing to avoid regulation, as well as of the nature of the interference contemplated, are relevant to such judgments. In regard to the size of the groups in the case of government safety regulation, there exist unambiguous survey data. In a 1974 poll, respondents were asked whether the government should "make sure that each packaged, canned, or frozen food is safe to eat." An overwhelming 97% agreed, a degree of unanimity hard to replicate for any government policy. In a 1976 poll, respondents were asked a similar question about government product safety standards and 85% agreed.[1] As for the extent of interference, it is not generally great. Those opposed to regulation are interfered with to the extent of having to pay some extra money for safety features they would have preferred to avoid. Their homes are not broken into. They are not restrained by physical force from moving around where they wish. Their fortunes are not decimated. My own conclusion is that it would be wrong to prevent the vast majority of Americans who prefer to turn the general run of decisions about product safety over to the government from doing so.

The figures on the percentages of those who wish to turn safety decisions over to the government also shed light on the earlier brief examination of whether decisions made by government safety regulators were likely to be sufficiently similar to those that consumers would make themselves, if fully informed, to make it rational for consumers voluntarily to hand such choices over to regulators. If government agencies did make decisions frequently that wildly departed from those that consumers would make themselves, one would expect the survey results to have been dramatically different. Instead, they show a broad vote of confidence for the efforts of government agencies regulating product safety. . . .

EXTERNAL EFFECTS AND THE OVERRULING OF A PERSON'S OWN CHOICE

John Stuart Mill affirmed in *On Liberty* that the restriction against interference with a person's authority to choose applied to acts that affected only the individual himself and not to those acts affecting others. Ever since Mill, however, this distinction has come under withering attack. Government intervention in people's choices may occur not out of a desire to overrule paternalistically an individual's choices insofar as they regard only himself, but out of a desire to protect others against the negative consequences of those choices. Thus, banning saccharin or requiring people to wear seatbelts might be justified on nonpaternalistic grounds even if people did not want to hand these decisions to the government, because of the effects bladder cancer or auto accidents have, not on the individual himself, but on others. The distinction between intervention on paternalistic grounds and intervention on the grounds that others must be protected against the negative consequences of a person's behavior is often lost in the general public debate on regulation, where opposition to both kinds of intervention tends to get lumped together as complaints against "government interference." Thus, the resentment of businessmen against OSHA or EPA regulations should not be confused with resentment against a bureaucrat who believes he knows what is good for a person better than the person does himself.

The discussions of external effects, such as pollution, in introductory economics textbooks tend to obscure the issue, because they imply that most actions lack external effects. That "no man is an island" dashes any attempt to make such neat categorizations. . . .

If a person becomes sick or is injured or if he dies because he purchased an unsafe product, clearly his action in buying the product had external effects on friends and loved ones. If a person is insured, other policyholders ultimately foot the bills. If a person is not insured and suffers great financial hardship, other members of society still end up paying. When the victim appears before us after a sad fate has befallen him, the rest of us pay cash to help the uninsured victim out—or pay in the form of the guilty feelings occasioned by turning our backs on the victim, even if we attempt the justification that the victim made his bed and now should have to lie in it. The fact that we end up either saving people from the really bad consequences of their choices or feeling guilty if we do not is an argument, based on external effects and not on paternalism, for intervening in the original choices. Consequently, we require people to provide for their old age through Social Security, give the poor in-kind rather than cash transfers, or mandate safety regulations.

None of this means that our every move should be subject to government restrictions. Almost everyone who has thought seriously about the implications of the ubiquity of external effects has come to the conclusion that society must establish which acts individuals have a right to do or refrain from doing, despite the harm the act may inflict on others, and which are too harmful to permit to go unhindered or be left undone, despite the fact that the individual would prefer to behave otherwise. . . .

To decide in a given case whether an individual should have the right to make decisions about what risks to take, despite the harm that the bad consequences of such decisions can cause others, raises difficult questions to which answers cannot be cranked out deductively. It will not do to argue, as is sometimes done, that external effects arguments must never be used to justify restricting risks because it would be possible to use such arguments to eradicate all exercises of liberty. For the fact is that *everyone,* even libertarians, recognizes that at some point the external effects of an individual's acts become great enough to justify taking away the individual's right to act. Thus, all agree that murder or assault are not rightful displays of liberty. We cannot escape a controversial balancing process in which the extent of the external effects that the person's actions produce, the importance of the act for the individual, and possible deontological considerations regarding *prima facie* duties, are weighed against one another. . . .

The purpose of this article has not been to defend or criticize any specific example of government safety regulation. Rather, I have attempted to defend the justifiability, in principle, of such regulation against the specific accusation that it inevitably involves paternalism and hence should be condemned. I have agreed with the general condemnation of paternalism, while suggesting nonpaternalistic justifications for such intervention and arguing that there are certain cases where cautious paternalistic intervention might be justified. . . .

NOTE

1. These figures are from Food and Drug Administration (1976). *Consumer Nutrition Knowledge Survey, Report I,* Washington, DC: FDA, p. 39.

Criteria for Government Regulations

Norman E. Bowie

In a penetrating analysis of law (*The Morality of Law*), Lon Fuller identified eight conditions that any legal system must fulfill if it is to be considered a good legal system.[1] These eight conditions include (1) laws must be general (laws are not made to apply to one individual), (2) laws must be publicized, (3) laws cannot be made retroactively, (4) laws must be understandable, (5) the set of laws should not contain rules that are contradictory, (6) laws must be within the power of citizens to obey them, (7) laws must maintain a certain stability through time, and (8) laws as announced must be in agreement with their actual administration.

Fuller's eight conditions for a good legal system have such a ring of self-evidence about them that explanatory comments can be kept to a minimum. However, in the course of supplying some explanatory comment, the extent to which government regulation violates these eight conditions for good law will become obvious. The condition of generality is clearly related to the analyses of justice and the universalizability required by Kant's categorical imperative. Rules are not directed toward a single person but rather are to apply to a class of persons. Relevantly similar persons are to be treated similarly. What is a reason in one case must be a reason in all similar cases.

Despite this requirement of generality, much regulatory law proceeds in an opposite direction. Fuller says,

> In recent history perhaps the most notable failure to achieve general rules has been that of certain of our regulatory agencies, particularly those charged with allocative functions. . . . [T]hey were embarked on their careers in the belief that by proceeding at first case by case they would gradually gain an insight which would enable them to develop general standards of decision. In some cases this hope has been almost completely disappointed; this is notably so in the case of the Civil Aeronautics Board and the Federal Communications Commission.[2]

If general rules are essential to good regulatory law as has been argued, then the case-by-case method is inadequate. If the government takes a position regarding water pollution from one of Bethlehem Steel's plants, the president of Bethlehem Steel should be able to conclude that the government will take a similar position on similar conditions at all Bethlehem's plants. Moreover, the president of Bethlehem Steel should be able to conclude that the same position will be taken when the same situation exists at other competing steel plants. If Fuller's description is right, the state of regulatory law is such that the president of Bethlehem Steel could *not* conclude that a similar position would be taken and hence much regulatory law is seriously deficient.

The second condition is that the laws be publicized. This condition goes hand in hand with the conditions of generality and stability. One cannot obey the law if one does not know what the law is. Regulatory law does conform—on the whole—to this condition. The regulations do appear in federal documents such as the *Federal Register.*

Adapted from Norman E. Bowie, *Business Ethics*, pp. 118–124, © 1982. Reprinted by permission of Prentice Hall, Englewood Cliffs, N.J.

However, any academic researcher who has worked with government documents knows that finding a rule or regulation is often no easy task. Large corporations have legal teams to assist them in knowing what the law is. However, as government regulations grow, the small business houses suffer a distinct handicap in their capability to know the law. To the extent the regulations change rapidly over time, the publicity requirement becomes harder and harder to meet.

Third, laws should not be made retroactively, and generally they are not. The reason for this requirement is clear. Laws are designed to guide behavior. A retroactive law violates the fundamental purpose of laws since it obviously cannot guide conduct. It punishes behavior that was legal at the time it was done. Business leaders complain that government regulators at least approach violating this condition when they threaten firms with penalties for environmental damage when there is no way for the firm to have known that some of its activities were causing environmental damage. A company should not be penalized for damage it caused to the earth's ozone layer when it produced fluorocarbons in the 1960s.

The fourth requirement of clarity is, to many business executives, the condition that government regulations most often violate. Loaded with jargon and bad grammer, these regulations often present a nightmare for highly trained corporate legal staffs and an impossible situation for small companies. An example to illustrate the point:

> 212.75 Crude Oil Produced and Sold from Unitized Properties.
> (b) Definitions. For purposes of this section—"Current unit cumulative deficiency" means (1) for months prior to June 1, 1979, the total number of barrels by which production and sale of crude oil from the unitized property was less than the unit base production control level subsequent to the first month (following the establishment of a unit base production control level for that unitized property) in which any crude oil produced and sold from that unit was eligible to be classified as actual new crude oil (without regard to whether the amount of actual new crude oil was exceeded by the amount of imputed new crude oil), minus the total number of barrels of domestic crude oil produced and sold in each prior month from that unitized property (following the establishment of a unit base production control level for that unitized property) which was in excess of the unit base production control level for that month, but which was not eligible to be classified as actual new crude oil because of this requirement to reduce the amount of actual new crude oil in each month by the amount of the current unit cumulative deficiency.[3]

Fifth, a system of laws that contains laws contradicting one another is inadequate because a situation covered by the contradictory laws requires the impossible. Fuller focuses on the federal Food, Drug, and Cosmetic Act.

> Section 704 of that act defines the conditions under which an inspector may enter a factory; one of these conditions is that he first obtain the permission of the owner. Section 331 makes it a crime for the owner of the factory to refuse "to permit entry or inspection as authorized by section 704." The Act seems, then, to say that the inspector has a right to enter the factory but that the owner has a right to keep him out by refusing permission.[4]

Actually, the instances of contradiction cited by businesspersons are not so obvious as those in the case given. Most contradictions in laws governing business practice result from two sources: (1) from contradictory rules issued by independent agencies responsible for the same area and (2) from contradictory rules issued by independent agencies on separate matters but when applied in a specfic case lead to contradiction.

To illustrate just how complex the issue of the contradictory nature of law can become, consider, for example, the recent Sears suit against a number of federal agencies or officers, including the attorney general, the secretary of Labor, the chairman of the Equal

Opportunity Commission (EOC), and seven other cabinet officers and federal agencies. The issue of contention is antidiscrimination statutes. Employers like Sears are not to discriminate on the basis of race, sex, age, or physical and mental handicaps. Yet the employer is required to give preference to veterans. But since veterans are overwhelmingly male, the required preference for veterans is in contradiction with the requirement that no preference be given to sex. Preferences for veterans ipso facto give preference to males. It is reported that

> The Company [Sears] asked the court to grant an injunction requiring the defendants "to coordinate the employment of anti-discrimination statutes" and to issue uniform guidelines that would tell employers "how to resolve existing conflicts between affirmative-action requirements based on race and sex and those based on veterans' status, age, and physical or mental handicaps."[5]

Without judging either Sears' motives for the suit or its behavior with respect to nondiscrimination, the Sears request for consistency is warranted in point of logic and good regulation.

Sixth, laws requiring the impossible violate the fundamental purpose of law—the guidance of human conduct. This point seems so obvious that it hardly needs comment. Yet a tradition is growing in legal circles that clearly violates this principle. Strict liability holds a person or corporation liable for an act even when they are not responsible for it. Fuller points out the absurdity of allowing strict liability to expand so that it covers all activities.

> If strict liability were to attend, not certain specified forms of activity, but all activities, the conception of a causal connection between the act and the resulting injury would be lost. A poet writes a sad poem. A rejected lover reads it and is so depressed that he commits suicide. Who "caused" the loss of his life? Was it the poet, or the lady who jilted the deceased, or perhaps the teacher who aroused

his interest in poetry? A man in a drunken rage shoots his wife. Who among those concerned with this event share the responsibility for its occurrence—the killer himself, the man who lent the gun to him, the liquor dealer who provided the gin, or was it perhaps the friend who dissuaded him from securing a divorce that would have ended an unhappy alliance?[6]

Hence, to conform to this requirement of good law, the government regulations of business must rest on an adequate theory that delineates a class of undesirable acts that can result from business activity and then assesses the extent to which business must be shown to be responsible for their acts before being held liable. It may well be, for example, that some activities (blasting) are so dangerous that strict liability should be invoked to discourage the activity in question. However, in many cases strict liability is not the appropriate legal category and business people are quite right in being concerned about its ever-growing application.

Another condition that seems constantly violated in the government regulation of business is Fuller's seventh requirement of constancy through time. Government regulations are in a constant state of flux. One political party replaces another in the White House and the rules of the game change. Let there be a change in the leadership of a major congressional committee and the rules change again.

During the early years of the environmental crisis, companies were forced or encouraged to abandon coal because it tended to be a highly polluting fuel. Now that the energy crisis is here, companies are being encouraged or forced to return to coal to save precious oil. The expenses involved in these transitions are staggering. Something must be done to control the anarchic flux so characteristic of the government regulation of business.

Finally, there should be agreement between the law and the way it is administered. It is one thing to discover what the law is. It is quite another to have the law enforced as written. Business people argue that the federal and state regulatory bureaucracies are filled with petty individuals whose only means of gaining self-respect is by blocking the legitimate plans or aims of business. The time and effort involved in fighting these people discourages the growth of small business and encourages large businesses to provide either a psychic or monetary bribe to clear the roadblocks. There has been much talk about protecting employee rights within the firm. Devices must also be found to protect the legitimate interests of individual businesses from the government bureaucracy.

To balance this criticism, the reader should know that Fuller's eight conditions for good law represent an ideal for a legal system. The reader should also realize that Fuller's ideal works best for statutes; it works somewhat less well for administrative decisions. No legal system can conform completely to Fuller's ideals. Take the condition that the law must be stable through time. Change, including change in the conditions that produced the law in the first place, requires changes in the law as well. Before OPEC and the oil crisis, cleaning up the atmosphere required regulations that discouraged the burning of coal. The oil embargo changed all that. Strategic considerations required encouragement for the use of coal. This shift in policy was expensive, but, given the changes in the world situation, the shift was necessary.

Fuller would agree here. Indeed, that is why he refers to his eight conditions as constituting a morality of the ideal rather than a morality of duty. However, Fuller is right in indicating that departures from these eight conditions do have costs, including the cost of undermining the law itself.

Others might argue that regulatory law is something of a misnomer. Regulatory "law" has less in common with law than it does with judicial decisions or executive decisions. What constitutes the disanalogy, Fuller's critics believe, is that judicial decisions or executive decisions are geared to specific situations and hence have less of the characteristics of generality than do statutes. Fuller might concede much of this point yet insist, correctly I believe, that his eight conditions still serve as an ideal for judicial and executive decisions as well. After all, Supreme Court *decisions* are viewed by everyone as establishing precedents. Perhaps the rule for the pricing of gas at the pumps need not be clear to everyone, but it should at least be clear to the oil companies, shouldn't it?

With these cautions in mind, Fuller's eight conditions for good law are fundamentally sound. Even when Fuller's eight conditions are recognized as an ideal, the fact that so much government regulatory policy stands in violation of them points out a serious inadequacy in the use of government regulation for achieving ethical corporate behavior. After all, government through its judicial system and through some regulation is, as we have seen, a requirement for a stable business environment. Both the law and business are rule-governed activities. When the rules that apply to business or that sustain and protect business violate the conditions for good law, business is harmed. Laws that are not stable do adversely affect incentives and efficiency. Laws that are not clear or that require the impossible, or that apply retroactively, or that are contradictory are unreasonable and unworkable. Both the business community and the public at large have every right to insist that the laws regulating business should conform to the criteria for good law.

NOTES

1. Lon Fuller, *The Morality of Law*, rev. ed. (New Haven, Conn.: Yale University Press, 1964), p. 39.
2. *Ibid.*, p. 46.
3. *Federal Register*, Vol. 44, no. 69, April 9, 1979.
4. Fuller, *The Morality of Law*, p. 67.
5. "Sears Turns the Tables," *Newsweek*, February 5, 1979, pp. 86–87.
6. Fuller, *The Morality of Law*, p. 76.

Why the Law Can't Do It

Christopher D. Stone

Wherever the market is inadequate as a control, one can, of course, act to shore it up by law. . . . If the majority of the people believe the market and present laws inadequate to keep corporations within socially desirable bounds, the society can, through its democratic processes, make tougher laws. . . . But I am . . . suggesting that even if the corporation followed the law anyway, it would not be enough. The first set of reasons involves what I shall call the "time-lag problem"; the second concerns limitations connected with the making of law; the third concerns limitations connected with the mechanisms for implementing the law.

THE TIME-LAG PROBLEM

Even if we put aside the defects in the impact of the sanctions, there still remains the problem that the law is primarily a reactive institution. Lawmakers have to appreciate and respond to problems that corporate engineers, chemists, and financiers were anticipating (or could have anticipated) long before—that the drugs their corporations are about to produce can alter consciousness or damage the gene pool of the human race, that they are on the verge of multinational expansion that will endow them with the power to trigger worldwide financial crises in generally unforeseen ways, and so on. Even if laws could be passed to deal effectively with these dangers, until they are passed a great deal of damage—some perhaps irreversible—can be done. Thus,

there is something grotesque—and socially dangerous—in encouraging corporate managers to believe that, until the law tells them otherwise, they have no responsibilities beyond the law and their impulses (whether their impulses spring from the id or from the balance sheet). We do not encourage human beings to suppose so. And the dangers to society seem all the more acute where corporations are concerned.

LIMITATIONS CONNECTED WITH THE MAKING OF LAW

To claim society's desires will be realized so long as the corporations "follow the edict of the populus" fails to take into account *the role of corporations in making the very law that we trust to bind them*. This is, incidentally, not an especially modern development or one peculiar to laws regulating corporations. The whole history of commercial law is one in which, by and large, the "legislation" has been little more than an acknowledgment of rules established by the commercial sector, unless there are the strongest and most evident reasons to the contrary. Thus, in many areas such as food, drug, and cosmetic regulation, and, more recently, with respect to the promulgation of safety rules by the Department of Transportation, the government effectively adopts the standards worked out with the industry. Such processes do not always bespeak, as is sometimes intimated, sinister sales of power. The real roots are more cumbersome, more bureaucratic,

Abridged from Christopher D. Stone, *Where the Law Ends: The Social Control of Corporate Behavior,* pp. 93–110. Copyright © 1975 by Christopher D. Stone. Reprinted by permission of Harper & Row, Publishers, Inc.

more "necessary," and therefore more difficult to remedy: The regulating body is considerably outstaffed and relatively uninformed; it knows that it has to "live with" the industry it is regulating; it does not want to set standards that it always will be having to fight to enforce. . . .

Even the specialized regulatory agencies, much less the Congress, cannot in their rule-making capacities keep technically abreast of the industry. Are employees who work around asbestos being subjected to high risks of cancer? What psychological and physical dangers lurk in various forms of manufacturing processes? What are the dangers to field workers, consumers, and the environment of various forms of pesticides? Congress and the various regulatory bodies can barely begin to answer these questions. The companies most closely associated with the problems may not know the answers either; but they certainly have the more ready access to the most probative information. It is their doctors who treat the employees' injuries; it is their chemists who live with and test the new compounds; it is their health records that gather absentee data. Granted, there are practical problems of getting corporations to gather and come forward with the relevant data, . . . But at this juncture my point is only this: Here, too, it is a lame argument that working within traditional legal strategies, we can keep corporations in line.

In many cases lawmaking is an unsatisfactory way to deal with social problems not because of a lack of "facts" in the senses referred to above, but because we, as a society, *lack consensus as to the values we want to advance.* For example, people do not want corporations to deplete natural resources "too fast," but desiring the luxuries that the resources can yield, differ on what "too fast" means. Then, too, we who live in the present do not know how to take into account the values that future generations might attach to the resources. Problems of this sort exist everywhere we look. Consider a drug that can benefit 99 percent of people who suffer from some disease, but could seriously injure 1 percent: Should it be banned from the market? People value inexpensive power. They also value a clean environment. These factors point toward construction of nuclear generating stations. But such stations put a risk on life. The problem ushered in is not merely a "factual" one in the narrow sense—for example, what is the probability over any time horizon of an accident that will cause such and such a magnitude of disaster. It is more complex still. For even if we could agree upon these "facts," how can we agree upon and factor into our decision the various values involved—the value of human life, the value of a relatively clean environment, those "fragile" values so easily lost in the shuffle of a technological society with its computers geared for the consumption of hard, quantifiable facts?

A closely related difficulty involves our increasing *lack of confidence as to causes and effects.* Let me explain this by a contrast. Suppose A shoots B, intending to kill him, and B dies. We place A on trial for murder. Why A? No one who has reflected upon the matter would be so naïve as to suppose that A was the "sole cause" of B's death either in any valid scientific sense or from a broader social perspective. As the defense attorney might remind us, "A was a product of a broken family, an intolerable social environment," and so on. What is more, by focusing on A as the legally responsible entity, we are overlooking the effect that a judgment of guilt will have on those other than A. His family will also be hurt by meting out "justice" to A. If he was a productive worker, the whole society will suffer to some degree. Thus, when we select A as the focus of legal responsibility, we are making simplifying judgments both on the causality side—supposing him to be the sole cause—and on the effect side—overlooking the effects on others. . . .

There are today, however, a whole host of major social problems that remain so for the reason that we cannot accept the simplified judgments as to causality and effect that traditional legal solutions demand. Take, as example of a major contemporary social dilemma, the problem of "inner-city blight." What entities can we single out for responsibility, either pragmatically or morally? The slum dwellers? Slum landlords? City employers who take their operations to other states? How complex, uncertain, and even counter-intuitive are the implications of any particular remedy that we may try. Worse, our uncertainties seem only to increase the more we develop methods and machinery to take into account the variety of factors we are increasingly capable of seeing are involved. A sort of legislative paralysis results—or worse, a legislative panic.

Even in those instances when the relevant facts can be established, and the relevant values are matters of consent, we may be able to agree upon what to do only in the most general way, inadequately for translation into viable legal rules. As the earth gets more and more crowded, and life more complex, increasingly such problems arise. For example, while we can all agree that bad odors ought to be held to a tolerable level in residential or mixed residential areas, it is not easy to translate this decision into enforceable legal machinery. How does one spell out a rule so that those bound by it know how to orient their behavior. . . .

The vagueness problem has even more serious ramifications than appear on first glance. For one thing, the administration of justice in this country depends upon most litigation being settled out of court, and the more vague a statute, the more in doubt an outcome, and thus the more likely we are to find our court dockets crowded with cases that neither side is prepared to concede. A related point is that when standards are vague, the persons against whom they are turned are apt to feel personally and arbitrarily selected out for persecution, victims of men, rather than of the laws. When people—or corporations—feel themselves to have had no fair warning, increased friction between industry and government is likely to result, a development that has numerous regrettable ramifications. (The vagueness of the antitrust laws, real and imagined, is a common point of complaint among businessmen and serves as a justification for the short shrift they would like to give laws and "government interference" generally.) What is more, if the language really is vague, the law is that much less likely to be an effective force in the face of competing, more definite constraints on the organization, such as the "need" to return profits, increase price-earnings ratios, and the like.

One can, of course, try to obviate the vagueness by seeking more and more precision in the law's language. But in doing so we risk making matters considerably worse. There is the possibility that once we have unleashed the regulators to make finer and finer regulations, the regulations become an end in themselves, a cumbersome, frustrating, and pointless web for those they entangle. Second, what all too often happens when legislatures try to turn vague value sentiments into tangible, measurable legal terms is that the rules they come up with have lost touch with the values they were originally designed to advance. There is a fascinating example of this in the area of water pollution. In their study of the attempt to reduce pollution in the Delaware River area, Bruce Ackerman and James Sawyer have shown that the regulators have emphasized dissolved oxygen content (D.O.) as a critical standard—the amount of D.O. in the water being taken as an inverse measure of how badly the water is polluted. What Ackerman and Sawyer show, however, is that if one looks at the values that lie behind efforts to minimize water pollution—boating and swimming, potable water, support of fish life—actually over a broad range of D.O. content, D.O. is an inadequate measure of whether or not any of those values are being advanced. Thus, while D.O. has the attractiveness of being traditionally recognized among sanitary engineers (it is "hard" and computerizable), gearing laws to it makes limited sense, at best. . . .

LIMITATIONS CONNECTED WITH IMPLEMENTING THE LAW

When we do push ahead even in the face of our doubts as to values, our uncertainty as to facts, and the myriad difficulties of fashioning our wants into legal language, further problems lie ahead. Each of them raises its own doubts as to the virtue of a society in which the outer bounds of a corporation's responsibility are established by the limits we can set down through law.

The fact is that a combination of factors, including the increased expectations of today's citizens and the increasingly technical nature of the society, have left our traditional legal mechanisms unsatisfactory to cope with the problems that currently concern people. Consider, for example, the law of torts, the ordinary rules for recovering damages against someone who has injured you. A model tort case is one in which Smith, who is walking across the street, is accidentally but negligently driven into by Jones. Smith falls, suffering internal injuries, and sues for damages. Now, I call this "a model" case because certain of its features make it so well suited to traditional legal recovery. Note that (a) Smith knows *the fact* that he has been injured; (b) Smith knows *who* has caused the injury; (c) one can assess, fairly well, the *nature and extent* of his injuries; and (d) the *technical inquiry* involved in analyzing causality is not too extensive—that is, simple laws of physics are involved, not beyond commonsense experience.

But contrast that model case—a case in which the tort laws may be fairly adequate to make restitution—with the sort of case that is increasingly of concern in the society today. The food we will eat tonight (grown, handled, packaged, distributed by various corporations) may contain chemicals that are killing us, or at least reducing our life expectancy considerably. But (a) we cannot know with certainty the fact that we are being injured by any particular product; (b) it is difficult determining who might be injuring us—that is, even if we know that our bod-

ies are suffering from a buildup of mercury, we are faced with an awesome task of pinning responsibility on any particular source of mercury; (c) we would have a difficult time proving the extent of our injuries (the more so proving the extent attributable to any particular source); and (d) the nature of the evidence that would have to be evaluated by the court is far more complex and technical than that in the "model" case above—perhaps too technical realistically to trust to courts or even agencies to handle. Thus, it seems inevitable that a certain percentage of harmful, even seriously harmful activity is not going to be contained by trusting to traditional legal mechanisms.

Then, too, at some point the costs of enforcing the law are going to transcend the benefits, and the law may not, on balance, be worth the effort. We can, for example, prohibit employers from discriminating on the basis of sex, and if we are using the law merely as a means of declaring social policy, it may make good sense to do so. But if we were to undertake serious systematic enforcement, the policing and prosecution costs (absent a strong sense by the employer that the law is right) would be questionably high. Some of the costs of falling back on law are obvious: administering court systems and staffing administrative agencies. . . . But there are other sorts of less direct "costs" hidden in such a system. There are various sorts of costs that arise from the attendant government-industry friction. A network of rules and regulations, backed by threats of litigation, breeds distrust, destruction of documents, and an attitude that "I won't do anything more than I am absolutely required to do."

The counterproductiveness of law can be extreme. I have already referred to the manner in which threatening directors and officers with legal liability impedes an ideal flow of information within the corporation, keeping potentially "tainting" knowledge away from those with most authority to step in and remedy the wrongdoing. But the law's bad effects on information are more pervasive still. To develop a system of total health care delivery demands not only a proper flow of information *within* pharmaceutical houses, but between the pharmaceutical houses and hospitals, doctors' offices, and coroners' laboratories. Information that doctors and hospital administrators should be regularly developing is, however, a potential source of medical malpractice liability. Because of the law, it may be best not to gather it and keep it on hand. . . .

Let me close by observing that in these and many criticisms of the federal agencies, I often find myself in strong agreement with the so-called "antis." But, in my mind, they fail to draw from their skepticism the correct implication for the corporate social-responsibility debate. If the agencies—or the other public control mechanisms—*were* effective, then it would be proper to brush aside the calls for corporate social responsibility by calling on the law to keep corporations in line. But the weaknesses of the agencies are simply a further argument that trust in our traditional legal machinery as a means of keeping corporations in bounds is misplaced—and that therefore something more is needed.

Cost-Benefit Analysis and Public Policy Formulation

Vincent Vaccaro

Unfortunately for many of us the mention of cost-benefit analysis conjures up a series of negative images: McNamara's whiz-kids and the Southeast Asia war, a Benthamic calculus in the hands of an uninspired bureaucrat or an analytical tool running roughshod over the analysts and the projects under review. Against such a hopelessly bleak backdrop, it almost seems ludicrous to ask whether cost-benefit analysis is adequate to serve as the basis for determining government policy.

Now having said this I shall attempt to discuss the role that cost-benefit analysis does and should play in determining government policy. At the very beginning, let it be clear that I do not believe that cost-benefit analysis alone is adequate as *the*, and I repeat *the*, (sole) basis for determining government policy. Certainly there are other factors and forms of analysis that are germane in determining what policy should prevail on one issue or another. However, cost-benefit analysis does provide "a conceptual structure and set of techniques for relating means to ends, for arranging the various costs associated with each course of action, and for describing, comparing, and assessing possible outcomes" and therefore warrants a central role in the formulation and execution of government policy. At this point, I hasten to add that the version of cost-benefit analysis

From Vincent Vaccaro, "Cost-Benefit Analysis and Public Policy Formulation" in *Ethical Issues in Government*, ed. Norman Bowie. Copyright © 1981 by Temple University Press. Reprinted by permission.

that I shall be discussing is cost-benefit analysis as *practiced* within governmental agencies (primarily at the federal level) and not as a theoretical construct abstracted from its application within the political process. . . .

I

First, make no mistake about it, cost-benefit analysis is "a formal procedure for comparing the costs and benefits of alternative policies."[1] The words are clear—the purpose of the procedure is to compare only one aspect of alternative policies, not the policies themselves. For that reason, it is inappropriate to expect this analytical tool to serve as *the* basis for comparing alternative policies.

My next three points concern the interpretation of data. The second one is that, although cost-benefit analysis does require that the alternatives be displayed and compared in economic terms, it in no way ignores non-economic considerations, and, in fact, the analyst is *expected* to appeal to non-economic criteria and standards at numerous points in the analysis. Properly done, cost-benefit analyses begin with the definition of the objective, followed by a searching out of hypothetical alternatives for accomplishing the objectives and then formulation of the assumptions or "givens." . . . These steps precede (in theory at least) any attempts to determine, quantify, display, or compare costs and benefits. Although most discussions of alternatives and assumptions normally found in cost-benefit analyses are devoted to eliminating non-competing alternatives or are devoted to structuring the data that will be considered (that is, the economic data), a good cost-benefit analyst will always include discussions of alternatives or assumptions that cannot be assessed by cost-benefit procedures. The exclusion of such alternatives or factors, rather than eliminating them from consideration by the policy-maker, in fact, flags them as alternatives or factors that must be considered simply because they have not been adequately evalu-

ated in the analysis. It is because cost-benefit theory is sensitive to identifying and clarifying critical non-economic issues that it is a valuable tool for those who must establish and implement our public policies and goals.

Third, the measurement of costs, but especially of benefits, involves interpretation of data in terms of economic theory. What constitutes a benefit? A cost? Whose benefit? Over what time scale? Such questions often depend for their answers upon a given theory or interpretation of economics. . . . Good cost-benefit analysts are extremely sensitive to the problems of "comparing apples and oranges" and have devised numerous methods and techniques that compare or at least measure (through cardinality as well as ordinality) apparent "incommensurables."[2] The important thing to note is that before employing any given cost-benefit technique—for example, option value or donor benefits[3]—a theoretical justification . . . must be presented and defended, and documentation of alternative measures or assumptions must be included. It is because of the requirement for more accurate measurement and complete documentation and justification that cost-benefit analyses are valuable to the policy-maker.

Fourth, the data available to the analyst may not be complete or the analyst may not be "satisfied" with what the data tells us. Here I am not talking about selecting data to prove a point. . . . There are times when a single figure may not accurately depict a given state of affairs or outcome of a course of action—economists will make the point in terms of single versus multiple indicies. Moreover, there may be a question about whether the data are somehow biased by the technique used in gathering or categorizing it—for example, for many public sector, regulatory issues, 'like urban transit systems, "comparisons of cost-related indicators have been impossible because of wide variations in accounting practices. Different procedures have been followed in assigning costs to different costs categories. Furthermore, estimates about the future or uncertainty about the appropriateness of a given measurement methodology may dictate that a range of values (based on various assumptions) be employed. In this way contingencies can be tested, various expected values for parameters displayed, and intuitive judgments introduced, using a technique called *a fortiori* analysis. Again, the analyst is expected to justify and document all such "interpretations." The introduction of such adjustments flags them as worthy of special consideration by the policy-maker....

II

Certainly cost-benefit analysis has some serious shortcomings, especially when it comes to government policy. Here are some of the major drawbacks or limitations in cost-benefit analysis as it is now used in determining or evaluating policy alternatives.

The first is a conceptual point and in my opinion it represents the most serious to overcome. Cost-benefit analysis is a formal procedure for analyzing policy alternatives involving the use or allocation of the resources of our economy. Thus, its purpose is to assist policy-makers in their fundamentally economic (not political) task of allocating scarce resources among competing alternatives. In other words, the primary objective in cost-benefit analysis is the achievement of allocative efficiency, which means that there is an "improvement" in the allocation of economic resources. Most cost-benefit theorists base their definition of efficiency on the Pareto criterion, any change in the social state is desirable if at least one person judges himself or herself to be better off because of the change, while no one else is made worse off by the change.

But this still leaves the question of who should benefit from the distribution unresolved. I shall briefly discuss two issues—distributional equity and the normative force of rights or entitlements. First, to the question of distributional equity.

It is a generally accepted principle underlying the words, if not always the actions, of public officials that those less fortunate economically, physically, intellectually, and so on should benefit from the actions of those more fortunately endowed. Because both allocative efficiency and distributional equity appear to be equally intuitive and compelling in our society, attempts have been made to accommodate both within welfare economics and cost-benefit analysis—for example, by introducing a theory of compensation or by weighting the desired equity formula in some way and *then* applying the criteria of allocative efficiency. These "shoe-horning" efforts have not provided a conceptually sound principle of distributional equity needed to co-function with the principle of allocative efficiency. Without meeting this conceptual requirement, cost-benefit analysis alone can in principle never serve as *the* basis for determining government policy in this country.

The question of the normative force of rights or entitlements has recently been raised in discussions of cost-benefit analysis. Simply put, allocative efficiency and its related criterion of Pareto optimality focus upon what constitutes the most economically efficient distribution, but allocative efficiency in no way ensures that those who are entitled to benefit (either morally or legally) from the policy or program will actually be the ones who receive the benefit. Allocative efficiency fails to consider the normative force of rights and entitlements in its calculus and therefore fails to satisfy the minimum criterion for social justice.

Although determinations regarding public policy must respect the normative force of rights and entitlements, I do not see this issue presenting a problem to cost-benefit analysis. Cost-benefit analysis again is "a conceptual structure and set of techniques for relating means to ends, for arranging the various costs associated with each course of action, and for describing, comparing, and assessing possible outcomes." Cost-benefit analysis is not conducted in a legal or moral vacuum. Questions or rights and entitlements and full consideration of their normative force can and should be considered as constraints and are generally introduced in steps 2 and 3 of the analysis. All too often, we tend to forget that cost-benefit analysis is an analytical tool that provides a map of how the policy will be *executed* should it be established, not simply what should be done, and for this reason cost-benefit analysis provides valuable information for the policy-maker (or legislator). Because moral and legal rights and entitlements are to be respected in the formulation of public policy (from the legislative, executive, and judicial viewpoints), their normative force is considered in evaluating costs and benefits of the various alternatives. Again, however, it is the decision-maker who decides, not the model; and the main focus of the public sector decision-maker is practical: will it work? . . .

How good are the studies being done? The quality of a study is directly related to three factors: the strength of the economic theory underlying cost-benefit analysis; the quality of the data available; and the quality of the analyst.

On the first point, as I have mentioned above, there are still many short-comings and weaknesses of cost-benefit analysis, but the conceptual foundation and critical issues regarding the concept of cost and benefits, the measurement of benefits, estimating the worth of aesthetics and quality of life, cost-estimating methodologies, and the like are being debated and greatly improved. I have presented some of what is underway in section I.

On the second, the availability of data—especially regarding cost—is critical. Unlike the problem of measuring benefits, which is still enmeshed in conceptual difficulties, the primary problem with estimating costs is accessibility. Most cost figures in coke emissions, car emissions, carcinogenic effects,

and the like belong to the industries being regulated or threatened with regulation. If the analyst must go to the industry to get the data, the question of its accuracy or completeness is always open. In cases such as the health effects of asbestos or benzine, the problem of projecting twenty or thirty years into the future or extracting data from the past rears its head.

On the third point, one of my pet concerns is: How good are the analysts? The entire gamut is covered, from exceptionally good to grossly incompetent. I think that it should be obvious by now that cost-benefit analysts must be innovative and creative thinkers who can deal effectively with economic and non-economic issues and not merely self-serving or obsequious, number-crunching drones. Some would suggest that outside consultants from highly respected research institutes would provide the safeguards needed (objectivity, professionalism, and perspective). And often they do. But I have come across an interesting example of how not to do a cost-benefit analysis. This study involved a proposed rapid transit system in a major U.S. city and was conducted by staff members of a major "think tank."[4] . . . My conclusion is simple: if we are going to use cost-benefit analysis as an effective tool in policy determination and formulation, we must attract and train intelligent and sensitive people to perform the analyses. The criteria used in selecting and developing analysts still leave a lot to be desired.

My last point is that all the work of the economic theorists, data gatherers, and cost-benefit analysts is useless if the policy-maker either cannot or does not take the time to read and understand the analysis. Many decision-makers, unfortunately, would like to see cost-benefit information expressed as a simple ratio on a one-page memo. The problem is that by themselves cost-benefit ratios do *not* provide sufficient guidance to enable one to pick out the best alternative. The proper way to view the cost-benefit ratio is in terms of the incremental ratio of costs to benefits of alternative policies. That is not a simple task by itself and does not include all the noneconomic issues "flagged" by the analyst, a point I raised in section I.

III

Several issues arise regarding the economic evaluation of public policy formulation that I shall now touch upon briefly. I shall not in this section attempt to do more than introduce some concerns and hope to provide a springboard for future discussions.

First, a need exists for determinations concerning those rights and principles that are fundamental to public policy formulation in the United States today. I have already discussed the issue of the adequacy of the Pareto criterion, the notion of distributional equity and the normative force of rights. In addition, there are a host of other issues that appear to be assuming the status of "informal" rights or principles, if I can coin a phrase: for example, the quality of the working environment, say, regarding benzine and coke emissions, the "no safe" principle regarding carcinogens in foods, esthetic integrity of rivers, forests, and the like, the quality of leisure or retirement, quality of life for the handicapped, and the "no benefit is too small or too costly" slogan regarding health care. Analysis of these concepts has barely begun. Likewise, it is about time that the United States formally establish certain national priorities, say, for air pollution abatement or minimum income, and require that these priorities be weighed in all regulatory or other cost-benefit analyses. Without some agreement about the meaning and relative importance of such issues, economic and other analytical methodologies will always produce "disputed" results. (National priorities are not that far removed from national needs, and "national needs" are defined in sixteen broad areas that provide a coherent and comprehensive basis for analyzing and understanding the U.S. budget for fiscal year 1980.)

The second regards the value of competing or supplemental (reinforcing) economic approaches, such as cost-effectiveness analysis, risk assessment, risk-benefit analysis, cost-benefit analysis, and to a limited extent inflationary impact assessment and regulatory analysis. Each approach has its own conceptual framework and evaluates policy alternatives in light of that framework. For example, cost-benefit analysis requires that decision-makers establish both societal goals and the means for achieving the goals as a basis for accomplishing cost-benefit comparisons. Cost-effectiveness analysis begins with the assumption that societal goals are established and reduces the *analytical* task to issues of cost and technical feasibility. Risk assessment, on the other hand, attempts to estimate how likely it is that some hazard will occur, how many people will be affected and in what way, and what steps can and to some extent should be taken to avert it. Its bottom line is an estimate of the extent to which the public fears or is willing to tolerate a particular risk (or is willing to tolerate lower levels of risk). Decisions must be made (presumably at the federal level) regarding what analytical technique or methodology is most appropriate for a given type of policy question.[5] Such (federal) decisions will also provide a basis for ensuring industry-wide, consistent collection of desired data.

A third issue deals with the need for noneconomic and quasi-economic techniques or approaches. Here, one might include technology assessment, regulatory analysis, legal analysis, environmental impact assessment, policy evaluation, and political impact assessment. In addition, even ethical analyses are being proposed, and, in my opinion, such ethical analyses will provide needed insight into establishing national priorities and may possibly provide guidance in determining weights to be assigned in ordering the priorities. Through discussion of each type of analysis, the strengths and weaknesses of each, and clarification of the interrelationship between and compatibility with the various methodologies mentioned above, it may someday be possible to reach agreement concerning what constitutes an adequate analysis of a public policy issue.

The last issue is one of talent. As I mentioned in section II, the quality of the policy analysts of whatever type depends as much upon the insight and creative judgment of the analyst as it does on the analytical methodology or the data. For this reason, policy analysts must have perspective, interdisciplinary interests, and an ability not merely to analyze but to put parts back together into a coherent whole. Policy analysis is demanding, because it requires the analyst to clarify objectives, make assumptions, choose to include or exclude information, select the proper analytical technique, and consume, interpret, and in certain cases translate qualitative information in one field into quantitative data in another. The pressures on the analyst are great, and the professional demands are tremendous. Unfortunately, too many "analysts" (considering the widespread effects of policy analysis) fall short of the minimum level of competence we would hope for at the federal level. Simply put, we appear to be more worried about the methodological techniques than the analysts applying them. Considering the stakes, the establishment of government policy and the multi-million-dollar price tag, neither can be ignored.

NOTES

1. Henry M. Peskin and Eugene P. Seskin, "Introduction and Overview," in Peskin and Seskin, *Cost Benefit Analysis*, p. 1. A similar definition is found in Peter G. Sassone and William A. Schaffer, *Cost-Benefit Analysis: A Handbook* (New York: Academic Press, 1978), p. 3: Cost-benefit analysis is "an *estimation* and *evaluation* of net benefits associated with alternatives for achieving defined public goals" (my emphasis).
2. For an interesting discussion of "measuring the incommensurable," see James Griffen, "Are There Incommensurable Values?" *Philosophy and Public Affairs* 7, no. 1 (Fall 1977): 39–59.
3. See the discussion of option value and donor benefits in Robert H. Haveman and Burton A. Weisbrod, "The Concept of Benefits in Cost-Benefit Analysis: With Emphasis on Water Pollution Control Activities," in Peskin and Seskin, eds., *Cost Benefit Analysis*, pp. 59–64.
4. I have not included any reference to the study or the institution, because I believe the quality of this particular study is the exception rather than the rule.
5. For instance, the cosmetics industry is vehemently opposed to the use of cost-benefit analysis as a basis for evaluating the industry's practices and policies. It believes that risk assessment is most appropriate and that prospective customers or users should be advised of health risks and then allowed to make their own choices (willingness to pay).

Cost-Benefit Analysis: An Inadequate Basis for Health, Safety, and Environmental Regulatory Decisionmaking

Michael S. Baram

INTRODUCTION

This Article critically reviews the methodological limitations of cost-benefit analysis, current agency uses of cost-benefit analysis under statutory requirements, the impact of recent Executive orders mandating economic balancing analyses for all major regulatory agency decisions, and agency efforts to structure their discretion in the use of cost-benefit analysis. The Article concludes that if the health, safety, and environmental regulators continue to use cost-benefit analysis, procedural reforms are needed to promote greater accountability and public participation in the decisionmaking process. Further, to the extent that economic factors are permissible considerations under enabling statutes, agencies should conduct cost-effectiveness analysis, which aids in determining the least costly means to designated goals, rather than cost-benefit analysis, which improperly determines regulatory ends as well as means. . . .

METHODOLOGICAL ISSUES IN REGULATORY USES OF COST-BENEFIT ANALYSIS

Inadequate Identification of Costs and Benefits of Proposed Action

. . . One of the first steps in cost-benefit analysis is identifying the implications of regulatory options. Forecasting techniques notoriously fail to identify the possible primary, secondary, and tertiary consequences of a proposed action—particularly if that action sets a standard with diffuse health or environmental consequences that extend geographically and temporally. For example, analysts have great difficulty estimating the specific social and economic costs and benefits of regulatory options for controlling carcinogens. Cost-benefit analysis "offers no protection against historically bad assumptions. . . . [F]oolproof techniques for forecasting unforeseen consequences are by definition nonexistent."

The problem of inadequate or impossible measurement of attributes is related to the deficiencies of forecasting techniques. For instance, the "skimpy science" of toxicity is an acknowledged problem for regulatory officials seeking to measure costs and benefits of possible regulatory options for the control of toxic substances. Without the knowledge, techniques, trained personnel, and funds to measure these factors adequately, gross error in estimation may result. Similarly, many environmental effects, such as changes in ecosystems, cannot be estimated with confidence because no acceptable method exists to measure these attributes.

Furthermore, characterization of attributes may be problematic. An attribute deemed a benefit by an agency official may pose the problem of beneficiaries who do

From Michael S. Baram, "Cost-Benefit Analysis: An Inadequate Basis for Health, Safety, and Environmental Regulatory Decisionmaking," *Ecology Law Quarterly* 8 (1980): 473–475, 477–492. Copyright © by Michael S. Baram. Reprinted by permission.

not desire the benefit or who do not even consider the attribute to be a benefit. For example, "cheap energy" is normally characterized as a benefit in a proceeding considering the construction of an energy facility. It may, however, be immaterial to those who have enough energy, or may be viewed as a cost to proponents of resource conservation.

Even if costs and benefits are identified, they may not be included in subsequent analysis for pragmatic reasons. Attributes may be too costly or too complex to measure. Exclusion may be based on a tenuous causal connection between the planned action and the possible attribute, as with the predicted probabilities of secondary or tertiary effects of a proposed agency action. Identified attributes also may be excluded for self-serving reasons. For example, if consideration of a possible disastrous consequence of a regulatory decision would tilt the outcome of the analysis against a favored agency action, it might be omitted from the final balancing process.

Quantifying the Value of Human Life and Other Traditionally Unquantifiable Attributes

Cost-benefit analysis works best when (1) a socially accepted method, such as market pricing, is available to measure the costs and benefits, and (2) the measurement can be expressed in dollars or some other commensurable unit. Regulatory agencies using cost-benefit analysis face a critical problem when confronted with attributes that defy traditional economic valuation.

Analysts are well aware of these problems. Some refrain from placing their own values on immeasurable attributes and redirect their analyses. More typically, analysts recommend cautious use of cost-benefit analysis. Inconclusive analyses of valuation difficulties in cost-benefit literature reflect the hope that the problem will fade or be forgotten. For instance, although Stokey and Zeckhauser maintain that the complexity and importance of measuring intangible costs and benefits should not be underestimated, they

ultimately conclude that perhaps quantification should be consciously postponed.

> In some cases, it may be best to avoid quantifying some intangibles as long as possible, carrying them along instead in the form of a written paragraph of description. Maybe we will find that the intangible considerations point toward the same decision as the more easily quantified attributes. Maybe one or a few of them can be adequately handled by a decision-maker without resort to quantification. We will find no escape from the numbers.... Ultimately the final decision will implicitly quantify a host of intangibles; there are no incommensurables when decisions are made in the real world.[1]

This use of cost-benefit analysis is morally and intellectually irresponsible.

Today, a number of agencies assign monetary values to human life. The Nuclear Regulatory Commission (NRC) uses a value of $1,000 per whole-body rem in its cost-benefit analysis. This figure, multiplied by the number of rems capable of producing different types of deaths, provides dollar values for human life. The Environmental Protection Agency's Office of Radiation Programs establishes its environmental radiation standards at levels that will not cost more than $500,000 for each life to be saved. The Consumer Product Safety Commission uses values ranging from $200,000 to $2,000,000 per life in its analyses.

But the fundamental issue is whether cost-benefit analysis is appropriate at all. Without an answer to this question from Congress or the courts, consideration turns to lesser issues: the proper method of valuation, the substantive basis for valuation (possibly relying on insurance statistics, jury awards, or potential lifetime earnings), and the extent agencies should articulate these issues and provide procedures for participation in the valuation process.

To date, agencies have expressed surprisingly little concern about these unresolved problems associated with cost-benefit analysis. Although officials deny valuing unquantifiable factors, these valuations are implicit in any cost-benefit based policy decision involving risks to human life. Responsible decisionmaking demands that implicit valuations be acknowledged and addressed explicitly. . . .

Improper Distribution of Costs and Benefits

Every regulatory decision on health, safety, or environmental problems results in costs and benefits that will be distributed in some pattern across different population sectors, and in many cases, over several generations. For example, a decision to allow the commercial distribution of a toxic substance may result in economic benefits to the industrial users, their shareholders and employees, and consumers. It may also result, however, in adverse health effects and property damage to plant employees and those living near the plant. In addition, future generations may suffer mutagenic health effects or the depletion or pollution of natural resources.

Analysts and decisionmakers using cost-benefit analysis recognize these implications. Nonetheless, in the absence of public policy directives, analysts frequently apply personal assumptions about the allocation of costs and benefits while calling for objective "fairness" in dealing with distributional problems. . . .

Such earnest analytical approaches to determining fair distributions of costs and benefits ignore constitutional precepts underlying public sector decisionmaking. Constitutional guarantees of due process, equal protection, property rights, and representative government should carry greater weight in solving the distributional problem than assumptions about fairness developed by economists and analysts.

Issues of temporal distribution, involving the allocation of costs and benefits for future generations, transcend even these constitutional values. Future generations possess neither present interests nor designated representatives to advance those interests. Our laws and values favor current benefits to those that accrue later. Cost-benefit analy-

sis also reflects a preference for current benefits over future ones. Distribution over time, therefore, like the discount rate, is essentially an ethical issue for the nation. The assumptions that analysts must make about temporal distributions in using cost-benefit analysis are inadequate precisely because analysts, and not society, have made them.

Promoting Self-Interest and Other Analytical Temptations

Users of cost-benefit analysis can easily play a "numbers game" to arrive at decisions that promote or justify agency actions reached on other grounds. The purportedly objective framework of cost-benefit analysis can be used to promote rather than to analyze options by manipulating the discount rate, assigning arbitrary values to identified costs and benefits, excluding costs that would tilt the outcome against the preferred option, and using self-serving assumptions about distributional fairness. Indeed, the very use of cost-benefit analysis leads some observers to conclude that the action under consideration is scheduled for approval. Even self-corrective measures are suspect. For example, the use of safety factors ostensibly chosen to avoid certain effects may prove to be a facile solution that does not alter the preferred analytical result if these factors are determined only *after* completing a preliminary analysis. Furthermore, these factors are usually based on technical estimates and do not properly consider the value-laden aspects of large, irreversible risks.

In addition, the "technology-forcing function" of regulatory programs can be stifled by limited technical and economic information. Governmental officials must often rely on the regulated industry for news of recent technological developments. Industry information is likely to be unduly pessimistic about the costs, reliability, and availability of new techniques. Thus, cost-benefit analysis based upon industrial information may become a mechanism for economically convenient regulation that tends to perpetuate the technological status quo. This result is particularly predictable when regulatory agencies have not defined their objectives. If such objectives were established initially, they would "drive" the regulatory process and more readily force development of new technology.

Special Problems of Accountability

The use of cost-benefit analysis raises new issues in addition to the usual problems of ensuring agency accountability to the courts, Congress, the President, and the public. Certainly the jargon, presumably objective numbers, and analytical complexities of cost-benefit analysis obscure the subjective assumptions, uncertain data, and arbitrary distributions and valuations of the decision-making process, thereby preventing meaningful review of agency activity. Agency uses of cost-benefit analysis tend to promote the role of experts and diminish the participatory and review roles of nonexperts.

Senator Muskie has voiced his concern about agencies including "questionable benefits" that can make projects appear "economically sound."[2] He has called for evaluating projects at different stages of completion "to find if the validity of benefits claimed at project authorization can be reaffirmed during and after construction."[3] No governmental agency has adopted this approach despite its obvious value in improving subsequent uses of cost-benefit analysis.

In its cost-benefit analysis of nuclear reactor licensing decisions, NRC estimates the population that will live near the reactor site in the future. Yet neither NRC nor any other governmental body attempts to control actual population growth in the areas surrounding nuclear plants. Thus the estimated cost-benefit basis for approving a proposed activity is not used as a planning tool for maintaining predicted costs and benefits once the activity is undertaken. The actual costs and benefits consequently may vary considerably from those projected in the analysis.

Additionally, the combination of fragmented regulatory jurisdiction over perva-sive problems and increased agency reliance on cost-benefit analysis ultimately leads to increased societal risk. For example, a trace metal such as mercury constitutes a health and environmental quality hazard. It is regulated by several agencies, including the Environmental Protection Agency (EPA), Occupational Safety and Health Administration (OSHA), Consumer Product Safety Commission (CPSC), and Food and Drug Administration (FDA). Each agency may permit some activity introducing an additional incremental amount of the pollutant into the environment because the minor amount of calculable human exposure or environmental harm in each instance is offset by a broad range of postulated societal benefits. Even though each agency may be making careful and objective decisions, without overall interagency accounting for the increasing risk to the general population and the environment from these many small decisions, the total societal risk will continue to aggregate.

The above taxonomy of methodological problems reveals the need for a "best efforts" approach, fostered by Congress and the President, and administered by the agencies and the courts, to exclude the use of cost-benefit analysis under certain conditions and to resolve rational and humanistic concerns. This best efforts approach should focus on: (1) improving the technical and objective quality of cost-benefit analysis; (2) establishing the limits and societal implications of cost-benefit analysis; (3) improving public participation; and (4) designing more effective measures for congressional and executive oversight of agency practices. . . .

NOTES

1. E. Stokey & R. Zeckhauser, *A Primer for Policy Analysis* (1978), p. 153.
2. Letter from Senator Edmund Muskie to Comptroller General Elmer Staats (August 5, 1977), reprinted in General Accounting Office, *Improved Formulation and Presentation of Water Resources Project Alternatives Provide a Basis for Better Management Decisions,* 18 (February 1, 1978), p. 19.
3. Id.

Why Efficiency Is Not Enough

Mark Sagoff

I

On February 19, 1981, President Reagan published Executive Order 12,291 requiring all administrative agencies and departments to support every new major regulation with a cost-benefit analysis establishing that the benefits of the regulation to society outweigh its costs.[1] The Order directs the Office of Management and Budget (OMB) to review every such regulation on the basis of the adequacy of the cost-benefit analysis supporting it. This is a departure from tradition. Traditionally, regulations have been reviewed not by OMB but by the courts on the basis of their relation not to cost-benefit analysis but to authorizing legislation.

A month earlier, in January 1981, the Supreme Court heard lawyers for the American Textile Manufacturers Institute argue against a proposed Occupational Safety and Health Administration (OSHA) regulation which would have severely restricted the acceptable levels of cotton dust in textile plants.[2] The lawyers for industry argued that the benefits of the regulation would not equal the costs. The lawyers for the government contended that the law required the tough standard. OSHA, acting consistently with Executive Order 12,291, asked the Court not to decide the cotton dust case, in order to give the agency time to complete the cost-benefit analysis required by the textile industry. The Court declined to accept OSHA's request and handed down its opinion on June 17, 1981.[3]

The Supreme Court, in a 5–3 decision, found that the actions of regulatory agencies which conform to the OSHA law need not be supported by cost-benefit analysis. In addition, the Court asserted that Congress in writing a statute, rather than the agencies in applying it, has the primary responsibility for balancing benefits and costs. The Court said:

> When Congress passed the Occupational Health and Safety Act in 1970, it chose to place pre-eminent value on assuring employees a safe and healthful working environment, limited only by the feasibility of achieving such an environment. We must measure the validity of the Secretary's actions against the requirements of that Act.[4]

The opinion upheld the finding of the Appeals Court that "Congress itself struck the balance between costs and benefits in the mandate to the agency."[5]

The Appeals Court opinion in *American Textile Manufacturers* vs. *Donovan* supports the principle that legislatures are not necessarily bound to a particular conception of regulatory policy. Agencies that apply the law, therefore, may not need to justify on cost-benefit grounds the standards they set. These standards may conflict with the goal of efficiency and still express our political will as a nation. That is, they may reflect not the personal choices of self-interested individuals, but the collective judgments we make on historical, cultural, aesthetic, moral, and ideological grounds.

The appeal of the Reagan Administration to cost-benefit analysis, however, may arise more from political than economic consider-

From **Mark Sagoff**, "At the Shrine of Our Lady of Fatima, or Why Political Questions Are Not All Economic," 23 *Arizona Law Review* (1981): 225–233. Copyright © 1981 by the Arizona Board of Regents. Reprinted by permission.

ations. The intention, seen in the most favorable light, may not be to replace political or ideological goals with economic ones but to make economic goals more apparent in regulation. This is not to say that Congress should function to reveal a collective willingness-to-pay just as markets reveal an individual willingness-to-pay. It is to suggest that Congress should do more to balance economic with ideological, aesthetic, and moral goals. To think that environmental or worker safety policy can be based exclusively on aspiration for a "natural" and "safe" world is as foolish as to hold that environmental law can be reduced to cost-benefit accounting. . . .

II

The labor unions won an important political victory when Congress passed the Occupational Safety and Health Act of 1970.[6] That Act, among other things, severely restricts worker exposure to toxic substances. It instructs the Secretary of Labor to set "the standard which most adequately assures, to the extent feasible . . . that no employee will suffer material impairment of health or functional capacity even if such employee has regular exposure to the hazard . . . for the period of his working life."[7]

Pursuant to this law, the Secretary of Labor, in 1977, reduced from ten to one part per million (ppm) the permissible ambient exposure level for benzene, a carcinogen for which no safe threshold is known. The American Petroleum Institute thereupon challenged the new standard in court.[8] It argued, with much evidence in its favor, that the benefits (to workers) of the one ppm standard did not equal the costs (to industry). The standard, therefore, did not appear to be a rational response to a market failure in that it did not strike an efficient balance between the interests of workers in safety and the interests of industry and consumers in keeping prices down.

The Secretary of Labor defended the tough safety standard on the ground that the law demanded it. An efficient standard might have required safety until it cost industry more to prevent a risk than it cost workers to accept it. Had Congress adopted this vision of public policy—one which can be found in many economics texts[9]—it would have treated workers not as ends-in-themselves but as means for the production of overall utility. And this, as the Secretary saw it, was what Congress refused to do.

The United States Court of Appeals for the Fifth Circuit agreed with the American Petroleum Institute and invalidated the one ppm benzene standard.[10] On July 2, 1980, the Supreme Court affirmed remanding the benzene standard back to OSHA for revision.[11] The narrowly based Supreme Court decision was divided over the role economic considerations should play in judicial review. Justice Marshall, joined in dissent by three other justices, argued that the Court had undone on the basis of its own theory of regulatory policy an act of Congress inconsistent with that theory. He concluded that the plurality decision of the Court "requires the American worker to return to the political arena to win a victory that he won before in 1970."[12]

To reject cost-benefit analysis, as Justice Marshall would, as a basis for public policy making is not necessarily to reject cost-effectiveness analysis, which is an altogether different thing. *"Cost-benefit analysis,"* one commentator points out, "is used by the decision maker to establish societal goals as well as the means for achieving these goals, whereas *cost-effectiveness analysis* only compares alternative means for achieving 'given' goals."[13] Justice Marshall's dissent objects to those who would make efficiency the goal of public policy. It does not necessarily object to those who would accomplish as efficiently as possible the goals Congress sets.[14]

III

When efficiency is the criterion of public safety and health one tends to conceive of social relations on the model of a market, ignoring competing visions of what we as a society should be like. Yet it is obvious that there are competing conceptions of how we should relate to one other. There are some who believe, on principle, that worker safety and environmental quality ought to be protected only insofar as the benefits of protection balance the costs. On the other hand, people argue, also on principle, that neither worker safety nor environmental quality should be treated merely as a commodity, to be traded at the margin for other commodities, but should be valued for its own sake. The conflict between these two principles is logical and moral, to be resolved by argument or debate. The question whether cost-benefit analysis should play a decisive role in policymaking is not to be decided by cost-benefit analysis. A contradiction between principles—between contending visions of the good society—cannot be settled by asking how much partisans are willing to pay for their beliefs.

The role of the *legislator,* the political role, may be more important to the individual than the role of *consumer.* The person, in other words, is not to be treated as merely a bundle of preferences to be juggled in cost-benefit analyses. The individual is to be respected as an advocate of ideas which are to be judged in relation to the reasons for them. If health and environmental statutes reflect a vision of society as something other than a market by requiring protections beyond what are efficient, then this may express not legislative ineptitude but legislative responsiveness to public values. To deny this vision because it is economically inefficient is simply to replace it with another vision. It is to insist that the ideas of the citizen be sacrificed to the psychology of the consumer. . . .

Nowhere are the rights of the moderns, particularly the rights of privacy and property, less helpful than in the area of the natural environment. Here the values we wish to protect—cultural, historical, aesthetic, and moral—are public values; they depend not so much upon what each person wants individually as upon what he or she believes we stand for collectively. We refuse to regard worker health and safety as commodities; we regulate hazards as a matter of right. Likewise, we refuse to treat environmental resources simply as public goods in the economist's sense. Instead, we prevent significant deterioration of air quality not only as a matter of individual self-interest but also as a matter of collective self-respect. How shall we balance efficiency against moral, cultural, and aesthetic values in policy for the workplace and the environment? No better way has been devised to do this than by legislative debate ending in a vote. This is not the same thing as a cost-benefit analysis terminating in a bottom line.

IV

It is the characteristic of cost-benefit analysis that it treats all value judgments other than those made on its behalf as nothing but statements of preference, attitude, or emotion, insofar as they are value judgments. The cost-benefit analyst regards as true the judgment that we should maximize efficiency or wealth. The analyst believes that this view can be backed by reasons; the analyst does not regard it as a preference or want for which he or she must be willing to pay. The cost-benefit analyst, however, tends to treat all other normative views and recommendations as if they were nothing but subjective reports of mental states. The analyst supposes in all such cases that "this is right" and "this is what we ought to do" are equivalent to "I want this" and "this is what I prefer." Value judgments are beyond criticism if, indeed, they are nothing but expressions of personal preference; they are incorrigible since every person is in the best position to know what he or she wants. . . . On this approach, the reasons that people give for their views, unless these people are welfare economists, do not count; what counts is how much they are willing to pay to satisfy their wants. Those who are willing to pay the most, for all intents and purposes, have the right view; theirs is the more informed opinion, the better aesthetic judgment, and the deeper moral insight. . . .

Economists likewise argue that their role as policymakers is legitimate because they are neutral among competing values in the client society. The political economist, according to James Buchanan, "is or should be ethically neutral: the indicated results are influenced by his own value scale only insofar as this reflects his membership in a larger group."[15] The economist might be most confident on the impartiality of his or her policy recommendations if he or she could derive them formally or mathematically from individual preferences. If theoretical difficulties make such a social welfare function impossible,[16] however, the next best thing, to preserve neutrality, is to let markets function to transform individual preference orderings into a collective ordering of social states. The analyst is able then to base policy on preferences that exist in society and are not necessarily his own.

Economists have used this impartial approach to offer solutions to many outstanding social problems, for example, the controversy over abortion. An economist argues that "there is an optimal number of abortions, just as there is an optimal level of pollution, or purity. . . . Those who oppose abortion could eliminate it entirely, if their intensity of feeling were so strong as to lead to payments that were greater at the margin than the price anyone would pay to have an abortion."[17] Likewise economists, in order to determine whether the war in Vietnam was justified, have estimated the willingness to pay of those who demonstrated against it.[18] Likewise it should be possible, following the same line of reasoning, to decide whether Creationism should be taught in the public schools, whether black and white people should be segregated, whether the death penalty should be enforced, and whether the square root of six is three. All of these questions depend upon how much people are willing to pay for their subjective prefer-

ences or wants—or none of them do. This is the beauty of cost-benefit analysis: no matter how relevant or irrelevant, wise or stupid, informed or uninformed, responsible or silly, defensible or indefensible wants may be, the analyst is able to derive a policy from them—a policy which is legitimate because, in theory, it treats all of these preferences as equally valid and good.

V

Consider, by way of contrast, a Kantian conception of value.[19] The individual, for Kant, is a judge of values, not a mere haver of wants, and the individual judges not for himself or herself merely, but as a member of a relevant community or group. The central idea in a Kantian approach to ethics is that some values are more reasonable than others and therefore have a better claim upon the assent of members of the community as such.[20] The world of obligation, like the world of mathematics or the world of empirical fact, is intersubjective, it is public not private, so that objective standards of argument and criticism apply. Kant recognizes that values, like beliefs, are subjective states of mind, but he points out that like beliefs they have an objective content as well; therefore they are either correct or mistaken. Thus Kant discusses valuation in the context not of psychology but of cognition. He believes that a person who makes a value judgment—or a policy recommendation—claims to know what is *right* and not just what is *preferred*. A value judgment is like an empirical or theoretical judgment in that it claims to be *true*, not merely to be *felt*.

We have, then, two approaches to public policy before us. The first, the approach associated with normative versions of welfare economics, asserts that the only policy recommendation that can or need be defended on objective grounds is efficiency or wealth-maximization. Every policy decision after that depends only on the preponderance of feeling or preference, as expressed in willingness to pay. The Kantian approach, on the other hand, assumes that many policy recommendations other than that one may be justified or refuted on objective grounds. It would concede that the approach of welfare economics applies adequately to some questions, e.g., those which ordinary consumer markets typically settle. How many yoyos should be produced as compared to how many frisbees? Shall pens have black ink or blue? Matters such as these are so trivial it is plain that markets should handle them. It does not follow, however, that we should adopt a market or quasi-market approach to every public question.

A market or quasi-market approach to arithmetic, for example, is plainly inadequate. No matter how much people are willing to pay, three will never be the square root of six. Similarly, segregation is a national curse and the fact that we are willing to pay for it does not make it better but only makes us worse. Similarly, the case for abortion must stand on the merits; it cannot be priced at the margin. Similarly, the war in Vietnam was a moral debacle and this can be determined without shadow-pricing the willingness to pay of those who demonstrated against it. Similarly, we do not decide to execute murderers by asking how much bleeding hearts are willing to pay to see a person pardoned and how much hard hearts are willing to pay to see him hanged. Our failures to make the right decisions in these matters are failures in arithmetic, failures in wisdom, failures in taste, failures in morality—but not market failures. There are no relevant markets to have failed. What separates these questions from those for which markets are appropriate is this. They involve matters of knowledge, wisdom, morality, and taste that admit of better or worse, right or wrong, true or false—and these concepts differ from that of economic optimality. Surely environmental questions—the protection of wilderness, habitats, water, land, and air as well as policy toward environmental safety and health—involve moral and aesthetic principles and not just economic ones. This is consistent, of course, with cost-effectiveness and with a sensible recognition of economic constraints.

The neutrality of the economist, . . . is legitimate if private preferences or subjective wants are the only values in question. A person should be left free to choose the color of his or her necktie or necklace—but we cannot justify a theory of public policy or private therapy on that basis. . . . The analyst is neutral among our "values"—having first imposed a theory of what value is. This is a theory that is impartial among values and for that reason fails to treat the persons who have them with respect or concern. It does not treat them even as persons but only as locations at which wants may be found. And thus we may conclude that the neutrality of economics is not a basis for its legitimacy. We recognize it as an indifference toward value—an indifference so deep, so studied, and so assured that at first one hesitates to call it by its right name. . . .

NOTES

1. See 46 *Fed. Reg.* 13193 (February 19, 1981). The Order specifies that the cost-benefit requirement shall apply "to the extent permitted by law."
2. *American Textile Mfgrs. Inst.* v. *Bingham,* 617 F.2d 636 (D.C. Cir. 1979) *cert.* granted *sub nom* [1980]; *American Textile Mfgrs.* v. *Marshall,* 49 U.S.L.W. 3208.
3. *Textile Mfgrs.* v. *Donovan,* 101 S.Ct.2478 (1981).
4. *Id.* U.S.L.W. (1981), 4733–34.
5. *Ibid.,* 4726–29.
6. Pub. L. No. 91-596, 84 Stat. 1596 (codified at 29 U.S.C. 651–78) (1970).
7. 29 U.S.C., 655(b)(5).
8. *American Petroleum Institute* v. *Marshall,* 581 F.2d 493 (1978) (5th Cir.), aff'd 100 S. Ct. 2844 (1980).
9. See, e.g., R. Posner, *Economic Analysis of Law,* parts I, II (1972, 1973). In *The Costs of Accidents* (1970), G. Calabresi argues that accident law balances two goals, "efficiency" and "equality" or "justice."
10. 581 F.2d 493 (1978).
11. 100 S.Ct. 2844 (1980).

12. *Id.* at 2903.
13. M. Baram, "Cost-Benefit Analysis: An Inadequate Basis for Health, Safety and Environmental Regulatory Decision Making" 8 *Ecological Law Quarterly* 473 (1980).
14. See 49 U.S.L.W. 4724–29 for this reasoning applied in the cotton dust case.
15. Buchanan, "Positive Economics, Welfare Economics, and Political Economy" 2 *J.L. and Econ.* 124, 127 (1959).
16. K. Arrow, *Social Choice and Individual Values* i–v (2d ed., 1963).
17. H. Macaulay and B. Yandle, *Environmental Use and the Market* 120–21 (1978).
18. Cicchetti, Freeman, Haveman, and Knetsch, "On the Economics of Mass Demonstrations: A Case Study of the November 1969 March on Washington, 61 *Am. Econ. Rev.* 719 (1971).
19. Kant, *Foundations of the Metaphysics of Morals* (R. Wolff, ed., L. Beck trans., 1969). I follow the interpretation of Kantian ethics of W. Sellars, *Science and Metaphysics* chap. VII (1968) and Sellars, "On Reasoning about Values" 17 *Am. Phil. Q.* 81 (1980).
20. See A. MacIntyre, *After Virtue* 22 (1981).

Licensee Responsibility to Review Records Before Their Broadcast

A number of complaints received by the Commission concerning the lyrics of records played on broadcasting stations relate to a subject of current and pressing concern: the use of language tending to promote or glorify the use of illegal drugs as marijuana, LSD, "speed," etc. This Notice points up the licensee's long-established responsibilities in this area.

Whether a particular record depicts the dangers of drug abuse, or, to the contrary, promotes such illegal drug usage is a question for the judgment of the licensee. The thrust of this Notice is simply that the licensee must make that judgment and cannot properly follow a policy of playing such records without someone in a responsible position (i.e., a management level executive at the station) knowing the content of the lyrics. Such a pattern of operation is clearly a violation of the basic principle of the licensee's responsibility for, and duty to exercise adequate control over, the broadcast material presented over his station. It raises serious questions as to whether continued operation of the station is in the public interest, just as in the case of a failure to exercise adequate control over foreign-language programs.

In short, we expect broadcast licensees to ascertain, before broadcast, the words or lyrics of recorded musical or spoken selections played on their stations. Just as in the case of the foreign-language broadcasts, this may also entail reasonable efforts to ascertain the meaning of words or phrases used in the lyrics. While this duty may be delegated by licensees to responsible employees, the licensee remains fully responsible for its fulfillment.

Thus, here as in so many other areas, it is a question of responsible, good faith action by the public trustee to whom the frequency has been licensed. No more, but certainly no less, is called for.

Action by the Commission February 24,

Public Notice of March 5, 1971, 28 F.C.C. 2d 409. Commission decision with statements by Robert E. Lee and H. Rex Lee, Federal Communications Commission.

1971. Commissioners Burch (Chairman), Wells and Robert E. Lee with Commissioner Lee issuing a statement, Commissioners H. Rex Lee and Houser concurring and issuing statements, Commissioner Johnson dissenting and issuing a statement, and Commissioner Bartley abstaining from voting.

STATEMENT OF COMMISSIONER ROBERT E. LEE

I sincerely hope that the action of the Commission today in releasing a "Public Notice" with respect to *Licensee Responsibility to Review Records Before Their Broadcast* will discourage, if not eliminate the playing of records which tend to promote and/or glorify the use of illegal drugs.

We are all aware of the deep concern in our local communities with respect to the use of illegal drugs particularly among the younger segment of our population. Public officials, at all levels of government, as well as all interested citizens are attempting to cope with this problem.

It is in this context that I expect the Broadcast Industry to meet its responsibilities of reviewing records before they are played. Obviously, if such records promote the use of illegal drugs, the licensee will exercise appropriate judgment in determining whether the broadcasting of such records is in the public interest.

CONCURRING STATEMENT OF COMMISSIONER H. REX LEE

While the title of the notice seemingly applies to the licensee's responsibility to review all records before they are broadcast, the notice itself is directed solely at records which allegedly use "language tending to promote or glorify the use of illegal drugs. . . ."

Although I am concurring, I would have preferred it if the Commission had not decided to restrict today's notice to so-called "drug lyrics." The Commission may appear to many young people as not being so concerned with other pressing broadcasting problem areas. And to many of these young people (and not just to that segment who use illegal drugs) the Commission may appear as "an ominous government agency" merely out to clamp down on *their* music.

A preferable approach would have been to repeat, with an additional reference to drug abuse of all kinds, our *1960 Program Policy Statement* wherein we stated:

> Broadcasting licensees must assume responsibility for all material which is broadcast through their facilities. *This includes all programs and advertising material which they present to the public....* This duty is personal to the licensee and may not be delegated. He is obligated to bring his positive responsibility affirmatively to bear upon all who have a hand in providing broadcast material for transmission through his facilities so as to assure the discharge of his duty to provide acceptable program schedule consonant with operating in the public interest in his community.[1] [Emphasis added.]

Because of the Commission's expressed concern with the drug problem, I would hope that we could initiate action with other appropriate Federal agencies to require a reassessment by pharmaceutical manufacturers, advertisers, and the media, looking toward the reform of advertising practices in the non-prescription drug industry. *Advertising Age* expressed its concern with the increased use of drugs—both the legal and illegal types—when it stated in an editorial:

> With an estimated $289,000,000 being spent annually on TV advertising of medicines, this serious question is being raised: Is the flood of advertising for such medicines so pervasive that it is convincing viewers that there is a medical panacea for any and all of their problems, medical and otherwise? Are we being so consistently bombarded with pills for this and pills for that and pills for the other thing that we have developed a sort of Pavlovian reaction which makes us reach for a pill everytime

we are faced with an anxious moment, be it of physical or psychic origin?[2]

Drug abuse *is* a serious problem in the United States. It is found in every sector of the population, not merely among the young who listen to hard rock music.

I believe the broadcasting industry has made a good start in helping to discourage illegal drug abuse. Many local radio and television stations and the four networks have broadcast documentaries and specials, carried spot announcements, helped to raise funds for local drug abuse clinics and information centers, and have helped to establish "tie-lines" and "switchboards" where all people can call for free medical and psycho-

logical help and guidance. These activities represent "communicating" in the best sense of the word.

My concurrence in this notice, therefore, should not be regarded as a reflection on the good start that I think most broadcasters have made in dealing with this problem. They must continue with even more determination and support from everyone.

NOTES

1. *Report and Statement of Policy re: Commission En Banc Programming Inquiry,* FCC 60–970, 20 R.R. 1901, 1912–1913 (July 27, 1960).
2. *Advertising Age* (May 11, 1970), p. 24.

American Textile Manufacturers Institute, Inc., v. Raymond J. Donovan, Secretary of Labor

... Congress enacted the Occupational Safety and Health Act of 1970 (the Act) "to assure so far as possible every working man and woman in the Nation safe and healthful working conditions...." The Act authorizes the Secretary of Labor to establish, after notice and opportunity to comment, mandatory nationwide standards governing health and safety in the workplace. In 1978, the Secretary, acting through the Occupational Safety and Health Administration (OSHA), promulgated a standard limiting occupational exposure to cotton dust, an airborne particle byproduct of the preparation and manufacture of cotton products, exposure to which induces a "constellation of respiratory effects" known as "byssinosis." This disease was one of the expressly recognized health

hazards that led to passage of the Occupational Safety and Health Act of 1970.

Petitioners in these consolidated cases, representing the interests of the cotton industry challenged the validity of the "Cotton Dust Standard" in the Court of Appeals for the District of Columbia Circuit pursuant to §6 (f) of the Act, 29 U. S. C. §655 (f). They contend in this Court, as they did below, that the Act requires OSHA to demonstrate that its Standard reflects a reasonable relationship between the costs and benefits associated with the Standard. Respondents, the Secretary of Labor and two labor organizations, counter that Congress balanced the costs and benefits in the Act itself, and that the Act should therefore be construed not to require OSHA to do so. They interpret the

452 U.S. 490 (1981). Majority opinion by Justice William J. Brennan, United States Supreme Court.

Act as mandating that OSHA enact the most protective standard possible to eliminate a significant risk of material health impairment, subject to the constraints of economic and technological feasibility. The Court of Appeals held that the Act did not require OSHA to compare costs and benefits. . . .

I

. . . In enacting the Cotton Dust Standard, OSHA interpreted the Act to require adoption of the most stringent standard to protect against material health impairment, bounded only by technological and economic feasibility. OSHA therefore rejected the industry's alternative proposal for a PEL of 500 $\mu g/m^2$ in yarn manufacturing, a proposal which would produce a 25% prevalence of at least Grade ½ byssinosis. The agency expressly found the Standard to be both technologically and economically feasible based on the evidence in the record as a whole. Although recognizing that permitted levels of exposure to cotton dust would still cause some byssinosis, OSHA nevertheless rejected the union proposal for a 100 $\mu g/m^2$ PEL because it was not within the "technological capabilities of the industry." Similarly, OSHA set PELS for some segments of the cotton industry at 500 $\mu g/m^2$ in part because of limitations of technological feasibility. Finally, the Secretary found that "engineering dust controls in weaving may not be feasible even with massive expenditures by the industry," and for that and other reasons adopted a less stringent PEL of 750 $\mu g/m^2$ for weaving and slashing.

The Court of Appeals upheld the Standard in all major respects. The court rejected the industry's claim that OSHA failed to consider its proposed alternative or give sufficient reasons for failing to adopt it. The court also held that the Standard was "reasonably necessary and appropriate" within the meaning of §3(8) of the Act, 29 U.S.C. §652(8), because of the risk of material health impairment caused by exposure to cotton dust. Rejecting the industry position that OSHA must demonstrate that the benefits of the Standard are proportionate to its costs, the court instead agreed with OSHA's interpretation that the Standard must protect employees against material health impairment subject only to the limits of technological and economic feasibility. The court held that "Congress itself struck the balance between costs and benefits in the mandate to the agency" under §6 (b) (5) of the Act, 29 U. S. C. §655 (b) (5), and that OSHA is powerless to circumvent that judgment by adopting less than the most protective feasible standard. Finally, the court held that the agency's determination of technological and economic feasibility was supported by substantial evidence in the record as a whole.

We affirm in part, and vacate in part.

II

The principal question presented in this case is whether the Occupational Safety and Health Act requires the Secretary, in promulgating a standard pursuant to §6 (b) (5) of the Act, 29 U. S. C. §655 (b) (5), to determine that the costs of the standard bear a reasonable relationship to its benefits. Relying on §§6 (b) (5), and 3(8) of the Act, 29 U. S. C. §§655 (b) (5), 652(8), petitioners urge not only that OSHA must show that a standard addresses a significant risk of material health impairment, but also that OSHA must demonstrate that the reduction in risk of material health impairment is significant in light of the costs of attaining that reduction. Respondents on the other hand contend that the Act requires OSHA to promulgate standards that eliminate or reduce such risks "to the extent such protection is technologically and economically feasible." To resolve this debate, we must turn to the language, structure, and legislative history of the Occupational Safety and Health Act. . . .

The legislative history of the Act, while concededly not crystal clear, provides general support for respondents' interpretation of the Act. The congressional reports and debates certainly confirm that Congress meant "feasible" and nothing else in using that term. Congress was concerned that the Act might be thought to require achievement of absolute safety, an impossible standard, and therefore insisted that health and safety goals be capable of economic and technological accomplishment. Perhaps most telling is the absence of any indication whatsoever that Congress intended OSHA to conduct its own cost-benefit analysis before promulgating a toxic material or harmful physical agent standard. The legislative history demonstrates conclusively that Congress was fully aware that the Act would impose real and substantial costs of compliance on industry, and believed that such costs were part of the cost of doing business. . . .

Not only does the legislative history confirm that Congress meant "feasible" rather than "cost-benefit" when it used the former term, but it also shows that Congress understood that the Act would create substantial costs for employers, yet intended to impose such costs when necessary to create a safe and healthful working environment. Congress viewed the costs of health and safety as a cost of doing business. Senator Yarborough, a cosponsor of the Williams bill, stated: "We know the costs would be put into consumer goods but that is the price we should pay for the 80 million workers in America." He asked:

"One may well ask too expensive for whom? Is it too expensive for the company who for lack of proper safety equipment loses the services of its skilled employees? Is it too expensive for the employee who loses his hand or leg or eyesight? Is it too expensive for the widow trying to raise her children on meager allowance under workmen's compensation and social security? And what about the man—a good hardworking man—tied to a wheel chair or hospital bed for the rest of his life? That is what we are dealing with when we talk about industrial safety. . . . We are talking about people's lives, not the indifference of some cost accountants."

Senator Eagleton commented that "[t]he costs that will be incurred by employers in meeting the standards of health and safety to be established under this bill are, in my view, *reasonable and necessary costs of doing business.*"

Other Members of Congress voiced similar views. Nowhere is there any indication that Congress contemplated a different balancing by OSHA of the benefits of worker health and safety against the costs of achieving them. Indeed Congress thought that the *financial costs* of health and safety problems in the workplace were as large or larger than the *financial costs* of eliminating these problems. In its statement of findings and declaration of purpose encompassed in the Act itself, Congress announced that "personal injuries and illnesses arising out of work situations impose a substantial burden upon, and are a hindrance to, interstate commerce in terms of lost production, wage loss, medical expenses, and disability compensation payment." The Senate was well aware of the magnitude of these costs:

"[T]he economic impact of industrial deaths and disability is staggering. Over $1.5 billion is wasted in lost wages, and the annual loss to the Gross National Product is estimated to be over $8 billion. Vast resources that could be available for productive use are siphoned off to pay workmen's compensation benefits and medical expenses."

V

. . . When Congress passed the Occupational Safety and Health Act in 1970, it chose to place pre-eminent value on assuring employees a safe and healthful working environment, limited only by the feasibility of achieving such an environment. We must measure the validity of the Secretary's actions against the requirements of that Act. For "[t]he judical function does not extend to substantive revision of regulatory policy. That function lies elsewhere—in Congressional and Executive oversight or amendatory legislation."

Accordingly, the judgment of the Court of Appeals is affirmed in all respects except to the extent of its approval of the Secretary's application of the wage guarantee provision of the Cotton Dust Standard at 29 CFR § 1910.1043 (f) (2) (v). To that extent, the judgment of the Court of Appeals is vacated and the case remanded with directions to remand to the Secretary for further proceedings consistent with this opinion. . . .

CASE 1. The Advertising Code Case

The Advertising Code of American Business was part of a program of industry self-regulation announced 28, September, 1971. This program arose in response to mounting public criticism of the advertising industry, to more aggressive action by federal regulatory agencies, and to fears of even greater government control in the future.

In announcing the new program of self-regulation, enforcement was emphasized. Complaints are received or initiated by the National Advertising Division (NAD) of the Council of Better Business Bureaus. During the first year, 337 complaints were placed on the table. Of these 337, investigations were completed on 184. Seventy-two of those complaints were upheld. In every case, the advertiser either agreed to withdraw the objectionable ad or to modify it. Six of the cases which were dismissed were appealed to a higher body, the National Advertising Review Board. Of the six cases, the NARB accepted the decision of the NAD in four cases, but agreed with two complaints. In these two cases, the challenged ads were withdrawn. All complaints were settled within several months. Supporters of the NAD applaud their time record for handling complaints as compared with frequent delays of several years in federal suits.*

---

*These figures may be found in Howard H. Bell's "Self-Regulation by the Advertising Industry," in *The Unstable Ground: Corporate Social Policy in a Dynamic Society*, ed. S. Prakash Sethi (Los Angeles: Melville Publishing Company, 1974).

The Advertising Code of American Business reads as follows:

1. *Truth.* Advertising shall tell the truth, and shall reveal significant facts, the concealment of which would mislead the public.
2. *Responsibility.* Advertising agencies and advertisers shall be willing to provide substantiation of claims made.
3. *Taste and Decency.* Advertising shall be free of statements, illustrations or implications which are offensive to good taste or public decency.
4. *Bait Advertising.* Advertising shall offer only merchandise or services which are readily available for purchase at the advertised price.
5. *Guarantees and Warranties.* Advertising of guarantees and warranties shall be explicit. Advertising of any guarantee or warranty shall clearly and conspicuously disclose its nature and extent, the manner in which the guarantor or warrantor will perform, and the identity of the guarantor or warrantor.
6. *Price Claims.* Advertising shall avoid price or savings claims which are false or misleading, or which do not offer provable bargains or savings.
7. *Unprovable Claims.* Advertising shall avoid the use of exaggerated or unprovable claims.
8. *Testimonials.* Advertising containing testimonials shall be limited to those of competent witnesses who are reflecting a real and honest choice.

Questions

1. How should rule 7 which forbids exaggerated claims be interpreted?

Adapted from "Advertising Code of American Business," 1971. Reprinted by permission of the American Advertising Federation and the author, Norman E. Bowie.

2. Is the set of rules comprehensive enough to forbid deceptive advertising?
3. Evaluate the described enforcement mechanism. Suggest improvements if you think any are needed.

4. Is the rule on "taste and decency" too broad and amorphous?

CASE 2. Regulating Insider Trading

Trading stocks on "insider information" has long been banned in the United States, and the Securities and Exchange Commission (SEC) has vigorously pursued rules against such trading since the Securities Exchange Act of 1934. Under the terms of this law, an insider is forbidden by law to use information obtained on the inside to buy or sell securities or to pass the information on to others so that they might benefit. In the important precedent case of *SEC* v. *Texas Gulf Sulphur,* a court held that "Anyone in possession of material inside information must either disclose it to the investing public, or, if he is disabled from disclosing it in order to protect a corporate confidence, or he chooses not to do so, must abstain from trading in or recommending the securities concerned while such inside information remains undisclosed."

However, "insider-trading" has proved difficult to define. An inside trader is someone who has material nonpublic information obtained by virtue of a relationship with the corporation and who trades in the stock of the corporation. Some believe that the information a trader has must be relevant to the price of the stock and should not include any inside-derived information that might have a bearing on one's purchase of the

stock. For example, one might have confidential information that could not be disclosed and yet would not likely affect the stock's price even if it were known. The SEC has said that one must *misappropriate* the nonpublic information, but a definition of "misappropriate" has proved difficult and tortuous.

In late 1985 and mid-1986 the financial world was stunned by two prominent insider trading "scandals" in a row. The first case involved a reporter, R. Foster Winans of the *Wall Street Journal.* He had taken advantage of his position as a reporter for personal financial gain (not very effectively) and had also helped his friends and associates gain financially (very effectively). Winans was one of the reporters who wrote the column "Heard on the Street," which frequently influences stock prices. A Winans-recommended stock jumped, on average, 6.5 percent on the day it was touted in his column. Winans and his friends enjoyed a trading advantage over members of the general public, who did not have access to the same information as did a surrogate for the public who was presumed to hold it in trust for the public until it was published. The *Journal* has a policy requiring that such information be held in trust and not acted upon in order to

---

This case was prepared by Tom L. Beauchamp and Norman Bowie based on Jonathan R. Macey, "SEC Vigilant on Insider Trading—But Is It Within Law?" *Wall Street Journal,* May 28, 1986, p. 34; "Insider Trading Case Reinforces Belief That Small Investor Is at a Disadvantage," *Wall Street Journal,* May 20, 1986, p. 2; "The War on Insider Trading," *Business Week* (May 26, 1986): 38; Daniel Seligman, "An Economic Defense of Insider Trading," *Fortune* (September 5, 1983): 47–48; "Greed on Wall Street," *Newsweek* (May 26, 1986): 44–46; "The Levine Case: New Names," *Newsweek* (July 14, 1986): 55; Larry Elkin, "Lawyers File Appeals for 3 in Winans Case," *Washington Post,* November 27, 1985, p. D2; "Ex-Reporter Says He Believed Leaks on His Journal Articles Weren't Illegal," *Wall Street Journal,* March 19, 1985, p. 12; "Those Hobnailed Boots: The SEC Has Put the Workings of the Market in Jeopardy," *Barron's* (June 2, 1986): 11; "Winans Says He Knew Leaks Would Bring Dismissal," *Wall Street Journal,* March 21, 1985, p. 10; Editorial, *Business Week* (April 29, 1985): 79, 128.

avoid conflict of interest—particularly in the tempting case of the "Heard on the Street" column—because of the opportunity to cause sharp movements in the price of a stock.

In spring 1986 a more consequential case erupted. Dennis Levine, a Managing Director who specialized in mergers and acquisitions at Drexel Burnham Lambert, was arrested for allegedly trading the securities of 54 companies (including major companies such as Nabisco and McGraw-Edison) on insider information in order to earn over $12.6 million. Levine was one of Wall Street's most successful figures and had taken home $3 million in salary and bonuses during the previous year. He had also just pulled off a major deal in his advising of Pantry Pride Inc. in its takeover of Revlon Inc.

Levine's walk on the wrong side of the Street evidently began on a trip to the Bahamas in 1980, where he deposited $170,000 at secret branches of a Swiss bank. He used code names and ultimately set up two dummy Panamanian corporations, which traded through the Bahamian bank. On or about March 22, 1984, Levine bought 75,000 shares of Jewell Companies, Inc. He sold them on June 5, 1984. In 1985, he bought 145,000 shares of American Natural Resources Co. on February 14, and sold them March 4. A continuous pattern of such trading developed, netting Levine the $12.6 million in a short period of time. On the basis of a tip, the SEC launched its investigation and built its case on the pattern of suspiciously well-timed stock trading.

The Levine case reinforced a view that is strongly held at the SEC: Insider trading is rampant on Wall Street. Repeatedly, the stock of a takeover target will jump in price immediately before a takeover offer is announced to the public. For example, just before Levine's arrest, General Electric acquired RCA. Immediately prior to the announcement the stock had jumped a dramatic 16 points. The SEC immediately began a massive investigation. It became clear then that the SEC is dedicated to major policing efforts in the attempt to contain insider trading. Since Levine's arrest, several other prominent Wall Street figures have been arrested.

The view that insider trading is rampant is widely held beyond the SEC as well. In reporting on the Winans case, *Business Week* pointed out in a cover story: "Executives do it. Bankers do it. Accountants, secretaries, and messengers do it. And so do printers, cabdrivers, waiters, housewives, hairdressers—and mistresses. Some do it on their own. Others work in rings with connections as far away as Switzerland and Hong Kong. But they all work the shadowy side of Wall Street by trading on inside information to make money in the stock market. Insider trading is running rampant, despite a major law enforcement crackdown and toughened penalties." *Business Week* maintained in an editorial in the same issue that "Insider trading violates a felt ethical sense," but was unable to offer a single reason for the conclusion that it is ethically improper.

The purpose of laws against insider trading—as the SEC interprets them—is essentially a moral one: to preserve fairness in the market place. If some investors have inside information not publicly available, they are thought to be unfairly advantaged. The underlying principles are that all investors should have equal access to information in a free market, that securities markets must operate on faith and trust, and that insider trading undermines public confidence in the marketplace. The United States Supreme Court has taken a slightly different view of the moral purpose from the SEC's. The Court has held that an inside trader must be one who has a fiduciary duty to retain confidential information; inside trading is therefore like stealing from an employer.

However, there is considerable moral ambiguity surrounding insider trading in general, and not every authority considers it unfair. Several scholars have argued that permitting insider trades would make the securities markets more efficient. The activities of the traders would be spotted and the market would respond more quickly to essential information. Ben R. Murphy, a partner in a merchant banking firm in Dallas, argues as follows: "My theory is that if we didn't have [insider trading laws] the market would eventually discount all the leaks and rumors and become more efficient. People would have to take a risk on believing the rumors or not." It is noteworthy that over $50 billion of securities trade daily on American exchanges, and no one is prepared to argue that even as much as 1 percent involves insider trading or any form of illegal transactions.

Jonathan Macey, Professor of Law at Emory University, has argued that a person who locates undervalued shares in a company through inside information can provide a valuable service to the market by the discovery, whether insider trading occurs or not. But in order to encourage such discovery, the person or institution must be allowed to profit. This is basically what stock analysts do; they all try to get information not yet public before their rivals do in order to reward clients who pay them for their activities. The amateur investing public has no chance against such professional knowledge and can only hope that the market price already reflects insider information. Macey concludes that "A complete ban on trading by those with confidential information about a company would be disastrous to the efficiency of the capital markets. If such a rule were enforced, nobody would have an incentive to engage in a search for undervalued firms, stock prices would not accu-

rately reflect company values, and, perhaps worst of all, investment capital would not flow to its most highly valued users. Thus, we would all be better off if the SEC would deescalate its war on insider trading."

The status of the law against insider trading is uncertain and very difficult to enforce. The leading investment journal, *Barron's*, has maintained that the SEC is "riding roughshod over due process of law," drying up the free flow of information, and harming the interests of those it is sworn to protect. *Barron's* adamantly insisted that Winans had done no legal wrong and that the SEC had twisted the idea of "misappropriation" of information to the breaking point in getting a conviction of Winans. Winans' only wrong, said *Barron's*, was the moral wrong of violating the *Wall Street Journal's* rules of ethics.

Questions

1. Does the fact that prohibitions against insider trading are difficult to enforce make any difference to determining whether they are immoral or should be made illegal?
2. Should the law have anything to say about insider trading? Should morality?
3. Would self-regulation be a better way to control insider trading than government regulation?
4. If permitting insider trading would indeed make markets more efficient, does that fact establish that we should permit such trading practices?

CASE 3. Flyover in Midland

On February 7, 1978, an aerial photography team commissioned by the EPA flew over and took detailed aerial photographs of the Midland, Michigan, plant of The Dow Chemical Company. The company had no knowledge that the flight was taking place.

This case was prepared by Norman E. Bowie based on articles by Edward M. Nussbaum and Garry L. Hamlin in *Chemical Engineering Progress* (April 1981), and from "The EPA's Eye in the Sky Has Companies Seeing Red," *Business Week* (October 28, 1985): 90.

Prior to February 1978 the EPA had been conducting an investigation to determine whether to approve a consent order, issued by the State of Michigan, under the Clean Air Act. The order had to do with emissions from Dow power plants at its Midland location. The EPA later admitted that they had had "the full cooperation of Dow, and Dow withheld nothing" that their inspectors had asked to see during their preliminary investigation in September 1977. In addition, one month later when the EPA requested schematic drawings of the power plants, Dow voluntarily provided them.

In December 1977 the EPA again requested access to the Midland plant, this time indicating that they intended to take pictures. In order to protect its trade secrets, it is Dow's policy not to allow cameras into its plants. After being informed of this policy, the chemical engineer, employed at the EPA's Region V office, apparently made comments that were interpreted by one of his subordinates to be an authorization for the flyover. Dow found out about the flyover a month after it occurred and promptly filed suit against the EPA in Federal Court.

Such flyovers are not unusual, however. The agency's Environmental Photographic Interpretation Center has a staff of 50 pilots, photographers, and map readers. The EPA maps hazardous waste dumps and takes high resolution pictures from small aircraft.

On April 19, 1982, the Eastern District of Michigan U.S. District Court ruled that the overflight violated the law. The EPA appealed and in 1984 won a victory in the U.S. Court of Appeals. The Court specifically rejected the company's argument that the EPA action amounted to a search that violated the company's constitutional right to privacy. As of this writing the case is on appeal to the U.S. Supreme Court.

Questions

1. Should the EPA be required to inform a corporation when a flyover is to be made? After a flyover has been made?
2. What obligations, if any, does the EPA have to protect a company's trade secrets?
3. Should the Freedom of Information Act apply to material gathered by the EPA on flyovers?
4. If a decision were to be made solely on moral grounds, how should a company's right to protect trade secrets be balanced against society's right to enforce environmental regulations?

CASE 4. Cost-Benefit Decision at Bluebird Smelter

Bluebird Smelter is owned by a large, national mining company and located in Bluebird, a town of 12,000 in western Montana. The smelter, which has been operating profitably for 35 years with 125 employees, processes copper ore arriving by railroad.

Bluebird Smelter is the only major industrial pollution source in the valley. On sunny days when the air is still and during periods of temperature inversion over the valley, the action of the sun on smelter emissions con-

tributes to photochemical smog similar to that in urban areas. Auto emissions and agricultural activities are also sources of photochemical oxidants, but smelter emissions are far more important.

A group of economists from a prestigious research institute in another city picked the Bluebird Smelter as a test case for a research project on the health effects of pollution. The figures they produced led to debate among the various local groups involved in

---

This case is extracted from a longer case by the same name. It was written by George A. Steiner and John F. Steiner for *Issues in Business and Society.* Our extracted case is used by permission of Random House, Inc.

TABLE 1. Annual Benefits and Costs of Bluebird Smelter

Benefits		Value
Payroll for 125 employees at an average of $15,000 each		$1,875,000
Benefits paid to workers and families at an average of $1,000 each		125,000
Income, other than wages and salaries, generated in the valley by the company		4,600,000
Local taxes and fees paid by the company		100,000
Social services to community and charitable contributions		20,000
	Total	$6,720,000
Costs		
Excess deaths of 5 persons at $1 million each*		$5,000,000
Other health and illness costs to exposed population		450,000
Crop and property damage from pollutants		1,000,000
Reduction of aesthetic value and quality of life		500,000
Lost revenues and taxes from tourism		500,000
	Total	$7,450,000

*Calculated on the basis of recent court decisions compensating victims of wrongful death in product liability cases in Western states. The figure reflects average compensation.

the controversy. The researchers looked at the operation of Bluebird Smelter in terms of costs and benefits to the community and to society. The following table shows their basic calculations.

The Earth Riders (a small local environmental group) seized upon the study, arguing that if total costs of smelter operation exceeded benefits, then a clear-cut case had been made for closing the plant. It was already operating at a loss; in this case a net social loss of $730,000. Thus, in the eyes of the environmentalists Bluebird Smelter was in social bankruptcy.

The smelter's managers and members of the Bluebird City Council, on the other hand, ridiculed the study for making unrealistic and overly simplistic assumptions. They questioned whether the costs were meaningful, citing estimates of the value of a human life that were much lower than $1 million, made by other economists. They argued that health risks posed by the smelter were less than those of smoking cigarettes, drinking, or riding motorcycles and that benefits to the community were great. They even suggested that important costs had

been left out of the calculations such as sociological and psychological costs to workers who would be laid off if the plant closed.

Questions

1. Analyze the costs and benefits enumerated in Table 1. Are there items that belong on the list but aren't included? Are there items on the list that should be taken off?
2. When making public policy decisions, do you think a dollar value should be placed on human life? If your answer is no, how do you decide whether to spend an extra $100 million on highway safety? If your answer is yes, how do you decide how much a human life is worth?
3. Suppose it is true that the health risks posed by the smelter were less than those of smoking cigarettes. Does that mean that the smelter should not be closed down? that cigarettes should be banned?
4. Is the decision whether or not to close Bluebird Smelter the kind of decision that should be made by cost-benefit analysis?

Suggested Supplementary Readings

Ackerman, Bruce A., and William T. Hassler. *Clean Coal, Dirty Air.* New Haven: Yale University Press, 1981.

Aharoni, Yair. *The Non-Risk Society.* Chatam, N.J.: Chatam Houst, 1981.

Andrews, Kenneth R. "Can the Best Corporations Be Made Moral?" *Harvard Business Review* 51 (May–June 1973): 57–64.

Baram, Michael S. *Alternatives to Regulation.* Lexington, Mass.: Lexington Books, 1981.

Barkdoll, Gerald L. "The Perils and Promise of Economic Analysis for Regulatory Decision-Making." *Food, Drug and Cosmetic Law Journal* 34 (1979).

Bator, Francis M. "The Anatomy of Market Failure." *The Quarterly Journal of Economics* 72 (August, 1958): 351–79.

Beach, John. "Code of Ethics: Court Enforcement Through Public Policy." *Business & Professional Ethics Journal* 4: 53–64.

Bell, Howard H. "Self-Regulation by the Advertising Industry." *California Management Review* 16 (Spring 1974): 58–63.

Blake, David H., William C. Frederick, and Mildred S. Myers. *Social Auditing: Evaluating the Impact of Corporate Progress.* New York: Praeger, 1976.

Coffee, John C., Jr. "No Soul to Damn: No Body to Kick: An Unscandalized Inquiry into the Problem of Corporate Punishment." *Michigan Law Review* 79 (1981): 386–459.

——. "Regulating the Market for Corporate Control." 84 *Columbia Law Review*: 1145–1296.

Cortle, Douglas M. "Innovative Regulation." *Economic Impact* 29 (1979).

Crandell, Robert W., and Lester B. Lave, eds. *The Scientific Basis of Health and Safety Regulation.* Washington, D.C.: Brookings Institute, 1981.

Eilbert, Henry, and I. R. Parket. "The Corporate Responsibility Officer: A New Position on the Organizational Chart." *Business Horizons* 16 (February 1973): 45–51.

Estes, Ralph. *Corporate Social Accounting.* New York: John Wiley and Sons, 1976.

Fischhoff, Baruch, Sarah Lichtenstein, Paul Slovic, Stephen L. Derby, and Ralph L. Kenney. *Acceptable Risk.* Cambridge: Cambridge University Press, 1981.

Fisse, Brent, and John Braithwaite. *The Impact of Publicity on Corporate Offenders.* Albany, N.Y.: State University of New York Press, 1983.

Fisse, Brent, and Peter A. French. *Corrigible Corporations and Unruly Law.* San Antonio, Tex.: Trinity University Press, 1985.

Green, Mark, and Norman Waitzman. *Business War On the Law: An Analysis of the Benefits of Federal Health/Safety Enforcement.* Washington, D.C.: The Corporate Accountability Research Group, 1979.

Hill, Ivan. *The Ethical Basis of Economic Freedom.* Chapel Hill, N.C.: American Viewpoint, 1976.

Hoffman, W. Michael, Jennifer Mills Moore, and David Fedo, eds. *Corporate Governance and Institutionalizing Ethics.* Lexington, Mass.: Lexington Books, 1984.

Johnson, M. Bruce, and Tibor R. Machan. *Rights and Regulation.* Cambridge, Mass.: Ballinger, 1982.

Machan, Tibor, and Bruce M. Johnson, eds. *Rights and Regulation: Ethical, Political, and Economic Issues.* Cambridge, Mass.: Ballinger, 1983.

MacLean, Douglas. "Risk and Consent: Philosophical Issues for Centralized Decisions." *Risk Analysis* 2 (1982): 59–67.

——. *Values at Risk.* Totowa, N.J.: Rowman and Allanheld, 1986.

Mishan, E. J. *Cost Benefit Analysis: An Introduction.* New York: Praeger, 1971.

Mitnick, Barry M. *The Political Economy of Regulation.* New York: Columbia University Press, 1980.

Poole, Robert W., Jr., ed. *Instead of Regulation.* Lexington, Mass.: Lexington Books, 1981.

Posner, Richard A. *Regulation of Advertising by the FTC.* Washington, D.C.: American Enterprise Institute for Public Policy Research, 1973.

Purcell, Theodore V., S. J. "Institutionalizing Ethics on Corporate Boards." *Review of Social Economy* 36 (April 1978): 41–54.

Rhoads, Steven E., ed. *Valuing Life: Public Policy Dilemmas.* Boulder, Col.: Westview Press, 1980.

"The Role and Composition of the Board of Directors of the Large Publicly Owned Corporation." Statement of the Business Roundtable, January, 1978.

Schwamm, Henri, and Dimitri Germides. *Codes of Conduct for Multinational Companies: Issues and Positions.* Brussels: European Center for Study and Information on Multinational Corporations, 1977.

Sethi, S. Prakash. "Getting a Handle on the Social

Audit." *Business and Society Review* 4 (Winter 1972–73): 31–38.

Shrader-Frechette, K. S. *Science Policy, Ethics and Economic Methodology.* Boston: D. Reidel, 1985.

Stone, Christopher D. *Where The Law Ends: The Social Control of Corporate Behavior.* New York: Harper & Row, 1975.

Weaver, Paul H. "Regulations, Social Policy, and Class Conflict." *The Public Interest* 50 (Winter 1978): 45–63.

Werther, William B., Jr. "Government Control vs. Corporate Ingenuity." *Labor Law Journal* 26 (June 1975): 360–67.

Wiedenbaum, Murray L. "The High Cost of Government Regulation." *Business Horizons* 18 (August 1975): 43–51.

CHAPTER FOUR

Protecting Consumers, Workers, and the Environment

INTRODUCTION

As we see in several sections of this book, the activities of business present risk of harm in many forms. In this chapter we will concentrate on risk to consumers, to workers, and to the environment. The focus will be less on the nature of the harms caused by business than on the *responsibilities* of business and the *methods* for correcting and avoiding harm that might be used to protect workers, consumers, and the environment. These methods include disclosure of information about risks as well as risk-reduction techniques.

In general, we are agreed as a society that government is constituted to protect citizens from risk to the environment, risk from external invasion, risk to health, risk from crime, risk from fire, the risk of highway accidents, and the like. It seems a natural extension that government is obligated by the social contract to protect citizens against risks to health, safety, and the environment. And indeed in the United States we have followed this rule for the protection of consumers, workers, and the environment: In the last two decades we have created the Occupational Safety and Health Administration (OSHA), the Environmental Protection Agency (EPA), the Consumer Product Safety Commission (CPSC), and the Nuclear Regulatory Commission

(NRC). At the same time, we have sharply increased the authority of other agencies charged with pertinent regulation, such as the Food and Drug Administration (FDA).

However, the extent to which government should restrain free-market business activities in the interest of health, safety, and the environment is not a matter about which we have settled convictions. For example, although almost everyone now agrees that the primary responsibilities for risk reduction and disclosure of information about risk are those of business rather than government, the role of government in effecting the process is still under examination.

THE RISK OF HARM

This chapter is unified by its concern with protecting against harm. A judge once noted that even businesses established to serve the public, "such as providers of food or shelter or manufacturers of drugs designed to ease or prolong life . . . must pay the freight" when they cause damage through their activities.[1] However, it is difficult to apply such a rule unless we have a shared conception of what counts as a "harm" and as a "risk" of harm.

The Nature of Harm. There are competing conceptions of harm, some of which are broad enough to encompass invasion of liberty, damage to or theft of property, damage to reputation, and more. No analysis will dispose of all controversy surrounding the nature of harm, but a satisfactory working definition for our purposes has been supplied by one of the authors in this chapter—Joel Feinberg (in the book from which his selection is drawn). Feinberg contends that a harm involves a thwarting, defeating, or setting back of a nontrivial interest:

> [Interests] can be blocked or defeated by events in impersonal nature or by plain bad luck. But they can only be 'invaded' by human beings, . . . singly, or in groups and organizations. . . . One person harms another in the present sense then by invading, and thereby thwarting or setting back, his interest. The test . . . of whether such an invasion has in fact set back an interest is whether that interest is in a worse condition than it would otherwise have been in had the invasion not occurred at all. . . . Not all invasions of interest are wrongs, since some actions invade another's interests excusably or justifiably, or invade interests that the other has no right to have respected.[2]

The specific kinds of interests Feinberg has in mind include property, privacy, confidentiality, reputation, health, and career. This broad definition based on nontrivial setbacks to interests is well suited to an analysis of the problems involving the harms that arise in business. However, questions about the *responsibility* for the harm, or the justifiability of causing the harm, or the violation of another's right should, under this analysis, be kept entirely separate from the question of whether *the harm occurred.* Causing a setback to interests in health, financial goals, or the environment can, as Feinberg notes, constitute a harm without necessarily being unjustifiable.

On a superficial level the moral problems involved in causing and avoiding harm seem uncomplicated. Almost everyone would agree that setting back another person's interests is blameworthy if there is little compensating benefit and the damage could easily be avoided. But business rarely confronts such a clear and relatively uncomplicated scenario. There usually are benefits that offset risk, and the risk of harm is often expensive to manage. Even in some of the most heated debates that we have witnessed over products thought to be harmful—for example, presweetened children's cereals—the product generally can show a substantial benefit for users. Moreover, in the workplace the risks of even the most dangerous chemicals are often extremely difficult to express and must be weighed against the benefits of the job and the product manufactured. This takes us directly to the subject of risk.

The Nature and Kinds of Risk. No one in management or daily life can escape risk decisions. We are constantly asking questions about how much risk is acceptable and how much can be reduced. Even as simple a decision as whether to extend an insurance policy is a decision about acceptable risk. There are many different kinds of risks—for example, risks of psychological harm, physical harm, legal harm, and economic harm. It is also meaningful to speak of risks of harm to the public, to the environment, and even to a person's sense of self-respect. Risks to consumers generally have to do with the risk of a manufactured product, whereas risks to workers are almost always risks of death, disease, injury, discomfort, and their psychological and economic aftermaths. At least three types of products and activities found in industrial manufacturing create a general need for protection against risk and for risk information. These types—which correspond to the three parts of this chapter—and some representative harms under each type are as follows:

Risks to consumers (and their families)
Tampons (toxic shock syndrome)
Prepared foods (cancer caused by food additives)
Nonprescription drugs (G. I. bleeding)
Cigarettes (lung cancer)
Radiation therapy (secondary cancers)
Children's clothes (burns due to flammability)
Oral contraceptives (pulmonary emboli; stroke)

Risks to workers (and their families)
Benzene (leukemia)
Asbestos (asbestosis)
Lead (destruction of reproductive capacities)
Microwaves (cataractogenic effects; decreased sperm count)
Petrochemicals (brain tumors; sterility)
Machines (ear damage from noises)
Construction (injury due to accident)
Cotton textiles (byssinosis)
Coal dust (black lung)
Hydrocarbons (childhood cancer in offspring)

Risks to the public and the environment
Coal-dust emissions (respiratory complications)
Carbon and other fuel emissions (respiratory complications)
Toxic chemicals (genetic defects)
Kepone (neurological disorders)
Agent Orange (birth defects; neurologic damage)
Nuclear power plants (radiation effects)
Acid rain (destruction of wildlife and forests)

There has been a growing concern in recent years that the answers given both by corporations and by government regarding acceptable risk are outdated and in need of new approaches. For example, we do not have an adequate grasp of the risks inherent in thousands of toxic chemicals, foods, drugs, sources of energy, machines, and environmental emissions—some of which may have serious and irreversible consequences. It has repeatedly been shown that intractable problems confront our demands for scientific evidence, testing for side-effects, and risk assessments. The *probability* of exposure to a risk may be known with some precision, while virtually nothing is known about the *magnitude* of harm; or the magnitude may be precisely expressible, while the probability is too indefinite to be calculated accurately. In many cases "wild guess" may best describe the accuracy with which risks of physical and chemical hazards may be determined—for example, for a worker who constantly changes locations, who works with multiple toxic substances, and whose physical condition is in part attributable to factors independent of the workplace, many of which can magnify the risks of workplace hazards.

In thinking about the need for risk information and risk reduction, it is often not useful to think of acceptable risk decisions in terms of a single best outcome. Several outcomes may arguably be equally appropriate in the circumstances. The choice to assume one risk rather than another almost always involves complicated value choices, a choice of which facts are to be considered relevant to the decision, some assumptions about probable consequences, and different conceptions of available options. (See the discussion of cost-benefit analysis in Chapter Three for further treatment of this problem.)

PRODUCT SAFETY AND RISK TO CONSUMERS

A consumer is a person or institution who uses a commodity or service. Businesses are consumers no less than individuals, and thus are as concerned about product safety and quality as their customers are. The carcinogenicity of industrial products, for example, is a consumer/business risk, as well as a risk in the workplace. It is a safe generalization that all of us are consumers of products that carry minor, significant, and unknown risks. Although automobiles and drugs are among the most thoroughly tested products, they can be lethal; and no household is complete without several dozen potentially hazardous products such as ovens, electrical lines, furniture cleaners, spray paints, insecticides, medicines, and video display terminals. Millions of people in North America are the victims of household and office accidents involving these products every year, and more of our young people die from failures and accidents involving products than from disease. Thousands of law suits are filed by businesses against other businesses each year because of product failure, hazard, and harm, and there are many related problems about deceptive marketing practices and inadequate warranties.

Some responsibility for the occurrence of

these harms rests primarily on the consumer, who may carelessly use products or fail to read clearly written instructions. But some risks can be described as inherent in the product—meaning that a cautious and reasonable judgment of acceptable risk has been made that the product cannot be made less risky without unduly increasing cost or limiting use. Still other problems of risk derive from use of cheap materials, careless design, poor construction, or new discovery about risk in a product already on the market. To assign responsibility to manufacturers for the latter defects and hazards is relatively easy. But we are concerned here with much more than liability for shoddy or defective products; we are concerned with all areas of product safety, consumer protection, and related judgments of acceptable risk and liability.

Disclosure of Risk Information. Some of these problems, for example, those involving risk inherent in a product where no further reduction in risk is feasible, seem best handled by responsible disclosures of information. Presumably in a market environment the consumer is in control, because the seller must satisfy consumers or fail to sell the product and be driven from the market. This principle works only if the consumer understands relevant information about risk and performance and chooses it without undue influence being exerted. But as the chapter on advertising and information disclosure indicates, serious questions exist about whether the information put in the hands of consumers, including information facilitating an understanding of hazards and other consequences of use, is adequate for making an informed and free choice. For example, are we told how a kerosene heater should be cleaned and stored and how often new filters should be installed? Are the side effects of a drug disclosed when a prescription is filled? In handling such questions, sellers may list only a minimal set of facts about known hazards, especially regarding technologically advanced products, because a seller is in the business of *selling* in the most cost-effective manner. Disclosure of information

costs money and risks loss of sales. Thus, the seller has an economic incentive to keep disclosure to a selective minimum.

These topics of disclosure and understanding have been under intense discussion in recent years. By the late 1970s a major right-to-know movement had taken hold in the United States as a response. Numerous laws were passed—most notably the Consumer Product Safety Act of 1972—to protect consumers by setting safety standards, examining consumer product marketing, providing for more adequate risk information, and upgrading the quality of warranty statements. Some of the themes of this consumer-protection movement (e.g., the obligations business has to advertise its products truthfully and to warranty a product nondeceptively) are discussed in other chapters. Other topics are discussed in the section of this chapter on provision of information to employees who work with hazardous products.

Product Safety and Quality Control. Another important strategy in addition to disclosure of risk information is *quality control,* including adequate research and testing designed to establish safety. If foods, for example, were certified as nutritious and free of harmful ingredients such as artificial coloring before being allowed on the market, then we would care much less about what is conveyed by advertisements or sales representatives. Food products present almost trivial harms in comparison to the massive product liability judgments seen in recent years against corporations such as Johns Manville (asbestos) and A. H. Robins (the Dalkon Shield). These judgments indicate a public consensus and legal judgment that corporations have a moral duty to research the safety of their products and pass adequate information on to the public in a timely, updated fashion. Higher standards of quality control would also protect manufacturers who produce quality products from those who produce inferior ones.

However, there are theoretical and practical problems in establishing and enforcing these standards. Significant costs are attached to consumer protection that drive up the cost of products and frequently drive companies out of the market. For example, some lawn mower prices almost doubled after new safety requirements were initiated in the 1970s; and several companies went under in the process. There are also problems—as we saw earlier—about how far the responsibility to market safe products extends and who should assume liability for accidents. And there are liberty issues at stake about the free market—for example, the freedom to put a new "junk food" on the market may be jeopardized (in theory the freedom to produce junk foods would be eliminated), and the freedom to buy cheap, substandard products would be lost (because they could not be marketed).

These problems about quality control raise important questions about liability and manufacturer warranties, discussed in this chapter in the case of *Henningsen* v. *Bloomfield Motors*. In this case, the court holds Chrysler as well as the dealer *liable* for an injury caused by a defective steering gear, without any evidence of *negligence*. The court argues that an implied warranty of suitability for use is owed the purchaser and points out that a major assumption behind "contracting" in the free market—bargaining among equals—can be brought into question when products prove to be defective. The consumer is not an equal when he or she purchases a major, essential product that is manufactured by few producers and has no industrywide, standard warranty. There may also be multiple manufacturers and suppliers of whom the consumer is unaware. The *Henningsen* case served to cast doubt on the effectiveness of disclaimers by manufacturers and quickly came to be applied to many products, such as glass doors, guns, and stoves.

Manuel Velasquez considers in his essay how to differentiate between the duties of consumers to themselves and the duties of manufacturers to consumers. He distinguishes three theories of the duties of business, showing that each strikes a different balance between the duties of the consumer and the duties of the manufacturer. The first theory rests on an account of the social contract between consumers and business (under which Velasquez situates the *Henningsen* case as a classic example), and the second provides a theory of *due care*. The third theory rests on an account of *strict liability,* a topic to which we now turn.

Liability for Harm. Some of these issues—especially those that fall under the *Henningsen* ruling—are commonly framed in terms of manufacturer liability. In Chapter One we saw that a business is morally blameworthy and perhaps legally liable for causing a harm if it is caused by carelessness resulting from failure to discharge a socially, legally, or morally imposed duty to take care or to behave reasonably toward others. Two important tests of reasonableness were discussed that apply here as well: that professionals should conform to the minimally acceptable standards practiced in the profession, and that they should perform any actions that a reasonably prudent person would perform in the circumstances. Sometimes when the utmost care has been exercised, an accident or lack of information or documents might still cause harm. But if due care has been exercised to make a product safe (and affected parties have been apprised of known risks), a business would seem not to be at *fault* for any harm caused, even if the business played some role in bringing the harm about.

This suggests the standard that a manufacturer can be held liable for unsafe or inefficacious products or unsafe workplaces only if it knew or *should have known* about the risks involved (or, of course, if a specific guarantee or warranty was provided). As attractive as this standard is, it does not take much ingenuity to imagine how difficult it would be to determine what an employer or manufacturer "should have known." A product or technique of manufacture can, after all, be so thoroughly researched and delayed that it will insure a loss rather than a profit to a manufacturer. Are we to hold businesses to this kind of economic risk? If so, how could one ever determine that enough research and development had been carried out? Can the whole problem be handled through adequate insurance to cover all affected parties? Or do we need to modify our conception of liability?

In recent years it has been suggested that we should hold manufacturers liable not only to a standard of prudent behavior but to the following even stronger standard: A manufacturer is liable for injuries caused to parties by defects in the manufacturing process even if the manufacturer exercised due diligence and still could not have reasonably foreseen the problem. This principle is generally referred to as *strict product liability*—that is, liability without fault, where questions of good faith, negligence, and absence of knowledge are not pertinent to a determination of liability. The advocates of this no-fault principle use primarily utilitarian arguments. They maintain that manufacturers are in the best position to pay and recover the costs of injury because they can pass the costs on through the price of the product and, moreover, will have the side benefit of increasing the manufacturer's objectivity, diligence, and prudence before putting a product on the market. This argument envisions a shift through strict liability from the traditional doctrine of "buyer beware" *(caveat emptor)* to "seller beware." The burden of responsibility for unknown hazards and risks inherent in the product is shifted to the manufacturer despite prudent manufacture.

This utilitarian justification is controversial and is challenged in this chapter by George Brenkert, who thinks it important to ask whether strict liability conforms to principles of justice—in particular whether it is just to ask manufacturers to bear the cost of injury merely because they are in the best position to do so. Brenkert maintains that in a free market society it is just to use strict liability because it is essential to maintain a consumer's equal opportunity to function. Using premises of compensatory justice and equal opportunity rather than utility, then, Brenkert argues

that it is just to place the burden of strict liability on manufacturers.

WORKER SAFETY, OCCUPATIONAL RISK, AND THE RIGHT TO KNOW

Critics of business and government have long argued that workers are routinely, and often knowingly, exposed to dangerous situations and never informed of the risks. For example, asbestos workers were not told for many years of the dangers of contracting asbestosis, construction workers have often been killed when flimsy rigging collapsed, and miners have perished from mine explosions. Although the Occupational Safety and Health Act of 1970 sought to assure safety in the workplace, there have been no significant declines in injury and fatality rates since the Act was passed. Government statistics show that there are approximately 6,000 fatal accidents and 5 million nonfatal accidents in the workplace each year in the United States. Disease statistics are either unknown or too unreliably gathered to be meaningful.

Although relatively little is known at present about the knowledge and comprehension of workers, there is evidence that in at least some industries ignorance is a causal factor in occupational illness or injury. A detailed study was done, for example, of the Hurley Reduction Works—a smelter owned by Kennecott Copper. It concluded that "the smelter's work force has little or no understanding of occupational health hazards, their evaluation, or prevention"—especially regarding airborne arsenic, sulfur dioxide, and copper dust, all of which appear in high to very high levels in the reverberators and converter areas.[3] The simple solution to such problems is, of course, to ban hazardous products from use. But to do so would be to shut down most industrial manufacture. For example, for more than 2,500 products that use asbestos there is no desirable substitute available.

The implications of worker ignorance about health hazards in many industries have been given compelling expression in testimony such as the following before an OSHA hearing by a worker exposed to the toxic agent DBCP:

> We had no warning that DBCP exposure might cause sterility, testicular atrophy, and perhaps cancer. If we had known that these fumes could possibly cause the damage that we have found out it probably does cause, we would have worn equipment to protect ourselves. As it was, we didn't have enough knowledge to give us the proper respect for DBCP.[4]

The moral justification for requiring disclosures of information by employers and occupational physicians is the principle of respect for autonomy discussed in Chapter One. True respect for autonomy demands that we allow persons the freedom to form their own judgments and perform whatever actions they autonomously choose. Many issues about workplace safety, ranging from manipulative underdisclosure of pertinent information to nonrecognition of a right to refuse hazardous work conditions, involve alleged failures to respect workers as agents with their own perspectives and rights to make free choices. The idea that a worker should be enabled to *decide* freely about hazardous work and agree to it means that the worker must do more than acquiesce in, yield to, or comply with an arrangement or a proposal. He or she must actively agree to the conditions through a substantial understanding of the circumstances and in substantial absence of control by others.

The main goal in regulating risks in the workplace has always been and probably always will be to determine an objective level of acceptable risk and then to ban or limit conditions of exposure above that level. However, this goal of safety is not the primary justification for disclosures of risk. Individuals need the information upon which the objective standard is based in order to determine whether the risk it declares acceptable is *acceptable to them*. Here, we might say, a subjective standard of acceptable risk seems

more appropriate than an objective standard established by "experts." As the worker's testimony quoted previously indicates, choosing a risk of testicular atrophy seems rightly a worker's personal choice, one not fully decidable by health and safety standards established for aggregated groups of workers. Even with objective standards, a situation of substantial ambiguity prevails, where the risks are uncertain by the assessment of the most informed expert, and the dose levels at which there is concern for health and safety can be made no clearer.

There seem to be problems about both the strategy of information disclosure and the strategy of protection if either is used in isolation. There are often no meaningful figures defining the relationship between the acceptability of a risk and the ease with which the risk can be eliminated or controlled. There also may be no consensus on which levels of probability of serious harm, such as death, constitute risks sufficiently high that steps ought to be taken to reduce or eliminate the risk or to provide information to those affected. In one essay in this chapter, June Fessenden-Raden and Bernard Gert present an analytical procedure rooted in a moral theory that can be used by government officials, employers, and employees in order to analyze the full range of occupational health problems. They try to show how to reduce areas of disagreement, eliminate irrelevant considerations from the decisionmaking process, and provide an impartial procedure for reasoning about the problems. This procedure considers the costs, risks, and benefits of proposals and in addition demands "universalizing" rules in order to control for biased reasoning.

Both the employer's responsibility to inform employees and the employee's right to refuse hazardous job assignments are the concern of the essay by Ruth Faden and Tom Beauchamp. They appeal to the principle of autonomy to support an appropriate standard of information disclosure and consider three possible standards for determining whether a refusal to work or a safety walkout is justified. They note that all the proposed standards justifying a safety walkout are similar to the standards requiring that workers be informed of hazards in the workplace.

ENVIRONMENTAL PROTECTION AND RISKS TO HEALTH

Controversy over protecting the environment and preventing the depletion of natural resources has mushroomed in the last two decades, a period that has caught business, government, and the general public unprepared to handle environmental problems of air pollution, ground-water contamination, and the like. The public has become increasingly concerned about the environmental impact of chemical dumping, supersonic transport, burning coal, nuclear power, the Alaska pipeline, and so on. In this debate, environmental deterioration has often been linked to corporate actions, and thus corporate responsibility has become a major part of the environmental issue.

In earlier times environmental issues were conceived in free-market terms: Natural resources were available to entrepreneurs who were free to use them as they saw fit. Any conflicts over proper environmental use were handled by relatively simple procedures that balanced conflicting interests. Those who polluted, for example, could be prosecuted and fined in order to protect the community's interests. It was assumed that the environment, once properly tended to, was sufficiently resilient to return to its former state. Recently this optimistic outlook has been vigorously challenged. The contention is that technology and increased production have affected the environment to the point where unrectifiable and uncontrollable global imbalances may emerge. Thus, whole sections of leading periodicals such as *National Geographic* now routinely devote sections to topics such as the dangers of acid rain. These articles often depict corporations as "externalizing" rather than internalizing costs of production by passing on the costs of cleaning up their environmental messes to the public.

Some writers depict the environment as analogous to a pasture where competing herdsmen graze so many cattle in the quest for profits (as it is economically rational for each cattleman to do) that eventually the common land is overgrazed and can no longer support even a single animal. As each businessperson pursues his or her own economic interest, collectively they work toward the ruin of all—"the tragedy of the commons," as Garrett Hardin puts it.[5] This analogy has been widely disputed in various sectors of business, which tend to see present environmental problems as sometimes involving tradeoffs that need not do irreversible damage to "the commons." However, almost everyone acknowledges that some tradeoffs involve additional tradeoffs that may only mortgage the future. For example, air-pollution scrubbers used in industry to remove sulfur dioxide from flue gas produce three to six tons of sludge for every ton of sulfur dioxide they remove. The sludge is then buried in landfills, creating a risk of water pollution. Thus, efforts to clean the air risk polluting the water.

Classic conflicts between public and private interests have emerged in these environmental debates. For example, there have been attempts to show that fluorocarbons in aerosol spray cans sufficiently damage the earth's ozone shield that serious repercussions may follow from continued use: for example, melting of polar ice caps, flooding of cities along the world's coasts, and radioactive contamination. The food industry has been charged with raping the land by its failure to balance high-level methods of food production with the land's actual lower-level capacity to produce. The timber industry has been accused of deforestation without replenishment. Responsibility for various forms of pollution has been laid at the door of the bottle and can industries, plastics industries, smelters, the chemical industry, and the oil industry. And in recent years industrial disposals of hazardous wastes that include mercury, benzene, and dioxin have been faulted for the contamination of groundwater, landfills, and even waste recovery plants.

Those who promote a new environmental ethic argue that we have a special problem in Western culture because of entrenched attitudes about nature as inferior to human life and therefore to be used chiefly for human enjoyment and betterment. Humans are thus conceived less as part of the ecosystem than as dwellers external to it. Others argue, however, that we need to view the environment in a different way only to the extent that doing so would improve our quality of life and continued existence, now and in the future. They argue that environmental concerns are valid only to the extent that they improve the human situation, and not because animals and plants have rights. This approach emphasizes the freedom of businesses to use the environment unless they harm other individuals in society by their activities.

The article in this chapter by Alasdair MacIntyre exhibits limited sympathy for some aspect of this thesis and emphasizes the vital role that industry can play in a situation of public choice about the environment. He faults moralizers who attempt to find a scapegoat for every social ill, and maintains that "the record of the electric power industry . . . is by and large an exemplary one" in abstaining from wrongdoing. Like Fessenden-Raden and Gert, MacIntyre believes we must learn to "reason together morally in an effective way." In the following essay, Joel Feinberg considers what kinds of questions a legislature should ask about the environment in order to minimize public harms within the limits of efficiency, equity, and fair play. He considers the setting of standards for the emission of industrial pollutants into the air and water (the precise problem in the *Reserve Mining* case discussed later), and argues that we need an authoritative regulatory scheme of allocational priorities to resolve the problem of accumulative harms—that is, those harms, like automobile emissions, caused not by isolable individuals but only by large

groups jointly. In the absence of such a scheme, he concludes, there is no nonarbitrary method for imputing accumulative harms to individual parties.

Feinberg is among a group of philosophers who argue that the morally relevant differences between human life and animal life are not sufficient to support the claim that only humans have interests that deserve protection. Some writers, including former Supreme Court Justice William O. Douglas (in *Sierra Club* v. *Morton*, 401 U.S. 907), have argued that plants and animals, and perhaps even other natural objects such as oceans and trees, should be given some form of legal standing so that others could institute such actions on their behalf—just as guardians now do for children, the comatose, and the retarded. Only granting such moral and legal standing to the objects in question, they argue, will provide sufficient environmental status to protect them. If natural objects had standing in court, they could then be defended against the actions of corporations. Corporations would often win, because they could show many clear rights to use the environment; but if these natural objects themselves had rights, corporations could simply use environmental entities in any way they please.

These problems obviously bear on more general problems of legitimate social and political control over industry. Many now believe that severe curbs on industry and severe judicial penalties provide the only viable ways to protect the environment, while others believe that the filing of environmental impact statements and other currently employed practices are sufficient. But almost everyone now believes that there will be in the future still further loss of the liberty for corporations to use the environment as they see fit. The heart of the environmental problem is how to balance the liberties of those who want to put the environment to work in the free market against rights to safe workplaces, to safe products, and to an environment free of contamination.

A classic legal case in this chapter that

bears on precisely this issue is a composite of two opinions presented as a single case, *Reserve Mining Company* v. *United States*. Both opinions were delivered by Judge Myron Bright (on separate dates). This case occurred during a critical transitional phase in American environmental law and is among the best demonstrations of the complexity and uncertainty of evaluating environmental hazards. Prior to this case, the courts had held that the burden of proof in demonstrating that hazardous environmental conditions exist rested with the *government,* rather than the burden being on *industry* to prove that the effects of its discharges are nonhazardous. Several cases in the mid-1970s, including this one, promoted a shift of perspective in the judiciary (a changing "environmental ethic"): The courts began to hold that the burden of proof was on industry rather than on government.

The Reserve Mining case began as a controversy over the effects of water pollution on aquatic life. However, on June 8, 1973, the focus shifted from fish to people—specifically, to the *public health* implications of Reserve Mining's discharge of asbestiform particles into the air and water. There appears to be some sympathy in Judge Bright's first opinion (of June 4, 1974) for the position that the government must prove that a hazardous condition prevails. However, in his second opinion he seems to conclude that the identical evidence proves that a public health hazard exists, and hence that the burden is on industry to take positive steps to end the pollution. Still, he sees the matter of proof as complex. The larger thesis spanning these two opinions is that the burden of proof is always heavier on the government if it seeks an injunction to stop an industry from producing its products on grounds of pollution. The burden is lighter on the government when it seeks only to force industry to reduce the amount of its discharge, thereby cleaning up the environment but without stopping production. This approach is utilitarian: Acceptance of an industry's pollution must be justified on a cost/benefit basis. If the pollution costs the community more than it profits the community, then the company must either cease production or improve the quality of its environmental discharges. However, if it benefits the community more than it places the community at risk, then the balance of justification tips in the direction of industry.

We have had a tendency in the United States to look to legal and regulatory approaches for the resolution of these vital social problems. However, it has become progressively clear that the combined effects of statutory law, case law, and regulatory guideline will not suffice. Problems regarding the quality of the environment and the adequacy of health and safety protections will require corporate initiatives and a keener sense of responsibility on everyone's part.

NOTES

1. Judge Henry Friendly, *Buckley* v. *New York Post,* 373 F.2d 175 (1967), p. 182.
2. Joel Feinberg, *Harm to Others* (New York: Oxford University Press, 1984), p. 34–35.
3. Manuel Gomez et al., "Kennecott/Hurley," in Vol. 3 of *At Work in Copper: Occupational Health and Safety in Copper Smelting* (New York: Inform, 1979), p. 132.
4. Occupational Safety and Health Administration, "Access to Employee Exposure and Medical Records—Final Rules," *Federal Register,* May 23, 1980, p. 35222.
5. See the discussion of these problems in F. R. Anderson et al., *Environmental Improvement Through Economic Incentives* (Baltimore: Johns Hopkins University Press, 1977).

The Ethics of Consumer Production

Manuel G. Velasquez

... Where ... does the consumer's duties to protect his or her own interests end, and where does the manufacturer's duty to protect consumers' interests begin? Three different theories on the ethical duties of manufacturers have been developed, each one of which strikes a different balance between the consumer's duty to himself or herself and the manufacturer's duty to the consumer: the contract view, the "due care" view, and the social costs view. The contract view would place the greater responsibility on the consumer, while the "due care" and social costs views place the larger measure of responsibility on the manufacturer. We will examine each of these views.

1. THE CONTRACT VIEW OF BUSINESS'S DUTIES TO CONSUMERS

According to the contract view of the business firm's duties to its customers, the relationship between a business firm and its customers is essentially a contractual relationship, and the firm's moral duties to the customer are those created by this contractual relationship. When a consumer buys a product, this view holds, the consumer voluntarily enters into a "sales contract" with the business firm. The firm freely and knowingly agrees to give the consumer a product with certain characteristics and the consumer in turn freely and knowingly agrees to pay a certain sum of money to the firm for the product. In virtue of having voluntarily entered this agreement, the firm then has a duty to provide a product with those characteristics, and the consumer has a correlative right to get a product with those characteristics.

The contract theory of the business firm's duties to its customers rests on the view that a contract is a free agreement that imposes on the parties the basic duty of complying with the terms of the agreement. ...

... Traditional moralists have argued that the act of entering into a contract is subject to several secondary moral constraints:

1. Both of the parties to the contract must have full knowledge of the nature of the agreement they are entering.
2. Neither party to a contract must intentionally misrepresent the facts of the contractual situation to the other party.
3. Neither party to a contract must be forced to enter the contract under duress or undue influence.

These secondary constraints can be justified by the same sorts of arguments that Kant[1] and Rawls[2] use to justify the basic duty to perform one's contracts. Kant, for example, easily shows that misrepresentation in the making of a contract cannot be universalized, and Rawls argues that if misrepresentation were not prohibited, fear of deception would make members of a society feel less free to enter contracts. But these secondary constraints can also be justified on the grounds that a contract cannot exist unless these constraints are fulfilled. For a contract is essentially a *free agreement* struck between

From Manuel G. Velasquez, "The Ethics of Consumer Production and Marketing," *Business Ethics: Concepts & Cases,* pp. 226–241, © 1982. Reprinted by permission of Prentice Hall, Englewood Cliffs, N.J.

two parties. Since an agreement cannot exist unless both parties know what they are agreeing to, contracts require full knowledge and the absence of misrepresentation. And since freedom implies the absence of coercion, contracts must be made without duress or undue influence.

The contractual theory of business's duties to consumers, then, claims that a business has four main moral duties: The basic duty of (1) complying with the terms of the sales contract, and the secondary duties of (2) disclosing the nature of the product, (3) avoiding misrepresentation, and (4) avoiding the use of duress and undue influence. By acting in accordance with these duties, a business respects the right of consumers to be treated as free and equal persons, that is, in accordance with their right to be treated only as they have freely consented to be treated.

The Duty to Comply

The most basic moral duty that a business firm owes its customers, according to the contract view, is the duty to provide consumers with a product that lives up to those claims that the firm expressly made about the product, which led the customer to enter the contract freely, and which formed the customer's understanding concerning what he or she was agreeing to buy. In the early 1970s, for example, Winthrop Laboratories marketed a painkiller that the firm advertised as "nonaddictive." Subsequently, a patient using the painkiller became addicted to it and shortly died from an overdose. A court in 1974 found Winthrop Laboratories liable for the patient's death because, although it had expressly stated that the drug was nonaddictive, Winthrop Laboratories had failed to live up to its duty to comply with this express contractual claim.[3]

As the above example suggests, our legal system has incorporated the moral view that firms have a duty to live up to the express claims they make about their products. The Uniform Commercial Code, for example, states in Section 2–314:

Any affirmation of fact or promise made by the seller to the buyer that related to the goods and becomes part of the basis of the bargain creates an express warranty that the goods shall conform to the affirmation or promise.

In addition to the duties that result from the *express* claim a seller makes about the product, the contract view also holds that the seller has a duty to carry through on any *implied* claims he or she knowingly makes about the product. The seller, for example, has the moral duty to provide a product that can be used safely for the ordinary and special purposes for which the customer, relying on the seller's judgment, has been led to believe it can be used. The seller is morally bound to do whatever he or she knows the buyer understood the seller was promising, since at the point of sale sellers should have corrected any misunderstandings they were aware of.[4] . . .

The express or implied claims that a seller might make about the qualities possessed by the product range over a variety of areas and are affected by a number of factors. Frederick Sturdivant classifies these areas in terms of four variables: "The definition of product quality used here is: the degree to which product performance meets predetermined expectation with respect to (1) reliability, (2) service life, (3) maintainability, and (4) safety."[5]

Reliability. Claims of reliability refer to the probability that a product will function as the consumer is led to expect that it will function. If a product incorporates a number of interdependent components, then the probability that it will function properly is equal to the result of multiplying together each component's probability of proper functioning. As the number of components in a product multiplies, therefore, the manufacturer has a corresponding duty to ensure that each component functions in such a manner that the total product is as reliable as he or she implicitly or expressly claims it will be. This is especially the case when malfunction poses health or safety hazards. The

U.S. Consumer Product Safety Commission lists hundreds of examples of hazards from product malfunctions in its yearly report.[6]

Service Life. Claims concerning the life of a product refer to the period of time during which the product will function as effectively as the consumer is led to expect it to function. Generally, the consumer implicitly understands that service life will depend on the amount of wear and tear to which one subjects the product. In addition, consumers also base some of their expectations of service life on the explicit guarantees the manufacturer attaches to the product.

A more subtle factor that influences service life is the factor of obsolescence.[7] Technological advances may render some products obsolete when a new product appears that carries out the same functions more efficiently. Or purely stylistic changes may make last year's product appear dated and less desirable. The contract view implies that a seller who knows that a certain product will become obsolete has a duty to correct any mistaken beliefs he or she knows buyers will form concerning the service life they may expect from the product.

Maintainability. Claims of maintainability are claims concerning the ease with which the product can be repaired and kept in operating condition. Claims of maintainability are often made in the form of an express warranty. Whirlpool Corporation, for example, appended this express warranty on one of its products:

> During your first year of ownership, all parts of the appliance (except the light bulbs) that we find are defective in materials or workmanship will be repaired or replaced by Whirlpool free of charge, and we will pay all labor charges. During the second year, we will continue to assume the same responsibility as stated above except you pay any labor charges.[8]

But sellers often also imply that a product may be easily repaired even after the expiration date of an express warranty. In fact, however, product repairs may be costly, or even impossible, due to the unavailability of parts.

Product Safety. Implied and express claims of product safety refer to the degree of risk associated with using a product. Since the use of virtually any product involves some degree of risk, questions of safety are essentially questions of *acceptable known levels of risk.* That is, a product is safe if its attendant risks are known and judged to be "acceptable" or "reasonable" by the *buyer* in view of the benefits the buyer expects to derive from using the product. This implies that the seller complies with his or her part of a free agreement if the seller provides a product that involves only those risks he or she says it involves, and the buyer purchases it with that understanding. The National Commission on Product Safety, for example, characterized "reasonable risk" in these terms:

> Risks of bodily harm to users are not unreasonable when consumers understand that risks exist, can appraise their probability and severity, know how to cope with them, and voluntarily accept them to get benefits they could not obtain in less risky ways. When there is a risk of this character, consumers have reasonable opportunity to protect themselves; and public authorities should hesitate to substitute their value judgments about the desirability of the risk for those of the consumers who choose to incur it. But preventable risk is not reasonable (a) when consumers do not know that it exists; or (b) when, though aware of it, consumers are unable to estimate its frequency and severity; or (c) when consumers do not know how to cope with it, and hence are likely to incur harm unnecessarily; or (d) when risk is unnecessary in that it could be reduced or eliminated at a cost in money or in the performance of the product that consumers would willingly incur if they knew the facts and were given the choice.[9]

Thus the seller of a product (according to the contractual theory) has a moral duty to provide a product whose use involves *no greater risks* than those the seller *expressly* communicates to the buyer or those the seller *implicitly* communicates by the implicit claims made when marketing the product for a use whose normal risk level is well known. If the label on a bottle, for example, indicates only that the contents are highly toxic ("Danger: Poison"), the product should not include additional risks from flammability. Or, if a firm makes and sells skis, use of the skis should not embody any unexpected additional risks other than the well-known risks which attend skiing (it should not, for example, involve the added possibility of being pierced by splinters should the skis fracture). In short, the seller has a duty to provide a product with a level of risk which is no higher than he or she expressly or implicitly claims it to be, and which the consumer freely and knowingly contracts to assume.

The Duty of Disclosure

An agreement cannot bind unless both parties to the agreement know what they are doing and freely choose to do it. This implies that the seller who intends to enter a contract with a customer has a duty to disclose exactly what the customer is buying and what the terms of the sale are. At a minimum, this means the seller has a duty to inform the buyer of any facts about the product that would affect the customer's decision to purchase the product. For example, if the product the consumer is buying possesses a defect that poses a risk to the user's health or safety, the consumer should be so informed. Some have argued that sellers should also disclose a product's components or ingredients, its performance characteristics, costs of operation, product ratings, and any other applicable standards.[10]

Behind the claim that entry into a sales contract requires full disclosure is the idea that an agreement is free only to the extent that one knows what alternatives are available: Freedom depends on knowledge. The more the buyer knows about the various products available on the market and the more comparisons the buyer is able to make among them, the more one can say that the buyer's agreement is voluntary.[11] . . .

A seller misrepresents a commodity when he or she represents it in a way deliberately intended to deceive the buyer into thinking something about the product that the seller knows is false. The deception may be created by a verbal lie, as when a used model is described as "new," or it may be created by a gesture, as when an unmarked used model is displayed together with several new models. That is, the deliberate intent to misrepresent by false implication is as wrong as the explicit lie.

The varieties of misrepresentation seem to be limited only by the ingenuity of the greed that creates them.[12] . . .

The Duty Not to Coerce

People often act irrationally when under the influence of fear or emotional stress. When a seller takes advantage of a buyer's fear or emotional stress to extract consent to an agreement that the buyer would not make if the buyer were thinking rationally, the seller is using duress or undue influence to coerce. An unscrupulous funeral director, for example, may skillfully induce guilt-ridden and grief-stricken survivors to invest in funeral services that they cannot afford. Since entry into a contract requires *freely* given consent, the seller has a duty to refrain from exploiting emotional states that may induce the buyer to act irrationally against his or her own best interests. For similar reasons, the seller also has the duty not to take advantage of gullibility, immaturity, ignorance, or any other factors that reduce or eliminate the buyer's ability to make free rational choices.

Problems with the Contractual Theory

The main objections to the contract theory focus on the unreality of the assumptions on which the theory is based. First, critics argue, the theory unrealistically assumes that manufacturers make direct agreements with consumers. Nothing could be farther from the truth. Normally, a series of wholesalers and retailers stand between the manufacturer and the ultimate consumer. The manufacturer sells the product to the wholesaler, who sells it to the retailer, who finally sells it to the consumer. The manufacturer never enters into any direct contract with the consumer. How then can one say that manufacturers have contractual duties to the consumer?

Advocates of the contract view of manufacturer's duties have tried to respond to this criticism by arguing that manufacturers enter into "indirect" agreements with consumers. Manufacturers promote their products through their own advertising campaigns. These advertisements supply the promises that lead people to purchase products from retailers who merely function as "conduits" for the manufacturer's product. Consequently, through these advertisements, the manufacturer forges an indirect contractual relationship not only with the immediate retailers who purchase the manufacturer's product but also with the ultimate consumers of the product. The most famous application of this doctrine of broadened indirect contractual relationships is to be found in a 1960 court opinion, *Henningsen* v. *Bloomfield Motors* [see pp. 242–246]. . . .

A second objection to the contract theory focuses on the fact that a contract is a two-edged sword. If a consumer can freely agree to buy a product *with* certain qualities, the consumer can also freely agree to buy a product *without* those qualities. That is, freedom of contract allows a manufacturer to be released from his or her contractual obligations by explicitly *disclaiming* that the product is reliable, serviceable, safe, etc. Many manufacturers fix such disclaimers on their products. The Uniform Commercial Code, in fact, stipulates in Section 2–316:

a. Unless the circumstances indicate otherwise, all implied warranties are excluded by expressions like "as is," "with all faults," or other language that in common understanding calls the buyer's attention to the exclusion of warranties and makes plain that there is no implied warranty, and

b. When the buyer before entering into the contract has examined the goods or the sample or model as fully as he desired, or has refused to examine the goods, there is no implied warranty with regard to defects that on examination ought in the circumstances to have been revealed to him.

The contract view, then, implies that if the consumer has ample opportunity to examine the product and the disclaimers and voluntarily consents to buy it anyway, he or she assumes the responsibility for the defects disclaimed by the manufacturer, as well as for any defects the customer may carelessly have overlooked. Disclaimers can effectively nullify all contractual duties of the manufacturer.

A third objection to the contract theory criticizes the assumption that buyer and seller meet each other as equals in the sales agreement. The contractual theory assumes that buyers and sellers are equally skilled at evaluating the quality of a product and that buyers are able to adequately protect their interests against the seller. This is the assumption built into the requirement that contracts must be freely and knowingly entered into: Both parties must know what they are doing and neither must be coerced into doing it. This equality between buyer and seller that the contractual theory assumes, derives from the laissez-faire ideology that accompanied the historical development of contract theory.[13] Classical laissez-faire ideology held that the economy's markets are competitive and that in competitive markets the consumer's bargaining power is equal to that of the seller. Competition forces the seller to offer the consumer as good or better terms than the consumer could get from other competing sellers, so the consumer has the power to threaten to take his or her business to other sellers. Because of this equality between buyer and seller, it was fair that each be allowed to try to out-bargain the other and unfair to place restrictions on either. In practice, this laissez-faire ideology gave birth to the doctrine of "caveat emptor": let the buyer take care of himself.

In fact, sellers and buyers do not exhibit the equality these doctrines assume. A consumer who must purchase hundreds of different kinds of commodities cannot hope to be as knowledgeable as a manufacturer who specializes in producing a single product. Consumers have neither the expertise nor the time to acquire and process the information on which they must base their purchase decisions. Consumers, as a consequence, must usually rely on the judgment of the seller in making their purchase decisions, and are particularly vulnerable to being harmed by the seller. Equality, far from being the rule, as the contract theory assumes, is usually the exception.

2. THE DUE CARE THEORY

The "due care" theory of the manufacturer's duties to consumers is based on the idea that consumers and sellers do not meet as equals and that the consumer's interests are particularly vulnerable to being harmed by the manufacturer who has a knowledge and an expertise that the consumer does not have. Because manufacturers are in a more advantaged position, they have a duty to take special "care" to ensure that consumers' interests are not harmed by the products that they offer them. The doctrine of "caveat emptor" is here replaced with a weak version of the doctrine of "caveat vendor": let the seller take care of the buyer. . . .

The "due care" view holds, then, that because consumers must depend upon the greater expertise of the manufacturer, the manufacturer not only has a duty to deliver a product that lives up to the express and implied claims about it, but in addition the manufacturer has a duty to exercise due care to prevent others from being injured by the product, *even if the manufacturer explicitly disclaims such responsibility and the buyer agrees to the disclaimer.* The manufacturer violates this duty and is "negligent" when there is a failure to exercise the care that a reasonable person could have foreseen would be necessary to prevent others from being harmed by use of the product. Due care must enter into the design of the product, into the choice of reliable materials for constructing the product, into the manufacturing processes involved in putting the product together, into the quality controls used to test and monitor production, and into the warnings, labels, and instructions attached to the product. In each of these areas, according to the due care view, the manufacturer, in virtue of a greater expertise and knowledge, has a positive duty to take whatever steps are necessary to ensure that when the product leaves the plant it is as safe as possible, and the customer has a right to such assurance. Failure to take such steps is a breach of the moral duty to exercise due care and a violation of the injured person's right to expect such care, a right that rests on the consumer's need to rely on the manufacturer's expertise. Edgar Schein sketched out the basic elements of the "due care" theory several years ago when he wrote:

> . . . a professional is someone who knows better what is good for his client than the client himself does. . . . If we accept this definition of professionalism . . . we may speculate that it is the *vulnerability of the client* that has necessitated the development of moral and ethical codes surrounding the relationship. The client must be protected from exploitation in a situation in which he is unable to protect himself because he lacks the relevant knowledge to do so. . . . [14]

The Duty to Exercise Due Care

. . . According to the due care theory, manufacturers exercise sufficient care when they take adequate steps to prevent whatever injurious effects they can foresee that the use of their product may have on consumers after having conducted inquiries into the way the product will be used and after having attempted to anticipate any possible misuses of the product. A manufacturer, then, is *not* morally negligent when others are harmed by a product and the harm was not one that the manufacturer could possibly have foreseen or prevented. Nor is a manufacturer morally negligent after having taken all reasonable steps to protect the consumer and to ensure that the consumer is informed of any irremovable risks that might still attend the use of the product. A car manufacturer, for example, cannot be said to be negligent from a moral point of view when people carelessly misuse the cars the manufacturer produces. A car manufacturer would be morally negligent only if the manufacturer had allowed unreasonable dangers to remain in the design of the car that consumers cannot be expected to know about or that they cannot guard against by taking their own precautionary measures.

What specific responsibilities does the duty to exercise due care impose on the producer? In general, the producer's responsibilities would extend to three areas:

Design. The manufacturer should ascertain whether the design of an article conceals any dangers, whether it incorporates all feasible safety devices, and whether it uses materials that are adequate for the purposes the product is intended to serve. The manufacturer is responsible for being thoroughly acquainted with the design of the item, and to conduct research and tests extensive enough to uncover any risks that may be involved in employing the article under various conditions of use....

Production. The production manager should control the manufacturing processes to eliminate any defective items, to identify any weaknesses that become apparent during production, and to ensure that short-cuts, substitution of weaker materials, or other economizing measures are not taken during manufacture that would compromise the safety of the final product. To ensure this, there should be adequate quality controls over materials that are to be used in the manufacture of the product and over the various stages of manufacture.

Information. The manufacturer should fix labels, notices, or instructions on the product that will warn the user of all dangers involved in using or misusing the item and that will enable the user to adequately guard himself or herself against harm or injury. These instructions should be clear and simple, and warnings of any hazards involved in using or misusing the product should also be clear, simple, and prominent....

Problems with "Due Care"

The basic difficulty raised by the "due care" theory is that there is no clear method for determining when one has exercised enough "due care." That is, there is no hard and fast rule for determining how far a firm must go to ensure the safety of its product. Some authors have proposed the general utilitarian rule that the greater the probability of harm and the larger the population that might be harmed, the more the firm is obligated to do. But this fails to resolve some important issues. Every product involves at least some small risk of injury. If the manufacturer should try to eliminate even low-level risks, this would require that the manufacturer invest so much in each product that the product would be priced out of the reach of most consumers. Moreover, even *attempting* to balance higher risks against added costs involves measurement problems: How does one quantify risks to health and life?

A second difficulty raised by the "due care" theory is that it assumes that the manufacturer can discover the risks that attend the use of a product before the consumer buys and uses it. In fact, in a technologically innovative society new products will continually be introduced into the market whose defects cannot emerge until years or decades have passed. Only years after thousands of people were using and being exposed to asbestos, for example, did a correlation emerge between the incidence of cancer and exposure to asbestos. Although manufacturers may have greater expertise than consumers, their expertise does not make them omniscient. Who, then, is to bear the costs of injuries sustained from products whose defects neither the manufacturer nor the consumer could have uncovered beforehand?

Thirdly, the due care view appears to some to be paternalistic. For it assumes that the *manufacturer* should be the one who makes the important decisions for the consumer, at least with respect to the levels of risks that are proper for consumers to bear. But one may wonder whether such decisions should not be left up to the free choice of consumers who can decide for themselves whether or not they want to pay for additional risk reduction.

3. THE SOCIAL COSTS VIEW OF THE MANUFACTURER'S DUTIES

A third theory on the duties of the manufacturer would extend the manufacturer's duties beyond those imposed by contractual relationships and beyond those imposed by the duty to exercise due care in preventing injury or harm. This third theory holds that a manufacturer should pay the costs of *any* injuries sustained through any defects in the product, *even when the manufacturer exercised all due care in the design and manufacture of the product and has taken all reasonable precautions to warn users of every foreseen danger.* According to this third theory a manufacturer has a duty to assume the risks of even those injuries that arise out of defects in the product that no one could reasonably have foreseen or eliminated. The theory is a very strong version of the doctrine of "caveat vendor": let the seller take care of the buyer.

This third theory, which has formed the basis of the legal doctrine of "strict liability," is founded on utilitarian arguments.[15] The utilitarian arguments for this third theory hold that the "external" costs of injuries resulting from unavoidable defects in the design of an artifact constitute part of the costs society must pay for producing and using an artifact. By having the manufacturer bear the external costs that result from these injuries as well as the ordinary internal costs of design and manufacture, all costs will be internalized and added on as part of the price of the product. Internalizing all costs in this way, according to proponents of this theory, will lead to a more efficient use of society's resources. First, since the price will reflect *all* the costs of producing and using the artifact, market forces will ensure that the product is not overproduced, and that resources are not wasted on it. (Whereas if some costs were not included in the price, then manufacturers would tend to produce more than is needed.) Secondly, since manufacturers have to pay the costs of injuries, they will be motivated to exercise greater care and to thereby reduce the number of accidents. Manufacturers will therefore strive to cut down the social costs of injuries, and this means a more efficient care for our human resources. In order to produce the maximum benefits possible from our limited resources, therefore, the social costs of injuries from defective products should be internalized by passing them on to the manufacturer, even when the manufacturer has done all that could be done to eliminate such defects. And thirdly, internalizing the costs of injury in this way enables the manufacturer to distribute losses among all the users of a product instead of allowing losses to fall on individuals who may not be able to sustain the loss by themselves.

Underlying this third theory on the duties of the manufacturer are the standard utilitarian assumptions about the values of efficiency. The theory assumes that an efficient use of resources is so important for society that social costs should be allocated in whatever way will lead to a more efficient use and care of our resources. On this basis, the theory argues that a manufacturer should bear the social costs for injuries caused by defects in a product, even when no negligence was involved and no contractual relationship existed between the manufacturer and the user.

Problems with the Social Costs View

The major criticism of the social costs view of the manufacturer's duties is that i[t] is unfair.[16] It is unfair, the critics charge, because it violates the basic canons of compensatory justice. Compensatory justice implies that a person should be forced to compensate an injured party only if the person could foresee and could have prevented the injury. By forcing manufacturers to pay for injuries that they could neither foresee nor prevent, the social costs theory (and the legal theory of 'strict liability' that flows from it) treats manufacturers unfairly. Moreover, insofar as the social costs theory encourages passing the costs of injuries on to all consumers (in the form of higher prices), consumers are also being treated unfairly.

A second criticism of the social costs theory attacks the assumption that passing the costs of all injuries on to manufacturers will reduce the number of accidents.[17] On the contrary, critics claim, by relieving consumers of the responsibility of paying for their own injuries, the social costs theory will encourage carelessness in consumers. And an increase in consumer carelessness will lead to an increase in consumer injuries.

The arguments for and against the social costs theory deserve much more discussion than we can give them here. The theory is essentially an attempt to come to grips with the problem of allocating the costs of injuries between two morally innocent parties: The manufacturer who could not foresee or prevent a product-related injury, and the consumer who could not guard himself or herself against the injury because the hazard was unknown. This allocation problem will arise in any society that, like ours, has come

to rely upon a technology whose effects do not become evident until years after the technology is introduced. Unfortunately, it is also a problem that may have no "fair" solution.

NOTES

1. Immanual Kant, *Groundwork of the Metaphysic of Morals*, trans. H.J. Paton (New York: Harper & Row, Publishers, Inc., 1964), pp. 90, 97; see also, Alan Donagan, *The Theory of Morality* (Chicago: The University of Chicago Press, 1977), p. 92.

2. John Rawls, *A Theory of Justice* (Cambridge: Harvard University Press, Belknap Press, 1971), pp. 344–50.

3. *Crocker* v. *Winthrop Laboratories, Division of Sterling Drug, Inc.,* 514 Southwestern 2d 429 (1974).

4. See Donagan, *Theory of Morality,* p. 91.

5. Frederick D. Sturdivant, *Business and Society* (Homewood, IL: Richard D. Irwin, Inc., 1977), p. 259.

6. U.S. Consumer Products Safety Commission, *1979 Annual Report* (Washington, DC: U.S. Government Printing Office, 1979), pp. 81–101.

7. A somewhat dated but still incisive discussion of this issue is found in Vance Packard, *The Wastemakers* (New York: David McKay Co., Inc., 1960).

8. Quoted in address by S.E. Upton (vice-president of Whirlpool Corporation) to the American Marketing Association in Cleveland, OH: 11 December 1969.

9. National Commission on Product Safety, *Final Report,* quoted in William W. Lowrance, *Of Acceptable Risk* (Los Altos, CA: William Kaufmann, Inc., 1976), p. 80.

10. See Louis Stern, "Consumer Protection via Increased Information," *Journal of Marketing* vol. 31, no. 2 (April 1967).

11. Lawrence E. Hicks, *Coping with Packaging Laws* (New York: AMACOM, 1972), p. 17.

12. See, for example, the many cases cited in George J. Alexander, *Honesty and Competition* (Syracuse, NY: Syracuse University Press, 1967).

13. See Friedrich Kessler and Malcolm Pitman Sharp, *Contracts* (Boston: Little, Brown and Company, 1953), p. 1–9.

14. Edgar H. Schein, "The Problem of Moral Education for the Business Manager," *Industrial Management Review*, 8 (1966): 3–11.

15. See, for example, Michael D. Smith, "The Morality of Strict Liability In Tort," *Business and Professional Ethics*, 3, no. 1 (December 1979): 3–5; for a review of the rich legal literature on this topic, see Richard A. Posner, "Strict Liability: A Comment," *The Journal of Legal Studies*, 2, no. 1 (January 1973): 205–21.

16. George P. Fletcher, "Fairness and Utility in Tort Theory," *Harvard Law Review*, 85, no. 3 (January 1972): 537–73.

17. Posner, *Economic Analysis of Law*, pp. 139–42.

Strict Products Liability and Compensatory Justice

George G. Brenkert

I

Strict products liability is the doctrine that the seller of a product has legal responsibilities to compensate the user of that product for injuries suffered because of a defective aspect of the product, even when the seller has not been negligent in permitting that defect to occur.[1] Thus, even though a manufacturer, for example, has reasonably applied the existing techniques of manufacture and has anticipated and cared for nonintended uses of the product, he may still be held liable for injuries a product user suffers if it can be shown that the product was defective when it left the manufacturer's hands.

To say that there is a crisis today concerning this doctrine would be to utter a commonplace which few in the business community would deny. The development of the doctrine of strict products liability, according to most business people, threatens many businesses financially. Furthermore, strict products liability is said to be a morally questionable doctrine, since the manufacturer or seller has not been negligent in permitting the injury-causing defect to occur. On the other hand, victims of defective products complain that they deserve full compensation for injuries sustained in using a defective product whether or not the seller is at fault. Medical expenses and time lost from one's job are costs no individual should have to bear by himself. It is only fair that the seller share such burdens.

In general, discussions of this crisis focus on the limits to which a business ought to be held responsible. Much less frequently, discussions of strict products liability consider the underlying question of whether the doctrine of strict products liability is rationally justifiable. But unless this question is answered it would seem premature to seek to determine the limits to which businesses ought to be held liable in such cases. In the following paper I discuss this underlying philosophical question and argue that there is a rational justification for strict products liability which links it to the very nature of the free enterprise system.

Used by permission of the author.

II

... To begin with, it is crucial to remember that what we have to consider is the relationship between an entity doing business and an individual. The strict liability attributed to business would not be attributed to an individual who happened to sell some product he had made to his neighbor or a stranger. If Peter sold an article he had made to Paul and Paul hurt himself because the article had a defect which occurred through no negligence of Peter's, we would not normally hold Peter morally responsible to pay for Paul's injuries. . . .

It is different for businesses. They have been held to be legally and morally obliged to pay the victim for his injuries. Why? What is the difference? The difference is that when Paul is hurt by a defective product from corporation X, he is hurt by something produced in a socioeconomic system purportedly embodying free enterprise. In other words, among other things:

1. Each business and/or corporation produces articles or services it sells for profit.
2. Each member of this system competes with other members of the system in trying to do as well as it can for itself not simply in each exchange, but through each exchange for its other values and desires.
3. Competition is to be "open and free, without deception or fraud."
4. Exchanges are voluntary and undertaken when each party believes it can benefit thereby. One party provides the means for another party's ends if the other party will provide the first party the means to its ends.
5. The acquisition and disposition of ownership rights—that is, of private property—is permitted in such exchanges.
6. No market or series of markets constitutes the whole of a society.
7. Law, morality, and government play a role in setting acceptable limits to the nature and kinds of exchange in which people may engage.

What is it about such a system which would justify claims of strict products liability against businesses? . . . In the free enterprise system, each person and/or business is obligated to follow the rules and understandings which define this socioeconomic system. Following the rules is expected to channel competition among individuals and businesses to socially positive results. In providing the means to fulfill the ends of others, one's own ends also get fulfilled.

Though this does not happen in every case, it is supposed to happen most of the time. Those who fail in their competition with others may be the object of charity, but not of other duties. Those who succeed, qua members of this socioeconomic system, do not have moral duties to aid those who fail. Analogously, the team which loses the game may receive our sympathy but the winning team is not obligated to help it to win the next game or even to play it better. Those who violate the rules, however, may be punished or penalized, whether or not the violation was intentional and whether or not it redounded to the benefit of the violator. Thus, a team may be assessed a penalty for something that a team member did unintentionally to a member of the other team but which injured the other team's chances of competition in the game by violating the rules.

This point may be emphasized by another instance involving a game that brings us closer to strict products liability. Imagine that you are playing table tennis with another person in his newly constructed table tennis room. You are both avid table tennis players and the game means a lot to both of you. Suppose that after play has begun, you are suddenly and quite obviously blinded by the light over the table—the light shade has a hole in it which, when it turned in your direction, sent a shaft of light unexpectedly into your eyes. You lose a crucial point as a result. Surely it would be unfair of your opponent to seek to maintain his point because he was faultless—after all, he had not intended to blind you when he installed that light shade. You would correctly object that he had gained the point unfairly, that you should not have to give up the point lost, and that the light shade should be modified so that the game can continue on a fair basis. It is only fair that the point be played over.

Businesses and their customers in a free enterprise system are also engaged in competition with each other. The competition here, however, is multifaceted as each tries to gain the best agreement he can from the other with regard to the buying and selling of raw materials, products, services, and labor. Such agreements must be voluntary. The competition which leads to them cannot involve coercion. In addition, such competition must be fair and ultimately result in the benefit of the entire society through the operation of the proverbial invisible hand.

Crucial to the notion of fairness of competition are not simply the demands that the competition be open, free, and honest, but also that each person in a society be given an equal opportunity to participate in the system in order to fulfill his or her particular ends. . . .

. . . Equality of opportunity requires that one not be prevented by arbitrary obstacles from participating (by engaging in a productive role of some kind or other) in the system of free enterprise, competition, and so on in order to fulfill one's own ends ("reap the benefits"). Accordingly, monopolies are restricted, discriminatory hiring policies have been condemned, and price collusion is forbidden.

However, each person participates in the system of free enterprise *both* as a worker/producer *and* as a consumer. The two roles interact; if the person could not consume he would not be able to work, and if there were no consumers there would be no work to be done. Even if a particular individual is only (what is ordinarily considered) a consumer, he or she plays a theoretically significant role in the competitive free enterprise system. The fairness of the system depends upon what access he or she has to information about goods and services on the market, the lack of coercion imposed on that person

to buy goods, and the lack of arbitrary restrictions imposed by the market and/or government on his or her behavior.

In short, equality of opportunity is a doctrine with two sides which applies both to producers and to consumers. If, then, a person as a consumer or a producer is injured by a defective product—which is one way his activities might arbitrarily be restricted by the action of (one of the members of) the market system—surely his free and voluntary participation in the system of free enterprise will be seriously affected. Specifically, his equal opportunity to participate in the system in order to fulfill his own ends will be diminished.

Here is where strict products liability enters the picture. In cases of strict liability the manufacturer does not intend for a certain aspect of his product to injure someone. Nevertheless, the person is injured. As a result, he is at a disadvantage both as a consumer and as a producer. He cannot continue to play either role as he might wish. Therefore, he is denied that equality of opportunity which is basic to the economic system in question just as surely as he would be if he were excluded from employment by various unintended consequences of the economic system which nevertheless had racially or sexually prejudicial implications. Accordingly, it is fair for the manufacturer to compensate the person for his losses before proceeding with business as usual. That is, the user of a manufacturer's product may justifiably demand compensation from the manufacturer when its product can be shown to be defective and has injured him and harmed his chances of participation in the system of free enterprise.

Hence, strict liability finds a basis in the notion of equality of opportunity which plays a central role in the notion of a free enterprise system. That is why a business which does *not* have to pay for the injuries an individual suffers in the use of a defective article made by that business is felt to be unfair to its customers. Its situation is analogous to that of a player's unintentional violation of a game rule which is intended to foster equality of competitive opportunity.

A soccer player, for example, may unintentionally trip an opposing player. He did not mean to do it; perhaps he himself had stumbled. Still, he has to be penalized. If the referee looked the other way, the tripped player would rightfully object that he had been treated unfairly. Similarly, the manufacturer of a product may be held strictly liable for a product of his which injures a person who uses that product. Even if he is faultless, a consequence of his activities is to render the user of his product less capable of equal participation in the socioeconomic system. The manufacturer should be penalized by way of compensating the victim. Thus, the basis upon which manufacturers are held strictly liable is compensatory justice.

In a society which refuses to resort to paternalism or to central direction of the economy and which turns, instead, to competition in order to allocate scarce positions and resources, compensatory justice requires that the competition be fair and losers be protected.[2] Specifically, no one who loses should be left so destitute that he cannot re-enter the competition. Furthermore, those who suffer injuries traceable to defective merchandise or services which restrict their participation in the competitive system should also be compensated.

Compensatory justice does not presuppose negligence or evil intentions on the part of those to whom the injuries might ultimately be traced. It is not perplexed or incapacitated by the relative innocence of all parties involved. Rather, it is concerned with correcting the disadvantaged situation an individual experiences due to accidents or failures which occur in the normal working of that competitive system. It is on this basis that other compensatory programs which alleviate the disabilities of various minority groups are founded. Strict products liability is also founded on compensatory justice.

An implication of the preceding argument is that business is not morally obliged to pay, as such, for the physical injury a person suffers. Rather, it must pay for the loss of equal competitive opportunity—even though it usually is the case that it is because of a (physical) injury that there is a loss of equal opportunity. Actual legal cases in which the injury which prevents a person from going about his or her daily activities is emotional or mental, as well as physical, supports this thesis. If a person were neither mentally nor physically harmed, but still rendered less capable of participating competitively because of a defective aspect of a product, there would still be grounds for holding the company liable.

For example, suppose I purchased and used a cosmetic product guaranteed to last a month. When used by most people it is odorless. On me, however, it has a terrible smell. I can stand the smell, but my co-workers and most other people find it intolerable. My employer sends me home from work until it wears off. The product has not harmed me physically or mentally. Still, on the above argument, I would have reason to hold the manufacturer liable. Any cosmetic product with this result is defective. As a consequence my opportunity to participate in the socioeconomic system is curbed. I should be compensated.

III

There is another way of arriving at the same conclusion about the basis of strict products liability. To speak of business or the free enterprise system, it was noted above, is to speak of the voluntary exchanges between producer and customer which take place when each party believes he has an opportunity to benefit. Surely customers and producers may miscalculate their benefits; something they voluntarily agreed to buy or sell may turn out not to be to their benefit. The successful person does not have any moral responsibilities to the unsuccessful person—at least as a member of this economic system. If, however, fraud is the reason one person does not benefit, the system is, in principle, undermined. If such fraud were universalized, the system would collapse. Accordingly, the person committing the fraud does have a responsibility to make reparations to the one mistreated.

Consider once again the instance of a person who is harmed by a product he bought or used, a product that can reasonably be said to be defective. Has the nature of the free enterprise system also been undermined or corrupted in this instance? Producer and consumer have exchanged the product but it has not been to their mutual benefit; the manufacturer may have benefited, but the customer has suffered because of the defect. Furthermore, if such exchanges were universalized, the system would also be undone.

Suppose that whenever people bought products from manufacturers the products turned out to be defective and the customers were always injured, even though the manufacturers could not be held negligent. Though one party to such exchanges might benefit, the other party always suffered. If the rationale for this economic system—the reason it was adopted and is defended—were that in the end both parties share the equal opportunity to gain, surely it would collapse with the above consequences. Consequently, as with fraud, an economic system of free enterprise requires that injuries which result from defective products be compensated. The question is: Who is to pay for the compensation?

There are three possibilities. The injured party could pay for his own injuries. However, this is implausible since what is called for is compensation and not merely payment for injuries. If the injured party had simply injured himself, if he had been negligent or careless, then it is plausible that he should pay for his own injuries. No compensation is at stake here. But in the present case the injury stems from the actions of a particular manufacturer who, albeit unwittingly, placed the defective product on the market and stands to gain through its sale.

The rationale of the free enterprise system would be undermined, we have seen, if such actions were universalized, for then the product user's equal opportunity to benefit from the system would be denied. Accordingly, since the rationale and motivation for an individual to be part of this socioeconomic system is his opportunity to gain from participation in it, justice requires that the injured product user receive compensation for his injuries. Since the individual can hardly compensate himself, he must receive compensation from some other source.

Second, some third party—such as government—could compensate the injured person. This is not wholly implausible if one is prepared to modify the structure of the free enterprise system. And, indeed, in the long run this may be the most plausible course of action. However, if one accepts the structure of the free enterprise system, this alternative must be rejected because it permits the interference of government into individual affairs.

Third, we are left with the manufacturer. Suppose a manufacturer's product, even though the manufacturer wasn't negligent, always turned out to be defective and injured those using his products. We might sympathize with his plight, but he would either have to stop manufacturing altogether (no one would buy such products) or else compensate the victims for their losses. (Some people might buy and use his products under these conditions.) If he forced people to buy and use his products he would corrupt the free enterprise system. If he did not compensate the injured users, they would not buy and he would not be able to sell his products. Hence, he could partake of the free enterprise system—that is, sell his products—only if he compensated his user/victims. Accordingly, the sale of this hypothetical line of defective products would be voluntarily accepted as just or fair only if compensation were paid the user/victims of such products by the manufacturer.

The same conclusion follows even if we consider a single defective product. The manufacturer put the defective product on the market. Because of his actions others who seek the opportunity to participate on an equal basis in this system in order to benefit therefrom are unable to do so. Thus, a result of his actions, even though unintended, is to undermine the system's character and integrity. Accordingly, when a person is injured in his attempt to participate in this system, he is owed compensation by the manufacturer. The seller of the defective article must not jeopardize the equal opportunity of the product user to benefit from the system. The seller need not guarantee that the buyer/user will benefit from the purchase of the product; after all, the buyer may miscalculate or be careless in the use of a nondefective product. But if he is not careless or has not miscalculated, his opportunity to benefit from the system is illegitimately harmed if he is injured in its use because of the product's defectiveness. He deserves compensation.

It follows from the arguments in this and the preceding section that strict products liability is not only compatible with the system of free enterprise but that if it were not at-

tributed to the manufacturer the system itself would be morally defective. And the justification for requiring manufacturers to pay compensation when people are injured by defective products is that the demands of compensatory justice are met.[3]

NOTES

1. This characterization of strict products liability is adapted from Alvin S. Weinstein et al., *Products Liability and the Reasonably Safe Product* (New York: John Wiley & Sons, 1978), ch. 1. I understand the seller to include the manufacturer, the retailer, distributors, and wholesalers. For the sake of convenience, I will generally refer simply to the manufacturer.
2. I have drawn heavily, in this paragraph, on the fine article by Bernard Boxhill, "The Morality of Reparation," reprinted in *Reverse Discrimination,* ed. Barry R. Gross (Buffalo, New York: Prometheus Books, 1977), pp. 270–278.
3. I would like to thank the following for providing helpful comments on earlier versions of this paper: Betsy Postow, Jerry Phillips, Bruce Fisher, John Hardwig, and Sheldon Cohen.

A Philosophical Approach to the Management of Occupational Health Hazards

June Fessenden-Raden and Bernard Gert

... Scientific knowledge about actual and potential occupational hazards is limited. Scientists sometimes interpret the same data differently. There is not yet enough data to

conclusively decide exactly how harmful some substances are, but the data that is available can be used to determine relative risks. Too often the result of the disagree-

Excerpted from June Fessenden-Raden and Bernard Gert, "A Philosophical Approach to the Management of Occupational Health Hazards," pp. 2–43, published by the Social Philosophy and Policy Center, Bowling Green State University, 1984. Used by permission.

ments and the many unknowns and uncertainties has been a postponed decision with a call for more data.

Workers, however, face health hazards now. It has been estimated that all workers at some time in their employment life encounter toxic material—most often without ever knowing about the hazard or the risks—with over 55,000,000 persons exposed on a regular basis. Although clearly there needs to be increased support for research in the area of occupational health, we cannot do nothing while we wait for more data. Even given this scientific uncertainty and disagreement, the appropriate role of government, employers, and employees in dealing with occupational health problems must be delineated now. The reduction of occupational health hazards by an agreed upon disciplined approach to these problems, an approach that goes beyond the traditional cost (risk) benefit analysis currently in vogue, is needed. Equally important is the question of what should be done when no exposure standards exist or the risks cannot be prevented.

This paper presents an analytical procedure based on a moral theory that can be used by government officials, employers, and employees when faced with analysis of an occupational health problem. The proposed philosophical-based analytical procedure will assist in determining the relevant facts and justifying the subsequent decision. While this approach will not provide unique answers in every case, we will show that it can (1) reduce the areas of disagreement, (2) eliminate irrelevant facts and reasonings from intruding into the decision-making process, and (3) provide a precise and objective procedure for reasoning about values and facts. . . .

Scope of the Problem

Many occupational-related maladies take 10, 20, even 40 years to develop, or may manifest themselves only in the next generation. The long lag time, the lack of exposure information and medical documentation, plus the impact of an individual's lifestyle, all serve to confuse and even mask the relationship between employment conditions and chronic diseases, birth defects, and reproductive maladies. Statistical inferences from retrospective epidemiological studies are notoriously unreliable. The true scope of employment-related health problems is just not known.

. . . Chemicals, natural and synthetic, are vital to our high quality of life and the U.S. economy. Also, it is known that most chemicals when used under normal conditions will not cause harm to the average healthy adult. In the workplace, unfortunately, conditions of exposure are not "normal"; that is, the concentration of the hazardous substance is often much higher than under so-called "normal" conditions.

Cardiovascular diseases and preventable deaths were found to be abnormally high among workers exposed to carbon monoxide, such as those employed in the veracose rayon industry. Blood and neurological disorders are associated with exposure to such chemicals as solvents (e.g. benzene, carbontetrachloride, and toluene) and heavy metals (e.g. lead, mercury, cadmium, beryllium) and are estimated to affect in excess of 500,000 workers.[1] Exposure to cotton dust has put nearly a million workers at risk of developing byssinosis (brown lung).[2] Hypersensitivity lung diseases, such as asthmas and allergic alveolitis caused by inhalation of chemical gases or fumes, occur not only among miners and factory workers, but are seen in high numbers among quite diverse groups such as artists, firefighters, and meat wrappers.[3] . . .

Six million workers are estimated to have been exposed to known or suspected carcinogens. It is variously estimated that from 5 to 20 percent of all cancers are occupationally related, with many of these concentrated among specific industries (e.g. those having asbestos and pesticide).[4] Using the American Cancer Society estimates of 835,000 new cancer cases for 1982,[5] that would mean from 41,750 to 167,000 new cancer cases are job-related and potentially preventable.

The U.S. Public Health Service in 1975 estimated that 390,000 new cases of occupational disease appear annually with as many as 100,000 deaths having been occupationally induced each year.[6] In excess of 800,000 cases of job-related skin disorders are diagnosed annually: the result of exposure to hazardous substances. It is also known that low levels of hazardous substances can cause subclinical changes, thus making some workers more susceptible to other illnesses. The true dimension of the occupational health problem is not known. And it will not be known until employees, employers, the medical profession, and the government are able to work cooperatively to recognize and correlate specific maladies to employment activities. Many occupational health specialists suggest that the workers most closely involved with an activity can often suggest the most practical ways of reducing the hazard. Paradoxically, in some cases, it is these employees that have not been made aware of the hazards. . . .

An Analytical Approach Based on Impartial Rationality

Since it is very difficult, often impossible, to prove that a health problem, especially if chronic, is the result of an employment-related exposure to a hazardous substance, and given the different self-interests, some procedure(s) must be available to justify the respective responsibilities of employees, employers, and government. This section presents and uses a morally-based analytical procedure that could be agreed upon and used to resolve disagreements, including determining the appropriate kinds and limits of government intervention as well as determining the responsibilities of employers and employees.

To morally justify breaking a moral rule (e.g. deprive of freedom or opportunity), it is first required that one determine[s] what facts are morally relevant to the specific violation. The first part of our proposed approach consists of four questions that provide a guideline for determining the morally relevant facts in each situation. These questions are:

1. What is (are) the moral rule(s) being violated?;
2. What is the amount of harm (its probability + severity) caused by the violation?;
3. What is the amount of harm avoided or prevented by the violation?; and
4. What are the rational desires of those toward whom the moral rule is being violated?

Once one has the answers to these four questions, one knows all of the morally relevant facts and can proceed to determine whether or not one regards that violation of a moral rule as morally justified.

The second part of the proposed procedure insures impartiality by requiring that a rational person use all, but only, the morally relevant facts determined as outlined in the four questions above, and then decide if the action described by these facts could be publicly advocated. If the rational desires of those toward whom the moral rule is being violated give their valid consent to the violation, this in itself provides moral justification for the violation, because all rational persons would agree to such a violation. But when people do not want the rule violated, we must consider whether at least some rational persons, given just these relevant facts provided by the answers to questions 2 and 3, would agree that the evil prevented by universally allowing the violation significantly outweighs the evil caused by such a universal violation[.] If no rational person would agree to the violation it is not morally justified. If some would, it is at least weakly justified. If all rational persons would agree to the violation, then the action is strongly justified and it would be morally wrong not to break the rule. While this procedure allows for moral disagreement, it should be able to reduce the points of disagreement and make clearer whether there is a disagreement on the facts of the case or on the ranking of the different evils.

When considering government intervention to regulate a hazardous substance, the procedure would be to first ask the four questions to determine the morally relevant facts, that is, to determine what counts as the same violation. Then one would decide if the regulation could be morally justified and determine if the violation could be publicly advocated (rationality is assumed). The four questions would be responded to as follows:

1. Regulations break the moral rule "Don't deprive of freedom or opportunity."
2. The amount of harm that regulation inflicts on both the employers and employees would be considered.
3. The amount of worker death, disability, and pain prevented by the regulation would be considered. Employer harm avoided, usually in terms of economic costs of worker absenteeism, medical and disability insurance, etc., would also be relevant.
4. The rational desires of those who are being deprived of freedom and opportunity (i.e. the regulated employers) would be considered.

... Recently several national management groups, as well as several unions, successfully convinced OSHA to reinstate a federal directive requiring a uniform hazard communication standard. The current plan would require labelling of over 300 hazardous chemicals, preparation of Material Data Sheets (MDS), and training programs. The unions supported the regulation as a means of informing workers. Some management groups desired such regulations even though they lost some freedom, because to have had separate states enacting different labelling and/or 'right-to-know' laws would have entailed complying with several different laws, resulting in a greater cost.

Employers who are conscious of the degradation of the environment by industrial pollution and who have diminished their own pollution output would be expected to favor certain clean water and clean air legislation. Without some federal mandate any pollution-conscious company could be put at a competitive disadvantage by an unconcerned company. Also, if there were only

state regulations that differed from state to state, a given company would be disadvantaged or advantaged depending on the specific regulations of the state in which the company operated. Thus, concerned companies and/or companies operating in several states would be expected to support national legislation. In these examples, that of setting speed limits, pollution containment measures, and the labelling of hazardous chemicals, the primary justification is that considerably more harm is prevented than is caused. However, it is also true in these cases that most of the persons affected by the regulations have a rational desire to have their freedom curtailed in order to gain the greater benefits of such limitations.

The procedure we have been discussing may seem to be the familiar cost-benefit analysis with risk assessment tacked on. It is, however, important to distinguish it from (1) standard utilitarian cost-benefit analysis, which attempts to convert all factors to common negotiable tender, and (2) risk assessment, which considers only facts relevant to risks. Both of these procedures share a common problem in that they do not take into account the distribution of goods and evils, the fairness of risk, or justice. Although cost-benefit analysis and risk assessment play a role in determining the relevant facts, our proposed procedure differs from both in that it claims that more facts are relevant (e.g. it regards as essential the determination of who pays what cost, who takes what risk, and who receives what benefit). When the same person or group receives the benefits and pays the costs or takes the risks, a simple balancing of benefits and costs or risks would result in the same conclusion as the procedure proposed above. There is, however, an insidious nature to traditional cost-benefit analysis that could allow a few to suffer great harm to benefit many others in some small way. Rational persons would hardly consent to such a risk for themselves unless coerced in some manner, and it would be immoral to subject anyone to such a risk for such a gain without his/her consent. It is essential, therefore, that any pre-scribed procedure not have this fault.

Our proposed analytical procedure does not merely consider the costs, risks, and benefits of a particular violation, but what would be the costs, risks, and benefits if this kind of violation were to be universally al-lowed, that is, if one publicly advocated this kind of violation? Universalizing increases impartially by moving from the particular to the general, which counterbalances the falli-bility of people. It seems quite natural for people to expect that one specific violation will not do much harm, but from past experi-ences it is known that people consistently underestimate the harm they cause and over-estimate the harm they prevent. By requiring that all cases of the "same kind" be consid-ered, rather than only one particular action, a decision-maker is forced to think about and describe a given case in more general terms, since "same kind" is determined com-pletely by the general factors given in an-swer to the four questions discussed above. The universalizing further supports imparti-ality by forcing one to take more seriously the fact that the harm prevented is only probable while some of the harm caused by a violation is certain. . . .

APPLICATION OF THE ANALYTICAL APPROACH

. . . Given the magnitude of current and fu-ture harms, nearly everyone would agree that exposure to asbestos should be con-trolled and that government intervention to establish exposure standards is justified. In-tuitively, most of us would reject allowing such a potentially significant harm to con-tinue unabated and feel government inter-vention to limit exposure justified. But is it?

Using our analytical approach to deter-mine if regulation of worker exposure to as-bestos is justified, we would first determine the relevant facts by answering the four questions:

1. What moral rule is being broken? As with all regulations, there is some deprivation of freedom.
2. What harms will the regulation cause? There will be increased economic costs for the em-ployers to bring their workplaces within estab-lished worker exposure limits. For the employ-ees, there is inconvenience when they must wear personal protection equipment and clothing.
3. What harms will the regulation prevent? The benefits are both economic—a lowering of fu-ture employer costs (e.g. insurance), and health-related—the prevention of significant pain, disability and premature death (e.g. as-bestosis, cancer).
4. What are the rational desires of the employees and employers? The employees would be ex-pected to be willing to give up some freedom for better health. It is also plausible to assume that given the magnitude of the asbestos-related maladies and the compensation costs, some employers would be willing to give up some freedom, although they may prefer vol-untary guidelines.

Given the above facts, some level of en-forceable regulation would be universally advocated by all impartial rational persons for all cases of this kind. It is, therefore, clearly morally justified for the government to intervene and provide the legal force to ensure that the employers do what is morally required (i.e. not to harm). . . .

Permissible Exposure Limits (PEL)

While employers and employees will prob-ably agree that some type of government regulation of asbestos is justified, they would be expected to disagree on the specifics of that regulation. Employees would want a regulation that set their health risks as low as possible; that is, they would advocate im-mediate implementation of an exposure standard for asbestos fibers that represented the lowest technically possible exposure level with minimal employee inconvenience (e.g. being required to wear special equip-ment). Employers would be expected to prefer an exposure guideline with the standard set at a level that would not require great technological retooling. Also they would want as much time as possible in which to comply with the standard. Once it has been determined that some exposure level regulation is justified, one can determine the justification of a specific exposure standard using the same procedure and answering the same four questions.

It is essential to know if available technology can lower the workplace asbestos concentration to the desired level or, if it is not available, what the feasibility of its development is, and over how long a period of time.

To fully understand the future harm prevented or avoided, unbiased scientific risk assessments must be available for each of the exposure conditions under consideration. For example, in determining what size asbestos particles should be excluded from the workplace, one would need to know that a majority of the asbestos fibers found at autopsy in human lungs were more than 5 μm in length. Moreover, seldom were fibers found more than 200 μm in length. The diameter of the fibers ranged from about 0.5 μm to 3.3 μm. Data have shown that fibers in these ranges of length and width can cause cancer and asbestosis. Applying our proposed procedure utilizing all available and relevant information, including uncertain information, one would opt for a regulatory standard rather than a guideline. Also the PEL fiber size selected would be the one to provide the maximum feasible protection from available technology within a reasonable time. Thus, in 1972 the OSHA standard excluding asbestos fibers of 5 μm or longer length from the work place would have been justified. Also, using this approach whenever new relevant facts become available concerning technology or health hazards the current standard or guideline must be reassessed. In fact, such evidence did become available and in 1976 OSHA lowered the PEL fiber length to 2 μm. Since then even more health hazard data has accumulated, and a lowering of the PEL fiber length to 0.5

μm with maximum diameter of 5 μm was proposed by NIOSH but not acted upon by OSHA. Results obtained using the proposed procedure would indicate that not only would OSHA be justified in lowering the PEL fiber size, but that morally, OSHA should select the reduced PEL fiber size for asbestos.[7] . . .

All impartial rational persons would agree that banning or restricting from the workplace toxic chemicals and materials that cause great harm is both appropriate and justified and should be pursued unless there is an overwhelming reason not to. The restriction on employer freedom by government regulatory intervention is justified when the evil(s) to be avoided or ameliorated are very great, much greater than the loss of freedom, and are such that it would be irrational for any impartial person not to favor the restriction of freedom in order to avoid the evil(s); though as noted above there can be legitimate disagreement on the extent of the restriction.

Unfortunately, not all regulatory determinations are ever this clear-cut; most involve some disagreement. Policy decisions often must be made where there is scientific uncertainty and disagreement on the interpretation of the data which lead to disagreement on the solution. It is with these cases that the analytical approach we have suggested could be helpful in establishing the relevant facts needed to propose a specific action (e.g. regulation). Once the irrelevant facts are excluded, we then ask, "Could that action be one that is advocated for all similar cases all of the time?" This, however, does not guarantee agreement on the specific solution, only that each proposed standard is one that could be justified given what was known at the time it was proposed. . . .

Utilizing this same approach there would be a general consensus that those substances with no known or suspected toxic properties, or only weakly toxic properties (e.g. sodium chloride), should be free from all regulation. Many other chemicals such as the approximately 400 listed by NIOSH/OSHA in the "Occupational Health Guidelines for Chemical Hazards",[8] will justifiably have guideline standards or strict governmental control. Most of the 40,000 substances listed in the NIOSH "Registry of Toxic Effects of Chemical Substances" will, however, fit into neither the control nor the no-control category.[9] For most of these substances, there will be considerable disagreement about their toxicity due to a limited amount of unbiased data, scientific uncertainty, or scientific disagreement. There are also thousands of chemicals that are not listed by NIOSH because no toxicity data exist, but which, nevertheless, may be toxic or hazardous in some other way (e.g. explosive or flammable), or for which only minimal data exist. To control these chemicals would unduly restrict freedom and cannot be justified.

The prevention of workplace health problems requires more than voluntary control programs and controlling employee exposure. Standards in and of themselves are not sufficient to prevent harm to some workers, therefore the actual and potential harms of any workplace must be made known to the workers, and this requirement must be [e]nforced by OSHA. . . .

SHARED RESPONSIBILITY

It is now recognized that informed employees and their supervisors are sometimes in a much better position than the government to solve many of the hazardous substances exposure problems. Both employers and employees have certain morally required responsibilities. Employers, because of their positions of management and control, are expected to assume the major share of the responsibility for providing a safe and healthful workplace.

Role of the Employer

The moral requirement not to harm imposes a duty on employers to (1) eliminate, wherever feasible, hazardous substances from the workplace; and whenever elimination is not feasible, to (2) control all hazardous substances so as to minimize worker exposure, (3) provide information to all employees, and (4) train employees so that they understand and appreciate the information provided. In this way no worker will ever be exposed to a hazardous substance without his/her valid consent. . . .

Several unions have tried to insure that employers provide as safe and healthful a workplace as possible via contract negotiations. For example, General Motors and the United Auto Workers have, through negotiation, established an occupational health advisory board consisting of a panel of experts who will work with the unions and company to improve health and safety.[10] This is a precedent-setting example of cooperation and sharing of responsibility. In some instances, unions have also been able to negotiate higher pay for more hazardous jobs. But even with unions, employee health and safety issues have a lower priority than employee compensation or job security, especially during economical[ly] hard times.

Role of the Employee

Learning what is harmful is helpful for avoiding harm. Thus, employee education and training should be a part of any job requirement. It is recognized that employees will not be uniformly interested in acquiring information, training, or understanding. However, employees cannot neglect the duties associated with their employment in order to be "macho" and show their fearlessness, or because the personal protective equipment is awkward and uncomfortable, or because they do not want to learn about, understand, or face the possible health hazards. The job requirement should be used to enforce what is morally required. The requirement not to harm imposes a responsibility on employees to act on relevant health hazard information in such a way that they will not cause harm to others. Employees cannot arbitrarily decide to ignore a prescribed procedure for handling a toxic substance and thereby expose another employee to an increased risk of cancer. That would clearly be causing harm and be immoral and punishable.

Employees must follow established health and safety procedures in their work practices even if they would seem to be the only ones who would be harmed if the procedures were not followed. First, it is very unlikely that the employee would be the only one placed at increased risk. Second, even if it were possible to directly harm no one else, every accident or illness, death, or disability, affects the employer's insurance and compensation costs. Indirectly, other workers, consumers of the goods or services, and taxpayers may be adversely affected by such actions: this justifies imposing a duty on employees to follow all health and safety regulations.

The assurance of competence may be done in several ways such as informal discussions in small groups or one-on-one discussions, or the process may be more formal and suitable oral or written tests may be given to measure employee understanding. Through the process of insuring competence, whether by testing or discourse, nonbelievers and slower learners could be identified, and special provision could be made for them to receive more education or information or have the information presented in a different format until it is adequately understood. Also, questions can be answered and misunderstandings cleared up.

Employees or prospective employees who refuse the information provided or cannot demonstrate that they understand the information (e.g. pass an informal test) could be considered incompetent for that job and justifiably be fired or not hired. Such employees would legitimately be considered unqualified for the job.

Those who fail to follow the procedures would be appropriately considered negligent. Further, employees should be encouraged to actively seek information whenever they have questions or concerns or suspect a possible hazard, to support proper monitoring and enforcement of health and safety practices and standards, and to suggest possible ways of better controlling a hazardous substance....

To summarize, this analytical procedure, based on impartial rationality, could be an agreed upon conceptual framework in which to consider all risk management decisions. The procedure can be used to resolve disagreements, including determining the appropriate limits of government intervention and the responsibilities of employers and employees in the risk management of occupational health hazards....

... As people become better educated they will be more able to make valid decisions about risks to themselves and their families. It would, therefore, seem to be a most opportune time in which to give legal standing to what is already morally required.

NOTES

1. NIOSH, National Occupational Hazard Survey, Vol. III, Survey Analysis and Supplemental Tables. Cincinnati: USHEW NIOSH Publ. No. 78–114, 1977.
2. Gemmill, Daphne, De J. and Edward C. Prest, "Occupational Lung Disease—We're Seeing Only the Tip of the Iceberg." *Amer. Lung Assoc. Bull.* 63 (August 1977): 12–16.
3. Anderson, J. Marion, "Prevention of Job-Related Lung Diseases." *Amer. Lung Assoc. Bull.* 65 (January 1979): 10–13.
4. "German Research." Jan. 11, 1982, as reported in *Occupational Safety and Health Letter* 12 (4): 5. Washington, D.C.: Environews, Inc., 1982.
5. Silverberg, Edwin, "Cancer Statistics, 1982." *CA-A Cancer J. for Clinicians* 32 (1982): 15–31.
6. Ashford, Nicolas A., *Crisis in the Workplace: Occupational Disease and Injury,* Cambridge: MIT Press, 1976: 10.
7. Levine, Richard J. (ed.), *Asbestos: An Information Resource,* Washington, D.C.: NIH, USPHS, U.S. Dept. of Health, Education, and Welfare, 1978, pp. 1–5.
8. Mackean, F. W., R. S. Stricoff, and L. J. Partridge, Jr. (eds.), *Occupational Health Guidelines for Chemical Hazards,* 3 volumes. Washington,

D.C. USDHHS and U.S. Dept. of Labor, NIOSH Publ. No. 81–123, 1981.

9. Lewis, R. J., Sr., and R. L. Tathen (ed.), *The Registry of Toxic Effects of Chemical Substances,* 2 volumes. Cincinnati: USHHS. NIOSH Publ. No. 80–111, 1981.

10. *Occupational Health and Safety Letter,* 12 (1982): 6–7. Washington, D.C.: Environews, Inc.

The Right to Risk Information and the Right to Refuse Health Hazards in the Workplace

Ruth R. Faden and Tom L. Beauchamp

In recent years, the right of employees to know about health hazards in the workplace has emerged as a major issue in occupational health policy.[1] This paper focuses on several philosophical and policy-oriented problems about the right to know and correlative duties to disclose. Also addressed are related rights, such as the right to refuse hazardous work and the right of workers to contribute to the development of safety standards in the workplace.

I

A general consensus has gradually evolved in government and industry that there is a right to know, and correlatively that there is both a moral and legal obligation to disclose relevant information to workers. The National Institute for Occupational Safety and Health (NIOSH) and other U.S. federal agencies informed the U.S. Senate as early as July 1977 that "workers have the right to know whether or not they are exposed to hazard-

ous chemical and physical agents regulated by the Federal Government."[2] The Occupational Safety and Health Administration (OSHA) promulgated regulations guaranteeing workers access to medical and exposure records in 1980,[3] and then developed regulations in 1983 and 1986 pertaining to the right to know about hazardous chemicals and requiring right-to-know training programs in many industries.[4] Legislation has also passed in numerous states and municipalities that are often more stringent than federal requirements.[5] For example, one of the earliest state bills, in New York, declared that employees and their representatives have a right to "*all* information relating to toxic substances"—a right that cannot be "waived as a condition of employment."[6] Many corporations—including Monsanto, DuPont, and Hercules—have also initiated right-to-know programs.

Although the general view that workers have some form of right to information about health hazards is now well established under law, there is no consensus about the

Copyright © 1982, 1987 by Ruth R. Faden and Tom L. Beauchamp. We are indebted to Ilise Feitshans for helpful comments and criticisms on the 1987 revision. Parts of the earlier article had appeared in the *Canadian Journal of Philosophy,* Supplementary Volume, 1982.

nature and extent of an employer's moral or legal obligation to disclose such information. Considerable ambiguity also attends the nature and scope of the right—that is, which protections and actions the right entails, and to whom these rights apply.[7] For example, there is often a failure to distinguish between disclosing already available information, seeking information through literature searches or new research, and communicating about hazards through educational or other training programs. It is also often unclear whether there exists an affirmative duty to disclose information about health hazards to workers or merely a duty to honor worker-initiated or physician-initiated requests for access to records. What corporations owe their workers' over and above the demands of federal and state requirements is likewise little discussed in the literature.

II

The belief that citizens and communities in general (and sometimes workers in particular) have a right to know about significant risks is reflected in a diverse set of recent laws and federal regulations in the United States. These include The Freedom of Information Act; The Federal Insecticide, Fungicide, and Rodenticide Amendments and Regulations; The Motor Vehicle and School Bus Safety Amendments; The Truth-in-Lending Act; The Pension Reform Act; The Real Estate Settlement Procedures Act; The Federal Food, Drug, and Cosmetic Act; The Consumer Product Safety Act; and The Toxic Substances Control Act. These acts commonly require manufacturers and other businesses to make available guidebooks, explanations of products, and warranties. Taken together, the implicit message of this corpus of legislation is that manufacturers and other businesses have a moral (and in some cases a legal) obligation to disclose information without which individuals could not adequately decide about matters of par-

ticipation, usage, employment, or enrollment.[8]

Recent legal developments in the employee's right-to-know controversy have been consistent with this general trend toward disclosure and have included a more sweeping notion of corporate responsibility to provide adequate information to workers than had previously prevailed. These developments could have a pervasive and revolutionary effect on major American corporations. Until the 1983 final OSHA Hazard Communication Standard went into effect in 1986,[9] workers did not routinely receive extensive information from many employers. Now some corporations are beginning to establish model programs. For example, the Monsanto Company has a right-to-know program in which it distributes information on hazardous chemicals at its 53 plants, screens its employees, and both notifies and monitors past and current employees exposed to carcinogenic chemicals. Hercules Inc. has training sessions using videotapes with frank discussions of workers' anxieties. The tapes include depictions of dangers and of on-the-job accidents. Those employees who have seen the Hercules film are then instructed how to read safety data and how to protect themselves.[10]

That such programs are needed in many corporations is evident from the sobering statistics on worker exposure and injury and on dangerous chemicals in the workplace. The annual Registry of Toxic Effects of Chemical Substances lists over 25,000 hazardous chemicals, at least 8,000 of which are present in the workplace. As OSHA pointed out in the preamble to its final Hazard Communication Standard, an estimated 25 million largely uninformed workers in North America (1 in 4 workers) are exposed to toxic substances regulated by the federal government. About 6,000 American workers die from workplace injuries each year, and perhaps as many as 100,000 deaths annually are caused in some measure by workplace exposure and consequent disease. One percent of the labor force is exposed to known carcinogens, and over 44,000 U.S. workers are exposed *fulltime* to OSHA-regulated carcinogens.[11]

III

The most developed models of general disclosure obligations and the right to know are presently found in the extensive literature on informed consent, which also deals with informed refusal. This literature developed largely in the context of fiduciary relationships between physicians and patients, where there are broadly recognized moral and legal obligations to disclose known risks (and benefits) associated with a proposed treatment or research maneuver.

No parallel obligation has traditionally been recognized in nonfiduciary relationships, such as that between management and workers. Risks in this environment have traditionally been handled largely by workmen's compensation laws that were originally designed for problems of accident in instances of immediately assessable damage. Duties to warn or to disclose are irrelevant under the "no-fault" conception operative in workmen's compensation, and thus these duties went undeveloped.

However, needs for information in clinical medicine and in the workplace have become more similar in light of recent knowledge about occupational disease—in particular, knowledge about the serious long-term risks of injury, disease, and death from exposure to toxic substances. In comparison to traditional accident and safety issues, these recently discovered risks to health in the workplace carry with them *increased* need for information on the basis of which a person may wish to take various actions, including choosing to forego employment completely, to refuse certain work environments within a place of employment, to request improved protective devices, or to request lowered levels of exposure.

Employee-employer relationships—unlike physician-patient relationships—are often confrontational, with few goals shared in common, and therefore with undisclosed risk to workers a constant danger. This danger of harm to employees and their relative powerlessness in the employer-employee relationship may not be sufficient to justify employer disclosure obligations in *all* industries, but few would deny that placing relevant information in the hands of workers seems morally appropriate in at least some cases. By what criteria, then, shall such disclosure obligations be determined?

One plausible argument is the following: Because large employers, unions, and government agencies must deal with multiple employees and complicated causal conditions, no standard should be *more* demanding than the so-called objective reasonable person standard. This is the standard of what a fair and informed member of the relevant community believes is needed. Under this standard, no employer, union, or other party should be held responsible for disclosing information beyond that needed to make an informed choice about the adequacy of safety precautions, industrial hygiene, long-term hazards, and the like, as determined by what the reasonable person in the community would judge to be the worker's need for information material to a decision about employment or working conditions.

It does not follow, however, that this general standard of disclosure is adequate for all individual disclosures. At least in the case of serious hazards—such as those involved in short-term, but concentrated doses of radiation—a *subjective* standard may be more appropriate.[12] In cases where disclosures to *individual* workers may be expected to have significant subjective impact that varies with each individual, the reasonable person standard should perhaps be supplemented by a standard that takes account of each worker's personal informational needs. A viable alternative might be to include the following as a component of all general disclosures under the reasonable person standard: "If you are concerned about the possible effect of hazards on your individual health, and you seek clarification or personal information, a company physician may be consulted by making an appointment." Perhaps the most satisfactory solution to the problem of a general standard is a compromise between a reasonable-person and a subjective standard: Whatever a reasonable person would judge material to the decision-making process should be disclosed, and in addition any remaining information that is material to an individual worker should be provided through a process of asking whether he or she has any additional or special concerns.[13]

This standard is indifferent as to which groups of workers will be included. Former workers, for example, often have as much or even more need for the information than do presently employed workers. The federal government has the names of approximately 250,000 former workers whose risk of cancer, heart disease, and lung disease has been increased by exposure to asbestos, polyvinyl chloride, benzene, arsenic, betanaphthy-alamine, and dozens of other chemicals. Employers have the names of several million such workers. Legislation has been in and out of the U.S. Congress to notify workers at greatest risk so that checkups and diagnosis of disease can be made before an advanced stage.[14] At this writing, neither industry nor the government has developed a systematic program, claiming that the expense of notification would be enormous, that many workers would be unduly alarmed, and that existing screening and surveillance programs should prove adequate to the task of monitoring and treating disease. Critics charge, however, that existing programs are far from adequate and that, in any event, there are duties to inform workers so that they can pursue potential problems at their own initiative.[15]

IV

Despite the apparent consensus on the appropriateness of having some form of right to know in the workplace, there are reasons why it will prove difficult to implement this right. There are, for example, complicated questions about the kinds of information to be disclosed, by whom, to whom, and under what conditions. Trade secrets have also been a long-standing thorn in the side of progress, because companies resist disclosing information about an ingredient or process that they claim is a trade-secret.[16]

There is also the problem of what to do if workers are inhibited from taking actions they otherwise would take because of economic or other constraints. For example, in industries where ten people stand in line for every available position, bargaining for increased protection is an unlikely event. However, we must set most of these problems aside here in order to consider perhaps the most perplexing difficulty about the right to know in the workplace: the right to refuse hazardous work assignments and to have effective mechanisms for workers to reduce the risks they face.

In a limited range of cases, it is possible for informed workers to reject employment because they regard health and safety conditions as unacceptable. This decision is most likely to be reached in a job market where workers have alternative employment opportunities or where a worker is being offered a new assignment with the option of remaining in his or her current job. More commonly, however, workers are not in a position to respond to information about health hazards by seeking employment elsewhere. For the information to be useful, it must be possible for workers to effect changes on the job.

The United States Occupational Safety and Health Act of 1970 (OSH Act)[17] confers a series of rights on employees that appear to give increased significance to the duty to disclose hazards in the workplace. Specifically, the OSH Act grants workers the right to request an OSHA inspection if they believe an OSHA standard has been violated or an imminent hazard exists. Under the Act, employees also have the right to "walk-around," that is, to participate in OSHA inspections of the worksite and to consult freely with the inspection officer. Most importantly, the OSH Act expressly protects employees who request an inspection or otherwise exercise their rights under the OSH Act from discharge or any discriminatory treatment in retaliation for legitimate safety and health complaints.[18]

While these worker rights under the OSH Act are important, they are not strong enough to assure that all workers have effective mechanisms for initiating inspections of suspected health hazards. Small businesses (those with fewer than ten workers) and federal, state, and municipal employees are not covered by the OSH Act. There are also questions about the ability of the Occupational Safety and Health Administration (OSHA) to enforce these provisions of the OSH Act. If workers are to make effective use of disclosed information about health hazards, they must have access to an effective and efficient regulatory system.

It is also essential that workers have an adequately protected right to refuse unsafe work. It is difficult to determine the extent to which this right is legally protected at the present time. Although the OSH Act does not grant a general right to refuse unsafe work,[19] provisions to this effect exist in some state occupational safety laws. In addition, the Secretary of Labor has issued a regulation that interprets the OSH Act as including a limited right to refuse unsafe work, a right that was upheld by the United States Supreme Court in 1980.[20] A limited right of refusal is also protected in the Labor-Management Relations Act (LMRA) and implicitly in the National Labor Relations Act (NLRA).[21]

Unfortunately, these statutory protections vary significantly in the conditions under which they grant a right to refuse and in the consequences they permit to follow from such refusals. For example, the OSHA regulation allows workers to walk off the job where there is a "real danger of death or serious injury," while the LMRA permits re-

fusals only under "abnormally dangerous conditions."[22] Thus, under the LMRA, the nature of the occupation determines the extent of danger justifying refusal, while under OSHA the character of the threat, or so-called "imminent danger," is determinative. By contrast, under the NLRA a walk-out by two or more workers may be justified for even minimal safety problems, so long as the action can be construed as a "concerted activity" for mutual aid and protection and there does not exist a no-strike clause in any collective bargaining agreements.[23] While the NLRA would appear to provide the broadest protection to workers, employees refusing to work under the NLRA may lose the right to be reinstated in their positions if permanent replacements can be found.[24]

The relative merits of the different statutes are further confused by questions of overlapping authority, called "preemption." It is not always clear (1) whether a worker is eligible to claim protection under a given law, (2) which law affords a worker maximum protections or remedies in a particular circumstance, and (3) whether or under what conditions a worker can seek relief under another law or through the courts, once a claim under a given law has not prevailed.

The current legal situation concerning the right to refuse hazardous work leaves many other questions unresolved as well. Consider, for example, whether a meaningful right to refuse hazardous work entails an obligation to continue to pay nonworking employees, or to award the employees back pay if the issue is resolved in their favor. On the one hand, workers without union strike benefits or other income protections would be unable to exercise their right to refuse unsafe work because of economic pressures. On the other hand, to permit such workers to draw a paycheck is to legitimate strike with pay, a practice generally considered unacceptable by management and by Congress. Also unresolved is whether the right to refuse unsafe work should be restricted to cases of obvious, imminent, and serious risks to health or life (the current OSHA and

LMRA position) or should be expanded to include lesser risks and uncertain risks—for example, exposure to suspected toxic or carcinogenic substances that although not immediate threats, may prove more dangerous over time. If "the right to know" is to lead to meaningful worker action, workers must be able to remove themselves from exposure to suspected hazards, as well as obvious or known hazards.

Related to this issue is the question of the proper standard for determining whether a safety walkout is justified. At least three different standards have been applied in the past: a good-faith subjective standard, which requires only a determination that the worker honestly believes that the health hazard exists; a reasonable person standard, which requires that the belief be reasonable under the circumstances as well as sincerely held; and an objective standard, which requires evidence—generally established by expert witnesses—that the threat actually exists. Although the possibility of worker abuse of the right to refuse has been a major factor in a current trend to reject the good faith standard, recent commentary has argued that this trend raises serious equity issues in the proper balancing of this concern with the needs of workers confronted with basic self-preservation issues.[25]

No less important is whether the right to refuse hazardous work should be protected only until a formal review of the situation is initiated (at which time the worker must return to the job) or whether the walkout should be permitted until the alleged hazard is at least temporarily removed. So long as the hazards covered under a right to refuse are restricted to risks that are obvious in the environment and that are easily established as health hazards, this issue is relatively easy to resolve. However, if the nature of the risk is less apparent, a major function of any meaningful right to refuse will be to call attention to an alleged hazard and to compel regulatory action. If this chain of events is set in motion, then requirements that workers continue to be exposed while OSHA or

the NLRB conduct investigations may be unacceptable to workers and certainly will be unacceptable if the magnitude of potential harm is perceived to be significant. However, compelling employers to remove suspected hazards during the evaluation period may also result in intolerable economic burdens. We therefore need a delineation of the conditions under which workers may be compelled to return to work while an alleged hazard is being evaluated, and the conditions under which employers must be compelled to remove immediately alleged hazards.

V

Legal rights will be of no practical consequence if workers remain ignorant of their options. It is doubtful that many workers, particularly nonunion workers, are aware that they have a legally protected right to refuse hazardous work, let alone that there are at least three statutory provisions protecting that right.[26] Even if workers were aware of such a right, it is unlikely that they could weave their way through the maze of legal options unaided. If there is to be a meaningful right to know in the workplace, there will also have to be an adequate program to educate workers about their rights and how to exercise them, as well as adequate legal protection of this and related worker rights.

It is to be hoped that many corporations will follow the model guidelines and programs established by Monsanto and Hercules on the right to know and will make these rights as meaningful as possible by confirming a right to (at least temporarily) refuse work under unduly hazardous conditions. Potentially effective programs of information and training in hazards are as important for managers as for the workers they manage. In several recent court cases executives of corporations have been tried—and in some cases convicted—for murder because of negligence in causing the deaths of workers by failing to warn them of hazards.

The Los Angeles District Attorney has announced that he will investigate all occupational deaths as possible homicides, and similar cases of criminal action have been prosecuted in Chicago.[27] A better system of corporate responsibility in disclosing risks thus stands to benefit management no less than employees.

NOTES

1. For developments in this area, see *Protecting Workplace Secrets, A Manager's Guide to Workplace Confidentiality* (New York: Joseph P. O'Reilly Executive Enterprises, 1985); Elihu D. Richter, "The Worker's Right to Know: Obstacles, Ambiguities, and Loopholes," *Journal of Health Politics, Policy and Law* 6 (1981): 340; George Miller, "The Asbestos Coverup," *Congressional Record,* May 17, 1979, pp. E2362–E2364, and "Asbestos Health Hazards and Company Morality," *Congressional Record,* May 24, 1979, pp. E2523–E2524; *The "Right to Know" Law: Special Report to the Governor and Legislature,* NY State Bureau of Toxic Substances, Department of Labor, March 1983.

2. NIOSH et al., "The Right to Know: Practical Problems and Policy Issues Arising from Exposures to Hazardous Chemical and Physical Agents in the Workplace," a report prepared at the request of the Subcommittee on Labor and Committee on Human Resources, U.S. Senate (Washington, D.C.: July 1977), 1, 5; Ilise L. Feitshans, "Hazardous Substances in the Workplace: How Much Does the Employee Have the Right to Know?" *Detroit Law Review III* (1985).

3. Occupational Safety and Health Administration, "Access to Employee Exposure and Medical Records—Final Rules," *Federal Register,* May 23, 1980, pp. 35212–35277. (Hereafter referred to as OSHA *Access* regulations.)

4. OSHA, *Access* regulations 29 CFR 1910.1200 et seq; printed in 48 FR 53278 (1983) and (1986). See also *United Steelworkers v. Auchter,* No. 83–3554 et al.; 763 F.2d 728 (3rd Cir. 1985).

5. See Barry Meier, "Use of Right-to-Know Rules Increasing," *Wall Street Journal,* May 23, 1986, p. 10; Vilma R. Hunt, "Perspective on Ethical Issues in Occupational Health," in *Bi-*

omedical Ethics Reviews 1984, ed. J. Humber and R. Almeder (Clifton, N.J.: Humana Press, 1984), p. 194; and "Bhopal Has Americans Demanding the Right to Know," *Business Week,* February 18, 1985.

6. State of New York, 1979–1980 Regular Sessions, 7103-D, Article 28, para. 880.

7. 762 F.2d 728.

8. On this point, cf. Harold J. Magnuson, "The Right to Know," *Archives of Environmental Health* 32 (1977): 40–44.

9. 29 CFRs 1910. 1200; 48 FR 53,280 (1983). See also Mary Melville, "Risks on the Job: The Worker's Right to Know," *Environment* 23 (1981): 12–20, 42–45.

10. Laurie Hays, "New Rules on Workplace Hazards Prompt Intensified On the Job Training Programs," *Wall Street Journal,* July 8, 1986, p. 31; Cathy Trost, "Plans to Alert Workers to Health Risks Stir Fears of Lawsuits and High Costs," *Wall Street Journal,* March 28, 1986, p. 15.

11. See 48 CFR 53, 282 (1983); Office of Technology Assessment, *Preventing Illness and Injury in the Workplace* (Washington, D.C.: Government Printing Office, 1985); "Suit Challenges OSHA Limits on Worker's Right to Know Standards," *The Nation's Health* (July 1984): 1; U.S. Department of Labor, *"An Interim Report to Congress on Occupational Disease"* (Washington, D.C.: Government Printing Office, 1980), pp. 1–2; NIOSH et al., "The Right to Know," pp. 3–9.

12. For an account that in effect demands a subjective standard for carcinogens, see Andrea Hricko, "The Right to Know," in *Public Information in the Prevention of Occupational Cancer: Proceedings of a Symposium,* 2–3 December, 1976, ed. Thomas P. Vogl (Washington, D.C.: National Academy of Science, 1977), esp. p. 72.

13. As more and more data are gathered regarding the effects of workplace hazards on particular predisposing conditions, the need for disclosure of such information can be identified through pre-employment physical examinations without the worker's needing to ask questions.

14. High Risk Occupational Disease Notification and Prevention Act, HR 1309.

15. See Trost, "Plans to Alert Workers," p. 15; Peter Perl, "Workers Unwarned," *Washington Post,* January 14, 1985, pp. A1, A6.

16. OSHA initially asserted that by regulating

the "worst" areas of illness, it had "preempted" (or replaced) state "Right-to-Know" laws when it promulgated OSHA's Hazard Communication Standard. OHSA also claimed that its broad definition of trade secret exemptions for employers superceded state trade secret laws. Connecticut, New York, and New Jersey joined with several other states and challenged both of these assertions in *United Steelworkers* v. *Auchter* (763 F.2d 728 (3rd Cir. 1985). The Steelworkers court held that OSH Act enabled the Secretary to promulgate *minimum* standards to protect workers, but that in the absence of coverage, states remain free to "fill the void" (between the need for regulation and actual hazards) with valid state laws. Consequently, insofar as OSHA's standard does not cover workers, there can be no "preemption" of state laws.

17. 29 U.S.C. S 651–658 (1970).
18. OSH Act 29 USC S 661 (c). Note, if the health or safety complaint is not determined to be legitimate, there are no worker protections.
19. Susan Preston, "A Right Under OSHA to Refuse Unsafe Work or A Hobson's Choice of Safety or Job?," *University of Baltimore Law Review* 8 (Spring 1979): 519–550.
20. The Secretary's interpretation of the OSH Act was upheld by the Supreme Court on February 26, 1980. *Whirlpool* v. *Marshall* 445 US 1 (1980).
21. Preston, "A Right Under OSHA to Refuse Unsafe Work," pp. 519–550.
22. 20 U.S.C. S143 (1976), and 29 CFR S 1977.12 (1978).
23. Nicholas Ashford and Judith P. Katz, "Unsafe Working Conditions: Employee Rights Under the Labor Management Relations Act and the Occupational Safety and Health Act," *Notre Dame Lawyer* 52 (June 1977): 802–837.
24. Preston, "A Right Under OSHA to Refuse Unsafe Work," p. 543.
25. Nancy K. Frank, "A Question of Equity: Workers' Right to Refuse Under OSHA Compared to the Criminal Necessity Defense," *Labor Law Journal* 31 (October 1980): 617–626.
26. In most states, these rights are not extended to public employees or domestic workers.
27. See *Illinois* v. *Chicago Magnet Wire Corporation*, No. 86–114, *Amicus Curiae* for The American Federation of Labor and Congress of Industrial Organizations; Jonathan Tasini, "The Clamor to Make Punishment Fit the Corporate Crime," *Business Week*, February 10, 1986, p. 73; Aric Press et al., "Murder in the Front Office," *Newsweek*, July 8, 1985; Bill Richards, "Ex-Officials Get 25-Year Sentences in Worker's Death," *Wall Street Journal,* July 2, 1985, p. 14; and *Illinois* v. *Chicago Magnet Wire Corporation*, No. 86–114, *Amicus Curiae* for The American Federation of Labor and Congress of Industrial Organizations.

Power Industry Morality

Alasdair MacIntyre

We are in one of those phases, recurrent in American history, in which morality has been rediscovered yet once again. It is characteristic of such phases that a hunt for scapegoats ensues, focusing our concerns in precisely the wrong way on precisely the wrong issues. Blaming and punishing individuals becomes a substitute for asking what

From Alasdair MacIntyre, "Power Industry Morality," *Symposium: A Report from The Edison Electric Institute,* Advertising Supplement to the *New York Review of Books,* 1981, pp. 7–9. Reprinted by permission of Pergamon Press.

it was in the structures of our common life that at the very least made possible and perhaps even positively engendered moral fault and failure.

The present fashionable concern with morality in general and the practice of scapegoating in particular concentrate their concern almost exclusively upon breaches of the kind of moral rule that tells us only what we ought not to do. Our very concern with an emphasis upon negative, prohibiting rules leads us to lose sight of what is, in fact, centrally important to morality and thus, in turn, to fail to give due importance to these self-same negative, prohibiting rules.

The record of the electric power industry, in abstaining from breaking such negative, prohibiting rules, is by and large an exemplary one. Paradoxically enough, insofar as I am inclined to question the moral resources of the electric power industry, it is because in one way its moral record is as good as it is. The morality of the industry has been essentially a negative one of proved abstinence from wrongdoing.

Since the end of the Great Depression, the electric power industry has inflexibly interpreted its legally mandated task, at the heart of which is the requirement to supply electric power on demand. The American electric power industry not only supplied power with a success unparalleled in human history, but actually participated in creating the demand that made that success necessary to the rest of American industry. All this was achieved in such a way that neither the more general question: "Growth for what?" nor the more specific question: "Electric power for what?" needed to be raised, let alone answered. Those questions implicitly were held to be questions only for consumers, just as questions of the legal constraints to be imposed on the provision and use of electric power were held to be questions for the Congress and for citizens.

The morality required and practiced by the industry was generally a strict morality of non-intervention in every area but that which it and others regarded as its own legit-imate realm. There was one positive aspect to the morality: its basic assumption, so firmly held as scarcely needing to be stated, was that the providing of electric power within the limits set by these negative constraints was an unqualified good.

Environmental concerns did not emerge until the very end of the period about which I am speaking; and the obvious connections between the provision of electric power and the possibilities both of providing employment for an increasing work force and of increasing the comfort of domestic life reinforced this assumption. The consequence was that a whole range of decisions came to be treated as purely or almost purely technical decisions to be handed over to the economists and the engineers: what types of plants should be built, where should they be sited, at what points should investment be made, what skills did the industry need. Congress provided the mandate, the consumer provided the data for prediction, the executives of the industry provided the commercial integrity and the skills for answering such questions, but the questions themselves were technical, not moral.

The electric power industry—and in this it has been no different from the rest of us in modern society—has allowed its moral perspectives to be defined too much in terms of the negative prohibiting and constraining rules and not enough in terms of positive goods that ought to inform its tasks. It is those goods that provide the distinctive moral dimension in any definition of the future tasks of the electric power industry. We can very happily take for granted the need to observe the requirements of the negative rules; what we do need is a more explicit assertion of the industry's positive moral tasks.

One positive moral task of the industry is to assume a large public responsibility in areas that it has hitherto treated with a scrupulous but, if I am right, partly misplaced respect as the responsibility either of the Congress or the executive branch of government or of the industrial, commercial and private consumer. That responsibility is to urge, cajole and compel our society to make certain choices and to make those choices in as open, as explicit and as rational a way as possible. There are two different kinds of reason why this responsibility falls to the electric power industry. The first is concerned with its unrivaled strategic position in the supply of power and with the scale and scope of its resources, especially the industry's accumulation of relevant knowledge and relevant skills. Both government and the general public have to learn what are the applications and consequences of alternative energy sources under specific local conditions of particular communities and environments. Engineering, economic, environmental and social considerations are going to have to be presented within a framework of political choice.

It is perhaps obvious that the members of the electric power industry are, as a group, uniquely well-fitted to present such choices. It would be required of them that they transcend their position as one special interest group among others. Would we then be asking them to become moral supermen? There is no simple, glib answer. But part of the complex answer is that we have asked no less from a variety of special interest groups in times of national crisis, especially during the Second World War.

The second type of reason for suggesting that the industry has this special and relatively new responsibility is that so far those who have been conveniently assigned this task by the democratic process have signally failed to discharge it in any but the most inadequate ways.

We have in our society only two institutionalized methods for coordinating individual preferences and transforming them into public choices: those of the market and its allied institutions, and those of government legislation, taxation and regulation. It is scarcely surprising that public debate has focused, explicitly and implicitly, on energy questions as elsewhere on the choice between those two, and that the form of public debate has been largely that of an indict-

ment of each of these methods by the proponents of the other. The sad fact of course is that both parties are right; both methods are grossly defective, and specifically so with respect to the kind of choices that our society now needs to formulate.

Consider first some defects of the mechanisms of the market. Markets only provide mechanisms for coordinating individual preferences once those preferences have been formulated and expressed in acts of consumption. The market, therefore, is of no help to us in those areas of life where we have to decide what our patterns of consumption are to be, how our preferences are to be ranked, how our desires are to be ordered. The debate on energy is centrally about investment; and it is a debate that has to be conducted within what Daniel Bell has felicitously called the "public household." We need to reason together in order to discover with what choices we want to enter the market. We are, that is to say, at a point in the argument where to tell us to rely on the mechanisms of the market is not so much mistaken as irrelevant.

There are weaknesses and defects in our system of political decision-making that correspond precisely to the weaknesses and defects of the market. It, like the market, is responsive to the pressures of the present much more rationally than to those of the future, partly because our ability to predict the future accurately is in general extraordinarily limited. And it, like the market, is far more effective at expressing already formulated choices on familiar issues than at formulating new possibilities of choice in unfamiliar areas. Neither the market nor the political system will provide the ordinary citizen with an adequate arena for formulating and expressing radically new choices of the kind that the energy debate thrusts upon us. And if public discussion that will enable ordinary citizens to formulate and express radically new choices does not take place, then the political and economic outcomes will inevitably be sadly defective.

But who is to begin the debate necessary

to supplement our conventional economic and political institutions? Who is to educate the educators? I see very few individuals or institutions who are both capable of taking up this task and who possess the resources and the strategic position to carry it through, apart from those individuals and institutions comprised by the electric power industry. Their work compels them to interact with both producers and consumers at essential points. They have a peculiar responsibility, which arises from the fact that if they do not discharge it, it is unlikely that anyone else will. If the industry does embark on this task, it will perhaps be accused of trying to pre-empt the democratic process; but if it does not take action that will render it liable to such accusations, the democratic process itself may fail us.

What then is the task, and why does it have moral dimensions? In order to answer this question, I shall have to state briefly and unoriginally what I take the energy crisis to be. There is no more of a shortage of available energy now than at any other time; what has suddenly become unavailable is energy at the kind of low price to us to which we had become accustomed. What we now have to debate is what we are prepared to pay for what and to whom and how are we going to pay for it. The major possibility that we confront is of a gigantic shift in patterns of investment. And if we invest massively in new energy sources or in new ways and to new extents in existing sources, then we shall necessarily be shifting our investment away from something else important to our lives. Hence the energy crisis is a crisis about our whole way of life and not just about energy.

It is not difficult to see that when we rethink the wide range of questions facing America as questions about energy, four different kinds of moral concern must arise. The first is a concern for complexity. Oversimplification, the sacrifice of complexity, is in fact a crucial form of the vice of untruthfulness. Yet this is not the only morally damaging harm that is likely to arise from oversimplification of the issues. Just because so many different kinds of issues of policy and practice interlock at the point of energy use, there is no simple way to assess the costs and benefits that will arise from any particular proposal. How, for example, are we to weigh as considerations relevant to the same proposal the harm of damage to the environment against the harm of making fewer jobs available to those who badly need work, and both against the harm of injury and death to a certain number of presently unidentifiable individuals? It is always much easier for us to consider these issues in a piecemeal, local way, in which some particular compromise—determined through bargaining by local circumstances and balance of power—will, in the short run, at least, satisfy the particular, local contending parties. Our whole political and legislative process is biased towards oversimplified statements of problems and, consequently, not only oversimplified but unjust solutions.

Because our culture possesses no general set of standards that will enable us to evaluate costs and benefits of very different types in a single rational argument, it is all the more important that our evaluations satisfy two minimal requirements of justice. The first is that everyone relevantly involved—and where energy is concerned that means everyone—should have a chance to say what is to count as a cost and what as a benefit. The second is that, so far as possible, those who receive the benefits should also be those who pay the costs and vice versa. Neither the former nor the latter principle has received anything like adequate attention in recent debates. When environmentalists urge policies that will significantly reduce the number of jobs that might otherwise be available, it is rarely, perhaps never, the case that they are able to show *either* that those who would lose their opportunities of work are the same people who would benefit from the environment *or* that those who would lose their opportunities to work have had a part in shaping the conception and criteria of costs and benefits involved. Environmentalists in the present have sometimes been as untrammeled in endangering other people's jobs as industrialists in the past were in endangering other people's investments. Equally, when opponents of nuclear power stations urge policies that will significantly increase our future dependence on coal, the lives that will be lost as a result of their policies are not their own. Justice demands not only that everyone have a voice and a vote, but that some people—the populations that will bear the relevant risks and dangers, or most of them—have more of a voice and more of a vote than others.

There is at least one further requirement that must be met if justice is to be served. Because the energy crisis is primarily a crisis about the investment of resources, ordinary citizens are going to have no opportunity to understand how the costs and benefits of different investment policies do and will impinge upon them, if the costs are systematically concealed by subsidy. For the inhabitants of most advanced countries, the cheapness of energy to the consumer in the past 50 years has disguised its true costs. Ordinary citizens respond to their everyday experience and, if their everyday experience conceals what they are really paying for energy in all sorts of disguised ways, then no amount of theoretical education is likely to succeed. Only if there is widespread perception of what the costs and benefits of different energy policies are can we decide both democratically and rationally how it is just to distribute costs and benefits.

Justice and truthfulness are not the only virtues central to determining energy production and use. Another is the ability to live with unpredictability.

We need to plan on a large scale, but we also have to recognize that our plans are for a future that is always apt to surprise us with its unexpectedness. In part, our social future is unpredictable because of the ways in which the future development of mathematics, science and technology are unpredictable. An obvious and obviously crucial example is the mathematics of Turing or of von Neumann, work essential to the development of modern computing science and engineering, and work whose outcome could not have been rationally predicted in advance.

In changing the social world and its national environment, we also change ourselves. No matter how sophisticated our social planning with respect to energy or to anything else, we can never rule out the possibility that in the course of implementing our plans we shall acquire views, interests and desires markedly different from those that led us to draw up and implement our original plans. Hence it is crucial that our planning is not so inflexible that it leaves our future selves—let alone successor generations—with no or few options acceptable to them because we were, at an early stage, too rigidly insistent on what is now acceptable to us.

It follows that there are great moral as well as practical dangers in making too many large-scale irreversible investment decisions that foreclose on future choices. This is especially a danger because the urgency of our immediate needs always tempts us towards short-term solutions.

Some of my statements about justice might seem supportive to the advocates of massive investment in nuclear power, while what I am now saying about the need for an ability to live with unpredictability may seem to endorse what some of their critics have said. But what matters at this juncture is not so much the particular policy implications of particular points; rather, it is the need to underline the fact that we ought not to expect moral considerations all to point in one single policy direction. There is a genuinely tragic dimension to the energy debate in that any particular policy direction is going to involve the sacrifice of some authentic goods for the sake of others. Our culture lacks any clear sense of how to handle tragic situations, situations that reveal our moral and human limitations in relation to the tasks imposed upon us.

Because we have never learned to face up to our moral limitations, we have lost to a large degree our vision of positive possibility. We have trudged for so long into a future of apparently limitless consumption that we do not now find it easy to remember who we are and what links us to others. The notion of possibility is always the notion of some future form of community that provides us now with standards and goals by which to diagnose our various forms of inadequacy and to set about remedying them. Just such a common vision—partial, not always coherent, but providing the essential sustenance for our constitution—was implicit in the founding of this republic.

What I am suggesting is this: that to press forward in the public arena the debate about energy, in such a way as to make its moral dimensions clear so far as possible to the whole society, will reveal to that society that it is, to a degree that a good deal of political rhetoric conceals from us, involved in a moral crisis as well as in an energy crisis. The prospect is a dismaying one and requires courage: we do not know how to reason together morally in an effective way. And this lack—just because it is something wanting in the social order as a whole—will never be remedied unless we face it as a society.

Environmental Pollution As a Public Accumulative Harm

Joel Feinberg

... One *could* say simply that air and water pollution, since they threaten a vital public interest, are harmful, and therefore should be prohibited. Henceforth, a hasty legislature might declare, anyone who pollutes the air or water is guilty of a felony and subject to not less than a year in prison and a $10,000 fine. Would this criminal statute be supported by the harm principle? It does satisfy the letter of the harm principle's minimal requirement: it cites the need to prevent harm as a reason for prohibitive legislation. But from the point of view of an actual legislature seriously grappling with a pressing public problem, it is utterly trivial and nearly vacuous to say so little. Since obviously it would also cause serious public dislocations to force the immediate closing of all industrial facilities that emit gases into the atmosphere or chemicals into the groundwater, or to ban all gasoline-powered motor vehicles, it is not in the spirit of the harm principle to fight one set of harms by blunt and sweeping measures that produce many harms of other kinds as side effects. Straightforward first-resort use of criminal sanctions would be much too crude, not to say socially harmful, an approach to a problem of this complexity. Rather, the question a legislature must ask, in the spirit of the harm principle, is this: In the effort to minimize public harms generally, within the limits of efficiency, equity, and fair play, what sort of regulative scheme should be devised?

Excerpted from *Harm to Others: The Moral Limits of the Criminal Law* by Joel Feinberg. Copyright © 1984 by Oxford University Press, Inc. Reprinted by permission of the author and the publisher.

Moreover, because of imputational obscurities, it would be impossible to know how to recognize a violation of the simpler kind of criminal regulation. Air and water pollution are paradigmatic accumulative harms. If there were only one automobile allowed to operate in the entire state of California, its exhaust fumes would soon be dissipated and no harm to the ambient air would even be worth mentioning. One hundred cars might begin to threaten the air quality but it is unlikely that they would bring it to the threshold of harmfulness. But somewhere between those minor exhaust emissions and those produced by millions of cars without catalytic converters the threshold of harm is reached. Similarly, it will do no harm to the public drinking water to drop a few ounces even of so deadly a poison as potassium cyanide into a reservoir. There is some threshold quantity, however (and a surprisingly large one), at which cyanide concentrations would be lethal. When a person (or company) emits a certain amount of sulfur dioxide into the air, well short of the threshold of harm, he has slightly increased the concentration of dangerous chemicals in the direction of harm, and in that sense his actions are "harmful." ... But that can hardly be the sense of "harm" in any formulation of the harm principle that can serve as a guide to legislators, since it would provide a "reason" for banning indispensable innocent activities, like car driving and fossil-fuel-fired electricity-generating plants, across the board.

Suppose, however, that some person (or company) emits the same small amount of the same gases, but in circumstances such that concentrations of those gases already present in the air are raised just above the threshold of actual harm. Has that person violated the statute (supposing it to be actually in the penal code) against "polluting the air"? With that question, a host of imputational difficulties are introduced. To be sure, the concentration levels were raised by his act above the permissible threshold, but that is mainly because countless other emitters had already made *their* independent contributions, many of them much larger than those of our hapless defendant, and made them with less care and for socially less valuable purposes. "Why pick on me for contributing so little to the harmful accumulation when so many others, for no better and often worse reasons, contributed so much more?" the indignant scapegoat might ask. "I was not the one who harmed the public interest; those others were the true culprits." The others, however, would have similar arguments in their own defense. And no one of the others, we must concede, caused all that harmful concentration. It will not help our confused legislators to say simply that they must make laws to prevent individuals from harming others, when there is no clear way of telling when a particular emission is the one that does the harm. (Of course, above the threshold, all subsequent emissions cause harm, as higher and higher concentrations are ever more injurious, at least up to a further threshold where things are so bad they cannot get worse. From the point of view of the dead, "overkill" is no worse than "kill.")

These legislative problems have a common form. In each case: (1) A threshold of harm is approached, reached, or exceeded through the joint and successive contributions of numerous parties. (2) These contributions are uneven in amount, and unequal in degree of care and in social value. (3) In respect to the harm of pollution, each contribution is "harmless" in itself except that it moves the condition of the environment to a point closer to the threshold of harm. (4) When these accumulations cross the harm-threshold, they constitute *public* harms in that they set back vital net interests shared by almost everyone. (5) Most of the activities that produce these contributions toward pollution are so beneficial in other ways that if they were to be prevented entirely, as a group, the resultant harm to the public would be as great or even greater than the harm they now produce. The legislative problem then is to control emissions so that the chemical accumulations remain below the harm-threshold, while restricting as little as possible the socially valuable activities that produce emissions as regrettable by-products. A satisfactory solution requires not a simple criminal prohibition, modeled say on the statute against homicide or burglary, but an elaborate scheme of regulation, administered by a state agency empowered to grant, withhold, and suspend licenses, following rules designed to promote fairness and efficiency.[1] The role of the criminal law would be a derivative one: to provide backup sanctions to enforce authoritative orders.

... When a legislature wishes to prevent a public accumulative harm like pollution, it must know precisely how to describe the prohibitable actions that harm the public interest, so that it can prohibit just those actions. But when the legislature does not know, and has no way of deciding, to just which actions to impute the harm in question, it has no way of formulating the desired statute that avoids vacuousness, arbitrariness, and legislative overkill. If there is no way after the fact to tell to which actions to impute the harm, then there can be no way before the fact for legislatures to decide which actions to prohibit because of their harm production. The harm principle in that case is of no use at all.

My thesis is that it is only against the background of such a regulative system as that suggested above that individual imputations of public accumulative harm make any sense. For A to harm the public interest is for A's wrongful conduct to cause a setback to that interest. In the context of industrial polluting, "wrongful" must mean unlawful as judged by a regulative agency applying rules for allocating permits in accordance with specified requirements of fairness and efficiency. In these contexts, no prior standard of wrongfulness exists. There is nothing inherently wrongful or right-violating in the activity of driving an automobile, generating electricity, or refining copper. These activities can be meaningfully condemned only as violations of an authoritative scheme of allocative priorities. To the more general question—does a legislature have a right to prohibit (say) copper-refining as such?—the only answer yielded by the unsupplemented harm principle is the unhelpful one, "Yes, but only if copper refining causes harm." How do we tell if a given refining operation causes harm? Only by determining whether its contribution to the accumulation of certain gases and materials in the ambient air is more than its permitted share. But we can only know its "permitted share" by reference to an actual allocative scheme, operative and in force.

In 1970, Congress passed the Clean Air Act Amendments which for the first time empowered the Environmental Protection Agency (EPA) to promulgate uniform national ambient air standards for seven pollutants.[2] These standards define for each region regulated the same maximal allowable concentration of each pollutant. In effect then, these standards define the threshold of public harm, as determined by scientists in the employ of the EPA. In the terminology favored by economists and legal commentators, they impose "ceilings" above which the total concentration of a given pollutant is not allowed to rise. In those defined regions in each of the fifty states where the ambient pollution concentration does not now exceed the ceiling, the EPA is to monitor a program of "prevention of significant deterioration" (PSD), assuring that the ceilings are never surpassed.[3] The law now requires each state to develop an implementation plan to protect the PSD ceilings by regulating future economic growth, requiring technical diminution devices, and the like. A key term in the accounting system defined by these requirements is the "PSD increment," which is (speaking very roughly) the allowable total increase, at a given time, in the actual concentration levels. The increment will be roughly the difference between those levels (the "baseline pollution concentration") and the imposed upper ceiling. The baseline, of course, varies (in the preferred terminology, "floats") with changes in the quantity of local emissions. The *available PSD increment* at a given time, therefore, is "the difference between this floating baseline and the local PSD ceiling."[4] Lewis Kontnik explains—

> Increases in local air pollution emissions effectively "consume" PSD increment since the ambient increase resulting from the new emissions will decrease the available increment. Conversely, a reduction in local emissions lowers the floating baseline, which increases the amount of PSD increment available. In other words, reductions in local emissions "liberate" increment. When this occurs, the Act allows the emission reduction and resulting liberation of increment by one source to then be used by another source to "offset" emission increases at a nearby location.[5]

The problem to be solved by each state in its own implementation plan is how to allocate the available increment among prospective new sources of air pollution, and this involves comparing such disparate sources of sulphur dioxide emission (say) as one huge industrial smokestack and 60,000 automobiles.

We can hardly pursue the problem here into its bewildering technicalities, but to appreciate what *kind* of moral problem it is, we should briefly glance at some of the potentially clashing goals of an "increment allocation mechanism." Kontnik classifies them under three headings: efficiency, equity, and feasibility. Even a cursory examination of specific objectives under these headings reveals that conflicts can occur both within and between these categories. Under "efficiency," the regulative agency must consider net productivity ("the total value of goods and services produced by the allocation of increment"), increase in employment, tax revenues generated, new capital investment, and minimal environmental impact apart from pollution. Under "equity," the agency must balance regional and local priorities, including the concerns of neighborhood groups, urban planners, and other "interest groups," and fairness (equal consideration)

to competing sources. "Existing sources seeking to continue or increase their present rates of air pollution emissions invite treatment different from that of new sources seeking to locate in an area," but "even though a satisfactory legal basis exists for the classification of sources, mechanisms that treat all sources evenly are preferable to those that do not."[6] Under "feasibility," consideration must be paid to political possibilities and dangers, as well as to legal, administrative, and technical costs of the allocation mechanism itself. Then heed must be paid to the requirements of both certainty (predictability) and flexibility in the allocation decisions.

. . . In short, responsible legislative consideration of the problem posed by the accumulative public harm of pollution involves the entire range of reasons bearing on policy decisions: the values of environmental protection, economic growth, regional fairness, and equal consideration of competing interests; maxims of justice; costs of administration; predictability without inflexibility, and the like, not to mention the debate between advocates of market mechanisms of various kinds and defenders of long-term governmental planning. We are a long way from the world of simple criminal prohibitions, like that which punishes "littering" by a fine of $100. The harm principle lends legitimacy to legislative efforts to solve the multidimensional problems of air and water pollution, but in its bare formulation without supplement, it offers no guide to policy.

REFERENCES

1. See Kenneth Culp Davis, *Discretionary Justice: A Preliminary Inquiry* (Urbana, Ill.: University of Illinois Press, 1971), especially Chap. IV, "Structuring Discretion."
2. The seven pollutants controlled under the 1970 Amendments are: sulfur dioxide, particulate matter, nitrogen dioxide, carbon monoxide, photochemical oxidents (as ozone), nonmethane hydrocarbons, and lead.

3. Problems of pollution control are not different in kind, but much more difficult politically, in those regions ("nonattainment areas") where ambient pollution concentrations exceed their assigned ceilings. See Lewis T. Kontnik, "Comment. Increment Allocation Under Prevention of Significant Deterioration: How

to Decide Who is Allowed to Pollute," *Northwestern Law Review,* Vol. 74 (Feb., 1980), pp. 936–969. I am heavily indebted to Kontnik's article in what follows.
4. *Ibid.,* p. 941.
5. *Loc. cit.*
6. *Ibid.,* p. 949.

Henningsen v. Bloomfield Motors, Inc. and Chrysler Corporation

Claus H. Henningsen purchased a Plymouth automobile, manufactured by defendant Chrysler Corporation, from defendant Bloomfield Motors, Inc. His wife, plaintiff Helen Henningsen, was injured while driving it and instituted suit against both defendants to recover damages on account of her injuries. Her husband joined in the action seeking compensation for his consequential losses. The complaint was predicated upon breach of express and implied warranties and upon negligence. At the trial the negligence counts were dismissed by the court and the case was submitted to the jury for determination solely on the issues of implied warranty of merchantability.* Verdicts were returned against both defendants and in favor of the plaintiffs. Defendants appealed and plaintiffs cross-appealed from the dismissal of their negligence claim. . . .

. . . The particular car selected was described as a 1955 Plymouth, Plaza "6," Club Sedan. The type used in the printed parts of

the [purchase order] form became smaller in size, different in style, and less readable toward the bottom where the line for the purchaser's signature was placed. The smallest type on the page appears in the two paragraphs, one of two and one-quarter lines and the second of one and one-half lines, on which great stress is laid by the defense in the case. These two paragraphs are the least legible and the most difficult to read in the instrument, but they are most important in the evaluation of the rights of the contesting parties. They do not attract attention and there is nothing about the format which would draw the reader's eye to them. In fact, a studied and concentrated effort would have to be made to read them. De-emphasis seems the motive rather than emphasis. . . . The two paragraphs are:

"The front and back of this Order comprise the entire agreement affecting this purchase and no other agreement or understanding of any nature concerning same has been made or entered into, or will be recognized. I hereby certify that no credit has been extended to me for the purchase of this motor vehicle except as appears in writing on the face of this agreement.

"I have read the matter printed on the

*["Merchantability": The articles shall be of the kind described and be fit for the purpose for which they were sold. Fitness is impliedly warranted if an item is merchantable. Ed.]

Atlantic Reporter 161 A2d 69, pp. 73–75, 78–81, 83–87, 93–96, 102. This opinion was written by Justice John J. Francis.

back hereof and agree to it as a part of this order the same as if it were printed above my signature.... "

The testimony of Claus Henningsen justifies the conclusion that he did not read the two fine print paragraphs referring to the back of the purchase contract. And it is uncontradicted that no one made any reference to them, or called them to his attention. With respect to the matter appearing on the back, it is likewise uncontradicted that he did not read it and that no one called it to his attention.

... The warranty, which is the focal point of the case, is set forth [on the reverse side of the page]. It is as follows:

"7. It is expressly agreed that there are no warranties, express or implied, *made* by either the dealer or the manufacturer on the motor vehicle, chassis, of parts furnished hereunder except as follows.

"'The manufacturer warrants each new motor vehicle (including original equipment placed thereon by the manufacturer except tires), chassis or parts manufactured by it to be free from defects in material or workmanship under normal use and service. Its obligation under this warranty being limited to making good at its factory any part or parts thereof which shall, within ninety (90) days after delivery of such vehicle *to the original purchaser* or before such vehicle has been driven 4,000 miles, whichever event shall first occur, be returned to it with transportation charges prepaid and which its examination shall disclose to its satisfaction to have been thus defective: *this warranty being expressly in lieu of all other warranties expressed or implied, and all other obligations or liabilities on its part,* and it neither assumes nor authorizes any other person to assume for it any other liability in connection with the sale of its vehicles.... '"[Emphasis added] ...

The new Plymouth was turned over to the Henningsens on May 9, 1955. No proof was adduced by the dealer to show precisely what was done in the way of mechanical or road testing beyond testimony that the manufacturer's instructions were probably fol-

lowed. Mr. Henningsen drove it from the dealer's place of business in Bloomfield to their home in Keansburg. On the trip nothing unusual appeared in the way in which it operated. Thereafter, it was used for short trips on paved streets about the town. It had no servicing and no mishaps of any kind before the event of May 19. That day, Mrs. Henningsen drove to Asbury Park [New Jersey]. On the way down and in returning the car performed in normal fashion until the accident occurred. She was proceeding north on Route 36 in Highlands, New Jersey, at 20–22 miles per hour. The highway was paved and smooth, and contained two lanes for northbound travel. She was riding in the right-hand lane. Suddenly she heard a loud noise "from the bottom, by the hood." It "felt as if something cracked." The steering wheel spun in her hands; the car veered sharply to the right and crashed into a highway sign and a brick wall. No other vehicle was in any way involved. A bus operator driving in the left-hand lane testified that he observed plaintiffs' car approaching in normal fashion in the opposite direction; "all of a sudden [it] veered at 90 degrees ... and right into this wall." As a result of the impact, the front of the car was so badly damaged that it was impossible to determine if any of the parts of the steering wheel mechanism or workmanship or assembly were defective or improper prior to the accident. The condition was such that the collision insurance carrier, after inspection, declared the vehicle a total loss. It had 468 miles on the speedometer at the time....

The terms of the warranty are a sad commentary upon the automobile manufacturers' marketing practices. Warranties developed in the law in the interest of and to protect the ordinary consumer who cannot be expected to have the knowledge or capacity or even the opportunity to make adequate inspection of mechanical instrumentalities, like automobiles, and to decide for himself whether they are reasonably fit for the designed purpose.... But the ingenuity of the Automobile Manufacturers Association, by means of its standardized form, has metamorphosed the warranty into a device to limit the maker's liability. To call it an "equivocal" agreement, as the Minnesota Supreme Court did, is the least that can be said in criticism of it.

The manufacturer agrees to replace defective parts for 90 days after the sale or until the car has been driven 4,000 miles, whichever is first to occur, *if the part is sent to the factory, transportation charges prepaid, and if examination discloses to its satisfaction that the part is defective....*

Chrysler points out that an implied warranty of merchantability is an incident of a contract of sale. It concedes, of course, the making of the original sale to Bloomfield Motors, Inc., but maintains that this transaction marked the terminal point of its contractual connection with the car. Then Chrysler urges that since it was not a party to the sale by the dealer to Henningsen, there is no privity of contract* between it and the plaintiffs, and the absence of this privity eliminates any such implied warranty.

There is no doubt that under early common-law concepts of contractual liability only those persons who were parties to the bargain could sue for a breach of it. In more recent times a noticeable disposition has appeared in a number of jurisdictions to break through the narrow barrier of privity when dealing with sales of goods in order to give realistic recognition to a universally accepted fact. The fact is that the dealer and the ordinary buyer do not, and are not expected to, buy goods, whether they be foodstuffs or automobiles, exclusively for their own consumption or use. Makers and manufacturers know this and advertise and market their products on that assumption; witness the "family" car, the baby foods, etc. The limitations of privity in contracts for the sale of goods developed their place in the law when marketing conditions were simple, when maker and buyer frequently met face to face on an equal bargaining plane and when many of the products were relatively uncomplicated and conducive to inspection by a buyer competent to evaluate their quality. With the advent of mass marketing, the manufacturer became remote from the purchaser, sales were accomplished through intermediaries, and the demand for the product was created by advertising media. In such an economy it became obvious that the consumer was the person being cultivated. Manifestly, the connotation of "consumer" was broader than that of "buyer." He signified such a person who, in the reasonable contemplation of the parties to the sale, might be expected to use the product. Thus, where the commodities sold are such that if defectively manufactured they will be dangerous to life or limb, then society's interests can only be protected by eliminating the requirement of privity between the maker and his dealers and the reasonably expected ultimate consumer. In that way the burden of losses consequent upon use of defective articles is borne by those who are in a position to either control the danger or make an equitable distribution of the losses when they do occur....

Under modern conditions the ordinary layman, on responding to the importuning of colorful advertising, has neither the opportunity nor the capacity to inspect or to determine the fitness of an automobile for use; he must rely on the manufacturer who has control of its construction, and to some degree on the dealer who, to the limited extent called for by the manufacturer's instructions, inspects and services it before delivery. In such a marketing milieu his remedies and those of persons who properly claim through him should not depend "upon the intricacies of the law of sales. The obligation of the manufacturer should not be based

---

*["Privity of contract": A contractual relation existing between parties that is sufficiently close to confer a legal claim or right. Ed.]

alone on privity of contract. It should rest, as was once said, upon 'the demands of social justice.'" . . .

In a society such as ours, where the automobile is a common and necessary adjunct of daily life, and where its use is so fraught with danger to the driver, passengers, and the public, the manufacturer is under a special obligation in connection with the construction, promotion, and sale of his cars. Consequently, the courts must examine purchase agreements closely to see if consumer and public interests are treated fairly. . . .

What influence should these circumstances have on the restrictive effect of Chrysler's express warranty in the framework of the purchase contract? As we have said, warranties originated in the law to safeguard the buyer and not to limit the liability of the seller or manufacturer. It seems obvious in this instance that the motive was to avoid the warranty obligations which are normally incidental to such sales. The language gave little and withdrew much. In return for the delusive remedy of replacement of defective parts at the factory, the buyer is said to have accepted the exclusion of the maker's liability for personal injuries arising from the breach of the warranty, and to have agreed to the elimination of any other express or implied warranty. An instinctively felt sense of justice cries out against such a sharp bargain. But does the doctrine that a person is bound by his signed agreement, in the absence of fraud, stand in the way of any relief? . . .

The warranty before us is a standardized form designed for mass use. It is imposed upon the automobile consumer. He takes it or leaves it, and he must take it to buy an automobile. No bargaining is engaged in with respect to it. In fact, the dealer through whom it comes to the buyer is without authority to alter it; his function is ministerial—simply to deliver it. The form warranty is not only standard with Chrysler but, as mentioned above, it is the uniform warranty of the Automobile Manufacturers Association. . . . Of these companies, the "Big Three" (General Motors, Ford, and Chrysler) represented 93.5% of the passenger-car production for 1958 and the independents 6.5%.[1] And for the same year the "Big Three" had 86.72% of the total passenger vehicle registrations. . . .

In the context of this warranty, only the abandonment of all sense of justice would permit us to hold that, as a matter of law, the phrase "its obligation under this warranty being limited to making good at its factory any part or parts thereof" signifies to an ordinary reasonable person that he is relinquishing any personal injury claim that might flow from the use of a defective automobile. Such claims are nowhere mentioned. . . .

In the matter of warranties on the sale of their products, the Automobile Manufacturers Association has enabled them to present a united front. From the standpoint of the purchaser, there can be no arms length negotiating on the subject. Because his capacity for bargaining is so grossly unequal, the inexorable conclusion which follows is that he is not permitted to bargain at all. He must take or leave the automobile on the warranty terms dictated by the maker. He cannot turn to a competitor for better security.

Public policy is a term not easily defined. Its significance varies as the habits and needs of a people may vary. It is not static and the field of application is an ever increasing one. A contract, or a particular provision therein, valid in one era may be wholly opposed to the public policy of another. Courts keep in mind the principle that the best interests of society demand that persons should not be unnecessarily restricted in their freedom to contract. But they do not hesitate to declare void as against public policy contractual provisions which clearly tend to the injury of the public in some way. . . .

In the framework of this case, illuminated as it is by the facts and the many decisions noted, we are of the opinion that Chrysler's attempted disclaimer of an implied warranty of the merchantability and of the obligations arising therefrom is so inimical to the public good as to compel an adjudication of its invalidity. . . .

The principles that have been expounded as to the obligation of the manufacturer apply with equal force to the separate express warranty of the dealer. This is so, irrespective of the absence of the relationship of principle and agent between these defendants, because the manufacturer and the Association establish the warranty policy for the industry. The bargaining position of the dealer is inextricably bound by practice to that of the maker and the purchaser must take or leave the automobile, accompanied and encumbered as it is by the uniform warranty. . . .

Under all of the circumstances outlined above, the judgments in favor of the plaintiffs and against the defendants are affirmed.

NOTE

1. Standard and Poor (Industrial Surveys, Autos, Basic Analysis, June 25, 1959), p. 4109.

Reserve Mining Co. v. United States

OPINION I (JUNE 4, 1974)

Reserve Mining Company is a jointly owned subsidiary of Armco Steel Corporation and Republic Steel Corporation which mines low-grade iron ore, called "taconite," near Babbitt, Minnesota. The taconite is shipped by rail to Reserve's "beneficiating" plant at Silver Bay, Minnesota, on the north shore of Lake Superior, where it is concentrated into "pellets" containing some 65 percent iron ore. The process involves crushing the taconite into fine granules, separating out the metallic iron with huge magnets, and flushing the residue into Lake Superior. Approximately 67,000 tons of this waste product, known as "tailings," are daily discharged into the lake.

The use of Lake Superior for this purpose was originally authorized by the State of Minnesota in 1947, and Reserve commenced operations in 1955. In granting this permit to Reserve, the State of Minnesota accepted Reserve's theory that the weight and velocity of the discharge would insure that the tailings would be deposited at a depth of approximately 900 feet in the "great trough" area of the lake, located offshore from Reserve's facility. The permit provides that:

> [T]ailings shall not be discharged . . . so as to result in any material adverse effects on fish life or public water supplies or in any other material unlawful pollution of the waters of the lake. . . .

Until June 8, 1973, the case was essentially a water pollution abatement case, but on

---

498 F.2d 1073 and 514 F.2d 492 (1975). Majority Opinion by Judge Myron H. Bright, Eighth Circuit Court of Appeals.

that date the focus of the controversy shifted to the public health impact of Reserve's discharge of asbestiform particles into the air and water.... On April 20, 1974, after 139 days of trial extending over a nine month period and after hearing more than 100 witnesses and examining over 1,600 exhibits, Judge Miles Lord of the United States District Court for the District of Minnesota entered an order closing Reserve's Silver Bay facility. In an abbreviated memorandum opinion, Judge Lord held that Reserve's water discharge violated federal water pollution laws and that its air emissions violated state air pollution regulations, and that both were common law nuisances. Most importantly to the question now before this court, Judge Lord concluded in Findings 9 and 10 of his opinion that:

> 9. The discharge into the air substantially endangers the health of the people of Silver Bay and surrounding communities as far away as the eastern shore of Wisconsin.
> 10. The discharge into the water substantially endangers the health of the people who procured their drinking water from the western arm of Lake Superior, including the communities of Silver Bay, Beaver Bay, Two Harbors, Cloquet, Duluth [Minnesota], and Superior, Wisconsin.

Defendants Reserve, Armco, and Republic noticed their appeal to this court and moved for a stay of the district court's injunction pending the appeal. Judge Lord denied this request and Reserve applied to us for a stay....

... The question now before us is whether, considering all facts and circumstances, the injunction order should be stayed pending Reserve's appeal. We grant the stay subject to certain conditions and limitations as stated herein.

Although there is no dispute that significant amounts of waste tailings are discharged into the water and dust is discharged into the air by Reserve, the parties vigorously contest the precise nature of the discharge, its biological effects, and, particularly with respect to the waters of Lake Supe-

rior, its ultimate destination. Plaintiffs contend that the mineral commingtonite-grunerite, which Reserve admits to be a major component of its taconite wastes and a member of the mineral family known as amphiboles, is substantially identical in morphology (or shape and form) and similar in chemistry to amosite asbestos, a fibrous mineral which has been found, in certain occupational settings, to be carcinogenic. The plaintiffs further argue that the mineral fibers discharged represent a serious health threat, since they are present in the air of Silver Bay and surrounding communities and, by way of dispersion throughout Lake Superior, in the drinking water of Duluth and other communities drawing water from the lake....

The suggestion that particles of the cummingtonite-grunerite in Reserve's discharges are the equivalent of amosite asbestos raised an immediate health issue, since inhalation of amosite asbestos at occupational levels of exposure is a demonstrated health hazard resulting in asbestosis and various forms of cancer. However, the proof of a health hazard requires more than the mere fact of discharge; the discharge of an agent hazardous in one circumstance must be linked to some present or future likelihood of disease under the prevailing circumstances. An extraordinary amount of testimony was received on these issues....

The theory by which plaintiffs argue that the discharges present a substantial danger is founded largely upon epidemiological studies of asbestos workers occupationally exposed to and inhaling high levels of asbestos dust. A study by Dr. Irving Selikoff of workers at a New Jersey asbestos manufacturing plant demonstrated that occupational exposure to amosite asbestos poses a hazard of increased incidence of asbestosis and various forms of cancer. Similar studies in other occupational contexts leave no doubt that asbestos, at sufficiently high dosages, is injurious to health. However, in order to draw the conclusion that environmental exposure to Reserve's discharges presents a health threat in the instant case, it must be shown either that the circumstances of exposure are at least comparable to those in occupational settings, or, alternatively, that the occupational studies establish certain principles of asbestos-disease pathology which may be applied to predicting the occurrence of such disease in altered circumstances.

Initially, it must be observed that environmental exposure from Reserve's discharges into air and water is simply not comparable to that typical of occupational settings. The occupational studies involve direct exposure to and inhalation of asbestos dust in high concentrations and in confined spaces. This pattern of exposure cannot be equated with the discharge into the outside air of relatively low levels of asbestos fibers....

... In order to make a prediction, based on the occupational studies, as to the likelihood of disease at lower levels of exposure, at least two key findings must be made. First, an attempt must be made to determine, with some precision, what that lower level of exposure is. Second, that lower level of exposure must be applied to the known pathology of asbestos-induced disease, i.e., it must be determined whether the level of exposure is safe or unsafe.

Unfortunately, the testimony of Dr. Arnold Brown[1] indicates that neither of these key determinations can be made. Dr. Brown testified that, with respect to both air and water, the level of fibers is not readily susceptible of measurement. This results from the relatively imprecise state of counting techniques and the wide margins of error which necessarily result, and is reflected in the widely divergent sample counts received by the court....

Even assuming that one could avoid imprecision and uncertainty in measuring the number of fibers at low levels, there remains vast uncertainty as to the medical consequences of low levels of exposure to asbestos fibers....

... In commenting on the statement, "This suggests that there are levels of asbestos exposure that will not be associated with any detectable risk," Dr. Brown stated:

> As a generalization, yes, I agree to that. But I must reiterate my view that I do not know what that level is....

A fair review of this impartial testimony by the court's own witnesses—to which we necessarily must give great weight at this interim stage of review—clearly suggests that the discharges by Reserve can be characterized only as presenting an unquantifiable risk, i.e., a health risk which either may be negligible or may be significant, but with any significance as yet based on unknowns. This conclusion is simply a logical deduction from the following facts: (1) that fiber levels are not at occupational levels; (2) that the low levels present cannot be expressed or measured as a health risk; and (3) that, in any event, threshold values and dose-response relationships are undetermined. In other words, it is not known what the level of fiber exposure is, other than that it is relatively low, and it is not known what level of exposure is safe or unsafe. Finally, no basis exists, save a theoretical one, for assuming that drinking water, otherwise pure but containing asbestos-like particles, is dangerous to health....

Considering all of the above, we think one conclusion is evident: although Reserve's discharges represent a possible medical danger, they have not in this case been proven to amount to a health hazard. The discharges may or may not result in detrimental health effects, but, for the present, that is simply unknown....

Our stay of the injunction rests upon the good faith preparation and implementation of an acceptable plan. Therefore, we grant a 70-day stay upon these conditions:

1. Reserve's plans shall be promptly submitted to plaintiff-states and to the United States for review and recommendations by appropriate

agencies concerned with environmental and health protection. Such plan shall be filed with the district court and submitted to all plaintiffs in no event later than 25 days from the filing of this order.

2. Plaintiffs shall then have an additional 20 days within which to file their comments on such plan.

OPINION II (APRIL 8, 1975)

On June 4, 1974, [this] court issued an opinion granting Reserve a 70-day stay of the injunction. *Reserve Mining Co.* v. *United States,* 498 F.2d 1073 (8th Cir. 1974). The court conditioned the stay upon Reserve taking prompt steps to abate its air and water discharges, and provided for further proceedings to review whether Reserve had proceeded with the good faith preparation and implementation of an acceptable plan. . . .

The initial, crucial question for our evaluation and resolution focuses upon the alleged hazard to public health attributable to Reserve's discharges into the air and water. . . .

In this preliminary review, we did not view the evidence as supporting a finding of substantial danger. We noted numerous uncertainties in plaintiff's theory of harm which controlled our assessment, particularly the uncertainty as to present levels of exposure and the difficulty in attempting to quantify those uncertain levels in terms of a demonstrable health hazard. . . .

We reached no preliminary decision on whether the facts justified a less stringent abatement order.

As will be evident from the discussion that follows, we adhere to our preliminary assessment that the evidence is insufficient to support the kind of demonstrable danger to the public health that would justify the immediate closing of Reserve's operations. We now address the basic question of whether the discharges pose any risk to public health

and, if so, whether the risk is one which is legally cognizable. . . .

As we noted in our stay opinion, much of the scientific knowledge regarding asbestos disease pathology derives from epidemiological studies of asbestos workers occupationally exposed to and inhaling high levels of asbestos dust. Studies of workers naturally exposed to asbestos dust have shown "excess" cancer deaths and a significant incidence of asbestosis. The principal excess cancers are cancer of the lung, the pleura (mesothelioma) and gastrointestinal tract ("gi" cancer).

Studies conducted by Dr. Irving Selikoff, plaintiffs' principal medical witness, illustrated these disease effects. Dr. Selikoff investigated the disease experience of asbestos insulation workers in the New York–New Jersey area, asbestos insulation workers nationwide, and workers in a New Jersey plant manufacturing amosite asbestos. Generally, all three groups showed excess cancer deaths among the exposed populations. . . .

Additionally, some studies implicate asbestos as a possible pathogenic agent in circumstances of exposure less severe than occupational levels. For example, several studies indicate that mesothelioma, a rare but particularly lethal cancer frequently associated with asbestos exposure, has been found in persons experiencing a low level of asbestos exposure.

Plaintiffs' hypothesis that Reserve's air emissions represent a significant threat to the public health touches numerous scientific disciplines, and an overall evaluation demands broad scientific understanding. We think it significant that Dr. Brown, an impartial witness whose court-appointed task was to address the health issue in its entirety, joined with plaintiffs' witnesses in viewing as reasonable the hypothesis that Reserve's discharges present a threat to public health. Although, as we noted in our stay opinion, Dr. Brown found the evidence insufficient to make a scientific probability statement as to whether adverse health consequences would in fact ensue, he expressed a public health concern over the continued long-term emission of fibers into the air. . . .

The . . . discussion of the evidence demonstrates that the medical and scientific conclusions here in dispute clearly lie "on the frontiers of scientific knowledge." . . .

As we have demonstrated, Reserve's air and water discharges pose a danger to the public health and justify judicial action of a preventive nature.

In fashioning relief in a case such as this involving a possibility of future harm, a court should strike a proper balance between the benefits conferred and the hazards created by Reserve's facility.

Reserve must be given a reasonable opportunity and a reasonable time to construct facilities to accomplish an abatement of its pollution of air and water and the health risk created thereby. In this way, hardship to employees and great economic loss incident to an immediate plant closing may be avoided. . . .

We cannot ignore, however, the potential for harm in Reserve's discharges. This potential imparts a degree of urgency to this case that would otherwise be absent from an environmental suit in which ecological pollution alone were proved. Thus, any authorization of Reserve to continue operations during conversion of its facilities to abate the pollution must be circumscribed by realistic time limitations. Accordingly, we direct that the injunction order be modified as follows.

A. The Discharge into Water

Reserve shall be given a reasonable time to stop discharging its wastes into Lake Superior. A reasonable time includes the time necessary for Minnesota to act on Reserve's present application to dispose of its tailings at Milepost 7. . . .

Upon receiving a permit from the State of Minnesota, Reserve must utilize every reasonable effort to expedite the construction of new facilities. . . .

B. Air Emissions

Pending final action by Minnesota on the present permit application, Reserve must promptly take all steps necessary to comply with Minnesota law applicable to its air emissions. . . .

We wish to make it clear that we view the air emission as presenting a hazard of greater significance than the water discharge. Accordingly, pending a determination of whether Reserve will be allowed to construct an on-land disposal site or will close its operations, Reserve must immediately proceed with the planning and implementation of such emission controls as may be reasonably and practically effectuated under the circumstances. . . .

Finally, this court deems it appropriate to suggest that the national interest now calls upon Minnesota and Reserve to exercise a zeal equivalent to that displayed in this litigation to arrive at an appropriate location for an on-land disposal site for Reserve's tailings and thus permit an important segment of the national steel industry, employing several thousand people, to continue in production. As we have already noted, we believe this controversy can be resolved in a manner that will purify the air and water without destroying jobs.

The existing injunction is modified in the respects stated herein.

NOTE

1. Dr. Brown, a research pathologist associated with the Mayo Clinic of Rochester, Minnesota, served the court both in the capacity of a technical advisor and that of an impartial witness.

EDITOR'S POSTSCRIPT—1987

For several years after this decision by the Eighth Circuit Court of Appeals, various courts witnessed arguments to show whether, as the Court of Appeals had put it, "the probability of harm is more likely than not." Neither side ever succeeded in providing definitive scientific evidence, and the focus of the controversy over Reserve Mining shifted to the problem of finding a satisfactory on-land disposal site. Reserve complained bitterly about the costs that would be involved in constructing on the site the state of Minnesota preferred. (Their separate cost estimates varied by $50–60 million.)

Every health question mentioned above by the Eight Circuit remained in dispute. Reserve repeatedly threatened to close down its Silver Bay facility permanently in the face of costs imposed by courts and the state. Finally, a bargain was struck: on July 7, 1978, Reserve agreed both to build a new facility to satisfy stringent conditions the state insisted upon for approval of the permits. The total investment in the new facility was set at $370 million. The company agreed to stop all discharges into Lake Superior by April 15, 1980. It faithfully carried out this promise and the new facility began operations in August, 1980.

Several scientific studies of health hazards had been completed by July, 1978, and subsequent studies were eventually completed. These studies, several of which were sponsored by Reserve, have not shown any significant increase in disease related to asbestos in the region or in workers at the plant. By mid-1982 studies had not shown a build-up of asbestiform bodies in lung tissue (of sufficient size to be detected), or in the bloodstream, among persons drinking the water from Lake Superior. Reserve's work force has not shown a significant problem of asbestosis or any similarly caused disease. On the other hand, just as government officials have never been able to show any increased incidence of disease as a result of the Silver Bay facility, so Reserve has no way of showing that there will not be latent and serious long-term effects in 15–20 years—as is commonly the case with asbestos-cased diseases.

T.L.B.

CASE 1. Protecting Consumers Against the Hazards of Smoking

The dangers of smoking cigarettes are now generally conceded by almost everyone except tobacco companies. Far less decided is how to protect the consumer and the potential consumer of cigarettes. A major source of marketing—perhaps *the* major source—is newspaper advertising. Newspapers are also a major source, and probably *the* major source, of information transmitted to the public about the dangers of smoking cigarettes. Newspapers thus have an interest in revenue from cigarette advertising and an

This case was prepared by Tom L. Beauchamp based on the following sources: Charles Trueheart, "The Tobacco Industry's Advertising Smoke Screen," *USA Today,* March 15, 1985, p. 3D; Kenneth E. Warner, "Cigarette Advertising and Media Coverage of Smoking and Health," *The New England Journal of Medicine* 312 (February 7, 1985): 384–388; Sam Zagoria, "Smoking and the Media's Responsibility," *Washington Post,* December 18, 1985, p. A26; Elizabeth Whelan, "Second Thoughts on a Cigarette-Ad Ban," *Wall Street Journal,* December 18, 1985, p. 28; Sam Zagoria, "Consumer Watchdogs," *Washington Post,* April 24, 1985, p. A24; Robert J. Samuelson, "Pacifying Media Hype," *Washington Post,* October 9, 1985, pp. F1, F12.

interest in informing the public about the dangers of what they advertise. No one needs to be reminded that most newspapers are businesses interested in making a profit but also interested in customer satisfaction.

The American Newspaper Publishers Association and the Magazine Publishers Association have appealed to First Amendment protections of the right to advertise and to present the facts as newspapers see fit in order to justify their view that this matter should be left up to each individual newspaper.

The New Republic once commissioned reporter David Owen to write an article on cancer and the cigarette lobby. He wrote a piece so blunt in stating the issues and laying blame that *The New Republic*'s editors killed it. According to *USA Today*, which investigated the incident, "In the candid (and no doubt regretted) words of Leon Wieseltier, the editor who assigned it, the threat of 'massive losses of advertising revenue' did it in."

The editors of *The New Republic* had been willing to report on the dangers of smoking and on the pressures brought by lobbyists, but were not willing to support the forcefulness with which Owen stated his case. Owen latter published his piece in the *Washington Monthly*, where he wrote that "The transcendent achievement of the cigarette lobby has been to establish the cancer issue as a 'controversy' or a 'debate' rather than as the clear-cut scientific case that it is." He went on to portray an industry that, among other things, uses newspapers and magazines to enhance its appeal by portraying the young smoker as healthy and sexy.

According to extensive research conducted by Kenneth E. Warner, this example of the burying of Owen's article is but one of many cases in which American news media refused to cover the story of the dangers of smoking for fear of loss of advertising revenue. This general problem prompted *Washington Post* ombudsman Sam Zagoria to chide newspapers for a failure to see the issues as moral rather than legal:

In this era of voluntarism, when the business community is constantly urging Congress and regulatory agencies to stand aside and "let us take care of this problem ourselves," couldn't the newspapers of the country agree—voluntarily and collectively—to refuse cigarette advertising? Couldn't they do what is right rather than only what is not prohibited by law? Most papers take great pride in the service they render to their communities, not only in providing information but also in philanthropic activities that provide scholarships and underwrite athletic tournaments. Is not helping some youngster avert the tortures of life-shortening lung cancer even a greater gift? . . . Is there any media group for social responsibility?

Only 6 out of 1,700 daily American newspapers, Zagoria notes (using statistics taken from the *New York State Journal of Medicine*), at present attempt wholeheartedly to report on the dangers of smoking.

During National Consumer Week in 1985, Zagoria took the position that the press has a "watchdog" role to play in consumer safety. Few journalists disagree with Zagoria's judgment that this role is a legitimate one for the media or that a newspaper can validly choose to emphasize reporting on the risks of smoking. However, Zagoria's contentions that the press has an *obligation* to promote the interests of consumers met a hostile reaction in journalism.

Questions

1. Has Zagoria confused the industry's responsibility and the government's responsibility to protect the public with that of the media's responsibilities, as many newspapers believe?

2. Should a newspaper refuse to accept ads for beer, firearms, or X-rated movies if a substantial portion of the public regards them as immoral or harmful?

3. Are stiff warnings on packages of cigarettes adequate to protect consumers? Potential consumers?

CASE 2. Union Carbide's MIC Plants in the United States and France

One of the most famous industrial accidents in the twentieth century happened on December 3, 1984, when a tragic toxic gas leak of methyl isocyanate (MIC) occurred at a Union Carbide Plant in Bhopal, India, killing at least 1,750 people and leaving thousands of others sick and incapacitated. That plant was closed and never reopened. In subsequent litigation, U.S. District Judge John F. Keenan called the case "the most significant, urgent, and extensive litigation ever to arise from a single event."

Although its own internal inspections and reports had warned of potential problems in controlling reactions and failures both in India and at a similar plant at Institute, West Virginia, Union Carbide took the position that potential problems had been handled and that both plants were operated in accordance with proper safety standards. It suggested sabotage as a likely, but not conclusive explanation of the "accident" in India and sharply criticized the way Indian supervisors had loosely implemented the company's safety standards.

Subsequent investigation indicated that there had been more than 70 generally small MIC leaks at the Institute plant from 1980–1984. That plant was closed for a five-month period after the Bhopal disaster, but reopened after presumably thorough inspections by Union Carbide, the State of West Virginia, EPA, and OSHA. Before reopening the plant, Union Carbide put in place $5 million in new safety equipment—introducing new safety monitors and a new cooling system that was thought to "solve" the problems that arose in India.

A year later, on April 1, 1986 Union Carbide was fined $1.3 million by the U.S. Labor Department for 221 safety violations at the Institute Plant. This was the largest such fine in history. OSHA inspectors charged that Union Carbide had intentionally under-reported the number of injuries at the plant and maintained defective safety equipment. Secretary of Labor Brock said the findings show a "laissez-faire attitude" toward worker safety. However, none of these violations involved the MIC unit, and no one had died. No units were closed.

Less well-discussed and investigated is a semi-obscure Union Carbide facility in Beziers, France, that uses large quantities of MIC in order to produce an insecticide. Beziers is also in a region of France that has one of the highest unemployment rates in that country. The French are well aware of the safety concerns that have arisen about Union Carbide facilities. However, workers have made it clear that they are much more concerned about losing their jobs than they are about injury from toxic gases. Shortly after Bhopal, Environment Minister Huguette Bouchardeau had the plant inspected and declared it safe. Local officials have made it clear that jobs at this facility are critical to the area's economic viability. Bouchardeau further noted that "in France, there are at least 300 companies that present comparable risks. If we reacted emotionally to the catastrophe [in India], there would be an industrial disaster in France."

Questions

1. If you worked in the West Virginia or French plants of Union Carbide, would you think you had been fairly treated by owners and inspectors? If not, on what moral basis do you believe you deserve certain changes?

2. Is the fact of high unemployment relevant

This case was prepared by Tom L. Beauchamp on the basis of numerous press reports and government documents.

to whether these plants should be allowed to operate? Is it true, as the French minister suggests, that we are always in a circumstance of trading off safety standards and employment?
3. Should these facilities be closed?

CASE 3. OSHA Noncompliance and Seniority

TMW Corporation produces three-quarters of the world's micro-synchronizers, an integral part of apartment vacuum systems. This corporation has plants mostly in the Midwest, although a few are scattered on both the East and West Coasts. The plants in the Midwest employ members of the Electronic Worker's Union under a contract which became effective last August and is in force for three years. This union is very strong and the employees will do anything to preserve and maintain the strong union benefits that have been won.

Last year an OSHA official came on a visit to the St. Louis plant and found several discrepancies with the standards established by the act. These included the absence of safety goggles on employees whose job it is to weld tiny wires together, and an automatic shut-off switch on the wire-splicing machine. TMW was issued warnings of the noncompliances, and was told if they were not corrected, the next step would be drastic fines.

The company immediately set about correcting the problems. They had to shut parts of the plants down in the midwest on a rotating basis to take care of the wire-splicing machines. The union members were quite upset because the employer laid off older employees, not the new trainees on the machines. They threatened a walkout.

Another company problem with the OSHA compliances was with the safety goggles. When told of the need to wear their goggles the welders refused, saying they were not able to see as well. They did not have to wear them before. The welders said they would take the responsibility of not wearing them now. The union backed the welders in their refusal.

Questions

1. Was the TMW Corporation wrong in the layoffs of the senior employees? Should the trainees be laid off instead?
2. If the union members walked off the job, would they have their jobs when the problem was settled?
3. Can the company force the welders to comply with the wearing of the safety goggles?
4. If an accident occurred to a welder because of the noncompliance with OSHA, would TMW be responsible, even though the welders and union said that they would assume the responsibility?
5. Could the OSHA official fine TMW for their employees not wearing the goggles? The union?

CASE 4. Velsicol Chemical Corporation

On December 24, 1975, the administrator of the Environmental Protection Agency of the United States Government, Russell E. Train, issued an order suspending some uses of the
pesticides heptachlor and chlordane. A Federal act seemed to give him authority to do so, but both the Secretary of the Department of Agriculture and the manufacturer of the

---

Case 3 was prepared by Professor Kenneth A. Kovach of George Mason University. Reprinted with permission.

Case 4 was prepared by Tom L. Beauchamp.

pesticides, Velsicol Chemical Corporation, joined hands in asking for a public hearing on the decision. Train and the EPA adduced considerable evidence to indicate that these pesticides, which were widely used in the environment to control pests, produced cancer in laboratory animals. Testing on laboratory animals was the sole basis for the inference that the pesticides posed a cancer threat to humans, although it also was conclusively demonstrated that residues of the chemical were widely present in the human diet and in the human tissues of those exposed.

Velsicol Chemical stood to lose a substantial amount of money unless existing stocks could be sold, and the EPA administrator did allow them to sell limited stock for use on corn pests (for a short period of time). The Environmental Defense Fund felt strongly that no sale should be permitted, and sought an injunction against continued sale. During the course of the public hearing, Velsicol argued both that its product should not be suspended unless the governmental agency could demonstrate that it is unsafe, and that any other finding would be a drastic departure from past federal policy.

However, both the agency and the judge argued that *the burden of proof is on the company* (i.e., the company must be able to prove that its product is safe). Since most issues about environmental and human safety turn on a demonstration of either safety or hazardousness, this burden-of-proof argument was strongly contested in the hearing. The judge found in favor of the agency largely because he believed the animal tests demonstrated a "substantial likelihood" of serious harm to humans. EPA officials subsequently considered backing down on this suspension ruling.

Questions

1. Should Velsicol have been allowed to sell its existing stock?
2. Why should the "burden of proof" be place on the company rather than the government (if it should)? Are there parallels between the burden-of-proof arguments in this case and in the *Reserve Mining* case?
3. Are there any respects in which Velsicol was treated unfairly by the government?

Suggested Supplementary Readings

Consumer Protection

Berenson, Conrad. "The Product Liability Revolution." *Business Horizons* 15 (October 1972).

Carruba, E. *Assuring Product Integrity.* Lexington, Mass.: Lexington Books, 1975.

Clasen, Earl A. "Marketing Ethics and the Consumer." *Harvard Business Review* (January–February 1967).

Fletcher, G. "Fairness and Utility in Tort Theory." *Harvard Law Review* 85 (January 1972): 537–573.

Gray, I. *Product Liability: A Management Response,* Chapter 6. New York: Amacom, 1975.

Luthans, Fred, et al., *Social Issues in Business,* part III. New York: Macmillan, 1984.

Owen, David G. "Rethinking the Policies of Strict Products Liability." *Vanderbilt Law Review* 33 (1980): 686.

Plant, Marcus L. "Strict Liability of Manufacturers for Injuries Caused by Defects in Products—An Opposing View." *Tennessee Law Review* 24 (1957): 945.

Posner, R. "Strict Liability: A Comment." *The Journal of Legal Studies* 2 (January 1973): 205–221.

Preston, I. *The Great American Blow-up: Puffery in Advertising and Selling.* Madison, Wis.: University of Wisconsin Press, 1975.

Prosser, William L. "The Assault Upon the Citadel (Strict Liability to the Consumer)." *The Yale Law Journal* 69 (1960): 119.

Weinstein, Alvin S., et al. *Products Liability and the Reasonably Safe Product.* New York: John Wiley and Sons, 1978.

Worker Protection

Daniels, Norman. *Just Health Care,* Chapter 8. New York: Cambridge University Press, 1985.

Eckholm, Eric. "Unhealthy Jobs." *Environment* 19 (June 1977): 29–38.

Gibson, Mary. *Worker's Rights.* Totowa, N.J.: Rowman and Allanheld, 1983.

Hunt, Vilma R. "Perspective on Ethical Issues in Occupational Health." In *Biomedical Ethics Reviews 1984,* Edited by R. Almeder and J. Humber. Clifton, N.J.: Humana Press, 1984.

Kasperson, Roger E. "Worker Participation in Protection: The Swedish Alternative." CENTED Reprint No. 33, Center for Technology, Environment, and Development, Clark University (January 1984).

Kaufman, Stuart, and Judson MacLaury. "Historical Perspectives." In *Protecting People at Work,* edited by Judson MacLaury, 16–31. Washington, D.C.: U.S. Department of Labor, 1980.

Murrary, Thomas, and Ronald Bayer. "Ethical Issues in Occupational Health." In *Biomedical Ethics Reviews 1984,* edited by R. Almeder and J. Humber. Clifton, N.J.: Humana Press, 1984.

"Occupational Health." Symposium, *The Hastings Center Report* 14 (August 1984).

Office of Technology Assessment. *Preventing Illness and Injury in the Workplace.* Washington, D.C.: U.S. Government Printing Office, 1985.

Sass, Robert. "The Worker's Right to Know, Participate, and Refuse Hazardous Work: A Manifesto Right." *Journal of Business Ethics* (April 1986).

Schottenfeld, David, and Joanna F. Haus. "Carcinogens in the Workplace." *CA-A Cancer Journal for Clinicans* 29 (1979): 144–168.

Settle, Russell F., and Burton A. Weisbrod. "Occupational Safety and Health and the Public Interest." In *Public Interest Law,* edited by Burton Weisbrod, et al. Berkeley: University of California Press, 1978.

Environmental Protection

Ackerman, Robert W. *The Social Challenge to Business.* Cambridge, Mass.: Harvard University Press, 1975.

Anderson, Frederick R., et al. *Environmental Improvement Through Economic Incentives.* Baltimore: Johns Hopkins University Press, 1977.

Blackstone, William T., ed. *Philosophy and Environmental Crisis.* Athens: University of Georgia Press, 1974.

Brunner, David L., et al., eds. *Corporations and the Environment: How Should Decisions be Made?* Stanford, Calif.: Committee on Corporate Responsibility, 1981.

Elliot, Robert, and Arran Gare, eds. *Environmental Philosophy.* University Park, Pa.: Pennsylvania State University Press, 1983.

Environmental Ethics. "An Interdisciplinary Journal Dedicated to the Philosophical Aspects of Environmental Problems," 1979 to present.

Gibson, Mary. *To Breathe Freely: Risk, Consent, and Air.* Totowa, N.J.: Rowman and Allanheld, 1985.

Goodpaster, K. E., and K. M. Sayre, eds. *Ethics and Problems of the 21st Century.* Notre Dame, Ind.: University of Notre Dame Press, 1979.

Hardin, Garrett, and John Baden. *Managing the Commons.* San Francisco: W.H. Freeman, 1977.

Leopold, Aldo. "The Land Ethic." In *A Sand County Almanac.* New York: Oxford University Press, 1966.

Partridge, Ernest, ed. *Responsibilities to Future Generations: Environmental Ethics.* Buffalo: Prometheus Books, 1981.

Regan, Tom, ed. *Earthbound: New Introductory Essays in Environmental Ethics.* New York: Random House, 1984.

Rolston, Holmes. "Is There an Ecologic Ethic?" *Ethics* 85 (January 1975).

Sagoff, Mark. "Economic Theory and Environmental Law." *Michigan Law Review* 79 (June 1981).

Sayre, Kenneth, ed. *Values in the Electric Power Industry.* Notre Dame, Ind.: University of Notre Dame Press, 1977.

Scherer, Donald, and Thomas Attig, eds. *Ethics and the Environment.* Englewood Cliffs, N.J.: Prentice-Hall, 1983.

Schumaker, E. F. *Small Is Beautiful.* New York: Harper and Row, 1973.

Shrader-Frechette, Kristin S. *Environmental Ethics.* Pacific Grove, Calif.: Boxwood Press, 1982.

Tribe, Laurence. "Ways Not to Think About Plastic Trees." *The Yale Law Journal* 83 (1974).

Velasquez, Manuel G. *Business Ethics: Concepts and Cases,* chapter 5. Englewood Cliffs, N.J.: Prentice-Hall, 1982.

CHAPTER FIVE

Rights and Obligations of Employers and Employees

INTRODUCTION

Traditionally, business firms are organized hierarchically, with production line employees at the bottom and the CEO at the top. Also, the interests of the stockholders are given priority over the interests of other stakeholders. However, much recent literature presents a challenge to these arrangements, especially to underlying classical economic assumptions whereby labor is treated as analogous to land, capital, and machinery, that is, as replaceable and as means to the end of profit. Employees want primarily to be treated as persons who make an essential contribution rather than as means to the end of profit. They want decent salaries and job security, but they also want appreciation from supervisors, the sense of accomplishment, and fair opportunities to display their talents. Many employees are also interested in participating in the future of the company, defining the public responsibilities of the corporation, evaluating the role and quality of management, and—most especially—helping to set the tasks assigned to the job.

Some corporations have recently invested considerable ingenuity in implementing increased worker participation, including reorganization to give employees more to say about their jobs and about company fringe benefits. Numerous corporations have revised their conception of employee relations by establishing explicit standards for hiring, firing, merit evaluation, retirement, grievance proceedings, and participative management by workers. These developments are now taking place in thousands of factories, offices, warehouses, and retail stores; and they seem destined to permanently alter traditional patterns of the employer/employee relationship.

To suggest that moral problems in employer/employee relations are all about employee *rights,* would, of course, be one-sided. No less important are employee *obligations:* Employees have moral obligations to respect the property of the corporation, to abide by employment contracts, and to operate within the bounds of procedural rules. Just as the employee has rights as well as obligations, so the employer has rights that the employee must respect as well as obligations to the employee. When these rights or obligations compete, they must be balanced in such a way that no party is given an undue advantage or an unjustified form of power. This chapter is concerned with these problems of rights, obligations, and balance.

THE STATUS AND SCOPE
OF EMPLOYEE RIGHTS

The movement to protect workers' rights through unions reached a peak in the United States around 1946, when 30 percent of the nonfarm work force was unionized. But, as employment shifted from manufacturing to services, unions declined rapidly in the 1970s and 1980s to about 16 percent of the work force. Many unions and scholars predicted that if unions ever declined in influence there would be a parallel decline in workers' rights. Yet as the power of unions declined, worker protections seemed to increase rather than decrease. Formerly, government had acted only as an external source of regulation, and unions negotiated directly with companies. But in recent years all three branches of the U.S. government have become entangled with problems of rights in the workplace.

What seems to be happening in American society is that workers are looking less to unions for collective action and more to the law. They have been looking, in particular, to courts and legislatures. More than any other factor in American society, these legal institutions have become the vanguard of worker protections, often imposing substantive terms of employment on employers. Paul Weiler, a labor law specialist at Harvard, has summed up the contemporary situation as follows: "Some business leaders think they will get a union-free environment, but what they may get is a legalized environment."[1]

The growing nexus of laws and court rulings includes, for example, right-to-know legislation and numerous new standards to provide for a safe and healthful workplace—as discussed in Chapter Four—and numerous statutes and court decisions pertaining to discrimination—as discussed in Chapter Six. Other laws cover minimum wage, maximum-hour work week, rights against discharge and discipline, privacy rights, mandatory retirement age, severance pay, and funding and other standards for pensions. These legislative developments provide a powerful layer of protection for workers on top of the antidis-crimination laws and labor legislation of the 1960s and 1970s.

Courts have at the same time begun to critically examine management's traditional rights to fire employees for reasons other than discrimination. Many now believe that in the future we will see the complete eclipse of the doctrine of "employment at will," which derives from English common law and which has been the prevailing rule in American society. According to this doctrine, employment is at the will of the employer. Unless there is a contract specifying otherwise, an employee may be fired for good cause or for no cause at all. In one precedent-setting nineteenth-century case, it was even said that the employee could be legitimately fired when reasons for the firing were morally wrong.[2] However, as the *Pierce* v. *Ortho Pharmaceutical Corporation* case in this chapter indicates, this view is beginning to break down. In this New Jersey case a physician employee appealed to moral conscience and protection of the public as the basis for a wrongful discharge.

Laws are now pending in several legislatures that would prohibit unjust dismissals by private employers. It seems certain that legislative and court actions will combine to recognize in at least some legal jurisdictions that even in the absence of explicit contracts, such as union-negotiated contracts, all employees have an *implicit* employment contract that courts can enforce. For example, on May 9, 1985, the New Jersey Supreme Court again struck at the state's long history of operating under the doctrine of employment at will. It held that Hoffmann–La Roche Inc. was bound by job security assurances that were implied in an employee manual and had to reinstate an employee who had been fired on grounds that his supervisor had lost confidence in his work. The handbook seemed to pledge that employees could be fired only for just cause, and then only if certain procedures were followed. Hoffmann–La Roche argued that the company manual gave company policy but that adherence to it was voluntary and not legally enforceable. The court said employers cannot have it both ways without acting unfairly and so illegally: Either the pledge is a meaningful right or not. Sears & Roebuck and other employers are now trying to combat such court decisions by having employees sign a form declaring that they can be fired "with or without just cause." And to avoid courtroom battles, several companies have developed internal procedures that examine every dismissal case as though there were a specific contract with a just-cause-for-firing provision in it.[3]

Courts in approximately half of the states in the United States have now handed down opinions that, in varying degrees, reverse a former strict adherence to the doctrine of employment at will. These developments piggyback on the well-accepted principle that the doctrine of employment at will in the common law can be superseded by contracts and by statutes. Most collective bargaining contracts, for example, provide for a formal grievance procedure that protects union members from an unjust dismissal. Civil servants are similarly protected, tenured college faculty members have job protection until age 70, and many kinds of employees have contracts that stipulate a minimum length of employment. Professional football coaches offer an example of the latter protection: If fired before their contracts expire, they are still paid for the term of their contract.

Although the idea that one can be legitimately fired for vindictive reasons or by abusive managers is fast fading from the American scene, the doctrine of employment at will has recently been upheld in some legal jurisdictions[4] and is being written into new proposed legislation in some states. Roughly 60 million workers still fall under the employment-at-will doctrine, and it is documented that many workers are still fired for unconscionable reasons. Some bring wrongful-discharge suits, but these costly suits are, for the most part, only affordable by white-collar workers. This raises still further questions about the *justice* of a system using the employment-at-will doctrine.

In the selection that opens this chapter, Patricia Werhane considers the arguments for and against the "employment-at-will" doctrine. She concludes that this doctrine cannot be justified, not only because it permits an employer to fire an employee for no reason or even for a morally wrong reason, but also because it violates the principle of equal treatment. Although employees of a given firm are all treated equally in that they are all equally employed at will, the employer is not committed to equality of treatment in giving specific causes for dismissal: One employee might be fired for tardiness, while a similarly tardy employee is retained.

One of the advantages of personnel policy, formal rules, and codes of ethics is that they promote substantive equality of treatment. Companies that have a proper personnel policy and procedures for terminating employees are constrained from simply mistreating or firing an employee in violation of official policies. Of course, it is one thing to say that a corporation should have a proper policy for terminating employees, and it is another to state what that policy should be and what makes it proper. As George Brenkert discusses, controversy has arisen over substantive company policies that infringe on an employee's privacy—for example, in the use of polygraphs. Other controversies involve attempts to control employee conduct off the job or to deny an employee Constitutional rights.[5]

But this does not mean that "tough" rules for employees are not in order. For example, the managers of day-care centers have an obligation to their customers to determine whether a potential employee has ever been convicted of child molesting, and an airline company has a right to know if its pilots are taking narcotics. Polygraphs might be appropriate in such cases. But even if an employer has a right to invade an employee's privacy in obtaining such information, there is always a question of appropriate *means*. For example, an employer might ask the employee if he or she takes drugs, might require that the employee submit to urinalysis, or might hire a private investigative firm to poke into intimate aspects of the employee's personal life. And, as Raymond Pfeiffer discusses, management might use unduly manipulative methods in the attempt to motivate employees.

As for restricting conduct off the job, the response of an employee tends to be that private life is just that: private. But this response may be unrealistic in many situations that might embarrass or otherwise negatively affect the company. Many employees cannot shed their company identity the way they shed their overcoats. For eample, what the president of the bank does in a private club off hours may affect the profits of the bank. How businesses should respond to employee conduct that reduces or is likely to reduce profit presents an unavoidable problem.

One solution to this problem might come through appeal to constitutional rights. The courts have never accorded extensive rights to *criticize* an employer to the employees of private organizations. However, the courts have extended rights of *privacy* to these employees in connection with the employment-at-will doctrine. For example, IBM lost an unjust dismissal case (*Rulon-Miller* v. *IBM*) after it fired an employee for dating the employee of a competitor firm, Qyx, which is owned by Exxon. IBM conceded that its employee, Gina Rulon-Miller, had an outstanding record but argued that the mere existence of an intimate relationship with a person from a rival firm created a conflict of interest. In still other cases the courts have awarded large sums to employees fired for refusing to take polygraph tests about private matters.[6]

THE RIGHT TO WORK, MEANINGFUL WORK, AND RIGHTS OF PRIVACY AND AUTONOMY

Some companies, including giants like Hewlett-Packard, have adopted voluntary initiatives to expand employee rights in the corporation—for example, rights to privacy and autonomy. These strategies include placing employees on corporate boards and other official decision-making committees and provid-

ing procedures to hear grievances. One controversial strategy is a no-layoff policy. For example, Materials Research Corporation of Orangeburg, New York, adopted a no-layoff policy in 1981. Immediately a recession set in, but the company kept on 100 excess employees at a cost of $4 million. So loyal are the 1,000 employees of this company that the turnover rate is less than 1 percent per month, which has cut personnel costs. Sheldon Weinig, Chairman and founder of the company, says, "If they do a first-class job, pursue further education, and are willing to work heavy overtime, they have a *job for life.*"[7]

At some more traditional companies, successful lawsuits are resulting in large awards in unjust-dismissal suits. The courts in California, for example, have been generous in giving damage awards. Like product liability suits, the number of cases, the size of the awards, and the publicity surrounding them are all increasing. These developments, in turn, have spurred legislators to work on (often sharply competing) unjust-dismissal bills to protect both employees and employers.[8] A number of bills that would prohibit firing employees except for just cause (e.g., for drunkenness, incompetence, and criminal behavior) are currently being introduced into legislatures. These bills are sometimes drafted in such broad language that they suggest that employees have a *right to a job* paralleling the rights that the Materials Research Corporation voluntarily conferred on its employees. Some employers are concerned that the legislation will have the effect of requiring them to retain even incompetent workers.

These legislative developments, the aforementioned voluntary corporate initiatives, and court verdicts have led to philosophical questions about the right to work, property rights in jobs, and meaningful work. Richard De George maintains in this chapter that employee rights include a worker's right to a job. The right to work is on the list of rights enumerated in the United Nations Universal Declaration of Human Rights, but has proved difficult to defend by philosophical argument. Indeed some contend that employees have no such right. A common approach is to base the right on the principle of respect for persons discussed in Chapter 1 (see pp. 38–39). The claim is that one can only be in a position to be respected as a person if one has certain rights, including the right to work. This claim must be defended by showing an intimate connection between work and being accorded proper respect. One argument to this effect is largely empirical; it makes a connection between having a job and having social status and self-esteem. In the United States a major measure of social status is size of income, and having a job is necessary to acquire virtually any significant status of this sort. In addition, *having a job* carries status independent of income level. Some jobs carry more status than others, but there is a threshold below which one is not respected by society; being on welfare carries such negative status. Some people who qualify for welfare seek low-paying jobs simply to avoid the stigma attached to welfare and therefore to gain social status and self-esteem.

Another argument for the right to a job depends on an analogy to expectations generated by investing precious time and resources. Many persons invest as much money and time in their education with the purpose of obtaining work as they do in purchasing and maintaining the home they own. They speak of their job as their *career,* and they may expect to have no more than one, two, or three careers in a lifetime. If a person faithfully invests time, money, and energy in educational training for a job and later in that job itself, can we speak of the person as having a right to that job that is analogous to the homeowner's property right to a home? This question remains controversial.

Other problems regarding work and employee status and esteem are similarly controversial. For example, even if we have some form of right to a job, it may still be asked whether we have a right either to decent working conditions or to what is sometimes called "meaningful work"—work an employee finds so valuable that monetary reward is not the sole or even primary reason for performing it. "Intrinsically valuable" work is worthwhile in and of itself—for example, artistic creativity fits this description even when the artist creates works for the market. However, much of the available work in the world of business is not so creative and must be performed under less than ideal conditions. If the criterion for meaningful work is that it be intrinsically valuable, meaningful work would be a practical impossibility for many.

Some less demanding criterion of "meaningful work" than "intrinsic value" therefore seems essential. In her article, Diana Meyers argues that meaningful work should be described as that which fosters self-respect. Because work occupies such a large portion of our time and may be central to our identity, it is important to identify conditions and rights in the workplace that are supportive of self-respect. Meyers believes that if workers have three rights—the right to employment, the right to equal opportunity, and the right to participate in job-related decisions—self-respect on the job would be adequately supported.

The final of her three rights deserves special attention. In the past ten years a loose consensus has formed that productivity would increase if employees had more to say about their jobs and the work environment and were allowed more protection of privacy and rights of autonomy. A number of strategies have been adopted to put this managerial principle into practice. For example, some have urged that employers change their typical attitude of looking at employees as lazy and as responding only to rewards and threats (Theory X); instead, an employer should assume that employees want to achieve and will do so if given the opportunity (Theory Y). If an employer adopts Theory Y, employees will be given increased responsibility, which will enable them to be more involved in work-related decisions. Perhaps a production process will be broken down into teams, with each team making decisions concerning their aggregate activities.

Although critics have charged that such programs are attempts to corrupt workers and that some practices are fundamentally manipulative—a charge assessed by Pfeiffer—these employee-involvement plans have generally been well received. Of course, this scheme of democratization—if acted on extensively—could shift control of the corporation from the owners or stockholders to the employees. Whereas classical theory is faulted for vesting all power in the *stockholders* at the expense of other stakeholders, the theory of worker democracy could be similarly criticized for empowering the *employees* at the expense of the other stakeholders, including the stockholders.

WHISTLEBLOWING AND THE DUTY OF LOYALTY

State legislatures in almost half of the fifty states have at this writing passed laws to protect corporate and government whistleblowers—those employees who refuse on moral grounds to engage in or condone legal or moral violations by an employer or who refuse to engage in a practice that runs against the public interest. Such actions and laws raise questions about whether and to what extent employees should have recourse to higher authorities in the company or should inform the public if asked to participate in an illegal, immoral, or questionable act (or if they witness such an action).

Despite the obviously good intentions of whistleblowers to protect the interests of others (sometimes at significant personal cost), many businesspersons hold that whistleblowers violate a duty of loyalty. This attitude is captured in some remarks by James M. Roche, former president of General Motors, that are quoted and assessed in the essay by Ronald Duska: "Some of the enemies of business now encourage an employee to be *disloyal* to the enterprise. They want to create suspicion and disharmony, and pry into the proprietary interests of the business. However this is labelled—industrial espionage, whistle blowing, or professional responsibility—it is another tactic for spreading disunity and creating conflict."[9]

Roche has a point in this respect: American corporations are today facing the most significant crisis of loyalty in their history. Interviews and empirical studies have repeatedly shown that many employees view their employer as a massive bureaucracy not deserving of their devotion and loyalty. James Walls, a marketing vice-president at Stanton Corporation, which administers honesty tests to the employees of its corporate clients, says that his test results show that "there's absolutely no doubt that corporate loyalty is lower today than it's ever been."[10] A wave of mergers, corporate cutbacks, and job reductions (nearly a half million between 1979 and 1985) have no doubt played a role in introducing these doubts that corporate organizations are stable and care about the welfare of employees.

Employees have both *legal* and *moral* obligations to be loyal to their employers. This is not surprising inasmuch as the employer has provided them a job, which is the primary vehicle for an employee to attain income and status. If the employer is loyal to the employee, loyalty may be conceived as a reciprocal obligation on the part of the employee. However, some aspects of this conception are challenged in the article by Duska. An issue featured in Chapter Two concerns whether the corporation, as distinguished from the individuals within the corporation, is the kind of entity that could be held morally responsible. Duska raises a related question: Can corporations properly be *an object of loyalty?* He argues that loyalty can apply only in a relationship that transcends self-interest and must be based on a stable relationship of trust and confidence. The relationship of an employee to a corporation is not that kind of relationship, in his view, because it is a relationship of mutual *self*-interest. In this form of relationship the employee does not have an obligation of loyalty to the employer.

If the classical theory is presumed, that the firm's sole concern is profit for its stockholders, then Duska's contention is plausible. But if a broader stakeholder theory is substituted (see pp. 61–62, especially Freeman's theory), the corporation does have genuine obligations to employees. Duska's argument seems progressively more problematic as firms increase the emphasis on the interests of all corporate stakeholders and provide devices for disclosure of wrongdoing. Some American companies are now actively encouraging conscientious objections and warnings by their employees. They use hotlines, ombudsmen, confidential questionnaires, and other mechanisms to encourage internal criticism of supervisors or activities. The idea is to arrange the workplace so that employees are not driven to external whistleblowing and can speak their minds free of intimidation. However, such corporations are still a small minority, and hostility toward whistleblowing remains the norm.

Another issue that demands attention is the nature of a duty of loyalty itself. That an employee *should* be loyal is a prima facie duty. Yet the object of one's loyalty must be deserving and morally appropriate if loyalty is to be the overriding obligation. The virtue of loyalty does not require that one accept blindly the person or cause to which one is loyal. Nor does it require that when loyalty conflicts with other duties—such as respecting another's autonomy—loyalty is always overriding. To be loyal to an employer thus does not require that the employer must be obeyed under all conditions.

Moreover, questions can be raised about whether loyalty and disloyalty are the right concepts to express the ideas of faithful service and lack of devotion in employment. We have seen previously that a corporation and its employees are bound by contractual understandings, which often require both parties to be honest, truthful, and trustworthy. But no one should expect that an employee has a duty of loyalty to remain with a company if presented with a better opportunity by a competing firm. New start-up companies are by definition composed of employees who left older companies for new ones. It seems wrong to describe such departures as acts of disloyalty. Most employment arrangements are motivated by opportunity, advancement, and salary, and termination of these arrangements need not amount to disloyalty. Even the acts of whistleblowers may have more to do

with maintaining personal moral integrity than with disloyalty.

However, the claims of whistleblowers are not always justified, just as denials of wrongdoing by employers are not always true. Whistleblowers may be trying to seize more power within the company or trying to cover up personal inadequacies that represent the real reason for discipline or dismissal. What is needed is a careful definition of whistleblowing and a set of conditions indicating precise considerations that should be taken into account to justify acts of whistleblowing. Sissela Bok makes a start in this direction in her essay. She explains why the stakes in a whistleblowing situation are so high, as well as why employers are often bitter when an employee has blown the whistle. She also analyzes the nature of whistleblowing and explores when whistleblowing is justified. (The *Pierce* v. *Ortho Pharmaceutical Corporation* case is also relevant to these issues in that it shows a physician's conscientious refusal to use a drug for clinical testing. However, it is more a resignation case than a whistleblowing case.)

TRADE SECRETS AND THE DUTY OF CONFIDENTIALITY

Conflict between employer and employee can also arise over proprietary information. Here issues concern what belongs to an employer and what belongs to an employee, especially when the "property" is so-called intellectual property and has become part of the employee's knowledge and thinking. Among the legal obligations of an employee to an employer under common law is the duty of confidentiality. An employee in possession of confidential information that could damage the economic interests of an employer if disclosed is under an an obligation of confidentiality that remains in force when the employee leaves the firm and takes employment elsewhere. However, under common law it is not a breach of any obligation owed to an employer to *plan* for a new competitive venture while still employed, even though the employee has an opportunity to observe (what will later be) a competitor's secrets, and even though the employee may leave with a wealth of experience in and knowledge about the competitor's processes, products, research, and financial matters.[11]

Under the law, an employee leaving a job cannot utilize or disclose a trade secret. For example, the formula for Coca-Cola is the property of the Coca-Cola Company. If an employee gave the formula to Pepsi, a trade secret would have been disclosed. However, other vital knowledge is not secret—for example, general knowledge about a field that a researcher in computer technology at Bell Laboratories obtains while employed there. If not framed carefully, what might be called "the Coca-Cola Model" of trade secrets disclosure may prove more misleading than illuminating. This model assumes that a company *owns* a formula, device, or process that has been *disclosed* in confidence to one or more employees. More typically in some industries, employees are instrumental in creating or advancing the formula, device, or process through their own ingenuity and skills. The more an employee creates or otherwise improves the confidential information or property, the more the employee seems to have a right to use it, and the less an employer seems to have a right to claim sole possession. In the *Futurecraft Corp.* v. *Clary Corp.* case at the end of this chapter, a judge argues that an employer's legitimate interest in protecting a secret is reduced to the extent that a former employee helped to develop the item.

Whenever an employee acts on this premise after having made a contribution to a corporation's formula, device, or process, a conflict of rights between employer and employee is imminent. The employer has a right to its intellectual property; the employee has a right to seek gainful employment that requires his or her abilities. The traditional rule in law and industry is that a former employer is entitled to retain proprietary information for purposes of competition. The former employee therefore must keep such information confidential. In reaching a judgment that there has been a trade secrets violation, the

courts have traditionally required only that there be proof that a former employee exploited the trade secret, resulting in damage to the company. In the event of conflict, the employee's interest in employment mobility yields to the former employer's interest in protecting the trade secret.

However, some courts have begun to look closely at the relative weights of the competing interests in many cases. A few courts have adopted what might be called a "balancing model" of trade secrets protection, according to which the employee's interest in mobility and opportunity should be weighed against the employer's rights in determining the scope of protection afforded to confidential information. Such courts have attempted to weigh a public policy favoring the protection of trade secrets against a competing public policy favoring the interest of an employee to use skills and knowledge acquired in a field in order to earn a livelihood.[12] These courts set forth the elements to be pleaded and proved in a trade secrets case as follows:

1. There must be true trade secrecy and established ownership;
2. The secret must have been disclosed, thereby breaching a duty of confidentiality, by an employee;
3. The employer's interest in maintaining the secret must outweigh both the interest of the employee in using the knowledge to earn a living and the interest of the public in having the knowledge transmitted.

The first element—true trade secrecy—raises questions about the definition of *trade secret*. The standard definition, as referred to in the selections in this section, is from "Restatement of Torts": A trade secret consists of any confidential formula, pattern, device, or compilation of information that is employed in a business and that gives the business the opportunity to gain a competitive advantage over those who do not know or use it. These secrets must be the particular secrets of an owner, not general secrets maintained in a trade. A trivial advance or difference in a known formula, process, or device is not a trade secret. However, because the quality or degree of innovation may itself be disputed, it can be controversial whether methods and processes that are merely skillful variations of general processes can qualify as trade secrets.

The mere *intent* of an employer to treat something as confidential is not sufficient to make it a trade secret, and there is no trade secrecy if a process can be ascertained either by the application of general skill and knowledge to a sold product or by what is called *reverse engineering,* that is, by an engineering examination that starts with a known product and works backward to discover the processes through which the product was produced. For example, a computer engineer might be able to discover how a computer head is made by examining the layers and types of film deposited on the head of a computer.[13] Furthermore, although trade secrecy requires that there be secret or confidential information, it is not necessarily an employee's disclosure that causes loss of secrecy. The company's own carelessness can be the source of the problem, and it is therefore expected that the company will take reasonable precautions to protect itself against discovery even by industrial spies. When the Kellogg Company stopped its famous plant tours in April 1986, the primary reason was a fear that the tours created a legitimate opportunity for industrial spies to take the tours and steal state-of-the-art manufacturing secrets.[14]

This third condition is the most significant, because it requires a balancing of the *competing equitable interests* of former employer and former employee, without antecedently presuming that the burden of proof is on the former employee to show that secrets were not taken. Although the courts have traditionally tended to treat the transfer of proprietary information as simple theft, under condition three a court could actually deny protection of trade secrets to a former employer despite the existence of a bona fide trade secret if the former employee had a demonstrable interest in the trade secret. Thus, if the employee would be absolutely foreclosed from competition, while the employer losing the trade se-

cret would be only minimally damaged, the court could in theory deny trade secret protection.[15] The rationale for this approach is the goal of not placing employees in a situation of servitude while at the same time not precluding technological transfer and progress in industry. Ex-employees cannot legitimately be hamstrung by overprotective employers, and the public interest cannot be thwarted by overprotective policies of secrecy. The *Futurecraft* case in this chapter expresses the view that there is a strong public policy interest against restraining the mobility of employees in highly technical, specialized fields even where there is a risk that employees may walk away from a former place of employment with secret information usable for purposes of competition.

The model of balancing the competing interests of employees and employers is a utilitarian and pragmatic model that has emerged through an American court system charged with weighing such competing interests. The model may not be better than the older model fashioned on the goal of protecting the employer's property, but one thing is clear from recent analyses of trade secrets: The issues about trade and proprietary information are more complex and more extensive in business than has been appreciated in the past. There are many types of obligations to a past employer that might be violated when a former employee takes a new position—including those established by contractual obligations, keeping promises, truthfulness, confidentiality, and loyalty—and any assessment of what a former employee owes to the employing company would involve a careful scrutiny of each of these obligations. Furthermore, problems of conflict of interest may be at work even before an employee leaves a place of employment. The employee may be involved for several months in planning a new venture that will be a competitor to the present employer. In such situations, employees have an interest in their new venture but simultaneously are under an obligation to maintain their interest in protecting the employer's rights.

When the employee leaves to become a

competitor, it seems only fair that the process or product used should be sufficiently independent of the former employer's product or process to show that there is a significant measure of innovation and product development. But here we encounter one of the most difficult problems about proprietary information. In many cases the information in question involves some deviation from the trade secrets, patents, and proprietary designs held by corporations, but not enough deviation in the opinion of the former employer to qualify as an independent product. Thus, in the handling of a trade secrets case, the degree of innovation itself becomes a complex, technical, and often central matter.

The article by Michael Baram as well as that by Robert Frederick and Milton Snoeyenbos discuss some of these issues. Baram tries to point to the notable lack of success the law has had in dealing with the knotty issues and attempts to sketch a management policy that protects a corporation's intellectual property while remaining sensitive to bona fide rights of employees. Frederick and Snoeyenbos probe the duty of confidentiality and the issue of a role for public utility.

NOTES

1. See John Hoerr et al., "Beyond Unions: A Revolution in Employee Rights Is in the Making," *Business Week*, July 8, 1985, p. 72.
2. *Payne* v. *Western*, 81 Tenn. 507 (1884).
3. See "Fear of Firing," *Forbes*, December 2, 1985, p. 90; Hoerr, "Beyond Unions," pp. 74–75.
4. See, for example, *Parnar* v. *Americana Hotels, Inc.*, 652 2d 625 (Hawaii, 1982).
5. See, for example, David W. Ewing, "Civil Liberties in the Corporation," *New York State Bar Journal* (1978).
6. See Susan Chace, "Rules and Discipline, Goals and Praise Shape IBMers' Taut World,"

Wall Street Journal, April 8, 1982, pp. 1, 18; Peter Perl, "Rights of Employees at High-Tech Firms in Dispute," *Washington Post*, March 12, 1984, Washington Business section, p. 3; "Fear of Firing," p. 90.
7. Hoerr, "Beyond Unions," p. 76 (italics added).
8. "Fear of Firing," p. 90; Hoerr, "Beyond Unions," p. 77.
9. James M. Roche, "The Competitive System, to Work, to Preserve, and to Protect," *Vital Speeches of the Day* (May 1971): 445. See the Duska essay in this chapter, pp. 299–303, and Alan L. Otten, "States Begin to Protect Employees Who Blow Whistle on Their Firms," *Wall Street Journal*, December 31, 1984, p. 11.
10. As quoted in Thomas F. O'Boyle, "Loyalty Ebbs at Many Companies As Employees Grow Disillusioned," *Wall Street Journal*, July 11, 1985, p. 27.
11. See *Restatement of Agency Second*, par. 393, comment e; *Metal Lubricants Co.* v. *Engineered Lubricants Co.* 411 F.2d 426, 429 (1969); *Cudahy Co.* v. *American Laboratories, Inc.* 313 F. Supp. 1339, at 1345–46 (1970).
12. See, for example, *Cambridge Filter* v. *Intern Filter Company, Inc.*, 548 F. Supp. 1301, at 1307 (1982).
13. See *Videotronics, Inc.* v. *Bend Electronics*, 564 F. Supp. 1471, at 1475 (Nev. 1983); *Sarkes Tarzian, Inc.* v. *Audio Devices, Inc.*, 166 F. Supp, at 265; *Aetna Building Maintenance Co.* v. *West*, 39 Cal.2d 198, 206 (1952); *Hollingsworth Solderless Terminal Co.* v. *Turley*, 622 F.2d 1324, at 1334; *Kewanee Oil Co.* v. *Bicron Corp.*, 416 U.S., at 476.
14. Damon Darlin, "Kellogg is Snapping Its 80-Year Tradition of Cereal Tours," *Wall Street Journal*, April 10, 1986, p. 1.
15. See Diane Louise Wear, "A Balanced Approach to Employer-Employee Trade Secrets Disputes in California," *Hastings Law Journal* 31 (January 1980): 671–695; and Russell B. Stevenson, Jr.," *Corporations and Information: Secrecy, Access, and Disclosure*, Chapter 2. (Baltimore: Johns Hopkins University Press, 1980).

Employee and Employer Rights in an Institutional Context

Patricia H. Werhane

The common law principle of Employment at Will (EAW) states that in the absence of a specific contract or law, an employer may hire, fire, demote, or promote any employee (not covered by contract or law) when that employer wishes. The theory is that employers have rights—rights to control what happens in the workplace. These include decisions concerning all business operations, extending of course to the hiring and placement of employees. Although EAW is a common-law doctrine, until recently it virtually dictated employment relationships.

What are the justifications for EAW? How would one defend this idea? EAW is sometimes justified on the basis of property rights. It is contended that the rights to freedom and to property ownership are valid rights and that they include the right to use freely and to improve what one owns. According to this view, an employer has the right to dispose of her business and those who work for that business (and thus affect it) as she sees fit. Instituting employee rights such as due process or the protection of whistle blowers, for example, would restrict an employer's freedom to do what she wishes with her business, thus violating property rights.

In the twentieth century, employer property rights have changed. Businesses are mainly corporations owned by a large number of changing shareholders and managed by employees who usually own little or no stock in the company. The board of directors represents the owner-shareholder interests, but most business decisions are in the hands of managers. Despite this division of ownership from management, however, proprietory ownership rights of employers have translated themselves into management rights. Contemporary management sees itself as having the rights to control business and therefore to control employment. From a utilitarian perspective, control of a company by its managers is thought of as essential for maximum efficiency and productivity. To disrupt this would defeat the primary purpose of free enterprise organizations. Moreover, according to its proponents, EAW preserves the notion of "freedom of contract," the right of persons and organizations to enter freely into binding voluntary agreements (e.g., employment agreements) of their choice.

That managers see themselves in the role of proprietors is, of course, too simple a description. In complex organizations there is a hierarchy of *at-will* relationships. Each manager is an at-will employee, but sees himself as proprietor of certain responsibilities to the organization and as being in control of certain other employees whom the manager can dismiss at will, albeit within certain guidelines of legal restraint. That manager, in turn, reports to someone else who is herself an at-will employee responsible to another segment of the organization. These at-will relationships are thought to preserve equal employee and employer freedoms because, just as a manager can demote or fire an at-will employee at any time, so too an

---

Used by permission of the author.

employee, any employee, can quit whenever he or she pleases for any reason whatsoever. Notice a strange anomaly here. Employees have responsibilities to their managers and are not free to make their own choices in the workplace. At the same time, employees are conceived of as autonomous persons who are at liberty to quit at any time.

Notice, too, that there is sometimes a sort of Social Darwinist theory of management functioning in many of these relationships. Managers are so-titled because it is felt that they are the most capable. By reason of education and experience and from the perspective of their position, they allegedly know what is best for the organization or the part of the organization they manage. This gives them the right to manage other employees. The employees they manage (who themselves may be managers of yet other employees) have roles within the organization to carry out the directives of their managers, and so on.

The employee-manager hierarchy of at-will employment relationships is both more complex and more simple in union-management relationships. It is more complex because often the relationship is specified or restricted by a number of well-defined rules for seniority, layoffs, dismissals, and so on. It is more simple because by and large union employees are *employees,* not managers. Their role responsibilities defined by hierarchical relationships are clear-cut, and those wishing to change or move up to management usually must give up union membership.

This oversimplified, crude, overstated, overview of hierarchical employment relationships in business may not currently exist in the ways I have described in any business. Yet such relationships are at least *implicit* in many businesses and perpetuated in the law by a continued management or employer-biased interpretation of the principle of EAW.

Despite the fact that the principle of EAW is defended on a number of grounds—including that it allegedly protects equal employee and manager freedoms, that it promotes efficiency, and that it preserves the notion of freedom of contract—EAW violates all of these for the following reasons. EAW does not preserve equal freedoms because in most employment relationships employer-managers are in positions of greater power than employees. This in itself does not undermine EAW, but the potential abuse of this power is what is at issue. Employees and managers allegedly have equal rights—rights to be fired or to quit at any time for any reason. But an at-will employee is seldom in a position within the law to inflict harm on an employer. Legally sanctioned at-will treatment by employers of employees can, however, harm employees. This is because when an employee is fired arbitrarily without some sort of grievance procedure, a hearing or an appeal, he cannot demonstrate that he was fired without good reason. Employees who have been fired have much more difficulty getting new jobs than those who have not been fired, even when that treatment was unjustified. Because arbitrarily fired employees are treated like those who deserved to lose their jobs, EAW puts such employees at an unfair disadvantage compared with other workers. The principle of EAW, then, does not preserve equal freedoms because it is to the advantage of the employer or manager and to the unfair disadvantage of the fired employee.

Worse, at-will practices violate the very right upon which EAW is allegedly based. Part of the appeal of EAW is that it protects the freedom of contract—the right to make employment agreements of one's choice. Abolishing EAW is coercive, according to its proponents, because this forces employers involuntarily to change their employment practices. But at-will employment practices too are or can be coercive. This is because when an employee is fired without sufficient reasons employers or managers place this person involuntarily in a personally harmful position unjustified by her behavior, a position that an employee would never choose. Thus the voluntary employment agreement according to which such practices are allowed is violated.

It is argued that EAW maximizes efficiency. But what is to prevent a manager from hiring a mentally retarded son-in-law or firing a good employee on personal grounds, actions that themselves damage efficiency? On a more serious level, if managers have prerogatives, these are based on a claim to the right to freedom—the freedom to conduct business as one pleases. But if this is a valid claim, then one must grant equal freedoms to everyone, including employees. Otherwise managers are saying that *they* have greater rights than other persons. This latter claim brings into question a crucial basis of democratic capitalism, namely that every person has *equal* rights, the most important of which is the equal right to freedom. The notion of equal rights does not necessarily imply that employees and managers have equal or identical prerogatives in business decision making or in managing a company. But what is implied is that the exercise of freedom requires a respect for the equal exercise of freedom by others, although the *kind* of exercises in each case may be different. EAW practices, then, are inconsistent practices because they do not preserve equal freedoms, they do not protect freedom of contract for both parties, and they do not guarantee efficiencies in the workplace. A number of thinkers contend that the principle should be abolished or disregarded in the law.

Interestingly, however, one can *defend* at least some employee rights from a consistent interpretation of the principle of EAW. This is because to be consistent the demands of EAW, principally the demand of management for the freedom to control business, require an equal respect for employee freedoms. In other words, if EAW is to be justified on the basis of the right to freedom, it can only be justified for that reason if it respects everyone's freedoms equally. Otherwise, managers' alleged freedoms are merely unwarranted licenses to do anything they please, even abridging employee rights, and thus have no moral or constitutional basis. Such equal respect for employee rights cannot always be interpreted as equal participation in management decisions. Extending

and respecting employee freedoms requires balancing equal but not necessarily identical liberties. The free exercise of management employment decisions, however, does seem to require that employees be given reasons, publicly stated and verfiable, for management decisions that affect employees, including hiring and firing. In this way voluntary choices in the job market are truly equal to management employment choices. Moreover, freedom of choice in management decision making requires allowing legitimate whistle blowing, conscientious objection, and even striking without employer retaliation when an employee is asked to perform illegal, immoral, and/or socially dangerous jobs, or when such practices occur in the workplace. I am suggesting that a proper interpretation of EAW is not inconsistent with granting some employee rights. It is the misinterpretation of EAW that has served as a basis for the exercise of management prerogatives at the expense of employee rights.

Employers and managers, of course, will not always be happy to grant these freedoms to employees, because such freedoms are often seen as giving employees too many rights. Others managers identify extending employee freedoms with participatory management programs that, they argue, would abridge management responsibilities. Neither of these consequences, however, necessarily follows from extending employee rights. On the other hand, continuing the present imbalance of freedoms in the workplace perpetuates injustices. Worse, from the perspective of management this is a highly risky policy in an age of employee enlightenment and a concern for employee rights. Many managers are sympathetic to arguments defending employee rights. However, they fear that instituting employee rights in the workplace entails government regulation of and intervention in the affairs of business, all of which is intrusive, expensive, and time-consuming. But there is no reason why businesses cannot voluntarily institute employment reforms, and in the climate of a surging interest in employee rights, such voluntary actions would help prevent government intervention and regulation.

Turning to a second moral justification for employee rights, balancing employee and employer freedoms in the workplace is also justified because of what I shall call the reciprocal nature of employment relationships. Employment relationships, which are by and large hierarchical role relationships, tend to be destructive of employee rights, yet this need not be so, and in fact quite the contrary is required. The reasons for this are the following. In the workplace both management and employees have role responsibilities that are a source of job accountability. A person holding a job is held accountable for a certain performance; it is sometimes not considered unjust to dismiss someone for failure to perform his or her job even if the employer pays poorly and sometimes even if the employer does not respect other employee rights. Employee job accountability in this context is usually described as first-party duties of the employee to a manager or to the organization for whom one works. However, this description is incomplete. There are, in addition, duties on the part of the manager or the institution to the employee who is held accountable. These obligations arise in part from the role responsibilities of the party to whom an employee is answerable and in part because of the nature of the relationship. These obligations, which are often neglected in an analysis of accountability, are reciprocal or correlative obligations implied by role responsibility to the employee in question. This notion of reciprocity, I shall argue, is crucial in employment relationships.

The notion of reciprocity in any social relationship is grounded on the basic fact that each party is a person or a group of persons. As the philosopher Carol Gould puts it,

Reciprocity may be defined as a social relation among agents in which each recognizes the other as an agent, that is, as equally free, and each acts with respect to the other on the basis of a shared understanding and a free agreement to the effect that the actions of each with respect to the other are equivalent.[1]

This does not mean that each party must treat the other in the same way in every respect, but rather that each treats the other with equal respect and as equal possessors of rights and benefits. Because they are social relationships between persons or between persons and institutions developed by persons, accountability relationships entail this notion of reciprocity.

Reciprocity in accountability relationships operates in part, as follows. If I am accountable for my actions to a certain group or institution because of my role in that group or institution, this accountability implicitly assumes a reciprocal accountability to me on the part of the institution to whom I am answerable. The obligations in each relationship are not necessarily contractual, but the strength of my role obligations depends at least in part on equally forceful, though obviously not identical, role obligations of the second party to me. And if no such reciprocal obligations exist, or if they are not respected, my accountability to that individual, group, or institution weakens.

What this brief analysis of role accountability suggests in the workplace is that when taking a job an employee has responsibilities connected with that job, responsibilities that are often only implicitly stated. At the same time, accountability does not consist merely of first-party duties of employees to employers or managers; it is also defined in reciprocal relationships with the party to whom one is accountable. The reason for this is that employee-employer relationships are both social and contractual arrangements. They are social because they are relationships entered into between persons or between persons and organizations created and run by persons. They are at least implicitly contractual ones voluntarily entered into and freely dissolvable by both parties. Therefore, if employees are accountable to managers or employers, managers or employers are also accountable for upholding their part of the agreement by being reciprocally accountable, albeit in different ways, to their employees.

The reciprocal nature of employee-employer relationships entails some important employee rights, in particular the rights to fair treatment and respect. What might constitute such fair treatment and respect? Obviously, fair pay or a living wage in exchange for work is an essential part of just treatment in the workplace. But if, in addition to working, employees are expected to respect and be fair to their employers, then employers have reciprocal obligations that go beyond merely offering fair pay. Employee respect demands from a manager a correlative respect for employee privacy, employee information, and for due process in the workplace, even for at-will employees.

Due process demands not that employees not be dismissed, but rather that any employer action meet impartial standards of reasonableness, the same sort of reasonableness expected of employees. Similarly, if an employee is to respect his or her employer and the decisions of that employer, the employer needs to honor the privacy of the employee as a human being, including protecting with confidentiality personnel information and respecting the privacy of employee activities outside the workplace. Respect for the employee also involves keeping the employee well-informed about his or her job, the quality of his or her work, and the stability of the company. This is a two-pronged responsibility. It entails not only the requirement that all employees are equally entitled to information, but the recognition that all employees actually in fact *have* such information. Employees have rights not merely to be informed but also to be communicated with in ways they understand.

The employee rights just enumerated—the rights to privacy, to employee information, and the right to due process—are moral rights that result from the nature of role accountability in the workplace. Like the right to freedom that is implied by a consistent interpretation of EAW, these rights are moral rather than legal rights, so employers need not respect them. But if the reciprocal requirements of employment accountability relationships are not met by employers or managers, those employers or managers undermine the basis for employee accountability in the workplace.

NOTE

1. Carol Gould, "Economic Justice, Self-Management and the Principle of Reciprocity," in *Economic Justice,* ed. Kenneth Kipnis and Diana T. Meyers (Totowa, N.J.: Rowman and Allanheld, 1985), pp. 213–214.

The Right to Work: Law and Ideology

Richard T. De George

Many people in the United States feel strongly about human rights. They champion human rights, criticize the violation of human rights abroad, and both support the U.S. Government's complaints about human rights violations in other countries and encourage a stronger policy on human rights than the Reagan administration has adopted. Yet listed in the Universal Declaration of Human Rights is the right to work—a right neither recognized nor respected in the United States, where unemployment is both accepted and expected. How are we to explain this apparent contradiction in attitudes, and what importance does it have for law?

I. THE HUMAN RIGHT TO WORK

The Universal Declaration of Human Rights, Article 23, states:

1. Everyone has the right to work, to free choice of employment, to just and favourable conditions of work and to protection against unemployment.
2. Everyone, without any discrimination, has the right to equal pay for equal work.
3. Everyone who works has the right to just and favourable remuneration ensuring for himself and his family an existence worthy of human dignity, and supplemented, if necessary, by other means of social protection.
4. Everyone has the right to form and to join trade unions for the protection of his interests.[1]

The right, as stated, requires both interpretation and defense. As every human right, it applies to all human beings simply by virtue of their being human. The right is appropriately implemented differently both in different societies and for people of different ages and circumstances. Infants as well as all other human beings have the right to work; but being physically and mentally incapable of working, they do not actively exercise the right. Adults in primitive societies exercise the right differently from those in advanced industrial societies. . . .

The derivation that hinges on the right of all human beings to respect provides the most solid basis for the right to work. To be a human being is a matter not only of being of a certain biological type but also of belonging to human society. A full, able-bodied, competent member of society has a role and plays a role in it. Each has a right to do so. No adult is "excess" or "expendable" and the recognition of this fact is part and parcel of what it means for people to have the right to respect. Work is the typical way by which human adults assert their independence and are able to assume their full share of responsibility in a community. Work involves the assumption of one's place in the community, whether it is work in the home, the fields, the factory, or the office. One's self respect as well as the respect of others is closely linked with what one does, how a person expresses himself through his actions, and the extent to which one assumes the full burden of and responsibility for one's life and one's part in the social whole. A person who is not allowed to work, is not allowed to take a rightful place in society as a contributing, mature, responsible adult. The right to work is in this way closely re-

From Richard T. De George, "The Right to Work: Law and Ideology," *Valparaiso University Law Review,* 19 (Fall 1984): 15–35. Reprinted by permission.

lated to the right to respect and derived from it for every society. It is for this reason that in many societies to deprive a person of a productive role in society is a form of ostracism, tantamount to punishment, and justifiable only for a serious social offense or crime.

The right to work can be interpreted as both a negative and as a positive right. As a negative right, no one, including the government, may legitimately prohibit someone who wishes to work from doing so, within the normal restrictions for negative rights, such as not infringing the similar, equal, or more important rights of others. As a positive right it requires at least that one's society provide one with the opportunity for full membership including the opportunity for participation in the productive activity of that society....

II. IDEOLOGY AND LABOUR LEGISLATION

How are we to understand the failure of the United States to recognize the right to work? It becomes intelligible when we understand the ideology behind U.S. labour legislation. The ideology has two main aspects. The first is linked historically with the conception of free enterprise that has grown up in the United States and can be understood in terms of both social conditions and ideas. The second is related to how labour legislation develops in the United States and is linked to the adversarial relation of labour and management and the power conflict that results from this. Ideology helps prevent recognition of the right to work; but the portion of the ideology in question is a carry-over from an earlier age, no longer reflects reality, and should properly be replaced.

The aspects of the free enterprise ideology that prevents recognition of the right to work in the United States has its roots in the nation's history. At the time the Constitution was adopted the country was young and growing. The Bill of Rights did not include the right to work, for that right had not emerged as a matter of concern, either in its negative or in its positive sense, except in the case of slavery. Slavery was a different and separate issue. The right to life, liberty, and the pursuit of happiness were paramount, although behind the scenes the right to property was strongly upheld. The main fear was of government intrusion, and the rights to be secured were primarily against the government. The right to life was not interpreted as the right to work. A number of factors make this intelligible and make it acceptable.

The availability of the frontier was both a safety valve and an opportunity for people who wished to strike out on their own. The population was relatively small, and the opportunities many. It was not true, as would later be the case, that the only way for most people to live was to sell their labour to entrepreneurs for wages. Together with the land and opportunities available went three other ideological components, the roots of which can be traced to the conditions of the times.

The first of these was the doctrine of self-reliance. It was a trait that was cherished, and had to be cherished if one were to survive in a new land, especially on its frontiers. Self-reliance, of course, did not preclude helping one's neighbour. Yet each person was expected to stand on his own feet, work, and fend for himself.

Joined to this was the doctrine of competitive individualism. The ideology of incipient capitalism, which developed in the eighteenth and nineteenth centuries, incorporated the notion of competition. In the competitive battle each person was ego-centered. The best succeeded. The experience of the immigrants to a new land, joined with the experience of the frontier, complemented the capitalistic emphasis on the individual and the concomitant notion of competition. Individualism was ideologically joined with competition to become "rugged individualism," according to which one competed and managed on one's own, whatever the outcome.

The third component comes from the

"Protestant work ethic." This complemented the other two components and fostered the developing capitalist ideology. Industriousness was a virtue. Each person was expected to do his fair share. The belief was that those who worked hard prospered. Prosperity was an indication of the virtue of industry. The lazy reaped their own reward in the way of poverty and difficulty. Each person, it was believed, had the opportunity to succeed, and success depended on individual initiative.

This ideology had its basis in reality. There was, of course, unemployment. But the general belief was that opportunities were available for the industrious, those willing to take a chance, seek their own fortune, and if necessary tame the wilderness. The right to work did not emerge as an issue. It became an issue only when the labour supply exceeded demand; and only with the development of large industry, which carried with it the growth of a working force dependent on others for jobs. But the frontier had disappeared; there are no longer abundant opportunities for the self-reliant; and although industriousness is still deserving of reward, the equation of poverty with laziness is clearly not justified. . . .

If ideology stands in the way of recognizing the right to work, the history of the development of labour legislation, resulting from this ideology, hinders its implementation. . . . Labour legislation in the United States has developed largely out of the relations between management and labor, especially in the collective bargaining process. As a consequence, unless an issue is in the interest of either labour (as represented by the unions) or management such that it arises in collective bargaining, it usually fails for lack of an advocate. If, moreover, an issue is opposed by either labour or management outside the collective bargaining situation and without the full support of the other side, it has formidable opposition to overcome and slight chance of either getting a full hearing or of finding its way into legislation. The issue of the right to work is such an issue. It is opposed to the interest of man-

agement, does not arise in collective bargaining, and is given less importance by unions than issues that more directly affect their members.

The right to work, even if understood as full employment, is clearly not in the interest of management. Unemployment guarantees the availability of people for at least some—usually lower level—jobs. It helps keep wages down and helps enforce labour discipline, since fear of loss of one's job is a real threat. Given a choice, it is in management's interest to have a pool of unemployed from which to choose. Management would, therefore, not be anxious to have legislation that would guarantee full employment or recognize a right to work. If, however, full employment included people in training programs and people who were employed by the government only as an employer of last resort, there would in fact be a pool of people from which to draw when the need presented itself in times of expansion; and the presence of training programs might also guarantee a larger pool of qualified people than would otherwise be the case. . . .

In general, organized labour supports full employment legislation. But . . . United States unions have not been as vocal as one would expect in support of the right to work specifically as a human right. In practice individual unions have often been more concerned with benefits for their members than with the rights of unemployed workers. Some have even fought for benefits resulting in the laying off of some of their own members.[2] Moreover, although full employment with no unemployed would put unions in a better bargaining position than otherwise, guaranteed full employment would also undercut to some extent the need for the protection of jobs by unions.

A good deal of labour legislation has to do with the relation of labour and management, the rights of organized labour, and the workers represented by the unions. Many of the unemployed are nonunion, unorganized, and unrepresented. Clearly the hardcore unemployed are of less concern to the unions than are union members, and in collective bargaining neither the unions nor management are concerned with the rights of the unemployed. While the history of labour legislation has been generated by collective bargaining and by the interests of the union on the one hand and management on the other, less than 30 percent of the American labour force belongs to a union, and the number of unionized workers has been diminishing for several years.

The history of labour legislation in the United States shows that negotiations between unions and management have not led to any serious consideration of the human right to work. Discussion of this right has not surfaced because in the context of collective bargaining this right is in the interest of neither organized labour nor management. While this fact makes the failure to notice this right understandable, it does not justify the absence of any legislation implementing the right of all to work and of those who desire it and are qualified. Consequently, the ideology underlying labour legislation should be brought out in the open and reevaluated. Similarly, the presuppositions of much of labour law jurisprudence that picture legislation as a means of arbitrating between contending factions—organized labour and management—should also be reexamined. This view is reinforced by the respective ideologies of both labour and management, who see themselves as opponents in an adversarial system. This opposition is fostered by collective bargaining. But since the right to work can sometimes be best implemented by collaboration rather than antagonism between management and labour, the ideology helps suppress implementation of the right to work.

The reexamination shows that the traditional ideology is partially defective. It is presupposed that organized labour and management are the only two contending parties. Since those who are outside of the organized labour force have no organized representative, their rights are systematically ignored and violated. The right to work is compatible with the best in the United States' tradition of free enterprise and of peaceful and productive labour relations. . . .

NOTES

1. I. Brownlie, *Basic Documents on Human Rights* 25 (2d ed. 1981).
2. The U.A.W., for instance, in 1982 insisted on higher wages for auto workers—twice the average for manufacturing workers—even as layoffs by auto manufacturers mounted.

Work and Self-Respect

Diana T. Meyers

MEANINGFUL WORK AND SELF-RESPECT

. . . Despite the remarkable diversity of their pursuits, people agree that self-respect helps to give life value. As John Rawls puts it, "Without it [self-respect], nothing may seem worth doing, or if some things have value for us, we lack the will to strive for them."[1] . . . A person who has self-respect is able to lead a more rewarding life than a person who is burdened by self-contempt. But how do

Reprinted by permission of the author.

people gain self-respect? Part of the explanation lies in our upbringings. Attentive, supportive parenting fosters self-respect. Yet since we have no control over this childhood experience, it is important to consider how as adults we can build upon this early care or, if necessary, overcome the lack of it. In this essay I shall argue that personal integrity is necessary for self-respect and that rights can promote self-respect by allowing for personal integrity. Applying these results to the work world, I shall urge that employers recognize certain work-related rights. For the right to employment, the right to equal opportunity, and the right to participate in job-related decisions encourage personal integrity. In so doing, these rights give persons the chance to make their work meaningful.

PERSONAL INTEGRITY AND SELF-RESPECT

... To have personal integrity, a person must have stable beliefs and feelings that he or she expresses in practice. Personal integrity contrasts both with fickleness and with hypocrisy. Lacking firm convictions and abiding affections, the chameleon-like person tailors his or her views to fit changing circumstances. And though the hypocrite has lasting convictions and emotional bonds, this individual belies them in his or her conduct. Because of their respective failings, neither the chameleon nor the hypocrite can have self-respect. . . .

... Saying that a self-respecting person's beliefs and feelings must be stable is not equivalent to saying that once formed they must never change. If Linda stops reciprocating Susan's friendship, Susan's warm feelings for Linda will gradually disappear, and rightfully so. Stability is not immutability. But if Susan never felt any ongoing affection for Linda, her friendship was not genuine in the first place, and stability could not be an issue.

A person whose beliefs and feelings shift constantly can still approve or disapprove of these fleeting attitudes. However, momentary self-satisfaction is not self-respect. Quite the contrary, self-respect is a steady self-acceptance that endures through occasional self-blame as well as occasional self-congratulation. This foundational valuation would not be possible if personal characteristics all varied wildly. . . .

SELF-RESPECT AND RIGHTS

Human rights are commonly characterized as rights that all persons have simply in virtue of being human. . . . What, then, is the contribution fundamental rights make to self-respect?

Rights give rights-holders prerogatives with regard to specified benefits. A person who has a property right in a piece of land may use the land as he or she pleases, and a person who has a right to free speech may voice whatever ideas he or she chooses. Although rights-holders are forbidden to violate others' rights while exercising their own, rights provide the persons who possess them with options. Even rights that do not explicitly confer liberties, such as the right to medical care or to decent housing, nonetheless afford persons a measure of discretion. Rights-holders may avail themselves of existing rights-implementing facilities; they may demand improved programs to deliver the objects of their rights; or they may decide not to take advantage of their rights at all.

The prerogatives rights afford are the key to the way rights support self-respect. We have seen that personal integrity is necessary for self-respect and that personal integrity requires that individuals form the lasting convictions and emotional ties on which they act. But without freedom persons are likely to adopt the views and attitudes the authorities prescribe. Moreover, persons with nonconformist ideas will be forced to hide them or to risk penalties in voicing them. Only when people are free to discover themselves and to express their distinctive personalities can personal integrity flourish. Because every right secures a measure of such freedom, each right serves to foster self-respect. . . .

RIGHTS AND MEANINGFUL WORK

In authorizing persons to exercise a range of prerogatives, rights invite rights-holders to act in accordance with their settled beliefs and feelings. Unlike duties, which impose requirements, rights issue permissions. Each of these permissions defines an arena in which individuals may set personal objectives and standards and seek to fulfill them. . . . Denial of persons' rights can crush self-respect. For this reason, it is important to consider how rights support self-respect in major areas of life. Since work consumes a large part of most people's lives, it is especially urgent to determine how rights figure in the workplace. . . .

. . . A variety of personally rewarding occupations are now considered to be work. Also, unionization and labor law have provided greater job security and better salaries for many employees, while public education has afforded many people a more egalitarian perspective on life. As a result, many people are not content to devote most of their time merely to earning a wage, and many workers have begun to demand more fulfilling work arrangements. Still, the problem of meaningful work has not been solved. Though meaningful work has become a widely discussed issue, many people remain unemployed or stuck in tedious jobs. I shall argue, however, that full implementation of three rights would make the work world much more conducive to self-respect.

The first difficulty a person encounters vis-à-vis work is finding employment. In our society, gainful employment is a badge of respectability, yet since World War II the official unemployment rate has never been lower than 2.8 percent and has ranged as high as 10.6 percent. Moreover, these government statistics do not include many individuals . . . because some have given up looking for jobs while others never wanted jobs. This distinction—the distinction between an unwilling, defeated drop-out from the job market and a willing, happy dependent on another person or the state—is crucial to the issue of self-respect. A willing dependent does not need employment to respect himself or herself, but enforced unemployment is a direct threat to an unwilling drop-out's personal integrity. This latter individual accepts conventional economic values, such as effort and self-sufficiency. But a surplus of job candidates combines with rigidity in the economic sphere to prevent him or her from acting on these beliefs. Structural unemployment compels its victims to jettison their values or sacrifice their self-respect.

The right to employment is primarily a right to a fairly remunerated position. However, in a society in which unemployment is chronic, . . . this right implies a right to be recognized as a member of the work force. As such, it provides rights-holders with two kinds of leverage. First, this right entitles persons to the training they need in order to find a niche in the job market. Second, it justifies a demand for innovation in job and income distribution patterns, such as part-time positions that pay decent wages and provide essential health and retirement benefits. Thus, the right to employment denies that a class of permanently jobless though able people is inevitable, and it authorizes rights-holders who have been excluded from the job market to stand up for their values.

The standard argument against the right to employment is that society cannot afford it. Training programs are costly; reliance on part-time labor is only feasible when it can be bought cheap; and the economy would falter because people would not strive to get ahead if jobs were guaranteed. The economic issues raised by this objection are too complex for adequate treatment here. Nevertheless, it should be said that it is an open question whether the proposed programs would be prohibitively expensive. In their support, it can be said that savings on welfare and increased productivity would help to offset these costs. Moreover, trimming the military budget could release funds to implement the right to employment. Finally, it must be stressed that the right to employment would not eliminate competition for jobs. Though everyone would be assured of some job, candidates would compete for the more interesting and better-paid positions. Accordingly, there is no reason to suppose that the right to employment would weaken the incentive to work.

At this point the problem of how to distribute the more desirable positions arises. The right to equal opportunity comes into play in education preparatory to work, in the search for employment, and in consideration for promotion and raises. At each of these stages, this right guarantees that no one's opportunities will be limited by discrimination on grounds of race, creed, sex, or other irrelevant characteristics. In other words, this right requires that the best qualified applicant be chosen for each available opening.

An obvious way in which the right to equal opportunity bears on self-respect is that this right shields persons from arbitrary and humiliating rejections. Victims of discrimination may perceive that they are not being judged fairly, yet it is difficult to avoid succumbing to self-doubt when one's endeavors meet with repeated failure. The right to equal opportunity removes this source of self-contempt. Moreover, in assuring all candidates that their credentials will be reviewed impartially and taken seriously, this right implicitly affirms that self-respect properly hinges on a person's effort and attainment, not on the accidents of a person's birth. In effect, this right calls on individuals to assess their abilities, envisage a suitable career, and strive to bring it about. The right to equal opportunity releases people from tradition-bound assumptions about the social niches befitting them and offers them the chance to work at jobs of their own choosing, if not their own design. Thus, a notable function of the right to equal opportunity is to guarantee the possibility of self-expression in the initial choice of an occupation.

It might be objected that self-respecting persons need not regard their jobs as reflections of their selves. Persons can gain self-respect from performing well a socially designated task. Perhaps insisting that one's work match one's personality is evidence of self-indulgence, not self-respect, for no viable economy can accommodate such adamant individualism. Whatever the merits of equal opportunity, the objection concludes, workers must accede to the time-honored compromises and strictures of the work world.

Of course, no right can promise that everyone's dreams will come true. Mature adults modulate their aspirations and expectations in light of a realistic appraisal of what is possible. Graceless weaklings do not yearn to be ballerinas; they turn to other enterprises. Nevertheless, if prejudice forces the members of one social group to discard otherwise sensible career plans, while many individuals who do not belong to groups that are discriminated against can pursue the careers they prefer, personal integrity in employment goals becomes a privilege of the advantaged class. Notoriously, there was never any good reason to bar the great black pitcher Satchel Paige from major league baseball. The right to equal opportunity prevents maldistribution of a central component of self-respect, namely, personal integrity in career direction.

Other rights protect personal integrity on the job. Prominent among them is the right to participate in job-related decisions. This is a right that is sometimes dismissed out of hand because it seems to conflict with the rights of business owners to delegate authority within their firms as they think best. However, there are various ways to implement this right, and some of them do not usurp property owners' legitimate prerogatives. Moreover, all these ways support personal integrity in the workplace.

First, it is important to recognize that

business owners are not entitled to wield absolute authority over workers during the workday. When laws or union contracts provide for such employee rights as the right to safe work conditions, rest periods, and job security, owners' rights are thereby eroded. Yet, since the compelling needs of employees plainly justify many of these arrangements, property rights must yield to them. Likewise, the right to participate in job-related decisions can be instituted in a manner that restricts but does not extinguish owners' rights. For example, the right to participate in job-related decisions could be interpreted as requiring procedures for consulting with all concerned employees and a reorganization of work activities. Consultation involves soliciting and paying attention to employees' views before making decisions. Reorganization may involve breaking up assembly lines, eliminating regimented, mass-production formats in offices, and replacing them with work groups each responsible for handling a particular project. Experience has shown that such reforms can improve efficiency.[2] Also, it is clear that these programs do not preempt owners' rights.

To actually democratize the workplace would be to grant employees the power to control, through their ballots, a firm's future course. Consultation procedures and reorganized work schedules do not redistribute economic power in so far-reaching a fashion and therefore are not tantamount to economic democracy. Nevertheless, a right ex-

acting these reforms could have a marked impact on employees' self-respect since both afford opportunities for constructive self-expression at the workplace.[3] In discussions with supervisors and in cooperation with a self-contained work unit, individuals would be encouraged to reflect on their occupations and to suggest changes. Workers' proposals must pass tests of practicality, but nothing would prevent workers from putting forth sound suggestions based on their own values and feelings. Insofar as allowance for employees' personal integrity can be incorporated into the workplace, self-respect can be promoted in this context. Clearly, the right to participate in job-related decisions serves this purpose.

... In authorizing employees to bring their convictions and feelings to bear on their occupations, these rights respect the unity and independence of persons. In recognizing the autonomy of employees, these rights make work a source of self-respect and, as such, a site of personal meaning.

NOTES

1. John Rawls, *A Theory of Justice* (Cambridge, Mass: Harvard University Press, 1971), p. 440.
2. *New York Times,* January 15, 1984, pp. 1, 20.
3. For a helpful related treatment of self-respect, see Thomas E. Hill, Jr., "Servility and Self-respect" in *Today's Moral Problems,* ed. Richard A. Wasserstrom (New York: Macmillan, 1979), pp. 133–147.

Privacy, Polygraphs and Work

George G. Brenkert

The rights of prospective employees have been the subject of considerable dispute, both past and present. In recent years, this dispute has focused on the use of polygraphs to verify the claims which prospective employees make on employment application forms. With employee theft supposedly amounting to approximately ten billion dollars a year, with numerous businesses suffering sizeable losses and even being forced into bankruptcy by employee theft, significant and increasing numbers of employers have turned to the use of polygraphs.[1] Their right to protect their property is in danger, they insist, and the use of the polygraph to detect and weed out the untrustworthy prospective employee is a painless, quick, economical, and legitimate way to defend this right. Critics, however, have questioned both the reliability and validity of polygraphs, as well as objected to the use of polygraphs as demeaning, affronts to human dignity, violations of self-incrimination prohibitions, expressions of employers' mistrust, and violations of privacy.[2] Though there has been a great deal of discussion of the reliability and validity of polygraphs, there has been precious little discussion of the central moral issues at stake. Usually terms such as "dignity," "privacy," and "property rights" are simply bandied about with the hope that some favorable response will be evoked. The present paper seeks to redress this situation by discussing one important aspect of the above dispute—the supposed violation of personal privacy. Indeed, the violation of "a right to privacy" often appears to be the central moral objection to the use of polygraphs. However, the nature and basis of this claim have not yet been clearly established.[3] If they could be, there would be a serious reason to oppose the use of polygraphs on prospective employees.

I

There are three questions which must be faced in the determination of this issue. First, is the nature of the information which polygraphing seeks to verify, information which can be said to violate, or involve the violation of, a person's privacy? Second, does the use of the polygraph itself as the means to corroborate the responses of the job applicant violate the applicant's privacy? Third, even if—for either of the two preceding reasons—the polygraph does violate a person's privacy, might this violation still be justified by the appeal to more weighty reasons, e.g., the defense of property rights? . . .

Upon what basis . . . do we maintain that certain information is rightfully private, that the knowledge of it by others constitutes a violation of one's right to privacy? There are two points to make here. First, there is no piece of information about a person which is by itself rightfully private. Information about one's financial concerns may be rightfully private vis-à-vis a stranger or a neighbor, but not vis-à-vis one's banker. The nature of one's sex life may be rightfully private with regard to most people, including future employers, but not to one's psychiatrist, sex therapist, or mate. Accordingly, the

From George G. Brenkert, "Privacy, Polygraphs and Work," *Business & Professional Ethics Journal*, 1 (Fall 1981): 19–34. Copyright © by George G. Brenkert. Reprinted by permission.

right to privacy involves a three place relation. To say that something is rightfully private is to say that A may withhold from or not share something, X, with Z. Thus to know whether some information, X, about a person or institution, A, is, or ought to be, treated as rightfully private, we must ask about the relationship in which A stands to Z, another person or institution. Because the threefold nature of this relation is not recognized, the view which we have argued is implausible, viz., that "none of us has a right over any fact to the effect that that fact shall not be known by others,"[4] is confused with the view which is plausible, viz., that there is no piece of information about people or institutions which is in itself private. It does not follow from this latter truth that the knowing of a piece of information by some particular person or institution may not be a violation of one's right to privacy—it may or may not be depending upon who or what knows it.

Second, then, to speak of the right to privacy is to speak of the right which individuals, groups, or institutions have that access to and information about themselves is limited in certain ways by the relationships in which they exist to others. In general, the information and access to which a person or institution is entitled with regard to another person and/or institution is that information and access which will enable the former to fulfill, perform, or execute the role the person or institution plays in the particular relationship. All other access and information about the latter is beyond the pale. Thus one cannot be a friend of another unless one knows more about another and has a special access to that person. Similarly, one cannot be a person's lawyer, physician, or barber unless one is entitled to other kinds of knowledge and access. . . .

II

In order to determine what information might be legitimately private to an individual who seeks employment we must consider the nature of the employer/(prospective) employee relationship. The nature of this relationship depends upon the customs, conventions and rules of the society. These, of course, are in flux at any time—and particularly so in the present case. They may also need revision. Further, the nature of this relationship will depend upon its particular instances—e.g., that of the employer of five workers or of five thousand workers, the kind of work involved, etc. In essence, however, we have a complex relationship in which an employer theoretically contracts with a person(s) to perform certain services from which the employer expects to derive a certain gain for himself. In the course of the employee's performance of these services, the employer entrusts him with certain goods, money, etc.; in return for such services he delivers to the employee a certain remuneration and (perhaps) benefits. The goals of the employer and the employee are not at all, on this account, necessarily the same. The employee expects his remuneration (and benefits) even if the services, though adequately performed, do not result in the end the employer expected. Analogously, the employer expects to derive a certain gain for the services the employee has performed even if the employee is not (fully) satisfied with his work or remuneration. On the other hand, if the employer is significantly unable to achieve the ends sought through the contract with the employee, the latter may not receive his full remuneration (should the employer go bankrupt) and may even lose his job. There is, in short, a complicated mixture of trust and antagonism, connectedness and disparity of ends in the relation between employer and employee.

Given this (brief) characterization of the relationship between employer and employee, the information to which the employer qua employer is entitled about the (prospective) employee is that information which regards his possible acceptable performance of the services for which he might be hired. Without such information the employer could not fulfill the role which present society sanctions. There are two aspects of the information to which the employer is entitled given the employer/employee relationship. On the one hand, this information will relate to and vary in accordance with the services for which the person is to be hired. But in any case, it will be limited by those services and what they require. In short, one aspect of the information to which the employer is entitled is "job relevant" information. Admittedly the criterion of job relevancy is rather vague. Certainly there are few aspects of a person which might not affect his job performance—aspects including his sex life, etc. How then does the "job relevancy" criterion limit the questions asked or the information sought? It does so by limiting the information sought to that which is directly connected with the job description. If a typist is sought, it is job relevant to know whether or not a person can type—typing tests are legitimate. If a store manager is sought, it is relevant to know about his abilities to manage employees, stock, etc. That is, the description of the job is what determines the relevancy of the information to be sought. It is what gives the employer a right to know certain things about the person seeking employment. Accordingly, if a piece of information is not "job relevant" then the employer is not entitled qua employer to know it. Consequently, since sexual practices, political beliefs, associational activities, etc. are not part of the description of most jobs, that is, since they do not directly affect one's job performance, they are not legitimate information for an employer to know in the determination of the hiring of a job applicant.[5]

However, there is a second aspect to this matter. A person must be able not simply to perform a certain activity, or provide a service, but he must also be able to do it in an acceptable manner—i.e., in a manner which is approximately as efficient as others, in an honest manner, and in a manner compatible with others who seek to provide the services for which they were hired. Thus, not simply one's abilities to do a certain job are rele-

vant, but also aspects of one's social and moral character are pertinent. A number of qualifications are needed for the purport of this claim to be clear. First, that a person must be able to work in an acceptable manner is not intended to legitimize the consideration of the prejudices of other employees. It is not legitimate to give weight in moral deliberations to the immoral and/or morally irrelevant beliefs which people hold concerning the characteristics of others. That one's present employees can work at a certain (perhaps exceptional) rate is a legitimate consideration in hiring other workers. That one's present employees have prejudices against certain religions, sexes, races, political views, etc. is not a morally legitimate consideration. Second, it is not, or should not be, the motives, beliefs, or attitudes underlying the job relevant character traits, e.g., honest, efficient, which are pertinent, but rather the fact that a person does or does not perform according to these desirable character traits. This is not to say, it should be noted, that a person's beliefs and attitudes about the job itself, e.g., how it is best to be done, what one knows or believes about the job, etc., are irrelevant. Rather it is those beliefs, attitudes and motives underlying one's desired character traits which are not relevant. The contract of the employer with the employee is for the latter to perform acceptably certain services—it is not for the employee to have certain underlying beliefs, motives, or attitudes. If I want to buy something from someone, this commercial relation does not entitle me to probe the attitudes, motives, and beliefs of the person beyond his own statements, record of past actions, and the observations of others. Even the used car salesman would correctly object that his right to privacy was being violated if he was required to submit to Rorschach tests, an attitude survey test, truth serums, and/or the polygraph in order to determine his real beliefs about selling cars. Accordingly, why the person acts the way in which he acts ought not to be the concern of the employer. Whether a person is a good working colleague simply because he is congenial, because his ego needs the approval of others, or because he has an oppressive superego is, in this instance, morally irrelevant. What is relevant is whether this person has, by his past actions, given some indication that he may work in a manner compatible with others.

Consequently, a great deal of the information which has been sought in preemployment screening through the use of polygraph tests has violated the privacy of individuals. Instances in which the sex lives, for example, of applicants have been probed are not difficult to find. However, privacy violations have occurred not simply in such generally atypical instances but also in standard situations. To illustrate the range of questions asked prospective employees and the violations of privacy which have occurred we need merely consider a list of some questions which one of the more prominent polygraph firms includes in its current tests:

Have you ever taken any of the following without the advice of a doctor? If Yes, please check: Barbiturates, Speed, LSD, Tranquilizers, Amphetamines, Marijuana, Others.
In the past five years about how many times, if any, have you bet on horse races at the race track?
Do you think that policemen are honest?
Did you ever think about committing a robbery?
Have you been refused credit or a loan in the past five years?
Have you ever consulted a doctor about a mental condition?
Do you think that it is okay to get around the law if you don't actually break it?
Do you enjoy stories of successful crimes and swindles?[6]

Such questions, it follows from the above argument, are for any standard employment violations of one's right to privacy. An employer might ask if a person regularly takes certain narcotic drugs, if he is considering him for a job which requires handling narcotics. An employer might ask if a person

has been convicted of a larceny, etc. But whether the person enjoys stories about successful larcenists, whether a person has ever taken any prescription drugs without the advice of a doctor, or whether a person bets on the horses should be considered violations of one's rightful privacy.

The upshot of the argument in the first two sections is, then, that some information can be considered rightfully private to an individual. Such information is rightfully private or not depending on the relationship in which a person stands to another person or institution. In the case of the employer/employee relationship, I have argued that that information is rightfully private which does not relate to the acceptable performance of the activities as characterized in the job description. This excludes a good many questions which are presently asked in polygraph tests, but does not, by any means, exclude all such questions. There still remain many questions which an employer might conceivably wish to have verified by the use of the polygraph. Accordingly, I turn in the next section to the question whether the verification of the answers to legitimate questions by the use of the polygraph may be considered a violation of a person's right to privacy. If it is, then the violation obviously does not stem from the questions themselves but from the procedure, the polygraph test, whereby the answers to those questions are verified.

III

A first reason to believe that use of the polygraph occasions a violation of one's right to privacy is that, even though the questions to be answered are job relevant, some of them will occasion positive, lying reactions which are not necessarily related to any past misdeeds. Rather, the lying reaction indicated by the polygraph may be triggered because of unconscious conflicts, fears and hostilities a person has. It may be occasioned by conscious anxieties over other past activities and observations. Thus, the lying reaction indicated by the polygraph need not positively identify actual lying or the commission of illegal activities. The point, however, is not to question the validity of the polygraph. Rather, the point is that the validity of the polygraph can only be maintained by seeking to clarify whether or not such reactions really indicate lying and the commission of past misdeeds. But this can be done only by the polygraphist further probing into the person's background and inner thoughts. However, inasmuch as the questions can no longer be restrained in this situation by job relevancy considerations, but must explore other areas to which an employer is not necessarily entitled knowledge, to do this will violate a person's right to privacy.

It has been suggested by some polygraphists that if a person has "Something Else" on his mind other than the direct answer to the question asked, a "something else" which might lead the polygraph to indicate a deceptive answer, the person might, if he so feels inclined,

> tell the examiner about this "outside troubling matter" . . . but as a special precaution obtain the examiner's promise that the disclosure of this information is secret and . . . request that the matter be held in strict confidence. The examiner will comply with your wishes. The examiner does not wish to enter into your personal problems since they tend to complicate the polygraph examination.[7]

What this suggests, however, is that a person go ahead, under the threat of the polygraph indicating that one is lying, and tell the polygraphist matters that are rightfully private. This is supposedly acceptable since one "requests" that it be held in strict confidence. But it surely does not follow that a violation of one's right to privacy does not occur simply because the recipient promises not to pass the information on. If, under some threat, I tell another person something which he has no right to know about me, but I then get his promise that he will treat the information confidentially and that it will

not be misused in any way, my right to privacy has still been violated.[8] Accordingly, whether the polygraphist attempts to prevent job applicants from producing misleading deceptive reactions by allowing them to reveal what else is on their minds or probes deceptive reactions once they have occurred to ascertain whether they might not be produced by job irrelevant considerations, he violates the right to privacy of the job applicant.

A second reason why the polygraph must be said to violate a job applicant's right to privacy relates to the monitoring of a person's physiological responses to the questions posed to him. By measuring these responses, the polygraph can supposedly reveal one's mental processes. Now even though the questions posed are legitimate questions, surely a violation of one's right to privacy occurs. Just because I have something which you are entitled to see or know, it does not follow that you can use any means to fulfill that entitlement and not violate my privacy. Consider the instance of two good friends, one of whom has had some dental work done which puts him in a situation such that he can tune in the thoughts and feelings of his friend. Certain facts about, and emotional responses of, his friend—aspects which his friend (we will assume) would usually want to share with him—simply now stream into his head. Even though the friendship relation generally entitles its members to know personal information about the other person, the friend with the dental work is not entitled to such information in this direct and immediate way. This manner of gaining this information simply eliminates any private reserves of the person; it wholly opens his consciousness to the consciousness of another. Surely this would be a violation of his friend's right to privacy, and his friend would rightfully ask that such dental work be modified. Even friends do not have a right to learn in this manner of each other's inner thoughts and feelings.

Such fancy dental work may, correctly, be

said to be rather different from polygraphs. Still the point is that though one is entitled to some information about another, one is not entitled to use any means to get it. But why should the monitoring by an employer or his agent of one's physiological responses to legitimate questions be an invasion of privacy—especially if one has agreed to take the test? There are several reasons.

First, the claim that one freely agrees or consents to take the test is surely, in many cases, disingenuous.[9] Certainly a job applicant who takes the polygraph test is not physically forced or coerced into taking the exam. However, it is quite apparent that if he did not take the test and cooperate during the test, his application for employment would either not be considered at all or would be considered to have a significant negative aspect to it. This is surely but a more subtle form of coercion. And if this be the case, then one cannot say that the person has willingly allowed his reactions to the questions to be monitored. He has consented to do so, but he has consented under coercion. Had he a truly free choice, he would not have done so. . . .

Second, it should be noted that even if a person voluntarily agreed to the polygraph test, it need not follow that there is not a violation of his privacy. It was argued in Section I that there are certain aspects of oneself which are obligatorily private, that is, which one ought to keep private. Accordingly, it may be wrong for one voluntarily to reveal various aspects of oneself to others, even though in so doing one would be responding to legitimate demands. For example, consider a person being interviewed by a health officer who is legitimately seeking information from the person about venereal diseases. Suppose that the person does not simply admit to having such a disease but also—instead of providing a corroborative statement from a physician—reveals the diseased organs. Further, suppose that the health officer is not shocked or offended in any way. The person has been asked legitimate questions, he has acted voluntarily, but

still he has violated his own privacy. This is not the kind of access to oneself one ought to afford a bureaucrat. Now it may well be that, analogously, one ought not to allow employers access to one's physiological reactions to legitimate questions, for the reason that such access also violates one's obligatory privacy. To act in this way sets a bad precedent, it signifies that those with power and authority may disregard the privacy of an individual in order to achieve aims of their own. Thus, even if a job applicant readily agreed to reveal certain aspects of himself in a polygraph test, it would not follow without more argument that he was not violating his own privacy.

Finally, if we value privacy not simply as a barrier to the intrusion of others but also as the way by which we define ourselves as separate, autonomous persons, individuals with an integrity which lies at least in part in the ability to make decisions, to give or withhold information and access, then the polygraph strikes at this fundamental value.[10] The polygraph operates by turning part of us over which we have little or no control against the rest of us. If a person were an accomplished yogi, the polygraph would supposedly be useless—since that person's physiological reactions would be fully under his control. The polygraph works because most of us do not have that control. Thus, the polygraph is used to probe people's reactions which they would otherwise protect, not expose to others. It uses part of us to reveal the rest of us. It takes the "shadows" consciousness throws off within us and reproduces them for other people. As such, the use of the polygraph undercuts the decision-making aspect of a person. It circumvents the person. The person says such and such, but his uncontrolled reactions may say something different. He does not know—even when honest—what his reactions might say. Thus it undercuts and demeans that way by which we define ourselves as autonomous persons—in short, it violates our privacy. Suppose one said something to another—but his Siamese and undetached twin, who was given to absolute truth and who correctly knew every thought, past action, and feeling of the person said: "No, he does not really believe that." I think the person would rightfully complain that his twin had better remain silent. Just so, I have a right to complain when my own feelings are turned on me. This subtle form of self-incrimination is a form of invading one's privacy. An employer is entitled to know certain facts about one's background, but this relationship does not entitle him—or his agents—to probe one's emotional responses, feelings, and thoughts.

Thus, it follows that even if the only questions asked in a polygraph test are legitimate ones, the use of the polygraph for the screening of job applicants still violates one's privacy. In this case, the violation of privacy stems from the procedure itself, and not the questions. Accordingly, one can see the lameness of the defense of polygraphing which maintains that if a person has nothing to hide, he should not object to the polygraph tests. Such a defense is mistaken at least on two counts. First, just because someone believes something to be private does not mean that he believes that what is private is wrong, something to be ashamed about or to be hidden. Second, the polygraph test has been shown to violate a person's privacy, whether one person has really something to hide or not—whether he is dishonest or not. Consequently, if the question is simply whether polygraphing of prospective employees violates their privacy the answer must be affirmative. . . .

NOTES

1. Cf. Harlow Unger, "Lie Detectors: Business Needs Them to Avoid Costly Employee Rip-Offs," *Canadian Business*, Vol. 51 (April, 1978), p. 30. Other estimates may be found in "Out-law Lie-Detector Tests?", *U.S. News & World Report*, Vol. 84, No. 4, (January 1978), p. 45, and Victor Lipman, "New Hiring Tool: Truth Tests," *Parade* (October 7, 1979), p. 19.
2. Both the AFL-CIO and the ACLU have raised these objections to the use of the polygraph for screening job applicants; cf. *AFL-CIO Executive Council Statements and Reports: 1956–1975* (Westport, Conn.: Greenwood Press, 1977), p. 1422. See also ACLU Policy #248.
3. See, for example, Alan F. Westin, *Privacy and Freedom* (New York: Atheneum, 1967), p. 238.
4. Judith Jarvis Thomson, "The Right to Privacy," *Philosophy and Public Affairs*, Vol. IV (Summer, 1975), p. 307.
5. This would have to be qualified for security jobs and the like.
6. John E. Reid and Associates, *Reid Report* (Chicago: By the author, 1978), passim.
7. John E. Reid and Associates, *The Polygraph Examination* (Chicago: By the author, n.d.), p. 7.
8. It should be further pointed out that the polygraphist/job-applicant relation is not legally or morally a privileged relation. What one tells one's physician one can expect to be treated confidentially. There is no similar expectation that one may entertain in the present case. At most one may hope that as another human being he will keep his promise. On the other hand, the polygraphist is an agent of the employer and responsible to him. There is and can be then no guarantee that the promise of the polygraphist will be kept.
9. The reasons why people do not submit to the polygraph are many and various. Some might have something to hide; others may be scared of the questions, supposing that some of them will not be legitimate; some may feel that they are being treated like criminals; others may fear the jaundiced response of the employer to the applicant's honest answers to legitimate questions; finally some may even object to the polygraph on moral grounds, e.g., it violates one's right to privacy.
10. Cf. Jeffrey H. Reiman, "Privacy, Intimacy, and Personhood," *Philosophy and Public Affairs*, Vol. VI (Fall, 1976).

Is Motivation Management Manipulative?

Raymond S. Pfeiffer

One of the great challenges confronting managers in contemporary workplaces is to find and effect ways of increasing the productive efficiency of their subordinates. Most industrial and management psychologists assume that this goal is laudable and clearly to the advantage of the workers. They write in terms of increasing workers' *satisfaction* in what they do; of *maximizing task involvement,* and *responsibility,* of improving worker *achievement,* recognition of that achievement, *participation, growth,* and *advancement.* In the language of the human potential movement, they affirm that good management is good for people.

Others have, however, referred to the various psychological approaches to management as if there were something sinister about them. Management consultant Peter Drucker states, "Most of the recent writers on industrial psychology . . . use terms like 'self-fulfillment,' 'creativity' and 'the whole person.' But what they mean is control through psychological manipulation." Again, he says, "Under this new psychological approach, persuasion replaces command. . . . Psychological manipulation replaces the carrot of financial rewards."[1] Critic of capitalism Harry Braverman has stated, "Industrial psychology and sociology . . . from their confident beginnings as 'sciences' were devoted to discovering the springs of human behavior the better to manipulate them in the interests of management." He refers to personnel administration as representing "a manipulation to habituate the worker" to the job as it has been set up in advance.[2] Such writers view the psychological approach to management as a less than forthright means of promoting productive efficiency.

It is, I take it, of significance that both Drucker and Braverman describe the effects of industrial psychology by use of the word "manipulation." My task is to explicate their claims. There is no attempt here to determine whether or not any actual management practices of individual managers are in fact manipulative. The present concern is with first the significance that is attached to the claim that a practice is manipulative; second, the extent to which recent industrial psychologists prescribe manipulative management practices; and third, the degree to which such a manipulative element is objectionable.

The concept of manipulation has been invoked with increasing frequency since World War II among writers on psychology, social criticism, sociology, and social and political philosophy.[3] Manipulation, such writers broadly agree, involves a subtle influence on a person's actions, beliefs, desires, feelings, or values, and this in turn inhibits rational deliberation. The manipulation may involve the falsification or omission of information, or it may involve a play on one's nonrational impulses. But it is widely characterized by an element of subtle and often deceptive persuasiveness.

This is an earlier version of the paper "Is Motivation Management Manipulative?" published in Gertrude Ezorsky, ed., *Moral Rights in the Workplace*. Reprinted by permission of the State University of New York Press and the author.

We can clarify and summarize the content of the various views on the subject in the form of a set of conditions necessary and sufficient for manipulation to occur.

1. There is an action of commission or omission performed by a party, A.
2. The action is intended by A to influence in a certain way the feelings, thoughts, desires, values, inclinations or actions of another party, B.
3. The action consists of at least one of the following:
   a) providing B with false information intended to influence B's feelings, thoughts, desires, values, inclinations, or actions, where A has access to the truth; or
   b) withholding from B information that would influence B's feelings, thoughts, desires, values, inclinations, or actions, where A has access to the truth; or
   c) inhibiting B's informed, deliberate use of his or her rational or deliberative capacities.
4. The action is subtle and its effects irresistible.[4]

The first condition covers acts of omission because one can be responsible for manipulating another or be an accomplice in the manipulation by purposefully refraining from action. One can, as the second condition indicates, influence a person merely by withholding information. The third condition depends on a broad construal of information including empirical data, impressions, value judgments, opinions, and even hints that, if B knew of them, could serve as evidence as to whether B ought to have the feelings, thoughts, desires, values, and inclinations or perform the actions that he or she subsequently does. Subtle cues, innuendo, tone of voice, or even body language could count as potentially relevant evidence under the appropriate circumstances. Condition 3c allows for manipulation to be a kind of influence based on powerful emotional appeals instead of distortion or withholding of evidence. This would permit some advertising to count as manipulative, as well as certain appeals by political leaders. The sub-tlety required by the fourth condition is relevant to B's perspective, not necessarily that of anyone else. The means of persuasion in question may be blatant to some observers, but subtle in its actual effect on B. It may even be obvious to B, but have an effect of which he or she is quite unaware. It may be subtle to the extent that B may not be fully aware of having missed a chance to proceed deliberately and rationally. We can, following Stanley Benn, say that the action is irresistible if a person in B's position "could not reasonably be expected to resist it."[5]

To manipulate someone is morally objectionable on two main grounds. First, it consists of a violation of the person's capacity to live autonomously, and second, it may, depending on the circumstances, produce results inimical to the interests of that party. The four criteria do not entail that all acts of manipulation are necessarily morally unjustifiable. Such final verdicts depend on an assessment of the particulars of each individual case. But cases of manipulation are usually identified for evaluative purposes and most frequently singled out as objects of blame.

The question at issue is whether the new psychology of worker management through the promotion of job motivation and satisfaction is, in principle, as laudable as it appears, or whether it contains a deletory manipulative element. I shall argue that it does contain such an element and that the charges of Drucker and Braverman are not merely hollow rhetoric.

The intent of management, according to the proponents of motivation management, should be to promote employee motivation on the job. Motivated behavior has been described as that which (1) contains a deep commitment to attaining an objective, (2) displays a high degree of effort, and (3) is to a significant extent free of inner psychological conflict.[6] In a work environment, the objective referred to in (1) would presumably be completion of the assigned tasks in an efficient manner. And management can only afford to encourage worker stimulation, satisfaction, and fulfillment to the extent that it promotes worker efficiency. Both the worker's effort and the freedom from conflict he or she feels are necessarily at the service of work efficiency. This reveals that the first two conditions of an act's being manipulatory are fulfilled. According to motivation management, the manager acts in order to influence the performance of the employee.

The third condition of manipulatory action is also fulfilled by motivation management. Such management involves the use of strategies designed to foster certain attitudes in the employee. The attitudes are promoted by the manager's projecting a positive approach toward the work. Moreover, the manager can hardly afford to express doubts or reservations about the work to the worker. Such expression would be viewed as indecisive, uninspiring, and indicative of poor leadership.

It is not a part of the doctrine of motivation management that the manager assists the workers to arrive at a motivated state as the result of a wholly free, fully informed, open, rational, analytic, or critical approach to the issues. Proponents of motivation management have shown no interest in promoting open discussion between manager and subordinate on such important issues as the following: whether or not the employee is in the job best suited to his or her abilities; the degree of commitment the manager has to helping the subordinate in his or her career; the degree to which the manager communicates honestly and openly to the subordinate; the extent to which the job and the organization make a positive contribution to the well-being of the community; the advantages and disadvantages of collective bargaining; the pros and cons of the subordinate's participating to a greater extent in decision making. A manager's deliberate and calculated avoidance of or pat responses to such issues represents an effort to limit the worker's informed use of his or her rational, deliberative decision-making capacities.

The fourth condition is that an action, to

be manipulatory, must achieve its effects in a way that is subtle from the perspective of the person being manipulated and also irresistible to that person. From the outset of a new job, even the dullest employee hopes, however unrealistically, to find the work interesting, stimulating, challenging, and rewarding. Thus, the worker wants to be motivated in his or her work, and the motivation manager patently plays right to this desire. The effectiveness of motivation management is thus based in part on its irresistibility.

The subtlety of motivation management is part and parcel with its irresistibility. It is subtle in the sense that the manager seeks to help and in many ways promote what appear to be the interests of the subordinate worker. The manager strives to gain the confidence of the worker to appear not as a task master, as one holding the carrot or stick, but instead as an ally of the worker, one who can assist the worker to meet his or her needs. Ideally, both manager and employee come to view productivity as merely a function of other factors, as if it will naturally increase as other needs are met. Thus, the manager's primary job, which is to improve productivity, is masked by his or her role as assistant to the employee, and the workplace loses an air of conflict.

The subtlety of motivation management is due in large part to the exploitation by the manager of the worker's very deep and pressing needs. The worker is under great pressure to accept the relationship offered by the manager. The failure to do so may well mark the worker as uncooperative, whereas the acceptance of this relationship is viewed as a healthy attitude characteristic of "teamwork."

We can summarize the charge that motivation management is manipulative as the thesis that the motivation manager seeks to create in the workers through a subtle, irresistible strategy a certain set of attitudes and ways of thinking about the workplace; and that this strategy is designed to reduce the likelihood of workers' discussing or thinking through certain issues in a rational, informed, independent manner. Now even if true, the charge can be meaningful or significant only if there really is something wrong with this manipulation. I shall examine the question of its objectionability by first noting two main ways in which one might object to cases of manipulation.

One might argue first that manipulation is objectionable when and to the extent that it interferes with the interests of the parties being manipulated. However, such interference might be justified by other considerations, such as the well-being of the larger society. Although employees under motivation management are prevented from acting in fully autonomous ways, this sacrifice might be outweighed by the greater social good of increased happiness and productivity. But even a forcefully established case to this effect might not justify manipulatory practices, for another objection could be brought to the fore.

The second objection is that manipulation is intrinsically objectionable to the extent that it violates a basic human right. This is the right to act in a fully self-determining, rational, or autonomous manner unless one forfeits this right by a well-informed, rationally made decision to do so. Commitment to the right to autonomous action together with acceptance of the argument that motivation management is manipulative are the elements of a strong ethical objection to motivation management.

One might defend motivation management in three main ways at this point. One might argue first that the sacrifice of worker autonomy by motivation management is warranted by the advantageous consequences for both the worker and society. The increase in productivity raises wages, lowers consumer costs, and promotes commerce and industry and the material well-being of the society at large. Moreover, it makes workers happier and more fulfilled, and meets more of their needs.

Second, one might press the claim that worker sacrifice of autonomy in motivation management is so slight as to be negligible. Far from being warped by such working environments, employees are instead helped to become productive, proud, and fulfilled, thus realizing their best potential in contributing to the well-being of society. Moreover, their abilities to exercise judgment and live in autonomous ways outside of the workplace are not compromised. They are free to think things through on their own: They are merely encouraged to take a positive attitude toward their work.

Third is the case that some manipulation is unavoidable in human relationships, and that the degree of it promoted by motivation management is no more objectionable than that promoted by governments, religions, and even marriages or friendships. Thus, the manipulatory dimension at issue is slight, overshadowed by the benefits of motivation management, and would probably be replaced by some other form of manipulation in the absence of it.

One might bolster each argument by appeal to the principle of free employment, by which workers are free to find new employers without opposition (e.g., blacklists). Such appeal is, however, of no consequence. If employees are in fact manipulated, then such manipulation is objectionable for violating their autonomy and possibly damaging their interests. To wrong one who is unaware under the supposed disclaimer that the person is free to go elsewhere is to give no defense at all.

Each of the three arguments rests on the judgment that greater human well-being results from motivation management than from any other management strategy. Such claims are broad and merit a lengthy discussion that is inappropriate here. It is helpful, however, to note in outline one answer that merits attention.

The thrust of the arguments could be thwarted by a management strategy that would effectively promote productivity in a nonmanipulative way. Two such strategies are worth noting here. One is known variously as workplace democracy or participatory management. Under such an arrangement, the employees themselves determine democratically what institutional policy is to be and how managers are to do their jobs.[7] This reduces significantly the opportunity for manipulative management, and such workplaces are characterized by a high degree of worker motivation and high productivity.[8] There is, however, a practical and ideological question as to whether this strategy presents a viable alternative to motivation management.

The question is whether such democratic organizations are viable in a capitalist economy. Since the employees at large determine institutional policy, it appears that they in effect own the institution. In any case, the role and power of management in such organizations is different from what it is in most capitalist institutions. Thus, democratic management may be fundamentally unacceptable to capitalist managers who wish to retain the capitalist power structure. However, it is worth noting that in recent years a number of capitalist firms have conducted experiments with such democratic approaches. Although many have been temporary, with limited lasting impact, this may indicate that the ideological conflict is not insurmountable.

A different approach has been developed by D. McClelland and his students. Their courses in achievement motivation training have sought to promote employee dispositions to seek challenge, responsibility, and evaluation of performance in the fulfillment of work goals. Their work represents an effort to promote motivation through the development of personal autonomy. They help the apparently unmotivated individual to understand the implications of the negative attitudes toward achievement he or she holds, and then offer the support and opportunity to make some personal changes of attitude. McClelland's achievement motivation training courses involve four main parts:

1. Participants are trained to examine themselves carefully—their behavior, their needs, and their feelings.
2. Participants are trained to be aware of the thoughts and actions of "motivated" individuals and are helped to learn how to think and behave like those individuals.
3. Participants are trained to set realistic goals that they can responsibly achieve.
4. Participants, in group setting, are supported in their attempt at personal change.[9]

The achievement motivation training courses provide an open forum for addressing any real concerns of the participants. Their awareness and understanding of themselves is nourished, and their motivation to be achievers is promoted solely to the extent that this motivation is of real personal benefit. That is, the courses are not designed specifically as means to promote increased productivity of a worker in a certain job slot, as are the strategies of motivation management. Whether or not graduates of their courses return to their jobs to perform more effectively in the eyes of management is immaterial to the success of the courses. This success is determined by the extent to which they promote in subjects the increased desire and effort to assume more responsibility, to take more risks, and to seek more evaluation of their own performance. If graduates sought better positions elsewhere and improved their performance in the new positions, these would count as successes for the course. They would, on the other hand, count as failures from the perspective of motivation management.[10]

A capitalist system of production includes two factors that exacerbate the conflict between worker well-being and productive efficiency. These are the power of management, on the one hand, and the pressure on management to maximize productivity, on the other. The magnitude of both this power and the pressure to produce, together with social pressures to promote worker well-being, naturally incline management toward a subtly effective and thus manipulative approach. Any replacement of this approach would, it seems, have to bring either high levels of productivity or limitation of the power of management. Achievement motivation training courses appear to produce the former results, and democratic work arrangements the latter. To grant both that such options merit further inquiry and development and that motivation management does contain a manipulative element as argued here is further support for the thesis that this element may in fact be eliminated from management practice and that objections to its presence warrant serious consideration.

NOTES

1. Peter F. Drucker, *Management* (London: Pan Books, 1979), pp. 229–230.
2. Harry Braverman, *Labor and Monopoly Capital* (New York: Monthly Review Press, 1974), p. 145.
3. Cf. Robert K. Merton, *Mass Persuasion* (New York: Harper, 1946), p. 86; Robert Dahl, *Modern Political Analysis,* 3rd ed. (Englewood Cliffs, N.J.: Prentice-Hall, 1976), p. 46; Peter Abel, "The Many Faces of Power and Liberty," *Sociology* 11 (1977): 20; C. E. Moustakas, "Honesty, Idiocy and Manipulation," *Journal of Humanistic Psychology* 2 (1962): 1–15; Lawrence Stern, "Freedom, Blame and Moral Community," *Journal of Philosophy* 71 (1974): 74; Stanley Benn, "Freedom and Persuasion," in *Ethical Theory and Business,* ed. T. L. Beauchamp and N. E. Bowie (Englewood Cliffs, N.J.: Prentice-Hall, 1988), pp. 413–420.
4. Raymond S. Pfeiffer, "The Concept of Interpersonal Manipulation in Social Critique and Psychological Research," *Philosophy and Social Criticism* 8 (1981): 211–215.
5. Cf. Benn, "Freedom and Persuasion," p. 515.
6. Karl W. Jackson and Dennis J. Shea, "Motivation Training in Perspective," in *Concepts and Controversy,* 2nd ed., ed. W. R. Nord (Santa Monica, Calif.: Goodyear, 1976), pp. 81–82.
7. A wide variety of arrangements are covered by this term. Cf. Daniel Zwerdling, *Workplace Democracy* (New York: Harper & Row, 1980), and Gerry Hunnius, G. David Garson, and John Cas *Worker's Control* (New York: Vintage Books, 1973).
8. Paul Blumberg, *Industrial Democracy* (New York: Schocken Books, 1968), p. 123; Karl Frieden, *Workplace Democracy and Productivity* (Washington D.C.: National Center for Economic Alternatives, 1980).
9. Jackson and Shea "Motivation Training," p. 89.
10. Cf. Jackson and Shea, "Motivation Training," pp. 92–93.

Whistleblowing and Professional Responsibility

Sissela Bok

"Whistleblowing" is a new label generated by our increased awareness of the ethical conflicts encountered at work. Whistleblowers sound an alarm from within the very organization in which they work, aiming to spotlight neglect or abuses that threaten the public interest.

The stakes in whistleblowing are high. Take the nurse who alleges that physicians enrich themselves in her hospital through

---

From Sissela Bok, "Whistleblowing and Professional Responsibility," *New York University Education Quarterly,* 11 (Summer 1980): 2–7. Reprinted with permission.

unnecessary surgery; the engineer who discloses safety defects in the braking systems of a fleet of new rapid-transit vehicles; the Defense Department official who alerts Congress to military graft and overspending: all know that they pose a threat to those whom they denounce and that their own careers may be at risk.

MORAL CONFLICTS

Moral conflicts on several levels confront anyone who is wondering whether to speak out about abuses or risks or serious neglect. In the first place, he must try to decide whether, other things being equal, speaking out is in fact in the public interest. This choice is often made more complicated by factual uncertainties: Who is responsible for the abuse or neglect? How great is the threat? And how likely is it that speaking out will precipitate changes for the better?

In the second place, a would-be whistleblower must weigh his responsibility to serve the public interest against the responsibility he owes to his colleagues and the institution in which he works. While the professional ethic requires collegial loyalty, the codes of ethics often stress responsibility to the public over and above duties to colleagues and clients. Thus the United States Code of Ethics for Government Servants asks them to "expose corruption wherever uncovered" and to "put loyalty to the highest moral principles and to country above loyalty to persons, party, or government."[1] Similarly, the largest professional engineering association requires members to speak out against abuses threatening the safety, health, and welfare of the public.[2]

A third conflict for would-be whistleblowers is personal in nature and cuts across the first two: even in cases where they have concluded that the facts warrant speaking out, and that their duty to do so overrides loyalties to colleagues and institutions, they often have reason to fear the results of carrying out such a duty. However strong this duty

may seem in theory, they know that, in practice, retaliation is likely. As a result, their careers and their ability to support themselves and their families may be unjustly impaired.[3] A government handbook issued during the Nixon era recommends reassigning "undesirables" to places so remote that they would prefer to resign. Whistleblowers may also be downgraded or given work without responsibility or work for which they are not qualified; or else they may be given many more tasks than they can possibly perform. Another risk is that an outspoken civil servant may be ordered to undergo a psychiatric fitness-for-duty examination,[4] declared unfit for service, and "separated" as well as discredited from the point of view of any allegations he may be making. Outright firing, finally, is the most direct institutional response to whistleblowers.

Add to the conflicts confronting individual whistleblowers the claim to self-policing that many professions make, and professional responsibility is at issue in still another way. For an appeal to the public goes against everything that "self-policing" stands for. The question for the different professions, then, is how to resolve, insofar as it is possible, the conflict between professional loyalty and professional responsibility toward the outside world. The same conflicts arise to some extent in all groups, but professional groups often have special cohesion and claim special dignity and privileges.

The plight of whistleblowers has come to be documented by the press and described in a number of books. Evidence of the hardships imposed on those who chose to act in the public interest has combined with a heightened awareness of professional malfeasance and corruption to produce a shift toward greater public support of whistleblowers. Public service law firms and consumer groups have taken up their cause; institutional reforms and legislation have been proposed to combat illegitimate reprisals.[5]

Given the indispensable services performed by so many whistleblowers, strong public support is often merited. But the new climate of acceptance makes it easy to over-look the dangers of whistleblowing: of uses in error or in malice; of work and reputations unjustly lost for those falsely accused; of privacy invaded and trust undermined. There comes a level of internal prying and mutual suspicion at which no institution can function. And it is a fact that the disappointed, the incompetent, the malicious, and the paranoid all too often leap to accusations in public. Worst of all, ideological persecution throughout the world traditionally relies on insiders willing to inform on their colleagues or even on their family members, often through staged public denunciations or press campaigns.

No society can count itself immune from such dangers. But neither can it risk silencing those with a legitimate reason to blow the whistle. How then can we distinguish between different instances of whistleblowing? A society that fails to protect the right to speak out even on the part of those whose warnings turn out to be spurious obviously opens the door to political repression. But from the moral point of view there are important differences between the aims, messages, and methods of dissenters from within.

NATURE OF WHISTLEBLOWING

Three elements, each jarring, and triply jarring when conjoined, lend acts of whistleblowing special urgency and bitterness: dissent, breach of loyalty, and accusation.

Like all dissent, whistleblowing makes public a disagreement with an authority or a majority view. But whereas dissent can concern all forms of disagreement with, for instance, religious dogma or government policy or court decisions, whistleblowing has the narrower aim of shedding light on negligence or abuse, or alerting to a risk, and of assigning responsibility for this risk.

Would-be whistleblowers confront the conflict inherent in all dissent: between conforming and sticking their necks out. The more repressive the authority they challenge, the greater the personal risk they take in speaking out. At exceptional times, as in times of war, even ordinarily tolerant authorities may come to regard dissent as unacceptable and even disloyal.[6]

Furthermore, the whistleblower hopes to stop the game; but since he is neither referee nor coach, and since he blows the whistle on his own team, his act is seen as a violation of loyalty. In holding his position, he has assumed certain obligations to his colleagues and clients. He may even have subscribed to a loyalty oath or a promise of confidentiality. Loyalty to colleagues and to clients comes to be pitted against loyalty to the public interest, to those who may be injured unless the revelation is made.

Not only is loyalty violated in whistleblowing, hierarchy as well is often opposed, since the whistleblower is not only a colleague but a subordinate. Though aware of the risks inherent in such disobedience, he often hopes to keep his job.[7] At times, however, he plans his alarm to coincide with leaving the institution. If he is highly placed, or joined by others, resigning in protest may effectively direct public attention to the wrongdoing at issue.[8] Still another alternative, often chosen by those who wish to be safe from retaliation, is to leave the institution quietly, to secure another post, and then to blow the whistle. In this way, it is possible to speak with the authority and knowledge of an insider without having the vulnerability of that position.

It is the element of accusation, of calling a "foul," that arouses the strongest reactions on the part of the hierarchy. The accusation may be of neglect, of willfully concealed dangers, or of outright abuse on the part of colleagues or superiors. It singles out specific persons or groups as responsible for threats to the public interest. If no one could be held responsible—as in the case of an impending avalanche—the warning would not constitute whistleblowing.

The accusation of the whistleblower, moreover, concerns a present or an imminent threat. Past errors or misdeeds occasion such an alarm only if they still affect current practices. And risks far in the future lack the immediacy needed to make the alarm a compelling one, as well as the close connection to particular individuals that would justify actual accusations. Thus an alarm can be sounded about safety defects in a rapid-transit system that threaten or will shortly threaten passengers, but the revelation of safety defects in a system no longer in use, while of historical interest, would not constitute whistleblowing. Nor would the revelation of potential problems in a system not yet fully designed and far from implemented.[9]

Not only immediacy, but also specificity, is needed for there to be an alarm capable of pinpointing responsibility. A concrete risk must be at issue rather than a vague foreboding or a somber prediction. The act of whistleblowing differs in this respect from the lamentation or the dire prophecy. An immediate and specific threat would normally be acted upon by those at risk. The whistleblower assumes that his message will alert listeners to something they do not know, or whose significance they have not grasped because it has been kept secret.

The desire for openness inheres in the temptation to reveal any secret, sometimes joined to an urge for self-aggrandizement and publicity and the hope for revenge for past slights or injustices. There can be pleasure, too—righteous or malicious—in laying bare the secrets of co-workers and in setting the record straight at last. Colleagues of the whistleblower often suspect his motives: they may regard him as a crank, as publicity-hungry, wrong about the facts, eager for scandal and discord, and driven to indiscretion by his personal biases and shortcomings.

For whistleblowing to be effective, it must arouse its audience. Inarticulate whistleblowers are likely to fail from the outset. When they are greeted by apathy, their message dissipates. When they are greeted by disbelief, they elicit no response at all. And when the audience is not free to receive or to act on the information—when censorship or fear of retribution stifles response—then the message rebounds to injure the whistleblower. Whistleblowing also requires the possibility of concerted public response: the idea of whistleblowing in an anarchy is therefore merely quixotic.

Such characteristics of whistleblowing and strategic considerations for achieving an impact are common to the noblest warnings, the most vicious personal attacks, and the delusions of the paranoid. How can one distinguish the many acts of sounding an alarm that are genuinely in the public interest from all the petty, biased, or lurid revelations that pervade our querulous and gossip-ridden society? Can we draw distinctions between different whistleblowers, different messages, different methods?

We clearly can, in a number of cases. Whistleblowing may be starkly inappropriate when in malice or error, or when it lays bare legitimately private matters having to do, for instance, with political belief or sexual life. It can, just as clearly, be the only way to shed light on an ongoing unjust practice such as drugging political prisoners or subjecting them to electroshock treatment. It can be the last resort for alerting the public to an impending disaster. Taking such clear-cut cases as benchmarks, and reflecting on what it is about them that weighs so heavily for or against speaking out, we can work our way toward the admittedly more complex cases in which whistleblowing is not so clearly the right or wrong choice, or where different points of view exist regarding its legitimacy—cases where there are moral reasons both for concealment and for disclosure and where judgments conflict. Consider the following cases[10]:

A. As a construction inspector for a federal agency, John Samuels (not his real name) had personal knowledge of shoddy and deficient construction practices by private contractors. He knew his superiors received free vacations and entertainment, had their homes remodeled and found jobs for their relatives—all courtesy of a private contractor. These superiors later approved a multimillion no-bid contract with the same "generous" firm.

Samuels also had evidence that other firms were hiring nonunion laborers at a low wage while receiving substantially higher payments from the government for labor costs. A former superior, unaware of an office dictaphone, had incautiously instructed Samuels on how to accept bribes for overlooking sub-par performance.

As he prepared to volunteer this information to various members of Congress, he became tense and uneasy. His family was scared and the fears were valid. It might cost Samuels thousand of dollars to protect his job. Those who had freely provided Samuels with information would probably recant or withdraw their friendship. A number of people might object to his using a dictaphone to gather information. His agency would start covering up and vent its collective wrath upon him. As for reporters and writers, they would gather for a few days, then move on to the next story. He would be left without a job, with fewer friends, with massive battles looming, and without the financial means of fighting them. Samuels decided to remain silent.

B. Engineers of Company "A" prepared plans and specifications for machinery to be used in a manufacturing process and Company "A" turned them over to Company "B" for production. The engineers of Company "B," in reviewing the plans and specifications, came to the conclusion that they included certain miscalculations and technical deficiencies of a nature that the final product might be unsuitable for the purposes of the ultimate users, and that the equipment, if built according to the original plans and specifications, might endanger the lives of persons in proximity to it. The engineers of Company "B" called the matter to the attention of appropriate officials of their employer who, in turn, advised Company "A." Company "A" replied that its engineers felt that the design and specifications for the equipment were adequate and safe and that Company "B" should proceed to build the equipment as designed and specified. The officials of Company "B" instructed its engineers to proceed with the work.

C. A recently hired assistant director of admissions in a state university begins to wonder whether transcripts of some applicants accurately reflect their accomplishments. He knows that it matters to many in the university community, including alumni, that the football team continue its winning tradition. He has heard rumors that surrogates may be available to take tests for a fee, signing the names of designated applicants for admission, and that some of the transcripts may have been altered. But he has no hard facts. When he brings the question up with the director of admissions, he is told that the rumors are unfounded and asked not to inquire further into the matter.

INDIVIDUAL MORAL CHOICE

What questions might those who consider sounding an alarm in public ask themselves? How might they articulate the problem they see and weigh its injustice before deciding whether or not to reveal it? How can they best try to make sure their choice is the right one? In thinking about these questions it helps to keep in mind the three elements mentioned earlier: dissent, breach of loyalty, and accusation. They impose certain requirements—of accuracy and judgment in dissent; of exploring alternative ways to cope with improprieties that minimize the breach of loyalty; and of fairness in accusation. For each, careful articulation and testing of arguments are needed to limit error and bias.

Dissent by whistleblowers, first of all, is expressly claimed to be intended to benefit the public. It carries with it, as a result, an obligation to consider the nature of this benefit and to consider also the possible harm that may come from speaking out: harm to persons or institutions and, ultimately, to the public interest itself. Whistleblowers must, therefore, begin by making every effort to consider the effects of speaking out versus those of remaining silent. They must assure themselves of the accuracy of their reports, checking and rechecking the facts before speaking out; specify the degree to which there is genuine impropriety; consider how imminent is the threat they see, how serious, and how closely linked to those accused of neglect and abuse.

If the facts warrant whistleblowing, how can the second element—breach of loyalty—be minimized? The most important question here is whether the existing avenues for change within the organization have been explored. It is a waste of time for the public as well as harmful to the institution to sound the loudest alarm first. Whistleblowing has to remain a last alternative because of its destructive side effects: it must be chosen only when other alternatives have been considered and rejected. They may be rejected if they simply do not apply to the problem at hand, or when there is not time to go through routine channels or when the institution is so corrupt or coercive that steps will be taken to silence the whistleblower should he try the regular channels first.

What weight should an oath or a promise of silence have in the conflict of loyalties? One sworn to silence is doubtless under a stronger obligation because of the oath he has taken. He has bound himself, assumed specific obligations beyond those assumed in merely taking a new position. But even such promises can be overridden when the public interest at issue is strong enough. They can be overridden if they were obtained under duress or through deceit. They can be overridden, too, if they promise something that is in itself wrong or unlawful. The fact that one has promised silence is no excuse for complicity in covering up a crime or a violation of the public's trust.

The third element in whistleblowing—accusation—raises equally serious ethical concerns. They are concerns of fairness to the persons accused of impropriety. Is the message one to which the public is entitled in the first place? Or does it infringe on personal and private matters that one has no right to invade? Here, the very notion of what is in the public's best "interest" is at issue: "accusations" regarding an official's

unusual sexual or religious experiences may well appeal to the public's interest without being information relevant to "the public interest."

Great conflicts arise here. We have witnessed excessive claims to executive privilege and to secrecy by government officials during the Watergate scandal in order to cover up for abuses the public had every right to discover. Conversely, those hoping to profit from prying into private matters have become adept at invoking "the public's right to know." Some even regard such private matters as threats to the public: they voice their own religious and political prejudices in the language of accusation. Such a danger is never stronger than when the accusation is delivered surreptitiously. The anonymous accusations made during the McCarthy period regarding political beliefs and associations often injured persons who did not even know their accusers or the exact nature of the accusations.

From the public's point of view, accusations that are openly made by identifiable individuals are more likely to be taken seriously. And in fairness to those criticized, openly accepted responsibility for blowing the whistle should be preferred to the denunciation or the leaked rumor. What is openly stated can more easily be checked, its source's motives challenged, and the underlying information examined. Those under attack may otherwise be hard put to defend themselves against nameless adversaries. Often they do not even know that they are threatened until it is too late to respond. The anonymous denunciation, moreover, common to so many regimes, places the burden of investigation on government agencies that may thereby gain the power of a secret police.

From the point of view of the whistleblower, on the other hand, the anonymous message is safer in situations where retaliation is likely. But it is also often less likely to be taken seriously. Unless the message is accompanied by indications of how the evidence can be checked, its anonymity, however safe for the source, speaks against it.

During the process of weighing the legitimacy of speaking out, the method used, and the degree of fairness needed, whistleblowers must try to compensate for the strong possibility of bias on their part. They should be scrupulously aware of any motive that might skew their message: a desire for self-defense in a difficult bureaucratic situation, perhaps, or the urge to seek revenge, or inflated expectations regarding the effect their message will have on the situation. (Needless to say, bias affects the silent as well as the outspoken. The motive for holding back important information about abuses and injustice ought to give similar cause for soul-searching.)

Likewise, the possibility of personal gain from sounding the alarm ought to give pause. Once again there is then greater risk of a biased message. Even if the whistleblower regards himself as incorruptible, his profiting from revelations of neglect or abuse will lead others to question his motives and to put less credence in his charges. If, for example, a government employee stands to make large profits from a book exposing the iniquities in his agency, there is danger that he will, perhaps even unconsciously, slant his report in order to cause more of a sensation.

A special problem arises when there is a high risk that the civil servant who speaks out will have to go through costly litigation. Might he not justifiably try to make enough money on his public revelations—say, through books or public speaking—to offset his losses? In so doing he will not strictly speaking have *profited* from his revelations: he merely avoids being financially crushed by their sequels. He will nevertheless still be suspected at the time of revelation, and his message will therefore seem more questionable.

Reducing bias and error in moral choice often requires consultation, even open debate[11]: methods that force articulation of the moral arguments at stake and challenge privately held assumptions. But acts of whistleblowing present special problems when it comes to open consultation. On the one hand, once the whistleblower sounds his alarm publicly, his arguments will be subjected to open scrutiny; he will have to articulate his reasons for speaking out and substantiate his charges. On the other hand, it will then be too late to retract the alarm or to combat its harmful effects, should his choice to speak out have been ill-advised.

For this reason, the whistleblower owes it to all involved to make sure of two things: that he has sought as much and as objective advice regarding his choice as he can *before* going public; and that he is aware of the arguments for and against the practice of whistleblowing in general, so that he can see his own choice against as richly detailed and coherently structured a background as possible. Satisfying these two requirements once again has special problems because of the very nature of whistleblowing: the more corrupt the circumstances, the more dangerous it may be to seek consultation before speaking out. And yet, since the whistleblower himself may have a biased view of the state of affairs, he may choose not to consult others when in fact it would be not only safe but advantageous to do so; he may see corruption and conspiracy where none exists.

NOTES

1. Code of Ethics for Government Service passed by the U.S. House of Representatives in the 85th Congress (1958) and applying to all government employees and office holders.
2. Code of Ethics of the Institute of Electrical and Electronics Engineers, Article IV.
3. For case histories and descriptions of what befalls whistleblowers, see Rosemary Chalk and Frank von Hippel, "Due Process for Dissenting Whistle-Blowers," *Technology Review* 81 (June–July 1979): 48–55; Alan S. Westin and Stephen Salisbury, eds., *Individual Rights in the Corporation* (New York: Pantheon, 1980);

Helen Dudar, "The Price of Blowing the Whistle," *New York Times Magazine,* 30 October 1979, pp. 41–54; John Edsall, *Scientific Freedom and Responsibility* (Washington, D.C.: American Association for the Advancement of Science, 1975), p. 5; David Ewing, *Freedom Inside the Organization* (New York: Dutton, 1977); Ralph Nader, Peter Petkas, and Kate Blackwell, *Whistle Blowing* (New York: Grossman, 1972); Charles Peter and Taylor Branch, *Blowing the Whistle* (New York: Praeger, 1972).

4. Congressional hearings uncovered a growing resort to mandatory psychiatric examinations.

5. For an account of strategies and proposals to support government whistleblowers, see Government Accountability Project, *A Whistleblower's Guide to the Federal Bureaucracy* (Washington, D.C.: Institute for Policy Studies, 1977).

6. See, e.g., Samuel Eliot Morison, Frederick Merk, and Frank Friedel, *Dissent in Three American Wars* (Cambridge: Harvard University Press, 1970).

7. In the scheme worked out by Albert Hirschman in *Exit, Voice and Loyalty* (Cambridge: Harvard University Press, 1970), whistleblowing represents "voice" accompanied by a preference not to "exit," though forced "exit" is clearly a possibility and "voice" after or during "exit" may be chosen for strategic reasons.

8. Edward Weisband and Thomas N. Franck, *Resignation in Protest* (New York: Grossman, 1975).

9. Future developments can, however, be the cause for whistleblowing if they are seen as resulting from steps being taken or about to be taken that render them inevitable.

10. Case A is adapted from Louis Clark, "The Sound of Professional Suicide," *Barrister,* Summer 1978, p. 10; Case B is Case 5 in Robert J. Baum and Albert Flores, eds., *Ethical Problems of Engineering* (Troy, N.Y.: Rensselaer Polytechnic Institute, 1978), p. 186.

11. I discuss these questions of consultation and publicity with respect to moral choice in chapter 7 of Sissela Bok, *Lying* (New York: Pantheon, 1978); and in *Secrets* (New York: Pantheon Books, 1982), Ch. IX and XV.

Whistleblowing and Employee Loyalty

Ronald Duska

. . . There are proponents on both sides of the issue—those who praise whistleblowers as civic heroes and those who condemn them as "finks." Maxwell Glen and Cody Shearer, who wrote about the whistleblowers at Three Mile Island say, "Without the *courageous* breed of assorted company insiders known as whistleblowers—workers who often risk their livelihoods to disclose information about construction and design flaws—the Nuclear Regulatory Commission itself would be nearly as idle as Three Mile Island. . . . That whistleblowers deserve both gratitude and protection is beyond disagreement."[1]

Still, while Glen and Shearer praise whistleblowers, others vociferously condemn them. For example, in a now infamous quote, James Roche, the former president of General Motors said:

Some critics are now busy eroding another support of free enterprise—the loyalty of a management team, with its unifying values

Reprinted by permission of the author.

and cooperative work. Some of the enemies of business now encourage an employee to be *disloyal* to the enterprise. They want to create suspicion and disharmony, and pry into the proprietary interests of the business. However this is labelled—industrial espionage, whistle blowing, or professional responsibility—it is another tactic for spreading disunity and creating conflict.[2]

From Roche's point of view, not only is whistleblowing not "courageous" and not deserving of "gratitude and protection" as Glen and Shearer would have it, it is corrosive and impermissible.

Discussions of whistleblowing generally revolve around three topics: (1) attempts to define whistleblowing more precisely, (2) debates about whether and when whistleblowing is permissible, and (3) debates about whether and when one has an obligation to blow the whistle.

In this paper I want to focus on the second problem, because I find it somewhat disconcerting that there is a problem at all. When I first looked into the ethics of whistleblowing it seemed to me that whistleblowing was a good thing, and yet I found in the literature claim after claim that it was in need of defense, that there was something wrong with it, namely that it was an act of disloyalty.

If whistleblowing is a disloyal act, it deserves disapproval, and ultimately any action of whistleblowing needs justification. This disturbs me. It is as if the act of a good Samaritan is being condemned as an act of interference, as if the prevention of a suicide needs to be justified.

In his book *Business Ethics,* Norman Bowie claims that "whistleblowing . . . violate(s) a *prima facie* duty of loyalty to one's employer." According to Bowie, there is a duty of loyalty that prohibits one from reporting his employer or company. Bowie, of course, recognizes that this is only a *prima facie* duty, that is, one that can be overriden by a higher duty to the public good. Nevertheless, the axiom that whistleblowing is disloyal is Bowie's starting point.[3]

Bowie is not alone. Sissela Bok sees "whistleblowing" as an instance of disloyalty:

> The whistleblower hopes to stop the game; but since he is neither referee nor coach, and since he blows the whistle on his own team, his act is seen as a *violation of loyalty.* In holding his position, he has assumed certain obligations to his colleagues and clients. He may even have subscribed to a loyalty oath or a promise of confidentiality. . . . Loyalty to colleagues and to clients comes to be pitted against loyalty to the public interest, to those who may be injured unless the revelation is made.[4]

Bowie and Bok end up defending whistleblowing in certain contexts, so I don't necessarily disagree with their conclusions. However, I fail to see how one has an obligation of loyalty to one's company, so I disagree with their perception of the problem and their starting point. I want to argue that one does not have an obligation of loyalty to a company, even a *prima facie* one, because companies are not the kind of things that are properly objects of loyalty. To make them objects of loyalty gives them a moral status they do not deserve and in raising their status, one lowers the status of the individuals who work for the companies. Thus, the difference in perception is important because those who think employers have an obligation of loyalty to a company fail to take into account a relevant moral difference between persons and corporations.

But why aren't companies the kind of things that can be objects of loyalty? To answer that we have to ask what are proper objects of loyalty. John Ladd states the problem this way, "Granted that loyalty is the wholehearted devotion to an object of some kind, what kind of thing is the object? Is it an abstract entity, such as an idea or a collective being? Or is it a person or group of persons?"[5] Philosophers fall into three camps on the question. On one side are the idealists who hold that loyalty is devotion to something more than persons, to some cause or abstract entity. On the other side are what

Ladd calls "social atomists," and these include empiricists and utilitarians, who think that at most one can only be loyal to individuals and that loyalty can ultimately be explained away as some other obligation that holds between two people. Finally, there is a moderate position that holds that although idealists go too far in postulating some super-personal entity as an object of loyalty, loyalty is still an important and real relation that holds between people, one that cannot be dismissed by reducing it to some other relation.

There does seem to be a view of loyalty that is not extreme. According to Ladd, "'loyalty' is taken to refer to a relationship between persons—for instance, between a lord and his vassal, between a parent and his children, or between friends. Thus the object of loyalty is ordinarily taken to be a person or a group of persons."[6]

But this raises a problem that Ladd glosses over. There is a difference between a person or a group of persons, and aside from instances of loyalty that relate two people such as lord/vassal, parent/child, or friend/friend, there are instances of loyalty relating a person to a group, such as a person to his family, a person to his team, and a person to his country. Families, countries, and teams are presumably groups of persons. They are certainly ordinarily construed as objects of loyalty.

But to what am I loyal in such a group? In being loyal to the group am I being loyal to the whole group or to its members? It is easy to see the object of loyalty in the case of an individual person. It is simply the individual. But to whom am I loyal in a group? To whom am I loyal in a family? Am I loyal to each and every individual or to something larger, and if to something larger, what is it? We are tempted to think of a group as an entity of its own, an individual in its own right, having an identity of its own.

To avoid the problem of individuals existing for the sake of the group, the atomists insist that a group is nothing more than the individuals who comprise it, nothing other

than a mental fiction by which we refer to a group of individuals. It is certainly not a reality or entity over and above the sum of its parts, and consequently is not a proper object of loyalty. Under such a position, of course, no loyalty would be owed to a company because a company is a mere mental fiction, since it is a group. One would have obligations to the individual members of the company, but one could never be justified in overriding those obligations for the sake of the "group" taken collectively. A company has no moral status except in terms of the individual members who comprise it. It is not a proper object of loyalty. But the atomists go too far. Some groups, such as a family, do have a reality of their own, whereas groups of people walking down the street do not. From Ladd's point of view the social atomist is wrong because he fails to recognize the kinds of groups that are held together by "the ties that bind." The atomist tries to reduce these groups to simple sets of individuals bound together by some externally imposed criteria. This seems wrong.

There do seem to be groups in which the relationships and interactions create a new force or entity. A group takes on an identity and a reality of its own that is determined by its purpose, and this purpose defines the various relationships and roles set up within the group. There is a division of labor into roles necessary for the fulfillment of the purposes of the group. The membership, then, is not of individuals who are the same but of individuals who have specific relationships to one another determined by the aim of the group. Thus we get specific relationships like parent/child, coach/player, and so on, that don't occur in other groups. It seems then that an atomist account of loyalty that restricts loyalty merely to individuals and does not include loyalty to groups might be inadequate.

But once I have admitted that we can have loyalty to a group, do I not open myself up to criticism from the proponent of loyalty to the company? Might not the proponent of loyalty to business say: "Very well. I agree with you. The atomists are short-sighted. Groups have some sort of reality and they can be proper objects of loyalty. But companies are groups. Therefore companies are proper objects of loyalty."

The point seems well taken, except for the fact that the kinds of relationships that loyalty requires are just the kind that one does not find in business. As Ladd says, "The ties that bind the persons together provide the basis of loyalty." But all sorts of ties bind people together. I am a member of a group of fans if I go to a ball game. I am a member of a group if I merely walk down the street. What binds people together in a business is not sufficient to require loyalty.

A business or corporation does two things in the free enterprise system: It produces a good or service and it makes a profit. The making of a profit, however, is the primary function of a business as a business, for if the production of the good or service is not profitable, the business would be out of business. Thus nonprofitable goods or services are a means to an end. People bound together in a business are bound together not for mutual fulfillment and support, but to divide labor to make a profit. Thus, while we can jokingly refer to a family as a place where "they have to take you in no matter what," we cannot refer to a company in that way. If a worker does not produce in a company or if cheaper laborers are available, the company—in order to fulfill its purpose— should get rid of the worker. A company feels no obligation of loyalty. The saying "You can't buy loyalty" is true. Loyalty depends on ties that demand self-sacrifice with no expectation of reward. Business functions on the basis of enlightened self-interest. I am devoted to a company not because it is like a parent to me; it is not. Attempts of some companies to create "one big happy family" ought to be looked on with suspicion. I am not devoted to it at all, nor should I be. I work for it because it pays me. I am not in a family to get paid, I am in a company to get paid.

The cold hard truth is that the goal of profit is what gives birth to a company and forms that particular group. Money is what ties the group together. But in such a commercialized venture, with such a goal, there is no loyalty, or at least none need be expected. An employer will release an employee and an employee will walk away from an employer when it is profitable for either one to do so.

Not only is loyalty to a corporation not required, it more than likely is misguided. There is nothing as pathetic as the story of the loyal employee who, having given above and beyond the call of duty, is let go in the restructuring of the company. He feels betrayed because he mistakenly viewed the company as an object of his loyalty. Getting rid of such foolish romanticism and coming to grips with this hard but accurate assessment should ultimately benefit everyone.

To think we owe a company or corporation loyalty requires us to think of that company as a person or as a group with a goal of human fulfillment. If we think of it in this way we can be loyal. But this is the wrong way to think. A company is not a person. A company is an instrument, and an instrument with a specific purpose, the making of profit. To treat an instrument as an end in itself, like a person, may not be as bad as treating an end as an instrument, but it does give the instrument a moral status it does not deserve; and by elevating the instrument we lower the end. All things, instruments and ends, become alike.

Remember that Roche refers to the "management team" and Bok sees the name "whistleblowing" coming from the instance of a referee blowing a whistle in the presence of a foul. What is perceived as bad about whistleblowing in business from this perspective is that one blows the whistle on one's own team, thereby violating team loyalty. If the company can get its employees to view it as a team they belong to, it is easier to demand loyalty. Then the rules governing teamwork and team loyalty will apply. One reason the appeal to a team and team loyalty works so well in business is that businesses are in competition with one another. Effective motivation turns business practices into a game and instills teamwork.

But businesses differ from teams in very important respects, which makes the analogy between business and a team dangerous. Loyalty to a team is loyalty within the context of sport or a competition. Teamwork and team loyalty require that in the circumscribed activity of the game I cooperate with my fellow players, so that pulling all together, we may win. The object of (most) sports is victory. But winning in sports is a social convention, divorced from the usual goings on of society. Such a winning is most times a harmless, morally neutral diversion.

But the fact that this victory in sports, within the rules enforced by a referee (whistleblower), is a socially developed convention taking place within a larger social context makes it quite different from competition in business, which, rather than being defined by a context, permeates the whole of society in its influence. Competition leads not only to victory but to losers. One can lose at sport with precious few consequences. The consequences of losing at business are much larger. Further, the losers in business can be those who are not in the game voluntarily (we are all forced to participate) but who are still affected by business decisions. People cannot choose to participate in business. It permeates everyone's lives.

The team model, then, fits very well with the model of the free market system, because there competition is said to be the name of the game. Rival companies compete and their object is to win. To call a foul on one's own teammate is to jeopardize one's chances of winning and is viewed as disloyalty.

But isn't it time to stop viewing corporate machinations as games? These games are not controlled and are not ended after a specific time. The activities of business affect the lives of everyone, not just the game players. The analogy of the corporation to a team and the consequent appeal to team loyalty, although understandable, is seriously misleading, at least in the moral sphere where competition is not the prevailing virtue.

If my analysis is correct, the issue of the permissibility of whistleblowing is not a real issue since there is no obligation of loyalty to a company. Whistleblowing is not only permissible but expected when a company is harming society. The issue is not one of disloyalty to the company, but of whether the whistleblower has an obligation to society if blowing the whistle will bring him retaliation.

NOTES

1. Maxwell Glen and Cody Shearer, "Going After the Whistle-blowers," *Philadelphia Inquirer,* Tuesday, August 2, 1983, Op-ed page, p. 11A.
2. James M. Roche, "The Competitive System, to Work, to Preserve, and to Protect," *Vital Speeches of the Day* (May 1971): 445.
3. Norman Bowie, *Business Ethics* (Englewood Cliffs, N.J.: Prentice-Hall, 1982), pp. 140–143.
4. Sissela Bok, "Whistleblowing and Professional Responsibilities," *New York University Education Quarterly* 2 (1980): 3, and here p. 294.
5. John Ladd, "Loyalty," *The Encyclopedia of Philosophy* 5: 97.
6. *Ibid.*

Trade Secrets: What Price Loyalty?

Michael S. Baram

In 1963, the Court of Appeals of Ohio heard an appeal of a lower court decision from The B.F. Goodrich Company. The lower court had denied Goodrich's request for an injunction, or court order, to restrain a former employee, Donald Wohlgemuth, from disclosing its trade secrets and from working in the space suit field for any other company.

This case, as it was presented in the Court of Appeals, is a fascinating display of management issues, legal concepts, and ethical dilemmas of concern to research and development organizations and their scientist and engineer employees. The case also represents an employer-employee crisis of increasing incidence in the young and vigorous R&D sector of U.S. industry. Tales of departing employees and threatened losses of trade secrets or proprietary information are now common.

Such crises are not surprising when one considers the causes of mobility. The highly educated employees of R&D organizations place primary emphasis on their own development, interests, and satisfaction. Graduates of major scientific and technological institutions readily admit that they accept their first jobs primarily for money and for the early and brief experience they feel is a prerequisite for seeking more satisfying futures with smaller companies which are often their own. Employee mobility and high personnel turnover rates are also due to the placement of new large federal contracts and the termination of others. One need only look to the Sunday newspaper employment advertisements for evidence as to the manner in which such programs are used to attract highly educated R&D personnel.

This phenomenon of the mobile employee seeking fulfillment reflects a sudden change in societal and personal values. It also threatens industrial reliance on trade secrets for the protection of certain forms of intellectual property. There are no union solutions, and the legal framework in which it occurs is an ancient structure representing values of an earlier America. The formulation of management responses—with cognizance of legal, practical, and ethical considerations—is admittedly a difficult task, but one which must be undertaken.

In this article I shall examine the basic question of industrial loyalty regarding trade secrets, using the Goodrich-Wohlgemuth case as the focal point of the challenge to the preservation of certain forms of intellectual property posed by the mobile employee, and then offer some suggestions for the development of sound management policies.

THE APPEALS CASE

Donald Wohlgemuth joined The B.F. Goodrich Company as a chemical engineer in 1954, following his graduation from the University of Michigan, and by 1962 he had become manager of the space suit division. As the repository of Goodrich know-how and secret data in space suit technology, he was

From Michael S. Baram. "Trade Secrets: What Price Loyalty?" *Harvard Business Review* (November/December 1968): 66–74. Reprinted by permission of the *Harvard Business Review*. Copyright © 1968 by the President and Fellows of Harvard College; all rights reserved.

indeed a key man in a rapidly developing technology of interest to several government agencies. Nevertheless, he was dissatisfied with his salary ($10,644) and the denial of his requests for certain additional facilities for his department.

A Goodrich rival, International Latex, had recently been awarded the major space suit subcontract for the Apollo program. Following up a contact from an employment agency hired by Latex, Wohlgemuth negotiated a position with Latex, at a substantial salary increase. In his new assignment he would be manager of engineering for industrial products, which included space suits. He then notified Goodrich of his resignation, and was met with a reaction he apparently did not expect. Goodrich management raised the moral and ethical aspects of his decision, since the company executives felt his resignation would result in the transfer of Goodrich trade secrets to Latex.

After several heated exchanges, Wohlgemuth stated that "loyalty and ethics have their price and International Latex has paid this price...." Even though Goodrich threatened legal action, Wohlgemuth left Goodrich for Latex. Goodrich thereupon requested a restraining order in the Ohio courts.

At the appeals court level, the Goodrich brief sought an injunction that would prevent Wohlgemuth from working in the space suit field for *any* other company, prevent his disclosure of *any* information on space suit technology to *anyone,* prevent his consulting or conferring with *anyone* on Goodrich trade secrets, and finally, prevent *any* future contact he might seek with Goodrich employees.

These four broad measures were rejected by the Ohio Court of Appeals. All were too wide in scope, and all would have protected much more than Goodrich's legitimate concern of safeguarding its trade secrets. In addition, the measures were speculative, since no clear danger seemed imminent. In sum, they represented a form of "overkill" that would have placed undue restraints on Wohlgemuth.

The court did provide an injunction restraining Wohlgemuth from disclosure of Goodrich trade secrets. In passing, the court noted that in the absence of any Goodrich employment contract restraining his employment with a competitor, Wohlgemuth could commence work with Latex. With ample legal precedent, the court therefore came down on both sides of the fence. Following the decision, Wohlgemuth commenced his career with Latex and is now manager of the company's Research and Engineering Department.

COMMON-LAW CONCEPTS

The two basic issues in crises such as the Goodrich-Wohlgemuth case appear irreconcilable: (1) the right of the corporation to its intellectual property—its proprietary data or trade secrets; and (2) the right of the individual to seek gainful employment and utilize his abilities—to be free from a master-servant relationship.

There are no federal and but a few state statutes dealing with employment restraints and trade secrets. The U.S. courts, when faced with such issues, have sought to apply the various common-law doctrines of trade secrets and unfair competition at hand to attain an equitable solution. Many of these common-law doctrines were born in pre-industrial England and later adopted by English and U.S. courts to meet employment crises of this nature through ensuing centuries of changing industrial and social patterns. In fact, some of the early cases of blacksmiths and barbers seeking to restrain departing apprentices are still cited today.

To the courts, the common legal solution, as in *Goodrich* v. *Wohlgemuth,* is pleasing because it theoretically preserves the rights of both parties. However, it is sadly lacking in practicality, since neither secrets nor individual liberty are truly preserved.

The trade secrets which companies seek to protect have usually become an integral portion of the departing employee's total capabilities. He cannot divest himself of his intellectual capacity, which is a compound of information acquired from his employer, his co-workers, and his own self-generated experiential information. Nevertheless, all such information, if kept secret by the company from its competition, may legitimately be claimed as corporate property. This is because the employer-employee relationship embodied in the normal employment contract or other terms of employment provides for corporate ownership of all employee-generated data, including inventions. As a result, a departing employee's intellectual capacity may be, in large measure, corporate property.

Once the new position with a competitor has been taken, the trade secrets embodied in the departing employee may manifest themselves quite clearly and consciously. This is what court injunctions seek to prohibit. But, far more likely, the trade secrets will manifest themselves subconsciously and in various forms—for example, as in the daily decisions by the employee at his new post, or in the many small contributions he makes to a large team effort—often in the form of an intuitive sense of what or what not to do, as he seeks to utilize his overall intellectual capacity. Theoretically, a legal injunction also serves to prohibit such "leakage." However, the former employer faces the practical problem of securing evidence of such leakage, for little will be apparent from the public activities and goods of the new employer. And if the new employer's public activities or goods appear suspicious, there is also the further problem of distinguishing one's trade secrets from what may be legitimately asserted as the self-generated technological skills or state of the art of the new employer and competitor which were utilized.

This is a major stumbling block in the attempt to protect one's trade secrets, since the possessor has no recourse against others who independently generate the same information. It is therefore unlikely that an injunction against disclosure of trade secrets to future employers prevents any "unintentional" transfer (or even intentional transfer) of information, except for the passage of documents and other physical embodiments of the secrets. In fact, only a lobotomy, as yet not requested nor likely to be sanctioned by the courts, would afford security against the transfer of most trade secrets.

Conversely, the departing employee bears the terrible burden of sensitivity. At his new post, subconscious disclosure and mental and physical utilization of what he feels to be no more than his own intellectual capacity may result in heated exchanges between companies, adverse publicity, and litigation. He is marked, insecure, and unlikely to contribute effectively in his new position. In fact, new co-workers may consider him to be a man with a price, and thus without integrity. Frequently, caution on the part of his new employer will result in transfer to a nonsensitive post where he is unlikely to contribute his full skills, unless he has overall capability and adaptability.

The fact that neither secrets nor individual liberty will be truly preserved rarely influences the course of litigation. Similarly, these practical considerations are usually negligible factors in the out-of-court settlements which frequently terminate such litigation, because the settlements primarily reflect the relative bargaining strengths of disputing parties.

Finally, there is the full cost of litigation to be considered. In addition to the obvious court costs and attorney's fees, there is the potentially great cost to the company's image. Although the drama enacted in court reflects legitimate corporate concerns, the public may easily fail to see more than an unequal struggle between the powerful corporate machine and a lonely individual harassed beyond his employment tenure. Prospective employees, particularly new and recent graduates whose early positions are stepping stones, may be reluctant to accept employment with what appears to be a vindictive and authoritarian organization.

Practical & Legal Aspects

Trade secrets are, of course, a common form of intellectual property. Secrecy is the most natural and the earliest known method of protecting the fruits of one's intellectual labors. Rulers of antiquity frequently had architects and engineers murdered, after completion of their works, to maintain secrecy and security. The medieval guilds and later the craftsmen of pre-industrial Europe and America imposed severe restraints on apprentices and their future activities.

Recognition and acceptance of the practice of protecting intellectual property by secrecy is found throughout Anglo-American common or judge-made law, but statutory protection has not been legislated. Perhaps the failure to do so is because of the recognition by the elected officials of industrial societies that secrecy is not in the public interest and that the widest dissemination of new works and advances in technology and culture is necessary for optimal public welfare. . . .

To summarize this common law briefly, virtually all information—ranging from full descriptions of inventions to plant layouts, shop knowhow, methods of quality control, customer and source lists, and marketing data—is eligible for protection as trade secrets. No standards of invention or originality are required. If such information is not known to the public or to the trade (or it is known but its utility is not recognized), and if such information is of value to its possessor, it is eligible for protection by the courts.

Further, and of greatest importance in terms of favorably impressing the courts, there must be evidence that the possesor recognized the value of his information and treated it accordingly. In the context of confidential relationships, "treatment" normally means that the possessor provided for limited or no disclosure of trade secrets.

This means many things: for example, total prohibition of disclosure except to key company people on a need-to-know basis; provision of the information to licensees, joint ventures, or employees having contractual restraints against their unauthorized disclosure or use; division of employee responsibilities so that no employee is aware of more than a small segment of a particular process; and use in labs of unmarked chemicals and materials.

There must also be evidence that particular efforts were expended for the purpose of preserving secrecy for the specific data claimed as trade secrets. General company policies indiscriminately applied to data and employees or licensees will not suffice in the legal sense to convince the courts of the presence of trade secrets.

When the possessor and his information do fulfill such criteria, court recognition and the award of compensation to damaged parties, or injunctive restraints to protect parties in danger of imminent or further damage, will follow. If there is evidence of (a) breach of confidential relationships (contracts or licenses) which were established to preserve the secrecy of company information, (b) unauthorized copying and sale of secrets, or (c) conspiracy to damage the possessor, the courts will act with greater certitude. But in many cases, such as in the Goodrich-Wohlgemuth litigation, no such evidence is present.

Finally, the courts will not move to protect trade secrets when an action is brought by one party against another who independently generated similar information, or who "reverse-engineered" the publicly sold products of the party petitioning the court, unless there is some contractual, fiduciary, or other relationship based on trust connecting the parties in court.

Other Considerations

In addition to the foregoing practical and legal aspects, basic questions of industrial ethics and the equitable allocation of rights and risks should be examined to provide management with intelligent and humane responses to employer-employee crises that involved intellectual property. The patent and copyright systems for the stimulation and protection of such property are premised on dissemination of information and subsequent public welfare. These systems reflect public concern with the proper use of intellectual property, which the common law of trade secrets lacks.

Will the courts continue to utilize common-law concepts for the protection of trade secrets, when such concepts are based solely on the rights of the possessors of secret information, and when the application of such concepts has a detrimental effect on both the rights of employees and the public welfare? Since current court practice places the burden of industrial loyalty solely on the employee, the skilled individual has to pay the price. In other words, the law restricts the fullest utilization of his abilities. And the detrimental effect on public welfare can be inferred from recent federal studies of technology transfer, which indicate that employee mobility and the promotion of entrepreneurial activities are primary factors in the transfer of technology and the growth of new industries.

The continuation of trade secret concepts for the preservation of property rights in secret information at the expense of certain basic individual freedoms is unlikely. The law eventually reflects changing societal values, and the mobile R&D employee who seeks career fulfillment through a succession of jobs, frequently in sensitive trade secret areas, is now a reality—one not likely to disappear. Thus it is probable that the courts will eventually adopt the position that those who rely on trade secrets assume the realities or risks in the present context of public concern with technological progress and its relationship to the public good, and with the rights of the individual. Resulting unintentional leakage of secret information through the memory of a departing employee is now

generally accepted as a reasonable price to pay for the preservation of these societal values. However, the courts will never condone the theft or other physical appropriation of secret information, nor are the courts likely to condone fraud, conspiracy, and other inequitable practices resulting in some form of unfair competition.

The failings of the statutory systems serve, not as justification for the inequitable application of medieval trade secret concepts, but as the basis for legislative reform. Injunctive restraints against the unintentional leakage of secrets and the harassment of departing employees through litigation should not be part of our legal system. This is especially true when there is a growing body of evidence that management can respond, and has intelligently done so, to such crises without detriment to the individual employee, the public good, or the company itself.

MANAGEMENT RESPONSE

How then shall managers of research and development organizations respond to the reality of the mobile employee and his potential for damage to corporate trade secrets?

Contractual Restraints

Initial response is invariably consideration of the use of relevant contractual prohibitions on employees with such potential. For a minority of companies, this means the institution of employment contracts or other agreements concerning terms of employment. For most, a review of existing company contracts, which at a minimum provide for employee disclosure of inventions and company ownership of subsequent patents, will be called for to determine the need for relevant restraints.

Contractual prohibitions vary somewhat, but they are clearly of two general types: (I) restraints against unauthorized disclosure and use of company trade secrets or proprietary information by employees during their employment tenure or at any time there-after; (2) restraints against certain future activities of employees following their employment tenure.

A restraint against unauthorized disclosure or use is normally upheld in the courts, provided it is limited to a legitimate company concern—trade secrets. But it is usually ineffective, due to the unintentional leakage and subconscious utilization of trade secrets, and the difficulties of "policing" and proving violation, as discussed earlier. In fact, several authorities feel that this type of restraint is ineffective unless coupled with a valid restraint against future employment with competitors. . . .

Courts have been naturally reluctant to extend protection to trade secrets when the freedom of an individual to use his overall capability is at stake. In addition, the former employer faces the practical difficulty of convincing almost any court that a prohibition of future employment is necessary, since the court will look for clear and convincing evidence that the ex-employee has, or inevitably will, exercise more than the ordinary skill a man of his competence possesses. A few states—such as California by statute and others by consistent court action—now prohibit future employment restraints.

It therefore appears that a contractual prohibition of future employment in a broad area, which prevents an ex-employee from using his overall capability, is invalid in most states. . . .

Internal Policies

Another response of R&D management to the mobile employee and his potential for damage to corporate trade secrets is the formulation of internal company policies for the handling of intellectual property of trade secret potential. Such policies may call for the prior review of publications and addresses of key employees, prohibition of consulting and other "moonlighting," dissemination of trade secrets on a strict "need

to know" basis to designated employees, and prohibitions on the copying of trade secret data. More "physical" policies may restrict research and other operational areas to access for designated or "badge" employees only and divide up operations to prevent the accumulation of extensive knowledge by any individual—including safety and other general plant personnel. Several companies I know of distribute unmarked materials—particularly chemicals—to employees.

Although internal policies do not necessarily prevent future employment with competitors, they can serve to prevent undue disclosures and lessen the criticality of the departure of key personnel. All must be exercised with a sophisticated regard for employee motivation, however, because the cumulative effect may result in a police state atmosphere that inhibits creativity and repels prospective employees.

Several farsighted R&D organizations are currently experimenting with plans which essentially delegate the responsibility for nondisclosure and nonuse of their trade secrets to the key employees themselves. These plans include pension and consulting programs operative for a specified post-employment period. In one company, for example, the pension plan provides that the corporate monies which are contributed to the employee pension fund in direct ratio to the employee's own contributions will remain in his pension package following his term of employment, provided he does not work for a competing firm for a specified number of years. In another company, the consulting plan provides that certain departing employees are eligible to receive an annual consulting fee for a given number of years following employment if they do not work for a competitor. The consulting fee is a preestablished percentage of the employee's annual salary at the time of his departure.

Obviously, such corporate plans are subject to employee abuse, but if limited to truly key employees, they may succeed without abuse in most cases. They not only have the merit of providing the employee with a choice, an equitable feature likely to incur employee loyalty, but they also have no apparent legal defects.

Another valid internal practice is the debriefing of departing employees. The debriefing session, carried out in a low-key atmosphere, affords management an excellent opportunity to retrieve company materials and information in physical form, to impart to the employee a sense of responsibility regarding trade secrets and sensitive areas, and to discuss mutual anxieties in full.

External Procedures

Several management responses relating to external company policies are worth noting, as they also serve to protect trade secrets in cases involving employee departures. Among several industries, such as in the chemical field, it is common to find gentlemen's agreements which provide mutuality in the nonhiring of competitor's key employees, following notice. Employees who have encountered this practice have not found the experience a pleasant one. This same practice is also found in other areas, such as the industrial machinery industry, that are in need of innovation; and it appears that the presence of such agreements helps to depict these industries in an unappealing fashion to the types of employees they need.

Another external response for management consideration is company reliance on trademarks. Given a good mark and subsequent public identification of the product with the mark, a company may be able to maintain markets despite the fact that its intellectual property is no longer a trade secret. Competitors may be hesitant about utilizing the former trade secrets of any company whose products are strongly identified with trademarks and with the company itself.

Some trade secrets are patentable, and management faced with the potential loss of such secrets should consider filing for patent protection. The application is treated confidentially by the U.S. Patent Office and some foreign patent offices up to the time of award. Moreover, if the application is rejected, the secrecy of the information is not legally diminished. In any case, the subject matter of the application remains secret throughout the two-to-three year period of time normally involved in U.S. Patent Office review.

CONCLUSION

A major concern of our society is progress through the promotion and utilization of new technology. To sustain and enhance this form of progress, it is necessary to optimize the flow of information and innovation all the way from conception to public use. This effort is now a tripartite affair involving federal agencies, industry, and universities. A unique feature of this tripartite relationship is the mobility of R&D managers, scientists, and engineers who follow contract funding and projects in accordance with their special competence. Neither the federal agencies nor the universities rely on trade secret concepts for the protection of their intellectual property. However, industry still does, despite the fact that trade secret concepts bear the potential ancillary effect of interfering with employee mobility.

It is becoming increasingly clear that new societal values associated with the tripartite approach to new technology are now evolving, and that the common law dispensed by the courts has begun to reflect these values. A victim of sorts is trade secret law, which has not only never been clearly defined, but which has indeed been sustained by court concepts of unfair competition, equity, and confidence derived from other fields of law. The day when courts restrict employee mobility to preserve industrial trade secrets appears to have passed, except—as we noted earlier—in cases involving highly charged factors such as conspiracy, fraud, or theft.

In short, it is now unwise for management to rely on trade secret law and derivative employee contractual restraints to preserve trade secrets. Companies must now carefully weigh the nature and value of their intellectual property, present and potential employees, competition, and applicable laws in order to formulate sound management policies.

Programmed Approach

Regarding the challenge to the preservation of trade secrets posed by the mobile employee, sophisticated management will place its primary reliance on the inculcation of company loyalty in key employees, and on the continual satisfaction of such key employees. For example, management might consider adopting the following five-step basis for developing an overall approach to the challenge:

1. Devise a program for recognition of employee achievement in the trade secret area. At present, this form of recognition is even more neglected than is adequate recognition of employee inventions.

2. Make an appraisal of trade secret activities. This should result in a limitation of (a) personnel with access to trade secrets, (b) the extent of trade secrets available to such personnel, and (c) information which truly deserves the label of trade secret.

3. Review in-house procedures and the use of physical safeguards, such as restrictions on access to certain specified areas and on employee writings for outside publication. Restrictions may tend to stifle creativity by inhibiting communication and interaction conducive to innovation. Striking the balance between too few and too many safeguards is a delicate process and depends on

employee awareness of what is being sought and how it will benefit them.

4. Appraise the legal systems available for the protection of intellectual property. Utility and design patents may be advisable in some cases. The copyright system now offers some protection to certain types of industrial designs and computer software. Trademarks may be adroitly used to maintain markets.

5. Recognize that all efforts may fail to persuade a key employee from leaving. To cope with this contingency, the "gentle persuasion" of a pension or consulting plan in the post-employment period has proved effective and legally sound. A thorough debriefing is a further safeguard. Other cases wherein employee mobility is accompanied by fraud, unfair competition, or theft will be adequately dealt with by the courts.

The problem of the departing employee and the threatened loss of trade secrets is not solved by exhortations that scientists and engineers need courses in professional ethics. Mangement itself should display the standards of conduct expected of its employees and of other companies.

Finally, let me stress again that success probably lies in the inculcation of company loyalty in key employees, not in the enforcement of company desires or in misplaced reliance on the law to subsidize cursory management. Better employee relations—in fact, a total sensitivity to the needs and aspirations of highly educated employees—requires constant management concern. In the long run, total sensitivity will prove less costly and more effective than litigation and the use of questionable contractual restraints.

Trade Secrets, Patents, and Morality

Robert E. Frederick and Milton Snoeyenbos

Suppose that company M develops a supercomputer that gives it a competitive advantage, but decides that, rather than marketing it, it will use the computer to provide services to users. In doing so, it keeps its technical information secret. If another company, N, were to steal the computer, N would be subject to moral blame as well as legal penalty. But suppose that, without M's consent, N obtained M's technical information, which thereby enabled N to copy M's computer. Should N then be subject to moral blame and legal penalty?

At first glance it seems that N should be held morally and legally accountable; but N has a line of defense which supports its position. Information, or knowledge, unlike a physical asset, can be possessed by more than one individual or firm at any one time. Thus, in obtaining M's information N did not diminish M's information; since M possesses exactly the same information it had before, N cannot be said to have stolen it. Furthermore, everyone regards the dissemination of knowledge as a good thing; it has obvious social utility. M's competitive advantage, moreover, was not a good thing, since it could have enabled M to drive other firms out of the computer service business; M might have established a monopoly. Thus, M has no right to keep the information to itself, and, in the interests of social utility, N had a right to obtain M's information. Hence, N should be praised rather than blamed for its act.

This defense of N raises the general question of whether a firm's use of trade secrets or patents to protect information is justifiable. If it is not, then N may at least be morally justified in using clandestine means to obtain M's information. If there is a justification for allowing trade secrets and patents, then, not only is N's act unjustifiable, but we also have a basis for saying that the release of certain information in certain contexts to N by an employee of M is unjustifiable. In this paper we argue that there are both consequentialist and nonconsequentialist reasons for allowing firms to protect *their* proprietary information via patents and trade secrets. On the other hand, an individual has a right to liberty and a right to use *his* knowledge and skills to better himself. These rights place certain constraints on what can qualify as a trade secret or patentable item of information. We begin with a discussion of present patent and trade secret law.

Patents differ significantly from trade secrets. A patent provides a legal safeguard of certain information itself, but the information must be novel. Some internal information generated by a firm may not neet the U.S. Patent Office's standards of inventiveness. Then, too, even if an item is patentable, there may be disadvantages to the firm in seeking and securing a patent on it and/or advantages to the firm in just trying to keep the information secret. There are legal costs in securing a patent, and patents have to be secured in every country in which one wishes to protect the information. In the U.S. a patent expires in 17 years, and, since it is not renewable, the information then becomes public domain. Furthermore, since a patent is a public document, it both reveals research directions and encourages competi-

Reprinted from *Business Ethics*, © 1983 by Milton Snoeyenbos, Robert Almeder, and James Humber, eds., with permission of Prometheus Books, Buffalo, New York.

tors to invent related products that are just dissimilar enough to avoid a patent infringement suit. So there are ample reasons for a firm to keep information secret and not attempt to secure a patent. If a firm can keep the information secret, it may have a long-term advantage over competitors. The disadvantage is that, unlike a patented device or information, the law provides no protection for a trade secret itself. A competitor can analyze an unpatented product in any way, and, if it discovers the trade secret, it is free to use that information or product. For example, if a firm analyzes Coca-Cola and uncovers the secret formula, it can market a product chemically identical to it, although, of course, it cannot use the name "Coca-Cola," since that is protected by trademark law.

It is, however, unlawful to employ "improper means" to secure another's trade secret. Legal protection of trade secrets is based on the agent's duty of confidentiality. Section 395 of the *Restatement of Agency* imposes a duty on the agent "not to use or communicate information confidentially given to him by the principal or acquired by him during the course of or on account of his agency ... to the injury of the principal, on his own account or on behalf of another ... unless the information is a matter of general knowledge." This duty extends beyond the length of the work contract; if the employee moves to a new job with another firm, his obligation to not disclose his previous principal's trade secrets is still in effect.

Since patents are granted by the U.S. Patent Office in accordance with the U.S. Patent Code, patent law cases are federal cases, whereas trade secrets cases are handled by state courts in accordance with state laws. Although there is no definition of "trade secret" adopted by every state, most follow the definition in Section 757 of the *Restatement of Torts*, according to which a trade secret consists of a pattern, device, formula or compilation of information used in business and designed to give the employer an opportunity to obtain an advantage over his com-

petitors who neither know nor use the information. On this definition virtually anything an employer prefers to keep confidential could count as a trade secret.

In practice, however, the *Restatement* specifies several factors it suggests that courts should consider in deciding whether information is legally protectable: (1) the extent to which the information is known outside the business, (2) the extent to which it is known to employees in the firm, (3) the extent to which the firm used measures to guard secrecy of the information, (4) the value of the information to the firm and to its competitors, (5) the amount of money the firm spent to develop the information, and (6) how easily the information may be developed or propery duplicated.

According to (1), (2), (4), (5), and (6), not all internally generated information will count legally as a trade secret. And, via (3), the firm must take measures to guard its secrets: " ... a person entitled to a trade secret ... must not fail to take all proper and reasonable steps to keep it secret. He cannot lie back and do nothing to preserve its essential secret quality, particularly when the subject matter of the process becomes known to a number of individuals involved in its use or is observed in the course of manufacturing in the plain view of others" (*Gallowhur Chemical Corp. v. Schwerdle*, 37 N. J. Super. 385, 397, 117 A2d 416, 423; *J. T. Healy & Son, Inc., v. James Murphy & Son, Inc.*, 1970 Mass. Adv. Sheets 1051, 260 NE2d 723 (Ill. App. 1959)). In addition to attempting to keep its information secret, the firm must inform its employees as to what data are regarded as secret: there "must be a strong showing that the knowledge was gained in confidence," (*Wheelabrator Corp. v. Fogle*, 317 F. Supp. 633 (D. C. La. 1970)), and employees must be warned that certain information is regarded as a trade secret (*Gallo v. Norris Dispensers, Inc.*, 315 F. Supp. 38 (D. C. Mo. 1970)). Most firms have their employees sign a document that (a) specifies what its trade secrets or types of trade secrets are, and (b) informs them that improper use of the trade secrets violates confidentiality and subjects them to litigation.

If a firm has information that really is a legitimate trade secret, if it informs its employees that this information is regarded as secret, and informs them that improper use violates confidentiality, then it may be able to establish its case in court, in which case it is entitled to injunctive relief and damages. But the courts also typically examine how the defendant in a trade secret case obtained the information. For example, if an employee transfers from company M to company N, taking M's documents with him to N, then there is clear evidence of a breach of confidentiality (or "bad faith") if the evidence can be produced by M. But trade secret law is equity law, a basic principle of which is that bad faith cannot be presumed. In equity law the maxim "Every dog has one free bite" obtains, i.e., a dog cannot be presumed to be vicious until he bites someone. Thus, if the employee took no producible hard evidence in the form of objects or documents, but instead took what was "in his head" or what he could memorize, then M may have to wait for its former employee to overtly act. By then it may be very difficult to produce convincing evidence that would establish a breach of confidentiality.

In considering possible justifications of patents and trade secrets, we have to take into consideration the public good or social utility, the firm's rights and interests, and the individual's rights and interests. Our aim should be to maximize utility while safeguarding legitimate rights.

As Michael Baram has noted, "A major concern of our society is progress through the promotion and utilization of new technology. To sustain and enhance this form of progress, it is necessary to optimize the flow of information and innovation all the way from conception to public use."[1] Given the assumption that technological progress is conducive to social utility, and that the dissemination of technological information is a major means to progress, the key issue is how to maximize information generation and dissemination.

One answer is to require public disclosure of all important generated information, and allow unrestricted use of that information. In some cases this is appropriate, e.g., government sponsored research conducted by a private firm is disclosed and can be used by other firms. Within a capitalistic context, however, it is doubtful that a general disclosure requirement would maximize social utility. The innovative firm would develop information leading to a new product only to see that product manufactured and marketed by another firm at a lower price because the latter firm did not incur research costs. The proposal probably would also result in less competition; only firms with strong financial and marketing structures would survive. Small, innovative firms would not have the protection of their technological advantages necessary to establish a competitive position against industry giants. If both research effort and competition were diminished by this proposal, then the "progress" Baram mentions would not be maximized—at least not in the area of marketable products.

In a market economy, then, there are reasons grounded in social utility for allowing firms to have some proprietary information. The laws based on such a justification should, in part, be structured with an eye to overall utility, and in fact they are so structured. Patents, for example, expire in 17 years. While the patent is in force it allows the firm to recoup research expenses and generate a profit by charging monopolistic prices. Patent protection also encourages the generation of new knowledge. The firm holding the patent, and realizing profits because of it, is encouraged to channel some of those profits to research, since its patent is of limited duration. Given that its patent will expire, the firm needs to generate new, patentable information to maximize profits. Competitors are encouraged to develop competing products that are based on new, patentable information.

Patent protection should not, however, extend indefinitely; it would not only extend indefinitely the higher costs that consumers admittedly bear while a patent is in force, but in certain cases, it could also stifle innovation. A firm holding a basic patent might either "sit on" it or strengthen its monopoly position. A company like Xerox, for example, with the basic xerography patent, might use its profits to fund research until it had built up an impenetrable patent network, but then cut reproductive graphics research drastically and rest relatively secure in the knowledge that its competitors were frozen out of the market. Patents allow monopoly profits for a limited period of time, but patent law should not be structured to forever legitimatize a monopoly.

Richard De George has recently offered another argument to the conclusion that the right to proprietary information is a limited right:

> Knowledge is not an object which one can keep locked up as long as one likes. . . . Whatever knowledge a company produces is always an increment to the knowledge developed by society or by previous people in society and passed from one generation to another. Any new invention is made by people who learned a great deal from the general store of knowledge before they could bring what they knew to bear on a particular problem. Though we can attribute them to particular efforts of individuals or teams, therefore, inventions and discoveries also are the result of those people who developed them and passed on their knowledge to others. In this way every advance in knowledge is social and belongs ultimately to society, even though for practical purposes we can assign it temporarily to a given individual or firm.[2]

Allowing the firm to use proprietary information has utility, but the right to such information is limited. In point of fact, although we have stressed the utility of allowing use of proprietary information, U.S. patent and copyright laws were enacted during the industrial revolution to reduce secrecy. Patent laws allow limited monopolies in return for public disclosure of the information on which the patent is based. Thus, patent laws provide information to competitors and encourage them to develop their own patentable information that not only generates new products, but also adds to the store of available knowledge.

If allowing limited use of proprietary information has utility, it is still an open question as to the proper limits of such use. Does the present 17 year patent limit maximize utility? This is an empirical question that we will not attempt to answer. Although most experts and industry representatives believe the present limit is about right, U.S. drug firms have recently argued that research and development time and Federal Drug Administration (FDA) testing and licensing requirements are so extensive that social disutility results, as well as disutility for innovative firms.

Although patents expire and the information protected can then be used by anyone, trade secrets can extend indefinitely according to present law. In 1623, the Zildjian family in Turkey developed a metallurgical process for making excellent cymbals. Now centered in Massachusetts, the family has maintained their secret to the present day, and they still produce excellent cymbals. Preservation of such secrets may well have utility for firms holding the secrets, but does it have social utility? Not necessarily, as the following case illustrates. Suppose that Jones, a shadetree mechanic, develops a number of small unpatentable improvements in the internal combustion engine's basic design. The result is an engine that is cheap, reliable, and gets 120 miles per gallon. With no resources to mass produce and market his engine, Jones decides to sell to the highest bidder. XYZ oil company, with immense oil reserves, buys the information. To protect its oil interests, it keeps the information secret. Now suppose it is in fact against XYZ's interests to divulge the information. Then, to calculate overall utility we have to weigh the social disutility of keeping the information secret against the social utility of keeping the existing oil industry intact. Although utility calculations are difficult, it seems clear that disutility would arise from allowing the information to be kept secret.

If the preservation of *some* secrets has social disutility, it also seems clear that requiring immediate disclosure of *all* trade secrets in a capitalistic context would have disutility as well. The arguments here parallel those we developed in discussing patents. Again, specification of the appropriate duration of a trade secret is a utility calculation. The calculation will, however, have to take into consideration the fact that the law provides no protection for the secret itself. The firm with a significant investment in a trade secret always runs the risk that a competitor may legitimately uncover the use the secret.

Allowing patents and trade secrets has obvious utility for the firm that possesses them, but the firm also has a *right* to at least the limited protection of its information. It has a *legal* right to expect that its employees will live up to their work contracts, and employees have a correlative duty to abide by their contracts. The work contract is entered into voluntarily by employer and employee; if a prospective employee does not like the terms of a (legitimate) trade secret provision of a contract, he does not have to take the job. The normal employment contract specifies that the firm owns all employee-generated information. Even if the employee transfers from firm M to firm N, M still owns the information produced when he was employed there, and the employee is obligated not to reveal that information.

The moral basis of contract enforceability, including contractual provisions for the protection of proprietary information, is twofold. First, as argued, allowing trade secrets has social utility in addition to utility for the firm. The institution of contract compliance is necessary for the systematic and orderly functioning of business, and a sound business environment is essential to general social utility. However, if only a few people broke their contracts, business would continue to survive. This leads to the second moral basis for adhering to the provisions of one's contract.

If an individual breaks his contract, then he must either regard himself as an exception to the rule banning contract-breaking, or he must believe, in Kant's terms, that a maxim concerning contract-breaking is universalizable. But if we agree that in moral matters everyone ought to adopt the moral point of view, and that point of view requires that one not make himself an exception to the rule, it follows that the person in question is not justified in breaking the rule. On the other hand, if he claims that breaking the contract is in accordance with a maxim, then we can properly demand to have the maxim specified. Clearly the maxim cannot be something like: "I will keep my promises, except on those occasions where it is not to my advantage to keep the promises." For if everyone followed this maxim, there would be no institution of promising or promise-keeping. Since the maxim is not universalizable, it cannot legitimately be appealed to as a sanction for action. Of course, other maxims are available, and the contract-breaker may claim that his act is in accordance with one of these maxims. But note that this reply at least tacitly commits the person to the moral point of view; he is agreeing that everyone ought to act only on universalizable maxims. The only dispute, then, is whether his maxim is in fact universalizable. If we can show him that it is not, he is bound to admit that he is not morally justified in breaking the contract. As a standard, then, contracts should be kept, and where an individual breaks, or contemplates breaking, a contract, the burden is on him to produce a universalizable maxim for his action.

Our analysis does not, however, imply that a person is morally obligated to abide by all contracts; some contracts, or provisions of certain contracts, may be morally and/or legally unacceptable. A person does have a right to liberty and a right to use his knowledge and skills to earn a living. Thus, firm M cannot legitimately specify that *all* knowledge an employee gains while at M is proprietary. This would prohibit the person from obtaining employment at another firm; in effect the work contract would amount to a master-slave relationship. As the *Restate-*

ment of Torts appropriately specifies, only certain information qualifies as a legitimate trade secret. Furthermore, the employee brings to his job certain knowledge and skills that typically are matters of public domain, and, on the job, the good employee develops his capacities. As the court noted in *Donahue* v. *Permacil Tape Corporation:* an ex-employee's general knowledge and capabilities "belong to him as an individual for the transaction of any business in which he may engage, just the same as any part of the skill, knowledge, information or education which was received by him before entering the employment.... On terminating his employment, he has a right to take them with him."[3]

Given that an individual's rights to liberty and to use his knowledge and skills to better himself are primary rights, and hence cannot be overriden by utility considerations, the burden clearly is on the firm to: (1) specify to employees what it regards as its trade secrets, and (2) make sure the secrets are legitimate trade secrets. In addition, a company can employ certain pragmatic tactics to protect its trade secrets. It can fragment research activities so that only a few employees know all the secrets. It can restrict access to research data and operational areas. It can develop pension and consulting policies for ex-employees that motivate them not to join competitors for a period of time. More importantly, it can develop a corporate atmosphere that motivates the individual to remain with the firm.

We began by sketching an argument that company N was justified in obtaining information about company M's computer without M's consent. Our conclusion is that N's argument is specious. Utility considerations justify allowing M to keep its information secret for a period of time, and any employee of M who divulges M's secret information to N is morally blameworthy because he violates his contractual obligations to M.

NOTES

1. Michael S. Baram, "Trade Secrets: What Price Loyalty?" *Harvard Business Review,* vol. 46, No. 6 (Nov.–Dec., 1968), pp. 66–74 [reprinted here, pp. 304–311].
2. Richard T. DeGeorge, *Business Ethics* (New York: Macmillan, 1982), p. 207.
3. Cited in Baram, p. 71.

Pierce v. Ortho Pharmaceutical Corporation

Plaintiff, a physician, employed in research by defendant pharmaceutical company, filed a complaint seeking damages resulting from the termination of her employment with defendant, even though such employment was pursuant to an "at-will" relationship. The trial judge granted defendant's motion for summary judgment on the ground that even if plaintiff were constructively discharged and did not actually resign from her employment, by reason of the fact that this was an employment at will, defendant nevertheless had the right to terminate it for any reason whatsoever. This appeal followed....

Plaintiff commenced employment with defendant in May 1971 as Associate Director of Medical Research. The terms of her employment were not fixed by contract. In

399 A.2d. Opinion by Judge Kole, Superior Court of New Jersey, Appellate Division.

March 1973 she became Director of Medical Research/Therapeutics, a section that studied nonreproductive drugs.

One of the projects pursued by plaintiff was development of loperamide, a liquid treatment for acute and chronic diarrhea to be used by infants, children, older persons and those unable to take a solid form of medication. The formulation contained a high concentration of saccharin, apparently 44 times higher than that which is permitted by the Food and Drug Administration in 12 ounces of an artificially sweetened soft drink. It does not appear, however, that there are any promulgated standards for use of saccharin in drugs. At least one of the experts, a Ph.D., employed by defendant indicated that he did not know of any preparation whose saccharin level was as high as that contained in the loperamide formula and that it was "not desirable" to use such an excessively high level for a pediatric formulation.

Plaintiff worked in conjunction with a project team on the loperamide development. At a meeting of the team on March 6, 1975 it was unanimously agreed that the existing loperamide formula, which had apparently been marketed in Europe, was unsuitable for use in the United States due to the unusually high saccharin content. At the time it was felt that an alternate formulation would require at least three months of development.

The team apparently began to receive pressure to proceed with clinical or human testing of the existing formula, and in late March 1975 it finally acceded to the demands of management in this regard. Plaintiff, however, given her status as the only medical person on the team and her responsibility for recommending the drug for clinical use, maintained her opposition to the high saccharin formula, especially in light of indications that an alternative formula would soon be available. She refused to submit a drug containing such a high level of saccharin for clinical testing, as she could not in good conscience give the formula to old people and children in light of saccharin's potential carcinogenic attributes. She felt that such refusal was required by the Hippocratic Oath.

After indicating that she was unable to pursue clinical testing for the foregoing reasons, plaintiff was relieved of this project and informed by her supervisor, also a physician, that she was being demoted. He advised her that notice of this demotion would be posted. She was also told that she was considered nonpromotable, irresponsible and lacking in judgment, and that she had exhibited unacceptable productivity, inability to work with marketing people and failure to behave as a Director. She had not received such criticism from her supervisor before.

Plaintiff thereafter resigned, feeling that she was being punished for refusing to perform a task which she considered to be unethical. The resignation was accepted.

This action followed. Plaintiff sought to recover damages resulting from the termination of her employment. Essentially, the complaint alleged that because of defendant's actions she sustained damage to her professional reputation, interruption of her career, forfeiture of interesting and remunerative employment, monetary loss, deprivation of retirement benefits, loss of four years' seniority, physical and mental distress, and pain and suffering, and other damage was sustained by her and the public; that defendant breached its contract in refusing to permit her to use her expertise, skills and best medical judgment; that defendant, by its actions, violated plaintiff's property right in the form of her expertise and skill in medical and pharmaceutical research; that defendant interfered with plaintiff's employment contract and relationships, and that defendant violated and interfered with plaintiff's right to object to the appropriate regulatory bodies, presumably with regard to the safety of loperamide, the drug with which plaintiff had previously been working.

The trial judge denied defendant's summary judgment motion to the extent that it was based on plaintiff's written resignation, since there was a fact issue as to whether she was, in fact, induced to resign by defendant's actions. This determination is not assailed on this appeal and was proper. However, the judge did grant the summary judgment predicated on his conclusion that under New Jersey law there was no showing that the rule relating to at-will private employees did not apply—namely, that such an employment may be terminated at the will of either employer or employee, with or without justification, in the absence of a contractual or statutory provision to the contrary. . . .

The trial judge held that even if the facts could be construed to indicate that plaintiff was constructively discharged—that is, she resigned by reason of wrongful acts of defendant employer—defendant, nonetheless, had the right to terminate her employment for any reason whatsoever. The judge acknowledged the existence in other jurisdictions of an exception to that rule as to termination of at-will employment when the motivation therefore contravened public policy. He stated that it may be that "public policy will develop to a degree that professionals, even though employees at will, will be permitted to resist what they consider to be a professionally unsound and unethical decision without fear of demotion or discharge." He was of the view that that question had to be decided by the Supreme Court, rather than a trial judge. In any event, he found plaintiff's case to be distinguishable from the out-of-state cases permitting relief on public policy grounds, and that "even if plaintiff's termination [is considered] in the light that it has been presented by the plaintiff, the most that can be said is that she was discharged because of a conflict in a medical viewpoint concerning the advisability of testing the drug loperamide."

We reverse and remand for a trial on all of the issues raised by the pleadings.

This case presents a novel question in this State relating to relief for wrongful discharge of an employee at will where the termination involves a claimed violation of public policy. . . . We note in this regard that a growing minority of jurisdictions has created an exception to the traditional employment at-will rule, which generally bars an action for wrongful discharge, so as to permit recovery where the employment termination contravenes a clear mandate of public policy. . . .

This new doctrine seems particularly pertinent to professional employees whose activities might involve violations of ethical or like standards having a substantial impact on matters of public interest, including health and safety.

Arguably, the time may have arrived to permit recovery, predicated either on a theory of contract or of tort, for the terminated at-will employee where the circumstances involving the discharge contravene a clear and important public policy. We do not now decide whether any such new doctrine should be adopted in this State or whether this case presents the appropriate vehicle in which to determine that question.

[1] We note that a public policy exception would represent a departure from the well-settled common law employment-at-will rule. If such a departure is to be made, care is required in order to insure that the reasons underlying the rule will not be undermined. Most notably in this regard, the employer's legitimate interests in conducting his business and employing and retaining the best personnel available cannot be unjustifiably impaired. Thus, it cannot change the present rule which holds that just or good cause for the discharge of an employee at will or the giving of reasons therefore are not required. [citations omitted] In addition the exception must guard against a potential flood of unwarranted disputes and litigation that might result from such a doctrine, based on vague notions of public policy. Hence, if there is to be such an exception to the at-will employment rule, it must be tightly circumscribed so as to apply only in cases involving truly significant matters of clear and well-defined public policy and substantial violations thereof. If it is to be established at all, its development must be on a case-to-case basis.

For these reasons, the adoption of any such new doctrine must be grounded in a specific factual and legal context resulting from a plenary hearing, at which the proofs and public policy considerations involved will be fully developed and taken into account in the final determination. As indicated, we express no views on this issue. The matter should be decided in the first instance by the trial court after a hearing.

We merely hold that the grant of the summary judgment here was premature and a determination of the significant novel question projected by plaintiff, with respect to which such judgment was granted, should have been based upon a full record at a trial. Only in this fashion may the trial court, and if necessary, an appellate court render an appropriate decision on the issue thus presented. . . .

[2] The present record cannot serve as the predicate for determining whether the exception should be adopted and, if so, whether it should be applied in this case. For example, we are satisfied that, using the standard applicable to a summary judgment motion, the court below erred in finding that, even if there were public policy reasons which might be relevant to plaintiff's discharge, "the most that can be said is that she was discharged because of a conflict in a medical viewpoint concerning the advisability of testing the drug loperamide." There is a genuine fact issue as to that matter. Moreover, the question of whether plaintiff resigned or was constructively discharged, which remains unresolved, appears to be so intertwined with that relating to whether a public policy exception should be adopted and applied here, that it is desirable that both issues be tried and determined at a plenary hearing.

Additionally, we note that the instant case seems to implicate (1) an endeavor to compel a physician to violate what appears to be a reasonably supportable ethical standard and (2) the safety of the public in connection with the testing of drugs. If the court decides that plaintiff was discharged, unless the proofs at trial indicate otherwise, the determination of whether relief should be granted by reason of a substantial violation of a clear matter of public policy would be limited to that factual pattern. In ruling on whether a public policy exception should be adopted and applied here, the court may have to determine whether a bona fide dispute between a physician and her superior, also a physician, as to medical ethics relating to a matter of public health and safety is an appropriate consideration under the facts developed at trial. The court may also wish to consider, in addition to the Hippocratic Oath relied on by plaintiff as the ethical standard to which she claims to have adhered, the statutory provisions as to licensing of, and governing, physicians. . . .

Reversed and remanded for trial. We do not retain jurisdiction.

Futurecraft Corp. v. Clary Corp.

This is an unfair competition action brought by Futurecraft Corporation (hereinafter referred to as Futurecraft) for an injunction, damages and an accounting against a former employee, Roderick Koutnik (hereinafter referred to as Koutnik) and Koutnik's new employer, Clary Corporation (hereinafter referred to as Clary), for the wrongful use and disclosure of certain valve designs claimed to be confidential to and the trade secrets of

205 C.A.2d 279. Opinion by Judge J. Fourt.

Futurecraft. Futurecraft appeals from a judgment in favor of both defendants entered by the court below after a trial limited by that court to the following issue: "What, if any, trade secret, embraced within the issues as established by the pleadings, stipulations and pretrial order, *became entrusted to the defendant Roderick Koutnik while he was an employee of the plaintiff?*" (Emphasis added.) . . .

. . . The basis of plaintiff's claim for relief is, as set forth in the opening brief, "(1) that the various *design features* are protectible trade secrets, as such, and (2) that, at any rate, Koutnik had expressly agreed that he would not utilize these designs (and particularly the paragraph V design) in competition with Futurecraft." (Emphasis added.)

Futurecraft and Clary are, and since at least 1953 or early 1954 have been, competitors in the design, manufacture and sale of valves and valve components for guided missiles and rockets for the defense program of the United States. Koutnik was employed by Futurecraft during three separate periods (part-time from 1949 to 1951, and full-time from July 1, 1951, to April 25, 1952, and from January 31, 1953, to March 17, 1956) for the purpose of inventing, designing and developing such valves and valve components.

Koutnik had been employed by the California Institute of Technology at its Jet Propulsion Laboratory from September 15, 1947, to May 11, 1951, and from April 28, 1952, to January 25, 1953.

The trial court stated in his memorandum of decision (footnote 1, par. IX) that when Koutnik entered the employ of Futurecraft, "he carried with him a good deal of knowledge concerning the art, science and mechanics of valve design and manufacture, and a good deal of skill in the application of that knowledge . . . [and that] [m]uch, probably most, of that knowledge had been acquired at the Jet Propulsion Laboratory of the California Institute of Technology. . . . "

The particular valve designs forming the subject matter of this action . . . consist of two types of valve mechanisms. . . . The in-

formation alleged by Futurecraft to be confidential to it consists of a number of specific design features of the respective valves. . . .

It is appropriately stated in appellant's opening brief:

" . . . this Court will be presented with two basically divergent approaches, or viewpoints, on this definitional problem. The defendants successfully urged the trial court to adopt a rigidly narrow and absolutist view, based upon a concept that a trade secret must be 'an item of private property' and that one can have no 'property rights' in an idea if someone else—anyone else—knows about it.

"In contrast to defendants' property rights concept, plaintiff urged below and urges here a more realistic, equitable and common sense approach (which is widely accepted and applied in other jurisdictions), based upon the Restatement view that a trade secret may consist of anything which is '. . . used in one's business, and which gives him an opportunity to obtain an advantage over *competitors who do not know or use it. . . .* ' (Emphasis added.) Rest., Torts, § 757, Comment b."

[1a] Before turning to the "definitional problem" of what constitutes a trade secret, it is well to mention a basic underlying problem, namely, the legal basis upon which plaintiff predicates its right to relief. This problem stems from the fact that ownership of a trade secret does not give the owner a monopoly in its use, but merely a proprietary right which equity protects against usurpation by unfair means. . . .

" ' . . . The employer thus has the burden of showing two things: (1) a legally protectable trade secret; *and* (2) *a legal basis,* either a covenant or a confidential relationship, *upon which to predicate relief.*' " (Emphasis added.)

The case of *Wexler* v. *Greenberg, supra,* 160 A.2d 430, deals primarily with the "legal basis . . . upon which to predicate relief" problem. In many respects the *Wexler* case aptly illustrates the situation presented in the case at bar.

In *Wexler,* defendant Greenberg was a

qualified chemist in the sanitation and maintenance field. In March of 1949 he was employed by plaintiff as its chief chemist and continued there for approximately eight years. In the performance of his duties he spent approximately half of his working time in plaintiff's laboratory where he would analyze and duplicate competitor's products and then use the resulting information to develop various new formulas. In August 1957 defendant Greenberg left plaintiff and went to work for defendant corporation. Plaintiff sought to enjoin the defendants from disclosing and using certain formulas and processes pertaining to the manufacture of certain sanitation and maintenance chemicals which plaintiff claimed to be its trade secrets. The Chancellor found that the formulas constituted trade secrets and that their appropriation was in violation of the duty that Greenberg owed to plaintiff by virtue of his employment and the trust reposed in him.

The Supreme Court of Pennsylvania assumed that certain of the formulas were trade secrets of the plaintiff but reversed and stated in pertinent part as follows:

"[2] We are initially concerned with the fact that the final formulations claimed to be trade secrets were not *disclosed to* Greenberg by the appellees during his service or because of his position. [Italics shown.] Rather, the fact is that these formulas had been developed by Greenberg himself, while in the pursuit of his duties as Buckingham's [i.e., plaintiff] chief chemist, or under Greenberg's direct supervision. We are thus faced with the problem of determining the extent to which a former employer, *without the aid of any express covenant* [italics shown], can restrict his ex-employee, a highly skilled chemist, in the uses to which this employee can put his knowledge of formulas and methods he himself developed during the course of his former employment because this employer claims these same formulas, as against the rest of the world, as his trade secrets. *This problem becomes particularly signifi-*

cant when one recognizes that Greenberg's situation is not uncommon. In this era of electronic, chemical, missile and atomic development, many skilled technicians and expert employees are currently in the process of developing potential trade secrets. Competition for personnel of this caliber is exceptionally keen, and the interchange of employment is commonplace. One has but to reach for his daily newspaper to appreciate the current market for such skilled employees. *We must therefore be particularly mindful of any effect our decision in this case might have in disrupting this pattern of employee mobility, both in view of possible restraints upon an individual in the pursuit of his livelihood and the harm to the public in general in forestalling to any extent widespread technological advances.*" (P. 433.) (Emphasis added.) . . .

"The usual situation involving misappropriation of trade secrets in violation of a confidential relationship is one in which an employer *discloses to his employee* a pre-existing trade secret (one already developed or formulated) so that the employee may duly perform his work. . . . In such a case the trust and confidence upon which legal relief is predicated stems from the instance of the employer's *turning over to the employee* the pre-existing trade secret. [Italics shown.] It is then that a pledge of secrecy is impliedly extracted from the employee, a pledge which he carries with him even beyond the ties of his employment relationship. Since it is conceptually impossible, however, to elicit an implied pledge of secrecy from the sole act of an employee turning over to his employer a trade secret which he, the employee, has developed, as occurred in the present case, the appellees must show a different manner in which the present circumstances support the permanent cloak of confidence cast upon Greenberg by the Chancellor. The only avenue open to the appellees is to show that the nature of the employment relationship itself gave rise to a duty of nondisclosure.

"The burden the appellees must thus meet brings to the fore a problem of accommodating competing policies in our law: the right of a businessman to be protected against unfair competition stemming from the usurpation of his trade secrets and the right of an individual to the unhampered pursuit of the occupations and livelihoods for which he is best suited. There are cogent socio-economic arguments in favor of either position. Society as a whole greatly benefits from technological improvements. Without some means of post-employment protection to assure that valuable developments or improvements are exclusively those of the employer, the businessman could not afford to subsidize research or improve current methods. In addition, it must be recognized that modern economic growth and development has pushed the business venture beyond the size of the one-man firm, forcing the businessman to a much greater degree to entrust confidential business information relating to technological development to appropriate employees. While recognizing the utility in the dispersion of responsibilities in larger firms, the optimum amount of "entrusting" will not occur unless the risk of loss to the businessman through a breach of trust can be held to a minimum.

"On the other hand, any form of post-employment restraint reduces the economic mobility of employees and limits their personal freedom to pursue a preferred course of livelihood. The employee's bargaining position is weakened because he is potentially shackled by the acquisition of alleged trade secrets; and thus, paradoxically, he is restrained, because of his increased expertise, from advancing further in the industry in which he is most productive. Moreover, as previously mentioned, society suffers because competition is diminished by slackening the dissemination of ideas, processes and methods." (Pp. 434–435.) . . .

The court concluded that Greenberg was privileged to disclose and use the formulas which he had developed—they being a part of the technical knowledge and skill that he had acquired by virtue of his employment (p.

437). Therefore, even though the formulas were plaintiff's trade secrets, Greenberg was privileged to use them.

It is apparent that the trial judge in the case at bar did give careful consideration to the "legal basis . . . upon which to predicate relief" problem even though he ultimately held that there was no trade secret. This is evident from the trial court's framing of the issue to be: "What, if any, trade secret . . . became entrusted to the defendant Roderick Koutnik while he was an employee of the plaintiff" and by what was stated in paragraph IX of the notice of decision. . . .

Appellant asserts in its reply brief that the fact that Koutnik utilized knowledge and skill which he obtained at Jet Propulsion Laboratory in developing the Paragraph V valve design is immaterial. While it might well be immaterial on the "definitional problem" of what constitutes a trade secret, it is material on the "legal basis . . . upon which to predicate relief" phase of the problem. In other words, as illustrated by the *Wexler* case, *supra,* plaintiff may well have a trade secret yet defendant Koutnik be privileged to use it by virtue of there being no covenant or breach of confidence. . . .

. . . The court cannot compel a man who changes employers to wipe clean the slate of his memory. . . . To grant plaintiff the relief prayed for would in effect restrain Koutnik from the pursuit of his profession. He would be deprived of the use of knowledge and skill which he gained which did not originate with plaintiff. . . .

Mr. Julian O. von Kalinowski in an excellent article entitled "Key Employees and Trade Secrets" in 47 Virginia Law Review 583 states in the conclusion of the article at page 599:

"Protection should be afforded when, and only when, the information in question has value in the sense that it affords the plaintiff [i.e., ex-employer] a competitive advantage over competitors who do not know of it [i.e., the trade secret], *and where the granting of such protection will not unduly hamstring the ex-em-*

ployee in the practice of his occupation or profession. This simple balancing process will invariably protect all of the pertinent interests—those of the former employer, of the former employee, and of the public." (Emphasis added.) ...

The appellant's remaining contentions either have already been dealt with or are without merit.

For the reasons stated the judgment is affirmed.

CASE 1. Jobs and Controversy

Philip Washburn, supervisor of urban affairs at a Pennsylvania plant of Mammoth Steel Corporation, was fired by his employer after local newspaper articles identified him as a member of the city's Civic League, a volunteer group that studied various social problems of the city where Mr. Washburn worked and lived. The newspaper described a report by the League that asserted that the relatively higher dropout rate among the city's black high school population was caused by limited local employment opportunities and that major employers in the area still had some way to go before they met reasonable affirmative action goals in both blue-collar and white-collar hiring and promotion. Mammoth Steel was the largest employer in the city and one of only two or three companies that could be called "major employers" there. A spokesman for Mammoth promptly issued a statement calling attention to Mammoth's "long-standing policy of nondiscrimination."

The president of Mammoth Steel later explained, in answer to a question raised at the annual stockholders meeting, that Mr. Washburn was not experienced in personnel matters and that the company believed there was a risk he might be regarded as speaking for Mammoth at the Civic League. Mr. Washburn, a white, 43-year-old father of three, whose job had involved the company's relations with various departments of the city government, replied to a reporter that he

had made it clear "several times" he was acting on his own, as a private citizen, in the Civic League.

At about the time Mr. Washburn's case came to public notice, the *Wall Street Journal* news staff learned of two similar incidents. One concerned a 32-year-old lawyer who resigned from the most prestigious law firm in a large, older Alabama city after he wrote a letter to the Alabama superintendent of education protesting a state move to make Bible reading a regular part of the state-required curriculum. The young lawyer argued that this would defy the U.S. Supreme Court's ban on classroom prayers in public schools. The state superintendent mailed a copy of his reply to the partners of the young man's law firm, "because," said the superintendent, "they're acquaintances of mine and I thought they should know about it."

The young man told the *Wall Street Journal* that "it was generally felt in the city that people shouldn't get involved in things like that. The feeling was enhanced if you were on the 'wrong' side of an issue. I wasn't asked to leave, but after that I decided I had a better future elsewhere." A partner in the law firm said it would be "professionally improper" for him to comment on the resignation.

Another such incident involved activity at the opposite end of the political spectrum. An executive of a Midwestern advertising agency resigned after his superiors ordered

This case was prepared by the Committee for Education in Business Ethics under a grant from the National Endowment for the Humanities.

him to quit making speeches on Communist propaganda techniques. "They said the talks were right-wing, controversial, and bad for the agency," he recalled. "I disagreed with the right-wing part. I quit because I felt no one could tell me what to do with my own time."

The *Wall Street Journal* saw these as a crop of events worth investigating and went in search of executives who would comment on the occurrences. Most of the business officials interviewed claimed that their companies placed no limits on outside views or group membership of employees other than the obvious one of frowning upon illegal activities. There was general agreement, also, that an employee is liable for dismissal if outside interests interfere with his work.

Some executives candidly admitted, however, that their views were more restrictive. Said an official of a large New York metals processor:

> We assume that people who hold higher jobs here won't do or say anything that might reflect negatively on the company, like speak for some radical political outfit or get tossed in jail for civil disobedience. If a customer doesn't like our product, okay. But we'd hate to lose out because someone doesn't like one of our men's ideas.

The chairman of the board of a large industrial conglomerate went further and told how his firm tried to avoid ever having to defend or dismiss an employee for community activity:

> We don't try to tell employees what they can or can't do off the job, but we pick them carefully to begin with. Among other things, we don't go looking for people who'll go out looking for trouble.

Questions

1. Should an employee have the right in his or her role of private citizen to criticize his or her employer?
2. Should an employee be fired for belonging to a group that is critical of his or her employer?
3. Should an employer have the right to forbid an employee from belonging to any civic or social group, for example, the American Civil Liberties Union or the Ku Klux Klan?
4. Should membership in civic or social groups be considered relevant in making hiring decisions?

CASE 2. Catching a Thief by Honesty Exams

Employee theft is a serious problem. The American Management Association estimates that as many as 20 percent of the firms that go out of business do so because of employee theft. Since the polygraph or lie detector has been restricted in at least twenty states, a number of firms have turned to honesty tests. As described in the *Wall Street Journal,* the tests are given in the employer's office, take about an hour, and are relatively cheap, at $6 to $14 a test. Among the questions on the test are the following: What's your favorite alcoholic drink? Which drugs have you tried? Did you ever make a false

---

Case prepared by Norman Bowie.

insurance claim? Do you blush often? Have you ever gotten really angry at someone for being unfair to you?[1] Let us assume that the questions are statistically correlated with employee theft, that the tests are administered by the test manufacturer, and that persons failing the test are given an opportunity to establish their innocence on other grounds.

Many employees answer the questions openly, and many provide damaging information. As one corporate spokesperson said, "You become amazed at how many people believe it is acceptable conduct to steal just a little bit, maybe 50 cents, maybe a dollar a day."

Nonetheless, the tests have come under severe criticism from some unions, some lawyers, and the American Civil Liberties Union. They criticize many of the questions as non-job-related and as violations of rights of privacy. Others find the use of the tests intimidating.

1. *Wall Street Journal*, August 3, 1981.

Questions

1. Does the test violate an employee's right to privacy? Could a test be devised that didn't?
2. Is it a violation of an employee's right to privacy if the lie detector is used to catch thieves, that is, if the questions asked the employee relate solely to thefts that have actually occurred?
3. Suppose that data analysis indicates that 80 percent of the employees who steal from their employers blush often but that only 10 percent of those who do not steal blush often. If an employee who takes the tests blushes, should we conclude he has stolen from the employer?
4. Would it violate employee rights for a firm to use one-way mirrors or management "plants" among employees in order to catch thieves?

CASE 3. Whistleblowing—Alpha Corporation

You are purchasing manager for Alpha Corporation. You are responsible for buying two $1 million generators. Your company has a written policy prohibiting any company buyer from receiving a gratuity in excess of $50 and requiring that all gratuities be reported. The company has no company policy regarding *whistleblowing*. A salesperson for a generator manufacturer offers to arrange it so that you can buy a $12,000 car for $4,000. The car would be bought from a third party. You decline the offer.

Questions

1. If you reported the offer to your superior, would your action count as whistleblowing?
2. If you reported the offer to your salesperson's superior, would your action count as whistleblowing or is it merely tattling?
3. Should Alpha Corporation have a rule requiring that you report such offers to your superior?
4. Should Alpha Corporation have a policy of informing a buyer's company when a buyer makes offers like those described in the case?

This case was prepared by the Committee for Education in Business Ethics under a grant from the National Endowment for the Humanities.

CASE 4. Old Secrets in a New Job

William Stapleton, a chemical engineer with considerable experience in offset printing processes, had been hired recently as an engineering supervisor in Western Chemical's Printing Products Division. Until then he had been employed as a research chemist by a competing firm and during the past two years had personally developed a new formula and manufacturing process for press blankets. The new blanket was now on the market and was gaining an increasing share of the market for Stapleton's former employer.

In the offset process, the rubber blanket cylinder on the press receives the image from the inked printing plate and transfers this image to the paper. The blanket is thus an important determinant of printing quality. Stapleton's formula and manufacturing process resulted in a blanket which not only produced superior quality but also gave longer wear, reducing the cost of materials and the cost of press down-time for blanket changes.

Western executives who had interviewed Stapleton had made no mention to him of the new offset blanket. They had indicated it was his managerial potential which interested them since the company was expanding and would soon need many more managers with scientific experience than were presently available. Stapleton had been anxious to move out of the laboratory and into management work for some time, but his former employer had not afforded him the opportunity.

The responsibilities of supervision and administration had brought Stapleton to grips with new kinds of problems, as he had hoped would be the case. One problem, however, currently sitting on his desk in the form of a memo from George Curtis, the Division's director of Engineering, was giving him particular concern. It read as follows:

> Please see me this afternoon for the purpose of discussing formulas and manufacturing processes for offset press blankets.

This was the first reference anyone had made to the use of specific past technical information in his new job. Stapleton realized he would have to decide immediately to what extent he would reveal data concerning the secret processes being used by his former employer.

Questions

1. Is the new formula and manufacturing process for press blankets the kind of trade secret that should be protected?
2. Suppose an employee knew quite a lot about the manufacturing process, but did not know the new formula. If the employee gave Western Chemical his knowledge of the manufacturing process, would that violate a legitimate trade secret?
3. Would Stapleton violate a trade secret if his new employer were in a noncompetitive industry?
4. Is Stapleton morally obligated to refuse the information to Western Chemical, even if his refusal would cost him his job?

Case prepared by William McInnes, S.J., Fairfield University. Reprinted by permission.

Suggested Supplementary Readings

Rights, Responsibilities, and the Employment Relationship

Blades, Lawrence E. "Employment At Will vs. Individual Liberty: On Limiting the Abusive Exercise of Employment Power." *Columbia Law Review* 67 (1967): 1404–1435.

Cherrington, David J. *The Work Ethic: Working Values and Values That Work.* New York: Amacom, 1980.

Doerfer, Gordon L. "The Limits of Trade Secret Law Imposed by Federal Patent and Antitrust Supremacy." *Harvard Law Review* 80 (1967): 1432–1462.

Donaldson, Thomas. *Corporations and Morality,* chapter 7. Englewood Cliffs, N.J.: Prentice-Hall, 1982.

Ewing, David W. *Freedom Inside the Organization: Bringing Civil Liberties to the Workplace.* New York: E. P. Dutton, 1977.

———."What Business Thinks About Employee Rights." *Harvard Business Review* 55 (September–October 1977).

Holloway, William J. "Fired Employees Challenging Terminable-At-Will Doctrine." *The National Law Journal* (February 19, 1979): 22.

Jackson, Dudley. *Unfair Dismissal: How and Why the Law Works.* Cambridge: Cambridge University Press, 1975.

Lansing, Paul, and Richard Pegnetter. "Fair Dismissal Procedures for Non-Union Employees." *American Business Law Journal* 20 (Spring 1982).

Linowes, David, F. "Is Business Giving Employees Privacy?" *Business and Society Review* 32 (Winter 1979–80): 47–49.

Mason, Ronald M. *Participatory and Workplace Democracy.* Carbondale, Ill.: Southern Illinois University Press, 1982.

Nickel, James. "Is There a Human Right to Employment?" *Philosophical Forum* 10 (Summer 1978–Winter 1979).

Powers, Charles W. "Individual Dignity and Institutional Identity: The Paradoxical Needs of the Corporate Employee." In *The Work Ethic In Business,* edited by W. Michael Hoffman and Thomas J. Wyly. Cambridge, Mass.: Oelgeschlager, Gunn & Hain, 1981.

"Protecting At-Will Employees Against Wrongful Discharge: The Duty to Terminate Only in Good Faith." *Harvard Law Review* 93 (June 1980): 1816–1844.

Snoeyenbos, Milton, et al., eds. *Business Ethics,* chapters 3–5. Buffalo: Prometheus Books, 1982.

Stevens, George E. "The Legality of Discharging Employees for Insubordination." *American Business Law Journal* 18 (Fall 1980): 371–389.

Summers, C. "Individual Protection Against Unjust Dismissal: Time for a Statute." *Virginia Law Review* 62 (April 1976): 481–532.

Werhane, Patricia. "Accountability And Employee Rights." *International Journal of Applied Philosophy* 1 (Spring 1983): 15–26.

———. *Persons, Rights, and Corporations.* Englewood Cliffs, N.J.: Prentice-Hall, 1985.

Westin, Alan F. and Stephan Salisbury. *Individual Rights in the Corporation. A Reader on Employee Rights.* New York: Pantheon, 1980.

Whistleblowing and the Duty of Loyalty

Baron, Marcia. *The Moral Status of Loyalty.* Module Series in Applied Ethics. Dubuque, Iowa: Kendall/Hunt, 1984.

Blumberg, Philip. "Corporate Responsibility and the Employee's Duty of Loyalty and Obedience." *Oklahoma Law Review* 24 (August 1971).

Bok, Sissela. "Whistleblowing and Professional Responsibility." *New York Education Quarterly* 4 (1980): 2–7.

Bowie, Norman. *Business Ethics,* chapter 7. Englewood Cliffs, N.J.: Prentice-Hall, 1982.

Bowman, James, et al., *Professional Dissent.* New York: Garland, 1983.

DeGeorge, Richard T. *Business Ethics,* chapter 9. New York: Macmillan, 1982.

Elliston, Frederick. "Anonymity and Whistleblowing." *Journal of Business Ethics* 1 (August 1982).

———. "Anonymous Whistleblowing: A Conceptual and Ethical Analysis." *Business and Professional Ethics Journal* 1 (Winter 1982).

Elliston, Frederick, et al., *Whistleblowing and Whistleblowing Research.* 2 Vols. New York: Praeger, 1985.

Hirschman, Albert L. *Exit, Voice, and Loyalty.* Cambridge, Mass.: Harvard University Press, 1970.

Ladd, John. "Loyalty." Vol. 5 in *The Encyclopedia of Philosophy.* New York: Free Press, 1967.

Nader, Ralph, Peter J. Petkas, and Kate Blackwell, eds. *Whistle Blowing: The Report of the Conference on Professional Responsibility.* New York: Grossman, 1972.

Peters, Charles, and Taylor Branch. *Blowing the Whistle: Dissent in the Public Interest.* New York: Pineger, 1972.

Peterson, James C., and Dan Farrell. *Whistleblowing.* Module Series in Applied Ethics. Dubuque, Iowa: Kendall/Hunt, 1985.

Walters, K. "Your Employees' Right to Blow the Whistle." *Harvard Business Review* 53 (July–August 1975): 26 ff.

Weisband, Edward, and Thomas M. Frank. *Resignation in Protest.* New York: Grossman, 1975.

Trade Secrets and the Duty of Confidentiality

American Law Institute, Restatement of Torts (1939), No. 757.

Bok, Sissela. "Trade and Corporate Secrecy." In *Secrets.* New York: Random House, 1983.

Doerfer, Gordon L. "The Limits of Trade Secret Law Imposed by Federal Patent and Antitrust Supremacy." *Harvard Law Review,* 80 (1967): 1432–1462.

Milgrim, Roger M. *Protecting and Profiting from Trade Secrets.* New York: Practicing Law Institute, 1979.

———. *Trade Secrets.* New York: Matthew Bender, 1978.

Novotny, Eric J. *Who Owns Your Ideas?* Module Series in Applied Ethics. Dubuque, Iowa: Kendall/Hunt, 1985.

Stevenson, Russell B. *Corporations and Information: Secrecy, Access, and Disclosure.* Baltimore, Johns Hopkins University Press, 1980.

CHAPTER SIX

Discrimination and Employment Practices

INTRODUCTION

For years blacks, women, and other minority groups faced barriers deliberately placed to limit their participation in some of America's most desirable institutions of education, business, and law. Even when the barriers were formally dropped, matters often did not improve for some groups. At this writing no black has ever been chief executive of a Fortune 500 company, and none seems close. Critics have charged that our systems of screening and promotion discriminate not intentionally *against* certain groups so much as unintentionally *in favor of* other groups. Because of the history of discrimination and its persistence in the United States, it is widely believed that justice demands making it easier for previously discriminated-against groups to obtain admission to educational institutions and jobs.

In recent years policies that use target goals, timetables, and quotas intended to ensure more equitable opportunities for women and minority groups have provoked sustained controversy. These policies seem to many citizens to be preferential treatment that discriminate in their own right and sometimes even create a situation of "reverse discrimination": By compensating for past discrimination against persons on the basis of race,

sex, nationality, or religion, a policy may require discrimination against many individuals who never discriminated in the past—namely white males. Although these policies seem unfairly discriminatory to some, others believe that they are absolutely essential to the elimination of discrimination.

Contemporary controversy has centered on whether pressure not to discriminate is appropriate through the use of *affirmative action* programs, *reverse dscrimination,* and the principle of *comparable worth*. It is sometimes said in popular literature that affirmative action is synonymous with reverse discrimination, and that both are preferential practices. Treatment of these terms as synonymous can, however, be misleading, as we shall see.

DEFINING THE PRIMARY CONCEPTS

Not all forms of discrimination in employment are unjustified. For example, federal regulations prohibit pilots or co-pilots from continuing in their jobs beyond age 60, on grounds that age is *relevant* to performance and safety. Here use of age to demote pilots is not a form of age bias or unjustified discrimination by an employer, because there is a good reason for age discrimination. However, in 1986, Trans-World Airlines, American Airlines, Western Airlines, and United Airlines were all sued for age bias on grounds that they not only demoted pilots at age 60 but forced them to retire.[1] Federal rules clearly state that a pilot may continue beyond 60 as a flight engineer, the third member of the cabin crew. The reason for the different rules for pilots and flight engineers is that age is relevant to a pilot's performance but not to the performance of a flight engineer. That is, age is an *irrelevant* property of the person in the case of a flight engineer. In most of the controversies discussed in this chapter, it is alleged that race, sex, age, religion, and so on, are irrelevant properties that some person X has *unjustifiably made relevant,* and therefore X is invidiously discriminating and must be stopped from doing so. The difference between relevant and irrelevant properties is essential to understanding the meanings of the basic concepts in this chapter.

Affirmative Action. The term *"affirmative action"* refers primarily to the taking of positive steps to hire persons from groups whose members were previously discriminated against using irrelevant properties in situations of admission and employment. Passive nondiscrimination is thus not sufficient to qualify as affirmative action. Federal requirements have, in the last two decades or so, imposed on business the responsibility to advertise jobs fairly and to promote the hiring of members of groups discriminated against in the past on the basis of irrelevant properties such as race, age, and sex. The projected means for the fulfillment of these responsibilities are generally called employment *goals.* A "goal" in this context is a targeted employment outcome (intended ultimately to eliminate the vestiges of discrimination) planned by an institution. Goals have often resulted from consultation with government officials, but may be entirely voluntary or negotiated with labor or courts.

A goal is commonly distinguished from a *quota,* which is construed as a hard and fast figure or proportion—usually expressed in percentages. For example, in a much-discussed case, in 1978 the city of Indianapolis voluntarily (through a consent-decree process) agreed to fill at least 25 percent of its police and firefighter training classes with black applicants and in 1979 agreed to appoint women to at least 20 percent of police training classes. Goals and quotas sound to many ears like identical items, but there is a crucial symbolic, even if not substantive difference between them. Goals have come largely to symbolize mandated or negotiated targets and timetables, whereas quotas have come to symbolize policies resulting in reverse discrimination. But this loose identification is of little help until we understand reverse discrimination and how it differs from both affirmative action and preferential hiring.

Reverse Discrimination. Writers on the subject of discrimination have used the term *reverse discrimination* in different ways. At a minimum this term means discrimination that favors a *less qualified* person or persons on the grounds that the group to which the person belongs was previously discriminated against. Some also assert or assume that, by definition, reverse discrimination occurs only as a result of policies involving blanket preferential treatment on the basis of sex or race for *whole groups* of persons who are members of those classes. However this blanket conception of reverse discrimination is questionable on at least two counts. First, properties other than race or sex—for example, religion or nationality—may be used. Second, and more importantly, there is no reason why (by definition) a policy of compensation resulting in a reversal of discrimination must apply to whole groups rather than more restrictedly to a select number of subsets of persons who are members of those groups. Suppose an industrywide preferential policy were adopted that gave a competitive advantage to the job applications of the class of *blacks earning less than $10,000 per year* (and that discriminated against competitive whites earning equivalent amounts) but did not give an advantage to blacks earning more than that figure. This policy would qualify as reverse discrimination (based on race), but the entire racial group would not have been given blanket preferential treatment.

In sum, reverse discrimination is a discriminatory action or practice based on a (normally) morally irrelevant property, on the grounds that the group to which the person belongs was previously discriminated against. Policies resulting in reverse discrimination may apply to individual persons or select subgroups and need not involve unqualified blanket preferential treatment. Finally, any morally irrelevant property could be used, not simply race and sex.

Preferential Hiring.   Both affirmative action programs and policies possibly productive of reverse discrimination involve *preferential hiring.* This concept refers to hiring that gives preference in recruitment and ranking to women, minority groups, and others previously discriminated against. This preference can be practiced by the use of goals or quotas or merely by choosing blacks, women, and so on, whenever their credentials are equal to those of other candidates. However, to some preferential hiring carries connotations of reverse discrimination or at least of quotas. Accordingly, the term's use may vary from one person to the next.

Comparable Worth.   In recent years much of the discussion about discrimination in the workplace has concerned the problem of gaps between wages paid to different sets of workers. The slogan "equal pay for equal work" has been a centerpiece of such discussions, and the gap between men's and women's pay has been the major topic. The term *comparable worth* has now come into vogue to refer to comparable pay for work of comparable value, where the criterion is the comparable *worth* of work, whether it is equal work or not. "Comparable jobs" thus does not refer to the "same jobs," and the issues are more complex than mere equality of pay for the same work. The essence of how levels of compensation are fairly attached to jobs is at

stake. Comparable worth has thus come to be used as a shorthand way of referring to a set of several diverse principles, which Robert Simon discusses in his essay. Each principle is an attempt to grasp the idea of "comparable pay for comparable worth," which functionally means adjusting pay scales so that persons in different jobs are paid similarly if the jobs require similar skills, knowledge, effort, stress, and responsibilities. The specific term *comparable worth* continues to be unpopular in the corporate environment, where systems of rating scales and employment practices modelled on this idea are generally referred to as schemes of *pay equity* or *internal equity* rather than comparable worth.

COMPENSATORY JUSTICE AND FEDERAL POLICIES

If a severe injustice has been done to a group of persons for discriminatory reasons, the balance of justice should be restored by *compensating* them for their loss. The *principle of compensatory justice* states that whenever an injustice has been committed, just compensation or reparation is owed the injured parties. Thus, if persons were injured by discrimination in the past—including women, blacks, North American Indians, and French Canadians—they should be recompensed for the past injustices. Compensatory policies such as affirmative action or equal opportunity programs have been designed to serve as the primary means to this end in the United States.

Ever since Franklin Roosevelt issued an executive order forbidding discrimination by war industries, American presidents have used executive orders to fight discriminatory practices. Presidents Kennedy and Johnson issued further orders, which were implemented by agencies such as the Labor Department through the use of numerical goals. Eventually regulatory practices turned into an extensive network of policies favoring preferential treatments and using numbers to judge whether practices were discriminatory. The merits and demerits of the executive orders and their implementation are now widely debated.

These rules and aspirations affect American business in profound ways. A 1983 survey indicated that the number of minority employees in 34,000 American companies went from 12 percent in 1967 to 19 percent in 1983. Another study of federal contractors indicated that those required to comply with Labor Department guidelines increased their minority employment rates by 20 percent between 1974 and 1980, while contractors not subject to the guidelines increased by only 12 percent. In a third survey, of 104 major American corporations, 95 percent indicated that they would keep their affirmative action goals and timetables even if the government no longer required them.[2]

Eastman Kodak and Rockwell International have made public statements to this effect, and a particularly instructive case history involves the Monsanto Chemical Company, which found itself in 1971 with few black or female employees. In that year the Labor Department (under the administration of President Nixon) determined to get serious about past executive orders. The Department notified corporate America that affirmative action would be enforced. Over the next 14 years Monsanto complied by tripling the number of minority employees, agressively promoting women and blacks into middle management positions, and eliminating racial hiring patterns in technical and craft positions. Monsanto attempted to achieve these goals without diluting the quality of employees, and today the firm says it has no intention of abandoning its affirmative action programs. The focus of these programs has now shifted from problems of how to *hire* by the numbers to how to *promote* minorities once they have been hired. (Nine blacks and six white women had moved into the company's top rank of 397 managers by the end of 1985.)[3]

No U.S. president opposed such preferential measures until Ronald Reagan, who campaigned against quotas and then sought to roll them back through speeches, courts, and agencies. The Justice Department was the ad-

ministration's vanguard, but others were intimately involved. In 1985 the Chairman of the United States Civil Rights Commission, Clarence Pendleton, reported to the President his conviction that the Commission had succeeded in making racial and group quotas a "dead issue" and had replaced public controversy over preferential treatment with a vision of the colorblind society that is an "opportunity society" rather than a "preference society."[4]

Although this boast seems questionable given the facts of current social debate and policies, it does present the two major competing primary positions now operative in American society on the proper means to achieving a nondiscriminatory society. One group believes the only means that will produce a colorblind society is preferential treatment. The other group believes we should guarantee opportunities to all citizens and must never stoop to the use of criteria favoring color (or sex, and so on), because this means to the end of a nondiscriminatory society is precisely what one is attempting to overcome, namely discrimination. These two competing positions agree that compensation is in order for *particular* victims of discrimination (as opposed to *quotas* or preferential treatment for *groups*).

Pendleton and Reagan vigorously attempted to promote equal opportunity for all, with special opportunity for none, during their period of rule. The chief federal officer in charge of enforcing this viewpoint during the critical Reagan years was Assistant Attorney General for Civil Rights in the U.S. Department of Justice, William Bradford Reynolds, who is one of the authors in this chapter. On the one hand, Reynolds pursued a number of important lawsuits that sought to overturn municipal preferential programs containing hiring goals—even if the programs were voluntary or had been enacted by negotiation. He contended that such programs discriminate against white males by setting hiring goals. On the other hand, Reynolds sued cities if they established barriers that make it difficult to hire blacks as city employees. For example, he sued seven nearly all-white Chicago suburbs on grounds that their residency requirements for jobs were merely a de facto way of keeping blacks out of municipal positions.

In general, Reynolds promotes the view that he and the Reagan administration stand in the tradition of Martin Luther King, Jr., and other civil rights leaders (particularly prior to President Johnson's executive order) who stand for equal opportunity in a color-blind society. His opponents, he believes, have distorted the idea of *equal opportunity* into that of *equal results*, meaning numerical outcomes that discriminate against whites. Similarly, he argues that the right to individual opportunity was distorted into the idea of group entitlements. He has vigorously opposed the principles that federal contractors—for example, private consulting firms—should (1) hire qualified women and minorities in proportion to their presence and availability in the labor pool and (2) use quotas to achieve racial and sexual hiring goals.

Every major civil rights organization in the United States and the majority of affected municipal authorities have denounced Reynold's perspective as historically inaccurate and morally unfair. They have argued that Reynolds and the Reagan administration offer only an abstract vision of a color-blind society of equal opportunity that is of no functional assistance in overcoming real-world discrimination, where white males have always been and still are preferred in the marketplace through bias. Strong resistance to the Reagan administration's proposed changes also appeared in the House Judiciary Committee in the U.S. Congress. In addition, the Department of Labor and the Department of Justice were in serious conflict over policy. Sixty-nine U.S. Senators subsequently went on record as supporting Labor's position that goals and timetables are needed to eliminate discrimination.[5]

This political and moral dispute is far from insignificant for American business. Approximately 15,000 companies employing 23 to 27 million workers at over 70,000 installations fall under the Labor Department's Office of Federal Contract Compliance Programs—the principal arm of federal policy for implementing affirmative action guidelines. It has been estimated that slightly more than 50 percent use goals and timetables for minority hiring. The Labor Department has continued to press for goals, especially in the case of recalcitrant employers.[6]

The articles in this chapter by Reynolds and by philosopher Thomas Nagel address the ethical issues that have emerged from these congressional, executive, and judicial determinations, including the moral and legal responsibilities of businesses to eradicate discrimination, and the problem of whether there should be hiring quotas. Perhaps the major moral issue to emerge is the following: If preferential policies require that, for example, a minority candidate be given preference over a white male otherwise *better qualified* (i.e., if the circumstances had been anonymous, then the white male would have been selected), is this action a justified instance of compensatory justice, *or* is the white male treated unjustly? In the attempt to answer this question, it has been argued variously that such practices of preferential treatment are (1) just, (2) unjust, or (3) not just but *permitted and encouraged* nonetheless by principles other than those of justice and equality.

(1) Those who claim that such compensatory measures are *just*, or perhaps required by justice, argue that the past lives in the present. The victims of past discrimination against blacks are still handicapped or discriminated against, while the families of past slave owners are still being unduly enriched by inheritance laws. Those who have inherited wealth that was accumulated by iniquitous practices have no more right to the wealth, it is argued, than do the sons of slaves, who have some claim to it as a matter of compensation. In the case of women, it is often argued that our culture is structured to equip them with a lack of self-confidence, that it prejudicially excludes them from much of the work force, and that it treats them as a low-paid auxiliary labor unit. The consequence is that only highly independent

women can be expected to compete with males on initially fair terms. Sometimes a slightly stronger argument is advanced: Compensation is said to be fair simply because it is *owed* to those who in the past suffered unjust treatment. For example, if veterans are owed preferential treatment because of their service and sacrifice to country, perhaps blacks and women are owed preferential treatment because of their economic sacrifices, systematic incapacitations, and consequent family and group losses.

(2) Those who claim that sweeping group compensatory measures are *unjust* argue variously that no criteria exist for measuring just compensation, that the extent of discrimination is presently minor (insufficiently pervasive to justify preferential treatment), and that none of those actually harmed in previous eras is now available to be compensated. Instead of providing compensation, they argue, we should continue to guide justice by strict equality and merit, while attacking the roots of discrimination. Also, some now successful but once underprivileged minority groups argue that their long struggle for equality is jeopardized by programs of "favoritism" to blacks and women. For example, persons of Irish descent could argue that they will now be unfairly burdened again, having already suffered as a group from discrimination. It is not absurd to suggest that *all* past oppressed groups—blacks and women being only two among a great many—should receive compensatory reparations. Are we not compounding initial injustices with a vastly complicated system of further injustices? Some of these arguments are developed in the articles in this chapter by Reynolds and George Sher.

(3) The third possible view is that some strong compensatory measures are *not just* because they *violate* principles of justice, and yet *are justifiable* nonetheless by appeal to moral principles other than justice. Thomas Nagel argues, for example, that "there is an element of individual unfairness" in strong affirmative action plans, but he holds that these plans are justified as a *means* to the end of

eradicating an intolerable social situation. Similarly, Tom Beauchamp argues that even the straightforward attempt to justify use of *reverse discrimination* can be justified as a means to the end of nondiscrimination, because of *current* discrimination.

THE MORAL PROBLEM OF REVERSE DISCRIMINATION

Although the U.S. Supreme Court has held that federal law permits private employers to set up plans that favor groups traditionally discriminated against, the moral justification, if any, for such plans and also the acceptability of reverse discrimination remain widely discussed topics. In several celebrated cases white males who were laid off or refused promotions have contested a corporate or municipal plan in the courts. Their case has been repeatedly and energetically defended in the editorial columns of the *Wall Street Journal*, as represented by the following summary statement. "The odd argument that nondiscrimination requires discrimination is on its last legs. As the great civil-rights leaders insisted years ago justice is best served when we are blind to color."[7]

Among writers who support policies of reverse discrimination, a conventional approach has been to argue that under certain conditions compensation owed for *past* wrongs justifies *present* policies productive of reverse discrimination. Beauchamp argues, however, that reverse discrimination is permitted in order to eliminate or alleviate *present* discriminatory practices against classes of persons, not to compensate classes for *past* wrongs. He introduces factual evidence for his claim of present, continuing discrimination, and this evidence in turn is used to support his claim that reverse discrimination is sometimes justified. Beauchamp's contention is that because massive social conditions of discrimination now prevail, policies producing reverse discrimination are needed to eliminate the ongoing discrimination. These policies are thus conceived as necessary for the protection of those harmed by intractable social attitudes and selection procedures. This argument—in the language introduced in the first chapter of this book—is utilitarian. However, Sher argues against utilitarian justifications and insists that only if an individual himself or herself has been treated unjustly can a legitimate appeal be made to compensatory justice. Sher and Beauchamp thus come into direct conflict over a fundamental issue in ethical theory: utilitarian versus nonutilitarian justifications (see Chapter One, pp. 25–31).

Sher and other opponents of this position argue that reverse discrimination violates fundamental and overriding principles of justice, and thus cannot be justified. One widely defended thesis is that policies productive of reverse discrimination violate principles of equality of opportunity and fair treatment by discriminating for or against a group, thus favoring them with special privileges and damaging the rule of law by replacing it with power struggles. As Reynolds puts it, justice is no longer color-blind or sex-blind, as it properly should be. Other arguments—some proposed by George Sher—include the following: (1) Some persons who are innocent of and not responsible for the past invidious discrimination (e.g., qualified young white males) pay the price; such treatment is discriminatory because persons are penalized solely on the basis of their race rather than for having harmed another. (2) Male members of minority groups such as Poles, Irish, Italians—themselves discriminated against in the past—will bear a heavy and unfair burden of the cost of compensating women and minority groups such as blacks. (3) Many individual members of any class selected for preferential treatment will themselves never have been unjustly treated and will not deserve preferential policies. (4) There are some relevant differences between the sexes that justify limited differential expectations and treatment. (Men are naturally better at some things, women at others.) (5) Compensation can be provided to *individuals* treated unfairly in the past without resort to reverse discrimination, which is the result of blanket treatment for groups. The last reason

(5) is presumably not only a reason against reverse discrimination but an alternative *policy*, as well.

As indicated by some precedential court cases in this chapter—*Griggs et al.* v. *Duke Power Company* and *United Steelworkers and Kaiser Aluminum* v. *Weber*—problems of preferential and discriminatory hiring are surprisingly complicated. *Griggs* was an early case in which workers at Duke Power Company were required to have credentials that were not essential for performance of the job. This decision established the much disputed but foundational premise in antidiscrimination law that a company should hire approximately the percentage of minority workers as there are minorities in the "relevant work force." This decision was attacked in December 1984 by the chairman of the Equal Employment Opportunities Commission, Clarence Thomas, on grounds that it has been wrongly stretched in some quarters of American society to the rule that blacks and women must be hired by companies *in proportion* to their numbers in the relevant work force, and that any company failing to do so is discriminatory. Thomas held that this rule surpasses reasonableness because there may be good and justifiable reasons why a group is proportionally underrepresented.[8]

In the *Steelworkers* v. *Weber* case (1979), a private employer's voluntary affirmative action plan with explicit hiring quotas giving blacks preference for admission to a craft training program was upheld despite the absence of evidence of past discrimination by the employer. Recently, the case of *Firefighters Local Union No. 1784* v. *Stotts* (*Firefighters* v. *Stotts,* for short) has received national attention. In this case the U.S. Supreme Court found that seniority rules can outweigh affirmative action gains in a layoff situation: "There was no finding that any of the blacks protected from layoff had been a victim of discrimination. . . . It is inappropriate to deny an innocent employee the benefits of his seniority in order to provide a remedy in a pattern or practice case such as this." The court does not deny the validity of affirmative action plans; it merely says these plans yield in the layoff situation to seniority systems.

This case occupies a prominent role in the essay by Reynolds, which was written shortly after the court announced its opinion. Reynolds, then Assistant Attorney General, interpreted the case as the dismantling of affirmative action. He saw the case as outlawing all affirmative action plans that contain specific numerical goals and as asserting that preferential remedies must apply only to actual victims of a jurisdiction's discriminatory hiring patterns. However, this interpretation has been disputed. The primary issue in *Firefighters* was layoffs, and the court said that *seniority* rather than *race* can legitimately be the criterion. Whether the court meant the opinion to extend beyond layoffs to hiring and promotion is not discussed specifically, and no criterion is set forth for *valid* affirmative action plans.

In a mid-1986 Supreme Court opinion involving Jackson, Michigan, school teachers, Justice Lewis Powell—writing for the majority—distinguished between hiring and layoffs, and noted that the court has allowed hiring goals to burden some "innocent persons" through affirmative action plans—thus suggesting (but not asserting) that reverse discrimination may be justified in hiring, but not in layoffs. Then, in July 1986 and March 1987 the Court came down in three cases in support of the permissibility of using specific numerical goals in affirmative action plans intended to combat a manifest imbalance in traditionally segregated job categories, even if the particular workers drawn from minorities were not themselves victims of past discrimination. In a case involving sheet metal workers in New York, a specific minority hiring goal of 29.23 percent had been established. The Supreme Court held that the kind of quotas involved in the 29 percent goal are justified when dealing with persistent or egregious discrimination. The Court argued that

even where the employer or union formally ceases to engage in discrimination, informal mechanisms may obstruct equal employment opportunities. An employer's reputation for dis-

crimination may discourage minorities from seeking available employment. In these circumstances, affirmative race-conscious relief may be the only means available to assure equality of employment opportunities and to eliminate those discriminatory practices and devices which have fostered racially stratified job environments to the disadvantage of minority citizens.

In reaction to this 1986 case the Attorney General of the United States said that his department "will continue to hold to the moral proposition that racial quotas are wrong," and his spokesperson reiterated the same principle after the March, 1987 decision.[9]

Under almost any criterion, these cases have not answered all questions that business might have about the role and place of preferential programs. For example, immediately after *Firefighters* v. *Stott* was decided, the Fluor Corporation, a large engineering and construction firm, announced that the court's opinion would not affect its rules or practices because layoffs are based strictly on performance and never on either affirmative action or seniority.[10] Moreover, many companies have minority-targeted programs aimed at contractors and not merely employees. For example, in 1979 the Southern California Edison Company established a Female and Minority Business Department program within its Procurement Division. As a result, by the end of 1984 the number of female and minority enterprises cleared to do business with the company increased by 150 percent (from 207 to 523). The value of the contracts awarded to the firms increased from $3.7 million in 1979 to $38.3 million in 1984.[11] This program is entirely voluntary and outside the bounds of all federal and state programs of affirmative action.

THE PROBLEM OF COMPARABLE WORTH

The claim that different jobs should be rated as comparable and that employees in those positions should be paid comparably in order to raise wages and offset discrimination has received as much discussion in recent years as any problem of employment discrimination. Federal law in the United States holds that workers in the same job cannot be paid differently merely because of race or sex. The equal pay act of 1963 specifies that employers must pay the same wages for substantially equal work in jobs requiring equal skill, effort, and responsibility unless the pay differential is based on merit, seniority, or the quality or quantity of production. Few would dispute these premises, but the principle of comparable worth extends to the notions of "same job" and "equal work" to "jobs of the same value." For example, San Francisco's Amfac has hired a consultant to ensure that the "french-fry cooker in Portland is paid the same as a sugar-cane worker in Hawaii,"[12] under the assumption that their jobs are of the same value to the corporation. The idea is that traditionally male jobs such as mining and trucking can be rated comparably to traditionally female jobs such as secretary and nurse, so that any unjustified differential in pay can be reduced. The objective is that women (the center of most of the discussion) should be paid according to their responsibilities, experience, contributions, and training—just as men are paid on these same bases. Jobs that are equal in value with respect to these characteristics are considered identical in value.

The U.S. Civil Rights Commission adopted a report in April 1985 that urged federal agencies to reject both the principle of comparable worth and the claim that sex *discrimination* explains the wage disparity between the sexes. The Commission's chairman, who once called the principle of comparable worth, "the looniest idea since 'Looney Tunes' came on the screen," held that employers should be held accountable for individual discriminatory acts or policies but not for combatting social attitudes and industry-preferred forms of evaluating the worth of jobs. Two months later the Equal Employment Opportunity Commission ruled unanimously that federal law does not require comparable

worth and that factual differences in pay scales are no grounds for asserting discrimination. Shortly thereafter Reynolds and the Justice Department filed its first "friend-of-the-court" brief in a comparable worth case, siding with the state of Illinois against nurses seeking higher pay on comparable worth grounds. In this context Reynolds argued that the comparable worth theory made "a mockery of the ideal of pay equity" and would necessarily depend on "subjective evaluations" by those who made judgments of comparability.[13]

Part of this dispute seems to be *conceptual*. As Robert Simon notes, there are different *meanings* attached to "comparable worth" and thus to principles that would implement it. The Reagan administration seemed to define "comparable worth" as requiring that *all jobs of the same value to society be paid equally*. This understanding would require a wholesale restructuring of wage scales across American society and would be extremely difficult to implement. However, many who favor comparable worth use a different definition based on the idea of pay equity as specified in the Equal Pay Act of 1963. In this conception, *all differentials in wages must be justified by nondiscriminatory and relevant considerations* such as seniority, merit pay, skills, and stress—but some differentials can be justified, and even large differentials can exist across society.

Corporate America has been generally negative about comparable worth in its public statements, as have been the *Wall Street Journal*'s editors and many associations such as the U.S. Chamber of Commerce and the National Association of Manufacturers. This negativism may, in part, stem from conceptual confusion over the definition of comparable worth. The opponents of comparable worth argue that it is a policy that cannot be reasonably implemented because it is beyond the capacity of even experts to determine objective values for different jobs, it would require massive federal intervention to enforce even if it could be implemented, it invites exorbitant contract disputes and unending litigation, it disturbs the flexibility and diversity essential to a free market in hiring and promotion (perhaps by using government wage-setting boards), and it neglects the fact that women have less work experience, less seniority, and a lower rate of unionization. Opponents have also pointed out that women often choose lower-paying positions in order to leave more flexibility for responsibilities at home.

By contrast, the proponents of comparable worth see the principle as an essential means to the elimination of a systematic underevaluation of the contribution made by women, with its consequent discrimination in pay scales. They argue that policies of comparable worth are not only essential to fairness but can be implemented, using models we already have available in schemes of ratings, pay scales, job evaluation systems, and the like. Their argument is that comparable worth introduces a broader element of fairness into employment practices and reduces or possibly eliminates institutionalized systems of injustice—or what Eleanor Smeal, president of NOW, has called "the ghetto of low wages."[14] Proponents often admit that unfairness cannot be completely eliminated, but they point out that unfairnesses can be carefully monitored and that comparable worth is an idea around which we can at least have a reasoned public discussion of sex-based wage discrimination. Rosemarie Tong and Robert Simon engage in just such a discussion in this chapter.

The possible avenues to *implementation* of comparable worth criteria have been disputed as vigorously as the meaning and merit of the concept. Presumably, implementation can proceed by (1) negotiation at the bargaining table, (2) internal development at corporations (without turning to the bargaining table), or (3) external imposition by governments. All three are under discussion and experiment at the present time. The first approach to comparable worth has been heavily promoted by the American Federation of State, County, and Municipal Workers (AFSCME), which won impressive precedential comparable worth pay adjustments in 1985 in Chicago, Los

Angeles, Iowa, Minnesota, Wisconsin, New York, and Connecticut. These changes were all achieved by labor negotiation rather than appeals in court. (However, AFSCME brought and lost a case against the state of Washington in the U.S. Court of Appeals that was considered a major blow to the cause of comparable worth.)

Despite the public skepticism generally voiced by American corporations, many have begun to move internally to develop explicit programs of comparable worth.[15] For example, major corporations such as AT&T, and BankAmerica, Chase Manhattan, IBM, Motorola, and Tektronix have introduced systems of job comparisons that will allow the cross-job evaluations essential for comparable worth. In these systems, various factors that express a job's "worth," such as years of education, degree of responsibility, necessary skill, amount of noise in the work environment, and physical labor, are rated on a point scale. Jobs with equal points are compensated equally. For example, AT&T worked with its unions to devise a plan in which fourteen measurements were adopted to evaluate by point ratings such factors as keyboard skills, job stress, and abilities to communicate. A labor-relations manager at AT&T, Kenneth Ross, has argued that such systems, when *internally developed*, give a company a competitive edge in hiring because the company can point to real internal equity.[16]

A similar set of potentially revolutionary changes that would be *externally* imposed on corporations are pending at many state legislatures. As this book goes to press, some thirty states in the United States are doing job studies or adjusting salary levels of mostly female positions and have bills pending that qualify for the designation "statutes promoting comparable worth," even though the term "comparable worth" is rarely used. Minnesota was the first to adopt such a plan for state employees. This state then sent directives to its municipalities to enact such plans. Other states began at the same time to evaluate pay scales systematically.[17] At the federal level, the shape of the future is less clear. The Carter administration had proposed regulations to require comparable worth policies for federal contractors, but the Reagan administration generally opposed such regulations. Meanwhile, Canada enacted a comparable worth law that covers all workers under federal jurisdiction, and in Great Britain such a law has been imposed on an unwilling Prime Minister.

One reason legislative activity has flourished in the United States is that salary studies and data continue to show that women are paid considerably less than men and that despite changes in civil rights laws and in the entry of women into a broader range of higher-paying professions and positions, the earnings *ratio* of women to men has not changed significantly over the past thirty years.

NOTES

1. Stephen Wermiel, "High Court Rules TWA Discriminated Against Pilots on the Basis of Their Age," *Wall Street Journal,* January 9, 1985, p. 5; Al Kamen, "Court Backs TWA Workers in Age-Discrimination Case," *Washington Post,* January 9, 1985, p. A2.
2. See Joe Davidson and Linda Watkins, "Quotas in Hiring are Anathema to President Despite Minority Gains," *Wall Street Journal,* October 24, 1985, pp. 1, 18.
3. Aric Press et al., "The New Rights War," *Newsweek,* December 30, 1985, pp. 66–69.
4. Juan Williams, "Quotas are a 'Dead Issue,' Rights Panel Chairman Says," *Washington Post,* January 30, 1985, p. A2.
5. Aric Press et al., "The New Rights War."
6. See Robert Pear, "Goals for Hiring Split Reagan Aides," *New York Times,* October 23, 1985, p. 1; Joann Lublin and Andy Pasztor, "Tentative Affirmative Action Accord," *Wall Street Journal,* December 11, 1985, p. 4; Paula Dwyer and Lee Walczak, "Affirmative Action: A Deal to Patch Up the Brock-Meese Feud," *Business Week,* January 27, 1986, p. 51.
7. "The Colorblind Vision," *Wall Street Journal,* March 11, 1985, p. 28.
8. Juan Williams, "EEOC Chief Cites Abuse of Racial Bias Criteria," *Washington Post,* December 4, 1984, p. A13.
9. The quotation is from the reprint of the Court's opinion in *"Sheet Metal Workers' Plan," New York Times,* July 3, 1986, p. B8. The quote from Attorney General Meese is found in Andy Pasztor and Stephen Wermiel, "Supreme Court Reaffirms Its Support for Affirmative Action in Employment," *Wall Street Journal,* July 3, 1986, p. 3. The later reiteration is found in Al Kamen, "Justice Department Surrenders in War on Hiring Goals," *Washington Post,* March 28, 1987, p. A4. For the social significance of the earlier opinion, see Stephen Wermiel and Joann S. Lublin, "Justice Labor Agencies Argue Meaning of High Court's Ruling on Hiring Goals," *Wall Street Journal,* May 30, 1986; Richard Licayo, "Accent on the Affirmative," *Time,* June 2, 1986; Stuart Taylor, Jr., "High Court Bars Layoff Method Favoring Blacks," *New York Times,* May 20, 1986, p. 1.
10. "Affirmative Action Ruling Pleases Firms, Angers Minorities, Women," *Wall Street Journal,* June 14, 1984, p. 33.
11. Southern California Edison Company, 1984 Report, p. 19.
12. "Labor Letter," *Wall Street Journal,* April 16, 1985, p. 1, col. 5.
13. Brief filed with the 7th U.S. Circuit Court of Appeals in Chicago. See Los Angeles Times Service, "U.S. Court Brief Assails 'Comparable Worth' Pay," *International Herald Tribune,* August 19, 1985, p. 3.
14. See James R. Dickenson, "NOW Leader at Ramparts: Smeal Vows Fight on Comparable Worth," *Washington Post,* September 6, 1985, p. A9.
15. See "Comparable Worth: It's Already Happening," *Business Week,* April 28, 1986, p. 52.
16. Cathy Trost, "Pay Equity, Born in Public Sector, Emerges as an Issue in Private Firms," *Wall Street Journal,* July 8, 1985, p. 15.
17. *Ibid.,* and see also Cathy Trost, "In Minnesota, 'Pay Equity' Passes Test, but Foes See Trouble Ahead," *Wall Street Journal,* May 10, 1985, p. 27.

Equal Opportunity, Not Equal Results

William Bradford Reynolds

No one disputes that "affirmative action" is a subject of vital significance for our society. The character of our country is determined in large measure by the manner in which we treat our individual citizens—whether we treat them fairly or unfairly, whether we ensure equal opportunity to all individuals or guarantee equal results to selected groups. As the Assistant Attorney General, I am faced daily with what seem to have emerged on the civil rights horizon as the two predominant competing values that drive the debate on this issue—that is, the value of equal opportunity and the value of equal results—and I have devoted a great deal of time and attention to the very different meanings they lend to the phrase "affirmative action."

Typically—to the understandable confusion of almost everyone—"affirmative action" is the term used to refer to both of these contrasting values. There is, however, a world of difference between "affirmative action" as a measure for ensuring equality of opportunity and "affirmative action" as a tool for achieving equality of results.

In the former instance, affirmative steps are taken so that all individuals (whatever their race, color, sex, or national origin) will be given the chance to compete with all others on equal terms; each is to be given his or her place at the starting line without advantage or disadvantage. In the latter, by contrast, the promise of affirmative action is that those who participate will arrive at the finish in prearranged places—places allocated by race or sex.

I have expressed on a number of occasions my conviction that the promise of equal results is a false one. We can never assure equal results in a world in which individuals differ greatly in motivation and ability; nor, in my view, is such a promise either morally or constitutionally acceptable. This was, in fact, well understood at the time that the concept of "affirmative action" was first introduced as a remedial technique in the civil rights arena. In its original formulation, that concept embraced only non-preferential affirmative efforts, in the nature of training programs and enhanced recruitment activities, aimed at opening wide the doors of opportunity to all Americans who cared to enter. Thus, President Kennedy's Executive Order 10925, one of the earliest to speak to the subject, stated that federal contractors should "take affirmative action to ensure that the applicants are employed, and that employees are treated during employment, without regard to their race, creed, color, or national origin."

This principle was understood by all at that time to mean simply that individuals previously neglected in the search for talent must be allowed to apply and be considered along with all others for available jobs or contracting opportunities, but that the hiring and selection decisions would be made from the pool of applicants without regard to race, creed, color, or national origin—and later sex. No one was to be afforded a preference, or special treatment, because of group membership; rather, all were to be treated equally as individuals based on personal ability and worth.

This administration's commitment is, of

From William Bradford Reynolds, "Equal Opportunity, Not Equal Rights," in Robert K. Fullinwider and Claudia Mills, eds., *The Moral Foundations of Civil Rights* (Totowa, N.J.: Rowman and Littlefield, 1986). Reprinted with permission.

course, to this "original and undefiled meaning"—as Morris Abram, Vice Chairman of the Civil Rights Commission, calls it—of "affirmative action." Where unlawful discrimination exists, we see that it is brought to an abrupt and uncompromising halt; where that discrimination has harmed any individual, we ensure that every victim of the wrongdoing receives "make-whole" relief; and affirmative steps are required in the nature of training programs and enhanced recruitment efforts to force open the doors of opportunity that have too long remained closed to far too many.

The criticism, of course, is that we do not go far enough. The remedial use of goals-and-timetables, quotas, or other such numerical devices—designed to achieve a particular balance as to race or sex in the work force—has been accepted by the lower federal courts as an available instrument of relief, and therefore, it is argued, such an approach should not be abandoned. There are several responses to this sort of argumentation.

The first is a strictly legal one and rests on the Supreme Court's recent decision in *Firefighters Local Union* v. *Stotts*, No. 82 – 206 (decided June 12, 1984). The Supreme Court in *Stotts* did not merely hold that federal courts are prohibited from ordering racially preferential layoffs to maintain a certain racial percentage, or that courts cannot disrupt bona fide seniority systems. To be sure, it did so rule; but the Court said much more, and in unmistakably forceful terms. As Justice Stevens remarked during his recent commencement address at Northwestern University, the decision represents "a far-reaching pronouncement concerning the limits on a court's power to prescribe affirmative action as a remedy for proven violations of Title VII of the Civil Rights Act." For the *Stotts* majority grounded the decision, at bottom, on the holding that federal courts are without *any* authority under Section 706(g)—the remedial provision of Title VII—to order a remedy, either by consent decree or after full litigation, that goes beyond enjoining the unlawful conduct and awarding "make-whole" relief for actual victims of the discrimination. Thus, quotas or other preferential techniques that, by design, benefit nonvictims because of race or sex cannot be part of Title VII relief ordered in a court case, whether the context is hiring, promotion, or layoffs.

A brief review of the opinion's language is particularly useful to understanding the sweep of the decision. At issue in *Stotts* was a district court injunction ordering that certain white firefighters with greater seniority be laid off before blacks with less seniority in order to preserve a certain percentage of black representation in the fire department's work force. The Supreme Court held that this order was improper because "there was no finding that any of the blacks protected from layoff had been a victim of discrimination."[1] Relying explicitly on Section 706(g) of Title VII, the Court held that Congress intended to "provide make-whole relief only to those who have been actual victims of illegal discrimination."[2] . . .

After *Stotts*, it is, I think, abundantly clear that Section 706(g) of Title VII does not tolerate remedial action by courts that would grant to nonvictims of discrimination—at the expense of wholly innocent employees or potential employees—an employment preference based solely on the fact that they are members of a particular race or gender. Quotas, or any other numerical device based on color or sex, are by definition victim-blind: they embrace without distinction and accord preferential treatment to persons having no claim to "make-whole" relief. Accordingly, whether such formulas are employed for hiring, promotion, layoffs, or otherwise, they must fail under any reading of the statute's remedial provision.

There are equally strong policy reasons for coming to this conclusion. The remedial use of preferences has been justified by the courts primarily on the theory that they are necessary to cure "the effects of past discrimination" and thus, in the words of one Supreme Court Justice, to "get beyond" racism."[3] This reasoning is twice flawed.

First, it is premised on the proposition

that any racial imbalance in the employer's work force is explainable only as a lingering effect on past racial discrimination. The analysis is no different where gender-based discrimination is involved. Yet, in either instance, equating "underrepresentation" of certain groups with discrimination against those groups ignores the fact that occupation selection in a free society is determined by a host of factors, principally individual interest, industry, and ability. It simply is not the case that applicants for any given job come proportionally qualified by race, gender, and ethnic origin in accordance with U.S. population statistics. Nor do the career interests of individuals break down proportionally among racial or gender groups. Accordingly, a selection process free of discrimination is no more likely to produce "proportional representation" along race or sex lines than it is to ensure proportionality among persons grouped according to hair color, shoe size, or any other irrelevant personal characteristic. No human endeavor, since the beginning of time, has attracted persons sharing a common physical characteristic in numbers proportional to the representation of such persons in the community. "Affirmative action" assumptions that one might expect otherwise in the absence of race or gender discrimination are ill-conceived.

Second, and more important, there is nothing *remedial*—let alone *equitable*—about a court order that *requires* the hiring, promotion, or retention of a person who has not suffered discrimination solely because that person is a member of the same racial or gender group as other persons who were victimized by the discriminatory employment practices. The rights protected under Title VII belong to individuals, not to groups. The Supreme Court made clear some years ago that [t]he basic policy of [Title VII] requires that [courts] focus on fairness to individuals rather than fairness to classes."[4] The same message was again delivered in *Stotts*. As indicated, remedying a violation of Title VII requires that the individual victimized by the unlawful discrimination be restored to his or her "rightful place." It almost goes without saying, however, that a person who is *not* victimized by the employer's discriminatory practices has no claim to a "rightful place" in the employer's work force. And, according preferential treatment to *nonvictims* in no way remedies the injury suffered by persons who have in fact been discriminated against in violation of Title VII.

Moreover, racial quotas and other forms of preferential treatment unjustifiably infringe on the legitimate employment interests and expectations of third parties, such as incumbent employees, who are free of any involvement in the employer's wrongdoing. To be sure, awarding retroactive seniority and other forms of "rightful place" relief to individual victims of discrimination also unavoidably infringes upon the employment interests and expectations of innocent third parties. Indeed, this fact has compelled some, including Chief Justice Burger, to charge that granting rightful place relief to victims of racial discrimination is on the order of "robbing Peter to pay Paul."[5]

The legitimate "rightful place" claims of identifiable victims of discrimination, however, warrant imposition of a remedy that calls for a sharing of the burden by those innocent incumbent employees whose "places" in the work force are the product of, or at least enhanced by, the employer's unlawful discrimination. Restoring the victim of discrimination to the position he or she would have occupied but for the discrimination merely requires incumbent employees to surrender some of the largesse discriminatorily conferred upon them. In other words, there is justice in requiring Peter, as a kind of third-party beneficiary of the employer's discriminatory conduct, to share in the burden of making good on the debt to Paul created by that conduct. But, an incumbent employee should not be called upon as well to sacrifice or otherwise compromise legitimate employment interests in order to accommodate persons *never wronged* by the employer's unlawful conduct. An order directing Peter to pay Paul in the absence of any proof of a debt owing to Paul is without remedial justification and cannot be squared with basic notions of fairness.

Proponents of the so-called remedial use of class-based preferences often counter this point with a two-fold response. First, they note that the effort to identify and make whole all victims of the employer's discriminatory practices will never be 100 percent successful. While no one can dispute the validity of this unfortunate point, race- and gender-conscious preferences simply do not answer this problem. The injury suffered by a discriminatee who cannot be located is in no way ameliorated—much less remedied—by conferring preferential treatment on other, randomly selected members of his or her race or sex. A person suffering from appendicitis is not relieved of the pain by an appendectomy performed on the patient in the next room.

Second, proponents of judicially imposed numerical preferences also argue that they are necessary to ensure that the employer does not return to his or her discriminatory ways. The fallacy in this reasoning is self-evident. Far from *preventing* future discrimination, imposition of such remedial devices *guarantees* future discrimination. Only the color or gender of the ox being gored is changed.

It is against this backdrop that the Court's decision in *Stotts* assumes so much significance in the "affirmative action" debate. The inescapable consequence of *Stotts* is to move government at the federal, state, and local levels noticeably closer to the overriding objective of providing all citizens with a truly equal opportunity to compete on merit for the benefits that our society has to offer—an opportunity that allows an individual to go as far as the person's energy, ability, enthusiasm, imagination, and efforts will allow and not be hemmed in by the artificial allotment given to his or her group in the form of a numerical preference. The promise is that we might now be able to bring an end to that stifling process by which government and society view its citizens as possessors of racial or gender characteristics, not

as the unique individuals they are; where advancements are viewed not as hard-won achievements, but as conferred "benefits."

The use of race or sex in an effort to restructure society along lines that better represent someone's preconceived notions of how our limited educational and economic resources should be allocated among the many groups in our pluralistic society necessarily forecloses opportunities to those having the misfortune—solely by reason of gender or skin color—to be members of a group whose allotment has already been filled. Those so denied, such as the more senior white Memphis firefighters laid off to achieve a more perfect racial balance in the fire department, are discriminated against every bit as much as the black Memphis firefighters originally excluded from employment. In our zeal to eradicate discrimination from society, we must be ever vigilant not to allow considerations of race or sex to intrude upon the decisional process of government. That was precisely the directive handed down by Congress in the Civil Rights Act of 1964, and, as *Stotts* made clear, the command has full application to the courts. Plainly, "affirmative action" remedies must be guided by no different principle. For the simple fact remains that wherever it occurs, and however explained, "no discrimination based on race [or sex] is benign. . . . no action disadvantaging a person because of color [or gender] is affirmative.[6]

NOTES

1. Slip opinion at p. 16.
2. Slip opinion at p. 17.
3. *University of California Regents* v. *Bakke,* 438 U.S. 265, 407 (Justice Blackmun, concurring).
4. *Los Angeles Department of Water & Power* v. *Manhart,* 435 U.S. 702, 708 (1978).
5. *Franks* v. *Bowman Transportation Co.,* 424 U.S. 747, 781 (1976) (Justice Burger, dissenting).
6. *United Steelworkers of America, AFL-CIO* v. *Weber,* 443 U.S. 193, 254 (1979) (Justice Rehnquist, dissenting).

A Defense of Affirmative Action

Thomas Nagel

The term "affirmative action" has changed in meaning since it was first introduced. Originally it referred only to special efforts to ensure equal opportunity for members of groups that had been subject to discrimination. These efforts included public advertisement of positions to be filled, active recruitment of qualified applicants from the formerly excluded groups, and special training programs to help them meet the standards for admission or appointment. There was also close attention to procedures of appointment, and sometimes to the results, with a view to detecting continued discrimination, conscious or unconscious.

More recently the term has come to refer also to some degree of definite preference for members of these groups in determining access to positions from which they were formerly excluded. Such preference might be allowed to influence decisions only between candidates who are otherwise equally qualified, but usually it involves the selection of women or minority members over other candidates who are better qualified for the position.

Let me call the first sort of policy "weak affirmative action" and the second "strong affirmative action." It is important to distinguish them, because the distinction is sometimes blurred in practice. It is strong affirmative action—the policy of preference—that arouses controversy. Most people would agree that weak or precautionary affirmative action is a good thing, and worth its cost in time and energy. But this does not imply that strong affirmative action is also justified.

I shall claim that in the present state of things it is justified, most clearly with respect to blacks. But I also believe that a defender of the practice must acknowledge that there are serious arguments against it, and that it is defensible only because the arguments for it have great weight. Moral opinion in this country is sharply divided over the issue because significant values are involved on both sides. My own view is that while strong affirmative action is intrinsically undesirable, it is a legitimate and perhaps indispensable method of pursuing a goal so important to the national welfare that it can be justified as a temporary, though not short-term, policy for both public and private institutions. In this respect it is like other policies that impose burdens on some for the public good.

THREE OBJECTIONS

I shall begin with the argument against. There are three objections to strong affirmative action: that it is inefficient; that it is unfair; and that it damages self-esteem.

The degree of inefficiency depends on how strong a role racial or sexual preference plays in the process of selection. Among candidates meeting the basic qualifications for a position, those better qualified will on the average perform better, whether they are doctors, policemen, teachers, or electricians. There may be some cases, as in preferential college admissions, where the immediate usefulness of making educational resources

Testimony before the Subcommittee on the Constitution of the Senate Judiciary Committee, June 18, 1981. Reprinted by permission of Professor Nagel.

available to an individual is thought to be greater because of the use to which the education will be put or because of the internal effects on the institution itself. But by and large, policies of strong affirmative action must reckon with the costs of some lowering in performance level: the stronger the preference, the larger the cost to be justified. Since both the costs and the value of the results will vary from case to case, this suggests that no one policy of affirmative action is likely to be correct in all cases, and that the cost in performance level should be taken into acocunt in the design of a legitimate policy.

The charge of unfairness arouses the deepest disagreements. To be passed over because of membership in a group one was born into, where this has nothing to do with one's individual qualifications for a position, can arouse strong feelings of resentment. It is a departure from the ideal—one of the values finally recognized in our society—that people should be judged so far as possible on the basis of individual characteristics rather than involuntary group membership.

This does not mean that strong affirmative action is morally repugnant in the manner of racial or sexual discrimination. It is nothing like those practices, for though like them it employs race and sex as criteria of selection, it does so for entirely different reasons. Racial and sexual discrimination are based on contempt or even loathing for the excluded group, a feeling that certain contacts with them are degrading to members of the dominant group, that they are fit only for subordinate positions or menial work. Strong affirmative action involves none of this: it is simply a means of increasing the social and economic strength of formerly victimized groups, and does not stigmatize others.

There is an element of individual unfairness here, but it is more like the unfairness of conscription in wartime, or of property condemnation under the right of eminent domain. Those who benefit or lose out because of their race or sex cannot be said to deserve their good or bad fortune.

It might be said on the other side that the beneficiaries of affirmative action deserve it as compensation for past discrimination, and that compensation is rightly exacted from the group that has benefited from discrimination in the past. But this is a bad argument, because as the practice usually works, no effort is made to give preference to those who have suffered most from discrimination, or to prefer them especially to those who have benefited most from it, or been guilty of it. Only candidates who in other qualifications fall on one or the other side of the margin of decision will directly benefit or lose from the policy, and these are not necessarily, or even probably, the ones who especially deserve it. Women or blacks who don't have the qualifications even to be considered are likely to have been handicapped more by the effects of discrimination than those who receive preference. And the marginal white male candidate who is turned down can evoke our sympathy if he asks, "Why me?" (A policy of explicitly *compensatory* preference, which took into account each individual's background of poverty and discrimination, would escape some of these objections, and it has its defenders, but it is not the policy I want to defend. Whatever its merits, it will not serve the same purpose as direct affirmative action.)

The third objection concerns self-esteem, and is particularly serious. While strong affirmative action is in effect, and generally known to be so, no one in an affirmative action category who gets a desirable job or is admitted to a selective university can be sure that he or she has not benefited from the policy. Even those who would have made it anyway fall under suspicion, from themselves and from others: it comes to be widely felt that success does not mean the same thing for women and minorities. This painful damage to esteem cannot be avoided. It should make any defender of strong affirmative action want the practice to end as soon as it has achieved its basic purpose.

JUSTIFYING AFFIRMATIVE ACTION

I have examined these three objections and tried to assess their weight, in order to decide how strong a countervailing reason is needed to justify such a policy. In my view, taken together they imply that strong affirmative action involving significant preference should be undertaken only if it will substantially further a social goal of the first importance. While this condition is not met by all programs of affirmative action now in effect, it is met by those which address the most deep-seated, stubborn, and radically unhealthy divisions in the society, divisions whose removal is a condition of basic justice and social cohesion.

The situation of black people in our country is unique in this respect. For almost a century after the abolition of slavery we had a rigid racial caste system of the ugliest kind, and it only began to break up twenty-five years ago. In the South it was enforced by law, and in the North, in a somewhat less severe form, by social convention. Whites were thought to be defiled by social or residential proximity to blacks, intermarriage was taboo, blacks were denied the same level of public goods—education and legal protection—as whites, were restricted to the most menial occupations, and were barred from any positions of authority over whites. The visceral feelings of black inferiority and untouchability that this system expressed were deeply ingrained in the members of both races, and they continue, not surprisingly, to have their effect. Blacks still form, to a considerable extent, a hereditary social and economic community characterized by widespread poverty, unemployment, and social alienation.

When this society finally got around to moving against the caste system, it might have done no more than to enforce straight equality of opportunity, perhaps with the help of weak affirmative action, and then wait a few hundred years while things gradually got better. Fortunately it decided instead to accelerate the process by both public and private institutional action, because there was wide recognition of the intractable character of the problem posed by this insular minority and its place in the nation's history and collective consciousness. This has not been going on very long, but the results are already impressive, especially in speeding the advancement of blacks into the middle class. Affirmative action has not done much to improve the position of poor and unskilled blacks. That is the most serious part of the problem, and it requires a more direct economic attack. But increased access to higher education and upper-level jobs is an essential part of what must be achieved to break the structure of drastic separation that was left largely undisturbed by the legal abolition of the caste system.

Changes of this kind require a generation or two. My guess is that strong affirmative action for blacks will continue to be justified into the early decades of the next century, but that by then it will have accomplished what it can and will no longer be worth the costs. One point deserves special emphasis. The goal to be pursued is the reduction of a great social injustice, not proportional representation of the races in all institutions and professions. Proportional racial representation is of no value in itself. It is not a legitimate social goal, and it should certainly not be the aim of strong affirmative action, whose drawbacks make it worth adopting only against a serious and intractable social evil.

This implies that the justification for strong affirmative action is much weaker in the case of other racial and ethnic groups, and in the case of women. At least, the practice will be justified in a narrower range of circumstances and for a shorter span of time than it is for blacks. No other group has been treated quite like this, and no other group is in a comparable status. Hispanic-Americans occupy an intermediate position, but it seems to me frankly absurd to include persons of oriental descent as beneficiaries of affirmative action, strong or weak. They are not a severely deprived and excluded minority, and their eligibility serves only to swell the numbers that can be included on affirmative action reports. It also suggests that there is a drift in the policy toward adopting the goal of racial proportional representation for its own sake. This is a foolish mistake, and should be resisted. The only legitimate goal of the policy is to reduce egregious racial stratification.

With respect to women, I believe that except over the short term, and in professions or institutions from which their absence is particularly marked, strong affirmative action is not warranted and weak affirmative action is enough. This is based simply on the expectation that the social and economic situation of women will improve quite rapidly under conditions of full equality of opportunity. Recent progress provides some evidence for this. Women do not form a separate hereditary community, characteristically poor and uneducated, and their position is not likely to be self-perpetuating in the same way as that of an outcast race. The process requires less artificial acceleration, and any need for strong affirmative action for women can be expected to end sooner than it ends for blacks.

I said at the outset that there was a tendency to blur the distinction between weak and strong affirmative action. This occurs especially in the use of numerical quotas, a topic on which I want to comment briefly.

A quota may be a method of either weak or strong affirmative action, depending on the circumstances. It amounts to weak affirmative action—a safeguard against discrimi-

nation—if, and only if, there is independent evidence that average qualifications for the positions being filled are no lower in the group to which a minimum quota is being assigned than in the applicant group as a whole. This can be presumed true of unskilled jobs that most people can do, but it becomes less likely, and harder to establish, the greater the skill and education required for the position. At these levels, a quota proportional to population, or even to representation of the group in the applicant pool, is almost certain to amount to strong affirmative action. Moreover it is strong affirmative action of a particularly crude and indiscriminate kind, because it permits no variation in the degree of preference on the basis of costs in efficiency, depending on the qualification gap. For this reason I should defend quotas only where they serve the purpose of weak affirmative action. On the whole, strong affirmative action is better implemented by including group preference as one factor in appointment or admission decisions, and letting the results depend on its interaction with other factors.

I have tried to show that the arguments against strong affirmative action are clearly outweighed at present by the need for exceptional measures to remove the stubborn residues of racial caste. But advocates of the policy should ackowledge the reasons against it, which will ensure its termination when it is no longer necessary. Affirmative action is not an end in itself, but a means of dealing with a social situation that should be intolerable to us all.

The Justification of Goals and Quotas in Hiring

Tom L. Beauchamp

During the past two decades, government and corporate policies aimed at hiring women and racial minorities by setting numerical goals have been sharply criticized on grounds that they discriminate in reverse, often against more qualified white males. My objective in this paper is to defend such policies. I agree with those critics who maintain that some policies have created situations of injustice. However, I do not agree with the presumption that when policies with numerical goals create *injustices* they are necessarily *unjustified.* Equal opportunity is but one principle of justice, and justice is but one demand of ethics. We need also to take account of principles of just compensation (compensatory justice) and the public interest (utility).

A policy can create or perpetuate injustices, such as violations of principles of equal opportunity, and yet be justified by other reasons. It would, for example, be an injustice in one respect for a bank to fire one of two branch managers with identical professional credentials while retaining the other; yet the financial condition of the bank or compensation owed the retained person might provide compelling reasons that justify the action. An established seniority system might justifiably be used to decide such a matter; indeed, a devoted employee with long service might be retained in preference to a younger person with better credentials and higher productivity. In some circumstances, when implementing schemes of hiring, promoting, and firing, equal opportunity and the blinded evaluations of persons will have to yield on the scales of justice to the weight of other principles.

I shall use this general line of argument in defense of numerical targets, goals, quotas, and timetables. I contend that goals and even quotas are congenial to management, not hostile to business, as academic and government agency officials generally seem to presume. I also believe that business' long-range interest and the public interest are best served by preferential hiring, advancement, and layoff policies.

TWO POLAR POSITIONS

The U.S. Supreme Court and numerous scholars in ethics and legal theory have struggled with these problems of principle and balance in combatting discrimination, at least since President Lyndon Johnson's 1965 executive order that announced a toughened federal initiative by requiring specific goals and timetables for equal employment opportunity. This struggle has led to two primary competing schools of thought on the justifiability of preferential programs.

The first school locates justice in the claim that we are all entitled to an equal opportunity and to constitutional guarantees of equal protection in a color-blind, nonsexist society. An entitlement of this sort is an

Heavily revised from Tom L. Beauchamp, "The Justification of Reverse Discrimination," in *Social Justice and Preferential Treatment,* W. Blackstone and R. Heslep, eds. Copyright © 1977, 1987 by the author.

entitlement that only individuals possess. Civil rights laws therefore should offer protection not to aggregate groups but only to specific individuals who have been demonstrably victimized by racial, sexual, religious, or other forms of discrimination. Hiring goals, timetables, and quotas violate these laws as well as our moral sense of justice, because they create new victims of discrimination. The U.S. Department of Justice has spearheaded this view in recent years, but it has found adherents in many quarters as well.

The second school believes that mandated goals and enforced hiring measures are essential to ensure fairness in hiring and to achieve meaningful results in the attempt to eradicate discrimination. This group believes it is too onerous to require the actual identification of individual victims of discrimination—an assignment that is generally impossible because of secrecy (and sometimes even unintentional discrimination). Even the victims may not know they are victims. As the editors of the *New York Times* put it, finding actual victims as the means of ending discrimination would be the "project of a century and [would] leave most victims of discrimination with only empty legal rights. [Many] are still victims of the myths of racial superiority that once infused the law itself." The *Times* joined the Supreme Court in calling for the "adequate remedy" of "race-conscious relief" in the form of goals and timetables to the extent necessary to achieve the end of a nondiscriminatory society.[1] The second group thus tends to see the first group as construing "equal opportunity" and "civil rights" so narrowly that those affected by discrimination can receive no practical aid in overcoming the phenomenon of prejudice. That is, the noble ideal of equal opportunity is viewed as but a theoretical postulate that has no practical application in the real world under the first group's policies.

These two groups are perhaps not as far apart as they appear at first glance. Edwin Meese, Attorney General during the Reagan administration and the most publicly visible proponent of the first viewpoint in recent memory, dismissed the seemingly enormous gulf between his views and those of the U.S. Supreme Court—which has endorsed the second viewpoint—by saying that the Court *accepted* his views that racial preferences are wrong and merely "carved out various exceptions to that general rule, even while affirming the rule itself." There is something to be said for Meese's bold statement (although I think not quite what he intended): The second group need not disagree with the first group if legal enforcement were adequate to identify discriminatory treatment and to protect its victims. If we lived in such a society, then the second group could easily agree that the first group's policies are preferable for that society.

But there are two reasons why no member of the second group will agree to this solution at the present time. First, there is the unresolved issue of whether those in contemporary society who have been advantaged by *past* discrimination deserve their advantages, and thus whether classes such as blacks and women deserve some of those advantages. This thorny issue is surpassed in importance, however, by the second reason, which is whether *present*, ongoing discrimination can be successfully, comprehensively, and fairly combatted by identifying and prosecuting the violators. I do not believe that the form of enforcement so essential to the first group's position is possible. But I do believe that the enforcement of goals and quotas is both possible and necessary. Two reasons now to be discussed lead me to the conclusion that the second position is preferable to the first.

THE DATA ON DISCRIMINATION

My argument rests on the hypothesis that invidious discrimination that affects hiring and promotion is present in our society—not everywhere, of course, but pervasively.

Such a claim requires empirical evidence; and like almost any broad generalization, the evidence is not entirely conclusive. However, I believe the claim can be adequately substantiated, as some representative samples of available data indicate.

Statistical imbalances in hiring and admission and promotion are often discounted because so many variables can be hypothesized to explain why, for nondiscriminatory reasons, an imbalance exists. We can all think of plausible nondiscriminatory reasons why almost half of the graduate students in the United States are women but the tenured Arts and Sciences graduate faculties often hover around 5 to 10 percent women—and in some of the most prestigious schools, even lower. Occasionally we are able to discover firm evidence supporting the claim that such skewed statistics are not random but are the result of discrimination. Quantities of such discriminatory findings, in turn, raise questions about the real reasons for suspicious statistics in those cases where we have not been able to determine these reasons.

An impressive body of statistics constituting prima facie evidence of discrimination has been assembled in recent years indicating that women with identical credentials are promoted at almost exactly one-half the rate of their male counterparts; that 69 percent or more of the white-collar positions in the United States are presently held by women, but only 10 percent or so of the management positions are held by women (and again their pay is significantly lower); that 87 percent of all professionals in the private business sector are Orientals, but they comprise only 1.3 percent of management; that in the population as a whole in the United States 3 out of 7 employees hold white-collar positions, but only 1 of 7 blacks holds such a position (and these positions are clustered in professions that have the fewest jobs to offer in top-paying positions); and that numerous major U.S. corporations have settled discrimination suits out of court for hundreds of millions of dollars.[2]

Such statistics are far from decisive indicators of discrimination. But further evidence concerning the reasons for the statistics can sometimes be discovered to prove a discriminatory influence.[3] Other facts support the general conclusion that racist and sexist biases have a powerful influence in the marketplace. For example, from 1965 to 1975 the number of blacks in college doubled, but from 1975 to 1985 it leveled off without increase. The number of blacks making more than $25,000 in constant-dollar salary also doubled from 1965 to 1975, but dropped from 1975 to 1985.[4] There is a ready reason for both statistics. Both the Grier Partnership and the Urban League produced separate studies completed in 1985 that show striking disparities in the employment levels of college-trained blacks and whites in the job market in Washington, D.C.—one of the best markets for blacks. Both studies found that college-trained blacks find far more frustration in landing a position and that discrimination is a major underlying factor.[5]

Another example of prevailing biases in marketplace transactions is found in real estate rentals and sales. In a 1985 statement, Lucius McKelvey, president of a large Cleveland real estate firm, publicly proclaimed what numerous real estate agents had already privately reported: "You'd be surprised at the number of professional people, white-collar people, who ask us to discriminate—it's discouraging." Surveys have shown that blacks face an 85 percent probability of encountering discrimination in rental housing and almost 50 percent in buying a house.[6]

These studies and dozens that replicate their findings indicate that we live in a discriminatory society whose laws will make little difference in practice unless the laws are tough and are gauged to change the practices and underlying attitudes. The law cannot wait for evidence of abuse confined to demonstrable individual victims without permitting the continuation of present injustices.

PROBLEMS OF PROOF
AND INTENTION

The central problems of proof and enforcement in individual cases can best be captured by taking a particular case that illustrates the difficulty in determining whether discrimination—especially intentional discrimination—is occurring.

In December 1974 a decision was reached by the Commission against Discrimination of the Executive Department of the State of Massachusetts regarding a case at Smith College; the two complainants were women who were denied tenure and dismissed by the English Department.[7] The women claimed sex discrimination and based their case on the following: (1) Women at the full professor level in the college declined from 54 percent in 1958 to 21 percent in 1972, and in the English Department from 57 percent in 1960 to 11 percent in 1972. These statistics compare unfavorably at all levels with data from Mt. Holyoke, a comparable institution (since both have an all-female student body and are located in western Massachusetts). (2) Thirteen of the department's fifteen associate and full professorships at Smith belonged to men. (3) The two tenured women had obtained tenure under "distinctly peculiar experiences," including a stipulation that one be only part-time and that the other not be promoted when given tenure. (4) The department's faculty members conceded that tenure standards were applied subjectively, were vague, and lacked the kind of precision that would avoid discriminatory application. (5) The women denied tenure were at no time given advance warning that their work was deficient. Rather, they were given favorable evaluations of their teaching and were encouraged to believe that they would receive tenure. (6) Some of the stated reasons for the dismissals were later demonstrated to be rationalizations, and one letter from a senior member to the tenure and promotion committee contradicted his own appraisal of teaching ability filed with the department. (7) The court accepted expert testimony that any deficiencies in the women candidates were also found in male candidates promoted and given tenure in the same period and that the women's positive credentials were at least as good as the men's.[8]

The commissioner's opinion found that "the Complainants properly used statistics to demonstrate that the Respondents' practices operate with a discriminatory effect." Citing *Parham* v. *Southwestern Bell Telephone Co.*, the commissioner argued that "in such cases extreme statistics may establish discrimination as a matter of law, without additional supportive evidence." But in this case the commissioner found abundant additional evidence in the form of the "historical absence of women," "word-of-mouth recruitment policies" that operate discriminatorily, and a number of "subtle and not so subtle, societal patterns" existing at Smith.[9] On December 30, 1974, the commissioner ordered the two women reinstated with tenure and ordered the department to submit an affirmative action program within sixty days.

There is little in the way of clinching proof that the members of the English Department held discriminatory attitudes. Yet so consistent a pattern of *apparently* discriminatory results must be regarded, according to this decision, as de facto discrimination. The commissioner's ruling and other laws explicitly state that "intent or lack thereof is of no consequence." If a procedure constitutes discriminatory treatment, then the parties discriminated against must be recompensed. If irresistible statistics and other sociological evidence of "social exclusion" and "subtle societal patterns" provide compelling evidence that quotas, goals, or strong court-backed measures are necessary to overcome the discriminatory pattern (as the Respondents' testimony in the case indicates),[10] I find this fact sufficient to justify the measures.

In early 1985 the U.S. Supreme Court came down with perhaps its clearest example of this general point in the case of *Alexander* v. *Choate*. The Court held unanimously—against the U.S. Justice Department and the state of Tennessee—that states may be held guilty of discriminating against the handicapped because such discrimination is "most often the product not of invidious animus, but rather of thoughtlessness and indifference—of benign neglect." The Court rightly held that discrimination would be "difficult if not impossible to ban if only *intentional* acts of discrimination qualified as discrimination."[11]

PROBLEMS OF ENFORCEMENT

The protective camouflage surrounding discriminatory attitudes makes enforcement difficult in both the particular case and in the general case of monitoring nondiscriminatory guidelines. This problem is lessened by having specific goals and quotas, which are easier to meet and to enforce. In this section I want to present two cases that show how difficult—indeed meaningless—enforcement can be in the absence of specified goals and tough-minded control.

The January 1975 Report of the United States Commission on Civil Rights contains a section of "compliance reviews" of various universities.[12] The commissioners reviewed four major campuses in the United States: Harvard, University of Michigan, University of Washington, and Berkeley. They concluded that there has been a pattern of inadequate compliance reviews, inordinate delays, and inexcusable failures to take enforcement action where there were clear violations of the executive order regulations.[13]

Consider the example of the "case history of compliance contracts" at the University of California at Berkeley. When the Office for Civil Rights (OCR) of HHS determined to investigate Berkeley (April 1971), after several complaints, including a class action sex discrimination complaint, the university refused to permit access to its personnel files and refused to permit the interviewing of faculty members without an administrator

present. Both refusals are, as the report points out, "direct violations of the Executive order's equal opportunity clause," under which Berkeley held contracts. A year and a half later, after negotiations and more complaints, the university was instructed to develop a written affirmative action plan to correct "documented deficiencies" of "pervasive discrimination." The plan was to include target goals and timetables wherever job underutilization had been identified.[14]

In January 1973 the university submitted a draft affirmative action plan that was judged "totally unacceptable." Throughout 1973 Berkeley received "extensive technical assistance" from the government to aid it in developing a better plan. No such plan emerged, and OCR at the end of the year began to question "the university's commitment to comply with the executive order." The university submitted other unacceptable plans, and finally in March 1974 a conciliation document was reached. However, the document was vague and the university and OCR continued for years to be in disagreement on the meaning of key provisions.

Berkeley is an instructive case study, because it was at the time among the most concerned institutions in the United States over issues of race and civil rights. If it and the other three universities studied by the Commission of Civil Rights have troubled histories in installing and monitoring antidiscrimination laws, one can imagine the problems found elsewhere. Consider, as a revealing example of far more egregious resistance, what is perhaps the most important Supreme Court case on the issues of quotas and reverse discrimination: the case of *Local 28* v. *Equal Employment Opportunity Commission*, generally known as *Sheet Metal Workers*.[15] Although this case was decided in 1986, the discriminatory actions of Local 28 of the Sheet Metal Workers International had been in and out of court since 1963. The record, says the Supreme Court, was one of complete "foot-dragging resistance" to the idea of hiring from minority groups into the apprenticeship training programs that supply workers for construction in the New York City metropolitan area. In 1964 the New York Commission for Human Rights investigated the union and concluded that it excluded nonwhites through an impenetrable barrier of hiring by discriminatory selection. The state Supreme Court concurred and issued a "cease and desist" order. The union ignored it. Eventually, in a 1975 trial, the U.S. District Court found a record "replete with instances of bad faith" and ordered a "remedial racial goal" of 29 percent nonwhite membership (based on the percentage of nonwhites in the local labor pool). Another court then found that the union had "consistently and egregriously violated" the law of the land (Title 7, in particular.) In 1982 and 1983 court fines and civil contempt proceedings were issued. In 1981, virtually nothing had been done to modify the discriminatory hiring practices after twenty-two years of struggle.

The Supreme Court held that one need not produce "identified victims" of discrimination and that goals such as the 29 percent quota are justified when "an employer or a labor union has been engaged in persistent or egregrious discrimination, or where necessary to dissipate the lingering effects of pervasive discrimination." I find the latter clause particularly suitable. Goals and quotas are needed where there are lingering effects of pervasive preference for particular groups (e.g. white male graduates of certain schools) or discriminatory attitudes that control hiring. Otherwise, goals and quotas are not needed, and no one should invoke them. But if these problems are not restricted to a few isolated cases involving Sheet Metal Workers Unions or Departments of English, then it makes sense to see goals and quotas as a basic tool for eradicating discriminatory practices.

The Supreme Court points out that the present laws in the United States were enacted by Congress to prevent "pervasive and systematic discrimination in employment." No one should expect that practices like those of the Sheet Metal Workers can easily be removed by exhortations or by finding "identified victims." The stronger the resistance, the tougher the rules must be.

I might add, however, that the Supreme Court has not said, nor have I, that there cannot be a case of reverse discrimination in which a white male has unjustifiably been excluded for consideration from employment and has a right to compensation. Certainly *unwarranted* discrimination in reverse is no better than unwarranted discrimination in forward speed. But the following should also be considered: There is an important distinction between real reverse discrimination and merely apparent reverse discrimination. Sometimes persons who appear to be displacing better applicants will be hired or admitted—on a quota basis, for example, but the appearance may be the result of discriminatory perceptions of the person's qualifications. In this case there will appear to be reverse discrimination, and this impression will be reinforced by knowledge that quotas were used. However, the allegation of reverse discrimination will be mistaken. On other occasions there will be genuine reverse discrimination, and on many occasions it will be impossible to determine whether this consequence occurs.

I have argued that real and not merely apparent reverse discrimination is justified. But it is justified only as a means to the end of ensuring nondiscriminatory treatment of all persons. If the use of goals and quotas functioned as a vindictive tool (and, let us suppose, the end of nondiscrimination had already been achieved), then no reverse discriminatory effects would be justified.

WHY CORPORATIONS SHOULD WELCOME GOALS AND QUOTAS

Little has been said thus far about the relevance of these arguments to employment in business, largely because we have been concentrating on public policy affecting all institutions. In conclusion, I turn to corporate policy, which I believe would be aided by the use of goals and targets in the late 1980s and early 1990s. Here I shall discuss only policies voluntarily adopted by corporations—that is, voluntary programs using target goals and quotas. These programs stand in contrast to agency-ordered objectives featured in some previous examples.

Because of this shift to voluntary programs, my argument may seem a trivial addition to the problems mentioned above; a corporation can either accept or reject a program at its discretion. However, the issue of voluntary goals and quotas is far from trivial, for two reasons. First, the Justice Department has sought in recent years to ban voluntary corporate programs using goals and quotas, on grounds that these policies result in reverse discrimination. Many corporations and municipalities have resisted these government moves, and some have flatly refused to ease their affirmative action goals. Second, I believe that the active good will of corporations will prove to be more important than any other development (with the possible exception of activity in the U.S. Supreme Court) in ending discrimination and prejudice in the American workplace; and the workplace more than any other environment will serve as the melting pot of American society.

I offer four reasons why it is in the interest of responsible businesses to use aggressive plans involving goals and quotas. The judgement that such plans are fair and justified—as I have argued previously—could be appended as a reason, but it is not the type of reason needed in the present context.

(1) First, to the extent that a corporation either discriminates or fails to look at the full range of qualified persons in the market, to that extent it will eventually wind up with a larger percentage of second-best employees. Corporations continue to report that they find fewer qualified workers for available positions than they formerly did, and that they have profited from rules of nonracial, nonsexist hiring.[16] Hal Johnson, a senior vice-president at Travelers Companies,

projects that, "In 1990 more of the work force is going to be minorities—Hispanics, blacks—and women. The companies that started building bridges back in the 1970s will be all right. Those that didn't won't."[17] The free market has its own way of eroding color and sexual barriers in the search for the best talent. No one would argue, for example, that baseball has poorer talent for dropping its color barrier. To find that talent in its best form, bridges had to be built that extended far into, for example, the population of Puerto Rico. Businesses will be analogously improved if they extend their boundaries and provide the proper training programs. Bill McEwen of Monsanto Corporation and spokesperson for the National Association of Manufacturers notes that this extension not only will happen but has been happening at NAM companies for twenty years:

> We have been utilizing affirmative action plans for over 20 years. We were brought into it kicking and screaming. But over the past 20 years we've learned that there's a reservoir of talent out there, of minorities and women that we hadn't been using before. We found that it works.[18]

Some corporations have found it difficult to find and keep these talented persons and therefore have developed incentives and special benefits, such as job-sharing, home work, flextime, extended maternity leave, and day-care centers in order to keep them. These companies include Gannett, General Foods, General Motors, IBM, Lotus Development, Mellon Bank, Mutual Life, Peat Marwick Mitchell, and Proctor & Gamble.[19]

(2) A second reason is that pulling the foundations from beneath affirmtive action hiring would open old sores, especially for municipalities and corporations who over a period of years have developed target goals and quotas either through a consent-decree process with courts or direct negotiations with representatives of minority groups such as PUSH and the NAACP. These plans—

which now cover over 20 million Americans employed by federal contractors alone—have been agonizingly difficult to develop in some cases and would be disintegrated by the principle that goals and timetables are impermissible. Removal might also stigmatize a business by signalling to minority groups a return to older patterns of discrimination.[20]

(3) Third, the risk of reverse discrimination suits would be minimized, not maximized, by the use of goals and quotas. This paradox has been explained by Peter Robertson of Organizational Resource Counselors:

> In a recent survey of chief executive officers by the management consulting firm for which I work, 95 percent indicated that they will use numbers as a management tool to measure corporate progress whether the government requires them or not. However, once the government requirements are gone, there would be a risk of so-called "reverse discrimination" suits alleging that employers have gone too far with affirmative action.[21]

Thus, government programs and court decisions that *allow* voluntary goals and quotas actually protect good-faith employers rather than undermining them. As Robertson points out, the president of the National Association of Manufacturers, Alexander Trowbridge, has been making exactly that point to affiliate manufacturers. It has also been reported that many corporations enthusiastically greeted the 1986 and 1987 pro-affirmative-action decisions in the U.S. Supreme Court, because they feared that if the Justice Department's argument had been victorious, then employers would have been exposed to reverse discrimination suits by white males because of the plans corporations already had in effect.[22]

(4) Finally, the editors of *Business Week* have offered the following general reason in favor of voluntary and negotiated goals and quotas: "Over the years business and regulators have worked out rules and procedures for affirmative action, including numerical yardsticks for sizing up progress, that both sides understand. It has worked and should be left alone."[23] The reason why it has worked is intrinsic to a businesslike approach to problems: Managers set goals and timetables for almost everything they hope to achieve—from profits to salary bonuses. From a manager's point of view, setting goals and timetables is simply a basic way of measuring progress. One survey of 200 major American corporations found that over 75 percent already use "voluntary internal numerical objectives to assess [equal employment opportunity] performance."[24] A side benefit of the use of such numerical objectives is to create a ready defense of one's practices for government investigators, unions, or minority group representatives who inquire into the company's historical record. Many corporations have also promoted their record through public reports and recruiting brochures. Such reports and brochures have been developed, for example, by Schering-Plough, Philip Morris, Exxon, AT&T, IBM, Westinghouse, and Chemical Bank.[25]

CONCLUSION

Early in this paper I acknowledged that all racial and sexual discrimination, including reverse discrimination, is prima facie immoral, because a basic principle of justice creates a duty to abstain from such treatment of persons. But no absolute duty is created come what may. The thesis I have defended is that considerations of compensatory justice, equal opportunity, and utility are *conjointly* of sufficient weight to neutralize and overcome the quite proper presumption of immorality in the case of some policies productive of reverse discrimination.

My conclusion is premised on balancing several moral principles as well as on empirical judgments about the actual state of discrimination in American society. With some basic changes, the presumption might turn in a different direction, and thus my claims are contingent on the social circumstances. Moreover, I agree with critics of the position I have defended that the introduction of preferential treatment on a large scale might in some measure produce economic advantages to some who do not deserve them, protracted court battles, jockeying for favored position by other minorities, congressional lobbying by power groups, a lowering of admission and work standards in vital institutions, reduced social and economic efficiency, increased racial hostility, and continued suspicion that well-placed women and minority group members received their positions purely on the basis of quotas. Conjointly these reasons consitute a strong case against policies that use numerical goals and quotas in hiring, promotion, firing, and layoffs. However, this powerful case is not strong enough to overcome the even more powerful case against it.

NOTES

1. "Their Right to Remedy, Affirmed," *New York Times,* July 3, 1986, p. A30.
2. See the date and comments in the following sources: Kenneth M. Davidson, Ruth B. Ginsburg, and Herma H. Kay, eds., *Sex-Based Discrimination: Text, Cases and Materials* (Minneapolis: West Publishing Company, 1974), esp. Ch. 3. Hereafter *Sex-Based Discrimination;* Irene Pave, "A Woman's Place is at GE, Federal Express, P&G . . . ," *Business Week,* June 23, 1986, pp. 75–76; Winifred Yu, "Asian Americans Charge Prejudice Slows Climb to Management Rank," *Wall Street Journal,* September 11, 1985, p. 35.
3. From *Discrimination Against Women: Congressional Hearings on Equal Rights in Education and Employment,* ed. Catharine R. Stimpson (New York: R. R. Bowker, 1973), 505–506.
4. See Juan Williams, "The Vast Gap Between Black and White Visions of Reality" and "Blacks Don't See It The Way Whites Do," *Washington Post,* March 31, 1985, pp. K1, K4.
5. As reported by Rudolf A. Pyatt, Jr., "Significant Job Studies," *Washington Post,* April 30, 1985, pp. D1-D2.

6. See "Business Bulletin," *Wall Street Journal,* February 28, 1985, p. 1.
7. *Maurianne Adams and Mary Schroeder* v. *Smith College,* Massachusetts Commission Against Discrimination, Nos. 72–S–53, 72–S–54 (December 30, 1974). Hereafter *The Smith College Case.*
8. 433 F.2d 421, 426 (8 cir. 1970).
9. *The Smith College Case,* pp. 23, 26.
10. *Ibid.,* pp. 26–27.
11. As reported by and quoted in Al Kamen, "Justices Attack Inadvertent Bias," *Washington Post,* January 10, 1985, p. A4.
12. *The Federal Civil Rights Enforcement Effort—1974,* 2: p. 276.
13. *Ibid.,* p. 281.
14. *Ibid.;* all the following text references are from pp. 281–286.
15. *Local 28* v. *Equal Employment Opportunity Commission,* U.S. 84–1656. All the following quotations are from this case.
16. See Pave, "A Woman's Place," p. 76.
17. As quoted in Walter Kiechel, "Living with Human Resources," *Fortune,* August 18, 1986, p. 100.
18. As quoted in Peter Perl, "Rulings Provide Hiring Direction: Employers Welcome Move," *Washington Post,* July 3, 1986, pp. A1, A11.
19. See Alex Taylor, "Why Women Managers are Bailing Out," *Fortune,* August 18, 1986, pp. 16–23 (cover story).
20. See Mary Thornton, "Justice Dept. Stance on Hiring Goals Resisted," *Washington Post,* May 25, 1985, p. A2; Linda Williams, "Minorities Find Pacts with Corporations Are Hard to Come By and Enforce," *Wall Street Journal,* August 23, 1985, p. 13; and Perl, "Rulings Provide Hiring Direction," pp. A1, A11.
21. Peter C. Robertson, "Why Bosses Like to Be Told to Hire Minorities," *Washington Post,* November 10, 1985, pp. D1–D2.
22. Perl, "Rulings Provide Hiring Direction," p. 1; Al Kamen, "Justice Dept. Surrenders in War on Hiring Goals," *Washington Post,* March 28, 1987, p. A4.
23. Editorial, "Don't Scuttle Affirmative Action," *Business Week,* April 5, 1985, p. 174.
24. Robertson, "Why Bosses Like to Be Told," p. 2.
25. *Ibid.*

Groups and Justice

George Sher

In this paper I want to discuss one argument in favor of preferential treatment for the members of groups whose past members have suffered discrimination. On the argument in question such preference is said to be justified by the fact that it compensates for injustices *done to the relevant groups themselves.* By focusing on wronged groups, and not on their individual members, the argument may seem to avoid the problem of justifying preference for group members who were not themselves the victims of discrimination. However, despite this apparent advantage, I believe the argument should be rejected. In particular, I shall argue that it fails because (a) racial and sexual groups are not enough like persons to fall under the principle of distributive justice, and (2) even if such groups did fall under it, that principle could not possibly justify preferential treatment for their current, nondeprived members.

I

There is some initial appeal to the claim that discriminated-against groups have received "less than their fair share" of good jobs, educational opportunities, and other benefits in the past, and so deserve more of these benefits than they ordinarily would as compensation now. We have a fairly firm grasp of what constitutes fair sharing among individuals, and it is not unnatural to think that this notion might extend to groups as well. But there are pitfalls here. What constitutes an individual's fair share is determined by a principle of distributive justice that seems to dictate an equal distribution of goods except when persons differ in need or merit. Hence, a person's fair share is inextricably bound up with, and cannot be determined without a knowledge of, his merits and needs. If our notion of fair share is to be extended to groups, then this connection will have to carry over. What constitutes a group's fair share will have to be bound up with that group's needs and merits in a manner at least strongly analogous to that in which an individual's fair share is bound up with his needs and merits. It seems to me, however, and I shall argue in this section, that racial and sexual groups simply do not *have* needs or merits of the appropriate sorts. If they do not, then the seemingly natural claim that discriminated-against groups were denied their fair share of goods will make no sense.

Consider, first, the sense of "need" that is relevant to the principle of distributive justice. To say in this sense that an entity needs a good is just to say that the good is necessary for the entity's well-being. Hence, only those entities that in principle can attain states of well-being can possibly have needs of the appropriate sorts. For human beings, this restriction poses no difficulty. Human beings are equipped, physiologically and psychologically, to benefit in indefinitely many ways. Hence, the only problem about determining their needs is to decide which levels of well-being should be considered minimally acceptable for them. But for ra-

Reprinted from George Sher, "Groups and Justice," *Ethics* 87 (1977): 174–181, by permission of The University of Chicago Press. © 1977 by The University of Chicago.

cial and sexual groups, the situation is dramatically different. Such groups, unlike their members, do not satisfy the preconditions for attaining any of the states of well-being with which we are familiar. They do not have single organized bodies, and so can neither sustain good bodily health nor suffer illness. They do not have nervous systems, and so cannot experience the various states of comfort and discomfort that these systems make possible. They do not have consciousness, and so cannot experience either amusement, happiness, interest, or self-esteem, or the less pleasant states that stand opposed to these. They do not even have the degree of legal or conventional organization that is shared by corporations, clubs, and other legal persons. Hence, they cannot increase or decrease their wealth or holdings as these other composite entities can. Because racial and sexual groups lack the sorts of organization that alone confer capacities to attain states of well-being, they can hardly have the sorts of needs that presuppose these capacities. Any statements that appear to attribute such needs to them must therefore be elliptical. Such statements either must attribute needs to some of the groups' members (in which case no additional properties will be attributed to the groups as wholes) or else must be ways of speaking about *average* degrees of need within the groups (in which case additional properties will in a sense be attributed to the groups as wholes, but those properties will not be relevant to the distribution of goods: An average need is no more a genuine need than an average citizen is a more genuine citizen).

It is also difficult to see how racial or sexual groups could satisfy any of the criteria for *merit* relevant to distributive justice. Those criteria are notoriously diverse. We sometimes tie merit to pure ability (however measured), but at other times we consider also, or instead, efforts expended, degrees of skill acquired, and goods produced. Despite this diversity, however, and whatever the logical and historical relations among them, our criteria for merit are at least unified by

one common presupposition. To satisfy any of them, an entity must in some sense be capable of *acting*. Skills and abilities are exercised only through actions. Hence, it would be senseless to speak of either the abilities or the skills of a nonagent. For similar reasons, nonagents can neither exert effort nor produce goods. Once again, this requirement hardly restricts our application of the criteria of merit among human beings. Persons are the source of our concept of action, and so of course it applies to them. The requirement does, however, seem to rule out our application of the criteria of merit to racial and sexual groups. These groups do not have the organization required to act at all. Hence, they cannot possibly perform the sorts of actions alone through which efforts are made, skills exercised, abilities demonstrated, and goods produced. Once again, therefore, it seems that any statements that appear to be about the merits of racial or sexual groups must really be about something else. Such statements must be about either the merits of individual group members or the average degrees of merit within groups.

These considerations show that racial and sexual groups cannot have the sorts of needs and merits that justify deviations from strictly equal distribution of goods. But even if no racial or sexual group can deserve *more* of any good than any other, it might still seem that each group can deserve the *same* amount of goods as every other. If this were so, then questions of fair sharing among racial and sexual groups could still arise. To suppose this, though, would be to overlook the common roots of the different elements of our concept of distributive justice. As Gregory Vlastos has made clear, both equal distribution under ordinary circumstances and unequal distribution when needs differ are ways of achieving the single goal of *equalizing benefits*.[1] The first is appropriate when each recipient would benefit equally from the good in question, the second when some would benefit more than others. If equal treatment and special treatment under special circumstances do both aim at equalizing benefits, then what is deserved in each case presupposes the capacity to benefit. Hence, the proper conclusion is not merely that racial and sexual groups do not qualify for exemptions from equal treatment, but rather, and more radically, that such groups do not fall under the principle of distributive justice at all.[2] There may indeed be circumstances in which justice dictates preference for each group member; but if there are, this must be because each group member has suffered deprivation in the past. In any such case, it will be the affected individuals, and not the group itself, to whom the principle of distributive justice applies.

II

Thus far the argument has been that racial and sexual groups lack the sorts of organization they would need to deserve goods, and so all talk of unjust distributions of goods among them is out of place. In this section I want to make a further point: Even if it *were* possible to distribute goods unjustly among these groups, a policy of preferential treatment extending to their undeprived members could not possibly compensate for such injustices.

It seems obvious enough that the principle of distributive justice cannot apply only to racial and sexual groups. If it is to apply to groups of these sorts, it will have to apply also to cultural, religious, and geographic ones. But having widened our horizons this far, why should we stop even here? There are really as many groups as there are combinations of people; and if we are going to ascribe claims to equal treatment to racial, sexual, and other groups with high visibility, it will be mere favoritism not to ascribe similar claims to all these other groups as well. Moreover, if all groups do have the same claim to equal treatment, then all groups must also have the same claim to compensation for unequal treatment. Any compensation that is deserved by a deprived racial or sexual group must also and equally be

deserved by any other similarly deprived group. Once these natural assumptions are granted, however, it is easily shown that any case for the preferential treatment of nondeprived members of deprived racial or sexual groups would be precisely matched, and so destroyed, by similar cases for the preferential treatment of all other undeprived individuals.

Suppose that G is a group composed of all the individuals with a given racial or sexual characteristic. Moreover, suppose that most, but not all, of these individuals have suffered the privations of discrimination in the past. Let Adams, Brown, and Carpenter be the nondeprived members of the G, and let Edwards, Frederics, and Gordon be a similar number of nondeprived members of non-G. If deprived groups do deserve compensation, and if preferential treatment of their undeprived members is a proper way of effecting such compensation, the past deprivation of G will justify preferential treatment for Adams, Brown, and Carpenter. However, since all deprived groups must deserve compensation if any do, and since the "mixed" group consisting of the deprived members of G plus Edward, Frederics, and Gordon (call this group M) was precisely as deprived as G itself, the case for preference for Adams, Brown, and Carpenter will be precisely matched by a similar case for preference for Edwards, Frederics, and Gordon. Moreover, since the same reasoning must justify preference for the nondeprived members of all other mixed groups—and since everyone belongs to one or another of these—the ultimate conclusion must be that all nondeprived individuals (as well, of course, as all deprived ones) deserve preferential treatment now. But this is plainly absurd. If everyone deserved preference, there would be no one to whom anyone deserved to be preferred, and so no one would deserve preference.

It might seem possible to avoid these difficulties by showing that Adams, Brown, and Carpenter deserve preference over Edwards, Frederics, and Gordon in a slightly different way. It seems no less reasonable that groups that were overprivileged in the past deserve less than their ordinary fair shares than it does that groups that were underprivileged deserve more. Hence, since non-G has been precisely as overprivileged as G has been underprivileged, it might seem that non-G's members, Edwards, Frederics, and Gordon, deserve less than equal treatment now, and so, indirectly, that Adams, Brown, and Carpenter deserve preference over them. But this argument is just as vulnerable to refutation by generalization as its twin. If discrimination is called for against the current members of any overprivileged groups, then it must be called for against the current members of all of them. And since the mixed group M was precisely as underprivileged as G in the past, its complement, non-M, must have been precisely as overprivileged as G's complement, non-G. Hence, any case for discrimination against Edwards, Frederics, and Gordon because of their membership in non-G will again be precisely matched by a parallel case for discrimination against Adams, Brown, and Carpenter because of their membership in non-M.

If these remarks are correct, then even granting that deprived racial and sexual groups were denied distributive justice will not establish that the current, nondeprived group members should be afforded preference now. However, there may appear to be a problem with my argument's pivotal claim that artificially constructed groups like M are as deserving of compensation as deprived racial or sexual groups like G. Even though M has undoubtedly suffered the same amount of deprivation as G, the fact remains that it was prejudice focused on the relevant racial or sexual characteristic, but no prejudice focused on the arbitrary characteristic of M-ness, that was responsible for the deprivation of the two groups. For this reason, G may still seem to be the group that is the more deserving of compensation. But if so, then there will indeed be a reason to afford Adams, Brown, and Carpenter preference over Edwards, Frederics, and Gordon.

However, I do not think this objection can be sustained. To see the difficulties it involves, consider first the claim that certain intentions on the part of discriminatory agents can increase their victims' degrees of desert. The most plausible version of this claim is that desert of compensation increases when discriminatory acts are performed with the intention of harming their victims. However, there are at least two reasons why the claim, thus interpreted, is not likely to establish that G deserves compensation more than M. First, many of those who discriminated in the past held stereotyped views of their victims. Blacks were perceived as possessing criminal tendencies and lacking industry, women as being unable to do a full day's work, and so on. In light of these stereotypes, it seems reasonable to suppose that much discrimination was practiced not with the intention of harming blacks or women, but rather only with the intention of denying goods to anyone with those legitimately desert-canceling characteristics that blacks and women were mistakenly thought to possess. To the extent that this is so, it is hard to see how the intention behind the discrimination could increase the desert of these groups now. Moreover, even when discrimination has been guided by the intent to do harm, the intention is hardly likely to have been to harm any racial or sexual group. Only a very sophisticated bigot could intend to harm a group as opposed to its members; and yet in the absence of any intention to harm G itself, the principle that discriminators' intentions to harm their victims increase those victims' degrees of desert will not distinguish G's desert from M's.

There is also a deeper difficulty with the claim that the intentions behind past discrimination make G more deserving of compensation than M. This difficulty emerges when we recall the point of compensating for breaches of distributive justice. To compensate someone for receiving less than his proper share of a given good is simply to restore to him, as far as is possible, the good of which he has been unjustly deprived, or which he has been unjustly prevented from attaining. Since this is so, his desert of compensation must depend on precisely the same considerations as those which determined his initial claim to that good. But, except perhaps in some freakish and irrelevant cases, initial claims to goods are never a function of the (future) intentions of disruptive agents. Hence, subsequent desert of compensation for unjust distribution can hardly be affected by those intentions either.[3] Because desert of compensation for unjust distribution is independent of the intentions of those who acted unjustly, the fact that the common members of G and M were deprived because they belonged to G but not because they belonged to M cannot possibly bear on the degrees to which the two groups deserve compensation. Thus, it remains true that no breach of distributive justice involving a group could call for a preferential policy extending to that group's current non-deprived members.[4] If past violations of distributive justice are to license preference for all current group members, this can only be because each of these individuals has himself or herself been treated unjustly.[5]

NOTES

1. Gregory Vlastos, "Justice and Equality," in *Social Justice*, ed. Richard B. Brandt (Englewood Cliffs, N.J.: Prentice-Hall, 1962), 31–72.
2. Vlastos actually argues that all justified exceptions to equal distribution, those based on differences in merit as well as those based on differences in need, have a common equalitarian

ground. If true, this claim would provide even stronger reason to reject the view that racial and sexual groups can qualify for distributive justice than what has been said so far. However, since Vlastos's argument concerning merit is rather intricate, and since the considerations already raised seem quite sufficient to disqualify those groups from deserving distributive justice, I will not pursue this point further.

3. This conclusion is borne out of our intuitions in simple cases. If A is deprived of a month's social security benefits by a malicious clerk while B is deprived of a similar amount by a merely careless clerk, our reaction is surely that despite the clear difference in the clerks' intentions, both A and B deserve precisely what has been withheld from them, perhaps including interest, and nothing more.

4. The argument of this section is related to, yet distinct from, an argument advanced by Robert Simon in his "Preferential Hiring: A reply to Judith Jarvis Thomson," *Philosophy and Public Affairs* 3 (Fall 1974): 312–320. Simon contends that (a) it is not obvious that the preferential treatment of group members could serve to compenste a wronged group and that (b) at least in the case of preferential hiring, this is unlikely because "preferential hiring policies award compensation to an arbitrarily selected segment of the group; namely those who have the ability and qualifications to be seriously considered for the jobs available" (p. 315). My contention, by contrast, is that even if all the members of a particular disadvantaged group were compensated, the procedure would still be arbitrary in that it would stop short of compensating the equally deserving members of other disadvantaged groups.

5. I have benefited from helpful discussion of these topics with Michael Levin and William E. Mann.

Comparable Pay for Comparable Work?

Robert L. Simon

"Equal pay for equal work" is one of the most defensible and most widely accepted principles to have been implemented in this country in the name of equal opportunity. However, implementation of the principle of equal pay for equal work has not significantly closed the gap between the pay men receive and the pay women receive in the marketplace. Thus, in 1955, women's earnings were about 60 percent of the earnings of men, and today women continue to make only about 60 cents for every dollar men make in the workplace.[1]

One fact that helps explain a significant portion of this gap between men's and women's earnings is the concentration of women in low-paying job categories. Roughly four-fifths of all women work in 25 of the 420 job categories listed by the Department of Labor.[2] Clearly, implementation of the principle of equal pay for equal work will not close the gap between the earnings of males and earnings of females so long as, on the average, men and women are not doing the *same* work.

Accordingly, the support of many advocates of pay equity has shifted from the principle of equal pay for equal work to a new principle: the principle of *comparable pay for work of comparable worth* (PCW). Proponents of PCW argue that if the jobs in which women are concentrated are equal in worth to traditionally male jobs but pay less, then unequal pay across these job categories is inequitable and unjust.

Such an approach is not entirely new. For example, systems of job evaluation have been employed by the federal government

and by many private employees to assess comparative pay of different job categories.[3] On a more intuitive level, who has not wondered whether some highly paid job category is really more important than a lower paid one? Is the work done by police officers of less worth than that performed by better paid corporate vice presidents in charge of advertising? Isn't the work of teachers equal in value to that of many lawyers, professional athletes, or entertainers?

Advocates of comparable worth want to generate a social policy from the sentiments that lie behind such questions. However, implementation of some version of PCW should take place only after extensive debate and consideration. If the difficulties PCW generates are not understood and faced, this principle is all too likely to become a purely political weapon that, while capable of generating intense feelings of discontent, is unlikely to result in more equity in the workplace. In the following pages we will explain and examine some of these difficulties in an effort to evaluate comparable worth as a social policy.

THE MEANING OF COMPARABLE WORTH

As we will see, many questions can be raised about the justice and fairness of various versions of PCW. However, before turning to such fundamental *moral* concerns, we must be clear about the notion of comparable worth itself. In particular, what does it *mean* to say that two jobs are of comparable

Reprinted by permission of the author, who gratefully acknowledges the National Endowment for the Humanities for a summer stipend that supported the work on this paper.

worth? How are we to tell when two jobs are comparable? These questions, sometimes blurred together under the heading "the measurement problem," are of fundamental importance. Principles such as PCW can guide conduct only if they are clear enough so that those to whom they apply can understand what is being required of them.

As suggested above, the measurement problem really has two distinct parts. The first is to explain what is meant by "comparable worth." The second is to formulate a criterion for measuring comparable worth, as so defined. Without solutions to these problems, enforcement of PCW would be arbitrary and inequitable. Jobs judged comparable by one conception of comparable worth would not be so judged by another. Even if there were agreement on a conception of comparable worth, different criteria of measurement would yield different rankings of job categories. But justice and equity cannot vary arbitrarily; they require consistent application of defensible principles so that similar cases are treated alike.

We can begin with the question of meaning. What does it mean to say that two jobs are of comparable worth? Unfortunately, comparable worth can be understood in a variety of ways, many of which are irrelevant to understanding what advocates have in mind. For example, if we take the worth of a job to refer to its *intrinsic moral worth,* jobs would be comparable only when their intrinsic moral worth was equivalent. To the extent that this notion is intelligible at all (for it is far from clear that jobs even have intrinsic moral worth, let alone different degrees of it), it might rest on intuitions that some jobs—for example modeling for pornographic pictures—seem less worthy than others—for example that of a dedicated physician.

However, this clearly is not what advocates of comparable worth have in mind, and for good reason. It is difficult to see how an overall ranking of the intrinsic moral worth of different jobs is to be derived, or what would make it defensible. Moreover, it

is doubtful if any one such ranking, even if it could be shown to be defensible, should be implemented in a pluralistic society in which the intuitions of many individuals and groups are likely to differ significantly.

If advocates of comparable worth do not mean to refer to the moral value of jobs, what do they mean? Perhaps the best clue is the reliance by advocates on job evaluation studies as measuring devices. These studies assess such factors as the degree of responsibility a job requires, the quality of working conditions, the training needed to do the work, the degree of skill required, and so forth. This list suggests that advocates of comparable worth conceive of the worth of a job as its "level of demand," where the demand a job makes on a worker is a function of the application of a variety of demand-making criteria. Different jobs are comparable when they make equivalent demands on the worker, as measured by a variety of demand-making factors. "Level of demand" here is being used as a technical term to refer to the aggregate of factors held to be criteria of what the job requires. So, in this view, secretaries are underpaid relative to truck drivers if and only if truck drivers make more than secretaries but their jobs are no more demanding.

The problem with this view is that there does not appear to be any one favored set of demand-making criteria specifying the "level of demand" of particular jobs. On the contrary, job evaluations themselves rest on controversial value judgments. For example, should enhanced responsibility be viewed as a burden that makes a job more difficult or as an asset that makes a job more stimulating? Is outdoor work more demanding than indoor work since workers may have to be on the job in inclement weather, or is it less demanding since workers get fresh air and are not chained to a desk? Even if we could arrive at uncontroversial answers to questions regarding criteria for the level of demand, how would we *weigh* such criteria in case of conflict? If librarians require more training than city bus drivers, but the bus drivers work under greater stress, which job is of greater worth? Clearly, each of these questions calls for complex evaluations which raise normative issues rather than ones that can be settled by straightforward observation of the "facts."

Conceptions of comparable worth can vary, then, according to the criteria for the level of demand that are employed and the weight assigned to each. Therefore, we should think of comparable worth not as one principle but as a related family of principles that differ from one another, often in significant respects. Thus, in any debate about comparable worth, it is important to make sure that all parties involved are considering the same conception.

Perhaps more importantly, if there is no way of showing that one conception of comparable worth is more defensible than others, application of any one conception rather than another seems arbitrary. Even if there is a defensible conception, if we can't tell what it is, implementation of comparable worth will be open to charges of inequity and unfairness. Jobs will be rated as comparable or noncomparable without a justified basis for doing so.

So far we have been talking only about the meaning of comparable worth. However, even if we could agree on the nature and weight of the criteria of comparable worth, application of such criteria also involves normative issues. For example, even if we agree that, all else being equal, greater responsibility entails a greater level of demand, how are we to measure responsibility? Is responsibility related to the number of people one supervises, the level of decision making one holds within a firm, the costs of misjudgment, or what? Thus, an airline mechanic may supervise few people but has a great deal of responsibility for people's lives. Is the mechanic's responsibility greater than that of top executives in the airline's office? How are we to tell?

The problems of meaning and measurement often are claimed to undermine completely the case for comparable worth. How can comparable worth be an instrument for securing social justice if there are no defensible criteria of comparability, no defensible assignments of weight to conflicting criteria, and no clear way to measure application of the criteria in controversial cases?

At this point advocates of comparable worth may agree that comparison of jobs does rest on arguable value judgments. It does not follow, they will point out, that such judgments must be entirely arbitrary or indefensible. For one thing, even though many judgments about comparability will be controversial, many more may not. For example, most of us would agree that normally a person who has the responsibility for evaluating the work of many employees has more responsibility than an employee who performs routine clerical tasks. Moreover, even if it is arguable in theory that a routine job should receive greater compensation than one that involves stimulating responsibilities, which presumably are their own reward, that is not the way the market traditionally has worked. Males with responsible jobs generally have received greater compensation than those performing routine tasks. Accordingly, proponents of comparable worth can argue that there are widely shared intuitions and inherited practices that can form a core of standards for evaluating conceptions of comparable worth. Although the core will have to be expanded in controversial ways to deal with difficult cases, advocates claim that it is equally controversial to rely on the market alone.

In other words, advocates of comparable worth can argue that starting with relatively uncontested judgments and practices, society, through debate, can work toward a *reflective equilibrium* on job comparability.[4] Such a reflective equilibrium will have been reached when the jobs we intuitively feel are comparable are shown to be so by principles we are willing to accept and which yield no conflicting or counterintuitive decisions in other cases. The process of reaching such a reflective equilibrium involves the mutual adjustment and readjustment of judgments and principles until they fit together in harmony. While a reflective equilibrium is reached, if at all, only after an extended process of consideration and debate, the process itself is likely to move us closer to consensus. In any case, advocates would argue that the results are likely to be less unjust and unfair than the way the market currently treats women.

Such an approach does at least show that problems of meaning and measurement are not necessarily unresolvable. However, whether the attempt to achieve reflective equilibrium constitutes a plausible response to such problems is unclear. First of all, since the process of achieving reflective equilibrium takes considerable time, it will be unclear at any given point in the process whether particular job comparisons are warranted. This would count substantially against attempts to impose standards of comparable worth in one giant leap; for example, through congressional action or Supreme Court decision. Without actually going through the process, we would have no reason to place confidence in the defensibility of the imposed standards.

Moreover, even if this problem could be avoided, perhaps by having individual firms autonomously adopt their own standards of comparable worth, greater problems remain. For one thing, there is no guarantee that a social consensus about comparability will emerge. Individuals may arrive at their own personal reflective equilibriums, but why should those individual systematizations be in agreement with one another? Perhaps even more importantly, even if such a social agreement were to emerge from individual reflection, what moral weight would it have? Why should it be equated with the dictates of equity and justice rather than being regarded as a socially determined political consensus reflecting persuasion and political tradeoffs? How are we to distinguish a mere consensus from rational convergence on a common and defensible point of view?[5]

While such objections surely have force, they may not be decisive. After all, while there is no guarantee that a defensible equilibrium will be reached, there is no guarantee in other areas of social policy either. To the extent that the process of open discussion and democratic decision making is itself justifiable, it is as defensible in the area of comparable worth as in other areas of policy making. At the very least, by encouraging free discussion and criticism of prevailing views, biases are likely to be detected and criteria of comparability are likely to be gradually improved by exposure to the light of rational examination.

Our discussion suggests, then, that although questions of meaning are fundamental, they may not be so severe as to entirely undermine the case for comparable worth. Of course, if there is no clear account of how comparable worth is to be understood, it is likely to become a political football employed simply to advance the interests of groups that would benefit by its implementation. That may or may not be good policy, but it should not be confused with social justice. Nevertheless, it is at least arguable that defensible standards of comparability, initially based on considered judgments and existing practice, will emerge from the democratic decision-making process. Surely the burden of proof may still be on advocates to show that a given conception of comparable worth is defensible. Nevertheless, there may exist a procedure that would enable them to meet the task. Although healthy scepticism about that procedure may be warranted, it has not been established by the arguments we have considered that comparable worth is a necessarily unintelligible notion to be thrown out on grounds of incomprehensibility alone.

COMPARABLE WORTH AND SOCIAL JUSTICE

As we have seen, women tend to work in only a few of the occupations listed by the Labor Department, and there tend to be very few males in these occupations. For example, 97 percent of registered nurses are female, 99 percent of secretaries are female, and 84 percent of elementary school teachers are female. Moreover, as the number of males in a job category increases, so does the pay.[6] For example, household workers, 95 percent of which are female, make about half the average salary of janitors, 85 percent of which are males. Secretaries make only about three-fourths the average salary of truck drivers, virtually all of whom are male.[7] As stated earlier, overall women's earnings tend to be about 60 percent of the earnings of men in the marketplace.

This suggests a rationale for comparable worth. Most advocates of some version of PCW do not view it as a principle of ideal social justice, which any society must implement if it is to be fully just. That is, proponents of comparable worth tend not to claim that the market principle of compensation, "to each according to supply and demand," is inherently unjust. However, they argue that when differences in wages reflect sex discrimination, then the market has not operated properly, and corrective application of PCW is called for. In other words, comparable worth probably is best thought of as a principle of *corrective justice*. The point of instituting comparable worth is to correct for a breakdown in the market involving discrimination against women. Hence, comparable worth need not be instituted across the board, but only in those areas where women have been victimized by unfair treatment.

What is the evidence that women have been discriminated against? The wage gap itself often is cited as evidence of overt discrimination against women by employers. But while it cannot be doubted that such overt discrimination exists, there is considerable disagreement over whether it explains a significant proportion of the wage gap. Broad generalizations of the form, "Women make only X percent of what men make," tend not to be helpful, since it is the significance of such statistical claims that is at issue.

Many labor economists cite such premarket factors as the greater tendency of women to interrupt their careers, sex differences in educational background, and the greater willingness of women to sacrifice career goals for family responsibilities as explanations for a significant part of the wage gap.[8] Thus, according to one recent study of a corporation, even when offered promotions and responsibilities commensurate with those of men, women tend to turn them down more often.[9] Many labor economists argue further that when women make the same market choices as men, they are similarly rewarded, as comparisons of the earnings of never-married working men and women suggest.[10] One typical statement by a labor economist asserts that "perhaps half of the overall 40 percent differential between the earnings of men and women is due to premarket factors."[11]

Statistics by themselves will not show whether the wage gap, as well as the disproportionate representation of women in certain job categories, results from discrimination, the choices women make, or some complex interaction between the two. According to the theory of rational choice, women make rational decisions, based on their own values, to subordinate career to family responsibilities to a greater extent than men. According to critics of such a view, women make such decisions only because their expected return on the market is much less than men because of discrimination, and hence they have less incentive to pursue careers.[12]

We cannot decide between these two views here, but several points can be made. First, even if overt discrimination does play some role in contributing to the wage gap, it is far from clear that comparable worth is an appropriate or necessary response. Existing equal opportunity legislation prohibits the kind of on-the-job discrimination by employers that is at issue. Second, even if on the job discrimination were eliminated, the wage gap would persist so long as women remain concentrated in lower-paying job categories. Such concentration does not seem to be caused primarily by employer discrimination, since it occurs when women first enter the job market and overt discrimination would take place after women were actually on the job.

However, advocates of comparable worth might plausibly distinguish overt on-the-job discrimination from the more systematic and covert discrimination that limits women's choices in the market. For example, until very recently, not only were many jobs held largely by males (such as that of bartender) deemed unsuitable for females, but such prejudices were upheld by the courts.[13] Since women saw that their opportunities in the job market were limited, it became rational for them to devote more time to family than to their careers. Women, in other words, are caught in a vicious circle. "Women stay home because of low wages; women earn low wages because they stay at home."[14] It is widespread social and economic barriers, ranging from guidance counselors who steer women into "acceptable" career paths to socially enforced stereotypes about unsuitable jobs for women, that keep women concentrated in low-paying job categories.

Such theories of covert discrimination seem more relevant to the case for comparable worth than appeals to overt discrimination by employers, since they call into question the legitimacy of the initial situation within which women first make economic choices. However, such approaches are not free from difficulty. For one thing, they run the risk of degenerating into the kind of feminist theories about socialization and conditioning that deny that women function as autonomous agents in the first place. It seems far too self-serving to dismiss the traditional preferences of many women as simply the products of conditioning while always assuming that preferences more to one's liking are the truly autonomous ones. Such a claim might sometimes be true, but it makes it all too easy, as one writer sympathetic to feminism points out, "to slide into the convenient idea that *whenever* women

make choices which feminists think they ought not to make, they must be conditioned, so giving feminists an excuse to discount those opinions.... The attempt to free women turns into a different way of coercing them."[15] Indeed, the picture of women as brainwashed puppets is unacceptable—and in fact is contradicted by the recent behavior of women in the work force who have integrated many predominantly male job categories.

However, advocates of the theory of covert discrimination need not dismiss the claim that women make autonomous choices. Indeed, the fact that women are moving into predominantly male job categories suggests that when given the same opportunities and the same expected return, many women will make market choices that are similar to those of men. In this view, the concentration of women in low-paying job categories does reflect women's choices, but their choices frequently don't reflect the values women would express in a fair and equal context for decision making. Rather, they are rational responses to the illegitimately confining set of incentives that women face.

This argument is not implausible, especially when it is shown to be compatible with some aspects of rational choice theory. However, its connection with comparable worth is not clear. Advocates assume that if covert discrimination is a principal factor underlying the wage gap, comparable worth is justified. But is that assumption correct?

For one thing, comparable worth does not seem to be a form of compensation for individual victims of discrimination. Comparable worth affects everyone in a benefited job category, whether or not they have individually suffered from discrimination. Indeed, not only does comparable worth ignore the important principle that compensation should be proportional to injury; it virtually stands it on its head. Older women, who have fewer years left to work but who presumably are most likely to have been victims of discrimination, will receive the fewest benefits. Younger women, particularly those just entering the job market, who are least likely to have been victims of discrimination, will work the greatest number of years under comparable worth and hence will receive the greatest benefits.

Advocates of comparable worth rightly will reply that their goal is not to compensate individuals for discrimination. But what then is the connection between comparable worth and alleged discrimination in the market? Perhaps it is that since the market wage scale is heavily influenced by sex discrimination, comparable worth provides an untainted and therefore fairer standard of compensation. It is not that market wages, set by supply and demand, are *inherently* unfair. Rather, it is that since women in our society have not been in a fair market, comparable worth should replace the wage standards set by a tainted pseudomarket procedure.

Before adopting such a procedure, however, we should be sure that adoption of some form of comparable worth does promote overall fairness. If the adoption of comparable worth would itself generate serious problems of justice and fairness, we would need to consider whether overall gains, in terms of social justice, outweigh losses before recommending adoption.

Consider, first, the problems that would arise if a single standard of comparable worth were promulgated through legislation or as the result of a major court decision. How would such a single standard be arrived at? On what basis would it be selected? What would justify the standard employed? If, as suggested earlier, judgments of comparability are all too likely to rest upon highly controversial and contestable value judgments, why should the new pay scale be any more equitable than the old one? If the standard cannot be justified, those who are disadvantaged by it will have no reason to accept the resulting wage scale as fair. Thus, even without considering the kinds of complications to be discussed below, it is doubtful whether clear gains in equity would be achieved by implementation of a single standard of com-

parable worth, at least so long as judgments of comparability lack a substantial basis.

Perhaps this difficulty can be avoided by implementing comparable worth on a piecemeal basis, in a long-term effort to reach a reflective equilibrium on comparability. In this view, individual firms, or perhaps individual localities, adopt their own internal comparable worth plans, and these need not be identical.

But this piecemeal approach also raises problems of justice and fairness. One such problem is that workers doing the same job in different firms might have their jobs evaluated totally differently. In Firm X security guards and secretaries might be regarded as comparable while in Firm Y they might not be regarded as comparable. Suppose that as a result of comparability rankings, secretaries in X were paid more than secretaries in Y, even though all the secretaries do the same work. Of course, secretaries in different firms are presently paid differently, just as assistant professors at Harvard may receive higher compensation than assistant professors at a less highly rated institution; but this would not be a result of a purely internal job evaluation scheme that might later be found to be in sharp conflict with our considered judgments.

Perhaps some initial arbitrariness must be expected as the price to be paid as we move toward a less arbitrary reflective equilibrium. After all, as advocates of comparable worth would claim, the market itself reflects inequity in the treatment of women. The temporary unfairness generated by piecemeal approaches to comparable worth may be less than the unfairness that would persist if the status quo were simply allowed to stand.

Even though such a rejoinder has force, other serious problems of equity remain. Some of these are not problems of pure theory, but may become particularly acute when some form of comparable worth is applied in the real world. For example, the piecemeal approach to comparable worth generates economic incentives for firms to select those evaluators whose conceptions of comparable worth create the least economic disadvantage. Each employer reasons that if other employers adopt comparable worth plans without regard to market advantage, she can do better by adopting a less disadvantageous plan. Indeed, even employers with some genuine commitment to comparable worth may have to act in such fashion as a defensive measure against other firms that use comparable worth to secure market gains. In either case, it is rational for the employer to select the conception of comparable worth that departs least from the wage structure the market would have dictated. We are left with the inequitable result that employers most seriously committed to comparable worth are most open to exploitation by less-committed competitors. Indeed, without a defensible standard of comparable worth, how are employers who take unfair advantage of the system even to be identified?

The evaluation of equity becomes even more complicated when other costs of comparable worth are considered. It is extremely likely, for instance, that implementation of some form of comparable worth will lead to an overall rise in wages. Thus, if the work of a firm's clerical staff is found to be comparable to that of higher-paid truckers, it is unlikely that pay cuts can be forced on the truckers. Instead, the salaries of the clerical workers will be raised to a comparable level. This means that the firm's overall costs of production will rise. These costs are generally passed on to consumers, but firms in weak positions may be unable to do this and in some cases may even be forced out of business.

Suppose that costs are passed on to consumers in the form of higher prices. It is by no means clear that such costs will be passed on equitably. If the firm produces necessities, the poor will pay a disproportionate share of the cost, since they spend a higher percentage of their income on necessities than do the more affluent. When the employer in question is the federal, state, or lo-

cal government, services may be cut in an effort to avoid tax hikes that pay increases would otherwise require. Again these cuts in services may disproportionately affect the relatively poor and powerless.

Perhaps most importantly, many economists argue that comparable worth may not help (and may even harm) the very group it is designed to benefit.[16] If comparable worth raises the employer's costs of doing business, it creates an incentive to reduce the number of employees whose salaries are above the market price. In other words, if comparable worth makes the cost of employing people in certain job categories excessive, employers will have an incentive to reduce the number of people holding such jobs. Since the jobs in question are those held predominantly by women, comparable worth may ultimately create fewer employment opportunities for women than would otherwise have existed.[17]

Of course, it is possible that such dire empirical consequences will not come about, or that negative consequences will be outweighed by gains. The issues here are in part empirical as well as conceptual and moral. The moral point, however, is that harmful or inequitable consequences must be given adequate weight in the evaluation of comparable worth and must not be ignored because of perhaps justified indignation about the economic situation of women in the market.

Finally, when considering questions of equity and fairness, we need to consider how much *weight* comparable worth should be given when it is in conflict with other values, such as efficiency. Suppose, for example, that a state's job evaluation plan finds that electrical engineers and city planners do comparable work but that the state is faced with a shortage of electrical engineers and a surplus of city planners. One way of luring talented engineers to the area, or of inducing students to study electrical engineering, is to raise the wages of the electrical engineers. But if in order to do so the state must also raise the wages of all workers in comparable jobs, not only may the costs be prohibitive but the incentive effects of higher wages would be lost. In spite of social needs, individuals would find it just as desirable to become city planners as electrical engineers. Comparable worth, then, is inefficient in so far as it limits our ability to use higher compensation to attract people to positions where they are needed.

Of course, some losses in efficiency may be warranted by gains in the overall justice of the system. Indeed, it is plausible to think that small gains in justice and fairness outweigh larger losses in overall efficiency, since it is normally wrong to make some people better off by treating others unjustly. On the other hand, losses in efficiency may become so great as to outweigh minor gains in justice or equity, or may themselves constitute an injustice if sufficiently great and distributed in unfair or questionable ways. Clearly, enormous losses in efficiency normally are not justified by small gains in the overall justice or fairness of a system. We have already seen that the costs of comparable worth may be borne disproportionately by the relatively poor and powerless or perhaps even by some of those women the policy was designed to help. But even if these costs are ignored, the inefficiencies generated by departure from the pricing system have to be balanced against whatever gains comparable worth may promote. Thus, before implementing any particular conception of comparable worth, we must decide *the degree to which implementation will be restricted in case of conflict with other values.* In other words, if comparable worth is not to be an absolute to be applied regardless of other costs, what tradeoffs should we be prepared to make?

It will be well to remember here that the line between such values as efficiency, on one hand, and equity and justice, on the other, is not always a sharp one. If the costs of inefficiency are borne disproportionately by the least advantaged and the least powerful, questions of equity and social justice are raised. Our discussion suggests that this may actually be the case with comparable worth.

At the very least, we need good reason to think the costs will be fairly distributed before we hop aboard the comparable worth bandwagon.

Finally, before concluding our discussion of equity and fairness, we need to consider in what sense comparable worth might be a "remedy" for the concentration of women in low-paying job categories. As we have seen, comparable worth is not a form of compensatory justice for individuals. Moreover, it is unlikely that it will eliminate such concentration; in fact, it may perpetuate it. Since institution of comparable worth would remove much of the economic incentive for women to follow the same career paths as men, by compensating "women's" work comparably to "men's" work, it could be argued that women would have less reason to leave traditional female career paths than under the present system.[18] As a matter of empirical fact, in recent years, there has been significant movement of women into some previously male-dominated jobs. In 1960, for example, only 9 percent of insurance adjusters were female, while in 1981, 58 percent were female. Similarly, recent figures reveal that 47 percent of bartenders now are women—a significant change from times when the courts refused even to allow women to be bartenders on the paternalistic grounds that women were too pure to be sullied by such work.[19] Gains in female representation also have been made in law, medicine, and business, although many other job categories tend to remain almost exclusively male. Would comparable worth remove financial incentives for even more sexual integration in the workplace?

We need to be careful of trying to have it both ways on this point. It is surely possible that higher pay for traditionally female jobs will draw more male candidates, contributing to sexual integration through the back door. In turn, increased competition may require more and more women to try for employment in traditionally male job categories. The empirical issues here are difficult, and no prediction is likely to be uncontroversial. But it is at least possible that comparable worth will result in a reduction of jobs in traditionally female employment categories, the consequent forcing out of women who are unprepared for or who prefer not to engage in traditionally male work, and only minimal male interest in traditionally female jobs. While this is undoubtedly a "worst possible case" scenario, is it any less probable than more favorable alternatives? On the other hand, if we don't promulgate a version of comparable worth, will more women in the work force be worse off than if we did? What kind of evidence do we need before we decide? Morally, what is the fairest way of distributing benefits and burdens? What should public policy be under conditions of uncertainty and even radical disagreement on such fundamental points?

CONCLUSIONS

What does our discussion suggest about the overall case for comparable worth? For one thing, it suggests that simplistic approaches and political analysis by slogan are to be rejected. Clarence Pendleton, Chair of the U.S. Civil Rights Commission in 1985, who referred to comparable worth as "looney tunes," surely is mistaken. On the other hand, unquestioning adherence to comparable worth simply because the intent of the policy is to benefit women, or because of support by some feminists, may also be unwarranted.

Just because the situation is complex, it does not follow that nothing sensible can be said about it. One thing rational analysis can do, even when no entirely satisfactory alternative is available, is to set out the costs of holding different positions. This not only puts each of us in a better position to see what objections need to be answered and to see which policy best coheres with our other moral judgments, it may also promote reasonable choice under conditions of uncertainty.

In particular, proponents of comparable worth face serious difficulties. For one thing, it is at best unclear whether jobs can be compared in the way required. Imposition of a single nationwide standard of comparability seems unjustified, given the difficulties of justification that we have explored. Alternatively, even if we might eventually achieve a societal reflective equilibrium on comparability through the piecemeal approach, we do not have one now. Hence, promulgation of some form of comparable worth will not necessarily promote more equity in the workplace, particularly at the start. Moreover, it also is unclear whether comparable worth will help women as a class, or whether it will only help some women perhaps at significant expense to others. Finally, comparable worth may assign costs to those least able to bear them and may encourage gerrymandering of individual comparable worth plans to secure market advantages.

Proponents of comparable worth may acknowledge these difficulties, but they reply that the overall costs, including any possible inequities, are less serious than those generated by present reliance on the market. Be that as it may, such a reply seems insufficient to justify adoption of comparable worth, at least at the present time. For one thing, as we have seen, the degree to which the wage gap is explained by discrimination, even of the covert variety, is controversial. But even leaving that point aside, is it sensible to adopt a new broad-scale social formula for setting wages without any guarantee, or even reasonable assurances, that gains in equity and social justice will result? Without such reasonable assurances, comparable worth looks more and more like a social policy that will benefit some groups at the expense of others rather than a requirement of social justice.

In short, we started out with the claim that comparable worth is needed to remedy the unjust treatment of women in the workplace. Our discussion suggests, however, that the burden of proof remains on advocates of comparable worth. That is, while the evidence we have considered warrants neither total rejection nor total acceptance of comparable worth, it does support a healthy scepticism. Unless there is good reason to believe that comparisons of jobs will be supportable, that the costs of implementation will be distributed fairly, and that some mechanism will be instituted to balance comparable worth against other values in case of conflict, adoption of comparable worth seems premature at best. Perhaps these problems can be resolved, but adoption of this policy in advance of a resolution would be unwarranted.

This does not mean that the plight of women in the job market should be ignored. Greater enforcement of equal opportunity legislation surely is needed. Where possible, work options such as "flex-time" and the institution of regulated day-care centers can help all workers, male or female, to reconcile responsibilities to both family and career. Greater sensivity among educators and guidance personnel can contribute to even greater sexual integration in the work force. Finally, the economic contribution that women make to their families can receive greater recognition and protection by law.

Accordingly, before we implement some version of comparable worth, we need to resolve the problems it presents. In view of the real difficulties facing it, we should not just assume that it is a clear requirement of justice and fairness in the workplace. Rather, we need to consider whether comparable worth really is a defensible remedy for social injustice rather than a device that will simply replace old problems with new ones while moving us no closer to the goals of fairness and justice that we all should seek.

NOTES

1. Ronald G. Ehrenberg and Robert S. Smith, *Modern Labor Economics* (Glenview, Ill.: Scott, Foresman and Company, 1982), 396. If a different base year is selected, different results are obtained. Thus, if 1964 is taken as the base, one finds a slight decrease in the gap by 1979. Clearly, great care must be taken in the use of statistics in this area.
2. "Paying Women What They're Worth," *Report from the Center for Philosophy & Public Policy* 3 (1983): 1–2.
3. For discussion, see Sharon P. Smith, *Equal Pay in the Public Sector: Fact or Fantasy* (Princeton: Princeton University Press, 1977).
4. The idea of reflective equilibrium is developed and applied to the justification of a theory of justice by John Rawls, in his *A Theory of Justice* (Cmbridge: Harvard University Press, 1971), especially pp. 46–48, 577–579.
5. R. M. Hare argues that appeal to reflective equilibrium amounts to little more than appeal to accepted beliefs in his "Rawls' Theory of Justice," *The Philosophical Quarterly*, 23 (1973): 144–155, 241–251.
6. Bureau of Labor Statistics, 1981, reprinted in "Paying Women What They're Worth."
7. Bureau of Labor Statistics, 1982, reprinted in "Paying Women What They're Worth."
8. For discussion, see Michael Evan Gold, *A Dialogue on Comparable Worth* (Ithaca: Cornell University Press, 1983), and Ehrenberg and Smith, *Modern Labor Economics,* 395–397.
9. See Carl Hoffmann and John Shelton Reed, "Sex Discrimination?—the XYZ Affair," *The Public Interest* 62 (1980): 21–39.
10. U.S. Bureau of Labor Statistics, *Handbook of Labor Statistics,* table 60. However, other figures show that some significant inequality of results persists even when never married men and women are compared; see Ehrenberg and Smith, *Modern Labor Economics,* pp. 397–398.
11. Ehrenberg and Smith, *Modern Labor Economics,* p. 39.
12. For discussion, see Gold, A Dialogue on Comparable Worth, pp. 14–16.
13. See, for example, *Goesaert* v. *Cleary,* 335 U.S. 464 (1948), upholding a Michigan law which provided that no woman (unless she was the wife or daughter of the male owner) could obtain a bartender's license.
14. Gold, *A Dialogue on Comparable Worth,* p. 14.
15. Janet Radcliffe Richards, *The Sceptical Feminist* (Boston: Routledge and Kegan Paul, 1980).
16. For discussion, see George Hildebrand, "The Market System," in *Comparative Worth,* ed. Robert Libernash, (Washington, D.C.: Equal Treatment Advisory Council, 1980), especially p. 106.

17. This point is debated throughout Gold, *A Dialogue on Comparable Worth.*
18. Conversely, higher salaries for traditionally female jobs may attract males to compete for such positions. However, this incentive effect may be less than expected if there is a stigma attached to men doing "women's work."
19. "More Women Work at Traditional Male Jobs," *New York Times,* No. 15, 1982, p. C26.

Three Incomparable Perspectives on Comparable Worth

Rosemarie Tong

Over twenty years have passed since Congress passed the Equal Pay Act of 1963 and the Civil Rights Act of 1964, but the gap between women's and men's wages has not decreased. All across the country women earn approximately 59 cents for every dollar men earn. Even when this wage differential is adjusted for such factors as women's "lesser seniority" or "sporadic participation" in the labor market, at least half of the gap between male and female wages goes unexplained.[1] Many social scientists now attribute this residual gap to job segregation according to sex. In 1983, 95 percent or more of all secretaries and registered nurses were female; and 80 percent or more of all child-care workers, billing clerks, librarians, waiters, and waitresses, and health technicians were female.[2] Since several studies have shown that the best single predictor for a job's compensation is not difference in education, labor force experience, or labor force commitment, but rather the sex of a worker performing that job,[3] it is not surprising that secretaries, 99 percent of whom are female, earn $12,000 annually, whereas truck drivers, 98 percent of whom are male, earn $16,300; or that child-care workers, 87 percent of whom are female, earn $7,900 annually, whereas mail carriers, 88 percent of whom are male, earn $21,000 annually.[4] Given that such wage differentials are numerous, we must ask ourselves why it is that workers in male-dominated jobs are paid more than workers in female-dominated jobs. Is it because men need more money than women? Or is it because man's work is intrinsically more valuable than women's work? Or, finally, is it because the market rewards the job choices of men more than those of women because it perceives the lines of work men choose as instrumentally more valuable than the lines of work women choose? Only when we ask such questions can we identify what, if anything, is unfair about the fact that women earn 59 percent as much as men and determine whether the pay equity movement—equal pay for women who hold jobs comparable in worth to those which men have traditionally occupied—is likely to remedy this unfairness (be it unfair).

Although there are a variety of ways in which to approach the issue of comparable worth, I would like to approach it from three different feminist perspectives. *Liberal* femi-

---

Reprinted by permission of the author.

nists believe that comparable worth is the latest stage in the evolution of equal employment policy, a stage that will see women, fully empowered by the law, march over the rainbow to claim their rightful share of that pot of gold men currently horde. *Socialist* feminists believe that comparable worth is a critical assault on the market basis of wages, the straw that will finally break the capitalist camel's back. And *radical* feminists believe that comparable worth is a major opportunity for society to re-evaluate value—to ask itself why it values certain jobs more than others. My purpose in examining these feminist perspectives is not so much to argue for or against comparable worth (even though I happen to support at least one version of the pay equity movement) as to suggest that its various proponents support it for reasons that may in the end be incompatible even if equally laudable.

MAN'S WORK VERSUS WOMAN'S WORK

That the kind of work men have traditionally done is intrinsically more valuable than the kind of work women have traditionally done or vice versa strikes me as a singularly indefensible claim. Imagine a world in which no one did the kind of work with which men have been associated or a world in which no one did the kind of work with which women have been associated. I doubt that either a world bereft of enterprise or a world devoid of nurturance appeals to many of us. Nevertheless, as Margaret Mead once wrote, "There are villages in which men fish and women weave and in which women fish and men weave, but in either type of village the work done by the men is valued higher than the work done by the women."[5] Mysteriously, even when woman's work is more essential for a group's survival than man's work, man's work is still more valued than woman's work for no other reason, it seems, then that it is *man's* work.

The biological, psychological, and cultural causes that ground the acceptance of this valuation by both men and women are so complex as to defy brief explanation. So strong are these biological, psychological, and cultural chains that many economic and political forces presumably strong enough to overwhelm them succumb to the proverbial fate of the irresistible force meeting the unmovable object. For example, one of the laws of capitalist development is to lower the cost of industrial labor as much as possible by paying all workers the same. Given that skilled men have consistently demanded high wages, we would suppose that capitalists would seek to hire women for lower wages—on the shaky grounds, I suppose, that women because they are women are unskilled—thereby forcing down men's wages. But so fierce has society's adherence been to the view that men should be paid higher wages than women that men—with the support of women—have been able to control the supply side of the law of supply and demand. In the past, not only were laws passed to exclude or restrict the labor of women, but unions did not press for higher wages for their female workers, and married women opted to stay at home, convinced either that "kinder, kirche, und kuche" was their destiny or that life at home was bound to be more pleasant than life in the factory. Whether or not married women willingly fled from the factory, married men used married women's conspicuous absence from the marketplace to press for a family or "head of household" wage.[6] Although the meeting of this demand made families better off, it made single men and single women worse off. Single men were, of course, deprived of "free" housekeepers, nurses, and female companionship; and single women were, of course, without a man to support them in a style to which they wanted to be accustomed. Admittedly, woman's desire to stay in man's castle lessened with an increase in her education and with an increase in everyone's consumer desires. But when married women started to seep back into the labor force, they tended to accept whatever wages were paid them since they were supposedly working for "extras" or for "personal enrichment." Not wanting to deprive their husbands of the satisfaction of bringing home the bacon, married women did not immediately ally with single women who were eating not cake but the crusts of bread the likes of Marie Antoinette would toss them. By the time married women realized that marriage is an ephemeral institution that can be ended either by death, or more frequently, by divorce, and by the time single women, "freed" by the sexual revolution, had children no man could or would support, the stage for the feminization of poverty had been set. Women were to be paid less than men no matter how worthy or needy of higher wages they were.

LIBERAL FEMINISTS

As liberal feminists became more aware of the discrepancies between men's and women's wages, they came to suspect that the discrepancies were due more to sex discrimination than any other factor. Using the rhetoric of merit, liberal feminists pressed first for equal pay for equal work and then for equal pay for comparable worth on the grounds that women are typically paid less than men for work that is no less demanding than man's work. So reasonable does it seem to pay, for example, janitors and household workers the same wage (whereas janitors are currently paid $11,400, household workers are currently paid $5,600), that we may initially wonder why or how anyone would, could, or should object to comparable worth.[7] Nevertheless, many critics were quick to object to comparable worth, arguing that it is not a meritocratic maneuver but a socialist plan and a particularly unworkable one at that. The three main arguments critics have advanced against comparable worth are (1) that comparable worth will destroy the free market system because salaries are and should be dictated by the

law of supply and demand, (2) that comparing dissimilar jobs is like comparing apples and oranges, and (3) that society will go bankrupt as it struggles to meet women's and minorities' demands for equal pay for comparable worth. If we examine these arguments as well as liberal feminists' responses to them, we will see that comparable worth, as conceived by liberal feminists, is compatible with the principles of the free market even if it is unworkable in its more ambitious forms.

The first argument, that comparable worth will destroy the free market starts off on high ground. The defender of the market argues that in a market economy income is distributed according to the kind of socially valuable choices people make. That is, beginning from different starting points, with a set of aptitudes and interests, individuals make personal choices about how to produce, consume, save, and invest. If society perceives these personal choices as beneficial to it, market mechanisms reward the persons who make them; and it is only fitting and proper that these "natural" economic forces not be countervailed by "artificial" political forces that would dare to benefit individuals who are not perceived by others as having made socially beneficial choices.[8] Hopefully, God did not really mean it when He said that the rain would fall on the "good" and "evil" alike or on the "wise" and "foolish" alike. Thus, if women are not being rewarded by the market, they are making the wrong job choices. Phyllis Schlafly suggests that women choose low-paying, dead-end jobs either because they favor "soft" jobs or because they are not willing to invest the time and energy high-paying, upwardly mobile jobs demand. She finds "intolerable" any suggestion that "people who are largely clerical workers and work in clean indoor offices that are heated in winter and air-conditioned in summer, nine to five, should be paid the same as policemen and firefighters who risk their lives on our behalf everyday in all kinds of inclement weather."[9] Schlafly believes that women—many of whom are part-time or intermittent workers—do not deserve to be paid as much as men—most of whom are full-time and continuous workers. Says Schlafly: "I think the majority of women want to be wives and mothers and they do not look at life as a full-time dedication to the work force. Now when you're a part-time or some-time worker, you simply aren't as valuable to your employer."[10]

Liberal feminists respond angrily to Schlafly's observations, arguing that Schlafly is failing to assign proper value to the job choices women currently make. We discover, they say, some very interesting things when jobs are evaluated in terms of "worth points" for the four components found in most jobs: (1) "knowledge and skills," defined as the "total amount of information or dexterity" needed to perform the job, (2) "mental demands," the extent to which the job requires decision making, (3) "accountability," the amount of supervision the job entails, and (4) "working conditions," such as whether the job is done inside a building or outdoors.[11] For example, in the Norman D. Willis and Associates' study for the state of Washington, we find that, on the average, compensation for female-dominated jobs was only 80 percent of that for male-dominated jobs. The following disparaties are not atypical:

A Food Service Worker I, at 93 points, earned an average salary of $472 per month, while a Delivery Truck Driver I, at 94 points, earned $792; a Clerical Supervisor III, at 305 points, earned an average of $794. A Nurse Practitioner II, at 385 points, had average earnings of $832, the same as those of a Boiler Operator with only 144 points. A Homemaker I, with 198 points and an average salary of $462, had the lowest earnings of all evaluated jobs.[12]

Given that registered nurses received many more "worth points" than boiler operators, we must ask ourselves why the state of Washington, up to the time of the Willis study, paid its nurses the same as its boiler operators. If it is the market's task to reward instrumentally valuable work, Washington nurses should have been better off than Washington boiler operators. If the market was failing to reward nurses because it had misperceived the value of women's work, then comparable worth is for the free market a blessing in disguise, an opportunity to pull the wool off its eyes and to live according to the law of supply and demand rather than to disobey it as it did in Milwaukee, where an increased demand for nurses was met not by paying American nurses more but by importing British nurses willing to work for low wages.[13] The argument that comparable worth will help rather than hinder the market is one that liberal feminists can make, or so think Helen Remick and Ronnie J. Steinberg. As these two women see it, comparable worth advocates are simply seeking to disentangle and remove the discrimination that is impeding the market's operation:

The laissez-faire doctrine underlying the free market ideology assumes that employers and employees bargain as equals. Comparable worth policy can contribute toward a more smoothly running marketplace. Ironically, by giving less powerful women the power resource of a legally backed right to be paid at a nondiscriminatory wage rate, comparable worth policy removes a market imperfection (i.e., inequality between employers and some employees) that impinges unfairly on groups with less market power. Theoretically at least, by interfering in the free market we re-establish *laissez-faire* as the organizing principle guiding social relations in the labor market.[14]

Of course, it is not clear that Remick and Steinberg are committed to a laissez-faire market, but even if they are not, they suggest to us that we do live not in an *ideal* market that keeps all of its promises but in an *actual* market that tends to blunder along with the flesh-and-blood people who control it. Thus the free market should welcome movements like that of comparable worth since it enables it to rid itself of the extraneous baggage that inhibits its optimal functioning.

But even when critics come to think that, in theory, comparable worth is not the trumpet that will bring down the walls of Jericho, they remain convinced that there is no practical way of implementing pay equity for women without leading to chaos in the productive process. Thus resistant critics dismiss the whole effort to compare a school food supervisor's work with an unemployment insurance actuary's work as a useless effort to compare apples and oranges. It does no good to explain to a resistant critic that if apples and oranges can be compared in terms of how many calories, vitamins, and minerals each has, then school food supervisor's work can be compared with unemployment insurance actuary's work in terms of certain functional tasks and characteristics that, from the employer's point of view, are functionally equivalent and, therefore, of equal value to him or her. Similarly, it does no good to explain to a resistant critic that employers have been using job evaluation as a tool for determining the relative worth of jobs for over fifty years. During World War II the War Labor Board used job evaluation in setting wages. Labor arbitrators routinely use job evaluation in determining whether one job should pay more than another. The majority of large employers use some form of job evaluation in wage setting. But if this is the case, says the resistant critic, it is paradoxical that women should favor job evaluation studies. After all, continues the critic, the standards and measures that have been used for identifying and assessing job worth have resulted in women being paid 59 cents for every dollar men make. To this point, the experienced liberal feminist replies that if comparable worth is to achieve its goals, then, *subjective* or discriminatory standards and measures will have to be replaced by their *objective* or nondiscriminatory counterparts. Of course, once the terms subjective and objective surface, resistant critics are provided with new ammunition for their cause. If X happens to value knowledge and skills more than working conditions and if Y happens to value just the opposite, then, observes the critic, to the degree that X

wishes to reward brains, to the same degree Y will wish to reward brawn. The standards and measures of X will reward brainy women who do nice inside jobs and the standards and measures of Y will reward brawny men who do all kinds of unpleasant, outdoor, all-weather, difficult, and heavy jobs. To this further point, the experienced liberal feminist will reply that an *objective* standard is not to be confused with an *absolute* standard. As the National Research Council of the National Academy of Sciences reasoned:

> Acceptance of a comparable worth approach—the attempt to measure the worth of jobs directly on the basis of their content—does not require an absolute standard by which the value or worth of all jobs can be measured. In the judgment of the committee, no such standard exists, nor, in our society, is likely to exist. The relative worth of jobs reflects value judgments as to what features of jobs ought to be compensated, and such judgments vary from industry to industry, even from firm to firm. Paying jobs according to their worth requires only that whatever characteristics of jobs are regarded as worthy of compensation by an employer should be equally so regarded irrespective of the sex, race, or ethnicity of job incumbents.[15]

In short, a firm is free to value brawn more than brains or vice versa provided it applies its standards of worth consistently, and provided job content is accurately and completely assessed both for jobs held by women, so that none of the brawny work they do is overlooked, and for jobs held by men, so that none of the brainy work they do is overlooked.

SOCIALIST FEMINISTS

When socialist feminists approach the comparable worth movement, the first question they tend to ask is whether comparable worth is a disappointing liberal tool that further legitimates the existing hierarchy of wages or a radical tool that challenges the market basis of wages and promises to re-evaluate value.[16] In phrasing this question, socialist feminists undercut many of the arguments liberal feminists make to allay the suspicions of critics concerned about the free market. Not surprisingly, socialist feminists believe that talk of *ideal* markets, where there is some sort of perfect correlation between job choice and reward, is just so much nonsense. We live, claim socialist feminists, in imperfect *actual* markets. And although life in actual markets is not necessarily nasty, brutish, and short, it can be pretty tough, depending on a person's socioeconomic starting point, his or her inherent capacities and abilities, and the twistings and turnings of luck. Did Norma Rae, for example, choose—as Phyllis Schlafly would argue—to be a textile worker because it was a soft indoor job that demanded little of her time and energy, or did she—as the socialist feminist would argue—show up at the plant because it offered the only available jobs in town and people took them regardless of the cost to their physical and psychological well-being? Consider, says the socialist feminist, that nearly half of all poor families are headed by women. Consider also that 93 percent of all welfare recipients are women and their children, that 70 percent of all Food Stamp recipients are women, and that 66 percent of all Legal Services and Medicaid recipients are women. Consider, finally, that if women were paid the wages that similarly qualified men earn, we could cut the number of poor families in half and thus the number of welfare recipients in half. Why, then, concludes the socialist feminist, be foolish? Pay women what men are paid for comparable jobs, and women will be able to support themselves and their families adequately. Or continue to pay women less than men are paid for comparable jobs, and continue to support poor women and their families on welfare.

Despite its brief appeal to equal pay for similarly skilled jobs, a close inspection of the above argument reveals that socialist feminists are more concerned about eliminating women's poverty than with convincing society that female-dominated jobs are as skilled as male-dominated jobs or vice versa. If men's wages have had more to do with the power of their unions and with the appeal of a "head of household" wage than with either the intrinsic value of truck driving or the instrumental value of meat cutting, then socialist feminists are correct to emphasize need over merit. But it is not clear that our society is ready to accept the rhetoric of need, especially when a woman uses it to ask for more bacon for her dependents. Our society is still such that it would prefer to hear that women's wages are being raised not because women need more money but because they merit more money; and this despite the fact that as we pay our truck drivers and meat cutters more each year, we do not believe for a minute either that their knowledge and skills, mental demands, and accountability have increased or that their working conditions have worsened. Thus, socialist feminists decorate their comparable worth arguments with meritocratic phrases in the hope that as women's wages go up, the hierarchy of wages will flatten.

RADICAL FEMINISTS

Radical feminists are simultaneously attracted to and repelled by the comparable worth movement. They are attracted to the comparable worth movement because it does not seek to solve the problem of job segregation simply by educating and training women so that they can enter "men's fields." What radical feminists have against this strategy is threefold. First, there just are not enough male-dominated jobs to go around. If women are encouraged to enter male occupations but men are not encouraged to enter female occupations, the male occupations will become so overcrowded that employers will have the luxury of dropping wages in these work areas. Second, there are many women who have made meaningful lives for themselves as nurses, teachers, secretaries, librarians, and the like. Not only is it hard to ask a woman whose identity is that of nurse or teacher to give up her "female" work for "male" work, it may not be in society's best interests that she do so. Many women who are currently teaching this nation's children have the brains to become investment bankers, but even if it may be in these women's "best" interest that they make such a career transition—assuming that money makes the world go around—I doubt that it is in the children's best interest. Of course, women should not be asked to sacrifice themselves on behalf of humanity—at least, not if men are not called on to make similar sacrifices.

Unfortunately, as it is currently described, comparable worth is not necessarily what radical feminists have dreamed of: a way of valuing work because it is woman's work and not despite the fact that it is woman's work. Some radical feminists have come to suspect that the standards and measures being developed to assess comparable worth are no more gender-neutral than the schema Lawrence Kohlberg devised to measure human (i.e., male) moral development.[17] Kohlberg's scale was constructed to recognize persons as moral if they spoke the language of abstract principles and rules rather than the language of concrete responsibilities for and attachments to human persons. Since men are more inclined to speak the former language than the latter, men consistently scored higher than women on Kohlberg's scale. Analogously, some comparable worth schemes use male standards and measures either to reinforce the prevailing wage hierarchy or, more intricately, to prove that women have really been doing manly activities all along. Thus these schemes either fail to reward women or reward women for what radical feminists would regard as wrong reasons.

CONCLUSION

As someone who is not committed to any one feminist point of view and who is searching to discover a unifying feminist theory that explains my disparate feminist practices, I do not think that comparable worth can bear the burden radical feminists would like it to bear. Paying female nurses the same as male doctors on the grounds that nurses can do anything doctors can do better may encourage nurses to denigrate those very capacities and skills that make good nurses so special. As far as I am concerned, caring is the most important duty a nurse can perform. It is not true to say that caring is something anyone can do. In order to care well for others, a person has to develop a whole range of psychological and spiritual resources that permit him or her to remain patient, calm, and helpful in stressful and unpleasant situations. If everyone were by "nature" a caring person, I doubt that so many people would send their sick, aged, and handicapped relatives to people—call them health care professionals if you must—who are apparently better copers and givers than they. Moreover, paying women in female-dominated occupations as much as men in comparable male-dominated occupations in itself is not guaranteed to make either men or women, who are not already convinced of the value of their work, suddenly value women's work. Even if the President of Williams College were paid as much as the President himself, this fact alone would not make the college community value her work as much as his. Finally, insisting that a transvaluation can be achieved through comparable worth is to permit a supposedly "male value," number of dollars earned per year, to become woman's standard of worth. It is to say that what woman does is worth just as much as what man does because she is paid as much as he. But why should value be measured in terms of dollars?

If comparable worth cannot bear the burden radical feminists would impose on it, neither can it bear the burden liberal feminists would impose on it. Liberal feminists bill comparable worth as a means to the end of eliminating gender discrimination in the marketplace. Although the Equal Pay Act is limited to equal pay for substantially equal work, liberal feminists see in Title VII of the Civil Rights Act of 1974 (which forbids, among other things, sex discrimination in compensation) an opportunity to improve women's salaries. If it can be shown that employers pay women less simply because they are women, then employers are discriminating against women and must be required to pay women what their work would receive in a gender-blind world. The main problem with this line of reasoning is, as Mark Killingsworth points out, that employer discrimination is not the whole story. Comments Killingsworth:

> There's an awful lot of discrimination that goes on before men and women or boys and girls ever get into the labor markets that shapes the choices that people make before employers ever get to them. Employers have to deal with the labor force as it gets created and as it enters the job market for the first time, and a lot of the differences between men's and women's outcomes in the labor market can be attributed to those kind of phenomena rather than to direct discrimination by employers.[18]

In other words, because women have been socialized in certain ways, women choose to cluster in certain occupations. Individual employers can pay women in these occupations what they are worth, but this will not end the more subtle and more persuasive forms of gender discrimination that cause women to enter these occupations in the first place. Nevertheless, less discrimination is better than more discrimination. Or is it? Australia adopted a comparable worth policy that had an unfortunate side effect. Increases in women's wages attributable to the policy reduced by one-third the rate of growth in female employment (below the rate that would have otherwise prevailed) relative to the rate of growth in men's employment.[19] Apparently, the price of gender justice can be higher than the price bargained for.

Of course, the Australian experience does not have to be our experience. Were we to follow the lead of Sweden[29] and also that of the socialist feminists, we would see that comparable worth for women has to be seen as one of several steps toward reducing the wage disparities that trouble many of us. Pockets of justice, in a sea of injustice, cannot withstand the tides of a market bent on having its way. In the present labor market, wages are not set according to the complexity or difficulty of the jobs involved, but rather according to such labor market factors as availability of qualified workers and bargaining power of unions. Comparable worth policy would replace the labor market dynamic of supply and demand with compensation according to the relative worth of jobs, as measured by job content. It would logically lead to a radical restructuring of the labor market, in which virtually all jobs were seen as equally valuable to society and worth equal compensation.

Although many Americans are willing to endorse comparable worth on liberal feminist or even radical feminist terms, they seem unwilling to endorse it on socialist feminist terms. But I cannot see how a successful comparable worth policy that avoids the pitfalls of the Australian experience can also avoid a certain amount of governmental intervention. To be sure, we all want to raise women's wages without reducing men's wages. But men's wages will have to be reduced in the long run if the wage gap between genders is to be closed. That is to say, if women now make 59 cents for every dollar men make, then men's wages will have to be held fairly constant as women first earn 69 cents, then 79 cents, then 89 cents, then 99 cents, then at last one dollar for every dollar men make. Smart men will not view this as an economic threat even if it initially shakes their egos. Most women do get married at some point or other; and although I know that two can eat as cheaply as one, dinner is likely to be better if a couple have between them $2.00 rather than $1.59 to spend on groceries. And if a woman chooses not to get married or if she finds herself divorced or widowed, she will still have the same $1.00

to spend that her male counterpart does, and this is only fair. If all of us are to receive a decent day's pay for a decent day's work, then wage disparities will have to be narrowed. There is only so much money to go around. We all can't have more than the other person has, but we all can have about the same as the other has. Assuming that that other guy or gal may be someone I care about, comparable worth, as understood by socialist feminists, makes sense to me and ought to be pursued as a policy option.

NOTES

1. "Paying Women What They're Worth," *QQ-Report from the Center for Philosophy and Public Policy* 3, (Spring 1983): 1.

2. Jan Rosenberg, "Judging on the Merits," *Commonweal* 112 (May 31, 1985): 337.

3. D. L. Treiman and H. I. Hartmann, *Women, Work and Wages: Equal Pay for Jobs of Equal Value* (Washington, D.C.: National Academy Press, 1981), 42.

4. Bureau of Labor Statistics, March 1982, cited in "Paying Women What They're Worth," p. 2.

5. Margaret Mead, "On Freud's View of Female Psychology," in *Women and Analysis,* ed. J. Strouse (New York: Grossman, 1974).

6. Andrew Hacker, "'Welfare': The Future of an Illusion," *The New York Review of Books* (February 21, 1985): 41.

7. Bureau of Labor Statistics, March 1982, cited in "Paying Women What They're Worth," p. 2.

8. "Paying Women What They're Worth," p. 2. See also Ronald Dworkin, "Neutrality, Equality, and Liberalism," in *Liberalism Reconsidered,* eds. Douglas MacLean and Claudia Mills (Totowa, N.J.: Rowman and Allanheld, 1983).

9. Face Off: "Should Nurses Be Paid as Much as Truck Drivers?" *Common Cause* (March/April 1983): 37.

10. *Ibid.,* p. 39.

11. Helen Remick, "Major Issues in *a priori* Application," in *Comparable Worth and Wage Discrimintion: Technical Possiblities and Political Realities,* ed. Helen Remick (Philadelphia: Temple University Press, 1984), 102.

12. *Ibid.,* p. 103.

13. "Paying Women What They're Worth," p. 4.

14. Helen Remick and Ronnie J. Steinberg, "Technical Possiblities and Political Realities: Concluding Remarks," in *Comparable Worth and Wage Discrimination,* p. 289.

15. Quoted in Ronnie J. Steinberg, "'A Want of Harmony': Perspectives on Wage Discrimination and Comparable Worth," in *Comparable Worth and Wage Discrimination,* p. 18.

16. Roslyn L. Feldberg, "Comparable Worth: Toward Theory and Practice in the United States," *Signs: Journal of Women and Culture in Society* 10 (Winter 1984): 311–313.

17. Lawrence Kohlberg, "Continuities and Discontinuities in Childhood and Adult Moral Development Revisited" (Unpublished paper, Harvard University, 1973).

18. Statement of Mark R. Killingsworth, Professor of Economics, Rutgers University, New Brunswick, New Jersey, *Women in the Work Force: Pay Equity,* Hearing before the Joint Economic Committee, Congress of the United States, 98th Congr. 2nd Sess., April 10, 1984, p. 87.

19. Mark R. Killingsworth, "The Economics of Comparable Worth: Analytical, Empirical, and Policy Questions," in *Comparable Worth: New Directions for Research,* ed. Heidi L. Hartmann (Washington, D.C.: National Academy Press, 1985), 106.

20. Robert Kuttner, *The Economic Illusion: False Choices Between Prosperity and Social Justice* (Boston: Houghton Mifflin, 1984), 179.

Griggs et al. v. Duke Power Company

In 1965 the Duke Power Company's Dan River Steam Station of Draper, North Carolina, employed 95 people, 14 of whom were black. As a result of Title VII of the Civil Rights Act of 1964, the company had just revised its employment and promotion requirements for this generating plant. These revisions were challenged by thirteen of the power company's black employees, who questioned in particular the requirements of a high school diploma and passing intelligence tests as a condition of employment and transfer to other positions in the plant.

The Dan River facility then consisted of five operating departments: Labor, Coal Handling, Operations, Maintenance, and Laboratory and Tests. Prior to July 2, 1965, when the Civil Rights Act went into effect, black workers were by design employed exclusively in the Labor Department. The highest paying job in this department paid less than the lowest paying job in the other four operating departments, which were staffed entirely by white employees. In 1955, the company had instituted requirements of a high school education for initial assignment to any department except Labor, regardless of the employee's race. The diploma was also required for a transfer from Coal Handling to one of the remaining three departments (Operations, Maintenance, or Laboratory and Tests). From 1955 until the suit brought by the thirteen black employees, white employees hired before the high school requirement was put into effect functioned well in the top four operating departments, and these employees continued to be granted promotions. Those white employees hired after the 1955 high school standard was instituted were, in principle, not offered the privileged opportunities that obtained for the previous white employees. However, the black employees in or entering the Labor Department were not affected.

Title VII of the Civil Rights Act became effective on July 2, 1965. It deals specifically with the equality of employment opportunities, and the removal of arbitrary barriers to minorities. With a clear intent to be in compliance, the Duke Power Company altered its employment and promotion requirements. While black employees were no longer restricted to the Labor Department, completion of high school was still required for transfer from Labor to any other department. This restriction also applied to Coal Handling, previously open only to the white, nongraduate employee.

Another employment requirement that applied to initial assignment in any department (except Labor) had also been initiated in July, 1965. In addition to a high school diploma, the prospective employee had to register satisfactory scores on two professionally prepared aptitude tests. Those currently employed with a high school education were, however, still eligible for transfer from Labor to the other departments without such testing. Two months later, in September 1965, the company further expanded its promotion opportunities to incumbent employees who lacked the high school background. These longstanding employees could now qualify for advancement from the Labor or Coal Handling departments by scoring satisfactorily on two intelligence and comprehensive tests (The Wonderlic Personnel Test and the Bennett Mechanical Comprehension Test).

This use of tests by employers was specifically in conformity to the requirements of Title VII, Section 703(h) of the Civil Rights

---

The first introductory half of this case was prepared by Nancy Blanpied and Tom L. Beauchamp. The second half is from *Griggs* et al. v. *Duke Power Co.*, 401 U.S. 424 (1970), United States Supreme Court. Majority opinion by Chief Justice Warren Burger.

Act. This section was specifically included to allow testing for qualified personnel and to protect employers from being forced to hire solely because of an applicant's minority status. However, the effect of the requirement constituted an implicit barrier to black advancement in the judgment of those who challenged Duke Power's arrangement.

The Wonderlic and Bennett scores required by the company for initial hiring and transfer were equivalent to the national median of high school graduates, which in effect statistically eliminated half of all high school graduates. The power company's statistical data on test scores had shown that 58 percent of all white applications passed, as compared to 6 percent of all black applicants. These test results were generally consistent with the 1960 North Carolina census statistics, which included data on the state's segregated education system. That census had shown that 34 percent of white males had completed their high school education, while only 12 percent of the black males had graduated.

The power company's intent to upgrade its requirement for employment and transfer included a program to finance two-thirds of the cost of high school tuition to interested employees. However, the company's own statistics indicated that (at least between July 2, 1965 and November 14, 1966) white employees who did not have to meet the high school and test requirements continued to do very well in promotions within the company. In August 1966, the first black employee to be promoted out of the Labor Department was a high school graduate who had been with the power company since 1953. He was assigned to the Coal Handling Department.

The Duke Power Company's *intent* to improve and advance the level of its employment was never the point of challenge or argument in this case. When the Supreme Court of the United States heard this case it focused on the *effects* of these new standards and whether they were ultimately discriminatory. The Supreme Court ruled in favor of the thirteen employees of the company—thereby reversing a District Court and partially reversing a Court of Appeals. The crucial parts of the Supreme Court Opinion, written by Chief Justice Warren Burger, are as follows:

> We granted the writ in this case to resolve the question whether an employer is prohibited by the Civil Rights Act of 1964, Title VII, from requiring a high school education or passing of a standardized general intelligence test as a condition of employment in or transfer to jobs when (a) neither standard is shown to be significantly related to successful job performance, (b) both requirements operate to disqualify Negroes at a substantially higher rate than white applicants, and (c) the jobs in question formerly had been filled only by white employees as part of a longstanding practice of giving preference to whites. . . .
>
> The objective of Congress in the enactment of Title VII is plain from the language of the statute. It was to achieve equality of employment opportunities and remove barriers that have operated in the past to favor an identifiable group of white employees over other employees. Under the Act, practices, procedures, or tests neutral on their face, and even neutral in terms of intent, cannot be maintained if they operate to "freeze" the status quo of prior discriminatory employment practices.
>
> The Court of Appeals' opinion, and the partial dissent, agreed that, on the record in the present case, "whites register far better on the Company's alternative requirements" than Negroes. This consequence would appear to be directly traceable to race. Basic intelligence must have the means of articulation to manifest itself fairly in a testing process. Because they are Negroes, petitioners have long received inferior education in segregated schools and this Court expressly recognized these differences in *Gaston County* v. *United States*, 395 U.S. 285 (1969). . . . Congress did not intend by Title VII, however, to guarantee a job to every person regardless of qualifications. In short, the Act does not command that any person be hired simply because he was formerly the subject of discrimination, or because he is a member of a minority group. Discriminatory preference for any group, minority or majority, is precisely and only what Con-

gress has proscribed. What is required by Congress is the removal of artificial, arbitrary, and unnecessary barriers to employment when the barriers operate invidiously to discriminate on the basis of racial or other impermissible classification.

... The Act proscribes not only overt discrimination but also practices that are fair in form, but discriminatory in operation. The touchstone is business necessity. If an employment practice which operates to exclude Negroes cannot be shown to be related to job performance, the practice is prohibited.

On the record before us, neither the high school completion requirement nor the general intelligence test is shown to bear a demonstrable relationship to successful performance of the jobs for which it was used. Both were adopted, as the Court of Appeals noted, without meaningful study of their relationship to job-performance ability. Rather, a vice president of the Company testified, the requirements were instituted on the Company's judgment that they generally would improve the overall quality of the work force.

The evidence, however, shows that employees who have not completed high school or taken the tests have continued to perform satisfactorily and make progress in departments for which the high school and test criteria are now used. The promotion record of present employees who would not be able to meet the new criteria thus suggests the possibility that the requirements may not be needed even for the limited purpose of preserving the avowed policy of advancement within the Company....

The Court of Appeals held that the Company had adopted the diploma and test requirements without any "intention to discriminate against Negro employees." We do not suggest that either the District Court or the Court of Appeals erred in examining the employer's intent; but good intent or absence of discriminatory intent does not redeem employment procedures or testing mechanisms that operate as "built-in headwinds" for minority groups and are unrelated to measuring job capability.

The Company's lack of discriminatory intent is suggested by special efforts to help the undereducated employees through Company financing of two-thirds the cost of tuition for high school training. But Congress directed the thrust of the Act to the *consequences* of employment practices, not simply the motivation. More than that, Congress has placed on the employer the burden of showing that any given requirement must have a manifest relationship to the employment in question.

The facts of this case demonstrate the inadequacy of broad and general testing devices as well as the infirmity of using diplomas or degrees as fixed measures of capability. History is filled with examples of men and women who rendered highly effective performance without the conventional badges of accomplishment in terms of certificates, diplomas, or degrees. Diplomas and tests are useful servants, but Congress has mandated the commonsense proposition that they are not to become masters of reality.

The company contends that its general intelligence tests are specifically permitted by § 703 (h) of the Act. That section authorizes the use of "any professionally developed ability test" that is not "designed, intended *or used* to discriminate because of race...." [Emphasis added.]

The Equal Employment Opportunity Commission, having enforcement responsibility, has issued guidelines interpreting § 703 (h) to permit only the use of job-related tests....

Nothing in the Act precludes the use of testing or measuring procedures; obviously they are useful. What Congress has forbidden is giving these devices and mechanisms controlling force unless they are demonstrably a reasonable measure of job performance. Congress has not commanded that the less qualified be preferred over the better qualified simply because of minority origins. Far from disparaging job qualifications as such, Congress has made such qualifications the controlling factor, so that race, religion, nationality, and sex become irrelevant. What Congress has commanded is that any tests used must measure the person for the job and not the person in the abstract.

The judgment of the Court of Appeals is, as to that portion of the judgment appealed from, reversed.

As a result of this opinion, testing was stopped at Duke Power Company.

United Steelworkers and Kaiser Aluminum v. *Weber*

Challenged here is the legality of an affirmative action plan—collectively bargained by an employer and a union—that reserves for black employees 50% of the openings in an in-plant craft-training program until the percentage of black craftworkers in the plant is commensurate with the percentage of blacks in the local labor force. The question for decision is whether Congress, in Title VII of the Civil Rights Act of 1964, 78 Stat 253, as amended, 42 USC §§ 2000e et seq. [42 USCS §§ 2000e et seq.], left employers and unions in the private sector free to take such race-conscious steps to eliminate manifest racial imbalances in traditionally segregated job categories. We hold that Title VII does not prohibit such race-conscious affirmative action plans.

I

In 1974, petitioner United Steelworkers of America (USWA) and petitioner Kaiser Aluminum & Chemical Corp. (Kaiser) entered into a master collective-bargaining agreement covering terms and conditions of employment at 15 Kaiser plants. The agreement contained, inter alia, an affirmative action plan designed to eliminate conspicuous racial imbalances in Kaiser's then almost exclusively white craftwork forces. Black craft-hiring goals were set for each Kaiser plant equal to the percentage of blacks in the respective local labor forces. To enable plants to meet these goals, on-the-job training programs were established to teach unskilled production workers—black and white—the skills necessary to become craft-

workers. The plan reserved for black employees 50% of the openings in these newly created in-plant training programs.

This case arose from the operation of the plan at Kaiser's plant in Gramercy, La. Until 1974, Kaiser hired as craft-workers for that plant only persons who had had prior craft experience. Because blacks had long been excluded from craft unions, few were able to present such credentials. As a consequence, prior to 1974 only 1.83% (5 out of 273) of the skilled craftworkers at the Gramercy plant were black, even though the work force in the Gramercy area was approximately 39% black.

Pursuant to the national agreement Kaiser altered its craft-hiring practice in the Gramercy plant. Rather than hiring already trained outsiders, Kaiser established a training program to train its production workers to fill craft openings. Selection of craft trainees was made on the basis of seniority, with the proviso that at least 50% of the new trainees were to be black until the percentage of black skilled craft-workers in the Gramercy plant approximated the percentage of blacks in the local labor force. See 415 F Supp 761, 764.

During 1974, the first year of the operation of the Kaiser-USWA affirmative action plan, 13 craft trainees were selected from Gramercy's production work force. Of these, seven were black and six white. The most senior black selected into the program had less seniority than several white production workers whose bids for admission were rejected. Thereafter one of those white production workers, respondent Brian Weber (hereafter respondent), instituted this class

---

443 U.S. 193, 61 L Ed 2d 480, 99 S. Ct. 2721 (1979), United States Supreme Court. Majority opinion by Justice William Brennan.

action in the United States District Court for the Eastern District of Louisiana.

The complaint alleged that the filling of craft trainee positions at the Gramercy plant pursuant to the affirmative action program had resulted in junior black employees, receiving training in preference to senior white employees, thus discriminating against respondent and other similarly situated white employees in violation of §§ 703(a)[1] and (d)[2] of Title VII. The District Court held that the plan violated Title VII, entered a judgment in favor of the plaintiff class, and granted a permanent injunction prohibiting Kaiser and the USWA "from denying plaintiffs, Brian F. Weber and all other members of the class, access to on-the-job training programs on the basis of race." App 171. A divided panel of the Court of Appeals for the Fifth Circuit affirmed, holding that all employment preferences based upon race, including those preferences incidental to bona fide affirmative action plans, violated Title VII's prohibition against racial discrimination in employment. 563 F2d 216 (1977). We granted certiorari. 439 US 1045, 58 L Ed 2d 704, 99 S Ct 720 (1978). We reverse.

II

We emphasize at the outset the narrowness of our inquiry. Since the Kaiser-USWA plan does not involve state action, this case does not present an alleged violation of the Equal Protection Clause of the Fourteenth Amendment. Further, since the Kaiser-USWA plan was adopted voluntarily, we are not concerned with what Title VII requires or with what a court might order to remedy a past proved violation of the Act. The only question before us is the narrow statutory issue of whether Title VII forbids private employers and unions from voluntarily agreeing upon bona fide affirmative action plans that accord racial preferences in the manner and for the purpose provided in the Kaiser-USWA plan....

Congress' primary concern in enacting the prohibition against racial discrimination in Title VII of the Civil Rights Act of 1964 was with "the plight of the Negro in our economy." 110 Cong Rec 6548 (1964) (remarks of Sen. Humphrey). Before 1964, blacks were largely relegated to "unskilled and semi-skilled jobs." Ibid. (remarks of Sen. Humphrey); id., at 7204 (remarks of Sen. Clark); id., at 7379–7380 (remarks of Sen. Kennedy). Because of automation the number of such jobs was rapidly decreasing.

Given this legislative history, we cannot agree with respondent that Congress intended to prohibit the private sector from taking effective steps to accomplish the goal that Congress designed Title VII to achieve. The very statutory words [were] intended as a spur or catalyst to cause "employers and unions to self-examine and to self-evaluate their employment practices and to endeavor to eliminate, so far as possible, the last vestiges of an unfortunate and ignominious page in this country's history."

It would be ironic indeed if a law triggered by a Nation's concern over centuries of racial injustice and intended to improve the lot of those who had "been excluded from the American dream for so long," 110 Cong Rec 6552 (1964) (remarks of Sen. Humphrey), constituted the first legislative prohibition of all voluntary, private, race-conscious efforts to abolish traditional patterns of racial segregation and hierarchy.

Our conclusion is further reinforced by examination of the language and legislative history of § 703(j) of Title VII. Opponents of Title VII raised two related arguments against the bill. First, they argued that the Act would be interpreted to *require* employers with racially imbalanced work forces to grant preferential treatment to racial minorities in order to integrate. Second, they argued that employers with racially imbalanced work forces would grant preferential treatment to racial minorities, even if not required to do so by the Act. See 110 Cong Rec 8618–8619 (1964) (remarks of Sen. Sparkman). Had Congress meant to prohibit all race-conscious affirmative action, as respondent urges, it easily could have answered both objections by providing that Title VII would not require or *permit* racially preferential integration efforts. But Congress did not choose such a course. Rather Congress added § 703(j) which addresses only the first objection. The section provides that nothing contained in Title VII "shall be interpreted to *require* any employer . . . to grant preferential treatment . . . to any group because of the race . . . of such . . . group on account of" a de facto racial imbalance in the employer's work force. The section does *not* state that "nothing in Title VII shall be interpreted to *permit*" voluntary affirmative efforts to correct racial imbalances. The natural inference is that Congress chose not to forbid all voluntary race-conscious affirmative action.

The reasons for this choice are evident from the legislative record. Title VII could not have been enacted into law without substantial support from legislators in both Houses who traditionally resisted federal regulation of private business. Those legislators demanded as a price for their support that "management prerogatives, and union freedoms . . . be left undisturbed to the greatest extent possible." . . .

III

We need not today define in detail the line of demarcation between permissible and impermissible affirmative action plans. It suffices to hold that the challenged Kaiser-USWA affirmative action plan falls on the permissible side of the line. The purposes of the plan mirror those of the statute. Both were designed to break down old patterns of racial segregation and hierarchy. Both were structured to "open employment opportunities for Negroes in occupations which have been traditionally closed to them." 110 Cong Rec 6548 (1964) (remarks of Sen. Humphrey).

At the same time, the plan does not unnecessarily trammel the interests of the white employees. The plan does not require

the discharge of white workers and their replacement with new black hirees. Cf. McDonald v. Santa Fe Trail Transp. Co., 427 US 273, 49 L Ed 2d 493, 96 S Ct 2574 (1976). Nor does the plan create an absolute bar to the advancement of white employees; half of those trained in the program will be white. Moreover, the plan is a temporary measure; it is not intended to maintain racial balance, but simply to eliminate a manifest racial imbalance. Preferential selection of craft trainees at the Gramercy plant will end as soon as the percentage of black skilled craftworkers in the Gramercy plant approximates the percentage of blacks in the local labor force. See 415 F Supp, at 763.

We conclude, therefore, that the adoption of the Kaiser-USWA plan for the Gramercy plant falls within the area of discretion left by Title VII to the private sector voluntarily to adopt affirmative action plans designed to eliminate conspicuous racial imbalance in traditionally segregated job categories. Accordingly, the judgment of the Court of Appeals for the Fifth Circuit is reversed.

NOTES

1. Section 703(a), 78 Stat 255, as amended, 86 Stat 109, 42 USC § 2000e-2(a) [42 USCS § 2000e-2(a)], provides:
   "(a) . . . It shall be an unlawful employment practice for an employer—"(1) to fail or refuse to hire or to discharge any individual, or otherwise to discriminate against any individual with respect to his compensation, terms, conditions, or privileges of employment, because of such individual's race, color, religion, sex, or national origin; or
   "(2) to limit, segregate, or classify his employees or applicants for employment in any way which would deprive or tend to deprive any individual of employment opportunities or otherwise adversely affect his status as an employee, because of such individual's race, color, religion, sex, or national origin."

2. Section 703(d), 78 Stat 256, 42 USC § 2000e-2(d) [42 USCS § 2000e-2(d)], provides:
   "It shall be an unlawful employment practice for any employer, labor organization, or joint

labor-management committee controlling apprenticeship or other training or retraining, including on-the-job training programs to discriminate against any individual because of his race, color, religion, sex, or national origin in admission to, or employment in, any program established to provide apprenticeship or other training."

Firefighters Local Union No. 1784 v. Stotts

I

In 1977 respondent Carl Stotts, a black holding the position of fire-fighting captain in the Memphis, Tennessee, Fire Department, filed a class action complaint in the United States District Court for the Western District of Tennessee. The complaint charged that the Memphis Fire Department and other city officials were engaged in a pattern or practice of making hiring and promotion decisions on the basis of race in violation of Title VII of the Civil Rights Act of 1964, 42 U.S.C. § 2000e *et seq.*, as well as 42 U.S.C. §§ 1981 and 1983. The District Court certified the case as a class action and consolidated it with an individual action subsequently filed by respondent Fred Jones, a black fire-fighting private in the Department, who claimed that he had been denied a promotion because of his race. Discovery proceeded, settlement negotiations ensued, and in due course, a consent decree was approved and entered by the District Court on April 25, 1980. The stated purpose of the decree was to remedy the hiring and promotion practices "of the Department with respect to blacks." 679 F.2d 541, 575–576 (CA6 1982) (Appendix). Accordingly, the City agreed to promote 13 named individuals and to provide backpay to 81 employees of the Fire Department. It also adopted the long-term goal of increasing the proportion of minority representation in each job classification in the Fire Department to approximately the proportion of blacks in the labor force in Shelby County, Tennessee. However, the City did not, by agreeing to the decree, admit "any violations of law, rule or regulation with respect to the allegations" in the complaint. *Id.,* at 574. The plaintiffs waived any further relief save to enforce the decree, *ibid.,* and the District Court retained jurisdiction "for such further orders as may be necessary or appropriate to effectuate the purposes of this decree." *Id.,* at 578.

The long-term hiring goal outlined in the decree paralleled the provisions of a 1974 consent decree, which settled a case brought against the City by the United States and which applied citywide. Like the 1974 decree, the 1980 decree also established an interim hiring goal of filling on an annual basis 50 percent of the job vacancies in the Department with qualified black applicants. The 1980 decree contained an additional goal with respect to promotions: the Department was to attempt to ensure that 20 percent of the promotions in each job classification be given to blacks. Neither decree contained provisions for layoffs or reductions in rank, and neither awarded any competitive seniority. The 1974 decree did require that for purposes of promotion,

---

104 S.Ct. 2576 (1984), United States Supreme Court. Opinion by Justice Byron White.

transfer, and assignment, seniority was to be computed "as the total seniority of that person with the City." *Id.*, at 572.

In early May, 1981, the City announced that projected budget deficits required a reduction of non-essential personnel throughout the City Government. Layoffs were to be based on the "last hired, first fired" rule under which city-wide seniority, determined by each employee's length of continuous service from the latest date of permanent employment, was the basis for deciding who would be laid off. If a senior employee's position were abolished or eliminated, the employee could "bump down" to a lower ranking position rather than be laid off. As the Court of Appeals later noted, this layoff policy was adopted pursuant to the seniority system "mentioned in the 1974 decree and . . . incorporated in the City's memorandum with the Union." 679 F.2d, at 549.

On May 4, at respondents' request, the District Court entered a temporary restraining order forbidding the layoff of any black employee. The Union, which previously had not been a party to either of these cases, was permitted to intervene. At the preliminary injunction hearing, it appeared that 55 then-filled positions in the Department were to be eliminated and that 39 of these positions were filled with employees having "bumping" rights. It was estimated that 40 least-senior employees in the fire-fighting bureau of the Department would be laid off and that of these 25 were white and 15 black. It also appeared that 56 percent of the employees hired in the Department since 1974 had been black and that the percentage of black employees had increased from approximately 3 or 4 percent in 1974 to 11½ percent in 1980.

On May 18, the District Court entered an order granting an injunction. The Court found that the consent decree "did not contemplate the method to be used for reduction in rank or lay-off," and that the layoff policy was in accordance with the City's seniority system and was not adopted with any intent to discriminate. Nonetheless, conclud-

ing that the proposed layoffs would have a racially discriminatory effect and that the seniority system was not a bona fide one, the District Court ordered that the City "not apply the seniority policy insofar as it will decrease the percentage of black lieutenants, drivers, inspectors and privates that are presently employed. . . . " On June 23, the District Court broadened its order to include three additional classifications. A modified layoff plan, aimed at protecting black employees in the seven classifications so as to comply with the court's order, was presented and approved. Layoffs pursuant to the modified plan were then carried out. In certain instances, to comply with the injunction, non-minority employees with more seniority than minority employees were laid off or demoted in rank.

On appeal, the Court of Appeals for the Sixth Circuit affirmed despite its conclusion that the District Court was wrong in holding that the City's seniority system was not bona fide . . .

II

The issue at the heart of this case is whether the District Court exceeded its powers in entering an injunction requiring white employees to be laid off, when the otherwise applicable seniority system would have called for the layoff of black employees with less seniority. We are convinced that the Court of Appeals erred in resolving this issue and in affirming the District Court.

A

[5,6] The Court of Appeals first held that the injunction did no more than enforce the terms of the agreed-upon consent decree. This specific-performance approach rests on the notion that because the City was under a general obligation to use its best efforts to increase the proportion of blacks on the force, it breached the decree by attempting to effectuate a layoff policy reducing the percentage of black employees in the Depart-

ment even though such a policy was mandated by the seniority system adopted by the City and the Union. A variation of this argument is that since the decree permitted the District Court to enter any later orders that "may be necessary or appropriate to effectuate the purposes of this decree," 679 F.2d, at 578 (Appendix), the City had agreed in advance to an injunction against layoffs that would reduce the proportion of black employees. We are convinced, however, that both of these are improvident constructions of the consent decree. . . .

. . . Had there been any intention to depart from the seniority plan in the event of layoffs or demotions, it is much more reasonable to believe that there would have been an express provision to that effect. . . . It is thus not surprising that when the City anticipated layoffs and demotions, it in the first instance faithfully followed its preexisting seniority system, plainly having no thought that it had already agreed to depart from it. . . .

B

[8] The Court of Appeals held that even if the injunction is not viewed as compelling compliance with the terms of the decree, it was still properly entered because the District Court had inherent authority to modify the decree when an economic crisis unexpectedly required layoffs which, if carried out as the City proposed, would undermine the affirmative action outlined in the decree and impose an undue hardship on respondents. This was true, the court held, even though the modification conflicted with a bona fide seniority system adopted by the City. The Court of Appeals erred in reaching this conclusion.

[9] Section 703(h) of Title VII provides that it is not an unlawful employment practice to apply different standards of compensation, or different terms, conditions, or privileges of employment pursuant to a bona fide seniority system, provided that such differences are not the result of an intention to discriminate because of race. It is clear that the City had a seniority system, that its proposed layoff plan conformed to that system, and that in making the settlement the City had not agreed to award competitive seniority to any minority employee whom the City proposed to lay off. The District Court held that the City could not follow its seniority system in making its proposed layoffs because its proposal was discriminatory in effect and hence not a bona fide plan. Section 703(h), however, permits the routine application of a seniority system absent proof of an intention to discriminate. *Teamsters* v. *United States,* 431 U.S. 324, 352, 97 S.Ct. 1843, 1863, 52 L.Ed.2d 396 (1977). Here, the District Court itself found that the layoff proposal was not adopted with the purpose or intent to discriminate on the basis of race. Nor had the City in agreeing to the decree admitted in any way that it had engaged in intentional discrimination. . . .

. . . If individual members of a plaintiff class demonstrate that they have been actual victims of the discriminatory practice, they may be awarded competitive seniority and given their rightful place on the seniority roster. . . . Mere membership in the disadvantaged class is insufficient to warrant a seniority award; each individual must prove that the discriminatory practice had an impact on him. . . . Even when an individual shows that the discriminatory practice has had an impact on him, he is not automatically entitled to have a non-minority employee laid off to make room for him. He may have to wait until a vacancy occurs, and if there are non-minority employees on layoff, the Court must balance the equities in determining who is entitled to the job. . . . Here, there was no finding that any of the blacks protected from layoff had been a victim of discrimination and no award of competitive seniority to any of them. Nor had the parties in formulating the consent decree purported to identify any specific employee entitled to particular relief other than those listed in the exhibits attached to the decree. . . .

CASE 1. Severance Pay at Westinghouse Electric

In the early 1980s, the Westinghouse Electric Corporation adopted a cost-saving policy pertaining to employees of retirement age (those *eligible* for retirement pension benefits) who have been *laid off by management.* Here "laid off" means that the employees were fired (at least temporarily) and did not voluntarily leave their positions. Westinghouse's policy, as is customary, was to provide severance pay to employees in the event that management determines they must lose their positions. Employees of retirement age and eligible for the corporation pension plan could, of course, elect to retire at the time of the layoff if they no longer wished to work.

Westinghouse's policy was framed as follows: No employee could receive both severance pay and retirement benefits. That is, laid-off union and management employees could not collect both severance pay and payments from the pension plan. They had to choose one or the other: An employee who did not retire could receive severance pay, and an employee who chose to retire (having been forced involuntarily into a loss of job) could not receive severance pay. No employee could receive the severance pay, look for a job, not find one, and then announce his intention to go on the company's retirement plan.

Management at Westinghouse thought this policy was justified for two reasons: (1) for cost control and (2) because employees would be "double dipping" if they received both severance pay and payments from a pension plan. The company also held that both the severance plan and the pension plan are voluntary programs not mandated by law.

Thirty-five employees at Westinghouse's Lester, Pennsylvania, plant objected to this justification and filed a lawsuit. They saw the issue as one of age discrimination. They held that severance pay is justified by rules about

being involuntarily laid off, whereas pension benefits are warranted by the rules of retirement plans.

U.S. District Judge Marvin Katz of Philadelphia found in March 1986 that Westinghouse's policy did indeed involve "blatant, willful age discrimination" against older employees. The judge held that the policy had the effect of giving "employees who are eligible for retirement no practical choice but to take retirement benefit and forgo severance pay." The judge saw the severance-pay provision as a short-term way for an employee to think through his or her situation and alternatives. Pension plans, by contrast, are provisions for long-term retirement. To penalize an older employee by forcing him or her to limit or give up one in order to claim the other is age-based discrimination.

Westinghouse said its policy was not based on age but rather on whether the employee was eligible for a pension, regardless of age. But Judge Katz held that "age and retirement are, in fact, so closely linked that a criterion based on one is a criterion based on the other." Westinghouse vigorously objected to this finding and appealed the judge's ruling.

Questions

1. Is Westinghouse discriminating on the basis of age? Is it immorally discriminating? Willfully discriminating?
2. If both the pension plan and the severance plan are voluntary, can Westinghouse be held either morally or legally at fault for violating someone's rights? Should the acceptability of the policy be left to the free market of competition for employees?
3. Is it unfair that an employee cannot choose to take severance pay first and then later, having received the severance pay while looking for a job, choose to go into retirement?

This case was prepared by Tom L. Beauchamp on the basis of reports in the *Wall Street Journal*, March 28, 1986, p. 4, and the *New York Times*, March 28, 1986, p. 9.

CASE 2. Sing's Chinese Restaurant

The Bali Hai Corporation started as a small Chinese restaurant in Boston, Massachusetts in 1959. The restaurant was an exact replica of a Chinese pagoda. Over the years, the restaurant, owned and managed by Arnold Sing, became known for its food and atmosphere. Customers were made to feel as if they were actually in China. In the last few years Sing decided to incorporate and open other similar restaurants throughout the country. Sing, who had come to the United States from China in the early 1940s, was very strict in keeping up his reputation of good food and atmosphere, and had a policy of hiring only waiters of Oriental descent. He felt this added to his customers' dining pleasure and made for a more authentic environment. For kitchen positions, though, Sing hired any applicants who were qualified.

About a year ago in Sing's Bali Hai of Washington, D.C. there was a shortage of waiters. An advertisement was placed in the paper for waiters, and the manager of the store was instructed by Sing to hire only Orientals. The manager was also reminded of

Bali Hai's commitment to a reputation of good food and atmosphere. Two young men, one black and one white, both with considerable restaurant experience, applied for the waiter's jobs. The manager explained the policy of hiring only Orientals to the young men, and he also told them he could get them work in his kitchen. The two men declined the positions and instead went directly to the area Equal Employment Office and filed a complaint. Sing's defense was that the policy was only to preserve the atmosphere of the restaurant. He said the Oriental waiters were needed to make it more authentic. Sing also added that he hired Blacks, Whites, and other races for his kitchen help.

Questions

1. Is Sing's defense a good one under the law? Why or why not?
2. Is Sing's defense a good one under the standards of morality? Why or why not?
3. Is this a case of "preferential hiring"? "Reverse discrimination"?

CASE 3. T. H. Sandy Sportswear

The Millers, Brad and Mary, moved to Tallahasse, Florida in order for Mary to attend Law School at Florida State University. Brad graduated from Georgetown University with a degree in Business Administration and worked in retail management for five years. Brad graduated with top honors from Georgetown and had excellent recommendations from his former employers.

Tallahassee, Florida is basically a college town, centering around two universities and

the Florida State Legislature. The two universities are Florida State University and Florida A & M University. There is only one large shopping mall and a few department stores in Tallahassee, and jobs in retail management are quite scarce.

Upon arriving in Tallahassee, Mary started classes at the Law School and Brad began looking for a job. There were absolutely no openings anywhere in town for retail managers, and Brad eventually had to

Case 2: Copyright © 1980 by Kenneth A. Kovach and reprinted with permission of the author. This case was prepared by Kenneth A. Kovach as a basis for class discussion rather than to illustrate either effective or ineffective handling of an administrative situation.

Case 3: Copyright © 1980 by Kenneth A. Kovach and reprinted with permission of the author. This case was prepared by Kenneth A. Kovach.

settle for a teller position at a local bank. Brad kept abreast of the retail job market in Tallahassee, and finally an opportunity came open.

T. H. Sandy, a women's discount sportswear retailer advertised in the local newspaper for a store manager. Brad immediately made an appointment for an interview and sent in a resume, as requested in the ad. Brad arrived early for his interview and was given an application form to complete. The application form was a long one and included a question concerning sex of applicant. While completing the application form, Brad noticed that all the employees of T. H. Sandy were female and all of the other applicants waiting to be interviewed were also female. Brad was finally called in for his interview, which he thought went very well. The interviewer told Brad that they had two more days of interviewing before a decision would be made and that he would be hearing from them in about a week. The next week Brad received a letter from T. H. Sandy informing him that he had not been chosen for the position and thanking him for his interest in the company. The letter gave no reason for their decision. Since this job was so important to Brad, he decided to visit the store and talk with the lady who had interviewed him.

In his meeting with the interviewer, Brad found out that the company had been very impressed with his experience and credentials, but had decided against hiring him because he was a male. The interviewer showed Brad a job description for the manager's position and pointed out that one of the duties of the manager was to supervise all areas of the store, including the dressing room. Because of this particular duty, the company felt that the position should be filled with a female. Brad left the store upset and discouraged.

After discussing the situation with his wife, who was now studying Fair Employment Legislation, Brad considered filing suit against T. H. Sandy for discrimination based on sex under Title VII of the Civil Rights Act of 1964.

Questions

1. Was T. H. Sandy's decision concerning Brad Miller in conflict with Title VII of the Civil Rights Act of 1964?
2. Is sex a bona fide occupational qualification in this situation?
3. Is Brad a "victim" of reverse discrimination?

CASE 4. Quotas for Sheet Metal Workers

Local 28 of the Sheet Metal Workers' International Association was sued by the city of New York in 1971 for persistent exclusion of minorities from membership. A series of district court rulings established a long record of discriminatory practices in hiring by the union as well as staunch resistance to attempts by the city to end those practices. Nepotism was found to be the basic system of recruiting, training, admission, and advancement; this system established an impenetrable barrier to nonwhite employment

that had never been passed by a nonwhite candidate. The union was ordered by the court to achieve a goal of 29 percent minority membership by the year 1981, later extended to 1982. The union was also fined enough money to set up a penalty fund to provide money for training and assistance for minority workers. In 1982 and again in 1983 the city and state charged that little had been done to achieve the mandated goal. The court found the union in contempt both times.

This case was written by Tom L. Beauchamp on the basis of the opinion by Justice Brennan in *Sheet Metal Workers' Plan,* as printed in the *New York Times,* July 3, 1986, p. B8.

The union maintained that the membership goal and the fund exeeded the boundaries of a justifiable remedy because they extended race-conscious preferences to individuals who are not the identified victims of unlawful discrimination. The Solicitor General of the United States supported the union in this claim in arguments before the Supreme Court. However, the Supreme Court held in July 1986 that in circumstances of egregious discrimination of this sort preferential treatment involving quotas could be justified even if it benefits individuals who are not the actual victims of discrimination in order to remedy the discriminatory situation. It found the quotas "appropriate equitable relief" under the objective of equal employment opportunity. However, it maintained that quotas could not be justified in every case "simply to create a racially balanced work force."

Questions

1. Does the filling of a 29 percent quota entail denial of equal employment opportunity to white applicants who have no history of discrimination?
2. Is reverse discrimination at work in this case? If so, is it justifiable?
3. Is the target goal of 29 percent appropriate equitable relief?

CASE 5. Comparable Worth in the Female Section?

Throughout the early 1970s the County of Washington, Oregon, established salary scales for its guards in the county jail such that female guards in the female section were paid (in various years and scales) one-third to one-eighth less than male guards of comparable rank and experience in the male section. (All salaries were less than $1000 per month, irrespective of rank, experience, or sex.)

The female guards complained that they were paid unequal wages for work substantially equal to that performed by male guards and that the underlying reason was sex discrimination. The women showed that the pay scale for males was set by the county's survey of outside markets. That survey showed that the average outside pay standard is that female correctional officials are paid about 95 percent as much as male correctional officials, but that on average the County of Washington paid only 70 percent as much. The county thus had scaled down the worth of the female guards' work below the outside market level. However, the county had not had difficulty hiring women in the local region at its pay scales.

The county said there were two major differences in the jobs for men and women: The male guards supervised more than ten times as many prisoners per guard as did the female guards, and the females, unlike the males, were required to spend part of their time on clerical jobs (considered less valuable by the county). The county therefore held that the females' jobs were not substantially equal to those of the male guards and merited less than equal pay. The county also objected to the idea that an outside authority such as the courts could evaluate their pay scales without placing virtually every employer at risk of scrutiny by the courts for not paying comparable wages.

Questions

1. Is this a "comparable worth" case or only a case involving alleged sex discrimination? Is it both?
2. Are there relevant differences between the male jobs and the female jobs that would justify a lower salary scale for women?

This case was prepared by Tom L. Beauchamp on the basis of facts presented in the United States Supreme Court opinion on *County of Washington* v. *Gunther*, 452 U.S. 161 (1980).

Suggested Supplementary Readings

Adelson, Joseph. "Living With Quotas." *Commentary* 65 (May 1978).

Amdur, Robert. "Compensatory Justice: The Question of Costs." *Political Theory* 7 (May 1979).

Axelsen, Diana. "With All Deliberate Delay: On Justifying Preferential Policies in Education and Employment." *Philosophical Forum* 9 (Winter–Spring 1977—1978).

Babcock, Barbara, *Sex Discrimination and the Law: Causes and Remedies*. Boston: Little, Brown and Company, 1975.

Beauchamp Tom L., and Terry Pinkard, eds. *Ethics and Public Policy*. 2nd ed., chapter 6. Englewood Cliffs, N.J.: Prentice-Hall, 1983.

Blackstone, William T. "An Assessment of the Ethical Pros and Cons of Reverse Discrimination." In *Philosophy and Public Policy*. Edited by Donnie E. Self. Norfolk, Va.: Teagle & Little, Inc., 1977.

——, and Robert Heslep, eds. *Social Justice and Preferential Treatment*. Athens: University of Georgia Press, 1977.

Blumrosen, Alfred. "Quotas, Common Sense, and Law in Labor Relations: Three Dimensions of Equal Opportunity." *Rutgers Law Review* 27 (Spring 1974).

——. "Strangers in Paradise: *Griggs* v. *Duke Power Co.* and the Concept of Employment Discrimination." *Michigan Law Review* 71 (1975).

Bowie, Norman E., and Robert L. Simon. *The Individual and the Political Order,* chapter 9. Englewood Cliffs, N.J.: Prentice-Hall, 1977.

Boyle, M. Barbara. "Equal Opportunities for Women in Smart Business." *Harvard Business Review* (May–June 1973).

Burstein, Paul. *Discrimination, Jobs, and Politics*. Chicago: University of Chicago Press, 1985.

Cohen Carl. "Why Racial Preference is Illegal and Immoral." *Commentary* 67 (June 1979).

Cohen, Marshall, Thomas Nagel, and Thomas Scanlon, eds. *Equality and Preferential Treatment*. Princeton, N.J.: Princeton University Press, 1977.

"Constitutionality of Remedial Minority Preferences in Employment." *Minnesota Law Review* 56 (1972).

Dworkin, Ronald. "How to Read the Civil Rights Act." *New York Review of Books* 26 (December 20, 1979).

Edwards, Harry T. "Race Discrimination in Employment: What Price Equality?" *University of Illinois Law Forum* 1976 (1976).

Epstein, E. M., and D. R. Hampton. *Black America and White Business*. Belmont, Calif.: Wadsworth, 1971.

Fiss, Owen. "A Theory of Fair Employment Laws." *University of Chicago Law Review* 38 (Winter 1971).

Fullinwider, Robert, *The Reverse Discrimination Controversy*. Totowa, N.J.: Rowman and Allanheld, 1980.

Glazer, Nathan. *Affirmative Discrimination: Ethnic Inequality and Public Policy*. New York: Basic Books, 1975.

Goldman, Alan. *Justice and Reverse Discrimination*. Princeton, N.J.: Princeton University Press, 1979.

Gross, Barry R. *Reverse Discrimination*. Buffalo, N.Y.: Prometheus Books, 1977.

Hook, Sidney. "Discrimination, Color Blindness, and the Quota System." In *Ethical Theory and Business*. 2nd ed. Edited by Tom L. Beauchamp and Norman Bowie. Englewood Cliffs, N.J.: Prentice-Hall, 1983.

Hughes, Graham. "The Right to Special Treatment." In *The Rights of Americans*. Edited by Norman Dorsen. New York: Pantheon Books, 1971.

Nagel, Thomas. "Equal Treatment and Compensatory Discrimination." *Philosophy & Public Affairs* 2 (Summer 1973).

Newton, Lisa. "*Bakke* and *Davis:* Justice, American Style." *National Forum: The Phi Kappa Phi Journal* 58 (Winter 1978).

Note. "*Weber* v. *Kaiser Aluminim & Chemical Corp.*: The Challenge to Voluntary Compliance Under the Title VII." *Columbia Journal of Law and Social Problems* 14 (1978).

Posner, Richard. "The *Bakke* Case and the Future of 'Affirmative Action'." *California Law Review* 67 (January 1979).

——. "The *DeFunis* Case and the Constitutionality of Preferential Treatment of Racial Minorities." *The Supreme Court Review*. Edited by Philip Kurland. Chicago: University of Chicago Press, 1975.

Remick, Helen. *Comparable Worth and Wage Discrimination*. Philadelphia: Temple University Press, 1984.

Sher, George. "Justifying Reverse Discrimination in Employment." *Philosophy & Public Affairs* 4 (Winter 1975).

———. "Reverse Discrimination, the Future, and the Past." *Ethics* 90 (October 1979).

Simon, Robert. "Preferential Hiring: A Reply to Judith Jarvis Thomson." *Philosophy & Public Affairs* 3 (1974).

Thomson, Judith Jarvis. "Preferential Hiring." *Philosophy & Public Affairs* 2 (1973).

U.S. Supreme Court. *Burwell* v. *Eastern Air Lines, Inc.,* 450 U.S. 965 (1981).

———. *DeFunis* v. *Odegaard.* 416 U.S. 312 (1974).

———. *Firefighters* v. *Cleveland,* 478 U.S. (1986).

———. *Frontiero* v. *Richardson.* 411 U.S. 677 (1973).

———. *McDonald* v. *Santa Fe Transportation Co.* 427 U.S. 273 (1976).

———. *McDonnell Douglas Corp.* v. *Green,* 411 U.S. 792 (1973).

———. *Regents of the Unviersity of California v. Allan Bakke.* 438 U.S. 265, 46 LW 4896 (1978).

———. *Sheet Metal Workers* v. *EEOC,* 478 U.S. (1986).

Velasquez, Manuel G. *Business Ethics: Concepts and Cases,* chapter 7. Englewood Cliffs, N.J.: Prentice-Hall, 1982.

Vitteritti, Joseph P. *Bureaucracy and Social Justice: Allocation of Jobs and Services to Minority Groups.* Port Washington, N.Y.: Kennikat Press. 1979.

Wasserstrom, Richard. "A Defense of Programs of Preferential Treatment." *National Forum: The Phi Kappa Phi Journal* 58 (Winter 1978), and a more inclusive article, "Racism, Sexism, and Preferential Treatment: An Approach to the Topics." *UCLA Law Review* 24 (1977).

CHAPTER SEVEN

Advertising and Disclosing Information

INTRODUCTION

Advertising is the most visible way in which businesses present information to the public, but it is not the only practice of communication in business, and perhaps not the most important one. Marketing, sales, government reports, annual reports containing financial audits, public relations presentations, warranties, and even public education and public health campaigns are vital means by which corporations communicate information. Usually we expect substantially complete disclosures, although sometimes information is justifiably suppressed or withheld (e.g., because trade secrets are at stake, or the information might be used for insider trading in the stock, or because only the board of directors is privy to the information).

A wide array of moral problems attend various methods of communication and nondisclosure. Some problems are commonplace; for example, vital information may be withheld or the truth otherwise distorted by a misleading presentation, lying, or bluffing. Other problems of information control are more subtle. These include the use of information to manipulate persons, using annual reports more as public relations devices than for the disclosure of financial soundness, giving calculated "news releases" to the press, avoid-

ing disclosures to workers that directly affect their health and welfare, and so on. Several related problems are considered in other chapters in this book. See Chapters Four (pp. 199–201) and Five (pp. 263–266).

Several moral problems with the communication and use of information concern *free choice:* Certain forms of withholding of information and advertising can rob a person of the capacity for free choice of a product, good, or service by manipulating or even coercing that person. Deceptive and misleading statements, especially as they affect consumers, limit freedom by restricting the range of choice and by causing a person to do what he or she otherwise would not do. Other problems, by contrast, are *harm*-based and may have little to do with issues of free choice. For example, when the Nestle Corporation was under pressure to suspend advertising and aggressive marketing of infant formula products in developing countries, the controversy centered less on a freedom-based worry about information deficiency or distortion than on a felt need to educate a population about breastfeeding and about risks and benefits in the use of infant formula so as to avoid harm to infants.

Harm-based issues will occasionally be

mentioned in this chapter, but the dominant focus will be restrictions on free choice, especially by manipulative influence that serves to constrain human freedom.

INFLUENCE AND FREEDOM OF CHOICE

A basic condition of freedom is that personal actions remain free of controls by alien influences that would deprive the person of autonomy and personal responsibility. Control over a person—whether over body or mind—is always exerted through some form of influence, but not all influences are controlling. Influences come from diverse sources. They include threats of physical harm, news conferences, promises of love and affection, economic incentives, reasoned argument, lies, and emotional appeals. Many such influences are easily resisted by most persons; others are irresistible by most. Some have a major effect on a person's abilities to perform actions, while others have trivial, if any, influence.

The word *influence* does not entail *control* of the person in the form of force or compulsion. "Influence" covers a broad array of human interactions. Many important life decisions are made in contexts replete with competing claims and interests, social demands and expectations, and express attempts by others to achieve their ends. Some of these influences are desired by those who are influenced, while others are detested.

In many cases, of course, we do not know and cannot easily study human reactions—in general or in particular—to the presentations made in advertising. Frank Dandrea, vice-president for marketing at the offices of the importer of Hennessy's Cognac (Schieffelin & Co.), reports that in their advertisements "The idea is to show a little skin, a little sex appeal, a little tension."[1] This is attempted, for example, by showing an encounter between a woman in a skimpy dress holding a brandy snifter and provocatively staring in response to a man's glance of interest. Hennessy uses sex and humor; other companies use rebates

and coupons. All this is an attempt to influence, and there is little question that their techniques do influence. But how they influence and the moral acceptability of these influences are not well understood.

Quite apart from the specifics of advertising, we do know that there is a continuum of controlling influence in our daily lives, running from coercion, which is at the most controlling end of the continuum, to persuasion and education, which are not *controlling* at all, even though they are influences. Coercion requires an intentional and successful influence through a threat of harm that one is unable to resist. Coercion, so understood, essentially negates freedom because it entirely controls action. Persuasion, by contrast, involves a successful appeal to reason in order to get a person to freely accept what is advocated by the persuader. (Benn offers a somewhat different analysis in his selection in this chapter.) Like *informing, persuading* is entirely compatible with free choice, even though both are forms of influence.

The great gray area of influence is *manipulation,* a catch-all category that includes any intentional and successful influence of a person by (noncoercively) shifting the *choices* available to the person or (nonpersuasively) modifying the person's *perceptions* of those choices. The essence of manipulation is getting people to do what the manipulator intends without resort to coercion or appeal to reasoned argument. In the case of *informational* manipulation, on which this chapter concentrates, information is managed so that the person does what the manipulator intends. Whether such uses of information necessarily compromise or restrict free choice is an unresolved and untidy issue, but one plausible view is that some manipulations—for instance the use of rewards such as free trips or lottery chances in direct mail advertising—are compatible with free choice, whereas others—such as deceptive offers or tantalizing ads aimed at young children—are not compatible with free choice.

Most real-world problems of advertising are somewhere between acceptable and unacceptable manipulation, and therefore firm determination of their justifiability often tends to be elusive. Consider two examples: Anheuser-Busch ran a television commercial for its Budweiser Beer showing some working men heading for a brew at day's end. The commercial begins with a shot of the Statue of Liberty in the background, includes a few close-up shots of a construction crew working to restore the Statue, and ends with the words, "This Bud's for you, you know America takes pride in what you do." This may seem innocent enough, but the Liberty–Ellis Island Foundation accused Anheuser-Busch of a "blatant attempt to dupe [i.e., manipulate] consumers" by getting them to believe that Budweiser was among the sponsors helping to repair Lady Liberty, thereby promoting its image and product through a false association. Moreover, Anheuser-Busch had refused such a sponsorship when invited by the Foundation; its rival Stroh Brewery Company had subsequently accepted an exclusive brewery sponsorship.[2]

A second and dilemmatic case comes from Kellogg's advertising for its All-Bran product. Kellogg ran a campaign linking its product to the prevention of cancer; as the apparent result, sales immediately jumped 41 percent for All-Bran (in the final quarter of 1984). Many food manufacturers advertise the low-salt, low-fat, low-calorie, or high-fiber content of their products, but Kellogg had gone further by citing a *specific product* as a way to combat a *specific disease*. It is illegal to make claims about the health benefits of a specific food product without FDA approval, and Kellogg did not have this approval; yet officials at both the National Cancer Institute and FDA found the ads perplexing. On the one hand, officials at these agencies believe that a high-fiber, low-fat diet containing products such as All-Bran does help prevent cancer. On the other hand, there is no direct association between eating a given product and preventing cancer, and certainly no single food product can function, like a drug, as a preventative or a remedy for a disease such as cancer. The Kellogg ad seemed to say, on a literal reading, that all one needs to do to prevent cancer is consume All-Bran. Such a claim is potentially misleading in several respects. The ad does not report how much fiber people should eat, nor does it note that persons can consume too much fiber to the neglect of other needed minerals. There is no direct scientific link between eating this product and preventing cancer, and there are many types of cancer, not all of which this product could be expected to affect. Does Kellogg promise a reward that is in effect manipulative, or is the ad, as Kellogg claims, basically a health-promotion campaign? Or is it both?

These examples help illustrate the broad categories on the continuum of controlling influences that are at work in this chapter: coercion, manipulation, and persuasion. Other forms of influence such as indoctrination and seduction might be mentioned, but in the end—especially for advertising—the difference between manipulation and persuasion will prove to be the most important matter. The central question is not whether we are *entirely* free of even manipulative influences, but whether we are *sufficiently* free to say that we remain autonomous—free to perform our own actions—rather than controlled by the actions of another.

FAIR AND UNFAIR INFLUENCE

One classic defense of American business practice is that it gives the public what it wants and freely chooses. In the American free enterprise system the consumer is king, and the market responds to consumer demands. This response to consumer demand allegedly represents one of the chief strengths of a market economy over a collectivist economy. In the latter economy, consumption patterns are severely constrained by government bureaucrats. In a competitive free-enterprise economy, freedom of consumer choice is unfettered by government constraints and hence is presumably free.

Much discussion about the morality of advertising, marketing, and sales focuses on the degree of freedom of choice. Consider, as an example, the following problem. The Federal Trade commission (FTC) in late 1984 and early 1985 "reconsidered" its rule prohibiting the advertising by supermarkets of items that they do not actually have on their shelves. The rule had been enacted in 1971 to combat frustration among shoppers who found empty shelves when goods were advertised and often wound up substituting more expensive items. FTC officials suggested that the rule may be unduly burdensome for the supermarket industry and that "market forces" would eliminate or curtail those who advertise abusively. However, consumer groups complained that relaxing the rule wou:d permit more expensive stores to lure shoppers by advertising low prices; many shoppers would then spend more than they would in a low-budget store. Mark Silbergeld of the Consumers Union argued that the Commission was acting in ignorance of the *real purpose* of supermarket advertising, which is to present a "come-on to get people into their stores."[3] On the one hand, if the advertisements do succeed in manipulating persons to greater monetary outlays through false or empty advertising, the purchases made by consumers may not be as free as they think or as supermarket companies suggest. On the other hand, shoppers can refuse to buy or to return in the future once they find the goods unavailable. Does such advertising, then, represent the deprivation of free choice, or is it rather an example of how free choice determines market forces? Can it function as both for different populations of persons?

Some critics of advertising, such as John Kenneth Galbraith in his article in this chapter, contend that the effectiveness of advertising actually may destroy the benefits of consumer sovereignty. Contrary to a popular myth, the market does not merely respond to consumer demand; rather it *creates* demand through advertising. If consumer preferences were taken as given, the only advertising that society would need would be strictly informational. But as every good market researcher knows, one must create or encourage a demand for one's product. A contemporary example of a morally questionable and heavily criticized practice is television advertising by cigarette companies in African and South American countries. The Third World is now the cigarette industry's chief area of growth (sales have stagnated in many industrialized nations), and the advertising has been highly successful in some countries (usually countries with no government constraints on the kind of advertising that may be used) where many citizens suffer from malnutrition.

Given human nature, Galbraith argues that the fact that business firms must often create a market for their products should come as no surprise. The necessity of creating demand can be anticipated from one of the "laws" of economic theory—specifically the law of diminishing marginal utility. Under the law of diminishing utility, a consumer's satisfaction from each additional unit of a product increases, but at a decreasing rate. Stripped of jargon, this means for example, that a child enjoys the third ice cream less than the first one. The law of diminishing marginal utility applies to material goods in general. Galbraith maintains that as our standard of living increases, luxuries become increasingly less important to us (by contrast to basic needs). In an affluent society, industry needs increasingly to create a demand for more goods and services. Advertising represents one (possibly manipulative) means for effecting this repeal of the law of diminishing marginal utility. Thus, no home will be complete without a personal computer to replace the typewriter, and no automobile satisfactory without a sophisticated stereo system. If business lived by the creed of consumer sovereignty, heavy advertising of such products would be unnecessary.

In a critique of Galbraith's views, Friedrich von Hayek accepts Galbraith's distinction between different levels of need, but is unwilling to accept the conclusions Galbraith draws from this distinction. Von Hayek argues that it is not true that culturally induced needs are of comparatively little value. If that were true, the products of music, painting, and literature would be of little value. Moreover, even though nonbasic needs may not *originate* with the consumer, that fact does not show that such needs were not *freely* adopted, or were in any unacceptable way manipulated. When a student develops the need to hear Beethoven rather than popular music, has his or her music teacher induced this need? Von Hayek in effect argues that consumers are of necessity *influenced,* but to be influenced is not to be *unduly* influenced and therefore unfree.

The underlying dispute here turns at least in part on different conceptions of the conditions of human freedom. Galbraith thinks that some advertising is unduly manipulative and even coercive, and hence undermines human freedom and consumer sovereignty. Von Hayek, on the other hand, agrees that advertising influences consumers but denies that it coerces or manipulates. This dispute about undue influence is a dispute about the moral acceptability of the influence. It is important not to be tendentious by presuming that manipulation is necessarily *unfair* or *immoral.* Although manipulation certainly has been analyzed by some philosophers as necessarily immoral, because it "uses" another person to one's own ends without the other's consent, the issues should be addressed without a presumption of immorality. The moral character of manipulating by presenting a desired reward differs markedly from the moral character of an act of deception that tricks persons into doing what they do not want to do. Both are manipulative, and thus questions of the moral justifiability of manipulation should be kept separate from questions about whether something is manipulative or questions about the conceptual nature of manipulation.

One difficulty with this whole discussion centers on the notion of autonomy. Under what conditions is a person autonomous or truly self-governing? Suppose that, as a result of advertising, a person purchases consumer goods at the expense of an adequate savings account or investment program for the future. If the consumer indicates that the decision represents what he or she genuinely wants to do, on what basis can an outsider deny that

the decision was freely made? Is the person deceived about his or her preferences? Suppose one buys a particular brand of toothpaste and cites as the reason for buying it that the toothpaste gives the mouth sex appeal. One might disagree with the reason the person had for buying the toothpaste, but it scarcely follows that the decision was not freely made, because the person after all did choose *on the basis of a reason.*

Stanley Benn's article focuses on the legitimate and illegitimate uses of influence and persuasion. Even if most advertising does not violate either negative or positive freedom, the standard persuasive techniques of advertising might nonetheless be morally inappropriate. Benn argues that the key is whether the advertiser treats human beings as rational and autonomous agents. Benn concludes with the provocative, but undeveloped, suggestion that nonrational persuasion is illegitimate if it influences people to choose on grounds that reflect a corrupt understanding of human nature. If Benn is right, a fair amount of advertising is morally suspect.

A somewhat different perspective is found in the essay by Tom Beauchamp, who argues that persuasion is always rational and never deprives persons of autonomy. He proposes the normative thesis that advertisements *should* be persuasive rather than—as they often are—manipulative. Whatever the merit in the distinction between persuasion and manipulation, it should be acknowledged that it is not possible to specify with precision where persuasion ends and manipulation begins. These concepts are too ill-formed, and no one has yet been able to provide exact boundaries between them that fit all cases.

DECEPTION, BLUFFING, AND INFORMATION DISCLOSURE

Manipulation can take many forms. For example, manipulators operate by offering rewards, threatening punishments, or by causing changes in mental processes through fear appeals and sly maneuvers intended to engender personal commitment. The most important type of manipulation discussed in this chapter is the manipulation of information, in which the manipulator modifies a person's perception of options by affecting the person's understanding of the situation in some way other than by providing information or using persuasion. Deception, bluffing, and the like are used by the manipulator to change not the person's *actual* options but only the person's *perception* of the options. The more a person is deprived of a relevant understanding in the circumstances, the more the person's free choice stands to be affected.

One does not need extensive experience in business to know that many deceptive practices, like bluffing, are both widely practiced and widely accepted. It is common knowledge that automobile dealers do not expect people to pay the sticker price for automobiles. A certain amount of haggling, quoting of competitors, and bargaining is part of the game. A similar situation prevails in real estate transactions, where the asking price for a house is seldom the selling price. Labor leaders overstate wage demands at bargaining sessions, and management also understates the wage increases it is willing to grant. The intent is to manipulate, however gently.

In his article "Is Business Bluffing Ethical?" Albert Carr recognizes that such practices are characteristic of business, which he takes to be analogous to the game of poker. Just as conscious misstatement, concealment of pertinent facts, exaggeration, and bluffing are morally acceptable in poker, they are also acceptable in business. What makes such practices acceptable, Carr seems to say, is that all parties understand the rules of the game. In advertising, for example, exaggeration and bluffing are understood to be part of the selling game.

But there are moral limits. Suppose that Pamela is willing to sell her home for $60,000 if that is the best price she can get. She asks $70,000. A potential buyer's initial offer is $60,000. She turns it down and tells him that $65,000 is her rock-bottom price. He purchases the home for $65,000. Many people would characterize her behavior as shrewd bluffing rather than an immoral lie. Most people would think more of her rather than less. However, suppose she manufactured the claim that another party had promised her they were in the process of writing up a contract for $65,000 for the house but she would sell it to him because both she and he were Baptists. In this case many people would maintain that she had told an immoral lie. It also would not improve the moral character of her action to have her brother pretend to make her an offer so that the prospective buyer would be pressured to buy. That would be a case of an immoral deception as well.

To decide whether information is unacceptably presented, the sophistication of the audience, the standard practice, as well as the intention of the informer all need to be considered. Manipulation and deception can result as much from what is not said as from what is said. For example, true information can be presented out of context and hence, can be misleading. The reasoning of Chief Justice Earl Warren in *FTC* v. *Colgate-Palmolive Co.* et al. demonstrates how the omission of some facts can be misleading while the omission of others is not misleading. At issue is a television commercial depicting someone shaving sandpaper that had been generously lathered with Rapid Shave. The FTC admitted that Rapid Shave could soften sandpaper so that it could be shaved, but the sandpaper needed to soak in Rapid Shave for approximately eighty minutes before it could be shaved. On the basis of this, the FTC declared the ad deceptive because the television viewer was not informed about the eighty-minute wait.

Colgate-Palmolive disagreed. It compared its "experiment" with the use of mashed potatoes instead of ice cream in television ice cream ads. Just as the television lights made the use of ice cream impossible—which ice cream ads do not disclose—so the working time made showing an actual experiment impossible. The court turned down the analogy on the grounds that the mashed potatoes prop was not used for additional proof of the quality of the product while the Rapid Shave commercial was attempting to provide such proof. Accordingly, the Rapid Shave decision could be generalized to make the following point: Whether or not undisclosed information is considered an example of immoral deception depends on whether the information is related to the cost, amount, or quality of the product.

Federal regulatory agencies that grapple with these questions tend to focus on the audience, the recipients of the information. Agencies like the Federal Trade Commission appeal to two competing standards: the reasonable consumer standard and the ignorant consumer standard. Ivan Preston describes the history behind the use of these two standards by the FTC and provides some analysis of the strengths and weaknesses of them. A decision establishing the appropriate standard has important implications for whether ads should be viewed as inherently deceptive or simply given to harmless exaggeration. Such standards are also relevant in determining whether certain types of manipulations are immoral.

For example, the ignorant consumer takes everything literally. He or she believes that when Old Froshingslosh beer advertises that the foam will be on the bottom, it will be on the bottom. It is generally agreed that requiring business practice to be so open and literal that even the ignorant consumer would not be deceived would stifle business and seriously affect productivity. On that point the conventional wisdom seems correct. However, the definition of the reasonable consumer is amorphous. Sometimes reasonable consumer is just a synonym for average consumer. Advertisements, like television programs, would have to be aimed at those with the reading ability of a twelve-year-old. At other times reasonable consumer is given a more normative definition. It is equated with what a consumer *should* know. In the legal context, what a rational person should do or should not do is ultimately decided by a jury of one's peers. If a person is sued for negligence, one of the big questions is whether or not the person took reasonable precautions; this is determined by what a reasonable man would do in those circumstances. Whether the manipulation of a piece of information is immoral depends in part on whether the audience should have been manipulated in that context. That question is decided by the standard you choose as an evaluative device.

Another way to handle the debate over where to draw the line between harmless exaggeration and immoral deception is to appeal to a criterion of public openness. A business practice may not be deceptive if that business *acknowledges* the rules it is playing by. Ads for automobiles and for real estate make it clear that the "asking price" is not the "real price." An ad for a home that says, "asking $120,000" virtually announces that the homeowner is in a mood to deal. Automobile ads for individual dealers often stress the fact that they will match any other deal in town. They explicitly acknowledge the bargaining aspect of automobile sales. Grocery store ads contain none of this bargaining language, and it is only rarely found in stock brokerage advertising (e.g., Pacific Brokerage Services advertises "Above 3,000 shares—Negotiable," while under 3,000 shares is always fixed). Deception of course reenters if a businessperson announces that he or she is playing by one set of rules when in fact he or she is playing by another; immorality also enters if one partner to a contract breaks his or her end of the deal. But as long as the rules of the game are known and people are in equal bargaining positions, then most people will accept consequences of business practice that they might not accept in other circumstances.

But as Carr points out, the criterion of public openness still allows for much bluffing, exaggeration, and nondisclosure. It is morally permissible to try to deceive others as long as everyone openly knows that such actions are permitted by the rules. In his article, Norman Bowie rejects the public openness criterion on both Kantian and utilitarian grounds. Bowie also argues that bluffing, "white lies," and lack of information disclosure interfere with markets, hurt productivity and hence competition, create instability, and in the long run threaten the business community itself.

The issue of what information ought to be disclosed is at least as prominent in sales as in advertising. In the extended case study, David Holley demonstrates that a business commitment to the market system requires a business commitment to certain kinds of information disclosure. As he puts it, the primary duty of salespeople is not to undermine the conditions of acceptable exchange.

The readings in this chapter raise a set of largely unresolved problems about the role of informing, persuading, and manipulating in advertising and sales. They also return us to the issues of corporate responsibility raised in Chapter Two. As several essays note, advertising agencies and the corporations for which they develop ads must ultimately bear the responsibility for the content and influence of those ads.

NOTES

1. As quoted in Amy Dunkin et al., "Liquor Makers Try the Hard Sell in a Softening Market," *Business Week,* May 13, 1985, p. 56.
2. "Anheuser-Busch Sued on Ad Showing Statue of Liberty," *Wall Street Journal,* November 28, 1984, p. 43.
3. See Sari Horwitz, "FTC Considers Letting Food Stores Advertise Out-of-Stock Items," *Washington Post,* December 27, 1984, p. E1.

The Dependence Effect

John Kenneth Galbraith

The theory of consumer demand, as it is now widely accepted, is based on two broad propositions, neither of them quite explicit but both extremely important for the present value system of economists. The first is that the urgency of wants does not diminish appreciably as more of them are satisfied or, to put the matter more precisely, to the extent that this happens it is not demonstrable and not a matter of any interest to economists or for economic policy. When man has satisfied his physical needs, then psychologically grounded desires take over. These can never be satisfied or, in any case, no progress can be proved. The concept of satiation has very little standing in economics. It is neither useful nor scientific to speculate on the comparative cravings of the stomach and the mind.

The second proposition is that wants originate in the personality of the consumer or in any case, that they are given data for the economist. The latter's task is merely to seek their satisfaction. He has no need to inquire how these wants are formed. His function is sufficiently fulfilled by maximizing the goods that supply the wants. . . .

The notion that wants do not become less urgent the more amply the individual is supplied is broadly repugnant to common

---

From John Kenneth Galbraith, *The Affluent Society.* Copyright 1958, 1969, 1976, 1984 by John Kenneth Galbraith. Reprinted by permission of Houghton Mifflin Company and Andre Deutsch, Ltd.

sense. It is something to be believed only by those who wish to believe. Yet the conventional wisdom must be tackled on its own terrain. Intertemporal comparisons of an individual's state of mind do rest on doubtful grounds. Who can say for sure that the deprivation which afflicts him with hunger is more painful than the deprivation which afflicts him with envy of his neighbor's new car? In the time that has passed since he was poor his soul may have become subject to a new and deeper searing. And where a society is concerned, comparisons between marginal satisfactions when it is poor and those when it is affluent will involve not only the same individual at different times but different individuals at different times. The scholar who wishes to believe that with increasing affluence there is no reduction in the urgency of desires and goods is not without points for debate. However plausible the case against him, it cannot be proved. In the defence of the conventional wisdom this amounts almost to invulnerability.

However, there is a flaw in the case. If the individual's wants are to be urgent they must be original with himself. They cannot be urgent if they must be contrived for him. And above all they must not be contrived by the process of production by which they are satisfied. For this means that the whole case for the urgency of production, based on the urgency of wants, falls to the ground. One cannot defend production as satisfying wants if that production creates the wants.

Were it so that a man on arising each morning was assailed by demons which instilled in him a passion sometimes for silk shirts, sometimes for kitchenware, sometimes for chamber-pots, and sometimes for orange squash, there would be every reason to applaud the effort to find the goods, however odd, that quenched this flame. But should it be that his passion was the result of his first having cultivated the demons, and should it also be that his effort to allay it stirred the demons to ever greater and greater effort, there would be question as to how rational was his solution. Unless re-

strained by conventional attitudes, he might wonder if the solution lay with more goods or fewer demons.

So it is that if production creates the wants it seeks to satisfy, or if the wants emerge *pari passu* with the production, then the urgency of the wants can no longer be used to defend the urgency of the production. Production only fills a void that it has itself created. . . .

The even more direct link between production and wants is provided by the institutions of modern advertising and salesmanship. These cannot be reconciled with the notion of independently determined desires, for their central function is to create desires—to bring into being wants that previously did not exist.[1] This is accomplished by the producer of the goods or at his behest. A broad empirical relationship exists between what is spent on production of consumers' goods and what is spent in synthesizing the desires for that production. A new consumer product must be introduced with a suitable advertising campaign to arouse an interest in it. The path for an expansion of output must be paved by a suitable expansion in the advertising budget. Outlays for the manufacturing of a product are not more important in the strategy of modern business enterprise than outlays for the manufacturing of demand for the product. None of this is novel. All would be regarded as elementary by the most retarded student in the nation's most primitive school of business administration. . . .

But such integration means recognizing that wants are dependent on production. It accords to the producer the function both of making the goods and of making the desires for them. It recognizes that production, not only passively through emulation, but actively through advertising and related activities, creates the want it seeks to satisfy.

The businessman and the lay reader will be puzzled over the emphasis which I give to a seemingly obvious point. The point is indeed obvious. But it is one which, to a singular degree, economists have resisted. They have sensed, as the layman does not, the damage to established ideas which lurks in these relationships. As a result, incredibly, they have closed their eyes (and ears) to the most obtrusive of all economic phenomena, namely modern want creation.

This is not to say that the evidence affirming the dependence of wants on advertising has been entirely ignored. It is one reason why advertising has so long been regarded with such uneasiness by economists. Here is something which cannot be accommodated easily to existing theory. More pervious scholars have speculated on the urgency of desires which are so obviously the fruit of such expensively contrived campaigns for popular attention. Is a new breakfast cereal or detergent so much wanted if so much must be spent to compel in the consumer the sense of want? But there has been little tendency to go on to examine the implications of this for the theory of consumer demand and even less for the importance of production and productive efficiency. These have remained sacrosanct. More often the uneasiness has been manifested in a general disapproval of advertising and advertising men, leading to the occasional suggestion that they shouldn't exist. Such suggestions have usually been ill received.

And so the notion of independently determined wants still survives. In the face of all the forces of modern salesmanship it still rules, almost undefiled, in the textbooks. And it still remains the economist's mission—and on few matters is the pedagogy so firm—to seek unquestioningly the means for filling these wants. This being so, production remains of prime urgency. We have here, perhaps, the ultimate triumph of the conventional wisdom in its resistance to the evidence of the eyes. To equal it one must imagine a humanitarian who was long ago persuaded of the grievous shortage of hospital facilities in the town. He continues to importune the passers-by for money for more beds and refuses to notice that the town doctor is deftly knocking over pedestrians with his car to keep up the occupancy.

And in unravelling the complex we should always be careful not to overlook the obvious. The fact that wants can be synthesized by advertising, catalysed by salesmanship, and shaped by the discreet manipulations of the persuaders shows that they are not very urgent. A man who is hungry need never be told of his need for food. If he is inspired by his appetite, he is immune to the influence of Messrs. Batten, Barton, Durstine and Osborn. The latter are effective only with those who are so far removed from physical want that they do not already know what they want. In this state alone men are open to persuasion.

The general conclusion of these pages is of such importance for this essay that it had perhaps best be put with some formality. As a society becomes increasingly affluent, wants are increasingly created by the process by which they are satisfied. This may operate passively. Increases in consumption, the counterpart of increases in production, act by suggestion or emulation to create wants. Or producers may proceed actively to create wants through advertising and salesmanship. Wants thus come to depend on output. In technical terms it can no longer be assumed that welfare is greater at an all-round higher level of production than at a lower one. It may be the same. The higher level of production has, merely, a higher level of want creation necessitating a higher level of want satisfaction. There will be frequent occasion to refer to the way wants depend on the process by which they are satisfied. It will be convenient to call it the Dependence Effect. . . .

The final problem of the productive society is what it produces. This manifests itself in an implacable tendency to provide an opulent supply of some things and a niggardly yield of others. This disparity carries to the point where it is a cause of social discomfort and social unhealth. The line which divides our area of wealth from our area of poverty is roughly that which divides privately produced and marketed goods and services from publicly rendered services. Our wealth in the first is not only in startling contrast with the meagerness of the latter, but our wealth in privately produced goods is, to a marked degree, the cause of crisis in the supply of public services. For we have failed to see the importance, indeed the urgent need, of maintaining a balance between the two.

This disparity between our flow of private and public goods and services is no matter of subjective judgment. On the contrary, it is the source of the most extensive comment which only stops short of the direct contrast being made here. In the years following World War II, the papers of any major city—those of New York were an excellent example—told daily of the shortages and shortcomings in the elementary municipal and metropolitan services. The schools were old and overcrowded. The police force was under strength and underpaid. The parks and playgrounds were insufficient. Streets and empty lots were filthy, and the sanitation staff was underequipped and in need of men. Access to the city by those who work there was uncertain and painful and becoming more so. Internal transportation was overcrowded, unhealthful, and dirty. So was the air. Parking on the streets had to be prohibited, and there was no space elsewhere. These deficiencies were not in new and novel services but in old and established ones. Cities have long swept their streets, helped their people move around, educated them, kept order, and provided horse rails for vehicles which sought to pause. That their residents should have a non-toxic supply of air suggests no revolutionary dalliance with socialism.

The contrast was and remains evident not alone to those who read. The family which takes its mauve and cerise, air-conditioned, power-steered, and power-braked car out for a tour passes through cities that are badly paved, made hideous by litter, blighted buildings, billboards, and posts for wires that should long since have been put underground. They pass on into a countryside that has been rendered largely invisible by commercial art. (The goods which the latter ad-

vertise have an absolute priority in our value system. Such aesthetic considerations as a view of the countryside accordingly come second. On such matters we are consistent.) They picnic on exquisitely packaged food from a portable icebox by a polluted stream and go on to spend the night at a park which is a menace to public health and morals. Just before dozing off on an air-mattress, beneath a nylon tent, amid the stench of decaying refuse, they may reflect vaguely on the curious unevenness of their blessings. Is this, indeed, the American genius? . . .

The case for social balance has, so far, been put negatively. Failure to keep public services in minimal relation to private production and use of goods is a cause of social disorder or impairs economic performance. The matter may now be put affirmatively. By failing to exploit the opportunity to expand public production we are missing opportunities for enjoyment which otherwise we might have had. Presumably a community can be as well rewarded by buying better schools or better parks as by buying bigger cars. By concentrating on the latter rather than the former it is failing to maximize its satisfactions. As with schools in the community, so with public services over the country at large. It is scarcely sensible that we should satisfy our wants in private goods with reckless abundance, while in the case of public goods, on the evidence of the eye, we practice extreme self-denial. So, far from systematically exploiting the opportunities to derive use and pleasure from these services, we do not supply what would keep us out of trouble.

The conventional wisdom holds that the community, large or small, makes a decision as to how much it will devote to its public services. This decision is arrived at by democratic process. Subject to the imperfections and uncertainties of democracy, people decide how much of their private income and goods they will surrender in order to have public services of which they are in greater need. Thus there is a balance, however rough, in the enjoyments to be had from private goods and services and those rendered by public authority.

It will be obvious, however, that this view depends on the notion of independently determined consumer wants. In such a world one could with some reason defend the doctrine that the consumer, as a voter, makes an independent choice between public and private goods. But given the dependence effect—given that consumer wants are created by the process by which they are satisfied—the consumer makes no such choice. He is subject to the forces of advertising and emulation by which production creates its own demand. Advertising operates exclusively, and emulation mainly, on behalf of privately produced goods and services.[2] Since management and emulative effects operate on behalf of private production, public services will have an inherent tendency to lag behind. Car demand which is expensively synthesized will inevitably have a much larger claim on income than parks or public health or even roads where no such influence operates. The engines of mass communication, in their highest state of development, assail the eyes and ears of the community on behalf of more beer but not of more schools. Even in the conventional wisdom it will scarcely be contended that this leads to an equal choice between the two.

The competition is especially unequal for new products and services. Every corner of the public psyche is canvassed by some of the nation's most talented citizens to see if the desire for some merchantable product can be cultivated. No similar process operates on behalf of the nonmerchantable services of the state. Indeed, while we take the cultivation of new private wants for granted we would be measurably shocked to see it applied to public services. The scientist or engineer or advertising man who devotes himself to developing a new carburetor, cleanser, or depilatory for which the public recognizes no need and will feel none until an advertising campaign arouses it, is one of the valued members of our society. A politician or a public servant who dreams up a new public service is a wastrel. Few public offences are more reprehensible.

So much for the influences which operate on the decision between public and private production. The calm decision between public and private consumption pictured by the conventional wisdom is, in fact, a remarkable example of the error which arises from viewing social behaviour out of context. The inherent tendency will always be for public services to fall behind private production. We have here the first of the causes of social imbalance.

NOTES

1. Advertising is not a simple phenomenon. It is also important in competitive strategy, and want creation is, ordinarily, a complementary result of efforts to shift the demand curve of the individual firm at the expense of others or (less importantly, I think) to change its shape by increasing the degree of product differentiation. Some of the failure of economists to identify advertising with want creation may be attributed to the undue attention that its use in purely competitive strategy has attracted. It should be noted, however, that the competitive manipulation of consumer desire is only possible, at least on any appreciable scale, when such need is not strongly felt.

2. Emulation does operate between communities. A new school or a new highway in one community does exert pressure on others to remain abreast. However, as compared with the pervasive effects of emulation in extending the demand for privately produced consumer's goods there will be agreement, I think, that this intercommunity effect is probably small.

The *Non Sequitur*
of the "Dependence Effect"

F. A. von Hayek

For well over a hundred years the critics of the free enterprise system have resorted to the argument that if production were only organized rationally, there would be no economic problem. Rather than face the problem which scarcity creates, socialist reformers have tended to deny that scarcity existed. Ever since the Saint-Simonians their contention has been that the problem of production has been solved and only the problem of distribution remains. However absurd this contention must appear to us with respect to the time when it was first advanced, it still has some persuasive power when repeated with reference to the present.

The latest form of this old contention is expounded in *The Affluent Society* by Professor J. K. Galbraith. He attempts to demonstrate that in our affluent society the important private needs are already satisfied and the urgent need is therefore no longer a further expansion of the output of commodities but an increase of those services which are supplied (and presumably can be supplied only) by government. Though this book has been extensively discussed since its publication in 1958, its central thesis still requires some further examination.

I believe the author would agree that his argument turns upon the "Dependence Effect" [pp. 405–409 of this book]. The argument of this chapter starts from the assertion that a great part of the wants which are still unsatisfied in modern society are not wants which would be experienced spontaneously by the individual if left to himself, but are wants which are created by the process by which they are satisfied. It is then represented as self-evident that for this reason such wants cannot be urgent or important. This crucial conclusion appears to be a complete *non sequitur* and it would seem that with it the whole argument of the book collapses.

The first part of the argument is of course perfectly true: we would not desire any of the amenities of civilization—or even of the most primitive culture—if we did not live in a society in which others provide them. The innate wants are probably confined to food, shelter, and sex. All the rest we learn to desire because we see others enjoying various things. To say that a desire is not important because it is not innate is to say that the whole cultural achievement of man is not important.

This cultural origin of practically all the needs of civilized life must of course not be confused with the fact that there are some desires which aim, not as a satisfaction derived directly from the use of an object, but only from the status which its consumption is expected to confer. In a passage which Professor Galbraith quotes, Lord Keynes seems to treat the latter sort of Veblenesque conspicuous consumption as the only alternative "to those needs which are absolute in the sense that we feel them whatever the situation of our fellow human beings may be." If the latter phrase is interpreted to exclude all the needs for goods which are felt only because these goods are known to be produced, these two Keynesian classes describe

From F. A. von Hayek, "The *Non Sequitur* of the 'Dependence Effect'," *Southern Economic Journal* (April 1961). Reprinted by permission.

of course only extreme types of wants, but disregard the overwhelming majority of goods on which civilized life rests. Very few needs indeed are "absolute" in the sense that they are independent of social environment or of the example of others, and that their satisfaction is an indispensable condition for the preservation of the individual or of the species. Most needs which make us act are needs for things which only civilization teaches us to exist at all, and these things are wanted by us because they produce feelings or emotions which we would not know if it were not for our cultural inheritance. Are not in this sense probably all our esthetic feelings "acquired tastes"?

How complete a *non sequitur* Professor Galbraith's conclusion represents is seen most clearly if we apply the argument to any product of the arts, be it music, painting, or literature. If the fact that people would not feel the need for something if it were not produced did prove that such products are of small value, all those highest products of human endeavor would be of small value. Professor Galbraith's argument could be easily employed without any change of the essential terms, to demonstrate the worthlessness of literature or any other form of art. Surely an individual's want for literature is not original with himself in the sense that he would experience it if literature were not produced. Does this then mean that the production of literature cannot be defended as satisfying a want because it is only the production which provokes the demand? In this, as in the case of all cultural needs, it is unquestionably, in Professor Galbraith's words, "the process of satisfying the wants that creates the wants." There have never been "independently determined desires for" literature before literature has been produced and books certainly do not serve the "simple mode of enjoyment which requires no previous conditioning of the consumer." Clearly my taste for the novels of Jane Austen or Anthony Trollope or C. P. Snow is not "original with myself." But is it not rather absurd to conclude from this that it is less important

than, say, the need for education? Public education indeed seems to regard it as one of its tasks to instill a taste for literature in the young and even employs producers of literature for that purpose. Is this want creation by the producer reprehensible? Or does the fact that some of the pupils may possess a taste for poetry only because of the efforts of their teachers prove that since "it does not arise in spontaneous consumer need and the demand would not exist were it not contrived, its utility or urgency, ex contrivance, is zero?"

The appearance that the conclusions follow from the admitted facts is made possible by an obscurity of the wording of the argument with respect to which it is difficult to know whether the author is himself the victim of a confusion or whether he skillfully uses ambiguous terms to make the conclusion appear plausible. The obscurity concerns the implied assertion that the wants of the consumers are determined by the producers. Professor Galbraith avoids in this connection any terms as crude and definite as "determine." The expressions he employs, such as that wants are "dependent on" or the "fruits of" production, or that "production creates the wants" do, of course, suggest determination but avoid saying so in plain terms. After what has already been said it is of course obvious that the knowledge of what is being produced is one of the many factors on which it depends what people will want. It would scarcely be an exaggeration to say that contemporary man, in all fields where he has not yet formed firm habits, tends to find out what he wants by looking at what his neighbours do and at various displays of goods (physical or in catalogues or advertisements) and then choosing what he likes best.

In this sense the tastes of man, as is also true of his opinions and beliefs and indeed much of his personality, are shaped in a great measure by his cultural environment. But though in some contexts it would perhaps be legitimate to express this by a phrase like "production creates the wants," the circumstances mentioned would clearly not justify the contention that particular producers can deliberately determine the wants of particular consumers. The efforts of all producers will certainly be directed towards that end; but how far any individual producer will succeed will depend not only on what he does but also on what the others do and on a great many other influences operating upon the consumer. The joint but uncoordinated efforts of the producers merely create one element of the environment by which the wants of the consumers are shaped. It is because each individual producer thinks that the consumers can be persuaded to like his products that he endeavours to influence them. But though this effort is part of the influences which shape consumers' tastes, no producer can in any real sense "determine" them. This, however, is clearly implied in such statements as that wants are "both passively and deliberately the fruits of the process by which they are satisfied." If the producer could in fact deliberately determine what the consumers will want, Professor Galbraith's conclusions would have some validity. But though this is skillfully suggested, it is nowhere made credible, and could hardly be made credible because it is not true. Though the range of choice open to the consumers is the joint result of, among other things, the efforts of all producers who vie with each other in making their respective products appear more attractive than those of their competitors, every particular consumer still has the choice between all those different offers.

A fuller examination of this process would, of course, have to consider how, after the efforts of some producers have actually swayed some consumers, it becomes the example of the various consumers thus persuaded which will influence the remaining consumers. This can be mentioned here only to emphasize that even if each consumer were exposed to pressure of only one producer, the harmful effects which are apprehended from this would soon be offset by the much more powerful example of his fellows. It is of course fashionable to treat this influence of the example of others (or, what comes to the same thing, the learning from the experience made by others) as if it amounted all to an attempt of keeping up with the Joneses and for that reason was to be regarded as detrimental. It seems to me that not only the importance of this factor is usually greatly exaggerated but also that it is not really relevant to Professor Galbraith's main thesis. But it might be worthwhile briefly to ask what, assuming that some expenditure were actually determined solely by a desire of keeping up with the Joneses, that would really prove? At least in Europe we used to be familiar with a type of persons who often denied themselves even enough food in order to maintain an appearance of respectability or gentility in dress and style of life. We may regard this as a misguided effort, but surely it would not prove that the income of such persons was larger than they knew how to use wisely. That the appearance of success, or wealth, may to some people seem more important than many other needs, does in no way prove that the needs they sacrifice to the former are unimportant. In the same way, even though people are often persuaded to spend unwisely, this surely is no evidence that they do not still have important unsatisfied needs.

Professor Galbraith's attempt to give an apparent scientific proof for the contention that the need for the production of more commodities has greatly decreased seems to me to have broken down completely. With it goes the claim to have produced a valid argument which justifies the use of coercion to make people employ their income for those purposes of which he approves. It is not to be denied that there is some originality in this latest version of the old socialist argument. For over a hundred years we have been exhorted to embrace socialism because it would give us more goods. Since it has so lamentably failed to achieve this where it has been tried, we are now urged to adopt it because more goods after all are not important. The aim is still progressively to increase the share of the resources whose use is determined by political authority and the coercion of any dissenting minority. It is not surprising, therefore, that Professor Galbraith's thesis has been most enthusiastically received by the intellectuals of the British Labour Party where his influence bids fair to displace that of the late Lord Keynes. It is

more curious that in this country it is not recognized as an outright socialist argument and often seems to appeal to people on the opposite end of the political spectrum. But this is probably only another instance of the familiar fact that on these matters the extremes frequently meet.

Freedom and Persuasion

Stanley I. Benn

I

Some time in the fifties, everyone became conscious of the menace of the hidden persuaders. Whether as commercial advertisers or as political propagandists, they formed, it was said, an invisible power elite, corrupting taste and manipulating opinion for private gain or sectional power. We learnt with alarm that having the sense of choosing freely was no guarantee that one really had a free choice; choices could be rigged by skillful operators who could make us want what they or their clients wanted us to want.

This scandal of our age seems to have been exaggerated. It is now the fashion to take a more sober view of the claims of the persuasion industry and its supporting "motivational research." Propaganda and advertising, we are assured, can shape beliefs and attitudes only within limits; people resist suggestions that run counter to their basic personality characteristics. So a film intended to counter a prejudice may actually reinforce it. Though authoritarian personalities can be readily switched from fas-

cism to communism, they make poor liberals. "Brain-washing" is effective only with alienated and anomic individuals—and its effects even on them are relatively short-lived once they leave the reinforcing environment.

All the same, although mass persuasive techniques are less successful in changing attitudes than the alarmists would have us suppose, they seem to be very effective in reinforcing already existing tendencies to change. Furthermore, all the research done so far has been on "campaign effects" i.e., on the kind of short-term effects which are typically the goals of publicity and advertising; little is known as yet of the long-term effects of mass persuasive influences. Besides, the reassurances that have been given amount only to saying that not much progress has been made so far. As yet, our minds cannot readily be made up for us unless we are initially indifferent (as, for instance, between one kind of soap and another, or, maybe, between one brand of authoritarianism and another); altering basic attitudes is very much more difficult. Propaganda may

From Stanley I. Benn, "Freedom and Persuasion," *The Australasian Journal of Philosophy,* 45, (December 1967): 259–261, 265–275. Reprinted by permission.

"boomerang"; human personality is not infinitely plastic; psychologists have much to learn about the formation of human attitudes, and propagandists about how to manipulate them. In much the same way one might have been assured at the end of the last century that fear of aerial warfare was fantastic—pioneers had barely succeeded in getting a heavier-than-air machine off the ground. For the fact remains that there are interested people who are spending a great deal to find out what makes a man believe and behave as he does, and who clearly live in hope that out of it will come more efficient ways of influencing both. Discovering why primitive techniques have only limited effectiveness is the first step to more effective ones.

My intention here, however, is not to assess the claims of the persuasion industry, but rather to examine what the expressions of alarm that these claims evoke presuppose about freedom and the social interactions of aims and influences, and to gain from this an insight into certain liberal ways of thinking about politics and society. . . .

. . . The classic discussions of political obligation have all been concerned with what constitutes a good reason for requiring a man to put aside his own wishes or opinions and to act instead in accordance with someone else's. The problem presented by propagandists, advertisers and public relations experts is quite different. They aim not at overruling contrary intentions by threats of coercion but, by persuasion, to create a willing—if possible an enthusiastic—accord. They seek to avoid or dissolve conflict, not to overrule it. . . .

. . . But liberalism has never taken much notice of how men come to want what they do want—or rather, the traditional target for liberal critics like Milton, Jefferson, and Mill, has been censorship, the monopolistic control of the supply of ideas, not the techniques used to persuade people to adopt some ideas rather than others. Pinning their faith to human rationality, they believed that to drive out error truth needed no special

privilege beyond the opportunity to be heard; the shoddy tricks of those who exploited credulity could not survive exposure to rational criticism. This faith never faced the challenge that there might be nonrational techniques for persuading a person to believe certain things or to adopt certain desired attitudes—that is, techniques for inducing him to want to do or be something that someone else had decided upon, even though arguments and evidence to the contrary remained fully accessible. Would the classical liberals have said that a person who was able to do what he wanted without interference, but whose preferences had been shaped by such techniques, was free because he was "left to do or be what he wanted to do or be, without interference by other persons"?

The classical liberals might have objected that the techniques of persuasion that modern liberals fear do in fact "interfere"—not, certainly, with a man's doing what he wants to do, but with his freely *deciding* what he wants to do. But making this move commits the liberal to some way of distinguishing forms of persuasion that interfere from those that do not. For in defining social and political freedom, the liberal relies on a conception of a free market in ideas, a conception which actually presupposes that men will attempt to influence one another's beliefs. Accordingly, he must allow that there are some ways at least of getting people to change their minds that are not in his sense interferences. . . .

II

The liberal emphasis on rationality may suggest that the distinction sought for, between persuasion that is consistent with autonomy and persuasion that is not, would be the distinction between rational and nonrational persuasion. This distinction can indeed be made, and, as I hope to show, can be useful, but it will not take us the whole way we have to go. Persuasion is rational in so far as the persuasiveness lies in the substance of the arguments rather than in the manner of presentation, the authority of the persuader, or some other special relationship by virtue of which one party is particularly susceptible to suggestions from the other. Rational persuasion, in short, is impersonal, in the sense that it is the argument not the person that persuades—the same argument advanced by anyone else would be as effective. Of course, not any kind of reason will do. To give as a reason the injury you will do to me if I reject your suggestions is to threaten me, not to use rational persuasion. However, some neutral or disinterested person with no control over your behavior would be using rational persuasion if *he* warned me of what you would do to me if I disobeyed you. The distinctive feature of rational persuasion is that it invites and responds to criticism. The would-be persuader is committed to changing his opinion too if the persuadee gives sufficient reason for rejecting it. Rational persuasion is therefore essentially a dialogue between equals. Although the man who warns me of the probable consequences of what I am doing may be trying to stop me doing it, and perhaps succeeds, he is not acting inconsistently with my autonomy; for though I might have preferred to remain ignorant of the inconvenient facts—or even to have gone on disregarding what I already really knew—still, he has not made my mind up for me, but, on the contrary, has made it more possible for me to make a rational decision for myself. Indeed, by offering reasons why I should make one decision rather than another, so far from abusing my rational autonomy he recognizes and respects it. It was because the liberal classics took this as the paradigm of persuasion that they never felt the necessity for defining the relation between persuasion and power.

I said above that the persuasion is rational *in so far as* it seeks to convince by giving reasons, and consequently in so far as it is impersonal. This is not to say that we can distinguish sharply between the case of pure rational persuasion and others. Most cases combine rational and nonrational elements; any argument, however good, can be spoilt by bad presentation, and its effect heightened by fitting eloquence. Still, we can envisage a case of successful persuasion in which the persuader is so distasteful to the persuadee, his presentation so graceless and his whole demeanour so repellent, that almost anyone else could have done it better. Unless the persuadee is over-compensating for his personal dislike, we shall have to attribute the persuader's success entirely to the rational merits of his argument.

The possibility of distinguishing rational and non-rational persuasion does not imply, however, that an instance of persuasion is an invasion of personal freedom or autonomy precisely to the extent that it involves nonrational elements, like appeals to emotion or prejudice. The pretty girl in the tooth paste advertisement may be captivating, but do her charms really make slaves of us? While, therefore, we can confidently say that rational persuasion is consistent with freedom, we still have to distinguish among different forms of non-rational persuasion those that are not.

A is not unfree merely because his conduct is influenced (i.e., affected) by someone else's actions or communications of some kind other than rational arguments. Suppose, for instance, that he confides in B a plan from which he has great hopes; B, while offering no criticism, treats it scornfully; A, discouraged, gives up. Should we say that A's freedom had been infringed? Has B interfered with A, because B's non-rational influence upon A has put him off? Or should we not rather say that A must have been unusually weak-minded to be put off so easily?

This example suggests that whether a man is really master of himself or whether he is being interfered with, does not depend solely on the kind of influence another man exerts, nor on its actual effects; it depends *also* on whether it would be reasonable to expect him, in the given conditions, to withstand influence of that kind.

I suggested earlier that to say that a man

was not free to do what he would certainly be punished for doing is not to say that no one, faced with the same consequence, has ever chosen to do such a thing, but rather that the choice is not one we could reasonably expect a man to make. Similarly a temptation or a provocation is not irresistible merely because someone has in fact failed to resist it; but neither is the fact that someone has resisted it proof that it is not irresistible. A temptation is said to be irresistible only if a man *could not reasonably be expected* to resist it, even though others might actually have resisted it in the past.

These are instances of a class of judgments which cannot be satisfactorily elucidated without using some standard of "the normal man." Judgments about freedom, influence, power, and interference are, I believe, of the same class. What does it mean to say that a man does not withstand an influence? It is not simply that he falls in with what is proposed. For the idea of withstanding it suggests some inner source of strength, some kind of disposition, interest, or motive for not falling in with it. It is not merely that the influence fails in its intent, but that it fails on account of something about the patient, not simply on account of the ineptitude of the agent. Consider the dialogue:

Customer: I want a cake of soap, please.
Shopkeeper: Which brand?
Customer: Which do you recommend?
Shopkeeper: *Pongo.* (Aside) It's no different from any of the others, and I make a quarter cent more profit per bar.
Customer: Very well, I'll take *Pongo.*

Clearly, he could have said no. But why should he have done so? To say that he failed to withstand the suggestion seems to presuppose, what is not the case in this example, that he had some contrary interest or disposition, that he knew, for instance, that he was allergic to *Pongo.* Even then, one would not say that the grocer's influence was irresistible. For any other customer in his place would have said: "No, not that one—I'm allergic to it."

Bribery raises similar issues. If A asks B for a service in return for a sum of money, there is no reason *prima facie* why B should be expected to refuse the offer; and if B accepts it, we should not say that he failed to withstand or resist it. If, however, he accepts, having an interest that could provide a counter-motive, or a duty, e.g., as a public official, not to do what A asks, one could properly say that he did not resist. Furthermore, if we wanted to plead irresistible temptation in his defence, we should have to argue that no one under the exceptional conditions in which B was placed (whatever they may have been) could *reasonably be expected* to resist. That a man has been provided with a counter-motive is not enough to make it impossible for him to do his duty, though it may sufficiently explain why he did not do it. In the absence of exceptional conditions, attempting to corrupt him does not deprive him of free choice. On the contrary, his freedom is an indispensable condition for his being held responsible should he give in to the temptation. Similarly one cannot plead by way of excuse that a man has been subject to non-rational persuasive influence, unless one can also maintain that no one, despite an interest counter to the suggestion, could reasonably have been expected not to fall in with it.

The problem for the liberal, then, is to establish tests by which to identify non-rational influences that a person could not reasonably be expected to resist, supposing that he has some interest in doing so. One such test is whether the patient can be aware of what is happening to him. For if one cannot know that an attempt is being made to manipulate one's preferences, and if one has no way of distinguishing a manipulated preference, one cannot be on one's guard against it. Subliminal suggestion would probably prove objectionable by this test (though there appear to be subconscious censors operating even here to inhibit out-of-character responses). An extension of the same principle would cover propaganda, supported and protected by censorship. For supposing the subject to have some initial disposition, presumed interest, or duty not to accept it, an apparently well-supported suggestion in the complete absence of any counter-evidence might fairly be called irresistible. Beyond these rather obvious criteria we should have to rely on the results of psychological research. If we want to discuss whether protection from mass persuasive techniques is necessary or even desirable, we must first have some idea of the kinds of influence that a person of normal firmness of purpose and with normal interests could reasonably be expected to withstand in a given situation. Moreover, there may be classes of persons, like children, who are peculiarly vulnerable to particular techniques, or to suggestions of particular kinds; principles of protection may very possibly have to use different norms for different purposes. Information like this is as important to the defenders of freedom as it is to the manipulators, and may well be among the fruits of psychologists' investigations into the effectiveness of advertising and propaganda techniques.

III

To what extent can such criteria for distinguishing forms of persuasion inconsistent with freedom suggest moral criteria for the use and control of persuasion and manipulative techniques? The liberal presupposition that every man has a right not to be interfered with unless he is doing something that itself interferes with the freedom or well-being of someone else, applies as much to the persuader as to the persuadee. Unless a form of persuasion itself interferes with the freedom or interests either of the persuadee or someone else, to interfere with it would be an invasion of the rights of the persuader. On the other hand, the persuadee can properly claim as a condition for *his* freedom, that he be protected from hidden manipulation aimed at political or economic exploitation. From these considerations we can

elicit, in the first place, criteria for any advertising or propaganda that is designed to promote the interests of the persuaders. We can say, provisionally, that there is no ground for objecting to such influences if they do not infringe the freedom of the persuadee, and constitute no threat to the interests of anyone else. It is up to the persuadee to determine whether his own interests would be served or impaired by letting himself fall in with what is suggested to him. It is not consistent, in other words, with liberal presuppositions about human nature and its characteristic excellence that he should be protected from every kind of influence that might lead him to do things against his own interests. If men allow themselves to be exploited, through lack of reasonable caution or of the exercise of normal critical judgment, they have only themselves to blame. As rational and autonomous beings, they are responsible within reason for safeguarding their own interests—*caveat emptor* applies to ideas and tastes as well as to goods. There is a case, of course, for protection against misrepresentation of both ideas and goods. But this is not to protect the consumer against freely choosing what is damaging to his own interests; it is rather that in determining where his interest lies he shall not be deliberately and unfairly deceived by a lack of information he cannot remedy or by false information that he cannot reasonably be expected to check. Lying newspapers are at least as objectionable as false statements of the weight of soap powder in a King Size packet. Though there may be no objection to manufacturers attracting customers by putting small amounts of soap in large packets, the consumer who wants to make a reasoned choice between brands is entitled to know the weight of soap he is buying without the inconvenience of carrying his own scales or insisting on having the alternative packages weighed before he decides. Of far greater importance is his right to be told the truth in news reports, on which he has to base rational judgments on public affairs, and which he simply cannot confirm for himself. Of course, insisting that newspapers tell the truth is far more problematic and politically hazardous than insisting on the truth about soap powders. Since governments are interested parties there are no doubt good reasons for leaving it to the reader to check one against the other.

Applying the criteria to techniques which, designed to get under the consumer's guard, may be incompatible with his autonomy, is rather more complicated. A practice which simply exploits the consumer (or the voter) presents no theoretical difficulty; if it is both an infringement of the consumer's freedom and an attack on his interest, it is indefensible. But how firmly can the liberal turn down a plea that a manipulative technique is being used in the general interest, or in the interests of the individual himself? *Pace* Mill, it is difficult to sustain unqualified the doctrine that "the sole end for which mankind are warranted, individually or collectively, in interfering with the liberty of action of any of their number is self-protection" and that "his own good ... is not a sufficient warrant."[1] Mill's equivocation in the matter of the unsafe bridge[2] is evidence of his own uneasiness; and one can have legitimate doubts about his plea that poisons and dangerous drugs be freely available without medical prescription. What kind of an interest, however, would justify interference for a man's own good?

Consider a possible advertiser's argument that, by persuading a consumer to want G (which the consumer can afford and the manufacturer can supply) he makes it possible for the former to satisfy his wants; moreover, creating a want he can also satisfy, he is acting in the consumer's own interests by maximizing his satisfactions. (If this be a man of straw, this particular kind of straw can still be illuminating.)

The argument would be mistaken, in my view, firstly in identifying the consumer's wants with his interests. Tobacco manufacturers who by advertising create tobacco customers, may cultivate their customer's wants but are questionably serving their interests.

And this is not because the experience might not be "really satisfying." For once the habit is formed, smoking undoubtedly satisfies a craving, and deprivation is so unpleasant that many smokers accept the risk of lung cancer rather than give it up. One has to recognize that people often want what is conspicuously bad for them, and that what satisfies their desires may not be in their interests. Suppose, however, the desire were for something reasonably harmless; what value would we attach to satisfying it, once it were seen as the deliberate creation of someone else? If the advertiser succeeds in producing a mass demand for a product that no one wanted before, is his product valuable and his activity worthwhile, simply because it now meets a demand? Or are we entitled to look critically at the sorts of things that men are encouraged to demand, and to decide that some demands may be unworthy of satisfaction?

Writers in the empirical, liberal tradition, and most notably, of course, writers in the utilitarian tradition, have been inclined to treat as a reason in favour of any performance or provision whatsoever that someone wanted it. Though this reason might be overridden in a given instance by other people's wishes, or by the expectation of harmful consequences, these would weigh as reasons against doing something that would still have been intrinsically worth doing simply as satisfying a desire. Moreover, if the thing were not done, there would be a presumption in favour of saying that the person desiring it had been deprived of a satisfaction, that the result had been to his disadvantage, and that he would have been better off had he got what he wanted. So *ceteris paribus* a world in which many desires were satisfied would seem to be a better world than one in which fewer were satisfied, whether because some remained unsatisfied or because people had fewer desires.

Though this view is persuasive when stated generally, I have difficulty in extending this presumption in favor of satisfying desires to desires demonstrably contrived by someone else, especially if contrived for his own purposes. That is not to say that no contrived desire would ever be worth satisfying; one might properly claim that some kind of experience for which one had induced a desire in someone else, for whatever purpose, was worth having, and that he would consequently be better off if his desire for it were satisfied. But this would be to recognize a distinction between experiences which were worth having, for which the corresponding desires would be worth satisfying, and those which were not. This is quite different from allowing a residual kind of worth in the satisfaction of any desire, simply as such and irrespective of its object.

It might be objected, as a general negative reason for satisfying desires, that a desire unsatisfied is a source of suffering. Certainly, if a drug addict had no hope of cure, what he suffered from his unsatisfied desire would be a strong reason, perhaps sufficient reason, for satisfying it. It is surely a mistake, however, to assimilate all desires to cravings; to be disappointed is not necessarily to suffer, or, at any rate, to suffer in the same sense in which deprived addicts suffer. Furthermore, there is something repugnant about saying that, in a case of deliberate torturing a saving factor in an otherwise totally deplorable situation is that the sadistic desires of the torturer have been satisfied. Malicious satisfaction makes a situation worse, not better.

The view I am challenging depends for its persuasiveness in part on a meaning shift in the word "satisfaction." I may get satisfaction from contemplating a picture or reading a novel, but this is not necessarily because a desire to look at a picture has been satisfied. On the other hand, if I desire X and get X my desire is satisfied but it may give me no satisfaction. I may discover that what I wanted was not worth having. And this may not be because I was misinformed about the nature of the thing; I may have got precisely what I desired and expected, yet still be no better off for having it. The quality of the life into which it enters may be no

better for it—it may have no function in my life, and add nothing to me as a person. My wanting it may have been factitious, in the sense that the desire arose from no integral tendency in my nature, no search for a mode of expression, no recognizable need. I could have set my heart on almost anything else, or on nothing at all, and have been no worse off. Now, if my desires were simply the contrivance of persuaders, they might very well be like this. In that case one would be led to ask whether the mere fact of a desire could really be a reason for satisfying it or whether what gives value to the satisfaction of a desire is the quality of the life of which it forms a part and in which it has a function. Satisfying a desire would be valuable then if it sustained or made possible a valuable kind of life. To say this is to reject the argument that in creating the wants he can satisfy, the advertiser (or the manipulator of mass emotion in politics or religion) is necessarily acting in the interests of his public. What their interests are depends now on some objective assessment of what constitutes excellence in human beings, not on what they happen, for whatever reason, to want. If this is true, advertising that presents consumption as a self-justifying activity, that attributes value to things, rather than to what they do to and for a person, is essentially corrupting in that it promotes a misconception of the nature of man. Misunderstanding what we are, we are misled about the nature of the enterprize in which as men we are engaged.

This does not mean that we ought to repudiate the cautious liberal approach to protection "in one's own interests." For everything depends on what one takes to be the characteristic human excellences. The liberal concept of man, as sustained by Kant and Mill, places at the top of the list a man's capacity for making responsible choices among alternative ways of life, for striving no matter how mistakenly or unsuccessfully to make of himself something worthy of his own respect. This is a creative enterprise calling for experiment, intelligent self-appraisal, and criticism. Consequently, it cannot be fostered by denying men the opportunity to make false starts and to learn from experience. Men have an overriding interest in liberty itself.

This account of human interests suggests an important qualification to my earlier provisional statement, that there was no ground for objecting to persuasion that did not infringe the freedom of the persuadee, and constituted no threat to the interests of anyone else, since it was for him to determine whether his own interests would be served or impaired by falling in with it. For we can now suggest a case for protecting a man from any influence, irresistible or not, which if successful would lead to a condition like drug addiction in which his ability to make further rational choices would be permanently and irremediably impaired. For though the mode of persuasion might not itself be an interference, nevertheless, if successful, it would impair freedom, understood as rational self-mastery.

I do not expect everyone to agree on the application of this criterion, on whether, for instance, it would rule out advertising by cigarette manufacturers, or advertising of the type mentioned earlier, which corrupts by promoting the worship of consumption for its own sake. It is arguable, on the one hand, that advertisements of this latter kind are not, taken severally, irresistible, nor would responding to them irremediably impair the individual's capacity for discovering for himself what kinds of things are valuable and why. Indeed, the very opposite might be the case. On the other hand, the cumulative influence of an environment filled with a variety of advertisements all with the same underlying message hidden by its very ubiquity may be more closely analogous to influences like subliminal suggestions that one cannot directly perceive than to a straightforward appeal to emotions.

The same basic principles on which I have relied for criteria justifying protection from persuasion also provide criteria for the use of irresistible manipulative techniques. Just as the sole ground for protecting a man from an influence which is not irresistible is that he should not risk impairing his capacity for choosing rationally and for making critical appraisals of his own experience and achievements, so the justification for manipulation must be that he is suffering from some impediment or handicap, which inhibits such activities, and which he could not remedy by his own efforts. This would justify, for instance, the use in psychotherapy of hypnosis and "truth-drugs"; for the aim of the treatment is not to dominate nor to mould the patient, but to restore his capacity for making his own rational appraisals of his environment, and for deciding for himself what would be his appropriate adjustment to it. Here again one has to rely heavily on conceptions of normality; for to be handicapped is to lack capacities that a man normally enjoys.

I have said that these criteria are not easy to apply, and there would be plenty of argument about any particular application. Nevertheless since we are bound to make decisions of this kind, it is well that we should be conscious of what we are about in making them.

NOTES

1. John Stuart Mill, *On Liberty*, Everyman Edition (New York: E. B. Dutton Company, 1910), pp. 72–73.
2. *Ibid.*, pp. 151–152.

Manipulative Advertising

Tom L. Beauchamp

Lake Jewelers recently closed after being in business in Detroit for 36 years. Arthur Lake, president of the Local Chamber of Commerce, was not as yet financially imperilled, but he said his business was gradually being ruined by the misleading advertisements of his competitors, a practice in which he refused to engage. Lake cited, in particular, "phony discounting," in which fake percentage markdowns are presented in advertisements as bargains (50–78 percent off), when in fact the prices are comparatively high for the value of the merchandise. The prices are advertised as markdowns from "suggested retail prices" that are imaginary or artificially inflated. Lake said that customers are "duped into thinking" they receive bargains and that "ethical" merchants find it extremely difficult to compete against such advertisements.[1] In this paper, I shall assess a range of criticisms that, like this one, accuse advertisers of manipulating customers, on the basis of incorrect information, into purchases that they otherwise would not make. I shall be concerned exclusively with problems about nondisclosure of information and about manipulations that limit free actions.

I shall neither deal with all forms of advertising nor range across a broad array of the industries that advertise. Instead, I shall concentrate late in the paper on contemporary advertising by banks, savings and loans, and brokerage houses. In particular, I shall feature the advertising war between these financial institutions for the investment of IRA funds. Through analysis of this single area of advertising, some broader compari-

sons and generalizations will be offered. Like all generalizations from particular case studies, we had best be careful not to overreach in generalizing across contexts without an underlying theory that supports the generalizations. In an attempt to avoid this pitfall, I shall begin with the rudiments of a theory of influence and return later to advertising by financial institutions.

THE CONTINUUM OF INFLUENCES

To determine whether advertising diminishes free choice, we need to specify how influences in general affect free choice. The antithesis of being free is being controlled by an alien influence that deprives one of self-imposed directedness and personal responsibility. I shall use the terms *freedom* and *free to act* in a restricted sense to refer to the absence of controlling external influences or constraints.

Coercion is the most frequently analyzed form of influence, at least in the philosophical and legal literature, but an examination of coercion does not cover all forms of controlling influence and does not touch on noncontrolling influence. Coercion is simply at one end of a continuum of influence, the end that entirely negates freedom and therefore entirely compromises free choice. At the other end of the continuum are forms of influence such as (rational) persuasion. Other points on the continuum include indoctrination, seduction, and the like. At one end point of the continuum are completely *controlling* influences—those that fully gov-

Reprinted by permission of the author.

ern or control a person's actions, rendering the person unfree and so rendering the person's choices and actions in no meaningful sense his or her own. At the other end are wholly *noncontrolling* influences—those that in no way undermine a person's free choice. The expression "*fully* free choice" specifies an ideal on the noncontrolling end of the continuum, but choosing freely admits of degrees that should be interpreted in terms of this continuum of controlling influences.

Many free choices may fall within the class of choices that only minimally satisfy the threshold conditions of freedom and thus are *minimally but not substantially* free. These include actions under powerful family and religious influences, purchases made under partial ignorance of the quality of the merchandise purchased, choices following swift moves by salespersons, and deference to an authoritative physician in circumstances of uncertainty. Many such actions (but not all) are *free,* yet fall short of our *ideals* of free action because of operative constraints. The important question is whether actions are *sufficiently* or *adequately* free.

From Coercion to Persuasion

There are many grey areas of overlap between categories of influence. However, we can frame at least some rough definitions of coercion, manipulation, and persuasion that express the basic distinctions between the categories. Although these definitions are not sufficiently rigorous to eliminate all hard cases, they are adequate for the objectives of this inquiry. I begin with coercion and persuasion, as opposite ends of the continuum of influence.

Coercion occurs if one party deliberately and successfully uses force or a credible threat of unwanted, avoidable, and serious harm in order to compel a particular response from another person. This response may involve getting someone to do something he or she does not want to do or keeping someone from doing something he or she wants to do.

Coercion is a rare occurrence in advertising. Some writers have paraded a long list of horror stories about coercion in modern society, and some of these stories involve advertising. In using the word *coercion,* these writers often are referring to virtually any kind of pressure or influence that inappropriately or unduly compromises the freedom of a person—such as through the medium of subliminal advertising. However, I am using coercion in a stricter sense, and—as we shall see—manipulation rather than coercion will turn out to be the major problem about such social interventions. For example, in my use of coercion, no matter how attractive or overwhelming an offer, coercion cannot be involved unless a threatening negative sanction is presented.

For advertising, the most difficult circumstance would be one in which ads are directed at an easily threatened population, such as the very poor or the politically dependent. Advertisements directed at a starving population that "offer" food and medical attention in return for marketable blood—as allegedly was done by Plasma International[2]—would constitute a threat and not a mere offer and so would be coercive, at least to some persons in some circumstances. But such circumstances are only rarely present in advertising as we know it in North America, and thus the problem of "coercive advertising" seems contrived. Manipulation is the more significant issue. However, before we turn to that category, we need to examine the nature of persuasion, which is on the other end of the continuum of influence from coercion.

Persuasion is a deliberate and successful attempt by one person to get another person by appeals to reason to freely accept beliefs, attitudes, values, intentions, or actions. The first person points out to the other that there are good reasons for accepting the desired perspective. In paradigmatic cases of persuasion, these good reasons are conveyed through language, by use of structured argument and verbal reasoning. However, good reasons can also be expressed through nonverbal communication, as, for example, by bringing forward visual evidence in support of a position.

"Rational" persuasion is often distinguished from "nonrational" persuasion. Because the above definition of persuasion restricts the category to influence by appeals to reason, *persuasion* will here be used to refer exclusively to rational persuasion. (Nonrational persuasion is a form of manipulation.) An example of self-proclaimed persuasive advertising is found in the advertisements of Kellogg Co., which has been attacked for its child-oriented advertisements of presweetened, ready-to-eat cereals. The company has responded (in effect) that its strategies are persuasive rather than manipulative. In 1973, Executive Vice President William E. LaMothe testified before the Senate Select Committee on Nutrition and Human Needs that Kellogg has adopted the following approach to advertising its products: "Our company is very conscious of the fact that social responsibilities go hand-in-hand with business responsibilities. The steps that we are taking to contribute to the improvement of the understanding of the need for breakfast and a complete and adequate breakfast reflect this consciousness."[3] I am not convinced that the company's purposes and programs were so noble, but any company that acted on the entailed principle that advertising should "contribute to the improvement of the understanding" of nutrition and tried by informational appeals to convince viewers to eat healthier breakfasts would be employing a policy of persuasion.

Stanley Benn has provided the most persuasive analysis of rational persuasion in the philosophical literature. Benn urges that persuasion is rational

> in so far as the persuasiveness lies in the substance of the argument rather than in the manner of presentation, the authority of the persuader, or some other special relationship by virtue of which one party is particularly susceptible to suggestions from the other.[4]

Benn correctly holds that the essence of rational persuasion is that it induces change by convincing a person through the merit of the reasons put forward. However, Benn oversteps when he argues that rational persuasion is necessarily impersonal in the sense that the reasons or "substance" of the argument" are persuasive regardless of who advances them or how they are presented.[5] This claim is overly restrictive. The credibility and expertise of the person advancing an argument can affect reasoned judgments about the correctness of the premises and the soundness of the argument. Acceding to an argument simply because one *likes the person* who presents the point of view—as in Pepsi's Michael Jackson television ads—or finds the person physically attractive—as in typical magazine advertising for Virginia Slims—can be distinguished from accepting an argument because the *person is an expert* and therefore likely to be correct. The same arguments may be more persuasive through appeals to reason if the reasons are presented by a professional speaker than by an inexperienced amateur, because authoritative judgment and communication skills may rationally persuade no less than sound arguments.

The problem of how the characteristics of the source of a communication affect a person's response points to a basic issue in distinguishing persuasion from manipulation. One often cannot tell from the description of an attempt to influence whether the influence is a case of persuasion or a case of manipulation. The central question in many instances is not what is done (said, suggested, etc.), but how or through what psychological processes the person responded to and was affected by the influence. This is directly relevant to problems of advertising appeals that tend to persuade or to mislead only *some* persons. A 1981 FTC staff report concerning children's television noted the following about young children six years and under:

> (1) They place indiscriminate trust in televised advertising messages; (2) they do not understand the persuasive bias in television advertising; and (3) the techniques, focus and themes

used in child-oriented television advertising enhance the appeal of the advertising message and the advertised product. Consequently, young children do not possess the cognitive ability to evaluate adequately child-oriented television advertising.[6]

Although children under six cannot understand the intent of a commercial message, the report argues, children *over* six often can. The idea seems to be that children under six are manipulated, whereas some over six can be persuaded. Nevertheless, many critics argue that such advertising is far more manipulative than persuasive;[7] and everyone must acknowledge the many questions that remain unanswered about the depth and manner of television advertising's influence on both children and adults. For example, there are questions about the *effect* of television advertising, about the ability of persons to *process cognitively* the advertising information, about the ability of various persons to *discriminate* between the content of the program and the commercial, and about the ability of persons to *resist* persuasive or manipulative appeals even if they understand them to be commercial in character.

There are also questions about what counts as a good reason, or even a reason at all. If advertiser A believes that the reasons in an ad are bad reasons, but knows that the persons at whom the advertisement is directed believes that they are good reasons, is this an attempt at persuasion by giving good reasons, or an attempt at manipulation by motivating purchases for bad reasons? Sometimes it seems irrelevant whether anyone except the consumer believes the reason to be a good reason. Thus, an advertiser may believe it is crazy to buy a soap merely because it smells good when the wrapper is opened, but if people value the soap for this reason, then why not feature the soap's aroma in an ad?

The cases can, of course, be made progressively more difficult to handle: If a person believes—based on an advertisement—that a good-tasting toothpaste enhances sex appeal, can this qualify as a good reason, or

as a reason at all? If a mother believes, quite falsely, that a tasty snack food will make her baby healthier, can this be a good reason? As the ads become progressively more deceptive or harmful it seems likely that we will progressively abstain from calling them "good reasons." Our criteria of "good reasons" will be tailored by some broader conception of legitimate and illegitimate influence.

Consumer protection groups and sometimes government officials tend to focus on the consumers' *response* to advertising and on its human effects, rather than on the *intention* of those who create the advertising. By contrast, those who defend controversial advertising focus more on the intentions of advertising agencies and manufacturers in marketing a product—namely, on the intent to sell a "good product." These different emphases show further inherent complications in the issues, for an advertisement created with good intentions can be misleading, nonrationally controlling, and the like.

In sum, persuasion is a nonclandestine form of interpersonal influence that appeals to reason by bringing forward in the mind of the persuadee good reasons to adopt an advocated position. Both parties are aware of the intent to influence and, at least in some cases, both parties are subject to change as a result of the reasoned exchange. The essence of persuasion is that it influences a person through the substance, the merit, and the soundness of the reasons presented or through reasonable appeals to authority. If this analysis of persuasion is correct, then persuasion and free action are entirely compatible. Actions based on reasons believed by the actor to be good reasons are distinguishable from coerced actions and from many, but not all, manipulated actions.

Again, it is important to recognize the imprecision at work in specifying where persuasion and manipulation merge. Fortunately, we have no need here to stipulate the needed precision into existence. For present purposes, it is sufficient to work with this general continuum analysis of the differences between coercion, manipulation, and persuasion.

Manipulation

If we move away from coercion at one end of the continuum and from persuasion at the other into the region of an attractive reward or nonthreatening negative inducement, we reach a third, and the most important, class of influences for our purposes: *manipulation.* Manipulation is a broad category that includes any successful attempt to elicit a desired response from another person by noncoercively altering the structure of available choices or by nonpersuasively altering the person's perceptions of those choices. Current literature that deals with influences falling between coercion and manipulation uses a wide variety of concepts to explicate this portion of the continuum between coercion and persuasion.[8] Thus, writers speak of incentives, strong offers, indoctrination, propaganda, emotional pressure, irrational persuasion, temptation, seduction, and deception. I am using the single word *manipulation* to describe various parts of this vast territory of forms of influence.

The major difference between persuasion and informational manipulation is that the latter always involves deception used to influence a person's choice or action, whereas persuasion is not based on deception. In being influenced by information, one is persuaded by an attempt to get one to believe what is *correct* (or sound, or backed by good reasons, etc.), and one is manipulated by an attempt to get one to believe what is *not correct* (false, unsound, not backed by good reasons, etc.).

We should, however, be cautious in using words like *misleading* and *deceptive,* which have both subjective and objective senses. People are often misled by their own bizarre inferences or by lack of concentration on what is presented. It does not follow that the presentation is misleading because it is misunderstood or because it led persons to be-

lieve what is false. The goal of eliminating all subjective interpretation that proves misleading is a noble ideal, but far too demanding as a standard for public presentations.

Some writers have held that manipulation involves eliciting a desired decision through more subtle means than coercion, but, like coercion, so that the facts are packaged and presented to leave the person with *no real choice.* Thus, to heighten an appeal to the point that a person can no longer resist the temptation is, on this criterion, a *manipulative* way of leaving a person without any real choice.[9] This understanding of manipulation is too narrow. Manipulated persons may have some genuine alternatives available, should they elect them, and some capacities for resisting an offer, should they have a reason to resist, even if one offer is known by the offerer to be clearly the most attractive and clearly the one that the other person ought to pursue. Unlike coercion, and despite attractive incentives, manipulation can be compatible with freedom. The manipulee may even arrange and welcome the manipulative influence. A part of the difficulty in assessing the moral acceptability of advertising is that a potentially manipulative advertisement may be directed at a group of otherwise free persons, some of whom find the appeal resistible and some of whom do not, when the influence attempt could have been persuasive but a manipulative appeal was elected instead.

MANIPULATION IN ADVERTISING

The Case of Contemporary IRA Advertising

This account of manipulation can now be turned directly to advertising appeals. I believe that contemporary advertising by many banks for IRA accounts, to which I turn first, is manipulative and not merely persuasive. I believe its being manipulative rather than persuasive is in many instances a good reason for finding it a morally deficient practice. I proceed now to an argument for these claims, providing first some background in this form of advertising, including a few recent examples.

The advertisements I examine share in common that they are for fixed-term IRA deposits that pay more than one rate over the term but that advertise the higher, shorter-duration rate of interest in very large type, while the lower rate is noted in far smaller type, as is the fact that the lower rate is effective for a far longer term. Also relegated to the smaller print, if mentioned at all, is any statement of effective annual yield or yield over the course of the account. The advertisements are, in my reading, designed to convey the message to a reader that the significant rate for the thrifty-minded is the one in large type, rather than either the effective annual yield or the underlying, lower rate. Of course, a reverse priority ranking would be more prudent. The ads also often present the rates as "tax-free" or "tax-exempt," but they are actually tax-deferred, and deposited monies are tax-deductible.

Consider some history and some examples drawn from newspapers in the Washington and Baltimore metropolitan regions. As the competition for IRA customers grew in recent newspaper advertisements, and as it became apparent to banks that the advertising campaigns were effective, the rates initially offered were adjusted to higher levels and greater attractiveness. For example, Chevy Chase first inched forward from 14 percent to 15 percent. Riggs National Bank, which advertises itself as "The Most Important Bank in the Most Important City in the World," also started out at 14 percent, but quickly saw the importance of the trends and rocketed up to 25 percent, then the highest rate in the area. Standard Federal started out with 15 percent, then quickly went to 17 percent, and finally to 25 percent, without otherwise changing its ads. Other banks were not about to lose customers and followed suit. Figure 1 is a representative depiction of the structure and language of these ads.

FIGURE 1.

How successfully do such ads work to influence customers to open new accounts? An official of the Riggs Bank interviewed by the *Washington Post* confirmed that the promotional rate brought in a large influx of customers from the start. But, after Riggs raised the promotional rate from 14 to 25 percent, three times as many depositors signed up for Riggs IRAs on the days the 25 percent rate was run than had signed up on the days the 14 percent rate had been run.[10]

Applicable federal regulations state that "No member bank shall make any advertisement, announcement, or solicitation relating to the interest paid on deposits that is inaccurate or misleading or that misrepresents its deposit contracts."[11] The staff of the Legal Division of the Federal Reserve System asked Riggs officials to comment on its compliance with the code in these advertisements. Riggs responded that it believed the advertisement was fully in compliance because all relevant terms of the account were explained in larger than normal newstype.[12]

This response seems to me, as to the staff of the Legal Division of the Federal Reserve System, thoroughly inadequate. More important than the short duration of the very high deposit rates is the inherent complication and confusion involved in interpreting the split rate in a context where there are no uniform practices, standardized rates, or conventional expectations. This is not a mere problem of chaos in a shifting industry. It is beyond the powers of most readers to compute average effectual annual yields over the life of the deposit, and yet this computation reveals the single most important information in this circumstance. It is thus beyond the powers of most readers to make significant comparisons across the different banks. The split rate, the method of compounding, and the term of the deposit make for too many complicated calculations, even among those few who might figure out how to make the basic computations.

For example, Riggs's 25 percent promotional, two-month rate is accompanied by an underlying rate of 10.87 percent for 28 months, while Chevy Chase's two-month 15 percent promotional rate is accompanied by an underlying rate of 11.5 percent for 28 months. The *undisclosed* data are that Chevy Chase has an average annual effective yield of 12.39 percent, while for Riggs the average annual effective yield is 12.31 percent. Fortunately, the term, the compounding method, and so on, are identical for these two banks, which makes comparisons relatively easy. But these variables are not stable in most of the advertising presented to the public.

The Manipulation of Investment Decisions

Each of the advertisements thus far considered is, in my judgment, manipulative, under a category earlier referred to as the "manipulation of information." Such ma-

nipulation is a deliberate act that elicits a response from a person by controlling the person's information about the nature or consequences of the response or about alternative responses (thereby altering the structure of actual choices available to the person or altering the person's perception of those choices). Manipulation of information affects freedom by deception that renders persons at least partially ignorant, thereby causally constraining relevant aspects of their decisions. Manipulation by deception includes such strategies as lying, withholding of information, and misleading exaggeration, all of which can produce false beliefs.

Deception used successfully to get people to do what the arranger of the environment intends is always manipulative, and I believe the IRA advertisements surveyed above satisfy this general description. Other investment advertising is still more deceptive and manipulative, well toward coercion on the continuum of influence.

Although manipulation of information usually involves controlling the quantity, content, or intensity of a person's beliefs, manipulation of information can also involve manipulating a person's response by managing the *order* in which information is presented. A popular term for one form of this kind of manipulation among salespersons is "low-balling."[13] This tactic typically involves revealing certain less favorable or unfavorable aspects of an agreement to a person only *after* the person has already made an *initial* decision to perform some action. The central feature of low-balling is that it always involves withholding information at a point in a (more or less) intentionally ordered interaction. Unlike most ordinary uses of withholding in order to deceive and manipulate, in low-balling the withheld information is revealed to the manipulee *before* the manipulee makes an *irrevocable* commitment by, for example, actually signing an agreement.

Low-balling is a prime example of the overlap between informational manipulation and psychological manipulation. Although low-balling induces compliance through a deceptive presentation of information, it does not work exclusively by virtue of rendering the manipulee *ignorant* of relevant information. Instead, ignorance is used to initiate certain psychological processes of commitment that are difficult to reverse even after the ignorance condition is removed. People have a strong psychological tendency to continue with an active decision, especially if an agreement has been reached, even after having become aware that the decision is more costly to execute than was originally thought. Moreover, the low-balling phenomenon is particularly interesting for the relationship between freedom and manipulation, because the claim has been well documented that the low-ball technique works best if the *initial* decision is perceived by the actor to be a free choice.[14]

Consider a parallel case from retail sales. A salesperson is concluding negotiations with a customer for the purchase of a set of automobile tires. After a quarter of an hour of discussion, the customer agrees to purchase two brand X tires for $150. After the sales clerk has written up the first half of a receipt and has a credit card in hand, he observes that the $150 price does not include three forms of tax, and then casually mentions that charges for mounting the tires and balancing the wheels are extra, as is the cost of an extended warranty policy that is highly recommended for these tires. The total charge for all goods and services, including sales tax, is $202.50. The clerk asks if the customer still wants the tires and, if so, which of the additional services is desired. Meanwhile, the clerk is poised to complete the receipt and credit card form.

At a minimum, any choice in these circumstances that would not have been made by a customer had he or she not been ignorant—at the most decisive moment of choice—of certain facts is not fully free, and probably not substantially free. The "but-for" causal principle upon which this judgment relies is grounded in the way ignorance causally affects the choice of outcome. Ignorance of information that is not causally

determinative on the "but-for" principle may still *diminish* the freedom of a choice. This is so even if (as a constraint) such ignorance is not sufficient to render choice fully unfree. This seems to me to be what occurs in a low-balling situation that can leave one in ignorance until the final moment when it is time to sign on the line.

An Objection in Defense of the Advertising Industry

It might be objected to this analysis that with persons of normal maturity, liberty, and resistibility, my criticism of advertising breaks down. Can we not expect persons to take care of themselves when hearing an advertisement no less than when shopping in a department store with attractive displays on every counter? Advertising and marketing have often been defended by a rules-of-the-game model: There are more or less established, well-delineated procedures or moves for marketing a product; the consumer world is well acquainted with these rules of the game, and consumers are generally in an equal bargaining position. Only an isolated innocent wholly unacquainted with the game of advertising would think otherwise. While abuse of subliminal persuasion or ads that are inherently offensive to large segments of the population are not permitted, it might be argued that sexual suggestion, strong pitches to young children in toy advertisements, and the attractiveness of high bank rates are simply parts of the game.

We can easily get upset about advertising directed at children, and other vulnerable parties, because the ordinary rules of the game are either suspended or violated; like a turkey at Thanksgiving, the unsuspecting child is sacrificed to the greed of the toymaker or cookie manufacturer. But is not advertising, placed in more favorable light, analogous to activities in which we all engage—for example, purchasing a house or bargaining over the price of a rug in an overpriced store? Here bluffing, overstatement, and even enticement are expected and invite similar countermoves; certainly these routines involve more than mere persuasion. Although abuse and contempt are not tolerated, deception is—so long as the rules of the game are known and the players are in a roughly equal bargaining position.

I think this defense of advertising overlooks that advertisers manipulate not only the weak and unwary, but even persons of normal discernment and resistibility. Advertisers know the art of subtle deception and manipulation. They can do it through high rates, charts, and a wide variety of other techniques that I have not here had an opportunity to survey.

In one of the more famous passages in the history of ethical theory, Immanual Kant demands that we treat other people as ends in themselves and not solely as means to the ends of others. This requirement of noninterference and the entailed attitude of respect seems easy to apply in some contexts. For example, in research involving human subjects it is a moral requirement that we enable or at least not prevent the subject's informed choice (consent or refusal) before involving subjects in the research. A parallel application in the context of advertising might seem no less compelling: Advertising should enable or at least not prevent an informed choice about purchase of the product or service being advertised. It should be persuasive in presentation, not manipulative. Rules of acceptable advertising should encompass more than the mere creation of a market; advertising is the dissemination of information from which consumers should be able to make an informed choice. If they are misled in the attempt to make an intelligent choice or are enticed into the choice by deception, the advertising has an enormous burden of justification—no matter the target population or the implicit rules of the game.

Much more of an innovative sort needs to be said along lines of obligations of communication than has been said by bureaucrats, courts, advertisers, and writers in ethics. We need to discuss openly how false assurances and manipulative maneuvers intended to encourage persons may seriously mislead them, how to present information persuasively, and the importance of advertising directed at vulnerable populations. Disclosure "requirements" and permissible styles of presentation should be discussed, with a focus on the entire communication process and not simply on "truthtelling." When implicit rules of games are inadequate, as they are at the present time in advertising, there ought to be external standards by reference to which the presuppositions behind the rules are challenged. When deep assumptions in the rules permit the nonunique, inessential, and less nutritious product to be advertised to children and adults alike as unique, essential, or highly nutritious—and when merchants like Arthur Lake, with whom we began this paper, are driven out of business by "competitive" advertising—we know that some assumptions about the rights of advertisers need to be thoroughly defended by good reasons, far better reasons than I have yet seen forthcoming.

NOTES

1. Walter B. Smith, "For Lake, Jewelry Has Lost Its Glitter," *Detroit News,* December 9, 1982, p. 3B.
2. T. W. Zimmerer and P. L. Preston, "Plasma International," in *Business and Society,* ed. Robert D. Hay, Edmund R. Gray, and James E. Gates (Cincinnati: South-Western, 1976).
3. William E. LaMothe, "Testimony," in Part 5—TV Advertising of Food to Children, Hearings before the Senate Select Committee on Nutrition and Human Needs, 93rd Congress, 1st Session, 1973, p. 258. The Kellogg Company has worked tirelessly to refute charges that its advertising makes false nutritional claims. Kellogg issued a pamphlet on "Advertising" in late 1979. In this pamphlet the company argued as follows:

> Kellogg's has been recognized an unprecedented seven times by *Family Health Magazine* for excellence in nutritional advertising. . . .
>
> For years we have placed great emphasis on creating honest and tasteful advertising for youngsters with messages that con-

vey the inherent nutritional value of our products. We present these messages in a way that is not only informative and interesting, but also appropriate for a child's level of understanding.

Our advertising serves not only as a product selling tool, it also stresses the importance of starting the day with a nutritious breakfast. Since 1973 Kellogg cereal advertisements for both children and adults have shown cereal and milk being eaten as a part of a complete breakfast. Our advertising improves a child's awareness of the need for a complete, nutritious breakfast.

4. Stanley I. Benn, "Freedom and Persuasion," *Australasian Journal of Philosophy* 45 (December 1967): 265.

5. *Ibid.*, pp. 265–266.

6. *FTC Final Staff Report and Recommendation in the Matter of Children's Advertising*, 43 *Federal Register* 17967, TRR No. 215–60, (1981), p. 3. See also Donald F. Roberts and Christine M. Bachen, "Mass Communication Effects," *Annual Review of Psychology* 32 (1981), section on Effects on Children and Adolescents, pp. 336, 338.

7. John Culkin, writing in the *Hastings Center Report*, concentrates on the unfairness of manipulating children as a means of selling to their parents. Culkin quotes a 1978 advertisement that appeared in *Broadcasting* magazine soliciting advertising for a Boston television station. The ad was entitled "Kid Power is Coming to Boston." It read as follows:

If you're selling, Charlie's mom is buying. But you've got to sell Charlie first.

His allowance is only 50 cents a week but his buying power is an American phenomenon. He's not only tight with his Mom, but he has a way with his Dad, his Grandma, and Aunt Harriet, too.

When Charlie sees something he likes, he usually gets it.

Culkin, "Selling to Children: Fair Play in TV Commercials," *Hastings Center Report* 8 (June 1978): 7–9.

8. Richard De George, *Moral Issues in Business* (New York: Macmillan, 1982), pp. 192–194.; Ruth Macklin, *Man, Mind and Morality: The Ethics of Behavior Control* (Englewood Cliffs, NJ: Prentice-Hall, 1982), p. 12; and Perry London, *Behavior Control* (New York: Harper and Row, 1969), p. 1. Perhaps the most sustained treatment of the concept of manipulation in the philosophical literature has been presented by Joel Rudinow. His analysis is restricted to intentional acts of psychological manipulation, generally involving the treatment of others instrumentally and, therefore, immorally. Joel Rudinow, "Manipulation," *Ethics* 88 (1978): 338–347.

9. President's Commission for the Study of Ethical Problems in Medicine and Biomedical and Behavioral Research, *Making Health Care Decisions* (Washington: Government Printing Office, 1982), vol. 1, 66–67.

10. L. Ross, "IRA Jungle Grows More Dense as Tax Time Draws Near," *Washington Post*, March 19, 1984, Business Section, p. 34. See also Mary W. Walsh, "Banks' Policies on Figuring and Advertising Deposit Interest Make Picking Rates Hard," *Wall Street Journal*, October 8, 1984, sec. 2, p. 33.

11. CFR Part 217, Sec. 217.6(g).

12. Legal Division (Messrs. Schwartz and Pilecki), Federal Reserve System, Division of Research and Statistics, Memo: Advertising Interest Rates on IRA Time Deposits (March 16, 1984).

13. Robert B. Cialdini et al., "Low-Ball Procedure for Producing Compliance: Commitment then Cost," *Journal of Personality and Social Psychology* 36 (1978): 463–476, esp. 464.

14. Low-balling is closely related to another technique for inducing compliance, known as the "foot-in-the-door technique." A longtime favorite of social psychologists, this procedure involves increasing compliance with a request by first inducing compliance with an initial smaller, but different, request. See J. L. Freedman and S. C. Fraser, "Compliance with Pressure, the Foot-in-the-Door Technique," *Journal of Personality and Social Psychology* 4 (1966): 195–202; P. Pliner et al., "Compliance without Pressure, Some Further Data on the Foot-in-the-Door Technique," *Journal of Experimental Social Psychology* 10 (1974): 17–22; and Mark Snyder and Michael R. Cunningham, "To Comply or Not Comply: Testing the Self-Perception Explanation of the 'Foot-in-the-Door' Phenomenon," *Journal of Personality and Social Psychology* 31 (1975): 64–67.

Reasonable Consumer
or Ignorant Consumer?
How the FTC Decides

Ivan L. Preston

INTRODUCTION

Is the Federal Trade Commission obligated to protect only reasonable, sensible, intelligent consumers who conduct themselves carefully in the marketplace? Or must it also protect ignorant consumers who conduct themselves carelessly?

Since its origin in 1914, the Commission has varied its answer to these questions. It has committed itself at all times to prohibit sellers' claims which would deceive reasonable people, but has undergone changes of direction on whether to ban claims which would deceive only ignorant people. At times it has acted on behalf of the latter by invoking the "ignorant man standard."[1] At other times it has been ordered by courts to ignore these people and invoke the "reasonable man standard." In still other cases it has chosen voluntarily to protect certain ignorant persons but not others.

The significance of the issue is that the FTC will rule against the fewest types of sellers' claims under the reasonable man standard, and against the most under the ignorant man standard. The latter guideline therefore means, in the eyes of many, the greatest protection for the consuming public. Some consumerists may feel, in fact, that such a standard should be mandatory on the grounds that a flat prohibition is needed against all sellers' deceptions which would deceive anyone at all.

The FTC, however, works under a constraint which makes it necessary to temper its allegiance to the ignorant man standard. The constraint is that the Commission may proceed legally only in response to substantial public interest.[2] Over the years the Commissioners have been sensitive to the argument that there is no public interest in prohibiting messages which would deceive only a small number of terribly careless, stupid or naive people. To explain the compelling nature of this argument, I would like to describe a deception of that sort.

AN EXAMPLE

In my hometown of Pittsburgh, Pennsylvania, there appears each Christmas-time a brand of beer called Olde Frothingslosh. This quaint item is nothing but Pittsburgh Brewing Company's regular Iron City Beer in its holiday costume, decked out with a specially designed label to provide a few laughs. The label identifies the product as "the pale stale ale for the pale stale male," and there is similar wit appended, all strictly nonsense. One of the best is a line saying that Olde Frothingslosh is the only beer in which the foam is on the bottom.

A customer bought some Olde Frothingslosh to amuse friends at a party and was disturbed to find the claim was nothing but a *big lie*: the foam was right up there on top where it always is! She wanted her money back from the beer distributor, couldn't get

From Ivan L. Preston, "Reasonable Consumer or Ignorant Consumer? How the FTC Decides," *Journal of Consumer Affairs*, 8 (Winter 1974): 131–143. Reprinted by permission.

it, and went to a lawyer with the intention of bringing suit. The true story ended right there because the lawyer advised her there was no chance of success. The reasonable man (woman! person!) standard would be applied to her suit, and her reliance on the belief about the foam would be judged unreasonable.

Had the ignorant man standard applied she would possibly have succeeded, which illustrates the difference the choice of standards makes. It also illustrates the essential weakness, in conjunction with definite strengths, possessed by a legal standard which sets out to protect everybody from everything. Many of the resulting prohibitions would eliminate only infinitesimal amounts of deception.

PROBLEMS OF THE IGNORANT MAN STANDARD

There are other reasons, too, for the FTC's cautious attitude toward the ignorant man standard. A pragmatic point is that the Commission does not have the resources to prosecute all cases, therefore those which are investigated might better be ones which endanger greater numbers of people. Another problem is that an extreme concern for the ignorant could lead to repression of much communication content useful to consumers, and could lead as well to possible violation of the First Amendment's freedom of speech guarantee.

Probably the most important objection to the ignorant man standard is that the reasonable man standard was traditional in the common law which preceded the development of the FTC in 1914. The common law held that to avoid being negligent a person must act as a reasonable person would act under like circumstances.[3] Mention of the reasonable or prudent person first appeared in an English case of 1837,[4] and has been in widespread use since.

In many of its applications the reasonable man concept has been applied to the defendant; did he, for example, act negligently in causing an accident which injured the plaintiff? In the law of misrepresentation, however, the concept is applied to the plaintiff, the deceived consumer. He brings a suit against the deceptive seller, and the question is whether he is guilty of contributory negligence which the deceiver may use as a defense. The rules require the plaintiff to assert and show that he relied upon the false representation, and that the damages he suffered were a result of such reliance. In addition, he must show that his reliance was justified—that is, his reliance must pass the test of the conduct of a reasonable man. He may not claim to have relied on a statement which sensible and prudent people would recognize as preposterous. If he does, he is guilty of contributory negligence which the deceiver may use as a reason for having the suit dismissed.[5]

This rule usually does not apply in the case of a fraudulent misrepresentation, where the deceiver consciously knows the representation was false and deliberately seeks to deceive with it. If that is shown, the person deceived is entitled to rely without having to justify the action as reasonable conduct.[6] But where the deceit is not intentional (or not so proved!) the reasonable man standard applies and the seller's falsity will not amount legally to deception where it is felt that the buyer should have known better than to rely on it. Various types of sellers' statements thereby escape legal liability under the reasonable man standard, beginning with those such as the Olde Frothingslosh claim which are physically impossible and therefore presumed obviously false. Also included are the exaggerations and superlatives called puffery—"The Greatest Show on Earth" and the claims that psychosocial values are present in products—"Ultra-Brite gives your mouth sex appeal."

THE TRANSITION TO THE IGNORANT MAN STANDARD

At the time the FTC was created, the only specific law on these matters was the common law just described. The FTC Act stated nothing explicitly about what persons the Commission was authorized to protect; it said only that proceedings must be in the interest of the public. The most obvious procedure therefore would have been to follow the common law precedents and embrace the reasonable man standard. Instead, the FTC did the unexpected and flaunted the reasonable man standard in many of its early cases. Neither that concept nor a replacement standard were discussed explicitly, but numerous early cases show that the Commission was applying an ignorant man standard or a close approximation of it. In 1919 it ordered a manufacturer to stop advertising that its automobile batteries would "last forever."[7] One might assume that no reasonable person even in that year would have relied upon this claim literally, especially when the same ads offered a service by which "the purchaser pays 50 cents per month and is entitled to a new battery as soon as the old one is worn out." The FTC saw the latter phrase, however, as confirming the falsity and deceptiveness rather than the sheer frivolousness of "last forever." The case indicates that the Commission was developing a policy of stopping deceptions which would deceive only a minority.[8]

The switch to the ignorant man standard appeared questionable legally; precedent did not support it. But before we describe the eventual court considerations of this matter, we should acknowledge that there was much argument against the reasonable man standard in common sense if not in law. The legal conception of the buyer who failed to be reasonable in the marketplace was that of a person who made a stupid purchase through his own fault—he should have known better. It was this conception with which common sense could disagree. Some so-called stupid choices may be made not through carelessness but through the impossibility of obtaining and assessing information even when great caution and intelligence are applied. The world of goods and services was once simple, but has become terribly technical. Many poor choices were

being made by persons who *couldn't* have known better.

These problems might have been incorporated into the reasonable man standard by adjusting that standard to the realities of the market. Consider a store scene in which a product was available at six cans for a dollar while one can was 16 cents. In considering whether a reasonable person would be deceived, the law might have taken into account that many people are slow at arithmetic, and that the bustle of a market and the need to make many other choices in the same few minutes rendered it unlikely they would fully use the mathematical capacity they possessed. The competence assumed of a "reasonable person" might have been reduced accordingly, and the traditional standard, altered in this way, might still have been applied.

Something bordering the opposite actually occurred in legal actions. The reasonable man came to be regarded as a *better* than average person, as someone who was never negligent and who therefore was entirely fictitious outside the courtroom.[9] He was "an ideal creature. . . . The factor controlling the judgment of [his] conduct is not what *is*, but *what ought to be*." The law, apparently, had created an unreasonable conception of the reasonable man.

It was this problem the FTC sought to correct. We do not know, because the point was not discussed as such, whether the Commission regarded its new conception as a move to the ignorant man standard or as a redefinition of the reasonable man standard by the method described above. But the practical effect was the same in either case—the Commission moved toward protecting the public from deceptions which regulators previously had ignored because they did not harm the fictitiously reasonable man.

COURT INTERPRETATIONS

Considerations of the reasonable and ignorant man standards eventually were made explicit through the intervention of appeals court decisions into FTC affairs. In 1924 the Commission outlawed a sales method which offered an encyclopedia "free" provided a purchaser paid $49 for two supplementary updating services.[10] The seller appealed and won a reversal on the grounds that no deception was involved.[11] "It is conceivable," the opinion stated, "that a very stupid person might be misled by this method of selling books, yet measured by ordinary standards of trade and by ordinary standards of the intelligence of traders, we cannot discover that it amounts to an unfair method of competition. . . . "

The FTC did not adopt the reasonable man standard as a result of this ruling; its subsequent activities reflected instead a posture of resistance. When it stubbornly invoked a similar restraint against a different encyclopedia company it was again reversed by an appeals court. Circuit Judge Learned Hand was most adamant in declaring that

> . . . a community which sells for profit must not be ridden on so short a rein that it can only move at a walk. We cannot take seriously the suggestion that a man who is buying a set of books and a ten years' extension service, will be fatuous enough to be misled by the mere statement that the first are given away, and that he is paying only for the second. Nor can we conceive how he could be damaged were he to suppose that that was true. Such trivial niceties are too impalpable for practical affairs, they are will-o-the-wisps which divert attention from substantial evils.[12]

This time, however, the FTC took the case to the U.S. Supreme Court, where a new justice delivering his first opinion told Learned Hand that the encyclopedia decision *was* a substantial evil. Hugo Black's opinion in *FTC* v. *Standard Education* of 1937 restored the Commission's use of the ignorant man standard:

> The fact that a false statement may be obviously false to those who are trained and experienced does not change its character, nor take away its power to deceive others less experi-

enced. There is no duty resting upon a citizen to suspect the honesty of those with whom he transacts business. Laws are made to protect the trusting as well as the suspicious. The best element of business has long since decided that honesty should govern competitive enterprises, and that the rule of *caveat emptor* should not be relied upon to reward fraud and deception.

Though Black mentioned the name of neither standard, his words suggest he was rejecting the reasonable man standard rather than proposing merely to adjust it. It was his words, above all, which led to the concept of an "ignorant man standard" for the FTC in place of what went before.

Just how *Standard Education* was supported by precedent is a curious question. Justice Black's opinion cited none. It affirmed that the sales method not merely had deceptive capacity but clearly deceived many persons,[13] and it also stated that the deception was committed knowingly and deliberately. This suggests the Supreme Court was invoking the common law notion that the reasonable man standard should not apply in case of deliberate deception. Something left unclarified, however, is what significance such a ruling should have for an agency such as FTC which routinely did not make findings of deliberate deception. Deliberate intent to deceive undoubtedly occurs in many cases where no one can prove it. The whole advantage of FTC procedure, in comparison with what went before, was that it could rule sellers' messages out of the marketplace *without* bothering with the traditional requirement of having to prove intent. What was the advantage, then, of obtaining the right to use the ignorant man standard only in conjunction with proven intent to deceive?

The result, strangely, was that the FTC, on the basis of *Standard Education,* began applying the ignorant man standard liberally without regard for determining intent, and in some cases without regard for the fact that intent to deceive was almost surely absent. The appeals courts, also via *Standard Education,* approved this procedure. The trend was thoroughly questionable but was pursued decisively, particularly by the Second Circuit Court of Appeals, the one which *Standard Education* had reversed. In *General Motors* v. *FTC*, involving a "6% time payment plan" which actually charged 11½% interest, the Second Circuit's Judge Augustus Hand concluded:

It may be there was no intention to mislead and that only the careless or the incompetent could be misled. But if the Commission, having discretion to deal with these matters, thinks it best to insist upon a form of advertising clear enough so that, in the words of the prophet Isaiah, "wayfaring men, though fools, shall not err therein," it is not for the courts to revise their judgment.

The influence of the *Standard Education* reversal was unmistakable on the one Hand— and on the other Hand as well. When Judge Learned Hand considered an appeal to the Second Circuit of the Commission's finding of deception in an admittedly untrue claim that "one Moretrench wellpoint is as good as any five others," he said:

It is extremely hard to believe that any buyers of such machinery could be misled by anything which was patently no more than the exuberant enthusiasm of a satisfied customer, but in such matters we understand that we are to insist upon the most literal truthfulness. *Federal Trade Commission* v. *Standard Education Society* .... [14]

It was clear that the Second Circuit's Hands were tied. Substitution of the ignorant man standard for the reasonable man standard proceeded in additional Second Circuit cases, and in others as well.[15] Under these liberal interpretations the FTC appeared during most of the 1940's to be knocking down right and left every advertising claim it thought had the slightest chance of deceiving even the most ignorant person. There was a good bit of unchecked exuberance in this spree, reaching an extreme when Clairol was forbidden to say that its

dye will "color hair permanently." The FTC thought the public would take this as a claim that all the hair a person grows for the rest of her life will emerge in the Clairol color. That expectation was based on the testimony of a single witness who said she thought somebody might think that—although she added that *she wouldn't*.

On Clairol's appeal the Second Circuit said it couldn't imagine *anybody* believing the claim, but in accordance with *Standard Education* it said it had to support the FTC. No hint was offered that the Clairol claim was used with intent to deceive, and no acknowledgment was made by the Second Circuit that *Standard Education* might have been intended by the Supreme Court to apply only where such intent was evident. We may speculate that if the Olde Frothingslosh matter had been appealed to the Second Circuit in the same year as the Clairol case, 1944, the purchaser might have recovered damages because the beer's foam wasn't on the bottom!

RETURN TO THE REASONABLE MAN STANDARD

We have now seen the development of a strong emphasis on the ignorant man standard. The next task is to describe how this emphasis came to be diluted, a matter which involved additional curious events. One of the arbitrary facts of life in U.S. law is that the various Circuit Courts of Appeal are sometimes inconsistent in their rulings. They need not take each other's decisions into account, so a case may be decided differently in one than in another. The Second Circuit was the one reversed by *Standard Education*, and we have seen that this court in subsequent cases applied the ignorant man standard assiduously. This included the prohibition of puffery in *Moretrench*, even though puffery had traditionally been called nondeceptive. With its long-standing immunity, puffery might have been expected to resist the courts even if nothing else did, but under the ignorant man standard the Second Circuit moved to eliminate this kind of falsity along with everything else.

But the time came, in 1946, when a puffery case was appealed to the Seventh Circuit rather than the Second, and the difference was significant. *Carlay* involved a claim that Ayds candy mints make weight-reducing easy, which FTC said was false. On appeal the Seventh Circuit, which had tended earlier to object to the ignorant man standard, said the claim of "easy" was "mere puffing or dealer's talk upon which no charge of misrepresentation can be based." The court cited previous non-FTC cases which had allowed puffery, and completely ignored the cases stemming from Justice Black and the Second Circuit, which would have supported the FTC's outlawing of "easy."

As a result the FTC had a contradiction on its hands. The Second Circuit told it to protect the ignorant man; the Seventh Circuit told it to permit puffery which could deceive the ignorant man. The contradiction might have been resolved by the Supreme Court, but was never considered there. The FTC's resolution was to allow puffery thereafter, which tended to dilute the ignorant man standard.

An example of the dilution occurred in *Bristol-Myers,* in which the Commission issued a complaint against the "Smile of Beauty" phrase used by Ipana tooth paste. Apparently it felt the line amounted to a claim that Ipana would straighten out people's crooked teeth. The complaint was issued in 1942, about the same time as the Clairol (*Gelb*) case and prior to *Carlay* which legitimized puffery. But the final decision was made in 1949, post-*Carlay,* and produced a change of mind in which the Commission decided that "the reference to beautification of the smile was mere puffery, unlikely, because of its generality and widely variant meanings, to deceive anyone factually."

The trend away from the extreme ignorant man standard had begun, but only slightly. Cases followed in which the FTC retained a strong protective stance on behalf of ignorant consumers. But in 1963 the FTC

finally commented that the standard could be carried too far. *Heinz W. Kirchner* was a case about an inflatable device to help a person stay afloat and learn to swim. Called Swim-Ezy, it was worn under the swimming suit and was advertised as being invisible. It was not invisible, but the FTC found it to be "inconspicuous," and ruled that that was all the claim of invisibility would mean to the public:

> The possibility that some persons might believe Swim-Ezy is not merely inconspicuous, but wholly invisible or bodiless, seems to us too far-fetched to warrant intervention.

But what about the few persons who would accept this far-fetched belief? The Commission made clear it no longer intended to protect such ignorant persons:

> True ... the Commission's responsibility is to prevent deception of the gullible and credulous, as well as the cautious and knowledgeable.... This principle loses it validity, however, if it is applied uncritically or pushed to an absurd extreme. An advertiser cannot be charged with liability in respect of every conceivable misconception however outlandish, to which his representations might be subject among the foolish or feebleminded.... A representation does not become "false and deceptive" merely because it will be unreasonably misunderstood by an insignificant and unrepresentative segment of the class of persons to whom the representation is addressed.

That is the position the FTC has followed since. It holds no longer to the strict ignorant man standard by which it would protect everyone from everything which may deceive them. It would rule out consideration, for example, of the Olde Frothingslosh claim which apparently fooled only one stray individual. Perhaps we may call the new stance a modified ignorant man standard which protects only those cases of foolishness which are committed by significant numbers of people.

Some observers may protest that any behaviors which are customary for a substantial portion of the population shouldn't be called "ignorant." They might rather call the new stance a modified reasonable man standard in which what is reasonable has been equated more closely than before with what is average or typical. Whatever the name, however, the FTC's present position appears to remain closer to the spirit and practice of the strict ignorant man standard of the 1940's than to the reasonable man standard of tradition.

NOTES

1. "Ignorant man standard" is my own term, which I feel is correctly blunt. The terms "credulous man standard" and "lowest standard of intelligence," which lack semantic punch, have been used elsewhere.
2. FTC Act, #5(b), 15 U. S. C. #45(b).
3. *Restatement of Torts (Second),* Section 283 (1965). Section 283A states that a child must act as would a reasonable person of like age, intelligence, and experience under like circumstances.
4. Vaughan v. Menlove, 3 Bing N.C. 468, 132 Eng. Rep. 490 (1837). For other cases and references see Reporter's Notes to Section 283 in *Restatement of Torts (Second) Appendix.*
5. The terminology "contributory negligence" is not always used, but the idea of denying recovery for unreasonable reliance on misrepresentations is based on that concept; William L. Prosser, *Torts,* 4th ed., p. 717 (1971).
6. Prosser, *ibid.,* p. 716.
7. FTC v. Universal Battery, 2 FTC 95 (1919).
8. See also FTC v. A. A. Berry, 2 FTC 427 (1920); FTC v. Alben-Harley, 4 FTC 31 (1921); FTC v. Williams Soap, 6 FTC 107 (1923); Alfred Peats, 8 FTC 366 (1925).
9. #283 *Restatement of Torts (Second),* comment c.
10. John C. Winston, 8 FTC 177 (1924).
11. John C. Winston v. FTC, 3 F.2d 961 (3rd Cir., 1925).
12. FTC v. Standard Education Society, 86 F.2d. 692 (2d Cir., 1936).
13. 302 U.S. 112, 58 S.C. 113 (1937), p. 117.
14. Moretrench v. FTC, 127 F.2d 792 (2d Cir., 1942). Turning to another literally untrue Moretrench claim, that its product had an advantage to which "contractors all over the world testify," Hand stated, "It is again hard to imagine how anyone reading it could have understood it as more than puffing; yet for the reasons we have just given, if the Commission saw fit to take notice of it, we may not interfere." This was the same judge who once had rejected similar claims on the grounds that "There are some kinds of talk which no man takes seriously, and if he does he suffers from his credulity.... Neither party usually believes what the seller says about his opinions, and each knows it. Such statements, like the claims of campaign managers before election, are rather designed to allay the suspicion which would attend their absence than to be understood as having any relationship to objective truth." Vulcan Metals v. Simmons, 248 F. 853 (2d Cir., 1918).
15. D.D.D. v. FTC, 125 F.2d 679 (7th Cir., 1942); Aronberg v. FTC, 132 F.2d 165, (7th Cir., 1942); Gulf Oil v. FTC, 150 F.2d 106 (5th Cir., 1945); Parker Pen v. FTC, 159 F.2d 509 (7th Cir., 1946). In the latter case the FTC's role was said to be to "protect the casual, one might say the negligent, reader, as well as the vigilant and more intelligent.... " A much-used quote, cited in *Aronberg* and *Gulf Oil,* above, and in *Gelb, op. cit.,* was from Florence v. Dowd, 178 F. 73 (2d Cir., 1910): "The law is not made for the protection of experts, but for the public—that vast multitude which includes the ignorant, the unthinking, and the credulous, who, in making purchases, do not stop to analyze, but are governed by appearances and general impressions." This was a pre-FTC case with evidence of deliberate deception.

Is Business Bluffing Ethical?

Albert Z. Carr

A respected businessman with whom I discussed the theme of this article remarked with some heat, "You mean to say you're going to encourage men to bluff? Why, bluffing is nothing more than a form of lying! You're advising them to lie!"

I agreed that the basis of private morality is a respect for truth and that the closer a businessman comes to the truth, the more he deserves respect. At the same time, I suggested that most bluffing in business might be regarded simply as game strategy—much like bluffing in poker, which does not reflect on the morality of the bluffer.

I quoted Henry Taylor, the British statesman who pointed out that "falsehood ceases to be falsehood when it is understood on all sides that the truth is not expected to be spoken"—an exact description of bluffing in poker, diplomacy, and business. I cited the analogy of the criminal court, where the criminal is not expected to tell the truth when he pleads "not guilty." Everyone from the judge down takes it for granted that the job of the defendant's attorney is to get his client off, not to reveal the truth; and this is considered ethical practice. I mentioned Representative Omar Burleson, the Democrat from Texas, who was quoted as saying, in regard to the ethics of Congress, "Ethics is a barrel of worms"[1]—a pungent summing up of the problem of deciding who is ethical in politics.

I reminded my friend that millions of businessmen feel constrained every day to say *yes* to their bosses when they secretly believe *no* and that this is generally accepted as permissible strategy when the alternative might be the loss of a job. The essential point, I said, is that the ethics of business are game ethics, different from the ethics of religion.

He remained unconvinced. Referring to the company of which he is president, he declared: "Maybe that's good enough for some businessmen, but I can tell you that we pride ourselves on our ethics. In 30 years not one customer has ever questioned my word or asked to check our figures. We're loyal to our customers and fair to our suppliers. I regard my handshake on a deal as a contract. I've never entered into price-fixing schemes with my competitors. I've never allowed my salesmen to spread injurious rumors about other companies. Our union contract is the best in our industry. And, if I do say so myself, our ethical standards are of the highest!"

He really was saying, without realizing it, that he was living up to the ethical standards of the business game—which are a far cry from those of private life. Like a gentlemanly poker player, he did not play in cahoots with others at the table, try to smear their reputations, or hold back chips he owed them.

But this same fine man, at that very time, was allowing one of his products to be advertised in a way that made it sound a great deal better than it actually was. Another item in

From Albert Z. Carr, "Is Business Bluffing Ethical?" *Harvard Business Review* (January/February 1968). Reprinted by permission of the *Harvard Business Review.* Copyright © 1968 by the President and Fellows of Harvard College; all rights reserved.

his product line was notorious among dealers for its "built-in obsolescence." He was holding back from the market a much-improved product because he did not want to interfere with sales of the inferior item it would have replaced. He had joined with certain of his competitors in hiring a lobbyist to push a state legislature, by methods that he preferred not to know too much about, into amending a bill then being enacted.

In his view these things had nothing to do with ethics; they were merely normal business practice. He himself undoubtedly avoided outright falsehoods—never lied in so many words. But the entire organization that he ruled was deeply involved in numerous strategies of deception.

PRESSURE TO DECEIVE

Most executives from time to time are almost compelled, in the interests of their companies or themselves, to practice some form of deception when negotiating with customers, dealers, labor unions, government officials, or even other departments of their companies. By conscious misstatements, concealment of pertinent facts, or exaggeration—in short, by bluffing—they seek to persuade others to agree with them. I think it is fair to say that if the individual executive refuses to bluff from time to time—if he feels obligated to tell the truth, the whole truth, and nothing but the truth—he is ignoring opportunities permitted under the rules and is at a heavy disadvantage in his business dealings.

But here and there a businessman is unable to reconcile himself to the bluff in which he plays a part. His conscience, perhaps spurred by religious idealism, troubles him. He feels guilty; he may develop an ulcer or a nervous tic. Before any executive can make profitable use of the strategy of the bluff, he needs to make sure that in bluffing he will not lose self-respect or become emotionally disturbed. If he is to reconcile personal integrity and high standards of honesty with the practical requirements of business, he must feel that his bluffs are ethically justified. The justification rests on the fact that business, as practiced by individuals as well as by corporations, has the impersonal character of a game—a game that demands both special strategy and an understanding of its special ethics.

The game is played at all levels of corporate life, from the highest to the lowest. At the very instant that a man decides to enter business, he may be forced into a game situation, as is shown by the recent experience of a Cornell honor graduate who applied for a job with a large company.

> This applicant was given a psychological test which included the statement, "Of the following magazines, check any that you have read either regularly or from time to time, and double-check those which interest you most. *Reader's Digest, Time, Fortune, Saturday Evening Post, The New Republic, Life, Look, Ramparts, Newsweek, Business Week, U.S. News & World Report, The Nation, Playboy, Esquire, Harper's, Sports Illustrated.*"

His tastes in reading were broad, and at one time or another he had read almost all of these magazines. He was a subscriber to The New Republic, an enthusiast for Ramparts, and an avid student of the pictures in Playboy. He was not sure whether his interest in Playboy would be held against him, but he had a shrewd suspicion that if he confessed to an interest in Ramparts and The New Republic, he would be thought a liberal, a radical, or at least an intellectual, and his chances of getting the job, which he needed, would greatly diminish. He therefore checked five of the more conservative magazines. Apparently it was a sound decision, for he got the job.

He had made a game player's decision, consistent with business ethics.

A similar case is that of a magazine space salesman who, owing to a merger, suddenly found himself out of a job:

This man was 58, and, in spite of a good record, his chance of getting a job elsewhere in a business where youth is favored in hiring practice was not good. He was a vigorous, healthy man, and only a considerable amount of gray in his hair suggested his age. Before beginning his job search he touched up his hair with a black dye to confine the gray to his temples. He knew that the truth about his age might well come out in time, but he calculated that he could deal with that situation when it arose. He and his wife decided that he could easily pass for 45, and he so stated his age on his résumé.

This was a lie: yet within the accepted rules of the business game, no moral culpability attaches to it.

THE POKER ANALOGY

We can learn a good deal about the nature of business by comparing it with poker. While both have a large element of chance, in the long run the winner is the man who plays with steady skill. In both games ultimate victory requires intimate knowledge of the rules, insight into the psychology of the other players, a bold front, a considerable amount of self-discipline, and the ability to respond swiftly and effectively to opportunities provided by chance.

No one expects poker to be played on the ethical principles preached in churches. In poker it is right and proper to bluff a friend out of the rewards of being dealt a good hand. A player feels no more than a slight twinge of sympathy, if that, when—with nothing better than a single ace in his hand—he strips a heavy loser, who holds a pair, of the rest of his chips. It was up to the other fellow to protect himself. In the words of an excellent poker player, former President Harry Truman, "If you can't stand the heat, stay out of the kitchen." If one shows mercy to a loser in poker, it is a personal gesture, divorced from the rules of the game.

Poker has its special ethics, and here I am not referring to rules against cheating. The man who keeps an ace up his sleeve or who marks the cards is more than unethical; he is a crook, and can be punished as such—kicked out of the game or, in the Old West, shot.

In contrast to the cheat, the unethical poker player is one who, while abiding by the letter of the rules, finds ways to put the other players at an unfair disadvantage. Perhaps he unnerves them with loud talk. Or he tries to get them drunk. Or he plays in cahoots with someone else at the table. Ethical poker players frown on such tactics.

Poker's own brand of ethics is different from the ethical ideals of civilized human relationships. The game calls for distrust of the other fellow. It ignores the claim of friendship. Cunning deception and concealment of one's strength and intentions, not kindness and openheartedness, are vital in poker. No one thinks any the worse of poker on that account. And no one should think any the worse of the game of business because its standards of right and wrong differ from the prevailing traditions of morality in our society. . . .

'WE DON'T MAKE THE LAWS'

Wherever we turn in business, we can perceive the sharp distinction between its ethical standards and those of the churches. Newspapers abound with sensational stories growing out of this distinction:

We read one day that Senator Philip A. Hart of Michigan has attacked food processors for deceptive packaging of numerous products.[2]
The next day there is a Congressional to-do over Ralph Nader's book, *Unsafe At Any Speed,* which demonstrates that automobile companies for years have neglected the safety of car-owning families.[3]
Then another Senator, Lee Metcalf of Montana, and journalist Vic Reinemer show in their book, *Overcharge,* the methods by which utility companies elude regulating government bodies to extract unduly large payments from users of electricity.[4]

These are merely dramatic instances of a prevailing condition; there is hardly a major industry at which a similar attack could not be aimed. Critics of business regard such behavior as unethical, but the companies concerned know that they are merely playing the business game.

Among the most respected of our business institutions are the insurance companies. A group of insurance executives meeting recently in New England was startled when their guest speaker, social critic Daniel Patrick Moynihan, roundly berated them for "unethical" practices. They had been guilty, Moynihan alleged, of using outdated actuarial tables to obtain unfairly high premiums. They habitually delayed the hearings of lawsuits against them in order to tire out the plaintiffs and win cheap settlements. In their employment policies they use ingenious devices to discriminate against certain minority groups.[5]

It was difficult for the audience to deny the validity of these charges. But these men were business game players. Their reaction to Moynihan's attack was much the same as that of the automobile manufacturers to Nader, of the utilities to Senator Metcalf, and of the food processors to Senator Hart. If the laws governing their businesses change, or if public opinion becomes clamorous, they will make the necessary adjustments. But morally they have in their view done nothing wrong. As long as they comply with the letter of the law, they are within their rights to operate their businesses as they see fit.

The small business is in the same position as the great corporation in this respect. For example:

In 1967 a key manufacturer was accused of providing master keys for automobiles to mail-order customers, although it was obvious that some of the purchasers might be automobile thieves. His defense was plain and straightforward. If there was nothing in the law to prevent him from selling his keys to anyone who ordered them, it was not up to him to inquire as to his customers' motives.

Why was it any worse, he insisted, for him to sell car keys by mail, than for mail-order houses to sell guns that might be used for murder? Until the law was changed, the key manufacturer could regard himself as being just as ethical as any other businessman by the rules of the business game.[6]

Violations of the ethical ideals of society are common in business, but they are not necessarily violations of business principles. Each year the Federal Trade Commission orders hundreds of companies, many of them of the first magnitude, to "cease and desist" from practices which, judged by ordinary standards, are of questionable morality but which are stoutly defended by the companies concerned.

In one case, a firm manufacturing a well-known mouthwash was accused of using a cheap form of alcohol possibly deleterious to health. The company's chief executive, after testifying in Washington, made this comment privately:

"We broke no law. We're in a highly competitive industry. If we're going to stay in business, we have to look for profit wherever the law permits. We don't make the laws. We obey them. Then why do we have to put up with this 'holier than thou' talk about ethics? It's sheer hypocrisy. We're not in business to promote ethics. Look at the cigarette companies, for God's sake! If the ethics aren't embodied in the laws by the men who made them, you can't expect businessmen to fill the lack. Why, a sudden submission to Christian ethics by businessmen who would bring about the greatest economic upheaval in history!"

It may be noted that the government failed to prove its case against him.

CAST ILLUSIONS ASIDE

Talk about ethics by businessmen is often a thin decorative coating over the hard realities of the game. . . .

The illusion that business can afford to be

guided by ethics as conceived in private life is often fostered by speeches and articles containing such phrases as, "It pays to be ethical," or, "Sound ethics is good business." Actually this is not an ethical position at all; it is a self-serving calculation in disguise. The speaker is really saying that in the long run a company can make more money if it does not antagonize competitors, suppliers, employees, and customers by squeezing them too hard. He is saying that oversharp policies reduce ultimate gains. That is true, but it has nothing to do with ethics. The underlying attitude is much like that in the familiar story of the shopkeeper who finds an extra $20 bill in the cash register, debates with himself the ethical problem—should he tell his partner?—and finally decides to share the money because the gesture will give him an edge over the s.o.b. the next time they quarrel.

I think it is fair to sum up the prevailing attitude of businessmen on ethics as follows:

We live in what is probably the most competitive of the world's civilized societies. Our customs encourage a high degree of aggression in the individual's striving for success. Business is our main area of competition, and it has been ritualized into a game of strategy. The basic rules of the game have been set by the government, which attempts to detect and punish business frauds. But as long as a company does not transgress the rules of the game set by law, it has the legal right to shape its strategy without reference to anything but its profits. If it takes a long-term view of its profits, it will preserve amicable relations, so far as possible, with those with whom it deals. A wise businessman will not seek advantage to the point where he generates dangerous hostility among employees, competitors, customers, government, or the public at large. But decisions in this area are, in the final test, decisions of strategy, not of ethics.

... If a man plans to make a seat in the business game, he owes it to himself to master the principles by which the game is played, including its special ethical outlook. He can then hardly fail to recognize that an occasional bluff may well be justified in terms of the game's ethics and warranted in terms of economic necessity. Once he clears his mind on this point, he is in a good position to match his strategy against that of the other players. He can then determine objectively whether a bluff in a given situation has a good chance of succeeding and can decide when and how to bluff, without a feeling of ethical transgression.

To be a winner, a man must play to win. This does not mean that he must be ruthless, cruel, harsh, or treacherous. On the contrary, the better his reputation for integrity, honesty, and decency, the better his chances of victory will be in the long run. But from time to time every businessman, like every poker player, is offered a choice between certain loss or bluffing within the legal rules of the game. If he is not resigned to losing, if he wants to rise in his company and industry, then in such a crisis he will bluff—and bluff hard. . . .

In the last third of the twentieth century even children are aware that if a man has become prosperous in business, he has sometimes departed from the strict truth in order to overcome obstacles or has practiced the more subtle deceptions of the half-truth or the misleading omission. Whatever the form of the bluff, it is an integral part of the game, and the executive who does not master its techniques is not likely to accumulate much money or power.

NOTES

1. *The New York Times,* March 9, 1967.
2. *The New York Times,* November 21, 1966.
3. New York, Grossman Publishers, Inc., 1965.
4. New York, David McKay Company, Inc., 1967.
5. *The New York Times,* January 17, 1967.
6. Cited by Ralph Nader in "Business Crime," *The New Republic,* July 1, 1967, p. 7.

Does It Pay to Bluff in Business?

Norman E. Bowie

I

Albert Carr has argued in an influential article[1] that the ethics of business is best understood on the model of the ethics of poker.

> Poker's own brand of ethics is different from the ethical ideals of civilized human relationships. The game calls for distrust of the other fellow. It ignores the claim of friendship. Cunning deception and concealment of one's strength and intentions, not kindness and openheartedness, are vital in poker.
>
> Most executives from time to time are almost compelled in the interests of their companies or themselves to practice some form of deception when negotiating with customers, dealers, labor unions, government officials, or even the departments of their companies. By conscious misstatements, concealment of pertinent facts, or exaggeration—in short, by bluffing—they seek to persuade others to agree with them.... A good part of the time the businessman is trying to do unto others as he hopes others will not do unto him.... A man who intends to be a winner in the business game must have a game player's attitude.

Although Carr's attitude is widely held, I think Carr's argument can be refuted. I begin with an appeal to Kant's ethics in order to show that unless business adheres to a minimum standard of justice, business practice would be impossible. In particular I will show that such practices as lying, cheating, and bribery are immoral and that business practice presupposes that such practices are immoral. I then consider a Carr-like two pronged rebuttal of the Kantian analysis—specifically that as a matter of fact business practice succeeds quite well with a certain amount of lying and cheating and that whatever the case against outright lying and cheating, in some institutions a certain amount of deception and nondisclosure of information might be morally permissible. In responding to this rebuttal, I appeal to utilitarian considerations to show that when Carr's poker model is adopted, bad consequences result. Deception and the nondisclosure of information are usually counterproductive in terms of long-term profit.

The first step of my argument is based on the moral philosophy of Immanuel Kant, particularly on Kant's first formulation of the categorical imperative.[2] Kant argues that a requirement of morality is consistency in action. Suppose that someone were to advocate discriminatory policies against Jews. To be consistent, that person would have to advocate discrimination even if he himself should turn out to be a Jew. Presumably, he would not be willing to be treated discriminatorily, and hence consistency in action requires that he not treat Jews in a discriminatory way. Morality is not simply a matter of treating others as you would like them to treat you. It is also a matter of not treating others in ways that you would not accept if you were they. Kant's point is that morality requires consistency of action and judgment when you are on both the receiving and the giving ends. Morality requires that you not make an exception of yourself, that you not engage in practices or follow rules that you could not recommend to everyone.

But suppose one were to reply to Kant as follows: "I don't care if other people try to

Used by permission of the author.

take advantage of the rules by making exceptions of themselves. If they can get away with it, more power to them." In the business context, such a person would be willing to participate in a business environment in which deception is expected. This is precisely the position of Carr. In situations like this, the Golden Rule fails us. The answer it gives depends on how the person contemplating a given action wants to be treated himself or herself. Suppose the way in which one wants to be treated is immoral in itself—suppose one doesn't care if others try to deceive him or her. Such a business person could be consistent in action and still behave unjustly. How could Kant reply?

Kant has a ready answer. Some contemplated actions would be self-defeating if they were universalized. Kant's categorical imperative strengthens the Golden Rule so that the person who is willing to allow others to behave unjustly is defeated. Kant's categorical imperative says, "I ought never to act except in such a way that I can also will that my maxim should become a universal law." To use one of Kant's examples, consider whether or not a businessperson should tell a lie. If the businessperson were to make the principle of her action a universal law, namely "lying is permissible," the act of lying would be self-defeating. For if lying were universally permitted, people would never know whether an assertion was true or false, and hence both the purpose of telling the truth and of lying would be defeated. Lying is possible only when it is not made universal.

Kant's point can apply specifically to business. There are many ways of making a promise. One of the more formal ways is by a contract. A contract is an agreement between two or more parties, usually enforceable by law, for the doing or not doing of some definite thing. The contract device is extremely useful in business. The hiring of employees, the use of credit, the ordering and supplying of goods, and the notion of warranty, to name but a few, all make use of the contract device. Indeed, the contract is

such an important part of business operation that it is often overlooked. This is a serious blunder. I maintain that, if contract breaking were universalized, then business practice would be impossible. If a participant in business were to universally advocate violating contracts, such advocacy would be self-defeating, just as the universal advocacy of lying and cheating were seen to be self-defeating.

But Carr could correctly point out that he never advocated the breaking of contracts. He simply advocates the nondisclosure of information, bluffing, and the calculated use of exaggeration. Does this narrow interpretation of Carr's thesis enable him to escape Kant's trap? Perhaps not.

Let us take a simple business transaction and move on to more complicated ones. In almost every case of a cash-for-product transaction, either the purchaser receives the good before paying or the purchaser pays before receiving the good. Seldom is the transfer simultaneous. What would happen to business if, in an attempt to receive something for nothing, it was common practice for the purchaser to claim that he or she had paid when he or she had not, in other words, to bluff. Or suppose the salesperson bluffed by claiming that the customer had not paid when he or she had paid. If such behavior were universalized, ordinary commerce would become self-defeating. The modern grocery or department store could not exist if such bluffing were universalized, and hence the bluffers have nothing to gain if bluffing is universally advocated.

Kant's argument is meant to show that rational agents cannot will that certain maxims be universally acted upon. If the principles were universally adopted, the behavior described by the principles would be self-defeating. The maxim, "It's morally permissible to lie" is a perfect example of just such a principle.

But does Kant's argument really apply in the bluffing example? There is nothing self-defeating about a world with no grocery stores or supermarkets. However, the observation misses Kant's larger point. A Kantian could argue that the acceptance of any practice requires acceptance of the rules that constitute the practice. To accept the practice without accepting the rules that underlie it is self-defeating. If you break the rules, consistency requires that you permit others to break the rules, and such universal rule breaking would undermine the practice. One purpose of the preceding discussion was to show how lying and bluffing undercut business practice. Since such actions cannot be universalized from the Kantian perspective, lying and bluffing by business persons is immoral.

II

Does this Kantian argument refute Carr's analysis? Many philosophers would think not. First, one does not need extensive experience in business to know that there are many types of deception, like bluffing, that are both widely practiced and widely accepted. A few examples suffice. It is common knowledge that automobile dealers do not expect people to pay the sticker price for automobiles. A certain amount of bargaining is taken for granted. The same is true for real estate prices. Unless a seller's market is in effect, the asking price for a house is seldom the selling price. At the initial bargaining session, labor leaders overstate wage demands, and management also understates the wage increases it is willing to grant. In all these instances, the final price or wage contract is arrived at through a process that does resemble the poker game Carr uses as an analogy. The price or wage contract does depend in part on the strength of one's hand and on one's bluffing ability. In the late 1970s, one did need to pay the sticker price for small foreign cars with good gas mileage.

Surely automobile dealers and sellers of homes cannot be accused of immoral behavior when they post prices above those that they are willing to accept. Surely the labor leader is not behaving immorally when he

overstates the wage increases his union expects to receive.

The point that Carr and his defenders is making is simply this: In the real world of everyday business practice, there is a great amount of bluffing, exaggeration and manipulation. Since everyone knows that such bluffing, and the like take place, business does quite well—the logic of Kant not withstanding. There is no danger of a collapse—either of credit or of capitalism as a whole. Practical experience confounds the philosopher's theory. The ethics of poker is still the appropriate model for business ethics.

Second, so long as Carr's argument is limited to the nondisclosure of information, bluffing, and the calculated use of exaggeration, Carr can escape the Kantian trap after all. Carr might concede that once one has agreed not to bluff, then it would be wrong to do so. However, Carr could maintain that his recommendations apply to the practice itself. In other words, he is making a recommendation regarding business practices. If bluffing and the like are accepted as a part of business practice, then there is nothing wrong with bluffing in business situations. Indeed it is because bluffing and exaggeration are accepted as part of the game that the examples Carr cites are not viewed as threatening to business practice.

III

What response can be made to Carr and his defenders? First Kant has set some limits. If lying or cheating were universalized, they surely would be self-defeating. The fact that some lying and cheating occur is quite beside the point. Kant is not claiming that people never lie; rather he is providing reasons why they shouldn't. Indeed nothing Carr has said counts against either Kant's point or Kant's argument. After all, even Carr admits that cheating in poker is not permitted. Where Carr disagrees with a Kantian is that if bluffing and the like were universally practiced in business, it would be self-defeating.

Perhaps utilitarianism can be of some assistance here. The task is to compare Carr's recommendation that business practice permit widespread bluffing, exaggeration, and the nondisclosure of information with an alternative conception of business that seeks to eliminate or sharply circumscribe such activities. Which conception of business practice would produce the greatest good for society? For business itself? Perhaps a more utilitarian perspective might break the impasse.

Wouldn't it be in the best interest of business to adopt the poker model of business ethics? I think not. Let us consider labor relations, where Carr's poker model is implicitly if not explicitly adopted. In collective bargaining the relationship between the employer and the employee is adversarial. Collective bargaining is competitive through and through. The task of the union is to secure as much in pay and benefits as possible. The task of the employer's negotiators is to keep the pay and benefits as low as possible.

In the resulting give-and-take, bluffing and deception are the rule. Management expects the union to demand a percentage pay increase it knows it won't get. The union expects the company to say that such a pay increase will force it to shut down the plant and move to another state. Such demands are never taken at face value although they are taken more seriously on the ninetieth day of negotiations than they are on the first day.

Recently the conventional view of collective bargaining practice has been under attack. One of the most prominent criticisms of current practice is its economic inefficiency. The adversarial relationship at the bargaining table carries over to the workplace. As a result of the hostility between employee and employer, productivity suffers and many American products are at a competitive disadvantage with respect to foreign products. Japanese labor-management relations are not so adversarial and this fact accounts for part of their success. This particular criticism of collective bargaining has received much attention in the press and in popular business magazines. The most recent manifestation of the recognition of the force of this criticism is the host of decisions General Motors has made to ensure that labor relations are different at its new assembly plant for the Saturn.

Second, the practice of bluffing and deception tends to undermine trust. As some American firms lost ground to foreign competition, the management of many of the firms asked for pay reductions, commonly called "give backs." Other managers in firms not threatened by foreign competition cited the "dangers" of foreign competition to request pay cuts for their employees—even though they were not needed. Use of this tactic will only cause future problems when and if the competitive threat really develops. This utilitarian point was not lost on participants in a labor-management relations seminar I attended.

Participant I: In the past, there was a relationship of mutual distrust.
Participant II: These are the dangers in crying "wolf." When the company is really in trouble, no one will believe them.
Participant III: To make labor/management participation teams work, you need to generate mutual trust. It only takes one bad deal to undermine trust.

These individuals are indicating that the practices of bluffing and deception have bad consequences in employer/employee relationships. These unfortunate consequences have been well documented by philosophers—most recently by Sissela Bok. Bok's critique of "white lies" and the use of placebos applies equally well to deception in the collective bargaining process.

Triviality surely does set limits to when moral inquiry is reasonable. But when we look more closely at practices such as placebo-giving, it becomes clear that all lies defended as "white" cannot be so easily dismissed. In the first place, the harmlessness of lies is notoriously disputable. What the liar perceives as harmless or even beneficial may not be so in the eyes of the deceived. Second, the failure to look at an entire practice rather than at their own isolated case often blinds liars to cumulative harm and expanding deceptive activities. Those who begin with white lies can come to resort to more frequent and more serious ones. Where some tell a few white lies, others may tell more. Because lines are so hard to draw, the indiscriminate use of such lies can lead to other deceptive practices. The aggregate harm from a large number of marginally harmful instances may, therefore, be highly undesirable in the end—for liars, those deceived, and honesty and trust more generally.[3]

However, there is more at stake here than the bad consequences of lying. Bluffing, exaggeration, and the nondisclosure of information also undermine a spirit of cooperation that is essential to business success. The poker model, with its permitted bluffing and the like, is a competitive model. What the model overlooks is the fact that the production of a good or service in any given plant or office is a cooperative enterprise. Chrysler competes with General Motors and Toyota but the production of Chrysler K cars in that assembly plant in Newark, Delaware, is a cooperative enterprise. Lack of cooperation results in poor quality vehicles.

Hence the competitive model of collective bargaining sets wages and working conditions for what at the local level is a cooperative enterprise. Labor-management negotiators forget the obvious truth that the production of goods and services cannot succeed on a purely competitive basis. There have to be some elements of cooperation somewhere in the system. Why shouldn't the collective bargaining process use cooperative rather than competitive techniques?

When bargaining is conducted industry-wide, as it is with automobiles, the competitive mode seems natural. Auto production is a competitive industry. But just because Chrysler is competitive with General Motors, why must Chrysler management be in a competitive relationship with its own employees? Indeed, couldn't it be argued that the fact that Chrysler's management does see itself in competition with its unionized employees undercuts its competitive position vis-à-vis other automobile producers? To use the language of competition, if Chrysler is at war with itself, how can it win the war against others?

As long as collective bargaining is essentially adversarial and characterized by bluffing and exaggeration on both sides, the cooperative aspect of business will be underemphasized. The costs of ignoring the cooperative aspect are great—both for society and for business itself.

Hence this distrust that so concerned the participants in the seminar is only in part a function of the deceit and bluffing that go on in collective bargaining. It is in large part a function of using the wrong model. We shouldn't look at collective bargaining as a game of poker.

With this discussion of collective bargaining as instance, let us evaluate Carr's proposal on utilitarian grounds. Should the stockholders applaud a chief executive officer whose operating procedure is analogous to the operating procedure of a poker player? In Carr's view, "A good part of the time the businessman is trying to do unto others as he hopes others will not do unto him." But surely such a practice is very risky. The danger of discovery is great, and our experience of the past several years indicates that many corporations that have played the game of business like the game of poker have suffered badly. Moreover, if business practice consisted essentially of these conscious misstatements, exaggerations, and the concealment of pertinent facts, it seems clear that business practice would be inherently unstable. Contemporary business practice presupposes such stability, and business can only be stable if the chief executive officer has a set of moral standards higher than those that govern the game of poker. The growth of the large firm, the complexity of business decisions, the need for planning and stability, and the undesirable effects of puffery, exaggeration, and deception all count against Carr's view that the ethics of business should be the ethics of a poker game.

NOTES

1. Albert Z. Carr, "Is Business Bluffing Ethical?" *Harvard Business Review,* 46 (January–February 1968): 143–153.
2. For a review of the essentials of Kant's moral philosophy see Chapter One.
3. Sissela Bok, *Lying: Moral Choice in Public and Private Life* (New York: Pantheon Books, 1978), pp. 19, 31.

A Moral Evaluation of Sales Practices

David M. Holley

A relatively neglected area in recent literature on business ethics is the ethics of sales practices. Discussions of the moral dimensions of marketing have tended to concentrate almost exclusively on obligations of advertisers or on the moral acceptability of the advertising system. By contrast, little attention has been given to the activities of individual salespersons.[1]

This neglect is surprising on several counts. First, efforts to sell a product occupy a good deal of the time of many people in business. Developing an advertising campaign may be a more glamorous kind of activity, but it is sales on the individual level that provides the revenue, and for most businesses the number of persons devoted to selling will far exceed the number devoted to advertising. Second, the activity of selling something is of intrinsic philosophical significance. It furnishes a paradigm case of persuasive communication, raising such

issues as deception, individual autonomy, and the social value of a marketing-oriented system for distributing goods and services. While the practice of advertising raises these same issues, the potential for manipulation of vulnerable consumers comes into much sharper focus at the level of individual sales.

In this paper I will attempt to develop a framework for evaluating the morality of various sales practices. Although I recognize that much of the salesforce in companies is occupied exclusively or primarily with sales to other businesses, my discussion will focus on sales to the individual consumer. Most of what I say should apply to any type of sales activity, but the moral issues arise most clearly in cases in which a consumer may or may not be very sophisticated in evaluating and responding to a sales presentation.

My approach will be to consider first the context of sales activities, a market system of production and distribution. Since such a

Used by permission of the author.

system is generally justified on teleological grounds, I describe several conditions for its successful achievement of key goals. Immoral sales practices are analyzed as attempts to undermine these conditions.

I

The primary justification for a market system is that it provides an efficient procedure for meeting people's needs and desires for goods and services.[2] This appeal to economic benefits can be elaborated in great detail, but at root it involves the claim that people will efficiently serve each other's needs if they are allowed to engage in voluntary exchanges.

A crucial feature of this argument is the condition that the exchange be voluntary. Assuming that individuals know best how to benefit themselves and that they will act to achieve such benefits, voluntary exchange can be expected to serve both parties. On the other hand, if the exchanges are not made voluntarily, we have no basis for expecting mutually beneficial results. To the extent that mutual benefit does not occur, the system will lack efficiency as a means for the satisfaction of needs and desires. Hence, this justification presupposes that conditions necessary for the occurrence of voluntary exchange are ordinarily met.

What are these conditions? For simplicity's sake, let us deal only with the kind of exchange involving a payment of money for some product or service. We can call the person providing the product the *seller* and the person making the monetary payment the *buyer*. I suggest that voluntary exchange occurs only if the following conditions are met:

1. Both buyer and seller understand what they are giving up and what they are receiving in return.
2. Neither buyer nor seller is compelled to enter into the exchange as a result of coercion, severely restricted alternatives, or other constraints on the ability to choose.

3. Both buyer and seller are able at the time of the exchange to make rational judgments about its costs and benefits.

I will refer to these three conditions as the knowledge, noncompulsion, and rationality conditions, respectively.[3] If the parties are uninformed, it is possible that an exchange might accidentally turn out to benefit them. But given the lack of information, they would not be in a position to make a rational judgment about their benefit, and we cannot reasonably expect beneficial results as a matter of course in such circumstances. Similarly, if the exchange is made under compulsion, then the judgment of personal benefit is not the basis of the exchange. It is possible for someone to be forced or manipulated into an arrangement that is in fact beneficial. But there is little reason to think that typical or likely.[4]

It should be clear that all three conditions are subject to degrees of fulfillment. For example, the parties may understand certain things about the exchange but not others. Let us posit a theoretical situation in which both parties are fully informed, fully rational, and enter into the exchange entirely of their own volition. I will call this an *ideal exchange*. In actual practice there is virtually always some divergence from the ideal. Knowledge can be more or less adequate. Individuals can be subject to various irrational influences. There can be borderline cases of external constraints. Nevertheless, we can often judge when a particular exchange was adequately informed, rational, and free from compulsion. Even when conditions are not ideal, we may still have an *acceptable exchange*.

With these concepts in mind, let us consider the obligations of sales personnel. I suggest that the primary duty of salespeople to customers is to avoid undermining the conditions of acceptable exchange. It is possible by act or omission to create a situation in which the customer is not sufficiently knowledgeable about what the exchange involves. It is also possible to influence the customer in ways that short-circuit the rational decision-making process. To behave in such ways is to undermine the conditions that are presupposed in teleological justifications of the market system. Of course, an isolated act is not sufficient to destroy the benefits of the system. But the moral acceptability of the system may become questionable if the conditions of acceptable exchange are widely abused. The individual who attempts to gain personally by undermining these conditions does that which, if commonly practiced, would produce a very different system from the one that supposedly provides moral legitimacy to that individual's activities.

II

If a mutually beneficial exchange is to be expected, the parties involved must be adequately informed about what they are giving up and what they are receiving. In most cases this should create no great problem for the seller[5], but what about the buyer? How is she to obtain the information needed? One answer is that the buyer is responsible for doing whatever investigation is necessary to acquire the information. The medieval principle of *caveat emptor* encouraged buyers to take responsibility for examining a purchase thoroughly to determine whether it had any hidden flaws. If the buyer failed to find defects, that meant that due caution had not been exercised.

If it were always relatively easy to discover defects by examination, then this principle might be an efficient method of guaranteeing mutual satisfaction. Sometimes, however, even lengthy investigation would not disclose what the buyer wants to know. With products of great complexity, the expertise needed for an adequate examination may be beyond what could reasonably be expected of most consumers. Even relatively simple products can have hidden flaws that most people would not discover until after the purchase, and to have the responsibility for closely examining every purchase would in-

volve a considerable amount of a highly treasured modern commodity, the buyer's time. Furthermore, many exchange situations in our context involve products that cannot be examined in this way—goods that will be delivered at a later time or sent through the mail, for example. Finally, even if we assume that most buyers, by exercising enough caution, can protect their interests, the system of *caveat emptor* would take advantage of those least able to watch out for themselves. It would in effect justify mistreatment of a few for a rather questionable benefit.

In practice the buyer almost always relies on the seller for some information, and if mutually beneficial exchanges are to be expected, the information needs to meet certain standards of both quality and quantity. With regard to quality, the information provided should not be deceptive. This would include not only direct lies but also truths that are intended to mislead the buyer. Consider the following examples:

1. An aluminum siding salesperson tells customers that they will receive "bargain factory prices" for letting their homes be used as models in a new advertising campaign. Prospective customers will be brought to view the houses, and a commission of $100 will be paid for each sale that results. In fact, the price paid is well above market rates, the workmanship and materials are substandard, and no one is ever brought by to see the houses.[6]
2. A used car salesperson turns back the odometer reading on automobiles by an average of 25,000 to 30,000 miles per car. If customers ask whether the reading is correct, the salesperson replies that it is illegal to alter odometer readings.
3. A salesperson at a piano store tells an interested customer that the "special sale" will be good only through that evening. She neglects to mention that another "special sale" will begin the next day.
4. A telephone salesperson tells people who answer the phone that they have been selected to receive a free gift, a brand new freezer. All they have to do is buy a year's subscription to a food plan.

5. A salesperson for a diet system proclaims that under this revolutionary new plan the pounds will melt right off. The system is described as a scientific advance that makes dieting easy. In fact, the system is a low-calorie diet composed of foods and liquids that are packaged under the company name but are no different from standard grocery store items.

The possibilities are endless, and whether or not a lie is involved, each case illustrates a salesperson's attempt to get a customer to believe something that is false in order to make the sale. It might be pointed out that these kinds of practices would not deceive a sophisticated consumer. Perhaps so, but whether they are always successful deceptions is not the issue. They are attempts to mislead the customer, and given that the consumer must often rely on information furnished by the salesperson, they are attempts to subvert the conditions under which mutually beneficial exchange can be expected. The salesperson attempts to use misinformation as a basis for customer judgment rather than allowing that judgment to be based on accurate beliefs. Furthermore, if these kinds of practices were not successful fairly often, they would probably not be used.

In the aluminum siding case, the customer is led to believe that there will be a discount in exchange for a kind of service, allowing the house to be viewed by prospective customers. This leaves the impression both that the job done will be of high quality and that the price paid will be offset by commissions. The car salesperson alters the product in order to suggest false information about the extent of its use. With such information, the customer is not able to judge accurately the value of the car. The misleading reply to inquiries is not substantially different from a direct lie. The piano salesperson deceives the customer about how long the product will be obtainable at a discount price. In this case the deception occurs through an omission. The telephone solicitor tries to give the impression that there has been a contest of some sort and

that the freezer is a prize. In this way, the nature of the exchange is obscured.

The diet-system case raises questions about how to distinguish legitimate "puffery" from deception. Obviously, the matter will depend to some extent on how gullible we conceive the customer to be. As described, the case surely involves an attempt to get the customer to believe that dieting will be easier under this system and that what is being promoted is the result of some new scientific discovery. If there were no prospect that a customer would be likely to believe this, we would probably not think the technique deceptive. But in fact a number of individuals are deceived by claims of this type.

Some writers have defended the use of deceptive practices in business contexts on the grounds that there are specific rules applying to these contexts that differ from the standards appropriate in other contexts. It is argued, for example, that deception is standard practice, understood by all participants as something to be expected and, therefore, harmless, or that it is a means of self-defense justified by pressures of the competitive context.[7] To the extent that claims about widespread practice are true, people who know what is going on may be able to minimize personal losses, but that is hardly a justification of the practice. If I know that many people have installed devices in their cars that can come out and puncture the tires of the car next to them, that may help keep me from falling victim, but it does not make the practice harmless. Even if no one is victimized, it becomes necessary to take extra precautions, introducing a significant disutility into driving conditions. Analogously, widespread deception in business debases the currency of language, making business communication less efficient and more cumbersome.

More importantly, however, people are victimized by deceptive practices, and the fact that some may be shrewd enough to see through clouds of misinformation does not alter the deceptive intent. Whatever may be said with regard to appropriate behavior among people who "know the rules," it is clear that many buyers are not aware of having entered into some special domain where deception is allowed. Even if this is naive, it does not provide a moral justification for subverting those individuals' capacity for making a reasoned choice.

Only a few people would defend the moral justifiability of deceptive sales practices. However, there may be room for much more disagreement with regard to how much information a salesperson is obligated to provide. In rejecting the principle of *caveat emptor*, I have suggested that there are pragmatic reasons for expecting the seller to communicate some information about the product. But how much? When is it morally culpable to withhold information? Consider the following cases:

1. An automobile dealer has bought a number of cars from another state. Although they appear to be new or slightly used, these cars have been involved in a major flood and were sold by the previous dealer at a discount rate. The salesperson knows the history of the cars and does not mention it to customers.
2. A salesperson for an encyclopedia company never mentions the total price of a set unless he has to. Instead he emphasizes the low monthly payment involved.
3. A real estate agent knows that one reason the couple selling a house with her company want to move is that the neighbors often have loud parties and neighborhood children have committed minor acts of vandalism. The agent makes no mention of this to prospective customers.
4. An admissions officer for a private college speaks enthusiastically about the advantages of the school. He does not mention the fact that the school is not accredited.
5. A prospective retirement home resident is under the impression that a particular retirement home is affiliated with a certain church. He makes it known that this is one of the features he finds attractive about the home. Though the belief is false, the recruiters for the home make no attempt to correct the misunderstanding.

In all these cases the prospective buyer lacks some piece of knowledge that might be relevant to the decision to buy. The conditions for ideal exchange are not met. Perhaps, however, there can be an acceptable exchange. Whether or not this is the case depends on whether the buyer has adequate information to decide if the purchase would be beneficial. In the case of the flood-damaged autos, there is information relevant to evaluating the worth of the car that the customer could not be expected to know unless informed by the seller. If this information is not revealed, the buyer will not have adequate knowledge to make a reasonable judgment. Determining exactly how much information needs to be provided is not always clear-cut. We must in general rely on our assessments of what a reasonable person would want to know. As a practical guide, a salesperson might consider, "What would I want to know if I were considering buying this product?"

Surely a reasonable person would want to know the total price of a product. Hence the encyclopedia salesperson who omits this total is not providing adequate information. The salesperson may object that this information could be inferred from other information about the monthly payment, length of term, and interest rate. But if the intention is not to have the customer act without knowing the full price, then why shouldn't it be provided directly? The admissions officer's failure to mention that the school is unaccredited also seems unacceptable when we consider what a reasonable person would want to know. There are some people who would consider this a plus, since they are suspicious about accrediting agencies imposing some alien standards (e.g., standards that conflict with religious views). But regardless of how one evaluates the fact, most people would judge it to be important for making a decision.

The real estate case is more puzzling. Most real estate agents would not reveal the kind of information described, and would not feel they had violated any moral duties in failing to do so. Clearly, many prospective customers would want to be informed about such problems. However, in most cases failing to know these facts would not be of crucial importance. We have a case of borderline information. It would be known by all parties to an ideal exchange, but we can have an acceptable exchange even if the buyer is unaware of it. Failure to inform the customer of these facts is not like failing to inform the customer that the house is on the sight of a hazardous waste dump or that a major freeway will soon be adjacent to the property.

It is possible to alter the case in such a way that the information should be revealed or at least the buyer should be directed another way. Suppose the buyer makes it clear that his primary goal is to live in a quiet neighborhood where he will be undisturbed. The "borderline" information now becomes more central to the customer's decision. Notice that thinking in these terms moves us away from the general standard of what a reasonable person would want to know to the more specific standard of what is relevant given the criteria of this individual. In most cases, however, I think that a salesperson would be justified in operating under general "reasonable person" standards until particular deviations become apparent.[8]

The case of the prospective retirement home resident is a good example of how the particular criteria of the customer might assume great importance. If the recruiters, knowing what they know about this man's religious preferences, allow him to make his decision on the basis of a false assumption, they will have failed to support the conditions of acceptable exchange. It doesn't really matter that the misunderstanding was not caused by the salespeople. Their allowing it to be part of the basis for a decision borders on deception. If the misunderstanding was not on a matter of central importance to the individual's evaluation, they might have had no obligation to correct it. But the case described is not of that sort.

Besides providing nondeceptive and relatively complete information, salespeople may be obligated to make sure that their communications are understandable. Sales presentations containing technical information that is likely to be misunderstood are morally questionable. However, it would be unrealistic to expect all presentations to be immune to misunderstanding. The salesperson is probably justified in developing presentations that would be intelligible to the average consumer of the product he or she is selling and making adjustments in cases where it is clear that misunderstanding has occurred.

III

The condition of uncompelled exchange distinguishes business dealings from other kinds of exchanges. In the standard business arrangement, neither party is forced to enter the negotiations. A threat of harm would transform the situation to something other than a purely business arrangement. Coercion is not the only kind of compulsion, however. Suppose I have access to only one producer of food. I arrange to buy food from this producer, but given my great need for food and the absence of alternatives, the seller is able to dictate the terms. In one sense I choose to make the deal, but the voluntariness of my choice is limited by the absence of alternatives.

Ordinarily, the individual salesperson will not have the power to take away the buyer's alternatives. However, a clever salesperson can sometimes make it seem as if options are very limited and can use the customer's ignorance to produce the same effect. For example, imagine an individual who begins to look for a particular item at a local store. The salesperson extolls the line carried by his store, warns of the deficiencies of alternative brands, and warns about the dishonesty of competitors, in contrast to his store's reliability. With a convincing presentation, a customer might easily perceive the options to be very limited. Whether or not the technique is questionable may depend on the accuracy of the perception. If the salesperson is attempting to take away a legitimate alternative, that is an attempt to undermine the customer's voluntary choice.

Another way the condition of uncompelled choice might be subverted is by involving a customer in a purchase without allowing her to notice what is happening. This would include opening techniques that disguise the purpose of the encounter so there can be no immediate refusal. The customer is led to believe that the interview is about a contest or a survey or an opportunity to make money. Not until the end does it become apparent that this is an attempt to sell something, and occasionally if the presentation is smooth enough, some buyers can be virtually unaware that they have bought anything. Obviously, there can be degrees of revelation, and not every approach that involves initial disguise of certain elements that might provoke an immediate rejection is morally questionable. But there are enough clear cases in which the intention is to get around, as much as possible, the voluntary choice of the customer. Consider the following examples:

1. A seller of children's books gains entrance to houses by claiming to be conducting an educational survey. He does indeed ask several "survey" questions, but he uses these to qualify potential customers for his product.
2. A salesperson alludes to recent accidents involving explosions of furnaces and, leaving the impression of having some official government status, offers to do a free safety inspection. She almost always discovers a "major problem" and offers to sell a replacement furnace.
3. A man receives a number of unsolicited books and magazines through the mail. Then he is sent a bill and later letters warning of damage to his credit rating if he does not pay.

These are examples of the many variations on attempts to involve customers in exchanges without letting them know what is happening. The first two cases involve deceptions about the purpose of the encounter. Though they resemble cases discussed earlier that involved deception about the nature or price of a product, here the salesperson uses misinformation as a means of limiting the customer's range of choice. The customer does not consciously choose to listen to a sales presentation but finds that this is what is happening. Some psychological research suggests that when people do something that appears to commit them to a course of action, even without consciously choosing to do so, they will tend to act as if such a choice had been made in order to minimize cognitive dissonance. Hence, if a salesperson successfully involves the customer in considering a purchase, the customer may feel committed to give serious thought to the matter. The third case is an attempt to get the customer to believe that an obligation has been incurred. In variations on this technique, merchandise is mailed to a deceased person to make relatives believe that some payment is owed. In each case, an effort is made to force the consumer to choose from an excessively limited range of options.

IV

How can a salesperson subvert the rationality condition? Perhaps the most common way is to appeal to emotional reactions that cloud an individual's perception of relevant considerations. Consider the following cases:

1. A man's wife has recently died in a tragic accident. The funeral director plays upon the husband's love for his wife and to some extent his guilt about her death to get him to purchase a very expensive funeral.
2. A socially insecure young woman has bought a series of dance lessons from a local studio. During the lessons, an attractive male instructor constantly compliments her on her poise and natural ability and tries to persuade her to sign up for more lessons.[9]

3. A life insurance salesperson emphasizes to a prospect the importance of providing for his family in the event of his death. The salesperson tells several stories about people who put off this kind of preparation.
4. A dress salesperson typically tells customers how fashionable they look in a certain dress. Her stock comments also include pointing out that a dress is slimming or sexy or "looks great on you."
5. A furniture salesperson regularly tells customers that a piece of furniture is the last one in stock and that another customer recently showed great interest in it. He sometimes adds that it may not be possible to get any more like it from the factory.

These cases remind us that emotions can be important motivators. It is not surprising that salespeople appeal to them in attempting to get the customer to make a purchase. In certain cases the appeal seems perfectly legitimate. When the life insurance salesperson tries to arouse the customer's fear and urges preparation, it may be a legitimate way to get the customer to consider something that is worth considering. Of course, the fact that the fear is aroused by one who sells life insurance may obscure to the customer the range of alternative possibilities in preparing financially for the future. But the fact that an emotion is aroused need not make the appeal morally objectionable.

If the appeal of the dress salesperson seems more questionable, this is probably because we are not as convinced of the objective importance of appearing fashionable, or perhaps because repeated observations of this kind are often insincere. But if we assume that the salesperson is giving an honest opinion about how the dress looks on a customer, it may provide some input for the individual who has a desire to achieve a particular effect. The fact that such remarks appeal to one's vanity or ambition does not in itself make the appeal unacceptable.

The furniture salesperson's warnings are clearly calculated to create some anxiety about the prospect of losing the chance to buy a particular item unless immediate action is taken. If the warnings are factually based, they would not be irrelevant to the decision to buy. Clearly, one might act impulsively or hastily when under the spell of such thoughts, but the salesperson cannot be faulted for pointing out relevant considerations.

The case of the funeral director is somewhat different. Here there is a real question of what benefit is to be gained by choosing a more expensive funeral package. For most people, minimizing what is spent on the funeral would be a rational choice, but at a time of emotional vulnerability it can be made to look as if this means depriving the loved one or the family of some great benefit. Even if the funeral director makes nothing but true statements, they can be put into a form designed to arouse emotions that will lessen the possibility of a rational decision being reached.

The dance studio case is similar in that a weakness is being played upon. The woman's insecurity makes her vulnerable to flattery and attention, and this creates the kind of situation in which others can take advantage of her. Perhaps the dance lessons fulfill some need, but the appeal to her vanity easily becomes a tool to manipulate her into doing what the instructor wants.

The key to distinguishing between legitimate and illegitimate emotional appeals lies in whether the appeal clouds one's ability to make a decision based on genuine satisfaction of needs and desires. Our judgment about whether this happens in a particular case will depend in part on whether we think the purchase likely to benefit the customer. The more questionable the benefits, the more an emotional appeal looks like manipulation rather than persuasion. When questionable benefits are combined with some special vulnerability on the part of the consumer, the use of the emotional appeal appears even more suspect.

In considering benefits, we should not forget to consider costs as well. Whether a purchase is beneficial may depend on its effects on the family budget. Ordinarily it is not the responsibility of a salesperson to inquire into such matters, but if it becomes clear that financial resources are limited, the use of emotional appeals to get the customer to buy more than she can afford becomes morally questionable. Occasionally we hear about extreme cases in which a salesperson finds out the amount of life insurance received by a widow and talks her into an unnecessary purchase for that amount, or in which the salesperson persuades some poor family to make an unwise purchase on credit requiring them to cut back on necessities. The salesperson is not responsible for making a rational calculation for the customer, but when a salesperson knowingly urges an action that is not beneficial to the consumer, that is in effect trying to get the consumer to make an irrational judgment. Any techniques used to achieve this end would be attempts to subvert the conditions of mutually beneficial exchange.

For obvious reasons, salespeople want as many customers as possible to make purchases, and therefore they try to put the decision to purchase in the best possible light. It is not the job of a salesperson to present all the facts as objectively as possible. But if playing on a customer's emotions is calculated to obscure the customer's ability to make rational judgments about whether a purchase is in her best interest, then it is morally objectionable.

V

I have attempted to provide a framework for evaluating the morality of a number of different types of sales practices. The framework is based on conditions for mutually beneficial exchange and ultimately for an efficient satisfaction of economic needs and desires. An inevitable question is whether this kind of evaluation is of any practical importance.

If we set before ourselves the ideal of a knowledgeable, unforced, and rational decision on the part of a customer, it is not diffi-

cult to see how some types of practices would interfere with this process. We must, of course, be careful not to set the standards too high. A customer may be partially but adequately informed to judge a purchase's potential benefits. A decision may be affected by nonrational and even irrational factors and yet still be rational enough in terms of being plausibly related to the individual's desires and needs. There may be borderline cases in which it is not clear whether acting in a particular way would be morally required or simply overscrupulous, but that is not an objection to this approach, only a recognition of a feature of morality itself.[10]

NOTES

1. In a survey of the major textbooks in the field of business ethics, I discovered only one with a chapter on sales practices: David Braybrooke's *Ethics in the World of Business,* Chapter 4 (Totowa, N.J.: Rowman and Allanheld, 1983). That chapter contains only a brief discussion of the issue; most of the chapter is devoted to excerpts from court cases and the quotation of a code of ethics for a direct-mail marketing association.

2. The classic statement of the argument from economic benefits is found in Adam Smith, *The Wealth of Nations* (1776) (London: Methusen and Co. Ltd., 1930). Modern proponents of this argument include Ludwig von Mises, Friedrich von Hayek, and Milton Friedman.

3. One very clear analysis of voluntariness making use of these conditions may be found in John Hospers' *Human Conduct: Problems of Ethics,* 2nd ed. (New York: Harcourt Brace Jovanovich, 1982), pp. 385–388.

4. I will refer to the three conditions indifferently as conditions for voluntary exchange or conditions for mutually beneficial exchange. By the latter designation I do not mean to suggest that they are either necessary or sufficient conditions for the occurrence of mutual benefit, but that they are conditions for the reasonable expectation of mutual benefit.

5. There are cases, however, in which the buyer knows more about a product than the seller. For example, suppose Cornell has found out

that land Fredonia owns contains minerals that make it twice as valuable as Fredonia thinks. The symmetry of my conditions would lead me to conclude that Cornell should give Fredonia the relevant information unless perhaps Fredonia's failure to know was the result of some culpable negligence.

6. This case is described in Warren Magnuson and Jean Carper, *The Dark Side of the Market-Place* (Englewood Cliffs, N.J.: Prentice Hall, 1968), pp. 3–4.

7. Albert Carr, "Is Business Bluffing Ethical?" *Harvard Business Review* 46 (January–February 1968): 143–153. See also Thomas L. Carson,. Richard E. Wokutch, and Kent F. Murrmann, "Bluffing in Labor Negotiations: Legal and Ethical Issues," *Journal of Business Ethics* 1 (1982): 13–22.

8. My reference to a reasonable person standard should not be confused with the issue facing the FTC of whether to evaluate advertising by the reasonable consumer or ignorant consumer standard as described in Ivan Preston, "Reasonable Consumer or Ignorant Consumer: How the FTC Decides," *Journal of Consumer Affairs* 8 (Winter 1974): 131–143. [reprinted in this volume, pp.

431–437]. There the primary issue is with regard to whom the government should protect from claims that might be misunderstood. My concern here is with determining what amount of information is necessary for informed judgment. In general I suggest that a salesperson should begin with the assumption that information a reasonable consumer would regard as important needs to be revealed and that when special interests and concerns of the consumer come to light they may make further revelations necessary. This approach parallels the one taken by Tom Beauchamp and James Childress regarding the information that a physician needs to provide to obtain informed consent. See their *Principles of Biomedical Ethics,* 2nd ed. (New York: Oxford University Press, 1983), pp. 74–79.

9. This is adapted from a court case quoted in Braybrooke, pp. 68–70.

10. This paper was written during a sabbatical leave from Friends University at the Center for the Study of Values, University of Delaware. I wish to thank Friends University for the leave and Dr. Norman Bowie for his hospitality during my stay at the Center.

Federal Trade Commission v. Colgate-Palmolive Co. et al.

The basic question before us is whether it is a deceptive trade practice, prohibited by § 5 of the Federal Trade Commission Act, to represent falsely that a televised test, experiment, or demonstration provides a viewer with visual proof of a product claim, regardless of whether the product claim is itself true.

The case arises out of an attempt by re-

spondent Colgate-Palmolive Company to prove to the television public that its shaving cream, "Rapid Shave," outshaves them all. Respondent Ted Bates & Company, Inc., an advertising agency, prepared for Colgate three one-minute commercials designed to show that Rapid Shave could soften even the toughness of sandpaper. Each of the commercials contained the same "sandpaper

380 U.S. 374 (1964), 85 S. Ct. 1035, 13 L Ed. 2nd 904. Majority opinion by Chief Justice Earl Warren, U.S. Supreme Court.

test." The announcer informed the audience that, "To prove RAPID SHAVE'S super-moisturizing power, we put it right from the can onto this tough, dry sandpaper. It was apply . . . soak . . . and off in a stroke." While the announcer was speaking, Rapid Shave was applied to a substance that appeared to be sandpaper, and immediately thereafter a razor was shown shaving the substance clean.

The Federal Trade Commission issued a complaint against respondents Colgate and Bates charging that the commercials were false and deceptive. The evidence before the hearing examiner disclosed that sandpaper of the type depicted in the commercials could not be shaved immediately following the application of Rapid Shave, but required a substantial soaking period of approximately 80 minutes. The evidence also showed that the substance resembling sandpaper was in fact a simulated prop, or "mockup," made of plexiglass to which sand had been applied. However, the examiner found that Rapid Shave could shave sandpaper, even though not in the short time represented by the commercials, and that if real sandpaper had been used in the commercials the inadequacies of television transmission would have made it appear to viewers to be nothing more than plain, colored paper. The examiner dismissed the complaint because neither misrepresentation—concerning the actual moistening time or the identity of the shaved substance—was in his opinion a material one that would mislead the public.

The Commission, in an opinion dated December 29, 1961, reversed the hearing examiner. It found that since Rapid Shave could not shave sandpaper within the time depicted in the commercials, respondents had misrepresented the product's moisturizing power. Moreover, the Commission found that the undisclosed use of a plexiglass substitute for sandpaper was an additional material misrepresentation that was a deceptive act separate and distinct from the misrepresentation concerning Rapid Shave's underly-

ing qualities. Even if the sandpaper could be shaved just as depicted in the commercials, the Commission found that viewers had been misled into believing they had seen it done with their own eyes. As a result of these findings the Commission entered a cease-and-desist order against the respondents.

An appeal was taken to the Court of Appeals for the First Circuit which rendered an opinion on November 20, 1962. That court sustained the Commission's conclusion that respondents had misrepresented the qualities of Rapid Shave, but it would not accept the Commission's order forbidding the future use of undisclosed simulations in television commercials. It set aside the Commission's order and directed that a new order be entered. On May 7, 1963, the Commission, over the protest of respondents, issued a new order narrowing and clarifying its original order to comply with the court's mandate. The Court of Appeals again found unsatisfactory that portion of the order dealing with simulated props and refused to enforce it. We granted certiorari, 377 U.S. 942, to consider this aspect of the case and do not have before us any question concerning the misrepresentation that Rapid Shave could shave sandpaper immediately after application, that being conceded. . . .

We are not concerned in this case with the clear misrepresentation in the commercials concerning the speed with which Rapid Shave could shave sandpaper, since the Court of Appeals upheld the Commission's finding on that matter and the respondents have not challenged the finding here. We granted certiorari to consider the Commission's conclusion that even if an advertiser has himself conducted a test, experiment or demonstration which he honestly believes will prove a certain product claim, he may not convey to television viewers the false impression that they are seeing the test, experiment or demonstration for themselves, when they are not because of the undisclosed use of mock-ups.

We accept the Commission's determination that the commercials involved in this case contained three representations to the public: (1) that sandpaper could be shaved by Rapid Shave; (2) that an experiment had been conducted which verified this claim; and (3) that the viewer was seeing this experiment for himself. Respondents admit that the first two representations were made, but deny that the third was. The Commission, however, found to the contrary, and, since this is a matter of fact resting on an inference that could reasonably be drawn from the commercials themselves, the Commission's finding should be sustained. For the purposes of our review, we can assume that the first two representations were true; the focus of our consideration is on the third, which was clearly false. The parties agree that § 5 prohibits the intentional misrepresentation of any fact which would constitute a material factor in a purchaser's decision whether to buy. They differ, however, in their conception of what "facts" constitute a "material factor" in a purchaser's decision to buy. Respondents submit, in effect, that the only material facts are those which deal with the substantive qualities of a product.[1] The Commission, on the other hand, submits that the misrepresentation of *any* fact so long as it materially induces a purchaser's decision to buy is a deception prohibited by § 5.

The Commission's interpretation of what is a deceptive practice seems more in line with the decided cases than that of respondents. This Court said in *Federal Trade Comm'n v. Algoma Lumber Co.,* 291 U.S. 67, 78: "[T]he public is entitled to get what it chooses, though the choice may be dictated by caprice or by fashion or perhaps by ignorance." It has long been considered a deceptive practice to state falsely that a product ordinarily sells for an inflated price but that it is being offered at a special reduced price, even if the offered price represents the actual value of the product and the purchaser is receiving his money's worth.[2] Applying respondents' arguments to these cases, it would appear that so long as buyers paid no more than the product was actually worth and the product contained the qualities ad-

vertised, the misstatement of an inflated original price was immaterial.

It had also been held a violation of § 5 for a seller to misrepresent to the public that he is in a certain line of business, even though the misstatement in no way affects the qualities of the product. As was said in *Federal Trade Comm'n v. Royal Milling Co.,* 288 U.S. 212, 216:

> If consumers or dealers prefer to purchase a given article because it was made by a particular manufacturer or class of manufacturers, they have a right to do so, and this right cannot be satisfied by imposing upon them an exactly similar article, or one equally as good, but having a different origin.

The courts of appeals have applied this reasoning to the merchandising of reprocessed products that are as good as new, without a disclosure that they are in fact reprocessed. And it has also been held that it is a deceptive practice to misappropriate the trade name of another.

Respondents claim that all these cases are irrelevant to our decision because they involve misrepresentations related to the product itself and not merely to the manner in which an advertising message is communicated. This distinction misses the mark for two reasons. In the first place, the present case is not concerned with a mode of communication, but with a misrepresentation that viewers have objective proof of a seller's product claim over and above the seller's word. Secondly, all of the above cases, like the present case, deal with methods designed to get a consumer to purchase a product, not with whether the product, when purchased, will perform up to expectations. We find an especially strong similarity between the present case and those cases in which a seller induces the public to purchase an arguably good product by misrepresenting his line of business, by concealing the fact that the product is reprocessed, or by misappropriating another's trademark. In each the seller has used a misrepresentation to break down what he regards to be an annoying or irrational habit of the buying public—the preference for particular manufacturers or known brands regardless of a product's actual qualities, the prejudice against reprocessed goods, and the desire for verification of a product claim. In each case the seller reasons that when the habit is broken the buyer will be satisfied with the performance of the product he receives. Yet, a misrepresentation has been used to break the habit and, as was stated in *Algoma Lumber,* a misrepresentation for such an end is not permitted.

We need not limit ourselves to the cases already mentioned because there are other situations which also illustrate the correctness of the Commission's finding in the present case. It is generally accepted that it is a deceptive practice to state falsely that a product has received a testimonial from a respected source. In addition, the Commission has consistently acted to prevent sellers from falsely stating that their product claims have been "certified." We find these situations to be indistinguishable from the present case. We can assume that in each the underlying product claim is true and in each the seller actually conducted an experiment sufficient to prove to himself the truth of the claim. But in each the seller has told the public that it could rely on something other than his word concerning both the truth of the claim and the validity of his experiment. We find it an immaterial difference that in one case the viewer is told to rely on the word of a celebrity or authority he respects, in another on the word of a testing agency, and in the present case on his own perception of an undisclosed simulation.

Respondents again insist that the present case is not like any of the above, but is more like a case in which a celebrity or independent testing agency has in fact submitted a written verification of an experiment actually observed, but, because of the inability of the camera to transmit accurately an impression of the paper on which the testimonial is written, the seller reproduces it on another

substance so that it can be seen by the viewing audience. This analogy ignores the finding of the Commission that in the present case the seller misrepresented to the public that it was being given objective proof of a product claim. In respondents' hypothetical the objective proof of the product claim that is offered, the word of the celebrity or agency that the experiment was actually conducted, does exist; while in the case before us the objective proof offered, the viewer's own perception of an actual experiment, does not exist. Thus, in respondents' hypothetical, unlike the present case, the use of the undisclosed mock-up does not conflict with the seller's claim that there is objective proof.

We agree with the Commission, therefore, that the undisclosed use of plexiglass in the present commercials was a material deceptive practice independent and separate from the other misrepresentation found. . . .

We turn our attention now to the order issued by the Commission. . . . The Court of Appeals has criticized the reference in the Commission's order to "test, experiment or demonstration" as not capable of practical interpretation. It could find no difference between the Rapid Shave commercial and a commercial which extolled the goodness of ice cream while giving viewers a picture of a scoop of mashed potatoes appearing to be ice cream. We do not understand this difficulty. In the ice cream case the mashed potato prop is not being used for additional proof of the product claim, while the purpose of the Rapid Shave commercial is to give the viewer objective proof of the claims made. If in the ice cream hypothetical the focus of the commercial becomes the undisclosed potato prop and the viewer is invited, explicitly or by implication, to see for himself the truth of the claims about the ice cream's rich texture and full color, and perhaps compare it to a "rival product," then the commercial has become similar to the one now before us. Clearly, however, a commercial which depicts happy actors delightedly eating ice cream that is in fact mashed potatoes or drinking a product appearing to be coffee but which is in fact some other substance is not covered by the present order.

The crucial terms of the present order—"test, experiment or demonstration ... represented ... as actual proof of a claim"—are as specific as the circumstances will permit. If respondents in their subsequent commercials attempt to come as close to the line of misrepresentation as the Commission's order permits, they may without specifically intending to do so cross into the area proscribed by this order. However, it does not seem "unfair to require that one who deliberately goes perilously close to an area of proscribed conduct shall take the risk that he may cross the line," *Boyce Motor Lines, Inc.* v. *United States,* 342 U.S. 337, 340. In commercials where the emphasis is on the seller's word, and not on the viewer's own perception, the respondents need not fear that an undisclosed use of props is prohibited by the present order. On the other hand, when the commercial not only makes a claim, but also invites the viewer to rely on his own perception for demonstrative proof of the claim, the respondents will be aware that the use of undisclosed props in strategic places might be a material deception. We believe that respondents will have no difficulty applying the Commission's order to the vast majority of their contemplated future commercials. If, however, a situation arises in which respondents are sincerely unable to determine whether a proposed course of action would violate the present order, they can, by complying with the Commission's rules, oblige the Commission to give them definitive advice as to whether their proposed action, if pursued, would constitute compliance with the order.

NOTES

1. Brief for Respondent Colgate, p. 16: "What [the buyer] is interested in is whether the actual product he buys will look and perform the way it appeared on his television set." *Id.,* at 17: "[A] buyer's real concern is with the truth of the substantive claims or promises made to him, not with the means used to make them." *Id.,* at 20: [T]he Commission's error was to confuse the substantive claim made for a product with the means by which such claim was conveyed."

    Brief for Respondent Bates, pp. 2–3: "If the viewer or reader of the advertisement buys the product, and it will do exactly what the portrayal in the advertisement asserts it will do, can there be any unlawful misrepresentation?" *Id.,* at 13–14: "What induces the buyer to purchase is the claim that the product will perform as represented in the portrayed test. That is the material claim." *Id.,* at 25: "It is not a representation in any way relating to the product or to its purchase, so that even if the strained suggestion that there is such an implied representation were realistic, the representation plainly would be immaterial."

2. Federal Trade Comm'n v. Standard Education Society, 302 U.S. 112, 115–117, Kalwajtys v. Federal Trade Comm'n, 237 F.2d 654, 656 (C. A. 7th Cir. 1956), cert. denied, 352 U.S. 1025.

Federal Trade Commission v. Sterling Drug, Inc.

The Federal Trade Commission, appellant here, instituted an action in the District Court for the Southern District of New York praying for a temporary injunction designed to prevent the dissemination of what the Commission alleged it had reason to believe was false and misleading advertising. Judge Dawson denied the injunction....

I

The controversy has its roots in the December 29, 1962 issue of the *Journal of the American Medical Association,* which carried an article written by two physicians and a medical statistician, titled "A Comparative Study of Five Proprietary Analgesic Compounds." The article analyzed the results of a study made of the efficacy as well as the unhappy after-effects of certain pain-relieving drugs, sold in pharmacies and supermarkets throughout the nation. These five were Bayer Aspirin, St. Joseph's Aspirin, Bufferin (aspirin with buffering agent), and two of the so-called "combination of ingredients" tablets, Anacin and Excedrin. Also used in the experiment, as a form of control, was a placebo, the name given a harmless nonmedicinal substance administered in the form of a pill for those pill-poppers whose ailment is without organic origin and whose pain seems to be relieved by following the ritual of downing a tablet irrespective of size, shape, or content which the user believes has qualities of medicinal value; the placebo utilized by the three researchers was composed of lactose, or milk sugar, and a conventional cornstarch binder. After investigating the efficacy of the five analgesic agents as pain relievers, the study noted, "The data failed to show any statistically significant difference among any of the drugs (that is, excluding the placebo) at any of the check points [fifteen minutes through four hours].... [T]here are no important differences among the compounds studied in rapidity of onset, degree, or duration of analgesia." Fifteen minutes after the drugs were administered, so-called "pain-relief scores" were computed, and Bayer earned a score of 0.94, while the next most effective drug at that point in time, Excedrin, earned a score of 0.90; the others were rated at 0.76 and lower. The chart on which these figures appeared indicated that the "standard error of mean," or the margin of statistical accuracy of the study, was 0.124. Upon investigating the incidence of stomach upset after the administration of the five drugs as well as the placebo, the researchers came to this conclusion: "Excedrin and Anacin form a group for which the incidence of upset stomach is significantly greater than is the incidence after Bayer Aspirin, St. Joseph's Aspirin, Bufferin, or the placebo. The rates of upset stomach associated with these last 4 treatments are not significantly different, one from the other." The accompanying table revealed that of the 829 doses taken of Bayer Aspirin, there were nine episodes of upset stomach, a rate of 1.1%; the placebo was administered in 833 cases, and caused stomach upset but seven times, a rate of 0.8%. The article concluded by stating, "This study was supported by a grant from the Federal Trade Commission, Washington, D.C."

---

317 Fed 669 (1963). Opinion by Judge Irving R. Kaufman, U.S. Court of Appeals Second Circuit.

It is not difficult to understand the heart-warming reception this article received in the upper echelons of Sterling and its Madison Avenue colleagues; no sooner were the results of the study published in the *Journal of the American Medical Association* when Sterling Drug and its advertising agencies decided to make the most of them. This decision, we may fairly assume, did not surprise Sterling's competitors. The public had long been saturated with various claims proved by the study to be of doubtful validity. One of the products had boasted in its advertisements that it "works twice as fast as aspirin," and "protects you against the stomach distress you can get from aspirin alone"; another, that it "does not upset the stomach" and "is better than aspirin"; and yet another, that it is "50% stronger than aspirin." Believing that the Judgment Day has finally arrived and seeking to counteract the many years of hard-sell by what it now believed to be the hard facts, Sterling and its codefendants prepared and disseminated advertising of which the following, appearing in *Life* Magazine and numerous newspapers throughout the country, is representative:

> Government-Supported Medical Team Compares Bayer Aspirin and Four Other Popular Pain Relievers.
>
> Findings reported in the highly authoritative *Journal of the American Medical Association* reveal that the higher priced combination-of-ingredients pain relievers upset the stomach with significantly greater frequency than any of the other products tested. While Bayer Aspirin brings relief that is as fast, as strong, and as gentle to the stomach as you can get.

This important new medical study, supported by a grant from the federal government, was undertaken to compare the stomach-upsetting effects, the speed of relief offered by five leading pain relievers, including Bayer Aspirin, aspirin with buffering, and combination-of-ingredients products. Here is a summary of the findings.

Upset Stomach

According to this report, the higher priced combination-of-ingredients products upset the stomach with significantly greater frequency than any of the other products tested, while Bayer Aspirin, taken as directed, is as gentle to the stomach as a plain sugar pill.

Speed and Strength

The study shows that there is no significant difference among the products tested in rapidity of onset, strength, or duration of relief. Nonetheless, it is interesting to note that within just fifteen minutes, Bayer Aspirin had a somewhat higher pain relief score than any of the other products.

Price

As unreasonable as it may seem, the products which are most likely to upset the stomach—that is, the combination-of-ingredients products—actually cost substantially more than Bayer Aspirin. The fact is that these products as well as the buffered product, cost up to 75% more than Bayer Aspirin.

II

In a proceeding such as this, the burden was upon the Commission, in seeking its temporary injunction against the advertising, to show that it had "reason to believe" that the advertisements were false and misleading, and that the injunction during the pendency of administrative proceedings which the Commission initiated against Sterling Drug in January 1963 "would be to the interest of the public."

The Commission alleged and sought to prove the appellees' advertisements falsely represented, directly and by implication: (a) that the findings of the medical research team were endorsed and approved by the United States Government; (b) that the publication of the article in the *Journal of the American Medical Association* is evidence of endorsement and approval thereof by the association and the medical profession; (c) that the research team found that Bayer Aspirin is not upsetting to the stomach and is as gentle thereto as a sugar pill; (d) that the research team found that Bayer Aspirin, after fifteen minutes following administration, affords a higher degree of pain relief than any other product tested. An injunction was alleged to be in the public interest, since the consuming public would otherwise unwarrantedly rely upon the advertising to their "irreparable injury," and since competitors of Sterling Drug might be encouraged to engage in similar advertising tactics in order to maintain competitive standing.

The legal principles to be applied here are quite clear. . . .

It is well established that advertising need not be literally false in order to fall within the proscription of the act. Gone for the most part, fortunately, are the days when the advertiser was so lacking in subtlety as to represent his nostrum as superlative for "arthritis, rheumatism, neuralgia, sciatica, lumbago, gout, coronary thrombosis, brittle bones, bad teeth, malfunctioning glands, infected tonsils, infected appendix, gall stones, neuritis, underweight, constipation, indigestion, lack of energy, lack of vitality, lack of ambition and inability to sleep. . . ." See *Federal Trade Commission* v. *National Health Aids, Inc.,* 108 F.Supp. 340, 342 (D. Md. 1952). The courts are no longer content to insist simply upon the "most literal truthfulness," *Moretrench Corp.* v. *Federal Trade Commission,* 127 F.2d 792 at 795, for we have increasingly come to recognize that "Advertisements as a whole may be completely misleading although every sentence separately considered is literally true. This may be because things are omitted that should be said, or because advertisements are composed or purposefully printed in such way as to mislead." . . . There are two obvious methods of employing a true statement so as to convey a false impression: one is the half truth, where the statement is removed from its context and the nondisclosure of its context renders the statement misleading, see *P. Lorillard Co.* v. *Federal Trade Commission,* 186 F.2d 52, 58 (4th Cir., 1950); a second is the ambiguity, where the statement in context has two or more commonly understood meanings, one of which is deceptive.

III

The Federal Trade Commission asserts here that the vice of the Bayer advertisement is of these types. It concedes that none of the statements made therein is literally false, but it contends that the half-truths and ambiguities of the advertisement give it "reason to believe" that our hypothetical, sub-intelligent, less-than-careful reader will be misled thereby. Thus, we are told that the reference in large type to a "Government-Supported Medical Team" gives the misleading impression that the United States Government endorsed or approved the findings of the research team. Surely the fact that the word "supported" might have alternative dictionary definitions of "endorsed" or "approved" is not alone sufficient to show reason to believe that the ordinary reader will probably construe the word in this manner. Most words *do* have alternative dictionary definitions; if that in itself were a sufficient legal criterion, few advertisements would survive. Here, no impression is conveyed that the *product itself* has its source in or is being endorsed by the Government; for this reason, the cases cited by the Commission are inapt. If the reader of the advertisement believes that the Government in some way vouched for the soundness of the study's conclusions, then this impression would have also been conveyed had the advertisement "told the whole story," relating in full detail the extent of the Commission's participation: it selected the research team, supported the study with a grant, and authorized the publication of the report. The capsulized expression "Government-Supported" can not, therefore, be characterized as misleading. The Commission indicated to us upon argument that it would have been equally unhappy had the advertisement stated that the medical team was "Government-Financed" or "Government-Subsidized." But surely the concise statement of an established fact, immediately thereafter expanded—"This important new medical study, supported by a grant from the federal government..."— cannot fairly be proscribed by the Commission; the alternatives are complete omission of the admittedly true statement or long-winded qualification and picayune circumlocution, neither of which we believe was in the contemplation of Congress.

The Commission's attack upon the use of the phrase "Findings reported in the highly authoritative *Journal of the American Medical Association*," as misleadingly connoting endorsement and approval, is similarly unfounded, for much the same reasons already discussed. To assert that the ordinary reader would conclude from the use of the word "authoritative" that the study was endorsed by the *Journal* and the Association is to attribute to him not only a careless and imperceptive mind but also a propensity for unbounded flights of fancy. This we are not yet prepared to do. If the reader's natural reaction is to think that the study, because of publication in the *Journal,* is likely to be accurate, intelligent and well-documented, then the reaction is wholly justified, and one which the advertiser has every reason to expect to seek to inculcate. We, as judges, know that an article on the law which has survived the rigorous selection and editing process of one of the major law publications is most probably more reliable and more thoroughly researched than the report of a recent trial or judicial decision carried in the *Podunk Daily Journal.* But we hardly think that there is "reason to believe" that either we or the lay observer would tend to construe the views expressed in the article as having secured the wholehearted endorsement and approval of the "authoritative" periodical in which it appears.

The Commission's third objection deals with the probable vulnerability of the ordinary reader to Bayer's representations concerning stomach upset. We pass without comment the Commission's claim that the Bayer advertisement represented that no other available analgesic product was more gentle to the stomach; clearly, any comparative statements made in the advertisement could only be understood to refer to the four other products tested. More seriously pressed upon us is the claim that the reader will be deceived by the statement that "Bayer Aspirin, taken as directed, is as gentle to the stomach as a plain sugar pill." "Sugar pill," we are told, is misleading terminology; the advertisement should have used the word "placebo." Again, we are confronted by a simple problem of communication. For how can we expect our hypothetically slow-witted reader to react when he reads that "Bayer Aspirin is as gentle to the stomach as a placebo"! Most likely, he will either read on, completely unaware of the significance of the statement, or impatiently turn the page. Perhaps he will turn to his neighbor, and in response to a request for a definition of the troublesome word be greeted with the plausible query, "A *what?*" (This assumes that the reader will have been able to muster the correct pronunciation of the word.) But, all this aside, the pill used as a control in this case was indeed constituted of milk sugar and the use of the term "sugar pill" was neither inaccurate nor misleading.

The Commission next shifts its focus to the words "as gentle as," alleging that it has reason to believe that the reader will conclude that Bayer is not in the slightest bit harmful to the stomach; this can be rectified, we are told, by stating that Bayer is "no more upsetting" than the placebo, which did in fact cause a very minor degree of stomach upset. Unlike the standard of the average reader which the Commission avidly endorses throughout these proceedings, it here would have us believe he is linguistically and syntactically sensitive to the difference between the phrases "as gentle as" and "no more upsetting than." We do not find that the Commission has reason to believe that this will be the case, and we therefore reject its contentions.

Finally, the Commission attacks the manner in which the Bayer advertisement treated results of the study on speed and effectiveness of pain relief. As we understand the Commission's argument, no objection is taken to the statement that "The study shows that there is no significant difference among the products tested in rapidity of onset, strength, or duration of relief." Indeed, no objection can properly be taken, for the statement reproduces almost verbatim one of the conclusions enumerated in the article. It is thought, however, that the advertisement improperly represents greater short-run pain relief with Bayer Aspirin by stating that "Nonetheless, it is interesting to note that within just fifteen minutes, Bayer Aspirin had a somewhat higher pain relief score than any of the other products." As we have seen, the statement is literally true, for Bayer's "score" after fifteen minutes was 0.94 while its closest competitor at that time interval was rated 0.90. The fact that the margin of accuracy of that scoring system was 0.124—meaning that the second-place drug might fare as well as or better than Bayer over the long run of statistical tests—does not detract from the fact that on this particular test, Bayer apparently fared better than any other product in relieving pain within fifteen minutes after its administration. It is true that a close examination of the statistical chart drawn up by the three investigators reveals that they thought the difference between all of the drugs at that time interval not to be "significantly different." But that is precisely what the Bayer advertisement stated in the sentence preceding its excursion into the specifics of the pain-relief scores. We cannot, therefore, conclude that Judge Dawson clearly erred in finding that

the Commission failed properly to carry its statutory burden of proof, however slim that burden might be. Not even the Commission contends that in a proceeding under section 13(a) the judge is merely a rubber stamp, stripped of the power to exercise independent judgment on the issue of the Commission's "reason to believe."

The Commission relies heavily, especially as to the pain-relief aspects of its case, upon *P. Lorillard Co.* v. *Federal Trade Commission*, 186 F.2d 52 (4th Cir., 1950). There, *Reader's Digest* sponsored a scientific study of the major cigarettes, investigating the relative quantities of nicotine, tars, and resins. It accompanied its conclusions with a chart which revealed that, although Old Gold cigarettes ranked lowest in these deleterious substances, the quantitative differences between the brands were insignificant and would have no effect in reducing physiological harm to the smoker. The tenor of the study is revealed by its cheery words to the smoker "who need no longer worry as to which cigarette can most effectively nail down his coffin. For one nail is just about as good as another." Old Gold trumpeted its dubious success, claiming that it was found lowest in nicotine, tars, and resins, and predicting that the reader upon examining the results of the study would say "From now on, my cigarette is Old Gold." The Court quite properly upheld a cease-and-desist order issued by the Commission. An examination of that case shows that it is completely distinguishable in at least two obvious and significant respects. Although the statements made by Old Gold were at best literally true, they were used in the advertisement to convey an impression diametrically opposed to that intended by the writer of the article. As the Court noted, "The company proceeded to advertise this difference as though it had received a citation for public service instead of a castigation from the *Reader's Digest.*" 186 F.2d at 57. Moreover, as to the specifics of brand-comparison, it was found that anyone reading the advertisement would gain "the very definite impression that Old Gold cigarettes were less irritating to the throat and less harmful than other leading brands of cigarettes.... The truth was exactly the opposite." 186 F.2d at 58. In the instant case, Sterling Drug can in no sense be said to have conveyed a misleading impression as to either the spirit or the specifics of the article published in the *Journal of the American Medical Association.*

CASE 1. Food Labels and the Art of Sales

All packaged foods in supermarkets contain a listing of the ingredients in the package as well as other information. Much of that information, including the list of ingredients, is required by law. However, sales research has indicated that what is said or not said on the label has an important effect on the sale of the product.

In 1983, the Kellogg Company changed the names of two of its cereals from Sugar Frosted Flakes and Sugar Smacks to Frosted Flakes and Honey Smacks, respectively. At about the same time C. W. Post changed the name of its cereal Super Sugar Crisp to Super Golden Crisp. Market research had shown some consumers reacted negatively to the word "sugar." However, the sugar and sweetener content of the cereal continued to be at least 50 percent.

Market research has also shown that some consumers react *positively* to the word "granola"; "granola bars" saw retail sales grow 290 percent from 1980 through 1985—the fastest growing segment of the candy bar market. Granola bars were first introduced into the market as health-food products, and the ingredients were fashioned for consumers concerned about nutrition. However, many complained that they tasted like cardboard. Manufacturers then changed the products by adding peanut butter, chocolate chips, marshmallows, and sugar. Although the bars gradually became more like candy bars than granola in nutritional value and sugar content, they are slightly more nutritious than conventional candy bars. They have a higher fiber content, slightly less fat, and a higher percentage of complex carbohydrates. Advertising has continued to present the product through a healthful image, carrying over the public's association of the word "granola" with "health food" or "healthy." Quaker Oats, General Mills, and Hershey Foods emphasize the "wholesomeness" and "goodness" of their granola bars in their advertising. In order to compete, conventional candy bar companies such as M & M/Mars have begun to advertise their products as healthy snacks. Cadbury advertises that its chocolate is made with milk.

The amount of sugar is not the only concern of consumers. Also important is the amount of protein and vitamins a food contains, as well as its fat content, sodium content, and calories. This information is found on the label, but the numbers found there are a function of serving size. The consumer's information is in protein, calories, and the like per serving. The larger the serving size, the higher the numbers are apt to be. As consumer concern about calories and sodium levels changes, reducing the size of the serving will lower the number of calories and the amount of sodium.

This case was written by Norman Bowie and Tom Beauchamp on information found in Lisa Belkin, "Food Labels: How Much They Do and Don't Say," *New York Times,* September 18, 1985, pp. C1, C8, and in Amy Dunkin, "How Sweet It Is For Granola Bars," *Business Week,* August 12, 1985, pp. 61–62.

Around 1982, the Campbell Soup Company reduced its serving size from 10 ounces to 8 ounces. A can of Campbell's soup that once held two servings now held two and one-half servings. As a result the calorie and sodium levels per serving fell. The size of the can had not changed. The Campbell Soup Company said that "people are eating less" and "most bowls hold eight ounces."

Questions

1. Are such marketing practices by candy, cereal, and soup companies manipulative? deceptive?
2. Should companies be permitted to change the name, contents, or serving size without changing the product or the amount of the product?
3. The term *sugar free* literally means free of sucrose. Since many people purchase sugar-free foods to assist them with weight loss, should a standard be required so that "sugar free" means "free of any high-calorie sweetener?"
4. Flexi-labeling permits wording like "contains one or more of the following." Hence, "contains sunflower seed oil, coconut oil, and/or palm oil" is legally permitted. Yet sunflower seed oil is a polyunsaturated fat, and the other two are saturated fats. Since many people believe that polyunsaturated fats are more healthy, should flexi-labeling be permitted?

CASE 2. Zeroing in on the Joneses

The technology now exists to tailor ads for individual families. Experiments are now under way in several cities to study the effectiveness of these ads and the initial results have been enthusiastically received by the advertising industry. Consumers in the test areas are asked if they would permit their purchases to be monitored at supermarket checkout counters. They are promised anonymity. They are often rewarded with food discounts and other inducements. They are also told that the ads they see on their cable TV may differ from those seen by their neighbors. Advertisers are then able to beam ads promoting competing products into the consumer's home. If the Joneses use brand X, the competitor can beam ads for brand Y into the Joneses home. The Civil Liberties Union takes a dim view of these developments. An ACLU spokesperson has characterized the experiments as "shocking," and an invasion of privacy.

Questions

1. Do you think such ads directed toward specific families undermine human freedom?
2. Even if you think they don't invade human freedom, do you find them objectionable on grounds of the invasion of privacy?
3. Does this individualized method of advertising undermine rational decision making?
4. Is the description of the experiment given to potential participants at the supermarket checkout counters deceptive?

Used by permission of the author, Norman E. Bowie.

CASE 3. What Does "List Price" Mean?

Giant Food, Inc. is a supermarket chain, which sells housewares and appliances in some of its stores. Its advertising in the Washington, D.C. area sometimes appeared in the form:

Sunbeam Mixmaster $24.00—
Manufacturer List Price $37.95

Regina Twin Brush Waxer $25.47—
Manufacturer List $66

The advertisments also contained the following note at the bottom of each page:

The manufacturer's list prices referred to in this advertisement are inserted to assist you in identification of the products and to allow you to compare accurately the selling prices offered here and elsewhere. The use of the term manufacturer's list, or similar terminology in our advertising, is not to imply that Giant has ever sold the advertised product at such list prices, or that the products are being offered for sale generally in the area at such list prices. Many reputable national brand manufacturers issue to retailers, from time to time, suggested retail list prices that are intended to afford reasonable profits to all retailers based upon their traditional costs of marketing. Giant's employment of self-service supermarket techniques enables it usually to sell below suggested list prices. Consumers, however, have come to recognize most brand merchandise by the list prices, rather than model numbers, consequently Giant includes these manufacturer's list prices so that you may make simple, intelligent comparisons between our selling prices and those of others.

According to buyers from three companies in the Washington area, their stores never sold at the list prices advertised by Giant. Thus where Giant had advertised a Sunbeam appliance as selling for $13.97 with a list of $21, the three stores charged the following prices for the same item: $16.49, $14.97 and $13.49.

Giant contended that at least some stores in the Washington area had advertised the product for sale at the manufacturer's list price. Furthermore, Giant's comparison shoppers had discovered stores which actually sold the advertised products at the list price. In addition the manufacturers themselves had used the list prices in *Life, Look,* and *McCall's.*

The Federal Trade Commission claimed that despite the note inserted by Giant, the term *manufacturer's list price* meant that this was the price at which the item was usually and customarily sold in that area.

The matter was taken to the U.S. Court of Appeals of the District of Columbia, which had to decide whether the FTC has the right—when an advertisement has two meanings, one of which is deceptive—to demand the termination of such advertising. The court was also expected to rule on whether the insertion itself tended to reinforce the deception.

Questions

1. Does the addition of the note make any difference in determining whether or not Giant Food Inc.'s ad is deceptive?
2. Would the placement of the note or the size of the type make any difference?
3. If advertisers use words which have two distinct meanings, does that make the ad deceptive?
4. In terms of determining deception, does it matter if only one store had sold the items at the manufacturer's list price? If one store had never sold at the manufacturer's list price? If Giant Food Inc., had never sold at the manufacturer's list price?

From Thomas Garrett, Raymond C. Baumhart, Theodore Purcell, and Perry Roets, eds., *Cases in Business Ethics,* pp. 151–152. Copyright © 1968 by Appleton-Century Crofts, New York. Reprinted by permission of Prentice-Hall, Inc.

CASE 4. The Case of the Giant Quart

Your company sells only in the state of New Wyoming. State law does not prohibit marketing your cola in "giant quarts." A quart is a standard measure, so a giant quart is the same size as an ordinary quart. A survey conducted by your firm indicates that 40 percent of cola buyers think that a giant quart is larger than a regular quart.

Questions

1. Would it be deceptive advertising to call your bottle a giant quart?

2. In deciding whether this ad is deceptive, does it make any difference what percentage of cola buyers think that a giant quart is larger than a regular quart?

3. Suppose a firm sold a half gallon of soda for 89¢. In ads, the half gallon size was called the giant size. The firm finds it necessary to increase the price of the soda to 99¢. With the new price comes a new name—the "giant economy" size. Is the use of the new name deceptive?

4. Should there be a standard according to product for large, extra large, giant, and family sizes?

Suggested Supplementary Readings

Arrington, Robert L. "Advertising and Behavior Control." *Journal of Business Ethics* 1 (February 1982): 3–12.

Bok, Sissela. *Lying: Moral Choice in Public and Private Life.* New York: Pantheon Books, 1978.

Business and Professional Ethics Journal 3 (Spring/ Summer 1984). The entire issue is devoted to ethical issues in advertising.

Carson, Thomas L., Richard E. Wokutch, and Kent F. Murrman. "Bluffing in Labor Negotiations: Legal and Ethical Issues." *Journal of Business Ethics* 1 (February 1982): 13–22.

Cialdini, Robert B., Rodney Bassett, John T. Cacioppo, and John A. Miller. "Low Ball Procedure for Producing Compliance: Commitment then Cost." *Journal of Personality and Social Psychology* 36 (1978): 463–476.

Classen, Earl A. "Marketing Ethics and the Consumer." *Harvard Business Review* 45 (January– February 1967): 79–86.

Divita, S. F., ed. *Advertising and the Public Interest.* Chicago: American Marketing Association, 1974.

Finn, David. "Struggle for Ethics in Public Relations." *Harvard Business Review* 38 (January– February 1959): 49–58.

Fried, Charles. *Right and Wrong,* chapter 3. Cambridge, Mass.: Harvard University Press, 1978.

Gardner, David M. "Deception in Advertising: A Conceptual Approach." *Journal of Marketing* 39 (January 1975): 40–46.

Goodpaster, Kenneth E. "Should Sponsors Screen for Moral Values?" *The Hastings Center Report* 13 (December 1983): 17–18.

Greyser, Stephen A. "Advertising: Attacks and Counters." *Harvard Business Review* 50 (March 10, 1972): 22–24.

Henry, Jules. *Culture Against Man.* New York: Random House, 1963.

Hentoff, Nat. "Would You Run This Ad?" *Business and Society Review* 14 (Summer 1975): 8–13.

Keane, John G. "On Professionalism in Advertising." *Journal of Advertising* 3 (Fall 1974): 6–12.

Leiser, B. "The Ethics of Advertising." In *Ethics, Free Enterprise, and Public Policy,* edited by Richard De George and Joseph Pichler, 173– 186. New York: Oxford University Press, 1978.

Lucas, John T., and Richard Gurman, *Truth in Advertising.* New York: American Management Association, 1972.

Millum, Trevor. *Images of Woman: Advertising in Women's Magazines.* Totowa, N.J.: Rowman and Littlefield, 1975.

Moskin, J. Robert, ed. *The Case for Advertising.* New York: American Association of Advertising Agencies, 1973.

Case 4 was prepared by the Committee for Education in Business Ethics under a grant from the National Endowment for the Humanities.

Murphy, Pat, and Ben M. Enis. "Let's Hear the Case Against Brand X." *Business and Society Review* 12 (Winter 1974–1975): 82–89.

Nelson, Philip. "Advertising and Ethics." *Ethics, Free Enterprise and Public Policy,* edited by Richard T. De George and Joseph A. Pichler, 187–198. New York: Oxford University Press, 1978.

Packard, Vance. *The Hidden Persuaders.* New York: Pocket Books, 1957.

Preston, Ivan L. *The Great American Blow-up: Puffery in Advertising and Selling.* Madison: University of Wisconsin Press, 1975.

Reilly, John H., Jr. "A Welfare Critique of Advertising." *American Journal of Economics and Sociology* 31 (July 1972): 283–293.

Sandage, C. H., and Vernon Fryburger. *Advertising Theory and Practice.* 9th ed. Homewood, Ill.: Richard D. Irwin, 1975.

Stuart, Frederick, ed. *Consumer Protection from Deceptive Advertising.* Hempstead, N.Y.: Hofstra University, 1974.

Sullivan, Roger J. "A Response to 'Is Business Bluffing Ethical?'" *Business and Professional Ethics Journal* 3 (Winter 1984): 1–18.

Truth in Advertising: A Symposium of the Toronto School of Theology. Toronto, 1975.

CHAPTER EIGHT

Obligations in Accounting, Finance, and Investment

INTRODUCTION

Few of you will design grand strategies for achieving corporate social responsibility or even design corporate policies on the environment or on affirmative action. But many of you will hold jobs in corporations, for example, as accountants, engineers, or quality-control experts. Nearly all of you will also be investors either directly as purchasers of stock or indirectly in pension plans where pension-plan managers have a fiduciary duty to invest wisely on your behalf. In this chapter, we will consider the special moral obligations that occur as a result of the jobs we hold. In particular, we will consider the obligations of accountants to the investing public and the obligations of managers to stockholders when faced with a hostile takeover. In both cases, special interest will be directed toward conflict-of-interest situations. We will also be concerned with whether corporations have an obligation not to invest in a racist country like South Africa and whether institutions (e.g. universities) or individuals should divest themselves of stock they own in companies that do have facilities in countries such as South Africa.

CONFLICT OF INTEREST

Conflict of interest involves either a conflict between role obligations and personal interests or a conflict between two role obligations. A key ingredient in a conflict-of-interest situation in business is the existence of a role that requires the exercise of judgment. A conflict of interest arises when a person in a business role (e.g., a supplier, director, or quality-control engineer) who must exercise a judgment upon which others appropriately rely is subject to influences, loyalties, and temptations that would cause those who rely on that person to receive less qualified judgment than they have a right to expect.

Among the types of conflict-of-interest cases to achieve recent notoriety are those involving (1) city councilmen who combine the role of public service with personal legal practice, consulting service, or real estate development in areas where the city does business; (2) government officials who regulate an industry or corporation in which they own stock; (3) advertising agencies that accept contracts to advertise the merchandise of two

472

competing companies; (4) executives who arrange contracts for a corporation with companies in which they own stock; (5) members of bank boards who arrange large loans and privileged treatment from the bank—by obtaining, for example, loans at below-market interest rates; and (6) brokerage firms that receive loans from banks yet must objectively evaluate the stock of those same banks for clients who seek promising investment opportunities.

One case that received wide attention in the financial press involved an Arizona State University scientist who agreed to testify on CBS News that there were questions concerning the safety of ingesting Nutra Sweet. Before testifying, the scientist and his attorney purchased "put" options[1] on the stock of G. D. Searle & Company, the manufacturer of Nutra Sweet. Both men expected Searle's stock to drop on the basis of the scientist's testimony. If it did, both individuals would make a large profit.[2] It is the role obligation of a scientist to provide unbiased information. Here the scientist's personal financial interest in Searle & Company stock compromises or at least potentially compromises (and gives the appearance of conflicting with) the obligation to provide objective information.

In the specific cases cited above, the individuals and firms accused of conflicts of interest generally denied any wrongdoing. They claimed that a conflict of interest is often in the eye of the beholder and that what appears to be a conflict is not a genuine conflict. That is, they held that one can maintain one's distance and not be compromised or corrupted by a "competing" or personal interest. To address such disputes, certain distinctions are needed. As Michael Davis points out in his essay, there are three different kinds of conflicts of interest: latent, potential, and actual. These distinctions help explain why a person accused of a conflict of interest often sees no problem. For example, the Arizona State professor believes he can do his job by giving an objective report on the safety of Nutra Sweet.

His benefiting from the results that will likely follow when his report is made is only a side effect. From his perspective, he need not do anything in the way of taking precautions beyond what his job as a scientist requires, and he has no intention of violating his obligations as a scientist.

What the Arizona State professor forgets is that from the public's point of view, he cannot escape a potential conflict of interest: Because he has a vested interest in the stock's going down, he could exaggerate his report if exaggeration were necessary to produce a drop in price. The public frequently tries to ensure that a person whose judgment they rely on not only is not acting from a conflict of interest but also could not be so motivated. In Davis' terminology, the public wants to avoid both actual and potential conflicts of interest.

Given the wide range of possibilities for conflicts of interest, how are they to be avoided? One strategy is ensuring that a full disclosure is made. As Davis reports, the American Bar Association's legal code permits lawyers to accept client opportunities that contain potential or latent conflicts of interest as long as full disclosure has been made to all relevant parties. For example, if a client wants to sue the local automobile dealer and the lawyer represents the dealer in other transactions, the lawyer must disclose that information to the client. If the client still wishes to retain the lawyer, the lawyer then may accept this client (unless the lawyer's connection with the local automobile dealer is germane to this case).

But full disclosure is not a sufficient condition for eliminating all conflicts of interest. The more intractable problem is whether full disclosure renders a conflict of interest justifiable as a result of the disclosure. For example, E. F. Hutton promoted its "Hutton Advantaged Properties: Limited Partnership" in a brochure (issued August 9, 1984) that contained, as is common practice in such brochures, a disclosure of conflict of interest. It said, in part, that "the activities of Hutton . . . and . . . Affiliates may now or in the future be in direct competition with the Partnership and the Local Partnership. SUCH ACTIVITIES MAY BE DETRIMENTAL TO THE SUCCESS OF THE PARTNERSHIP.'' The fact that this warning was issued in bold print before selling the partnership speaks in Hutton's favor, but it can still be asked whether having such a conflict is morally acceptable. Indeed, full disclosure may sometimes only erode public confidence. For example, full disclosure by the professor may erode public confidence in the accuracy of his analysis of Nutra Sweet.

Traditionally, there have been three other means of avoiding or resolving conflicts of interest: (1) reduction in the opportunities for conflicts of interest, (2) legislation, and (3) codes or other formal guidelines. Each of these means has a role to play, but each has disadvantages. Consider the first approach. Many cases could be avoided if persons could not serve on multiple boards of directors. Such a policy would reduce opportunities for conflict of interest and could be written into codes or formal policies. However, as David C. David, former dean of the School of Business Administration at Harvard said, there is the problem that "the men with the conflicts usually make excellent directors."[3] A case in point occurred on May 31, 1985, when Mr. Bernard Katz resigned from the board of Helionetics, Inc., in Irvine, California. Helionetics sought to buy two companies in which Mr. Katz owned 45 percent and 35 percent of the stock. To avoid conflict of interest he resigned. However, Helionetics opposed the resignation because it wanted to retain his strategic knowledge and experience.[4]

The second traditional approach is legislation, much of which focuses on disclosure requirements. The federal government forbids some employees from taking similar jobs in the private sector for three years after leaving government. The purpose of the legislation is to prevent a former government employee from using knowledge obtained while working for the government to gain an unfair competitive advantage for a private firm. One difficulty with this approach is that it tends to discourage talented people from entering government service. For example, if you are an expert in defense weaponry, you know before you accept a federal position that *later* your services will be most needed in the private arms-manufacturing sector, where the major opportunities for advancement exist. To be prohibited from working in that industry for three years after leaving government service is a disincentive to accepting federal employment.

Codes of ethics represent another alternative. In conflict-of-interest cases, one interest must yield to another, and codes can set such priorities as to which interest must be overriding. The corporate codes of ethics discussed in Chapter Three all have extensive provisions to avoid conflicts of interest (see pp. 123–125). As discussed there, codes of ethics can indicate areas in which the scramble for increased profits would not be permitted and can help in writing fair rules of the game. Their function may be vital in the absence of international legislation or multinational business and trade agreements. But codes of ethics do have limitations, and it is often prudent to leave moral elbow room to assess each case as it comes along rather than adopting hidebound rules. For example, one might adopt a rule that a corporate executive with a firm that is under federal or state environmental-protection rules should not be appointed to a government position involving regulation of the environment. The conflict of interest is obvious and the rule seems reasonable, but should such a rule be administered without exception?

To answer this question, consider the following case that occurred in Virginia. A du Pont executive, Richard L. Cook, was appointed to the state's highest environmental post and was allowed to maintain ties to the chemical giant with the understanding that he would return to du Pont after a one-year stint with the state. The conflict appeared serious in that du Pont had been accused of mercury contamination in Virginia and had recently settled out of court for $1.8 million. The Environmental Defense Fund had also been in direct conflict with du Pont over its activities. Yet when it came to Mr. Cook *all* parties were agreed—including the Environmental Defense Fund—that Mr. Cook was the best person for the job, even under the unusual arrangement with its inherent conflict of interest. His moral integrity and concern for the environment overrode objections to any conflict of interest. This case indicates not only that codes may not serve us well if too tightly regimented, but also that having a conflict of interest that justifiably leads to moral suspicion is not always determinative of what should be prohibited.[5]

OBLIGATIONS AND CONFLICTING INTERESTS IN ACCOUNTING

A conflict-of-interest situation encountered by accountants is of special relevance to this chapter. The purpose of an audit by a certified public accountant of a publicly held company is to provide an objective report on a corporation's assets and liabilities. In carrying out this purpose, the CPA serves the investing public. Yet two significant factors can be perceived as compromising the objectivity of a CPA audit. First, there is ambiguity as to who represents the CPA's client. The audit is of the firm and the information is for the investing public, but the firm hires and fires the CPA's company. Is the investing public the client, or is the firm the client? The traditional view is that the firm under audit is the client. If so, the CPA's personal interest in having his or her firm rehired can conflict with the CPA's role obligation to provide objective information. Second, certified public accounting firms are diversifying in order to maintain business. One of the most lucrative of the new activities is corporate consulting. The accounting firms give advice to corporations, some of which presumably is implemented. The same accounting firms then audit the corporations they advise. Again, the personal interest of the accounting firm in securing consulting arrangements conflicts with the role obligation to give an impartial report.

These problems have deeply troubled accounting firms in recent years—exploding in a variety of controversies about the moral and legal responsibilities of accounting firms. In the mid-1980s accounting firms began to be sued by shareholders and "public interest" lawyers because a number of banks and financial companies encountered severe problems shortly after accounting firms had declared them healthy. Major trouble spots included Continental Illinois National Bank, Financial Corporation of America, and Baldwin-United. State and federal courts were also moving to widen the accountant's responsibilities to the public. In March 1984, the U.S. Supreme Court, in deciding a case against Arthur Young & Co., declared that the public responsibility of auditors transcends all obligations to the client and requires total independence of special indebtedness to the client.[6]

Regulation to enforce proper accounting measures has long been controversial. Although the Securities and Exchange Commission has quite limited powers in these matters and has traditionally kept its distance, in July 1984, SEC Chairman John Shad announced that the SEC would step up its investigation of accounting abuses, especially those involving shares of stock that were sold on the basis of faulty financial information produced by disclosure fraud. In May 1986, a bill was introduced in Congress that would require independent auditors of publicly held companies to report possible fraud by clients. Yet, SEC commissioners went on record as having grave reservations about such a bill, because they thought that independent professional auditors would be immediately transformed into state-regulated examiners and would be asked to assume a position of investigator that they are not qualified to handle. The commissioners favored the traditional system in which auditors must only report to management any fraud they discover or suspect and may then resign if management fails to respond.[7]

In this chapter a nontraditional view of the accounting profession is presented by accountants William Hamilton and William Callahan. They argue that if accountants wish to remain private-sector employees like attorneys and physicians, they must be willing to be held legally liable for their work. If they do not wish to be held accountable in this way, they should become public employees (employees of the state).

Self-regulation no less than government regulation has proved controversial. In November 1985, the United States' fifth-largest accounting firm, Price Waterhouse, made the highly unusual proposal that the accounting profession create its own self-regulatory body but one that would also be under the oversight of the Securities and Exchange Commission. The group would, for example, draw up guidelines to improve fraud detection, examine liability exposure, and perform peer review with less secrecy surrounding client information than has been customary in the past (although the SEC would be shielded from confidential material). However, both the SEC and the other major firms gave the idea a cool reception, saying that they were troubled by problems of invasion of confidential information, excessive regulation, and duplication of work already being done by the trade group.[8]

On occasion, attempts at both self-regulation and legal redress can combine to send contradictory signals to the accounting profession. An accountant's obligation to keep a confidence is an excellent case in point. In his article, John Beach shows that the accountant is caught in a Catch-22 situation. The American Institute of Certified Public Accountants' code of ethics has a specific regulation that client information be kept confidential, and aggrieved parties have successfully sued accountants or accounting firms that breach confidentiality. On the other hand, accounting firms have been successfully sued because their failure to provide confidential information has damaged persons who rely on the accuracy of the information accountants supply. Beach argues that this problem cannot be corrected merely by modifying the code of ethics (by self-regulation).

Although many accountants continue to hold to the view that they can only be expected to abide by established professional standards, cannot be expected to uncover well-embedded fraud, and should not publicly disclose confidential information, many others (including some in the profession) insist that if accountants accept the role obligation of certifying annual reports as correct, then their standards of due diligence in pursuing information must at least be tough enough to keep corporations honest.

HOSTILE TAKEOVERS AND DEFENSIVE STRATEGIES

Another apparent conflict-of-interest situation can occur during attempts by managers either to promote or to thwart hostile takeovers. In a bitter takeover battle of the late 1970s, Harold McGraw publicly raised a conflict-of-interest charge against Roger H. Mosley, President of American Express. At the time, American Express was trying to gain control of McGraw-Hill Publishing Company. Specifically, McGraw-Hill charged Mosley with using information obtained as a member of the board of directors of McGraw-Hill to assist American Express in its takeover bid and also with obtaining the financing for the acquisition of McGraw-Hill from the bank with which McGraw-Hill had done most of its business over the past fifty years.[9] Mosley's personal and corporate interest in McGraw-Hill's success stands in conflict with his role obligation to promote the interests of American Express.

The more common, and now much discussed, conflict-of-interest problem involves managers who seek to *thwart* hostile takeovers. On the one hand, a manager has a fiduciary duty to increase profits for the benefit of stockholders, and thus if a takeover offer would enhance stockholder wealth it would seem that the managers have a moral duty to accept it. On the other hand, takeovers often cause the dismissal of managers in the firm taken over, and it may not be in the interest of these managers to accept the takeover bid. A conflict of interest is apparent between the personal career interests of managers and the financial interests of stockholders, which management is obligated to promote.

Is the conflict of interest actual, latent, or potential? On the basis of the information provided thus far, a potential conflict is the most that can be claimed. If the takeover bid is contrary to the interests of current managers, then the conflict of interest is latent. The conflict of interest becomes actual when the takeover attempt is in the interest of the corporate stakeholders and management tries to defend its position by such strategies as poison pills, greenmail, and a scorched earth policy.[10] However, the mere fact that a defensive strategy is in the self-interest of the managers of the threatened company is not sufficient for claiming that the strategy is wrong or blameworthy. First, a takeover bid may not be in the long-term interests of the stockholders. Second, as Lisa Newton argues in her article in this chapter, takeover bids are often not in the interests of the corporation or its stakeholders. Hostile takeovers have frequently been criticized as harmful to employees, and a proponent of this criticism can argue that no actual conflict of interest occurs when management takes defensive measures against hostile takeover bids.

In *Johnson* v. *Trueblood,* a federal court used partially moral premises to reject the argument that self-interest on the part of management in a decision affecting stockholders necessarily invalidates the management's action.

It is frequently said that directors are fiduciaries. Although this statement is true in some senses, it is also obvious that if directors were held to the same standard as ordinary fiduciaries the corporation could not conduct business. For example, an ordinary fiduciary may not have the slightest conflict of interest in any transaction he undertakes on behalf of the trust. Yet by the very nature of corporate life a director has a certain amount of self-interest in everything he does. The very fact that the director wants

to enhance corporate profits is in part attributable to his desire to keep shareholders satisfied so that they will not oust him.

The business judgment rule seeks to alleviate this problem by validating certain situations that otherwise would involve a conflict of interest for the ordinary fiduciary. The rule achieves this purpose by postulating that if actions are arguably taken for the benefit of the corporation, then the directors are presumed to have been exercising their sound business judgment rather than responding to any personal motivations.[11]

The court implicitly recognizes the distinction between a latent conflict of interest and an actual conflict of interest and accepts a defensive strategy by management so long as this strategy can be defended on sound business grounds. Hence, the mere fact that a latent conflict of interest exists is not sufficient to show that the anti-takeover defenses are wrongful.

Much of the controversy surrounding hostile takeovers (especially the greenmail situation) centers on the so-called "business judgment rule" mentioned by this court. This rule provides that board-room decisions are justifiable (free of criticism and liability) if made in good faith with a reasonable corporate business purpose. Boards have not traditionally had the burden of proof in court to show that they acted prudently; rather, dissatisfied shareholders have had that burden. However, radical takeover defenses have forced some rethinking of both the rule and the placement of the burden of proof. Corporate directors have generally warned that significant modification of this rule could have the consequence of spawning large numbers of takeover attempts and paralyzing boards in their attempts to defend their companies. Critics of the rule, however, believe that there need to be new ways to force directors to justify their decisions and to subject them to legal liability.

Thus, the recent discussion of takeovers, takeover defenses, greenmail, and the like has raised important moral issues about directors' responsibilities, the nature of fiduciary duties to stockholders, and the concept of a prudent business decision. The courts have begun, in some decisions, to erode the past wall of protection for corporate directors. For example, in June 1984, a federal appeals court barred the Norlin Corporation from issuing 49 percent of its stock to a Panamanian subsidiary and from using an employee stock plan in order to fight a takeover attempt. The judge ruled that beneath the surface of these business maneuvers was an attempt to entrench management and that the burden of proof that the move was in the shareholders' interest rested with Norlin.[12]

The debate about hostile takeovers and defenses often centers on disputes between those who think that such takeovers are generally in the public interest and those who deny that they are in the public interest. Much of the debate reflected in the readings in this chapter is rule-utilitarian in nature. (Chapter One provided an analysis of rule utilitarianism as the theory that a society should adopt those rules and practices that lead to the greatest good for the greatest number; see pp. 29–31.) On rule-utilitarian grounds, Craig Lehman defends takeovers while criticizing strategies like greenmail and poison pills, whereas Lisa Newton uses some rule-utilitarian arguments to support the opposite position.

This debate involves more than the factual question of whether hostile takeovers produce overall social benefit. Questions of justice arise as well. The paying of greenmail involves treating one class of stockholders differently from another, because the raider is paid a premium for stock to ensure that the raider will exit. Usually no other stockholder can receive a parallel increase in the value of stock. However, Unocal Corporation reversed the greenmail situation in 1985 by paying all stockholders a premium, except for the stock of the raider—in this case Mesa Petroleum. In deciding on behalf of Unocal—in the *Unocal* v. *Mesa* decision included in this chapter—the Delaware Supreme Court supported Unocal on the grounds that the Mesa takeover bid was *coercive*. What made the bid coercive was Mesa's two-tiered stock offer. For the first 64 million shares of Unocal

stock, Mesa offered $54 a share. For the remaining shares, Mesa would offer securities allegedly worth $54 a share, but the backing on the remaining shares was through what both the market and the court pejoratively term "junk bonds."[13] In passing moral judgment, the court argued, "It is now well recognized that such offers are a classic coercive measure designed to stampede shareholders into tendering at the first tier, even if the price is inadequate, out of fear of what they will receive at the back end of the transaction."[14] The court ruled that the Unocal move was a fair defensive strategy, given the coercive nature of Mesa's offer.

INVESTMENT CONFLICTS AND MORAL CONSTRAINTS ON INVESTMENT

The stock market is one of the distinctive features of the American capitalist system. When Americans think of investment, they think of various kinds of securities and the Wall Street stock exchanges. But there is much more to investment than putting money into the stock and bond markets. Consider the traditional model of a venture. Suppose you or a friend have a great idea for a product, but you do not have enough money to manufacture the product. You need to sell your idea to others so that they are willing to back your idea with their money in the hope of future profit. If you succeed in selling your idea, they will invest in you. Such investment is often referred to as venture capital. It enables the new Silicon Valley firms, for example, to get their products designed, their plants built, and their products marketed.

Big companies like General Motors and IBM need money as well—for growth, the introduction of new products, and the construction of new plants. These companies offer stock and bonds to the public to finance their expansion. The public then invests in these companies in the expectation of regular dividend payments, the appreciation of the value of the stock, or both. The issuance of stock and bonds allows a significant percentage of

Americans to have a stake in the success of business—either directly through the personal ownership of securities or indirectly through the investment decisions of a pension fund manager. Many of us are in this respect investors in the future of American business.

When a company like General Motors or IBM introduces a new product or builds a new plant, it too is investing. When General Motors recently selected a small town in Tennessee as the site of a new automobile assembly plant, General Motors was investing resources in that community in the belief that its resources would best be used in that community to return a profit rather than in the other communities that sought the new plant. In this chapter, *investment* can have two references—either to the commitment of resources by businesses themselves or to purchases of securities by individuals or their surrogates.

Conflict of Interest in the World of Investment. Investment, like the worlds of accounting and finance, is ripe for problems of conflict of interest. The brokerage industry, for example, is plagued at its very heart with a conflict of interest: A stockbroker makes a living by selling securities to a client on a commission basis while at the same time standing in a fiduciary relationship to the client. The more trades the better for the stockbroker, but seldom so for the client. (Financial planners and money managers, by contrast, largely escape the conflict by charging flat fees or percentage of profits for recommendations or services.)

Investment bankers have a dual role with dual obligations: They bring together buyers and sellers of businesses and sources of financing. They may also serve both as advisor to corporations and as an investor in their stock. Large brokerage houses frequently buy the shares of a company in order to hold them for a profit and at the same time recommend that company to clients. Sensing a moral taint, firms such as Salomon Brothers and Kidder, Peabody & Company have strict rules against such activities on grounds that one's primary commitment is to clients and that such activity

compromises objectivity in making recommendations.[15] Most firms, however, have not adopted these restraints.

The problem extends to a number of areas in investment banking, as can be illustrated by the following case: In a proposed buyout of Levitz Furniture, Drexel Burnham Lambert, Inc., was retained by Levitz's independent directors to evaluate bids. After advising the directors that several bids they received were inadequate, Drexel resigned as advisor and submitted its own bid, which was higher than the others that it had evaluated. A natural question is how firms can serve as objective investment advisors and submit competitive bids of their own. For its part, Drexel acknowledged that the role obligations of a buyer are in conflict with the role obligations of an appraiser, but insisted that by changing roles one changes one's role obligations.[16]

Clearly problems of impartiality when counseling either a company in which one has invested or a competitor seeking objective advice are inherent in some of the roles assumed in modern investing. These problems raise profound questions about the kinds of constraints that should be placed on investing practices where there is potential for conflict of interest.

Moral Constraints on Investment. The articles in this chapter focus primarily on some special moral constraints that may be required for those who either directly or indirectly invest in South Africa. With respect to investment by American business, John Akers, President of IBM, said in 1986:

> The economic activity there is worse than it was a year ago, the economic pressure in the United States is heightened, and Mr. Botha is too slow. If we cannot have as successful a business remaining in South Africa as we would have leaving, then I think we have no choice than to leave. If we elect to leave it will be a business decision. What other kind of decision would it be? We are not in business to conduct moral activity, we are not in business to conduct socially responsible action. We are in business to conduct business.[17]

Akers' comments were issued during a period of vast uncertainty in American business about remaining in South Africa. Pieter Botha, South Africa's President, had failed to deliver on a number of promises for racial reforms, and major U.S. corporations that had previously defended policies of gradual change found themselves in a far more hostile and uncertain environment. Major companies such as Phibro-Salomon, Inc., ITT Corporation, General Foods Corporation, General Electric, and USG had just announced that they would sell out and leave. Others such as Diamond Shamrock and Eaton Corporation were selling their subsidiaries and leaving. In addition, Chase Manhattan bank and other smaller banks had established a policy of no more loans to South Africa; a long list of U.S. states, municipalities, and universities had decided to divest holdings of companies with South African operations; and the U.S. Congress had approved a package of economic sanctions against South Africa.

Shortly after Akers' statement, on July 11, 1986, the *Wall Street Journal* asserted (in a front-page news story) that

> It is a no-win situation [for American business firms]. The deteriorating economy has devastated most companies' profits in South Africa. The black population grows ever more hostile to U.S. companies' presence. The Sullivan Principles, which have provided a moral framework for doing business in a repressive state, are under attack as ineffective. While South Africa burns, companies are viewed as doing too little too late. Staying in South Africa will require them to spend many more millions than they ever expected and plunge them more deeply into South Africa's messy internal affairs.[18]

Critics of investment in South Africa argue that South Africa is such a racist society that business should not exploit black workers and perpetuate racism even if it were profitable to do so. Behind this criticism is the notion that the parties to a business contract must meet minimum standards of morality—a test that critics believe businesses entangled with South Africa fail.

Supporters of investment in South Africa argue that if we should not invest in South Africa because it is a brutal racist society, then we should not invest in Uganda or the Soviet Union either, because they are brutal racist societies as well. Consistency demands such a uniform policy, but those urging divestment are seldom willing to go that far.

Supporters of investment also argue that failure to invest in South Africa hurts the oppressed and eliminates all opportunity for internal reform. This point has been sufficiently persuasive so that companies with operations in South Africa have endorsed "The Sullivan Principles" to guide their operations. This code of principles was named for the Reverend Leon Sullivan, pastor of the Zion Baptist Church of Philadelphia and the first black director of General Motors. The Sullivan Code requires that U.S. firms with affiliates in the Republic of South Africa subscribe to the following principles in their operations:

1. nonsegregation of the races in all eating, comfort, and work facilities;
2. equal and fair employment practices for all employees;
3. equal pay for all employees doing equal or comparable work for the same period of time;
4. initiation of and development of training programs that will prepare in substantial numbers, blacks and other nonwhites, for supervisory, administrative, clerical, and technical jobs;
5. increasing the number of blacks and other nonwhites in management and supervisory positions;
6. improving the quality of employees' lives outside the work environment in such areas as housing, transportation, schooling, recreation, and health facilities.

Action in accordance with some of these principles puts a company in violation of South African law. Nonetheless, most American companies operating in South Africa are signatories.

It is now widely agreed that compliance with the Sullivan Code constitutes a moral minimum for companies with operations in South Africa. However, many argue that as time passes and there is little, if any, sign of reform on the part of the South African government, merely subscribing to the Sullivan Principles will not be enough and a new moral minimum will have to be established. As we go to press, Reverend Sullivan himself set a deadline of May 1987 for government reform. Failure to achieve reform will result in his call for all U.S. companies to cease operations in South Africa. Although there is nothing sacred about his deadline, the purpose of the Sullivan Code was to enable businesses to set an example and to help achieve reform. If no real reform occurs, a major rationale for the Sullivan Code disappears.

It should also be noted that the Sullivan Code provides no warrant for companies without facilities and operations in South Africa doing business with the South African government. To argue that the mere doing of business with the South African government benefits the oppressed is a difficult case to make. The opposite seems likely to be the case—except perhaps in isolated cases such as supplying health-care goods.

Thus far we have concentrated on the investment decisions of businesses as to whether they should build plants in South Africa, but what about the investment decisions of portfolio managers? Should they not buy, or even sell off, stocks of companies that do have operations or do business with the South African government? How one answers that question depends in part on the answer to the question of whether or not American companies should be in South Africa. If compliance with the Sullivan Code is morally permissible, then it seems that buying or holding stock in companies that subscribe to the Sullivan Principles is also morally permissible.

However, if a person is a portfolio manager, the moral issue is more complicated. A portfolio manager has clients—those who own the stocks in the portfolio or those who benefit from the returns on the stocks in the portfolio. It can be argued that the portfolio manager has a fiduciary duty to maximize the return on the portfolio. (We addressed this issue earlier when we discussed the duties of

portfolio managers with respect to tender offers.) Some have argued that divesting in the stock of companies with operations in South Africa need not diminish the rate of return to the portfolio. Others argue that even if the rate of return is diminished, the portfolio manager has other duties that override the fiduciary duty to maximize the return on the portfolio. Discussion of these issues is found in the article by Joseph Murphy.

The disinvestment question is an intensely felt issue. Not since the 1960s has an issue so galvanized public debate, especially on America's campuses. However, our task here is the dispassionate assessment of arguments. In the concluding article, Richard De George examines the arguments on both sides of this controversial issue with the intent of just such dispassionate analysis.

NOTES

1. A put is an option contract that gives the buyer the right to sell some multiple of 100 shares of a given stock at a certain price within a specified period of time. If the stock drops in price, the buyer realizes a profit.
2. See Bruce Ingersoll, "SEC's Probe of Searle Options Raises Questions on Ethics, Inside Trades," *Wall Street Journal*, February 27, 1984, p. 29.
3. Quoted in Joseph Margolis, "Conflict of Interest and Conflicting Interests," in *Ethical Theory and Business*, ed. Tom L. Beauchamp and Norman Bowie, (Englewood Cliffs, N.J.: Prentice-Hall, 1979), 235.
4. See Jennifer Hull, "Helionetics's Katz Resigns as Director to Avoid Conflict," *Wall Street Journal*, May 21, 1985, p. 8.
5. See Sandra Sugawara, "Virginia's New Point Man on Ecology," *Washington Post*, December 5, 1974, pp. B1, B9.
6. See Lee Berton, "Investors Call CPAs to Account," *Wall Street Journal*, January 28, 1985, editorial page.
7. Cynthia S. Grisdela, "SEC to Oppose Bill That Forces Auditors to Report Possible Fraud by Their Clients," *Wall Street Journal*, June 20, 1986, p. 4.
8. Lee Berton, "Price Waterhouse Is Urging For-

mation of Group to Regulate Accounting Firms," *Wall Street Journal*, November 20, 1985, p. 10.

9. "Open Letter to American Express Company from Harold McGraw of McGraw-Hill Publishers," *Wall Street Journal*, January 18, 1979, 14–15.

10. A poison pill is a provision activated in a takeover attempt that makes the target company too expensive to swallow. Greenmail is the offer or payment of a premium over market value to an outside shareholder; this offer is not available to other shareholders and is authorized by management for the purpose of avoiding a battle for control of the company. A scorched earth policy is a policy of defensive measures that makes a target company financially unattractive to a potential hostile raider.

11. *Johnson v. Trueblood*, 629 F.2d 287 (1980) at 292.

12. George Aguilar, "Business Judgment Doctrine Is Being Challenged in U.S.," *Wall Street Journal*, August 14, 1984.

13. Junk bonds are below–investment grade securities. They can be used as a financial device by corporate raiders to back tender offers for stock purchasers whose economic worth is alleged to be below the market value of the bond. However, most of the U.S. companies (over 90 percent) who issue bonds issue "junk" by this definition, because they are below "investment grade."

14. *Unocal v. Mesa Petroleum Co.*, 493 A.2d at 956.

15. See Fred R. Bleakley, "Wall St.'s Merchant Bankers," *New York Times*, November 19, 1984, p. 25.

16. See David A. Vise, "Investment Bankers Throw Own Money Into the Ring," *Washington Post*, December 30, 1984, F1, F6.

17. See Thomas B. Morgan, "Why I'm Unloading My I.B.M. Shares," *New York Times*, April 29, 1986, op-ed page. IBM replied that the quote was misleadingly used out of context. "Letters," *New York Times*, June 3, 1986.

18. Dennis Kneale, "U.S. Firms Operating in South Africa Debate Whether to Stay or Go," *Wall Street Journal*, July 11, 1986, p. 1.

Conflict of Interest

Michael Davis

I. THE LAWYER'S ANALYSIS

. . . The lawyer's analysis of conflict of interest is to be found in the American Bar Association's *Code of Professional Responsibility* as well as in numerous articles, books, court opinions, and opinions of various bar ethics committees.[1] The *Code's* statement of the analysis, while not particularly subtle, is all we need here.

The *Code* understands a conflict of inter-est to require only (a) one relatively formal role (with occupants), the role of being someone's lawyer, and (b) at least one interest tending to interfere with acting properly in that role. The *Code* understands a lawyer's role to be exercising "professional judgment . . . , within the bounds of the law, solely for the benefit of his client and free of compromising influences and loyalties."[2] The emphasis is on the lawyer's judgment within *that* role. The lawyer's professional judgment must be "independent." The lawyer must be

From Michael Davis, "Conflict of Interest," *Business & Professional Ethics Journal* 1 (Summer 1982): 17–23, 27. Used by permission of the author.

able to commit his legal training, knowledge, and sagacity fully to his client (within the bounds of the law and what the client wants done). Let us consider this analysis in detail. . . .

"Interest" is just short-hand for any influence, loyalty, or other concern capable of compromising a lawyer's ability to act for the benefit of his client (within the bounds of his role as a lawyer). Such concerns might include the temptation to turn the lawyer-client relation to the lawyer's advantage, the possibility of using confidence gained in one lawyer-client relation for the benefit of another client, or the necessity of sacrificing one of two clients whose interests have come in conflict. "Interest" does not, however, include *any* factor that might make judgment unreliable. For lawyers, all talk of conflict of interest presupposes a competent professional. Judgment made unreliable by ignorance of the law, poor training, drunkenness, or the like is incompetent, a failing of *"professional* judgment" rather than of *"independent* judgment." Conflict of interest is a problem of professional judgment, a problem of arranging things so that competent judgment can function as it ordinarily does. The "conflict" of conflict of interest is a collision between competent judgment and something that might make that judgment unable to function as the lawyer's role requires.

The ABA *Code of Professional Responsibility* implicitly distinguishes at least three kinds of conflict of interest. Some interests are such that they are certain to affect adversely the advice given or services rendered the prospective client. These create (what we may call) "actual" conflicts of interest. Other interests create only a "reasonable probability" of such adverse effects. Such interests create (what we may call) "latent" conflicts ("latent" because the conflict is already there, requiring only a change of circumstance to become actual). Other interests are such that a lawyer can "reasonably foresee" that an actual conflict may arise (even though there is not even a latent conflict yet). Such interests create (what we may call)

"potential" conflicts ("potential" because circumstances must change for such conflicts even to become latent). The boundaries of these three sorts of conflict are, of course, rather indefinite. The distinction is nevertheless useful.

. . . Suppose that a lawyer is considering becoming a candidate for Congress, that among his clients is an Indian tribe with a claim against the federal government, that the lawyer can foresee the Indians some day becoming dissatisfied with the slow pace of adjudication, and that under such circumstances it might be reasonable for them to try to get Congress to act on their claim directly. Such a lawyer already has a potential conflict of interest. He can reasonably foresee that he may some day have to choose between his client and his constituency. He may already have begun to feel the tug of constituent interests. There is already some reason for his client to be wary of depending upon his advice should the question of taking the claim to Congress arise. If the lawyer were then to run for Congress and win, the potential conflict would become latent. There would now be a reasonable probability that the lawyer-Congressman would have to advise on a question in which his interests as Congressman made his judgment as lawyer unreliable. But, so long as the Indians have no reason to become dissatisfied with the pace of adjudication, he does not have an actual conflict. He is not yet in a situation in which he will have to advise on the question of taking the claim to Congress. To be in a situation requiring advice on that question is to have a conflict of interest par excellence, an actual conflict.

The *Code* does not treat these three sorts of conflict of interest the same. The differences are instructive. . . . The *Code* looks with distrust upon *all* conflicts of interest, even those that are merely potential. For example, not only should a lawyer not accept proffered employment if his personal interests or desires will affect adversely the advice given or services rendered the prospective client, he should also not accept such employment if there is even a reasonable probability that they will have that effect.³ A lawyer should not draw up a will in which he is named a beneficiary, or take a case where there is much chance that he will be called as a witness concerning any controversial point, or agree in advance to accept as payment for services any publication rights relating to the subject of employment.

The *Code* flatly condemns not only actual conflicts of interest but also latent conflicts. The *Code* sets a lower standard only for potential conflicts. A lawyer may properly accept a client even if he can reasonably foresee that an actual conflict may arise. He may accept, but only if he explains the situation to the client and the client consents to continuing the relationship with the lawyer nonetheless.⁴ Thus, if a lawyer has a financial interest in a company competing with a client's, the lawyer may agree to draft contracts for that company only after making full disclosure of the potential conflict and receiving the client's permission to go ahead nevertheless. . . .

The *Code* also distinguishes between (what we may call) *having* a conflict of interest (potential, latent, or actual) and *acting* in a conflict-of-interest situation. . . . The *Code* expressly allows a lawyer to act in situations of potential conflict as noted above. . . . Such action is quite proper if there is full disclosure and the client consents nonetheless. The *Code*'s approach to acting in other conflict-of-interest situations is more complex. While it condemns most acting in situations of actual (or latent) conflict, it exempts much of it from discipline if the lawyer makes full disclosure and his client retains him nonetheless.⁵ . . .

The way the *Code* does that tells much about what the *Code* takes to be wrong with having a conflict of interest. What the *Code* says in effect is that while a lawyer *should* provide independent professional judgment, he *must* at least not betray the trust a client properly puts in him. If a lawyer has a conflict of interest (actual or latent), he must either refuse the proffered employment . . . or let the client know that he cannot trust

the lawyer to exercise his professional judgment as independently as lawyers ordinarily do. . . . To have a conflict of interest is bad, but to have one without putting the client on notice is worse. To be a lawyer is (the *Code* seems to say) to occupy a role traditionally understood to guarantee independent (professional) judgment. That guarantee is worth preserving. A conflict of interest makes the lawyer's judgment less reliable, endangering the client's interests whether the client is willing to tolerate the danger or not. So, a lawyer *should* (all else equal) divest. But, if a lawyer does not at least warn his client of the conflict, he does more than weaken a guarantee worth preserving. He presents himself as having a judgment more reliable than in fact it is. He invites a trust the invitation itself betrays. No matter how well things happen to turn out, the lawyer would not have behaved as his client had a right to expect him to behave. The lawyer would have taken risks his client did not know of, risks a client has a right to decide whether or not to take. If the lawyer does not realize he has a conflict (and that certainly is possible), he has failed to perform competently. Lawyers are supposed to recognize conflicts. If, however, the lawyer knows he has a conflict and chooses not to tell the client, having the conflict becomes an intentional wrong. The best analogue is . . . lying or promise-breaking. Disclosure and consent cannot end the conflict (because they cannot make judgment more reliable). But they can prevent automatic betrayal (because they allow the client to adjust his reliance to fit the circumstances).

The *Code* also distinguishes between what we may call "real" conflict of interest, whether actual, latent, or potential, and apparent conflict. An apparent conflict of interest is not a conflict of interest strictly speaking, but the mere appearance of such a conflict. The lawyer who merely has an apparent conflict will always know enough to show the conflict in question to be a mere appearance. A lawyer who (questions of confidentiality aside) cannot show that a conflict of interest is a mere appearance has a real conflict, not an apparent one. Consider, for example, our would-be congressman. If he knows that Congress lacks the power to do what his Indian clients might ask of him were he to win election, he has no conflict of interest, not even a potential one. Should any would-be constituent question him about possible conflicts, he could show that none existed. If, however, he did not know the limit of Congress's powers, he would (until informed otherwise) have a conflict of just the sort discussed earlier. His mistaken belief in the powers of Congress could affect the independence of his judgment on matters his Indian clients might put before him, just as any other conflict of interest could (assuming his mistake does not threaten his professional competence).

Since an apparent conflict of interest is only apparent, we might suppose that nothing is wrong with having such a "conflict." A cursory reading of the *Code* would give that impression. There is no provision expressly prohibiting "apparent conflict of interest." Indeed, there is nothing even resembling a discussion of the subject in the Canon concerned with professional judgment. Apparent conflicts are, however, something lawyers should avoid, and the *Code* says so in a way that explains what is wrong with them.

The *Code*'s discussion of apparent conflict of interest occurs under the Canon "A Lawyer Should Avoid Even the Appearance of Professional Impropriety." What is wrong with merely appearing to have a conflict of interest is what is wrong with merely appearing to engage in any form of wrongdoing. It has the same effect "real" wrongdoing has, once discovered, by justifying precautions costing time, money, the ability to maintain relationships of trust, or the like. The only difference in this respect between real conflicts of interest and merely apparent ones is that precautions adopted because of an apparent conflict are in fact unnecessary. So, to appear to be in a conflict of interest when one is not is to risk putting people to unnecessary expense. And knowingly to appear so

is wrong for much the same reason any misrepresentation risking harm to others is (whether or not harm is in fact done).

II. GENERALIZING THE LAWYER'S ANALYSIS

That is enough of the lawyer's analysis for our purposes. Its main components should now be familiar: (a) the role of being someone's lawyer and (b) an interest tending to interfere with proper exercise of judgment required in that role. To generalize the analysis so that it covers all of business and professional ethics, we need to replace being-someone's-lawyer with the appropriate category of which being-someone's-lawyer is a special case. If we take being-someone's-lawyer to be (as seems reasonable) a special case of relationships-between-persons-requiring-one-to-exercise-judgment-in-the-other's-service, we get the following generalization of the lawyer's analysis:

I. A person has a conflict of interest if (a) he is in a relationship with another requiring him to exercise judgment in that other's service and (b) he has an interest tending to interfere with the proper exercise of judgment in that relationship.

This formulation is too rough to be final. But it is good enough to start with. Let us consider it term by term to see what it entails. . . .

The generalized analysis does not, as formulated, refer to "role" at all, only to "relationship" of a certain kind. That is no accident. Though "lawyer" is a traditionally defined role, there is no reason to limit conflict of interest to traditionally defined roles. . . . Quite informal roles, mere relationships among persons, can, it seems, involve relatively clear conflicts of interest. For example: Suppose that I have been raising black angus bulls with the intention of competing with you in the next cattle show. Suppose too that you do not know of my intention, that you ask me to look after your bulls while you are away, and that I agree. Taking care of cattle requires exercise of judgment now and then. If your bull looks a bit weak, I may have to decide whether it is better to check its temperature now or wait till morning. If the wind picks up and the sky starts to cloud over, I may have to decide whether it would be better to bring the bulls in from the field now or wait a little longer to be sure there will be a storm. And so on. Given my interest in beating you at the next cattle show, I may not be as good a judge of such things as I would otherwise be. My own interests would tend to make my judgment on such questions less reliable than it would otherwise be. I have, then, a conflict of interest as soon as I agree to put myself in your service. If it is not too likely that I will have to exercise judgment while looking after your bulls, the conflict will be potential. But, even so, it will be there, informal role or not. . . .

What is judgment? Judgment must, of course, be something that lawyers exercise, but something too that not only lawyers exercise. For our purposes, judgment may be thought of as the capacity to make correctly decisions not as likely to be made correctly by a simple clerk with a book of rules and access to all the facts (and only the facts) the actual decision-maker has. Judgment implies discretion. A policeman does not need judgment (in this sense) to decide whether to issue me a speeding ticket once I have been clocked well over the limit, pulled over, and found to have no valid excuse. A bank president does not need judgment to decide whether she (as president) should embezzle the bank's money. And so on. For questions such as these, such persons cannot have a conflict of interest, however hard the question may be for them. In contrast, a critic needs judgment to decide how good a play or actor is. A member of Congress needs judgment to decide how to vote on a certain bill. And so on. Such persons can be subject to a conflict of interest in any situation where they are charged with deciding such questions.

Judgment is, of course, always judgment relative to certain questions, not judgment in the abstract. A conflict of interest is always a situation where someone is charged with deciding something or other. Acting in a situation of conflict is always deciding *that* something or other. For example: A bank president should exercise judgment in deciding to whom the bank should make loans. She can, then, have a conflict of interest when deciding such questions even if she cannot have a conflict when deciding whether to embezzle or not.

There will be borderline cases. A relationship can be defined by tradition, rule, or express agreement. Such relationships are likely to be relatively well-defined. But relationships can also grow up more or less haphazardly. Much can be left unsaid and ill-defined. Such relationships, not the well-defined ones, are the ones likely to turn up near the border. If we allow "role" its full elasticity, we will allow for relationships in which it may be impossible to know whether the role requires judgment and so, impossible to say whether a situation involving that role constitutes a conflict of interest. Such inchoate relationships are, however, not common. Even most informal roles are not *that* informal.

The more common reason for doubt about whether a particular situation constitutes a conflict of interest is lack of information. . . . For example, . . . "Is it a conflict of interest to recommend to one's own company a contract with another firm in which one holds substantial stock?" The answer depends in part on whether the recommendation requires judgment. Many such recommendations may be so routine that making them could be left to any clerk. Deciding to make such recommendations, like deciding whether or not to embezzle, would involve no exercise of judgment and so, would not involve a conflict of interest. . . .

[In addition to what is being decided, we need to know] what is "proper" in the role. If it were not part of serving the company to forego serving oneself where one cannot serve both, an executive could not have a conflict of interest even when faced with deciding whether to recommend a contract disadvantageous to the company but beneficial to himself. The term "proper" is relatively well-defined for lawyers. The *Code* specifies that role in detail, amplifying what tradition leads us to expect anyway. For most roles, however, there is no such code and tradition is not so settled. Still, insofar as a role is defined at all, it justifies certain expectations just as surely as does being a lawyer. For our purposes, what is proper in a role is just what is ordinarily expected of persons in that role, those expectations themselves being justified by express agreement, ongoing practice, rule, or the like. Even so informal a role as looking after someone's bulls while the owner is away justifies certain expectations, for example, that I will act for your benefit while looking after your bulls. We may then identify what is proper in the role

of recommending contracts by asking people who know about such things what they would expect of a person in such a role, what they generally rely on people in that role to be and do. . . .

NOTES

1. For a recent general discussion, see Geoffrey C. Hazard, Jr., *Ethics in the Practice of Law* (New Haven, CT: Yale University Press, 1978), especially Chapter 5. For a recent survey of the literature, see Robert H. Aronson, "Conflict of Interest," *Washington Law Review*, vol. 58 (1977), pp. 807–858.
2. American Bar Association, *Code of Professional Responsibility* (Chicago: National Center for Professional Responsibility, 1980), EC 5–1.
3. Ibid., EC 5–2.
4. Ibid., EC 5–3.
5. Ibid., DR 5–101(A) and DR 5–105(A).

The Accountant as a Public Professional

William F. Hamilton and William D. Callahan

INTRODUCTION

This article argues that the independent auditor owes a duty of care to the financial public. This public relies on the auditor's opinion that the examined financial statements were prepared in conformity with generally accepted accounting principles and that the numbers in the financial statements were stated fairly on the basis of tests made according to generally accepted auditing standards. This relationship of the outside, independent auditor to the financial public makes the auditor's position somewhat unique when compared to that of other professionals: An auditor's real client is not the party that engages him and pays for the rendered professional services; instead it is the generally unidentified immediate users of the audited financial statements, the financial public. Thus, the public accountant is a "public professional," not merely in the sense that the outside accountant performs a socially useful function, as must all professionals, but that in contrast to other professionals (e.g., physicians, lawyers, and dentists), the outside accountant's actual "clients" are the numerous and often un-

Used by permission of the authors.

identified members of the financial public. This social position of the accountant creates numerous problems for the profession that we hope to touch on in this short essay. Specifically, the accountant's relationship to his client and the financial public creates problems with respect to the profession's accountability for economic harm suffered by members of the financial public who, through audit failures, rely to their detriment on erroneous or misleading financial statements. The courts are now struggling with the so-called duty of accountants to immediate third-party users; the conclusion, we believe, is foregone. Without legislative intervention such a duty will likely become recognized in one form or another. The accounting profession, we suggest, is therefore faced with a choice: Either accept liability to immediate third-party users for audit failures or accept the social position of salaried state officials rather than that of independent, licensed professionals. The financial public will not allow the accounting profession to maximize its fees while avoiding responsibility for its professional performance.

I. CURRENT FERMENT: INTERNAL AND EXTERNAL CHALLENGE

From the U.S. Supreme Court to Congress and the Securities and Exchange Commission (SEC) and indeed within the accounting profession itself, a general state of ferment, change, and uncertainty regarding the profession is evident. In dicta that run counter to common law principles traditionally thought to govern the scope of an accountant's legal liability, the U.S. Supreme Court noted in its often quoted 1984 decision:

> By certifying the public reports that collectively depict a corporation's financial status, the independent auditor assumes a public responsibility transcending any employment re-

lationship with the client. The independent public accountant performing this special function owes allegiance to the corporation's creditors and stockholders as well as to the investing public. This "public watchdog function" demands that the accountant maintain total independence from the client at all times and requires complete fidelity to the public trust.[1]

The Supreme Court's unanimous opinion pierces the fiction that an outside accountant is merely a servant of the paying client. The Supreme Court has clearly stated—at least from the perspective of the federal judiciary—that the scope of a public accountant's liability is to be measured by the accountant's role as a public professional. As lawyers well know and accountants are quickly learning, responsibility means liability: Litigation against accountants has expanded and dramatically increased in the past ten years.[2]

The theme of the outside accountant as a public professional is not confided to jurisprudence. Recently SEC Commissioner Charles C. Cox addressed the American Institute of Certified Public Accountants' National Conference on current SEC developments and bluntly stated that "the profession is not accounting, but is rather public accounting" and that "the major lesson of 1985 is that a public accounting belongs unequivocally to the public," although possession is entrusted to the accountants.[3]

In October 1985, the *Journal of Accountancy* featured an article by Robert J. Sack, CPA, Chief Accountant of the SEC Division of Enforcement, entitled "Commercialism in the Profession: A Threat to Be Managed."[4] Mr. Sack noted that CPA professionalism is vital to the capital system, but that the threat of commercialism is the most dangerous of the profession's current problems because it is the "antithesis of the 'public first' attitude." Mr. Sack has argued that increased competition coupled with a changing market makes the profession increasingly vulnerable to pressure from client at the expense of the financial public. "The concern about commercialism today is a concern that the profession may be tempted to put present business interests ahead of the longer-term public interest."[5]

In September 1985, George Anderson, a former chairman of the AICPA, noted in his article "A Fresh Look at Standards of Professional Conduct" that "a crisis of confidence and credibility is confronting the accounting profession."[6] Finally, there are the more sensational accounts of the alleged crises, changes, and developments in the profession, such as Mark Steven's *The Accounting Wars: How Today's CPAs are Fighting for Business, Money and Survival.*[7]

II. THE RENAISSANCE IDEA OF A PROFESSION

One of the more interesting modern meditations on the relationship of the professional to society and the body politic is found in Alfred North Whitehead's *Adventures of Ideas.*[8] The concept of a profession engenders at least two principles: *independence* and *freedom of thought.* For Whitehead, ancient societies were based on crafts, static communal organizations, and rigid customs. The genius of the modern world is the liberation of practice and inquiry based on freedom of thought. "[A]ncient society was a coordination of crafts . . . whereas modern society is a coordination of professions."[9]

The concept of a profession is thus necessarily linked to the liberty of thought, the exchange of ideas among those interested, and separation from the compulsive apparatus of the state. It is the professions—as autonomous independent social agencies—that are entitled to act "without immediate reference to the state." Each profession, with its own telos, goals, and, more importantly, internal standards, receives a license or empowerment from the state to act in limited domains. A profession is a grant, a charter, and economically speaking, a monopoly.

III. ACCOUNTANTS AS PUBLIC PROFESSIONALS

There appears to be little or no current outside challenge to the accounting profession's formation and determination of professional standards and principles. The profession's organized societies, such as the American Institute of Certified Public Accountants (AICPA), in conjunction with university departments and the Financial Accounting Standards Board (FASB) are providing a rigorous and disciplined, albeit developing, theoretical analysis and examination of accounting principles and practices. It is not the articulation, development, and promulgation of accounting principles, but the execution of these principles and practices on which criticism is focused. The financial public is not demanding legislation of generally accepted accounting or auditing principles. This is the job of the duly constituted professional committees, the FASB, and the accounting professional as a whole. Should the political currents, however, begin to move in this direction, they should be opposed by the profession as a whole with the greatest vigor. Such intervention offends the theoretical and practical activity underlying the very essence of the profession. The public may—and indeed must—participate in the evaluation of the profession's field exercise and the accomplishment of its general goals; however, the public, *qua* public, is barred from injecting its opinions into the on-going theoretical or practical activities of the profession.

Accountants, however, must be flexible and open to change and suggestion in the area of public oversight and scrutiny of the profession. The general community must be convinced not only that accountants have properly constructed the basic framework of principles and practices through which the sophisticated demands of modern financial statement users are met, but that those principles and practices have been properly applied by the individual professionals who have accepted the responsibility of performance thereunder. Field work *must* be satisfactory. The financial public is not required to tolerate audit failures. This means that accountants must not be defensive regarding public supervision; nor is it in the profession's interest to attempt to ward off outside inspection by protests of adequate internal investigation, education, and controls. The latter should not be abandoned; however, the public will not be content with mere internal peer review because of the generally recognized institutional difficulty of policing one's own. This need for outside scrutiny is especially strong in the accounting profession because there is a built-in conflict of interest between the accountant and clients: Though the accountant's professional responsibilities to the financial public demand independence, the accountant is nonetheless paid by his client. This creates an immediate, apparent, and striking conflict of interest that can only be mitigated by complete, open inspection and disclosure. Because the accounting profession operates under a tremendous handicap by having this initial conflict at the very core of its professional activity, it must not resist outside scrutiny of its practice.

The public's most powerful weapon in the vindication of individual rights is the law courts. Until recently, legal action against accountants was unusual. (Even as this article is drafted, a special committee on accountants' legal liability reported to the AICPA on initiatives being undertaken to return to that halcyon era, among them the act of fully restoring the concept of privity.)[10] This resulted primarily from the lingering influence of certain legal decisions written by noted legal scholars prior to the securities legislation of 1933 and 1934.[11] Prior to the 1933–34 legislative scheme of openness, disclosure, and fairness in the financial markets, the audit was purchased by a client principally to uncover internal theft and embezzlement.[12] Such clients rarely brought suit against their accountants.

Today, however, the real victims of audit failures are creditors and other users of financial statements who, in relying on the auditor's professional opinion, have extended financial considerations to the debtor or purchased into the corporation on whose financial statements the accountant has expressed his opinion. However, until recently, the judicial system accepted the fiction that the principal relationship in the accounting profession was that between the accountant and his client, and barred suits against accountants by users of audited financial statements. This legal rigidity is now in retreat. Three state supreme courts have adopted an attitude of accountants' liability to immediate third-party users.[13] It is beyond controversy that the contemporary audit client obtains the accountant's opinion to influence others, and the accountant is aware of this purpose when rendering professional services.

This fact is inherent in the meaning of the expression "public accounting." Whereas most professionals render services directly to the client primarily for the client's benefit, the accountant, although paid by the client, renders services to the financial public in the sense that the accountant knows that others will be relying on his audit opinions in making their financial decisions. In contrast, the physician, for example, provides services to his patients, and his malpractice risk is limited to the harm his opinion or activity may cause to the patient, his paying client. The accountant, however, not only provides audit services to the client, but expects that creditors, investors, and other users will rely on his opinion. Indeed, one of the principal purposes and goals of modern accounting is to make useable information available to the financial public in a form that will serve as a predicate for rational decision making.

The jurisprudential block to extending liability to accountants was created and in part influenced by the linguistic nature of the tortious acts involved. The accountant puts his opinion—in standard form—in writing. Accountants use language unchanged since 1948 to describe the nature of their procedures ("We have examined the financial statements of XYZ Corporation ... in accordance with generally accepted auditing standards") and their conclusions arising from those procedures ("The accompanying financial statements present fairly XYZ's financial condition and results of its operations ... in accordance with generally accepted accounting principles consistently applied"). Accountants mean to leave themselves wiggle room; after all, an opinion, however clean, is not a warranty. Or is it? Clearly it contains a warranty that accepted standards of performance were adhered to during the conduct of the audit examination. Certainly it is a warranty that the accountant has adequately determined the financial statements to be free from material error. Undisputably it is a warranty that all financial disclosures necessary for fair presentation of the financial statements have been made. But does the warranty process extend beyond those areas? And for how long? Does it extend to all into whose hands the audited financial might ultimately fall?

To illustrate: Implicit in the accountant's notion of fair presentation is the belief that his client will continue in business as a "going concern" and that all assets reported in financial statements eventually will be converted into cash in a process that assures the perpetual life of his client. Partly on the belief that his client's future will be an extension of the present, the accountant issues his standard-form opinion, stating that the financial statements present fairly his client's financial position and results of operations. What then if the business should fail three, or six, or nine months after the accountant's work is concluded? At what point, if any, can the accountant breathe a sigh of relief and content himself in the knowledge that his client's subsequent failure was caused by intervening events that occurred after his work was completed and that nothing could have been overlooked in his audit which, had it been known at the time, might have caused him to have formed a different opinion about his client's financial statements?

The next judicial concern is the nature of the injury. Courts have traditionally been less solicitous of economic injury suffered by investors, corporations, and creditors than of personal injury suffered by individuals at the hands of negligent physicians or defective products. If a defective product is manufactured, law will permit any harmed purchaser—and generally any innocent bystander—to sue the manufacturer for damages. Consider, for example, the purchaser of a used automobile who is injured when an axle snap causes him suddenly to veer into a pole, striking a pedestrian. In most jurisdictions, both the driver and the pedestrian would have an action against the manufacturer should the cause of the accident turn out to be a vehicle defect. Similarly, if an architect designs an unsafe building and a passerby is hurt by a falling facade, the architect will quickly find herself sued for personal injury. However, in the majority of jurisdictions, if an accountant negligently audits a company and issues a clean opinion, the accountant cannot be sued by a commercial bank that lent money in reliance upon audited financial statements provided to the bank. Yet it is precisely this issue, that of implied fitness for use, that stands between the accountants and the return to public favor they now seek.

IV. THE FUTURE

The current state of affairs should be an embarrassment to the accounting profession. The legal precepts under which accountants have operated for decades amount to a form of immunity, excusing them from liability to the financial public, except if actual fraud, or a presumption thereof, can be proved. This era is quickly coming to an end. The current "legal crisis" of the accounting profession is in reality nothing more than the accounting profession's being brought into line with the liability risks of other businesses and fee-accepting professions. But where should the line be drawn? How should we balance the historic concept of a professional—one capable of thought and of independence who performs to standards set out by his governing council—with the needs for redress, often staggering, imposed by modern business society. Clearly the accounting profession's response to date— largely to assert that its internal controls provide adequate safeguards against malpractice—have been inadequate, for audit failures can and do occur. Education, supervision, and instruction within the profession are designed to avoid problems and, in the worse case, to discipline members by revoking their licenses. Internal controls, however, are of little use to the damaged creditor. Such victims can only seek redress in the courts. So long as redress is blocked, public antipathy toward accountants will rise.

If the accounting profession wishes to continue to function, as do doctors and attorneys, in the "private sector" and are to regain their once-esteemed role in financial society, accountants must be willing to stand behind their opinions and be prepared, if necessary, to make restitution for damages caused by audit failures. Doing so, and doing so willingly, will restore public confidence in ways that self-serving statements (accompanied by whatever degree of committee formation) never could. This is especially so since the spectacular rise of the accounting professional is a result of public laws' requiring annual and regular audits for use by an informed investing public.

There is, however, an alternative for the profession. The profession—or the public— may decide that because accountants are public professionals, they should be state-salaried employees. This is precisely the current position of professionals who by law do not have legal "duty" to those to whom they provide their services, and whose practices do not create private legal actions by those receiving their services. Without a waiver, sovereign immunity bars such actions that in any event typically are brought against the state and not the individual servant. This revision of status would not be the horror envisioned by some. Independent federal and state agencies could be established and salaries and stipends rendered respectable. Rigorous testing, examination, and work product review would assure quality and prestige. Of course, mechanisms would be needed to ward against overt political manipulation and to protect professional integrity, but these could be implemented.

The public accounting profession is thus on the horns of a dilemma: If it persists in blocking legal action by foreseeable users of audited financial statements, then the erosion of public confidence it so fears will continue; if it accepts the regulatory approach to discharging its public responsibilities, its members may have to accept standards of financial reward less opulent than those now enjoyed. Whatever its decision, it must choose or a choice will be made for it, for a disgruntled financial public has already served notice that it will no longer permit public accountants to shield themselves from professional liability while maximizing profits.

NOTES

1. *United States* v. *Arthur Young & Co.,* 79 L.Ed.2d 826, 836, 104 S.Ct. 1495 (1984).
2. Newton N. Minow, "Accountants' Liability and the Litigation Explosion," *Journal of Accountancy* 157 (September 1984): 70–88.
3. Charles Cox, "Public Accounting: Whose Profession Is It Anyway," 1986 Thirteenth Annual AICPA National Conference on SEC Development. January 7, 1986. (Available through the U.S. Securities and Exchange Commission, Washington, D.C. 20549.)
4. Robert J. Sack, "Commercialism in the Profession: A Threat to be Managed," *Journal of Accountancy* 160 (October 1985): 125–134.
5. *Ibid.,* p. 126.
6. George Anderson, "A Fresh Look at Standards of Professional Conduct," *Journal of Accountancy* 160 (September 1985): 91–106.
7. Mark Stevens, *The Accounting Wars* (New York: Macmillan, 1985).
8. Alfred North Whitehead, *Adventures in Ideas* (New York: Macmillan, 1933).

9. *Ibid.*, p. 57.
10. *The CPA Letter* 66 (March 24, 1986).
11. *Ultramares* v. *Touche Ross,* 255 N.Y. 170, 174 N.E. 441 (1931).
12. *International Mortgage Co.* v. *Butler,* No. G001099, slip opinion. February 20, 1986 (Cal. 4th Appeal District).

13. *H. Rosenblum, Inc.* v. *Alder,* 93 N.J. 324, 461 A.2d 138 (1983); *Citizens State Bank* v. *Timm Schmidt & Co.,* 335 N.W. 2d 361 (Wis. 1983); *International Mortgage Co.* v. *Butler,* No. G001099, February 20, 1986 (Cal. 4th District App.).

Code of Ethics: The Professional Catch 22

John E. Beach

In October of 1981, a jury in Ohio found an accountant guilty of negligence and breach of contract for violating the obligation of confidentiality mandated in the accountant's code of ethics and awarded the plaintiffs approximately $1,000,000. At approximately the same time, a jury in New York awarded a plaintiff in excess of $80,000,000 based in part on the failure of an accountant to disclose confidential information.

INTRODUCTION

A particularly difficult problem arises if an accountant learns that a client's negative financial situation or fraudulent activity jeopardizes the financial health of another. The dilemma facing the accountant is one of conflict of obligations. First, the accountant has the professional duty of integrity[1] and an ethical (and possible common law—see section VI) duty to prevent harm. On the other hand, the accountant has a professional duty not to disclose confidential client information. The accountant who discloses information regarding a client's negative financial position or fraudulent intent in order to prevent harm to others apparently satisfies these former duties. However, disclosures may well be at the expense of the accountant's professional duty of confidentiality to the client. It may, in fact, be impossible to honor both duties in a given situation.

. . . This article is divided as follows. Section I examines the reasons for the particular code's existence. In Sections II and III the target code section is applied to two actual cases and then these cases are set against one another in Section IV. The professional reaction to the cases is discussed in Section V and suggests an alternative approach to the problem which is offered in Section VI. However, any cure may be worse than the disease itself. In the long run, short of creating an absolute privilege regarding information obtained during the course of an accounting engagement, the courts are going to determine the relative rights of the parties regarding the obligations of confidentiality. As with most dilemmas, any resolution will

Reprinted by permission of the publisher from John E. Beach, "Code of Ethics: The Professional Catch 22," in *Journal of Accounting and Public Policy* 3 (1984): 311–323. Copyright 1984 by Elsevier Science Publishing Co., Inc.

no doubt be left until the problem reaches crisis proportions. Hopefully, however, this article will stir those in positions of responsibility to at least begin a thoughtful examination of the topic.

I. THE CODE: ITS EXISTENCE

The American Institute of Certified Public Accountants (AICPA) recognizes itself as an association of professionals who, collectively and individually, have a duty to the public. The Institute announced that this responsibility is "a distinguishing mark of a professional . . . " (AICPA, ET Sec. 51.01 "Introduction") and accordingly "all true professions have deemed it essential to promulgate codes of ethics and to establish a means of ensuring their observance" (AICPA, ET Sec. 51.01 "Introduction"). . . .

As it is difficult at best for the average person to adequately assess the quality of the service rendered by an accountant, it seems appropriate that a code exist that gives assurances of fair and honest treatment. In truth, the Institute and its members are probably in the best position to determine the proper level of responsibility owed to the public and clients. The *Code* of the Institute, in an attempt to establish this proper posture, " . . . *emphasizes* the profession's responsibility to the public . . . " (AICPA, ET Sec. 51.04) and "*stresses* the . . . responsibility to clients and colleagues . . . " (AICPA, ET Sec. 51.05). This is accomplished within the *Code* as it deals with the issue in separate sections by identifying both "Concepts of Professional Ethics" and "Rules of Conduct." The "Concept" section is designed as a philosophical essay. It suggests behavior above and beyond that considered the minimum standard of care but it "is not intended to establish enforceable rules" (AICPA, ET Sec. 50, Preface). On the other hand, the "Rules" "consist of enforceable ethical standards" (AICPA, ET Sec. 50, Preface). A member who is found guilty of violating a rule is subject to disciplinary action by the body through its trial board (AICPA, ET Sec. 92.01).

Enforcement is not left to AICPA itself. The *Code* may also be enforced by the individual state boards of accountancy through their respective corrective processes. This is possible as the *Code* has been adopted, or used as a model in the adoption of rules, by the boards and are therefore a part of the administrative law which governs the accountants' activity. Corrective action may be taken in the courts as well as through the imposition of money judgments against the professional whose violation of the code has caused injury.

II. RULE 301 AND ALEXANDER GRANT

A "Concept" found within the AICPA *Code* clearly states "it is fundamental that the CPA hold in strict confidence all information concerning a client's affairs which he acquires in the course of his engagement" (AICPA, ET Sec. 54.02). This is later followed by Rule 301, which reads:

> *Confidential client information.* A member shall not disclose any confidential information obtained in the course of a professional engagement except with the consent of the client.

The idea that such information should be held in confidence finds expression not only as a matter of ethical concern, but in an enforceable rule of the AICPA (and the state boards). The accountant is therefore under the affirmative duty not to disclose confidential information.

It would seem appropriate at this time to apply Rule 301 to a specific fact situation. Consider a recent case involving Alexander Grant and Consolidata Services.[2] The plaintiff, Consolidata Services (CDS) was a bookkeeping and payroll processing firm. The defendant, Alexander Grant and Company (AG), is a major accounting firm that provided tax and other services to CDS. On January 28, 1978, a meeting was held between representatives of AG and the president of CDS to discuss an outstanding debt for past accounting services. At that time, the current financial status of CDS was made known to the AG representatives and it was determined that CDS was $150,000 short of cash in its payroll accounts. AG asked CDS to disclose this cash problem to its clients. CDS refused. On February 6, 1978, at another meeting between the parties, AG again insisted on disclosure. CDS once more refused and specifically asked AG not to disclose the information. The next day, AG, without notifying CDS, began calling mutual clients and advised them not to send additional payroll funds to CDS. Ten days later, CDS terminated its operations and closed down its office. It subsequently sued AG, alleging that the unauthorized disclosure was the precipitating factor in the closing of the business. The jury agreed and awarded substantial compensatory and punitive damages. The decision has been upheld in part by the Court of Appeals of Ohio. The case is now under appeal in the Ohio supreme court.

In rendering its decision, the Court reasoned that a mere breach of an ethical concept established by the board of accountancy does not in itself provide a cause of action (a conclusion with which I vigorously disagree). However, the court did find a present duty through another theory.

> As has been pointed out by both parties, the statutory and case law in Ohio, as well as in other states, is void of any discussion concerning such a cause of action; and, therefore, this case appears to be one of first impression in the United States. However, this court recognizes that the legal basis upon which such liability could be established exists. It is implied in every contractual relationship between an accountant and his client that a general duty exists not to make extra-judicial disclosures of information acquired in the course of their professional relationship; and that a breach of that duty by an accountant may give rise to a cause of action (Wagenheim 1983, p. 3398). . . .
> There is " . . . credence to the proposition that it is within the expectations of both parties . . . that these restrictions not be violated. . . . As a result, there is a legal obligation existing in every accountant-client relationship . . . , unless specifically excluded, that all information communicated . . . by its client in con-

fidence should not be disclosed without the client's prior consent" (Wagenheim 1983, p. 3401).

In essence, the court said that the rules had become a part of the contract between the accountant and client.

From this case, one might reach the following conclusion:

> A specific requirement or prohibition found within a code of ethics establishes the minimum legal requirement regarding the subject. That standard is incorporated by reference into the contract between the accountant and client. Failure to adhere to the duty expressed in the standard is a breach of contract.

III. THE OTHER SIDE OF THE COIN WITH ARTHUR ANDERSEN

The above conclusion states a neat and concise rule that can be easily understood. As applied to Rule 301, the code obligation of confidentiality becomes legally binding. Though adherence to Rule 301 is capable of 100% compliance, it is not at all certain that such a high degree of compliance is always desirable or ethical. The accountant " . . . must not let his regard for the client's interest . . . override his obligation to the public to maintain his independence, integrity, and objectivity. The discharge of this dual responsibility to both clients and the public requires a high degree of ethical perception and conduct" (AICPA, ET Sec. 54.01). The ethical concept suggests that there may well be a possible overriding concern—that being the welfare of others. Although this concern for others is a compelling argument, it flies in the face of the specific rule, i.e., Rule 301.

The following facts will set the stage for another look at the rule (Fund of Funds 1982, 545 F. Supp. 1314).[3] The plaintiff, Fund of Funds (FOF), purchased a considerable number of natural resource properties from one John King and/or King-related corporate entities. It appears that the properties in question were considerably overvalued at the time of sale and later revalued. The defendant, Arthur Andersen and Company (AA), was engaged by FOF as its auditors. AA was apparently aware of the pricing policies of the King group before all the properties in question had been purchased by FOF. Additionally, AA was also involved in the later revaluation of the properties. The facts indicate that AA was also the auditor of the various King group entities.

The plaintiff alleged that AA was aware of the irregularities in the pricing practices of the King group and that AA did not reveal this information, to the detriment of FOF. Additionally, it was alleged that AA was in possession of information regarding fraud practiced by the King group in the revaluation of the properties in question and again failed to disclose pertinent information. Therefore, FOF contended that AA was guilty of both common law fraud and breach of contract in its auditing capacity by not informing FOF of all material information within AA's knowledge or material information that AA should have reasonably discovered regarding the values of the natural resource interests. The plaintiff reasoned that as AA had also audited King, it had or should have had facts at its disposal that could have, if known to the plaintiff, prevented the alleged financial injury.

AA's defense was based on the grounds that it had properly performed all aspects of the contractual relationship with FOF and it had not fraudulently, knowingly, or recklessly failed to discover and/or disclose material information. Additionally, for the purpose of argument, it urged that even if it had information regarding the alleged overvaluation (AA claims that it had no such information), " . . . that the duty of confidentiality prohibited disclosure . . . " (Fund of Funds).

The judge instructed the jury on the elements of breach of contract. The jury was presented with, among others, the following questions on the *Special Verdict Form:*

1. "Are defendants liable of common law Fraud?"

2. "Are defendants liable for breach of contract?" (Fund of Funds, Jury Charge)

The answer that the jury returned to both questions was "yes." One might conclude that the jury felt that AA had the contractual duty to disclose information, confidential or not. This leaves the unsettling conclusion that disclosure of confidential information may in some cases be required and the rule barring such activity must take a back seat to other overriding considerations. . . .

The code prohibition found in Rule 301 raises the ethical and legal duty of the accountant above that required of citizens generally. This duty runs to the client. If the particular accountant/client relationship were isolated, there would be no problem. But in the real world, relationships between various individuals and groups of individuals sometimes mesh, sometimes stand alone, sometimes run parallel courses, and occasionally come together violently. This latter possibility is what we have here. The extraordinary duty of confidentiality has collided with and been checked by the duty to disclose information based on a contractual obligation. The source of the accountant's dilemma arises out of ethical, legal, and code demands. Accordingly, the accountant may owe conflicting duties to different clients in related transactions, and to clients and members of the public. If that be the case, the profession is in a "no win" situation.

IV. THE DILEMMA: A "CATCH 22"

Consider the facts of the Alexander Grant case to be as they were, but now, for purposes of argument, the conclusion will be modified as follows:

1. XYZ Inc. (a fictitious organization), a client of both Consolidata and AG, regularly transmitted payroll funds to CDS;
2. At the point in time when AG learned of CDS's precarious financial position, AG remained silent and did not disclose any confidential information to XYZ or any other client of CDS;
3. CDS, being insolvent, terminated its business

operations while holding payroll funds of XYZ. These funds were not disbursed to XYZ's employees. XYZ Inc. was then required to meet its payroll obligation at severe economic hardship;

4. XYZ Inc. is now simply one of the many creditors of CDS in line with little or no hope of recovering its loss; and

5. XYZ Inc. sues AG for this loss based on the theory that AG owed XYZ (a) a general contractual duty to disclose information in its possession that could prevent economic injury, and (b) a common law duty to prevent harm if possible as this ethical concern so pervades the common law, it overrides Rule 301.

The shoe, so to speak, is now on the other foot. The court or jury in this hypothetical case would be faced with a different type of claimant than the one found in the actual Grant case. Now, not asked to find liability for an affirmative act in violation of Rule 301, that is, the disclosure of confidential client information, it would be asked to find liability for an act of omission, that is, for failure to disclose confidential information that could have prevented harm. By applying the reasoning of the FOF case to the present facts, there is the distinct possibility liability could be found. The clear implication is that there is a conflict regarding duties. The disclosure of confidential information to the detriment of a client is an actionable wrong, but so too is the failure to disclose confidential information to the detriment of a third party. The accountant is damned if he does, and damned if he doesn't! (See the argument in section VI regarding duty based on recognized position of public trust.)

V. REACTION AND IMPLICATION

Reactions to the dilemma faced by the accountant regarding issues of confidentiality were reported in the *Wall Street Journal* in an article on the Alexander Grant case (Yao 1981). There, in response to the actual finding of liability in favor of CDS, an unnamed SEC attorney was reported to have said that

Alexander Grant should have called all the customers of Consolidata instead of simply those who were also clients of the accounting firm. Such an obligation would dictate that an almost impossible effort be mounted in cases where an accountant learns of facts that suggest financial harm to others. This is as broad a position as one could take regarding the duty of the accountant to clients and members of the general public. It certainly suggests that the SEC attorney considered Rule 301 merely as a guideline subject to the specifics of a particular situation. The basis of this view originates at its source. The SEC has numerous rules that mandate disclosure for the purpose of protecting the public. However, the facts in the Grant case go only to the code obligation itself. These specific federal regulations are of significance but they were not at issue in that case. The issue was confined to the common law interpretation of the code as it pertained to a specific contractual engagement.

The AICPA's general counsel is reported to have expressed concern for the public welfare, as the Wagenheim decision struck a balance between public interest and confidentiality, apparently in favor of the latter (Yao 1981). The impression that immediately comes to mind suggests that "enforceability" of the "Rules" is relative. Yet, as has oft been said, "You can't have your cake and eat it too." One cannot profess a canon of confidentiality as a shield to the client and at the same time, in the parenthetical recesses of the mind, harbor the vague exception that will strip away the protection so specifically granted. As presently stated, it cannot be used as the accountant deems fit in each situation according to whose ox is then being gored.

The conceptual issue here, while having been exemplified by the obligation of confidentiality, has to do with a code that contains statements of absolute obligation. It may seem surprising that those who draft such codes are prone to the absolute. It is difficult to visualize an absolute rule, without possible exception, suitable for every occasion. There are those who would say that one should never kill another person regardless of the circumstances. Yet, when faced with the rule, "Thou shalt not kill," I believe that the majority of people would take the life of another if doing so appeared to be the only way of protecting their own or the life of a loved one. Is one supposed to keep the commandment of Rule 301 at the expense of severe financial injury to others, or are there exceptions to this rule? . . .

At present, the AICPA *Code* recognizes exceptions to Rule 301 in practice-related incidents (where disclosure is called for by GAAP and GAAS), legally compelled disclosure, AICPA reviews, and in disciplinary proceedings (AICPA, Rule 301). Might it not be deemed desirable to amend the AICPA *Code* to allow disclosure of information in circumstances similar to those recognized by the ABA and ICA? The judge in Wagenheim stated:

> Although the duty of confidentiality implied in the accountant-client relationship is favored, this court recognizes that such a duty is not absolute. Overriding public interests may exist to which confidentiality must yield. . . . (Wagenheim 1983, p. 3403).

If one believes that failure to disclose information for the protection of others is unethical, then such an amendment would be the appropriate course of action for the AICPA. . . .

VI. CATCH 22 TO CATCH 22, FROM FRYING PAN TO THE FIRE

Let us now consider the possibility of the AICPA amending Rule 301 to include the following: ". . . Information may be disclosed to prevent the client from causing imminent serious physical or financial injury." The code duty of confidentiality would no longer be absolute and the accountant could disclose "confidential" information in certain circumstances. Given this power to disclose, the question arises as to a duty to do so. Precendent suggests that the duty to dis-

close does not arise with the code itself, and if it does exist, it does so through other theories of law. "As a general rule, the law imposes no duty on one person actively to assist the preservation of the person or property of another. . . . Those duties which are dictated merely by good morals, or humane considerations, are not within the domain of the law" (American Jurisprudence 1968, Negligence, Sec. 41). If there is no contractual relationship that would require disclosure of possible economic peril, it might appear that there is no legal duty to become involved. Yet in the FOF case, the jury apparently felt an ethical obligation could exist that required disclosure. This certainly suggests that juries are inclined to find for an individual where a loss has been sustained that could have been prevented.

It was suggested by the SEC attorney quoted earlier that even under the current law, the accountant may have an obligation to inform even those with whom he has no contractual relationship. Such a duty could be based on a general obligation to the public. As noted above, one is generally not required to volunteer. However, there may be precedent to support the theory that such a duty does exist due to an individual's particular position within society. If a duty to the general public is found because of one's station, failure to disclose would then be actionable (American Jurisprudence 1968, Negligence, Sec. 44).

Individuals in positions of public trust do in fact have a duty to the general public regarding the prevention of harm. Certainly one will recognize that members of the medical profession have such a duty regarding both public and individual health. Recently, a number of cases have held members of the medical profession liable for failure to warn or to protect individuals specifically known to be in peril by the probable conduct of a patient.[4] In some of these cases, the duty to prevent harm was extended to any person foreseeably endangered by the patient.[5] In these cases, the potential harm was known to the medical practitioner through information that, by definition, was confidential. Although the obligation of confidentiality did exist, a broader duty was recognized, that being the duty to prevent harm from being visited upon innocent individuals. The physician-patient relationship imposes affirmative duties on the physician for the benefit of persons other than the patient.[6]

Because of the accountants importance to the economic well-being of individuals and the public generally, they likewise hold a position of public trust. The accountant's position regarding economic health parallels that of medical professionals regarding physical health.[7] That is, the duties of the accountant go to the public generally, to third parties, and to clients. A common law duty may thereby be imposed upon the accountant to disclose information, confidential or not, that would tend to protect the well-being of persons known to be in peril. As the duty to disclose certain information may exist, a code power to disclose would operate as a mandate, not merely a suggestion, primarily because of the accountant's position of public trust.

Given the possibilities of both the power and the obligation to disclose, one might consider additional areas of potential conflict. By way of example, one must recognize that legal duties usually arise in such situations regarding not only what the professional actually knew, but what a reasonable professional *should know* through the exercise of due care. Therefore, the obligation would exist to disclose information that may or may not actually be in the "hands" of an accountant. Additionally, reasonable people may disagree as to the appropriate definitions of the words "imminent" and "serious." Considering all of the factors, the position of the accountant would be much as that of the football coach on Monday morning when asked to explain certain decisions made during the game that led to unfortunate results. The person questioning the coach has both the benefit of hindsight and the time to weigh the correctness of the decision in light of the results. A person questioning an accountant regarding the appropriateness of disclosure or nondisclosure in a particular situation is similarly situated. The accountant, as the football coach, is called upon to make decisions in the "heat of the battle" and must proceed without benefit of knowing what the precise result will be. In other words, given the power by code amendment to disclose in certain situations, a determination of the correctness of doing or not doing so becomes the province of the judge or jury (American Jurisprudence, Negligence, Sec. 172). Leaving this question for later argument in the courts should cause the accountant to wince.

If such an amendment is deemed necessary, a possible way by which the problem could be eased is through the inclusion of limiting language. This has been done in other situations where there was the potential of questioning of events after the fact.[8] By restating the exception as follows, the situation might (only might) be eased: ... except the accountant, using reasonable professional judgment as to the facts as they appear at the time, may disclose information in order to prevent the client from causing imminent serious financial injury to others." Yet then again, who is to define "reasonable professional judgment."

CONCLUSION

The promulgation of a code of ethics or the review of one already in existence should be performed only with extreme care. Consideration must be given every section as to both benefit and cost. The examination of just one section of a particular code, Rule 301 of the AICPA *Code of Professional Ethics*, points out the problems that exist for the client, members of the profession, and the general public. It can therefore be concluded that codes of ethics may well be fraught with pitfalls for the unwary. To write a code avoiding all problems is quite impossible in light of the conflicting interests addressed. If a code is to exist, it must be drawn carefully, not written simply to put up a good facade. Putting it on paper for this latter reason can be more dangerous than not having a code at all. . . .

The interesting question raised has to do with a conflict of legitimate expectations. On the one hand, the client expects the professional to keep information confidential. In opposition to that position is the right of other individuals to their reasonable expectations, i.e., the right to proceed in their activities without unreasonable fear of injury. If the policy-makers are inclined to the former, they could institute a policy of absolute privilege, thereby protecting both the client and the accountant. If the policy-makers lean to the latter position, they will let the matter alone, allowing the courts to develop the law as changing times and conditions dictate. This author is inclined to take the latter position.

NOTES

1. *AICPA Professional Standards, Vol. 2.* ET, Section 52, "Independence, Integrity, and Objectivity." Therein it states, "A certified public accountant should maintain his integrity and objectivity . . . "
2. Appellate *Wagenheim, J. S. (Consolidata Services, Inc.)* v. *Alexander Grant & Co.,* 1983. 10th District, Court of Appeals, Ohio 3393.
3. This case is limited in that it did not go beyond the trial court level. There was a jury decision and a lengthy judicial determination (cited here) regarding AA's motion for a new trial and a judgment notwithstanding the verdict. (The parties settled before the matter reached the appellate level.) Yet, as noted in the CDS case, this is a developing area of the law and therefore any judicial statement must be considered as having at least some significance. The case itself is extremely involved and included allegations of SEC violations as well as wrongs based on the common law rules of fraud and contract. The discussion here will attempt to isolate the common law allegations as the issues of confidentiality are so limited.
4. *Tarasoff* v. *Regents of the University of California.* 1976. 551 P2d 334.
5. *Petersen* v. *Washington.* 1983. 57 P2d 230 (W).
6. *Lipari* v. *Sears, Roebuck & Co.* 1980. 497 F. Supp. 185.
7. *Kemmerlin* v. *Wingate.* 1979. 261 SE2d 56, (S. C.).
8. The Uniform Commercial Code 2-704(2) states, "Where the goods are unfinished, an aggrieved seller may, in the exercise of reasonable commercial judgment for the purpose of . . . " The "Official Comments" to that section note that discretion is vested in the seller to exercise ". . . reasonable commercial judgment as to the facts as they appear at the time. . . . " The burden shifts to the opposing party "to show the unreasonable nature" in the exercise of commercial judgment.

REFERENCES

AICPA Professional Standards. New York. American Institute of Certified Public Accountants, Vol. 2.

American Jurisprudence 2d. 1968 (updated). Jurisprudence Publishers Inc.

Carey, J. L., and Doherty, W. O. 1966. *Ethical Standards of the Accounting Profession,* New York, American Institute of Certified Public Accountants.

Fund of Funds v. *Arthur Andersen & Co.,* Federal District Court, S.D.N.Y., "Jury Charge," pp. 13, 14.

Yao, M. 1981. Client's suit against Alexander Grant spotlights "The accountant's dilemma." *The Wall Street Journal,* October 27, p. 8.

The Hostile Takeover: An Opposition View

Lisa Newton

I. RIGHTS AND CONSEQUENCES

Given the nature and prestige of the players, we might be tempted to think that the *hostile takeover* is just one more game businessmen play. But the business literature on the subject sounds atypically harsh notes, describing this activity in the unbusinesslike language of threat and attacks, followed by occasionally desperate and increasingly sophisticated defenses—the junk-bond bust-up takeover versus the Pac-Man, Poison Pill, Crown Jewel Option defenses ranged against the two-tier tender offer and finally the launching of the golden parachutes.

In this colorful literature, the most noticeable feature of a corporate takeover is its terrible human cost. *Fortune* magazine entitled a 1984 article, "Help! My Company Has Just Been Taken Over," and began the article with the story of the suicide of a corporate executive precipitated by his termination following a takeover. "There are more mergers than ever these days," the author warns, "and their human toll is higher than ever too."[1] A more recent *New York Times* article, entitled "'People Trauma' in Mergers" documents the anxiety and feelings of betrayal experienced by employees—increasingly, down to the hourly level—when the prospect of takeover looms into view. Trust is broken, loyalty ebbs, and, if none of the above is of any interest to managers, productivity plummets.[2] The fact that these alarms come from publications inside the business world is significant; outsiders might be expected to see human effects more clearly than the economic realities that underlie the takeover activity, yet here are the insiders suddenly concluding that the realities of profit may actually be less important than the injuries to the people caught up in it against their will. The hostile corporate takeover is simply *not* business as usual. It is assault with a deadly weapon; and the question seems to be, how can it be right?

Let us backtrack for the moment. A practice requires moral scrutiny if it regularly derogates from human dignity, causes human pain, or with no apparent reason treats one class of human beings less well than another. Any practice that regularly throws people out of work does at least the first two of those (work being possibly the largest factor in self-worth and the major instrument to creature satisfactions), and unless we find the raider's urgent need for self-aggrandizement as a worthy reason for dismembering working units, it probably does the third also. To be sure, all manner of evil things can happen to people in non-takeover situations; part of the fun of being alive is the risk, and part of being in business is knowing that your livelihood may depend on the next quarter's earnings. But as a general moral principle, if I, by my voluntary act and for my own profit, increase the riskiness of your life, no matter how high the base risk and no matter how small the increment by which I raise it for you, then I owe you an explanation. The hostile takeover regularly disemploys at least some people who would not have been unemployed absent the take-

Used by permission of the author.

over; that makes it, by the above, a proper candidate for moral scrutiny, without presumption one way or another on the results of the scrutiny.

A further problem, if it is a problem, is that a takeover deliberately destroys something—a company, corporation, an instance of human association. In the other cases, it can be said that the association itself "decided" to do something to make itself better, or more efficient. But when it is taken over, it does nothing—it is killed, and the atmosphere of the threat of death hangs over the entire proceeding, from the raider's first phone call to the final resolution (usually the acquisition of the company by some party other than the raider). Does it make any difference, that a company is destroyed? Is that an evil over and above all the other disruptions that takeovers occasion? Or is it, strictly speaking, meaningless, beyond the sufferings of the individuals?

We have, in short, two very separate and distinct questions. First, does the hostile corporate takeover serve some ordinary and necessary role in the economy? Whatever the present injuries, is the practice justified in the long run as improving the economic condition of the greatest number? That very pragmatic question is accompanied by a second, metaphysical one: Is the corporation the type of thing whose demise could or should be regretted? Could it have some right to live, to persevere in existence—a right appropriately exercised in management's series of "defenses"? Ordinarily we assume that only individual human beings have dignity, worth, or rights (beyond the uninteresting legal "rights" bestowed on the corporation to permit it to conduct business). But that assumption fits poorly with the fact that people will willingly die for their associations when they will not willingly sacrifice their lives for personal interests; that fact needs further examination before we dismiss the association as a merely instrumental good. We will pursue, then, two separate and logically independent lines of inquiry: First, on straightforward utilitar-

ian reasoning, does the business practice that we know as the *hostile takeover* serve the public interest by performing some useful role in the economy, or are there good utilitarian reasons for limiting or prohibiting it? Second, does the corporation have some right to exist that is violated by any business practice that ends its existence without the consent of its present governors? Along the line of the first inquiry, we will argue, first, that the hostile takeover is damaging to the economy (and the people in it) in the short and middle run and, second, that this practice is a deadly symptom of a long-term process in our relation to material goods, a loss of "ownership," which ought to be noted and, as far as possible, reversed. On the line of the second inquiry, we will argue that "the association," usually the political association, has been invested with dignity since Aristotle's day, and that its right to self-defense is firmly grounded in individual rights of undisputed worth. Therefore the corporation, acting through its present management, has the right and (sometimes) the duty to defend itself when its existence is threatened, apart from any arguments about immediate effects on the wealth of individuals.

II. RESPONSIBLE OWNERSHIP PROFITS

Takeovers are generally defended on the utilitarian grounds that they are in the public interest. The "takeover" is simply capital flowing from one sector of the economy to a more profitable one, in this instance, to buy up the stock of a company the value of whose assets is significantly greater than the value of its outstanding stock. Where stock is undervalued, an inefficiency exists in the economy; whether through management ineptness or other market conditions, the return on the shareholder's investment is not as high as it could be. It would be maximized by selling off the assets and distributing the proceeds among the owners; but then, by the above, it is management's duty to do that.

The takeover merely does the job that the managers were supposed to do, and the prospect of a takeover, should the stock become undervalued, is an excellent incentive to management to keep the shareholders' interest in mind.

Moreover, defenses against takeovers often involve managers in apparent conflicts of interest. They are protecting their jobs rather than meeting their fiduciary obligations to stockholders. Theory in this instance concurs with current case law; there should be no regulation of takeovers beyond (not very rigorous) anti-trust scrutiny, and defensive moves on the part of management are morally and probably legally illegitimate. To be sure, people get hurt in takeovers, but the shareholders profit, and control of the corporation belongs by statute to them. Against these considerations, what arguments can be raised that unregulated takeover activity is harmful, wrong, contrary to the public interest, and ought to be stopped by new legislation?

The best approach to a response may be to peel an onion: All of the evils seem to be related, differing primarily in the level of analysis suited to elicit them. Beginning with the surface, then, we may note the simple disruption caused by hostile takeover activity: The raider's announcement that a certain percentage of shares of a company have been purchased, more to follow, immediately puts the company in play in a deadly game from which it will not emerge intact. Productive activity, at least at the upper levels of the target (where salaries are highest), stops. Blitzkrieg raider tactics are met with poison pills, sales of crown jewels and other defenses—often of questionable legality. Orderly planning disappears. Employees, terrified for their jobs, spend their days in speculation and the search for another job.[3] Other bidders emerge from the Midwest, from abroad, from next door. Nobody sleeps. All the players hire lawyers, financiers, banks, and start paying them incredible amounts of money. (In the takeover of Revlon by Pantry Pride in the fall of 1985, the investment

bankers' share alone came to over $100 million, legal fees to over $10 million, and the negotiated "golden parachutes" to $40 million. Added up, the costs of the takeover—not one penny of which went to shareholders—came to close to 9 percent of the $1.83 billion deal.)[4] However the game ends, people are exhausted, betrayed, out of work, and demoralized. The huge debt incurred by the acquiring company, secured by the assets of the target (by the infamous *junk bonds*), requires the immediate dismemberment of the company for financial survival (more on this later), and financial health, under those circumstances, is out of the question. And all this to what end?

"Hostile takeovers create no new wealth," Andrew Sigler pointed out to the House Committee on Energy and Commerce, "They merely shift ownership, and replace equity with large amounts of debt." He continues:

> More and more companies are being pushed—either in self-defense against the raiders or by the raiders once they achieve control—into unhealthy recapitalizations that run contrary to the concepts of sound management I have learned over thirty years. This type of leveraging exposes companies to inordinate risks in the event of recession, unanticipated reverses, or significant increases in interest rates. . . . Generation after generation of American managers have believed that there *must* be a solid equity basis for an enterprise to be successful in the long term. This long-term equity base absorbs—in exchange for the expectation of higher returns—the perils of depression, product failure, strikes, and all the other dangers that characterize business in a free economy. That healthy conservatism is now being replaced by a new game in which the object is to see how far that equity base can be squeezed down by layers of debt. And too much of this debt is carrying interest rates far in excess of those a prudent manager can possibly be comfortable with.[5]

At a second level, then, the takeover has two deleterious effects on the management of corporations: First, when the takeover materializes, equity is inevitably transformed into debt, leaving the company terribly vulnerable to foreseeable reverses; second, anticipating takeover attempts, management may well be tempted to aim for short-term profits and engage in aggressive accounting practices to show higher current earnings. These practices may weaken the company and deceive long-term investors, but they will be reflected in a higher stock price and thus one more resistant to attack.[6] As Peter Drucker put it, "Fear of the raider and his unfriendly takeover bid is increasingly distorting business judgment and decisions. In company after company the first question is no longer: Is this decision best for the business? But, will it encourage or discourage the raider?"[7] Fear of the raider may encourage the managers of a company to put up their own money as well as to incur debts well beyond prudence, to take the company privately in a "leveraged buyout." All the same risks, including bankruptcy in the event of any reversal, attend the buyout as attend the takeover.[8] Nor is it clear that the damaging effects of these maneuvers are limited to the domestic scene: As Harold Williams (chairman of the Securities and Exchange Commission during the Carter administration) points out,

> The pursuit of constantly higher earnings can compel managers to avoid needed write-downs, capital programs, research projects, and other bets on the long term. The competitiveness of U.S. corporations has already been impaired by the failure to make long-term commitments. To compound the problem because of fears of takeovers is a gift to foreign competitors that we cannot afford.[9]

The alarms, confusions, and pains first noted as the result of hostile takeover activity, are then compounded by what seems to be very imprudent business practice. But imprudent for whom? Do the target shareholders, at least, get some profit from the takeover—and if they do, does that not justify it? Michael Jensen, one of a new breed of scholar known as the "shark defenders," ar-

gues that they do and that does. He dismisses worries about shareholders' welfare as "folklore," and insists that "science" shows otherwise.[10] His evidence for this claim is interesting:

> More than a dozen studies have painstakingly gathered evidence on the stock price effect of successful takeovers.... According to these studies, companies involved in takeovers experience abnormal increases in their stock prices for approximately one month surrounding the initial announcement of the takeover.... The evidence shows that target company shareholders gain 30% from tender offers and 20% from mergers.[11]

But isn't the raider's effect pure artifice? Let his initiative be withdrawn—because of government opposition, or because he has agreed to purchase no more stock for whatever reason—and the same studies show that the stock immediately reverts to its previous value.[12] So it was not, really, that the company's stock was too low. It was rather that the flurry of activity, leading to speculation that the stock might be purchased at an enormous premium, fueled the price rise all by itself. Or could it be that certain professional investors find out about the raid before the public does, buy the target's stock at the lowest point, sending it up before the announcement, wait for the announcement, ride the stock to the top, then sell off before the defense moves, government action, or "targeted repurchase" (see the section on "greenmail," below) stop the takeover bid and send the stock back down to its true market value? As Jensen's figures confirm,[13] that value is often a bit *lower* than the starting value of the stock; after all those payouts we are dealing with a much poorer company. Nothing but evil, for all concerned except professional fund managers and investment bankers, seems to come of this takeover activity.

Hence, at the first level there is disruption and tens of millions of dollars' worth of unproductive expense; at the second level there is very dubious business practice. At a third, there is the betrayal of the stakeholders. Current laws, as discussed earlier, force the directors of the target company to consider only shareholder rights and interests, to the probable disadvantage of the other stakeholders: employees, retirees, creditors, host communities, customers, and suppliers. But each of these has helped to build the company to its present state, relying on the company's character and credit-worthiness; the employees and retirees, especially, have worked in expectation of future benefits that may depend in part on the good faith of management, good faith that can hardly be presumed in a raider.[14] The mid-career, upper middle-level managers are especially vulnerable to redundancy and the least likely to be able to transfer their acquired skills and knowledge elsewhere.

Some elimination of positions resulting from duplication is inevitable in any merger, of course, hostile or otherwise, and when carried out under normal conditions succeeds at least in making the company more efficient, even if the cost to the individual is very high. But only some of the people-cutting in these extravagant takeovers stems from real redundancy. Companies are paying such high takeover prices that they have to engage in deep cost-cutting immediately, even to the elimination of personnel crucial to continued operations. The "efficiency" achieved may not serve the company well in the long run, but the raider's calculations rarely run very long. As a consequence, middle-management employees (who are, on the whole, not stupid, and read the same business publications as we do) seem to have taken all this into account and reoriented their work lives accordingly:

> Management turnover at all levels is on the rise and employee loyalty is at a low, according to consultants, executive recruiters and the companies themselves. And there is growing evidence, they say, that merger mania is an important reason for both problems, spreading fear about layoffs and dissatisfaction with other changes in the corporate environment. These problems, in turn, promise to make it harder for companies to realize the anticipated efficiencies that many of them pointed to in justifying their acquisitions.... Critics of the takeover binge maintain that the short shrift given to 'people issues' ... [is] one reason why perhaps half to two-thirds of mergers and acquisitions ultimately fail.[15]

Do we owe anything to people who have worked for a company and who may actually love the company and may be devastated by its dismemberment or transformation? At present, our law does not recognize, or even have any language to describe, the rights possessed by those who have contributed to the growth of an association, have participated in it and loved it, and now see it threatened. The fact that such rights are by no means absolute does not mean they are not there. Classical political theory has the vocabulary to discuss them, under the rubric of the "just war"; discussion of the implications of that doctrine for the hostile takeover issue will occupy the final section of this paper. Rights or no rights, and prudential considerations (as discussed earlier) aside, the condition of the stakeholders ought not, in charity, to be ignored; yet our institutions make no provision for them. Here we have, in the center of the most civilized sector of the civilized world, an open wound, a gap of institutional protection most needed by those who have worked hardest, which we struggle to paper over with the "unemployment benefits" fashioned for different people in different circumstances. Law and business practice seem to require a callousness toward human need and human desert that is incompatible with our notions of justice.

Inevitable disruption, mandated imprudence, and legally required injustice are the first three levels of palpable wrong in the hostile takeover phenomenon. It may be that the fourth layer, the last under consideration in this section, has more worrisome implications than all of the above. The thesis is simple: At primary risk in all of this is our concept of ownership. For all of human history, we have been able to trust property owners (individuals or groups) to take care of their property, because it was in their interest to do so, and outside of military and government property, that was how the property of the world was cared for. With the corporate takeover, that may no longer be the case for the kind of property that looms so large in Western economies, the publicly held corporation. And this development is very alarming.

To begin with the concepts: Ordinarily we use the concepts of *ownership* and *property* interchangeably; even etymologically, they are indistinguishable. But the concept does have two distinct aspects: the primary aspect of a legally protected complex of rights and duties obtaining between the owner and other *persons* and the less prominent aspect of a diffuse set of nonlegal duties, or imperatives, incumbent upon the owner to take care of the *owned thing,* itself. This duty of care has a history of its own; the duty to the thing, analogous to the duty of *stewardship* when the property of others is in question, attaches naturally to the legal owner.

Ownership has the longest history of any concept still extant in the West, certainly longer than its ultimate derivative, *personhood.* Aristotle assumed that the union of man and property, along with the union of man and woman, lay at the foundation of the household and hence of all society. Ownership is presupposed, and discussed, throughout the earliest books of the Bible. The list of *what* was owned was very short: animals, people (slaves), land, tools, buildings, and personal effects. Except for the last item, all were essential to survival, and all required care. The duty arises from that fact.

Whether ownership is single or shared, the duty corresponds to personal interest. If I own a sheep, it is very much in my interest, and incumbent upon me, to take care of the beast and see that it thrives. If you and I together own a sheep, the same interest applies to both of us, the same imperative follows, and we shall divide up the responsibilities of caring for it. If you and I and 998 others own it, enormous practical difficulties attend that care. But however small my interest in that sheep, it is still in my interest that the animal should thrive. Similarly, partial ownership in a whole herd of sheep, or a farm, or a factory, or a business that owns several factories, does not necessitate a change in the notion of *ownership.*

Liquidation consumes something that is owned, or turns it into money that can be spent on consumption. The easiest way to liquidate a sheep is to eat it. The way to liquidate most owned things is to sell them. Then you no longer own the thing, and your responsibilities terminate; but so, of course, does all future good you might have gotten of the thing. Part of the cultural evolution of ownership has been the elaboration of a tension between retention and liquidation, saving and spending, with the moral weight of the most successful cultures on the side of thrift and preservation. The business system probably depends as much on Ben Franklin's "A penny saved is a penny earned" as it does on Adam Smith's "invisible hand." The foreseen result of the *hand,* we may remember, was to increase the wealth, the assets, of a nation. For the herdsman it is self-evident that if you slaughter or sell all your sheep, you will starve in the next year; for Smith, it was equally self-evident that it is in a businessman's interest, whatever business he may be in, to save his money and invest it in clearing more land, breeding more beasts, or building more plants, to make more money in the future. Hence the cleared land, the herds, and the factories—the assets of the nation—increase without limit, and all persons, no matter how they participate in the economy, in fact share in this increased wealth. Presupposed is the willingness of all players in the free enterprise game to acquire things that need care if they are to yield profit, hence to render that care, and to accept that responsibility, over the long run. Should that willingness disappear, and the population suddenly show a preference for liquidation, all bets are off for the wealth of the nation.

And the problem is, of course, that the developments of ownership made possible in the last century create excess tendencies toward liquidation. If several thousand of us jointly own several thousand shares of stock, we may in theory bear the traditional responsibilities of owners for those companies, but we shall surely not *feel* them. And if we purchased those shares not for the sake of investing in the companies, but for the sake of having money available to us at some future time (say, in a pension fund), we will have acquired them for a purpose that is directly contrary to our concerns as owners. We will be involved in a conflict of interest and obligation with ourselves: On the one hand, we should be protecting and nurturing the company(s) we (partially) own, plowing profit back into improvements in plant on occasion, even if that means no profit this year; on the other, if it seems we could get more money if the company were liquidated and the proceeds shared around, we should work toward that end. Suppose that we several thousand owners hire a fund manager to make sure our pension fund provides us with as much pension as possible. That manager, hired with those instructions, is not an owner, and has *no* responsibility toward the companies. On the contrary, his entire obligation is to us and the increase of our money. Where liquidation serves that purpose, it is his job to bring it about. Ownership, for such a manager, is no more than present legal title to property, a way station between sums of money, and its whole moral framework has become totally irrelevant. To complete the picture, let only the tax structure subsidize that liquidation in cases of takeover:

> Accounting procedures and tax laws ... shift much of the cost of acquisitions to taxpayers through the deductibility of interest payments and the revaluation of assets in ways that reduce taxes ... I suspect that many of the acquisitions that proved profitable for acquirers did so largely because of tax benefits and the proceeds from busting up the target company. If liquidation is subsidized by the tax system, are we getting more liquidations than good business would dictate?[16]

The answer is probably yes.

Institutional investors—those gargantuan funds—now own up to 70 percent of the stock of the publicly owned corporations. It must be unprecedented in human history that majority ownership of such entities lies with "owners" whose interests may be best served by the destruction of the object owned. In the case of companies that own large holdings of natural resources, forests, or oil reserves, it is usually the case that the assets sold separately will yield more than the companies' stock. (As Minow and Sawyier grimly put it, under current practices such companies "are worth more dead than alive.")[17] Any company, in fact, that regularly works for the long term (funding research and development, for example), can be profitably liquidated: Whatever those raiders may be, they do not need to be geniuses to figure out which companies to attack. The only limits on the process of liquidation of the country's assets by the managers hired by those investors, or by the raiders that cater to their own interests, might be the success of new and inventive defenses.

The evils of the takeover market, then, go to the philosophical base of our market system, striking at the root of moral habits evolved over 2500 years. The corporate raiders have yet to make their first widget, grow their first carrot, or deliver their first lunch. *All* they do is turn money into money, cantilevering the profit off the shell of responsible ownership. No doubt capital is more productively lodged in some places than others, but it follows from no known economic theory that it is more beneficial to the world when lodged in T. Boone Pickens's bank account than when lodged wherever it was before he got it. Possibly it will end up facilitating some industrial projects—he has no intention of keeping it in a mattress, after all—but only in those that promise quick profits. We need not look to him to revitalize our smokestack industries and make them competitive on the world markets. The whole productive capacity of the American economy seems at the mercy of moneymen on the rampage, with all productive companies under threat of being taken over, taken apart, and eradicated. Surely this condition cannot be healthy or good.

In sum: This section has tried to provide a series of pragmatic arguments that the present rash of corporate takeover activity is harmful to the stakeholders, to the economy, and to the general public, from all of which it would follow that regulation is justified. In the next section we attempt to provide a defense for the proposition that a corporation has a real right to exist, hence to resist takeover.

III. THE ASSOCIATION AS WORTH KEEPING

Individuals may be hurt by the corporate takeover. The corporation, on the other hand, is usually killed. Does this fact add anything to the list of injuries, or is it simply a shorthand way of saying that the individuals are no longer part of it? Does the corporation have a right to life—a right to persevere in existence, as itself, under its own laws and practices, at least to the extent that would give it a presumptive right to mount a defense against hostile takeover?

The disutility of unregulated takeover activity, implying the desirability of some regulation in the public interest, was the theme of the last section. In this section we ask a different question: Can the corporation be seen as an entity analogous to an individual human being, with rights, including the right to defend itself (through the actions of its officers) regardless of the utilities involved in each case? The law is unsympathetic to defensive moves in takeover situations, suggesting that the right in question here is not derivable from any acknowledged legal rights or present powers of the corporation. It must be found, if it is to be found anywhere, as a logical derivation from other recognized rights of the corporation or, more likely, of the individuals who make it up.

We may begin the inquiry by noting that over the last decade, philosophical students of the corporation have been moving cau-

tiously in the direction of grounding their moral discourse, in the assumption that the corporation is a moral individual like other moral individuals.

It is possible, however, that a corporation may be capable of assuming moral responsibility and still not have rights, but it is not likely. Our attribution of rights rests heavily on the attribution of moral agency, which alone confers worth or dignity on the human, and moral agency is the condition for attribution of moral responsibility. In the literature, the development continues, and recent work (e.g., Patricia Werhane's *Persons, Rights, and Corporations*) accepts that corporations have, indeed, moral rights, even if only "secondarily."[18]

There is, however, one body of literature precisely on the point of our question, albeit not one that deals with "the corporation" as this paper understands the corporation. Since Saint Augustine, the right of a nation to defend itself against foreign aggression has been recognized. While the political association, as Aristotle and Augustine understood it, may seem an odd model for Phillips Petroleum and Continental Group, it is possible that the literature articulating any collectivity's right of defense may help us formulate one for the modern corporation.

The queerness of attributing a "right" to a collectivity rather than to an individual was not generally noticed in discussions of the Just War, most likely because its recognition predates the theory of individual rights by several centuries; nations had rights long before we did. But if we are to make sense of this right in a modern political context, it must be restated in terms compatible with individual rights theory. Michael Walzer undertakes this task in *Just and Unjust Wars*. For Walzer, the right of the political association to exist comes from the general right of *social contract*—the right of people to join together in any voluntary association, preeminently the state, the association charged with the whole governance of a people. (This is the right primarily challenged in *aggression*, which threatens to abrogate it permanently.)

Like Burke before him, Walzer does not understand the agreement that binds the state as a set of real "contracts."

> What actually happens is harder to describe. Over a long period of time, shared experiences and cooperative activity of many different kinds shape a common life. . . . The moral standing of any particular state depends on the reality of the common life it protects and the extent to which the sacrifices required by that protection are willingly accepted and thought worthwhile.[19]

Again,

> The right of a nation or people not to be invaded derives from the common life its members have made . . . and not from the legal title they hold or don't hold.[20]

So the fact of the common life, which has been made by the participants in it, is the immediate source of the right to defend it, presumably necessarily mediated by the desire of participants to defend it. Walzer is likely correct that the right of the state to defend itself stems from the right of a people to create a common life, to adorn and embellish it, to examine and reform it, and by spending themselves on it, to make it valuable—a variety of the rather prosaic right of association. And the reason why people exercise that right in the formation of permanent associations, which build up a history for themselves, is that associations extend individual life in dimensions that the individual otherwise cannot control—in time, in space, in power. To the limited and partial individual, participation in an association provides immortality, global reach, and collective power. The individual needs the association for these benefits, and in this way the right of association is grounded in human nature. When my association is attacked, my basic security in these insecurity-ridden areas is very much endangered, and that is why I so justifiably resent any attacks on it.

Has this argument any validity for the corporation? Here the relatively recent moves to articulate the internal order of a corporation precisely as a historical culture, with a set of values and commitments all its own, may have some relevance. It would be tempting to argue that a corporation that has, as have the best companies of the recent literature, earnestly pursued excellence in all respects, taken care of its employees, stayed close to its customers, produced the highest quality product, and really cared about its communities, has somehow earned the right to exist, while the others have not.[21] Temptation must be resisted: the difficulties of discerning the "excellent" companies from the others are insurmountable. But maybe we don't have to make that judgment: If a corporation, even in theory, can be the kind of collectivity that the state is, and can serve the purposes in human life that a state can serve, then good or bad, it shares in the state's presumptive right to defend itself.

To summarize this section: The association provides those individuals who voluntarily and fully participate in it with goods they can not get elsewhere—social recognition, material reward, and above all the extension of the limited self in space, time, and power. These are the reasons why the right of association exists and is exercised, and why the result of that exercise has, derived from that right, the right to stay in being and to expect its officers to mount a defense for it should that turn out to be necessary. But that is all we need to establish the right to defend itself against hostile takeover attempts.

That conclusion does not entail, of course, that present officers may do anything they like in the course of a defense; as Walzer points out, there are standards of justice in war as well as standards to determine if a war as a whole is just. (At present, for instance, the payment of greenmail to a raider—a premium price to obtain his stock and only his stock, to persuade him to go away and leave the company alone—raises questions of acceptable practice in the event of a takeover, more than the poison pills,

ESOPs, and Crown Jewel Options designed to make a company significantly poorer in the event of takeover.)

CONCLUSION

We have argued that as a matter of right, and as a matter of utility, the takeover game should be ended. Capital is not unlimited; in a country rapidly losing out to foreign competition in part because of outdated plant, and declining in its quality of urban life in part because of obsolete and crumbling infrastructure, there are plenty of worthwhile uses for capital. Law that turns the attentions of the restless rich away from cannibalizing productive corporations, toward investing in the undercapitalized areas of the economy, would be a great public service.[22]

NOTES

1. Myron Magnet, "Help! My Company Has Just Been Taken Over," *Fortune*, July 9, 1984, pp. 44–51. See also Joel Lang, "Aftermath of a Merger," *Northeast Magazine*, April 21, 1985, pp. 10–17.
2. Steven Prokesch, "'People Trauma' in Mergers," *New York Times*, November 19, 1985.
3. *Ibid.*
4. *Wall Street Journal*, November 8, 1985.
5. Testimony of Andrew C. Sigler, Chairman and Chief Executive Officer of Champion International Corporation, representing the Business Roundtable, before hearings of the Subcommittee on Telecommunications, Consumer Protection and Finance of the House Committee on Energy and Commerce, Thursday, May 23, 1985.
6. Some of these considerations I owe to con-

versations and correspondence with S. Bruce Smart, Jr.
7. Drucker, *Wall Street Journal*, January 5, 1983.
8. Leslie Wayne, "Buyouts Altering Face of Corporate America," *New York Times*, November 23, 1985.
9. Harold M. Williams, "It's Time for a Takeover Moratorium," *Fortune*, July 22, 1985, pp. 133–136.
10. Michael Jensen, "Takeovers: Folklore and Science," *Harvard Business Review* 62 (November–December 1984): 109–121.
11. P. 112. The footnote on the studies cites, for a summary of these studies, Michael C. Jensen and Richard S. Ruback, "The Market for Corporate Control: The Scientific Evidence," *Journal of Financial Economics* (April 1983). The studies are cited individually in the same footnote; *ibid.*, p. 120.
12. *Ibid.*, p. 116.
13. *Ibid.*
14. Another point owed to conversations and correspondence with S. Bruce Smart, Jr.
15. Prokesch, "'People Trauma' in Mergers."
16. Williams, "It's Time for a Takeover Moratorium," pp. 133–136.
17. Newton Minow and David Sawyier, "The Free Market Blather Behind Takeovers" Op-ed, *The New York Times*, December 10, 1985.
18. Patricia H. Werhane, *Persons, Rights, and Corporations* (Englewood Cliffs, N.J.: Prentice-Hall, 1985), p. 61.
19. Michael Walzer, *Just and Unjust Wars* (New York: Basic Books, 1977), p. 54.
20. *Ibid.*, p. 55.
21. Criteria freely adapted from Thomas J. Peters and Robert H. Waterman, Jr., *In Search of Excellence* (New York: Harper and Row, 1982).
22. In developing the ideas for this paper, I have profited enormously from conversations with Lucy Katz, Philip O'Connell, Stuart Richardson, Mark Shanley, Andrew Sigler, S. Bruce Smart, Jr., and C. Roger Williams.

Takeovers and Takeover Defenses: Some Utilities of the Free Market

Craig Lehman

An intriguing phenomenon in recent financial reporting has been the emergence and elaboration of a great variety of good versus evil metaphors to describe corporate takeover struggles. "Raiders" attack the peace-loving corporate settlers; the greedy thugs of arbitrage demand "greenmail"; beleaguered Fortune 500 damsels pray for the intervention of a "white knight." My favorite image, however, is the one that describes the embattled organization's deployment of "shark repellent." It's *Jaws* all over again: We visualize the frail, innocent corporation being threatened with "dismemberment" to satisfy the shark's blind, insatiable appetite, and surely, we are supposed to think, *any* act or device that protects it against this kind of threat is justified.

I want to dwell on this last metaphor, however. For it seems to me that there is a good deal to be said *for* takeovers, and that much of it can be worked out by simply thinking about the shark metaphor in a little more detail. For instance, sharks play a valuable role in the ecology of the ocean; they help weed out the weak and poorly adapted, and in so doing contribute to conditions in which new species can flourish. Similarly for takeovers: They are often precipitated by weak, poorly adapted management, and they provide a mechanism whereby productive assets can be transferred to the hands of new, more entrepreneurial managers who are capable of making them work more efficiently. Second, sharks, or some predator like them, are probably inevitable, in a biological sense;

there is an obvious role for predators in nature. It is unreasonable to blame sharks for doing what they do; and unless we are prepared to attempt to change the whole ecology of the ocean, we have to accept the role they play within that framework. By the same token, it is difficult for me to see how there could be anything like the institution of the publicly traded, shareholder-owned corporation without takeover bids. If someone wants an economic system in which the corporation's shareholders *cannot* generally decide to sell their assets to others who desire to purchase them—in which, in other words, shareholders are not free to exercise a fundamental right of *ownership*—then they are certainly proposing to tamper with a basic element of the capitalist ecology, and we should be very skeptical until we see a cautious, thoroughly worked-out environmental impact report.

Consider too the concept of *shark repellent*. In certain cases, there is obviously nothing objectionable about this. If there is a practical way to do it, I would be happy to see sharks kept out of lagoons frequented by small children. If my life raft were being circled by sharks, I would have no qualms about trying to shoot or club them. In general, I'm not much worried about the "rights" of either animals like sharks or fictitious legal "persons" like shell corporations set up to acquire stock in takeovers. But as a matter of public policy, it would be unwise to allow individuals to employ any shark repellent they choose, no matter how drastic. Suppose

Used by permission of the author.

the Resort Owner's Association engages in a systematic poisoning campaign, for instance; we might well wonder whether the damage to the environment is worth whatever marginal safety is gained for human beings. Equally, there is reason to be skeptical that "poison pills" and other anti-takeover devices are compatible with preserving the virtues of our economic environment. If managers can do whatever they please to repel corporate takeover bids that threaten their jobs, then one of capitalism's main methods for holding corporate power accountable is eliminated. If investors who see the potential for more productive management of an enterprise are blocked from buying up a controlling interest and carrying out their plans, then we interfere with one of the important mechanisms whereby our economic system achieves efficiencies. In general, while tampering with the balance of nature often seems to promise the alleviation of some immediate and easily perceived harm, we must be very careful not to pay the price of giving up a larger systemic benefit.

But enough of metaphor. To describe the content of this paper in plain philosophical language, I will be discussing moral issues in corporate takeovers from a fundamentally rule-utilitarian perspective. I will examine both takeovers and takeover defenses—"shark repellents"—and point out what I believe are some of the main utilities and disutilities of various practices. I will be defending an economic system in which the takeover process is not directly regulated or restricted, while condemning many but not all forms of management-instituted takeover defenses.

It is important to appreciate the significance of the concept of a *practice* in the view just sketched.[1] The publicly traded, shareholder-owned corporation—like promising, punishment, marriage, and somewhat like an ecosystem—is an *institution*, involving an interrelated set of established rules and customs. Institutions and the practices involved in them have to be evaluated in terms of the results they produce as an entire and ongo-

ing system. Of course, no evidence should be disregarded, but one cannot look at the beneficial or harmful results of a single takeover, or promise, or punishment, or marriage, or shark attack, and form any meaningful conclusions about the overall utility of the institution in which the event occurred. Rather, the focus must be on the *patterns* of effects that the institution brings about, and any proposed changes must be evaluated in the light of their impact on all parts of the system. Accordingly, my discussion of takeovers and takeover defenses will concentrate on a few global effects of takeover bids and takeover defenses and will emphasize some of their broader but less immediately obvious consequences. In Part I, I discuss three of the main positive utilities associated with takeovers, and in Part II, I point out some of the disutilities associated with unrestricted private deployment of several varieties of "shark repellent." A brief concluding note introduces some reservations.

I

I will begin by discussing three main systemic utilities of takeovers: their role in the process of capital reallocation, their role in shareholder control of management, and their role in opening up opportunities for new, more entrepreneurial management. These are actually closely related, as we will see when we turn to some contemporary examples, but I will begin with an idealized and simplified discussion of the contribution takeovers make to the process of capital allocation.

Capital allocation is important because manufacturers need capital to build factories, purchase inventories of raw materials, and staff offices before they can make a single sale. If the market is to respond efficiently to increasing demand for some products and decreasing demand for others—and capitalism's defenders claim that this is one of the system's major virtues—then capital must be free to flow in and out of the various sectors of the economy.

This can happen in a variety of ways. Suppose, for instance, that widgets are the product of the future, but that right now there is only one widget manufacturer: The megatrend has not yet arrived. So right now the stock of Widget Corporation (which represents ownership of widget-producing assets and a flow of future earnings from widget sales) may well be selling for less than it is worth, according to various theories of securities valuation. As the boom in widgets becomes more visible and finally arrives, however, the price of Widget Corporation stock will be bid up, and eventually it will become high enough that some investors will prefer to put up capital for new widget-producing facilities (or alternative technologies), rather than paying a premium for the stream of earnings from the current facilities. Thus the realization of asset values is the first step in a larger process that eventually leads to a greater supply of the products consumers desire, at a price constrained by competitive pressures. This is one of the basic and fundamental utilities of a capitalistic system.

One way in which takeovers are part of this picture is that they can *speed* the process of asset value realization and capital flow. If individual investors who see the value of owning widget-producing assets start buying up the stock of Widget Corporation, it may be several years before the stock is fully priced and there is an economic incentive to bankroll new widget facilities. (Common advice to asset-oriented investors is to be very patient.) But if Behemoth Corporation or Octopus Investors Group devour all the stock of Widget Corporation in one gulp, there is no "pure play" left in widgets; those who want to make a killing in this area will have to put their capital into new facilities. Takeovers can thus *accelerate* the process of asset value realization and capital flow. In any case, however, capital flow is capital flow whether it comes from the treasury of a large, established corporation or the investments of individuals. If a low-growth,

"smokestack"-type company uses some of its capital to buy a high-tech company instead of building another factory, that represents capital reallocation as surely as if individual investors had decided to sell the securities of the smokestack company and purchase those of the high-tech company.

In the illustration just given, a takeover was part of the flow of capital *into* a growing industry; the electronics-computers-telecommunications industry would be a rich source of examples of this sort (General Motors' recent acquisition of Electronic Data Systems, for instance). Indeed, many small electronics firms are started up with the hope of someday being bought out by a major company. But takeovers can also facilitate the flow of capital out of mature or moribund industries; this more closely resembles the case with the recent highly publicized takeover bids for oil companies.

The key phenomenon here is that some parts of the oil business have become far less profitable than others over the last decade or so. Excess capacity coupled with lagging demand has resulted in the bankruptcy of many independent refineries; the neighborhood, full-service, brand-name gasoline retailer is fast becoming an anachronism; exploration and development, particularly in the United States, have become increasingly expensive and difficult. On the other hand, proven reserves represent a steady and relatively certain cash flow, in many ways comparable to owning the shares of an electrical utility company. For instance, the argument goes, large fixed assets that are a dependable source of revenue can be borrowed against heavily to increase current income. Thus, while there were once strong incentives to vertical integration in the oil industry, capital is now demonstrating its natural tendency to flow into the areas that yield a high return and to flow out of the sectors in which supply exceeds demand.[2]

If something like this sketch is even roughly correct, then a number of recent events in the oil industry—not just takeovers—become comprehensible. All of T.

Boone Pickens's proposed takeover deals have been predicated on disposing of refining or retailing operations, increasing debt, and putting more of the cash flow from oil reserves directly into shareholders' hands. But Pickens hasn't been the only one to have this idea. Atlantic Richfield, under no immediate takeover pressure, has sold refineries, shut down East Coast marketing operations, incurred additional debt, and raised its dividend payment. Exxon, probably too big to be taken over, has nevertheless been buying back its own shares, which increases the return to shareholders and also says that the company thinks that refining and exploration (as well as electric motors and office equipment) are *not* the best way to spend its money. Chevron, the "white knight" that rescued Gulf from Pickens, did so not because it had a multibillion-dollar urge to be chivalrous; it saw the same value in Gulf's reserves that Pickens did, and upon acquiring Gulf promptly sold off some major refining and marketing operations. And Unocal, a Pickens takeover target for a while, responded by increasing debt, buying back stock, raising its dividend, and offering shareholders units in a trust.

In this light, many oil company takeovers (as well as many takeovers in other industries where assets are more valuable unbundled than conglomerated) are seen simply as manifestations of the market trying to reallocate capital; current management may think bigger is better, but the capital markets have in effect been demanding that organizations with inefficient divisions grow smaller and devote resources only to operations in which they can achieve an acceptable return on investment. Capitalism thus turns out to have a built-in mechanism that counteracts the drive toward bigness for its own sake, and the takeover appears in a new light, as a way in which the market can discipline managers who have failed to heed public demands for a reallocation of capital. "Villains" such as Pickens, Carl Icahn, or Sir James Goldsmith are recast as inevitable and impersonal outgrowths of market pressures.

Finally, from this perspective, the takeover also appears far less important than recent coverage has made it out to be. For if it is really just one mechanism among many by which capital is reallocated, with about the same effects as other mechanisms, there is no reason to single it out for moral censure: The complaint should be with the whole system. What, for example, is the moral difference between Arco voluntarily closing down refineries and service stations in response to current market conditions, and Pickens taking over a company with less astute management and doing it for them? In either case, there has simply been a response to the market's demand that resources not be squandered on the additional refined products and old-fashioned gasoline stations that consumers no longer want. The objection would seem to be to our system's relentless demand for efficient capital allocation, not to takeovers in particular.

Of course, the system as a whole can be questioned, but establishing that one interlocking set of economic practices produces greater on-balance utility than another is a much larger undertaking than simply identifying unfortunate human consequences of selected takeovers and deploring them. Shark attacks have unfortunate human consequences too, but the problem is to find an environmentally acceptable way to eliminate the threat they pose while still allowing human beings the pleasure of swimming in the ocean.

As noted earlier, the capital-reallocation and shareholder-control functions of takeovers have tended to converge in recent instances. There have been few recent takeover bids (or proxy battles, or leveraged buyouts) in which someone has *not* been proposing to sell off at least some of an organization's assets, and frequently this has been the central issue. In a way, this is not very surprising; the rational agent's allocation of resources in the free market environment is at the heart of capitalist economic theory. Nevertheless, shareholder control of management is a logically independent reason for favoring a basically unconstrained take-over environment. The arguments in favor of procedures that allow society to remove less able or morally corrupt figures from the governmental power structure are well known and are appreciated in political philosophy. A mechanism that enables large, crisscrossing constituencies of shareholders to exercise a similar kind of social control in the corporate sphere can claim very plausibly to produce similar benefits.

A final systemic utility of takeovers is the entrepreneurial opportunities many of them provide. True, General Electric's recent acquisition of RCA will not do much for entrepreneurship, but that is because the two companies have been described as a "perfect fit." *Most* takeovers result in the sale of overlapping or inefficient divisions. Indeed, one senses that much of the moral concern about recent takeovers is actually directed at "bust-up" takeovers, in which most of a corporation's divisions are sold off. But look at the other side of this coin, says the advocate of free markets. These divisions will tend to be bought up by more entrepreneurial investors, people who have "an idea" and are convinced that they know how to make a go of the business even when the previous owner couldn't. And, of course, many times they are correct; one recent example is Weirton Steel, which was (let us not forget) *taken over* by its employees. This defense of a free-market takeover environment has its roots in the views of the economist Joseph Schumpeter, who glorified the entrepreneur as "the fundamental impulse that sets and keeps the capitalist engine in motion," but who also spoke of a process of "creative destruction" as "the essential fact about capitalism."[3]

II

So three large and interrelated patterns of utility are claimed for a free-market takeover environment: enhancement of the market's ability to efficiently reallocate capital, social control of corporate management, and creation of new opportunities for entrepreneurs. This is like pointing out the major contributions that sharks make to the maintenance of the oceanic ecology. But the shark analogy led to a mixed conclusion about shark repellent: sometimes plainly justifiable, sometimes excessive, damaging to the environment, and (from a public-policy perspective) deserving of prohibition. The problem is to work out what an analogous stance would amount to in the case of corporate shark repellent.

Let us begin this discussion by briefly characterizing some of the main tactics that are at issue.

1. Perhaps the most dramatic and widely discussed shark repellent is the "poison pill." In its classic and most common form, the poison pill is a new issue of preferred stock declared by the board of a company threatened with a takeover. This preferred stock has a very special characteristic: In the event that the company attempting the takeover succeeds, holders of the acquired company's new preferred stock will be entitled to buy shares of the acquiring company at a huge discount—typically, half its market price. Since this makes the takeover prohibitively expensive, it theoretically provides the target company with absolute protection against being acquired.

2. Supermajority requirements, staggered board terms, noncumulative voting, and two-class common stock form a group of functionally similar repellents. All of them in some way alter the corporation's voting and representation rules to make it more difficult for the would-be acquirer to take control of the target company. Supermajority requirements, like certain provisions in the Constitution, make a greater-than-50 percent majority necessary for the acquirer to take control. Staggered terms on the board of directors, similar to the way in which only one-third of the U.S. Senate is elected every two years, keep an acquiring company from taking control until at least two regular board elections have been held (quite possibly an unaccept-

able delay). Noncumulative voting rules out the possibility of a shareholder's concentrating all his votes for one board candidate; it makes it more difficult for a minority shareholder who is also a potential acquirer to get representation on the target company's board of directors. Two-class common stock gives a subset of shares (typically held by established interests) heavier weight or even sole voting authority, again making it more difficult for an acquirer to take control. This list is not exhaustive; many other "mechanical" adjustments of corporate charters are possible.

3. A close relative of the preceding repellents is the tactic of issuing new common stock. Rather than tampering with the formal structure of the corporation, this changes the balance of power by diluting the influence of a certain block of shares, that is, the shares of the potential acquirer. Deployment of this repellent has, however, been limited by recent court decisions.[4]

4. Probably the most drastic of all shark repellents is (to mix metaphors) the "scorched-earth" defense, in which management deliberately makes the company less financially attractive to a potential acquirer, for example, by selling off desirable assets, draining cash by making wise or unwise acquisitions of its own, or by incurring large debts. One man's scorched earth may be another man's prudent strategy, however; it is unclear that all anti-takeover measures described as scorched-earth defenses actually damage the company. Nevertheless, the recent success of other types of anti-takeover measures has diminished the attractiveness of "scorched earth" except as a last resort.[5]

5. Whether or not the "golden parachutes" should qualify as shark repellent depends on one's interpretation of the basic metaphor: Who is it that is being threatened by the sharks? If the answer is "management," then golden parachutes *are* shark repellent, for they protect a firm's current managers against harm by guaranteeing them lucrative, even eight-figure[6] payoffs if the firm is acquired and they lose their jobs.

On the other hand, from the shareholders' perspective, golden parachutes do nothing to deter an acquirer; shareholders who are opposed to a proposed takeover should actually fear the worst when golden parachutes are issued.

6. One other tactic often described as shark repellent is what I will call, for neutrality's sake, the premium-price selective buyback. Suppose a potential acquirer has bought up a significant block of a company's outstanding shares (say, five or ten percent) and is thought to be contemplating an all-out takeover bid; one way to keep this from happening is for management to buy back the potential acquirer's shares at a premium over the market price. This is often called payment of "greenmail," but whether the implication of blackmail-like deliberate coercion is correct depends on the intentions of the acquirer. If there is no intention to take over the company, but only to extort the premium, then the term seems apt; but the selective buyback might also deter a serious buyer for whom taking the buyback premium simply made even better financial sense than pressing ahead with the acquisition. In fact, this is probably the typical case; after all, if an acquirer cannot muster the financial resources for a credible takeover bid, no one will be concerned to buy their shares back in the first place. It is also doubtful that buyback premiums could ever be large enough to permanently repel serious offers for large companies that were thought to embody substantial unrealized asset values. Accordingly, allegations of "greenmail" seem to be receiving less and less attention as the players in the current takeover environment become more sophisticated.

Now, for someone who is impressed by the capital-reallocation, management-discipline, and entrepreneurship utilities of a free-market takeover environment, the use of any of these shark repellents should seem morally suspect. For any of them (with the exception of golden parachutes) are capable of blocking takeover bids that might otherwise succeed, and this means that the market will not be deciding whether a takeover is desirable. When one concentrates on anti-takeover measures adopted by entrenched but weak managements that have been mis-allocating corporate resources and underre-warding shareholders, one is almost tempted to think that shark repellent should be for-bidden altogether.

Nevertheless, the shark analogy should not lead us to draw this conclusion. Of course, predators weed out the weak, but they sometimes devour the strong and de-serving too. A shark repellent that could save the strong and deserving corporation while not damaging the economic environ-ment would be a blessing.

And indeed essentially utilitarian argu-ments have been made in favor of the occa-sional use of all kinds of shark repellents.[7] Let us change our example and concentrate on the case of a well-managed company that, because it engages in long-term thinking and long-term projects, has temporarily gotten it-self into a financial position in which partial or total liquidation might look profitable. A T. Boone Pickens has begun to acquire shares and is assumed to intend drastic re-structuring if he succeeds. Management re-sponds by taking its case to the shareholders: It points to the solid evidence of past per-formance, reiterates a coherent plan for con-tinuing development, and asks for a suitable arsenal of shark repellents. The sharehold-ers agree, and the repellents serve their purpose. Three years later, management is vindicated: Growth of all the company's divi-sions is back on track and profitability is at a record high. When we think of this kind of example, the case against shark repellent seems far less open-and-shut.

Can any general conclusions be drawn from these examples? One difference that seems worth noting in the latter case is that the deployment of shark repellent was ap-proved in advance by shareholders.[8] For phi-losophers who approach moral questions from a contractarian perspective, this will in itself be a justification, but there are utilitar-ian reasons to favor shareholder-mandated

shark repellents as well. If we grant the gen-eral claim that market decisions about the proper allocation of capital tend to maxi-mize utility, then this deployment of shark repellent is arguably just another market de-cision about capital allocation, namely, a decision *not* to allocate it as the potential ac-quirer would. If the utility judgments of indi-vidual shareholders are the ultimate source of the market's wisdom in allocating capital, then they should be attended to just as seri-ously when the decision is *against* realloca-tion.

This claim can only be made, however, about cases in which shareholder permission to deploy shark repellent is requested in ad-vance. If the shark repellent is employed unilaterally by management, if it comes into use at precisely the time the first concrete takeover activity begins, and particularly if recent performance has been poor, there is good reason to believe that shareholders might disagree with the use of shark repel-lent. Exactly how often this happens is a dif-ficult empirical question, but alleged cases are frequently discussed in the financial press.

A corollary of the proposition that shark repellents should be approved in advance by shareholders is that shark repellents should be fixed policies, announced in advance by management, rather than spur-of-the-mo-ment exercises of "business judgment." For instance, in the middle of its recent battle against a takeover bid by Pickens, Unocal suddenly announced that it would buy back 29 percent of its shares at a very attractive above-market price, but with one caveat: Pickens (by this point an owner of millions of shares) would be excluded from the offer. The Delaware Supreme Court ruled that this was a valid exercise of "business judgment" (an area in which courts have generally re-fused to interfere), and so Pickens, would-be acquirer of a company that had just incurred a huge debt but unable to recapture any of the payout for which the debt was incurred, came to a standstill agreement with manage-ment and abandoned his bid.[9]

But what happened to the market's (not to mention Pickens's) ability to efficiently allocate capital in this case? Suppose that, in truth, the capital invested in Unocal *could* be utilized more efficiently—producing more goods, services, and jobs—if the company was broken up. Then we, the public, lost by letting Pickens be thwarted. If Unocal's half-million shareholders had prudently examined the situation, decided that a breakup was not in their best interests, and told management to go ahead and deploy shark repellent, then the collective wisdom of these capital allocators would give us some confidence in the efficiency of the result. But this is exactly what we can never know if the deployment of shark repellent is an unchecked and spontaneous exercise of business judgment (as a very large number of shark repellent measures are).

Thus we arrive at a provisional position according to which there is a presumption in favor of a free-market takeover environment and against shark repellent measures, *except* when they are announced to and approved in advance by shareholders. But our now well-used shark analogy tells us to go a step further. Even if a majority of the local citizenry—resort owners and scuba divers and fishermen—approved a systematic poisoning campaign to eliminate sharks, those responsible for public policy would still need to think about what was in the best long-run interests of the community and its environment and whether it wasn't important to protect at least some interests of the anti-repellent minority. By the same token, there may be public-policy reasons for forbidding various kinds of corporate shark repellent, even when they are approved by a majority of a company's stockholders. (The argument has only been that the collective wisdom of shareholders is an important source of evidence about what allocations of capital will produce the greatest total utility, not that ownership is the sole basis of the right to decide how productive assets shall be allocated.)

One issue concerns formal or mechanical devices like supermajority requirements that give a minority of shareholders the right to veto a takeover bid. If we are impressed by the utilities of letting the shareholders decide whether to accept takeover bids, then it is unclear why we should allow a minority of a corporation's shareholders to interfere with that process. Perhaps the reply will be that that objection has already been answered: If shareholders *vote* to let a minority veto a takeover bid, they have in effect agreed that the minority shall speak for them in capital reallocation decisions. Analogously, it might be argued, if 59 Senators fail to obtain the three-fifths majority needed for cloture, there is no undermining of the principle of majority control, because 60 Senators had to vote for the cloture rule in the first place. By voting for it, they in effect agreed to let the 41 percent minority's position prevail the next time there was a cloture vote. But there is a large difference between the typical governmental supermajority requirement and the typical corporate supermajority shark repellent. Governmental supermajority rules are typically *instituted* by a supermajority; the typical corporate rule can be instituted by only a bare majority of stockholders. The argument that the pro-takeover minority voted to tie its own hands is not available in the usual case. This being so, it is not obvious that public policy should acquiesce and permit a minority-veto arrangement. Suppose, for instance, that 51 percent of the shareholders of a company authorize a supermajority provision that requires an 80 percent vote of shareholders to replace management. Subsequently, a tender offer is made, and it is so favorable that 76 percent of shareholders subscribe: a large majority, but not 80 percent. This result is inconsistent with a public policy predicated on listening to what the shareholders themselves have to say about takeover bids; in this case, for instance, the judgment of that 25 percent who never did favor shark repellent and who now favor a takeover bid is artificially kept from contributing to the collective wisdom of the market.

It might be objected here that supermajority provisions are, after all, consistent with a public policy that looks to shareholder judgment as the best way to settle takeover bids. Shareholders know (or should know) perfectly well that simple majorities prevail in corporate decision, so if they go ahead, buy stock, and then find themselves in the minority on the question of instituting an 80 percent supermajority provision, they have in effect concurred with the resulting anti-takeover measures. I would reply that the collective shareholder judgment we want to utilize concerns concrete, individual takeover offers, but the objection raises a larger issue. For it is a fiction to suppose that a typical shareholder vote on shark repellent measures accurately represents the judgment of the corporate constituency, particularly if it passes by only a small majority; management has a huge advantage in shareholder voting. For instance, proxies can be voted for management and its slate of directors by simply signing at the bottom, but dissenters must cast their votes for specific opposition policies or persons. Management has easy access to the shareholders, and can expend corporate funds to advocate its position. Finally, management can count on the habitual, uncritical support of the "Aunt Agatha" type of shareholder whose stock certificate has been locked in her safe deposit box for the last thirty years. (Note that citizens whose interest in public affairs is approximately equivalent to Aunt Agatha's interest in corporate affairs generally just don't vote, while the corporate sign-and-mail system tends to result in the unconcerned voting for the incumbents.) Thus, there are broader reasons for contemplating public policies that restrict even shareholder-mandated shark repellents.

In concluding this section, I want to argue that one device that is sometimes called a shark repellent is quite compatible with the complete health of our economic environment: the "fair price" amendment. This provides that in the event of a takeover bid, the acquirer must pay all shareholders the same amount, in the same form (e.g., cash, stock, bonds, etc.). In many recent takeover battles, for example, would-be acquirers such as Pickens have made "two-tier" bids: they have offered an attractive cash payment for 51 percent of the shares, and announced their intention to complete the purchase of the company with packages of low-grade securities that were difficult to appraise and not worth their stated value in the opinion of many experts. Now it is difficult to see the utility of a practice that puts extra pressure on investors to hurry up and sell their stock to a potential acquirer so that they won't get stuck with less valuable securities if the deal goes through. There are, I have argued, large social benefits to a system that encourages investors to sit back and coolly decide between current management and an acquirer's bid, but there is no obvious reason to tip the scales in *favor* of the acquirer by allowing him to make an offer that applies this kind of pressure. Put another way, we want to encourage investors to think about the relative merits of different management teams and their plans, but there is no obvious value in forcing them to become sophisticated arbitrage speculators, able to accurately estimate which takeover bids will be favorably received and which not, what a package of "junk bonds" is worth, and so on.

Finally, it should be noted that "fair price" amendments are really very weak shark repellents, for they will not deter serious takeover offers. Recently, for instance, Pantry Pride acquired Revlon with a bid of $58 per share in cash for all shares outstanding; this kind of transaction would not be affected by a prohibition on two-tier bids. At most, a fair-price amendment repels only undercapitalized or coercive acquirers.

In closing, I want to admit to a few reservations about the theses of this paper. First, of course, several controversial theses are simply assumed, rather than argued for: most notably the truth of rule-utilitarianism and the appropriateness of the analogy between ecosystems and economics. Many will find my discussion of the disutilities of a free market in takeovers insufficient, though I have tried to at least sketch my grounds for skepticism about the preferability of alternative practices. But a complete discussion of these issues is beyond the scope of this essay.

I also want to concede the force of two serious objections. The first would be that while I have resolutely pretended that takeovers are purely a reflection of free-market forces, the bust-up, liquidation-oriented takeover has artificial advantages in its favor, advantages that must be compensated for in some way. Fiduciaries such as pension-fund managers are required by law to maximize returns (within certain safety constraints), which puts tremendous pressure on them to accept tender offers.[10] Tax policies—for example, the deductibility of interest payments on the bonds that finance many takeovers, as well as numerous more complex provisions—make it artificially cheap to buy a company.[11] The disinflationary environment may be further tipping the scales.[12] According to this objection, then, factors that artificially mitigate in favor of takeovers may justify restrictions that would not be necessary in a true free market.

I am in agreement with the factual premise of this objection; it does seem likely that some tax provision or other mitigates in favor of takeovers. But I see no reason to suppose that this demonstrates the wisdom of further interventions to "even things out." If that is inevitable—if the only solution to the problem is letting the politicians and lawyers and interest groups add layer upon layer of offsetting regulations until they reach a more-or-less equitable but completely unprincipled standoff—then I am afraid that philosophers will have little to contribute to public policy discussion, because understanding the offsetting effects of pro-takeover and anti-takeover distorting factors will involve such a huge amount of technical expertise in law, tax policy, and the like that they, like other ordinary citizens, will not be able to get to the heart of the matter. But why should they have to? Why not try to make public policy more equitable and efficient by gradually peeling away systematic biases in favor of any interest? One possible reaction to the observation that there are pro-takeover biases built into our economic institutions is simply to deplore them along with the anti-takeover biases discussed earlier, and argue against any distortions that cannot be defended in their own right. On this view, then, the objective of public policy should be more than the proverbial "level playing field"; it should be a level playing field built on ground where underlying structural deformities have been detected and eliminated insofar as possible. Nevertheless, the existence of some "tilt" in the current economic environment is hard to deny.

The other serious objection I want to discuss concerns the financing of many (but not all) recent takeovers by high-yielding but low-grade "junk bonds." The technical issues involved here cannot be quickly or easily summarized; suffice it to say that many sober and responsible economists think that the enormous amounts of debt accumulated in the last few years of takeover activity have put dangerous stresses on our economic system.[13] The more extreme among them point to parallels with the collapse of 1929. Now suppose these economists are right. Wouldn't this be a conclusive argument against the free-market takeover policies that have been advocated in this essay?

The answer must surely be yes, if we grant the views of these economists for the sake of argument. They are definitely arguable: For instance, the general Wall Street hilarity that greeted Ted Turner's no-cash, junk-bond-financed bid for CBS certainly shows that the market has some built-in checks against excessively leveraged buyout proposals. But let us suppose someone can make the case for the factual premise. What impresses me about the excessive-debt objection is its form. It is, of course, rule-utilitarian. We are presented with a reason for thinking that a practice might have serious long-run disutilities. The utilities of takeovers are not ignored, and the evil identified is not simplistically blamed on the greed of wicked financiers. The point is simply that a beneficial practice threatens to undermine even more beneficial economic institutions. We are led to contemplate important and difficult questions about private debt and public policy, questions that raise great difficulties for free-market economics. As I indicated, resolution of these issues goes far beyond the scope of this essay. But it is primarily through further consideration of partly technical issues such as these that I believe most future progress in moral assessment of takeover policies will be made.[14]

NOTES

1. The classic source here is John Rawls, "Two Concepts of Rules," *Philosophical Review* 64 (1955): 3–32.
2. Richard B. Schmitt, "Despite Raider's Lust, Oil Industry is Facing Retrenchment Period," *Wall Street Journal,* June 7, 1985, p. 1. Also see "Oil's Inevitable Restructuring" (letter from T. Boone Pickens to the *Wall Street Journal*), January 8, 1985, p. 37.
3. Joseph Schumpeter, *Capitalism, Socialism, and Democracy* (New York: Harper and Row, 1942), especially chapter 7.
4. George C. Aguilar, "Business-Judgment Rule Draws Criticism as More Firms Take Anti-Takeover Steps," *Wall Street Journal,* August 10, 1984, p. 27.
5. Daniel Hertzberg, "Takeover Targets Find Loading Up on Debt Can Fend Off Raiders," *Wall Street Journal,* September 10, 1985, p. 1.
6. Daniel Hertzberg and Hank Gilman, "Revlon

Officials to Get Payments if Buyout Occurs," *Wall Street Journal,* October 11, 1985, p. 43.
7. See, e.g., William J. Carney, "Pols Poking Holes in Golden Parachutes," *Wall Street Journal,* April 16, 1984, p. 32; John Boland, "Missing the Bottom Line on Greenmail," *Wall Street Journal,* July 25, 1984, p. 26; J. Gregory Dees, "The Ethics of Greenmail," in James E. Post, ed., *Research in Corporate Social Performance and Policy,* 8 (1986).
8. This is the position of raider Sir James Goldsmith. See "Hostile Takeovers Easier to Swallow than Poison Pills," *Wall Street Journal,* February 11, 1985, p. 22.
9. Ed Leefeldt, "A Sweet Way to Foil Takeover Bids," *Wall Street Journal,* September 4, 1985, p. 24; James B. Stewart, and Laurie P. Cohen, "Pickens-Unocal Truce Poses Possibility that Golden Era for Raiders is Ending," *Wall Street Journal,* May 22, 1985, p. 2.
10. Peter Drucker, "Taming the Corporate Takeover," *Wall Street Journal,* October 30, 1984, p. 30.
11. Martin Lipton, "Takeover Abuses Mortgage the Future," *Wall Street Journal,* April 5, 1985, p. 16.
12. Alan Greenspan, "Takeovers Rooted in Fear," *Wall Street Journal,* September 27, 1985, p. 28.
13. See, e.g., Felix Rohatyn, "Junk Bonds and Other Securities Swill," *Wall Street Journal,* April 18, 1985, p. 30; Senator Pete J. Domenici, "Fools and Their Takeover Bonds," *Wall Street Journal,* May 14, 1985, p. 28. For an opposing view, see William Carney, "Junk Bonds Don't Merit a Black-Hat Image," *Wall Street Journal,* April 29, 1985, p. 24; Frederick H. Joseph, "High-Yield Bonds Aren't Junk," *Wall Street Journal,* May 31, 1985, p. 22.
14. I am grateful to William Irvine and Edwin Hettinger for comments and suggestions on an earlier draft of this paper.

The Apartheid Debate on American Campuses

Joseph Murphy

IBM ON THE RUN?

"The economic activity there is worse than it was a year ago, the economic pressure in the United States is heightened, and Mr. Botha is too slow. If we cannot have as successful a business remaining in South Africa as we would have leaving, then I think we have no choice than to leave. If we elect to leave it will be a business decision. What other kind of decision would it be? We are not in business to conduct moral activity, we are not in business to conduct socially responsible action. We are in business to conduct business."

—John Akers
President, IBM
April 21, 1986

At first glance, it might seem odd that the issue of apartheid should have emerged as a critical political issue on American campuses in the mid-1980s. So many concerns closer to home have more direct impact on daily life in academia: the Reagan Administration's efforts to reduce aid to students, the impetus for more vocationally oriented programs and less attention to the liberal arts, and the diminished enforcement of affirmative action mandates are just a few. Why in this context have student and faculty activists chosen to focus their attention on the repressive policies of a nation 8,000 miles from our shores?

The answer to that has several elements. First and most important is the fact that the South African government's official policy of racial separatism and enforced discrimination is so blatantly cruel and so morally repugnant as to make it a nondebatable moral issue, one on which Americans covering a broad ideological spectrum can unite. With no significant exception, spokesmen for all of our major national institutions deplore apartheid; even Jerry Falwell admits that it is a bad thing. We can argue vehemently over tactics of opposition (or even whether a foreign regime's policies are within our legitimate sphere of moral or political influence), but that apartheid is abhorrent is a subject on which there is rare consensus.

Second, apartheid is a highly visible sin. We read about it daily in *The New York Times*. We see an average of three graphic reports per week on the nightly news. The policy is easily described and its impacts are clearly depicted. In that sense, South African racial struggles are more immediate to us than are many of our own domestic conflicts over abstract propositions about budgets and priorities. We see how the Botha government's edicts affect people in black villages in a way that we cannot see how the Reagan Administration's budget cuts affect minority or low-income people in the ghettoes of the United States; as we all learned in the 1960s, police confrontations make good news footage and subtle acts of repression do not.

Finally, and perhaps more subtly, we sense that apartheid is one of those issues about which we just might be able to do

From Joseph Murphy, "The Apartheid Debate on American Campuses," *Business and Society Review* 57 (Spring 1986): 113–117. Reprinted with permission.

something—although we are not at all clear or united about what that something is. We deplore repression in Eastern Europe, but we sense that Americans have little leverage to exercise there. In South Africa, whether because of some shared linkage with Anglo-Saxon political and juridical traditions or because of a common set of material interests and lifestyle patterns among our two nations' elites, or simply because of U.S. business involvement, we perceive some possibility that we are in a position to exercise influence for change.

Thus, that rare contemporary phenomenon: an evil at once clear-cut, visible, and conceivably amenable to remedy. To those of us who talk about ethics and think about ideas, apartheid offers a compelling opportunity to translate moral conviction into political action. It is in this context not ironic but perfectly logical that the question of what we ought to do about South Africa should assume so great a place of importance on the American higher education community's agenda. . . .

. . . [M]any of us feel that we are under moral obligation . . . to take all legitimate steps within our power to dissociate our institutions from the practitioners of racial discrimination in South Africa and to make that practice costly to the point that even its advocates accept pragmatic arguments for change. It was out of a desire to fulfill this obligation that leaders of the American academic community began a few years ago to turn their specific attention to the issue of using investment leverage in the battle against apartheid. . . .

. . . [U]niversities control large endowments. They seek to use those endowments for worthy purposes, ranging from scholarship aid to the disadvantaged to construction of new facilities. The greater the return on investment of endowment assets, the more worthy purposes may be served. The more profitable the corporations in which endowment monies are placed, the greater the return on investment. Our standard investment policy is to generate more re-

sources to help us fulfill our basic educational mission; it is not to change the realities of the world. My own university's pre-1984 investments in such corporations as Burroughs, Citicorp, Coca-Cola, and General Electric, all of which did business in South Africa and all of which made us and their other shareholders a lot of money, were guided by that policy.

The question that we at the City University of New York and our colleagues across the nation confronted in the early 1980s was whether conditions in South Africa were such as to warrant deviation from that basic and traditional approach to investment practice. As we approached the question of divestiture, we found ourselves grappling with four basic arguments against selling off our stock; only if we could respond cogently to each could we justify taking what we all recognized as a serious and unprecedented action. Essentially the antidivestiture arguments were as follows:

- Divestiture is a wrong-headed approach to resolution of the South African problem. American corporations actually represent progressive, integration-fostering elements in the South African economy. Those opposed to apartheid should encourage American investment, not seek to prevent it.

  In support of this proposition, advocates present evidence showing that more than 100 U.S. firms in South Africa follow the Sullivan Principles of nondiscrimination in and around the workplace. Black South Africans employed by U.S. businesses enjoy wage levels, benefits, and opportunities for advancement far in excess of those available to blacks elsewhere in that nation's economy. Presumably, over time, the advocates argue, South African firms will be forced by market pressure and moral example to offer black and coloured workers terms of employment similar to those provided by U.S. corporations.
- Even if American firms are not now acting as progressive influences, their shareholders (including universities and other institutional investors) can use leverage to force implementation of nondiscriminatory practices and adherence to the Sullivan Principles.

Approximately 250 U.S. corporations doing business in South Africa have not accepted the Sullivan Principles, although many claim to act in a nondiscriminatory manner nonetheless. Conceivably, colleges could use proxy votes in shareholder resolutions, moral argument, and threats of disinvestment to force corporations to change their ways—to pull out of South Africa entirely or to adopt rigidly enforced codes of nondiscrimination. Once a university sells its stock in a firm, this leverage is gone.

- Whether or not corporations discriminate is of no legitimate concern to the university. Those charged with investing college funds have one basic responsibility: to maximize return on capital outlay. To take *any* action for political or moral cause is to abandon the university's proper fiduciary role.

  In Milton Friedman's memorable phrase, "The social responsibility of the corporation is to make a profit." By implication, the investor's responsibility is to garner a positive return. Social policy is for voters and their representatives in Congress to determine—not for corporate directors or college trustees who are, after all, playing with other people's money.

- Divestiture hurts those in our institutions most dependent on marginal dollars—primarily the economically disadvantaged. To vent moral outrage at policies abroad by hurting those at home least able to sustain the blow is bad policy.

  Given the recent pattern of federal aid cutbacks to students and to campuses, American higher education depends increasingly on revenue from investment. Endowment-earnings dollars can provide low-income students with tuition assistance, work-study support, living stipends, and other aid. Selling off profitable but morally unpalatable securities in exchange for holdings more ethically pure but less financially remunerative will force us to spend less than we otherwise would on socially and educationally desirable programs. Divestiture may mean less help to the needy. It will hurt not the trustees who make the decision but those who depend on the aid.

Each of these contentions was advanced with sincerity and each had some intellectual merit. Each deserved a detailed response. For CUNY in 1984, that response ran along these lines:

- Divestiture is not wrong-headed. Our analysis of the South African situation showed the positive impact exerted by U.S. corporations to be limited at best and far outweighed by the negative effects of corporate participation in the economy of a repressive state. Some 100,000 South African blacks were employed by U.S. firms, in a nation whose population included 27 million nonwhites. Of those 100,000 people, a significant number worked for firms refusing to sign the Sullivan Principles. There has been little evidence of South African firms following an American lead toward progressive workplace policy. While not ignoring the benefits U.S. employment offered some blacks, we could not avoid the conclusion that the U.S. corporate presence in South Africa represented basic recognition of the legitimacy of the white regime. American corporations pay South African taxes and abide by South African laws. In so doing they tacitly accept the right of a minority regime to govern a disfranchised majority.

- American firms' shareholders have found it difficult to use leverage to force implementation of nondiscriminatory practices. Marginal success in this effort (and there has been some) has had no significant impact on the overall situation in South Africa. Moreover, this approach would not work for CUNY. The practical obstacles to such an effort were formidable. In no firm did the City University hold more than a negligible proportion of outstanding stock; our proxy votes might have symbolic significance but they would lack real clout. We did not possess the energy, the manpower, or the expertise necessary to lead the battle on controversial shareholder resolutions, and we were not in a position to allocate staff resources away from educational programs to such an effort. We had no effective precedents to guide us in this approach in any event.

  Some individuals argued that we possessed sufficient moral authority to force corporations in which we owned stock to answer for their actions. Harvard, Yale, and other universities have indeed used institutional prestige and media access to force a public accounting of South African activities; where the corporate response to university probing was unsatisfactory, those institutions have fulfilled a public commitment to sell stock. The option to try this approach was open to us as well.

We rejected it on pragmatic grounds. As a public institution dependent on support from all segments of the community, the City University could not easily engage in a protracted public debate with a specific business firm. Our moral authority is not, moreover, universally recognized and accepted; as a competitor with other social service agencies for public funding, we are suspected of political motives in most of what we do. To cut and cut cleanly seemed the more practical course.

- In unusual circumstances, our proper fiduciary role may indeed encompass taking some actions for political or moral cause. We are not discussing here a close question, on which a fiduciary's prescribed political neutrality might make sense and in which trustees bring ideological considerations to bear at the risk of misplaying their part in institutional guidance.

There are some questions—South Africa currently among them—that are not close. Would 1930's investments in firms supplying German armaments have been appropriate had stock analysts predicted a high rate of return from those firms? No, because such investments would have run counter to clearly defined and well-understood definitions of the larger social interest. Would current investment in corporations operating on the borderline of environmental regulations be justifiable if the likely appreciation and dividend rates looked good? No again, because the element of risk to us as a culpable partner in environmental disaster would be uncomfortably great.

So, too, with investments in most South African operations. The long-term risks of involvement in tainted enterprises are unacceptably large. We are not willing to use our endowment dollars in such a way as to make us accomplices in activities that prop up a regime whose activities run counter to the broad interests and ideological goals of our society. We cannot take the chance that the firms in which we invest will escape the consequences of a revolutionary overthrow of apartheid. As fiduciaries, we could in good judgment conclude that divestiture represented a prudent and responsible course of behavior.

- Divestiture might adversely impact on some in our own institution. It can nevertheless be jus-

tified on the basis of the greater good it will yield to the university and all those we serve—including the disadvantaged. In this sense the decision to divest is conceptually similar to all other policy decisions we as institutional leaders are called upon to make.

Fortunately for all of us whose colleges opted to divest in the mid-1980s, however, the "lower rate of return" issue has proved to be fairly moot. . . . We might not be as lucky if we have to grapple with a similar issue at some point in the future. Then our choice would boil down to a high profit with bad firms or a lower profit with good ones—and the latter option would mean fewer scholarships, fewer remedial programs, less enrichment activity, and reduction in other desirable campus enterprises. By what right do we forego those things—or, more accurately, force our students to forego them—as we pursue some higher social value?

I would answer that we do so by the same right that we cite as we set institutional priorities in all other areas. We deem that an extra course in ethics is more valuable than extra computer terminals, even though computer training might make our students more marketable and able to command higher salaries; we adopt the course and essentially impose its cost on our students. We spend scarce dollars to bring controversial spokespeople to campus and presumably force some of our enrollees to forego extra tuition support that the funds paid to those spokespeople might have been used to provide. We engage in costly social service activities that benefit the communities that surround our campus, cutting back on intramural enrichment activities in order to do so. We make these choices partly because we believe that they are intrinsically right and socially worthy and partly because they enable us to establish and protect our identity as moral, responsible institutional members of society. That identity is an essential asset in assuring for ourselves a continued, meaningful existence. . . .

. . . Those who advocate total divestiture must still demonstrate that the policy is a sensible, productive, appropriate, and ultimately prudent course for all institutional investors to follow. Those who oppose divestiture must refute those claims. In our view, and in the view of a list of divesting institutions, which grows longer each month, the weight of argument is on the side of those who would opt to break all links with a social system whose philosophy and whose deeds shock the conscience of the world.

U.S. Firms in South Africa

Richard T. De George

The situation in South Africa illustrates a third aspect of the morality of multinationals, and one of the major difficulties in multinational operations.

The Union of South Africa practices a policy of racial segregation, discrimination, and oppression known as *apartheid*. The practice is condemned as immoral by many in the United States and in other countries throughout the world. It is justified and defended by many whites in South Africa as the morally allowable lesser of two evils.

Under apartheid, the blacks in South Africa suffer extreme repression. Although they constitute the overwhelming majority of the population, they are allowed to live on only 13 percent of the land. The other 87 percent is reserved for the whites, who constitute only 17 percent of the population. The whites control the gold and diamond mines, the harbors, and the industrial areas. Blacks who wish to work in these areas are required to live in townships outside of the major cities. Because only males are allowed in the townships, the workers are separated from their families for the major part of the year. The blacks cannot vote, own property, organize politically, or join unions. They are systematically paid less than whites for the same work. They are not allowed to hold managerial positions of even the lowest kind. They are forced to use segregated eating, dressing, and toilet facilities.

United States companies began moving into South Africa as early as the 1880s. At that time, these firms employed only whites and sold their products almost exclusively to the white community. The white community was the economically advanced and productive sector of the country, and supplied the market for goods. The blacks lived in their own sections of the country, in their traditional tribal ways. The whites set up and controlled the government. The blacks did not take part in any governmental activities, were not educated, and were not considered able to run the government or to have any impact on it. A colonial type of paternalism was exercised by the whites over the blacks.

Whatever one considers [about] the morality of such colonial paternalism, it is understandable how and why companies from the United States initially saw their market as the white community, and their employees as coming from that same community. The intent of these companies was to expand their markets and make a profit, and South Africa was a ripe market to develop. With time and the changes of over half a century, colonialism fell out of favor in other parts of Africa; the native inhabitants took over the reins of power in country after country, and ran their own affairs. In South Africa, however, blacks did not succeed in gaining power and have been kept from doing so by the legal enforcement of apartheid.

Reprinted with permission of Macmillan Publishing Company from Richard T. De George, "U.S. Firms in South Africa," *Business Ethics* (2nd ed). Copyright © 1986 by Macmillan Publishing Company.

Some changes, however, did take place finally. Factories, as they expanded, found that there were not enough whites to fill the jobs available, and blacks were found able and willing to work in these factories. Fear of their achieving control was, in part, what motivated the government to draw up and enforce the apartheid laws. But as blacks entered the labor market, they also had money to buy goods and so represented a potential market for goods.

American-controlled multinationals moved into South Africa in greater numbers, to take advantage of the low wages they could pay blacks and the large market that South Africa represented. The profits earned by American South African subsidiaries were often twice as much as the profits earned by the home-based mother company. Many black-dominated countries in Africa have placed embargoes on goods manufactured by U.S. companies operating in South Africa. But the local market is sufficient to make operation of subsidiaries in South Africa profitable for IBM, Ford, General Motors, Goodyear, Firestone, Exxon, Mobil, Kellogg's, Eli Lilly, Kodak, Control Data, and over 300 other U.S. companies.

Despite the protestations of the whites in South Africa, most people acknowledge that apartheid is immoral. It is blatant racial segregation, discrimination, and oppression. Let us assume the majority view (i.e., apartheid is immoral). The moral issues that have surfaced have been of two kinds, related though separable. One is the question of whether it is moral for U.S. multinationals to operate in South Africa. The other is whether U.S. investors, especially university endowment associations and churches, should invest in companies that operate in South Africa.

U.S. MULTINATIONALS IN SOUTH AFRICA

U.S. multinationals would not open subsidiaries in South Africa unless it were profitable to do so. South Africa has four conditions that make it attractive to U.S. companies. First, it has a stable government. U.S. companies are reluctant to open plants in countries with unstable governments, for fear of losing their investments because of nationalization or constant domestic turmoil. U.S. companies therefore have an interest in helping preserve stable governments. They tend not to care whether the government is repressive or dictatorial. That, they claim, is a local, political matter. And from a business point of view, a strong, stable government is a guarantee of the safety of their investment. Second, South Africa has a large potential market. Its population is 28 million people. Even though only 17 percent of the population is white, that represents a market of close to 5 million people; and the other 23 million form a pool that can be increasingly tapped. The U.S. companies are the chief suppliers of consumer goods and of advanced technology. Third, South Africa has a large and cheap supply of labor. The standard of living of the blacks is extremely low, and the scale paid them by South African firms is about one-fourth the wages paid to white workers. As more blacks are brought into the work force, the market for manufactured goods grows. Fourth, South Africa is rich in minerals. It can provide from within its own borders, the materials necessary for manufacturing, as well as ship to the parent U.S. companies raw materials needed for production in the United States.

All four conditions supply both the reasons why multinationals want to locate subsidiaries in South Africa and the reasons why critics of such firms charge them with immoral exploitation and with supporting repressive regimes.

United States firms have not been unaware of the charges of immorality. A few of them have responded to the charges by withdrawal. Polaroid is one such company. Citibank and the First Pennsylvania Bank no longer give loans to the South African government. But most of the other companies have not moved out. They have felt the moral pressure from stockholders and from other vocal groups in the United States, however, and have responded in a number of cases by adopting a set of principles drawn up in 1977 by Leon Sullivan, a black Philadelphia minister and a director of General Motors. The principles, known as the *Sullivan Code,* aim to end apartheid in the companies that adopt the code. The code calls for desegregation of eating, toilet, and work facilities; equal pay for all people doing comparable jobs within the plant; equal opportunity for advancement regardless of race; apprenticeships and training of nonwhites; promotion of blacks and other minorities to supervisory positions; improvement of living conditions; and support of unionization by nonwhites.

The Sullivan Code, its supporters argue, works to break down apartheid from within and so is more effective than simply casting moral stones at the system from outside the country. It helps nonwhites get training they could not get without the multinationals. It serves to increase the pay of the nonwhites to the level of the whites doing similar work. All of this is illegal; it violates South African law. But the South African government has not complained or sought to prevent the adoption of the Sullivan Code by American companies.

The critics of the Sullivan Code claim that it is not an effective way of breaking down apartheid. If it were, it would not be allowed by the South African government. The American firms pay taxes, and so provide revenue essential to the government to support and enforce its practice of repression throughout the country. The Sullivan Code, its critics claim, serves as a smoke screen behind which American companies can hide. They can sign the Code and claim to adhere to it, but in fact not do so, or do so only in token fashion. The Code, moreover, takes pressure off the companies to withdraw from the country, and gives them a moral excuse for continuing their profitable and exploitative operations.

The Sullivan Code was proposed in 1977. The fact that many U.S. firms adopted the Sullivan Code so readily, at least in principle, indicates two things: such companies respond, to some extent, to moral pressure applied in the United States, and they can operate profitably (even if less profitably) while observing the Code. But if we admit that U.S. companies act immorally when following the apartheid laws, are they morally permitted to operate in South Africa even if they follow the Sullivan Code? The question is not whether an American company follows the Sullivan Code completely; but rather, *if* a company diligently enforced the Sullivan Code in all its detail, would its continued operation in South Africa be morally justifiable? If we assume that the Sullivan Code negates all of the immoral aspects of apartheid, then a company that implements the Code would not be guilty of racial segregation, discrimination, or exploitation (unless white employees were also exploited). To that extent its operation would not be immoral. But through its taxes, the company helps support the government, which in turn enforces apartheid in the South African firms and in all other aspects of life within the country. Is such support of a repressive government morally justifiable?

Let us attempt to analyze the question from a utilitarian point of view. What are the consequences of the American firms operating within the country as opposed to withdrawing from the country? The critics of the American firms claim that if the firms left South Africa, much of the revenue needed to support the government would disappear. Furthermore, a wholesale withdrawal of American firms would leave the country in chaos. The government would not be able to keep the peace or run the economy. Because of the subsequent turmoil, blacks would have the opportunity to stage an effective revolution; they would seize control of the government and put an end to apartheid. As a result, they claim, the repression of the blacks would be ended. The 23 million nonwhites would benefit incomparably more than the 5 million whites would suffer. The whites would suffer loss of their special position; but the blacks would gain respect as persons, which they have been denied for a century. The American firms would not be substantially harmed by withdrawal, and after the revolution they might even return to South Africa to operate within a moral rather than an immoral context.

The foregoing scenario, however, is disputed by those who are in favor of continuing American operations in South Africa. In the first place, they say, consider the benefits to the South African blacks and other minorities. The U.S. firms are the only places where they can get work at wages comparable to whites. They are the only firms at which they can learn skills and rise to supervisory positions. Hence, those who work for American companies that follow the Sullivan Code gain much more by working for American-owned plants than they would if these firms left South Africa. Second, a wholesale U.S. withdrawal would not bring the results claimed by the critics of the U.S. companies. As the American companies left the country, they would be replaced by firms from other countries, most likely by Japanese or German firms. And these firms are less likely to follow the Sullivan Code. The South African government would continue to receive from these firms the revenue it needs. Hence, the government would not be affected, but the workers would be harmed. Therefore, by withdrawal of U.S. companies, less good would be achieved than by their continued presence.

A third reason they give is that the violation of the apartheid laws by U.S. companies is the first step in the process of abolishing these laws. It is admittedly a small step, but it is a first step. It sets the stage for a gradual change in the laws. Breaking down the laws from within the country is more effective than simply condemning the laws from outside the country. The spokesmen for an American presence also claim that if (counter to what they predict) a revolution does take place, there is little reason to believe that such a revolution would produce more good on the whole than a continuation of the present system. The blacks have not been educated or trained in the skills required to run the economy or the country.

There is little reason to believe that a stable black government would be formed, or that whatever government is formed would be less repressive than the present government, even though the repression might express itself differently. They also say that many black leaders fear what might happen if the American companies were to leave. Defenders of a continued American presence argue that, on utilitarian grounds, more good is achieved by the U.S. firms remaining in South Africa, and following the Sullivan Code, than would be achieved by their departure.

Which scenario is the more likely? Which side's predictions of what would happen as a result of U.S. withdrawal should be believed? The evidence is not sufficiently clear to make a dogmatic judgment of the morality of American companies in South Africa. What is clear, however, is that any company operating in South Africa without adopting and fully enforcing the Sullivan Code practices apartheid, and hence acts immorally.

Investing in Multinationals

Thus far we have focused on the morality of practices of multinationals which are outside of the control of the United States government. But American-controlled multinationals are not beyond control of the American parent company. These companies are controlled by their respective boards of directors, which are in turn subject to the interests of the shareholders. American shareholders could, at least in theory, determine the practices of the U.S. multinationals.

Concerning those U.S. multinationals that operate in South Africa, we can raise two moral issues: (1) Is it morally permissible for people or groups to hold stock in corporations that engage in immoral practices? And (2) Should churches and universities, in particular, divest themselves of the stock of corporations that operate in South Africa?

The answer to the first question is that every person has a moral obligation *not* to engage in immoral practices. Is it, then, immoral for anyone to own stock in a company that engages in immoral practices? The simplest answer would be a flat yes. By owning part of a firm, a shareholder supplies the capital for its operation. If it operates immorally, the shareholder is helping it to do so. The answer to the foregoing question would apply clearly to a company that had as its end some immoral purpose. For instance, no one could morally invest in Murders, Inc., if its purpose was to provide excellent hit men for those who wished to kill people they did not like. But few if any companies have as their purpose something that is outrightly immoral, and the typical investor would not invest in such a firm if it did exist.

What makes a firm immoral? Is it enough that someone within the firm acts immorally? Is a firm immoral only if it habitually acts immorally? Is a firm immoral if one of its practices is immoral? The questions cannot be answered with a simple yes or no. Clearly, a firm is not immoral simply if someone within the firm acts immorally. If an employee of a firm, for instance, were to embezzle funds from the company, we would say that the employee and not the company was immoral. If a company made it a practice to exploit its workers, to discriminate against women and blacks, to overcharge its customers—and if it did all these things as a matter of ordinary practice—we could well say the company was immoral. It would therefore be immoral to invest in such a company because such an investment would help promote the company's immoral practices.

But what are the moral responsibilities of an investor? Must he investigate from a moral point of view the activities of a company in which he is interested in investing? Is such a rule practical and reasonable, or does it ask too much of the typical, small investor? It is not always easy to obtain information about the immoral activities of companies. If a company's activities are questionable, it is unlikely to publicize this or include it in its annual report. No moral audit is required of companies to help potential investors. The Council on Economic Priorities, and a few other groups, monitors corporate performance on social issues. Those who do not want to purchase stock in munitions firms can learn which firms make munitions. Those who do not wish to purchase stock in firms that operate in South Africa can find out the names of those firms. And those who wish to purchase stock in firms that operate in South Africa only if the firms follow the Sullivan Code can learn which firms do so. But this sort of information is not always easily available to the small shareholder, and in the absence of such information, an investor must make do with information that is available to him in the newspapers—legal suits, and the like. A moral investor should not support a firm that engages in immoral practices. But the lengths to which one must go to determine which practices are immoral and which companies engage in the immoral practices are matters of judgment, with much room for discretion and disagreement.

We come now to the second question: Should churches and universities, in particular, divest themselves of the stock of corporations that operate in South Africa?

Individuals should not support firms that engage in immoral practices; it therefore follows that institutions also should not invest in such firms. Because corporate bodies usually make larger investments than individuals, they have a correspondingly greater responsibility concerning the investments they make. Critics have claimed that churches and universities should take the lead in ethical investment practices because they are appropriate models for moral behavior.

The critics of multinationals operating in South Africa have focused primarily on church and university investments. They have attempted to persuade these groups to divest themselves of their investments in American companies operating in South Africa. Their arguments are based on two premises. The first is that companies operating in South Africa are engaged in immoral practices, even if they follow the Sullivan principles, because they help the government through their taxes. Secondly, they argue that the churches and universities can force the U.S. companies out of South Africa by selling their stock in protest.

We have already seen that those firms that do not follow the Sullivan Code principles act immorally. Because it is immoral to support apartheid, both institutional and private investors who own stock in such companies should divest themselves of it. Many universities have done so by eliminating from their portfolios investments in banks that grant loans to the government of South Africa. Such banks do not help to break down apartheid by hiring blacks, promoting them, or by doing any of the things the Sullivan Code requires; the banks help the government without attacking apartheid in any way, and thereby help to support apartheid. Because this is immoral, many universities have protested this action by divestiture of their stock.

Two arguments that oppose such action have been raised, but neither is very convincing. One argument claims that no investor can be sure that a company in which he is investing is not engaged in immoral practices. No one can investigate all companies, therefore it is unreasonable to expect investors to be guided by moral considerations. The argument is not convincing. We grant that no one is required to find out what he cannot in practice determine; however, when it is clear that a company is engaging in an immoral practice, and when this is brought to one's attention, then one should act on that information. For instance, to refuse to act on information concerning company *A* simply because one may not know whether company *B* is acting immorally is to choose, knowingly, to participate in an immoral practice.

The second argument is that, for most American companies, their South African operations constitute a very small part of the company's total activities. Hence, if on the whole the companies operate morally, a small immorality in a minor portion of their operations should not be blown out of proportion. The companies, the defenders say, are on the whole moral. The corporate investors claim that they have obligations to their respective institutions, that is, to invest their funds to produce the greatest return. They must weigh this obligation against the obligation not to support a company that engages in an immoral practice but only in a small area of its total operation. The equation, they claim, often comes out in favor of retaining their invested shares. The counter claim, however, is that they would lose so little if they did divest themselves of the shares of those companies that not to do so is to condone the immoral practice.

The situation is far less clear, however, when we consider those firms that follow the Sullivan Code. Nor is it clear that the universities and churches could effect the withdrawal of these companies from South Africa by selling their stock in protest. If they were to sell their stock and drive the price of the stock down, it would simply be purchased by traders who would be delighted to get it at a lower price, confident that it will soon rise again, in line with its actual worth. Some of the institutional shareholders claim that they are more effective voting from within the company than they would be if they voiced their disapproval as outsiders. But the fact is that they have not been effective as insiders when they have sought to force a company to leave South Africa.

During the 1970s and the early part of the 1980s, and to the present time, groups on campuses around the country have sought to get their local endowment associations to divest themselves of companies operating in South Africa. These groups have in some cases been successful and in others unsuccessful; and they show how pressure might be brought to bear on university endowment associations. But they have not accomplished much in the way of effecting withdrawal of companies from South Africa. One reason is that their protest has been in some ways too broad and in others too narrow. It has been too broad because they have tarred with the same brush all U.S. corporations operating in South Africa, instead of concentrating on those corporations that do not adopt the Sullivan Code principles. Their protest has been too narrow because it has focused only on divestiture by university endowment associations, groups which even together could not force a change in policy. If Ford Motor Company and IBM are immoral, then the attack should not stop with refusal by a university to own stock in the company. Ford is helped more by millions of students and their families, who buy Ford cars, than by some endowment associations owning Ford stock. IBM is helped more by universities buying or renting IBM computers, and by offices and individuals buying IBM typewriters, than by endowment associations owning IBM stock. If a practice is immoral, there are more effective ways to influence a company than by symbolic divestiture. But what are we to do if all the major car makers operate in South Africa, or if we prefer IBM computers or typewriters to those of other companies? This question gets to the crux of the issue. Those seriously interested in stopping immorality, and who wish to protest the immoral practice of a company, should not only urge other people to make sacrifices and take action, but they themselves should be willing to do the same.

Multinationals can be held accountable by their shareholders if the shareholders are truly interested in holding them accountable. Shareholders can demand to know what practices the companies follow in their subsidiaries abroad. If immoral practices are discovered in an operation abroad, and if enough people in the United States refuse to purchase the product of the manufacturer in question until the immoral practice is stopped, then it is safe to assume that the practice will be changed when the economics of the situation demand it.

The structures for controlling multinationals and for preventing practices that harm people have been slow in coming. They require international cooperation both on the part of governments and people—organized either as workers or as consumers. Multinationals are helping to bind the world closer together. As they do so, they help prepare the way for collective efforts by those affected by their actions. Those interested in morality on the international level can be effective only if they act collectively. Morality is not a matter of individual activity only. Our obligations expand, as our effective role in the world expands. But moral issues on the international level, though complex, are amenable to careful analysis from a moral point of view.

Unocal Corporation v. Mesa Petroleum Co.

We confront an issue of first impression in Delaware—the validity of a corporation's self-tender for its own shares which excludes from participation a stockholder making a hostile tender offer for the company's stock.

The Court of Chancery granted a preliminary injunction to the plaintiffs, Mesa Petroleum Co., Mesa Asset Co., Mesa Partners II, and Mesa Eastern, Inc. (collectively "Mesa")[1], enjoining an exchange offer of the defen-

---

493 A2d 946. Opinion by Justice J. Moore, Supreme Court of Delaware.

dant, Unocal Corporation (Unocal) for its own stock. The trial court concluded that a selective exchange offer, excluding Mesa, was legally impermissible. We cannot agree with such a blanket rule. The factual findings of the Vice Chancellor, fully supported by the record, establish that Unocal's board, consisting of a majority of independent directors, acted in good faith, and after reasonable investigation found that Mesa's tender offer was both inadequate and coercive. Under the circumstances the board had both the power and duty to oppose a bid it perceived to be harmful to the corporate enterprise. On this record we are satisfied that the device Unocal adopted is reasonable in relation to the threat posed, and that the board acted in the proper exercise of sound business judgment. We will not substitute our views for those of the board if the latter's decision can be "attributed to any rational business purpose." *Sinclair Oil Corp.* v. *Levien,* Del.Supr., 280 A.2d 717, 720 (1971). Accordingly, we reverse the decision of the Court of Chancery and order the preliminary injunction vacated.

I

The factual background of this matter bears a significant relationship to its ultimate outcome.

On April 8, 1985, Mesa, the owner of approximately 13% of Unocal's stock, commenced a two-tier "front loaded" cash tender offer for 64 million shares, or approximately 37%, of Unocal's outstanding stock at a price of $54 per share. The "back-end" was designed to eliminate the remaining publicly held shares by an exchange of securities purportedly worth $54 per share. However, pursuant to an order entered by the United States District Court for the Central District of California on April 26, 1985, Mesa issued a supplemental proxy statement to Unocal's stockholders disclosing that the securities offered in the second-step merger would be highly subordinated, and that Unocal's capitalization would differ signifi-

cantly from its present structure. Unocal has rather aptly termed such securities "junk bonds."[2]

Unocal's board consists of eight independent outside directors and six insiders. It met on April 13, 1985, to consider the Mesa tender offer. Thirteen directors were present, and the meeting lasted nine and one-half hours. The directors were given no agenda or written materials prior to the session. However, detailed presentations were made by legal counsel regarding the board's obligations under both Delaware corporate law and the federal securities laws. The board then received a presentation from Peter Sachs on behalf of Goldman Sachs & Co. (Goldman Sachs) and Dillon, Read & Co. (Dillon Read) discussing the bases for their opinions that the Mesa proposal was wholly inadequate. Mr. Sachs opined that the minimum cash value that could be expected from a sale or orderly liquidation for 100% of Unocal's stock was in excess of $60 per share. In making his presentation, Mr. Sachs showed slides outlining the valuation techniques used by the financial advisors, and others, depicting recent business combinations in the oil and gas industry. The Court of Chancery found that the Sachs presentation was designed to apprise the directors of the scope of the analyses performed rather than the facts and numbers used in reaching the conclusion that Mesa's tender offer price was inadequate.

Mr. Sachs also presented various defensive strategies available to the board if it concluded that Mesa's two-step tender offer was inadequate and should be opposed. One of the devices outlined was a self-tender by Unocal for its own stock with a reasonable price range of $70 to $75 per share. The cost of such a proposal would cause the company to incur $6.1–6.5 billion of additional debt, and a presentation was made informing the board of Unocal's ability to handle it. The directors were told that the primary effect of this obligation would be to reduce exploratory drilling, but that the company would nonetheless remain a viable entity.

The eight outside directors, comprising a

clear majority of the thirteen members present, then met separately with Unocal's financial advisors and attorneys. Thereafter, they unanimously agreed to advise the board that it should reject Mesa's tender offer as inadequate, and that Unocal should pursue a self-tender to provide the stockholders with a fairly priced alternative to the Mesa proposal. The board then reconvened and unanimously adopted a resolution rejecting as grossly inadequate Mesa's tender offer. Despite the nine and one-half hour length of the meeting, no formal decision was made on the proposed defensive self-tender.

On April 15, the board met again with four of the directors present by telephone and one member still absent. This session lasted two hours. Unocal's Vice President of Finance and its Assistant General Counsel made a detailed presentation of the proposed terms of the exchange offer. A price range between $70 and $80 per share was considered, and ultimately the directors agreed upon $72. The board was also advised about the debt securities that would be issued, and the necessity of placing restrictive covenants upon certain corporate activities until the obligations were paid. The board's decisions were made in reliance on the advice of its investment bankers, including the terms and conditions upon which the securities were to be issued. Based upon this advice, and the board's own deliberations, the directors unanimously approved the exchange offer. Their resolution provided that if Mesa acquired 64 million shares of Unocal stock through its own offer (the Mesa Purchase Condition), Unocal would buy the remaining 49% outstanding for an exchange of debt securities having an aggregate par value of $72 per share. The board resolution also stated that the offer would be subject to other conditions that had been described to the board at the meeting, or which were deemed necessary by Unocal's officers, including the exclusion of Mesa from the proposal (the Mesa exclusion). Any such conditions were required to be in accordance with the "purport and intent" of the offer.

Unocal's exchange offer was commenced on April 17, 1985, and Mesa promptly challenged it by filing this suit in the Court of Chancery. On April 22, the Unocal board met again and was advised by Goldman Sachs and Dillon Read to waive the Mesa Purchase Condition as to 50 million shares. This recommendation was in response to a perceived concern of the shareholders that, if shares were tendered to Unocal, no shares would be purchased by either offeror. The directors were also advised that they should tender their own Unocal stock into the exchange offer as a mark of their confidence in it. . . .

II

The issues we address involve these fundamental questions: Did the Unocal board have the power and duty to oppose a takeover threat it reasonably perceived to be harmful to the corporate enterprise, and if so, is its action here entitled to the protection of the business judgment rule?

Mesa contends that the discriminatory exchange offer violates the fiduciary duties Unocal owes it. Mesa argues that because of the Mesa exclusion the business judgment rule is inapplicable, because the directors by tendering their own shares will derive a financial benefit that is not available to *all* Unocal stockholders. Thus, it is Mesa's ultimate contention that Unocal cannot establish that the exchange offer is fair to *all* shareholders, and argues that the Court of Chancery was correct in concluding that Unocal was unable to meet this burden.

Unocal answers that it does not owe a duty of "fairness" to Mesa, given the facts here. Specifically, Unocal contends that its board of directors reasonably and in good faith concluded that Mesa's $54 two-tier tender offer was coercive and inadequate, and that Mesa sought selective treatment for itself. Furthermore, Unocal argues that the board's approval of the exchange offer was made in good faith, on an informed basis, and in the exercise of due care. Under these circumstances, Unocal contends that its directors properly employed this device to protect the company and its stockholders from Mesa's harmful tactics.

III

We begin with the basic issue of the power of a board of directors of a Delaware corporation to adopt a defensive measure of this type. Absent such authority, all other questions are moot. Neither issues of fairness nor business judgment are pertinent without the basic underpinning of a board's legal power to act.

[1] The board has a large reservoir of authority upon which to draw. Its duties and responsibilities proceed from the inherent powers conferred by 8 *Del.C.* § 141(a), respecting management of the corporation's "business and affairs". Additionally, the powers here being exercised derive from 8 *Del.C.* § 160(a), conferring broad authority upon a corporation to deal in its own stock. From this it is now well established that in the acquisition of its shares a Delaware corporation may deal selectively with its stockholders, provided the directors have not acted out of a sole or primary purpose to entrench themselves in office. *Cheff* v. *Mathes,* Del.Supr., 199 A.2d 548, 554 (1964). . . .

[2] Finally, the board's power to act derives from its fundamental duty and obligation to protect the corporate enterprise, which includes stockholders, from harm reasonably perceived, irrespective of its source. . . . Thus, we are satisfied that in the broad context of corporate governance, including issues of fundamental corporate change, a board of directors is not a passive instrumentality.

[3, 4] Given the foregoing principles, we turn to the standards by which director action is to be measured. In *Pogostin* v. *Rice,* Del.Supr., 480 A.2d 619 (1984), we held that the business judgment rule, including the standards by which director conduct is

judged, is applicable in the context of a takeover. *Id.* at 627. The business judgment rule is a "presumption that in making a business decision the directors of a corporation acted on an informed basis, in good faith and in the honest belief that the action taken was in the best interests of the company." *Aronson* v. *Lewis,* Del.Supr., 473 A.2d 805, 812 (1984) (citations omitted). A hallmark of the business judgment rule is that a court will not substitute its judgment for that of the board if the latter's decision can be "attributed to any rational business purpose." *Sinclair Oil Corp.* v. *Levien,* Del.Supr., 280 A.2d 717, 720 (1971).

[5–8] When a board addresses a pending takeover bid it has an obligation to determine whether the offer is in the best interests of the corporation and its shareholders. In that respect a board's duty is no different from any other responsibility it shoulders, and its decisions should be no less entitled to the respect they otherwise would be accorded in the realm of business judgment. *See also Johnson* v. *Trueblood,* 629 F.2d 287, 292–293 (3d Cir.1980). There are, however, certain caveats to a proper exercise of this function. Because of the omnipresent specter that a board may be acting primarily in its own interests, rather than those of the corporation and its shareholders, there is an enhanced duty which calls for judicial examination at the threshold before the protections of the business judgment rule may be conferred.

This Court has long recognized that:

> We must bear in mind the inherent danger in the purchase of shares with corporate funds to remove a threat to corporate policy when a threat to control is involved. The directors are of necessity confronted with a conflict of interest, and an objective decision is difficult.

Bennett v. *Propp,* Del.Supr., 187 A.2d 405, 409 (1962). In the face of this inherent conflict directors must show that they had reasonable grounds for believing that a danger to corporate policy and effectiveness existed because of another person's stock ownership. *Cheff* v. *Mathes*, 199 A.2d at 554–55. However, they satisfy that burden "by showing good faith and reasonable investigation. ..." *Id.* at 555. Furthermore, such proof is materially enhanced, as here, by the approval of a board comprised of a majority of outside independent directors who have acted in accordance with the foregoing standards....

IV

A

[9] In the board's exercise of corporate power to forestall a takeover bid our analysis begins with the basic principle that corporate directors have a fiduciary duty to act in the best interests of the corporation's stockholders. *Guth* v. *Loft, Inc.*, Del. Supr., 5 A.2d 503, 510 (1939). As we have noted, their duty of care extends to protecting the corporation and its owners from perceived harm whether a threat originates from third parties or other shareholders. But such powers are not absolute. A corporation does not have unbridled discretion to defeat any perceived threat by any Draconian means available.

[10–12] The restriction placed upon a selective stock repurchase is that the directors may not have acted solely or primarily out of a desire to perpetuate themselves in office. *See Cheff* v. *Mathes*, 199 A.2d at 556; *Kors* v. *Carey*, 158 A.2d at 140. Of course, to this is added the further caveat that inequitable action may not be taken under the guise of law. *Schnell* v. *Chris-Craft Industries, Inc.*, Del.Supr., 285 A.2d 437, 439 (1971). The standard of proof established in *Cheff* v. *Mathes* and discussed *supra* at page 16, is designed to ensure that a defensive measure to thwart or impede a takeover is indeed motivated by a good faith concern for the welfare of the corporation and its stockholders, which in all circumstances must be free of any fraud or other misconduct. *Cheff* v.

Mathes, 199 A.2d at 554–55. However, this does not end the inquiry.

B

[13, 14] A further aspect is the element of balance. If a defensive measure is to come within the ambit of the business judgment rule, it must be reasonable in relation to the threat posed. This entails an analysis by the directors of the nature of the takeover bid and its effect on the corporate enterprise. Examples of such concerns may include: inadequacy of the price offered, nature and timing of the offer, questions of illegality, the impact on "constituencies" other than shareholders (i.e., creditors, customers, employees, and perhaps even the community generally), the risk of nonconsummation, and the quality of securities being offered in the exchange. *See* Lipton and Brownstein, *Takeover Responses and Directors' Responsibilities: An Update*, p. 7, ABA National Institute on the Dynamics of Corporate Control (December 8, 1983). While not a controlling factor, it also seems to us that a board may reasonably consider the basic stockholder interests at stake, including those of short term speculators, whose actions may have fueled the coercive aspect of the offer at the expense of the long term investor. Here, the threat posed was viewed by the Unocal board as a grossly inadequate two-tier coercive tender offer coupled with the threat of greenmail.

[15] Specifically, the Unocal directors had concluded that the value of Unocal was substantially above the $54 per share offered in cash at the front end. Furthermore, they determined that the subordinated securities to be exchanged in Mesa's announced squeeze out of the remaining shareholders in the "back-end" merger were "junk bonds" worth far less than $54. It is now well recognized that such offers are a classic coercive measure designed to stampede shareholders into tendering at the first tier, even if the price is inadequate, out of fear of what they will receive at the back end of the transaction. Wholly beyond the coercive aspect of an in-

adequate two-tier tender offer, the threat was posed by a corporate raider with a national reputation as a "greenmailer."[3]

[16] In adopting the selective exchange offer, the board stated that its objective was either to defeat the inadequate Mesa offer or, should the offer still succeed, provide the 49% of its stockholders, who would otherwise be forced to accept "junk bonds," with $72 worth of senior debt. We find that both purposes are valid.

However, such efforts would have been thwarted by Mesa's participation in the exchange offer. First, if Mesa could tender its shares, Unocal would effectively be subsidizing the former's continuing effort to buy Unocal stock at $54 per share. Second, Mesa could not, by definition, fit within the class of shareholders being protected from its own coercive and inadequate tender offer.

Thus, we are satisfied that the selective exchange offer is reasonably related to the threats posed. It is consistent with the principle that "the minority stockholder shall receive the substantial equivalent in value of what he had before." *Sterling* v. *Mayflower Hotel Corp.,* Del.Supr., 93 A.2d 107, 114 (1952). *See also Rosenblatt* v. *Getty Oil Co.,* Del.Supr., 493 A.2d 929, 940 (1985). This concept of fairness, while stated in the merger context, is also relevant in the area of tender offer law. Thus, the board's decision to offer what it determined to be the fair value of the corporation to the 49% of its shareholders, who would otherwise be forced to accept highly subordinated "junk bonds," is reasonable and consistent with the directors' duty to ensure that the minority stockholders receive equal value for their shares.

V

[17] Mesa contends that it is unlawful, and the trial court agreed, for a corporation to discriminate in this fashion against one shareholder. It argues correctly that no case has ever sanctioned a device that precludes a raider from sharing in a benefit available to all other stockholders. However, as we have noted earlier, the principle of selective stock repurchases by a Delaware corporation is neither unknown nor unauthorized. *Cheff* v. *Mathes,* 199 A.2d at 554. . . . The only difference is that heretofore the approved transaction was the payment of "greenmail" to a raider or dissident posing a threat to the corporate enterprise. All other stockholders were denied such favored treatment, and given Mesa's past history of greenmail, its claims here are rather ironic.

However, our corporate law is not static. It must grow and develop in response to, indeed in anticipation of, evolving concepts and needs. Merely because the General Corporation Law is silent as to a specific matter does not mean that it is prohibited. *See Providence and Worcester Co.* v. *Baker,* Del.Supr., 378 A.2d 121, 123–124 (1977). In the days when *Cheff, Bennett, Martin* and *Kors* were decided, the tender offer, while not an unknown device, was virtually unused, and little was known of such methods as two-tier "front-end" loaded offers with their coercive effects. Then, the favored attack of a raider was stock acquisition followed by a proxy contest. Various defensive tactics, which provided no benefit whatever to the raider, evolved. Thus, the use of corporate funds by management to counter a proxy battle was approved. *Hall* v. *Trans-Lux Daylight Picture Screen Corp.,* Del.Supr., 171 A. 226 (1934); *Hibbert* v. *Hollywood Park, Inc.,* Del.Supr., 457 A.2d 339 (1983). Litigation, supported by corporate funds, aimed at the raider has long been a popular device.

More recently, as the sophistication of both raiders and targets has developed, a host of other defensive measures to counter such ever mounting threats has evolved and received judicial sanction. These include defensive charter amendments and other devices bearing some rather exotic, but apt, names: Crown Jewel, White Knight, Pac Man, and Golden Parachute. Each has highly selective features, the object of which is to deter or defeat the raider.

Thus, while the exchange offer is a form

of selective treatment, given the nature of the threat posed here the response is neither unlawful nor unreasonable. If the board of directors is disinterested, has acted in good faith and with due care, its decision in the absence of an abuse of discretion will be upheld as a proper exercise of business judgment.

[18] To this Mesa responds that the board is not disinterested, because the directors are receiving a benefit from the tender of their own shares, which because of the Mesa exclusion, does not devolve upon *all* stockholders equally. *See Aronson* v. *Lewis,* Del.Supr., 473 A.2d 805, 812 (1984). However, Mesa concedes that if the exclusion is valid, then the directors and all other stockholders share the same benefit. The answer of course is that the exclusion is valid, and the directors' participation in the exchange offer does not rise to the level of a disqualifying interest. The excellent discussion in *Johnson* v. *Trueblood,* 629 F.2d at 292–293, of the use of the business judgment rule in takeover contests also seems pertinent here.

[19] Nor does this become an "interested" director transaction merely because certain board members are large stockholders. As this Court has previously noted, that fact alone does not create a disqualifying "personal pecuniary interest" to defeat the operation of the business judgment rule. *Cheff* v. *Mathes,* 199 A.2d at 554.

[20] Mesa also argues that the exclusion permits the directors to abdicate the fiduciary duties they owe it. However, that is not so. The board continues to owe Mesa the duties of due care and loyalty. But in the face of the destructive threat Mesa's tender offer was perceived to pose, the board had a supervening duty to protect the corporate enterprise, which includes the other shareholders, from threatened harm.

[21] Mesa contends that the basis of this action is punitive, and solely in response to the exercise of its rights of corporate democracy.[4] Nothing precludes Mesa, as a stockholder, from acting in its own self-interest. . . . However, Mesa, while pursuing its own interests, has acted in a manner which a board consisting of a majority of independent directors has reasonably determined to be contrary to the best interests of Unocal and its other shareholders. In this situation, there is no support in Delaware law for the proposition that, when responding to a perceived harm, a corporation must guarantee a benefit to a stockholder who is deliberately provoking the danger being addressed. There is no obligation of self-sacrifice by a corporation and its shareholders in the face of such a challenge.

Here, the Court of Chancery specifically found that the "directors' decision [to oppose the Mesa tender offer] was made in the good faith belief that the Mesa tender offer is inadequate." Given our standard of review under *Levitt* v. *Bouvier,* Del.Supr., 287 A.2d 671, 673 (1972), and *Application of Delaware Racing Association,* Del.Supr., 213 A.2d 203, 207 (1965), we are satisfied that Unocal's board has met its burden of proof. *Cheff* v. *Mathes,* 199 A.2d at 555.

VI

[22] In conclusion, there was directorial power to oppose the Mesa tender offer, and to undertake a selective stock exchange made in good faith and upon a reasonable investigation pursuant to a clear duty to protect the corporate enterprise. Further, the selective stock repurchase plan chosen by Unocal is reasonable in relation to the threat that the board rationally and reasonably believed was posed by Mesa's inadequate and coercive two-tier tender offer. Under those circumstances the board's action is entitled to be measured by the standards of the business judgment rule. Thus, unless it is shown by a preponderance of the evidence that the directors' decisions were primarily based on perpetuating themselves in office, or some other breach of fiduciary duty such as fraud, overreaching, lack of good faith, or being uninformed, a Court will not substitute its judgment for that of the board.

In this case that protection is not lost merely because Unocal's directors have tendered their shares in the exchange offer. Given the validity of the Mesa exclusion, they are receiving a benefit shared generally by all other stockholders except Mesa. In this circumstance the test of *Aronson* v. *Lewis,* 473 A.2d at 812, is satisfied. *See also Cheff* v. *Mathes,* 199 A.2d at 554. If the stockholders are displeased with the action of their elected representatives, the powers of corporate democracy are at their disposal to turn the board out. *Aronson* v. *Lewis,* Del.Supr., 473 A.2d 805, 811 (1984). . . .

. . . The decision of the Court of Chancery is therefore REVERSED, and the preliminary injunction is VACATED.

NOTES

1. T. Boone Pickens, Jr., is President and Chairman of the Board of Mesa Petroleum and President of Mesa Asset and controls the related Mesa entities.
2. Mesa's May 3, 1985 supplement to its proxy statement states:

   (i) following the Offer, the Purchasers would seek to effect a merger of Unocal and Mesa Eastern or an affiliate of Mesa Eastern (the "Merger") in which the remaining Shares would be acquired for a combination of subordinated debt securities and preferred stock; (ii) the securities to be received by Unocal shareholders in the Merger would be subordinated to $2,400 million of debt securities of Mesa Eastern, indebtedness incurred to refinance up to $1,000 million of bank debt which was incurred by affiliates of Mesa Partners II to purchase Shares and to pay related interest and expenses and all then-existing debt of Unocal; (iii) the corporation surviving the Merger would be responsible for the payment of all securities of Mesa Eastern (including any such securities issued pursuant to the Merger) and the indebtedness referred to in item (ii) above, and such securities and indebtedness would be repaid out of funds generated by the operation of Unocal; (iv) the indebtedness incurred in the Offer and the Merger would result in Unocal being much more highly leveraged, and the capitalization of the corporation surviving the Merger would differ significantly from that of Unocal at present; and (v) in their analyses of cash flows provided by operations of Unocal which would be available to service and repay securities and other obligations of the corporation surviving the Merger, the Purchasers assumed that the capital expenditures and expenditures for exploration of such corporation would be significantly reduced.

3. The term "greenmail" refers to the practice of buying out a takeover bidder's stock at a premium that is not available to other shareholders in order to prevent the takeover. The Chancery Court noted that "Mesa has made tremendous profits from its takeover activities although in the past few years it has not been successful in acquiring any of the target companies on an unfriendly basis." Moreover, the trial court specifically found that the actions of the Unocal board were taken in good faith to eliminate both the inadequacies of the tender offer and to forestall the payment of "greenmail."

4. This seems to be the underlying basis of the trial court's principal reliance on the unreported Chancery decision of *Fisher* v. *Moltz,* Del.Ch. No. 6068 (1979), published in 5 Del.J.Corp.L. 530 (1980). However, the facts in *Fisher* are thoroughly distinguishable. There, a corporation offered to repurchase the shares of its former employees, except those of the plaintiffs, merely because the latter were then engaged in lawful competition with the company. No threat to the enterprise was posed, and at best it can be said that the exclusion was motivated by pique instead of a rational corporate purpose.

Consolidata Services, Inc. v. Alexander Grant & Company

. . . Consolidata Services, Inc. (hereinafter referred to as CDS), was established in Ohio in 1970 by the plaintiff, Joel Wagenheim, and initially was created to provide bookkeeping services to small and medium-sized businesses. Later, it expanded its operations and commenced handling company payroll distributions. CDS continued to provide payroll services until it was forced into receivership in February of 1978. Wagenheim was also the co-signor or guarantor on a variety of notes on behalf of CDS. Even though he later relinquished all control in the corporation in 1976, Wagenheim maintained a security interest in the stock of CDS as collateral for the sale of his ownership interest, and remained available as a consultant to the management of CDS.

With each new payroll client of CDS, it was initially required that a deposit be given to insure that there would always be a sufficient amount of money to cover the payroll checks distributed should the cash advanced for each month be delayed. The deposits were not kept separately and the service contracts specifically provided that the customers had no right to any interest on the deposit while it was held by CDS. Also, the contracts placed no restrictions on the use of the deposits by CDS except that, upon termination of their contractual relationship, the deposits would be returned within 30 days.

Alexander Grant & Company (hereinafter called Alexander Grant), the defendant, is a major accounting firm that provided tax and other business related services to both CDS and Wagenheim. Many of the clients who used CDS's payroll services were also clients of Alexander Grant (hereinafter referred to as mutual clients) and, in fact, many had chosen Alexander Grant upon the recommendation of CDS and vice versa.

On January 23, 1978, a meeting was held between several representatives from Alexander Grant and the president of CDS, Tom Ryan, to discuss an outstanding debt owed by CDS to the defendant for past services and to discuss arrangements for the rest of the year. At the meeting, Ryan provided the representatives with a financial statement from CDS for the latter part of 1977 showing its financial status. From the statement, Alexander Grant's accountants determined that CDS was $150,000 short of cash in their payroll accounts based upon the payroll funds received and amounts owed as shown in the statement. Acting on the advice of their in-house counsel, the accountants from Alexander Grant contacted Ryan and asked that CDS immediately disclose its cash flow problems to its clients before any further funds were received. Ryan refused to make the disclosure and suggested that Wagenheim be contacted and advised of the problem.

On February 6, 1978, another meeting was held between the Alexander Grant representatives, and Ryan, but this time with Wagenheim also present. At the meeting, the representatives from Alexander Grant again insisted that the disclosure be made. Wagenheim refused to authorize the disclosure and asked Alexander Grant not to do so. Wagenheim also asked that he be given some time to formulate a plan to raise the missing money, and that if it later became necessary,

482 N.E.2d 955, 19 Ohio App. 3d 7. Opinion by Judge J. Strausbaugh, Tenth Appellate District, Ohio Court of Appeals.

he personally would notify the clients of the problem. It is unclear from the testimony whether the defendant actually agreed to wait and give the plaintiffs some additional time to solve the problem of the money deficiency. Soon after the meeting, Ryan, at the advice of his counsel, resigned as the sole officer and director of CDS.

The next day, without notifying either Wagenheim or anyone at CDS, the defendant began to call its mutual clients and advise them not to send additional payroll funds to CDS, and to retain their payroll records. Several other mutual clients who had no funds on deposit with CDS were also called. Some of those contacted called CDS to inquire why such advice had been given by defendant and were then told that CDS had a cash flow problem but was attempting to devise a solution. Most of the clients refused to continue their relationship with CDS and, subsequently, cancelled their contracts. Ten days after the phone calls were made, CDS terminated its operations and closed down its office. There was no evidence presented that prior to the phone calls CDS had ever failed to fulfill its payroll obligations to its clients or had ever been unable to return any of its customers' deposits. On February 9, 1978, the plaintiffs each received a letter from the defendant stating that Alexander Grant was terminating their relationship and that its accounting services would no longer be provided in the future.

On February 6, 1979, both Wagenheim and CDS filed their respective complaints against the defendant.... [O]n October 6, the jury returned a verdict in favor of plaintiffs, awarding $350,000 in compensatory damages to CDS, and $220,000 in compensatory damages and $750,000 in punitive damages to Wagenheim. The defendant then moved for judgment notwithstanding the verdict or, in the alternative, a new trial. The defendant's motion was again denied by the court in an order issued and filed on November 29, 1982. From the trial court's denial of its motion for judgment notwith-

standing the verdict and/or a new trial, the defendant brings this appeal raising the following ... assignments of error: ...

"4. The judgment in favor of CDS is contrary to law.
"A. The duty of confidentiality is not absolute.
"B. The disclosure was made to protect third parties and did not violate any duty of nondisclosure...."

We shall consider first defendant's fourth assignment of error, since much of this dispute centers around its outcome. The defendant asserts in its fourth assignment of error that the judgment in favor of CDS was contrary to law, and that no cause of action exists placing liability upon an accountant for the disclosure of confidential information obtained from a client during their association in order to protect the interests of certain third parties.

As has been pointed out by both the parties, the statutory and case law in Ohio, as well as in other states, is void of any discussion concerning such a cause of action; and, therefore, this case appears to be one of first impression in the United States. However, this court recognizes that the legal basis upon which such liability could be established exists. It is implied in every contractual relationship between an accountant and his client that a general duty exists not to make extrajudicial disclosures of information acquired in the course of their professional relationship; and that a breach of that duty by an accountant may give rise to a cause of action.

A client should be entitled to freely disclose information concerning his financial status to his accountant without fear that such information will be exposed to the public. When the plaintiff, CDS, contracted with the defendant for the performance of certain accounting services, the defendant was under a general duty not to disclose information about the financial status of the plaintiff obtained as a result of their relationship. This is not to say that a client enjoys an absolute right, but rather that he possesses a limited right against such a disclosure, subject to exceptions prompted by the supervening interests of the public.

For instance, the disclosure of confidential information would not be prohibited when it is necessary and relevant to the resolution of a litigated issue. . . .

A contractual relationship exists between an accountant and his client and, as such, an accountant's liability to his client is determined by the extent of their contractual relationship and the duties imposed by law upon accountants. 1 American Jurisprudence 2d, Accountants, Section 10. After reviewing the evidence in a light most favorable to the plaintiffs and with deference to the actions of the trial court below as is necessary in this appeal, we find that an accountant-client relationship existed between Alexander Grant and CDS and continued, as such, up to the time that the defendant notified the plaintiff by letter, on February 9, 1978, terminating their relationship. While no express written service agreement was ever signed, no such express written contract was needed. The defendant and CDS maintained an ongoing business relationship whereby services were rendered on a continual basis. As in the legal profession, the relationship that an accountant establishes with his client does not cease merely because the specific services provided at that time have been completed. The meeting between the representatives from Alexander Grant and Ryan on the 23rd of January was conducted in furtherance of their professional relationship for purposes of discussing the payment of an overdue debt and to make other arrangements for future services. At that meeting, a financial statement from CDS was given to the defendant's representatives and the sensitive information concerning the financial status of CDS was disclosed.

The legal obligations that flow from an accountant's business relationships necessarily arise from an understanding between the parties of the objectives to be achieved and the expectations that govern their achievement. As has been created in both the legal and medical professions, the State Accountancy Board has promulgated its own code of professional conduct, and with the recognition of those duties therein expressed comes the recognition that such conduct is expected by the public.

Chapter 4701–11 of the Ohio Admin. Code sets forth the ethical standards adopted by the State Accountancy Board and modeled after those standards established by the American Institute of Certified Public Accountants. Rule 4701–11–02(A), Confidential Client Information, states:

> (A) A certified public accountant or public accountant shall not disclose any confidential information obtained in the course of a professional engagement except with the consent of the client.

Indeed, a mere breach of the ethical concepts established by the accountancy board does not provide a cause of action for misconduct; however, these standards do give credence to the proposition that it is within the expectations of both parties involved that these restrictions will not be violated. This is consistent also with the fact that the personnel manual for Alexander Grant states:

> Alexander Grant & Company subscribes fully to the Code of Professional Ethics of the American Institute of Certified Public Accountants, and to the codes of societies of the various states in which we practice.

In essence, there is a reasonable expectation that Alexander Grant in providing accounting services to the public will conduct itself in a professional manner consistent with those standards established within the state. As a result, there is a legal obligation existing in every accountant-client relationship in which it participates, unless specifically excluded, that all information communicated to the defendant by its clients in confidence should not be disclosed without the client's prior consent.

Although not cited by either party, R.C. 4701.19 provides:

All statements, records, schedules, working papers, and memoranda made by a certified public accountant or public accountant incident to or in the course of professional service to clients by such accountant, except reports submitted by a certified public accountant or public accountant to a client, shall be and remain the property of such accountant, in the absence of an express agreement between such accountant and the client to the contrary. *No such statement, record, schedule, working paper or memorandum shall be sold, transferred or bequeathed, without the consent of the client or his personal representative or assignee, to anyone other than one or more surviving partners or new partners of such accountant.* [Emphasis added.]

R.C. 4701.19 expresses the policy of this state that information contained within the written materials prepared by an accountant for his client may not be relinquished by the sale or transfer of these documents without the prior consent of the client. Based upon the reasonable expectations of the parties involved, and the public policy against such action, a duty is imposed by law upon an accountant not to wrongfully disclose information given to him in confidence by his client. The preservation of a client's confidential information is not a mere ethical duty, it is a legal duty as well. The unauthorized disclosure of any secrets or other confidential information obtained during the professional association of an accountant and his client will give rise to an action for breach of contract.

While the defendant did not specifically disclose any confidential communications concerning CDS to its clients, the advice that it gave was based upon such information. Because of its superior knowledge, the warnings given by Alexander Grant were heeded with almost no hesitation by its clients and reasonably so. Thus, by using the confidential information obtained from CDS, and advising its clients to cease any further business dealings with the plaintiff, its actions were equivalent to, or perhaps even worse than, a complete disclosure of CDS's financial status to the mutual clients; because,

without a complete disclosure, the mutual clients were unable to make an independent evaluation as to what course of action should be pursued.

Although the duty of confidentiality implied in an accountant-client relationship is favored, this court recognizes that such a duty is not absolute. Overriding public interests may exist to which confidentiality must yield. The defendant asserts that the disclosures were necessary and justified because they were made to protect the overriding interests of the mutual clients. The defendant cites the insolvency of CDS, the absence of any officers or directors after Ryan's resignation, and certain questionable activities within the corporation as the basis for the disclosures. It claims that, as of February 6, 1978, CDS's financial situation was serious, and in order to keep its clients from sustaining any further financial losses than they were already exposed to, Alexander Grant felt that it was necessary to advise them to cease any further dealings with CDS. The defendant was also aware of the fact that CDS would, in all probability, be forced to close down if a majority of the clients contacted followed its advice. In effect, the defendant made a conscious decision to sacrifice one client for the protection and advancement of others.

The mere fact that CDS was insolvent does not in itself justify the disclosure of that corporation's financial status by the defendant to CDS's clients, without some further investigation into the business activities of the corporation to determine if, indeed, a fraud was being committed upon the mutual clients and if they were in immediate danger of suffering significant financial losses from a continued association with CDS. "There is substantial authority to the effect that mere silence as to one's financial status, solvency, and credit does not amount to fraud." 37 American Jurisprudence 2d, Fraud and Deceit, Section 171.... In this case, although there was some evidence presented by defendant that it knew or could reasonably have believed that CDS was irretrievably insolvent and had no reasonable expectation of fulfilling its contractual obligations with its payroll clients, we find that there was sufficient evidence in the record that CDS could have regained its solvency and obtained the cash needed to balance the accounts of its payroll clients.

As for the additional factors cited by the defendant, Ryan's resignation could not in itself or even in conjunction with the other factors cited have reasonably justified Alexander Grant's decision to call the mutual clients. Ryan had only resigned the day before.

No investigation was conducted as to who would replace him or when a replacement would be chosen or how the business would be affected. The defendant also claimed that CDS's books were inaccurate and incomplete and that certain questionable loans had been made to individuals within the corporation. However, no further testimony was given or evidence presented to substantiate these claims or show their severity. Accordingly, the defendant's fourth assignment of error is overruled. . . .

CASE 1. The Dual Reporters

Maxwell Newton publishes a newsletter called "Maxwell Newton's Daily New York Money Market Report." In 1985, 60 subscribers paid $7,500 to receive the newsletter. Newton also writes a column on economics and finance for Rupert Murdoch newspapers, including the *New York Post*. Newton is quoted as saying that he earns "more than twice" as much for his newsletter as he earns from Murdoch.

Jack Anderson's syndicated column appears in 900 newspapers around the world. Twice monthly he publishes *Jack Anderson's Washington Letter*. The cost of a subscription to this publication is $48.

Mr. Ben Weberman is the economics editor of *Forbes*. He is also the editor and publisher of *Reporting on Governments*. Subscribers pay $250 a year for information on government economic policy. Mr. Weberman's publication is in its twenty-eighth year. When it began Mr. Weberman was not employed by *Forbes;* he was employed by the *New York Herald Tribune*.

As a *Forbes* employee, Mr. Weberman is an exception. James W. Michaels, *Forbes* editor, is quoted as saying that members of the *Forbes* staff are not allowed to write for newsletters, because it creates too many conflicts

of interest. He charges that such dual reporting creates the potential for divided loyalties and is unfair. "How does a person you're interviewing know whether what he or she says is going to appear in *Forbes* or in some insider newsletter?"

The editor of *Forbes* is not alone in his concern. Other critics point out that the editor of a newspaper can't know if her journalists are giving their best stories to the newspaper rather than saving them for the journalist's private newsletter.

Many journalists deny any conflict of interest. Jack Anderson argues that his syndicated columns are designed for a mass audience, while his newsletter is for the specialist. Syndicated columnists Rowland Evans and Robert Novak, publishers of two newsletters, agree. They point out that newsletters contain details that editors would not print.

Questions

1. Is a financial reporter who publishes a newsletter in finance-related matters involved in a conflict of interest? Explain.

Case prepared by Norman Bowie from a report by Tom Herman, entitled "Some News Reporters Put Out Newsletters As a Lucrative Sideline," *Wall Street Journal*, May 22, 1985, pp. 1, 29.

2. Evaluate the Evans/Novack argument that they are not involved in a conflict of interest because their newsletters publish details that their editors would not print.
3. Suppose a reporter has part ownership in a private newsletter. She also helps manage it, but she does not write for it. Is she involved in a conflict of interest?

4. Some newspapers and magazines require that reporters get permission to write for or publish independent newsletters. Does the granting of the permission remove any potential conflict of interest?

CASE 2. An Accounting Firm Discovers Marketing

Reliability Accounting is a large regional certified public accounting firm located in a large midwestern city. It has been in business for sixty years and has made a reputation as a highly reliable auditor. Recently, Reliability Accounting has lost several long-term clients to large, national accounting firms who solicited them. Until recently, the "stealing of clients" was considered unethical. In addition, many other clients are asking if Reliability can provide other nonauditing, accounting services. The most requested services are consulting services. In the last three years the big eight accounting firms had a 33 percent rise in consulting fees as compared with a 14 percent rise in accounting fees.

Reliability is concerned that if it does not expand its services, it will be forced to merge in order to survive. Reliability knows that many accounting firms with similar characteristics have already merged. As it considers the consulting services it might offer, Reliability does not have an easy decision. One competing firm ran a two-day "Trade Fair" for its 500 partners. Twenty-seven products were "on display" including pension consulting, cost-sale analysis, and litigation support.

The senior partner at Reliability Accounting is deeply troubled by this planned expansion into consulting services. How can the integrity of the audit be maintained if

Reliability is providing all these services to the same company it audits? Won't Reliability be in the position of auditing and otherwise evaluating its own advice? As Michael Barrett, chief counsel from the House Subcommittee holding hearings on the accounting industry has said, "We're very concerned that the more hats an accounting firm wears for its clients, the more the firm is in the client's pocket." The senior partner is actively considering a statement opposing the proposed expansion.

Questions

1. Is a certified public accounting firm that offers consulting services in addition to auditing involved in a position of conflict of interest?
2. To whom does a certified public accounting firm owe its allegiance: the client that hires it or the investing public?
3. What institutional safeguards could be implemented that might lessen potential conflict of interest?
4. Should the fact that everyone else is providing such consulting services and that Reliability Accounting might not survive if it does not justify engaging in the new practices?

Case prepared by Norman E. Bowie from a report by Lee Berton, "CPA Firms Diversify, Cut Fees, Steal Clients in Battle for Business," *Wall Street Journal*, September 20, 1985, p. 4.

CASE 3. *Coastal Corporation v. Houston Natural Gas*

On the morning of Friday, January 27, 1984, Coastal Corporation announced a tender offer for 45 percent of the stock of Houston Natural Gas (HNG) at $68 per share. The two companies had been adversaries for over twenty years. Unbeknownst to HNG, Coastal had previously purchased enough shares to give Coastal 5.7 percent of the stock in HNG at the time of its tender. This 5.7 percent, coupled with the 45 percent of the tender, would give Coastal control of HNG.

The tender offer was a so-called two-tier offer; that is, Coastal would pay cash for 45 percent of the stock, and any stock over that 45 percent would be exchanged for "paper" comprised of "debt or equity securities" issued by Coastal on a pro rata basis. This type of "paper" is commonly referred to as "junk bonds."

At the time, Houston Natural Gas was the largest intrastate pipeline in the United States, with interests in coal, industrial gases, and marine transportation. HNG was considered to be a conservative company and took pride in the fact that it had never curtailed a customer because of lack of supply or deliverability.

Houston Natural Gas had an estimated 19,500 shareholders, 10,200 employees, 1982 fiscal year revenues of $2.96 billion, and a debt capitalization of less than 24 percent. Forty-eight percent of the stock in HNG was owned by institutional investors. The reserve base of HNG was well above the industry average. Houston Pipe Line, an HNG "cash cow," was one of the most profitable pipelines (or for that matter, oil and gas companies) in the United States, with a book value of $370 million and a yearly income of $250 million; that is, it recouped its investment every eighteen months.

Coastal Corporation was an oil and gas exploration and production company with major interest in oil refining and gas transmission. Coastal had 5,800 employees and 1982 revenues of $5.8 billion.

Coastal was run almost single-handedly by its founder, Oscar Wyatt, a former drilling-bit salesman who had built the oil and gas conglomerate from scratch in a generation. Wyatt was one of the most hated oilmen in Texas. In January 1984, he was in the process of suing the Houston Chronicle for likening him to J. R. Ewing of the popular television series "Dallas."

The reason for the enmity toward Wyatt dated back almost twenty years. Wyatt had secured gas-supply contracts to several Texas utilities by undercutting his opponents (primarily HNG) and promising consumers twenty years of gas at prices that seemed too good to be true. In the severe Texas winter of 1972–73, Coastal was unable to meet its obligations and had to purchase large volumes of high-priced gas from other pipelines. Coastal passed the cost of the higher-priced gas to its customers in violation of contractual terms; the customers sued and won. Further, Coastal was prohibited from ever reentering the lucrative unregulated Texas intrastate gas market. In the view of many Texas politicians and newspapers, Coastal, not OPEC, became the villain of the energy crisis.

When the rumors of possible takeover surfaced, HNG contracted with First Boston Corporation to be its financial advisor and to determine the value of the corporation to the shareholders. First Boston would call the plays in HNG's response to the takeover. When the tender offer was announced, HNG obtained a $1.5 billion line of credit to engage Coastal in battle.

On January 31, 1984, on First Boston's advice, HNG embraced the "Pac-Man" or "Bear-Hug" defense—so called because if a

Case prepared by Sheila Billingsley, Rice University, and edited by Norman E. Bowie. Copyright © Sheila Billingsley. Reprinted with permission.

company is trying to "eat another up," the company being pursued will turn around and try to "eat the aggressor up." HNG made a counter-tender for all 20.8 million shares of Coastal at $42 per share—a total offer of $924 million. HNG reserved the right to cancel this offer should Coastal drop its tender for HNG stock.

HNG filed suits against Coastal. HNG alleged that HNG customers would flee should Wyatt purchase HNG, thereby irreparably harming the shareholders. The language of the suits was vitriolic. "Coastal has a notorious reputation as an unreliable gas supplier." "Mr. Wyatt lacks the integrity and good reputation required to properly manage HNG." The suits also cited HNG's ownership of 50,000 shares of Valero as prohibiting a purchase by Coastal.

On February 2, the Coastal board rejected the tender offer by HNG, stating that "Houston Natural's efforts to ward off Coastal represents a flagrant disregard for the rights of Houston Natural Gas Stockholders . . . nothing short of a last-ditch effort to preserve management's position." HNG dismissed this claim as "rhetoric."

On February 5, HNG tendered for 20 percent or 8 million shares of its own stock at $69 per share giving two reasons for the tender:

1. to make it unattractive for Coastal to gain control;
2. to give shareholders a partial cash alternative to Coastal's offer.

This self-tender would substantially raise the debt capitalization of HNG from 24 percent to 36–38 percent.

Later, HNG raised its tender for Coastal stock from $42 to $50 per share contingent on Coastal dropping its bid for HNG.

The battle was becoming very expensive. HNG went to its lenders and increased its bank credit lines to $1.8 billion. HNG was in effect "hocking" all of its assets and granting the lenders a first mortgage. Additional terms for this increased line of credit were:

1. HNG could not pay any dividend after July 31 if it still owed more than $1.2 billion.
2. HNG could make no capital expenditures in the future beyond $75 million. ($300–$400 million had been HNG's capital expenditure average.)

These terms were "onerous" by design as a signal to Coastal's lenders that they would be financing the acquisition of a company with very little control over its own destiny. If HNG was the collateral to be received by Coastal's bankers, that collateral wouldn't be worth much. This policy—to bloat with debt and, thereby, make a company less attractive—is called a "scorched earth" policy.

On February 10, Texas Attorney General Jim Mattox obtained a temporary restraining order against Coastal prohibiting Coastal from proceeding in its takeover attempt against HNG.

Apparently Wyatt, and for that matter the professional arbitrageurs, had overlooked an important restriction in the Texas Railroad Commission Order that Coastal had signed in 1979. This order, according to Mattox, implicitly, if not explicitly, prohibited Coastal from being able to control gas supplies to its former subsidiary, Valero. HNG owned 50,000 shares of Valero stock and was the principal supplier to Valero; thus, Coastal's acquisition of HNG would result in a violation of that order.

On February 12, there was Wall Street speculation of a settlement between Coastal and HNG; on February 13, both companies requested that trade in their stocks be suspended. Later that day, a settlement was announced. Wyatt emerged with a before-tax profit of $42 million and received lucrative contract concessions. HNG stock plunged nearly $10 at the opening on the New York Stock Exchange February 14, following the announcement of the settlement. *Forbes* estimated that the arbitrageurs had paper losses of $200 million and controlled over 50 percent of the shares.

On March 23, a suit was filed by Prudential-Bache (P-B) against HNG and its Board. P-B had purchased 90,000 shares of HNG at $60 per share in speculation of a takeover. P-B sought an unspecified amount of actual and punitive damages plus $100,000 in legal fees. In addition, they sought a temporary injunction to prevent HNG from buying its own stock on the open market at a price below the price offered by Coastal.

Elements of the suit were:

1. The directors had breached their fiduciary responsibility and have damaged both HNG and its estimated 19,500 shareholders.
2. Friendly tender offers by at least three corporate suitors (including Transco) were kept from shareholders. These suitors entered into secret agreements not to acquire shares of HNG.
3. By rejecting Coastal's original tender offer, "The Board of Directors engaged in wrongful conduct: designed solely to perpetuate themselves and current management of HNG in positions of power and control in HNG at any cost and to the detriment of the corporation and its shareholders. This scheme resulted in the 'waste' of HNG's corporate assets and exposed the company to lawsuits and other actions designed to depress the value of HNG's stock.
4. HNG was charged with disposing of some of its most profitable assets in an effort to protect itself from future takeover attempts.

In 1985, HNG was merged with InterNorth (now Enron). Shareholders were paid $70 per share for their HNG stock.

In February 1986 the P-B suit against HNG and its directors was dismissed.

Questions

1. Arbitrageurs, short-term shareholders who purchased stock in HNG to make a "quick profit" when the company went through its death throes, claimed that they should have been considered in the decisions of management to the same degree as the long-term shareholders who purchased the stock of a viable corporation. These long-term shareholders "voted" for the management of HNG by purchasing the stock and had the right to sell their stock at any time they felt that management was not acting in their best interests. The arbitrageurs, on the other hand, voted against the management by purchasing the stock. Does HNG management's fiduciary responsibility apply equally to these two factions?
2. Does a long-term management team, with justifiable pride in its loyalty to employees and customers, have the right to keep its "good corporation" out of the hands of a "bad man"?
3. As part of the settlement, Coastal was paid a premium for its HNG stock. There was speculation that this premium was paid because HNG did not want to continue its tender for Coastal stock. Was it more ethical to pay a premium to Coastal than to proceed with a problematic acquisition?
4. HNG was an attractive takeover candidate for two reasons: (1) above average reserves, (2) low debt capitalization. A corporation can ward off predators by ensuring that the book value of the firm and the market value are very close to each other. This can only be accomplished by having a highly leveraged firm. Is it ethical to leverage a firm to capacity and thereby expose it to more risk solely to "repel the sharks"?

CASE 4. Bluebonnet College

Bluebonnet College is a private four-year liberal arts college in a south-central state. Most of its operating budget comes from student tuition. Its student population peaked in 1975 at 3,500. Over the past ten years student enrollment has gradually declined to 3,000. Bluebonnet College has a moderately selective admissions policy and a faculty of 200. Tuition is currently $6,000 and has been rising at about 8 percent per year. The college attracts aspiring artists, preprofessionals, and students whose parents prefer small, rural, and somewhat conservative institutions. The college has a modest endowment of $20 million. It has few large benefactors.

However, Mr. Smith, an elderly business executive, is an active board member who indicated that he has planned to leave most of his estate to Bluebonnet. Mr. Smith is a "local boy who has made good." He is the senior vice-president of a well-known multinational. This multinational has a manufacturing plant in South Africa and is a subscriber to the Sullivan principles. A small group of activist students demonstrates against Mr. Smith whenever he is on campus for a board meeting. Mr. Smith has challenged his critics to a debate on the merits of his company's operation in South Africa.

In the meantime, the faculty of Bluebonnet has approved a resolution asking the board to sell all stock of companies having facilities in or doing business with the government of South Africa. A private consulting firm has informed the president of Bluebonnet that such a decision to divest would reduce the yield from endowment by about 2 percent, from 10 to 8 percent, over each of the next five years and create a one-time brokerage charge of about $50,000. The drop in yield would cost Bluebonnet about $400,000 in investment income for each of the next five years. Since Bluebonnet has an extremely tight budget, the $450,000 decrease in income would have to be made up through an increase in tuition of about $150.

Mr. Smith opposes the faculty resolution. He insinuates that the faculty is hypocritical in asking the college to divest while simultaneously not asking the board of its pension fund to divest. Moreover, Mr. Smith points out that the college only has stock in companies that subscribe to the Sullivan principles.

Questions

1. If you were a student at Bluebonnet, would you be among those protesting against Mr. Smith's company? Explain your answer.
2. Should the board of trustees at Bluebonnet vote to divest itself of any stock of companies that have facilities in South Africa? In companies that have no facilities in South Africa but do business with the South African government?
3. In making its decision, should the board be concerned with the fact that many students who themselves would not vote to divest would pay an additional $150 in tuition?
4. Should the board take into consideration the fact that all companies in which the college has stock are subscribers to the Sullivan principles?

Used by permission of the author, Norman Bowie.

Suggested Supplementary Readings

American Institute of Certified Public Accountants. *Code of Professional Ethics*. New York: American Institute of Certified Public Accountants, 1972.

Beard, Edmund. "Conflict of Interest and Public Service." In *Ethics, Free Enterprise and Public Policy*, edited by Richard De George. New York: Oxford University Press, 1978.

Boulle, L. J. *Constitutional Reform and Apartheid*. New York: St. Martin's Press, 1983.

Briloff, A. "Codes of Conduct: Their Sound and Their Fury." In *Ethics, Free Enterprise, and Public Policy*, edited by Richard De George and Joseph Pichler, pp. 264–287. New York: Oxford University Press, 1978.

Briloff, Abraham J. *The Truth About Corporate Accounting*. New York: Harper & Row, 1979.

Business and Society Review. "South Africa: Is There a Peaceful Path to Pluralism." A Symposium Issue, 57 (Spring 1986).

Carey, J., and W. Doherty. *Ethical Standards of the Accounting Profession*. New York: American Institute of Certified Public Accountants, 1966.

Carmichael, D. and R. Swieringa. "The Compatibility of Auditing Independence and Management Services—An Identification of Issues." *The Accounting Review* 43 (October 1968): 697–705.

Causey, D. *Duties and Liabilities of Public Accountants*. Homewood, Ill.: Dow Jones-Irwin, 1982.

Commons, Dorman L. *Tender Offer: The Sneak Attack in Corporate Takeovers*. Berkeley: University of California Press, 1985.

Downie, R. S. *Roles and Values: An Introduction to Social Ethics*. London: Methuen & Co. Ltd., 1971.

Elbinger, Lee. "Are Sullivan's Principles Folly In South Africa?" *Business and Society Review* 30 (Summer 1979): 35–40.

Emmett, Dorothy. *Rules, Roles and Relations*. Boston: Beacon Press, 1966.

Harvard Law Review. "Greenmail: Targeted Stock Repurchases and The Manager Entrenchment Hypothesis." *Harvard Law Review* 98 (1985): 1045–1065.

Jensen, Michael C. "Takeovers: Folklore and Science." *Harvard Business Review* 62 (November–December 1984): 109–121.

Kanter, Rosabeth. *Men and Women of the Corporation*. New York: Basic Books, 1977.

Knight, Sharen D., and Deborah Knight. *The Concerned Investor's Guide: Non-Financial Corporate Data*. Arlington, Va.: Resource Publishing Group Inc., 1983.

Loeb, S., ed. *Ethics in the Accounting Profession*. Santa Barbara: Wiley, 1978.

Meyers, D. *U.S. Business in South Africa: The Economic, Political, and Moral Issues*. Bloomington: Indiana University Press, 1980.

McGuire, J. "Conflict of Interest: Whose Interest? And What Conflict?" In *Ethics, Free Enterprise, and Public Policy*, edited by Richard De George and Joseph Pichler, pp. 214–231. New York: Oxford University Press, 1978.

Parker, Frank J. *South Africa: Lost Opportunities*. Lexington, Mass.: Lexington Books, 1983.

Powers, Charles W., ed. *People/Profits: The Ethics of Investments*. New York Council on Religion and International Affairs, 1972.

Seidman, A., and N. Seidman. *South Africa and U.S. Multinational Corporations*. Westport, Conn.: Lawrence Hill, 1978.

Simon, John G., Charles Powers, and Jon P. Gunnemann. *The Ethical Investor*. New Haven, Conn.: Yale University Press, 1972.

Stettler, Howard F. "Two Proposals for Strengthening Auditor Independence." *MSU Business Topics* 28 (Winter 1980): 37–41.

Stevens, Mark. *The Accounting Wars*. New York: Macmillan, 1985.

Stock, Robert J. "Commercialism In The Profession: A Threat To Be Managed." *Journal of Accountancy* 128 (October 1985): 132–134.

Talbert, William L. "Who Should Set Accounting Standards?" *Atlanta Economic Review* 28 (September/October 1978): 12–17.

Vaughn, Robert G. *Conflict of Interest Regulation in the Federal Executive Branch*. Lexington, Mass.: Lexington Books, 1979.

Windal, F., and R. Corley. *The Accounting Professional: Ethics, Responsibility and Liability*. Englewood Cliffs, N.J.: Prentice-Hall, 1980.

CHAPTER NINE

Theories of Economic Justice

INTRODUCTION

The many economic disparities between individuals and nations have generated heated controversy over our systems for distributing and taxing income and wealth. Some of the most sustained political conflicts in the United States concern whether individuals and corporations are overtaxed, whether wealthy corporations and their stockholders deserve their abundant profits, and whether executives deserve the generous salaries they often receive. In 1985 the Chairman of the U.S. Congress House Ways and Means Committee said that the most important goal of a revised tax structure is *fairness*—more important than lowering tax rates or reducing the national debt.[1] But is this thesis correct and, if so, what are economic fairness and fairness in a tax code?

Several well-reasoned and systematic answers to such questions have been advanced, all of which are based on a theory of economic justice—that is, a theory of how economic goods and services should be distributed. In Chapter One we examined general theories of justice, and became familiar with the existence of rival theories (see pp. 41–44). The various problems of economic justice featured in this chapter emphasize the major distinctions, principles, and methods of

moral argument employed in contemporary philosophy. The first four authors attempt to answer the question, "Which general system of social and economic organization is most just?" The final articles concern the justification and justice of systems of taxation—in particular, moral problems about how to choose a just *tax base* (what is taxed), a just *tax rate*, and a just set of *tax exemptions*.

THEORIES OF DISTRIBUTIVE JUSTICE

We saw in Chapter One that the notion of justice is kin to the notions of fairness, desert, and entitlement. It was also noted that the expression "distributive justice" refers to the proper distribution of social benefits and burdens, often using "material" principles of distributive justice (see pp. 43–44). Each principle states a relevant property on the basis of which burdens and benefits should be distributed. The list of candidates for the position of "relevant properties" includes rights, individual effort, societal contribution, and merit.

The diversity of these principles indicates that justice is an enormously broad normative concept suited to accommodate several different principles and theories of justice. Consider the following example: A university professor hires three male students to help move the furniture in her house to a new location, promising each student the standard hourly wage for local professional movers. One student turns out to be capable of lifting large items by himself and is both more efficient and more careful than either of the other students. The second, the professor learns during conversation, is desperately in need of money because of a severe financial crisis that threatens the student's enrollment for the next semester. The third student carelessly breaks two vases and scars a table, fulfilling the conditions of the agreement in an undistinguished manner. The first student deserves greater compensation on the basis of *merit or performance;* the second *needs* a larger share of the money to be divided among them, though for no reason related to performance; and the third deserves less on the basis of performance but deserves an *equal share* on the basis of the agreement (if one overlooks the unnegotiated problem of carelessly marred or broken items). The professor is therefore somewhat at a loss about what reward to offer each student at the end of the day. Justice in general provides no solution, because the professor will have to accept one or more material principles of justice. Moreover, although we attach some weight to each of the possible material principles, none clearly outweighs the others.

Theories of distributive justice have been devised to give general guidelines for structuring society in accordance with a scheme of social justice. *Egalitarian* theories emphasize equal access to primary goods, *Marxist* theories emphasize fair financial return for labor and collective control of distribution, *libertarian* theories emphasize rights to social and economic liberty and deemphasize collective control, and *utilitarian* theories emphasize a mixed use of such criteria so that both the public and individual interests are maximized. The acceptability of any such general theory of justice is determined by the quality of its moral argument that some one or more selected (material) principles ought to be given priority. However, there may be principles of justice pertaining to *taxation* no less than *distribution,* as Baruch Brody and J. R. Lucas discuss in this chapter.

The utilitarian theory follows the main lines of the explanation of utilitarianism in Chapter One (see pp. 25–31), where economic justice is viewed as one among a number of problems concerning how to maximize value. The ideal economic distribution, utilitarians argue, is any arrangement that would have this maximizing effect. According to Peter Singer, this thesis leads to a position opposed to libertarianism: A heavy element of political planning and economic distribution is said to be morally required in order that justice be done to individuals. Brody's deontological analysis in this chapter is directly opposed to this conclusion in principle, but Brody does acknowledge some place for redistribution of goods and wealth through taxation that benefits those who are genuinely needy, and thus *in practice* his views may not be as diametrically opposed to Singer's as it first appears. Because utilitarianism as a general normative theory was thoroughly explored in Chapter One, detailed considerations will be given in this introduction only to egalitarian, libertarian, and Marxist theories.

THE EGALITARIAN THEORY

Some idea of equality in the distribution of social benefits and burdens has had an important place in most influential moral theories. For example, in utilitarianism different people are equal in the value accorded their wants, preferences, and happiness (see pp. 26–28), and in Kantian theories all persons are considered equally worthy and equally deserving of respect as ends in themselves (see pp. 37–39). In egalitarian theory, the question arises whether people should be considered equal in some respects (e.g., in their basic political and moral rights and obligations), yet unequal for the purpose of justly distributing certain social goods such as wealth and burdens such as taxation.

Radical and Qualified Egalitarianism. In its radical form, egalitarianism is the theory that individual differences are not significant in an account of social justice. Distributions of burdens and benefits in a society are just to the extent they are equal, and deviations from absolute equality in distribution is unjust. For example, the fact that roughly 20 percent of the wealth in the United States is owned by 5 percent of the population, while the poorest 20 percent of the population controls 5 percent of the wealth, makes American society unjust by this radical egalitarian standard, no matter how relatively deserving the people at both extremes might be (as judged by some non-egalitarian standard of desert). For strict egalitarians, membership in the human community is the sole respect in which people are to be compared in determining who has basic political rights. However, most egalitarian accounts of justice are more guardedly formulated, so that mere membership in the human species does not entitle people to equal shares of *all* social benefits and so that desert does justify differences in distribution. When structuring social arrangements, egalitarianism so qualified points only to *some* basic equalities among individuals that take priority over their differences. For example, Brody points out that egalitarians generally prefer *progressive* rates on a tax base rather than *proportional* (each unit taxed the same) rates. This may seem odd since a proportional rate treats everyone equally. However, qualified egalitarians reason that progressive rates tax the wealthy more and thus distribute wealth more evenly. The idea is to move from inequality to greater equality.

Rawls's Theory. In recent years a qualified egalitarian theory in the Kantian tradition has enjoyed wide currency in deontological ethics. John Rawls's *A Theory of Justice* (1971) has as its central contention that we should distribute all economic goods and services equally except in those cases in which an une-qual distribution would actually work to everyone's advantage, or at least would benefit the worst off in society. Rawls presents this egalitarian theory as a direct challenge to utilitarianism on grounds of social justice. His objection to utilitarianism is that social distributions produced by maximizing utility could entail violations of basic individual liberties and rights expressive of human equality and deserving protection as a matter of social justice (see Chapter One, pp. 32–33). Utilitarianism, being indifferent as to the *distribution* of satisfactions among individuals (but not of course to the *total* satisfaction in society) would, in Rawls's view, permit the infringement of some peoples' rights and liberties if the infringement genuinely promised to produce a proportionately greater utility for others.

Rawls therefore turns to a hypothetical social contract procedure strongly indebted to what he calls the "Kantian conception of equality." According to this account, valid principles of justice are those to which we would all agree if we could freely and impartially consider the social situation from a standpoint (the "original position") outside any actual society. Impartiality is guaranteed in this situation by a conceptual device Rawls calls the "veil of ignorance." This notion stipulates that in the original position, each person is ignorant of all his or her particular fortuitous characteristics. For example, the person's sex, race, IQ, family background, and special talents or handicaps are unrevealed in this hypothetical circumstance. The veil of ignorance prevents people from promoting principles of justice that are biased toward their personal combinations of fortuitous talents and characteristics—for example, the various combinations of need, merit, experience, and sexual advantage that lead different parties to promote competing material principles.

Rawls argues that under these conditions people would unanimously agree on two fundamental principles of justice. The first requires that each person be permitted the maximum amount of equal basic liberty compatible with a similar liberty for others. The second stipulates that once this equal basic liberty is assured, inequalities in social primary goods (e.g., income, rights, and opportunities) are to be allowed only if they benefit everyone (so long as everyone has fair equality of opportunity). Rawls considers social institutions to be just if and only if they conform to these principles of the social contract. In a later essay in this chapter, Lucas also uses a form of social contract, one based on the tradition emanating from John Locke rather than from Kant. He tries to "make sense of taxes as a sort of bargain in which the taxpayer surrenders his individual quid in return for a share of the collective quo." In the process he argues against egalitarianism, as well as against the strong forms of utilitarianism and libertarianism found in other articles in the chapter.

Rawls's theory makes equality a basic characteristic of the original position from which the social contract is forged. Equality is built into that hypothetical position in the form of a free and equal bargain among all parties, where there is equal ignorance of all individual characteristics and of the advantages that persons have or will have in their daily lives. Although Rawls believes that people in such a position would choose to make the possession of basic liberties the first commitment of their social institutions, he rejects radical egalitarianism, arguing that if there were inequalities that render *everyone* better off by comparison to being equal, then these inequalities would actually be desirable (again, so long as they were consistent with equal liberty and fair opportunity).

Rawls formulates what is called the *difference principle* so that inequalities would be justifiable only if they maximally enhance the position of the *"representative* least advantaged" person—that is, a hypothetical individual particularly unfortunate in the distribution of fortuitous characteristics or social advantages. Rawls is unclear about the range of types of individuals who might qualify under this category, but we can imagine that a worker who has been incapacitated from ex-

posure to asbestos would qualify. Formulated in this way, the difference principle could allow, for instance, extraordinary economic rewards to business entrepreneurs, venture capitalists, and even corporate takeover artists (perhaps raiders who use "greenmail"—see Chapter Eight, pp. 476–78) if the resulting economic stimulation were to produce improved job opportunities and working conditions for the least advantaged members of society, or greater benefits for pension funds holding stock for the working class. Brody's deontological theory leads to the similar conclusion that persons in need of financial aid would be the primary beneficiaries of our tax system.

The difference principle rests on the moral viewpoint that because inequalities of birth, historical circumstance, and natural endowment are undeserved, persons in a cooperative society should correct them by making more equal the unequal situation of naturally disadvantaged members. The system should also strive for equality through its tax code. According to a 1984 Yankelovich poll, 80 percent of Americans believe that their tax system benefits the rich and is unfair to the ordinary working person because of the distribution of income it establishes.[2] A defender of Rawls's theory might take this finding as one form of evidence that our system needs modification by his principles. However, this claim has been vigorously challenged by libertarian theories.

THE LIBERTARIAN THEORY

What makes libertarian theories *libertarian* is the priority afforded to distinctive processes, procedures, and mechanisms for ensuring that liberty rights are recognized in economic practice—typically the rules and procedures governing economic acquisition and exchange in capitalist or free-market systems.

The Role of Individual Freedom. The libertarian theory finds its intellectual foundations in classical writers such as John Locke and

Adam Smith, and these foundations still supply the underlying rationale for many parts of the social and economic systems in English-speaking nations. As Adam Smith depicted capitalist economic systems, self-interested individuals exhibit behavior patterns that collectively further the interests of the larger society (see Chapter One, p. 20). Such a system presumes a model of economic behavior that attributes a substantial degree of economic freedom to individual agents, who freely enter and withdraw from economic arrangements in accordance with their beliefs about their best interests.

This theory is often expressed in editorials and popular writings both as a justice-based rationale for taxation and as a means of defending the free market. For example, in two editorials concerning ''Principles of Tax Reform,'' the editors of the *Wall Street Journal* argued as follows:

> The key word is ''incentives.'' This . . . means allowing people to keep more of what they make, and leaving it to their ingenuity and the forces of the market to determine how they make it. The surest way to improve incentives is to pick out the highest rates in the tax code and pare them. . . .
>
> Contrary to all the impassioned rhetoric in the Washington community about 'fairness,' most of what the federal government does simply extracts money from the middle class to transfer it to selected interests. . . . [3]

The *Journal*'s editorials typically defend classical free-market principles of libertarianism, often by appeal to economic theorists who make libertarian appeals to fairness.

In seeing free action as central to justice in economic distribution (more central than equality or utilitarian efficiency), libertarian writers often accept an individualist conception of economic production and value and assume that it is possible to recognize meaningful distinctions between individual contributions to production. The industrious and entrepreneurial business executive, for instance, contributes more to his or her company's success than the similarly exemplary assembly-line worker or secretary, and the executive therefore deserves—on grounds of justice—a greater share of the profits.

Although the underlying assumptions of libertarianism correspond closely to economic presuppositions in free-market societies, many philosophers maintain that, however great the differences between particular people's contributions initially appear to be, all individual contributions shrink to insignificance once the broader context of production is appreciated. They hold that (1) the alleged contribution that anyone makes simply reflects a diversity of formative influences, including family background, education, and interaction with professional associates, and (2) economic value is generated through an essentially communal process that renders differences between individual contributions morally negligible. The initiative and ideas of the business executive would be only one among many factors contributing to a corporation's success.

Libertarian theorists, however, explicitly reject the conclusion that egalitarian patterns of distribution represent a normative ideal. People may be equal in a host of morally significant respects (e.g., entitled to equal treatment under the law and equally valued as ends in themselves), but the libertarian contends that it would be a basic violation of *justice* to regard people as deserving of equal economic returns. In particular, people are seen as having a fundamental right to own and dispense with the products of their labor as they choose, even if exercise of this right leads to large inequalities of wealth in society.

Equality and utility principles, from this libertarian perspective, sacrifice basic liberty rights to the larger public interest by using one set of individuals to benefit another set of individuals. All nonlibertarian theories coercively extract financial resources through taxation. Because no moral grounds would justify the sacrifice of liberty rights, the libertarian views utilitarianism and egalitarianism as perverted theories of justice that use one set of individuals as means to the end of benefiting another set of individuals. However, a libertarian is not opposed to utilitarian or egalitarian modes of distribution *if* they have been *freely chosen* by a group. What makes them right is precisely the free choice of the members of the group.

Nozick's Theory. The libertarian theory is defended in this chapter in the article by Robert Nozick, who refers to his social philosophy as an "entitlement theory" of justice. Nozick promotes the minimal or "night-watchman" state, according to which government action is justified only if it *protects* the rights or entitlements of citizens. He argues that a theory of justice should work to protect our rights not to be coerced and should not propound a thesis intended to "pattern" society through arrangements such as those found in socialist and (impure) capitalist countries in which governments take pronounced steps to redistribute the wealth acquired by individuals acting in accordance with free-market laws. Here the wealthy are taxed at a progressively higher rate than those who are less wealthy, with the proceeds underwriting state support of the indigent through welfare payments and unemployment compensation.

The goal of interference by the state is presumably the redistribution of economic benefits that would otherwise concentrate in a few hands through the unchecked exercise of individual rights in the marketplace. In the United States, for example, there has long been a tendency to use the tax code to effect social goals such as the alleviation of poverty and the support of the arts rather than simply conceiving the tax code as a source of revenue for essential services. Nozick resolutely resists such social engineering, and his libertarian theory invites consideration of whether such governmental intrusion is what *justice demands,* as distinct from what *some persons prefer.*

Nozick's entitlement theory relies on three principles: those of *acquisition, transfer,* and *rectification.* His libertarian position rejects *all* distributional patterns imposed by material principles of justice and thus is committed to a form of *procedural* justice. That is, for Nozick there is no pattern of just distribution independent of the procedures of acquisition, transfer, and rectification. This claim has been at the center of philosophical controversy over the libertarian account, and many competing theories of justice are reactions to such an uncompromising libertarian commitment to pure procedural justice. Brody maintains that there must be "limits on the rights of the private owner" and on the system of free exchange even in a free-market economy. His views, however, are fundamentally sympathetic to libertarianism, inasmuch as he gives priority in his system to liberty, property, free exchange of goods, and a dominantly procedural conception of justice.

Consideration will now be given to the most revolutionary competing theory: the Marxist theory.

THE MARXIST THEORY

Much of the discussion of business ethics in this text is premised on a system of free-market exchanges and limited government regulation. In discussions of the ethics of advertising in Chapter Seven or hiring in Chapter Six, for example, a competitive free market is assumed. In this way the person discussing advertising ethics or voluntary affirmative action plans is in the same position as a judge sentencing a convicted criminal: Both operate from *within* a given social framework of the terms of cooperation, and this framework establishes roles, obligations, and opportunities.

Some philosophers insist that the most important questions about ethics and business do not arise *within* capitalism, because they concern *external criticisms* directed at the competitive market economy itself. Rather than discussing advertising ethics or hiring programs viewed from within the capitalist framework, these philosophers assess the merits and demerits of the capitalist economic system. Perhaps the strongest and certainly the best-known challenge to capitalism comes from the political and social philosophy of Marxism. In this chapter the essay by Milton Fisk reflects this Marxist perspective, largely by criticizing operative assumptions in contemporary American business and society.

Like egalitarians, Marxists criticize the disparities in income and wealth, as well as class status, in modern free-market societies. But for Marxists, unlike many egalitarians and utilitarians, modern welfare provisions, graduated income-tax scales, and political rights do not amount to a just society.

Marx's Theory. Karl Marx's criticisms of capitalism focus on the notion of commodities and the "voluntary" exchange of private property. In his book *Capital,* Marx attempts to explain how the capitalist makes a profit, especially how labor is used to make a profit. He argues that a commodity's value is determined by the amount of labor invested in producing it. But if the commodity were exchanged for its full value, and that value was returned to laborers, there would be no profit. Profit comes only because the worker *sells* his or her labor power to the capitalist, who purchases the labor just like any other commodity. The worker produces "surplus labor," as Marx calls it, and this labor becomes the capitalist's profit. That is, the laborer works *more* than is necessary to produce something with the value of the commodity at the price it is sold. Why does a worker work more than necessary? Because there are more workers than are needed, so each can be replaced if he or she does not work more. The capitalist system seeks to gain greater and greater profit, which involves a constant increase in surplus value. The laborer becomes nothing but labor power; all other human values are tossed aside.

Marx knows that according to capitalist principles it is fair to pay a laborer what the laborer agrees to, but Marx in effect argues that capitalist justice is unjust. The classical capitalist justification for profit taking is based on the freedom of the free market: The laborer is free to sell or withhold labor, and hence is free not to work for an unfair wage. Marx does not accept this basic premise. His view is that in order to subsist, workers *must* sell their labor. They are *coerced* by the de-

mands of the capitalist system to do so as a means of existence. (On the meaning of "coercion," see Chapter Seven, pp. 399–400.) Marx believes that capitalist-based standards of justice (especially as found in libertarian theories) show the corruption in the system at its very core. His views on justice are, then, entirely revolutionary: He is not interested in distributive justice in the sense of distributing what is already there in the system, but rather in an entirely new social arrangement for property, labor, human relationships, and so on.

A major part of this restructuring would involve institutionalizing a new vision of the worker's relation to other workers. Marx held that workers have little, if any, need for what they themselves produce. They produce only for their "share" of the money that their products represent (their salary). Because what they produce is simply a means to obtain a salary, workers are "alienated" from their product; they work simply in order to acquire other products. Moreover, the worker's only interest in others occurs when they produce something the worker values; otherwise they are valueless to the worker. In this way free-market exchange based on private property corrupts workers' relations both to their products and to their fellow workers.

Marxist Critiques of the Free Market. Many contemporary Marxist critiques of free-market theories challenge the adequacy of all capitalist-based accounts of justice. As Fisk points out, the Marxist critic finds both libertarians and egalitarians naive in their assumption that true freedom of choice in economic matters is compatible with systems of private property and capitalist exchange. Marxists argue that through manipulation and coercion the dominant social class has led the working class to desire certain useless products of industry. The inevitable frustration and alienation of the working class have been successfully redirected away from the ruling class into the abuse of some of the products of the consuming society, such as racing cars, guns, and power tools. This critique is a direct challenge to the notion of consumer sovereignty. The purchases of the affluent consumer society are not *free* purchases at all, because the products of advanced capitalist societies are antithetical to the nature of free choice. (This particular challenge to the notion of consumer choice is considered in the discussion of advertising in Chapter Seven.

The Marxist also sees exploitation, coercion, and even extortion in international arrangements controlled by many capitalist institutions. A favorite example of Marxists at the present time is the crushing debt of Latin America and the Third World, which is largely a debt owed to banks in capitalist nations. Whereas a libertarian would look first to contractual obligations made between borrower and lender, the Marxist argument is that misfortune combined with a capitalist-controlled lending system have created an unprecedented situation where countries such as Argentina, Brazil, Nigeria, and Mexico are plagued with runaway poverty and hyperinflation and cannot both repay these debts and stabilize their economies in order to make social progress.

Defenders of the free market clash with these Marxist arguments in many circumstances, even though both might agree that the justice of economic arrangements can be decided only if we take into account historical details of ownership and growth that alone enable us to determine whether existing inequalities and property ownership are *deserved*. Consider the example of the "ITT-Chile Affair" (1970–71). The Marxist candidate for President of Chile, Dr. Salvadore Allende, proposed to nationalize ITT's $150 million investments in the Chile Telephone Company. Allende's view was that the company's exploitative history nullified its property claims and justified a government takeover. ITT, however, took the position that the property it had developed through its own careful planning and growth would be expropriated without compensation in Allende's plan. ITT's central defense was an argument from justice: Allende's actions were unfair to the company and its stockholders, who deserved by entitlement what they owned.

The Marxist thus would not deny that historical details figure prominently in an adequate account of justice in economic distribution. Indeed, Fisk uses historical appeals to mount a further challenge to the justice of existing economic arrangements in capitalist countries. In what sense, Marxists ask, did former Vice-President Nelson Rockefeller, as the descendant of the wealthy capitalist John D. Rockefeller, deserve his privileged social status and accompanying enhancement of economic choice? And how do the indigent workers' children employed by the Rockefeller estate deserve their correspondingly disadvantaged position? And how could one overlook the history of capitalist exploitation of workers in Chile in assessing what ITT deserves? Marxists believe that no theory of justice besides Marxism has anything approximating an adequate answer to these questions. For example, Brody's attempt to use taxation as the means of redistributing wealth to the needy would be regarded by Marxists as a small island of humanity in a sea of injustice.

CONCLUSION

Rawls, Nozick, and their utilitarian and Marxist opponents all capture some of our intuitive convictions about justice, and each exhibits strengths as a theory of justice. Rawls's difference principle, for example, describes a widely shared belief about justified inequalities. Nozick's theory makes a strong appeal in the domains of property rights and liberties. Utilitarianism is widely used in the Western nations in the development of public policy, and Marxist theory in some form is the prevailing model of justice in many nations around the earth because of its apparent protection of vulnerable workers. The views on taxation expressed by Brody and Lucas are clearly relevant to our system of state support and financial aid.

Perhaps, then, there are several equally valid, or at least equally defensible, theories of justice and just taxation. We noted in Chapter One that morality is a *social* institution; it may be that justice in society is social in this sense and so is dependent upon the standards acknowledged in a culture. There could, on this analysis, be libertarian societies, egalitarian societies, utilitarian societies, and Marxist societies—as well as societies based on mixed theories or derivative theories of taxation and redistribution. However, this possibility raises other problems in ethical theory discussed in Chapter One—in particular relativism and moral disagreement (see pp. 11–13)—and before this conclusion is accepted, the details of the arguments in the selections in this chapter should be carefully assessed.

NOTES

1. See Jeffrey H. Birnbaum, "Tax Revision Plan Must Convince Public That System Is Fair, Rostenkowski Says," *Wall Street Journal,* March 27, 1985, p. 23.
2. See Barry Sussman, "Flat-Tax Plan Appeals to Most, Polls Show," *Washington Post,* December 4, 1984.
3. "Principles of Tax Reform," *Wall Street Journal,* April 21, 1986, p. 22; "Decision Time," *Wall Street Journal,* November 27, 1984, p. 28.

An Egalitarian Theory of Justice

John Rawls

THE ROLE OF JUSTICE

Justice is the first virtue of social institutions, as truth is of systems of thought. A theory however elegant and economical must be rejected or revised if it is untrue; likewise laws and institutions no matter how efficient and well-arranged must be reformed or abolished if they are unjust. Each person possesses an inviolability founded on justice that even the welfare of society as a whole cannot override. For this reason justice denies that the loss of freedom for some is made right by a greater good shared by others. It does not allow that the sacrifices imposed on a few are outweighed by the larger sum of advantages enjoyed by many. Therefore in a just society the liberties of equal citizenship are taken as settled; the rights secured by justice are not subject to political bargaining or to the calculus of social interests. The only thing that permits us to acquiesce in an erroneous theory is the lack of a better one; analogously, an injustice is tolerable only when it is necessary to avoid an even greater injustice. Being first virtues of human activities, truth and justice are uncompromising.

These propositions seem to express our intuitive conviction of the primary of justice. No doubt they are expressed too strongly. In any event I wish to inquire whether these contentions or others similar to them are sound, and if so how they can be accounted for. To this end it is necessary to work out a theory of justice in the light of which these assertions can be interpreted and assessed. I shall begin by considering the role of the

Excerpted from John Rawls, *A Theory of Justice* (Cambridge, Mass.: Harvard University Press, 1971), pp. 3–4, 11–15, 18–19, 60–62, 64–65, 100–104, 274–277. Reprinted by permission of Oxford University Press and The Belknap Press of Harvard University Press, © 1971 by The President and Fellows of Harvard College.

principles of justice. Let us assume, to fix ideas, that a society is a more or less self-sufficient association of persons who in their relations to one another recognize certain rules of conduct as binding and who for the most part act in accordance with them. Suppose further that these rules specify a system of cooperation designed to advance the good of those taking part in it. Then, although a society is a cooperative venture for mutual advantage, it is typically marked by a conflict as well as by an identity of interests. There is an identity of interests since social cooperation makes possible a better life for all than any would have if each were to live solely by his own efforts. There is a conflict of interests since persons are not indifferent as to how the greater benefits produced by their collaboration are distributed, for in order to pursue their ends they each prefer a larger to a lesser share. A set of principles is required for choosing among the various social arrangements which determine this division of advantages and for underwriting an agreement on the proper distributive shares. These principles are the principles of social justice: they provide a way of assigning rights and duties in the basic institutions of society and they define the appropriate distribution of the benefits and burdens of social cooperation. . . .

THE MAIN IDEA OF THE THEORY OF JUSTICE

My aim is to present a conception of justice which generalizes and carries to a higher level of abstraction the familiar theory of the social contract as found, say, in Locke, Rousseau, and Kant. In order to do this we are not to think of the original contract as one to enter a particular society or to set up a particular form of government. Rather, the guiding idea is that the principles of justice for the basic structure of society are the object of the original agreement. They are the principles that free and rational persons concerned to further their own interests would accept in an initial position of equality as defining the fundamental terms of their association. These principles are to regulate all further agreements; they specify the kinds of social cooperation that can be entered into and the forms of government that can be established. This way of regarding the principles of justice I shall call justice as fairness.

Thus we are to imagine that those who engage in social cooperation choose together, in one joint act, the principles which are to assign basic rights and duties and to determine the division of social benefits. Men are to decide in advance how they are to regulate their claims against one another and what is to be the foundation charter of their society. Just as each person must decide by rational reflection what constitutes his good, that is, the system of ends which it is rational for him to pursue, so a group of persons must decide once and for all what is to count among them as just and unjust. The choice which rational men would make in this hypothetical situation of equal liberty, assuming for the present that this choice problem has a solution, determines the principles of justice.

In justice as fairness the original position of equality corresponds to the state of nature in the traditional theory of the social contract. This original position is not, of course, thought of as an actual historical state of affairs, much less as a primitive condition of culture. It is understood as a purely hypothetical situation characterized so as to lead to a certain conception of justice. Among the essential features of this situation is that no one knows his place in society, his class position or social status, nor does any one know his fortune in the distribution of natural assets and abilities, his intelligence, strength, and the like. I shall even assume that the parties do not know their conceptions of the good or their special psychological propensities. The principles of justice are chosen behind a veil of ignorance. This ensures that no one is advantaged or disadvantaged in the choice of principles by the outcome of natural chance or the contingency of social circumstances. Since all are similarly situated and no one is able to design principles to favor his particular condition, the principles of justice are the result of a fair agreement or bargain. For given the circumstances of the original position, the symmetry of everyone's relations to each other, this initial situation is fair between individuals as moral persons, that is, as rational beings with their own ends and capable, I shall assume, of a sense of justice. The original position is, one might say, the appropriate initial status quo, and thus the fundamental agreements reached in it are fair. This explains the propriety of the name "justice as fairness": it conveys the idea that the principles of justice are agreed to in an initial situation that is fair. The name does not mean that the concepts of justice and fairness are the same, any more than the phrase "poetry as metaphor" means that the concepts of poetry and metaphor are the same.

Justice as fairness begins, as I have said, with one of the most general of all choices which persons might make together, namely, with the choice of the first principles of a conception of justice which is to regulate all subsequent criticism and reform of institutions. Then, having chosen a conception of justice, we can suppose that they are to choose a constitution and a legislature to enact laws, and so on, all in accordance with the principles of justice initially agreed upon. Our social situation is just if it is such that by this sequence of hypothetical agreements we would have contracted into the general system of rules which defines it.

. . . It may be observed, however, that once the principles of justice are thought of as arising from an original agreement in a situation of equality, it is an open question whether the principle of utility would be acknowledged. Offhand it hardly seems likely that persons who view themselves as equals, entitled to press their claims upon one another, would agree to a principle which may require lesser life prospects for some simply for the sake of a greater sum of advantages enjoyed by others. Since each desires to protect his interests, his capacity to advance his conception of the good, no one has a reason to acquiesce in an enduring loss for himself in order to bring about a greater net balance of satisfaction. In the absence of strong and lasting benevolent impulses, a rational man would not accept a basic structure merely because it maximized the algebriac sum of advantages irrespective of its permanent effects on his own basic rights and interests. Thus it seems that the principle of utility is incompatible with the conception of social cooperation among equals for mutual advantage. It appears to be inconsistent with the idea of reciprocity implicit in the notion of a well-ordered society. Or, at any rate, so I shall argue.

I shall maintain instead that the persons in the initial situation would choose two rather different principles: the first requires equality in the assignment of basic rights and duties, while the second holds that social and economic inequalities, for example inequalities of wealth and authority, are just only if they result in compensating benefits for everyone, and in particular for the least advantaged members of society. These principles rule out justifying institutions on the grounds that the hardships of some are offset by a greater good in the aggregate. It may be expedient but it is not just that some should have less in order that others may prosper. But there is no injustice in the greater benefits earned by a few provided that the situation of persons not so fortunate is thereby improved. The intuitive idea is that since everyone's well-being depends upon a scheme of cooperation without which no one could have a satisfactory life, the division of advantages should be such as to draw forth the willing cooperation of everyone taking part in it, including those less well situated. Yet this can be expected only if reasonable terms are proposed. The two principles mentioned seem to be a fair agreement on the basis of which those better endowed, or more fortunate in their social position, neither of which we can be said to

deserve, could expect the willing cooperation of others when some workable scheme
is a necessary condition of the welfare of all.
Once we decide to look for a conception of
justice that nullifies the accidents of natural
endowment and the contingencies of social
circumstance as counters in quest for political and economic advantage, we are led to
these principles. They express the result of
leaving aside those aspects of the social
world that seem arbitrary from a moral
point of view. . . .

THE ORIGINAL POSITION
AND JUSTIFICATION

. . . The idea here is simply to make vivid to
ourselves the restrictions that it seems reasonable to impose on arguments for principles of justice, and therefore on these principles themselves. Thus it seems reasonable
and generally acceptable that no one should
be advantaged or disadvantaged by natural
fortune or social circumstances in the choice
of principles. It also seems widely agreed
that it should be impossible to tailor principles to the circumstances of one's own
case. We should insure further that particular inclinations and aspirations, and persons' conceptions of their good, do not affect the principles adopted. The aim is to
rule out those principles that it would be rational to propose for acceptance, however
little the chance of success, only if one knew
certain things that are irrelevant from the
standpoint of justice. For example, if a man
knew that he was wealthy, he might find it
rational to advance the principle that various taxes for welfare measures be counted
unjust; if he knew that he was poor, he would
most likely propose the contrary principle.
To represent the desired restrictions one
imagines a situation in which everyone is deprived of this sort of information. One excludes the knowledge of those contingencies
which sets men at odds and allows them to
be guided by their prejudices. In this man-

ner the veil of ignorance is arrived at in a
natural way. . . .

TWO PRINCIPLES OF JUSTICE

I shall now state in a provisional form the
two principles of justice that I believe would
be chosen in the original position. . . .

The first statement of the two principles
reads as follows.

> First: each person is to have an equal right to
> the most extensive basic liberty compatible
> with a similar liberty for others.
>
> Second: social and economic inequalities
> are to be arranged so that they are both (a)
> reasonably expected to be to everyone's ad-
> vantage, and (b) attached to positions and of-
> fices open to all. . . . [The Difference Prin-
> ciple]

By way of general comment, these principles primarily apply, as I have said, to the
basic structure of society. They are to govern
the assignment of rights and duties and to
regulate the distribution of social and economic advantages. As their formulation suggests, these principles presuppose that the
social structure can be divided into two
more or less distinct parts, the first principle
applying to the one, the second to the other.
They distinguish between those aspects of
the social system that define and secure the
equal liberties of citizenship and those that
specify and establish social and economic inequalities. The basic liberties of citizens are,
roughly speaking, political liberty (the right
to vote and to be eligible for public office)
together with freedom of speech and assembly; liberty of conscience and freedom of
thought; freedom of the person along with
the right to hold (personal) property; and
freedom from arbitrary arrest and seizure as
defined by the concept of the rule of law.
These liberties are all required to be equal
by the first principle, since citizens of a just
society are to have the same basic rights.

The second principle applies, in the first approximation, to the distribution of income and wealth and to the design of organizations that make use of differences in authority and responsibility, or chains of command. While the distribution of wealth and income need not be equal, it must be to everyone's advantage, and at the same time, positions of authority and offices of command must be accessible to all. One applies the second principle by holding positions open, and then, subject to this constraint, arranges social and economic inequalities so that everyone benefits.

These principles are to be arranged in a serial order with the first principle prior to the second. This ordering means that a departure from the institutions of equal liberty required by the first principle cannot be justified, or compensated for, by greater social and economic advantages. The distribution of wealth and income, and the hierarchies of authority, must be consistent with both the liberties of equal citizenship and equality of opportunity.

It is clear that these principles are rather specific in their content, and their acceptance rests on certain assumptions that I must eventually try to explain and justify. A theory of justice depends upon a theory of society in ways that will become evident as we proceed. For the present, it should be observed that the two principles (and this holds for all formulations) are a special case of a more general conception of justice that can be expressed as follows.

> All social values—liberty and opportunity, income and wealth, and the bases of self-respect—are to be distributed equally unless an unequal distribution of any, or all, of these values is to everyone's advantage.

Injustice, then, is simply inequalities that are not to the benefit of all. Of course, this conception is extremely vague and requires interpretation.

As a first step, suppose that the basic structure of society distributes certain primary goods, that is, things that every rational man is presumed to want. These goods normally have a use whatever a person's rational plan of life. For simplicity, assume that the chief primary goods at the disposition of society are rights and liberties, powers and opportunities, income and wealth. These are the social primary goods. Other primary goods such as health and vigor, intelligence and imagination, are natural goods; although their possession is influenced by the basic structure, they are not so directly under its control. Imagine, then, a hypothetical initial arrangement in which all the social primary goods are equally distributed: everyone has similar rights and duties, and income and wealth are evenly shared. This state of affairs provides a benchmark for judging improvements. If certain inequalities of wealth and organizational powers would make everyone better off than in this hypothetical starting situation, then they accord with the general conception.

Now it is possible, at least theoretically, that by giving up some of their fundamental liberties men are sufficiently compensated by the resulting social and economic gains. The general conception of justice imposes no restrictions on what sort of inequalities are permissible; it only requires that everyone's position be improved. . . .

Now the second principle insists that each person benefit from permissible inequalities in the basic structure. This means that it must be reasonable for each relevant representative man defined by this structure, when he views it as a going concern, to prefer his prospects with the inequality to his prospects without it. One is not allowed to justify differences in income or organizational powers on the ground that the disadvantages of those in one position are outweighed by the greater advantages of those in another. Much less can infringements of liberty be counterbalanced in this way. Applied to the basic structure, the principle of utility would have us maximize the sum of expectations of representative men (weighted by the number of persons they represent, on the classical view); and this would permit us to compensate for the losses of some by the gains of others. Instead, the two principles require that everyone benefit from economic and social inequalities. . . .

THE TENDENCY TO EQUALITY

I wish to conclude this discussion of the two principles by explaining the sense in which they express an egalitarian conception of justice. Also I should like to forestall the objection to the principle of fair opportunity that it leads to a callous meritocratic society. In order to prepare the way for doing this, I note several aspects of the conception of justice that I have set out.

First we may observe that the difference principle gives some weight to the considerations singled out by the principle of redress. This is the principle that undeserved inequalities call for redress; and since inequalities of birth and natural endowment are undeserved, these inequalities are to be somehow compensated for. Thus the principle holds that in order to treat all persons equally, to provide genuine equality of opportunity, society must give more attention to those with fewer native assets and to those born into the less favorable social positions. The idea is to redress the bias of contingencies in the direction of equality. In pursuit of this principle greater resources might be spent on the education of the less rather than the more intelligent, at least over a certain time of life, say the earlier years of school.

Now the principle of redress has not to my knowledge been proposed as the sole criterion of justice, as the single aim of the social order. It is plausible as most such principles are only as a prima facie principle, one that is to be weighed in the balance with others. For example, we are to weigh it against the principle to improve the average standard of life, or to advance the common good. But whatever other principles we hold, the claims of redress are to be taken into account. It is thought to represent one of the elements in our conception of justice. Now the difference principle is not of course the principle of redress. It does not require society to try to even out handicaps as if all were expected to compete on a fair basis in the same race. But the difference principle would allocate resources in education, say, so as to improve the long-term expectation of the least favored. If this end is attained by giving more attention to the better endowed, it is permissible; otherwise not. And in making this decision, the value of education should not be assessed only in terms of economic efficiency and social welfare. Equally if not more important is the role of education in enabling a person to enjoy the culture of his society and to take part in its affairs, and in this way to provide for each individual a secure sense of his own worth.

Thus although the difference principle is not the same as that of redress, it does achieve some of the intent of the latter principle. It transforms the aims of the basic structure so that the total scheme of institutions no longer emphasizes social efficiency and technocratic values. . . .

. . . The natural distribution is neither just nor unjust; nor is it unjust that men are born into society at some particular position. These are simply natural facts. What is just and unjust is the way that institutions deal with these facts. Aristocratic and caste societies are unjust because they make these contingencies the ascriptive basis for belonging to more or less enclosed and privileged social classes. The basic structure of these societies incorporates the arbitrariness found in nature. But there is no necessity for men to resign themselves to these contingencies. The social system is not an unchangeable order beyond human control but a pattern of human action. In justice as fairness men agree to share one another's fate. In designing institutions they undertake to avail themselves of the accidents of nature and social circumstance only when doing so is for the common benefit. The two principles are a fair way of meeting the arbitrariness of fortune; and while no doubt imperfect in other ways, the institutions which satisfy these principles are just. . . .

There is a natural inclination to object that those better situated deserve their greater advantages whether or not they are to the benefit of others. At this point it is necessary to be clear about the notion of desert. It is perfectly true that given a just system of cooperation as a scheme of public rules and the expectations set up by it, those who, with the prospect of improving their condition, have done what the system announces that it will reward are entitled to their advantages. In this sense the more fortunate have a claim to their better situation; their claims are legitimate expectations established by social institutions, and the community is obligated to meet them. But this sense of desert presupposes the existence of the cooperative scheme; it is irrelevant to the question whether in the first place the scheme is to be designed in accordance with the difference principle or some other criterion.

Perhaps some will think that the person with greater natural endowments deserves those assets and the superior character that made their development possible. Because he is more worthy in this sense, he deserves the greater advantages that he could achieve with them. This view, however, is surely incorrect. It seems to be one of the fixed points of our considered judgments that no one deserves his place in the distribution of native endowments, any more than one deserves one's initial starting place in society. The assertion that a man deserves the superior character that enables him to make the effort to cultivate his abilities is equally problematic, for his character depends in large part upon fortunate family and social

circumstances for which he can claim no credit. The notion of desert seems not to apply to these cases. Thus the more advantaged representative man cannot say that he deserves and therefore has a right to a scheme of cooperation in which he is permitted to acquire benefits in ways that do not contribute to the welfare of others. There is no basis for his making this claim. From the standpoint of common sense, then, the difference principle appears to be acceptable both to the more advantaged and to the less advantaged individual. . . .

BACKGROUND INSTITUTIONS FOR DISTRIBUTIVE JUSTICE

The main problem of distributive justice is the choice of a social system. The principles of justice apply to the basic structure and regulate how its major institutions are combined into one scheme. Now, as we have seen, the idea of justice as fairness is to use the notion of pure procedural justice to handle the contingencies of particular situations. The social system is to be designed so that the resulting distribution is just however things turn out. To achieve this end it is necessary to get the social and economic process within the surroundings of suitable political and legal institutions. Without an appropriate scheme of these background institutions the outcome of the distributive process will not be just. Background fairness is lacking. I shall give a brief description of these supporting institutions as they might exist in a properly organized democratic state that allows private ownership of capital and natural resources. . . .

In establishing these background institutions the government may be thought of as divided into four branches.[1] Each branch consists of various agencies, or activities thereof, charged with preserving certain social and economic conditions. These divisions do not overlap with the usual organization of government but are to be understood as different functions. The allocation branch, for example, is to keep the price system workably competitive and to prevent the formation of unreasonable market power. Such power does not exist as long as markets cannot be made more competitive consistent with the requirements of efficiency and the facts of geography and the preferences of households. The allocation branch is also charged with identifying and correcting, say by suitable taxes and subsidies and by changes in the definition of property rights, the more obvious departures from efficiency caused by the failure of prices to measure accurately social benefits and costs. To this end suitable taxes and subsidies may be used, or the scope and definition of property rights may be revised. The stabilization branch, on the other hand, strives to bring about reasonably full employment in the sense that those who want work can find it and the free choice of occupation and the deployment of finance are supported by strong effective demand. These two branches together are to maintain the efficiency of the market economy generally.

The social minimum is the responsibility of the transfer branch. . . . The essential idea is that the workings of this branch take needs into account and assign them an appropriate weight with respect to other claims. A competitive price system gives no consideration to needs and therefore it cannot be the sole device of distribution. There must be a division of labor between the parts of the social system in answering to the common sense precepts of justice. Different institutions meet different claims. Competitive markets properly regulated secure free choice of occupation and lead to an efficient use of resources and allocation of commodities to households. They set a weight on the conventional precepts associated with wages and warnings, whereas the transfer branch guarantees a certain level of well-being and honors the claims of need. . . .

It is clear that the justice of distributive shares depends on the background institutions and how they allocate total income, wages and other income plus transfers. There is with reason strong objection to the competitive determination of total income, since this ignores the claims of need and an appropriate standard of life. From the standpoint of the legislative stage it is rational to insure oneself and one's descendants against these contingencies of the market. Indeed, the difference principle presumably requires this. But once a suitable minimum is provided by transfers, it may be perfectly fair that the rest of total income be settled by the price system, assuming that it is moderately efficient and free from monopolistic restrictions, and unreasonable externalities have been eliminated. Moreover, this way of dealing with the claims of need would appear to be more effective than trying to regulate income by minimum wage standards, and the like. It is better to assign to each branch only such tasks as are compatible with one another. Since the market is not suited to answer the claims of need, these should be met by a separate arrangement. Whether the principles of justice are satisfied, then, turns on whether the total income of the least advantaged (wages plus transfers) is such as to maximize their long-run expectations (consistent with the constraints of equal liberty and fair equality of opportunity).

Finally, there is a distribution branch. Its task is to preserve an approximate justice in distributive shares by means of taxation and the necessary adjustments in the rights of property. Two aspects of this branch may be distinguished. First of all, it imposes a number of inheritance and gift taxes, and sets restrictions on the rights of bequest. The purpose of these levies and regulations is not to raise revenue (release resources to government) but gradually and continually to correct the distribution of wealth and to prevent concentrations of power detrimental to the fair value of political liberty and fair equality of opportunity. For example, the progressive principle might be applied at the beneficiary's end.[2] Doing this would encourage the wide dispersal of property which is a necessary condition, it seems, if the fair value of the equal liberties is to be maintained.

NOTES

1. For the idea of branches of government, see R. A. Musgrave, *The Theory of Public Finance* (New York: McGraw-Hill, 1959), Ch. I.
2. See Meade, *Efficiency, Equality and the Ownership of Property,* pp. 56f.

The Entitlement Theory

Robert Nozick

The term "distributive justice" is not a neutral one. Hearing the term "distribution," most people presume that some thing or mechanism uses some principle or criterion to give out a supply of things. Into this process of distributing shares some error may have crept. So it is an open question, at least, whether *re*distribution should take place; whether we should do again what has already been done once, though poorly. However, we are not in the position of children who have been given portions of pie by someone who now makes last minute adjustments to rectify careless cutting. There is no *central* distribution, no person or group entitled to control all the resources, jointly deciding how they are to be doled out. What each person gets, he gets from others who give to him in exchange for something, or as a gift. In a free society, diverse persons control different resources, and new holdings arise out of the voluntary exchanges and actions of persons. . . .

The subject of justice in holdings consists of three major topics. The first is the *original acquisition of holdings,* the appropriation of unheld things. This includes the issues of how unheld things may come to be held, the process, or processes, by which unheld things may come to be held, the things that may come to be held by these processes, the extent of what comes to be held by a particular person, and so on. We shall refer to the complicated truth about this topic, which we shall not formulate here, as the principle of justice in acquisition. The second topic concerns the *transfer of holdings* from one person to another. By what processes may a person transfer holdings to another? How may a person acquire a holding from another who holds it? Under this topic come general descriptions of voluntary exchange, and gift and (on the other hand) fraud, as well as reference to particular conventional details fixed upon in a given society. The complicated truth about this subject (with placeholders for conventional details) we shall call the principle of justice in transfer. (And we shall suppose it also includes principles governing how a person may divest himself of a holding, passing it into an unheld state.)

If the world were wholly just, the following inductive definition would exhaustively cover the subject of justice in holdings.

From Robert Nozick, *Anarchy, State, and Utopia* (New York: Basic Books, Inc., Publishers, 1974), pp. 149–154, 156–157, 159–163, 168, 174–175, 178–179, 182. Copyright © 1974 by Basic Books, Inc., Publishers, New York. Reprinted by permission of Basic Books, Inc., and Basil Blackwell Publisher.

1. A person who acquires a holding in accordance with the principle of justice in acquisition is entitled to that holding.
2. A person who acquires a holding in accordance with the principle of justice in transfer, from someone else entitled to the holding, is entitled to the holding.
3. No one is entitled to a holding except by (repeated) applications of 1 and 2.

The complete principle of distributive justice would say simply that a distribution is just if everyone is entitled to the holdings they possess under the distribution. . . .

Not all actual situations are generated in accordance with the two principles of justice in holdings: the principle of justice in acquisition and the principle of justice in transfer. Some people steal from others, or defraud them, or enslave them, seizing their product and preventing them from living as they choose, or forcibly exclude others from competing in exchanges. None of these are permissible modes of transition from one situation to another. And some persons acquire holdings by means not sanctioned by the principle of justice in acquisition. The existence of past injustice (previous violations of the first two principles of justice in holdings) raises the third major topic under justice in holdings: the rectification of injustice in holdings. If past injustice has shaped present holdings in various ways, some identifiable and some not, what now, if anything, ought to be done to rectify these injustices? . . .

HISTORICAL PRINCIPLES AND END-RESULT PRINCIPLES

The general outlines of the entitlement theory illuminate the nature and defects of other conceptions of distributive justice. The entitlement theory of justice in distribution is *historical;* whether a distribution is just depends upon how it came about. In contrast, *current time-slice principles* of justice hold that the justice of a distribution is determined by how things are distributed (who has what) as judged by some *structural* principle(s) of just distribution. A utilitarian who judges between any two distributions by seeing which has the greater sum of utility and, if the sums tie, applies some fixed equality criterion to choose the more equal distribution, would hold a current time-slice principle of justice. As would someone who had a fixed schedule of trade-offs between the sum of happiness and equality. According to a current time-slice principle, all that needs to be looked at, in judging the justice of a distribution, is who ends up with what; in comparing any two distributions one need look only at the matrix presenting the distributions. No further information need be fed into a principle of justice. It is a consequence of such principles of justice that any two structurally identical distributions are equally just. . . .

Most persons do not accept current time-slice principles as constituting the whole story about distributive shares. They think it relevant in assessing the justice of a situation to consider not only the distribution it embodies, but also how that distribution came about. If some persons are in prison for murder or war crimes, we do not say that to assess the justice of the distribution in the society we must look only at what this person has, and that person has, and that person has, . . . at the current time. We think it relevant to ask whether someone did something so that he *deserved* to be punished, deserved to have a lower share. . . .

PATTERNING

. . . Almost every suggested principle of distributive justice is patterned: to each according to his moral merit, or needs, or marginal product, or how hard he tries, or the weighted sum of the foregoing, and so on. The principle of entitlement we have sketched is *not* patterned. There is no one natural dimension or weighted sum or combination of a small number of natural dimensions that yields the distributions generated in accordance with the principle of entitlement. The set of holdings that results when some persons receive their marginal products, others win at gambling, others receive a share of their mate's income, others receive gifts from foundations, others receive interest on loans, others receive gifts from admirers, others receive returns on investment, others make for themselves much of what they have, others find things, and so on, will not be patterned. . . .

To think that the task of a theory of distributive justice is to fill in the blank in "to each according to his ＿＿＿" is to be predisposed to search for a pattern; and the separate treatment of "from each according to his ＿＿＿" treats production and distribution as two separate and independent issues. On an entitlement view these are *not* two separate questions. Whoever makes something, having bought or contracted for all other held resources used in the process (transferring some of his holdings for these cooperating factors), is entitled to it. . . .

So entrenched are maxims of the usual form that perhaps we should present the entitlement conception as a competitor. Ignoring acquisition and rectification, we might say:

> From each according to what he chooses to do, to each according to what he makes for himself (perhaps with the contracted aid of others) and what others choose to do for him and choose to give him of what they've been given previously (under this maxim) and haven't yet expended or transferred.

This, the discerning reader will have noticed, has its defects as a slogan. So as a summary and great simplification (and not as a maxim with any independent meaning) we have:

> *From each as they choose, to each as they are chosen.*

HOW LIBERTY UPSETS PATTERNS

It is not clear how those holding alternative conceptions of distributive justice can reject the entitlement conception of justice in holdings. For suppose a distribution favored by one of these non-entitlement conceptions

is realized. Let us suppose it is your favorite one and let us call this distribution D_1; perhaps everyone has an equal share, perhaps shares vary in accordance with some dimension you treasure. Now suppose that Wilt Chamberlain is greatly in demand by basketball teams, being a great gate attraction. (Also suppose contracts run only for a year, with players being free agents.) He signs the following sort of contract with a team: In each home game, twenty-five cents from the price of each ticket of admission goes to him. (We ignore the question of whether he is "gouging" the owners, letting them look out for themselves.) The season starts, and people cheerfully attend his team's games; they buy their tickets, each time dropping a separate twenty-five cents of their admission price into a special box with Chamberlain's name on it. They are excited about seeing him play; it is worth the total admission price to them. Let us suppose that in one season one million persons attend his home games, and Wilt Chamberlain winds up with $250,000, a much larger sum than the average income and larger even than anyone else has. Is he entitled to this income? Is this new distribution D_2, unjust? If so, why? There is *no* question about whether each of the people was entitled to the control over the resources they held in D_1; because that was the distribution (your favorite) that (for the purposes of argument) we assumed was acceptable. Each of these persons *chose* to give twenty-five cents of their money to Chamberlain. They could have spent it on going to the movies, or on candy bars, or on copies of *Dissent* magazine, or of *Monthly Review.* But they all, at least one million of them, converged on giving it to Wilt Chamberlain in exchange for watching him play basketball. If D_1 was a just distribution, and people voluntarily moved from it to D_2, transferring parts of their shares they were given under D_1 (what was it for if not to do something with?), isn't D_2 also just? If the people were entitled to dispose of the resources to which they were entitled (under D_1), didn't this include their being entitled to give it to, or exchange it with, Wilt

Chamberlain? Can anyone else complain on grounds of justice? Each other person already has his legitimate share under D₁. Under D₁, there is nothing that anyone has that anyone else has a claim of justice against. After someone transfers something to Wilt Chamberlain, third parties *still* have their legitimate shares; *their* shares are not changed. By what process could such a transfer among two persons give a rise to a legitimate claim of distributive justice on a portion of what was transferred, by a third party who had no claim of justice on any holding of the others *before* the transfer? To cut off objections irrelevant here, we might imagine the exchanges occurring in a socialist society, after hours. After playing whatever basketball he does in his daily work, or doing whatever other daily work he does, Wilt Chamberlain decides to put in *overtime* to earn additional money. (First his work quota is set; he works time over that.) Or imagine it is a skilled juggler people like to see, who puts on shows after hours. . . .

The general point illustrated by the Wilt Chamberlain example is that no end-state principle or distributional patterned principle of justice can be continuously realized without continuous interference with people's lives. Any favored pattern would be transformed into one unfavored by the principle, by people choosing to act in various ways; for example, by people exchanging goods and services with other people, or giving things to other people, things the transferrers are entitled to under the favored distributional pattern. To maintain a pattern one must either continually interfere to stop people from transferring resources as they wish to, or continually (or periodically) interfere to take from some persons resources that others for some reason chose to transfer to them. . . .

Patterned principles of distributive justice necessitate *re*distributive activities. The likelihood is small that any actual freely-arrived-at set of holdings fits a given pattern; and the likelihood is nil that it will continue to fit the pattern as people exchange and give. From the point of view of an entitlement theory, redistribution is a serious matter indeed, involving, as it does, the violation of people's rights. (An exception is those takings that fall under the principle of the rectification of injustices.) . . .

LOCKE'S THEORY OF ACQUISITION

. . . [Let us] introduce an additional bit of complexity into the structure of the entitlement theory. This is best approached by considering Locke's attempt to specify a principle of justice in acquisition. Locke views property rights in an unowned object as originating through someone's mixing his labor with it. This gives rise to many questions. What are the boundaries of what labor is mixed with? If a private astronaut clears a place on Mars, has he mixed his labor with (so that he comes to own) the whole planet, the whole uninhabited universe, or just a particular plot? Which plot does an act bring under ownership? . . .

Locke's proviso that there be "enough and as good left in common for others" is meant to ensure that the situation of others is not worsened. . . .

. . . I assume that any adequate theory of justice in acquisition will contain a proviso similar to [Locke's]. . . .

I believe that the free operation of a market system will not actually run afoul of the Lockean proviso. . . . If this is correct, the proviso will not . . . provide a significant opportunity for future state action.

Rich and Poor

Peter Singer

One way of making sense of the non-consequentialist view of responsibility is by basing it on a theory of rights of the kind proposed by John Locke or, more recently, Robert Nozick. If everyone has a right to life, and this right is a right *against* others who might threaten my life, but not a right *to* assistance from others when my life is in danger, then we can understand the feeling that we are responsibile for acting to kill but not for omitting to save. The former violates the rights of others, the latter does not.

Should we accept such a theory of rights? If we build up our theory of rights by imagining, as Locke and Nozick do, individuals living independently from each other in a 'state of nature', it may seem natural to adopt a conception of rights in which as long as each leaves the other alone, no rights are violated. I might, on this view, quite properly have maintained my independent existence if I had wished to do so. So if I do not make you any worse off than you would have been if I had had nothing at all to do with you, how can I have violated your rights? But why start from such an unhistorical, abstract and ultimately inexplicable idea as an independent individual? We now know that our ancestors were social beings long before they were human beings, and could not have developed the abilities and capacities of human beings if they had not been social beings first. In any case we are not, now, isolated individuals. If we consider people living together in a community, it is less easy to assume that rights must be restricted to rights against interference. We

might, instead, adopt the view that taking rights to life seriously is incompatible with standing by and watching people die when one could easily save them. . . .

THE OBLIGATION TO ASSIST

The Argument for an Obligation to Assist

The path from the library at my university to the Humanities lecture theatre passes a shallow ornamental pond. Suppose that on my way to give a lecture I noticed that a small child has fallen in and is in danger of drowning. Would anyone deny that I ought to wade in and pull the child out? This will mean getting my clothes muddy, and either cancelling my lecture or delaying it until I can find something dry to change into; but compared with the avoidable death of a child this is insignificant.

A plausible principle that would support the judgment that I ought to pull the child out is this: if it is in our power to prevent something very bad happening, without thereby sacrificing anything of comparable moral significance, we ought to do it. This principle seems uncontroversial. It will obviously win the assent of consequentialists; but non-consequentialists should accept it too, because the injunction to prevent what is bad applies only when nothing comparably significant is at stake. Thus the principle cannot lead to the kinds of actions of which non-consequentialists strongly disapprove— serious violations of individual rights, injus-

From Peter Singer, "Rich and Poor," in *Practical Ethics* (New York: Cambridge University Press, 1979), pp. 166, 168–179. Reprinted with permission of the publisher.

tice, broken promises, and so on. If a non-consequentialist regards any of these as comparable in moral significance to the bad thing that is to be prevented, he will automatically regard the principle as not applying in those cases in which the bad thing can only be prevented by violating rights, doing injustice, breaking promises, or whatever else is at stake. Most non-consequentialists hold that we ought to prevent what is bad and promote what is good. Their dispute with consequentialists lies in their insistence that this is not the sole ultimate ethical principle: that it is *an* ethical principle is not denied by any plausible ethical theory.

Nevertheless the uncontroversial appearance of the principle that we ought to prevent what is bad when we can do so without sacrificing anything of comparable moral significance is deceptive. If it were taken seriously and acted upon, our lives and our world would be fundamentally changed. For the principle applies, not just to rare situations in which one can save a child from a pond, but to the everyday situations in which we can assist those living in absolute poverty. In saying this I assume that absolute poverty, with its hunger and malnutrition, lack of shelter, illiteracy, disease, high infant mortality and low life expectancy, is a bad thing. And I assume that it is within the power of the affluent to reduce absolute poverty, without sacrificing anything of comparable moral significance. If these two assumptions and the principle we have been discussing are correct, we have an obligation to help those in absolute poverty which is no less strong than our obligation to rescue a drowning child from a pond. Not to help would be wrong, whether or not it is intrinsically equivalent to killing. Helping is not, as conventionally thought, a charitable act which it is praiseworthy to do, but not wrong to omit; it is something that everyone ought to do.

This is the argument for an obligation to assist. Set out more formally, it would look like this.

First premise: If we can prevent something bad without sacrificing anything of comparable significance, we ought to do it.

Second premise: Absolute poverty is bad.

Third premise: There is some absolute poverty we can prevent without sacrificing anything of comparable moral significance.

Conclusion: We ought to prevent some absolute poverty.

The first premise is the substantive moral premise on which the argument rests, and I have tried to show that it can be accepted by people who hold a variety of ethical positions.

The second premise is unlikely to be challenged. Absolute poverty is, as [Robert] McNamara put it, 'beneath any reasonable definition of human decency' and it would be hard to find a plausible ethical view which did not regard it as a bad thing.

The third premise is more controversial, even though it is cautiously framed. It claims only that some absolute poverty can be prevented without the sacrifice of anything of comparable moral significance. It thus avoids the objection that any aid I can give is just 'drops in the ocean' for the point is not whether my personal contribution will make any noticeable impression on world poverty as a whole (of course it won't) but whether it will prevent some poverty. This is all the argument needs to sustain its conclusion, since the second premise says that any absolute poverty is bad, and not merely the total amount of absolute poverty. If without sacrificing anything of comparable moral significance we can provide just one family with the means to raise itself out of absolute poverty, the third premise is vindicated.

I have left the notion of moral significance unexamined in order to show that the argument does not depend on any specific values or ethical principles. I think the third premise is true for most people living in industrialized nations, on any defensible view of what is morally significant. Our affluence means that we have income we can dispose of without giving up the basic necessities of life, and we can use this income to reduce absolute poverty. Just how much we will think ourselves obliged to give up will depend on what we consider to be of comparable moral significance to the poverty we could prevent: colour television, stylish clothes, expensive dinners, a sophisticated stereo system, overseas holidays, a (second?) car, a larger house, private schools for our children.... For a utilitarian, none of these is likely to be of comparable significance to the reduction of absolute poverty; and those who are not utilitarians surely must, if they subscribe to the principle of universalizability, accept that at least *some* of these things are of far less moral significance than the absolute poverty that could be prevented by the money they cost. So the third premise seems to be true on any plausible ethical view—although the precise amount of absolute poverty that can be prevented before anything of moral significance is sacrificed will vary according to the ethical view one accepts.

Objections to the Argument

Taking Care of Our Own. Anyone who has worked to increase overseas aid will have come across the argument that we should look after those near us, our families and then the poor in our own country, before we think about poverty in distant places.

No doubt we do instinctively prefer to help those who are close to us. Few could stand by and watch a child drown; many can ignore a famine in Africa. But the question is not what we usually do, but what we ought to do, and it is difficult to see any sound moral justification for the view that distance, or community membership, makes a crucial difference to our obligations.

Consider, for instance, racial affinities. Should whites help poor whites before helping poor blacks? Most of us would reject such a suggestion out of hand, [by appeal to] the principle of equal consideration of interests: people's needs for food has nothing to do with their race, and if blacks need food more than whites, it would be a violation of the principle of equal consideration to give preference to whites.

The same point applies to citizenship or nationhood. Every affluent nation has some relatively poor citizens, but absolute poverty is limited largely to the poor nations. Those living on the streets of Calcutta, or in a drought-stricken region of the Sahel, are experiencing poverty unknown in the West. Under these circumstances it would be wrong to decide that only those fortunate enough to be citizens of our own community will share our abundance.

We feel obligations of kinship more strongly than those of citizenship. Which parents could give away their last bowl of rice if their own children were starving? To do so would seem unnatural, contrary to our nature as biologically evolved beings—although whether it would be wrong is another question altogether. In any case, we are not faced with that situation, but with one in which our own children are well-fed, well-clothed, well-educated, and would now like new bikes, a stereo set, or their own car. In these circumstances any special obligations we might have to our children have been fulfilled, and the needs of strangers make a stronger claim upon us.

The element of truth in the view that we should first take care of our own, lies in the advantage of a recognized system of responsibilities. When families and local communities look after their own poorer members, ties of affection and personal relationships achieve ends that would otherwise require a large, impersonal bureaucracy. Hence it would be absurd to propose that from now on we all regard ourselves as equally responsible for the welfare of everyone in the world; but the argument for an obligation to assist does not propose that. It applies only when some are in absolute poverty, and others can help without sacrificing anything of comparable moral significance. To allow one's own kin to sink into absolute poverty would be to sacrifice something of comparable significance; and before that point had been reached, the breakdown of the system of family and community responsibility would be a factor to weigh the balance in favour of a small degree of preference for family and community. This small degree of preference is, however, decisively outweighed by existing discrepancies in wealth and property.

Property Rights. Do people have a right to private property, a right which contradicts the view that they are under an obligation to give some of their wealth away to those in absolute poverty? According to some theories of rights (for instance, Robert Nozick's) provided one has acquired one's property without the use of unjust means like force and fraud, one may be entitled to enormous wealth while others starve. This individualistic conception of rights is in contrast to other views, like the early Christian doctrine to be found in the works of Thomas Aquinas, which holds that since property exists for the satisfaction of human needs, 'whatever a man has in superabundance is owed, of natural right, to the poor for their sustenance'. A socialist would also, of course, see wealth as belonging to the community rather than the individual, while utilitarians, whether socialist or not, would be prepared to override property rights to prevent great evils.

Does the argument for an obligation to assist others therefore presuppose one of these other theories of property rights, and not an individualistic theory like Nozick's? Not necessarily. A theory of property rights can insist on our *right* to retain wealth without pronouncing on whether the rich *ought* to give to the poor. Nozick, for example, rejects the use of compulsory means like taxation to redistribute income, but suggests that we can achieve the ends we deem morally desirable by voluntary means. So Nozick would reject the claim that rich people have an 'obligation' to give to the poor, in so far as this implies that the poor have a right to our aid, but might accept that giving is something we ought to do and failure to give, though within one's rights, is wrong—for rights is not all there is to ethics.

The argument for an obligation to assist can survive, with only minor modifications, even if we accept an individualistic theory of property rights. In any case, however, I do not think we should accept such a theory. It leaves too much to chance to be an acceptable ethical view. For instance, those whose forefathers happened to inhabit some sandy wastes around the Persian Gulf are now fabulously wealthy, because oil lay under those sands; while those whose forefathers settled on better land south of the Sahara live in absolute poverty, because of drought and bad harvests. Can this distribution be acceptable from an impartial point of view? If we imagine ourselves about to begin life as a citizen of either Kuwait or Chad—but we do not know which—would we accept the principle that citizens of Kuwait are under no obligation to assist people living in Chad?

Population and the Ethics of Triage. Perhaps the most serious objection to the argument that we have an obligation to assist is that since the major cause of absolute poverty is overpopulation, helping those now in poverty will only ensure that yet more people are born to live in poverty in the future.

In its most extreme form, this objection is taken to show that we should adopt a policy of 'triage'. The term comes from medical policies adopted in wartime. With too few doctors to cope with all the casualties, the wounded were divided into three categories: those who would probably survive without medical assistance, those who might survive if they received assistance, but otherwise probably would not, and those who even with medical assistance probably would not survive. Only those in the middle category were given medical assistance. The idea, of course, was to use limited medical resources as effectively as possible. For those in the first category, medical treatment was not strictly necessary; for those in the third category, it was likely to be useless. It has been suggested that we should apply the same policies to countries, according to their prospects of becoming self-sustaining. We would not aid countries which even without our help will soon be able to feed their populations. We would not aid countries which, even with our help, will not be able to limit their population to a level they can feed. We would aid those countries where our help might make the difference between success and failure in bringing food and population into balance.

Advocates of this theory are understandably reluctant to give a complete list of the countries they would place into the 'hopeless' category; but Bangladesh is often cited as an example. Adopting the policy of triage would, then, mean cutting off assistance to Bangladesh and allowing famine, disease and natural disasters to reduce the population of that country (now around 80 million) to the level at which it can provide adequately for all.

In support of this view Garrett Hardin has offered a metaphor: we in the rich nations are like the occupants of a crowded lifeboat adrift in a sea full of drowning people. If we try to save the drowning by bringing them aboard our boat will be overloaded and we shall all drown. Since it is better that some survive than none, we should leave the others to drown. In the world today, according to Hardin, 'lifeboat ethics' apply. The rich should leave the poor to starve, for otherwise the poor will drag the rich down with them. . . .

Anyone whose initial reaction to triage was not one of repugnance would be an unpleasant sort of person. Yet initial reactions based on strong feelings are not always reliable guides. Advocates of triage are rightly concerned with the long-term consequences of our actions. They say that helping the poor and starving now merely ensures more poor and starving in the future. When our

capacity to help is finally unable to cope— as one day it must be—the suffering will be greater than it would be if we stopped helping now. If this is correct, there is nothing we can do to prevent absolute starvation and poverty, in the long run, and so we have no obligation to assist. Nor does it seem reasonable to hold that under these circumstances people have a right to our assistance. If we do accept such a right, irrespective of the consequences, we are saying that, in Hardin's metaphor, we would continue to haul the drowning into our lifeboat until the boat sank and we all drowned.

If triage is to be rejected it must be tackled on its own ground, within the framework of consequentialist ethics. Here it is vulnerable. Any consequentialist ethics must take probability of outcome into account. A course of action that will certainly produce some benefit is to be preferred to an alternative course that may lead to a slightly larger benefit, but is equally likely to result in no benefit at all. Only if the greater magnitude of the uncertain benefit outweighs its uncertainty should we choose it. Better one certain unit of benefit than a 10% chance of 5 units; but better a 50% chance of 3 units than a single certain unit. The same principle applies when we are trying to avoid evils.

The policy of triage involves a certain, very great evil: population control by famine and disease. Tens of millions would die slowly. Hundreds of millions would continue to live in absolute poverty, at the very margin of existence. Against this prospect, advocates of the policy place a possible evil which is greater still: the same process of famine and disease, taking place in, say, fifty years time, when the world's population may be three times its present level, and the number who will die from famine, or struggle on in absolute poverty, will be that much greater. The question is: how probable is this forecast that continued assistance now will lead to greater disasters in the future?

Forecasts of population growth are notoriously fallible, and theories about the factors which affect it remain speculative. One theory, at least as plausible as any other, is that countries pass through a 'demographic transition' as their standard of living rises. When people are very poor and have no access to modern medicine their fertility is high, but population is kept in check by high death rates. The introduction of sanitation, modern medical techniques and other improvements reduces the death rate, but initially has little effect on the birth rate. Then population grows rapidly. Most poor countries are now in this phase. If standards of living continue to rise, however, couples begin to realize that to have the same number of children surviving to maturity as in the past, they do not need to give birth to as many children as their parents did. The need for children to provide economic support in old age diminishes. Improved education and the emancipation and employment of women also reduce the birthrate, and so population growth begins to level off. Most rich nations have reached this stage, and their populations are growing only very slowly.

If this theory is right, there is an alternative to the disasters accepted as inevitable by supporters of triage. We can assist poor countries to raise the living standards of the poorest members of their population. We can encourage the governments of these countries to enact land reform measures, improve education, and liberate women from a purely child-bearing role. We can also help other countries to make contraception and sterilization widely available. There is a fair chance that these measures will hasten the onset of the demographic transition and bring population growth down to a manageable level. Success cannot be guaranteed; but the evidence that improved economic security and education reduce population growth is strong enough to make triage eth-

ically unacceptable. We cannot allow millions to die from starvation and disease when there is a reasonable probability that population can be brought under control without such horrors.

Population growth is therefore not a reason against giving overseas aid, although it should make us think about the kind of aid to give. Instead of food handouts, it may be better to give aid that hastens the demographic transition. This may mean agricultural assistance for the rural poor, or assistance with education, or the provision of contraceptive services. Whatever kind of aid proves most effective in specific circumstances, the obligation to assist is not reduced.

One awkward question remains. What should we do about a poor and already overpopulated country which, for religious or nationalistic reasons, restricts the use of contraceptives and refuses to slow its population growth? Should we nevertheless offer development assistance? Or should we make our offer conditional on effective steps being taken to reduce the birthrate? To the latter course, some would object that putting conditions on aid is an attempt to impose our own ideas on independent sovereign nations. So it is—but is this imposition unjustifiable? If the argument for an obligation to assist is sound, we have an obligation to reduce absolute poverty; but we have no obligation to make sacrifices that, to the best of our knowledge, have no prospect of reducing poverty in the long run. Hence we have no obligation to assist countries whose governments have policies which will make our aid ineffective. This could be very harsh on poor citizens of these countries—for they may have no say in the government's policies—but we will help more people in the long run by using our resources where they are most effective.

Economic Justice

Milton Fisk

Defenders of the capitalist form of society do not defend a right to economic equality. Economic inequality is, they argue, to everyone's advantage. Yet some of these defenders of capitalism are also supporters of liberal democracy. They must then recognize limits to economic inequality beyond which even capitalism should not go. Vast concentrations of economic wealth are sources of political power that strangle the basic liberties of a democratic society. But many defenders of capitalist society maintain that in the US at least these limits to economic inequality have not been reached.

The purpose of this [paper] is to show that the arguments justifying the existing high degree of economic inequality fall apart. To show this it will not be necessary to defend, or to reject, the right to complete economic equality. Nonetheless, this [paper] points in an egalitarian direction. For it shows also that the degree of economic inequality inevitable within even a reformed capitalist society cannot be justified from the perspective of working-class morality.

I. ECONOMIC INEQUALITY

According to many writers on US society, the stage of widespread affluence has been reached within the US. There is, on the one hand, a reduced level of economic inequality, and there is, on the other hand, an elimination of the lower classes as a majority in favour of a large and prosperous middle class. The misery and inequality that characterized nineteenth- and early twentieth-century capitalism have been redeemed with the arrival of the 'affluent society'. This picture, however, conceals the urgent problem of economic inequality within the US. As Gabriel Kolko notes in his pathbreaking dissenting work on income distribution, 'The predominantly middle-class society is only an image in the minds of isolated academicians.'[1]

First let us look at the distribution of before-tax personal, as opposed to corporate, income during the period 1910–70 to get some idea as to whether there has been a significant trend toward equality. To do this we can consider families as broken up into five groups of equal size, ranging from those with the highest to those with the lowest income. (People living in families make up roughly 90 per cent of the US population.) *In the sixty-year period considered, families in the highest fifth received between* 40 *and* 45 *per cent of all family income.* That is, they received at least two times more than they would have if every family received the same income. Despite variations from year to year, there is no overall trend in this period toward a significantly smaller share of the national income for the richest fifth. The middle fifth has received between 15 and 18 percent of all family income. This means that it received over the entire sixty-year period less than it would have if income were egalitarian. For this group the trend, within these narrow limits, has been for a slight rise in its share of income, but after World War II that rise stopped completely. Finally, what about the

From Milton Fisk, *Ethics and Society* (New York: New York University Press, 1980), pp. 224–235. Reprinted by permission of The Harvester Press, Ltd. and New York University Press.

families in the poorest quintile? That group has received between 4 and 6 per cent of the national personal income, which runs up to five times less than it would receive under equality. The overall trend has been for families in this bottom group to get proportionately the same during the sixty-year period. As regards income in the US, then, there is significant and continuing inequality.[2] The top fifth as a whole takes six to ten times more of the national family income than does the bottom fifth. (Data for non-family persons shows even greater inequality.)

Our data has so far been taken on before-tax income. Will not taxation make the picture one of greater equality? It does change the picture as regards equality but only in an insignificant way. Many taxes are regressive: they are a larger fraction of lower than of higher incomes. Social security taxes, property taxes, and sales taxes are all regressive. It cannot be expected that these would provide a shift toward equality. But even the federal income tax, which is progressive, has failed to do more than decrease by two per cent the share of national income of the top fifth. The increase in the share of the bottom fifth resulting from federal income taxes has remained a fraction of a per cent. Moreover, the percentage of all taxes coming from the non-owning classes has been rising steadily since World War II. Taxes have, then, failed to equalize income significantly.[3]

We are dealing with a society in which private ownership of the means of production is a fundamental feature. Some personal income comes from ownership, to be sure, but one cannot say exactly how wealth is distributed simply on the basis of knowing how income is distributed. For one thing, a significant but variable share of returns from ownership is invested in new means of production and does not appear as dividend income. Nonetheless, in a capitalist society we can predict that wealth, like income, is unevenly distributed. It is highly concentrated in the hands of a very few owners: they own the plants, the trucks, the warehouses, the mines, the office buildings, the large estates,

and the objects of art. The poor are often net holders of 'negative wealth' because of their debts. *Between 1810 and 1969, the concentration of wealth has remained remarkably constant; the top one per cent as regards wealth has held between 20 and 30 per cent of all the wealth in the US.* In 1962 the poorest 20 per cent held less than one-half of one per cent of the nation's wealth.[4]

Nonetheless, some currency has been given to the view that corporate ownership has become widespread and that workers are now significant owners. Stock ownership is, indeed, more widespread, but this has not seriously affected the high degree of concentration of stock ownership in the hands of the wealthiest.

By 1962, the wealthiest one per cent of the population still held 72 per cent of the nation's corporate stock. In that year, the wealthiest one per cent also held 48 per cent of the nation's bonds, 24 per cent of the loans, and 16 per cent of the real estate.[5] Clearly then wealth is even less equitably distributed than income in the US, and the inequality has been one of long duration. Pensions for workers account for nearly ten per cent of corporate stock. This may provide workers with security after retirement, but it does not give them the power of wealth holders. The reason is that they have no control over these pension funds, which merely add power to the financial institutions that manage them. . . .

A large prosperous middle class has by no means replaced the struggling lower classes as the majority class. With more than half of the people living below the modest but adequate budget of the BLS, the underbelly of US capitalist society is a deprived majority, just as it was fifty years ago. 'In advanced capitalist societies, the costs of staying out of poverty (i.e. of satisfying invariant subsistence needs) grows as the economy grows. Consequently, there is no long-term tendency in advanced capitalist societies for the incidence of poverty to decrease significantly as the economy grows.'[6] The economic inequality of US society is not just relative inequality, for it is an inequality that means deprivation for a sizeable chunk of the society.

II. OWNERSHIP AND PRODUCTIVITY

There are several strategies used by spokespersons of the ruling class to defend the situation of inequality described above. The first defence rests on the rights of ownership. The second rests on the need for inequality in order to increase productivity. In the next section, a third strategy will be discussed: it rests on the notion of a fair wage.

According to the *first defence* of inequality, those who have put their hard-earned money into a business enterprise have the right to appropriate the fruits of that enterprise and divide them according to their own decisions. Thus the product that workers have made is controlled by owners and not by the workers. Owners are within their rights to divide the product in such a way that inequality is great and poverty widespread. An entire web of ideology has been woven on this basic frame of the rights of ownership. Part of that web is the system of law, backed by police force, entitling the owner to the fruits of the worker. From the perspective of members of the working class, there are several holes in this defence. These holes show that what is built on the frame of ownership rights is indeed only ideology.

On the one hand, if ownership rights lead to continued inequality and poverty, then from a working-class perspective there simply are no such rights. The attitude that ownership of the means of production is sacred merely protects the owners at the expense of those who suffer the resulting inequality. A right is more than such an attitude; it must be justified and indeed justified from a class standpoint. Economic inequality can be justified by ownership rights only if there are such rights. There may well be such rights from the perspective of the ruling class. Yet the continued inequality and poverty resulting from ownership are evidence favouring the view that relative to the working class owners have no legitimate right to the fruits of enterprise.

On the other hand, the basis given for the justification of the owner's right to the fruits of enterprise is not adequate. That basis was the hard work of the investor. Investment, however, is an on-going process in a viable firm. The initial investment is followed by many subsequent investments. Let us grant that the owner has worked hard—whether in the form of the honest toil of the self-employed person or in the form of the forcible plunder of the syndicated criminal—to accumulate the initial investment. But when the plant is rebuilt or expanded, the new investment will be possible only because of the hard work of the workers. Once new investment has been made, there is no longer the same basis for saying that the original owner has the right to control the entire product of the new investment. The logic of 'hard work' applies here too. If the owner worked hard to accumulate the initial investment, it is equally true that the workers worked hard to make the new investment possible. Thus, in a viable firm, the workers should, on the logic of hard work, have a right to appropriate an ever increasing share of the product. The capitalist's own logic backfires! . . .

According to the *second defence* of inequality, significant inequality with poverty at the bottom is a necessary condition for making the society as affluent as it is. In a widely published newspaper article entitled 'Morality and the Pursuit of Wealth' appearing in July 1974, the President of the US Chamber of Commerce, Arch Booth, said the realization of equality by the transfer of wealth from the haves to the have-nots would lessen the 'work incentive of the most productive members of society' and endanger 'the ability of the economic system to accumulate capital for new productive facilities'. Booth's solution is to let the rich keep on investing in productive facilities thereby increasing the share the poor get through better wages and higher employment.

There is one glaring fallacy in this argument. It is the logical fallacy of an 'incomplete disjunction'. The disjunction Booth offers us is that *either* we have a forced redistribution of income within capitalism *or* we let the income of the non-owners rise naturally by increasing investment. But the disjunction needs to be expanded to include at least one more alternative: beyond capitalism, it is possible to expand productive facilities through the investment of collective rather than of private capital. In one form of collective ownership, workers would manage the investment of collective capital in order to advance their interests. In this case, the inequality in both wealth and income needed for growth under private capitalism becomes unnecessary. Without significant inequality, private capitalism would lack the centres of economic power needed to put large amounts of labour to work in order to produce a surplus for growth. The model here for a system of collective ownership of the means of production is not that of nationalized industry run by a bunch of officials who are not controlled by workers. This would be the bureaucratic model found in places like the USSR which are no longer private capitalist societies. Rather, the model is that of a workers' democracy in which democracy extends down to the workplace and in which workplaces are coordinated by a council of representatives from each. This socialist alternative is sufficient to make Booth's disjunction incomplete. . . .

III. A FAIR WAGE

A *third strategy* for defending the inequality and the poverty that is to be found today in the US introduces the concept of compensation for work. The defence is that labour is sold on the free market and, on the whole, the free market determines a *just* price for things. Thus, since inequality and poverty are, in part, a result of the free market for labour, there is no *right* to economic equality or even to a 'modest budget'. A free market must not involve the use of power by those who exchange their goods and services

within it to coerce those with whom they exchange.

This argument seems to leave open the possibility that wages should mount and thus that the worker should come closer to the owner in economic status. But in fact this possibility is not open. As pointed out in Section I, the range of inequality and the degree of poverty in the US have remained remarkably constant. The majority of the people are at or below the level of existence provided by the modest budget. Because of the greater power and organization of the owning class, the wages and salaries of workers remain at a level that allows them merely to perform their jobs well and to raise a new generation of workers. (Differences between the wages of, say, industrial and clerical workers need to be viewed against the background of a general pull toward this subsistence level.) To perform well and to reproduce themselves they have been forced to purchase the ever more elaborate and hence more expensive means of satisfying survival needs and the needs specific to their jobs. Short-term variations in the supply of and demand for labour are only part of this long-term pattern of compensating workers at a subsistence level. At this level, there is nothing much left over for savings and investments that might narrow the gap between them and the owning class. . . .

What, then, is a fair wage from the perspective of the working class? Suppose we are calves who face the prospect of going to slaughter as one-year-olds. The farmers who send us to slaughter find that this is the age at which to realize a maximum profit on us. So one year is the 'fair' time, from the perspective of the farmers, for calves to enjoy themselves before slaughter. An inquisitive calf poses the quesion, 'What is the true "fair" time for cattle to live before slaughter? Is it two years, or even three?' A selfish calf who has no regard for the farmer and the future of cattle farming generally shouts, 'Stop quibbling; we should demand a moratorium on beef eating. An end to the slaughter of cattle!' Similarly, Marx said that the slogan, 'A fair day's wage for a fair day's work!' should be replaced by the slogan, 'An end to the wage system!'[7] Instead of the wage system, work should be done in such a way that the workers' compensation is not just a function of the greater power of a non-working ruling class.

The wage system is a system that in advanced industrial countries has been central to the domination of lower classes by a ruling class. Through that system people are set to work in order to preserve or increase the control of wealth by and, thus, the power of a minority class. They are thus given from what they produce only what is needed to reproduce their labour. When part of the product of workers is used in this way to perpetuate and strengthen the domination of a non-working class, workers are properly said to be 'exploited'. Acceptance of the wage system and plans to reform it from within do not face up to the key role wages play in domination. When workers themselves decide how they are to be compensated out of what they produce, the wage system has ceased to exist and along with it exploitation. . . .

The struggle for higher income begins the organization of people for the collective action that is needed to abolish the wage system itself. This long-term perspective has for some time been forgotten by trade unions everywhere. Their leaders advocate accommodation with the existing system of domination of working people. These leaders talk about a fair wage but they mean only the wages and benefits they think they can wheedle out of the owners. Their conception of fairness and rights is no longer a class conception. A class conception makes overthrowing the wage system a right of working people.

IV. A JUST DISTRIBUTION

Let us leave defences of present economic inequality and take up a proposal for limiting inequality. If capitalist arguments justifying present inequality fail, then where is the line to be drawn for an acceptable degree of inequality? Our problem is how to distribute a product that has come about through the combined efforts of people in different roles. Since isolated producers are the exception, we cannot start with the assumption that there is a product to which an individual producer is 'entitled' because he or she is 'responsible' for that product.[8] In deciding on a principle of just distribution there are two factors to be considered.

On the one hand, there is the average amount of goods per individual in the population, and, on the other hand, there is the degree of inequality with which goods are actually parceled out to individuals. Increasing the average amount of goods per individual might increase the inequality of distribution, whereas decreasing the inequality in distribution might decrease the average per individual. In capitalism we saw that inequality of wealth is a condition of economic growth. Also, inequality of income within the working class weakens solidarity, making possible a greater surplus and hence greater growth. If strict equality means poverty all around, we might recoil from strict equality and look for a balance between a large average amount and considerable equality. But so far we have no clue as to where to strike this balance.

John Rawls has recently proposed an interesting way of balancing a high average amount of goods with a low degree of inequality.[9] The idea is that we are to avoid demanding such a low degree of inequality that the worst off are penalized by getting less than they would with a higher degree of inequality. We are to avoid only those high degrees of inequality that are arrived at by preventing the worst off from getting the most they could get.

Rawls formuated this in his Principle of Difference which tells us to 'maximize the expectations of the least favoured position'. . . .

[But] Rawls talks about distribution without relating it to production. He assumes wrongly that the validity of his principle is absolute, rather than relative to circumstances within production. One thing is certain: in capitalist society there is not the least chance that the Rawlsian scheme could be put into practice. The reason is simply that the organization of production in a capitalist society centres around increasing productive facilities through the making of profits. The class of owners would not advance the interests characteristic of their class by agreeing to maximize the expectations of the least favoured. Given its power, this class would block the realization of the scheme.

Suppose, though, that some mode of production would allow for distribution in accordance with the Principle of Difference. Should not one simply choose to bring about such a mode of production? Certainly—if the Principle of Difference is valid. But its validity is relative to production in the following way. Validity in general is relative to classes, and classes are essential roles in a given mode of production. One should, then, choose to realize the principle only if it is valid relative to one's class. Nonetheless, that class might have to change the existing mode of production in order to realize the new distribution. Even though the capitalist mode of production excludes the application of the Principle of Difference, it may be a valid principle for one of the lower classes within capitalism.

A distributional plan is not just because it is elegant or intuitive but because it answers to needs arising in production. Not only the actual but also the just distribution is dependent on production.

NOTES

1. Gabriel Kolko, *Wealth and Power in America* (Praeger, New York, 1962), p. 108.
2. These data are based on tables in Kolko, *Wealth and Power in America*, p. 14, and in Frank Ackerman and Andrew Zimbalist, "Capitalism and inequality in the United States," in *The Capitalist System*, 2nd ed., p. 298.
3. Kolko, *Wealth and Power in America*, Ch. II, and Ackerman and Zimbalist "Capitalism and inequality in the United States," in *The Capitalist System*, 2nd ed., p. 303. In Sweden, by contrast, taxes change the ratio of the bottom third to that of the top third from 38 to 48 percent.
4. Lititia Upton and Nancy Lyons, *Basic Facts: Distribution of Personal Income and Wealth in the United States* (Cambridge Institute, 1878 Massachusetts Ave., Cambridge, Mass., 1972), p. 6, and Ackerman and Zimbalist, "Capitalism and inequality in the United States," in *The Capitalist System*, 2nd ed., p. 301.
5. Upton and Lyons, *Basic Facts*, p. 31.
6. Bernard Gendron, "Capitalism and Poverty," *Radical Philosophers' Newsjournal*, 4, January 1975, p. 13. This essay appears as Ch. XII of Gendron's *Technology and the Human Condition* (St. Martin's Press, New York, 1977).
7. Karl Marx, *Wages, Price, and Profit* (1865) (Foreign Language Press, Peking, 1970), Ch. XIV.
8. On entitlement, see Robert Nozick, *Anarchy, State, and Utopia* (Basic Books, New York, 1974), Ch. VII.
9. Rawls, *A Theory of Justice*, pp. 78–80.

Taxation and the Distribution of Wealth

Baruch Brody

. . . It should be clear that the choice of a tax base is really a choice between competing views of fairness and justice, and that the choice of different tax bases has different implications for the degree of equality and meritocracy we will have in our society. Therefore, the choice of a tax base is not a purely economic decision, and any proper moral theory on the distribution of wealth must address the issues surrounding this question.

Tax rates generally can be classified in three categories: proportional, progressive, and regressive. A *proportional tax* rate is one that taxes each unit of the tax base at the same amount, or at the same percentage. Sales taxes are proportional taxes, because every item of expenditure is taxed the same percent. A *progressive tax* rate is a tax rate in which additional units are taxed at a higher rate than earlier units. In theory, at least, the personal income tax is a progressive tax, because the tax rate rises for higher income levels. The third type of tax rate is a *regressive tax*. Here, the additional units are taxed at a lower rate than earlier units. The social security tax is an example, since earnings above a certain level (currently $32,400) are exempt from this tax.

The value implications of the choice between a progressive, proportional, or regressive rate of taxation are just as powerful as those concerning the choice of a tax base. Egalitarians, for example, greatly prefer progressive rates on a tax base of either income or wealth. Their reasoning is that progressive rates, as opposed to proportional rates,

increase the amount of money paid to the government by those who have the most income or wealth. In this way, society's wealth can be distributed more equally and, thus, more fairly. Meritocrats, on the other hand, oppose progressive tax rates, particularly on a tax base of income. They claim that such taxes penalize those who are successful by taking money away from those who deserve it. So, meritocrats often prefer proportional taxes. Others object to progressive tax rates on the grounds that everyone should be taxed equally and that it is unfair to tax some income or wealth at a higher rate than other income or wealth. Again, you can see that these questions are not purely economic. . . .

UTILITARIANISM AND TAXATION

. . . Most discussions about which tax base to use reflect views as to which base is fairer. Some people consider ability to pay as the foundation of fairness, and they therefore argue for income or wealth as the tax base. Others emphasize that consumption takes from our common resources, and they therefore feel expenditure is the proper basis for taxation. The utilitarian, owing to his monolithic approach, does not look at the choice of a tax base in this way. Instead, he chooses the tax base which will best promote his utilitarian goals.

To see how this works, we need to examine the implications of choosing one or another of the various tax bases. If we

From Baruch Brody, *Ethics and Its Applications* (Orlando: Harcourt Brace Jovanovich, 1983), pp. 82–88, 96–101, 106–115. Copyright © 1983 by Harcourt Brace Jovanovich, Inc. Reprinted by permission of the publisher.

choose to tax income, then everybody who receives an income must give up some of what they earn. The more we tax, the less each person gets to keep and the more attractive the alternative of leisure becomes. Thus, a tax on income, at any rate of taxation, is an incentive not to work. And the higher the tax rate, the greater that incentive. Suppose we choose to tax wealth. The same reasoning leads to the conclusion that we are then offering incentives not to accumulate wealth. If we spend our money, we have no wealth on which to pay tax. But if we save it, we are taxed on the wealth we have accumulated. The higher the rate of taxation, the greater the incentive not to save. In short, taxes based on either income or wealth reduce the very incentives that utilitarians strive to promote. Consequently, they suggest that we base our taxes on consumption. Such taxes can be used as the basis for producing the redistribution of wealth that utilitarianism calls for without lessening the incentives that it wishes to maintain.

This idea requires some explanation. Generally, those who are interested in achieving greater equality in the distribution of wealth oppose heavy reliance on consumption taxes. They have in mind the sales tax with which we are all familiar. The reason they oppose such taxes is that they tend to be proportional, and proportional taxes do not go very far toward promoting greater equality in the distribution of wealth. However, the consumption tax which utilitarians favor is not this traditional sales tax. Their basic idea is to devise a method for seeing how much a person has spent each year on the consumption of goods and then use that consumption as a basis for taxation. There is no reason why the resulting consumption tax cannot be as progressive as the utilitarian wants it to be.

This leads us to the second major decision, the choice of a tax rate. As with their analysis of the tax base, utilitarians have their own special approach to deciding on the proper tax rate. It is based on their desire to strike the proper balance between egalitarianism and meritocracy. In order to

decrease the inequality in the distribution of wealth, utilitarians advocate progressive tax rates. Their argument runs as follows: by imposing an increasingly higher tax rate as the amount of consumption increases, we take an ever-increasing amount of money from those who have the most wealth. This is certainly a way to cut back on the amount of inequality in society; however, if the tax rate becomes too high, it will begin to lessen people's incentives to work. After all, we work and save with the eventual goal of consuming, and if the tax rate on consumption is too high, then we have less incentive to work and save.

You can see that utilitarians approach the question of taxation from their basic perspective of distributing society's wealth so as to maximize the satisfaction of human desires. They feel that we can only do this by having a greater degree of equality than is normally found in societies while maintaining a sufficient level of inequality to provide the proper incentives. One way to do this is through a progressive rate of taxation on consumption. The progressive feature is to ensure that the tax makes a major contribution toward leveling out inequalities in society, while the use of consumption as the tax base is to help keep down the impact the tax makes on the incentives to work and save.

Many people think of the inheritance tax as an ideal tax from the utilitarian point of view. For one thing, since it doesn't tax wealth until the owner of the wealth dies, it would seem to provide little disincentive to work and save. Second, since inherited wealth contributes to the inequality of wealth in society, it would seem that a tax on inheritance would do a good deal toward lessening that inequality. Why, then, does the utilitarian oppose the use of an inheritance tax?

We can answer this question only by understanding that this argument rests on a fundamental confusion. It supposes that inheritance taxes have no impact on people's desires to work and save because it also supposes that people have no interest in what will happen to the money they have earned and saved once they die. Obviously, this cannot be true, for otherwise, people would not make wills, buy life insurance, set up trust funds, and do all the other things they do to ensure that their money is spent the way they want it to be after they die. For such people, leaving money to others is best viewed as a form of consumption, and, presumably, it should be taxed at the same rate. Utilitarians see no reason for taxing inheritances in a special way.

UTILITARIANISM AND GOVERNMENT REDISTRIBUTIVE PROGRAMS

... It is clear from what we have seen so far that utilitarians support the legitimacy of massive redistributive programs. They do this not because they believe that the recipients have a right to aid and that the government is obligated to provide that aid. After all, utilitarian theory makes no appeal to rights. For this same reason, they also are not moved by the taxpayers' argument that they have a right to keep the money they make instead of having it taken away in taxes to fund programs they do not want. Utilitarians support government redistributive programs because they believe that the outcome of having these programs—namely, a much greater equality in the distribution of wealth—is desirable because it increases the satisfaction of human desires. In other words, utilitarians accept these programs as legitimate because of the results they produce.

Why can't we simply have programs of private charity which voluntarily redistribute wealth? The utilitarian answer to this question is quite straightforward: Some people will give charity, but many more will not. . . .

THE BASIS OF OUR DEONTOLOGICAL ANALYSIS

Most analyses of the distribution of wealth end with the conclusion that there is some special pattern of wealth distribution re-

quired by sound moral principles. For example, the egalitarian concludes that morality requires as much equality as possible in the distribution of wealth. The meritocrat concludes that morality requires that wealth be distributed according to people's efforts and contributions. The utilitarian requires that wealth be distributed in a way which produces as much equality as possible while still maintaining adequate incentives to work and save.

The theory which I will present [now is] *a* deontological approach to the value problems concerning the distribution of wealth, not *the only* deontological approach. This warning is particularly important in connection with the distribution of wealth, for different deontologists have arrived at very different conclusions about this problem. [This theory] belongs to a minority of theories which does not believe that morality requires a definite pattern for the distribution of wealth. Instead, this theory, and others like it, claims that morality requires only that wealth be obtained by proper processes. These processes may lead to widely different distributions of wealth, and any one of these distributions is acceptable as long as it comes about through a proper process.

A simple example may help illustrate this concept. Jones believes that he and his wife have a right of ownership of the house they live in. Why does he believe this? Because he knows that he and his wife bought that property from someone who had a right to it. The legitimacy of the Joneses' right to that bit of wealth depends on the process through which they acquired that property and not on some predetermined pattern for the proper distribution of wealth.

Let's develop this idea a little more fully. We need to distinguish between two types of legitimate property rights: derivative property rights and original property rights. A *derivative property right* is a property right acquired by legitimate means (e.g., purchase, gift, inheritance) from someone who previously had the rights to that property. An *original property right* is a right acquired in a legitimate fashion on some property which was not previously owned. Thus, our theory can be restated roughly this way: Distribution of wealth is legitimate if it consists of original property rights and/or of derivative property rights.

How does this differ from the utilitarian approach [just] discussed . . . ? The utilitarians view property holdings as legitimate if they contribute to the general satisfaction of human desires. To deontologists, property holdings are legitimate because the individuals who own them have a right to them (independent of the general satisfaction of human desires). A legitimate distribution of wealth can take many forms; some will promote the general satisfaction of human desires more than others. But all legitimate distributions are based on original or derivative property rights.

It follows that a theory like ours must depend very heavily on some theory as to how original property rights can be legitimately acquired. Suppose there is some property which is not owned by anyone and which everyone is thus free to use—How can someone acquire, in a legitimate fashion, a right to that property? Drawing upon the ideas of John Locke, these theorists would say that a person may legitimately acquire that original property right by expending his labor so as to increase the value of that piece of property. The basic notion is that we have a right to the increased value which our labor produces; thus, by increasing the value of unowned property, we have a legitimate right to that property.

An example may help bring out this point. Suppose that in the mid-nineteenth century nobody had any special claim to the land on which the Joneses' house now rests. Suppose, further, that someone came along and began to farm an area which includes that land. His labor improved the land, and thereby increased its value. After a few years he built a house there. Through this process he acquired in a legitimate fashion original property rights to the land and house. All subsequent owners, including the Joneses, have held derivative property rights on that

land and house, acquired successively by legitimate means, one from another, all the way back to that initial settler.

There is one major difficulty with this account, one that was already noted by contemporaries of John Locke. The objection might be stated like this: Granted that the settler who improved the land has a right to the increased value he produced through his labor, why should it follow that he then has a right to the whole property? After all, since the natural resource had its own initial value, much of the value of the property, and much of his resulting wealth, is independent of his labor. If we allow the settler to own the whole property and not merely the additional value he produced, we are giving him more wealth than he is entitled to. We are allowing him to expropriate the initial value of that resource.

To address this difficulty, we must imagine a group of people meeting to consider the question of how to allow those who labor on unowned natural resources to receive the value produced by their labor, given that such value is mixed up with the initial value of the original resources. One proposed solution to this problem is to negotiate an agreement that: (a) allows the original worker on the property to form property rights over the initial value of the natural resources as well as over the value he has added; (b) compensates those who lose the right to use those natural resources; and (c) offers that compensation in the form of a socially recognized right to a minimum level of support if one becomes indigent.

Think of it this way: The natural resources of the earth are leased to those who develop them, or to those to whom the leases get transferred. In return, the lease holders owe a rental to everyone. That rental is collected as taxes and used to fund a program of redistribution which aids those who are indigent. As with an insurance fund, while all are equally covered, not all receive payouts. In this program, only those who are needy may receive payouts. Since it would be reasonable for such people to agree to such a scheme of original acquisitions of property rights, we may conclude that such a scheme of property rights is legitimate.

In short, this theory says the following: Any distribution of wealth is legitimate providing it consists of legitimately acquired original property rights or legitimately acquired derivative property rights. Original property rights are legitimately acquired if they are based on labor performed on unowned natural resources which improves the value of those resources. An additional condition for legitimacy is that those who acquire the original property rights, or those to whom these rights are transferred, must pay taxes to help finance a scheme of social insurance which redistributes wealth to those who are needy. . . .

DEONTOLOGY AND TAXATION

. . . When people acquire original property rights, they simultaneously acquire certain obligations to pay taxes. The amount of their obligation is based on the initial value of the undeveloped property; that is, its value before any labor was performed on it. Thus, we may think of these bits of property as coming with a certain tax liability. As the holders of these original rights transfer their property to other people, those people also acquire the tax liability. In this way, at least in theory, we know what the basis of taxation ought to be.

The same considerations suggest what the rate of taxation ought to be. It ought to be proportional to the initial value of the originally acquired property. The intuitive idea is this: For each unit of initial value you acquire through original property rights, you owe a unit of taxes to help society compensate those who are needy. This theory gives rise to a proportional tax.

Although this scheme is easy to state in principle, it is extremely difficult to apply in practice, for over the centuries, we have lost track of who owes what taxes. What we need to do is find a tax base and a tax rate which

will reasonably approximate what should in theory be the proper taxes. It has been suggested that a proportional tax on wealth is the best approximation. Taxes on consumption are totally unrelated to our theoretical ideal. A wealthy miser would be taxed very little by a consumption tax, but he would owe a great deal if he were taxed on the basis of his property and its accompanying obligations. And the more extensive his property, the more substantial his tax bill. Similarly, a foolish investor, who earns very little income on his substantial wealth, would be taxed very little by a tax based on income. But a tax based on wealth would give him a substantial tax bill. These sorts of considerations suggest that the best we can do in the real world to approximate our ideal scheme is to tax people proportionally to their wealth.

It is interesting to note that neither the utilitarian analysis . . . nor the deontological analysis of this section lends any support to the current practice of progressive income taxes. The reader might well want to consider whether there is any moral basis for defending our current tax scheme.

It is also interesting to note certain practical differences between this proportional tax on wealth and the progressive tax on consumption advocated by the utilitarian approach. Particularly if the rate of progression advocated by the utilitarian is quite high, the utilitarian system of taxes is likely to lead to a greater redistribution of wealth than is our proportional tax on wealth. This is not surprising. The utilitarian analysis begins with a stronger positive feeling in favor of equalizing wealth. In fact, the only reason for stopping short of complete equalization is because of the need to preserve incentives. Since the deontological approach begins with no such feeling in favor of equalization, it winds up with less redistribution. Second, the utilitarian approach offers people a substantial incentive for avoiding consumption. The more you consume, the more you will be taxed. This bias against consumption seems to accept indirectly the idea (offered by other advocates of taxes on consumption) that the consumer is taking away what belongs to society in general and must pay a tax for doing so. The deontological approach, which sees the individual property holder as really owning his property if he acquires it legitimately, views consumption differently. If the wealth really is yours, then you have a perfect right to consume it— if that is what you want—and society has no right to discourage that consumption through taxation. As long as you pay the taxes you owe on your wealth, society should be neutral about the way in which you use the rest of it.

To summarize, our deontological theory suggests that the proper way to fund government programs of redistribution is through a proportional tax on wealth. Such a tax seems to be the best approximation of an ideal tax in which each taxpayer would pay his appropriate share based on the initial value of all originally acquired property rights which have been transferred to him. . . .

Towards a Theory of Taxation

J. R. Lucas

"Towards a Theory of Taxation" is a proper theme for an Englishman to take when giving a paper in America. After all it was from the absence of such a theory that the United States derived its existence. The Colonists felt strongly that there should be no taxation without representation, and George III was unable to explain to them convincingly why they should contribute to the cost of their defense. Since that time, understanding has not advanced much. . . . Taxes are regularly levied, in America as elsewhere, on those who have no say on whether they should be levied or how they should be spent. I am taxed by the Federal Government on my American earnings and by state governments on my American spending, but I should be hard put to it to make out that it was unjust. Florida is wondering whether to follow California in taxing multinational corporations on their world-wide earnings. There is some debate on whether such a move is expedient: but nobody to my knowledge has suggested that, in order to make it just, multinational corporations, or their overseas shareholders, should be given representation in the state legislature. Indeed, were anyone to make such a suggestion, he would be laughed out of court, so dead is the contention that representation is a necessary condition of taxes being justly levied. And yet I do not want to bury the Colonists' argument utterly. They had a point. Although the main issues in an adequate theory of taxation are those of justice, there is also room for a quasi-Lockean approach in which we try to make sense of taxes as a sort of bargain in which the taxpayer surrenders his individual quid in return for a share of a collective quo. . . .

It is often thought that the State should redistribute from rich to poor not because it is Wrong to be Rich, but because Equality is a Good Thing. I have argued against egalitar-

From J. R. Lucas, "Towards a Theory of Taxation," in Ellen Frankel Paul, Fred D. Miller, Jr., and Jeffrey Paul, eds., *Liberty and Equality* (Oxford: Basil Blackwell, 1985), pp. 161–165, 169–173. Used by permission.

ianism at length elsewhere and shall not weary you with repetition. In the context of taxation, however, there is one variant of the egalitarian argument which is superficially attractive. It seems natural to regard the relief of poverty as a possible aim of public policy—one does not have to be an egalitarian to regard poverty as a bad thing, and only extreme advocates of [laissez] faire would say that it should be no concern of the State. But then we seem to have a [license] for Robin Hood. Whenever there is a choice we should always devote public funds to the fashionable minority group of the moment rather than reduce the higher rate tax demands on the Duke of Westminster. It is this contention that I want to controvert, and in particular the second half. As regards the first half, it has been increasingly recognized that there are limits to what can be achieved by public expenditure in the way of relieving poverty. No matter how much we spend, the poor will always be with us. But although this is a reason for doubting the efficacy of egalitarian policies, there are always going to be some expenditures which look like they might do some good for some poor people; and unless there is some counter argument for not taxing the rich to the limit, the plea of poverty will win the day.

Some thinkers seek to block the Robin Hood argument by claiming that taxation ought not to be redistributive. This claim is ambiguous. In one sense, taxation cannot help but be redistributive. The tax collector takes money from me, and distributes it to soldiers, sailors, and civil servants. Even if there were no welfare payments as such, much of my money would go on expenditures which benefited others much more than myself: airports and the M25 for the rich, the health service for the ill, public education for the uneducated. We cannot lay down that taxation should not be redistributive in this sense. But even if it is permissible for taxation to have redistributive effects, some people would still argue that it should not be *intended* to redistribute resources. It is, they argue, contrary to the nature of the

State that it should extract from an unwilling individual taxes for any other purpose than the protection of his rights against criminals at home or aggressors from abroad. Such a theory of the State is difficult to refute because it is difficult to formulate coherently. I do not think that any such theory of a Minimum State can be sustained. I have argued the point elsewhere, but only cursorily.[1] For our present purpose, I do not claim that no such theory could be put forward, but only that other theories of the State are put forward and acted on, and that for these, too, a theory of contributive justice is needed. Most people do not believe in the Minimum State. They want to engage in collective action, *e.g.,* in sending a man to the moon, and see no reason why they should not act collectively through the mechanism of the nation-state. And if they engage in collective action generally, then they can choose as a permissible goal of collective action the relief of poverty, which will be redistributive not only in effect but—at least in one obvious sense—in intention too. Of course, there may still be reasons for being chary of adopting redistributive policies because they are inherently divisive and often give rise to abuse. But keeping pork barrels out of politics is a counsel of prudence rather than the imperative of political morality. Many redistributive policies at present practiced are unwise, and some are plain wrong. But I cannot see that there is, or even could be, a cogent argument, either of justice or of expediency, for holding that the relief of poverty or the amelioration of misfortune is not a proper object of public concern or public expenditure; I can, however, see arguments, both of justice and of expediency, for saying that the tax burden should be fairly borne by the whole community and not put disproportionately upon the shoulders of the rich.

Aristotle considers the allocation of benefits and burdens together under the title of distributive justice. But the cases are not all similar. When benefits are being distributed, I am not likely to shirk my share, and if I do, no great problem arises: if I do not want my piece of cake, there are plenty of others who will take it up for me. With burdens, however, each person is naturally reluctant to bear them, and so is tempted to shirk and may actually do so. Fare-dodging, free-riding, tax-evasion, and generally not pulling one's weight, are endemic problems when in pursuit of a collective goal we have to call on individuals to make unwelcome sacrifices as their contribution towards it. These problems ought to be considered quite separately from those of distributive justice, and I propose the name "contributive justice" instead. . . .

Although the State needs to have some coercive power at its disposal in order to bring sanctions to bear on those who will not otherwise keep their covenants, it cannot rely on the sword alone, but must secure a general measure of agreement to its general aims. Although I want to be assured that those who break the law will be punished, so that I am not being a mug when I myself forbear to break it, my own reason for keeping the law is not primarily that I shall be punished if I break it, but that I see the rationality of my, and everyone else's, keeping it, and am reasonably assured of others' actually doing so.

The fiscal application is clear. Taxes must be not simply what I can make others pay on pain of punishment, but what I can see good reason to pay as a matter of enlightened self-interest and reasonable identification with my fellow members of the State, and in reasonable confidence of their paying too. If these conditions are satisfied, then I will be fairly well disposed to pay my share. . . .

The case has become very different with taxation, especially income tax. I can still remember the time when it was thought to be a moral duty to pay one's taxes, and tax evasion was a serious social crime. Nobody thinks that now. A generation of high and avowedly punitive taxation has eroded the moral basis of fiscal policy, and has developed in Great Britain an Italian attitude towards the Inland Revenue. The rot set in from the top. Rich men felt—were encouraged to feel by some Chancellors—that they

were being unfairly taxed, and ceased to feel any moral obligation to contribute to the Exchequer the very large amounts demanded of them. They became less scrupulous about declaring unconsidered trifles, and understandably eager to rearrange their affiars so as to minimize the tax man's exactions. For forty years successive Finance Acts have sought to block up one loophole after another, but have by and large been defeated by the fact that people who run things have to have discretion, and cannot be stopped, except by moral considerations, from using their discretion to their own advantage. . . .

Some collective goods, although in principle available to all, are in practice enjoyed only by a minority. Only a small proportion of citizens avail themselves of consular services. Many poor people never go abroad at all. Only a minority of people go to university or have children who go to university. Public libraries and municipal museums are open to all, but not patronized by all. If all public expenditure were financed by a poll tax, it would be unfair on the poor, who would be paying for facilities for the rich which the poor either had no opportunity of using or no wish to use. . . .

Those with large houses in plush neighborhoods, or with large incomes, or large cars, can reasonably be asked to contribute more because typically they benefit more. Different people will avail themselves of different goods, but each will avail himself of some, and there will not be any general category of exploited taxpayers who have to pay a lot and do not receive a fair return. Although each would like to opt out of some items of public provision, which do not benefit him personally, he would suffer more by others opting out of the provisions which do benefit him. Granted reasonable efficiency of collective action, he gains on the swings what he loses on the roundabouts, and the package as a whole is one that it is in his enlightened self-interest to accept. . . .

If there is a system of representation, although we cannot tell each individual taxpayer that he wants the benefits he is asked to pay for, we can tell him that he is a member of a group which by and large wants them. So the question of whether the benefit should be provided is answered, moderately well. The only question left is whether the burden is being fairly shared. Here, it seems to me, we can make use of a presumption of equality. If the community calls on me to bear an equal share of the cost of carrying out a collective decision, even though it is one I may have opposed, I have no complaint. If the share is heavier than that asked of others, contributive justice requires that we consider all those also being asked to contribute the same amount, and ask whether they as a class are benefiting as much as they are having to pay. If they are, they are getting a good Lockean bargain, and are not being too badly done by. If super-tax payers as a whole are getting a lot of opera, foreign consular services, and national parks, which it would cost them more to provide for themselves by private subscription, then they are not being milked by the tax man. But if they are being asked to pay more without there being any justification in terms of benefits enjoyed or available for enjoyment, then their complaint that they are being unfairly "taxploited" stands.

The duties levied on alcohol, tobacco, and gasoline can be partly justified by the fair bargain argument. Consumers of these commodities are disproportionately heavy consumers of health services, which in most countries are at least partly funded out of general taxation. Drinkers and drivers also occupy a disproportionate amount of the time of the police and the judiciary. Large sums of money are spent on roads. The road lobby in Britain frequently makes out that all the money raised by road taxes should be spent on roads. The argument is fallacious, because it ignores the other costs imposed on the community by road users. But the fact that it is put forward at all, shows that there is felt to be something in the fair bargain argument. . . .

With regard to direct taxes, the fair bargain argument justifies proportionate taxation, as opposed to a simple poll tax. It might yield a partial justification of progressive taxation, although the main justification, in so far as it is justifiable, must rely on the third underlying principle of fiscal fairness, which is that the burdens should be equal not in monetary but in real terms: The widow's mites cost her much more than the rich man's largesse. And so we conclude that taxes should be not only proportionate but progressive. . . .

NOTE

1. J. R. Lucas, *The Principles of Politics* (Oxford 1966) (pbk. ed. 1985), Section 67, pp. 287–295.

CASE 1. Baseball Economics

On Wednesday, 9 December, 1981 the Baltimore Orioles' great pitcher, Jim Palmer, gave a newspaper interview in Portland, Oregon. He was highly critical of the system of economic incentives in baseball. He argued that money now controlled almost all decisions by management and players alike, and many players, he said, "make a lot more money than they should." The salaries are often determined through "panic" on the part of management, he said, which plans at all cost against a situation in which star players leave and join other teams at increased salary levels. He noted that players now make $300,000–400,000 in their second year, and sign multi-year contracts. This kind of security, he argued, leads players to relax and lose their concentration on skilled performance.[1]

On the same day that Palmer gave his in-

Used by permission of the author.

terview in Portland, Baseball Commissioner Bowie Kuhn was testifying before a Congressional Subcommittee on courts, civil liberties, and the administration of justice on issues surrounding cable television. Kuhn described the possible introduction of massive cable television broadcasts of baseball as economically intolerable for the sport. Both gate receipts and network television revenues would decline, he held, and this would be a disaster for a sport already "treading on financial quicksand." Kuhn supported this judgment with figures to show that only nine of baseball's twenty-six teams had made a profit in the previous year. He argued that the aggregate loss was $25 million. He further argued that cable television would bring competing sporting events into a city without the consent or agreement of anyone in baseball management.

Ted Turner, who owns both Turner Broadcasting System (cable television) and the Atlanta Braves baseball team, also testified at the same time as Kuhn. "If baseball is in trouble," he said, "it is because they are paying the baseball players a million and a half dollars a year." From Turner's perspective, "there isn't one single example of a proven economic harm from cable television. They just want total control to the detriment of the American public." Replied Kuhn, "We were prepared to negotiate with the cable people, but they had no interest."[2]

By 1985 the average salary of a major-league baseball player had risen to over $350,000 per season, and 36 of the 650 players made over a million dollars per season.[3] Both the players and their sports agents generally argued that salaries are purely a function of negotiating in the free market.

NOTES

1. See "Money Has Changed the Game," *Baltimore Sun* (Thursday, December 10, 1981), Sports Section, 1.
2. See "Kuhn Hits Cable T.V.," *Washington Post* (Thursday, December 10, 1981), Sports Section, 1.
3. See William Bulkeley, "Sports Agents Help Athletes Win—And Keep—Those Super Salaries," *Wall Street Journal*, March 25, 1985, p. 31.

Questions

1. If Jim Palmer were claiming that players' high salaries constitute an injustice in the American economic system, would he be right? Would Nozick agree with your answer?
2. Do Bowie Kuhn's comments derive from a libertarian or utilitarian theory of justice? Does he stand opposed to a pure free-market conception of justice?
3. If Peter Singer's proposals were followed, what would be the obligations of major league baseball players to help the poor both within and outside of their own country? Is this a Marxist theory in disguise as utilitarianism?
4. Would it be unjust to place a baseball player making 1½ million dollars per year in a 70 percent tax bracket? Would it be unjust to place anyone in business in a 70 percent bracket?

CASE 2. Libby, McNeil, & Libby on Cyclamates

In 1969 the Food and Drug Administration banned cyclamates, a sweetening agent, from the market. As with later controversies about saccharin, the evidence as to the dangers presented by cyclamates were much discussed at the time. What some persons regarded as telling animal studies were regarded by others as inconclusive. Nonetheless, by FDA criteria cyclamates presented an unacceptable level of risk.

Copyright © 1987 by Tom L. Beauchamp, and reprinted with permission.

Over the next sixteen months, Libby, McNeil, & Libby sold approximately 300,000 cases of cyclamate-sweetened fruit to customers in West Germany, Spain, and other countries. James Nadler, Libby's vice-president for international business, was quoted by *The Wall Street Journal* as giving the following justification for the sales: "Fortunately the older civilizations of the world are more deliberate about judging momentary fads that are popular in the United States from time to time."[1] *The Wall Street Journal* article went on to note that such sales are commonly considered acceptable practice in American business. The *Journal* cited such products as Parke, Davis, & Co.'s Chloromycetin and Merck's Indocin, both of which are marketed abroad without the cumbersome warnings as to side effects that are required in the United States.

Elsewhere in this same *Journal* issue it was noted that this traffic is not simply unilateral from the United States. A number of drugs produced by Ciba-Geigy, Ltd., are banned in Sweden but marketed in the United States. Of course in all cases these drugs could not be marketed unless there were at least an implicit recognition and acceptance within the country into which they are imported.

In direct reply to vice-president Nadler's comment on cyclamates, Robert L. Heilbroner offered the following critical comment: "The momentary fad to which [Nadler] was referring was the upshot of nineteen years of increasingly alarming laboratory findings concerning the effects of cyclamates on chick embryos—effects that produced grotesque malformations similar to those induced by thalidomide."[2]

NOTES

1. *The Wall Street Journal* (February 11, 1971).
2. Robert L. Heilbroner, "Controlling the Corporation," in *In the Name of Profit*, Robert L. Heilbroner, et al. (Garden City, N.Y.: Doubleday and Co., Inc., 1972). Heilbroner relies on evidence discussed in James Turner, *The Chemical Feast* (New York: 1970), p. 12.

Questions

1. Does Heilbroner seem to be accusing Libby of an injustice in marketing its product? If so, is it an implicit appeal to a utilitarian conception of justice?
2. Do you think Singer would agree with Heilbroner?
3. What might Nozick say about Libby's actions in this case?
4. Should drug companies print the above-mentioned warnings when marketing their products abroad? If so, does justice demand that they do so?

CASE 3. Cocaine as a Business

Roberto U. is a pure libertarian in moral and political philosophy who was deeply impressed by his reading of Robert Nozick's account of justice. He lives in Los Angeles and teaches philosophy at a local university. Roberto is also a frequent user of cocaine, which he enjoys immensely and often provides to friends at parties. Neither he nor any of his close friends is addicted. Over the years Roberto has tired of teaching philosophy and now has an opportunity, through old friends who live in Peru, to become a middleman in the cocaine business. He is disquieted about the effects cocaine has on some persons, but he has never witnessed these effects first hand, and he is giving his friends' offer serious consideration.

Roberto's research has told him the fol-

Written by Tom L. Beauchamp using facts in a *Wall Street Journal* story of June 30, 1986, pp. 1, 16. The *Journal* story was based on interviews with DEA officials, pilots, distributors, and lawyers.

lowing: Selling cocaine is a multi-billion-dollar industry. Peruvian President Alan Garcia once described it as Latin America's "only successful multinational." It can be and has been analyzed in traditional business categories; it has its own entrepreneurs, small organizations, giants, growth phases, and the like. Its profit margins have narrowed in some markets, while expanding in others. It often seeks new markets in order to expand its product line. For example, in the mid-1980s "crack"—a potent form of cocaine that is smoked—was moved heavily into new markets in Europe. Between the mid-1960s and the mid-1980s the demand for cocaine grew dramatically because of successful supply and marketing. Middlemen first in Miami and then in Los Angeles were established to increase already abundant profits. Heavy investments were made in airplanes, efficient modes of production, training managers, and regular schedules of delivery and distribution. In 1986 media presentations of the drug began to shift from a recreational drug to a killer, especially after the deaths of two prominent athletes. There was a severe downturn in cocaine consumption.

Roberto sees the cocaine industry—correctly—as not subject to taxes, tariffs, or government regulations other than those pertaining to its illegality. It is a pure form of the free market in which supply and demand control transactions. This fact about the business appeals to Roberto, as it seems perfectly suited to his libertarian viewpoint. He is well aware that there are severe problems of coercion and violence in some parts of the industry, but he is quite certain that the wealthy clientele that he would supply in Los Angeles neither abuses the drug nor redistributes it to others who might be harmed. He is confident that his Peruvian associates are honorable and that he can escape problems of violence, coercion, and abusive marketing. However, he has just read a newspaper story that Cocaine-use emergencies—especially those involving cocaine-induced heart attacks—have tripled in the last five years. This and this alone gives him pause before entering the cocaine business. He sees these health emergencies as *unfortunate* but not as *unfair*. So his humanity but not his theory of justice gives him pause.

Questions

1. Would a libertarian—as Roberto thinks—say that the cocaine business is just so long as no *coercion* is involved and the system is a pure function of supply and demand?
2. Does *justice* demand that cocaine be outlawed, or is this not a problem of justice at all? Are questions of justice even meaningful when the activity is beyond the boundaries of law?
3. Is the distinction Roberto draws between what is unfortunate and what is unfair relevant to a decision about whether an activity is just?

CASE 4. Covering the Costs of Health Care

Medicare—which is often pejoratively referred to by its critics as "socialized medicine"—was passed into law in the United States to provide coverage for health-care costs in populations that could not afford adequate coverage, especially the elderly. Then, as now, health-care technology was rapidly being developed and costs were skyrocketing. Health-care costs in the United States have increased from $1 billion in 1965

This case was written by Tom L. Beauchamp based largely on statistics and statements found in *Payment for Physician Services*, Office of Technology Assessment, U.S. Congress (Government Printing Office), 1986.

to over $70 billion in 1985. During the 1980s, Medicare expenditures for physicians rose an average of 16 percent per year. These payments are expected to increase 14 percent per year in the next decade.

These costs and federal payments for physicians' services are under intense study by the U.S. Congress. In recent years Congress has not been able to propose any formula for containing costs on which its members could agree except to freeze payment levels on physicians' fees to Medicare beneficiaries for fifteen months (in The Deficit Reduction Act of 1984). However, the members of Congress do agree that Medicare's payment policies have fueled unacceptable increases in expenditures for health-care services.

Medicare has generally been successful in meeting its goals of providing health care for the elderly, although for those with chronic diseases or in need of long-term care, health-care costs can still exceed Medicare's provisions and can wipe out a family's assets. For example, there have been cases in which hospital and nursing-care bills put families in debt for life and resulted in liens being placed on their homes for failure to pay.

It has been demonstrated that there is substantial variation across the United States in payment rates for services. Urban, specialist, and in-patient services are typically much higher than are rural, generalist, and ambulatory services. It has been widely argued that these differentials are independent of quality of services, depending more on urban location, the high costs of specialists, and the like.

Recent statistics indicate that the elderly, who were targeted for the Medicare program, have more after-tax income than do citizens under 65. They also have more needs for health care. By the year 2030 it is projected that there will be more than 60 million people over age 65—roughly double the present number. A quarter-million millionaires in the United States are presently eligible for Medicare coverage.

Questions

1. Is a nation obligated to provide quality health care for the elderly who otherwise could afford no care?
2. Is a nation obligated to provide quality health care for the elderly irrespective of ability to pay—for example, on egalitarian grounds of justice?
3. Is Medicare justifiable on either utilitarian or egalitarian premises of justice? Do Rawls's principles tell us anything about how health care should be distributed?
4. Would a Marxist approve of Medicare even if he or she did not think the system is socialized enough? Are libertarians and Marxists necessarily in opposition on the question of state-supported systems of health-care coverage?

Suggested Supplementary Readings

Concepts and Principles of Justice

Benn, Stanley I. "Justice." In vol. 4 of *The Encyclopedia of Philosophy,* edited by Paul Edwards, 298–302. New York: Macmillan and Free Press, 1967.

Bowie, Norman E. *Towards a New Theory of Distributive Justice.* Amherst: University of Massachusetts Press, 1971.

Buchanan, Allen. *Ethics, Efficiency, and the Market.* Totowa, N.J.: Rowman and Allanheld, 1985.

Feinberg, Joel. "Justice and Personal Desert." In *Nomos 6: Justice,* edited by Carl J. Friedrich and John W. Chapman, 68–97. New York: Atherton Press, 1963.

Kipnis, Kenneth, and Diana T. Meyers. *Economic Justice.* Totowa, N.J.: Rowman and Allanheld, 1985.

Rescher, Nicholas. *Distributive Justice.* Indianapolis: Bobbs-Merrill, 1966.

Sterba, James. *The Demands of Justice.* Notre Dame, Ind.: University of Notre Dame Press, 1980.

———, ed. *Justice: Alternative Political Perspectives.* Belmont, Calif.: Wadsworth, 1980.

Egalitarian Theories

Barry, Brian. *The Liberal Theory of Justice, a Critical Examination of the Principal Doctrines in a Theory of Justice by John Rawls.* Oxford, England: Clarendon Press, 1973.

Blocker, H. Gene, and Elizabeth Smith, eds. *John Rawls' Theory of Social Justice: An Introduction.* Athens: Ohio University Press, 1980.

Daniels, Norman, ed. *Reading Rawls: Critical Studies of a Theory of Justice.* New York: Basic Books, 1975.

Lekachman, Robert. "Economic Justice in Hard Times." In *Ethics in Hard Times,* edited by A. L. Caplan and D. Callahan, 91–116. New York: Plenum Press, 1981.

MacIntyre, Alasdair. "Justice: A New Theory and Some Old Questions." *Boston University Law Review* 52 (1972): 330–334.

Rawls, John. "Reply to Alexander and Musgrave." *Quarterly Journal of Economics* 88 (1974): 633–655.

Vlastos, Gregory. "Justice and Equality." In *Social Justice,* edited by Richard B. Brandt. Englewood Cliffs, N.J.: Prentice-Hall, 1962.

Libertarian Theories

Dworkin, Gerald, Gordon Bermant, and Peter G. Brown, eds. *Markets and Morals.* Washington, D.C.: Hemisphere Publishing Corp, John Wiley, 1977.

Friedman, Milton. *Capitalism and Freedom.* Chicago: University of Chicago Press, 1962.

Hayek, Friedrich. *Individualism and Economic Order.* Chicago: University of Chicago Press, 1948.

———. *The Mirage of Social Justice.* Vol. 2, *Law, Legislation, and Liberty.* Chicago: University of Chicago Press, 1976.

Loevinsohn, Ernest. "Liberty and the Redistribution of Property." *Philosophy and Public Affairs* 6 (1977): 226–239.

Machan, Tibor, ed. *The Libertarian Reader.* Totowa, N.J.: Rowman and Allanheld, 1982.

Mack, Eric. "Liberty and Justice." In *Justice and Economic Distribution,* edited by John Arthur and William Shaw, 83–93. Englewood Cliffs, N.J.: Prentice-Hall, 1978.

Nagel, Thomas. "Libertarianism Without Foundations." *Yale Law Journal* 85 (1975).

Paul, Jeffrey, ed. *Reading Nozick: Essays on Anarchy, State, and Utopia.* Totowa, N.J.: Rowman and Allanheld, 1981.

Scanlon, Thomas M. "Nozick on Rights, Liberty, and Property." *Philosophy and Public Affairs* 6 (1976): 3–25.

Utilitarian Theories

Braybrooke, David. "Utilitarianism with a Difference: Rawls' Position in Ethics." *Canadian Journal of Philosophy* 3 (1973): 303–331.

Brock, Dan W. "Contractualism, Utilitarianism, and Social Inequalities." *Social Theory and Practice* 1 (1971): 33–44.

———. "Recent Work in Utilitarianism." *American Philosophical Quarterly* 10 (1973): 241–276.

Goldman, Alan H. "Business Ethics: Profits, Utilities, and Moral Rights." *Philosophy and Public Affairs* 9 (1980): 260–286.

Lyons, David. "Rawls versus Utilitarianism." *Journal of Philosophy* 69 (1972): 535–545.

Mill, John Stuart. In *Utilitarianism; On Liberty; Representative Government,* edited by A. D. Lindsay. London: E. P. Dutton, 1976.

Posner, Richard A. *The Economics of Justice.* 2d ed. Cambridge, Mass.: Harvard University Press, 1983.

Singer, Peter. "Famine, Affluence, and Morality." *Philosophy and Public Affairs* 1 (1972).

———. "The Right to Be Rich or Poor." *New York Review of Books* 6 (March 1976): 19–24.

Taylor, Paul W. "Justice and Utility." *Canadian Journal of Philosophy* 1 (1972): 327–350.

Socialist and Marxist Theories

Brenkert, George G. *Marx's Ethics of Freedom.* London: Routledge and Kegan Paul, 1983.

Buchanan, Allen. *Marx and Justice.* Totowa, N.J.: Rowman and Allanheld, 1982.

Cohen, G. A. "The Labor Theory of Value and the Concept of Exploitation." *Philosophy and Public Affairs* 8 (1979): 338–360.

Elster, Jon. *Making Sense of Marx.* London: Cambridge University Press, 1985.

Engels, Friedrich. "Socialism: Utopian and Scientific." Reprinted in *Essential Works of Marxism,* edited by Arthur Mendel, 45–82. New York: Bantam Books, 1961.

Gallie, W. B. "Liberal Morality and Socialist Morality." In *Philosophy, Politics, and Society,* edited by Peter Laslett, 116–133. Oxford, England: Blackwell Press, 1956.

Heilbroner, Robert L. *The Nature and Logic of Capitalism.* New York: W. W. Norton, 1986.

Macpherson, C. B. *The Life and Times of Liberal Democrats.* New York: Oxford University Press, 1977.

Marx, Karl. *Economic and Philosophical Manuscripts.* In *Karl Marx: Early Writings,* edited by T. B. Bottomore. London: C. A. Watts, 1963.

Miller, David. *Social Justice.* Oxford: Clarendon Press, 1976.